Harnessing AutoCAD®

Release 14

Harnessing AutoCAD®

Release 14

Thomas A. Stellman
and
G. V. Krishnan

Autodesk.
Press

International Thomson Publishing

Albany • Bonn • Boston • Cincinnati • Detroit • London • Madrid
Melbourne • Mexico City • New York • Pacific Grove • Paris • San Francisco
Singapore • Tokyo • Toronto • Washington

NOTICE TO THE READER

Trademarks

Cover: Background image reprinted with permission from and under the copyright of Autodesk, Inc. "Ancient Jerusalem's Cardo Arc" photo by Evan N. Lauber.

COPYRIGHT © 1998
Delmar Publishers Inc.   The ITP logo is a trademark under license
Autodesk Press imprint   Printed in the United States of America
an International Thomson Publishing Company

For more information, contact:

Autodesk Press   International Thomson Editores
3 Columbia Circle, Box 15-015   Campos Eliseos 385, Piso 7
Albany, New York 12212-5015   Colonia Polanco
                                                11560 Mexico D. F. Mexico

International Thomson Publishing Europe
Berkshire House 168-173   International Thomson Publishing GmbH
High Holborn   Königswinterer Strasse 418
London, WC1V7AA   53227 Bonn Germany
United Kingdom

Thomas Nelson Australia   International Thomson Publishing France
102 Dodds Street   Tour Maine-Montparnesse
South Melbourne, 3205   33, Avenue du Maine
Victoria, Australia   75755 Paris Cedex 15, France

Nelson Canada   International Thomson Publishing - Japan
1120 Birchmont Road   Hirakawacho Kyowa Building, 3F
Scarborough, Ontario   2-2-1 Hirakaw-cho Chiyoda-ku
Canada, M1K 5G4   Tokyo 102 Japan

International Thomson Publishing Southern Africa
Building 18, Constantia Park   International Thomson Publishing Asia
240 Old Pretoria Road   221 Henderson Road
P.O. Box 2459   S#05 -10 Henderson Building
Halfway House, 1685 South Africa   Singapore 0315

4 5 6 7 8 9 10 XXX 03 02 01 00 99 98

Library of Congress Cataloging-in-Publication Data

Stellman, Thomas A.
    Harnessing AutoCAD release 14 / by Thomas A. Stellman, G.V. Krishnan.
        p. cm.
    Includes index.
    ISBN: 0-7668-0124-1
    1. Computer graphics. 2. AutoCAD (Computer file). I. Krishnan, G.V. II. Title

T385.S7522 1998
620'.0042' 02855369–dc21   97-25352
                                                             CIP

BRIEF CONTENTS

CONTENTS

CHAPTER 2   FUNDAMENTALS I

CHAPTER 3   FUNDAMENTALS II

CHAPTER 4   FUNDAMENTALS III

CHAPTER 5   FUNDAMENTALS IV

CHAPTER 6   FUNDAMENTALS V

CHAPTER 7   DIMENSIONING

CHAPTER 8   PLOTTING/PRINTING

CHAPTER 11   EXTERNAL REFERENCES

CHAPTER 12   DRAWING ENVIRONMENTS

CHAPTER 13   UTILITY COMMANDS

CHAPTER 16   RENDERING

CHAPTER 17   THE TABLET AND DIGITIZING

APPENDIX B   ALPHABETICAL LISTING OF AUTOCAD COMMANDS

APPENDIX C   AUTOCAD TOOLBARS

APPENDIX D   SYSTEM VARIABLES

APPENDIX E   HATCH AND FILL PATTERNS

APPENDIX F   FONTS

APPENDIX G   LINETYPES

INTRODUCTION

HARNESSING THE POWER OF AUTOCAD

When AutoCAD version 1.7 arrived in 1984, it was not just a simple drawing program. AutoCAD was only about two years old and already a giant in the fledgling personal computer world. Granted, you could get more power and features in a mainframe CAD system—but the cost was far beyond the reach of the average drafter. And it took at least one full semester with a lot of study and hands-on practice to begin to harness the power of AutoCAD.

Today, you can learn to do more with AutoCAD in less time than it took in 1984. Why? Because many of the things that used to take several commands and manipulations can be done with just one of the commands introduced since then. And AutoCAD in the Windows 95/NT platform has made the commands much easier to use. However, to truly master AutoCAD Release 14 takes much longer than it did to master Release 1.7 simply because there are so many more features and so much more capability.

Due to the original programmers' foresight, the core AutoCAD design/drafting program remains basically as it was in the first versions. AutoCAD Release 1.7 is singled out because that is when Object Snap was introduced. The importance of the Object Snap feature (described in detail in this text) cannot be emphasized enough. Once you have learned how to use this feature, try to imagine making mechanical or architectural drawings without it! Other features introduced since Release 1.7 include splines, custom linetypes, multilines, AutoLISP with its user programmability, 3D graphics, 2D regions, rendering, associative dimensioning and hatching, and many enhancements to the selection, editing, and management of objects, plus many others.

Whether you're new to AutoCAD or a seasoned user upgrading your skills, Harnessing AutoCAD will show you how to reign in the power of AutoCAD to improve your professional skills and increase your productivity.

HIGHLIGHTS AND FEATURES OF THIS NEW EDITION

- New features are covered in depth.
- Competency-based objectives at the beginning of each chapter have been thoroughly reviewed and revised when necessary.
- Toolbars, dialog boxes, and menu illustrations have been completely redone to match AutoCAD Release 14 interface.
- New step-by-step comprehensive project exercises have been added to all chapters where appropriate.
- Where chapter exercises pertain to skills and concepts for a specific discipline, the discipline is identified by an icon.

- End-of-chapter questions provide a test of key chapter concepts.
- Comments and suggestions from instructors and reviewers have been incorporated.
- Some topics and subject matter have been rearranged in an even more logical and practical manner
- Hands-on exercises and step-by-step examples appear earlier in the text than in previous editions.
- The dimensioning chapter (Chapter 7) has been completely revised and rearranged.

RELEASE 14 ENHANCEMENTS

AutoCAD Release 14 Features	Function
Lightweight polyline	Saves memory storage; and functions automatically unless it requires splines or is a 3D polyline.
Hatch no longer an anonymous "block"	New method of handling hatch patterns reduces the memory required in most cases
New methods of loading certain applications	Reduction in the waiting time for applications to be usable; makes more memory available for other operations
Paper space regenerations during display operations no longer required	Transparent and real-time panning and zooming are now available in paper space
AutoSnap®	Facilitates cycling through multiple running Osnap modes, identifying the one you want, and invoking it without having to move the cursor
Tracking	Facilitates moving through nonselected point(s) to a selected point
Direct Distance	Lets you specify a point by using your pointing device to determine the desired angle and entering the distance from the keyboard
Hybrid raster/vector drawings more accessible	Improves the usability of hybrid raster/vector drawings
Standardized File Open and Save dialog boxes	Now conforms to Windows 95/NT format
Drawing Wizards in Start Up dialog box	Drawing sessions are started faster and more easily
Demand-loaded reference files	Improves file-loading and display speeds
Configurable cursor size	Can be configured from 1 to 100 percent of the screen
Extended rendering capabilities	Full photorealistic capabilities, including texture maps
Internet access	You can access the Internet directly from AutoCAD and upload or download AutoCAD drawings
Preference dialog box	Easy-to-use graphical user interface
Profiles tab user Preferences	Allows multiple user configurations and preferences

HOW TO USE THIS BOOK

Overview

The first chapter of this text provides an overview of the AutoCAD program, its interface, the commands, special features and warnings, and Release 14 enhancements. Specific commands are described in detail throughout the book, along with lessons on how to use them.

Fundamentals

Harnessing AutoCAD contains five chapters devoted to teaching the fundamentals of AutoCAD. Fundamentals I introduces some of the basic commands and concepts, and Fundamentals II through V continue to build logically on that foundation until the student has a reasonable competency in the most basic functions of AutoCAD.

Intermediate

After mastering the fundamentals, you move on to the intermediate topics, which include dimensioning, plotting and printing, hatching and boundaries, blocks and attributes, external references, and drawing environments. Other chapters teach students to make the most of AutoCAD using utility commands, scripts and slides, 3D commands, rendering, and the digitizing tablet.

Advanced

For the advanced AutoCAD user, this book offers a chapter on customizing AutoCAD (including toolbar customization) and AutoLISP. These two chapters teach you to make AutoCAD more individualized and powerful as you tailor them to your special needs.

Appendices

There are seven appendices in the back of this book. Appendix A is an introduction to hardware and software requirements of AutoCAD. Appendix B is a quick reference of AutoCAD commands with a brief description of their basic functions, and Appendix C provides a visual reference of AutoCAD toolbars.

Appendix D lists system variables, including default setting, type, whether or not it is read-only, and an explanation of the system variables. To see hatch and fill patterns, fonts, and linetypes provided with the AutoCAD program, refer to Appendices E, F, and G.

STYLE CONVENTIONS

In order to make this text easier for you to use, we have adopted certain conventions that are used throughout the book:

Convention	Example
Command names are capitalized	the MOVE command
Pull-down menu names appear with the first letter capitalized	Draw pull down menu
Toolbar menu names appear with the first letter capitalized	Standard toolbar
A key icon appears when you should respond by striking a key on your keyboard	`Enter` ENTER or RETURN `Shift` Shift `Esc` Escape `Ctrl` Control `F9` F key
Command sequences are indented. User inputs are indicated by **boldface**. *(Instructions are indicated by italics and are enclosed in parentheses)*	Command: **move** Select Objects: **G** Enter group name: *(Enter group name)*

HOW TO INVOKE COMMANDS

Methods of invoking a command are summarized in a table

Standard toolbar	Select Redo (see Figure 3–75)
Pull-down menu	Edit > Redo
Command: prompt	**Redo** `Enter`

EXERCISE ICONS

Step-by-step Project Exercises are identified by the special icon shown in the following table. Exercises that give you practice with types of drawings that are often found in a particular discipline are identified by the icons shown in the following table. Exercises that are cross-discipline—that is, the skills used in the exercise are applicable to most or all disciplines—do not have a special icon designation.

Type of Exercise	Icon	Type of Exercise	Icon
Project Exercises		Electrical	
Mechanical		Piping	
Architectural		Civil	

ONLINE COMPANION™

The Online Companion™ is your link to AutoCAD on the Internet. We've compiled supporting resources with links to a variety of sites. Not only can you find out about training and education, industry sites, and the online community, we also point to valuable archives compiled for AutoCAD users from various Web sites. In addition, there are pages specifically for users of Harnessing AutoCAD. These include an owner's page with updates, a swap bank where you can share your drawings with other AutoCAD students, and a page where you can send us your comments. You can find the Online Companion at:

http://www.autodeskpress.com/onlinecompanion.html

When you reach the Online Companion page, click on the title Harnessing AutoCAD.

WE WANT TO HEAR FROM YOU!

Many of the changes to the look and feel of this new edition were made by way of requests from users of our previous editions. We'd like to hear from you as well! If you have any questions or comments, please contact

The CADD Team
c/o Autodesk Press
3 Columbia Circle
P.O. Box 15015
Albany, NY 12212-5015

ABOUT THE AUTHORS

Thomas A. Stellman received a B.A. degree in architecture from Rice University and has over 20 years of experience in the architecture, engineering, and construction industry. He has taught at the college level for over ten years and has been teaching courses in AutoCAD since the introduction of version 1.4 in 1984. He conducts seminars covering both introductory and advanced AutoLISP. In addition, he develops and markets third-party software for AutoCAD. He currently is a CADD consultant, AutoLISP programmer, and project coordinator for Testengeer, Inc., in Port Lavaca, Texas.

G.V. Krishnan is director of the Applied Business and Technology Center, University of Houston—Downtown, a Premier Autodesk Training Center. He has used AutoCAD since the introduction of version 1.4 and writes about AutoCAD from the standpoint of a user, instructor, and general CADD consultant to area industries. Since 1985 he has taught courses ranging from basic to advanced levels of AutoCAD, including customizing, 3D AutoCAD, solid modeling, and AutoLISP programming.

The authors would like to thank Matthew Whiteacre of Texas A&M for contributing review questions to this text.

ACKNOWLEDGMENTS

We would like to thank and acknowledge the many professionals who reviewed the manuscript to help us publish this AutoCAD Release 14 text. A special acknowledgment is due the following instructors, who reviewed the chapters in detail:

Katherine L. Amen
University of Advancing computer Technology, Phoenix, AZ

John F. Cawley
Moraine Park Technical College, West Bend, WI

John Horstketter
Spokane Community College, Spokane, WA

Neil A. Jacobson
St. Paul Technical College, St. Paul, MN

Bruce Mack
Cleveland Community College, Kings Mountain, NC

Stephen I. Ossias
Porter and Chester Institute, Chicopee, MA

Michael Stewart
University of Arkansas at Little Rock, Little Rock, AR

Katherine A. Walker
Pennsylvania College of Technology, Williamsport, PA

A special thank you for his careful and thoughtful technical editing to:

Matthew Whiteacre
Texas A&M, TX

The authors would like to acknowledge and thank the following staff members of Delmar Publishers:

Publisher: Alar Elken
Acquisitions Editor: Sandy Clark
Developmental Editor: Margaret Gantz
Production Coordinator: Jennifer Gaines
Art & Design Coordinator: Mary Beth Vought
Editorial Assistant: Christopher Leonard

The authors also would like to acknowledge and thank the following people:

Copyediting: Elliot Simon
Composition: John Shanley, Phoenix Creative Graphics

• • • • • • • • • • • • • • • •

CHAPTER

1

GETTING STARTED

• •

INTRODUCTION

The designer/drafter will find that AutoCAD is now faster and smoother than ever to use. Release 14 has shifted the program into high gear. And new features like AutoSnap, Tracking, and Direct Distance make designing/drafting less work and more pleasurable.

Release 14 takes less time during file-handling operations. Regenerating and redrawing operations are faster. Modifying commands operate more quickly. And all of this is accomplished while requiring less computer memory.

The improvements that AutoCAD Release 14 brings include the following:

✓ A new object called a *lightweight polyline* saves memory storage and functions automatically unless it requires splines or is a 3D polyline.
✓ The hatch is no longer an anonymous "block." The new AutoCAD method of handling hatch patterns reduces the memory required in most cases.
✓ New methods of loading applications that are called by certain commands has reduced the waiting time for those applications to be usable and also makes more memory available for other operations.
✓ Paper space no longer requires regenerations during display operations. Transparent and real-time panning and zooming are now available in paper space.
✓ AutoSnap®, new in Release 14, makes it easy to cycle through multiple running Osnap modes, to identify the one you want, and to invoke it

without having to move the cursor (and your eyes) away from the working area in the drawing.

✓ Tracking, also new in Release 14, lets you move through nonselected point(s) to a selected point. You can "make tracks" to a desired point by invoking the Tracking mode and then specify one or more points relative to previous point(s) "on the way to" the actual point for which a command is prompting.

✓ Direct Distance lets you specify a point by using your pointing device to determine the desired angle and then entering the distance from the keyboard. This is especially useful in conjunction with tracking and with Ortho set to ON.

✓ Hybrid raster/vector drawings are more accessible and usable in Release 14.

✓ Release 14 has standardized the File Open and Save dialog boxes to conform to a Windows 95/NT 4.0 format.

✓ The Start Up dialog box with Drawing Wizards makes it faster and easier to get started in your drawing session.

✓ Reference files can be made demand-loaded, improving file-loading and display speeds considerably.

✓ Cursor size is configurable from 1 to 100 percent of the screen.

✓ Rendering capablities are extended to provide full photorealistic capabilities, including texture maps.

✓ You now have access to the Internet within AutoCAD.

✓ The new Preference dialog box provides an easy-to-use graphical user interface.

✓ Multiple user configurations and preferences can be set up by means of the new Profiles tab under Preferences.

AutoCAD Release 14, like the new model automobile in the showroom, doesn't look a lot different from the last model. But once "behind the wheel," you will discover a noticeable improvement in performance and comfort. The programmers have paid attention to the needs of designers/drafters by incorporating true user-friendly innovations that are, not necessarily flashy, but that save time while still being enjoyable to use.

AutoCAD COMMANDS

As much as possible, AutoCAD divides commands into related categories. For example, Draw is not a command, but a category of commands used for creating primary objects such as lines, circles, arcs, text (lettering), and other useful objects that are visible on the screen. Categories include Modify, View, and another group listed under Format for controlling the electronic drawing environment. The commands under Format are also referred to as *drawing aids,* and *utility commands* throughout the book. Learning the program can progress at a better pace if the concepts and commands are mentally grouped into their proper categories. This not only helps you find them when you need them, but also helps you grasp the fundamentals of computer-aided drafting more quickly.

STARTING AUTOCAD

Design/drafting is what AutoCAD (and this book) is all about. So how do you get into AutoCAD? Choose the Start button (Windows 95 and Windows NT 4.0 operating system), select the AutoCAD R14 program group, and then select the AutoCAD R14 program. AutoCAD displays the Start Up dialog box, similar to Figure 1–1.

Whenever you begin a new drawing, whether by means of one of the two available wizards or one of the available templates or by starting from scratch, AutoCAD creates a new drawing called *DRAWING.DWG*. You can begin working immediately and save the drawing to a file name later, using the SAVE or SAVEAS command.

Starting a New Drawing with the Wizards

If from the Start Up dialog box you select the **Use a Wizard** option, as shown in Figure 1–1, AutoCAD leads you through the basic steps of setting up a drawing, using either the Quick Setup or the Advanced Setup. The initial drawing settings correspond to those in either the template *ACAD.DWT* (English units) or the template *ACADISO.DWT* (metric units), based on the current setting of the MEASURE system variable in the registry. When MEASURE is set to 0, the drawing settings are based on the template *ACAD.DWT*; when it is set to 1, the drawing settings are based on the template *ACADISO.DWT*. Depending on which wizard you select, you can then set the values of such variables as limits, units, and angle direction.

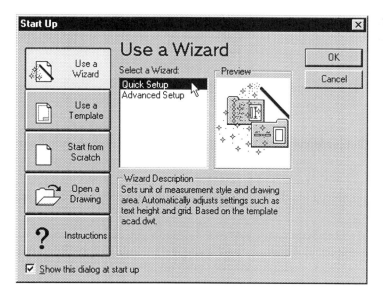

Figure 1–1 Start Up dialog box

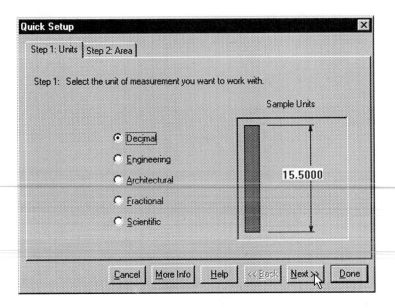

Figure 1-2 Quick Setup dialog box: Units tab

Quick Setup The Quick Setup dialog box has two tabs: the Units tab and the Area tab (Figure 1-2).

The **Units** tab (Figure 1-2) applies to how the linear units of the drawing are entered. They also determine how the linear units are reported in the status bar. When you select one of the radio buttons, an example of how linear units will be written is displayed in the Sample Units graphics box. AutoCAD allows you to choose from several formats for the display and entry of the coordinates and distances. For example, you can choose feet and fractional inches for architectural drafting. Other options include scientific notation and engineering formats. Selection of Decimal units allows you draw in inches, feet, millimeters, or whatever units you require. This enables you to draw with real-world values and eliminates the possibility of scaling errors. Once the drawing is complete, you can plot it at whatever scale you like. As mentioned earlier, drawing to real-world size is an advantage of AutoCAD that some overlook. You can plot a drawing at several different scales, thereby eliminating the need for separate drawings at different scales.

The **Area** tab (Figure 1-3) allows you to set your drawing area's width (left-to-right dimension) and length (bottom-to-top dimension), also known as the *limits*. You may set the limits to accommodate your drawing. For example, if you are drawing a printed circuit board that is 8 inches wide by 6 inches long, you can choose a decimal drawing unit and set the width to 8 and length to 6. If the drawing exceeds your original plans or the drawing limits

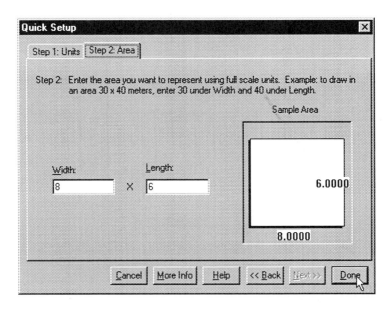

Figure 1–3 Quick Setup dialog box: Area tab

become too restrictive, you can change the drawing limits. A detailed description of how to set up limits appears later in the chapter.

Choose the Done button to close the Quick Setup dialog box. AutoCAD automatically adjusts the scale factors for dimension settings and text height. The adjusted settings are based on the full-scale size of the objects you draw. The dimension variables that are adjusted include DIMASZ, DIMCEN, DIMDLI, DIMEXE, DIMEXO, DIMGAP, and DIMTXT. Refer to Chapter 7, "Dimensioning," for a detailed discussion of dimension variable settings. In addition, AutoCAD adjusts the linetype scale, and hatch pattern scale.

Advanced Setup The Advanced Setup dialog box has seven tabs: Units, Angle, Angle Measure, Angle Direction, Area, Title Block, and Layout.

The **Units** tab and **Area** tab settings are the same as for the Quick Setup wizard.

In the **Angle** tab (Figure 1–4) you can set the type of units in which angular input and reporting is given. When you select one of the radio buttons, an example of how the angular units will be written is displayed in the Sample Angle graphics box. You can select the format used for the display and entry of angles. Degrees in decimal form are a common choice. However, you might also select gradient, radians, degrees/minutes/seconds, or surveyor's units. The Precision: text box lets you set the number of decimal places or

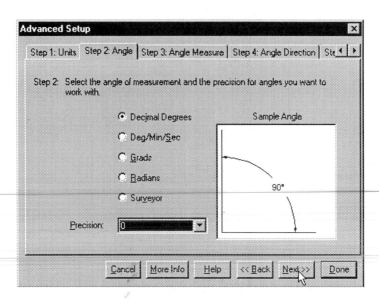

Figure 1–4 Advanced Setup dialog box: Angle tab

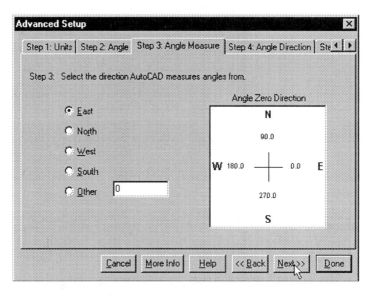

Figure 1–5 Advanced Setup dialog box: Angle Measure tab

the degrees, minutes, seconds or decimal precision of seconds to which angles are reported.

The **Angle Measure** tab (Figure 1–5) tab lets you set zero degrees for your drawing relative to the universally accepted map compass, where North is up on the drawing and East is 90 degrees clockwise from North.

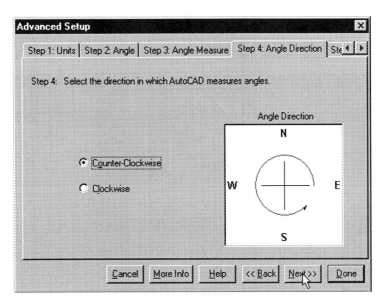

Figure 1–6 Advanced Setup dialog box: Angle Direction tab

The **Angle Direction** tab (Figure 1–6) lets you set the direction (clockwise or counterclockwise) in which angle values increase.

The **Block** tab (Figure 1–7) lets you set the description and the file name of a predrawn title block for use in your drawing. When you select one of the radio buttons, an example of the selected title block is displayed in the Sample Title Block graphics box.

The **Layout** tab (Figure 1–8) lets you select whether or not to use advanced paper space layout capabilities. Instructions on the use of paper space that affect decisions as to how to start the drawing when the paper space option is selected are given in Chapter 12.

Choose the Done button to close the Advanced Setup dialog box. As with the Quick Setup wizard, AutoCAD automatically adjusts the scale factors for dimension settings and text height. The adjusted settings are based on the full-scale size of the objects you draw.

> **NOTE:** The Wizards let you set up the drawing parameters that most commonly vary from one drawing to the next. It is convenient to have those variables accessible in a single place, and lessens the chance of forgetting one. You should note, however, that the Wizards' Area tab does not permit you to use a point other than 0,0 as a lower left corner of the limits.

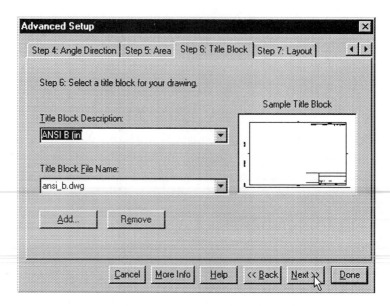

Figure 1–7 Advanced Setup dialog box: Title Block tab

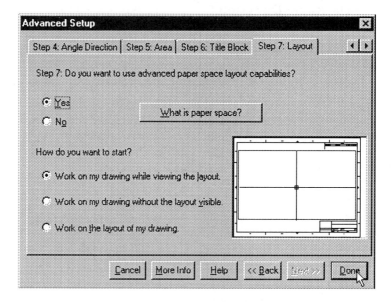

Figure 1–8 Advanced Setup dialog box: Layout tab

Any settings you changed in the wizard can be changed again later by invoking the UNITS and LIMITS commands. Detailed discussions of the UNITS and LIMITS commands are provided later in the chapter.

Starting a New Drawing with a Template

If from the Start Up dialog box you select the **Use a Template** option, as shown in Figure 1–9, AutoCAD lists the available templates. An AutoCAD template is a drawing file with a file extension of .*DWT* instead of .*DWG*.

The **Preview** section of the Use a Template dialog box lets you see a small view of the template that is highlighted in the **Select a Template:** list box. If a description has been saved with the selected template, it will be displayed in the **Template Description** section. To begin your drawing in the identical setup as the selected template, either choose OK or double-click the highlighted template in the Select a Template: list box. You can also choose the More files... option from the text box to invoke the Select Template dialog box to select a template file from a different folder.

When you use the appropriate template to create a new drawing, AutoCAD copies all the information from the template drawing to the new drawing. The most common use of drawing templates is to enable you to start with a border and title block already drawn, layers and styles already created, and the system variables set to values that suit the drawing you intend to make. For example, a template for a house floor plan might have the limits set for drawing the floor plan to draw at a full scale and to plot at a scale of 1/4" = 1'-0" on a 24"×18" sheet, the units set to architectural, and the border and title block drawn to full scale. Dimension variables might be saved in the desired style, and separate layers might be set for drawing walls, doors, windows, cabinetry, plumbing, dimensions, text, and any other object you wish to have kept on its own layer. You can even use an existing .*DWG* drawing file as a template to create a new drawing.

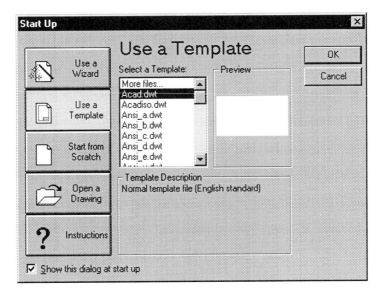

Figure 1–9 Start Up dialog box: Use a Template option

Starting a New Drawing from Scratch

If from the Start Up dialog box you select the **Start from Scratch** option, as shown in Figure 1–10, AutoCAD provides you two suboptions: English and Metric. The **English** suboption sets the units to feet and inches settings; the **Metric** suboption sets the units to metric settings. By default the limits are set to 0,0 for the lower left corner and 12,9 for the upper right corner. If necessary, you can change the settings at the beginning of the drawing session or at any time during the drawing session.

Opening an Existing Drawing from the Start Up Dialog Box

If from the Start Up dialog box you select the **Open a Drawing** option, as shown in Figure 1–11, AutoCAD lists the drawing files available from the current folder. If you need to open a drawing from a different folder, then select More files... in the Select a File: list box. AutoCAD displays a Select File dialog box. Select the appropriate folder and drawing to open.

After making any necessary changes, choose the OK button. AutoCAD closes the Start Up dialog box and displays the AutoCAD screen.

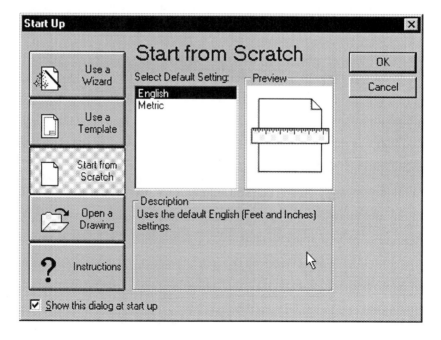

Figure 1–10 Start Up dialog box: Start from Scratch option

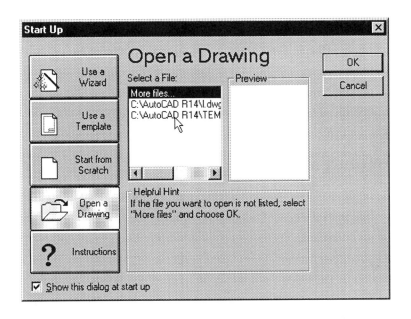

Figure 1–11 Start Up dialog box: Open a Drawing option

AutoCAD SCREEN

The AutoCAD screen (Figure 1–12) consists of the following elements: graphics window, status bar, title bar, toolbars, pull-down menus, and command window.

Graphics Window

The graphics window is where AutoCAD places the objects you create. In this window, AutoCAD displays the cursor, indicating your current working point. As you move your pointing device (usually a mouse or puck) around on a digitizing tablet, mouse pad, or other suitable surface, the cursor mimics your movements on the screen. When AutoCAD prompts you to select a point, the cursor is in the form of crosshairs. It changes to a small pick box when you are required to select an object on the screen. AutoCAD uses combinations of crosshairs, boxes, dashed rectangles, and arrows in various situations so you can quickly see what type of selection or pick mode to use.

Status Bar

The status bar at the bottom of the screen displays the cursor's coordinates and important information on the status of various modes.

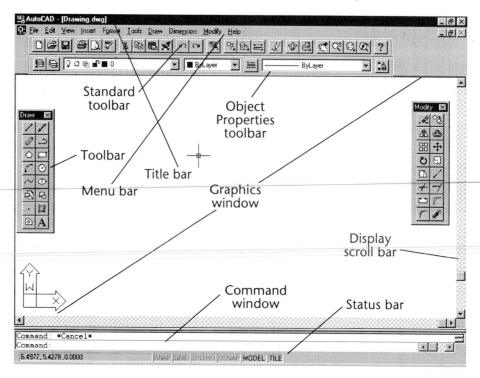

Figure 1–12 The AutoCAD screen

Title Bar

The title bar displays the current drawing name for the AutoCAD application window.

Toolbars

The toolbars contain tools, represented by icons, from which you can invoke commands. Click a toolbar button to invoke a command, and then select options from a dialog box or respond to the prompts on the command line. If you position your pointer over a toolbar button and wait a moment, the name of the tool is displayed, as shown in Figure 1–13. This is called the ToolTip. In addition to the ToolTip, AutoCAD displays on the status bar a very brief explanation of the function of the command.

Figure 1–13 Toolbar with a ToolTip displayed

Some of the toolbar buttons have a small triangular symbol in the lower right corner of the button indicating that there are *flyout* buttons underneath that contain subcommands. Figure 1–14 shows the Zoom flyout located in the Standard Toolbar. When you pick a flyout option, it remains on top to become the default option.

You can display multiple toolbars on screen at once, change their contents, resize them, and dock or float them. A *docked* toolbar attaches to any edge of the graphics window. A *floating* toolbar can lie anywhere on the screen and can be resized.

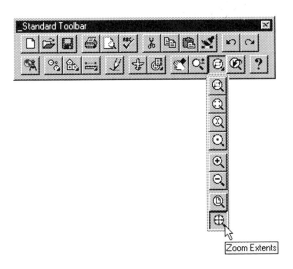

Figure 1–14 Display of the Zoom flyout located in the Standard Toolbar

Docking and Undocking a Toolbar To *dock* a toolbar, position the cursor on the caption, and press the pick button on the pointing device. Drag the toolbar to a dock location to the top, bottom, or either side of the graphics window. When the outline of the toolbar appears in the docking area, release the pick button. To *undock* a toolbar, position the cursor anywhere on the border of the toolbar and drag and drop it outside the docking regions. To place a toolbar in a docking region without docking it, hold down ⌐Ctrl⌐ as you drag. By default, the Standard toolbar and the Object Properties toolbar are docked at the top of the graphics window (see Figure 1–12). Figure 1–15 shows the Standard toolbar and the Object Properties toolbar docked at the top of the graphics window, the Draw toolbar docked on the left side of the graphics window, and the Modify toolbar docked on the right side of the graphics window.

Resizing a Floating Toolbar If necessary, you can resize a floating toolbar. To resize a floating toolbar, position the cursor anywhere on the border of the toolbar, and drag it in the direction you want to resize. Figure 1–16 shows different combinations of resizing of the Draw toolbar.

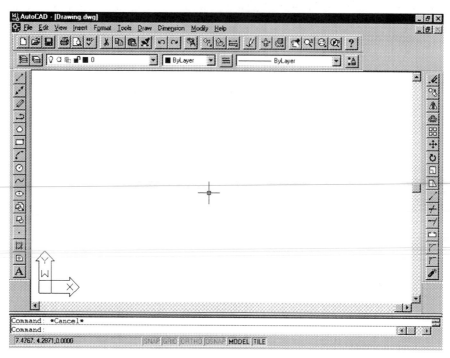

Figure 1–15 Docking of toolbars in the graphics window

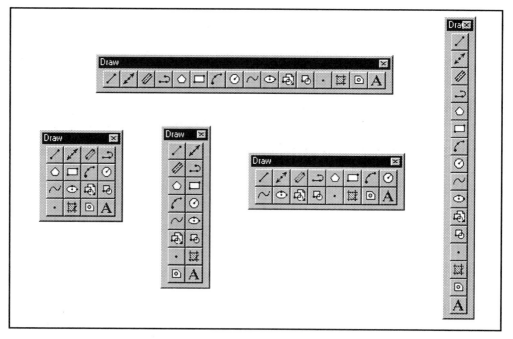

Figure 1–16 Draw toolbar in different resizing positions

Closing a Toolbar To close a toolbar, position the cursor on the X located in the upper right corner of the toolbar, as shown in Figure 1–17, and press the pick button on your pointing device. The toolbar will disappear from the graphics window.

Figure 1–17 Positioning the cursor to close a toolbar

Opening a Toolbar AutoCAD Release 14 comes with 18 toolbars in the ACAD group, three toolbars in the AC_BONUS group, and one toolbar in the INET group. To open any of the available toolbars, invoke the TOOLBAR command from:

Pull-down menu	View > Toolbars...
Command: prompt	**toolbar** Enter

AutoCAD displays the Toolbars dialog box, similar to Figure 1–18.

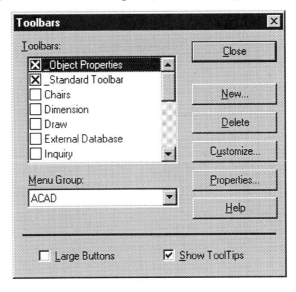

Figure 1–18 Toolbars dialog box

To open a toolbar, first select the name of the toolbar from the **Toolbars:** list box and then set the check box to ON. AutoCAD displays the selected toolbar. The **Show ToolTips** check box controls whether or not to display the ToolTips. The **Large**

Buttons check box controls the size (large vs. regular) at which buttons are displayed. The default display size is 16 × 15 pixels. Setting the Large Buttons check box to ON displays the icons at 24 × 22 pixels.

Figure 1–19 shows the command icons available in the Standard Toolbar; Figure 1–20 shows the commands available in the Object Properties toolbar. Appendix C lists all the toolbars available in AutoCAD.

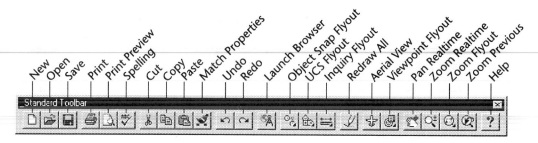

Figure 1–19 Standard Toolbar

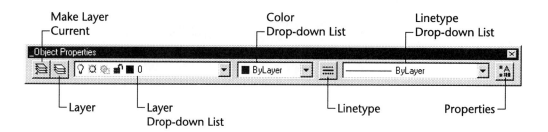

Figure 1–20 Object Properties toolbar

Pull-down Menus

The pull-down menus are available from the menu bar at the top of the screen. To select any of the available commands, move the crosshairs cursor into the menu bar area and press the pick button on your pointing device, which pops that menu bar onto the screen (see Figure 1–21). Selecting from the list is a simple matter of moving the cursor until the desired item is highlighted and then pressing the designated pick button on the pointing device. If a menu item has an arrow to the right, it has a cascading submenu. To display the submenu, move the pointer over the arrow and press the pick button. Menu items that include ellipses (...) display dialog boxes. To select one of these, just pick that menu item.

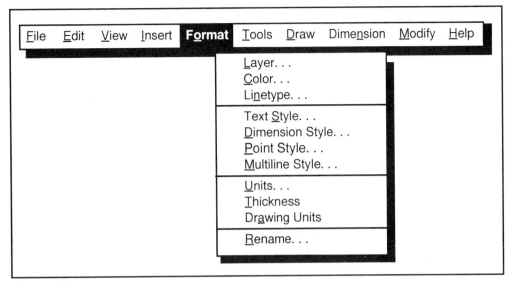

Figure 1–21 Example of a pull-down menu

Command Window

The command window is a window in which you enter commands and in which AutoCAD displays prompts and messages. The command window can be a floating window with a caption and frame. You can move the floating command window anywhere on the screen and resize its width and height with the pointing size.

There are two components to the command window: the single command line where AutoCAD prompts for input and you see your input echoed back, as shown in Figure 1–22, and the command history area, which shows what has transpired in the current drawing session. One display of the single Command Line remains at the bottom of the screen.

The command history area can be enlarged like other windows by picking the top edge and dragging it to a new size. You can also scroll inside the enlarged area to see previous command activity by using the scroll bars (see Figure 1–23).

By default, the F2 key causes the command history text box to switch between being displayed and being hidden. When the text box is displayed, you can scroll through the command history.

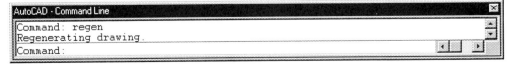

Figure 1–22 Single Command Line window

Figure 1–23 Command history

When you see "Command:" displayed in the Command Window, it signals that AutoCAD is ready to accept a command. After you enter a command name or select a command from one of the menus or toolbars, the prompt area continues to inform you of the type of response(s) that you must furnish, until the command is either completed or terminated. For example, when you pick the LINE command, the prompt displays "From point:"; after selecting a starting point by appropriate means, you will see "To point:" asking for the endpoint of the line.

Each command has its own series of prompts. The prompts that appear when a particular command is used in one situation may differ from the prompts or sequence of prompts when invoked in another situation. You will become familiar with the prompts as you learn to use each command.

When you type the command name or give any other response by typing from the keyboard, make sure to press ⏎ or the Spacebar. The ⏎ sends the input to the program for processing. For example, after you type LINE, you must press ⏎ or the Spacebar in order for AutoCAD to start the part of the program that lets you draw lines. If you type in **LIN** and press ⏎ or the Spacebar, you will get an error message, unless someone has customized the program and created a command alias or command named "LIN." Likewise, typing in **LINEZ** and pressing ⏎ or the Spacebar is not a standard AutoCAD command.

The Spacebar has the same function as ⏎ except when you are typing in strings of words, letters, or numbers in response to the TEXT command.

To repeat the previous command, you can press ⏎ or the Spacebar at the "Command:" prompt. A few commands when repeated in this manner, skip some of their normal prompts and assume default settings.

Terminating a Command There are three ways to terminate a command:

■ Complete the command sequence and return to the "Command:" prompt.
■ Use the ⎋ key to terminate the command before it is completed.
■ Invoke another command from one of the menus, which automatically cancels any command in progress.

INPUT METHODS

There are several ways to input an AutoCAD command: from the keyboard, toolbars, pull-down menus, the side screen menu, dialog boxes, the cursor menu, or the digitizing tablet.

Keyboard

To enter a command from the keyboard, simply type the command name at the "Command:" prompt and then press ⏎ or the Spacebar (⏎ and the Spacebar are interchangeable except when entering a space in a text string).

If at the "Command:" prompt you want to repeat a command you have just used, press ⏎, the Spacebar, or the return button on your pointing device. You can also repeat a command by using the up-arrow and down-arrow keys to display the commands you previously typed from the keyboard. Use the up-arrow key to display the previous line in the command history; use the down-arrow key to display the next line in the command history. Depending on the buffer size, AutoCAD stores all the information you typed from the keyboard in the current session.

AutoCAD also allows you to use certain commands transparently, which means they can be entered on the command line while you are using another command. Transparent commands frequently are commands that change drawing settings or drawing tools, such as GRID, SNAP, and ZOOM. To invoke a command transparently, enter an apostrophe (') before the command name while you are using another command. After you complete the transparent command, the original command resumes.

Toolbars

The toolbars contain tools that represent commands. Click a toolbar button to invoke the command, then select options from a dialog box or follow the prompts on the command line.

Pull-down Menus

The pull-down menus are available from the menu bar at the top of the screen. You can invoke almost all of the available commands from the pull-down menus. You can choose menu options in one of the following ways:

■ First click the menu name to display a list of available commands, and then click the appropriate command.
■ Hold down the Alt and then enter the underlined letter in the menu name. For example, to invoke the LINE command, first hold down the Alt while pressing **D** (that is, Alt + D) to open the Draw menu, and then press **L**.

The default menu file is *ACAD.MNU*. You can load a different menu file by invoking the MENU command.

Side Screen Menu

The side screen menu provides another, traditional way to enter AutoCAD commands. By default, the side screen menu is turned off in AutoCAD Release 14. While this book does not refer to the side screen menu, traditional DOS users of AutoCAD may be more comfortable using it. To display the side screen menu, type **preferences** at the "Command:" prompt and press Enter or the Spacebar. AutoCAD displays the Preferences dialog box, as shown in Figure 1–24.

Select the Display tab, and set the check box for **Display AutoCAD screen menu in drawing window** to ON. Choose **OK** to close the dialog box and save the settings. AutoCAD displays the side screen menu, as shown in Figure 1–25.

Moving the pointing device to the right will cause the cursor to move into the screen menu area. Moving the cursor up and down in the menu area will cause selectable items to be highlighted. When the desired item is highlighted, you can choose that item by pressing the designated pick button on the pointing device. If the item is a command, either it will be put into action or the menu area will be changed to a list of actions that are options of that command. The screen menu is made up of menus and submenus. At the top of every screen menu is the word *AutoCAD*. When selected, it will return you to what is called the *root menu*. The root menu is the menu that is displayed when you first enter AutoCAD. It lists the primary classifications of commands or functions available.

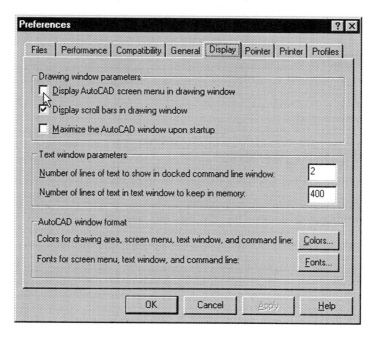

Figure 1–24 Preferences dialog box

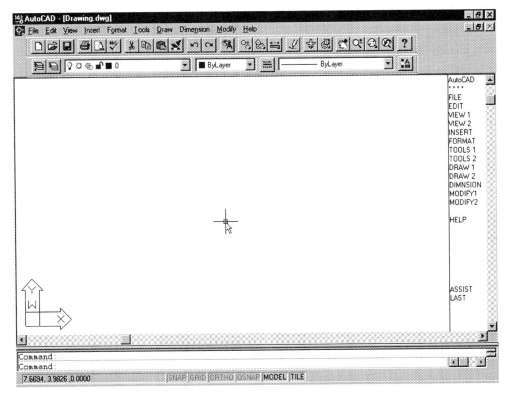

Figure 1-25 AutoCAD screen window with side screen menu

Dialog Boxes

Several commands, when invoked, cause a dialog box to appear. These dialog boxes display the lists and descriptions of options, long rectangles for receiving your input data, and, in general, are more convenient and more user-friendly method of communicating with the AutoCAD program for that particular command.

AutoCAD Release 14 has brought a notable increase in the number of commands and responses that could be input through dialog boxes. Release 14 has added more and refined the existing ones. The commands that include ellipses (...), such as PLOT... and HATCH... display dialog boxes. In addition, you can type at the "Command:" prompt the commands that begin with *DD* (for "dynamic dialog") to cause a dialog box to appear when invoked. Figure 1-26 shows the dialog box that appears when you invoke the DDINSERT command. Setting the FILEDIA system variable to 0 permits most commands to be operated through keyboard/prompt interaction instead of dialog boxes. For a detailed discussion of different dialog box components, see the section on "Using Dialog Boxes."

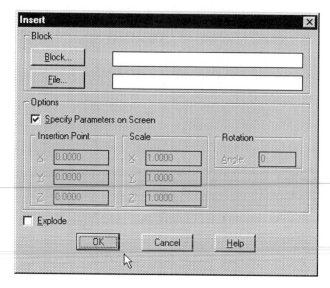

Figure 1–26 Dialog box invoked from the DDINSERT command

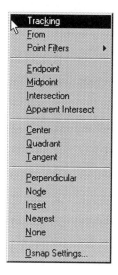

Figure 1–27 Cursor menu

Cursor Menu

The AutoCAD cursor menu (see Figure 1–27) appears at the location of the cursor by pressing the middle button on a three-or-more-button mouse. On a two-button mouse you can invoke this feature by pressing Shift + (the return button). On a two-button mouse, the return button is usually the right button. The menu includes the handy Object Snap mode options along with the *X,Y,Z*/filters. The reason that the Object Snap modes and tracking are in such ready access will become evident when you learn the significance of these functions.

Digitizing Tablet

The most common input device, after the mouse, is the digitizing tablet. It combines the screen cursor control of a mouse with its own printed menu areas for selecting items. One powerful feature of the tablet (not related to entering commands) is that it allows you to lay a map or other picture on the tablet and trace over it with the puck (the specific pointing device for a digitizing tablet), thereby transferring the objects to the AutoCAD drawing.

USING DIALOG BOXES

When a dialog box appears, the crosshairs cursor changes to an arrow, pointing up and to the left. You can use the arrow keys on your keyboard to make selections in the dialog box, but it is much easier to use your pointing device. Another way to make selections in a dialog box is to use keyboard equivalents. You can move the cursor from one field to another by pressing the ⌧Tab key when the cursor is not in the edit box.

Edit Box

An edit box is an area that accepts one line of text entry. It is normally used to specify a name, such as a layer name or even a file name, including the drive and/or directory path. Edit boxes often function as an alternate to selecting from a list of names when the desired name is not in the list box. Once the correct text is keyed in, enter it by pressing ⌧Enter.

Moving the pointer into the edit box causes the text cursor to appear in a manner similar to the cursor in a word processor. The text cursor, in combination with special editing keys, can be used to facilitate changes to the text. You can see both the text cursor and the pointer at the same time, making it possible to click the pointer at a character in the edit box and relocate the text cursor to that character.

Right and Left Arrows < > These move the cursor right or left (respectively) across text without having any effect on the text.

Backspace This deletes the character to the left of the cursor and moves the cursor to the space previously occupied by the deleted character.

⌧Delete **Key** This deletes the character at the location of the cursor, causing any text to the right to move one space to the left.

Buttons

Actions are immediately initiated when you click on or otherwise choose one of the dialog buttons.

Default Buttons If a button (like the **OK** button in most cases) is surrounded by a heavy line, then it is the default button and pressing ⏎ is the same as clicking that button.

Buttons with Ellipses (...) Buttons with ellipses display a second dialog box, called a subdialog or child dialog box.

> *NOTE:* When a subdialog box appears, you must respond to the options in the subdialog box before the underlying dialog box can continue.

Screen Action Buttons Buttons that are followed by an arrow (<) require a graphic response, such as selecting an object on the screen or picking/specifying coordinates.

Disabled Buttons Buttons with action that is not currently acceptable will be disabled. They appear grayed out.

Character Equivalents A button with a label that has an underlined character can be activated by pressing on the keyboard the combination of ⌥ Alt + that character.

Radio Buttons Radio buttons are options when only one of two or more selections can be active at a time (see Figure 1–28). Selecting one radio button will deactivate any other in the group, like selecting a station button on the radio.

Check Boxes

A check box acts as a toggle. When clicked or otherwise selected, the check box switches the named setting between ON and OFF, as shown in Figure 1–29. A check in the check box means the option is set to ON; no check (an empty box) means the option is set to OFF.

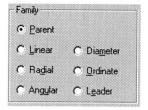

Figure 1–28 Radio buttons

Figure 1–29 Check boxes

List Boxes and Scroll Bars

List boxes make it easy to view, select, and enter a name from a list of existing items, such as file names and fonts. Move the pointer to highlight the desired selection. When you click on the item, it appears in the edit box. You accept this item by clicking or otherwise selecting OK or by double-clicking on the item. For example, Figure 1–30 shows the list box from the Standard File dialog box.

List boxes are accompanied by scroll bars to facilitate moving long lists left to right and right to left in the list box.

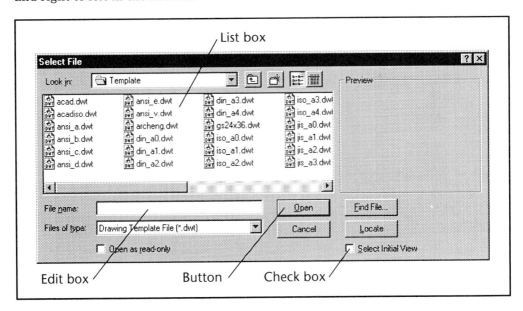

Figure 1–30 List box from the Standard File dialog box

Some boxes that have multiple options available are really just unexpanded list boxes. They will have a down arrow on the right side. Selecting the down arrow displays the expanded list.

> **NOTE:** Many dialog boxes have a **Help...** button. If you are not sure how to use the feature in the dialog box, choose the **Help...** button for a brief explanation of the dialog box.

GETTING HELP

When you are in the graphics window, AutoCAD provides a context-sensitive help facility to list its commands and what they do. The HELP command provides online assistance within AutoCAD. When an invalid command is entered, AutoCAD prints a message to remind you of the availability of the help facility.

Whenever you need AutoCAD help, invoke the HELP command from:

Standard Toolbar	Select the Help command (see Figure 1–31)
Pull-down menu	Help > AutoCAD Help Topics
Command: prompt	? or **HELP** Enter

Figure 1–31 Invoking the Help command from the Standard Toolbar

AutoCAD displays the Help Topics: AutoCAD Help dialog box, similar to Figure 1–32.

The HELP command can be invoked while you are in the middle of another command. This is referred to as a *transparent command*. To invoke a command transparently (if it is one of those that can be used that way), simply prefix the command name with an apostrophe. For example, to use HELP transparently, type **'help** or **'?** in response to any prompt that is not asking for a text string. AutoCAD displays help for the current command. Often the help is general in nature, but sometimes it is specific to the command's current prompt.

As an alternative, press F1 to bring up help. When you ask for help in the middle of a command, AutoCAD displays context-sensitive help. For example, if you press F1 in the middle of the LINE command, AutoCAD automatically selects the help information that describes how to use the LINE command.

Help flips to an independent window, so you probably will need to press the switch-task key combination Alt + Tab to switch back to the AutoCAD graphics window.

Figure 1–32 Help Topics: AutoCAD Help dialog box

The **Contents** tab of the Help Topics: AutoCAD Help dialog box (Figure 1–32) has a list of subjects prefixed by a closed-book icon. You may scroll through the list, pressing ⏎ when the item on which you need help is highlighted, or you may double-click that item in the text box. This causes the subject's icon to become an open book, and below the selected subject, a sublist will be displayed, indented, containing items that may be prefixed by a closed book or a ? button, similar to Figure 1–33. Items with closed-book icons lead to sublists, and ? buttons display a window containing the help available on the highlighted item.

The **Index** tab provides help on a particular item. First begin typing the desired topic in the top edit box, as shown in Figure 1–34. These items might be a command name, a concept, such as *color*, or maybe just a symbol, such as an asterisk or a backslash. The initial character(s) typed in will highlight the topic in the lower text box whose initial characters match the string of characters. You may scroll through the list, choosing the Display button when the item on which you need help is highlighted, or you may double-click that item in the text box. AutoCAD then displays a window containing the help available on the highlighted item.

The **Find** tab of the Help Topics: AutoCAD Help dialog box creates a list of indexed words from the *User's Guide* that can be searched. You may scroll through the list, pressing ⏎ when the word on which you need help is highlighted, or you may

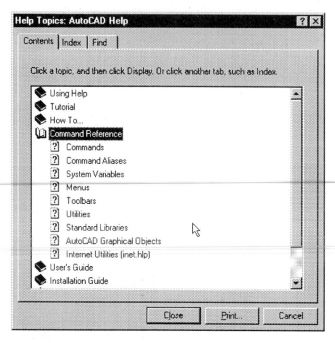

Figure 1–33 Contents tab of the Help Topics: AutoCAD Help dialog box

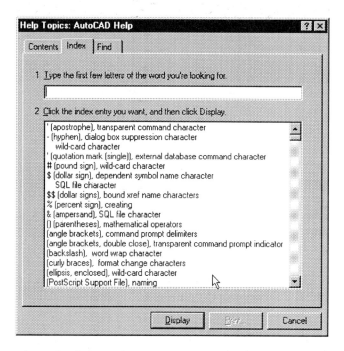

Figure 1–34 Index tab of the Help Topics: AutoCAD Help dialog box

Figure 1–35 Find tab of the Help Topics: AutoCAD Help dialog box

double-click that item in the text box as shown in Figure 1–35. A list of topics about the highlighted word is then displayed in the text box. You may scroll through this sublist, pressing Enter when the topic on which you need help is highlighted, or you may double-click that item in the text box.

You can also view an interactive presentation of a "Quick Tour" of AutoCAD R14 functionality by selecting Quick Tour... from the pull-down menu Help. A guided tour of two topics is provided: *Introducing AutoCAD 14* and *Drawing with AutoCAD*. Each topic has menus from which to select the part of AutoCAD through which you wish to be guided.

In addition, you can view an interactive presentation of "What's New" in AutoCAD Release 14 by selecting What's New from the pull-down menu Help. A menu of 11 topics is provided. Each topic has menus from which to select items covering the main "What's New" topic. When a menu item is selected, a view of the AutoCAD screen is displayed. You are then shown a video teaching you how to perform the task you wish to learn. The demonstration covers placing the cursor, pressing the buttons, and what happens on the screen as a result. You will see events such as pull-down menus being displayed, commands being invoked, and objects being created and modified in the drawing.

NOTE: The Quick Tour and the What's New options are accessible from each other. While you are in one, there is a button you can select to switch to the other.

BEGINNING A NEW DRAWING WITH THE NEW COMMAND

The NEW command allows you to begin a new drawing. If you are working on a drawing that is not saved and you invoke the NEW command, AutoCAD first prompts you to save the current drawing before it allows you to begin a new drawing.

Invoke the NEW command from:

Standard Toolbar	Select the New command (see Figure 1–36)
Pull-down menu	File > New...
Command: prompt	new Enter

Figure 1–36 Invoking the New command from the Standard Toolbar

AutoCAD displays the Create New Drawing dialog box, similar to Figure 1–37.

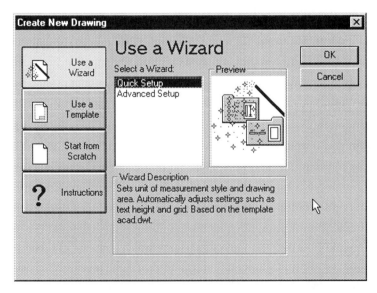

Figure 1–37 Create New Drawing dialog box

The options provided in the Create New Drawing dialog box are the same as in the Start Up dialog box explained earlier is this chapter. The only option missing in the Create New Drawing dialog box is the Open a Drawing option. For a detailed description of all of the options available in the Create New Drawing dialog box, refer to the "Starting AutoCAD" section earlier in this chapter.

OPENING AN EXISTING DRAWING WITH THE OPEN COMMAND

The OPEN command allows you to open an existing drawing. If you are working on a drawing that is not saved and you invoke the OPEN command, AutoCAD first prompts you to save the current drawing before it allows you to open another drawing.

Invoke the OPEN command from:

Standard Toolbar	Select the OPEN command (see Figure 1–38)
Pull-down menu	File > Open
Command: prompt	**open** Enter

Figure 1–38 Invoking the Open command from the Standard Toolbar

AutoCAD displays the Select File dialog box, similar to Figure 1–39. The dialog box is almost identical to the Standard File dialog box, except that it includes check boxes for selecting an initial view and for setting read-only mode. In addition, when you click on the file name, AutoCAD displays a bitmap image in the Preview box.

The Select Initial View list box permits you to specify a view name in the named drawing to be the startup view. If there are named views in the drawing, an M or P beside their name will tell if the view is model or paper space, respectively.

You may open a drawing in the read-only mode, which permits you to view the drawing but not save it with its current name. However, you can edit and save it under a different name by invoking the SAVEAS command.

Choosing the **Find File...** button causes the Browse/Search dialog box to be displayed. Various drives and directories are searched using search criteria. The Browse/Search dialog box combines the usual Windows file/path search of files by name (and normally with the .*DWG* extension) with small pictures of the drawings on the specified path to enable you to distinguish visually and select the drawing you wish to open.

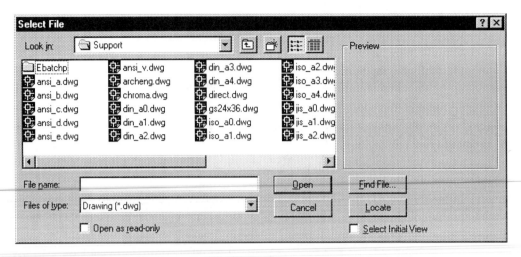

Figure 1–39 Select File dialog box

Browse The Browse tab, as shown in Figure 1–40, displays bitmap images of the drawings on the specified path.

> **File Name:** permits you to read the names of the available drawings and change the currently selected drawing.
>
> **Directories:** permits you to read the names of the available directories and change the currently selected directory.
>
> **Drives:** permits you to read the names of the available drives and change the currently selected drive.
>
> **List Files of Type:** permits you to read the available file types and change the current file type.
>
> **Size:** permits you to change the size of the bitmap images.

Select the appropriate drawing file to open from the Browse section.

Search The Search tab, as shown in Figure 1–41, permits you to search a specific path or paths and then displays bitmap images of the drawings that meet the search criteria and are on the specified path(s). It also displays each drawing's name and path.

> **Files**: permits you to read a list of files that meet the search criteria.
>
> **Search Pattern:** permits you to specify a criterion by which to search for files with the specified file type.
>
> **File Types:** permits you to specify the file type.

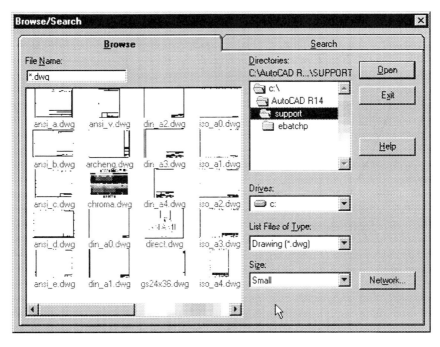

Figure 1–40 Browse tab of the Browse/Search dialog box

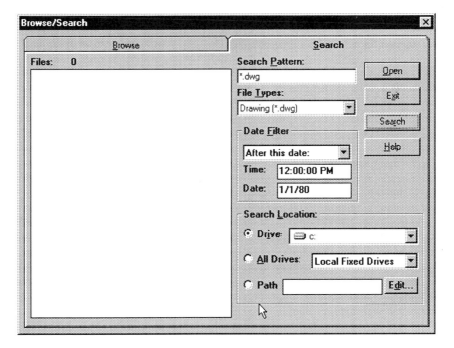

Figure 1–41 Search tab of the Browse/Search dialog box

Date Filter: permits you to tell AutoCAD whether to search forward or backward from a specified date and time.

The **Time:** edit field permits you to specify the time from which to search forward or backward.

The **Date:** edit field permits you to specify the date from which to search forward or backward.

Search Location: permits you to specify the drive/path on which AutoCAD will search.

All Drives: causes AutoCAD to search all available drives.

Path: permits you to specify drive/directory paths for searching.

Edit...: permits you to edit the path.

Select the appropriate drawing file to open from the Search section.

> **NOTE:** You can open and edit an AutoCAD Release 12 or Release 13 drawing. If necessary, you can save the drawing in AutoCAD Release 12 or Release 13 format by using the SAVEAS command.

CHANGING UNITS

DDUNITS and UNITS are the two commands you can invoke to change the linear and angular units in AutoCAD. The DDUNITS command allows you to set units through the AutoCAD **Units Control** dialog box. With this format, you use the cursor to select the choices listed in the dialog box. The UNITS command allows you to set units at the "Command:" prompt level.

The DDUNITS and UNITS commands let you set the display format measurement and precision of your drawing units. You can change them as often as you wish while drawing. The DDUNITS and UNITS commands allow you to change any one or all of the following:

Unit display format	Angle display precision
Unit display precision	Angle base
Angle display format	Angle direction

Invoke the DDUNITS command from:

Pull-down menu	Format > Units...
Command: prompt	**ddunits** [Enter]

AutoCAD displays the Units Control dialog box, similar to Figure 1–42.

Units The Units area of the **Units Control** dialog box allows you to change the units of linear measurement. Select one of the five radio buttons for the report format you prefer. For the selected report format, choose the precision from the popup list.

The engineering and architectural report formats produce feet-and-inches displays. These formats assume each drawing unit represents 1 inch. The other formats (scientific, decimal, and fractional) make no such assumptions, and they can represent whatever real-world units you like.

Drawing a 150-ft-long object might, however, differ depending on the units chosen. For example, if you use decimal units and decide that 1 unit = 1 foot, then the 150-ft-long object will be 150 units long. If you decide that 1 unit = 1 inch, then the 150-ft-long object will be drawn $150 \times 12 = 1800$ units long. In architectural and engineering units modes, the unit automatically equals 1 inch. You may then give the length of the 150-ft-long object as 150' or 1800" or simply 1800.

Angles The Angles area of the Units Control dialog box allows you to set the drawing's angle measurement. Select one of the five radio buttons for the angle format you prefer. For the selected format, choose the precision from the popup list.

Direction To control the direction of angles, pick the **Direction...** button; a Direction Control subdialog box appears, similar to the one in Figure 1–43.

AutoCAD, by its default setting, assumes that 0 degrees is to the right (East, or 3 o'clock) (see Figure 1–44), and that angles increase in the counterclockwise direction.

You can change measuring angles to start with any direction by selecting one of the five radio buttons.

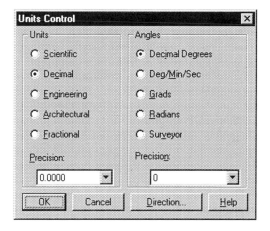

Figure 1–42 Units Control dialog box

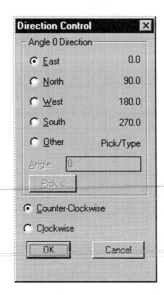

Figure 1-43 Direction Control subdialog box

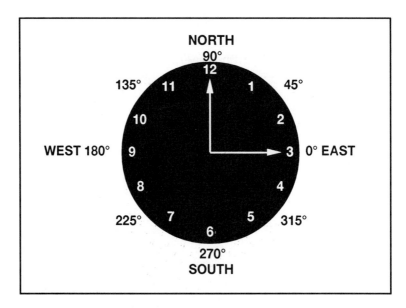

Figure 1-44 Default angle setting direction

You can also show AutoCAD the direction you want for angle 0 by specifying two points. This can be done by selecting the radio button for **Other** and choosing the **pick <** button. AutoCAD prompts you for two points and sets the direction for angle 0.

Finally, select the direction in which the angles are measured, clockwise or counter-clockwise. This can be done by selecting one of the two radio buttons for the direction in which angles are measured. If you accept the default, the angles are measured in the counterclockwise direction (see Figure 1–45).

Once you are satisfied with all of the settings in the **Units Control** dialog box, choose the **OK** button to set the appropriate settings to the current working drawing and close the dialog box.

Invoke the UNITS command from:

Command: prompt	**units** Enter

When you invoke the UNITS command, the screen flips to text mode (unless you are operating at a dual-monitor station). Remember, you flip (toggle) back and forth between the text screen and graphics screen by pressing F2. The text screen displays the following:

Report formats: **(Examples)**
1. Scientific   1.55E+01
2. Decimal   15.50
3. Engineering   1'-3.50"
4. Architectural   1'-3 1/2"
5. Fractional   15 1/2

Enter choice, 1 to 5 <default>:

Choose the report format you prefer. To illustrate the various report formats, the menu shows a distance of 15.5 drawing units displayed in each format. The current format has its corresponding number displayed where <default> is shown.

Once you have selected the report format, AutoCAD asks for the precision. If you select 1, 2, or 3, the following prompt appears:

Number of digits to right of decimal point (0 to 8) <default>:

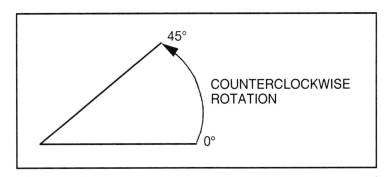

Figure 1–45 The default, counterclockwise-angle direction of angle measurement

For 4 or 5, the following prompt is displayed:

Denominator of smallest fraction to display
(1, 2, 4, 8, 16, 32, or 64) <default>:

After you have selected the report format and precision, AutoCAD prompts for an angle format:

Systems of angle measure:	(Examples)
1. Decimal degrees	45.0000
2. Degrees/minutes/seconds	45d0'0"
3. Grads	50.0000g
4. Radians	0.7854r
5. Surveyor's units	N 45d0'0" E

Enter choice, 1 to 5 <default>:

The menu illustrates the various formats by showing how an angle of 45 degrees would be displayed in each format.

Angle Display Precision After you specify the angle format, AutoCAD prompts you for the precision with which angles should be displayed.

Number of fractional places for display of angles (0 to 8) <default>:

You can specify a precision of up to eight places. If you are working with degrees/minutes/seconds, the number you enter determines the accuracy of the minutes and seconds. If you specify 0, for example, only degrees are displayed; if you specify 1 or 2, minutes also are displayed; 3 or 4 displays degrees, minutes, and seconds; and 5 to 8 will display additional fractional seconds (one to four decimal places).

Next, AutoCAD prompts for the direction for angle 0. The following prompt appears:

Direction for angle 0:

East	3 o'clock	=	0
North	12 o'clock	=	90
West	9 o'clock	=	180
South	6 o'clock	=	270

Enter direction for angle 0 <current>:

You can change measuring angles starting in any direction by supplying the starting direction to this prompt. Note that you always respond to this prompt with an angle specified in the default mode. For example, if you want to make North (12 o'clock) 0 degrees, then at the prompt type **90** and press Enter. You can also show AutoCAD the direction you want for angle 0 by specifying two points.

The final prompt controls the direction in which the angles are measured, clockwise or counterclockwise:

Do you want angles measured clockwise? <n>:

If you answer with **y** or **yes**, AutoCAD measures angles in the clockwise direction; if you answer **n** or **no**, AutoCAD measures angles in the counterclockwise direction.

NOTE: When AutoCAD prompts for a distance, displacement, spacing, or coordinates, you can always reply with numbers in integer, decimal, scientific, or fractional format. If engineering or architectural report format is in effect, you can also input feet, inches, or a combination of feet and inches. However, feet-and-inches input format differs slightly from the report format because it cannot contain a blank. For example, a distance of 75.5 inches can be entered in the feet/inches/fractions format as 6'3-1/2". Note the absence of spaces and the hyphen in the unconventional location between the inches and the fraction. Normally, it will be displayed in the status area as 6'-3 1/2.

If you wish, you can use the SETVAR command to set the UNITMODE system variable to 1 (default UNITMODE setting is 0) to display feet-and-inches output in the accepted format. For example, if you set UNITMODE to 1, AutoCAD displays the fractional value of 45 1/4 as you enter it: 45-1/4. The feet input should be followed by an apostrophe (') and inches with a trailing double quote (").

When engineering or architectural report format is in effect, the drawing unit equals 1 inch, so you can omit the trailing double quote (") if you like. When you enter feet-and-inches values combined, the inches values should immediately follow the apostrophe, without an intervening space. Distance input does not permit spaces because the Spacebar functions the same as Enter.

CHANGING THE LIMITS OF THE DRAWING

The LIMITS command allows you to place an imaginary rectangular drawing sheet in the CAD drawing space. But, unlike the limitations of the drawing sheet of the board drafter, you can move or enlarge the CAD electronic sheet (the limits) after you have started your drawing. The LIMITS command does not affect the current display on the screen. The defined area determined by the limits governs the portion of the drawing indicated by the visible grid (see GRID command on p. 3-1). Limits are also factors that determine how much of the drawing is displayed by the ZOOM All command (see ZOOM All on p. 3-39).

The limits are expressed as a pair of 2D points in the World Coordinate System, a lower left and an upper right limit. For example, to set limits for an A-size sheet, set lower left as 0,0 and upper right as 11,8.5 or 12,9; for a B-size sheet set lower left as 0,0 and upper right as 17,11 or 18,12. Most architectural floor plans are drawn at a scale of 1/4" = 1'-0". To set limits to plot on a C-size (22" × 17") paper at 1/4" = 1'-0", the limits are set lower left as 0,0 and upper right as 88',68' (4 × 22, 4 × 17).

Invoke the LIMITS command from:

Pull-down menu	Format > Drawing Limits
Command: prompt	**limits** Enter

AutoCAD prompts:

Command: limits Enter
ON/OFF/<Lower left corner> <current>: *(press Enter to accept the current setting, specify the lower left corner, or select an option)*
Upper right corner <current>: *(press Enter to accept the current setting, or specify the upper right corner)*

The response you give for the upper right corner gives the location of the upper right corner of the imaginary rectangular drawing sheet.

There are two additional options available for the LIMITS command. When AutoCAD prompts for the lower left corner, you may respond with the ON or OFF options. The ON/OFF options determine whether or not you can specify a point outside the limits when prompted to do so. When you select the ON option, limits checking is on and you cannot start or end an object outside the limits, nor can you specify displacement points required by the MOVE or COPY command outside the limits. You can, however, specify two points (center and point on circle) that draw a circle, part of which might be outside the limits. The limits check is simply an aid to help you avoid drawing off the imaginary rectangular drawing sheet. Leaving the limits checking ON is a sort of safety net to keep you from inadvertantly specifying a point outside the limits. On the other hand, limits checking is a hindrance if you need to specify such a point.

When you select the OFF option (default), AutoCAD disables limits checking, allowing you to draw the objects and specify points outside the limits.

Whenever you change the limits, you will not see any change on the screen unless you use the All option of the ZOOM command. ZOOM All lets you see the entire newly set limits on the screen. For example, if your current limits are 12 by 9 (lower left corner 0,0 and upper right corner 12,9) and you change the limits to 42 by 36 (lower left corner 0,0 and upper right corner 42,36), you still see the 12 by 9 area. You can draw the objects anywhere on the limits 42 by 36 area, but you will see on the screen the objects that are drawn only in the 12 by 9 area. To see the entire limits, invoke the ZOOM command using the All option.

Invoke the ZOOM command from:

Pull-down menu	<u>V</u>iew > <u>Z</u>oom > <u>A</u>ll
Command: prompt	**zoom** Enter

AutoCAD prompts:

Command: **zoom** Enter
All/Center/Dynamic/Extents/Left/Previous/Vmax/Window/<Scale(X/XP)>:
    all Enter

You see on the screen the entire limits or current extents (whichever is greater). If objects are drawn outside the limits, ZOOM All displays all objects. (For a detailed explanation of the ZOOM command, see p. 3-35).

Whenever you change the limits, you should always invoke ZOOM All to see on the screen the entire limits or current extents.

For example, the following command sequence shows steps to change limits for an existing drawing (see Figures 1-46a and 1-46b).

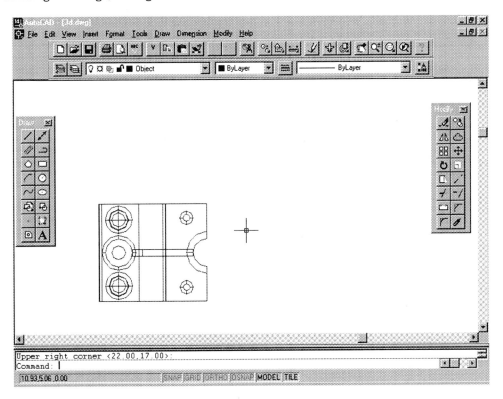

Figure 1-46a The limits of an existing drawing before being changed by the LIMITS command

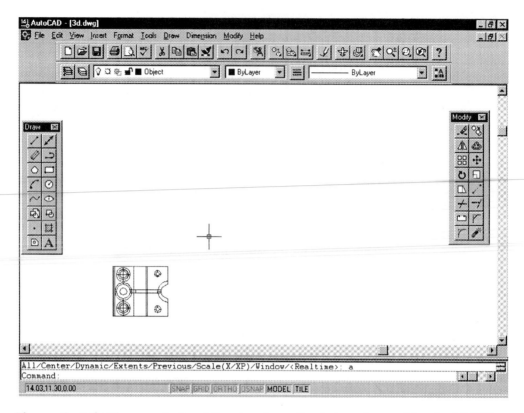

Figure 1–46b The new limits of the drawing, after being changed by the LIMITS command

Command: **limits** Enter
ON/OFF/<lower left corner><0.00,0.00>: Enter
Upper right corner <22.00,17.00>: **42,36** Enter
Command: **zoom** Enter
All/Center/Dynamic/Extents/Left/Previous/Vmax/Window/<Scale(X/XP)>:
    all Enter

SAVING A DRAWING

While working in AutoCAD, you should save your drawing once every 10–15 minutes without exiting AutoCAD. By saving your work periodically, you are protecting your work from possible power failures, editing errors, and other disasters. This can be done automatically by setting the SAVETIME system variable to a specific interval (in minutes). In addition, you can also manually save by using the SAVE, SAVEAS, and QSAVE commands.

The SAVE command saves an unnamed drawing with a file name. If the drawing is already named, then it works like the SAVEAS command.

The SAVEAS command saves an unnamed drawing with a file name or renames the current drawing. If the current drawing is already named, then AutoCAD exits the drawing (without saving the changes since the last save) to the current drawing name, prompts for a new file name, and sets the current drawing to the new file name you specified. If the current drawing is already named and you accept the current default file name, AutoCAD saves the current drawing and continues to work on the updated drawing. If you specify a file name that already exists in the current folder, AutoCAD displays a message warning you that you are about to overwrite another drawing file. If you do not want to overwrite it, specify a different file name. The SAVEAS command also allows you to save in various formats, including: Release 12 format, Release 13 format, and drawing template.

The QSAVE command saves an unnamed drawing with a file name. If the drawing is named, AutoCAD saves the drawing without requesting a file name.

Invoke the SAVE command from:

Command: prompt	**save** ⏎

AutoCAD displays the Save Drawing As dialog box, similar to Figure 1–47.

Select the appropriate folder in which to save the file, and type the name of the file in the **Save In:** edit field. The file name can contain up to 255 characters (Windows 95 and Windows NT 4.0 operating system), including embedded spaces and punctuation. Following are the examples of valid filenames:

> this is my first drawing
>
> first house
>
> machine part one

AutoCAD automatically appends *DWG* as a file extension. If you save it as a template file, then AutoCAD appends *DWT* as a file extension.

Invoke the SAVEAS command from:

Pull-down menu	File > Save As...
Command: prompt	**saveas** ⏎

AutoCAD displays the Save Drawing As dialog box. Select the appropriate folder in which to save the file, and type the name of the file in the **Save In:** edit field. The file name can contain up to 255 characters (Windows 95 and Windows NT 4.0 operating system), including embedded spaces and punctuation. Select the format type you want to save to from the **Save as type:** option menu.

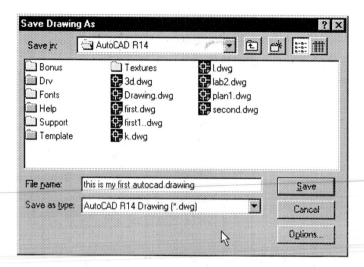

Figure 1–47 Save Drawing As dialog box

If you want to save the current drawing to the given file name, then select the **Save** button without changing the file name. AutoCAD displays a message to warn you that you are about to overwrite another drawing file. Select **Yes** to save to the current file name.

Invoke the QSAVE command from:

Standard toolbar	Select the Save command (see Figure 1–48)
Pull-down menu	File > Save
Command: prompt	qsave [Enter]

Figure 1–48 Invoke the Save command from Standard Toolbar

If the drawing is unnamed, then AutoCAD displays the Save Drawing As dialog box. Select the appropriate folder in which to save the file, and type the name of the file in the **Save In:** edit field. The file name can contain up to 255 characters (Windows 95 and Windows NT 4.0 operating system), including embedded spaces and punctuation. If the drawing is named, AutoCAD saves the drawing without requesting a file name.

EXITING AUTOCAD

The EXIT or QUIT command allows you to exit AutoCAD. The EXIT or QUIT command exits the current drawing if there have been no changes since the drawing was last saved. If the drawing has been modified, AutoCAD displays the Drawing Modification dialog box to prompt you to save or discard the changes before quitting.

Invoke the EXIT command from:

Pull-down menu	File > Exit
Command: prompt	**exit** Enter

If the drawing has been modified, AutoCAD displays the Drawing Modification dialog box to prompt you to save or discard the changes before exiting.

Invoke the QUIT command from:

Command: prompt	**quit** Enter

If the drawing has been modified, AutoCAD displays the Drawing Modification dialog box to prompt you to save or discard the changes before quitting.

REVIEW QUESTIONS

1. If you executed the following commands in order: LINE, CIRCLE, ARC, and ERASE; what would you need to do to re-execute the CIRCLE command?
   a. press {pgup} {pgup} {pgup}
   b. press {downarrow} {downarrow} {downarrow}
   c. press {uparrow} {uparrow} {uparrow}
   d. press {pgdn} {pgdn} {pgdn}
   e. press {leftarrow} {leftarrow} {leftarrow}

2. In a dialog box, when there are a set of mutually exclusive options (a list of several from which you must select exactly one), these are called:
   a. Edit boxes
   b. Check boxes
   c. Radio buttons
   d. Scroll bars
   e. List boxes

3. If you lost all pull down menus, what command could you use to load the standard menu?
   a. LOAD   d. MENU
   b. OPEN   e. PULL
   c. NEW

4. What is the extension used by AutoCAD for template drawing files used by the setup wizard?
   a. DWG   d. TEM
   b. DWT   e. WIZ
   c. DWK

5. If you performed a ZOOM-All and your drawing shrunk to a small portion of the screen, one possible problem might be:
   a. Out of computer memory
   b. Mis-placed drawing object
   c. Grid and Snap set incorrectly
   d. This should never happen in AutoCAD

6. What is an external tablet used to input absolute coordinate address to AutoCAD by means of a puck or stylus called?
   a. Digitizer
   b. Input pad
   c. Coordinate tablet
   d. Touch screen

7. The menu which can be made to appear at the location of the cross hairs is called:
   a. Mouse menu
   b. Cross hair menu
   c. Cursor menu
   d. None of the above, there is no such menu

8. In order to save basic setup parameters (such as snap, grid, etc.) for future drawings, you should:
   a. create an AutoCAD Macro
   b. create a prototype file
   c. create a new configuration file
   d. modify the ACAD.INI file

9. To cancel an AutoCAD command, press:
   a. {ctrl} + {a}
   b. {ctrl} + {x}
   c. {alt} + {a}
   d. {esc}
   e. {ctrl} + {enter}

10. The SAVE command:
    a. saves your work
    b. does not exit you out of AutoCAD
    c. is a valuable feature for periodically storing information to disk
    d. all of the above

2

FUNDAMENTALS I

• •

INTRODUCTION

This chapter introduces some of the basic commands and concepts in AutoCAD that can be used to complete a simple drawing. The project drawing used in this chapter is relatively uncomplicated, but for the newcomer to AutoCAD it presents ample challenge. It has fundamental problems that provide useful material for lessons in drawing setup, and in creating and editing objects. Also introduced are several different drawing aids to make your drafting and design layout quicker, easier, and more accurate. These can be created by using certain commands from the toolbars and pull-down menus. When you learn how to access and use the commands, how to find your way around the screen, and how AutoCAD makes use of coordinate geometry, you can apply these skills to the chapters containing more advanced drawings and projects.

After completing this chapter, you will be able to:

✓ Construct geometric figures with LINE, RECTANG, CIRCLE and ARC commands
✓ Use coordinate systems
✓ Use various object selection methods
✓ Use the ERASE command

DRAW COMMANDS

AutoCAD gives you an ample variety of drawing elements, called *objects*. It also provides you with many ways to generate each object in your drawing. You will learn about the properties of these objects as you progress in this text. It is important to keep in mind that the examples in this text of how to generate the various lines, circles, arcs, and other objects are not always the only methods available. You are invited, even challenged, to find other more expedient methods to perform tasks demonstrated in the lessons. You progress at a better rate if you make an effort to learn as much as possible as soon as possible about the descriptive properties of the individual objects. When you become familiar with how the CAD program creates, manipulates, and stores the data that describes the objects, you are then able to create drawings more effectively.

Drawing Lines

The primary drawing object is the *line*. A series of connected straight line segments can be drawn by invoking the LINE command and then selecting the proper sequence of endpoints. AutoCAD connects the points with a series of lines. The LINE command is one of the few AutoCAD commands that automatically repeats in this fashion. It uses the ending point of one line as the starting point of the next, continuing to prompt you for each subsequent ending point. To terminate this continuing feature you must give a null response (press Enter). Even though a series of lines is drawn using a single LINE command, each line is a separate object, as though it had been drawn with a separate LINE command.

You can specify the endpoints using either 2D (X,Y) or 3D (X,Y,Z) coordinates, or a combination of the two. If you enter 2D coordinates, AutoCAD uses the current elevation as the Z element of the point (zero is the default). This chapter is concerned only with 2D points whose elevation is zero. (3D concepts and nonzero elevations are covered in later chapters.)

Invoke the Line Command from:

Draw toolbar	Select the Line command (see Figure 2–1)
Pull-down menu	Draw > Line
Command: prompt	**line** Enter

Figure 2–1 Invoking the LINE command from the Draw toolbar

AutoCAD prompts:

Command: **line** Enter
From point:

Where to Start The first point of the first object in a drawing normally establishes where all of the points of other objects must be placed. It is like the cornerstone of a building. Careful thought should go into locating the first point.

You can specify the starting point of the line by absolute coordinates or by using your pointing device (mouse or puck). After specifying the first point, AutoCAD prompts:

    To point:

Where to from Here? In addition to the first point's being the cornerstone, the direction of the first object is also critical to where all other points of other objects are located with respect to one another.

You can specify the end of the line by means of absolute coordinates, or relative coordinates or by using your pointing device to specify the end of the line on the screen. Again, AutoCAD repeats the prompt:

    To point:

You can enter a series of connected lines. To save time, the LINE command remains active and prompts for a new "To point:" after each point you specify. When you have finished entering a connected series of lines, give a null reply (press Enter) to terminate the LINE command.

If you are placing points with a cursor instead of providing coordinates, a rubber-band line is displayed between the starting point and the crosshairs. This helps you see where the resulting line will go. In Figure 2–2 the dotted lines represent previous cursor positions.

Most of the AutoCAD commands have a variety of options. For the LINE command, three options are available: Continue, Close, and Undo.

Continue Option When you invoke the LINE command and respond to the "From point:" prompt with a null response, AutoCAD automatically sets the start of the line to the end of the most recently drawn line or arc. This provides a simple method for constructing a tangentially connected line in an arc-line continuation.

The subsequent prompt sequence depends on whether a line or arc was more recently drawn. If the line is more recent, the starting point of the new line will be set as the ending point of that most recent line, and the "To point:" prompt appears as usual. If an arc is more recent, its end defines the starting point and the direction of the new line. AutoCAD prompts for:

    Length of the line:

Specify the length of the line to be drawn, and then AutoCAD continues with the normal "To point:" prompt.

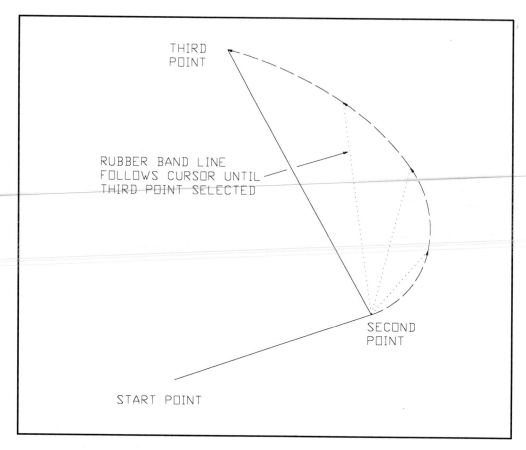

THIRD
POINT

RUBBER BAND LINE
FOLLOWS CURSOR UNTIL
THIRD POINT SELECTED

SECOND
POINT

START POINT

Figure 2–2 Placing points with the cursor rather than with keyboard coordinates input

The following command sequence shows an example using the Continue option (see Figure 2–3).

```
Command: line
From point: (pick point 1)
To point: (pick point 2)
To point: (pick point 3)
To point: Enter
Command: (invoke the LINE command)
From point: (to continue the line from point 3, press Enter or the Spacebar)
To point: (pick point 4)
To point: (pick point 5)
To point: Enter
```

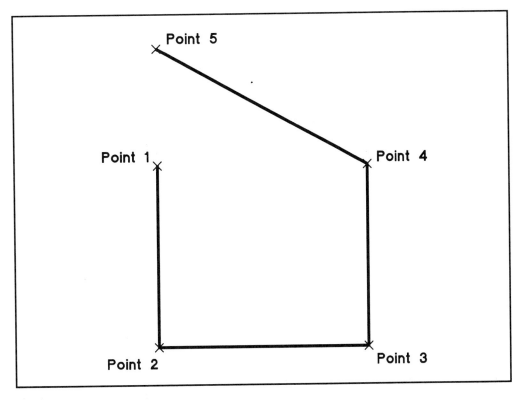

Figure 2-3 Invoke the LINE command's Continue option

Close Option   If the sequence of lines you are drawing forms a polygon, then you can use the Close option to join the last and first points automatically. AutoCAD draws the closing line segment if you respond to the "To point:" prompt with a **C** or **close** and press Enter. AutoCAD performs two steps when you select the Close option. The first step closes the polygon, and the second step terminates the LINE command (equivalent to a null response) and brings you back to the "Command:" prompt.

The following command sequence shows an example of using the Close option (see Figure 2-4).

Command: **line** Enter
From point: *(pick point 1)*
To point: *(pick point 2)*
To point: *(pick point 3)*
To point: *(pick point 4)*
To point: *(pick point 5)*
To point: **C** Enter

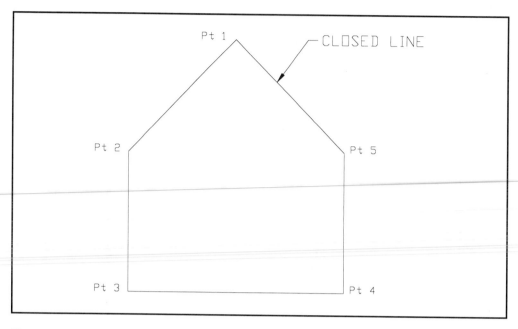

Figure 2–4 Using the LINE command's Close option

Undo Option When drawing a series of connected lines, you may wish to erase the most recent line segment and continue from the end of the previous live segment. You can do so and remain in the LINE command without exiting by using the Undo option. Whenever you wish to erase the most recent line segment, at the "To point:" prompt, enter **U** or **undo** and press Enter. If necessary, you can enter multiple U's; this will erase the most recent line segment one at a time. Once you are out of the LINE command, it is too late to use the Undo option of the LINE command to erase the most recent line segment.

The following command sequence shows an example using the Undo option (see Figure 2–5).

Command: **line** Enter
From point: *(pick point 1)*
To point: *(pick point 2)*
To point: *(pick point 3)*
To point: *(pick point 4)*
To point: *(pick point 5)*
To point: **u** Enter
To point: **u** Enter
To point: *(pick revised point 4)*
To point: *(pick revised point 5)*
To point: *(pick point 6)*
To point: Enter

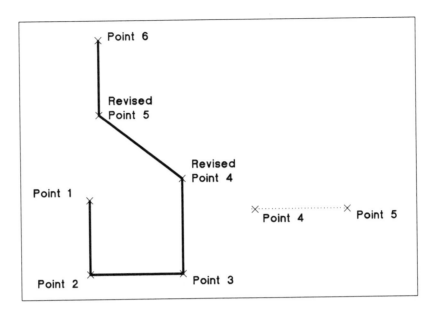

Figure 2–5 Using the LINE command's Undo option

Drawing Rectangles

When it is necessary to create a rectanglular box, you can use the RECTANG command.

Invoke the RECTANG command from:

Draw toolbar	Select the Rectangle command (see Figure 2-6)
Pull-down menu	Draw > Rectangle
Command: prompt	rectang Enter

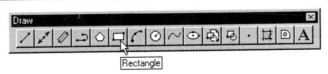

Rectangle

Figure 2–6 Invoking the RECTANG command from the Draw toolbar

AutoCAD prompts:

Command: **rectang** Enter
Chamfer/Elevation/Fillet/Thickness/Width/<First Corner>: *(place a point to define the start point of the rectangle)*
Other corner: *(place a point to define the opposite corner of the rectangle)*

Width Option The Width option allows you set the width for the rectangle to be drawn. The default width is set to 0.0.

Chamfer Option The Chamfer option sets the chamfer distance for the rectangle to be drawn. Refer to Chapter 4 for a detailed explanation on the usage of CHAMFER command and its available settings.

Fillet Option The Fillet option sets the fillet radius for the rectangle to be drawn. Refer to Chapter 4 for a detailed explanation on the usage of FILLET command and its available settings.

Elevation Option The Elevation option specifies the elevation of the rectangle to be drawn. Refer to Chapter 15 for a detailed explanation on the of Elevation setting.

Thickness Option The Thickness option specifies the thickness of the rectangle to be drawn. Refer to Chapter 15 for a detailed explanation on the Thickness setting.

Drawing Wide Lines

When it is necessary to draw thick lines, the TRACE command may be used instead of the LINE command. Traces are entered just like lines except that the line width is set first. To specify the width, you can type a distance or select two points and let AutoCAD use the measured distance between them. When you draw using the TRACE command, the previous TRACE segment is not drawn until the next endpoint is specified.

Invoke the TRACE command from:

Command: prompt	trace Enter

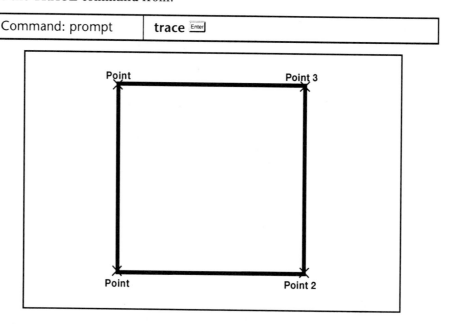

Figure 2–7 Placing wide connected lines using the TRACE command

AutoCAD prompts:

> Command: **trace**
> Trace width <current>: *(specify the trace width and press* Enter *)*

For example, the following command sequence shows placement of connected lines using the TRACE command (see Figure 2–7).

> Command: **trace** Enter
> Trace width <current>: **.05** Enter
> From point: *(pick point 1)*
> To point: *(pick point 2)*
> To point: *(pick point 3)*
> To point: *(pick point 4)*
> To point: Enter

COORDINATE SYSTEMS

In accordance with the conventions of the Cartesian coordinate system, horizontal distances increase in the positive X direction, toward the right, and vertical distances increase in the positive Y direction, upward. Distances perpendicular to the XY plane that you are viewing increase toward you in the positive Z direction. This set of axes defines the *World Coordinate System*, abbreviated as *WCS*.

The significance of the WCS is that it is always in your drawing; it cannot be altered. An infinite number of other coordinate systems can be established relative to it. These others are called *user coordinate systems (UCSs)* and can be created with the UCS command. Even though the WCS is fixed, you can view it from any angle, side, or rotation without changing to another coordinate system.

AutoCAD provides what is called a *coordinate system icon* to help you keep your bearings among different coordinate systems in a drawing. The icon will show you the orientation of your current UCS by indicating the positive directions of the X and Y axes. Figure 2–8 shows some examples of coordinate system icons.

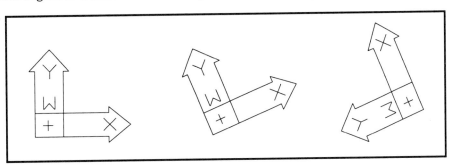

Figure 2–8   Examples of the UCS icons

Computer-aided drafting permits you always to draw an object at its true size and then make the border, title block, and other nonobject associated features fit the object. The completed combination is reduced (or increased) to fit the plotted sheet size you require when you plot.

A more complicated situation is when you wish to draw objects at different scales on the same drawing. This can be handled easily by one of several methods with the more advanced commands provided in AutoCAD.

Drawing a schematic that is not to scale is one situation where the graphics and computing power are hardly used to their potential. But even though the symbols and the distances between them have no relationship to any real-life dimensions, the sheet size, text size, line widths, and other visible characteristics of the drawing must be considered in order to give your schematic the readability you desire. Some planning, including sizing, needs to be applied to all drawings.

When AutoCAD prompts for the location of a point, you can use one of several available point entry techniques, including absolute rectangular coordinates, relative rectangular coordinates, relative polar coordinates, spherical coordinates, and cylindrical coordinates.

Absolute Rectangular Coordinates

The rectangular coordinates method is based on specifying a point's location by giving its distances from two intersecting perpendicular axes in a two-dimensional (2D) plane or from three intersecting perpendicular planes for three-dimensional (3D) space. Each point's distance is measured along the X axis (horizontal), Y axis (vertical), and Z axis (toward or away from the viewer). The intersection of the axes, called the *origin* $(X,Y,Z = 0,0,0)$ divides the coordinates into four quadrants for 2D or eight sections for 3D (see Figure 2–9).

Points are located by absolute rectangular coordinates in relation to the origin. You specify the reference to the WCS origin or UCS origin. In AutoCAD, by default the origin (0,0) is located at the lower left corner of the drawing, as shown in Figure 2–10.

As mentioned earlier, the horizontal distance increases in the positive X direction from the origin, and the vertical distance increases in the positive Y direction from the origin. You specify a point by typing its X,Y,Z coordinates in decimal, fractional, or scientific notation separated by commas.

For example, the following command sequence shows placement of connected lines as shown in Figure 2–11 by absolute coordinates (see Figure 2–12):

```
Command: line  Enter
From point: 2,2  Enter
To point: 2,4  Enter
To point: 3,5  Enter
To point: 5,5  Enter
To point: 5,7  Enter
```

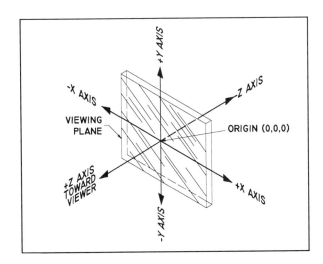

Figure 2–9 Specifying rectangular coordinates using the intersections of the *X*, *Y*, and *Z* axes

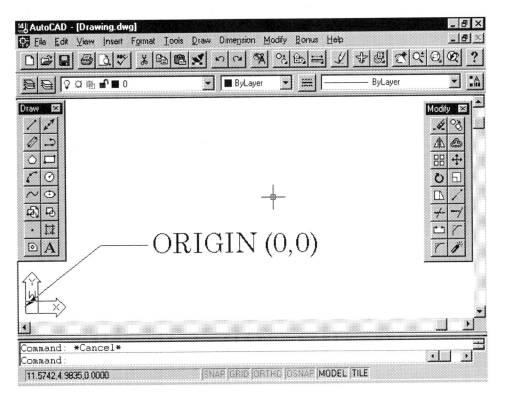

Figure 2–10 Default location of the AutoCAD origin

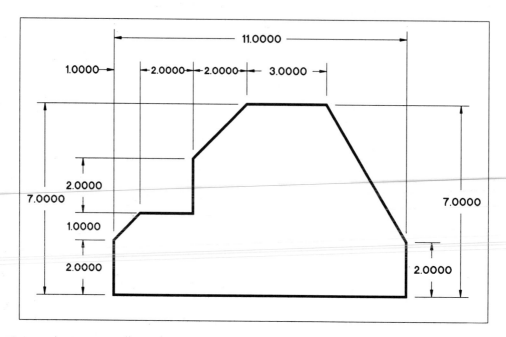

Figure 2–11   Placing connected lines

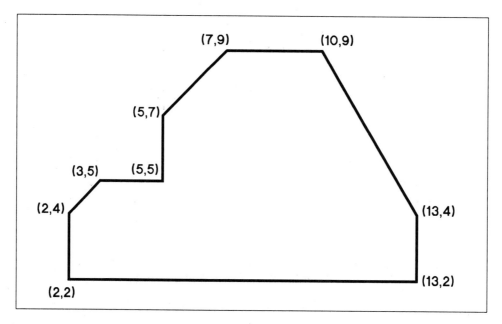

Figure 2–12   Placing connected lines using absolute coordinates

To point: **7,9** Enter
To point: **10,9** Enter
To point: **13,4** Enter
To point: **13,2** Enter
To point: **2,2** Enter
To point: Enter

Relative Rectangular Coordinates

Points are located by relative rectangular coordinates in relation to the last specified position or point, rather than the origin. This is like specifying a point as an offset from the last point you entered. In AutoCAD, whenever you specify relative coordinates, the **@** ("at" symbol) must precede your entry. This symbol is selected by holding the Shift key and simultaneously pressing the **2** key at the top of the keyboard.

The following command sequence shows placement of connected lines as shown in Figure 2–11 by relative rectangular coordinates (see Figure 2–13):

Command: **line** Enter
From point: **2,2** Enter
To point: **@0,2** Enter
To point: **@1,1** Enter
To point: **@2,0** Enter

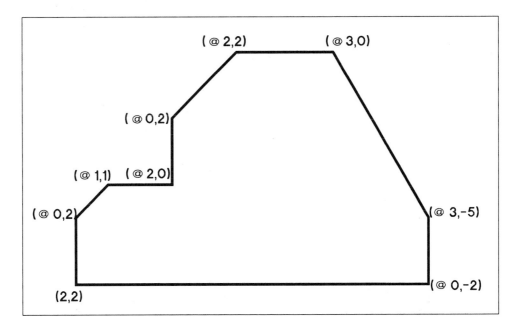

Figure 2-13 Placing connected lines using relative rectangular coordinates

To point: **@0,2** `Enter`
To point: **@2,2** `Enter`
To point: **@3,0** `Enter`
To point: **@3,-5** `Enter`
To point: **@0,-2** `Enter`
To point: **2,2** `Enter`
To point: `Enter`
Command:

Relative Polar Coordinates

Polar coordinates are based on a distance from a fixed point at a given angle. In AutoCAD, a polar coordinate point is determined by distance from previous point and angle measured from the zero degree. In AutoCAD, by default the angle is measured in the counterclockwise direction. It is important to remember that points located using polar coordinates are always positioned relative to the previous point and not the origin (0,0). You can specify a point by entering its distance from the previous point and its angle in the *XY* plane, separated by < (not a comma). This symbol is selected by holding the `Shift` key and simultaneously pressing the "," key at the bottom of the keyboard.

The following command sequence shows placement of connected lines as shown in Figure 2–11 by using a combination of polar and rectangular coordinates (see Figure 2–14).

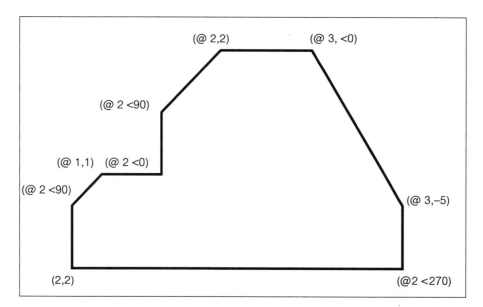

Figure 2–14 Placing connected lines using a combination of polar and rectangular coordinates

Command: **line** `Enter`
From point: **2,2** `Enter`
To point: **@2<90** `Enter`
To point: **@1,1** `Enter`
To point: **@2<0** `Enter`
To point: **@2<90** `Enter`
To point: **@2,2** `Enter`
To point: **@3,0** `Enter`
To point: **@3,-5** `Enter`
To point: **@2<270** `Enter`
To point: **2,2** `Enter`
To point: `Enter`

If you are working in a UCS and would like to enter points in reference to the WCS, enter coordinates preceded by an * (asterisk). For example, to specify the point with an X coordinate of 3.5 and Y coordinate of 2.57 in reference to the WCS, regardless of the current UCS, enter:

*3.5,2.57

In the case of relative coordinates, the * (asterisk) will be preceded by the **@** symbol. For example:

@*4,5

This represents an offset of 4,5 from the previous point in relation to the WCS.

Coordinate Display

The Coordinates Display is a report in the status toolbar at the bottom of the screen. It has three settings. On most systems the `F6` function key toggles between the three settings. The three settings are as follows:

1. This setting causes the display to report the location of the cursor when the prompt is in the "Command:" status or when you are being prompted to select the first point selection of a command. It then changes to a relative polar mode when you are prompted for a second point that could be specified relative to the first point. In this case the report is in the form of the direction/distance. The direction is given in terms of the current angular units setting and the distance in terms of the current linear units setting.
2. This setting is similar to the previous one, except that the display for the second location is given in terms of its coordinates, rather than relative to the first point.
3. This setting is used to save either the location in the display at the time you toggle to this setting or the last point entered. It does not change dynamically with the movement of the cursor and will not change until you select a new point.

EXERCISES 2–1 THROUGH 2–4

Exercise 2–1

Type of shape	Input Methods
Single Line Sequence	• Absolute rectangular coordinates • Relative rectangular coordinates • Relative polar coordinates

The points that determine the shape in this exercise can be entered by any one of the three listed methods. This is *not* always the case, as you will see in the next few exercises. Also, all of the lines that determine the shape are sequentially connected; that is, the ending point of each line can be used as the starting point of one other line. That means that this figure can be drawn without exiting the LINE command once it is invoked. Again, this is *not* the case with most shapes.

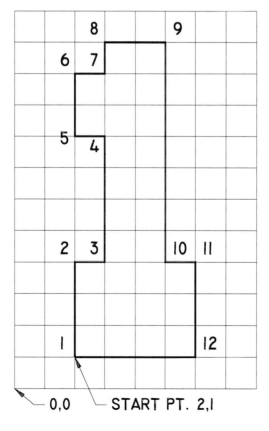

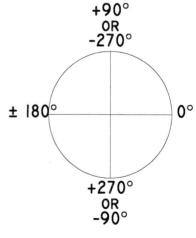

Points of Interest

■ With rectanglar coordinates, the distances are entered as horizontal (*X*) and vertical (*Y*) displacements.

■ Absolute rectangular coordinates are *X* and *Y* displacements from the origin (0,0).

■ Relative rectangular coordinates are *X* and *Y* displacements from the last point entered.

■ @ represents the last point entered.

■ Relative polar coordinates are a combination of a direction and a distance from the last point entered.

■ Substituting rectangular coordinate input with polar coordinate input (or vice versa) is not always done easily without the application of trigonometric functions.

Drawing Setup	Use Quick Setup wizard, set Units to Decimal, set Area to 9 x 13.

Invoke the LINE command and then respond to the "From point:" prompt as shown for each method.

Point by Point

Absolute	Relative Rectangular	Relative Polar
1. From point: **2,1** Enter	1. From point: **2,1** Enter	1. From point: **2,1** Enter
2. To point: **2,4** Enter	2. To point: **@0,3** Enter	2. To point: **@3<90** Enter
3. To point: **3,4** Enter	3. To point: **@1,0** Enter	3. To point: **@1<0** Enter
4. To point: **3,8** Enter	4. To point: **@0,4** Enter	4. To point: **@4<90** Enter
5. To point: **2,8** Enter	5. To point: **@-1,0** Enter	5. To point: **@1<180** Enter
6. To point: **2,10** Enter	6. To point: **@0,2** Enter	6. To point: **@2<90** Enter
7. To point: **3,10** Enter	7. To point: **@1,0** Enter	7. To point: **@1<0** Enter
8. To point: **3,11** Enter	8. To point: **@0,1** Enter	8. To point: **@1<90** Enter
9. To point: **5,11** Enter	9. To point: **@2,0** Enter	9. To point: **@2<0** Enter
10. To point: **5,4** Enter	10. To point: **@0,-7** Enter	10. To point: **@7<270** Enter
11. To point: **6,4** Enter	11. To point: **@1,0** Enter	11. To point: **@1<0** Enter
12. To point: **6,1** Enter	12. To point: **@0,-3** Enter	12. To point: **@3<270** Enter
13. To point: **2,1** Enter	13. To point: **@-4,0** Enter	13. To point: **@4<180** Enter
14. Command: Enter	14. Command: Enter	14. Command: Enter

Exercise 2–2

Type of shape	Input Methods
Multiple line sequences	• Absolute rectangular coordinates • Relative rectangular coordinates • Relative polar coordinates

As in Exercise 2–1, the points that determine the shapes in this exercise can be entered by any one of the three listed methods here. But because these are three separate shapes, all lines are not sequentially connected. The LINE command must be invoked at least three times.

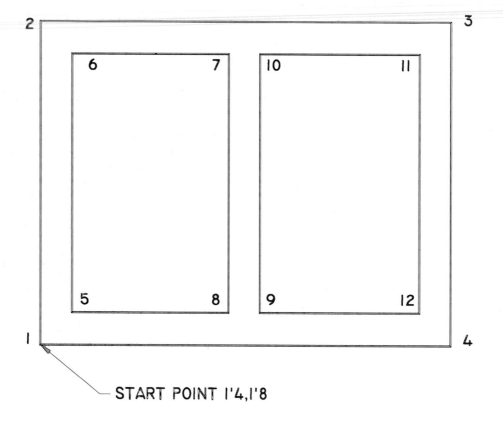

START POINT 1'4,1'8

Points of Interest

■ Steps 5, 11, and 17 in the following tables illustrate how you can use the Close option of the LINE command to draw the last segment of a closed sequence of lines and exit the LINE command at the same time.

■ In the "Relative Rectangular" column, steps 7 and 13 are examples of how you can use the @ (last point) symbol to establish a starting point, similar to the manner in which it is used to respond to the "To point:" prompt.

Drawing Setup	Use Quick Setup Wizard, set Units to Architectural, set Area to 8' x 6'.

Invoke the LINE command and then respond to the "From point:" prompt as shown for each method. Steps 6 and 12 use automatic reinvoking of the previously used command by pressing `Enter`. In this case the LINE command is the previously used command.

Absolute	Relative Rectangular	Relative Polar
1. From point: **1'4,1'8** `Enter`	1. From point: **1'4,1'8** `Enter`	1. From point: **1'4,1'8** `Enter`
2. To point: **1'4,5'** `Enter`	2. To point: **@0,3'4** `Enter`	2. To point: **@3'4<90** `Enter`
3. To point: **5'8,5'** `Enter`	3. To point: **@4'4,0** `Enter`	3. To point: **@4'4<0** `Enter`
4. To point: **5'8,1'8** `Enter`	4. To point: **@0,-3'4** `Enter`	4. To point: **@3'4<-90** `Enter`
5. To point: **c** `Enter` *(for Close)*	5. To point: **c** `Enter` *(for Close)*	5. To point: **c** `Enter` *(for Close)*
6. Command: `Enter`	6. Command: `Enter`	6. Command: `Enter`
7. From point: **1'8,2'** `Enter`	7. From point: **1'8,2'** `Enter`	7. From point: **1'8,2'** `Enter`
8. To point: **1'8,4'8** `Enter`	8. To point: **@0,2'8** `Enter`	8. To point: **@2'8<90** `Enter`
9. To point: **3'4,4'8** `Enter`	9. To point: **@1'8,0** `Enter`	9. To point: **@1'8<0** `Enter`
10. To point: **3'4,2'** `Enter`	10. To point: **@0,-2'8** `Enter`	10. To point: **@2'8<270** `Enter`
11. To point: **c** `Enter`	11. To point: **c** `Enter`	11. To point: **c** `Enter`
12. Command: `Enter`	12. Command: `Enter`	12. Command: `Enter`
13. From point: **3'8, 2'** `Enter`	13. From point: **3'8, 2'** `Enter`	13. From point: **3'8, 2'** `Enter`
14. To point: **3'8,4'8** `Enter`	14. To point: **@0,2'8** `Enter`	14. To point: **@2'8<90** `Enter`
15. To point: **5'4, 4'8** `Enter`	15. To point: **@1'8,0** `Enter`	15. To point: **@1'8<0** `Enter`
16. To point: **5'4,2'** `Enter`	16. To point: **@0,-2'8** `Enter`	16. To point: **@2'8<270** `Enter`
17. To point: **c** `Enter`	17. To point: **c** `Enter`	17. To point: **c** `Enter`

Exercise 2–3

Type of shape	Input Methods
Multiple line sequences	• Absolute rectangular coordinates for the first line segment of the first sequence • Relative polar coordinates for the remaining segments of the first sequence • Relative polar coordinates for entering the starting point of the second and third separate single line sections of the shape

Unlike the cases of Exercises 2–1 and 2–2, all of the points that determine the figure in this exercise cannot be entered with complete accuracy by all three of the methods listed (see Important Point below). Except for points A1, A2, A5, and A8, the points in the shape in this exercise can be accurately specified only by polar coordinates. For example, the coordinates of point A3 (2 units at 240° from point A2) are 5,1.267949192431. This is derived from the X coordinate of 6 − 2 cos 240° and the Y coordinate of 5 − 2 sin 240°. Even though the X coordinate happens to be a round number in this case, it is an exception rather than the rule. Keying in numbers like 1.267949192431 takes time and is subject to error. Any fewer digits might cause problems when endpoints of sequences are expected to end exactly at some other point. You cannot see the difference on a plot, but some of the computer functions that depend on this type of accuracy might not perform as expected. So not only is it easier to enter the polar coordinates @2<240, it is also quicker, more accurate, and less subject to error.

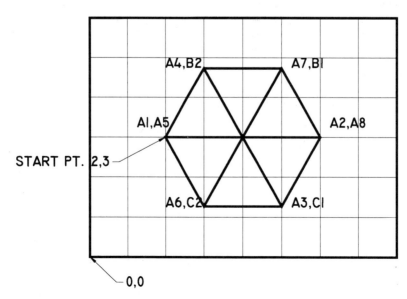

The LINE command must be invoked at least three times. And in order to enter the starting point for the second separate part of the shape (the line from B1 to B2), the last segment of the first sequence needs to end where shown, at point A8.

Important Point

AutoCAD has more advanced commands and features to make drawing these early exercises more easily than used here.

Points of Interest

■ Steps 11 and 15 in the following illustrate how you can specify starting points of lines (in this case points B1 and C1) by using the @ symbol and polar coordinate "distance and direction" data. Remember, the @ symbol means "last point."

■ This method is possible because we ended the previous lines in predetermined points (A8 and B2) whose direction and distance from B1 and C1 we knew. If we had wanted to start segment B1 at B2, it would have been difficult to establish it from A8 by means of polar coordinates.

■ Only the second point can be entered easily and accurately by means of any of the three methods (absolute, relative rectangular, or relative polar coordinates).

Drawing Setup	Use Quick Setup wizard, set Units to Decimal, set Area to 12 x 9.

Invoke the LINE command and then respond to the "From point:" prompt as shown. Steps 10 and 14 reinvoke the LINE command for separate sequences.

Point by Point

1. From point: **2,3** [Enter] *(specify starting point of line A1-A2)*
2. To point: **@4<0** [Enter] *(specify endpoint of line A1-A2)*
3. To point: **@2<240** [Enter] *(specify endpoint of line A2-A3)*
4. To point: **@4<120** [Enter] *(specify endpoint of line A3-A4)*
5. To point: **@2<240** [Enter] *(specify endpoint of line A4-A5)*
6. To point: **@2<300** [Enter] *(specify endpoint of line A5-A6)*
7. To point: **@4<60** [Enter] *(specify endpoint of line A6-A7)*
8. To point: **@2<300** [Enter] *(specify endpoint of line A7-A8)*
9. To point: [Enter] *(exit the LINE command)*
10. Command: [Enter] *(automatic recall of LINE command for B1 to B2)*
11. From point: **@2<120** [Enter] *(specify starting point of line B1-B2)*
12. To point: **@2<180** [Enter] *(specify endpoint of line B1-B2)*
13. To point: [Enter] *(exit the LINE command)*
14. Command: [Enter] *(automatic recall of LINE command for C1 to C2)*
15. From point: **@4<300** [Enter] *(specify starting point of line C1 to C2)*
16. To point: **@2<180** [Enter] *(specify endpoint of line C1 to C2)*
17. To point: [Enter] *(exit the LINE command)*

Fundamentals I

Exercise 2–4

Type of shape	Input Methods
Single line sequence	• Absolute rectangular coordinates for the first line segment of the sequence • Relative polar coordinates for the remaining segments

Important Point

AutoCAD has more advanced commands and features to make drawing these early exercises more easily than used here. These methods are pabulum. Solid food will come later.

Points of Interest

Steps 9 and 10 in the following can be substituted by simply entering the Close option.

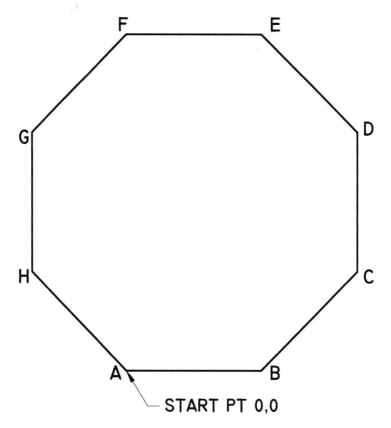

START PT 0,0

Drawing Setup	Use Start from Scratch option, set Units to Architectural and Limits to –4'–4",–1'–8" for lower left corner and 10'–0",11'–4" for upper right corner.
Useful Point	Don't forget to Zoom All after setting the limits.

Invoke the LINE command and respond to the "From point:" as shown below.

Point by Point

1. From point: **0,0** Enter *(specify starting point of line A-B)*
2. To point: **@4'<0** Enter *(specify endpoint of line A-B)*
3. To point: **@4'<45** Enter *(specify endpoint of line B-C)*
4. To point:**@4'<90** Enter *(specify endpoint of line C-D)*
5. To point: **@4'<135** Enter *(specify endpoint of line D-E)*
6. To point: **@4'<180** Enter *(specify endpoint of line E-F)*
7. To point: **@4'<225** Enter *(specify endpoint of line F-G)*
8. To point: **@4'<270** Enter *(specify endpoint of line G-H)*
9. To point: **@4'<315** Enter *(specify endpoint of line H-A)*
10. To point: Enter *(exit the LINE command)*

Drawing Circles

The CIRCLE command offers five different options for drawing circles: Center-Radius (default), Center-Diameter, 2 Point, 3 Point, and Tangent, Tangent, Radius (TTR).

Center-Radius Option Draws a circle based on a center point and a radius. Invoke the CIRCLE command from:

Draw toolbar	Select the Circle command (see Figure 2–15)
Pull-down menu	Draw > Circle > Center, Radius
Command: prompt	circle Enter

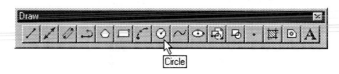

Figure 2–15 Invoking the CIRCLE command from the Draw toolbar

AutoCAD prompts:

> Command: **circle** Enter
> 3P/2P/TTR/<Center point>: *(place a point, or specify the coordinates to define the center of the circle)*
> Diameter/<Radius>: *(specify the radius of the circle)*

The following command sequence shows an example (see Figure 2–16):

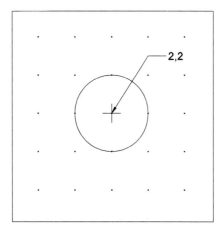

Figure 2–16 A circle drawn with the CIRCLE Command's default options: Center, Radius

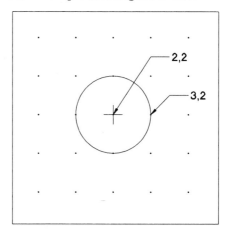

Figure 2–17 A circle drawn with the Center-Radius option by specifying the distance

Command: **circle** [Enter]
3P/2P/TTR/<Center point>: **2,2** [Enter]
Diameter/<Radius>: **1** [Enter]

The same circle can be generated as follows (see Figure 2–17):

Command: **circle** [Enter]
3P/2P/TTR/<Center point>: **2,2** [Enter]
Diameter/<Radius>: **3,2** [Enter]

In the last example, AutoCAD used as the value for the radius of the circle the distance between the center point and the second point given.

Center-Diameter Option   Draws a circle based on a center point and a diameter. Invoke the Center-Diameter option from:

Pull-down menu	Draw > Circle > Center, Diameter
Command: prompt	**circle** [Enter]

AutoCAD prompts:

Command: **circle** [Enter]
3P/2P/TTR/<Center point>: *(place a point, or specify the coordinates to define the center of the circle)*
Diameter/<Radius>: **d** [Enter]
Diameter: *(specify the diameter of the circle)*

The following command sequence shows an example:

Command: **circle** [Enter]
3P/2P/TTR/<Center point>: **2,2** [Enter]
Diameter/<Radius>: **d** [Enter]
Diameter: **2** [Enter]

The same circle can be generated as follows (see Figure 2–18):

Command: **circle** [Enter]
3P/2P/TTR/<Center point>: **2,2** [Enter]
Diameter/<Radius>: **d** [Enter]
Diameter: **4,2** [Enter]

> **NOTE:** Specifying a point causes AutoCAD to use the distance to the point specified from the previously selected center as the value for the diameter of the circle to be drawn.

Fundamentals I

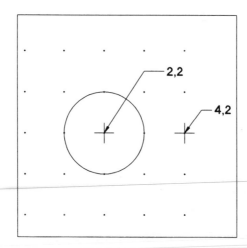

Figure 2–18 A circle drawn using the Center-Diameter option

Three-Point Circle Option The Three-Point circle option draws a circle based on three points on the circumference.

Invoke the Three-Point circle option from:

Pull-down menu	Draw > Circle > 3 Points
Command: prompt	circle [Enter]

AutoCAD prompts:

Command: **circle** [Enter]
3P/2P/TTR/<Center point>: **3p** [Enter]
First point: *(specify a point or a coordinate)*
Second point: *(specify a point or a coordinate)*
Third point: *(specify a point or a coordinate)*

The following command sequence shows an example (see Figure 2–19).

Command: **circle** [Enter]
3P/2P/TTR/<Center point>: **3P** [Enter]
First point: **2,1** [Enter]
Second point: **3,2** [Enter]
Third point: **2,3** [Enter]

> **NOTE:** The **3P** response allows you to override the Center Point default.

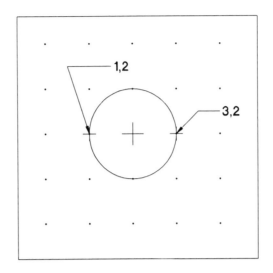

Figure 2–19   A circle drawn with the Three-Point option

Two-Point Circle Option   The Two-Point Circle option draws a circle based on two endpoints of the diameter.

Invoke the Two-Point circle option from:

Pull-down menu	Draw > Circle > 2 Points
Command: prompt	circle Enter

AutoCAD prompts:

    Command: **circle** Enter
    3P/2P/TTR/<Center point>: **2p** Enter
    First point on diameter: *(specify a point or a coordinate)*
    Second point on diameter: *(specify a point or a coordinate)*

The following command sequence shows an example (see Figure 2–20).

    Command: **circle** Enter
    3P/2P/TTR/<Center point>: **2P** Enter
    First point on diameter: **1,2** Enter
    Second point on diameter: **3,2** Enter

> **NOTE:**   The **2P** response allows you to override the Center Point default.

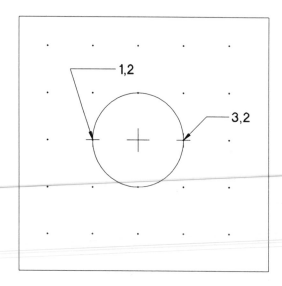

Figure 2–20 A circle drawn with the Two-Point option

Tangent, Tangent, Radius (TTR) Option This option draws a circle tangent to two objects (either lines, arcs, or circles) with a specified radius.

Invoke the Tangent, Tangent, Radius option from:

Pull-down menu	Draw > Circle > Tan, Tan, Radius
Command: prompt	circle Enter

AutoCAD prompts:

Command: **circle** Enter
3P/2P/TTR/<Center point>: **ttr** Enter
Enter Tangent spec: *(select the first object)*
Enter second Tangent spec: *(select the second object)*
Radius <current>: *(specify a distance or press* Enter *)*

For specifying the "tangent-to" objects, it normally does not matter where on the objects you make your selection. However, if more than one circle can be drawn to the specifications given, AutoCAD will draw the one whose tangent point is *nearest* to the selection made.

> **NOTE:** Until it is changed, the radius/diameter you specify in any one of the options becomes the default setting for subsequent circles to be drawn.

Drawing Arcs

The ARC command makes an arc and offers eleven combinations to draw an arc:

1. Three-point (3 points)
2. Start, center, end (S,C,E)
3. Start, center, included angle (S,C,A)
4. Start, center, length of chord (S,C,L)
5. Start, end, included angle (S,E,A)
6. Start, end, direction (S,E,D)
7. Start, end, radius (S,E,R)
8. Center, start, end (C,S,E)
9. Center, start, included angle (C,S,A)
10. Center, start, length of the chord (C,S,L)
11. Continuation from line or arc (LinCont or ArcCont)

Methods 8, 9, and 10 are just rearrangements of methods 2, 3, and 4 respectively.

Three-Point Arc Option   This option draws an arc using three specified points on the arc's circumference. The first point specifies the start point, the second point specifies a point on the circumference of the arc, and the third point is the arc endpoint. You can specify a three-point arc either clockwise or counterclockwise.

Invoke the Three-Point arc option from:

Draw toolbar	Select the Arc command (see Figure 2-21)
Pull-down menu	Draw > Arc > 3 Points
Command: prompt	arc Enter

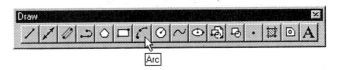

Arc

Figure 2–21   Invoking the ARC command from the Draw toolbar

AutoCAD prompts:

> Command: **arc** Enter
> Center/<Start point:>: *(place a point, or specify the coordinates to define the start point of the arc)*
> Center/End/<Second point>: *(place a point, or specify the coordinates to define a point on the circumference of the arc)*
> Endpoint: *(place a point, or specify the coordinates to define the endpoint of the arc)*

The following command sequence shows an example (see Figure 2–22).

Command: **arc** Enter
Center/<Start point>: **1,2** Enter
Center/End/<Second point>: **2,1** Enter
Endpoint: **3,2** Enter

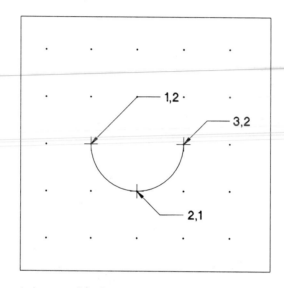

Figure 2–22 An arc drawn with the ARC command's default option: 3 Points

Start, Center, End Option (or S,C,E for short)   This option draws an arc using three specified points. The first point specifies the start point, the second point specifies the center point of the arc to be drawn, and the third point is the arc endpoint.

Invoke the Start, Center, End option from:

Pull-down menu	Draw > Arc > Start, Center, End
Command: prompt	**arc** Enter

AutoCAD prompts:

Command: **arc** Enter
Center/<Start point:>: *(place a point, or specify the coordinates to define the start point of the arc)*
Center/End/<Second point>: **c** Enter
Center: *(place a point, or specify the coordinates to define the center point of the arc to be drawn)*

Angle/Length of Chord/<Endpoint>: *(place a point, or specify the coordinates to define the endpoint of the arc)*

The following command sequence shows an example (see Figure 2–23).

Command: **arc** Enter
Center/<Start point>: **1,2** Enter
Center/End/<Second point>: **c** Enter
Center: **2,2** Enter
Angle/Length of chord/<Endpoint>: **2,3** Enter

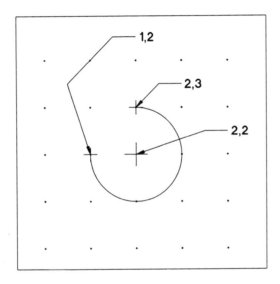

Figure 2–23   An arc drawn with the Start, Center, End (S,C,E) option

Arcs drawn by this method are always drawn counterclockwise from the starting point. The radius is determined by the distance between the center point and the starting point. Therefore, the point specified in response to "Endpoint" needs only to be on the same radial line of the desired endpoint. For example, specifying the point 2,2.5 or 2,4 draws the same arc.

An alternative to thise method is to specify the center point first, as follows (see Figure 2–24):

Command: **arc** Enter
Center/<Start point>: **c** Enter
Center: **2,2** Enter
Start point: **1,2** Enter
Angle/Length of chord/<Endpoint>: **2,3** Enter

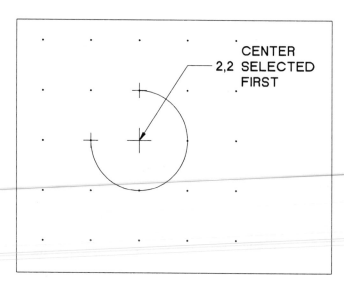

Figure 2–24 An arc drawn by specifying the center point first

Start, Center, Angle Option (or S,C,A for short) This option draws an arc similar to the Start, Center, End option method, but it places the endpoint on a radial line at the specified angle from the line between the center point and the start point. If you specify a positive angle as the included angle, an arc is drawn counterclockwise; for a negative angle, the arc is drawn clockwise.

Invoke the Start, Center, Angle option from:

Pull-down menu	Draw > Arc > Start, Center, Angle
Command: prompt	arc Enter

AutoCAD prompts:

Command: **arc** Enter
Center/<Start point:>: *(place a point, or specify the coordinates to define the start point of the arc)*
Center/End/<Second point>: **c** Enter
Center: *(place a point, or specify the coordinates to define the center point of the arc to be drawn)*
Angle/Length of chord/<Endpoint>: **a** Enter
Included Angle: *(specify the included angle of the arc to be drawn)*

The following command sequence shows an example (see Figure 2–25).

Command: **arc** Enter
Center/<Start point>: **1,2** Enter

Center/<Endpoint>: **c** Enter
Center: **2,2** Enter
Angle/Length of chord/<Endpoint>: **a** Enter
Included angle: **270** Enter

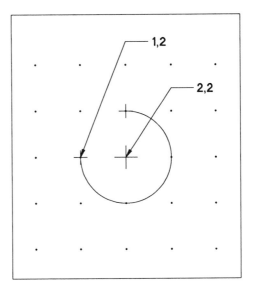

Figure 2–25   An arc drawn with the Start, Center, Angle (S,C,A) option

> **NOTE:** If a point directly below the specified center were selected (in the previous example) in response to the "Included angle:" prompt, AutoCAD would read the angle of the line (from zero) (270 degrees) as the included angle for the arc. In Figure 2–25, the point selected in response to the "Included angle:" prompt causes AutoCAD to read the angle between the line it establishes from the center and the zero direction (east in the default coordinate system). It does *not* measure the angle between the line the point establishes from the center and the line established from the center to the start point.

Start, Center, Length of Chord Option (or S,C,L for short)   This method uses the specified chord length as the straight-line distance from the start point to the endpoint. With any chord length (equal to or less than the diameter length) there are four possible arcs that can be drawn: a major arc in either direction and a minor arc in either direction. Therefore, all arcs drawn by this method are counterclockwise from the start point. A positive value for the length of chord will cause AutoCAD to draw the minor arc; a negative value will result in the major arc.

Invoke the Start, Center, Length of chord Option from:

Pull-down menu	Draw > Arc > Start, Center, Length
Command: prompt	arc [Enter]

AutoCAD prompts:

Command: **arc** [Enter]
Center/<Start point:>: *(place a point, or specify the coordinates to define the start point of the arc)*
Center/End/<Second point>: **c** [Enter]
Center: *(place a point, or specify the coordinates to define the center point of the arc to be drawn)*
Angle/Length of chord/<Endpoint>: **l** [Enter]
Length of chord: *(specify the length of the chord of the arc to be drawn)*

The following command sequence shows an example of drawing a minor arc, as shown in Figure 2–26.

Command: **arc** [Enter]
Center/<Start point>: **1,2** [Enter]
Center/<Endpoint>: **c** [Enter]
Center: **2,2** [Enter]
Angle/Length of chord/<Endpoint>: **l** *(letter l, not number 1)* [Enter]
Length of chord: **1.414** [Enter]

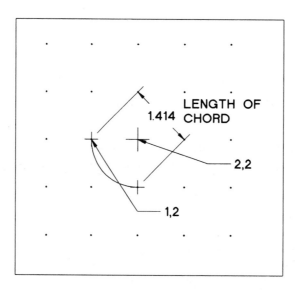

Figure 2–26 A minor arc drawn with the Start, Center, Length of chord (S,C,L) option.

The following command sequence shows an example of drawing a major arc, as shown in Figure 2–27.

Command: **arc** Enter
Center/<Start point>: **1,2** Enter
Center/<Endpoint>: **c** Enter
Center: **2,2** Enter
Angle/Length of chord/<Endpoint>: **l** *(letter l, not number 1)* Enter
Length of chord: **-1.414** Enter

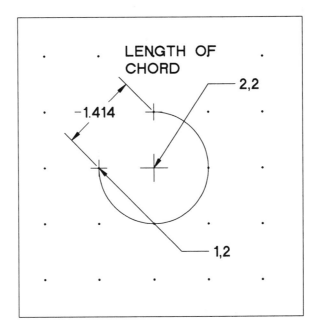

Figure 2–27 A major arc drawn with the Start, Center, Length of chord (S,C,L) option

Start, End, Angle Option (or S,E,A for short) This option draws an arc similar to the Start, Center, Angle option method, and places the endpoint on a radial line at the specified angle from the line between the center point and the start point. If you specify a positive angle for the included angle, an arc is drawn counterclockwise; for a negative angle the arc is drawn clockwise.

Invoke the Start, End, Angle option from:

Pull-down menu	Draw > Arc > Start, End, Angle
Command: prompt	**arc** Enter

AutoCAD prompts:

Command: **arc** [Enter]
Center/<Start point:>: *(place a point, or specify the coordinates to define the start point of the arc)*
Center/End/<Second point>: **e** [Enter]
Endpoint: *(place a point, or specify the coordinates to define the endpoint of the arc to be drawn)*
Angle/Direction/Radius/<Endpoint>: **a** [Enter]
Included Angle: *(specify the included angle of the arc to be drawn)*

The arc shown in Figure 2–28 is drawn using the following sequence:

Command: **arc** [Enter]
Center/<Start point>: **3,2** [Enter]
Center/End/<Second point>: **e** [Enter]
End point: **2,3** [Enter]
Angle/Direction/Radius/<Endpoint>: **a** [Enter]
Included angle: **90** [Enter]

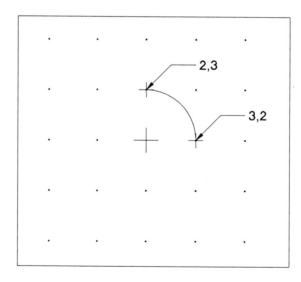

Figure 2–28   An arc drawn counterclockwise with the Start, End, Included Angle (S,E,A) option

The arc shown in Figure 2–29 is drawn with a negative angle using the following sequence:

Command: **arc** [Enter]
Center/<Start point>: **3,2** [Enter]

Center/End/<Second point>: **e** Enter
End point: **2,3** Enter
Angle/Direction/Radius/<Endpoint>: **a** Enter
Included angle: -**270** Enter

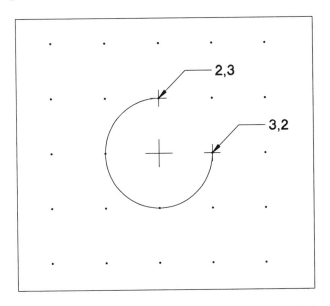

Figure 2–29 An arc drawn clockwise with the Start, End, Included Angle (S,E,A) option

Start, End, Direction Option (or S,E,D for short) This method allows you to draw an arc between selected points by specifying a direction in which the arc will start from the selected start point. Either the direction can be keyed in or you can select a point on the screen with your pointing device. If you select a point on the screen, AutoCAD uses the angle from the start point to the selected point as the starting direction.

Invoke the Start, End, Direction option from:

Pull-down menu	Draw > Arc > Start, End, Direction
Command: prompt	arc Enter

AutoCAD prompts:

Command: **arc** Enter
Center/<Start point:>: *(place a point, or specify the coordinates to define the start point of the arc)*
Center/End/<Second point>: **e** Enter

Endpoint: *(place a point, or specify the coordinates to define the endpoint of the arc to be drawn)*
Angle/Direction/Radius/<Endpoint>: **d** Enter
Direction from start point: *(specify the direction from the start point of the arc to be drawn)*

The arc shown in Figure 2–30 is drawn using the following sequence:

Command: **arc** Enter
Center/<Start point>: **3,2** Enter
Center/End/<Second point>: **e** Enter
Endpoint: **2,3** Enter
Angle/Direction/Radius/<Center point>: **d** Enter
Direction from start point: **90** Enter

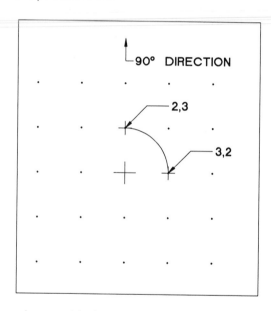

Figure 2–30 An arc drawn with the Start, End, Direction (S,E,D) option

Start, End, Radius Option (or S,E,R for short) This method allows you to specify a radius after selecting the two endpoints of the arc. As with the Chord Length method, there are four possible arcs that can be drawn: a major arc in either direction and a minor arc in either direction. Therefore, all arcs drawn by this method are counterclockwise from the start point. A positive value for the radius causes AutoCAD to draw the minor arc; a negative value results in the major arc.

Invoke the Start, End, Radius option from:

Pull-down menu	<u>D</u>raw > <u>A</u>rc > Start, End, <u>R</u>adius
Command: prompt	**arc** Enter

AutoCAD prompts:

> Command: **arc** Enter
> Center/<Start point:>: *(place a point, or specify the coordinates to define the start point of the arc)*
> Center/End/<Second point>: **e** Enter
> Endpoint: *(place a point, or specify the coordinates to define the endpoint of the arc to be drawn)*
> Angle/Direction/Radius/<Endpoint>: **r** Enter
> Radius: *(specify the radius of the arc to be drawn)*

The following command sequence shows an example of drawing a minor arc, as shown in Figure 2–31.

> Command: **arc** Enter
> Center/<Start point>: **1,2** Enter
> Center/End/<Second point>: **e** Enter
> Endpoint: **2,3** Enter
> Angle/Direction/Radius/<Center point>: **r** Enter
> Radius: **-1** Enter

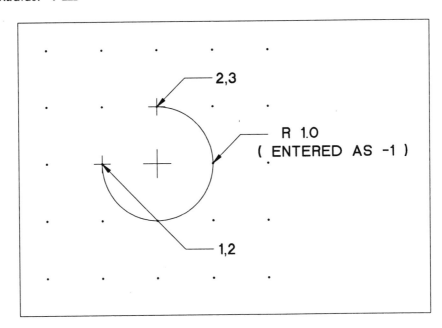

Figure 2–31 A minor arc drawn with the Start, End, Radius (S,E,R) option

The following command sequence shows an example of drawing a major arc, as shown in Figure 2–32.

Command: **arc** Enter
Center/<Start point>: **2,3** Enter
Center/End/<Second point>: **e** Enter
Endpoint: **1,2** Enter
Angle/Direction/Radius/<Center point>: **r** Enter
Radius: **1** Enter

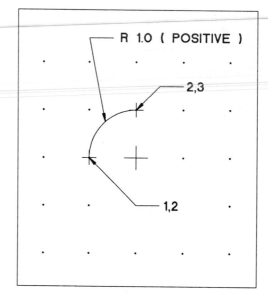

R 1.0 (POSITIVE)

2,3

1,2

Figure 2–32   A major arc drawn with the Start, End, Radius (S,E,R) option

Center, Start, End Option (or C,S,E for short)   This method is similar to the Start, Center, End (S,C,E) method, except in this option the beginning point is the center point of the arc rather than the start point.

Center, Start, Angle Option (or C,S,A for short)   This method is similar to the Start, Center, Angle (S,C,A) method, except in this option the beginning point is the center point of the arc rather than the start point.

Center, Start, Length Option (or C,S,L for short)   This method is similar to the Start, Center, Length (S,C,L) method, except that the beginning point is the center point of the arc rather than the start point.

Line-Arc and Arc-Arc Continuation Option   You can use an automatic Start point, Endpoint, Starting direction method to draw an arc by pressing Enter as a response to the first prompt of the ARC command. After pressing ⏎, the only other input is to select or specify the endpoint of the arc you wish to draw. AutoCAD uses the endpoint of the previous line or arc (whichever was drawn last) as the start point of the new arc. AutoCAD then uses the ending direction of that last drawn object as the starting direction of the arc. Examples are shown in the following sequences and figures.

The start point of the existing arc is 2,1 and the endpoint is 3,2 with a radius of 1. This makes the ending direction of the existing arc 90 degrees, as shown in Figure 2–33.

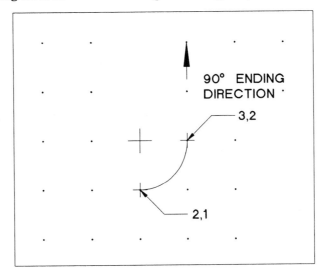

Figure 2–33 An arc drawn with a start point (2,1), an endpoint (3,2), and a radius of 1.0

The following command sequence continues drawing an arc, from the last-drawn arc, as shown in Figure 2–34 (arc-arc continuation).

    Command: **arc** ⏎
    Center/<Start point>: ⏎
    Endpoint: **2,3** ⏎

The arc, as shown in Figure 2–33, is drawn clockwise instead, with its start point at 3,2 to an endpoint of 2,1 (see Figure 2–35).

The following command sequence will draw the automatic Start point, Endpoint, Starting direction arc, as shown in Figure 2–36.

    Command: **arc** ⏎
    Center/<Start point>: ⏎
    Endpoint: **2,3** ⏎

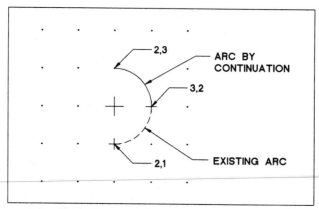

Figure 2–34   An arc drawn by means of the Arc-Arc Continuation method

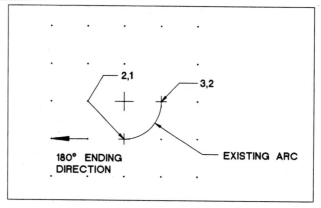

Figure 2–35   An arc drawn clockwise with start point (3,2) and endpoint (2,1)

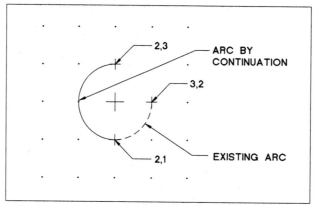

Figure 2–36   An arc drawn by means of the automatic Startpoint-Endpoint-Starting direction method

In the last case, the direction used is 180 degrees. The same arc would have been drawn if the last "line-or-arc" drawn was a line starting at 4,1 and ending at 2,1.

> **NOTE:** This method uses the last drawn of either an arc or a line. If you draw an arc, then draw a line, then draw a circle, and then use this continuation method, AutoCAD will use the line as the basis for the start point and direction. This is because the line was the last of the "line-or-arc" objects drawn.

OBJECT SELECTION

Many AutoCAD modify and construct commands prompt you to select one or more objects for manipulation. When you select one or more objects, AutoCAD highlights them by displaying them with broken lines. The group of objects selected for the manipulation is called the *selection set*. There are several different ways of selecting the objects for manipulation. The selection options include: Window, Window Polygon (WP), Crossing, Crossing Polygon (CP), Box, Fence, All, Last, Previous, Group Add, Remove, Single, Multiple, and Undo.

All modify and construct commands require a selection set, for which AutoCAD prompts:

Select objects:

AutoCAD replaces the screen crosshairs with a small box called the *object selection target*. With the target cursor, select individual objects for manipulation. Using your pointing device (or the keyboard's cursor keys), position the target box so it touches only the desired object or a visible portion of it. The object selection target helps you point to the object without having to be very precise. Every time you select an object, the "Select objects:" prompt reappears. To indicate your acceptance of the selection set, give a Null reply at the "Select objects:" prompt.

Sometimes, it is difficult to select objects or that are close together or lie directly on top of one another. You can use the pick button to cycle through these objects, one after the other, until you reach the one you want.

To cycle through objects for selection, at the "Select Objects" prompt, hold down the Ctrl key. Select a point as near as possible to the object. Press the pick button on your pointing device repeatedly until the object you want is highlighted, and press Enter key to select the object.

Window Option   The Window option in the selection of the objects allows you to designate all the objects contained completely in a rectangular area or dynamically manipulated window.

The window can be placed by placing a point at the appropriate location to the "Select Objects:" prompt and moving the cursor toward the right of the first data point. AutoCAD prompts:

Other corner: *(place a point, or specify the coordinates to define the opposite corner of the window)*

You can also define a window for selection of objects, by typing **w** to the "Select Objects:" prompt, and AutoCAD prompts:

First corner: *(place a point, or specify the coordinates to define the first corner of the window)*
Other corner: *(place a point, or specify the coordinates to define the opposite corner of the window)*

If there is an object that is partially inside the rectangular area, then that object is not included in the selection set. You can select only objects currently visible on the screen. To select a partially visible object, you must include all its visible parts within the window. See Figure 2-37, in which only the lines will be included, *not* the circles, because a portion of each of the circles is outside the rectangular area.

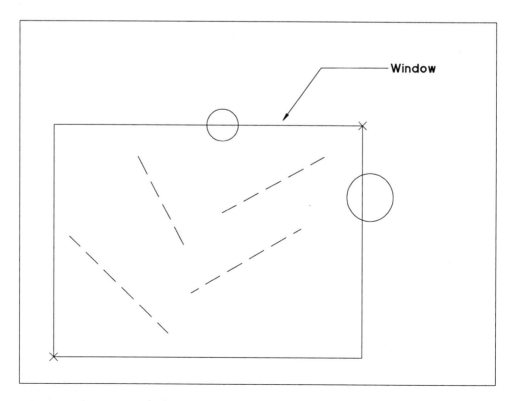

Figure 2–37 Selecting objects by means of the Window option

Crossing Option   The Crossing option in the selection of the objects allows you to designate all the objects contained completely in a rectangular area as well as the objects that are crossing the window.

The crossing can be placed by placing a point at the appropriate location to the "Select Objects:" prompt and moving the cursor toward the left of the first data point. AutoCAD prompts:

> Other corner: *(place a point, or specify the coordinates to define the opposite corner of the crossing)*

You can also define a crossing for the selection of objects, by typing **c** to the "Select Objects:" prompt, and AutoCAD prompts:

> First corner: *(place a point, or specify the coordinates to define the first corner of the window)*
> Other corner: *(place a point, or specify the coordinates to define the opposite corner of the window)*

See Figure 2-38, in which all the lines and circles are included, though parts of the circles are outside the rectangle.

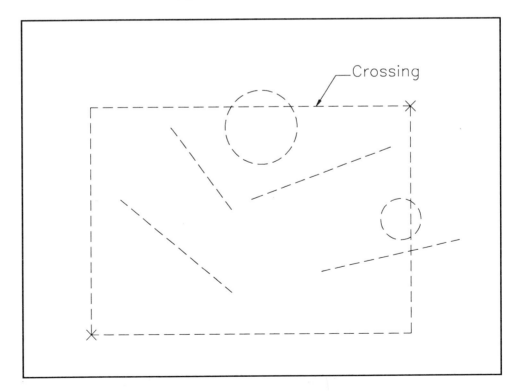

Figure 2–38   Selecting objects by means of the Crossing option

Previous Option The Previous option enables you to perform several operations on the same object or group of objects. AutoCAD remembers the most recent selection set and allows you to reselect it with the Previous option. For example, if you moved several objects and now wish to copy them elsewhere, you can invoke the COPY command and respond to the "Select objects:" prompt with **p** to select the same objects again. (There is a command called SELECT that does nothing but create a selection set; you can then use the Previous option to refer to this set in subsequent commands.)

Last Option The Last option is an easy way to select the most recently created object currently visible. Only one object is designated, no matter how often you use the Last option when constructing a particular selection set. The Last option is invoked by typing **l** at the "Select Objects:" prompt.

The WPolygon, CPolygon, Fence, All, Group, Box, Auto, Undo, Single, Multiple, Add, and Remove options are explained in Chapter 5.

MODIFY OBJECTS

AutoCAD not only allows you to draw objects easily, but also allows you to modify the objects you have drawn. Of the many modifying commands available, the ERASE command probably will be the one you use most often. Everyone makes mistakes, but in AutoCAD it is easier to erase them. Or, if you are through with an object that you have created for construction of other objects, you may wish to erase it.

Erasing Objects

To erase objects from a drawing, invoke the ERASE command from:

Modify toolbar	Select the Erase command (see Figure 2–39)
Pull-down menu	Modify > Erase
Command: prompt	erase Enter

Figure 2–39 Invoking the ERASE command from the Modify toolbar

Command: **erase** Enter
Select objects: *(select objects to be erased, and then press the Spacebar or* Enter *)*

You can use one or more available object selection methods. After selecting the object(s), press Enter (null response) in response to the next "Select objects:" prompt to complete the ERASE command. All the objects that were selected will disappear.

The following command sequence shows an example of erasing individual objects as shown Figure 2–40.

> Command: **erase** Enter
> Select objects: *(pick line 2, the line is highlighted)* 1 selected, 1 found
> Select objects: *(pick line 4, the line is highlighted)* 1 selected, 1 found
> Select objects: Enter

The following command sequence shows an example of erasing a group of objects as shown in Figure 2–41 by the Window option:

> Command: **erase** Enter
> Select objects: *(pick a point)*
> Other corner: *(pick a point for the diagonally opposite corner)* 4 found
> Select objects: Enter

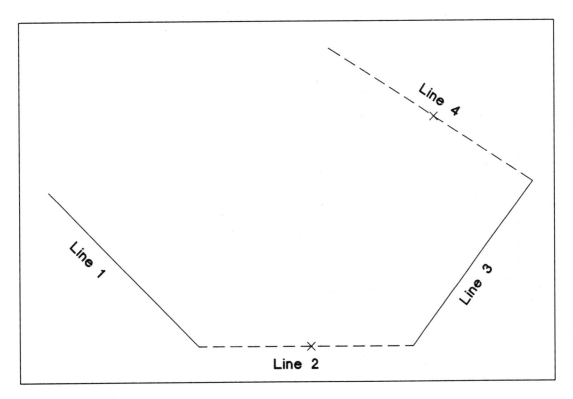

Figure 2–40 Selection of individual objects to erase

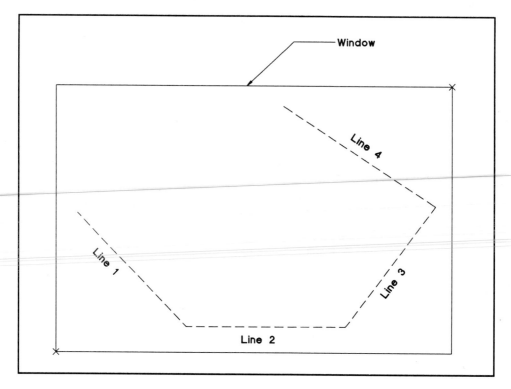

Figure 2–41 Erasing a group of objects

OOPS Command

The OOPS command restores objects that have been unintentionally erased. Whenever the ERASE command is used, the last group of objects erased is stored in memory. The OOPS command will help you to restore the objects; it can be used at any time. It only restores the objects erased by the most recent ERASE command. See Chapter 3 on the UNDO command, if you need to step back further than one ERASE command.

To restore objects erased by the last ERASE command, invoke the OOPS command from:

Command: prompt	**oops** ⏎ᴱⁿᵗᵉʳ

AutoCAD restores the objects erased by the last ERASE command.

The following example shows the command sequence for using the OOPS command in conjunction with the ERASE command:

Command: **erase** ⏎ᴱⁿᵗᵉʳ
Select objects: *(specify a point)*

Other corner: *(specify a point for the diagonally opposite corner)*
Select objects: Enter
Command: **oops** Enter *(will restore the erased objects)*

PROJECT EXERCISE

This project exercise provides point-by-point instructions for setting up the drawing, laying out the border, and then creating the objects shown in Figure P2–1. In this exercise you will apply the skills acquired in Chapters 1 and 2 to drawing basic architectural, mechanical, electronic, and piping objects.

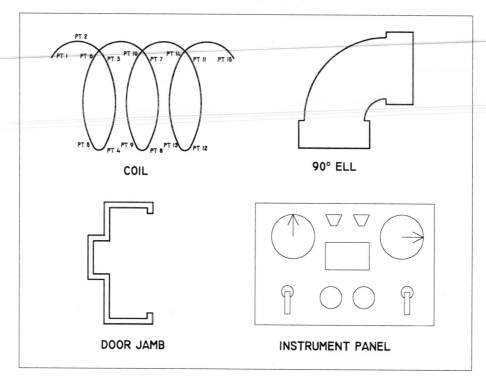

Figure P2–1   Completed project drawing

In this project you will:

- Apply the "Use a Wizard" option of the Create a New Drawing dialog box.
- Set the Units used for the drawing.
- Set the Limits for the drawing Area
- Use the LINE, RECTANG, CIRCLE, and ARC commands.

> **NOTE:** As you complete each step in the project procedure, place a check mark by the step to help you keep up with where you are in the project.

Set Up the Drawing and Draw a Border

This procedure describes the steps required to set up the drawing and to draw the border.

Step 1   Invoke the AutoCAD program.

Example: Under Microsoft Windows 95, find the AutoCAD program in the Start > Programs menu and select it.

Step 2   To create a new drawing, invoke the NEW command from the Standard toolbar, as shown in Figure P2–2 or select New from the pull-down menu File.

Figure P2–2   Invoking the NEW command from the Standard toolbar

Step 3   AutoCAD displays the Create New Drawing dialog box, as shown in Figure P2–3. Click the "Use a Wizard" button, and then select the Quick Setup and choose the OK button to close the dialog box.

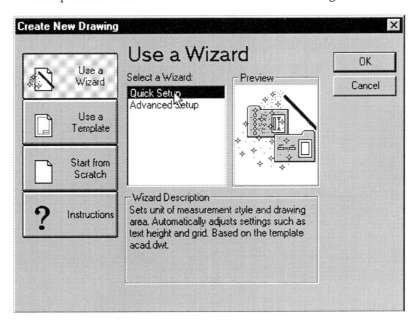

Figure P2–3   Create New Drawing dialog box

Step 4 AutoCAD displays the Quick Setup dialog box with the display of the Step 1: Units tab, as shown in Figure P2–4. Select the "Decimal" radio button, and choose the Next>> button.

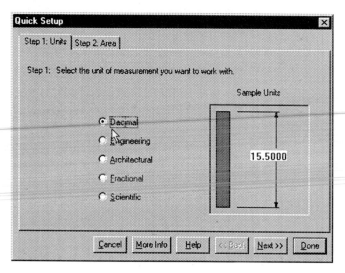

Figure P2–4 Quick Setup dialog box with Step 1: Units tab

Step 5 AutoCAD displays the Quick Setup dialog box with the display of the Step 2: Area tab, as shown in Figure P2–5. Under the Width: edit field enter **11**, and under the Length: edit field enter **8.5**. Choose the Done button to close the Quick Step dialog box.

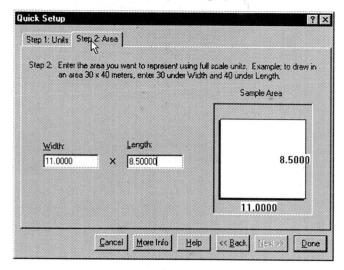

Figure P2–5 Quick Setup dialog box with Step 2: Area tab

Step 6   To draw the border, invoke the RECTANG command from the Draw toolbar, as shown in Figure P2–6, or type **rectang** at the "Command:" prompt and press Enter.

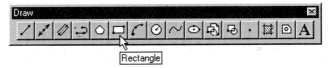

Figure P2–6   Invoking the RECTANG command from the Draw toolbar

AutoCAD prompts:

> Command: **rectang** Enter
> Chamfer/Elevation/Fillet/Thickness/Width/<First Corner>: **0.25,0.25** Enter
> Other corner: **10.75,8.25** Enter

AutoCAD draws a rectangle border as shown in Figure P2–7.

Figure P2–7   Completed border outline

Step 7   To save the current status of the drawing, invoke the Save command from the pull-down menu File or type **save** at the "Command:" prompt. AutoCAD displays the Save Drawing As dialog box. Type **PROJ2** as the name of the drawing in the File name: edit box, and click the Save button to save the drawing and close the Save Drawing As dialog box. Make sure you are saving the drawing in the appropriate directory.

Draw the Door Jamb

This procedure describes the steps required to draw the door jamb shown in Figure P2–8. The door jamb is drawn with the LINE command using rectangular coordinates and polar coordinates.

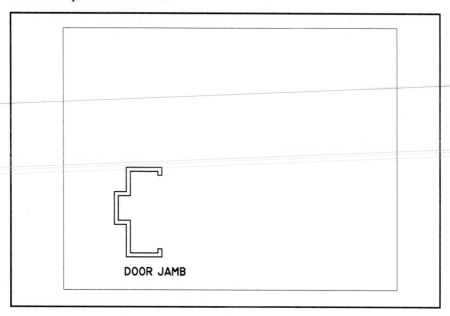

Figure P2–8 Door Jamb

Step 1   To draw the door jamb, invoke the LINE command from the Draw Toolbar, as shown in Figure P2–9, or type **line** and press ⏎ key at the "Command:" prompt.

Figure P2–9   Invoking the LINE command from the Draw toolbar

AutoCAD prompts:

> Command: **line** ⏎
> From point: **2,1.5** ⏎
> To point: **2,2.5** ⏎
> To point: **1.625,2.5** ⏎
> To point: **1.625,3.5** ⏎
> To point: **2,3.5** ⏎
> To point: **2,4.25** ⏎
> To point: **3.125,4.25** ⏎
> To point: **3.125,4** ⏎

To point: **3,4** `Enter`
To point: **@0.125<90** `Enter`
To point: **@0.875<180** `Enter`
To point: **@0.75<270** `Enter`
To point: **@0.375<180** `Enter`
To point: **@0,-0.75** `Enter`
To point: **@0.375,0** `Enter`
To point: **@0,-1** `Enter`
To point: **@0.875,0** `Enter`
To point: **@0,0.125** `Enter`
To point: **@0.125,0** `Enter`
To point: **@0,-0.25** `Enter`
To point: **@-1.125,0** `Enter`
To point: *(press the* `Enter` *to terminate the command sequence)*

Step 2   To save the current status of the drawing, invoke the Save command from the pull-down menu File or type **save** at the "Command:" prompt. AutoCAD saves the current status of the drawing.

Draw the Instrument Panel

This procedure describes the steps required to draw the instrument panel shown in Figure P2–10. The instrument panel is drawn with the LINE, RECTANG, CIRCLE, and ARC commands.

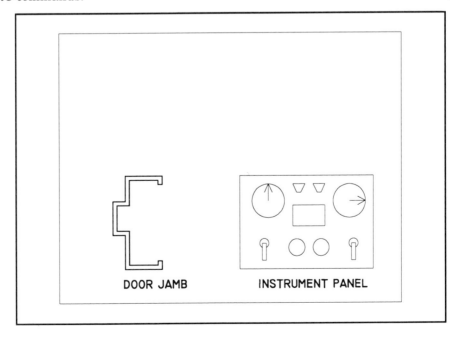

DOOR JAMB   INSTRUMENT PANEL

Figure P2–10   Door jamb and instrument panel

Step 1 To draw the main outline of the instrument panel and the central rectangle, invoke the RECTANG command from the Draw Toolbar or type **rectang** and press Enter at the "Command:" prompt.

AutoCAD prompts:

Command: **rectang** Enter
Chamfer/Elevation/Fillet/Thickness/Width/<First Corner>: **5.75,1.25** Enter
Other corner: **9.875,4** Enter

Command: (press the Enter to repeat the RECTANG command)
Chamfer/Elevation/Fillet/Thickness/Width/<First Corner>: **7.375,2.5** Enter
Other corner: **8.375,3.125** Enter

Step 2 To draw the trapezoidal shapes located in the top of the instrument panel, invoke the LINE command from the Draw Toolbar or type **line** and press Enter at the "Command:" prompt.

AutoCAD prompts:

Command: **line** Enter
From point: **7.375,3.75** Enter
To point: **@.375<0** Enter
To point: **7.625,3.5** Enter
To point: **@.125<180** Enter
To point: **c** Enter

Command: (press Enter to repeat the LINE command)
LINE From point: **8.000,3.75** Enter
To point: **@.375<0** Enter
To point: **8.25,3.5** Enter
To point: **@.125<180** Enter
To point: **c** Enter

Step 3 To draw the circular guages with the arrow pointers located in the top of the instrument panel, first invoke the CIRCLE command from the Draw Toolbar as shown in Figure P2–11, or type **circle** and press Enter at the "Command:" prompt.

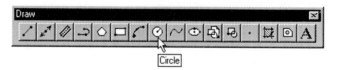

Figure P2–11 Invoking the CIRCLE command from the Draw toolbar

AutoCAD prompts:

Command: **circle** Enter
3P/2P/TTR/<Center point>: **6.625,3.25** Enter
Diameter/<Radius>: **@.5<0** Enter

Command: *(press* Enter *to repeat the CIRCLE command)*
CIRCLE 3P/2P/TTR/<Center point>: **9.125,3.25** Enter
Diameter/<Radius> <0.5000>: **@.5<0** Enter

To draw the arrow pointers, invoke the LINE command from the Draw Toolbar or type **line** and press Enter at the "Command:" prompt.

AutoCAD prompts:

Command: **line** Enter
From point: **6.5,3.5** Enter
To point: **6.625,3.75** Enter
To point: **6.75,3.5** Enter
To point: *(press* Enter *to terminate the command sequence)*

Command: *(press* Enter *to repeat the LINE command)*
LINE From point: **6.625,3.25** Enter
To point: **6.625,3.75** Enter
To point: *(press* Enter*to terminate the command sequence)*

Command: *(press* Enter *to repeat the LINE command)*
LINE From point: **9.375,3.375** Enter
To point: **9.625,3.25** Enter
To point: **9.375,3.125** Enter
To point: *(press* Enter *to terminate the command sequence)*

Command: *(press* Enter *to repeat the LINE command)*
LINE From point: **9.125,3.25** Enter
To point: **9.625,3.25** Enter
To point: *(press* Enter*to terminate the command sequence)*

Step 4   To draw the two circles located in the bottom of the instrument panel, first invoke the CIRCLE command from the Draw Toolbar or type **circle** and press Enter at the "Command:" prompt.

AutoCAD prompts:

Command: **circle** Enter
3P/2P/TTR/<Center point>: **7.5,1.875** Enter
Diameter/<Radius> <0.5000>:**.25** Enter

Command: *(press* Enter *to repeat the circle command)*
CIRCLE 3P/2P/TTR/<Center point>: **8.25,1.875** Enter
Diameter/<Radius> <0.2500>:**.25** Enter

Step 5   To draw the switches located in the bottom of the instrument panel, first invoke the RECTANG command from the Draw toolbar or type **rectang** at the "Command:" prompt.

Fundamentals I

AutoCAD prompts:

> Command: **rectang** [Enter]
> Chamfer/Elevation/Fillet/Thickness/Width/<First Corner>: **6.4375,1.5** [Enter]
> Other corner: **6.5625,2** [Enter]
>
> Command: (press [Enter] to repeat the RECTANG command)
> Chamfer/Elevation/Fillet/Thickness/Width/<First Corner>: **9.1875,1.5** [Enter]
> Other corner: **9.3125,2** [Enter]

Invoke the ARC command from the Draw Toolbar, as shown in Figure P2–12, or type **arc** at the "Command:" prompt.

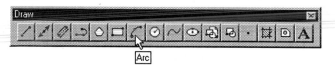

Figure P2–12   Invoking the ARC command from the Draw toolbar

AutoCAD prompts:

> Command: **arc** [Enter]
> Command: _arc Center/<Start point>: **6.5625,1.875** [Enter]
> Center/End/<Second point>: (type **c** and press [Enter] for Center option selection)
> Center: **6.5,2** [Enter]
> Angle/Length of chord/<End point>: **6.4375,1.875** [Enter]
>
> Command: (press [Enter] to repeat the circle command)
> ARC Center/<Start point>: **9.3125,1.875**
> Center/End/<Second point>: (type **c** and press [Enter] for Center option selection)
> Center: **9.25,2** [Enter]
> Angle/Length of chord/<End point>: **9.1875,1.875** [Enter]

Step 6   To save the current status of the drawing, invoke the Save command from the pull-down menu File or type **save** at the "Command:" prompt. AutoCAD saves the current status of the drawing.

Draw the 90° Ell

This procedure describes the steps required to draw the 90-degree ell shown in Figure P2–13. The 90-degree ell is drawn with the LINE and ARC commands.

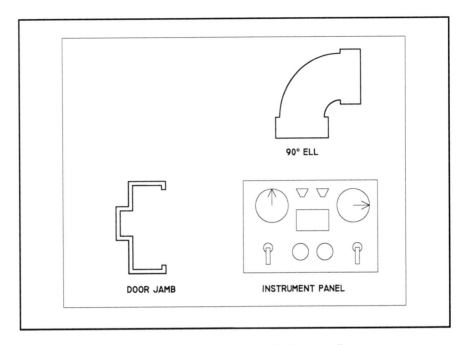

Figure P2–13 Door jamb, instrument panel, and 90-degree ell

Step 1   To draw the lower lines of the 90-degree ell, invoke the LINE command from the Draw toolbar or type **line** and press ⏎ at the "Command:" prompt.

AutoCAD prompts:

> Command: **line** ⏎
> From point: **8.25,5.875** ⏎
> To point: **@.125<0** ⏎
> To point: **@.625<-90** ⏎
> To point: **@1.625<180** ⏎
> To point: **@.625<90** ⏎
> To point: **@.125<0** ⏎
> To point: *(press ⏎ to terminate the command sequence)*

Step 2   To draw the large outer arc, invoke the ARC command from the Draw toolbar or type **arc** and press ⏎ at the "Command:" prompt.

AutoCAD prompts:

> Command: **arc** ⏎
> Center/<Start point>: **6.875,5.875** ⏎
> Center/End/<Second point>:   *(type **c** and press ⏎ for Center option selection)*

Center: @1.875<0 [Enter]
Angle/Length of chord/<End point>: *(type* **a** *and press* [Enter] *for Included angle option selection)*
Included angle: **-90** [Enter]

Step 3   To draw the upper lines of the 90-degree ell, invoke the LINE command from the Draw toolbar or type **line** and press [Enter] at the "Command:" prompt.

AutoCAD prompts:

Command: **line** [Enter]
From point: **8.75,7.75** [Enter]
To point: **@.125<90** [Enter]
To point: **@.625<0** [Enter]
To point: **@1.625<-90** [Enter]
To point: **@.625<180** [Enter]
To point: **@.125<90** [Enter]
To point: *(press* [Enter] *to terminate the command sequence)*

Step 4   To draw the smaller outer arc, invoke the ARC command from the Draw toolbar or type **arc** and press [Enter] the "Command:" prompt.

AutoCAD prompts:

Command: **arc** [Enter]
Center/<Start point>: *(type* **@** *and press* [Enter] *to select the last point as the start point)*
Center/End/<Second point>: *(type* **c** *and press* [Enter] *for center option selection)*
Center: **@.5<-90** [Enter]
Angle/Length of chord/<End point>: **@.5<180** [Enter]

Step 5   To save the current status of the drawing, invoke the Save command from the pull-down menu File or type **save** at the "Command:" prompt. AutoCAD saves the current status of the drawing.

Draw the Coil

This procedure describes the steps required to draw the coil shown in Figure P2–14. The coil is drawn with the ARC command.

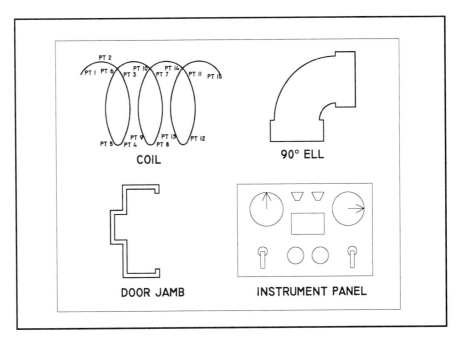

Figure P2–14 Door jamb, instrument panel, 90-degree ell, and coil

Step 1   To draw the coil, invoke the ARC command from the Draw toolbar or type **arc** and press Enter at the "Command:" prompt.

AutoCAD prompts:

Command: **arc** Enter
Center/<Start point>: **1,7.25** Enter
Center/End/<Second point>: **1.625,7.625** Enter
End point: **2.25,7.25** Enter

Command: (press Enter to repeat the ARC command)
ARC Center/<Start point>: (press Enter to continue from the previous point)
End point: **2.25,5.25** Enter

Command: (press Enter to repeat the ARC command)
ARC Center/<Start point>: (press Enter to continue from the previous point)
End point: **2,5.25** Enter

Command: (press Enter to repeat the ARC command)
ARC Center/<Start point>: (press Enter to continue from the previous point)
End point: **2,7.25** Enter

Command: (press Enter to repeat the ARC command)
ARC Center/<Start point>: (press Enter to continue from the previous point)
End point: **3.25,7.25** Enter

(Take a breath. This completes the first loop of the coil. Even though the Three-Point option was used for the leading arc of the first loop, the leading arc of the second loop, which is the trailing arc of the first loop, was drawn with the arc-arc continuation method.)

> Command: *(press* Enter *to repeat the ARC command)*
> ARC Center/<Start point>: *(press* Enter *to continue from the previous point)*
> End point: **3.25,5.25** Enter

> Command: *(press* Enter *to repeat the ARC command)*
> ARC Center/<Start point>: *(press* Enter *to continue from the previous point)*
> End point: **3,5.25** Enter

> Command: *(press* Enter *to repeat the ARC command)*
> ARC Center/<Start point>: *(press* Enter *to continue from the previous point)*
> End point: **3,7.25** Enter

> Command: *(press* Enter *to repeat the ARC command)*
> ARC Center/<Start point>: *(press* Enter *to continue from the previous point)*
> End point: **4.25,7.25** Enter

(Take another breath. This completes the second loop and starts the last loop of the coil.)

> Command: *(press* Enter *to repeat the ARC command)*
> ARC Center/<Start point>: *(press* Enter *to continue from the previous point)*
> End point: **4.25,5.25** Enter

> Command: *(press* Enter *to repeat the ARC command)*
> ARC Center/<Start point>: *(press* Enter *to continue from the previous point)*
> End point: **4,5.25** Enter

> Command: *(press* Enter *to repeat the ARC command)*
> ARC Center/<Start point>: *(press* Enter *to continue from the previous point)*
> End point: **4,7.25** Enter

> Command: *(press* Enter *to repeat the ARC command)*
> ARC Center/<Start point>: *(press* Enter *to continue from the previous point)*
> End point: **5.25,7.25** Enter

Step 2   To save the current status of the drawing, invoke the Save command from the pull-down menu File or type **save** at the command: prompt. AutoCAD saves the current status of the drawing.

Congratulations! You have just successfully applied several AutoCAD concepts in creating the drawing.

EXERCISES 2–5 THROUGH 2–8

Exercise 2–5

Type of shape	Input Methods
Multiple circles	• Absolute rectangular coordinates • Center-Radius option for circles

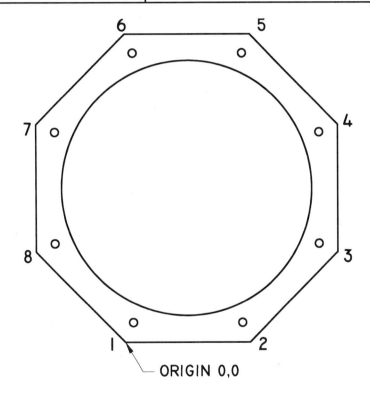

Points of Interest

■ The main octagon in this figure was drawn precisely by using the relative polar coordinate point entry method. However, only the coordinates of the bottom line are nice, round units. The other endpoints around the polygon cannot easily be entered exactly from the keyboard.

■ The most significant point of this figure is probably its center. The relative distance/direction from the center to the endpoints of the bottom line are calculated by trigonometry. Therefore, at this level we will simply enter "very close" coordinates for the center. We will do the same for the "bolt circle" (circle of circles).

Important Points

■ Advanced features like the ARRAY command may be used to make the drawing exact if necessary.

■ Note that arcs can be drawn both clockwise and counterclockwise with the three-point option. This is not the case with all options of the ARC command.

Drawing Setup	Open the drawing made in Exercise 2–4.
Power Point	Each center of the smaller circles can be established relative to the previous one drawn. But in order to start the first small circle, its center must be established by its absolute coordinates or by its relation to another point. We know that it is 2" distance at 68.5° from the left end of the bottom line (the origin 0,0). So, in order to make the origin the "last point," we will just start a line there and then not complete it. This will establish it as the point used by the "@" symbol. The next chapter will eliminate this trickery with the Tracking feature, new in AutoCAD Release 14.

Point by Point

Invoke the CIRCLE command, AutoCAD prompts:

Command: **circle**
3P/2P/TTR/<Center point>: **2'0,4'10** Enter *(center point of the large circle)*
Diameter/<Radius>: **48** Enter *(radius of the large circle)*

Invoke the LINE command, AutoCAD prompts:

Command: **line**
From point: **0,0** Enter *(establish the last point at 0,0)*
To point: *(press* Esc *to terminate the command sequence)*

Invoke the CIRCLE command, AutoCAD prompts:

Command: **circle**
3P/2P/TTR/<Center point>:**@8<67.5** Enter) *(center point of the first small circle)*
Diameter/<Radius>: **1.5** Enter *(radius of the first small circle)*
Command: *(press* Enter *to invoke the CIRCLE command again)*
3P/2P/TTR/<Center point>:**@42<0** Enter *(center point of the second small circle)*
Diameter/<Radius>: **1.5** Enter *(radius of the second small circle)*
Command: *(press* Enter *to invoke the CIRCLE command again)*
3P/2P/TTR/<Center point>:**@42<45** Enter *(center point of the third small circle)*
Diameter/<Radius>: **1.5** Enter *(radius of the second third circle)*
Command: *(press* Enter *to invoke the CIRCLE command again)*
3P/2P/TTR/<Center point>:**@42<90** Enter *(center point of the fourth small circle)*
Diameter/<Radius>: **1.5** Enter *(radius of the fourth small circle)*

(Draw the fifth through eighth small circles by continuing with the method explained above in the previous circles but adding 45 degrees to the angle each time)

Exercise 2–6

Type of shapes	Input Methods
Multiple line/arc sequences	• Absolute rectangular coordinates • Relative rectangular coordinates • Relative polar coordinates

Some—but not all—of the points that determine the shape in this exercise can be entered by any one of the three listed methods. This exercise is primarily to emphasize when the line-arc continuation and the arc-line continuation options can be applied and when they cannot.

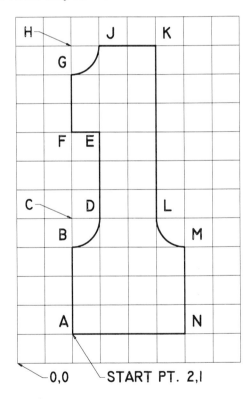

Points of Interest

■ The default line-line continuation of the LINE command does not require that lines drawn subsequent to the previous line segment start in the same direction that the previous line ends.

■ In line-line continuation you may proceed in any desired direction with the continuing line.

■ In line-arc and arc-line continuations the connecting line/arc must start in the same direction that the previous arc/line ends.

■ Invoking the Start-Center-End option (for arcs B-D and G-J in this exercise) requires:

1. Either overriding the default Start–Second point–End method by selecting St,C,End from the pull-down menu.

Drawing Setup	Use Quick Setup Wizard, set Units to Decimal, set Area to 9 x 13.

Point by Point

Invoke the LINE command, AutoCAD prompts:

Command: **line**
From point: **2,1** Enter *(starting point of line A-B)*
To point: **2,4** Enter *(end point of the line A-B)*
To point: Enter *(exit the LINE command)*

Invoke the ARC command, AutoCAD prompts:

Command: **arc**
Center/<Start point>: **2,4** Enter *(starting point of the arc B-D)*
Center/End/<Second point>: *(type c and press* Enter *for Center option selection)*
Center: **2,5** Enter *(arc center for the arc B-D)*
Angle/Length of chord/<End point>: **3,5** Enter *(end point of the arc B-D)*

Invoke the LINE command, AutoCAD prompts:

Command: **line**
From point: Enter *(invoke the continuation option)*
Length of line: **3** Enter *(length of the line D-E)*
To point: **2,8** Enter *(end point of the line E-F)*
To point: **2,10** Enter *(end point of the line F-G)*
To point: Enter *(exit the LINE command)*

Invoke the ARC command, AutoCAD prompts:

Command: **arc**
Center/<Start point>: **2,10** Enter *(starting point of the arc G-J)*
Center/End/<Second point>: *(type c and press* Enter *for Center option selection)*
Center: **2,11** Enter *(arc center for the arc G-J)*
Angle/Length of chord/<End point>: **3,11** Enter *(end point of the arc G-J)*

Invoke the LINE command, AutoCAD prompts:

Command: **line**
From point: **3,11** Enter *(start point of the line J-K)*
To point: **5,11** Enter *(end point of the line J-K)*
To point: **5,5** Enter *(end point of the line K-L)*
To point: Enter *(exit the LINE command)*

Invoke the ARC command, AutoCAD prompts:

Command: **arc**
Center/<Start point>: Enter *(invoke the continuation option to start the arc at L)*
End point: **6,4** Enter *(endpoint of the arc L-M)*

Invoke the LINE command, AutoCAD prompts:

Command: **line**
From point: **6,4** Enter *(start point of the line M-N)*
To point: **6,1** Enter *(end point of the line M-N)*
To point: **2,1** Enter *(end point of the line N-A)*
To point: Enter *(exit the LINE command)*

Exercise 2–7

Type of shapes	Input Methods
Single line sequence Multiple arcs	• Absolute rectangular coordinates • Three-point option for arcs

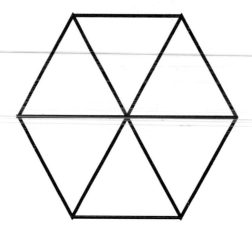

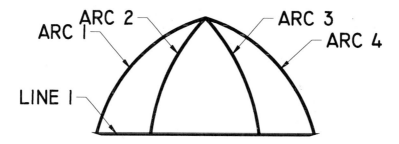

ARC 1   ARC 2   ARC 3   ARC 4

LINE 1

Points of Interest

■ The top view of this tent-shaped object gives some clues to its true shape, but not enough. A side view is required.

■ In the front view the two outside arcs are represented in their true 2-dimensional appearance. However, the two inner arcs represent arcs that are rotated 60°. Their true representation would be ellipses. Since we have not covered ellipses, we will use arcs to give close approximations.

Important Points

■ Advanced features like the ELLIPSE command and 3D drawing may used to make the drawing exact if necessary.

■ Note that arcs can be drawn both clockwise and counterclockwise with the three point option. This is not the case with all options of the ARC command.

Drawing Setup	Open the drawing created in Exercise 2–3

Point by Point

Invoke the LINE command, AutoCAD prompts:

> Command: **line**
> From point: **4,0.5** Enter *(starting point of line 1)*
> To point: **8,0.5** Enter *(end point of the line 1)*
> To point: Enter *(exit the LINE command)*

Invoke the ARC command, AutoCAD prompts:

> Command: **arc**
> Center/<Start point>: **4,0.5** Enter *(starting point of the arc 1)*
> Center/End/<Second point>: **5,2** Enter *(second point of the arc 1)*
> End point: **6,2.5** Enter *(end point of the arc 1)*
>
> Command: *(press* Enter *to invoke the ARC command again)*
> Center/<Start point>: **5,0. 5** Enter *(starting point of the arc 2)*
> Center/End/<Second point>: **5.5,1.875** Enter *(second point of the arc 2)*
> End point: **6,2.5** Enter *(end point of the arc 2)*
>
> Command: *(press* Enter *to invoke the ARC command again)*
> Center/<Start point>: **7,0.5** Enter *(starting point of the arc 3)*
> Center/End/<Second point>: **6.5,1.875** Enter *(second point of the arc 3)*
> End point: **6,2.5** Enter *(end point of the arc 3)*
>
> Command: *(press* Enter *to invoke the ARC command again)*
> Center/<Start point>: **8,0.5** Enter *(starting point of the arc 4)*
> Center/End/<Second point>: **7,2** Enter *(second point of the arc 4)*
> End point: **6,2.5** Enter *(end point of the arc 4)*

Fundamentals I

Exercise 2–8

Type of shape	Input methods
Multiple line/arc sequences	• Absolute rectangular coordinates • Relative rectangular coordinates • Relative polar coordinates

- This exercise is to be done without line-arc or arc-line continuation. Later, you will learn to use the command that draws Polylines; its options facilitate polyline-polyarc-polyline continuation.
- Some architectural illusionism is introduced.

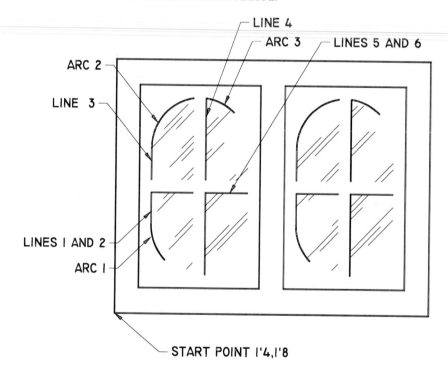

Drawing Setup	Open the drawing created in Exercise 2–2.

Point by Point

Invoke the LINE command, AutoCAD prompts:

Command: **line**
From point: **2'5,3'3** Enter *(starting point of line 1)*
To point: **1'10,3'3** Enter *(end point of the line 1)*

To point: **1'10,2'10** Enter *(end point of the line 2)*
To point: Enter *(exit the LINE command)*

Invoke the ARC command, AutoCAD prompts:

Command: **arc**
Center/<Start point>: **1'10,2'10** Enter *(starting point of the arc 1)*
Center/End/<Second point>: *(type c and press* Enter *for Center option selection)*
Center: **2'6,2'10** Enter *(arc center for the arc 1)*
Angle/Length of chord/<End point>: *(type a and press* Enter *for included angle option selection)*
Included angle: **45** Enter *(arc included angle for the arc 1)*

Invoke the LINE command, AutoCAD prompts:

Command: **line**
From point: **1'10,3'5** Enter *(starting point of line 3)*
To point: **1'10,3'10** Enter *(end point of the line 3)*
To point: Enter *(exit the LINE command)*

Invoke the ARC command, AutoCAD prompts:

Command: **arc**
Center/<Start point>: **1'10,3'10** Enter *(starting point of the arc 2)*
Center/End/<Second point>: *(type c and press* Enter *for Center option selection)*
Center: **2'6,3'10** Enter *(arc center for the arc 2)*
Angle/Length of chord/<End point>: *(type a and press* Enter *for included angle option selection)*
Included angle: **-82.82** Enter *(arc included angle for the arc 2)*

Invoke the LINE command, AutoCAD prompts:

Command: **line**
From point: **2'7,3'5** Enter *(starting point of line 4)*
To point: **2'7,4'6** Enter *(end point of the line 4)*
To point: Enter *(exit the LINE command)*

Invoke the ARC command, AutoCAD prompts:

Command: **arc**
Center/<Start point>: **2'7,4'6** Enter *(starting point of the arc 3)*
Center/End/<Second point>: *(type c and press* Enter *for Center option selection)*
Center: **2'6,3'10** Enter *(arc center for the arc 21)*
Angle/Length of chord/<End point>: *(type a and press* Enter *for included angle option selection)*
Included angle: **-45** Enter *(arc included angle for the arc 2)*

Invoke the LINE command, AutoCAD prompts:

Command: **line**
From point: **2'7,2'2** Enter *(starting point of line 5)*
To point: **2'7,3'3** Enter *(end point of the line 5)*
To point: **3'2,3'3** Enter *(end point of the line 6)*
To point: Enter *(exit the LINE command)*

(Second window: repeat the preceding points, adding 2'-0" to each X coordinate; slashed (glass) lines can be drawn freehand with LINE command)

EXERCISES 2–9 THROUGH 2–24

Create the drawings (orthographic projections) according to the settings given in the following table:

Settings	Value
1. Units	Decimal
2. Limits	
lower left corner	0,0
Upper right corner	12,9

NOTE: Grid lines in the drawings are spaced 0.25 units apart.

Exercise 2–9

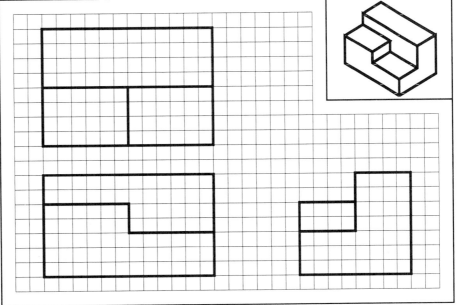

Exercise 2–10

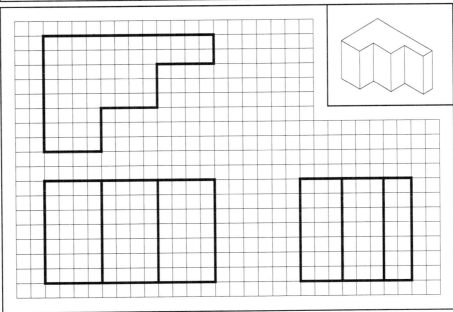

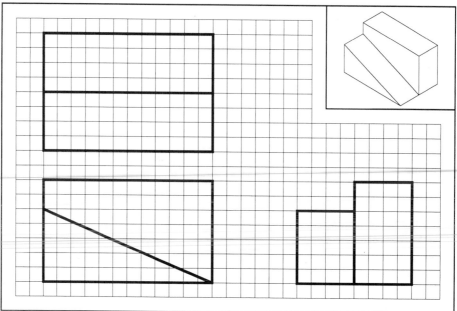

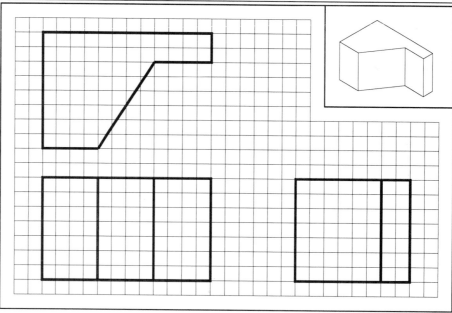

Exercise 2–13

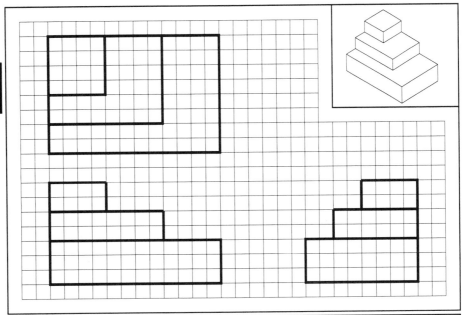

Exercise 2–14

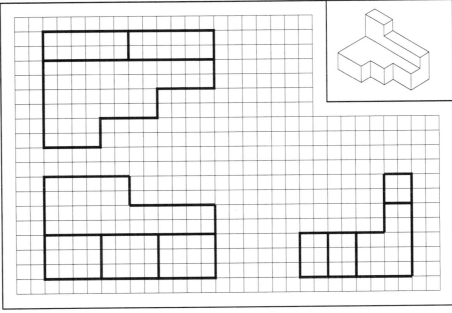

**Exercise
2–15**

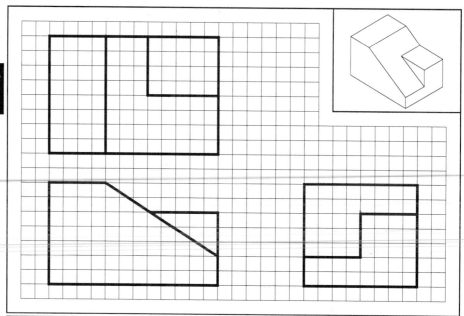

**Exercise
2–16**

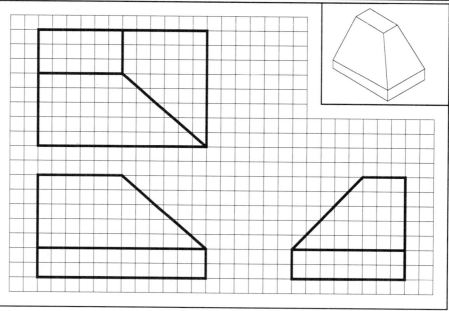

**Exercise
2–17**

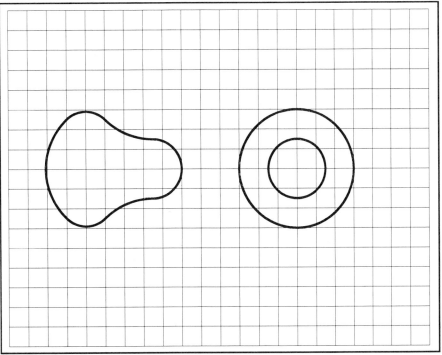

**Exercise
2–18**

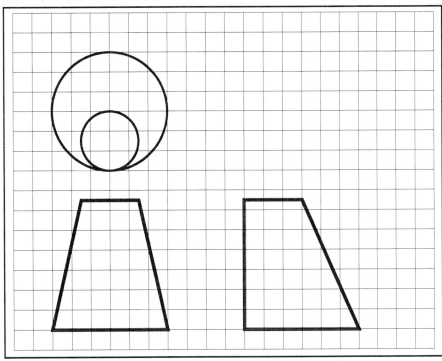

Exercise 2–19

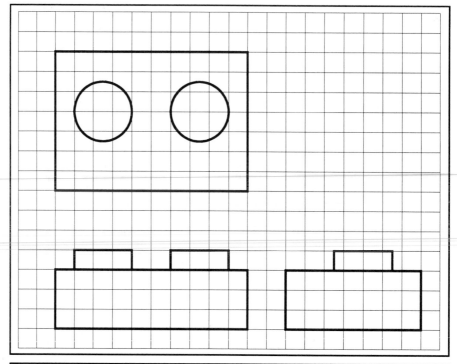

Exercise 2–20

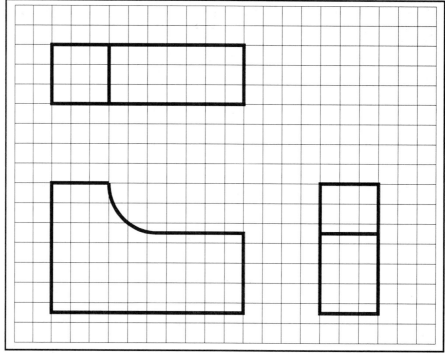

Exercise 2–21

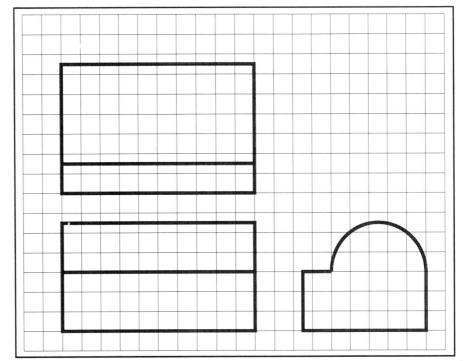

Exercise 2–22

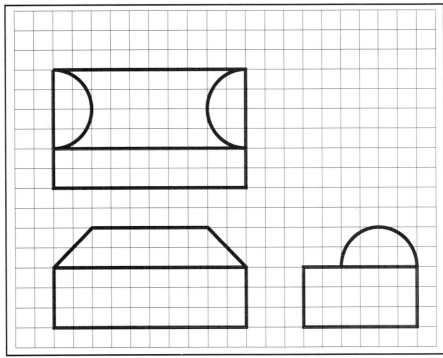

**Exercise
2–23**

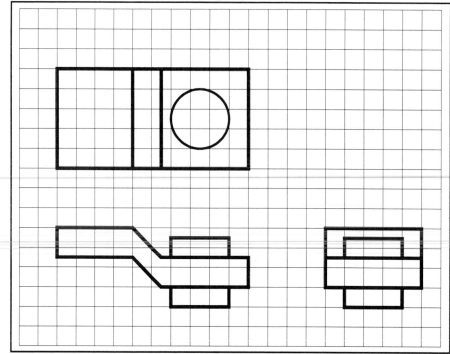

**Exercise
2–24**

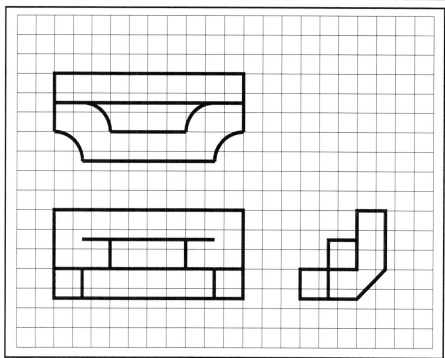

REVIEW QUESTIONS

1. The RECTANG command requests what information when drawing a rectangle?
   a. an initial corner, the width and the height
   b. the coordinates of the four corners of the rectangle
   c. the coordinates of diagonally opposite corners of the rectangle
   d. the coordinates of three adjacent corners of the rectangle

2. When drawing a trace line, after selecting the second point:
   a. nothing appears on the screen
   b. you are prompted for the trace width
   c. the segment is drawn and the command terminates
   d. the first segment is DRAWN and you are prompted for the next point

3. To draw multiple connected line segments, you must invoke the line command multiple times?
   a. True
   b. False

4. The file extension .BAK stands for:
   a. backup drawing file
   b. binary file
   c. binary attribute file
   d. drawing file
   e. both b and c

5. The HELP command cannot be used:
   a. while in the LINE command
   b. while in the CIRCLE command option TTR
   c. to list commands
   d. for a text string

6. Points are located by relative rectangular coordinate in relation to:
   a. the last specified point or position
   b. the global origin
   c. the lower left corner of the screen
   d. all of the above

7. Polar coordinates are based on a distance from:
   a. the global origin
   b. the last specified position at a given angle
   c. the center of the display
   d. all of the above

8. To enter a command from the keyboard, simply enter the command name at the "Command:" prompt:
   a. in lower-case letters
   b. in upper-case letters
   c. either a or b or mixed case
   d. commands cannot be entered via the keyboard

9. The "C" option used in the LINE command at the "From Point:" prompt will:
   a. Continue the line from the last line or arc that was drawn
   b. Close the previous set of line segments
   c. AutoCAD displays an error message

10. A rectangle generated by the RECTANG command will always have horizontal and vertical sides.
    a. True
    b. False

11. Which of the following coordinates will define a point at the screen default origin?
    a. 000   d. 112
    b. 00   e. @0,0
    c. 0,0 0,0

12. A flip screen can be accomplished by:
    a. pressing {enter} twice
    b. entering {ctrl} and {enter} at the same time
    c. pressing the {esc} key
    d. pressing the {F2} function key
    e. both B and C

13. To draw a line a length of eight feet, four and five-eights inches in the 12 o'clock direction from the last point selected, type:
    a. @8'4-5/8<90
    b. 8'-4-5/8<90
    c. @8-45/8<90
    d. 8'-45/8<90
    e. None of the above

14. By default, what direction does a positive number indicate when specifying angles in degrees?
    a. Clockwise
    b. Counter-clockwise
    c. Has no impact when specifying angles in degrees
    d. None of the above

15. When erasing objects, if you select a point which is not on any object, AutoCAD will:
    a. Terminate the ERASE command
    b. delete the selected objects and continue with the ERASE command
    c. allow you to drag a window to select many objects within the area
    d. ignore the selection and continue with the ERASE command

16. Regarding the ARC options, what does "S.C.E." mean?
    a. Start, Center, End
    b. Second, Continue, Extents
    c. Second, Center, End
    d. Start, Continue, End

17. The number of different methods by which a circle can be drawn is:
    a. 1
    b. 3
    c. 5
    d. 7
    e. None of the above

18. When using the ERASE command, AutoCAD deletes each object from the drawing as you select it.
    a. True
    b. False

19. Once an object is erased from a drawing, which of the following command could restore it to the drawing?
    a. OOPS
    b. RESTORE
    c. REPLACE
    d. CANCEL

20. When drawing a circle with the two-point option, the distance between the two points is equal to:
    a. the circumference
    b. the perimeter
    c. the shortest chord
    d. the radius
    e. the diameter

21. A circle may be created by any of the following options, except:
    a. 2P
    b. 3P
    c. 4P
    d. Cen,Rad
    e. TTR

3

FUNDAMENTALS II
• •

INTRODUCTION

AutoCAD provides various tools to make your drafting and design work easier. The following drawing tools will assist you in creating drawings rapidly, while ensuring the highest degree of precision.

After completing this chapter, you will be able to:

✔ Use and control accuracy enhancement tools (e.g., GRID, SNAP, ORTHO, and Object Snap).
✔ Use Tracking and Direct Distance.
✔ Use display control commands (e.g., ZOOM, PAN, REDRAW, and REGEN).
✔ Use layering techniques.
✔ Use the UNDO and REDO commands.

ACCURACY ENHANCEMENTS

GRID Command

The GRID command displays a visible array of dots with row and column spacings that you specify. AutoCAD creates a grid that is similar to a sheet of graph paper. You can turn the grid display ON and OFF at will, and you can change the dot spacing. The grid is a drawing tool and is not part of the drawing; it is for visual reference and is never plotted. In the World Coordinate System, the grid fills the area defined by the limits.

The grid has several uses within AutoCAD. First, it shows the extent of the drawing limits. For example, if you set the limits to 42×36 units and grid spacing is set to 0.5 units, then you will have 85×73 dots in the X and Y directions, respectively. This will give you a better sense of the drawing's size relative to the limits than if it were on a blank background.

Second, using the grid with the SNAP command (discussed in the next section) is helpful when you create a design in terms of evenly spaced units. For example, if your design is in multiples of 0.5 units, then you can set grid spacing as 0.5 to facilitate point entry. You could check your drawing visually by comparing the locations of the grid dots and the crosshairs. Figure 3–1 shows a drawing with a grid spacing of 0.5 units, with limits set to 0,0 and 17,11.

Invoke the GRID command from:

Command: prompt	grid Enter

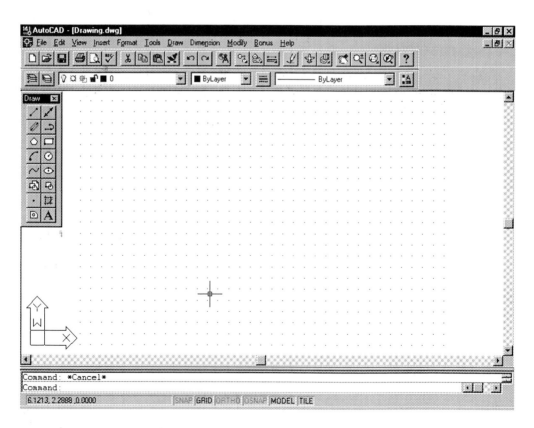

Figure 3–1 A grid spacing of 0.5 units, with limits set to (0,0) and (17,11)

AutoCAD prompts:

Command: **grid** Enter
Grid spacing (X) or ON/OFF/Snap/Aspect <current>: *(specify a grid spacing value or select one of the available options)*

You can accept the current value by pressing the Spacebar or Enter. If necessary, you can enter a new value representing a new grid spacing.

The grid is set to ON automatically when you either accept the default grid spacing or enter a new grid spacing value. It is often useful to set the grid spacing equal to the snap resolution or a multiple of it. To specify the grid spacing as a multiple of the snap value, enter **X** after the value. For example, to set up the grid value as three times the current snap value (snap = 0.5 units), enter **3X** for the prompt, which is the same as setting it to 1.5 units.

ON Option The ON option turns on the grid and has the same effect as accepting the default gridspace value.

OFF Option The OFF option turns off the grid.

Snap Option The Snap option provides a simple means of locking the grid spacing to the current snap resolution.

Aspect Option The Aspect option allows you to set different *X* and *Y* values for the grid. When you select the Aspect option, AutoCAD prompts for the *X* and *Y* values. This is handy if you are dealing with modules of unequal dimensions. For example, suppose you want a horizontal grid spacing of 0.5 and vertical spacing of 0.25. Enter the following:

Command: **grid** Enter
Grid spacing (X) or ON/OFF/Snap/Aspect <0>: **A** Enter
Horizontal spacing (X)<0>: **0.5** Enter
Vertical spacing (Y)<0>: **0.25** Enter

The Aspect option provides the Grid dot spacing as shown in Figure 3–2.

If the spacing of the visible grid is set too small, AutoCAD displays the following message and does not show the dots on the screen:

Grid too dense to display

To display the grid, invoke another GRID command and specify a larger spacing.

NOTE: You can also control the grid display by pressing the function key F7, Ctrl + G combination, or double-click the GRID on the status bar.

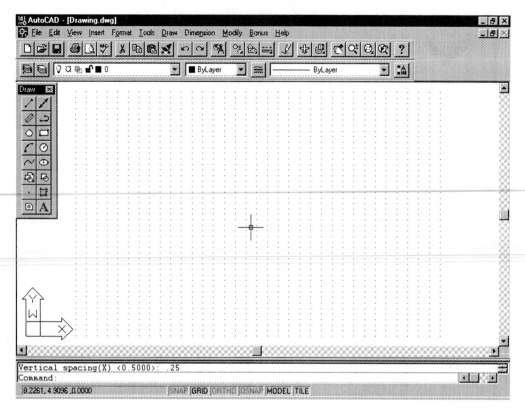

Figure 3-2 Display after setting the grid aspect to 0.5 for horizontal and 0.25 for vertical spacing

SNAP Command

The SNAP command provides an invisible reference grid. When set to ON, the Snap feature forces the cursor to lock in to the nearest point on the specified snap grid. Using the SNAP command, you can enter points quickly, letting AutoCAD ensure that they are placed precisely. You can always override the snap spacing by entering absolute or relative coordinate points via the keyboard or by simply turning off the Snap mode. When the Snap mode is set to OFF, it has no effect on the cursor. When it is set to ON, you cannot pick a point with the pointing device that is not on one of the specified snap locations.

Invoke the SNAP command from:

Command: prompt	**snap** Enter

AutoCAD prompts:

> Command: **snap** Enter
> Snap spacing or ON/OFF/Aspect/Rotate/Style <current>: *(specify a snap spacing value, or select one of the available options)*

You can accept the current value by pressing the Spacebar or Enter. If necessary, you can enter a new value representing a new snap spacing.

The grid is set to ON automatically when you either accept the default snap spacing or enter a new snap spacing value. It is often useful to set the grid spacing equal to the snap resolution or a multiple of it. When the snap mode is on, the word **SNAP** appears in the status bar at the bottom of your screen (see Figure 3–3).

ON Option The ON option sets the snap to ON and has the same effect as accepting the default snap space value.

OFF Option The OFF option sets the snap to OFF mode.

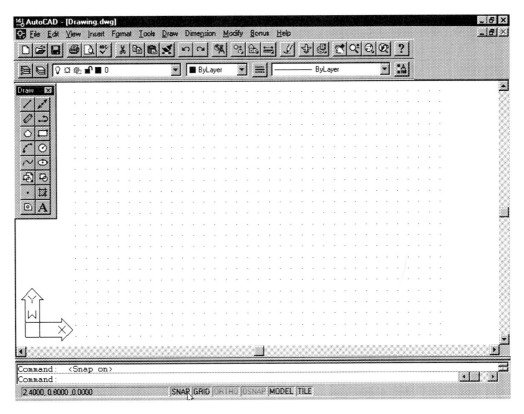

Figure 3–3 The status of Snap mode displayed on the status bar

Aspect Option The Aspect option acts the same as in GRID Command. That is, it allows you to set X and Y spacings to different values.

Rotate Option The Rotate option allows you to rotate both the visible grid and the invisible snap grid at any angle. It is a simple version of the more complicated User Coordinate System. It permits you to set up a Snap grid with an origin (X coordinate, Y coordinate of 0,0) and angle of rotation that you specify with respect to the default origin and Zero-East system of direction. In conjunction with the X and Y spacing of the Snap grid, the ROTATE option can make it easier to draw certain shapes.

The plot plan in Figure 3–4 is an example of where the ROTATE option of the SNAP command can be applied. The property lines are drawn using surveyor's units of angular display. In this example, the decimal linear units and the surveyor's angular units are selected. The limits are set up with the lower left corner at -20',-10' and the upper right corner at 124',86'. The sequence for drawing the property lines is as follows:

Command: **snap** Enter
Snap spacing or ON/OFF/Aspect/Rotate/Style <0'-0.5">: *(type r and press* Enter *for the Rotate option)*
Base point <0'-0.0",0'-0.0">: *(press* Enter *to accept the default value)*

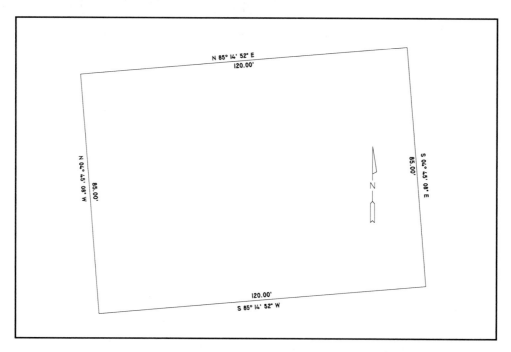

Figure 3–4 Example drawing where the Rotate option of the SNAP command can be used

Rotation angle <0r>: **4d45'08"** [Enter]
Command: **line** [Enter] *(invoke the LINE command)*
From point: **0,0** [Enter] *(select the starting point)*
To point: **85'** [Enter] *(point selected with the cursor north of the first point)*
To point: **120'** [Enter] *(with the cursor east of the last point)*
To point: **85'** [Enter] *(with the cursor south of the last point)*
To point: **c** *(completes the property line)*

Figure 3-5 shows the property lines drawn.

Style Option The Style option permits you to select one of the two available formats, Standard and Isometric. *Standard* refers to the normal rectangular type of grid (default) and *Isometric* refers to a grid and snap designed for Isometric drafting purposes (see Figure 3–6).

You can switch the isoplanes from left (90- and 150- degree angles), top (30- and 150- degree angles), and right (30- and 90-degree angles) by holding the [Ctrl] + [E] combination or [F5].

> **NOTE:** You can also control the snap display by pressing the [F9], [Ctrl] + [B] combination, or double-click the SNAP on the status bar.

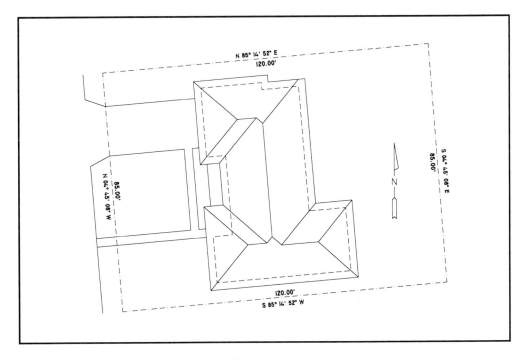

Figure 3–5 Layout of the property lines

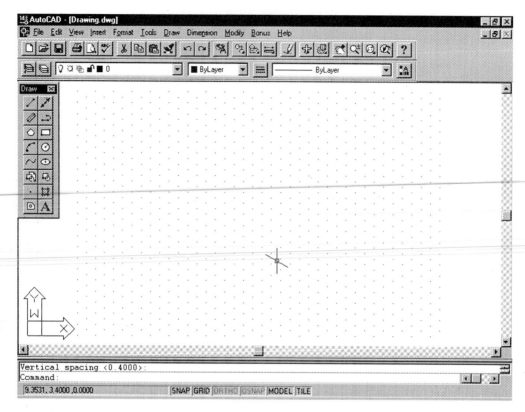

Figure 3-6 Setting the snap for isometric drafting

ORTHO Command

The ORTHO command lets you draw lines parallel to the X and Y axes; the lines are therefore perpendicular to each other. This mode is helpful when you need to draw lines that are exactly horizontal or vertical. It also forces lines to be parallel to one of the three isometric axes when the snap style is set to Isometric.

Invoke the ORTHO command from:

Command: prompt	ortho [Enter]

AutoCAD prompts:

Command: **ortho** [Enter]
ON/OFF: *(select one of the two available options to control the status of Ortho)*

You can accept the current setting by pressing the Spacebar or [Enter]. If necessary, you can change the status of the Ortho.

The ORTHO command has only two options, ON and OFF. The ON option sets the Ortho mode to ON, while the OFF option sets the Ortho mode to OFF. When the Ortho mode is set to ON, the word **ORTHO** appears in the status bar at the bottom of the screen (see Figure 3–7).

When Ortho mode is active, you can draw lines and specify displacements only in the horizontal or vertical directions, regardless of the cursor's on-screen position. The direction in which you draw is determined by the change in the X value of the cursor movement compared to the change in the cursor's distance to the Y axis. AutoCAD allows you to draw horizontally if the distance in X is greater than the distance in Y; conversely, if the change in Y is greater than the change in X, then it forces you to draw vertically. Ortho mode does not affect keyboard entry of points.

> **NOTE:** You can also control the status of the Ortho by pressing [F8], [Ctrl] + [O] key combination, or double-click the ORTHO on the status bar.

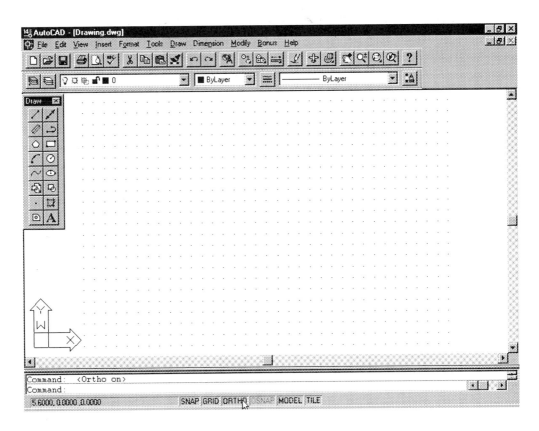

Figure 3–7 The status of Ortho mode displayed on the Status bar

Drawing Aids Dialog box

The Drawing Aids dialog box can be used to set the accuracy enhancement tools discussed earlier. If necessary, you can change the grid and snap setting in addition to changing the setting for Ortho, Solid Fill, Quick Text, Blips, Highlight, Hatch, and Groups in the Drawing Aids dialog box.

To open the Drawing Aids dialog box , invoke the DDRMODES command from:

Pull-down menu	Tools > Drawing Aids...
Command: prompt	**ddrmodes** Enter

AutoCAD displays the Drawing Aids dialog box as shown in Figure 3–8.

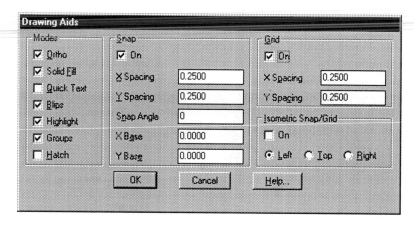

Figure 3–8 The Drawing Aids dialog box

Detailed explanations are provided in later chapters regarding the settings for Ortho, Solid Fill, Quick Text, Blips, Highlight, and Groups. Figure 3–8 shows grid spacing set to 0.25, snap to 0.25, with Grip, Snap, and Ortho set to ON.

Object Snap

The Object Snap (or Osnap, for short) feature lets you specify points on existing objects in the drawing. For example, if you need to draw a line from an endpoint of an existing line, you can use the Object Snap mode called ENDpoint, place the cursor so that it touches the line nearest endpoint, then AutoCAD snaps to the endpoint of the existing line for the starting point of the new line. This feature is similar to the basic SNAP command, which locks to invisible reference grid points.

You can invoke an object snap mode whenever AutoCAD prompts for a point.

Object Snap modes can be invoked while executing an AutoCAD command that prompts for a point, such as the LINE, CIRCLE, MOVE, and COPY commands.

Object Snap modes are invoked in two ways. One way is to respond to a prompt for a point with the name of the particular Object Snap mode desired. This is a one-time-only usage.

The second way is to use the OSNAP command and respond with the name of one or more Object Snap modes. This causes AutoCAD to use the mode(s) specified anytime you are requested to specify a point. This proves very helpful in dimensioning.

Invoke one of the available Osnap modes from:

Object Snap toolbar	Select one of the available Object Snap modes (see Figure 3–9)
Standard toolbar	Object Snap flyout
Command: prompt	Type the first three letters of one of the available Object Snap modes and press Enter whenever an AutoCAD "command:" prompt requests a point

Figure 3–9 Object Snap toolbar

Whenever you use object snap, AutoCAD displays a geometric shape (marker) and snap tip when you move your target box over a snap point. By displaying a geometric shape on the snap points with snap tip, you can see the point that will be selected and the object snap mode in effect. AutoCAD displays the geometric shape depending on the snap mode selected. (AutoCAD lists the geometric shape next to the name of the Object Snap mode in the Object Snap dialog box).

If necessary, you can turn off the display of the marker shapes and snap tip. To do so, open the Object Snap dialog box from:

Pull-down menu	Tools > Object Snap Settings. . .
Command: prompt	**ddosnap** Enter

AutoCAD displays the Object Snap settings box, as shown in Figure 3–10.

Select the AutoSnap page, and AutoCAD displays the available settings for the display of the geometric shape and snap tip, as shown in Figure 3–11.

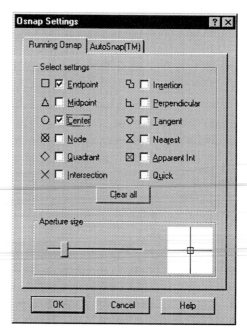

Figure 3–10 Object Snap settings box

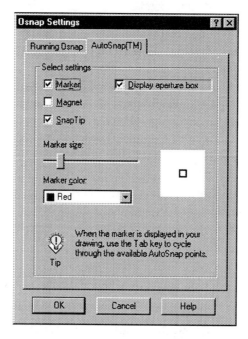

Figure 3–11 Object Snap settings box—AutoSnap settings

The **Marker** toggle controls the display of the geometric shape that is displayed when the target box moves over a snap point.

The **Magnet** locks the target box onto the snap point. The Magnet toggle controls the on/off of the magnet lock.

The **SnapTip** toggle controls the display of the Tooltip–like flag that displays the name of the snap mode.

The **Marker size** slide bar controls the size of the geometric shape (marker).

The **Marker color** option menu allows you to set the current color of the geometric shape.

The **Image** tile shows the current size of the marker.

The **Display aperture box** check box controls the display of the aperture box. Whenever you are in an Object Snap mode, a target is added to the crosshairs (see Figure 3–12) to indicate the area within which AutoCAD searches for Object Snap modes.

After making the necessary changes to the AutoSnap settings, choose the OK button to close the Object Snap dialog box.

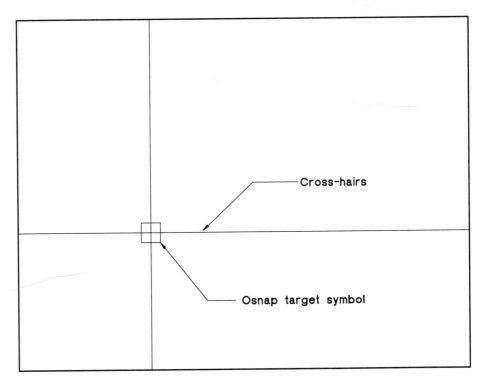

Figure 3–12 The crosshairs cursor with the aperture target in Object Snap mode

The following section explains the available Object Snap modes, with examples:

Object Snap—ENDpoint mode The ENDpoint mode allows you to snap to the closest endpoint of a line, arc, elliptical arc, mline, polyline segment, or ray, or to the closest corner of a trace, solid, or 3Dface.

Making sure you are in the appropriate AutoCAD command, invoke the Object Snap—ENDpoint mode from:

Object Snap toolbar	Select the ENDpoint mode (see Figure 3–13)
Standard toolbar	Object Snap flyout
Command: prompt	Type **END** and press [Enter] whenever an AutoCAD "command:" prompt requests a point

Figure 3–13 Invoke the Object Snap ENDpoint mode from the Object Snap toolbar

For example, to connect a line to the endpoint of an existing line, as shown in Figure 3–14, the following command sequence is used:

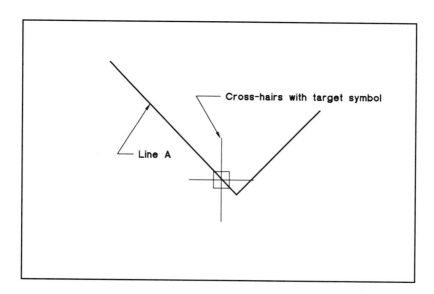

Figure 3–14 Connecting a line to another line's endpoint using the ENDpoint object snap

Command: **line** [Enter]
From point: **endpoint of** *(move the aperture cursor near the end of Line A and specify it)*
To point: *(specify a point)*
To point: [Enter]

Object Snap—MIDpoint Mode The MIDpoint mode allows you to snap to the midpoint of a line, arc, elliptical arc, mline, polyline segment, xline, solid, or spline.

Making sure you are in the appropriate AutoCAD command, invoke the Object Snap—MIDpoint mode from:

Object Snap toolbar	Select the MIDpoint mode (see Figure 3–15)
Standard toolbar	Object Snap flyout
Command: prompt	Type **MID** and press [Enter] whenever an AutoCAD "command:" prompt requests a point

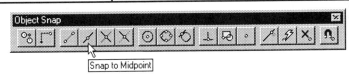

Figure 3–15 Invoking the Object Snap—MIDpoint mode from the Object Snap toolbar

For example, to connect a line to the midpoint of an existing line, as shown in Figure 3–16, the following command sequence is used:

Command: **line** [Enter]
From point: **Midpoint of** *(move the aperture cursor to anywhere on Line A and specify it)*
To point: *(specify a point)*
To point: [Enter]

Object Snap—CENter Mode The CENter mode allows you to snap to the center of an arc, circle, ellipse, or elliptical arc.

Making sure you are in the appropriate AutoCAD command, invoke the Object Snap—CENter mode from:

Object Snap toolbar	Select the CENter mode (see Figure 3–17)
Standard toolbar	Object Snap flyout
Command: prompt	Type **CEN** and press [Enter] whenever an AutoCAD "command:" prompt requests a point.

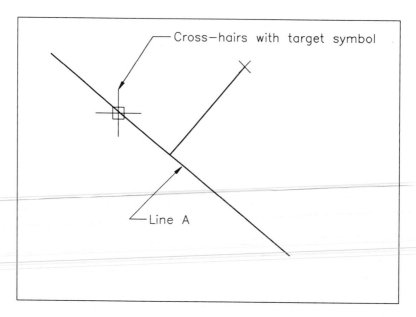

Figure 3-16 Connecting a line to another line's midpoint using the MIDpoint object snap

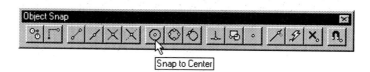

Figure 3-17 Invoking the Object Snap—CENter mode from the Object Snap toolbar

For example, to draw a line to the center of a circle, as shown in Figure 3–18, the following command sequence is used:

Command: **Line** Enter
From point: *(specify point p)*
To point: **cent** Enter
    of *(specify point P1 on circle)*

Object Snap - QUAdrant Mode The QUAdrant mode allows you to snap to the one of the quadrant points of a circle, arc, ellipse or elliptical arc. The quadrant points are located at 0 degrees, 90 degrees, 180 degrees, and 270 degrees from the center of the circle or arc, as shown in Figure 3–19. The quadrant points are determined by the zero degree direction of the current coordinate system.

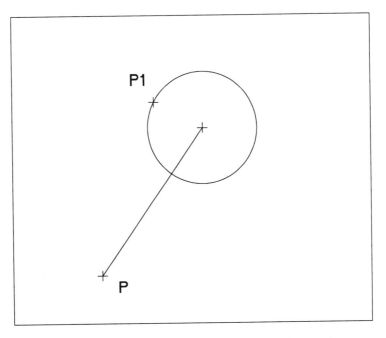

Figure 3–18 Selecting a point with the CENter Object Snap mode

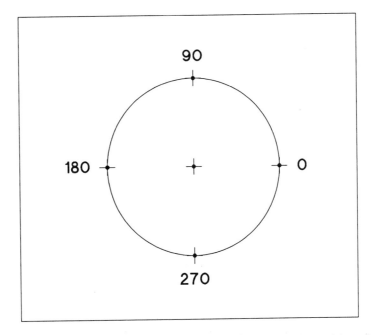

Figure 3–19 The quadrant points recognized by the QUADrant Object Snap mode

Making sure you are in the appropriate AutoCAD command, invoke the Object Snap—QUAdrant mode from:

Object Snap toolbar	Select the QUAdrant mode (see Figure 3–20)
Standard toolbar	Object Snap flyout
Command: prompt	Type **QUA and press** Enter whenever an AutoCAD "command:" prompt requests a point.

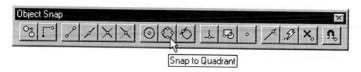

Figure 3–20 Invoking the Object Snap—QUAdrant mode from the Object Snap toolbar

In Figure 3–21 a line is drawn to a quadrant as follows:

Command: **line** Enter
From point: *(specify point A)*
To point: **qua** Enter
    of *(specify point A1)*

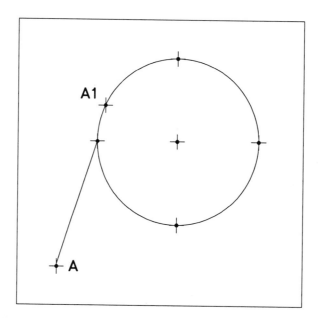

Figure 3–21 Drawing a line to a circle's quadrant point (Method 1)

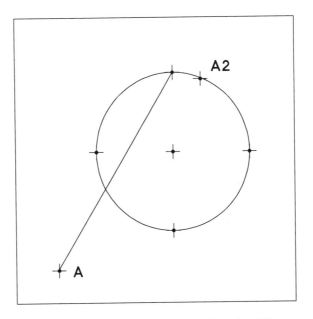

Figure 3–22 Drawing a line to a circle's quadrant (Method 2)

A line can also be drawn to a quadrant as follows (see Figure 3–22):

Command: **line** Enter
From point: *(specify point A)*
To point: **qua** Enter
    of *(specify point A2)*

> **NOTE:** Special precautions should be taken when attempting to se-
> lect circles or arcs in blocks or ellipses that are rotated at an angle
> that is not a multiple of 90 degrees. When a circle or an arc in a block
> is rotated, the point of that QUAdrant Osnap mode is also rotated.
> But when a circle/arc not in a block is rotated, the QUAdrant Osnap
> points stay at the 0, 90, 180, 270 degree points.

Object Snap—PERpendicular Mode The PERpendicular mode allows you to snap
to a point perpendicular to a line, arc, circle, elliptical arc, mline, polyline, ray, solid,
spline, or xline.

Making sure you are in the appropriate AutoCAD command, invoke the Object Snap—PERpendicular mode from:

Object Snap toolbar	Select the PERpendicular mode (see Figure 3–23)
Standard toolbar	Object Snap flyout
Command: prompt	Type **PER** and press Enter whenever an AutoCAD "command:" prompt requests a point

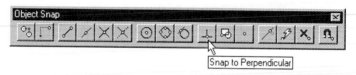

Figure 3–23 Invoking the Object Snap—PERpendicular mode from the Object Snap toolbar

The following command sequence demonstrates how you can draw lines using the PERpendicular object snap mode.

From inside the circle:

Command: **line** Enter
From point: *(specify point A)*
To point: **per** Enter
   to *(specify near-side point AN, as shown in Figure 3–24)*

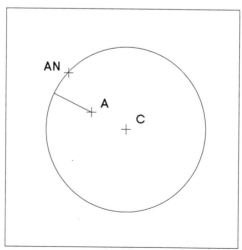

Figure 3–24 Specifying a line's endpoint perpendicular to a circle (from inside the near side of the circle) with the PERpendicular Object Snap mode

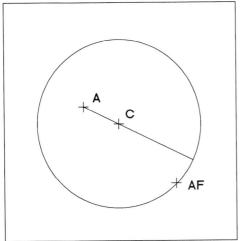

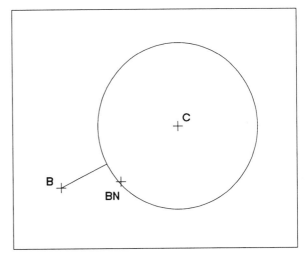

Figure 3–25 Specifying a line's end-point perpendicular to a circle (from inside the far side of the circle) with the PERpendicular Object Snap mode

Figure 3–26 Specifying a line's endpoint perpendicular to a circle (from outside the near side of the circle) with the PERpendicular Object Snap mode

Command: **line** [Enter]
From point: *(specify point A)*
To point: **per** [Enter]
   to *(specify far-side point AF, as shown in Figure 3–25)*

From outside the circle:

Command: **line** [Enter]
From point: *(specify point B)*
To point: **per** [Enter]
   to *(specify near-side point BN, as shown in Figure 3–26)*

Command: **line** [Enter]
From point: *(specify point B)*
To point: **per** [Enter]
   to *(specify far-side point BF, as shown in Figure 3–27)*

When drawing a line perpendicular to another line, the point that AutoCAD establishes can be off the line selected (in response to the "perpendicular to" prompt) and the new line will still be drawn to that point. In Figure 3–28 lines from both A and B can be drawn perpendicular to line L.

Applying the PERpendicular osnap mode to an arc works in a manner similar to a circle. Unlike drawing a perpendicular to a line, the point established must be on the arc.

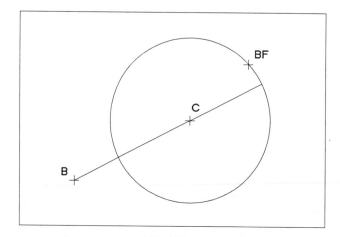

Figure 3-27 Specifying a line's endpoint perpendicular to a circle (from outside the far side of the circle) with the PERpendicular Object Snap mode

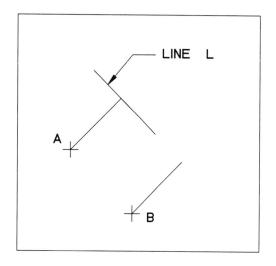

Figure 3-28 Using the PERpendicular Osnap mode, a line is drawn perpendicular to another line

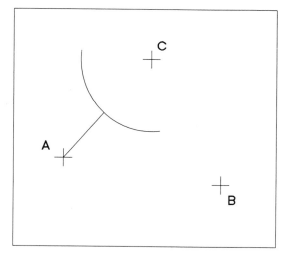

Figure 3-29 Using the PERpendicular Osnap mode, a line is drawn perpendicular to an arc

In Figure 3-29 a line is drawn perpendicular to an arc from A but not from B.

Object Snap–TANgent mode The TANgent mode allows you to snap to the tangent of an arc, circle, ellipse, or elliptical arc.

Make sure you are in the appropriate AutoCAD command, invoke the Object Snap - TANgent mode from:

Object Snap toolbar	Select the TANgent mode (see Figure 3–30)
Standard toolbar	Object Snap flyout
Command: prompt	Type **TAN** and press Enter whenever an AutoCAD "command:" prompt requests a point

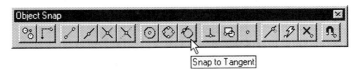

Figure 3–30 Invoking the Object Snap—TANgent mode from the Object Snap toolbar

The following command sequence draws a line from point A tangent to a point on the circle, as shown in Figure 3–31.

Command: **line** Enter
From point: *(specify point A)*
To point: **tan** Enter
   to *(specify point AL toward left semicircle)*

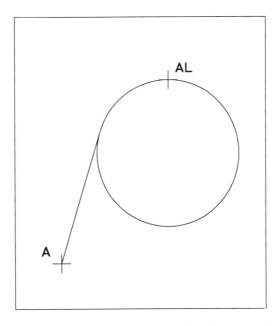

Figure 3–31 Using the TANgent Osnap mode, a line is drawn from a point outside a circle tangent to a left point on the circle

Fundamentals II

A line can also be drawn from point A tangent to a point on the circle, as shown in Figure 3–32.

> Command: **line** Enter
> From point: *(specify point A)*
> To point: **tan** Enter
>   to *(specify point AR toward right semicircle)*

With the TANgent Osnap mode you can select an arc also. Like the PERpendicular Osnap mode, the tangent point must be on the arc selected (see Figure 3–33).

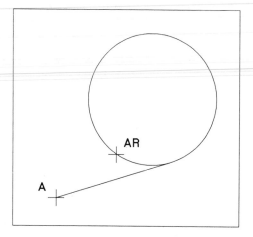

Figure 3–32 Using the TANgent Osnap mode, a line is drawn from a point outside a circle tangent to a right point on the circle

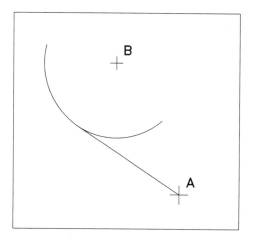

Figure 3–33 Using the TANgent Osnap mode, a line is drawn tangent to a point on an arc

Object Snap—INTersection Mode The INTersection mode allows you to snap to the intersection of an arc, circle, ellipse, elliptical arc, line, mline, polyline, ray, spline, or xline. An example with valid intersection points are shown in Figure 3–34.

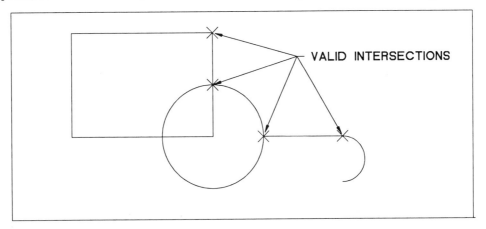

Figure 3–34 Valid intersections that can be selected using Object Snap— INTersection mode

Making sure you are in the appropriate AutoCAD command, invoke the Object Snap—INTersection mode from:

Object Snap toolbar	Select the INTersection mode (see Figure 3–35)
Standard toolbar	Object Snap flyout
Command: prompt	Type **INT and press** Enter whenever an AutoCAD "command:" prompt requests a point

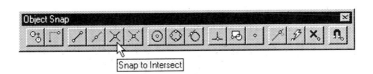

Figure 3–35 Invoking the Object Snap—INTersection mode from the Object Snap toolbar

AutoCAD prompts you to select two objects to establish the intersection point.

Object Snap—APParent Intersection Mode The APParent intersection mode allows you to snap to the apparent intersection of an arc, circle, ellipse, elliptical arc, line, mline, polyline, ray, spline, or xline, which may or may not actually intersect in 3D space.

Making sure you are in the appropriate AutoCAD command, invoke the Object Snap—APParent intersection mode from:

Object Snap toolbar	Select the APParent intersection mode (see Figure 3–36)
Standard toolbar	Object Snap flyout
Command: prompt	Type **APP** and press ⏎Enter whenever an AutoCAD "command:" prompt requests a point

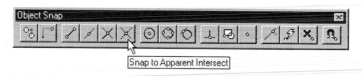

Figure 3–36 Invoking the Object Snap—APParent intersection mode from the Object Snap toolbar

AutoCAD prompts you to select two objects to establish the apparent intersection point.

> **NOTE:** The INTersection and APParent Intersection modes should not be in effect at the same time.

Object Snap—NODe The NODe mode allows you to snap to a point object.

Making sure you are in the appropriate AutoCAD command, invoke the Object Snap—NODe mode from:

Object Snap toolbar	Select the NODe mode (see Figure 3–37)
Standard toolbar	Object Snap flyout
Command: prompt	Type **NOD** and press ⏎Enter whenever an AutoCAD "command:" prompt requests a point

Figure 3–37 Invoking the Object Snap NODe mode from the Object Snap toolbar

Object Snap—NEArest Mode The NEArest Object Snap mode lets you select any object (except text and shape) in response to a prompt for a point, AutoCAD snaps to the point on that object nearest the cursor.

Making sure you are in the appropriate AutoCAD command, invoke the Object Snap—NEArest mode from:

Object Snap toolbar	Select the NEArest mode (see Figure 3-38)
Standard toolbar	Object Snap flyout
Command: prompt	Type **NEA** and press ⏎ whenever an AutoCAD "command:" prompt requests a point

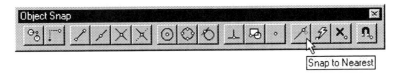

Figure 3–38 Invoking the Object Snap NEArest mode from the Object Snap toolbar

Object Snap—INSert Mode The INSert mode allows you to snap to the insertion point of a block, text string, attribute, or shape.

Make sure you are in the appropriate AutoCAD command, invoke the Object Snap - INSert mode from:

Object Snap toolbar	Select the INSert mode (see Figure 3–39)
Standard toolbar	Object Snap flyout
Command: prompt	Type **INS** and press ⏎ whenever an AutoCAD "command:" prompt requests a point

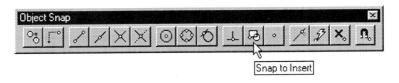

Figure 3–39 Invoking the Object Snap INSert mode from the Object Snap toolbar

Object Snap—Quick Mode The Quick mode allows you to snap to the first snap point found. Quick snap must be used in conjunction with other Object Snap modes.

Fundamentals II

Making sure you are in the appropriate AutoCAD command, invoke the Object Snap—Quick mode from:

Object Snap toolbar	Select the Quick mode (see Figure 3–40)
Standard toolbar	Object Snap flyout
Command: prompt	Type **Quick,** *(plus another Snap mode)* and press ⏎ whenever an AutoCAD "command :" prompt requests a point

Figure 3–40 Invoking the Quick mode from the Object Snap toolbar

Make sure to select another Snap mode after selecting Quick Snap mode.

Running Object Modes

As mentioned earlier, you can set one or more Object Snap modes to the OSNAP command (called a Running Object Snap mode) and AutoCAD always uses the mode(s) specified when you are requested to specify a point.

Invoke the OSNAP command from:

Object Snap toolbar	Select the Object Snap Settings (see Figure 3–41)
Command: prompt	**OSNAP** ⏎

Figure 3–41 Invoking the Object Snap Settings from the Object Snap mode toolbar

AutoCAD displays the Osnap Settings dialog box ,as shown in Figure 3–42.

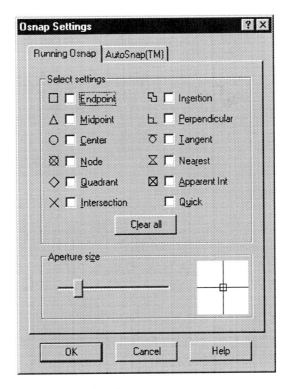

Figure 3-42 Object Settings dialog box

Select the appropriate Snap modes in the Object Settings dialog box.

To clear the existing Object Snap mode settings, click the **"Clear all"** button. In addition, you can set the aperture size from the dialog box. Click the **OK** button to close the dialog box.

> **NOTE:** You can control the status of the current Osnap settings by double-clicking the Osnap in the status bar. If it is set to ON, the current Osnap settings will be in effect. If it is set to OFF, it is the same as using the None option.

Direct Distance Option

The Direct Distance option for specifying a point relative to another point can be used with a command like LINE to permit a variation of the Relative Coordinates mode. In the case of the Direct Distance option, the distance is keyed in and the direction is determined by the current location of the cursor. This option is very useful when you know the exact distance but specifying the exact angle is not as easy as placing the cursor on a point that is at the exact angle desired.

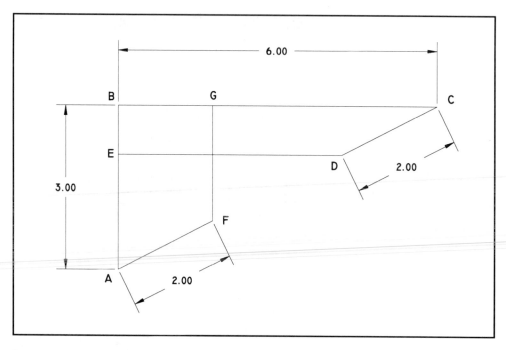

Figure 3–43 Example of a direct distance application

Figure 3–43 shows a shape that can be drawn more easily by using the Direct Distance option along with setting the Snap and Ortho modes to ON and OFF at the appropriate times. Points A, B, and C are on the Snap grid (X,Y coordinates 3,3 for A, 3,6 for B, and 9,6 for C). By setting the Snap mode to ON with the value set to 1 or perhaps 0.5, the cursor can be placed on the required points to draw lines A-B and B-C. After drawing lines A-B and B-C (with Ortho set to either ON or OFF), the cursor should be placed on point A (with Ortho set to OFF).

If you have exited the LINE command after drawing line B-C, you must invoke the LINE command and specify C as the first point before moving the cursor to A. The rubber-band line indicates that the next line is drawn from C to A, as shown in Figure 3–44. However, you wish to draw a line only 2 units long but in the same direction as a line from C to A. With the cursor placed on A, type in **2** and press Enter.

AutoCAD draws the line of 2 units, and Point D is established. To draw a line from D to E without exiting the LINE command, first set Ortho and Snap to ON, and then place the cursor on line A-B. The rubber-band line will indicate line D-E, as shown in Figure 3–45. In this case, you do not know the distance, but you do know that the line terminates on line A-B. Therefore, simply press the pick button on the cursor, and line D-E is drawn. You do not have to specify point D as the starting point of the line. Using the line-line continuation after drawing line C-D does that for you.

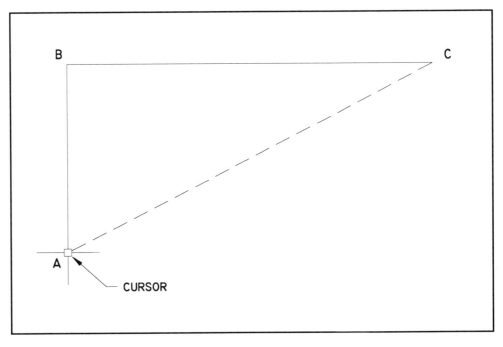

Figure 3–44 Drawing a line from C by means of the Direct Distance option

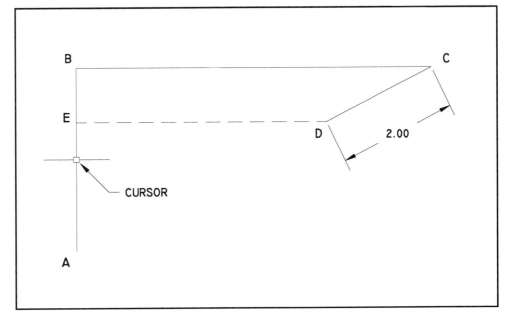

Figure 3–45 Drawing a line from D to E

Line A-F can be drawn in a similar manner as line C-D was drawn. Unlike line C-D, line A-F is not a continuation of another line. However, the starting point, A, can be selected with the Snap set to ON. After starting point A has been specified, place the cursor on point C and key in **2**. From line A-F, line F-G can be drawn in a similar manner as line D-E was drawn. This example shows an application of the Direct Distance option in which the distance was keyed in and the direction was controlled by the cursor.

Tracking Option

TRACKING, or moving through nonselected point(s) to a selected point, could be called a command "enhancer." It can be used whenever a command prompts for a point. If the desired point can best be specified relative to some known point(s), you can "make tracks" to the desired point by invoking the Tracking option and then specifying one or more points relative to previous point(s) "on the way to" the actual point that the command is prompting for. These intermediate tracking points are not necessarily associated with the object being created or modified by the command. The primary significance of tracking points is that they are being used to establish a *path* to the point you wish to designate as the response to the command prompt. Some of the objects in the partial plan shown in Figure 3–46 can be drawn more easily by means of Tracking.

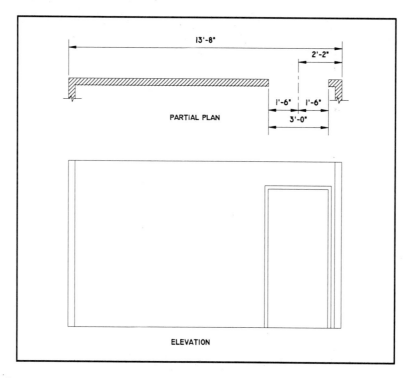

Figure 3–46 Example of a partial plan to demonstrate the Tracking option

The following example will use Tracking to draw lines A and B in the Partial Plan in Figure 3–47, leaving the 3'-0" door opening in the correct place. By means of Tracking, we can draw the lines with the given dimension information without having to calculate the missing information.

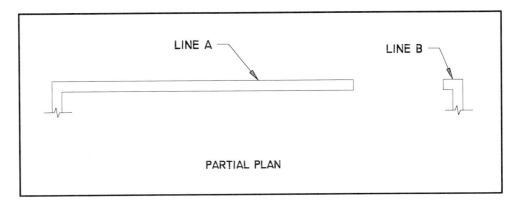

Figure 3–47 Lines A and B to be drawn with the help of the Tracking option

In Figure 3–48, line A from TK1/SP1 (tracking point 1 and starting point 1) to EP1 (ending point 1) and line B from SP2 (starting point 2) to TK2/EP2 (tracking point 2 and ending point 2) can be drawn by using the TRACKING command enhancer. Invoke the LINE command and AutoCAD prompts:

Command: **line** Enter
From point: **0,12'** Enter *(specify point TK1/SP1)*
To point: **tk** Enter *(invoke the Tracking feature)*
First tracking point: *(specify point SP1/TK1 again as the first tracking point)*

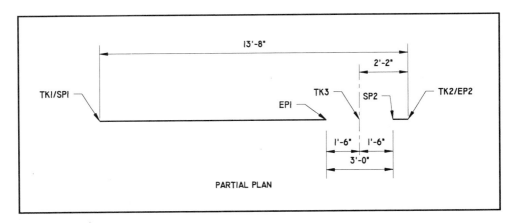

Figure 3–48 Various points to be drawn with the help of the Tracking option

Fundamentals II

Next point (Press ENTER to end tracking): **@13'8,0** Enter *(locates the second tracking point, TK2, as shown in Figure 3–48)*
Next point (Press ENTER to end tracking): **@2'2<180** Enter *(locates the third tracking point, TK3, as shown in Figure 3–48)*
Next point (Press ENTER to end tracking): **@1'6<180** Enter *(locates the fourth tracking point, EP1, as shown in Figure 3–48)*
Next point (Press ENTER to end tracking): *(press Enter to exit Tracking; by this you are designating the point to which you have "made tracks" as the response to the prompt that was in effect when you entered Tracking)*
To point: *(press Enter to exit the LINE command)*

Once the Tracking option is invoked, you establish a path to EP1 by specifying the initial tracking point, TK1, and then each subsequent point relative to the previous point, that is, TK2 relative to TK1, TK3 relative to TK2, and EP1 relative to TK3. The first track in this case is specified by the Relative Rectangular method, and the next two are Relative Polar. Also, because the tracking points are all on one horizontal line, you could use the direct distance feature by placing the cursor in the correct direction (with ORTHO set to ON) and keying in the distance.

> **NOTE:** If you knew the coordinates of one of the intermediate track-ing points, then it probably should be the initial tracking point. The idea behind Tracking is to establish a point by means of a path from and through other points. Thus, the shortest path is the best. If the coordinates of TK2 were known, or if you could specify it by some other method, it could become the initial tracking point. Keep this in mind as you learn to use Object Snap. You don't necessarily need to know the coordinates if you can use Object Snap to select a point from which a tracking path could be specified.

The line from SP2 to TK2/EP2 can be started and ended in a similar manner as the line from TK1/SP1 to EP1 was started, with some minor modifications. The se-quence (which involves using Tracking twice) is as follows:

Command: **line** Enter *(invoke the LINE command)*
From point: **tk** Enter *(invoke the Tracking option)*
First tracking point: **0,12'** Enter *(specify point TK1/SP1 as the first tracking point)*
Next point (Press ENTER to end tracking): **@13'8,0** Enter *(locates the second tracking point, TK2, as shown in Figure 3–48)*
Next point (Press ENTER to end tracking): **@2'2<180** Enter *(locates the third tracking point, TK3, as shown in Figure 3–48)*
Next point (Press ENTER to end tracking): **@1'6<0** Enter *(locates the fourth tracking point, SP2, as shown in Figure 3–48)*
Next point (Press ENTER to end tracking): *(press Enter to exit Tracking; AutoCAD establishes point SP2)*

> To point: **tk** [Enter] *(invoke the Tracking option again)*
> First tracking point: *(specify point TK1/SP1 as the first tracking point)*
> Next point (Press ENTER to end tracking): **@13'8,0** [Enter] *(locates the second tracking point, TK2/EP2, as shown in Figure 3–48)*
> Next point (Press ENTER to end tracking): *(press* [Enter] *to exit Tracking, AutoCAD establishes point EP2)*
> To point: *(press* [Enter] *to terminate the LINE command)*

This example shows an application of the Tracking option in which the points were established in reference to some known points.

DISPLAY CONTROL

There are many ways to view a drawing in AutoCAD. These viewing options vary from on-screen viewing to hard-copy plots. The hard-copy options are discussed in Chapter 8. Using the display commands, you can select the portion of the drawing to be displayed, establish 3D perspective views, and much more. By letting you see your drawing in different ways, AutoCAD gives you the means to draw faster, more easily, and more accurately.

The commands that are explained in this section are like utility commands. They make your job easier and help you to draw more accurately.

ZOOM Command

The ZOOM command is like a zoom lens on a camera. You can increase or decrease the viewing area, although the actual size of objects remains constant. As you increase the visible size of objects, you view a smaller area of the drawing in greater detail. As you decrease the visible size of objects, you view a larger area. This ability provides a closeup view for better accuracy and detail.

Invoke the ZOOM command from:

Zoom toolbar	Select one of the available options (see Figure 3–49)
Pull-down menu	View > Zoom
Command: prompt	**zoom** [Enter]

Figure 3–49 Zoom toolbar

AutoCAD prompts:

Command: **zoom**
All/Center/Dynamic/Extents/Previous/Scale(X/XP)/Window/<Realtime>:
   (select one of the available options)

Default Option The default option of the ZOOM command is a zoomed window. After the ZOOM command presents its long list of options, simply specify two points on the screen that represent a rectangle. AutoCAD enlarges the view to fit the rectangle. See the related Window option.

Realtime Option The Realtime option lets you zoom interactively to a logical extent. Once you invoke the command, the cursor changes to a magnifying glass with a "±" symbol. To zoom in, hold the pick button and move vertically toward the top of the window. To zoom out, hold the pick button and move vertically toward the bottom of the window. To discontinue the zooming, release the pick button.

The current drawing window is used to determine the zooming factor. If you move the cursor by holding the pick button from the midpoint of the window up or down to the top or bottom of the window, respectively, the zoom factor is set to 100%. If the cursor is moved by holding the pick button from the bottom of the window to the top of the window vertically, the zoom-in factor would be 200%. Conversely, holding the pick button from the top of the window and moving vertically to the bottom of the window, sets the zoom-out factor would be 200%.

When you reach the zoom-out limit, the cursor changes to a "+" symbol, indicating that you can no longer zoom out. Similarly, when you reach the zoom-in limit, the cursor changes to "–" symbol, indicating that you can no longer zoom in.

Invoke the ZOOM Realtime command from:

Standard toolbar	Select Zoom Realtime (see Figure 3–50)
Pull-down menu	View > Zoom > Realtime
Command: prompt	zoom Enter

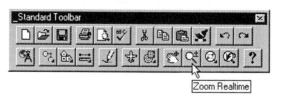

Figure 3–50 Invoking the Zoom Realtime option from the Standard toolbar

AutoCAD prompts:

Command: **zoom** Enter
All/Center/Dynamic/Extents/Previous/Scale(X/XP)/Window/<Realtime>: Enter
Press ESC or ENTER to exit, or right-click to activate pop-up menu.

To exit the ZOOM Realtime option, press [Esc] or [Enter] key. You can also exit by selecting Exit from the pop-up menu that is displayed when you press the right button on your pointing device. In addition, you can perform other operations related to ZOOM and PAN by selecting appropriate commands from the pop-up menu.

Scale Option   The ZOOM Scale command lets you enter a display scale (or magnification) factor. The scale factor, when entered as a number (it must be a numerical value and must not be expressed in units of measure), is applied to the area covered by the drawing limits. For example, if you enter a scale value of 3, each object appears three times as large as in the full view. A scale factor of 1 displays the entire drawing (the full view), which is defined by the established limits. If you enter a value less than 1, AutoCAD decreases the magnification of the full view. For example, if you enter a scale of 0.5, each object appears half its size in the full view while the viewing area is twice the size in horizontal and vertical dimensions. When you use this option, the object in the center of the screen remains centered.

See Figures 3–51a and 3–51b for the difference between a full view and a 0.5 zoom.

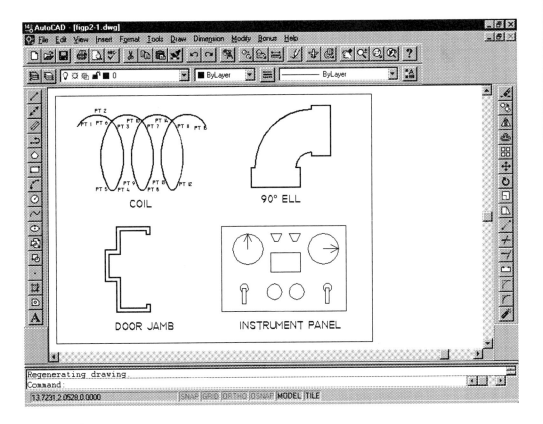

Figure 3–51a A drawing at ZOOM All (full view)

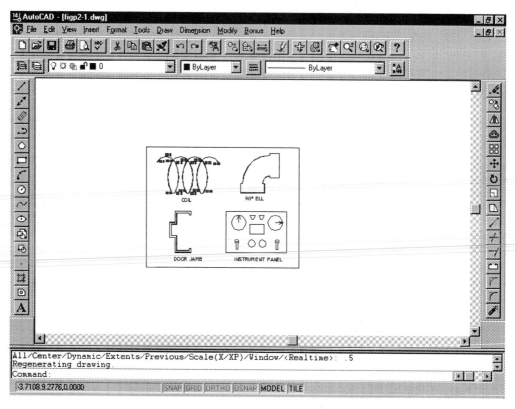

Figure 3-51b The same drawing after setting ZOOM to 0.5

Invoke the ZOOM Scale command from:

Zoom toolbar	Select Zoom Scale (see Figure 3–52)
Pull-down menu	View > Zoom > Scale
Command: prompt	zoom Enter

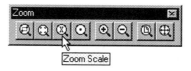

Zoom Scale

Figure 3-52 Invoking the Zoom Scale command from the Zoom toolbar

AutoCAD prompts:

Command: **zoom** Enter
All/Center/Dynamic/Extents/Previous/Scale(X/XP)/Window/<Realtime>:
    (specify the scale factor)

If you enter a number followed by X, the scale is determined relative to the current view. For instance, entering **2X** causes each object to be displayed two times its current size on the screen.

The scale factor XP option is explained in Chapter 12, because it is related to paper and model space units.

All Option The ZOOM All command lets you see the entire drawing. In a plan view, it zooms to the drawing's limits or current extents, whichever is larger. If the drawing extends outside the drawing limits, the display shows all objects in the drawing.

Invoke the ZOOM All command from:

Zoom toolbar	Select Zoom All (see Figure 3–53)
Pull-down menu	View > Zoom > All
Command: prompt	zoom Enter

Figure 3–53 Invoking the Zoom All command from the Zoom toolbar

AutoCAD prompts:

Command: **zoom** Enter
All/Center/Dynamic/Extents/Previous/Scale(X/XP)/Window/<Realtime>: **a** Enter

Center Option The ZOOM Center command lets you select a new view by specifying its center point and the magnification value or height of the view in current units. A smaller value for the height increases the magnification; a larger value decreases the magnification.

Invoke the ZOOM Center command from:

Zoom toolbar	Select Zoom Center (see Figure 3–54)
Pull-down menu	View > Zoom > Center
Command: prompt	zoom Enter

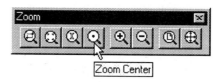

Figure 3–54 Invoking the Zoom Center command from the Zoom toolbar

AutoCAD prompts:

Command: **zoom** [Enter]
All/Center/Dynamic/Extents/Previous/Scale(X/XP)/Window/<Realtime>: **c** [Enter]
Center point: *(specify the center point)*
Magnification or Height <current height>: *(specify the magnification or height)*

The following command sequence produces the example of the ZOOM Center option shown in Figure 3–55.

Command: **zoom** [Enter]
All/Center/Dynamic/Extents/Previous/Scale(X/XP)/Window/<Realtime>: **c** [Enter]
Center point: **8,6** [Enter]
Magnification or Height <current height>: **4**

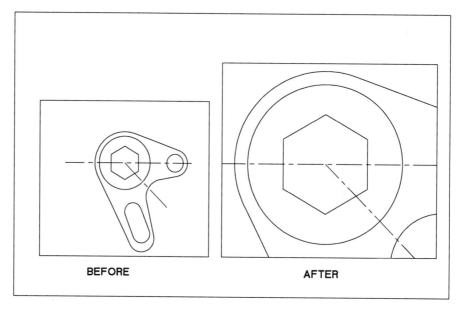

BEFORE AFTER

Figure 3–55 Using the Zoom Center command

In addition to providing coordinates for center point, you can also specify the center point by placing a point on the view window. The height can also be specified in terms of the current view height by specifying the magnification value followed by an X. A response of 3X will make the new view height three times as large as the current height.

Dynamic Option The AutoCAD ZOOM Dynamic command provides a quick and easy method to move to another view of the drawing. With ZOOM Dynamic, you can see the entire drawing and then select the location and size of the next view via simple cursor manipulations. Using ZOOM Dynamic is one means by which you can visually select a new display area that is not entirely within the current display.

Invoke the ZOOM Dynamic command from:

Zoom toolbar	Select Zoom Dynamic (see Figure 3–56)
Pull-down menu	View > Zoom > Dynamic
Command: prompt	zoom Enter

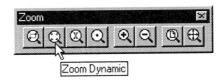

Zoom Dynamic

Figure 3–56 Invoking the Zoom Dynamic command from the Zoom toolbar

AutoCAD prompts:

Command: **zoom**
All/Center/Dynamic/Extents/Previous/Scale(X/XP)/Window/<Realtime>: **d**

The current viewport is then transformed into a selecting view that displays the drawing extents, as shown in the example in Figure 3–57.

When the selected view is displayed, you see the drawing extents marked by a white or black box, the current display marked by a green or magenta dotted box, and the generated area marked at the corners in red. A new view box, the same size as the current display, appears. Its location is controlled by the movement of the pointing device. Its size is controlled by a combination of the pick button and cursor movement. When the new view box has an X in the center, the box pans around the drawing in response to cursor movement. After you press the pick button on the pointing device, the X disappears and an arrow appears at the right edge of the box. The new view box is now in Zoom mode. While the arrow is in the box, moving the cursor left decreases the box size; moving the cursor right increases the size.

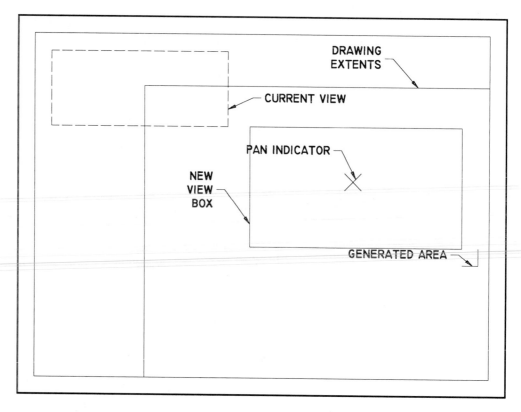

Figure 3–57 Using the Zoom Dynamic command to display the drawing extents

When the desired size has been chosen, press the pick button again to pan, or press Enter to accept the view defined by the location/size of the new view box. Pressing Esc cancels the ZOOM Dynamic and returns you to the current view.

Extents Option The ZOOM Extents command lets you see the entire drawing on screen. Unlike the All Option, the Extents Option uses only the drawing extents and not the drawing limits. See Figures 3–58a and 3–58b, which illustrate the difference between the options All and Extents.

Invoke the ZOOM Extents command from:

Zoom toolbar	Select Zoom Extents (see Figure 3–59)
Pull-down menu	View > Zoom > Extents
Command: prompt	**zoom** Enter

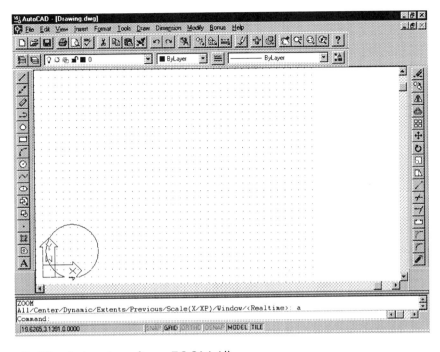

Figure 3–58a A drawing after a ZOOM All

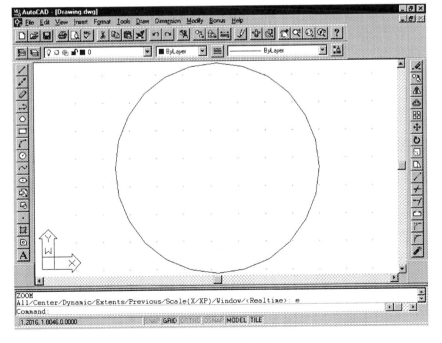

Figure 3–58b The same drawing after a ZOOM Extents

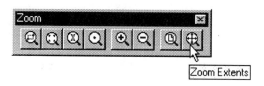

Figure 3–59 Invoking the Zoom Extents command from the Zoom toolbar

AutoCAD prompts:

Command: **zoom** Enter
All/Center/Dynamic/Extents/Previous/Scale(X/XP)/Window/<Realtime>: **e**
Enter

Previous Option The ZOOM Previous command displays the last displayed view. While editing or creating a drawing, you may want to zoom into a small area, back out to view the larger area, and then zoom into another small area. To do this, AutoCAD saves the coordinates of the current view whenever it is being changed by any of the zoom options or other view commands. So you can return to the previous view by entering the Previous option, which can restore the previous 10 views.

Invoke the ZOOM Previous command from:

Pull-down menu	View > Zoom > Previous
Command: prompt	zoom Enter

AutoCAD prompts:

Command: **zoom** Enter
All/Center/Dynamic/Extents/Previous/Scale(X/XP)/Window/<Realtime>: **p**
Enter

Window Option The ZOOM Window command lets you specify an area of the drawing you wish to see by placing two opposite corner points of a rectangular window. The center of the area selected becomes the new display center, and the area inside the window is enlarged to fill the display as completely as possible.

You can enter two opposite corner points to specify an area by means of coordinates or the pointing device (see Figures 3–60a and 3–60b).

Invoke the ZOOM Window command from:

Zoom toolbar	Select Zoom Window (see Figure 3–61)
Pull-down menu	View > Zoom > Window
Command: prompt	zoom Enter

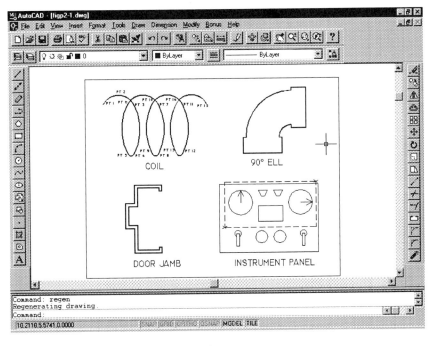

Figure 3-60a Specifying a ZOOM Window area

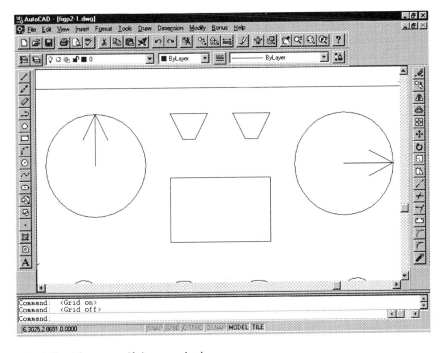

Figure 3-60b After specifying a window area

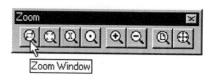

Figure 3–61 Invoking the Zoom Window command from the Zoom toolbar

AutoCAD prompts:

Command: **zoom** [Enter]
All/Center/Dynamic/Extents/Previous/Scale(X/XP)/Window/<Realtime>: **w** [Enter]
First corner: *(specify a point to define the first corner of the window)*
Other corner: *(specify a point to define the diagonally opposite corner of the window)*

PAN Command

The PAN command lets you view a different portion of the drawing in the current view without changing the magnification. You can move your viewing area to see details that are currently off screen. Imagine that you are looking at your drawing through the display window and that you can slide the drawing left, right, up, and down without moving the window.

Invoke the PAN command from:

Pull-down menu	View > Pan > Point

AutoCAD prompts:

Command: **pan** [Enter]
Displacement:

You must specify both the direction to move the view of the drawing and how far to move it. You can designate two points, in which case AutoCAD computes the displacement from the first point to the second.

For example, the following command sequence views a different portion of the drawing by placing two data points as shown in Figure 3–62.

Command: **pan** [Enter]
Displacement: *(specify first displacement point)*
Second point: *(specify second displacement point)*

AutoCAD calculates the distance and direction between the two points and pans the drawing accordingly. Sometimes it is useful to pan in exactly the horizontal or the

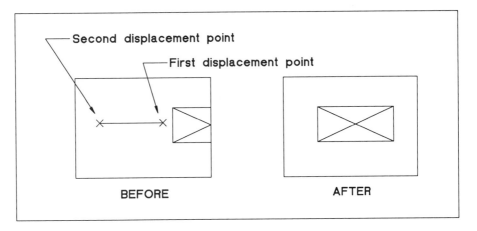

Figure 3–62 Moving the view with the PAN command by specifying two displacement points

vertical direction. In that case, set Ortho mode to ON before invoking the PAN command to constrain cursor movement to the X or Y axis directions. You can enter a single coordinate pair indicating the relative displacement of the drawing with respect to the screen. If you give a null response to the "Second point" prompt, you are indicating that the coordinates provided represent the displacement of the drawing with respect to the origin. If you provide the coordinates for the second point instead of giving a null response, then AutoCAD computes the displacement from the first point to the second.

For example, the following command sequence views a different portion of the drawing 2 units to the left and 0.75 units up, as shown in Figure 3–63.

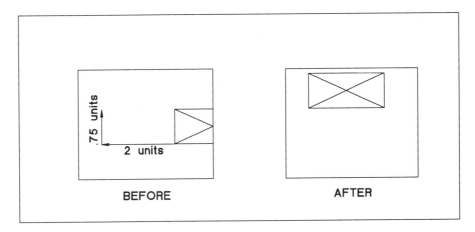

Figure 3–63 Moving the view with the PAN command by specifying a pair of coordinates

Command: **pan** Enter
Displacement: **-2,.75** Enter
Second point: Enter

Pan Realtime Command The Pan Realtime command lets you pan interactively to the logical extent (edge of the drawing space). Once you invoke the command, the cursor changes to a hand cursor. To pan, hold the pick button on the pointing device to lock the cursor to its current location relative to the viewport coordinate system, and move the cursor in any direction. Graphics within the window are moved in the same direction as the cursor. To discontinue the panning, release the pick button.

When you reach a logical extent (edge of the drawing space), a line-bar is displayed on the hand cursor on the side. The line-bar is displayed at the top, bottom, or left or right side of the drawing, depending upon whether the logical extent is at the top, bottom, or side of the drawing.

Invoke the PAN Realtime command from:

Standard toolbar	Select Pan Realtime (see Figure 3–64)
Pull-down menu	View > Pan > Real Time
Command: prompt	pan Enter

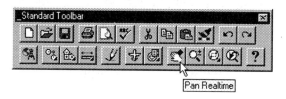

Figure 3–64 Invoking the Pan Realtime command from the Standard toolbar

AutoCAD prompts:

Command: **pan** Enter
Press Esc or Enter to exit, or right-click to activate pop-up menu.

To exit PAN Realtime, press Esc or Enter. You can also exit by selecting Exit from the pop-up menu that is displayed when you press the right button on your pointing device. In addition, you can perform other operations related to ZOOM and PAN by selecting the appropriate commands from the pop-up menu.

Aerial View

The DSVIEWER command is used to activate the Aerial View, which provides a quick method of visually panning and zooming. By default, AutoCAD displays the

Aerial View window, with the entire drawing displayed in the window, as shown in Figure 3–65. You can select any portion of the drawing in the Aerial View window by visually panning and zooming; in turn, AutoCAD displays the selected portion in the view window (current viewport).

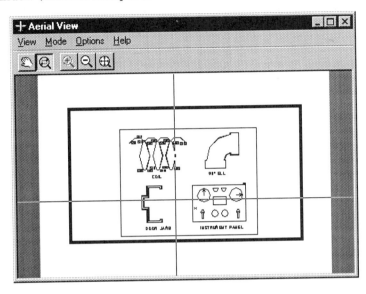

Figure 3–65 The Aerial View dialog window

Invoke the DSVIEWER command from:

Standard toolbar	Select Aerial View (see Figure 3–66)
Pull-down menu	View > Aerial View
Command: prompt	**dsviewer** Enter

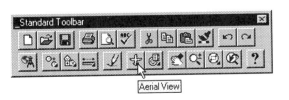

Figure 3–66 Invoking the Aerial View command from the Standard toolbar

AutoCAD displays the Aerial View window. Three option menus are provided to pan and zoom visually.

View Menu The View menu in the Aerial View window has three options available. Option **Zoom In** causes the view to appear closer, enlarging the details of objects, but covering a smaller area. Option **Zoom Out** causes the view to appear farther away, decreasing the size of details of objects, but covering a larger area. Option **Global** causes the entire drawing to be viewable in the Aerial View window. You can also select the three options from the toolbar provided in the Aerial View window.

Mode Menu The Mode menu in the Aerial View window has two options available. Selection of the **Pan** mode option causes the view to move in response to slide bar movements. Selection of the **Zoom** mode option changes the view by increasing or decreasing the magnification of the area in the Aerial View window. You can also change the mode selection from the toolbar provided in the Aerial View window.

Options Menu The Options Menu in the Aerial View window has three options available. **Auto Viewport** causes the active viewport to be displayed in model space. **Dynamic Update** toggles whether the view is updated or not in response to editing. The Real Time Zoom controls whether or not the AutoCAD window updates in real time when you zoom using the Aerial View.

REDRAW Command

The REDRAW command is used to refresh the on-screen image. You can use this command whenever you see an imcomplete image of your drawing. If you draw two lines in the same place and erase one of the lines, it appears as if both the lines are erased. By invoking the REDRAW command, the second line will reappear. Also, you can use the REDRAW command to remove the blip marks on the screen. A redraw is considered a screen refresh as opposed to a database regeneration.

Invoke the REDRAW command from:

Pull-down menu	View > Redraw
Command: prompt	redraw Enter

AutoCAD prompts:

Command: **redraw** Enter

REGEN Command

The REGEN command is used to regenerate the drawing's data on the screen. In general, you should use the REGEN command if the image presented by REDRAW does not correctly reflect your drawing. REGEN goes through the drawing's entire database and projects the most up-to-date information on the screen; this command will give you the most accurate image possible. Because of the manner in which it functions, a REGEN takes significantly longer than a REDRAW.

There are certain AutoCAD commands for which REGEN takes place automatically unless REGENAUTO is set to OFF.

The REGEN command does not have any options.

Invoke the REGEN command from:

Pull-down menu	View > Regen
Command: prompt	**regen** Enter

AutoCAD prompts:

Command: **regen** Enter

WILD CARDS AND NAMED OBJECTS

AutoCAD lets you use a variety of wild cards for specifying selected groups of named objects when responding to prompts during commands. By placing one or more of these wild cards in the string (your response), you can specify a group that includes (or excludes) all of the objects with certain combinations or patterns of characters.

The types of objects associated with a drawing that are referred to by name include blocks, layers, linetypes, text styles, dimension styles, named User Coordinate Systems, named views, shapes, and named viewport configurations.

The wild card characters include the two commonly used in DOS (* and ?) as well as eight more that come from the UNIX operating system. Here is a table listing the wild cards and their use.

Wild Card	Use
# (pound)	Matches any numeric digit
@ (at)	Matches any alphanumeric character
. (period)	Matches any character except alphanumeric
* (asterisk)	Matches any string. It can be used anywhere in the search pattern: the beginning, middle, or end of the string.
? (question mark)	Matches any single character
~ (tilde)	Matches anything but the pattern
[...]	Matches any one of the characters enclosed
[~...]	Matches any character not enclosed
- (hyphen)	Specifies single-character range
' (reverse quote)	Reads characters literally

The following table shows some examples of wild card patterns.

Pattern	Will match or include . . .	But not . . .
ABC	Only ABC	
~ABC	Anything but ABC	
?BC	ABC through ZBC	AB, BC, ABCD, XXBC
A?C	AAC through AZC	AC, ABCD, AXXC, ABCX
AB?	ABA through ABZ	AB, ABCE, XAB
A*	Anything starting with A	XAAA
A*C	Anything starting with A and ending with C	XA, ABCDE
*AB	Anything ending with AB	ABCX, ABX
AB	AB anywhere in string	AXXXB
~*AB*	All strings without AB	AB, ABX, XAB, XABX
[AB]C	AC or BC	ABC, XAC
[A-K]D	AD, BD, through KD	ABC, AKC, KD

CREATING AND MODIFYING LAYER SYSTEM

AutoCAD offers a means of grouping objects in layers in a manner similar to the manual drafter's separating complex drawings into simpler ones on individual transparent sheets superimposed in a single stack. Under these conditions, the manual drafter would be able to draw on the top sheet only. Likewise, in AutoCAD you can draw only on the current layer. However, AutoCAD permits you to transfer selected objects from one layer to another (neither of which needs to be the current layer) with commands called CHANGE, CHPROP and several others. (Let's see the manual drafter try that!)

A common application of the layer feature is to use one layer for construction (or layout) lines. You can create geometric constructions with objects, such as lines, circles, and arcs. These generate intersections, endpoints, centers, points of tangency, midpoints, and other useful data that might take the manual drafter considerable time to calculate with a calculator or to hand-measure on the board. From these you can create other objects using intersections or other data generated from the layout. Then the layout layer can be turned off (making it no longer visible). The layer is not lost, but can be recalled (turned on) for viewing later as required.

The same drawing limits, coordinate system, and zoom factors apply to all layers in a drawing. There is a limit of 32,000 layers in a drawing, more than enough for any drawing need. There is no limit to the number of objects per layer.

To draw an object on a particular layer, first make sure that that layer is set as the "current layer." There is one, and only one, current layer. Whatever you draw will be placed on the current layer. The current layer can be compared to the manual drafter's top sheet on the stack of transparencies. To draw an object on a particular layer, that layer must first have been created; if it is not the current layer, you must make it the current layer.

You can always move, copy, or rotate any object, whether it is on the current layer or not. When you copy an object that is not on the current layer, the copy is placed on the layer that the original object is on. This is also true with the mirror or an array of an object or group of objects.

A layer can be visible (on) or invisible (off). Only visible layers are displayed or plotted. Invisible layers are still part of the drawing; they are just not displayed or plotted. You can turn layers on and off at will, in any combination. It is possible to turn off the current layer. If this happens and you draw an object, it will not appear on the screen; it will be placed on the current layer and will appear on the screen when that layer is turned on (provided you are viewing the area in which the object was drawn). This is not a common occurrence, but it can cause concern to both the novice and the more experienced operator who has not faced the problem before. Do not turn off the current layer; the results can be very confusing. When the TILEMODE system variable is set to OFF, you can make specified layers visible only in certain viewports. For additional information see Chapter 12.

Each layer in a drawing has an associated name, color, and linetype. The name of a layer may be up to 31 characters long. It may contain letters, digits, and the special characters dollar ($), hyphen (-), and underscore (_) but no blank spaces. Always give a descriptive name appropriate to your application, such as floor-plan or plumbing. The first several characters of the current layer's name are displayed in the layer list box located in the Object Properties toolbar (see Figure 3-67). You can change the name of a layer any time you wish, and you can delete unused layers.

One color can be assigned to any number of layers in a drawing. You can assign to a layer any one of the 256 available colors. If your graphics monitor is monochrome, all color numbers will produce the same visual effect. Even in this case, color numbers are useful, because they can be assigned to different pens on a pen plotter to plot in different line weights and colors. This works even for single-pen plotters; you can instruct AutoCAD to pause for pen changes.

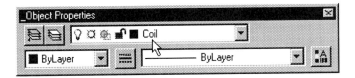

Figure 3-67 The current layer name is displayed in the list box located in the Object Properties toolbar

Fundamentals II

A *linetype* is a repeating pattern of dashes, dots, and blank spaces. AutoCAD adds the capability of including the repeated objects in the custom linetypes. The assigned linetype is used to draw all objects on the layer. The following are some of the linetypes that are provided in AutoCAD in a library file called *ACAD.LIN*:

Border	Dashdot	Dot
Center	Dashed	Hidden
Continuous	Divide	Phantom

See Appendix G for examples of each of these linetypes. Linetypes are another means of conveying visual information. You can assign the same linetype to any number of layers. In some drafting disciplines, conventions have been established giving specific meanings to particular dash-dot patterns. If a line is too short to hold even one dash-dot sequence, AutoCAD draws a continuous line between the endpoints. When you are working on large drawings, you may not see the gap between dash-dot patterns in a linetype, unless the scaling for the linetype is set for a large value. This can be done by means of the LTSCALE command. This command is discussed in more detail later in this chapter.

Every drawing will have a layer called layer 0 (zero). By default, layer 0 is set to ON and assigned the color white and the linetype continuous. Layer 0 cannot be renamed or deleted.

If you need additional layers, you must create them. By default, each new layer is assigned the the color white and linetype continuous. If necessary, you can always reassign the color and linetype of the new layer.

Setting up and Controlling Layers by Means of the Layer & Linetype Properties Dialog Box

The Layer & Linetype Properties dialog box or command line version of the layer can be used to set up and control layers.

To open the Layer & Linetype Properties dialog box, invoke the LAYER command from:

Object Properties toolbar	Select Layers (see Figure 3–68)
Pull-down menu	Format > Layer...
Command: prompt	**layer** Enter

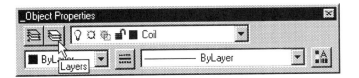

Figure 3–68 Invoking the DDLMODES command from the Object Properties toolbar

AutoCAD displays the Layer & Linetype dialog box, as shown in Figure 3–69.

Select the Layer tab, and AutoCAD lists the available layer names in the Layer & Linetype dialog box. By default, AutoCAD provides one layer called 0 that is set to ON and is assigned the color white and the linetype continuous.

Creating New Layer(s) To create new layer(s), click the **"New"** button. AutoCAD then creates a new layer by assigning the name *Layer1* and setting it to ON, with the color white and the linetype continuous. The name is listed in the layer list box. To rename the layer, click on the name, type a new name, and press Enter.

Fundamentals II

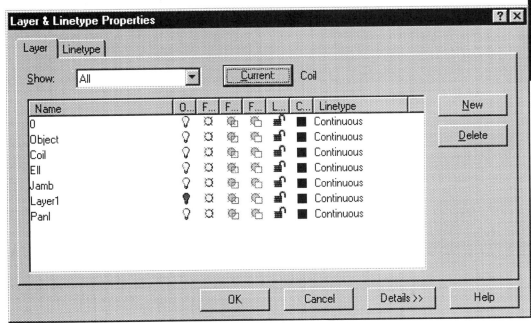

Figure 3–69 The Layer & Linetype Properties dialog box

> **NOTE:** The layer name can not contain wild-card characters (such as
> * and !) or spaces. You cannot duplicate existing names.

Making a Layer Current To make a layer current, first select the layer name in
the layer list box, and then click the **"Current:"** button located on the top right side
of the dialog box. The current layer name appears next to the **"Current:"** button.

Showing Layer(s) The **Show:** list box determines which layers are displayed in
the layer list box. You can list the layers by their state, name, color, and linetype.

By default, AutoCAD is set to list all the available layers in the list box. In addition,
you can set it to list all the layers that are in use, all the layers that are unused, all
the layers that belong to external reference drawing file(s), all the layers except
those that belong to external reference drawing file(s), and the layers that satisfy
the condition set forth in the **Set Layer Filters** dialog box.

The **Set Layer Filters** dialog box, shown in Figure 3–70, allows you to filter layers
with respect to their name, color, linetype, whether they are set to ON or OFF,
frozen or thawed, and locked or unlocked. To open the **Set Layer Filters** dialog box,
select **Set Filter Dialog...** from the Show option menu.

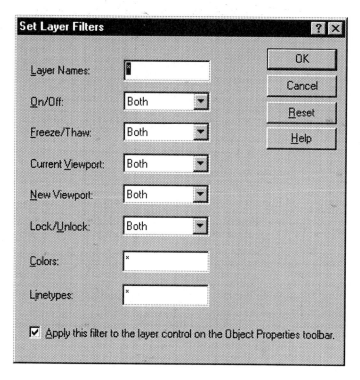

Figure 3–70 Set Layer Filters dialog box

Deleting Layer(s) To delete unused layer(s), first select one or more layers from the list box, and then click the **"Delete"** button. AutoCAD deletes all the selected layers from the current drawing.

> *Note:* You cannot delete layers that contain objects. To select more than one layer, hold down ⌜Ctrl⌟ and select the layer(s) from the list box. To select all the layers, click the right button; a button menu appears. Select the **Select All** option, and AutoCAD selects all the layers. To clear the selection, click the right button and select the **Clear All** option.

Controlling the Visibility of Layer(s) When you turn off a layer, the objects are not displayed on the view window and they are not plotted. The objects are still in the drawing, but they are made invisible. And they are still calculated during regeneration of the drawing, even though they are invisible.

To change the setting for the visibility of layer(s), click the icon corresponding to the layer name located under the **On** column (second column from the left). The icon is a toggle setting for ON/OFF of layers.

Instead of turning the layers off, you can freeze the layers. The layers that are frozen will be not be visible in the view window, nor will be they be plotted. In this respect, frozen layers are similar to layers that are off. However, layers that are simply turned off still go through a screen regeneration each time the system regenerates your drawing, whereas the layers that are frozen are not considered during a screen regeneration. If you want to see the frozen layer later, you simply thaw it, and automatic regeneration of the screen takes place.

To change the setting for the visibility of layer(s) by freezing/thawing, click the icon corresponding to the layer name located under the **Freeze in All Viewports** column (third column from the left). The icon is a toggle setting for FREEZE/THAW of layers.

> *NOTE:* To select more than one layer, hold down ⌜Ctrl⌟ and select the layer(s) from the list box. To select all of the layers, click the right button and select the **Select All** option from the menu. To clear the selection, click the right button and select the **Clear All** option from the menu.

> *NOTE:* The columns under **Freeze in Current Viewport** and **Freeze in New Viewports** are applicable only when the TILEMODE system variable is set to OFF. For a detailed explanation of the settings refer to Chapter 12.

Fundamentals II

Locking/Unlocking Layers Objects on locked layers are visible in the view window but cannot be modified by means of the modifying commands. However, it is still possible to draw on a locked layer by making it the current layer, changing the linetypes and colors, freezing them, and using any of the inquiry commands and Object Snap modes on them.

To change the setting for the Lock/Unlock of layer(s), click the icon corresponding to the layer name located under the **Lock** column (sixth column from the left). The icon is a toggle setting for Lock/Unlock of layers.

Changing the Color of Layer(s) By default, AutoCAD assigns the color white to a newly created layer. If necessary, you can change the color.

To change the assigned color, click the corresponding icon to the layer name located under the **Color** column (seventh column from the left). AutoCAD displays the Select Color dialog box, which allows you to change the color of the selected layer(s). You can select one of the 256 colors. Use the cursor to pick the color you want, or enter its name or number in the **Color:** edit box. Select the **OK** button to accept the color selection. To cancel the selection, select the **Cancel** button.

Changing the Linetype of Layer(s) By default, AutoCAD assigns the linetype continuous to a newly created layer. If necessary, you can change the linetype.

To change the assigned linetype, click the linetype name corresponding to the layer name located under the **Linetype** column (eighth column from the left). AutoCAD displays the Select Linetype dialog box, which allows you to change the linetype of the selected layer(s). Select the appropriate linetype from the list box, and select the **OK** button to accept the linetype selection. To cancel the selection, select the **Cancel** button.

> **NOTE:** AutoCAD lists in the Select Linetype dialog box only the linetypes that are loaded in the current drawing. To load additional linetypes in the current drawing, choose the **"Load..."** button, and AutoCAD displays the Load or Reload Linetypes dialog box. AutoCAD lists the available linetypes from the default linetype file ACAD.LIN. Select all the linetypes that need to be loaded, and select the OK button to load the linetypes into the current drawing. If necessary, you can change the default linetype file ACAD.LIN to another file by clicking the **File...** button and selecting the appropriate linetype file. You can also load the linetypes into the current drawing from the Linetype tab in the Layer and Linetype Properties dialog box.

The details section of the Layer & Linetype Properties dialog box displays an extension of the dialog box with alternate access to property settings. To display the details section choose the **Details>>** button.

If necessary, you can drag the widths of the column headings to see additional characters of the layer name, full legend for each symbol and color name or number in the list box. If you want to sort the order in which layers are displayed in the list box, choose the column headings. The first selection puts the layers in descending order (Z to A, then numbers), and a second selection puts the layers in ascending order (Numbers, A to Z). Choosing the status column headers lists the frozen or locked layers first in the list.

After making the necessary changes, choose the OK button to keep the changes and close the dialog box. To discard the changes, chose the Cancel button and close the dialog box.

Changing Layer Properties from the Object Properties Toolbox

You can also toggle on/off, freeze/thaw, lock/unlock, or freeze/thaw for the current viewport in paper space, in addition to making a layer current from the layer list box provided in the Object Properties toolbar. Click on the appropriate icon next to the layer name you wish to toggle, as shown in Figure 3–71.

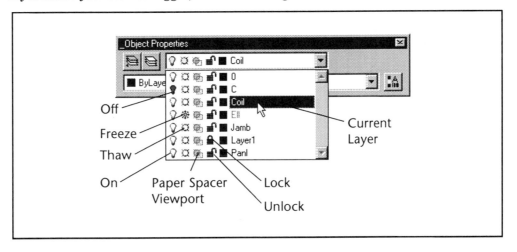

Figure 3–71 Layer list box in the Object Properties toolbar

Making an Object's Layer Current

AutoCAD allows you to select an object in the drawing to make its layer the current layer. To do so, invoke the command from:

Object Properties toolbar	Select Make Object's Layer Current (See Figure 3–72)

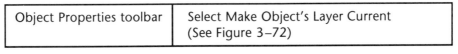

Figure 3–72 Invoking the Make Object's Layer Current from the Object Properties toolbar

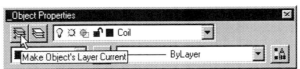

AutoCAD prompts:

> Select object whose layer will become current: *(select the object in the drawing to make its layer current)*

AutoCAD makes the selected object's layer current.

Setting Up and Controlling Layers by means of the Command Version of the LAYER Command

Invoke the command version of the LAYER command from:

Command: prompt	-layer Enter

AutoCAD prompts:

> Command: **layer** Enter
> ?/Make/Set/New/ON/OFF/Color/LType/Freeze/Thaw/LOck/Unlock: *(select one of the available options)*

? Option The ? option lists the names of layers defined in the current drawing, showing their on/off/frozen/thaw/lock/unlock state, color, and linetypes. When you select this option, AutoCAD prompts:

> Layer name(s) to list <*>:

You can enter a list of layer names, using wild cards if you wish, or press the Spacebar or Enter to accept the default to list all layer names.

Make Option The Make option effectively does three things. When this option is invoked, AutoCAD prompts you for a layer name. Once you enter a name, Make does the following:

1. Searches for the layer to determine whether it exists.
2. Creates it if the layer does not exist, and assigns the color white and the linetype continuous.
3. Sets the newly made layer to be the current layer.

When you select this option, AutoCAD prompts:

> New current Layer <default>:

If the layer you selected exists and is presently turned off, AutoCAD turns it on automatically, using the color and linetype previously assigned to that layer, and makes it the current layer.

Set Option The Set option tells AutoCAD on which layer you want to draw (making the current layer). When you select this option, AutoCAD prompts:

Current Layer <default>:

Enter the layer's name (it must be an existing layer) and press the Spacebar or Enter. This layer becomes the current layer. The first several characters of the layer name are displayed in the Object Properties layer list box.

New Option The New option allows you to create new layers. When you select this option, AutoCAD prompts:

New Layer name(s):

You can enter more than one name at a time by separating the names with a comma. If you need to separate characters in the name, use the underscore (_) instead of pressing the Spacebar (in AutoCAD, pressing the Spacebar is the same as pressing Enter). Each layer thus created is automatically turned on and assigned the color white and linetype continuous.

OFF Option The OFF option allows you to turn off selected layers. When you select this option, AutoCAD prompts:

Layer name(s) to turn off:

The list should contain only existing layer names. The names may include wild-card characters. When you turn off a layer, its associated objects will not be displayed in the new window and they are not plotted. The objects still exist in the drawing; they are just invisible. And they are still calculated during the regeneration of the drawing, even though they are not visible.

ON Option The ON option allows you to turn on layers that have been turned off. When you select this option, AutoCAD prompts:

Layer name(s) to turn on:

This list should contain only existing layer names. The name may include wild-card characters. Each designated layer is turned on using the color and linetype previously associated with it. Turning a layer on does *not* cause it to be the current layer.

Color Option The Color option allows you to change the color associated with that specific layer. When you select this option, AutoCAD first prompts:

Color:

Reply with one of the standard color names or with a legal color number from 0 and 255. After you specify the color, AutoCAD prompts:

Layer name(s) to color n <default>:

Fundamentals II

(This prompt will actually have the code number of the color selected in place of the "n" shown here.)

Reply with the names of existing layers, separated by commas. The names may include wild-card characters. The specified layers are given the color you designated and are then automatically turned on if they are off. If you would prefer to assign the color but to turn the layers off, precede the color with a minus sign (-).

Linetype Option The Linetype option allows you to change the linetype associated with a specific layer. When you select this option, AutoCAD prompts:

Linetype (or ?) <continuous>:

Reply with the name of an existing defined linetype. AutoCAD then asks for a list of layer names to which the linetype should be applied. For example, if you had replied to the first prompt with the linetype named *HIDDEN*, the next prompt would be:

Layer names(s) for linetype hidden <default>:

Reply with the names of existing layers, separated by commas. The names may include wild-card characters.

Freeze and Thaw Options The layers that are frozen will not be visible on the display, nor will they be plotted. In this respect, Freeze is similar to OFF. However, layers that are simply turned off still go through a screen regeneration each time the system regenerates your drawing. If you want to see the frozen layer later, you simply Thaw it, and automatic regeneration of the screen takes place. The layers that are frozen will not be regenerated.

When you select the Freeze option, AutoCAD prompts:

Layer name(s) to Freeze:

You can enter more than one name at a time by separating the names with a comma.

When you select the Thaw option, AutoCAD prompts:

Layer name(s) to Thaw:

You can enter more than one name at a time by separating the names with a comma.

LOck and Unlock Options Objects on locked layers are visible on the display but cannot be modified with the modify commands. When you select the Lock option, AutoCAD prompts:

Layer name(s) to Lock:

You can enter more than one name at a time by separating the names with a comma.

When you select the Unlock option, AutoCAD prompts:

Layer name(s) to UnLock:

You can enter more than one name at a time by separating the names with a comma.

Whenever you give a null response to the LAYER command, it returns you to the "Command:" prompt.

SETTING THE LINETYPE SCALE FACTOR

The linetype scale factor allows you to change the relative lengths of dashes and spaces between dashes and dots linetypes per drawing unit. The definition of the linetype instructs AutoCAD on how many units long to make dashes and the spaces between dashes and dots. As long as the linetype scale is set to 1.0, the displayed length of dashes and spaces coincides with the definition of the linetype. The LTSCALE command allows you to set the linetype scale factor.

Invoke the LTSCALE command from:

Command: prompt	Itscale Enter

AutoCAD prompts:

Command: **Itscale** Enter
New scale factor <current>: *(specify the scale factor)*

You can also specify the linetype scale factor in the Details section of the Linetype tab of the Layer & Linetype Properties dialog box.

Changing the linetype scale affects all linetypes in the drawing. If you want dashes that have been defined as 0.5 units long in the DASHED linetype to be displayed as 10 units long, you set the linetype scale factor to 20. This also makes the dashes that were defined as 1.25 units long in the CENTER linetype display as 25 units long and the short dashes (defined as 0.25 units long) display as 5 units long. Note that the 1.25-unit-long dash in the CENTER linetype is 2.5 times longer than the 0.5-unit-long dash in the DASHED linetype. This ratio will always remain the same, no matter what the setting of LTSCALE. So if you wish to have some other ratio of dash and space lengths between different linetypes, you will have to change the definition of one of the linetypes in the ACAD.LIN file.

Remember that linetypes are for visual effect. The actual lengths of dashes and spaces are bound more to how they should look on the final plotted sheet than to distances or sizes of any objects on the drawing. An object plotted full size can probably use an LTSCALE setting of 1.0. A 50'-long object plotted on an 18" × 24" sheet might be plotted at a 1/4" = 1'-0" scale factor. This would equate to 1 = 48. An LTSCALE setting of 48 would make dashes and spaces plot to the same lengths as the full-size plot with a setting of 1.0. Changing the linetpe scale factor causes the drawing to regenerate.

U, UNDO, AND REDO COMMANDS

The UNDO command undoes the effects of the previous command or group of commands, depending on the option employed. The U command reverses the most recent operation, and the REDO command is a one-time reversal of the effects of the previous U and UNDO commands.

U Command

The U command undoes the effects of the previous command by displaying the name of that command. Pressing Enter after using the U command undoes the next-previous command, and continues stepping back with each repetition until it reaches the state of the drawing at the beginning of the current editing session.

When an operation cannot be undone, AutoCAD displays the command name but performs no action. An operation external to the current drawing, such as plotting or writing to a file, *cannot* be undone.

Invoke the U command from:

Standard toolbar	Select Undo (see Figure 3–73)
Pull-down menu	Edit > Undo
Command: prompt	u Enter

Figure 3–73 Invoking the Undo command from the Standard toolbar

AutoCAD reverses the most recent operation.

For example, if the previous command sequences drew a circle and then copied it, two U commands would undo the two previous commands in sequence, as follows:

    Command: u Enter
    COPY
    Command: Enter
    CIRCLE

Using the U command after commands that involve transparent commands or subcommands causes the entire sequence to be undone. For example, when you set a dimension variable and then perform a dimension command, a subsequent U command nullifies the dimension drawn and the change in the setting of the dimension variable.

UNDO Command

The UNDO command permits you to select a specified number or marked group of prior commands for undoing.

Invoke the UNDO command from:

Command: prompt	**undo** `Enter`

AutoCAD prompts:

Command: **undo** `Enter`
Auto/Control/BEgin/End/Mark/Back/<Number>: *(select one of the available options)*

Control Option The Control option controls the number of available options. By limiting the number of options, you can free up the memory and disk space that is otherwise being used to save undoing operation information. AutoCAD prompts as follows when the Control option is selected:

Command: **undo** `Enter`
Auto/Control/BEgin/End/Mark/Back/<Number>: **c** `Enter`
All/None/One <All>: *(select one of the three available options)*

Selection of the **All** option (the default setting of the UNDO command) enables all Undo options. The **None** option disables the U and UNDO commands but not the Control option of the UNDO command that re-enables various options. And the **One** option reverses the most recent operation.

Number Option The Number option allows you to enter a number (such as 3) at the full prompt (when Control is set to All) as follows:

Command: **undo** `Enter`
Auto/Control/Begin/End/Mark/Back/<Number>: **3** `Enter`

This sequence causes the three previous operations to be undone. This is similar to using the U command three times in a row. The advantage of UNDO Number over multiple U's is that multiple screen regenerations will not occur, thus saving time.

Mark and Back Options If you are at a point in the editing session at which you would like to experiment but would still like the option of undoing the experiment, you can mark that point. An example of the use of the Mark and Back options is as follows:

Command: **line** `Enter` *(draw a line)*
Command: **circle** `Enter` *(draw a circle)*
Command: **undo** `Enter`
Auto/Control/Begin/End/Mark/Back/<Number>: **m** `Enter`

Command: **text** `Enter` *(enter text)*
Command: **arc** `Enter` *(draw an arc)*
Command: **undo** `Enter`
Auto/Control/Begin/End/Mark/Back/<Number>: **b** `Enter`

The Back option returns you to the state of the drawing that has the line and the circle. Following this UNDO Back with a U removes the circle. Another U removes the line. Another U displays the following prompt:

Everything has been undone

Using the Back option when no Mark has been established will prompt:

This will undo everything. OK? <Y>

Responding **Y** undoes everything done since the current editing session was begun or since the last SAVE command.

NOTE: The default is Y, think twice before pressing `Enter` in response to the "This will undo everything" prompt.

Begin and End Options AutoCAD's U and UNDO commands treat the operations between an UNDO Begin and an UNDO End as one command. A Begin option entered after another Begin option (before an UNDO End) will automatically invoke an UNDO End option, thereby grouping the operations since that prior Begin option. If the UNDO Control has been set to None or One, the Begin option will not work. Using the U command is permissible after Begin and before an UNDO End, to undo operations, but only back to the UNDO Begin.

The Begin and End options are normally intended for use in strings of menu commands where a menu pick involves several operations.

Auto Option The Auto option causes multiple operations invoked by a single menu pick to be treated as one command by the U or UNDO command. UNDO Begin should be placed at the beginning of a menu string, with UNDO End at the end of the string. It has no effect if the UNDO Control has been set to None or One, however.

The effects of the following commands *cannot* be undone:

AREA, ATTEXT, DBLIST, DELAY, DIST, DXFOUT, END, FILES, FILMROLL, GRAPHSCR, HELP, HIDE, ID, IGESOUT, LIST, MSLIDE, PLOT, PRPLOT, QUIT, REDRAW, REDRAWALL, REGENALL, RESUME, SAVE, SHADE, SHELL, STATUS, and TEXTSCR.

REDO Command

The REDO command permits one reversal of a prior U or UNDO command. This will undo the undo. To undo the undo, the REDO command should be used immediately after the U or UNDO command.

Invoke the REDO command from:

Standard toolbar	Select Redo (see Figure 3–74)
Pull-down menu	<u>E</u>dit > <u>R</u>edo
Command: prompt	**redo** Enter

Figure 3–74 Invoking the REDO command from the Standard toolbar

AutoCAD reverses the prior U or UNDO command.

The REDO command does not have any options.

PROJECT EXERCISE

This project exercise provides point-by-point instructions for setting up the drawing with layers and then creating the objects shown in Figure P3–1. In this exercise you will apply the skills acquired in Chapters 1, 2, and 3.

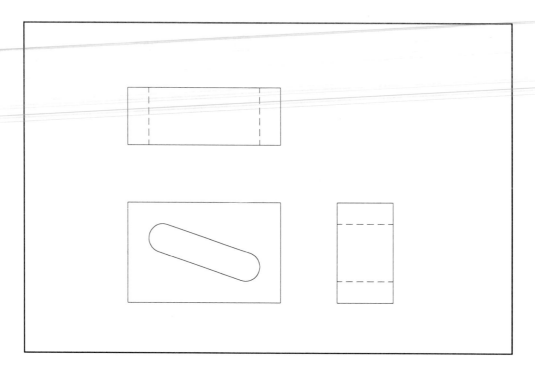

Figure P3–1 Completed project drawing

In this project you will:

■ Set up the drawing, including setting up the layers.
■ Use the LINE, and RECTANGLE commands with Object Snap mode

Set Up the Drawing and Draw a Border

Step 1   Start the AutoCAD program.

Step 2   To create a new drawing, invoke the NEW command from the Standard toolbar or select New from the pull-down menu File.

AutoCAD displays the Create New Drawing dialog box. Click the "Use a Wizard" button, and then select the Quick Setup and choose the OK button to close the dialog box.

AutoCAD displays the Quick Setup dialog box with the display of the Step:1 Units tab. Select "Decimal" radio button and choose the Next>> button.

AutoCAD displays Quick Setup dialog box with the display of the Step 2: Area tab. Under Width: edit field enter **18** and under the Length edit field enter **12**. Choose the Done button to close the Quick Setup dialog box.

Step 3 Invoke the LAYER command from the Object Properties toolbar, or select Layer... from the pull-down menu Format. AutoCAD displays the Layer & Linetype Properties dialog box.

Create four layers, rename them as shown in the table, and assign appropriate colors and linetypes.

Layer Name	Color	Linetype
Border	Cyan	Continuous
Object	Green	Continuous
Hidden	Blue	Hidden
Const	Red	Continuous

Set Border as the current layer, and close the Layer & Linetype Properties dialog box.

Step 4 To draw the border, invoke the RECTANG command from the Draw toolbar or type **rectang** at the "Command:" prompt and press Enter. AutoCAD prompts:

> Command: **rectang** Enter
> Chamfer/Elevation/Fillet/Thickness/Width/<First corner>: **0.25,0.25** Enter
> Other corner: **17.75,11.75** Enter

AutoCAD draws a rectangle border.

Draw the Objects

Step 1 From the Object Properties toolbar select the Layer Control down-arrow icon to display the layer list box. Select the OBJECT layer as the current layer.

Step 2 Invoke the LINE command from the Draw toolbar, and draw two rectanglular boxes.

Respond to the prompts in the command area as follows:

Command: **line**
From point: **2,7.5**
To point: **7.5,7.5**
To point: **7.5,9.5**
To point: **2,9.5**
To point: **c**

Command:(Press [Enter] to invoke the LINE command again)
From point: **9.5,2**
To point: **11.5,2**
To point: **11.5,5.5**
To point: **9.5,5.5**
To point: **c**

Step 3   Invoke the RECTANG command again from the Draw toolbar to draw a
rectangle by invoking appropriate object snaps.

Command: rectang
Chamfer/Elevation/Fillet/Thickness/Width/<First corner>: *(invoke the App
    Int object snap, and select line 1 and line 4 as shown Figure P3–2)*
Other corner: *(invoke the App Int object snap, and select the line 2 and
    line 3 as shown Figure P3–2)*

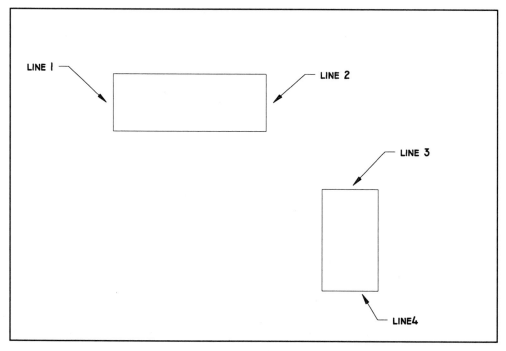

Figure P3–2   Identifying the lines to draw a rectangle

After drawing the rectangle, the drawing should look like Figure P3–3.

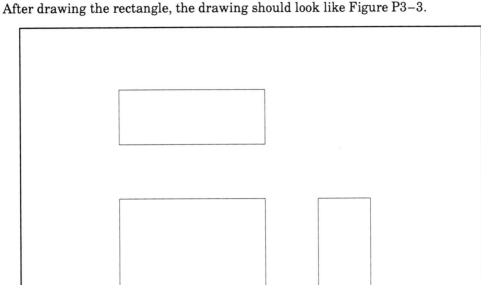

Figure P3–3 Completed drawing

Step 4 From the Object Properties toolbar select the Layer Control down-arrow icon to display the layer list box. Select the CONST layer as the current layer.

Step 5 Invoke the CIRCLE command from the Draw toolbar and draw two circles.

Respond to the prompts in the command area as follows:

Command: _circle 3P/2P/TTR/<Center point>: **3.25,4.25** `Enter`
Diameter/<Radius> <0.00>: **.5** `Enter`

Command: `Enter`
CIRCLE 3P/2P/TTR/<Center point>: **6.25,3.25** `Enter`
Diameter/<Radius> <0.50>: **.5** `Enter`

Step 6 Invoke the LINE command from the Draw toolbar and draw series of lines by invoking appropriate object snaps.

Command: _line
From point: *(invoke the QUAdrant object snap, and select a point QUA 1 as shown in Figure P3–4)*
To point: *(invoke the PERpendicular object snap, and select line 5, as shown in Figure P3–4)*
To point: `Enter`

Command: Enter
LINE
From point: *(invoke the QUAdrant object snap, and select a point QUA 2
as shown in Figure P3-4)*
To point: *(invoke the PERpendicular object snap, and select line 5, as
shown in Figure P3-4)*
To point: Enter

Command: Enter
Command: LINE
From point: *(invoke the QUAdrant object snap, and select a point QUA 3
as shown in Figure P3-4)*
To point: *(invoke the PERpendicular object snap, and select line 6, as
shown in Figure P3-4)*
To point: Enter

Command: Enter
LINE
From point: *(invoke the QUAdrant object snap, and select a point QUA 4
as shown in Figure P3-4)*
To point: *(invoke the PERpendicular object snap, and select line 6, as
shown in Figure P3-4)*
To point: Enter

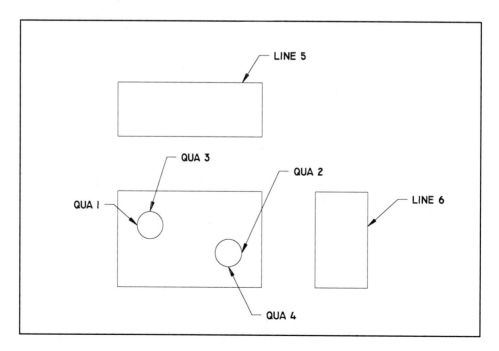

Figure P3-4 Identifying the points to draw additional lines

The drawing should look like Figure P3–5.

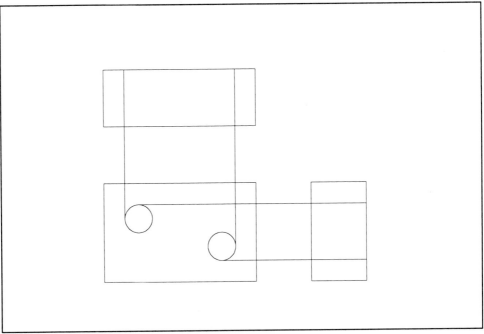

Figure P3–5   Completed drawing

Step 7   From the Object Properties toolbar select the Layer Control down-arrow icon to display the layer list box. Select the HIDDEN layer to make it the current layer.

Step 8   Invoke the LINE command from the Draw toolbar. Draw a series of lines by invoking appropriate object snaps.

> Command: _line
> From point: *(invoke the INTersection object snap, and select point 1 as shown in Figure P3–6)*
> To point: *(invoke the INTersection object snap, and select point 2 as shown in Figure P3–6)*
> To point: Enter
> Command:

Draw three additional lines:

From:	To:
point 3	point 4
point 5	point 6
point 7	point 8

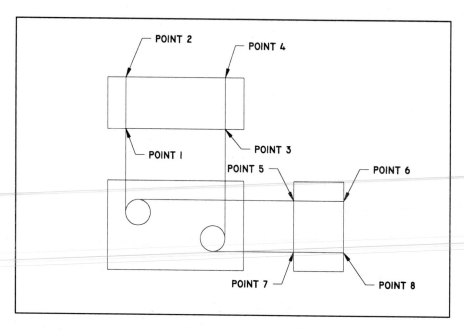

Figure P3–6   Identifying the points to draw additional lines

Step 9   Invoke the ERASE command from the Modify toolbar, and erase line 7, line 8, line 9, and line 10, as shown in Figure P3–7.

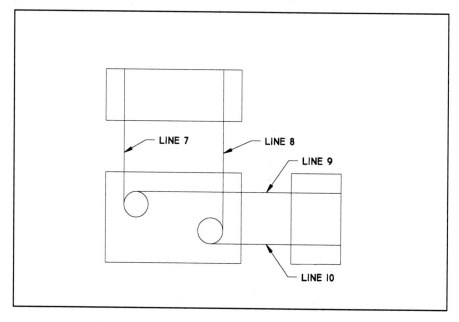

Figure P3–7   Identifying the lines to erase

The completed drawing should look like Figure P3–8.

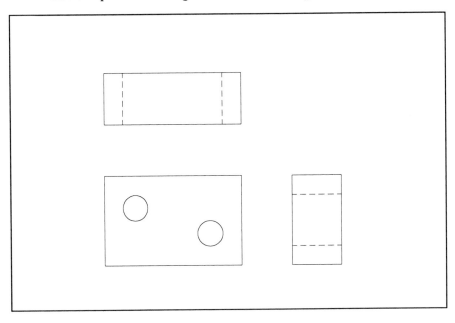

Figure P3–8 Completed drawing

Step 10   From the Object Properties toolbar select the Layer Control down-arrow icon to display the layer list box. Select the OBJECT layer to make it the current layer.

Step 11   Invoke the LINE command from the Draw toolbar and draw a series of lines.

Command: _line
From point: *(invoke the TANgent object snap, and select a point in the upper half of circle 1 as shown in Figure P3–9)*
To point: *(invoke the TANgent object snap, and select a point in the upper half of circle 2 as shown in Figure P3–9)*
To point: Enter

Command: Enter
LINE
From point: *(invoke the TANgent object snap, and select a point in the lower half of circle 1 as shown in Figure P3–9)*
To point: *(invoke the TANgent object snap, and select a point in the lower half of circle 2 as shown in Figure P3–9)*
To point: Enter
Command:

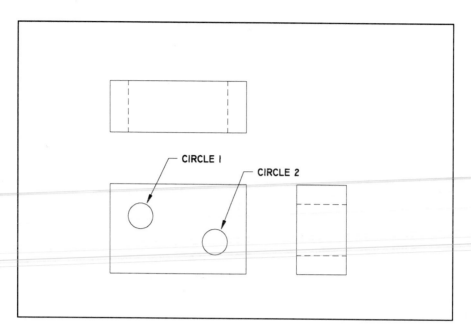

Figure P3–9 Identifying the object snap points to draw additional lines

Step 12   Invoke the ARC 3-Points command from the Draw toolbar.

> Command: _arc Center/<Start point>: *(invoke the ENDpoint object snap, and select endpoint 1 as shown in Figure P3–10)*
>
> Center/End/<Second point>: *(invoke the NEArest object snap, and select a point on circle 1 where indicated in Figure P3–10)*
>
> End point: *(invoke the ENDpoint object snap, and select endpoint 2 as shown in Figure P3–10)*

> Command: Enter
>
> ARC Center/<Start point>: *(invoke the ENDpoint object snap, and select endpoint 3 as shown in Figure P3–10)*
>
> Center/End/<Second point>: *(invoke the NEArest object snap, and select a point on circle 2 where indicated in Figure P3–10)*
>
> End point: *(invoke the ENDpoint object snap, and select endpoint 4 as shown in Figure P3–10)*

Step 13   From the Object Properties toolbar select the Layer Control down-arrow icon to display the layer list box. Set the CONST layer to off.

The completed drawing should look like Figure P3–11.

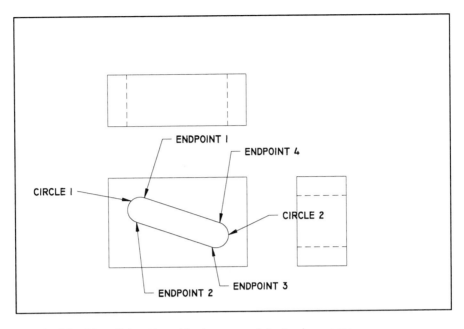

Figure P3–10 Identifying the object snap points to draw arcs

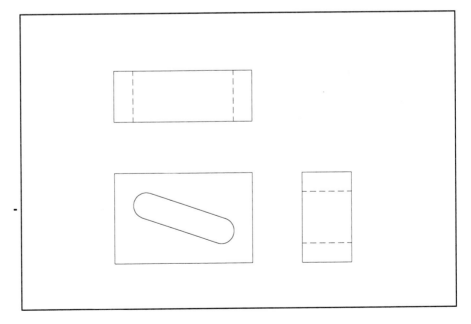

Figure P3–11 Completed drawing

Step 14 Invoke the SAVE... command from the File pull-down menu.

EXERCISES 3-1 THROUGH 3-6

Exercise 3-1

Create the drawing according to the settings given in the following table:

Settings	Value
1. Units	Decimal with two decimal places
2. Limits	Lower left corner:0,0
	Upper right corner: 18,12
3. Grid	0.25
4. Snap	0.25
5. Layers	*NAME* *COLOR* *LINETYPE*
	Solid Red Continuous
	Hidden Blue Hidden

Hint	To draw the border, use the RECTANGLE command with diagonally opposite corners at coordinates 0.25, 0.25 and 16.75,11.75

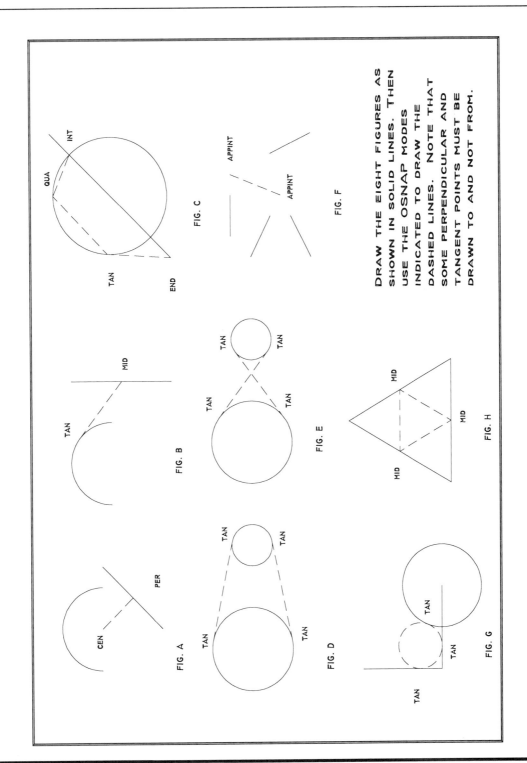

DRAW THE EIGHT FIGURES AS SHOWN IN SOLID LINES. THEN USE THE OSNAP MODES INDICATED TO DRAW THE DASHED LINES. NOTE THAT SOME PERPENDICULAR AND TANGENT POINTS MUST BE DRAWN TO AND NOT FROM.

FIG. A

FIG. B

FIG. C

FIG. D

FIG. E

FIG. F

FIG. G

FIG. H

Exercise 3–2

Create the drawing according to the settings given in the following table:

Settings	Value		
1. Units	Decimal with two decimal places		
2. Limits	Lower left corner: 0,0		
	Upper right corner: 17,11		
3. Grid	0.50		
4. Snap	0.25		
5. Layers	*NAME*	*COLOR*	*LINETYPE*
	Border	Red	Continuous
	Object	Green	Continuous
	Center	Blue	Center

Hints	Use the LINE and CIRCLE commands to complete the drawing. Make sure to draw the objects in the appropriate layers. Do not dimension the drawing.
	A good place to start is the center of the three circles. With the radius of 4 units, the center could be at coordinates 5,5.

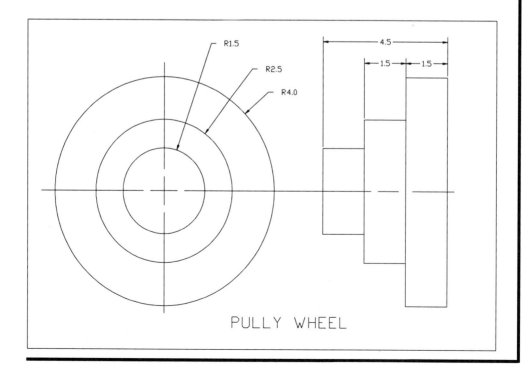

R1.5
R2.5
R4.0
4.5
1.5
1.5

PULLY WHEEL

Exercise 3-3

Create the drawing according to the settings given in the following table:

Settings	Value		
1. Units	Decimal with two decimal places		
2. Limits	Lower left corner: 0,0		
	Upper right corner: 22,17		
3. Grid	0.50		
4. Snap	0.25		
5. Layers	*NAME*	*COLOR*	*LINETYPE*
	Border	Red	Continuous
	Object	Green	Continuous
	Center	Blue	Center

Hints	Use the LINE and CIRCLE commands to complete the drawing. Make sure to draw the objects in the appropriate layers. Do not dimension the drawing.
	A good place to start is the center of the three circles. With the radius of 5.5 units, the center could be at coordinates 7,7.

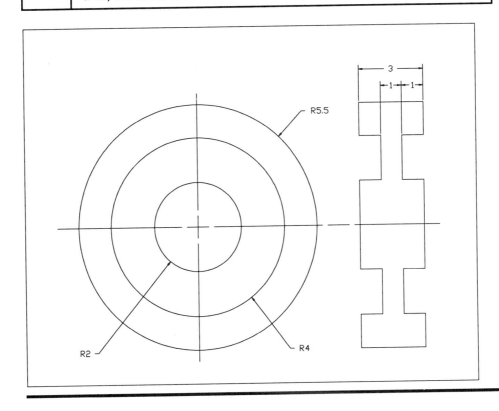

Exercise 3–4

Create the drawing according to the settings given in the following table:

Settings	Value		
1. Units	Decimal with two decimal places		
2. Limits	Lower left corner: 0,0		
	Upper right corner: 24,18		
3. Grid	1.00		
4. Snap	0.50		
5. Layers	*NAME*	*COLOR*	*LINETYPE*
	Border	Red	Continuous
	Object	Green	Continuous
	Center	Blue	Center

Hints	Use the LINE and CIRCLE and ARC commands to complete the drawing. Make sure to draw the objects in the appropriate layers. Do not dimension the drawing.
	A good place to start is the center of the large circle. The large circle is 4.5 units from the bottom of the plate and 8.5 units from the left side, so its center could be at coordinates 10,6.

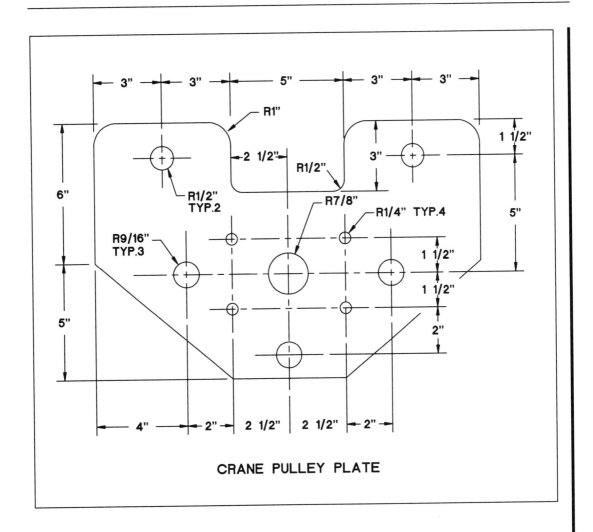

CRANE PULLEY PLATE

Exercise 3-5

In the following exercise the outline of the house shown in Figure Ex3–5a will be drawn. Create the drawing according to the settings given in the following table:

Settings	Value
1. Units	Linear UNITS set to Architectural
	Angular UNITS set to Surveyor's
2. Limits	Lower left corner: -20',-10'
	Upper right corner: 124',86'
3. Grid	5'
4. Snap	Set to Rotated snap at an angle of 4d45'08".

Hint	To draw the property lines, you can use the steps in the example following the text section on the Direct Distance Option regarding the Rotate option of the SNAP command. Do not draw the text; that is for reference only. After invoking the LINE command, begin tracking at TK1 (0,0) (refer to Figure Ex3–5b). Turn Ortho ON and track through point TK2 to TK3/A by forcing the cursor in the right direction and entering the proper distance (35.3' with the cursor to the East for TK2, and 7.1' with the cursor to the North for TK3/A). Draw the first line, A-B, by forcing the cursor to the North and entering the distance of 16.4'. Continue the lines around the outline of the house without exiting the LINE command. Each line's length can be entered when the cursor is forced in the right direction, thus using the DIRECT DISTANCE option for the endpoint of each line.

Point of Interest

■ It is important to realize that using the Rotate option of the SNAP command to establish a new snap origin and snap angle does not change the *X* and *Y* coordinates of the points on the screen. Nor does it change input angles. These can be done with the more complicated UCS command. This means that if you use Absolute Coordinate entry, AutoCAD will use the coordinates based on the origin and angle of rotation of the coordinate system in effect before changing the snap origin and/or angle of rotation. Also, Relative Rectangular or Polar Coordinate input is based on the unrotated system of coordinates. For example, if the snap origin and angle were changed to 4,4 (*X,Y* coordinates) and 45 degrees, respectively, and you were specifying a point relative to a point at the new snap origin as @4,0 or @4<0, the specified point would be at the *X,Y* coordinates of 8,4. They would not be 4 units distance at 45 degrees from 4,4 as you might expect. A rotated snap grid with a relocated origin is for use primarily in conjunction with the Snap and/or Ortho set to ON. Otherwise, SNAP Rotate is not that functional, as you will learn with experience.

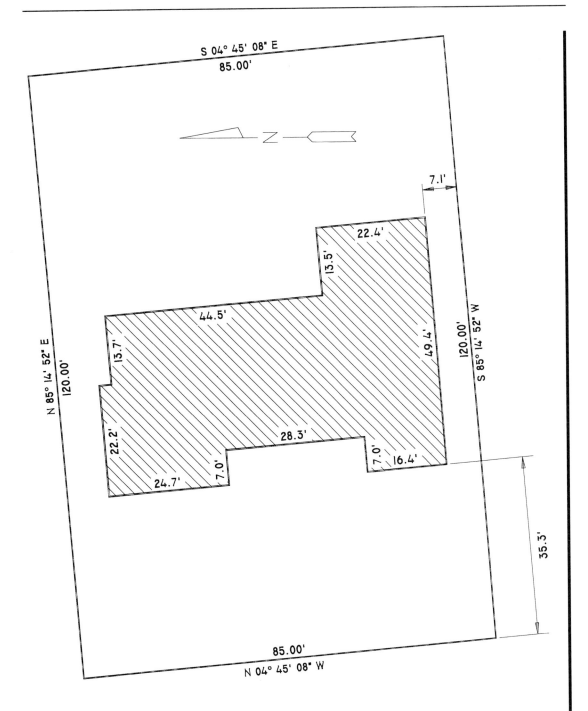

Figure Ex3–5a Outline of a house

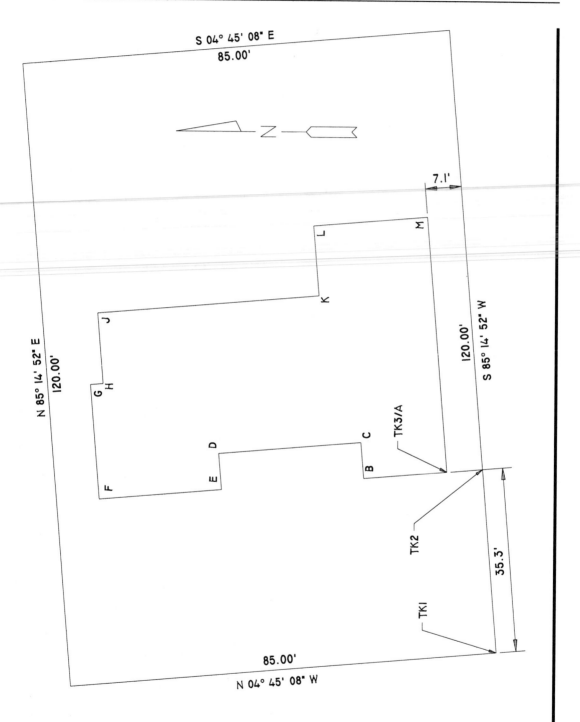

Figure Ex3–5b Outline of a house with dimensions

Exercise 3-6

Create the drawing according to the settings given in the following table:

Settings	Value
1. Units	Decimal
2. Limits	Lower left corner: -2,-2
	Upper right corner: 10,7
3. Grid	1.0
4. Snap	1.0

Hints	Draw a sequence of lines from A (7,1) through B, C, and D to E (3,4) with the Snap set to 1 (or 0.50, 0.25, or 0.125) and set to ON. Using the SNAP Rotate option, select point E as the new origin and point A to designate the rotation angle. Using the Continue option of the LINE command, draw the lines from E through F and G and back to point A. Points F and G can be specified only with the Snap rotated as explained and the Snap set to ON.

Point of Interest

■ This exercise seems simple enough. However, it is not too often that two systems of coordinates share the same common points like A and E in this exercise. This is because E-A is a 5-unit hypotenuse of a right triangle whose base and altitude are 4 and 3 units.

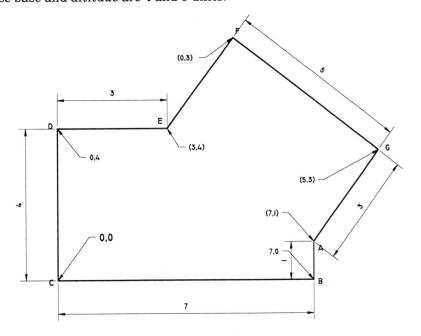

REVIEW QUESTIONS

1. The invisible grid which the crosshairs lock onto is called:
   a. SNAP
   b. GRID
   c. ORTHO
   d. Cursor Lock

2. To globally change the sizes of the dashes for all dashed lines, you should adjust:
   a. Line Scale
   b. LTSCALE
   c. SCALE
   d. Layer Scale

3. To reverse the effect of the last 11 commands, you could:
   a. Use the UNDO command
   b. Use the U command multiple times
   c. Either A or B
   d. It is not possible, AutoCAD only retains the last 10 commands

4. The following are AutoCAD tools available, except:
   a. GRID   d. TSNAP
   b. SNAP   e. OSNAP
   c. ORTHO

5. If you just used the U command, what command would restore the drawing to the state before the U command?
   a. RESTORE
   b. U
   c. REDO
   d. OOPS

6. Which of the following can not be modified in the Drawing Aids dialog box?
   a. Snap   d. Limits
   b. Grid   e. All of the above
   c. Ortho

7. If the spacing of the visible grid is set too small, AutoCAD responds as follows:
   a. does not accept the command
   b. produces a "Grid too dense to display" message
   c. produces a display that is distorted
   d. automatically adjusts the size of the grid so it will display
   e. displays the grid anyway

8. The smallest number that can be displayed in the denominator when setting units to architectural units is:
   a. 8   d. 128
   b. 16   e. none of the above
   c. 64

9. All of the following are considered valid options of the LAYER command, except:
   a. On   d. Lock
   b. Use   e. Set
   c. Make

10. Which of the following is not a valid option of the Layer Control dialog box ?
    a. Close   d. Freeze
    b. Lock   e. Color
    c. On

11. After having drawn a 3-point circle, you want to begin a line at the exact center of the circle. hat tool in AutoCAD would you use?
    a. Snap
    b. Object Snap
    c. Entity Snap
    d. Geometric Calculator

12. How many previous Zooms are available with the previous option of the ZOOM command?
    a. 4   c. 8
    b. 6   d. 10

13. The assignment of a specific color to a specific layer is permitted by the LAYER command option:
    a. Set   d. Make
    b. New   e. both C and D
    c. Color

14. In general, a REDRAW is quicker than a REGEN
    a. True
    b. False

15. When a layer is ON and THAWed:
    a. the objects on that layer are visible on the monitor
    b. the objects on that layer are not visible on the monitor
    c. the objects on that layer are ignored by a REGEN
    d. the drawing REDRAW time is reduced
    e. the objects on that layer cannot be selected

16. To ensure the entire limits of the drawing are visible on the display, you should perform a ZOOM-
    a. All
    b. Previous
    c. Extents
    d. Limits

17. A layer where objects may not be edited or deleted, but are still visible on the screen and may be OSNAPed to is considered:
    a. Frozen
    b. Locked
    c. On
    d. unSet
    e. fiXed

18. The LAYER command will allow you to:
    a. assign colors
    b. assign linetypes
    c. list previously created layers
    d. selectively turn ON and OFF the layers
    e. all of the above

FUNDAMENTALS III

• •

INTRODUCTION

After completing this chapter, you will be able to:

✓ Draw construction lines using the XLINE and RAY commands
✓ Construct geometric figures with polygons, ellipses, and polylines
✓ Create text, using appropriate styles and sizes, to annotate drawings
✓ Use the construct commands: COPY, ARRAY, OFFSET, MIRROR, FILLET, and CHAMFER
✓ Use the modify commands MOVE, TRIM, BREAK, and EXTEND

DRAWING CONSTRUCTION LINES

AutoCAD provides a powerful tool for drawing lines (XLINE and RAY Commands) that extend infinitely in one or both directions. These lines have no effect, however, on the ZOOM Extent command. They can be moved, copied, and rotated like any other objects. If necessary, you can trim the lines, break them anywhere with the BREAK command, draw an arc between two construction lines with the FILLET command, and draw a chamfer between two construction lines with the CHAMFER command.

The construction lines can be used as reference lines for creating other objects. To keep the construction lines from being plotted, you can draw them on a layer that can be turned off during plotting.

XLINE Command

The XLINE command allows you to draw lines that extend infinitely in both directions from the point selected when being created.

Invoke the XLINE command from:

Draw toolbar	Select the Construction Line command (see Figure 4–1)
Pull-down menu	Draw > Construction Line
Command: prompt	xline [Enter]

Figure 4–1 Invoking the XLINE command from the Draw toolbar

AutoCAD prompts:

Command: **xline** [Enter]
Hor/Ver/Ang/Bisect/Offset/<From point>: *(select one of the available options)*

From Point Option When you specify a point to define the root of the construction line, this point becomes the conceptual midpoint of the construction line. AutoCAD prompts:

Through point: *(specify a point through which the construction line should pass)*

AutoCAD draws a line that passes through two points and extends infinitely. AutoCAD continues to prompt for additional points to draw construction lines. To terminate the command sequence, press [Enter] or the Spacebar.

Horizontal Option The Horizontal option allows you to draw a construction line through a point that you specify and is parallel to the **X** axis of the current UCS.

Vertical Option The Vertical option allows you to draw a construction line through a point that you specify and is parallel to the **Y** axis of the current UCS.

Angle Option The Angle option allows you to draw a construction line at a specified angle. AutoCAD prompts:

Reference/<Enter angle(current)>: *(specify an angle at which to place the construction line)*
Through point: *(specify a point through which the construction line should pass)*

AutoCAD draws the construction line through the specified point, using the specified angle.

The **Reference** option allows you to draw a construction line at a specific angle for a selected reference line. The angle is measured counterclockwise from the reference line.

Bisect Option The Bisect option allows you to draw a construction line through the first point bisecting the angle determined by the second and third points, with the first point being the vertex. AutoCAD prompts:

> Angle vertex point: *(select a point for the vertex of an angle to be bisected and through which the construction line will be drawn)*
> Angle start point: *(select a point to determine one boundary line of an angle)*
> Angle endpoint: *(select a point to determine second boundary line of angle)*

The construction line lies in the plane determined by the three points.

Offset Option The Offset option allows you to draw a construction line parallel to and at the specified distance from the line object selected and on the side selected. AutoCAD prompts:

> Offset distance or Through <current>: *(specify an offset distance, enter t for through, or press* Enter *to accept the default value)*
> Select a line object: *(select a line, pline, ray, or xline)*
> Side to offset? *(specify a point to draw a construction line parallel to the selected object)*

The **Through** option allows you to specify a point through which a construction line is drawn to the line object selected.

RAY Command

The RAY command allows you to draw lines that extend infinitely in one direction from the point selected when the line is being created.

Invoke the RAY command from:

Pull-down menu	Draw > Ray
Command: prompt	**ray** Enter

AutoCAD prompts:

> Command: **ray** Enter
> From point: *(specify the start point to draw the ray)*
> Through point: *(specify a point through which you want the ray to pass)*
> Through point: *(specify a point to draw additional rays or press* Enter *to terminate the command sequence)*

The ray is drawn starting at the first point and extending infinitely in one direction through the second point. AutoCAD continues to prompt for through points until you provide a null response to terminate the command sequence.

DRAWING POLYGONS

AutoCAD allows you to draw 2D polygons (edges with equal length) with the POLYGON command. The number of sides can be anywhere from 3 (which forms an equilateral triangle) to 1024. AutoCAD draws a polygon as a polyline with zero width and no tangent information. If necessary, with the help of the PEDIT command you can modify the polygon, such as changing its width.

Invoke the POLYGON command from:

Draw toolbar	Select the Polygon command (see Figure 4–2)
Pull-down menu	Draw > Polygon
Command: prompt	**polygon** Enter

Figure 4–2 Invoking the POLYGON command from the Draw toolbar

AutoCAD prompts:

Command: **polygon** Enter
Number of sides <current>: (specify the number of sides for the polygon to be drawn)
Edge/<Center of Polygon>: (select one of the two available options)

Center of Polygon Option The Center of Polygon option first prompts you for a center point of the polygon to be drawn. Then you are prompted with two options: Inscribed in circle and Circumscribed about circle.

With the **Inscribed in circle** option, the radius of the circle that is specified is measured from the center of the polygon to a vertex between edges. For example, the following command sequence shows steps in drawing a six-sided polygon (see Figure 4–3).

Command: **polygon** Enter
Number of sides: **6** Enter

Edge/Center of polygon>: **3,3** `Enter`
Inscribed in circle/Circumscribed about circle (I/C): **I** `Enter`
Radius of circle: **2** `Enter`

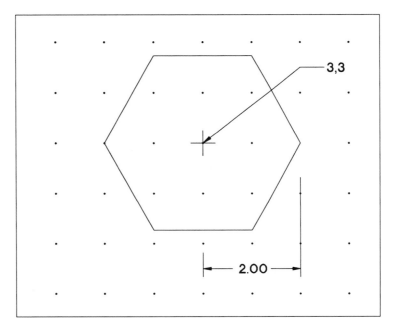

Figure 4–3 Polygon drawn with six sides by selecting the Circumscribed about circle option

AutoCAD draws a polygon with six sides, centered at 3,3, whose edge vertices are 2 units from the center of the polygon.

Specifying the radius with a value draws the bottom edge of the polygon at the current snap rotation angle. If instead, you specify the radius with your pointing device or by means of coordinates, AutoCAD determines the rotation and size of the polygon.

The following command sequence is an example of drawing a polygon by specifying the radius with relative coordinates.

Command: **polygon** `Enter`
Number of sides: **6** `Enter`
Edge/Center of polygon>: **3,3** `Enter`
Inscribed in circle/Circumscribed about circle (I/C): **I** `Enter`
Radius of circle: **@2<90** `Enter`

With the **Circumscribed about circle** option, the radius of the circle that is specified is measured from the center of the polygon to the midpoints of the edges of

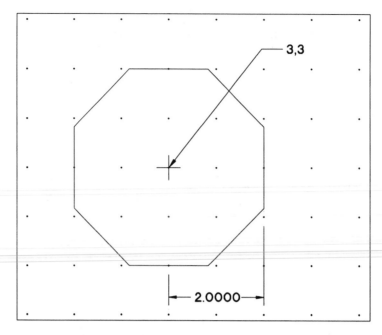

Figure 4-4 Polygon drawn with eight sides by selecting the Circumscribed about circle option

the polygon. For example, the following command sequence shows steps in drawing an eight-sided polygon (see Figure 4-4).

> Command: **polygon** [Enter]
> Number of sides: **8** [Enter]
> Edge/Center of polygon>: **3,3** [Enter]
> Inscribed in circle/Circumscribed about circle (I/C): **c** [Enter]
> Radius of circle: **2** [Enter]

AutoCAD draws a polygon with eight sides, centered at 3,3, whose midpoint of sides are 2 units from the center of the polygon.

Specifying the radius with a value draws the bottom edge of the polygon at the current snap rotation angle. If instead, you specify the radius with your pointing device or by means of coordinates, AutoCAD determines the rotation and size of the polygon.

Edge Option The Edge option allows you to draw a polygon by specifying the endpoints of the first edge.

For example, the following command sequence shows steps in drawing a six-sided polygon (see Figure 4-5).

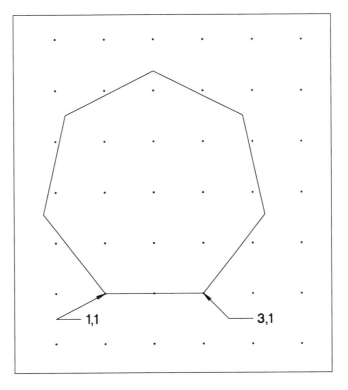

Figure 4–5 Polygon drawn with seven sides by selecting the Circumscribed about circle option

Command: **polygon** Enter
Number of sides: **7** Enter
Edge/Center of polygon>: **e** Enter
First endpoint of edge: **1,1** Enter
Second endpoint of edge: **3,1** Enter

DRAWING ELLIPSES

AutoCAD allows you to draw an ellipse or an elliptical arc with the ELLIPSE command. Invoke the ELLIPSE command from:

Draw toolbar	Select the Ellipse command (see Figure 4–6)
Pull-down menu	Draw > Ellipse
Command: prompt	**ellipse** Enter

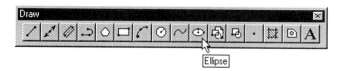

Figure 4-6 Invoking the ELLIPSE command from the Draw toolbar

AutoCAD prompts:

> Command: **ellipse** `Enter`
> Arc/Center/<Axis endpoint 1>: *(select one of the available options)*

Drawing an Ellipse by Defining Axis Endpoints This option allows you to draw an ellipse by defining the endpoints of the axes. AutoCAD prompts for two endpoints of the first axis. The first axis can define either the major or the minor axis of the ellipse. Then AutoCAD prompts for an endpoint of the second axis as the distance from the midpoint of the first axis to the specified point.

For example, the following command sequence shows steps in drawing an ellipse by defining axis endpoints (see Figure 4-7).

> Command: **ellipse** `Enter`
> Arc/Center/<Axis endpoint 1>: **1,1** `Enter`
> Axis endpoint: **5,1** `Enter`
> <Other Axis distance>/Rotation: **3,2** `Enter`

AutoCAD draws an ellipse whose major axis is 4.0 units long in a horizontal direction and whose minor axis is 2.0 units long in a vertical direction, as shown in Figure 4-7.

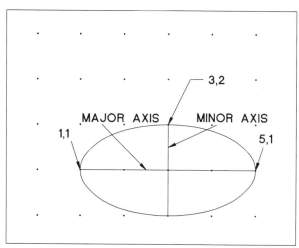

Figure 4-7 An ellipse drawn by specifying the major and minor axes

Drawing an Ellipse by Defining the Center of the Ellipse This option allows you to draw an ellipse by defining the center point and axis endpoints. First, AutoCAD prompts for the ellipse center point. Then AutoCAD prompts for an endpoint of an axis as the distance from the center of the ellipse to the specified point. The first axis can define either the major or the minor axis of the ellipse. Then AutoCAD prompts for an endpoint of the second axis as the distance from the center of the ellipse to the specified point.

For example, the following command sequence shows steps in drawing an ellipse by defining the ellipse center point.

> Command: **ellipse** `Enter`
> Arc/Center/<Axis endpoint 1>: **c** `Enter`
> Center of ellipse: **3,1** `Enter`
> Axis endpoint: **1,1** `Enter`
> <Other Axis distance>/Rotation: **3,2** `Enter`

AutoCAD draws an ellipse similar to previous example, with major axis 4.0 units long in a horizontal direction and minor axis 2.0 units long in a vertical direction.

Drawing an Ellipse by Specifying the Rotation Angle AutoCAD allows you to draw an ellipse by specifying a rotation angle after defining two endpoints of one of the two axes. The rotation angle defines the major-axis-to-minor-axis ratio of the ellipse by rotating a circle about the first axis. The greater the rotation angle value, the greater the ratio of major to minor axes. AutoCAD draws a circle if you set the rotation angle to 0 degrees.

For example, the following command sequence shows steps in drawing an ellipse by specifying the rotation angle.

> Command: **ellipse** `Enter`
> Arc/Center/<Axis endpoint 1>: **3,-1** `Enter`
> Axis endpoint 2: **3,3** `Enter`
> <Other Axis distance>/Rotation: **r** `Enter`
> Rotation around major axis: **30** `Enter`

See Figure 4–8 for examples of ellipses with various rotation angles.

Drawing an Elliptical Arc with the Arc option The Arc option allows you to draw an elliptical arc. After you specify the major and minor axis endpoints, AutoCAD prompts for the start and end angle points for the elliptical arc to be drawn. Instead of specifying the start angle or the end angle, you can toggle to the Parameter option, which prompts for the Start parameter and End parameter point locations. AutoCAD creates the elliptical arc using the following parametric vector equation:

$$p(u) = c + a^x + \cos(u) + b^x \sin(u)$$

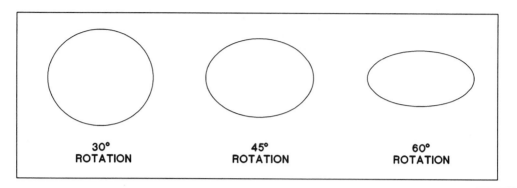

Figure 4-8 Ellipses drawn with different rotation angles

where C is the center of the ellipse and a and b are its major and minor axes, respectively. Instead of specifying the end angle, you can also specify the included angle of the elliptical arc to be drawn.

For example, the following command sequence shows steps in drawing an elliptical arc.

> Command: **ellipse** `Enter`
> Arc/Center/<Axis endpoint 1>: **a** `Enter`
> <Axis endpoint>/Center: **1,1** `Enter`
> Axis endpoint 2: **5,1** `Enter`
> <Other Axis distance>/Rotation: **3,2** `Enter`
> Parameter/<Start angle>: **3,2** `Enter`
> Parameter/Included/<end angle>: **1,1** `Enter`

AutoCAD draws an elliptical arc with the start angle at 3,2 and the ending angle at **1,1**.

Isometric Circles (or Isocircles) Option By definition, Isometric Planes (*iso* meaning "same" and *metric* meaning "measure") are all being viewed at the same angle of rotation (see Figure 4-9). The angle is approximately set to 54.7356 degrees. AutoCAD uses this angle of rotation automatically when you wish to represent circles in one of the isoplanes by drawing ellipses with the Isocircle option. Normally, a circle 1 unit in diameter being viewed in one of the isoplanes will project a short axis dimension of 0.577350 units. One of its diameters parallel to an isoaxis will project a dimension of 0.816497 units. A line drawn in isometric that is parallel to one of the three main axes will also project a dimension of 0.816497 units. We would like these lines and circle diameters to project a dimension of exactly 1.0 unit. Therefore, to automatically increase the entire projection by a fudge factor of 1.22474 (the reciprocal of 0.816497) in order to be able to use true dimensioning parallel to one of the isometric axes. This means that circles 1 unit in diameter will be measured along one of their isometric diameters rather than along their long axis. This facilitates using true lengths as the lengths of distances projected from lines parallel to one of the isometric axes. So a 1-unit-diameter isocircle will project a long axis that is 1.224744871 units and a short axis that is 0.707107 (0.577350 × 1.22474) units. These "fudge" factors are built into AutoCAD isocircles.

The Isometric Circle method is available as one of the options of the ELLIPSE command when you are in the isometric Snap mode.

> Command: **ellipse** Enter
> Arc/Center/Isocircle/<Axis endpoint 1>: **i** Enter
> Center of circle: *(select the center of the isometric circle)*
> <Circle radius>/Diameter: *(enter the radius or override with d)*

If you override the last prompt default by typing **d**, the following prompt will appear:

> Circle diameter: *(enter the desired diameter)*

> **NOTE:** The Iso and Diameter options will work only when you are in the isometric Snap mode.

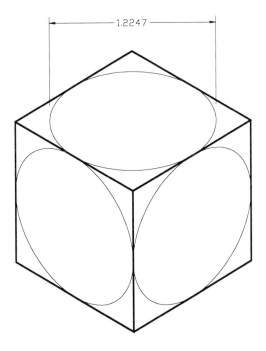

Figure 4–9 Ellipses drawn using the Isocircle option of the ELLIPSE command

Drawing Polylines

The *poly* in polyline refers to a single object with multiple connected straight-line and/or arc segments. The polyline is drawn by invoking the PLINE command and then selecting a series of points. In this respect, PLINE functions much like the LINE command. However, when completed, the segments act like a single object when operated on by modify commands. You specify the endpoints using only 2D *(X,Y)* coordinates.

The versatile PLINE command also draws lines and arcs of different widths, linetypes, tapered lines, and a filled circle. The area and perimeter of a 2D Polyline can be calculated.

In AutoCAD Release 14, by default polylines are drawn as optimized polylines. The optimized polyline provides most of the functionality of 2D polylines but with much improved performance and reduced drawing file size. The vertices are stored as an array of information on one object. When you use the PEDIT command to edit the polyline to spline fitting or curve fitting, the polyline loses its optimization feature and vertices are stored as separate entities, but it still behaves as a single object when operated on by modify commands.

> **NOTE:** If you open a AutoCAD Release 13 drawing containing polylines, they are transparently converted to optimized polylines, unless the 2D polyline is a curve-fit or splined polyline.

Invoke the PLINE command from:

Draw toolbar	Select the Polyline command (see Figure 4–10)
Pull-down menu	Draw > Polyline
Command: prompt	**pline** Enter

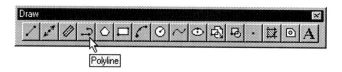

Figure 4–10 Invoking the Polyline command from the Draw toolbar

AutoCAD prompts:

Command: **pline** Enter
  From point: *(specify the start point of the polyline by means of coordinates or by using your pointing device)*

Current line-width is <current>
Arc/Close/Halfwidth/Length/Undo/Width/<Endpoint of line>: *(select one of the available options)*

Where to from Here? The default option, <Endpoint of line>, assumes you are going to enter straight-line segments. Therefore, it expects another point to be given to complete the line segment. You can specify the end of the line by means of absolute coordinates, relative coordinates, or by using your pointing device to specify the end of the line on the screen. After you do, AutoCAD repeats the prompt:

Arc/Close/Halfwidth/Length/Undo/Width<Endpoint of line>:

Having drawn a connected series of lines, you can give a null reply (press Enter) to terminate the PLINE command. The resulting figure is recognized by AutoCAD modify and construct commands as a single object.

The following command sequence presents an example of connected lines, as shown in Figure 4–11, drawn by means of the PLINE command.

Command: **pline** Enter
From point: **2,2** Enter
Current line-width is 0.0000
Arc/Close/Halfwidth/Length/Undo/Width/<Endpoint of line>: **4,2** Enter
Arc/Close/Halfwidth/Length/Undo/Width/<Endpoint of line>: **5,1** Enter
Arc/Close/Halfwidth/Length/Undo/Width/<Endpoint of line>: **7,1** Enter
Arc/Close/Halfwidth/Length/Undo/Width/<Endpoint of line>: **8,2** Enter
Arc/Close/Halfwidth/Length/Undo/Width/<Endpoint of line>: **10,2** Enter
Arc/Close/Halfwidth/Length/Undo/Width/<Endpoint of line>: **10,4** Enter
Arc/Close/Halfwidth/Length/Undo/Width/<Endpoint of line>: **9,5** Enter
Arc/Close/Halfwidth/Length/Undo/Width/<Endpoint of line>: **8,5** Enter
Arc/Close/Halfwidth/Length/Undo/Width/<Endpoint of line>: **7,4** Enter
Arc/Close/Halfwidth/Length/Undo/Width/<Endpoint of line>: **5,4** Enter
Arc/Close/Halfwidth/Length/Undo/Width/<Endpoint of line>: **4,5** Enter
Arc/Close/Halfwidth/Length/Undo/Width/<Endpoint of line>: **3,5** Enter
Arc/Close/Halfwidth/Length/Undo/Width/<Endpoint of line>: **2,4** Enter
Arc/Close/Halfwidth/Length/Undo/Width/<Endpoint of line>: **c** Enter

Close and Undo Options The Close and Undo options work similarly to the corresponding options for the LINE command.

Width Option After selecting a starting point, you may enter a **W** to specify a starting and an ending width for a wide segment. When you select this option, AutoCAD prompts:

Starting width <default>: *(specify the starting width)*
Ending width <default>: *(specify the ending width)*

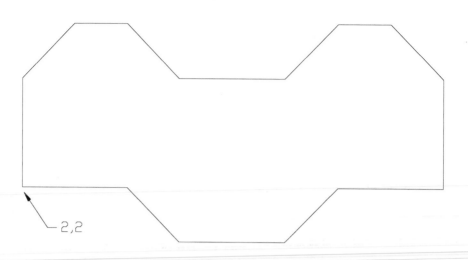

Figure 4–11 Example of connected line segments drawn by means of the PLINE command

You can specify a width by entering a value at the prompt or by selecting a width determining points on the screen. When you specify points on the screen, AutoCAD uses as the starting width the distance from the starting point of the polyline to the point selected. You can accept the default value for the starting width by providing a null response, or type in a new value. The starting width you enter becomes the default for the ending width. If necessary, you can change the ending width to another width, which results in a tapered segment or an arrow. The ending width, in turn, becomes the uniform width for all subsequent segments until you change the width again.

The following command sequence presents an example of connected lines with tapered width, as shown in Figure 4–12, drawn by means of the PLINE command.

```
Command: pline [Enter]
From point: 2,2 [Enter]
Current line-width is 0.0000
Arc/Close/Halfwidth/Length/Undo/Width/<Endpoint of line>: w [Enter]
Starting width <current>: 0 [Enter]
Ending width <0.0000>: .25 [Enter]
Arc/Close/Halfwidth/Length/Undo/Width/<Endpoint of line>: 2,2.5 [Enter]
Arc/Close/Halfwidth/Length/Undo/Width/<Endpoint of line>: 2,3 [Enter]
Arc/Close/Halfwidth/Length/Undo/Width/<Endpoint of line>: w [Enter]
Starting width <0.2500>: [Enter]
Ending width <0.2500>: 0 [Enter]
Arc/Close/Halfwidth/Length/Undo/Width/<Endpoint of line>: 2,3.5 [Enter]
Arc/Close/Halfwidth/Length/Undo/Width/<Endpoint of line>: w [Enter]
Starting width <0.0000>: [Enter]
```

Ending width <0.0000>: **.25** `Enter`
Arc/Close/Halfwidth/Length/Undo/Width/<Endpoint of line>: **2.5,3.5** `Enter`
Arc/Close/Halfwidth/Length/Undo/Width/<Endpoint of line>: **3,3.5** `Enter`
Arc/Close/Halfwidth/Length/Undo/Width/<Endpoint of line>: **w** `Enter`
Starting width <0.2500>: `Enter`
Ending width <0.2500>: **0** `Enter`
Arc/Close/Halfwidth/Length/Undo/Width/<Endpoint of line>: **3.5,3.5** `Enter`
Arc/Close/Halfwidth/Length/Undo/Width/<Endpoint of line>: **w** `Enter`
Starting width <0.0000>: `Enter`
Ending width <0.0000>: **.25** `Enter`
Arc/Close/Halfwidth/Length/Undo/Width/<Endpoint of line>: **3.5,3** `Enter`
Arc/Close/Halfwidth/Length/Undo/Width/<Endpoint of line>: **3.5,2.5** `Enter`
Arc/Close/Halfwidth/Length/Undo/Width/<Endpoint of line>: **w** `Enter`
Starting width <0.2500>: `Enter`
Ending width <0.2500>: **0** `Enter`
Arc/Close/Halfwidth/Length/Undo/Width/<Endpoint of line>: **3.5,2** `Enter`
Arc/Close/Halfwidth/Length/Undo/Width/<Endpoint of line>: **w** `Enter`
Starting width <0.0000>: `Enter`
Ending width <0.0000>: **.25** `Enter`
Arc/Close/Halfwidth/Length/Undo/Width/<Endpoint of line>: **3,2** `Enter`
Arc/Close/Halfwidth/Length/Undo/Width/<Endpoint of line>: **2.5,2** `Enter`
Arc/Close/Halfwidth/Length/Undo/Width/<Endpoint of line>: **w** `Enter`
Starting width <0.2500>: `Enter`
Ending width <0.2500>: **0** `Enter`
Arc/Close/Halfwidth/Length/Undo/Width/<Endpoint of line>: **c** `Enter`

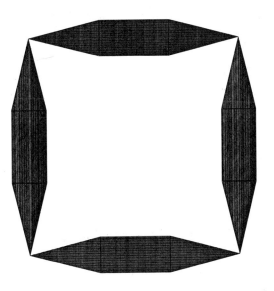

Figure 4–12 Example of connected line segments with tapered width drawn by means of the PLINE command

Halfwidth Option The Halfwidth option is similar to the width option, including the prompts, except it lets you specify the width from the center of a wide polyline to one of its edges. In other words, you specify half of the total width. For example, it is easier to input 1.021756 as the halfwidth than to figure out the total width by doubling. You can specify a halfwidth by selecting points on the screen in the same manner used to specify the full width.

Arc Option The Arc option allows you to draw a polyline arc. When you select the Arc option, AutoCAD displays another submenu:

> Angle/CEnter/CLose/Direction/Halfwidth/Line/Radius/Second pt/Undo/
>   Width/<Endpoint of arc>:

If you respond with a point, it is interpreted as the endpoint of the arc. The endpoint of the previous segment is the starting point of the arc, and the starting direction of the new arc will be the ending direction of the previous segment (whether the previous segment is a line or an arc). This resembles the ARC command's Start, End, Direction (S,E,D) option, but requires only the endpoints to be specified or selected on the screen.

The CLose, Width, Halfwidth, and Undo options are similar to the corresponding options for the straight-line segments described earlier.

The Angle option lets you specify the included angle by prompting:

> Included angle: *(specify an angle)*

The arc is drawn counterclockwise if the value is positive, clockwise if it is negative. After the angle is specified, AutoCAD prompts for the endpoint of the arc.

The CEnter option lets you override with the location of the center of the arc and AutoCAD prompts:

> Center point: *(specify the center point)*

When you provide the center point of the arc, AutoCAD prompts for additional information:

> Angle/Length/<Endpoint>: *(select one of the available options)*

If you respond with a point, it is interpreted as the endpoint of the arc. Selecting A (angle) or L (length) allows you to specify the arc's included angle or chord length.

The Direction option lets you override the direction of the last segment, and AutoCAD prompts:

> Direction from starting point: *(specify the direction)*

If you respond with a point, it is interpreted as the starting point of the direction and AutoCAD prompts for the endpoint for the direction.

The Line option reverts to drawing straight-line segments.

The Radius option allows you to specify the radius by prompting:

> Radius: *(specify the radius of the arc)*

After the radius is specified, you are prompted for the endpoint of the arc.

The Second point option causes AutoCAD to use the three-point method of drawing an arc by prompting:

> Second point: *(specify second point)*

If you respond with a point, it is interpreted as the second point and then you are prompted for the endpoint of the arc. This resembles the ARC command's Three-point option.

Length Option The Length option continues the polyline in the same direction as the last segment for a specified distance.

DRAWING TEXT

You have learned how to draw the geometric shapes that make up your design. Now it is time to learn how to annotate your design. When you draw on paper, adding descriptions of the design components and the necessary shop and fabrication notes is a tedious, time-consuming process. AutoCAD provides several text commands and tools (including a spell checker) that greatly reduce the tedium of text placement and reduce the time it takes.

Text is used to label the various components of your drawing and to create the necessary shop or field notes needed for fabrication and construction of your design. AutoCAD includes a large number of text fonts. Text can be stretched, compressed, obliqued, mirrored, or drawn in a vertical column by applying a style. Each text string can be sized, rotated, and justified to meet your drawing needs. You should be aware that AutoCAD considers a text string (all the characters that comprise the line of text) as one object.

> ***NOTE:*** If you do not know how to type, you can place text quickly and easily after a period of learning the keyboard and developing typing skills. If you create drawings that require a lot of text entry, it may be worth your time to learn to type with all ten fingers ("touch-typing"). There are several computer programs that can help you teach yourself to type, and almost all colleges offer typing classes. If you do not have time to learn touch-typing, there is no need to worry, many "two-finger" typists productively place text in their drawings.

Creating a Single Line of Text

The TEXT command allows you to create a single line of text in the current style. If necessary, you can change the current style. To modify a style or to create a new style, refer to Chapter 6.

Invoke the TEXT command from:

Command: prompt	**text** (ENTER)

AutoCAD prompts:

Command: **text** Enter
Justify/Style/<Start point>: (select one of the available options)

Start Point Option The Start Point option is the default option. It allows you to select a point in the drawing window where you want the text to begin. By default, this point indicates the lower left corner of the text. If necessary, you can change the location of the justification point. You can specify the starting point in absolute coordinates or by using your pointing device. After you specify the starting point, AutoCAD prompts:

Height <default>: (specify the text height)

This allows you to select the text height. You can accept the default text height by giving a null response, or you can type in the appropriate text height. Next, AutoCAD prompts:

Rotation angle <default>: (specify the rotation angle)

This allows you to place the text at any angle in reference to 0 degrees (default is 3 o'clock, or east, measured in the counterclockwise direction). The default value of the rotation angle is 0 degrees, and the text is placed horizontally at the specified start point. The last prompt is:

Text: (type the desired text and press Enter)

If you need to place another line of text, go back to the TEXT command and give a null response to the "Start point:" prompt; AutoCAD skips the prompts for height and rotation angle and displays the text prompt. The text is placed directly beneath the previous line of text.

For example, the following command sequence shows placement of left-justified text by providing the starting point of the text, as shown in Figure 4–13.

Command: **text** Enter
Justify/Style/<Start point>: (pick point)
Height <.20>: .25 Enter

Sample Text Left Justified

└─ **Start Point**

Figure 4-13 Using the TEXT command to place left justified text by specifying a start point

> Rotation angle <0>: `Enter`
> Text: **Sample Text Left Justified** `Enter`

Justify Option The Justify option allows you to place text in one of the 14 available justification points. When you select this option, AutoCAD prompts:

> Align/Fit/Center/Middle/Right/TL/TC/TR/ML/MC/MR/BL/BC/BR: *(select one of the available options)*

Type in the option by means of which you would like to place the text.

The **Center** option allows you to select the center point for the baseline of the text. *Baseline* refers to the line along which the bases of the capital letters lie. Letters with descenders, such as g, q, and y, dip below the baseline. After providing the center point, enter the text height and rotation angle.

For example, the following command sequence shows placement of center-justified text, by providing the center point of the text, as shown in Figure 4-14.

> Command: **text** `Enter`
> Justify/Style/<Start point>: **j** `Enter`
> Align/Fit/Center/Middle/Right/TL/TC/TR/ML/MC/MR/BL/BC/BR: **c** `Enter`
> Height <.20> **.25** `Enter`
> Rotation angle <0>: `Enter`
> Text: **Sample Text Center Justified** `Enter`

The **Middle** option allows you to center the text both horizontally and vertically at a given point. After providing the middle point, enter the text height and rotation angle.

For example, the following command sequence shows placement of middle-justified text by providing the middle point of the text, as shown in Figure 4-14.

> Command: **text** `Enter`
> Justify/Style/<Start point>: **j** `Enter`
> Align/Fit/Center/Middle/Right/TL/TC/TR/ML/MC/MR/BL/BC/BR: **m** `Enter`
> Height <.20> **.25** `Enter`

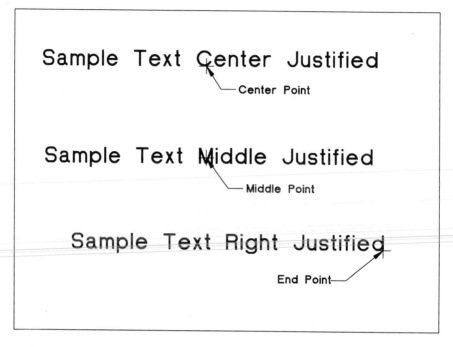

Figure 4–14 Using the TEXT command to place text by specifying a center point (center justified), a middle point (middle justified), or an endpoint (right justified)

Rotation angle <0>: `Enter`
Text: **Sample Text Middle Justified** `Enter`

The **Right** option allows you to place the text in reference to its lower right corner (right justified). Here, you provide the point where the text will end. After providing the right point, enter the text height and rotation angle.

For example, the following command sequence shows placement of right-justified text, as shown in Figure 4–14.

Command: **text** `Enter`
Justify/Style/<Start point>: **j** `Enter`
Align/Fit/Center/Middle/Right/TL/TC/TR/ML/MC/MR/BL/BC/BR: **r** `Enter`
Height <.20> **.25** `Enter`
Rotation angle <0>: `Enter`
Text: **Sample Text Right Justified** `Enter`

Other options are combinations of the previously mentioned options:

TL   top left

TC   top center

TR	top right
ML	middle left
MC	middle center
MR	middle right
BL	bottom left
BC	bottom center
BR	bottom right

The **Align** option allows you to place the text by designating the endpoints of the baseline. AutoCAD computes the text height and width so that the text just fits proportionately between two points.

For example, the following command sequence shows placement of text using the Align option as shown in Figure 4–15.

Command: **text** Enter
Justify/Style/<Start point>: **j** Enter
Align/Fit/Center/Middle/Right/TL/TC/TR/ML/MC/MR/BL/BC/BR: **a** Enter
First text line point: *(specify the first point)*

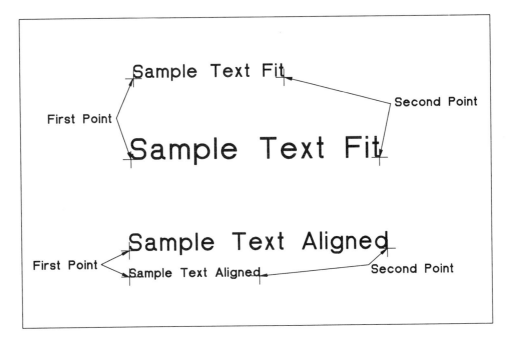

Figure 4–15 Using the Align and Fit option of the TEXT command to place text

Second text line point: *(specify the second point)*
Text: **Sample Text Aligned** `Enter`

The **Fit** option is similar to the Align option, but in the case of the Fit option AutoCAD uses the current text height and adjusts only the text's width, expanding or contracting it to fit between the points you specify.

For example, the following command sequence shows placement of text using the Fit option as shown in Figure 4–15.

Command: **text** `Enter`
Justify/Style/<Start point>: **j** `Enter`
Align/Fit/Center/Middle/Right/TL/TC/TR/ML/MC/MR/BL/BC/BR: **f** `Enter`
First text line point: *(specify the first point)*
Second text line point: *(specify the second point)*
Height <default): **0.25** `Enter`
Text: **Sample Text Fit** `Enter`

Style Option The Style option allows you to select one of the available styles in the current drawing. To modify a style or to create a new style, refer to Chapter 6.

Creating Multiple Lines of Text

The DTEXT command allows you to create multiple lines of text in the current style. In addition, AutoCAD lets you see the text on the screen as you type it in from the keyboard.

The prompt sequence is the same as for the TEXT command. After you select your Start point with any of the justification points, you will be prompted to enter a text height and a rotation angle. A box cursor appears on the screen at the starting point you have selected. After you enter the first line of text and press `Enter`, you will notice the box cursor drop down to the next line, anticipating that you wish to enter more text. If this is the case, type the next line of text string; when you are through with typing text strings, press `Enter` at the "Text:" prompt to terminate the command sequence.

> **NOTE:** Canceling the DTEXT command by pressing `Esc` or by invoking another command before completing the text will delete all text entered during this command.

If you are in the DTEXT command and notice a mistake (or simply want to change a value or word), backspace to the text you want to change. This, however, deletes all of the text you backspaced over to get to the point you want to change. If this involves erasing several lines of text, it may be faster to use the CHANGE or DDEDIT command to make changes to the text string.

One feature of DTEXT that will speed up text entry on your drawing is the ability to move the crosshairs cursor to a new point on the drawing while staying in the DTEXT command. As you move the crosshairs cursor to a new point on your drawing and specify the point with your pointing device, you will notice the cursor box move to this new point, allowing you to enter a new string of text and move the cursor to the next point to enter more text. However, you must remember to give a null response to the "Text:" prompt to terminate the command.

Invoke the DTEXT command from:

Command: prompt	**dtext** Enter

AutoCAD prompts:

Command: **dtext** Enter
Justify/Style/<Start point>: *(select one of the available options)*

The available options for the DTEXT command are similar to the options explained earlier for the TEXT command.

CREATING OBJECTS FROM EXISTING OBJECTS

AutoCAD not only allows you to draw objects easily, but also allows you to create additional objects from existing objects. This section discusses six important commands that will make your job easier: COPY, ARRAY, OFFSET, MIRROR, FILLET, and CHAMFER.

Copying Objects

The COPY command places copies of the selected objects at the specified displacement, leaving the original objects intact. The copies are oriented and scaled the same as the original. If necessary, you can make multiple copies of selected objects. Each resulting copy is completely independent of the original and can be edited and manipulated like any other object.

Invoke the COPY command from:

Modify toolbar	Select the Copy object command (see Figure 4–16)
Pull-down menu	Modify > Copy
Command: prompt	**copy** Enter

Figure 4–16 Invoking the Copy command from the Modify toolbar

AutoCAD prompts:

Command: **copy** Enter
Select objects: *(select the objects and then give a null response to complete the selection)*
<Base point or displacement>/Multiple: *(specify a point or type **m** to select multiple copies)*
Second point of displacement: *(specify a point for displacement, or press* Enter *for a null response)*

You can use one or more object selection methods to select the objects. If you specify two data points, AutoCAD computes the displacement and places a copy accordingly. If you provide a null response to the second point of displacement, AutoCAD considers the point provided as the second point of a displacement vector with the origin (0,0,0) as the first point, indicating how far to copy the objects and in what direction.

The following command sequence shows an example of copying a group of objects selected by means of the Window option, as shown in Figure 4–17, by placing two data points:

Command: **copy** Enter
Select objects: *(specify a point to place one corner of a window)*
Other corner: *(specify a point to place the opposite corner of the window)*

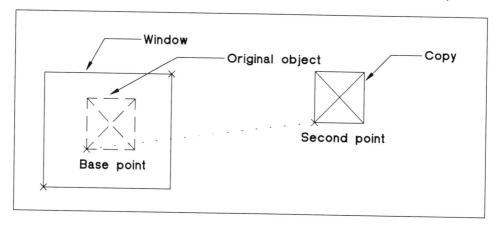

Figure 4–17 Using the COPY Window option to copy a group of objects by specifying two points

Select objects: Enter

<Base point or displacement)/Multiple: *(specify the base point as shown in Figure 4–17)*

Second point of displacement: *(specify the second point as shown in Figure 4–17)*

Creating Multiple Copies To make multiple copies, first invoke the COPY command, and respond to the "Base point" prompt by entering **m,** for multiple. The "Base point" prompt then reappears, followed by repeated "Second point" prompts, and a copy of the selected objects is made at a location determined by each displacement you enter. Each displacement is relative to the original base point. When you have made all the copies you need, give a null response to the "Second point" prompt to terminate the command sequence.

The following command sequence shows an example of placing multiple copies of a group of objects selected by means of the Window option, as shown in Figure 4–18.

Command: **copy** Enter

Select objects: *(specify a point to place one corner of the window)*

Other corner: *(specify a point to place the opposite corner of the window)*

Select objects: Enter

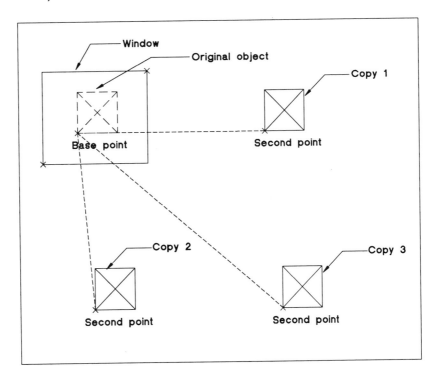

Figure 4–18 Using the COPY Window option to make multiple copies of a group of objects

<Base point or displacement>/Multiple: *(type* **m** *and press* <kbd>Enter</kbd> *)*
Multiple base point: *(pick base point as shown in Figure 4–18)*
Second point of displacement: *(specify the second point for copy 1 as shown in Figure 4–18)*
Second point of displacement: *(specify the second point for copy 2 as shown in Figure 4–18)*
Second point of displacement: *(specify the second point for copy 3 as shown in Figure 4–18)*
Second point of displacement: <kbd>Enter</kbd>
Command:

Creating a Pattern of Copies

The ARRAY command is used to make multiple copies of selected objects in either rectangular or polar arrays (patterns). In the *rectangular array,* you can specify the number of rows, the number of columns, and the spacing between rows and columns (row and column spacing may differ). The whole rectangular array can be rotated at a selected angle. In the *polar array,* you can specify the angular intervals, the number of copies, the angle that the group covers, and whether or not the objects maintain the orientation as they are arrayed.

Rectangular Array Invoke the ARRAY command from:

Modify toolbar	Select the Array command (see Figure 4–19)
Pull-down menu	Modify > Array
Command: prompt	array <kbd>Enter</kbd>

Figure 4–19 Invoking the Array command from the Modify toolbar

AutoCAD prompts:

Command: **array** <kbd>Enter</kbd>
Select objects: *(select the objects and then give a null response to complete the selection)*
Rectangular or Polar array (R/P) <current>: *(type* **r,** *for rectangular array, and press* <kbd>Enter</kbd> *)*
Number of rows (---) <1>: *(specify a nonzero integer)*
Number of columns (|||) <1>: *(specify a nonzero integer)*
Unit cell or distance between rows (---): *(specify a distance between rows, or place two points to measure the distance between rows)*

Distance between columns (|||): *(specify a distance between columns, or place two points to measure the distance between columns)*

Any combination of whole numbers of rows and columns may be entered (except both 1 row and 1 column, which would not create any copies). AutoCAD includes the original object in the number you enter. Row and column spaces can be different from each other. They can be entered separately when prompted, or you can select two points that specify the opposite corners of a rectangle called a *unit cell*. AutoCAD uses the width of the unit cell as the horizontal distance(s) between columns and the height as the vertical distance(s) between rows.

A positive number for the column and row spacing causes the elements to array toward the right and upward, respectively. Negative numbers for the column and row spacing cause the elements to array toward the left and downward, respectively.

AutoCAD creates rectangular arrays along a baseline defined by the current snap rotation. By default, the snap rotation is set to 0 degrees, so that rows and columns are orthogonal with respect to the X and Y drawing axes. The Rotate option of the SNAP command allows you to change the rotation angle and creates a rotated array.

The following command sequence shows an example of placing a rectangular array with 4 rows and 6 columns, as shown in Figure 4–20.

Command: **array** `Enter`
Select objects: *(select objects)*
Rectangular or Polar array (R/P): **r** `Enter`
Number of rows (---)<1>: **4** `Enter`
Number of columns (|||)<1>: **6** `Enter`
Unit cell or distance between rows <--->: **1** `Enter`
Distance between columns <|||>: **1.5** `Enter`

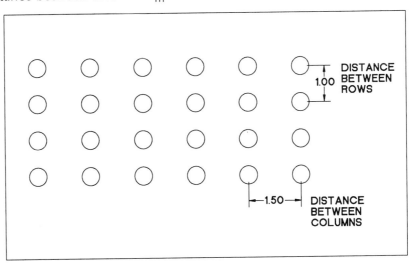

Figure 4–20 Using the ARRAY command to place a rectangular array

Polar Array Invoke the ARRAY command from:

Modify toolbar	Select the Array command (see Figure 4–21)
Pull-down menu	Modify > Array
Command: prompt	**array** Enter

Array

Figure 4–21 Invoking the Array command from the Modify toolbar

AutoCAD prompts:

Command: **array** Enter
Select objects: *(select the objects and then give a null response to complete the selection)*
Rectangular or Polar array (R/P) <current>: *(type p, for polar array, and press Enter)*
Center point of array: *(specify a point around which you want the array to form)*
Number of items: *(specify a positive integer, including the original item, or press Enter)*
Angle to fill (+=CCW, -=CW)<360>: *(specify an angle or press Enter)*
Angle between items (+=CCW, -=CW): *(specify an angle between items; this prompt appears only if a null response is provided for Angle to fill)*
Rotate object as they are copied <Y>: *(type y, for yes to Rotate as they are copied, or n, for no to Rotate as they are copied)*

If you specify the number of items for an array, you must specify *either* the angle to fill *or* the angle between items. If you provide a null response to the number of items, then you must specify the angle to fill *and* the angle between items.

The following command sequence presents an example of placing a rotated polar array as in Figure 4–22.

Command: **array** Enter
Select objects: *(select objects)*
Rectangular or Polar array (R/P): **p** Enter
Center point of array: *(specify the center point as shown in Figure 4–22)*
Number of items: **8** Enter
Angle to fill (+=CCW, -=CW) <current>: **360** Enter
Rotate objects as they are copied? <Y>: Enter

Figure 4–22 shows both nonrotated and rotated polar arrays.

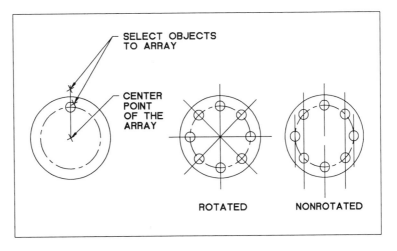

Figure 4–22 Using the ARRAY command to place rotated and nonrotated polar arrays

Creating Parallel Lines, Parallel Curves and Concentric Circles

The OFFSET command creates parallel lines, parallel curves, and concentric circles relative to existing objects, as shown in Figure 4–23. Special precautions must be taken when using the OFFSET command to prevent unpredictable results from occurring when using the command on arbitrary curve/line combinations in polylines.

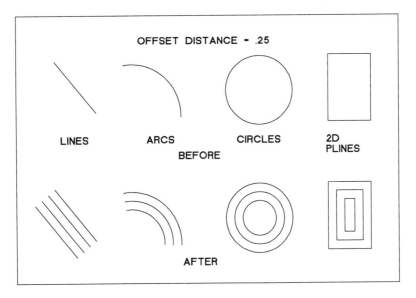

Figure 4–23 Examples created using the OFFSET command

Invoke the OFFSET command from:

Modify toolbar	Select the Offset command (see Figure 4–24)
Pull-down menu	Modify > Offset
Command: prompt	offset Enter

[Offset]

Figure 4–24 Invoking the OFFSET command from the Modify toolbar

AutoCAD prompts:

Command: **offset** Enter
Offset distance or Through <current>: *(specify offset distance, or enter **t**, for through)*
Select object to offset: *(select an object to offset)*
Side to offset?: *(pick a point to one side of the object to offset)*
Select object to offset: *(continue selecting additional objects for offset, and pick the side of the object to offset, or press Enter to terminate the command sequence)*

If instead of specifying the offset distance you select the Through option, AutoCAD prompts for a through point. Specify a point, and AutoCAD creates an object passing through the specified point.

Valid Objects to Offset Valid objects include the line, spline curve, arc, circle, and 2D polyline. If you select another type of object, such as text, you will get the following error message:

Cannot offset that object.

The object selected for offsetting must be in a plane parallel to the current coordinate system. Otherwise you will get the following error message:

Object not parallel with UCS.

Offsetting Miters and Tangencies The OFFSET command affects single objects in a manner different from a polyline made up of the same objects. Polylines whose arcs join lines and other arcs in a tangent manner are affected differently than polylines with nontangent connecting points. For example, in Figure 4–25 the seven lines are separate objects. When offset to the side shown, there are gaps and overlaps at the ends of the newly created lines.

In Figure 4–26, the lines have been joined together (see PEDIT in Chapter 5) as a single polyline. See how the OFFSET command affects the corners where the new polyline segments join.

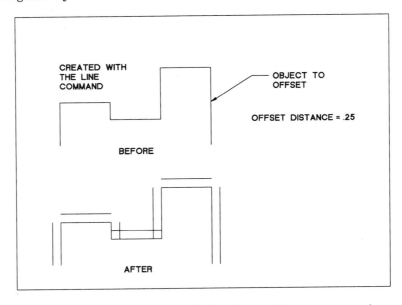

Figure 4–25 Using the OFFSET command with single objects as opposed to polylines

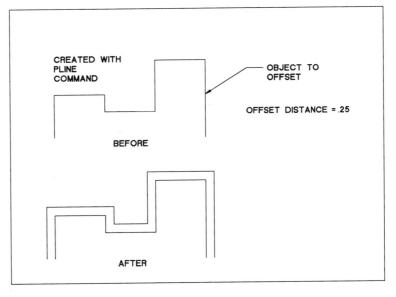

Figure 4–26 Using the OFFSET command with polylines

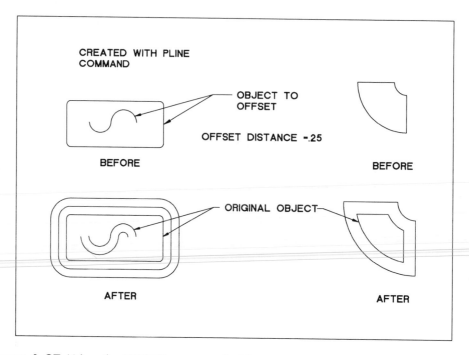

CREATED WITH PLINE
COMMAND

OBJECT TO
OFFSET

OFFSET DISTANCE -.25

BEFORE

BEFORE

ORIGINAL OBJECT

AFTER

AFTER

Figure 4–27 Using the OFFSET command with nontangent arc and/or line segments

NOTE: The results of offsetting polylines with arc segments that connect other arc segments and/or line segments in dissimilar (nontangent) directions might be unpredictable. Examples of offsetting such polylines are shown in Figure 4–27.

If you are not satisfied with the resulting new polyline configuration, you can use the PEDIT command to edit it. Or, you can explode the polyline and edit the individual segments.

Creating a Mirror Copy of Objects

The MIRROR command creates a copy of selected objects in reverse, that is mirrored about a specified line. Invoke the MIRROR command from:

Modify toolbar	Select the Mirror command (see Figure 4–28)
Pull-down menu	Modify > Mirror
Command: prompt	**mirror** [Enter]

Figure 4–28 Invoking the Mirror command from the Modify toolbar

AutoCAD prompts:

Command: **mirror** Enter
Select objects: *(select the objects and then give a null response to complete the selection)*
First point of mirror line: *(specify a point to define the first point of the mirror line)*
Second point: *(specify a point to define the second point of the mirror line)*
Delete old objects: <N>: *(type **y**, for yes to delete the original objects, or **n**, not to delete the original objects, that is, to retain them)*

The first and second points of the mirror line become the endpoints of an invisible line about which the selected objects will be mirrored.

The following command sequence shows an example of mirroring a group of selected objects by means of the Window option, as shown in Figure 4–29:

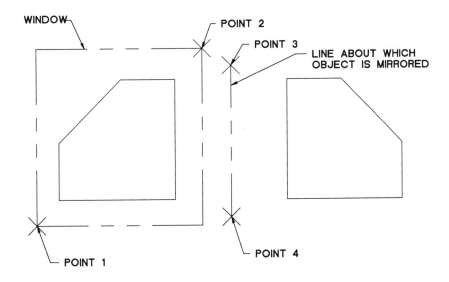

Figure 4–29 Mirroring a group of objects selected by means of the Window option

Fundamentals III

Command: **mirror** `Enter`
Select objects: *(pick Point 1 to place one corner of a window)*
Second corner: *(pick Point 2 to place the opposite corner of the window)*
Select objects: `Enter`
First point of mirror line: *(pick point 3, as shown in Figure 4–29)*
Second point: *(pick point 4, as shown in Figure 4–29)*
Delete old objects?<N>: `Enter`

The text as mirrored is located relative to other objects within the selected group. But the text will or will not retain its original orientation, depending on the setting of the system variable called MIRRTEXT. If the value of MIRRTEXT is set to 1, then text items in the selected group will have their orientations and location mirrored. That is, if their characters were normal and they read left to right in the original group, in the mirrored copy they will read right to left and the characters will be backwards. If MIRRTEXT is set to 0 (zero), then the text strings in the group will have their locations mirrored, but the individual text strings will retain their normal, left-to-right, character appearance. The MIRRTEXT system variable, like other system variables, is changed by the SETVAR command or by typing **MIRRTEXT** at the "Command:" prompt, as follows:

Command: **setvar** `Enter`
Variable name or ?: **mirrtext** `Enter`
New Value for MIRRTEXT <1>: **0** `Enter`

This setting causes mirrored text to retain its readability. Figures 4–30a and 4–30b show the result of the MIRROR command when the MIRRTEXT variable is set to 1 and 0, respectively.

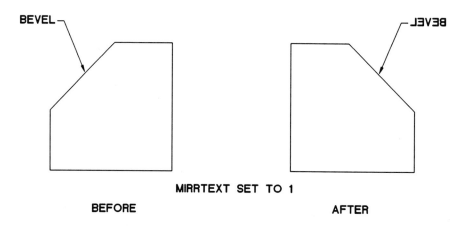

Figure 4–30a The MIRROR command with the MIRRTEXT variable set to 1

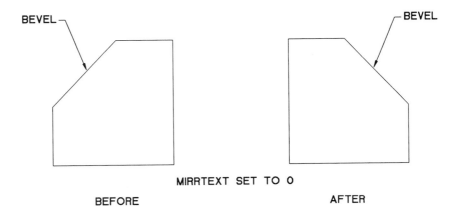

MIRRTEXT SET TO 0

BEFORE   AFTER

Figure 4-30b The MIRROR command with the MIRRTEXT variable set to 0

Creating a Fillet Between Two Objects

The FILLET command fillets (rounds) the intersecting ends of two arcs, circles, lines, elliptical arcs, polylines, rays, xlines, or splines with an arc of a specified radius.

If the TRIMMODE system variable is set to 1 (default), then the FILLET command trims the intersecting lines to the endpoints of the fillet arc. And if TRIMMODE is set to 0 (zero), then FILLET command leaves the intersecting lines at the endpoints of the fillet arc.

Invoke the FILLET command from:

Modify toolbar	Select the Fillet command (see Figure 4–31)
Pull-down menu	Modify > Fillet
Command: prompt	**fillet** Enter

Fillet

Figure 4-31 Invoking the Fillet command from the Modify toolbar

AutoCAD prompts:

Command: **fillet** Enter
(TRIM mode) Current fillet radius = <current>
Polyline/Radius/Trim/<Select first object>: *(select one of the two objects to fillet, or select one of the available options)*

By default, AutoCAD prompts you to select an object. If you select an object to fillet, then AutoCAD prompts:

Select second object: *(select the second object to fillet)*

AutoCAD joins the two objects with an arc having the specified radius. If the objects selected to be filleted are on the same layer, AutoCAD creates the fillet arc on the same layer. If not, AutoCAD creates the fillet arc on the current layer.

AutoCAD allows you to draw a fillet between parallel lines, xlines, and rays. The first selected object must be a line or ray, but the second object can be a line, xline, or ray. The diameter of the fillet arc is always equal to the distance between the lines. The current fillet radius is ignored and remains unchanged.

Radius Option The Radius option allows you to change the current fillet radius. The following command sequence sets the fillet radius to 0.5 and draws the fillet between two lines, as shown in Figure 4–32.

Command: **fillet**
(TRIM mode) Current fillet radius = <current>
Polyline/Radius/Trim/<Select first object>: **r**
Enter fillet radius <current>: **0.25**
Command: Enter *(to repeat the FILLET command)*
(TRIM mode) Current fillet radius = **0.25**
Polyline/Radius/Trim/<Select first object>: *(select the first object, as shown in Figure 4–32)*
Select second object: *(select the second object to fillet, as shown in Figure 4–32)*

If you select lines or arcs, AutoCAD extends these lines or arcs until they intersect, or trims them at the intersection, keeping the selected segments if they cross. The

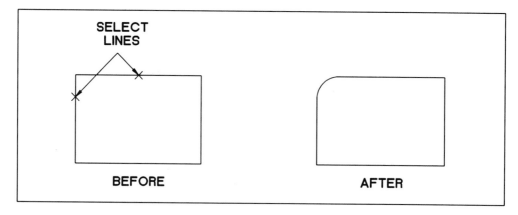

Figure 4–32 Fillet drawn with a radius of 0.25

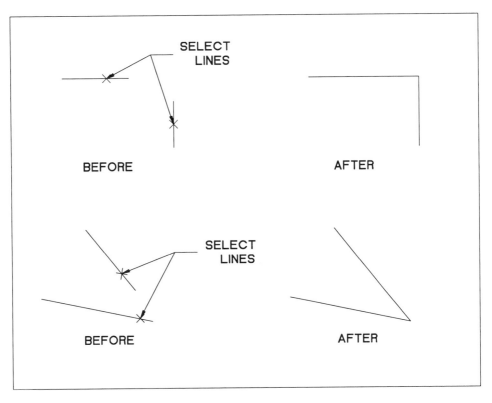

Figure 4–33 Fillet drawn with a radius of 0

following command sequence sets the fillet radius to 0 and draws the fillet between two lines as shown in Figure 4–33.

Command: **fillet** [Enter]
(TRIM mode) Current fillet radius = <current>
Polyline/Radius/Trim/<Select first object>: **r** [Enter]
Enter fillet radius <current>: **0** [Enter]
Command: [Enter] *(to repeat the FILLET command)*
(TRIM mode) Current fillet radius = **0.00**
Polyline/Radius/Trim/<Select first object>: *(select the first object as shown in Figure 4–33)*
Select second object: *(select the second object to fillet as shown in Figure 4–33)*

Polyline Option With the polyline option, AutoCAD draws fillet arcs at each vertex of a 2D polyline where two line segments meet. The following command sequence sets the fillet radius to 0.5 and draws the fillet at each vertex of a 2D polyline, as shown in Figure 4–34:

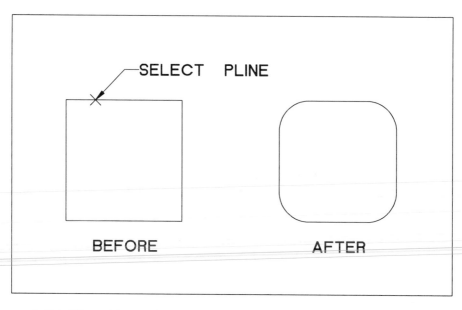

Figure 4–34 Fillet with a radius of 0.50 drawn to a polyline

Command: **fillet** Enter
(TRIM mode) Current fillet radius = <current>
Polyline/Radius/Trim/<Select first object>: **r** Enter
Enter fillet radius <current>: **0.5** Enter
Command: Enter *(to repeat the FILLET command)*
(TRIM mode) Current fillet radius = **0.5**
Polyline/Radius/Trim/<Select first object>: **p** Enter
Select 2D polyline: *(select the polyline as shown in Figure 4–34)*

Trim Option The Trim option (Trim/No Trim) controls whether or not AutoCAD trims the selected edges to the fillet arc endpoints. This option is similar to setting the TRIMMODE system variable from 1 to 0 or 0 to 1.

Creating a Chamfer Between Two Objects

The CHAMFER command allows you to draw an angled corner between two lines. The size of the chamfer is determined by the settings of the first and the second chamfer distances. If it is to be a 45-degree chamfer, then the two distances are set to the same value.

If the TRIMMODE system variable is set to 1 (default), then the CHAMFER command trims the intersecting lines to the endpoints of the chamfer line. And if TRIMMODE is set to 0 (zero), then CHAMFER leaves the intersecting lines at the endpoints of the chamfer line.

Invoke the CHAMFER command from:

Modify toolbar	Select the Chamfer command (see Figure 4–35)
Pull-down menu	Modify > Chamfer
Command: prompt	**chamfer** Enter

Figure 4–35 Invoking the Chamfer command from the Modify toolbar

AutoCAD prompts:

Command: **chamfer** Enter
(Trim mode) Current chamfer Dist1 = <current>, Dist2 = <current>
Polyline/Distance/Angle/Trim/Method/<Select first line>: *(select one of the two lines to chamfer, or select one of the available options)*

By default, AutoCAD prompts you to select the first line to chamfer. If you select a line to chamfer, then AutoCAD prompts:

Select second line: *(select the second line to chamfer)*

AutoCAD draws a chamfer to the selected lines. If the selected lines to be chamfered are on the same layer, AutoCAD creates the chamfer on the same layer. If not, AutoCAD creates the chamfer on the current layer.

Distance Option The Distance option allows you to set the first and second chamfer distances. The following command sequence sets the first chamfer and second chamfer distance to 0.5 and 1.0, respectively, and draws the chamfer between two lines as shown in Figure 4–36.

Command: **chamfer** Enter
(Trim mode) Current chamfer Dist1 = <current>, Dist2 = <current>
Polyline/Distance/Angle/Trim/Method/<Select first line>: **d** Enter
Enter first chamfer distance <current>: **0.5** Enter
Enter second chamfer distance <current>: **1.0** Enter
Command: Enter *(to repeat the CHAMFER command)*
(Trim mode) Current chamfer Dist1 = **0.5**, Dist2 = **1.0**
Polyline/Distance/Angle/Trim/Method/<Select first line>: *(select the first line, as shown in Figure 4–36)*
Select second line: *(select the second line, as shown in Figure 4–36)*

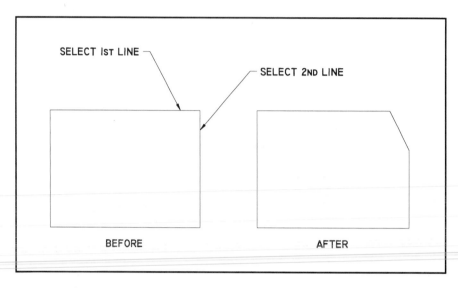

Figure 4–36 Chamfer drawn with distances of 0.5 and 1.0

Polyline Option With the Polyline option, AutoCAD draws chamfers at each vertex of a 2D polyline where two line segments meet. The following command sequence sets the chamfer distances to 0.5 and draws the chamfer at each vertex of a 2D polyline, as shown in Figure 4–37.

> Command: **chamfer** Enter
> (Trim mode) Current chamfer Dist1 = <current>, Dist2 = <current>
> Polyline/Distance/Angle/Trim/Method/<Select first line>: **d** Enter
> Enter first chamfer distance <current>: **0.5** Enter
> Enter second chamfer distance <current>: **0.5** Enter
> Command: Enter *(to repeat the CHAMFER command)*
> (Trim mode) Current chamfer Dist1 = **0.5**, Dist2 = **0.5**
> Polyline/Distance/Angle/Trim/Method/<Select first line>: **p** Enter
> Select polyline: *(select the polyline, as shown in Figure 4–37)*

Angle Option The Angle option is similar to the Distance option, but instead of prompting for the first and second chamfer distances, AutoCAD prompts for the first chamfer distance and an angle from the first line. This is another method by which to create the chamfer line.

Method Option The Method option controls whether AutoCAD uses two distances or a distance and an angle to create the chamfer line.

Trim Option The Trim option (Trim/No Trim) controls whether or not AutoCAD trims the selected edges to the chamfer line endpoints. This option is similar to setting the TRIMMODE system variable from 1 to 0 or from 0 to 1.

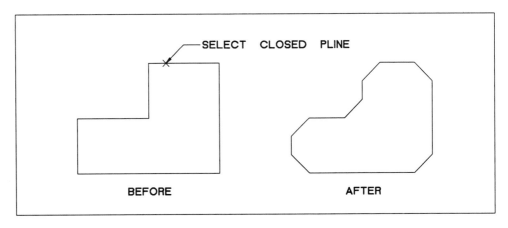

Figure 4–37 Chamfer with distances of 0.5 drawn on a polyline

> **NOTE:** The CHAMFER command set to a zero distance operates the same way the FILLET command operates set to zero radius.

MODIFYING OBJECTS

In this section, four additional Modify commands are explained: MOVE, TRIM, BREAK, and EXTEND. (The ERASE command was explained in Chapter 2.)

Moving Objects

The MOVE command lets you move one or more objects from their present location to a new one without changing orientation or size.

Invoke the MOVE command from:

Modify toolbar	Select the Move command (see Figure 4–38)
Pull-down menu	Modify > Move
Command: prompt	move ⏎

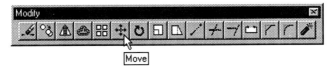

Figure 4–38 Invoking the Move command from the Modify toolbar

Fundamentals III

AutoCAD prompts:

> Command: **move** Enter
> Select objects: *(select the objects and then give a null response to complete the selection)*
> Base point or displacement: *(specify a point)*
> Second point of displacement: *(specify a point for displacement, or press* Enter *for a null response)*

You can use one or more object selection methods to select the objects. If you specify two data points, AutoCAD computes the displacement and moves the selected objects accordingly. If you specify the points on the screen, AutoCAD assists you in visualizing the displacement by drawing a rubber-band line from the first point as you move the crosshairs to the second point. If you provide a null response to the second point of displacement, then AutoCAD interprets the base point as relative X,Y,Z displacement.

The following command sequence shows an example of moving a group of objects, selected by means of the Window option, by relative displacement, as shown in Figure 4–39.

> Command: **move** Enter
> Select objects: *(pick Point 1 to place one corner of a window)*
> Other corner: *(pick Point 2 to place the opposite corner of the window)*
> Select objects: Enter
> Base point or displacement: **2,3** Enter
> Second point of displacement: Enter

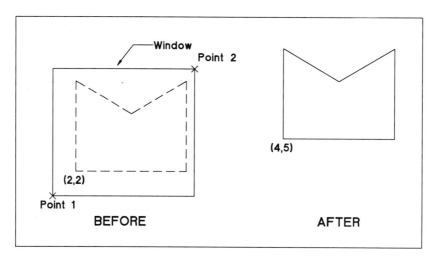

Figure 4–39 Using the MOVE Window option to move a group of objects by means of vector displacement

The following command sequence shows an example of moving a group of objects selected by the Window option and moving the objects by picking two data points, as shown in Figure 4–40.

Command: **move**
Select objects: *(pick Point 1 to place one corner for a window)*
Other corner: *(pick Point 2 to place the opposite corner of the window)*
Select objects: `Enter`
Base point or displacement: *(pick base point)*
Second point of displacement: *(pick second point)*

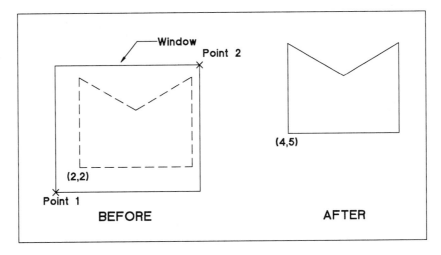

Figure 4–40 Using the MOVE Window command to move a group of objects by specifying two data points

Trimming Objects

The TRIM command is used to trim the portion of the object(s) that is drawn past a cutting edge or from an implied intersection defined by other objects. Objects that can be trimmed include lines, arcs, elliptical arcs, circles, 2D and 3D polylines, xlines, rays, and splines. Valid cutting edge objects include lines, arcs, circles, ellipses, 2D and 3D polylines, floating viewports, xlines, rays, regions, splines, and text.

Invoke the TRIM command from:

Modify toolbar	Select the Trim command (see Figure 4–41)
Pull-down menu	Modify > Trim
Command: prompt	**trim** `Enter`

Figure 4-41 Invoking the Trim command from the Modify toolbar

AutoCAD prompts:

Command: **trim**
Select cutting edge(s):
Select objects: *(select the objects and then give a null response to complete the selection)*
<Select object to trim>/Project/Edge/Undo: *(select object(s) to trim, press* Enter *to terminate the selection process, or select one of the available options)*

The TRIM command initially prompts you to "Select cutting edge(s):" After selecting one or more cutting edges to trim, press Enter. You are then prompted to "Select object to trim:" Select one or more objects to trim and then press Enter to terminate the command.

> **NOTE:** Don't forget to press Enter after selecting the cutting edge(s). Otherwise, the program will not respond as expected. In fact, TRIM continues expecting more cutting edges until you terminate the edge selecting mode.

Edge Option The Edge option determines whether objects that extend past a selected cutting edge or to an implied intersection are trimmed. AutoCAD prompts as follows when the Edge option is selected:

Extend/No extend <current>: *(select an option or press* Enter *)*

The Extend selection extends the cutting edge along its natural path to intersect an object in 3D (implied intersection).

The No Extend selection specifies that the object is to be trimmed only at a cutting edge that intersects it in 3D space.

Undo Option The Undo option reverses the most recent change made by TRIM.

Project Option The Project option specifies the projection mode AutoCAD uses when trimming objects. By default, it is set to the current UCS.

Figure 4-42 shows examples of using the TRIM command.

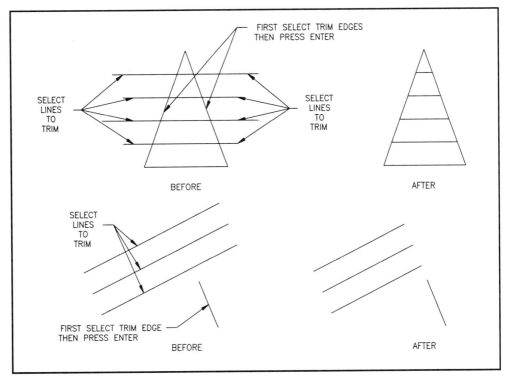

Figure 4–42 Examples of using the TRIM Command

Erasing Parts of Objects

The BREAK command is used to remove parts of objects or to split an object in two parts, and it can be used on lines, xlines, rays, arcs, circles, ellipses, splines, donuts, traces, 2D and 3D polylines.

Invoke the BREAK command from:

Modify toolbar	Select the Break command (see Figure 4–43)
Pull-down menu	Modify > Break
Command: prompt	**trim** Enter

Figure 4–43 Invoking the Break command from the Modify toolbar

AutoCAD prompts:

Command: **break** [Enter]
Select object: *(select an object)*
Enter second point (or F for first point): *(specify the second break point, or type f to redefine the first break point)*

AutoCAD erases the portion of the object between the first point (the point where the object was selected) and second point. If the second point is not on the object, then AutoCAD selects the nearest point on the object. If you need to erase an object to one end of a line, arc, or polyline, then specify the second point beyond the end to be removed.

If instead of specifying the second point you enter **f**, AutoCAD prompts for the first point and then for the second point.

An object can be split into two parts without removing any portion of the object by selecting the same point as the first and second points. You can do so by entering @ to specify the second point.

If you select a circle, then AutoCAD converts it to an arc by erasing a piece, moving counterclockwise from the first point to the second point. For a closed polyline, the part is removed between two selected points, moving in direction from the first to the last vertex. And in the case of 2D polylines and traces with width, the BREAK command will produce square ends at the break points.

See Figure 4–44 for examples of applications of the BREAK command.

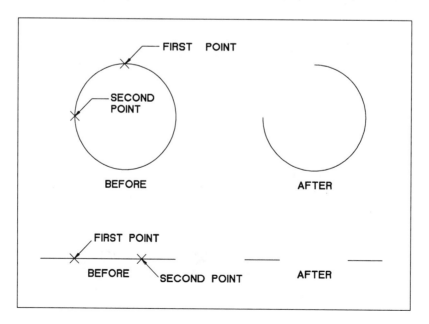

Figure 4–44 Examples of applications of the BREAK command

Extending Objects to Meet Another Object

The EXTEND command is used to change one or both endpoints of selected lines, arcs, elliptical arcs, open 2D and 3D polylines, and rays to extend to lines, arcs, elliptical arcs, circles, ellipses, 2D and 3D polylines, rays, xlines, regions, splines, text string, or floating viewports.

Invoke the EXTEND command from:

Modify toolbar	Select the Extend command (see Figure 4–45)
Pull-down menu	Modify > Exten<u>d</u>
Command: prompt	**extend** Enter

[Extend]

Figure 4–45 Invoking the Extend command from the Modify toolbar

AutoCAD prompts:

Command: **extend** Enter
Select boundary edges:
Select objects: *(select the objects and then give a null response to complete the selection)*
<Select object to extend>/Project/Edge/Undo: *(select the object(s) to extend, press* Enter *to terminate the selection process, or select one of the available options)*

The EXTEND command initially prompts you to "Select boundary edges:". After selecting one or more boundary edges, press Enter to terminate the selection process. Then AutoCAD prompts you to "Select object to extend:" (default option). Select one or more objects to extend to the selected boundary edges. After selecting the required objects to extend, press Enter to complete the selection process.

The EXTEND and TRIM commands are very similar in this method of selecting. With EXTEND you are prompted to select the boundry edge to extend to; with TRIM you are prompted to select a cutting edge.

Edge Option The Edge option determines whether objects are extended past a selected boundary or to an implied edge. AutoCAD prompts as follows when the Edge option is selected:

Extend/No extend <current>: *(enter an option or press* Enter *)*

The Extend selection extends the boundary object along its natural path to intersect another object in 3D space (implied edge).

The No Extend selection specifies that the object is to extend only to a boundary object that actually intersects it in 3D space.

Undo Option The Undo option reverses the most recent change made by the EXTEND command.

Project Option The Project option specifies the projection AutoCAD uses when trimming objects. By default, it is set to the current UCS.

Figure 4–46 shows examples of the use of the EXTEND command.

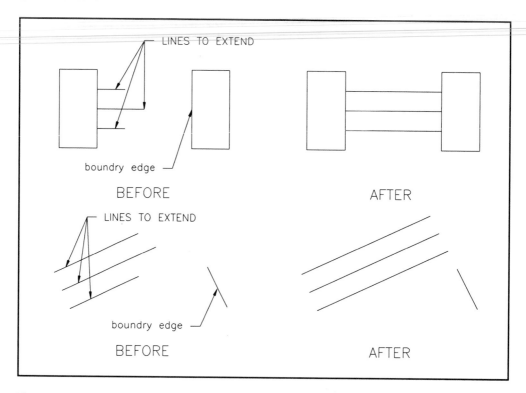

Figure 4–46 Examples of applications of the EXTEND command

PROJECT EXERCISE

This project exercise provides point-by-point instructions for setting up the drawing with layers and then creating the objects shown in Figure P4–1.

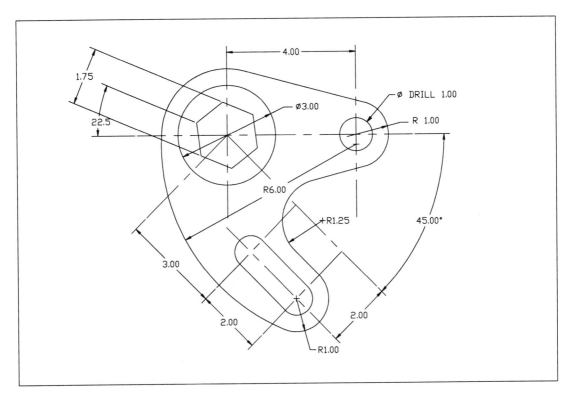

Figure P4–1 Completed project drawing

In this project you will:

- Set up the drawing, including Limits and Layers
- Use the LINE, RECTANG, POLYGON and CIRCLE commands to create objects
- Use the Osnap modes of int, tan, ttr, and per
- Use the TRIM, OFFSET, BREAK, MIRROR, and ERASE commands to modify objects or create new objects from existing ones

Set Up the Drawing and Draw a Border

Step 1   Start the AutoCAD program.

Step 2   To create a new drawing, invoke the NEW command from the Standard toolbar or select New from the pull-down menu File.

AutoCAD displays the Create New Drawing dialog box. Click the "Use a Wizard" button, select the Quick Setup, and choose the OK button to close the dialog box.

AutoCAD displays the Quick Setup dialog box with the display of the Step:1 Units tab. Select the "Decimal" radio button and choose the Next>> button.

AutoCAD displays the Quick Setup dialog box with the display of the Step 2: Area tab. Under the Width: edit field enter **18**, and under the Length edit field enter **12**. Choose the Done button to close the Quick Setup dialog box.

Step 3   Invoke the LAYER command from the Object Properties toolbar, or select Layer... from the pull-down menu Format. AutoCAD displays the Layer & Linetype Properties dialog box.

Create three layers, and rename them as shown in the following table, assigning appropriate color and linetype.

Layer Name	Color	Linetype
Border	Red	Continuous
Centerline	Green	Center
Object	Blue	Continuous

Set Border as the current layer, and close the Layer & Linetype Properties dialog box.

Step 4   Open the Drawing Aids dialog box from the pull-down menu Tools, and set Grid to 0.5 and Snap to 0.5, and then set the grid to ON.

Step 5   Invoke the RECTANG command to draw the border (17" by 11") as shown in Figure P4–2.

Command: **rectang** [Enter]
Chamfer/Elevation/Fillet/Thickness/Width/<First Corner>: **.5,.5** [Enter]
Other corner: **@17,11** [Enter]

Figure P4–2 Border for a mechanical drawing

Step 6   Begin the layout of the drawing by drawing the centerlines as shown in Figure P4–3. Set the CENTERLINE layer as the current layer. Invoke the LINE command from the Draw toolbar and draw lines 1, 2, 3, and 4.

Command: **line** Enter
From point: **4,8** Enter
To point: **@8.5<0** Enter
To point: Enter
Command: Enter
LINE From point: **7,5.5** Enter
To point: **@5<90** Enter
To point: Enter
Command: Enter
LINE From point: **7,8** Enter
To point: **@3.5<225** Enter
To point: Enter
Command: Enter
LINE From point: **7,8** Enter
To point: **@6.5<315** Enter
To point: Enter

Fundamentals III

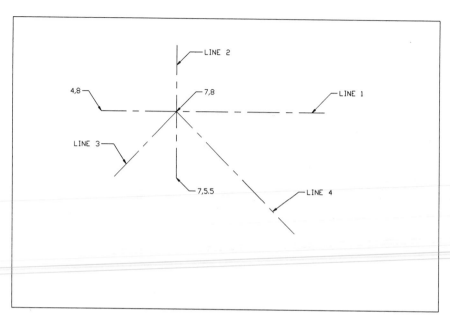

Figure P4–3 Placement of centerlines

Step 7   Use the OFFSET command to construct the additional centerlines necessary for completion of the project. Invoke the OFFSET command from the Modify toolbar, and construct centerlines 2A, 3A, 3B, and 4A as shown in Figure P4–4.

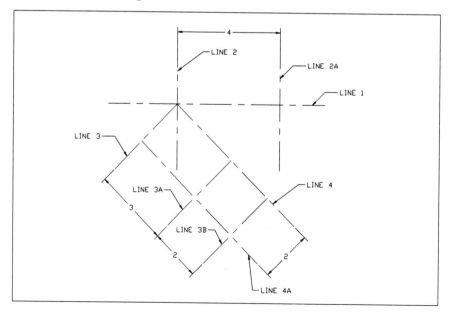

Figure P4–4 Placement of additional centerlines

Command: **offset** [Enter]
Offset distance or Through<Through>: **4** [Enter]
Select object to offset: *(select line 2)*
Side to offset? *(pick to the right of line 2 to construct line 2A, as shown in Figure P4–4)*
Select object to offset: [Enter]
Command: [Enter]
OFFSET
Offset distance or through<4.00>: **3** [Enter]
Select object to offset: *(select line 3)*
Side to offset? *(pick a point to the right of line 3 to construct line 3A, as shown in Figure P4–4)*
Select object to offset: [Enter]
Command: [Enter]
OFFSET
Offset distance or through<3.00>: **2** [Enter]
Select object to offset: *(select line 3A)*
Side to offset? *(pick a point to the right of line 3A to construct line 3B, as shown in Figure P4–4)*
Select object to offset: *(select line 4)*
Side to offset? *(pick a point below line 4 to construct line 4A, as shown in Figure P4–4)*
Select object to offset: [Enter]

Step 8   Erase lines 3 and 4, as shown in Figure P4–4, by invoking the ERASE command from the Modify toolbar.

Command: **erase** [Enter]
Select objects: *(select lines 3 and 4)*

Your drawing will appear as shown in Figure P4–5.

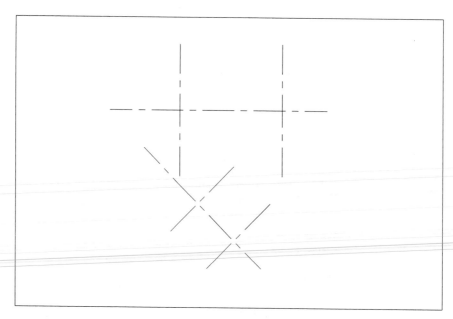

Figure P4–5 Drawing after lines 3 and 4 have been erased

Step 9   The intersection of the centerlines you laid out in the previous steps will provide the center points for the circles. Set the OBJECT layer as the current layer. Invoke the CIRCLE command from the Draw toolbar (Circle Center Radius), and draw the three circles shown in Figure P4–6.

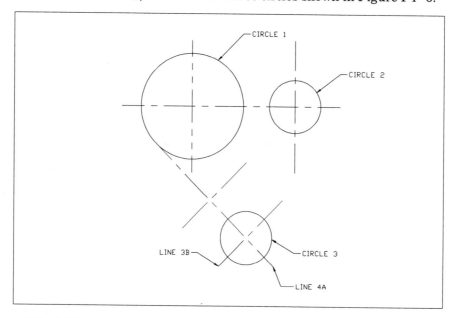

Figure P4–6 Placement of circles

Command: **circle** Enter
3P/2P/TTR/<Center point>: **7,8** Enter
Diameter/<Radius>: **2** Enter
Command: Enter
Circle 3P/2P/TTR/<Center point>: **11,8** Enter
Diameter/<Radius><2.00>: **1** Enter
Command: Enter
Circle 3P/2P/TTR/<Center point>: *(use the Object snap tool "intersection" to snap to the intersection of lines 3B and 4A to identify the center of circle 3)*
Diameter/<Radius><1.00>: Enter

Step 10 Invoke the LINE command from the Draw toolbar, and draw line 5 tangent to two circles (use the Osnap tool "tangent") as shown in Figure P4–7.

Command: **line** Enter
From point: *(invoke the tan object snap and select the upper part of circle 1)*
To point: *(invoke the tan object snap and select the upper part of circle 2)*
To point: *(press Enter to terminate the command sequence)*

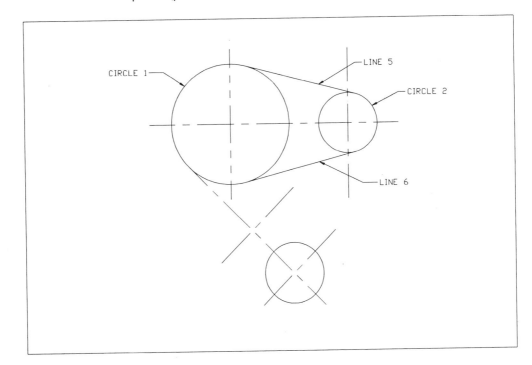

Figure P4–7 Lines 5 and 6 drawn tangent to two circles

Step 11   Invoke the MIRROR command to create line 6 from line 5 as shown in Figure P4-7.

>   Command: **mirror** Enter
>   Select objects: *(select line 5)*
>   Select objects: *(press* Enter *to terminate the selection of objects)*
>   First point of mirror line: **7,8** Enter
>   Second point: **11,8** Enter
>   Delete old objects? <N>: Enter

Step 12   Invoke the LINE command and draw line 1A using the Object snap modes intersection and perpendicular as shown in Figure P4-8.

>   Command: line Enter
>   From point: *(invoke the intersection object snap, and select the intersection of line 3B and circle 3)*
>   To point: *(invoke the perpendicular object snap, and select line 3A)*
>   To point: *(press* Enter *to terminate the command sequence)*

Your drawing will appear as shown in Figure P4-8.

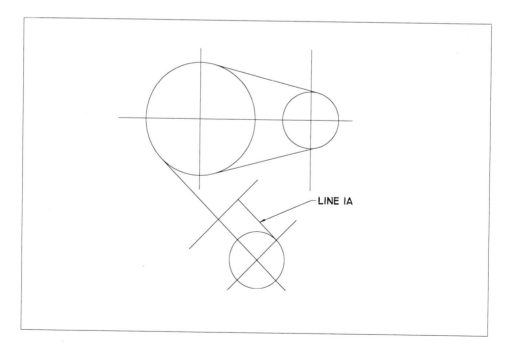

Figure P4-8 Drawing after changing the layer of line 1A

Step 13 Draw two circles, circle 4 and circle 5, as shown in Figure P4–9 by invoking the CIRCLE command's Tan Tan Radius option.

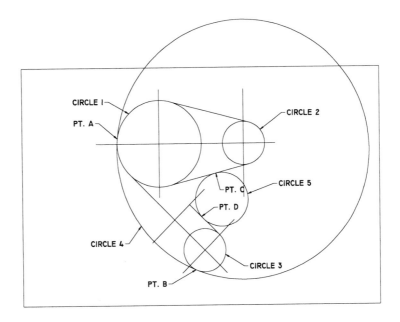

Figure P4–9 Placement of circle 4 and circle 5 tangent to two objects

> Command: **circle** `Enter`
> 3P/2P/TTR/<Center point>: **ttr** `Enter`
> Enter Tangent spec: *(select circle 1 at point A, as shown in Figure P4–9)*
> Enter second Tangent spec: *(select circle 3 at point B, as shown in Figure 4–9)*
> Enter second Tangent spec: Radius: <1.0000>: **6** `Enter`

Invoke the CIRCLE command again:

> Command: **circle** `Enter`
> 3P/2P/TTR/<Center point>: **ttr** `Enter`
> Enter Tangent spec: *(select the line at point C, as shown in Figure P4–9)*
> Enter second Tangent spec: *(select the line at point D, as shown in Figure 4–9)*
> Enter second Tangent spec: Radius: <6.0000>: **1.25** `Enter`

Your drawing will appear as shown in Figure P4–9.

Step 14 Invoke the TRIM command from the Modify toolbar to modify the two circles previously drawn in Step 13.

> Command: **trim** ⌅
> Select cutting edge(s)...
> Select objects: *(select circle 1, circle 2, line 1, and line 2, as in Figure P4–10, as the cutting edges, and press* ⌅*)*
> <Select object to trim>/Undo: *(select circle 3 at point A, as shown in Figure P4–10)*
> <Select object to trim>/Undo: *(select circle 4 at point B, as shown in Figure P4–10)*
> <Select object to trim/Undo: *(press* ⌅ *to complete the command sequence)*

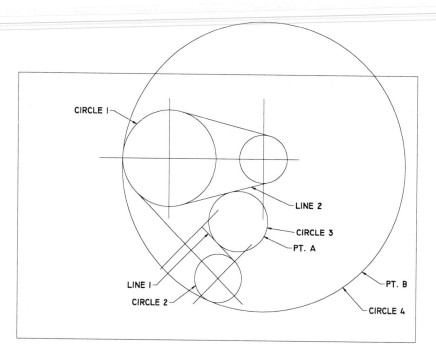

Figure P4–10 Drawing indicating the objects as the cutting edges

Your drawing will appear as shown in Figure P4–11.

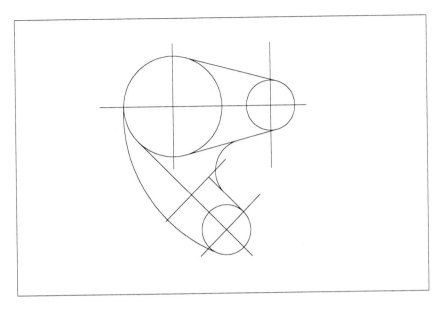

Figure P4-11 Circles modified with the TRIM command

Step 15   Use the TRIM command to modify the circles and lines to achieve the layout shown in Figure P4–12. Invoke the TRIM command and select lines 1, 2, 3, and 4 as cutting edges as shown in Figure P4–13. Select circles 1, 2, and 3, as shown in Figure P4–13, as objects to trim.

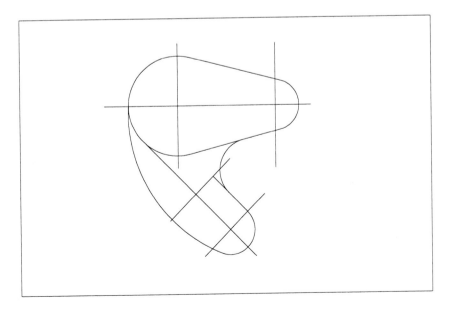

Figure P4-12 Drawing as it will look after modifying the circles and lines

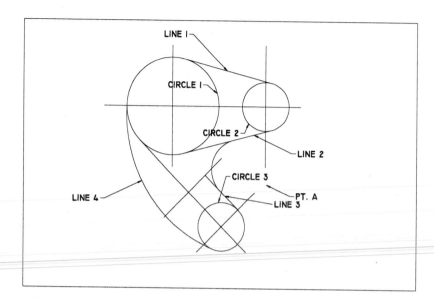

Figure P4–13 Drawing showing the selection of the objects as cutting and trim edges

Step 16   Continue to use the TRIM command to modify the figure to achieve the layout shown in Figure P4–14. Invoke the TRIM command again and select arcs 1, 2, and 3 as cutting edges, as shown in Figure P4–15. Select lines 1, 2, 3, and 4 to trim, as shown in Figure P4–15. Your drawing will appear as shown in Figure P4–14.

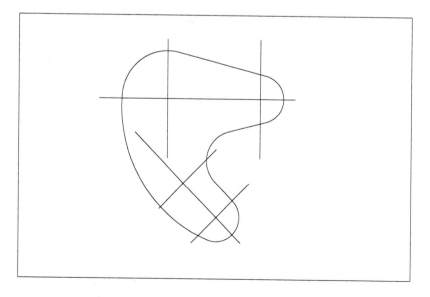

Figure P4–14 Drawing as it will look after modifying the arcs and lines

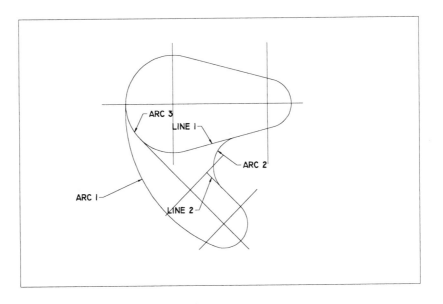

Figure P4–15 Drawing showing the selection of the objects as cutting and trim edges

Step 17   Draw the circles necessary to complete the design. Invoke the CIRCLE command and draw circles with points 1, 2, and 3 as center points and with a radius of 0.5. Draw another circle with center point at point 4 and with a radius of 1.5, as shown in Figure P4–16.

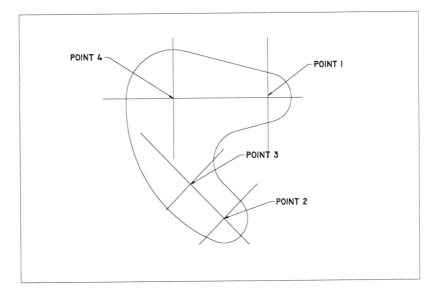

Figure P4–16 Drawing showing the center points to draw the circles

> **NOTE:** Make sure to use the object snap tool intersection when selecting the center points.

After drawing the circles, your drawing will appear as shown in Figure P4–17.

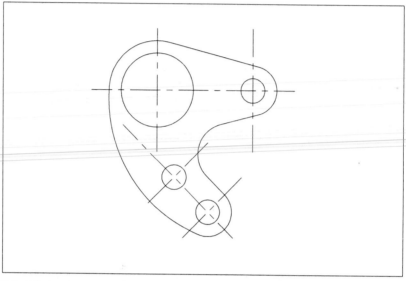

Figure P4–17 Design with the circles

Step 18 Draw lines A and B, needed to form the slot, by invoking the LINE command, as shown in Figure P4–18.

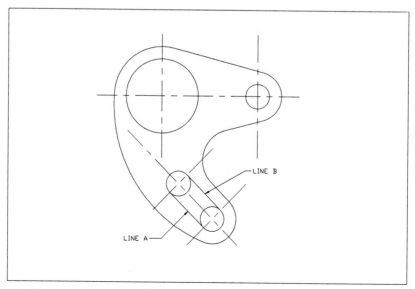

Figure P4–18 Lines drawn to form the slot

NOTE: Use the object snap tool intersection to snap to the intersection of the centerlines and the circle, as shown in Figure P4–18.

Step 19 Invoke the TRIM command and select lines A and B as cutting edges. Next, select the small circles as objects to trim at points 1 and 2, as shown in Figure P4–19.

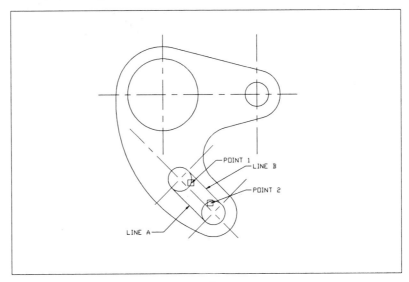

Figure P4–19 Trim edges and circles to trim

Your drawing will appear as shown in Figure P4–20.

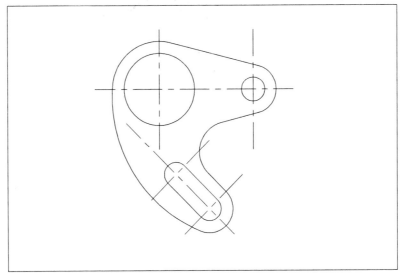

Figure P4–20 Drawing after the circles have been trimmed

Step 20 Invoke the POLYGON command from the Draw toolbar to draw the polygon shown in Figure P4–21.

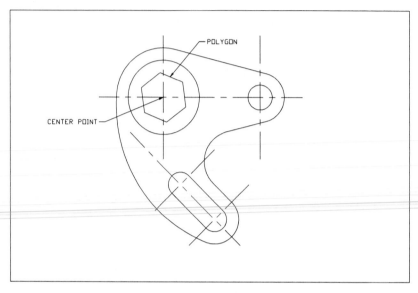

Figure P4–21 Design with a six-sided polygon

Command: **polygon** Enter
Number of sides<4>: **6** Enter
Edge <Cener of polygon>: *(select center point as in Figure P4–21)*
Inscribed in circle/Circumscribed about circle(I/C): **c** Enter
Radius of circle: **@0.875<67.5** Enter

Your drawing will appear as shown in Figure P4–21.

Step 21 Invoke the BREAK command from the Modify toolbar and select points 1 and 2, as shown in Figure P4–22, to break the centerline.

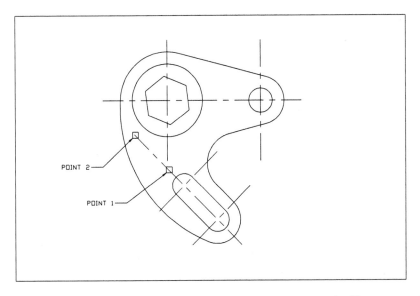

Figure P4–22 Showing the points where the BREAK command will remove part of the centerline

Your drawing will appear as shown in Figure P4–23 after removing the specified portion of the centerline.

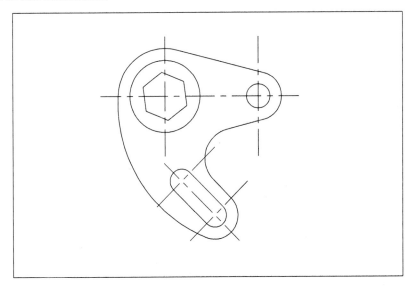

Figure P4–23 Drawing with the specified portion of the centerline removed

Step 22 Save the drawing as Ch4.DWG.

Congratulations! You have just successfully applied several AutoCAD concepts in creating a rather complex mechanical drawing.

EXERCISES 4–1 THROUGH 4–4

Exercise 4–1

Create the accompanying drawing of the finishing unit vent piping according to the settings given in the following table.

Settings	Value		
1. Units	Decimal with 4 decimal places		
2. Limits	Lower left corner: 0,0		
	Upper right corner: 12,9		
3. Grid	0.125		
4. Snap	0.0625		
5. Layers	*NAME*	*COLOR*	*LINETYPE*
	Construction	Cyan	Continuous
	Border	Red	Continous
	Pipes	Green	Continuous
	Sources	Magenta	Continuous
	Text	Blue	Continuous

Hints	Plan ahead before drawing the layout.
	The border can be drawn from coordinates .125,.125 to 11.875,8.875 using the RECTANG command.
	Set Construction as the current layer. Draw a horizontal construction line (xline) through a point whose *Y* coordinate is 1.0.
	Use the ARRAY command with the Rectangular option to make eight copies of the construction line, at a spacing of 0.875 units. Don't forget to array 9 objects (the original is included in the count). The drawing should look like Figure Ex4–1a.
	Set Sources as the current layer. Draw a circle (0.5 dia.) for one of the sources and a rectangle (0.5 × 0.5) for a pipe ID, and then copy them using the Multiple option of the COPY command.
	The alphanumeric characters can be drawn in their respective circles and boxes using the TEXT and DTEXT command. Select the M (middle) or MC (middle center) mode of justification, and then make the center of the circle/box the insertion point of the character.
	After you have finished drawing, either the Construction layer can be turned OFF or the construction lines can be erased. Your completed drawing should look like the drawing of the finishing unit vent piping.

Fundamentals III

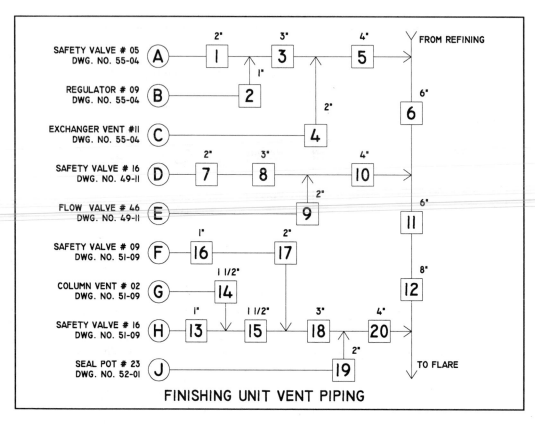

Figure Ex4–1 Completed drawing

Figure Ex4–1a Construction lines

Exercise 4–2

Create the structural steel framing plan shown, according to the settings given in the following table.

Settings	Value		
1. Units	Architectural		
2. Limits	Lower left corner: -10'-0",-10'-0"		
	Upper right corner: 50'-0",35'-0"		
3. Grid	12"		
4. Snap	6"		
5. Layers	*NAME*	*COLOR*	*LINETYPE*
	Construction	Cyan	Continuous
	Border	Red	Continuous
	Columns	Green	Continuous
	Beams	Magenta	Continuous
	Text	Blue	Continuous

Hints	
	Plan ahead before drawing the layout. The columns and beams in the structural steel framing plan can be drawn by using the PLINE command, and the text objects can be drawn with the TEXT and DTEXT command. Construction lines can be drawn by using the XLINE and RAY commands combined with the ARRAY command.
	Draw the border from coordinates -9'-6",-9'-6" to 49'-6",34'-6" using the RECTANG command.
	Draw a vertical construction line by means of the XLINE command through a point whose *X* coordinate is 0'-0".
	Copy the vertical construction line using the Multiple option of the COPY command.
	Draw two horizontal directional construction lines by means of the RAY command from the point whose coordinates are 24'-0",0'-0". One of the lines is drawn to the left and the other to the right. Use the ARRAY command with the Rectangular option set to four rows for the left construction ray, at a spacing of 8'-0", and five rows of the right construction ray, at a spacing of 6'-0". The drawing should look like Figure Ex4–2a.
	Using the PLINE command, draw the columns with a width of 2" and the beams with a width of 1". Draw the beams from intersection to intersection of the construction lines, and then, using the BREAK command, remove the sections of the polylines either 6" or 12" (make sure Snap is set to ON) from the intersections, depending on which way the column is oriented.
	After you have finished drawing, either the Construction layer can be turned OFF or the the construction lines can be erased. Your completed drawing should look like the finished framing plan. Do *not* dimension the drawing.

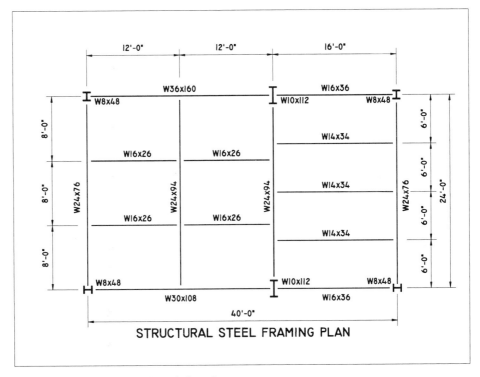

Figure Ex4–2 The completed drawing

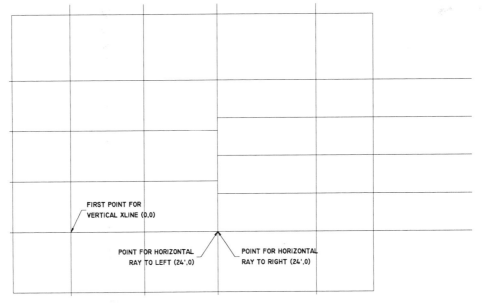

Figure Ex4–2a Construction line layout

Exercise 4–3

Create the drawing shown of the sleeve block according to the settings given in the following table.

Settings	Value		
1. Units	Decimal		
2. Limits	Lower left corner: 0,0		
	Upper right corner: 12,9		
3. Grid	0.50		
4. Snap	0.25		
5. Layers	*NAME*	*COLOR*	*LINETYPE*
	Object	Green	Continuous
	Center	Red	Center
	Hidden	Magenta	Hidden
	Text	Blue	Continuous

Hints	The object lines for the sleeve block can be drawn by using the LINE, POLYGON, and CIRCLE commands, and the text objects can be drawn with the TEXT or DTEXT command. The arcs can be created using the FILLET command. Do *not* dimension this drawing. Use the TEXT command to label the views only.
	Use two circles and two lines as the basis of the slot. Then use the TRIM command to remove the inner halves of the circles, leaving the outer arcs that, with the two lines, comprise the slot.
	Other arcs (.5 and .125 radii) can be created by using the FILLET command with the correctly specified radius.
	You will probably have to object snap to the "intersections" of the apexes of the hexagon in the top view and draw lines perpendicular to the base of the front view in order to locate them correctly. Then use the TRIM command to remove the unwanted portions of the lines.

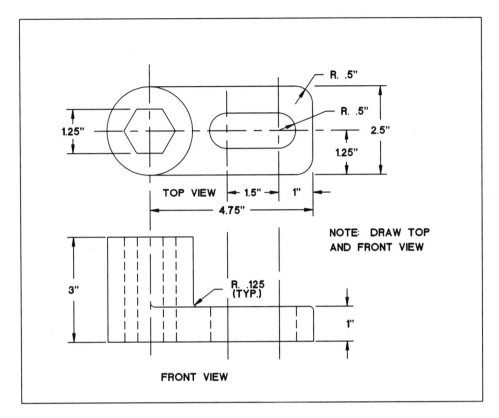

Figure Ex4–3 Sleeve block

Within the figure:

R. .5"

R. .5"

1.25"

2.5"

1.25"

TOP VIEW ← 1.5" → 1"

4.75"

NOTE: DRAW TOP
AND FRONT VIEW

3"

R. .125
(TYP.)

1"

FRONT VIEW

Exercise 4–4

Create the drawing shown of the input-output card according to the settings given in the following table.

Settings	Value		
1. Units	Decimal		
2. Limits	Lower left corner: 0,0		
	Upper right corner: 12,9		
3. Grid	0.25		
4. Snap	0.25		
5. Layers	*NAME*	*COLOR*	*LINETYPE*
	Object	Green	Continuous
	Center	Red	Center
	Hidden	Magenta	Hidden
	Text	Blue	Continuous

Hints	
	The input-output card can be created using the PLINE, LINE, and CIRCLE commands, and the text objects can be drawn with the TEXT or DTEXT command. Do *not* dimension the drawing.
	Create a circle with radius 0.01 in the lower left corner of the array of dots, and then, using the ARRAY command, create an array of 15 rows and 25 columns.
	The internal circuits can be drawn using the PLINE command, with the narrower segments set at 0.04 and the wider, "connection" end set at 0.10. This change should be done without exiting the PLINE command.
	The wide-line circles at the ends of the circuits can be created by using the PLINE command with the Arc option, drawing two half-circles with a line width of 0.02 and a radius of 0.0625. Be sure to note the starting direction. The snap resolution will have to be set to 0.03125.

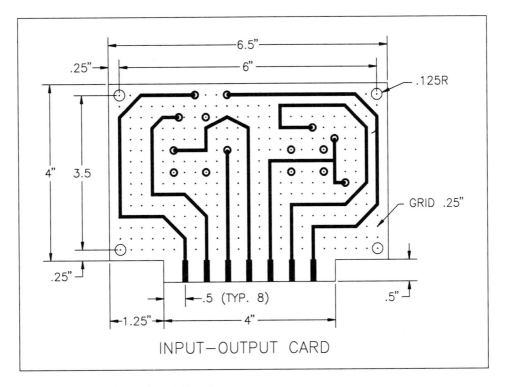

Figure Ex4–4 Completed drawing

Exercises 4–5 and 4–6

Create the drawings shown of the brackets and clamps according to the settings given in the following table.

Settings	Value		
1. Units	Architectural		
2. Limits	Lower left corner: 0,0		
	Upper right corner: 12'-0",9'-0"		
3. Grid	4"		
4. Snap	0.5"		
5. Text Height	0.375"		
5. Layers	NAME	COLOR	LINETYPE
	Object	Green	Continuous
	Center	Red	Center
	Hidden	Magenta	Hidden
	Text	Blue	Continuous

Hint	To lay out the views, you need to estimate the dimensions of the spaces between the objects. Then add up the total of the objects and estimated distances between to determine the spaces left over around the whole grouping.

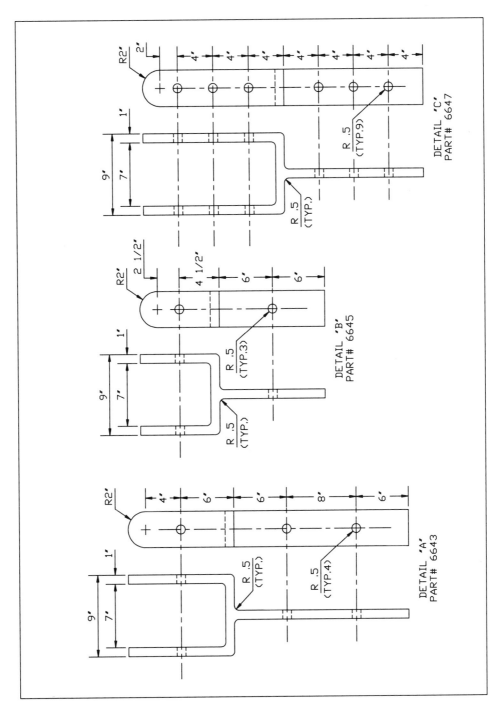

Figure Ex4–5 Brackets

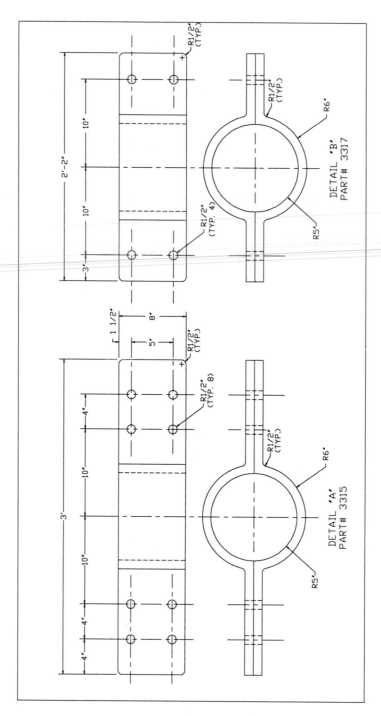

Figure Ex4–5 Clamps

REVIEW QUESTIONS

1. In order to draw two RAYs with different starting points, you must use the RAY command twice.
   a. True
   b. False

2. When you place XLINE's on a drawing, they
   a. may effect the limits of the drawing
   b. may effect the extents of the drawing
   c. always appear as construction lines on layer 0
   d. can be constructed as offsets to an existing line
   e. none of the above

3. Filleting two non-parallel, non-intersecting line segments with a zero radius will:
   a. return an error message
   b. have no effect
   c. create a sharp corner
   d. convert the lines to RAY's

4. Objects can be TRIMed at the points where they intersect existing objects.
   a. True
   b. False

5. The default justification for text is:
   a. TL
   b. BL
   c. MC
   d. BR
   e. None of the above

6. Which command allows you to change the location of the objects and allows a duplicate to remain in tact
   a. CHANGE
   b. MOVE
   c. COPY
   d. MIRROR

7. The maximum number of sides accepted by the POLYGON command is:
   a. 8
   b. 32
   c. 128
   d. 1024
   e. infinite (limited by computer memory, but VERY large)

8. Portions of objects can be erased or removed by using the command:
   a. ERASE
   b. REMOVE
   c. BREAK
   d. EDIT
   e. PARERASE

9. Ellipses are drawn by specifying:
   a. The major and minor axes
   b. The major axis and a rotation angle
   c. Any three points on the ellipse
   d. Any of the above
   e. Both A and B

10. Which of the following commands can be used to place text on a drawing:
    a. TEXT
    b. DTEXT
    c. MTEXT
    d. All of the above
    e. None of the above

11. Two lines are drawn. Then the first line is erased and the second line is moved. Executing the OOPS command at the "Command:" prompt will:
    a. restore the erased line
    b. execute the LINE command automatically
    c. replace the second line at its original position
    d. restore both lines to their original positions
    e. none of the above

12. To efficiently MOVE multiple objects, which option would be more efficient?
    a. Objects   d. Add
    b. Last   e. Undo
    c. Window

13. While using the TEXT command, AutoCAD will display the text you are typing:
    a. in the command prompt area
    b. in the drawing screen area
    c. Both A and B
    d. Neither A or B

14. While using the DTEXT command, AutoCAD will display the text you are typing:
    a. in the command prompt area
    b. in the drawing screen area
    c. Both A and B
    d. Neither A or B

15. The MOVE command allows you to:
    a. move objects to new locations on the screen
    b. dynamically drag objects on the screen
    c. move only the objects that are on the current layer
    d. move an object from one layer to another
    e. Both A and B

16. To create a rectangular ARRAY of objects, you must specify:
    a. the number of items and the distance between them
    b. the number of rows, the number of items, and the unit cell size
    c. the number of rows, the number of columns, and the unit cell size
    d. none of the above

17. A polyline:
    a. can have width
    b. can be exploded
    c. is one object
    d. all of the above

18. Polylines are:
    a. made up of line and arc segments, each of which is treated as an individual object
    b. are connected sequences of lines and arcs
    c. both A and B
    d. none of the above

19. To create an arc which is concentric with an existing arc, you could use what command?
    a. ARRAY
    b. COPY
    c. OFFSET
    d. MIRROR

20. The following are all options of the PLINE command except:
    a. Undo
    b. Halfwidth
    c. Arc
    d. Ltype
    e. Width

FUNDAMENTALS IV

• •

INTRODUCTION

After completing this chapter, you will be able to:

✓ Construct geometric figures with the DONUT, SOLID, and POINT commands
✓ Create freehand line segments with the SKETCH command
✓ Use advanced object selection methods and object selection modes to modify objects
✓ Use the modify commands LENGTHEN, STRETCH, ROTATE, SCALE, PEDIT (edit Polyline), Change Properties, and Match Properties

CONSTRUCTING GEOMETRIC FIGURES

Drawing Solid-Filled Circles

The DOUGHNUT (or DONUT) command lets you draw solid-filled circles and rings by specifying outer and inner diameters of the filled area. The fill display depends on the setting of the FILLMODE system variable.

Invoke the DONUT command from:

Pull-down menu	Draw > Donut
Command: prompt	**donut** Enter

AutoCAD prompts:

Command: **donut** Enter
Inside diameter <current>: *(specify a distance, or press* Enter *to accept the current setting)*
Outside diameter <current>: *(specify a distance, or press* Enter *to accept the current setting)*
Center of doughnut: *(specify a point to draw the donut)*

You may specify the inside and outside diameters of the donut to be drawn by picking two points at the appropriate distance apart on the screen, and AutoCAD will measure the distance and set the diameters.

You can select the center point by specifying its coordinates or by picking it with your pointing device. After you select the center point, AutoCAD prompts for the center of the next donut and continues prompting for subsequent center points. To terminate the command, enter a null response.

> **NOTE:** Be sure the FILLMODE system variable is set to ON (a value of 1). Check at the "Command:" prompt by typing **Fill** and pressing Enter. If FILLMODE is set to OFF (value of 0), then the PLINE, TRACE, DONUT, and SOLID commands display the outline of the shapes. With FILLMODE set to ON, the shapes you create with these commands appear solid. If FILLMODE is reset to ON after it has been set to OFF, you must use the REGEN command in order for the screen to display as filled any unfilled shapes created by these commands. Switching between ON and OFF affects only the appearance of shapes created with the PLINE, TRACE, DONUT, and SOLID commands. Solids can be selected or identified by picking the outlines only. The solid area is not recognized as an object.

For example, the following command sequence shows placement of a solid-filled circle, as shown in Figure 5–1, by use of the DONUT command.

Command: **donut** Enter
Inside diameter <.5>: **0** Enter
Outside diameter <1>: **1** Enter
Center of doughnut: **3,2** Enter
Center of doughnut: Enter

The following command sequence shows placement of a filled circular shape, as shown in Figure 5–1, by use of the DONUT command.

Command: **donut** Enter
Inside diameter <0.0>: **0.5** Enter

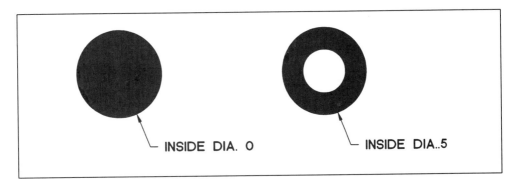

Figure 5–1 Using the DONUT command to place a solid-filled circle and a filled circular shape

Outside diameter <0.0>: **1** Enter
Center of doughnut: **6,2** Enter
Center of doughnut: Enter

Drawing Solid-Filled Polygons

The SOLID command creates a solid-filled straight-sided area whose outline is determined by points you specify on the screen. Two important factors should be kept in mind when using the SOLID command: (1) the points must be selected in a specified order or else the four corners generate a bowtie instead of a rectangle; (2) the polygon generated has straight sides. (Closer study reveals that even filled donuts and PLINE-generated curved areas are actually straight sided, just as arcs and circles generate as straight-line segments of small enough length to appear smooth.)

Invoke the SOLID command from:

Surfaces toolbar	Select the 2D Solid command (see Figure 5–2)
Pull-down menu	Draw > Surfaces > 2D Solid
Command: prompt	**solid** Enter

Figure 5–2 Invoking the SOLID command from the Surfaces toolbar

AutoCAD prompts:

Command: **solid** Enter
First point: *(specify a first point)*
Second point: *(specify a second point)*
Third point: *(specify a third point diagonally opposite the second point)*
Fourth point: *(specify a fourth point, or press* Enter *)*

When you specify a fourth point, AutoCAD draws a quadrilateral area. If instead you press Enter, AutoCAD creates a filled triangle.

For example, the following command sequence shows how to draw of a quadrilateral area such as shown in Figure 5–3.

Command: **solid** Enter
First point: *(pick point 1)*
Second point: *(pick point 2)*
Third point: *(pick point 3)*
Fourth point: *(pick point 4)*

To create the solid shape, the odd-numbered picks must be on one side and the even-numbered picks on the other side. If not, you get an effect such as shown in Figure 5–4.

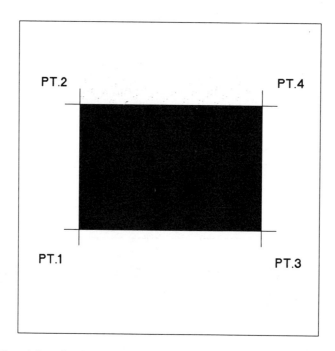

Figure 5–3 The pick order for crating a quadrilateral area with the SOLID command

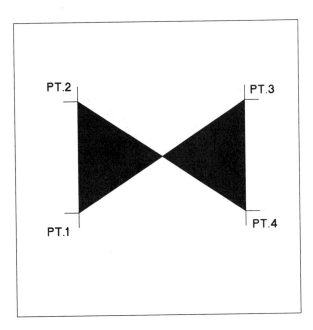

Figure 5–4 Results of using the SOLID command when odd/even points are not specified correctly

You can use the SOLID command to create an arrowhead, or triangle, shape such as shown in Figure 5–5. Polygon shapes can be created with the SOLID command by keeping the odd picks along one side and the even picks along the other side of the object, as shown in Figure 5–6.

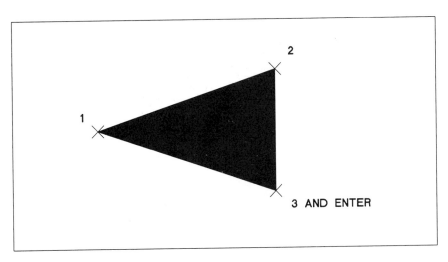

Figure 5–5 Using the SOLID command to create a solid triangular shape

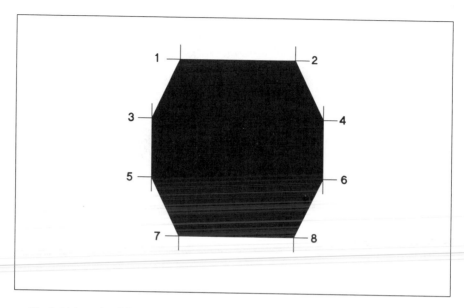

Figure 5-6 Using the SOLID command to create a polygonal shape

Drawing Point Objects

The POINT command draws points on the drawing, and these points are drawn on the plotted drawing sheet with a single "pen down." You can enter such points to be used as reference points for object snapping when necessary. When the drawing is finished, simply erase them from the drawing or freeze their layer. Points are entered by specifying coordinates or with the pointing device. You can specify a three-dimensional location for a point and object snap to a point by using the Node option of the Object snap (Osnap) feature.

Invoke the POINT command from:

Draw toolbar	Select the Point command (see Figure 5-7)
Pull-down menu	Draw > Point
Command: prompt	point [Enter]

Figure 5-7 Invoking the Point command from the Draw toolbar

AutoCAD prompts:

Command: **point** Enter
Point: *(specify a point)*

You can place as many points as you need. To terminate the command sequence, press Esc.

Point Modes When you draw the point, it appears on the display as a blip (+) if the BLIPMODE system variable is set to ON (default is ON). After a REDRAW command, it appears as a dot (.). You can make the point appear as a +, x, 0 or | by changing the PDMODE system variable. This can be done by entering PDMODE at the "Command:" prompt and entering the appropriate value. You can also change the PDMODE value by using the icon menu, as shown in Figure 5–8, invoked by typing DDPTYPE at the "Command:" prompt and pressing Enter. The default value of PDMODE is zero, which means the point appears as a dot. If PDMODE is changed, all previous points remain the same until you regenerate the drawing. After a screen regeneration, all points appear as the last PDMODE value entered.

Point Size The size that the point appears on the screen depends on the value to which the PDSIZE system variable is set. If necessary, you can change the size via the PDSIZE command. The default for PDSIZE is zero (one pixel in size). Any positive value larger than this will increase the size of the point accordingly.

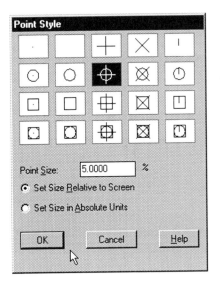

Figure 5–8 The Point Style icon menu lets you select the shape and size of the point object

DRAWING SKETCH LINE SEGMENTS

The SKETCH command creates a series of freehand line segments. It is useful for freehand drawings, contour mapping, and signatures. The sketched lines are not added to the drawing until they are recorded.

Invoke the SKETCH command from:

Command: prompt	sketch Enter

AutoCAD prompts:

Command: **sketch** Enter
Record increment <current>: *(specify a distance, or press Enter to accept the current value)*

You may also respond by specifying two points, either keyed in or specified on the screen, causing AutoCAD to use the distance between the points as the record increment distance. Once a record increment is specified, AutoCAD displays the following list of options:

Sketch   Pen   eXit   Quit   Record   Erase   Connect

You can use any of the available options while you are in the SKETCH command. They are accessible either as single-key entries or as a mouse/puck button, provided your mouse/puck has the number of buttons corresponding to the option. The following table shows the optional subcommands, their key, button number, and function. Normal button functions are not available while in the SKETCH mode.

Command Character	Pointer Button	Function
P	Pick	Raise/lower pen
.(period)	1	Line to point
R	2	Record lines
X, Spacebar, or Enter	3	Record lines and exit
Q, or Ctrl + C	4	Discard lines and exit
E	5	Erase
C	6	Connect

P (Pen Up and Down) An imaginary pen follows the cursor movement. When the pen is down, AutoCAD sketches a connected segment whenever the cursor moves the specified increment distance from the previously sketched segment. When the pen is up, the pen follows the cursor movement without drawing.

The pen is raised (up) and lowered (down) either by pressing the pick button on the mouse/puck or by pressing **P** on the keyboard. When you invoke a "PEN UP," the current location of the pen will be the endpoint of the last segment drawn, which will be shorter than a standard increment length.

A "PEN UP" does not take you out of the SKETCH mode. Nor does a "PEN UP" permanently record the lines drawn during the current SKETCH session.

. (Period; Line-to-Point) While the pen is up, you cause AutoCAD to draw a straight line from the last segment to the current cursor location and return to the "PEN UP" status by typing . (period) at the keyboard. This is convenient for long, straight lines that might occur in the middle of irregular shapes.

R (Record) Lines being displayed while the cursor is moved (with the pen down) are temporary. They will appear green (or red if the current color for that layer or object is green) on color monitors until they are permanently recorded. These temporary segments are subject to being modified with special SKETCH options until you press **R** to record the latest lines. These may include several groups of connected lines drawn during "PEN DOWN" sequences separated by "PEN UPs." When the Record option is invoked by pressing either **R** Enter or the third mouse/puck button, the total number of recorded segments is reported as follows:

    nnn lines recorded

E (Erase) Prior to any group(s) of connected lines being recorded with the Record option, you may use the E (Erase) option to remove any or all of the lines from the last segment back to the first. The sequence of prompts is as follows:

    Erase:
    Select end of delete

The pen is automatically set to UP, and you may then use the cursor to remove segments, starting from the last segment. When you are satisfied with the lines remaining, press **P** or the pick button to accept the erasure. To abort the erasure and return to the SKETCH mode, press **E** again (or any other option) and the following will be displayed:

    Erase aborted

C (Connect) Whenever a disconnect occurs (pen UP or erase), you can reconnect and continue sketching from the point of the last disconnect as long as you have not exited the SKETCH command. The sequence is as follows:

    Connect:
    Move to endpoint of line.

At this prompt you can move the cursor near the end of the last segment. When you are within a specified increment length, sketching begins, connected to that last endpoint. This option is meaningless if invoked during "PEN DOWN." A message also tells you:

> No last point known

if no last point exists. The Connect option can be canceled by pressing **C** a second time.

X (Record and Exit) The X option exits SKETCH mode after recording all temporary lines. This can also be accomplished by pressing either [Enter] or the Spacebar.

Q (Quit) The Q option exits SKETCH mode without recording any temporary lines. It is the same as pressing [Esc].

OBJECT SELECTION

As mentioned earlier, all the modify commands initially prompt you to select objects. In most modify commands, the prompt allows you to select any number of objects. In some of the modify commands, however, AutoCAD limits your selection to only one object, for instance, the BREAK, PEDIT, DIVIDE, and MEASURE commands. In the case of the FILLET and CHAMFER commands, AutoCAD requires you to select two objects. And, whereas in the DIST and ID commands AutoCAD requires you to select a point, in the AREA command AutoCAD permits selection of either a series of points or an object.

Compared to the basic object selection option, the options covered in this section give you more flexibility and greater ease of use when you are prompted to select objects for use by the modify commands. The options that are explained in this section include Wpolygon (WP), Cpolygon (CP), Fence, All, Multiple, Box, Auto, Undo, Add, Remove, and Single. Additional options are explained in Chapter 2.

WPolygon (WP) Option

The WPolygon option is similar to the Window option, but it allows you to define a polygon-shaped window rather than a rectangular area. You define the selection area as you specify the points about the objects you want to select. The polygon is formed as you select the points. The polygon can be of any shape but may not intersect itself. The polygon is formed as you specify points and includes rubber-band lines to the graphics cursor. When the selected points define the desired polygon, press [Enter]. Only those objects that are totally inside the polygon shape are selected. To select the WPolygon option, type **WP** and press [Enter] at the "Select Objects:" prompt. The Undo option lets you undo the most recent polygon pick point.

CPolygon (CP) Option

The CPolygon option is similar to the WPolygon option, but it selects all objects within or crossing the polygon boundary. If there is an object that is partially inside the polygon area, then the whole object is included in the selection set. To select the CPolygon option, type **CP** and press ⏎ at the "Select Objects" prompt.

Fence (F) Option

The Fence option is similar to the CPolygon option, except you do not close the last vector of the polygon shape. The selection fence selects only those objects it crosses or intersects. Unlike the WPolygons and CPolygons, the fence can cross over and intersect itself. To select the Fence option type **F** and press ⏎ at the "Select Objects:" prompt.

All Option

The All option selects all the objects in the drawing, including objects on frozen or locked layers. After selecting all the objects, you may use the Remove (R) option to remove some of the objects from the selection set. The All options must be spelled out in full (ALL) and not applied as an abbreviation as you may do with the other options.

Multiple Option

The Multiple option helps you overcome the limitations of the Point, Window, and Crossing options. The Point option is time-consuming for use in selecting many objects. AutoCAD does a complete scan of the screen each time a point is picked. By using the Multiple modifier option, you can pick many points without delay and when you press ⏎, AutoCAD applies all of the points during one scan.

Selecting one or more objects from a crowded group of objects is sometimes difficult with the Point option. It is often impossible with the Window option. For example, if two objects are very close together and you wish to point to select them both, AutoCAD normally selects only one no matter how many times you select a point that touches them both. By using the Multiple option, AutoCAD excludes an object from being selected once it has been included in the selection set. As an alternative, use the Crossing option to cover both objects. If this is not feasible, then the Multiple modifier may be the best choice.

Box Option

The Box option is usually employed in a menu macro to give the user a double option of Window and Crossing, depending on how and where the picks are made on the screen. It must be spelled out in full (BOX) and not applied as an abbreviation as you may do with the others e.g., W for Window. Because of this, you normally would not go to the trouble to use the Box option from the keyboard when a single key (W or C) provides a decidedly faster selection.

When the Box modifier is invoked as a response to a prompt to select an object, the options are applied as follows:

If the picks are made left to right (the first point is to the left of the second), then the two points become diagonally opposite corners of a rectangle that is used as a Window option. That is, all visible objects totally within the rectangle are part of that selection.

If the picks are right to left, then the selection rectangle becomes the Crossing option. That is, all visible objects that are within or partially within the rectangle are part of that selection.

Auto Option

The Auto option is actually a triple option. It includes the Point option with the two Box options. If the target box touches an object, then that object is selected as you would in using the Point option. If the target box does not touch an object, then the selection becomes either a Window or Crossing option, depending on where the second point is picked in relation to the first.

> **NOTE:** The Auto option is the default option when you are prompted to "Select Objects:".

Undo Option

The Undo option allows you to remove the last item(s) selected from the selection set without aborting the "Select Objects:" prompt and then to continue adding to the selection set. It should be noted that if the last option to the selection process includes more than one object, the Undo option will remove all the objects from the selection set that were selected by that last option.

Add Option

The Add option lets you switch back from the Remove mode in order to continue adding objects to the selection set by whatever and however many options you wish to use.

Remove Option

The Remove option lets you remove objects from the selection set. The "Select Objects:" prompt always starts in the Add mode. The Remove mode is a switch from the Add mode, not a standard option. Once invoked, the objects selected by whatever and however many options you use will be removed from the selection set. It will be in effect until reversed by the Add option.

Single Option

The Single option causes the object selection to terminate and the command in progress to proceed after you use only one object selection option. It does not matter if one object is selected or a group is selected with that option. If no object is selected and the point selected cannot be the first point of a Window or Crossing rectangle, AutoCAD will not abort the command in progress; however, once there is a successful selection, the command proceeds.

OBJECT SELECTION MODES

AutoCAD provides six selection modes that will enhance object selection. You can toggle on/off one or more object selection modes from the Object Selection Settings dialog box. By having the appropriate selection mode set to ON, you have various methods that give you more flexibility and greater ease of use in the selection of the objects.

To open the Object Selection Settings dialog box, invoke the DDSELECT command from:

Pull-down menu	Tools > Selection...
Command: prompt	**ddselect** Enter

AutoCAD displays the Object Selection Settings dialog box as shown in Figure 5–9.

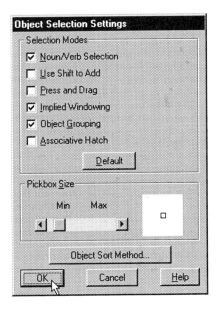

Figure 5–9 Object Selection Settings dialog box

You can toggle any one or more combinations of the settings provided under the selection modes or reset the settings to the original defaults by selecting the **Default** button. Noun/Verb Selection, Implied Windowing, and Object Grouping are the defaults.

Noun/Verb Selection

The Noun/Verb Selection feature allows the traditional verb-noun command syntax to be reversed for most modifying commands. When the Noun/Verb Selection is set to ON, you can select the objects first at the "Command:" prompt and then invoke the appropriate modifying command you want to use on the selection set. For example, instead of invoking the COPY command followed by selecting the objects to be copied, with Noun/Verb Selection set to ON, you can select the objects first and then invoke the COPY command, and AutoCAD skips the object selection prompt.

When Noun/Verb Selection is set to ON, the cursor at the "Command:" prompt changes to resemble a running-Osnap cursor. Whenever you want to use the Noun/Verb selection feature, first create a selection set at the "Command:" prompt. Subsequent modify commands you invoke execute using the objects in the current selection set without prompting for object selection. To clear the current selection set, press [Esc] at the "Command:" prompt. This clears the selection set, so any subsequent editing command will once again prompt for object selection.

> **NOTE:** Another way to set Noun/Verb Selection is to use the PICKFIRST system variable. TRIM, EXTEND, BREAK, CHAMFER, and FILLET are the commands not supported by the Noun/Verb selection feature.

Use Shift to Add

The Use Shift to Add feature controls how you add objects to an existing selection set. When Use Shift to Add is set to ON, it activates an additive selection mode in which the [Shift] key must be held down while adding more objects to the selection set. For example, if you first pick an object, it is highlighted. If you pick another object, it is highlighted and the first object is no longer highlighted. The only way you can add objects to the selection set is to select objects by holding down the [Shift] key. Similarly, the way to remove objects from the selection set is to select the objects by holding down the [Shift] key.

When Use Shift to Add is set to OFF (default), objects are added to the selection set by just picking them individually or by using one of the selection options; AutoCAD adds the objects to the selection set.

> **NOTE:** Another way to select objects with this method is to set the PICKADD system variable appropriately.

Press and Drag

The Press and Drag feature controls the manner by which you draw the selection window with your pointing device. When Press and Drag is set to ON, you can create a selection window by holding down the pick button and dragging the cursor diagonally while you create the window.

When Press and Drag is set to OFF (default), you need to use two separate picks of the pointing device to create the selection window. In other words, pick once to define one corner of the selection window, and pick a second time to define its diagonal corner.

> **NOTE:** Another way to control how selection windows are drawn is to set the PICKDRAG system variable appropriately.

Implied Windowing

The Implied Windowing feature allows you automatically to create a selection window when the "Select objects:" prompt appears. When Implied Windowing is set to ON (default), it works like the Box option explained earlier. If Implied Windowing is set to OFF, you can create a selection window by using the Window or Crossing selection set methods.

> **NOTE:** Another way to control the Implied Windowing option is to set the PICKAUTO system variable appropriately.

Object Grouping

The Object Grouping feature controls the automatic group selection. If Object Grouping is set to ON, then selecting an object that is a member of a group selects the whole group. Refer to Chapter 6 for a detailed description of how to create groups.

Associative Hatch

The Associative Hatch feature controls which objects will be selected when you select an associative hatch. If Associative Hatch is set to ON, then selecting an associative hatch also selects the boundary objects. Refer to Chapter 9 for a detailed description of hatching.

Fundamentals IV

In addition, you can adjust the size of the pickbox using the slider bar provided in the dialog box. Also, you can set the sorting of objects for processing in the order in which they were created in the drawing.

MODIFY COMMANDS

In this section, nine modify commands are described: LENGTHEN, STRETCH, CHANGE, CHPROP, MATCH PROPERTIES, MODIFY, ROTATE, SCALE, and PEDIT. Additional modify commands were explained in Chapters 2 and 3.

Lengthening Objects

The LENGTHEN command is used to increase or decrease the length of line objects or the included angle of an arc.

Invoke the LENGTHEN command from:

Modify toolbar	Select the Lengthen command (see Figure 5–10)
Pull-down menu	Modify > Lengthen
Command: prompt	lengthen [Enter]

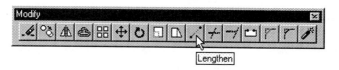

Figure 5–10 Invoking the Lengthen command from the Modify toolbar

AutoCAD prompts:

Command: **lengthen** [Enter]
DElta/Percent/Total/DYnamic/<Select object>: *(select an object or select one of the available options)*

When you select an object, AutoCAD displays its length in the current units display and, where applicable, the included angle of the selected object.

Delta Option The Delta option changes the length or, where applicable, the included angle from the endpoint of the selected object closest to the pick point. A positive value results in an increase in extension; a negative value results in a trim. When you select the Delta option, AutoCAD prompts:

Angle/<Enter delta length (current)>: *(specify positive or negative value)*
<Select object to change>/Undo: *(select an object, and its length is changed on the end nearest the selection point)*

<Select object to change>/Undo: *(select additional objects; when done,
    press* Enter *to exit the command sequence)*

Instead of specifying the delta length, if you select the Angle option, AutoCAD prompts:

Enter delta angle <current>: *(specify positive or negative angle)*
<Select object to change>/Undo: *(select an object, and its included angle is
    changed on the end nearest the selection point)*
<Select object to change>/Undo: *(select additional objects; when done,
    press* Enter *to exit the command sequence)*

The Undo option reverses the most recent change made by the LENGTHEN command.

Percent Option The Percent option sets the length of an object by a specified percentage of its total length. It will increase the length/angle for values greater than 100 and decrease them for values less than 100. For example, a 12-unit-long line will be changed to 15 units by using a value of 125. A 12-unit-long line will be changed to 9 units by using a value of 75. When you select the Percent option, AutoCAD prompts:

Enter percent length (current)>: *(specify positive nonzero value and press* Enter *)*
<Select object to change>/Undo: *(select an object, and its length is
    changed on the end nearest the selection point)*
<Select object to change>/Undo: *(select additional objects; when done,
    press* Enter *to exit the command sequence)*

Total Option The Total option changes the length/angle of an object to the value specified. When you select the Total option, AutoCAD prompts:

Angle/<Enter total length (current)>: *(specify distance, or enter A, for
    angle, and then specify an angle for change)*

The options and prompts are similar to those for the Delta option.

Dynamic Option The Dynamic option changes the length/angle of an object in response to the cursor's final location relative to the endpoint nearest to where the object is selected. When you select the Dynamic option, AutoCAD prompts:

<Select object to change>/Undo: *(select an object to change the endpoint)*
<Select object to change>/Undo: *(reposition the object if necessary, or press
    Enter to exit the command sequence).*

The options and prompts are similar to those for the Delta option.

Stretching Objects

The STRETCH command allows you to stretch the shape of an object without affecting other crucial parts that remain unchanged. A common example is to stretch a square into a rectangle. The length is changed while the width remains the same.

AutoCAD stretches lines, polyline segments, rays, arcs, elliptical arcs, and splines that cross the selection window. The STRETCH command moves the endpoints that lie inside the window, leaving those outside the window unchanged. If the entire object is inside the window, then the STRETCH command operates like the MOVE command.

Invoke the STRETCH command from:

Modify toolbar	Select the Stretch command (see Figure 5–11)
Pull-down menu	Modify > Stretch
Command: prompt	stretch Enter

Figure 5–11 Invoking the Stretch command from the Modify toolbar

AutoCAD prompts:

Command: **stretch** Enter
Select objects: *(select the objects for stretching by crossing window or crossing polygon, and press* Enter *to terminate object selection)*
Base point or displacement: *(specify a base point or press* Enter *)*
Second point of displacement: *(specify the second point of displacement or press* Enter *)*

If you provide the base point and second point of displacement, AutoCAD stretches the selected objects the vector distance from the base point to the second point. If you press Enter at the prompt for the second point of displacement, then AutoCAD considers the first point as the X,Y displacement value.

Figure 5–12 shows some examples of using the STRETCH command.

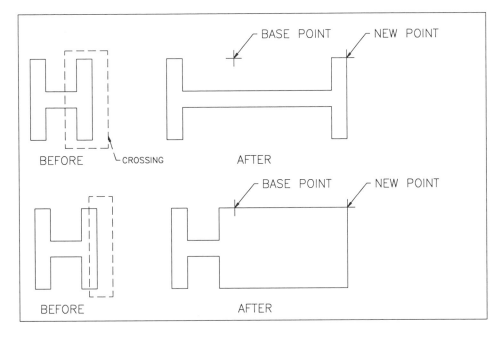

Figure 5-12 Examples of using the STRETCH command

Rotating Objects

The ROTATE command changes the orientation of existing objects by rotating them about a specified point, labeled as the base point. Design changes often require that an object, feature, or view be rotated. By default, a positive angle rotates the object in the counterclockwise direction, and a negative angle rotates in the clockwise direction.

Invoke the ROTATE command from:

Modify toolbar	Select the Rotate command (see Figure 5–13)
Pull-down menu	Modify > Rotate
Command: prompt	**rotate** Enter

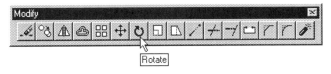

Figure 5-13 Invoking the Rotate command from the Modify toolbar

AutoCAD prompts:

> Command: **rotate** Enter
> Select objects: (*select the objects to rotate and press* Enter *to complete the selection*)
> Base point: (*specify a base point about which selected objects are to be rotated*)
> <Rotation angle>/Reference: (*specify a positive or negative rotation angle, or enter **r** to select the Reference option*)

The base point can be anywhere in the drawing. If the base point selected is on the selected object itself, then the selected base point becomes an anchor point for rotation. The Rotation Angle determines how far an object rotates around the base point.

The following command sequence shows an example of rotating a group of objects selected by the Window option, as shown in Figure 5–14.

> Command: **rotate** Enter
> Select objects: (*select the objects to rotate as shown in Figure 5–14 and press* Enter *to complete the selection*)
> Base point: (*pick the base point as shown in Figure 5–14*)
> <Rotation angle>/Reference: **45** Enter

AutoCAD rotates the selected objects by 45 degrees, as shown in Figure 5–14.

Reference Angle Option If an object has to be rotated in reference to the current orientation, you can use the Reference option to do that. Specify the current orientation as reference the angle, or show AutoCAD the angle by pointing to the two endpoints of a line to be rotated, and specify the desired new rotation. AutoCAD

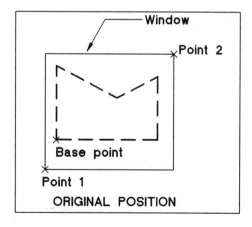
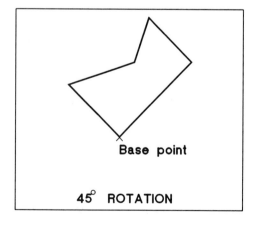

Figure 5–14 Rotating a group of objects by means of the ROTATE command

automatically calculates the rotation angle and rotates the object appropriately. This method of rotation is very useful when you want to straighten an object or align it with other features in a drawing.

The following command sequence shows an example of rotating a group of objects selected by the Window option in reference to the current orientation, as shown in Figure 5–15.

> Command: **rotate** `Enter`
> Select objects: *(select the objects to rotate, as shown in Figure 5–15)*
> Base point: *(pick the base point, as shown in Figure 5–15)*
> <Rotation angle>/Reference: **R** `Enter`
> Reference angle: **60** `Enter`
> New angle: **30** `Enter`

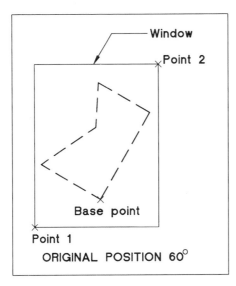

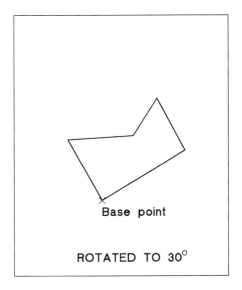

Figure 5–15 Rotating a group of objects by means of the ROTATE command in reference to the current orientation

Scaling Objects

The SCALE command lets you change the size of selected objects or the complete drawing. Objects are made larger or smaller; the same scale factor is applied to the X, Y, and Z directions. To enlarge an object, specify a scale factor greater than 1. For example, a scale factor of 3 makes the selected objects 3 times larger. To reduce the size of an object, use a scale factor between 0 and 1. Do not specify a negative scale factor. For example, a scale factor of 0.75 would reduce the selected objects to three-quarters of their current size.

Invoke the SCALE command from:

Modify toolbar	Select the Scale command (see Figure 5–16)
Pull-down menu	Modify > Scale
Command: prompt	scale Enter

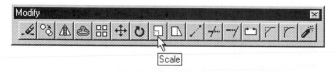

Figure 5–16 Invoking the Scale command from the Modify toolbar

AutoCAD prompts:

Command: **scale** Enter
Select objects: *(select the objects to scale and press* Enter *to complete the selection)*
Base point: *(specify a base point about which selected objects are to be scaled)*
<Scale factor>/Reference: *(specify a scale factor, or enter* **r** *to select the Reference option)*

The base point can be anywhere in the drawing. If the base point selected is on the selected object itself, then the selected base point becomes an anchor point for scaling. The scale factor multiplies the dimensions of the selected objects by the specified scale.

The following command sequence shows an example of enlarging a group of objects by a scale factor of 3, as shown in Figure 5–17.

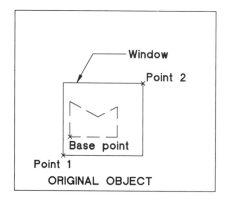
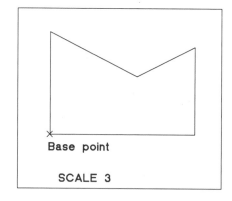

Figure 5–17 Enlarging a group of objects by means of the SCALE command

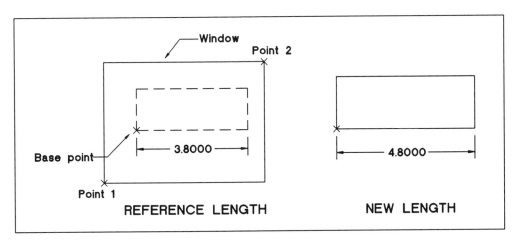

Figure 5-18 Enlarging a group of objects by means of the SCALE command in reference to the current dimension

> Command: **scale** `Enter`
> Select objects: *(select the objects to enlarge, as shown in Figure 5-17, and press `Enter` to complete the selection)*
> Base point: *(pick the base point, as shown in Figure 5-17)*
> <Scale factor>/Reference: **3** `Enter`

AutoCAD enlarges the selected objects by a factor of 3, as shown in Figure 5-17.

Reference Scale Option You can use the Reference option to scale objects relative to the current dimension. Specify the current dimension as a reference length, or select two endpoints of a line to be scaled, and specify the desired new length. AutoCAD will automatically calculate the scale factor and enlarge or shrink the object appropriately.

The following command sequence shows an example of using the SCALE command to enlarge a group of objects selected by means of the Window option in reference to the current dimension, as shown in Figure 5-18.

> Command: **scale** `Enter`
> Select objects: *(select the objects to enlarge, as shown in Figure 5-18)*
> Base point: *(pick the base point, as shown in Figure 5-18)*
> <Scale Factor>/Reference: **R** `Enter`
> Reference length: **3.8** `Enter`
> New length: **4.8** `Enter`

Modifying Polylines

The PEDIT command allows you to modify polylines. In addition to using such modify commands as MOVE, COPY, BREAK, TRIM, and EXTEND, you can use the

PEDIT command to modify polylines. The PEDIT command has special editing features for dealing with the unique properties of polylines and is perhaps the most complex AutoCAD command, with several multioption submenus totaling some 70 command options.

Invoke the PEDIT command from:

Modify II toolbar	Select the Edit Polyline command (see Figure 5–19)
Pull-down menu	Modify > Object > Polyline
Command: prompt	**pedit** Enter

Figure 5–19 Invoking the Edit Polyline command from the Modify II toolbar

AutoCAD prompts:

Command: **pedit** Enter
Select polyline: *(select polyline, line, or arc)*

If you select a line or an arc instead of a polyline, you are prompted as follows:

Object selected is not a polyline.
Do you want it to turn into one? <Y>

Responding **Y** or pressing Enter turns the selected line or arc into a single-segment polyline that can then be edited. Normally this is done in order to use the Join option to add other connected segments that, if not polylines, will also be transformed into polylines. It should be emphasized at this time that in order to join segments together into a polyline, their endpoints must coincide. This occurs during line-line, line-arc, arc-line, and arc-arc continuation operations or by using endpoint Object Snap mode.

The second prompt does not appear if the first segment selected is already a polyline. It may even be a multisegment polyline. After the object selection process, you will be returned to the multioption prompt as follows:

Close/Join/Width/Edit vertex/Fit/Spline/Decurve/Ltype gen/Undo/eXit
<x>: *(select one of the available options)*

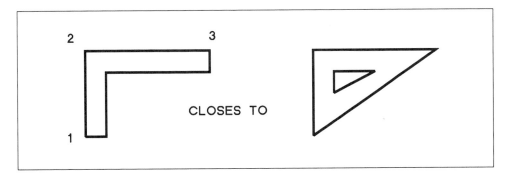

Figure 5–20 Using the PEDIT command Close option with polylines

Figure 5–21 Using the PEDIT command Close option with polyacrs

Close Option The Close option performs in a manner similar to the Close option of the LINE command. If, however, the last segment was a polyline arc, then the next segment will be similar to the arc-arc continuation, using the direction of the last polyarc as the starting direction and drawing another polyarc, with the first point of the first segment as the ending point of the closing polyarc.

Figures 5–20 and 5–21 show some examples of the application of the Close option.

Open Option The Open option deletes the segment that was drawn with the Close option. If the polyline had been closed by drawing the last segment to the first point of the first segment without using the Close option, then the Open option will not have a visible effect.

Join Option The Join option takes selected lines, arcs, and/or polylines and combines them with a previously selected polyline into a single polyline if all segments are connected at sequential and coincidental endpoints.

Width Option The Width option permits uniform or varying widths to be specified for polyline segments.

Edit Vertex Option A *vertex* is the point where two segments join. When you select the Edit Vertex option, the visible vertices are marked with an X to indicate which one is to be modified. You can modify vertices of polylines in several ways. When you select the Edit vertex option, AutoCAD prompts you with additional suboptions:

Command: **pedit** Enter
Select polyline: *(select a polyline)*
Close/Join/Width/Edit vertex/Fit curve/Spline curve/Decurve/Undo/
    eXit<X>: **e** Enter
Next/Previous/Break/Insert/Move/Regen/Straighten/Tangent/Width/eXit
    <N>:

Next and Previous: Whether or not you have modified the marked vertex, when you wish to move the mark to the next or previous vertex, you can use the N (Next) or P (Previous) option.

Break: The Break option establishes the marked vertex as one vertex for the Break option and then prompts:

Next/Previous/Go/eXit <N>:

The choices of the Break option permit you to step to another vertex for the second break point, or to initialize the break, or to exit the option. If two vertices are selected, you may use the Go option to have the segment(s) between the vertices removed. If you select the endpoints of a polyline, this option will not work. If you select the Go option immediately after the Break option, the polyline will be divided into two separate polylines. Or, if it is a closed polyline, it will be opened at that point.

Insert: The Insert option allows you to specify a point and have the segment between the marked vertex and the next vertex become two segments meeting at the specified point. The selected point does not have to be on the polyline segment.

For example, the following command sequence shows the application of the Insert option as shown in Figure 5–22.

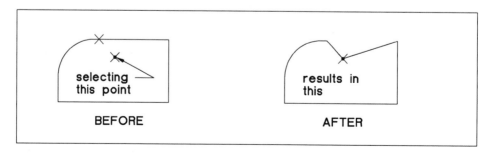

Figure 5–22 Using the PEDIT command Insert option

Command: **pedit** Enter
Select polyline: *(select the polyline as shown in Figure 5–22)*
Close/Join/Width/Edit vertex/Fit curve/Spline curve/Decurve/
   Undo/eXit<X>: **e** Enter
Next/Previous/Break/Insert/Move/Regen/Straighten/Tangent/
   Width/eXit <N>: **i** Enter
Enter location of new vertex: *(select a new vertex)*

Move: The Move option allows you to specify a point and have the marked vertex be relocated to the selected point.

For example, the following command sequence shows the application of the Move option as shown in Figure 5–23.

Command: **pedit** Enter
Select polyline: *(select the polyline as shown in Figure 5–23)*
Close/Join/Width/Edit vertex/Fit curve/Spline curve/Decurve/
   Undo/eXit<X>: **e** Enter
Next/Previous/Break/Insert/Move/Regen/Straighten/Tangent/
Width/eXit<N>: **m** Enter
Enter new location: *(specify the new location)*

Regen: The Regen option regenerates the polyline without having to cancel the PEDIT command to invoke the REGEN command at the "Command:" prompt.

Straighten: The Straighten option establishes the marked vertex as one vertex for the Straighten option and then prompts:

Next/Previous/Go/eXit <N>:

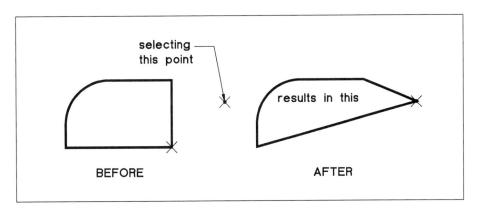

Figure 5–23 Using the PEDIT command Move option

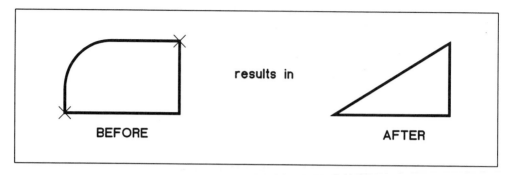

Figure 5–24 Using the PEDIT command Straighten option

These choices of the Straighten option permit you either to step first to another vertex for the second point or to exit the option. When the two vertices are selected, you may use the Go option to have the segment(s) between the vertices replaced with a single straight-line segment.

For example, the following command sequence shows the application of the Straighten option as shown in Figure 5–24.

> Command: **pedit** Enter
> Select polyline: *(select the polyline as shown in Figure 5–24)*
> Close/Join/Width/Edit vertex/Fit curve/Spline curve/Decurve/
> Undo/   eXit <X>: **e** Enter
> Next/Previous/Break/Insert/Move/Regen/Straighten/Tangent/
>   Width/eXit <N>: **s** Enter
> Next/Previous/Go/eXit <N>: **n** Enter
> Next/Previous/Go/eXit <N>: **n** Enter
> Next/Previous/Go/eXit <N>: **x** Enter

Tangent: The Tangent option permits you to assign to the marked vertex a tangent direction that can be used for the curve fitting option. The prompt is as follows:

> Direction of tangent:

You can either specify the direction with a point or type in the coordinates at the keyboard.

Width: The Width option permits you to specify the starting and ending widths of the segment between the marked vertex and the next vertex. The prompt is as follows:

> Enter new width for all segments <current>:

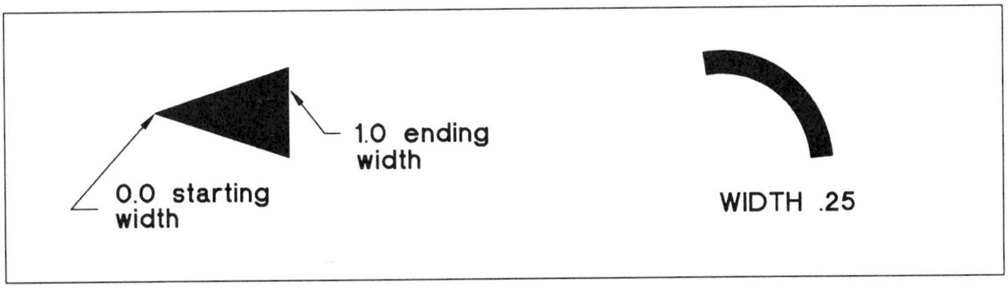

Figure 5–25 Using the PEDIT command Width option

For example, the following command sequence shows the application of the Width option as shown in Figure 5–25.

Command: **pedit** Enter
Select polyline: *(select a polyline)*
Close/Join/Width/Edit vertex/Fit curve/Spline curve/Decurve/
Undo/   eXit <X>: **e** Enter
Next/Previous/Break/Insert/Move/Regen/Straighten/Tangent/
     Width/eXit <N>: **w** Enter
Enter new width for segments<default>: **0.25** Enter

eXit: The eXit option exits from the Vertex editing option and returns to the PEDIT multioption prompt.

Fit Curve Option   The Fit Curve option draws a smooth curve through the vertices, using any specified tangents.

Spline Curve Option The Spline Curve option provides several ways to draw a curve based on the polyline being edited. These include Quadratic B-spline and Cubic B-spline curves.

Decurve Option The Decurve option returns the polyline to the way it was drawn originally.

See Figure 5–26 for differences between fit curve, spline, and decurve.

Undo Option The Undo option reverses the latest PEDIT operation.

eXit Option The eXit option exits the PEDIT command.

Changing Properties of Objects

The DDCHPROP command allows you to change properties of objects, such as color, layer, linetype, and thickness, by using a dialog box.

Invoke the DDCHPROP command from:

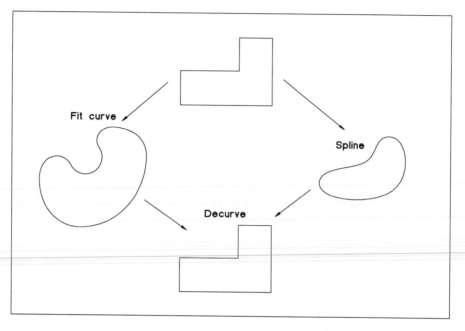

Figure 5-26 Comparing PEDIT command Fit Curve, Spline Curve, and Decurve options

Command: prompt	**ddchprop** Enter

AutoCAD prompts:

Command: **ddchprop** Enter
Select objects: *(select objects and press* Enter *to complete the selection)*

AutoCAD displays the Change Properties dialog box, as shown in Figure 5-27. Make the necessary changes in the dialog box by choosing the appropriate buttons for Color, Layer, and Linetype. If necessary you can also change the Linetype Scale and Thickness. Choose the OK button to accept the changes and close the Change Properties dialog box.

Similar to the DDCHPROP command, the DDMODIFY command can change properties of a selected object. In addition to changing properties, you can also modify the characteristics of line, circle, ellipse, arc, polyline, spline, solid, multiline, xline, ray, point, text, hatch, block insertion, attribute definition, external reference, shape, text, viewport, and dimension. Depending on the object selected, AutoCAD displays the appropriate dialog box. You can select only one object at a time.

Invoke the DDMODIFY command from:

Command: prompt	**ddmodify** Enter

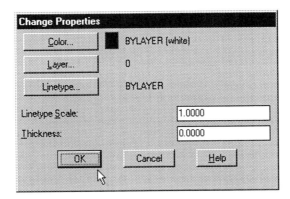

Figure 5–27 Change Properties dialog box

AutoCAD prompts:

> Command: **ddmodify** ⏎
> Select one object to modify: *(select an object to modify)*

AutoCAD displays the appropriate dialog box. Make the necessary changes, and choose the OK button to accept the modifications.

Every DDMODIFY dialog box has a Properties section, as shown in Figure 5–28. It permits you to control the selected object's color, layer, linetype, linetype scale, and thickness.

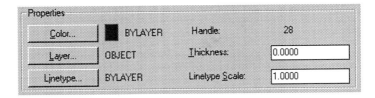

Figure 5–28 Properties section of the Modify dialog box

The **Color...** button displays the Select Color dialog box, from which you can change the color of the selected object.

The **Layer...** button causes the Select Layer dialog box to be displayed. The desired layer may be selected from the list box or by entering its name in the Set Layer Name: edit box for the selected object.

The **Linetype...** button displays the Select Linetype dialog box, from which you can select the linetype for the selected object.

The **Handle:** field displays the selected object's handle. However, it cannot be changed from this dialog box.

The **Thickness:** edit field displays the current thickness of the selected object. If necessary, you can change the value by typing in the new value in the Thickness: edit field.

The **Linetype Scale:** edit field displays the current linetype scale factor of the selected object. If necessary, you can change the value by typing in the new value in the Linetype Scale: edit field.

Following are the salient features of the various dialog boxes that are displayed by AutoCAD for the type of objects selected.

Modify Line When you select a line, AutoCAD displays the Modify Line dialog box, as shown in Figure 5–29.

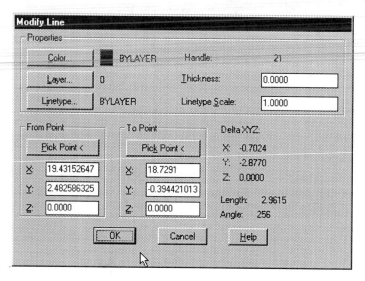

Figure 5–29 Modify Line dialog box

The **From Point** and **To Point** sections of the dialog box allow you to change the starting and ending points of the selected line object, respectively.

The **Delta XYZ:** section displays the change in *X,Y,* and *Z* coordinate distances between the starting point and the ending point of the selected line. The **Length:** and **Angle:** sections display the length of the line and the angle of the line, respectively, of the selected line object.

Modify Polyline When you select a 2D polyline, 3D polyline, or 3D polygon mesh, AutoCAD displays the Modify Polyline dialog box, as shown in Figure 5–30.

The **Polyline Type:** field displays the type of polyline selected. AutoCAD displays the coordinates of the first vertex in the **Vertex Listing** section of the dialog box. The **Next** button allows you to cycle through the vertices. The **Fit/Smooth** section permit you to select the type of line or surface curve fitting.

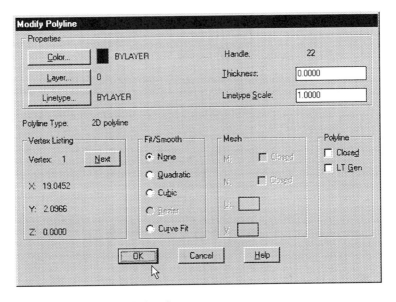

Figure 5-30 Modify Polyline dialog box

The **Mesh** section of the dialog box is enabled when a 3D polygon mesh is selected. Selection of M Closed/N Closed opens or closes the mesh in the M/N directions, respectively. The U/V edit fields permit you to control the accuracy of the surface approximation.

The **Polyline** section is enabled when a 2D or 3D polyline is selected. Closed selection permits you to open or close the polyline. LT Gen selection permits you to control the manner in which linetype patterns are assigned to the selected 2D polyline.

Modify Circle When you select a circle, AutoCAD displays the Modify Circle dialog box, as shown in Figure 5-31.

The **Center** section of the dialog box allows you to change the location of the center of the selected circle object. The **Radius:** edit field permits you to change the radius of the selected circle. The **Diameter:, Circumference:,** and **Area:** fields display the selected circle object's diameter, radius, and area, respectively.

Modify Arc When you select an arc, AutoCAD displays the Modify Arc dialog box, as shown in Figure 5-32.

The **Center** section of the dialog box allows you to change the location of the center of the selected arc object. The **Radius:** edit field permits you to change the radius of the selected arc. The **Start Angle:** and **End Angle:** edit fields permit you to change the start angle and end angle of the selected arc, respectively. The **Total Angle:** and **Arc Length:** fields display the selected arc object's total angle and arc length, respectively.

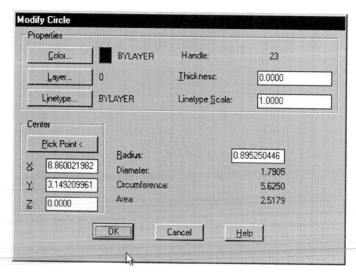

Figure 5-31 Modify Circle dialog box

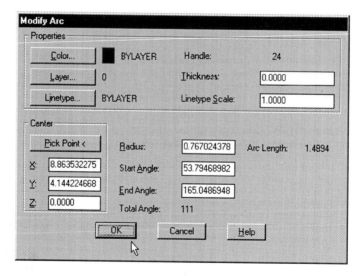

Figure 5-32 Modify Arc dialog box

Modify Ellipse When you select an ellipse, AutoCAD displays the Modify Ellipse dialog box, as shown in Figure 5-33.

The **Center** section of the dialog box allows you to change the location of the center of the selected ellipse object. The **Major Radius:** and **Minor Radius:** edit fields permit you to change the major and minor radii of the selected ellipse, respectively. The **Start Angle:** and **End Angle:** edit fields permit you to change the start angle

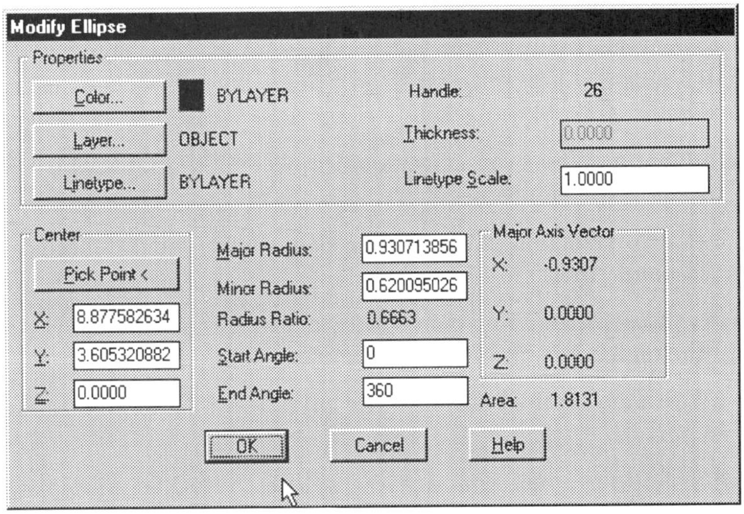

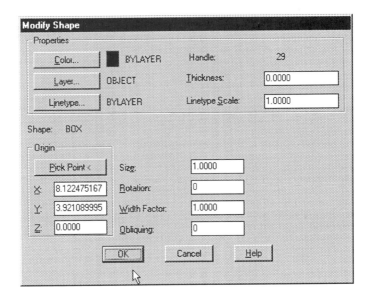

Figure 5–33 Modify Ellipse dialog box

and end angle of the selected ellipse. The **Radius Ratio:** and **Area:** fields display the radius ratio and area of the selected ellipse object, respectively. The **Major Axis Vector** displays the major axis direction of the selected ellipse object.

Modify Shape When you select a shape, AutoCAD displays the Modify Shape dialog box, as shown in Figure 5–34.

Figure 5–34 Modify Shape dialog box

The **Shape:** field displays the name of the selected shape. The **Origin** section of the dialog box allows you to change the shape's insertion point. The **Size:**, **Rotation:**, **Width Factor:**, and **Obliquing:** edit fields permit you to specify the size, rotation, width factor, and obliquing angle of the selected shape, respectively.

Modify Point When you select a point, AutoCAD displays the Modify Point dialog box, as shown in Figure 5-35.

The **Location** section of the dialog box allows you to change the location of the selected point object.

Modify Multiline When you select a multiline, AutoCAD displays the Modify Multiline dialog box, as shown in Figure 5-36.

The **MLine Style:** field displays the current multiline's style. You can change only the properties.

Modify Spline When you select a spline, AutoCAD displays the Modify Spline dialog box, as shown in Figure 5-37.

The **Control Points** section of the dialog box displays the information about the control points of the selected spline object. The **Next** button allows you to cycle through the vertices. The **Degree:** and **Properties:** fields display the degree and data point information of the spline, respectively. The **Data Points** section of the dialog box displays the information about the data points of the selected spline object. The **Next** button allows you to cycle through the vertices.

Modify Trace When you select a trace, AutoCAD displays the Modify Trace dialog box, as shown in Figure 5-38.

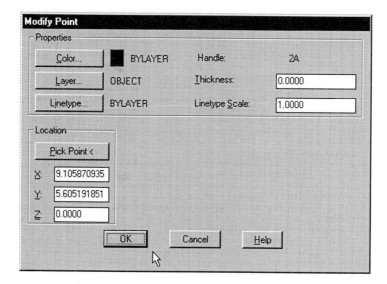

Figure 5-35 Modify Point dialog box

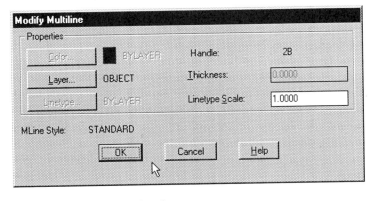

Figure 5–36 Modify Multiline dialog box

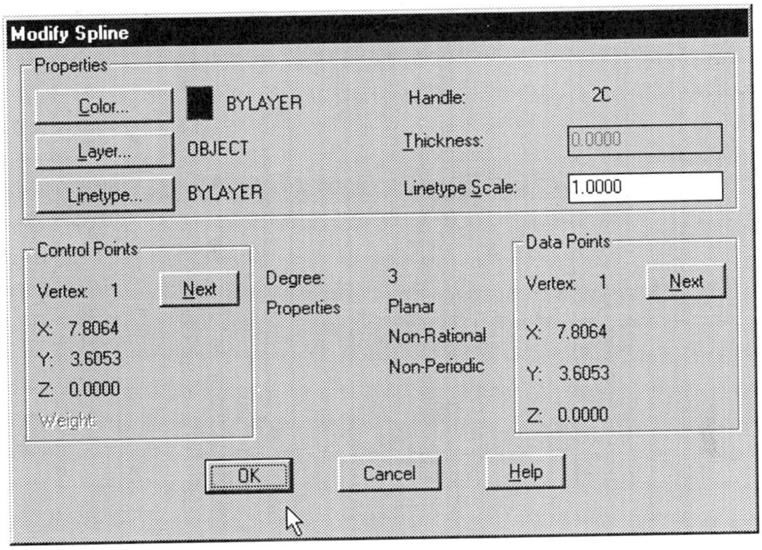

Figure 5–37 Modify Spline dialog box

The **Point 1, Point 2, Point 3,** and **Point 4** sections of the dialog box permit you to change the location of any of the four corner points by selecting a point on the screen or by entering its coordinates.

Modify Solid When you select a solid, AutoCAD displays the Modify Solid dialog box, as shown in Figure 5–39.

The **Point 1, Point 2, Point 3,** and **Point 4** sections of the dialog box permits you to change the location of any of the four corner points by selecting a point on the screen or by entering its coordinates.

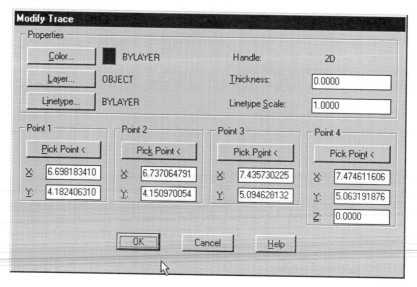

Figure 5–38 Modify Trace dialog box

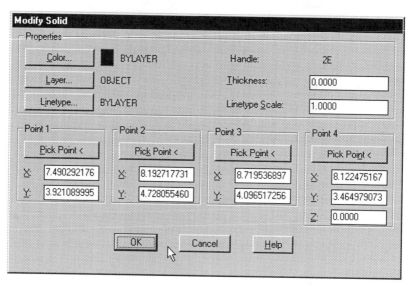

Figure 5–39 Modify Solid dialog box

Modify Ray When you select a ray, AutoCAD displays the Modify Ray dialog box, as shown in Figure 5–40.

The **Start Point** and **Second Point** sections of the dialog box allow you to change the starting point and the second point of the selected ray object, respectively.

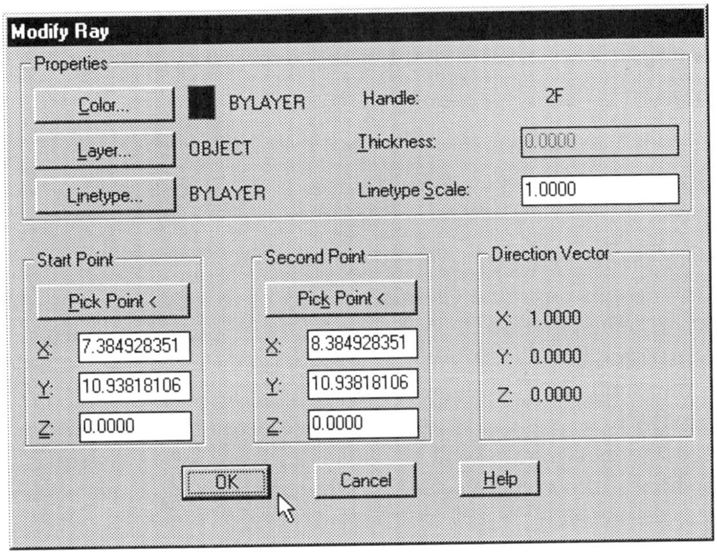

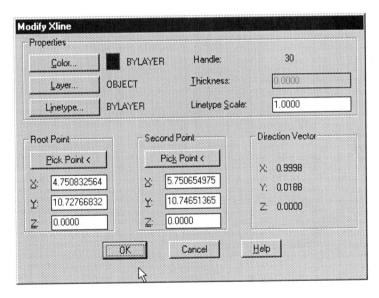

Figure 5-40 Modify Ray dialog box

Figure 5-41 Modify Xline dialog box

The **Direction Vector** section displays the change in *X*, *Y*, and *Z* coordinate values between the starting point and the ending point of the selected ray.

Modify Xline When you select an xline, AutoCAD displays the Modify Xline dialog box, as shown in Figure 5-41.

The **Root Point** and **Second Point** sections of the dialog box allow you to change the root point and second point of the selected xline object, respectively.

The **Direction Vector** section displays the change in X, Y, and Z coordinate values between the starting point and the ending point of the selected ray.

Modify Text When you select text, AutoCAD displays the Modify Text dialog box, as shown in Figure 5–42.

The **Text:** edit field displays the selected text; if necessary you can edit the characters in the edit box. The **Origin** section of the dialog box allows you to change the insertion point of the selected text. The **Height:**, **Rotation:**, **Width Factor:**, and **Obliquing:** edit fields permit you to change the height, rotation, width factor, and obliquing angle of the selected text, respectively. The **Justify:** list box allows you to change the existing justification of the selected text. The **Style:** list box allows you to change the existing style of the selected text. The **Upside Down** and **Backward** check boxes allow you to specify whether text is typed upside down and/or backwards, respectively.

Modify MText When you select paragraph or leader text, AutoCAD displays the Modify MText dialog box, as shown in Figure 5–43.

The **Contents:** section of the dialog box displays the selected paragraph text. The **Insertion Point** section of the dialog box allows you to change the insertion point of the selected paragraph text. The **Full editor...** button causes the Edit MText dialog box to be displayed. For a detailed explanation of the Edit MText dialog box, see the section on MTEXT.

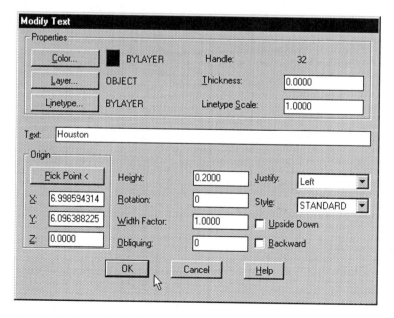

Figure 5–42 Modify Text dialog box

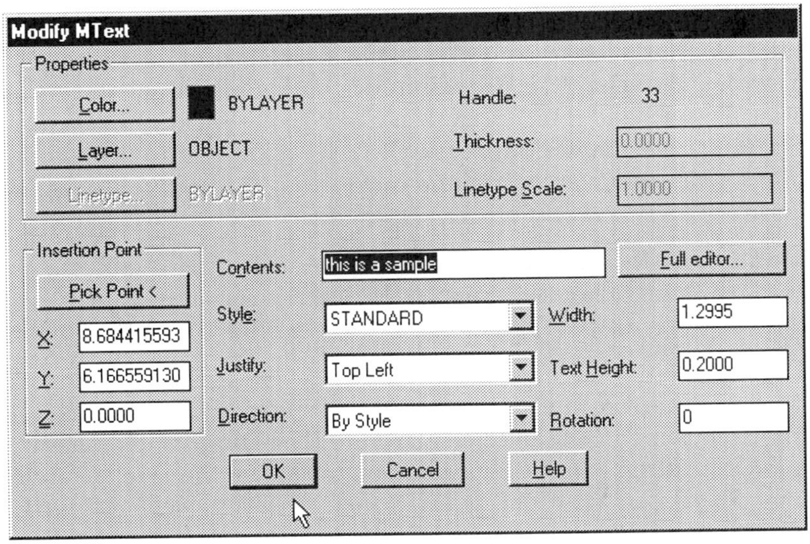

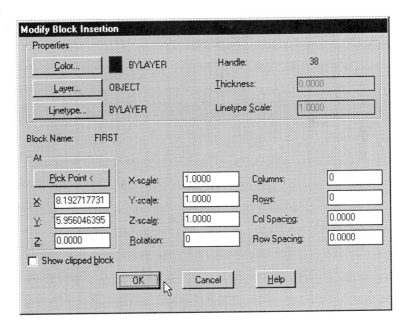

Figure 5–43 Modify MText dialog box

Figure 5–44 Modify Block Insertion dialog box

Modify Block Insertion When you select a block, AutoCAD displays the Modify Block Insertion dialog box, as shown in Figure 5–44.

The **Block Name:** field displays the name of the selected block. The **At** section of the dialog box allows you to change the insertion of the selected block. The **X-scale:**, **Y-scale:**, **Z-scale:**, and **Rotation:** edit fields allow you to change the X scale, Y scale, Z scale, and rotation angle of the selected block. The **Columns:**, **Rows:**, **Col Spacing:**, and **Row Spacing:** edit fields allow you to change the number of columns, rows, column spacing, and row spacing, respectively, when using a rectangular array-inserted set of blocks.

Modify Attribute Definition When you select an attribute, AutoCAD displays the Modify Attribute Definition dialog box, as shown in Figure 5–45.

The **Tag:** edit field permits you to change the attribute tag. The **Prompt:** and **Default:** edit fields permit you to change the prompt and default value, respectively, for the selected attribute. The **Origin** section allows you to change the insertion point for the selected attribute. The **Height:**, **Rotation:**, **Width Factor:**, and **Obliquing:** edit fields permit you to change the height, rotation, width factor, and obliquing angle of the selected text, respectively. The **Justify:** list box allows you to change the existing justification of the attribute text. The **Style:** list box allows you to change the existing style of the selected attribute text. In addition, the Modify Attribute Definition dialog box allows you to change the settings of the attribute modes. See Chapter 10 for a detailed explanation of blocks and attributes.

Modify Hatch When you select an associative hatch, AutoCAD displays the Modify Hatch dialog box, as shown in Figure 5–46.

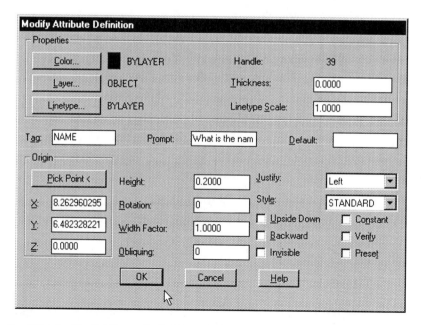

Figure 5–45 Modify Attribute Definition dialog box

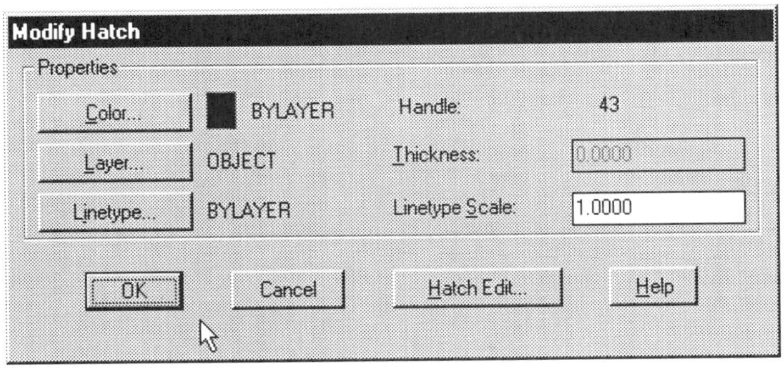

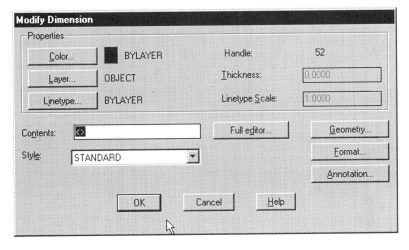

Figure 5–46 Modify Hatch dialog box

Figure 5–47 Modify Dimension dialog box

The **Hatch Edit...** button causes the Hatch Edit dialog box to be displayed. For a detailed explanation of the Hatch Edit dialog box, refer to Chapter 9.

Modify Dimension When you select a dimension or geometric tolerance, AutoCAD displays the Modify Dimension dialog box, as shown in Figure 5–47.

The **Contents...** edit field permits you to edit the dimension text. The **Style:** list box permits you to specify the dimension text style for the selected dimension. The **Geometry...** button displays the Geometry subdialog box. For a detailed explanation of the Geometry subdialog box, refer to Chapter 7. The **Format...** button displays the Format subdialog box. For a detailed explanation of the Format subdialog box, refer to Chapter 7. The **Annotation...** button displays the Annotation subdialog box. For a detailed explanation of the Annotation subdialog box, refer to Chapter 7.

Modify Leader When you select a leader, AutoCAD displays the Modify Leader dialog box, as shown in Figure 5–48.

The **Edit...** button causes the Edit MText dialog box to be displayed, permitting you to edit the leader text. The **Style:** list box permits you to specify the dimension text style for the selected leader. The **Geometry...**, **Format...**, and **Annotation...** buttons operate as just described in the previous section on Modify Direction. The **Type** section permits you to specify the leader type. The **Arrow** check box permits you to control whether or not an arrow is placed at the beginning of the leader.

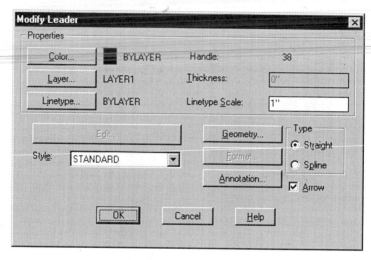

Figure 5–48 Modify Leader dialog box

Modify External Reference When you select an external reference (xref), AutoCAD displays the Modify External Reference dialog box, as shown in Figure 5–49.

The **Xref Name:** and **Path:** fields display the xref name and path, respectively. The **At** section of the dialog box allows you to change the insertion of the selected external reference. The **X-scale:**, **Y-scale:**, **Z-scale:**, and **Rotation:** edit fields allow you to change the X scale, Y scale, Z scale, and rotation angle of the selected external reference. The **Columns:**, **Rows:**, **Col Spacing:**, and **Row Spacing:** edit fields allow you to change the number of columns, number of rows, column spacing, and row spacing, respectively, when using a rectangular array of the selected xref.

Modify Region When you select a region, AutoCAD displays the Modify Region dialog box, as shown in Figure 5–50.

AutoCAD allows you to modify only the Properties of the selected region.

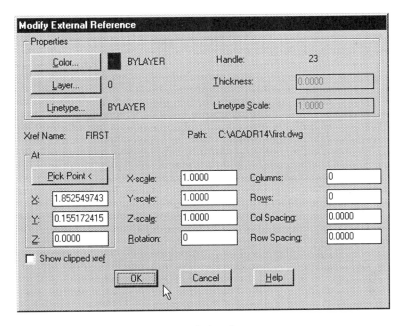

Figure 5–49 Modify External Reference dialog box

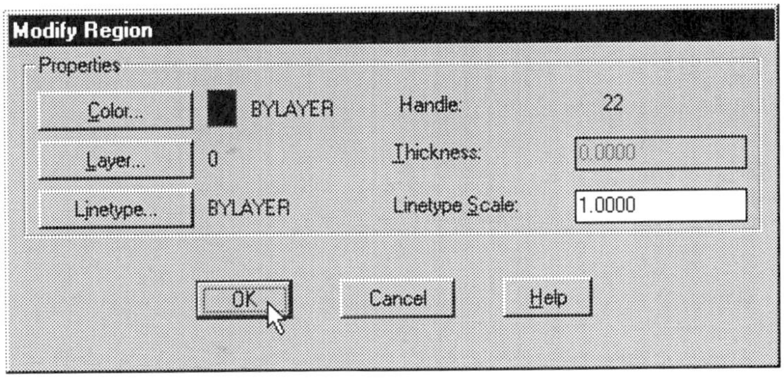

Figure 5–50 Modify Region dialog box

Modify 3D Solid When you select a 3D solid, AutoCAD displays the Modify 3DSolid dialog box, as shown in Figure 5–51.

AutoCAD allows you to modify only the Properties of the selected 3DSolid.

Modify 3D Face When you select a 3D face, AutoCAD displays the Modify 3D Face dialog box, as shown in Figure 5–52.

The **Point 1, Point 2, Point 3,** and **Point 4** sections of the dialog box permit you to change the location of any of the four vertices by selecting a point on the screen or by

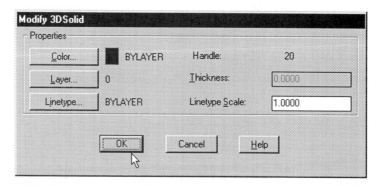

Figure 5–51 Modify 3DSolid dialog box

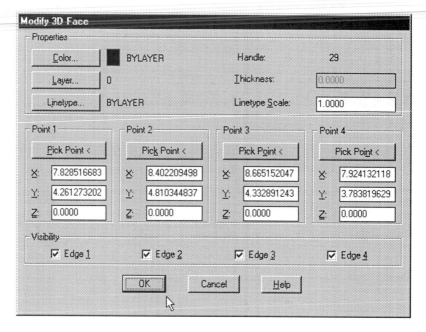

Figure 5–52 Modify 3D Face dialog box

entering its coordinates. The **Edge 1, Edge 2, Edge 3,** and **Edge 4** check boxes allow you to control the visibility of the four edges. If the SPLFRAME system variable is set to 1 (On), all edges are visible, regardless of the visibility setting.

The AutoCAD AI_PROPCHK command allows you to modify objects in a manner similar to the DDCHPROP and DDMODIFY commands. With the AI_PROPCHK command, if you select only one object, it will work like the DDMODIFY command; if you select more than one object, it will work like the DDCHPROP command.

Invoke the AI_PROPCHK command from:

Object Properties toolbar	Select the Properties command (see Figure 5–53)
Pull-down menu	Modify > Properties
Command: prompt	**ai_propchk** [Enter]

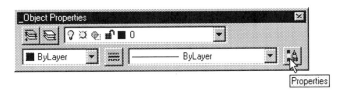

Figure 5–53 Invoking the Properties command from the Object Properties toolbar

AutoCAD prompts:

Command: **ai_propchk** [Enter]
Select objects: *(select the object(s) to modify and press* [Enter] *to terminate object selection)*

Depending on the number of objects selected and the type of object selected, AutoCAD displays the appropriate dialog box.

Matching Properties

The MATCHPROP command allows you to copy selected properties from one object to one or more other objects.

Invoke the MATCHPROP command from:

Standard toolbar	Select the Match Properties command (see Figure 5–54)
Pull-down menu	Modify > Match Properties
Command: prompt	**matchprop or painter** [Enter]

Figure 5–54 Invoking the Match Properties command from the Standard toolbar

AutoCAD prompts:

> Command: **matchprop** [Enter]
> Select Source Object: *(select the object whose properties you want to copy)*
> Settings/<Select Destination Object(s)>: *(select the destination objects and press [Enter] to terminate the selection, or press s to select the Settings option to display the Property Settings)*

Selection of the Settings option displays the Property Settings dialog box, similar to Figure 5–55. Use the Settings option to control which object properties are copied. By default, all object properties in the Property Settings dialog box are set to ON for copying. When the toggle button is set to ON, AutoCAD changes the settings of the destination object to that of the source object.

Choose the OK button to close the Property Settings dialog box. AutoCAD continues with the "Select Destination Object(s):" prompt. Press [Enter] to complete the object selection.

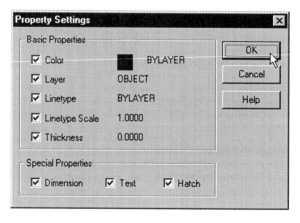

Figure 5–55 Property Settings dialog box

PROJECT EXERCISE

This project exercise provides point-by-point instructions for setting up the drawing with layers and then creating the objects shown in the accompanying figure.

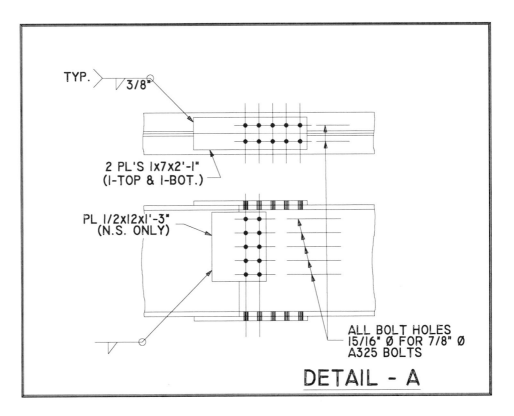

Figure P5-1 Completed project drawing (but with dimensions added for reference)

In this project you will:

- Set up the drawing, including Limits and Layers.
- Use the SKETCH, SOLID, and DONUT commands to create objects.
- Use the COPY command to create objects from other objects.
- Use the ROTATE, STRETCH, and CHPROP commands to modify objects.
- Use the TEXT or DTEXT command to create text objects.

Set Up the Drawing and Draw a Border

Step 1   Start the AutoCAD program.

Step 2   To create a new drawing, invoke the NEW command from the Standard toolbar or select New from the pull-down menu File.

AutoCAD displays the Create New Drawing dialog box. Click the "Use a Wizard" button, then select the Quick Setup, and choose the OK button to close the dialog box.

AutoCAD displays the Quick Setup dialog box with the display of the Step:1 Units tab. Select the Architectural radio button and choose the Next>> button.

AutoCAD displays the Quick Setup dialog box with the display of the Step 2: Area tab. Under the Width: edit field enter **9'**, and Under the Length edit field enter **7'**. Choose the Done button to close the Quick Setup dialog box.

Step 3   Invoke the LAYER command from the Object Properties toolbar, or select Layer... from the pull-down menu Format. AutoCAD displays the Layer & Linetype Properties dialog box.

Create six layers, and rename them as shown in the following table, assigning appropriate color and linetype.

Layer Name	Color	Linetype
Border	Red	Continuous
Object	White	Continuous
Solid-Donut	White	Continuous
Center	Red	Center
Hidden	Magenta	Hidden
Const	Blue	Continuous

Set Border as the current layer, and close the Layer & Linetype Properties dialog box.

Creating Objects

Step 4   Make the Border layer current, and draw the border using a Polyline, with a width of 0.5" from 0'-2",0-2" to 0'-2",6'-10" to 8'-10",6'-10" to 8'-10",0'-2", and then close back to 0'-2",0-2".

Step 5   Make the Object layer current and draw the bottom plate using the RECTANG command from 3'-4",1'-6" to 5'-5",1'-7". Your drawing should look like Figure P5–2.

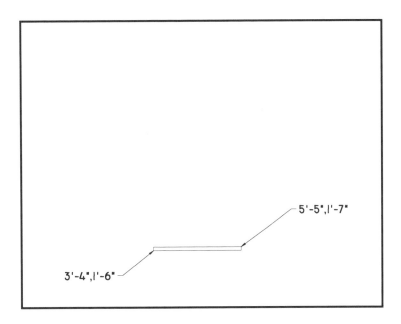

Figure P5–2 Bottom plate

Step 6   Copy the rectangle twice, with displacements of 0'-0",2'-1" and 0'-0",3'-1".
See Figure P5–3.

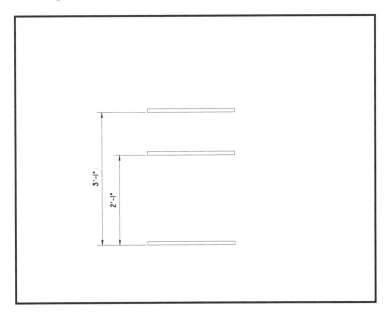

Figure P5–3 Setting of the base

Step 7 Stretch the top rectangle with a displacement of 0",6" to change it from a 2'-1" x 1" rectangle to a 2'-1" x 7" rectangle. See Figures P5–4 and P5–5.

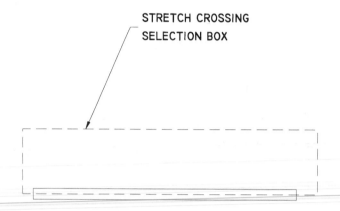

STRETCH CROSSING
SELECTION BOX

Figure P5–4 Display with the stretch crossing

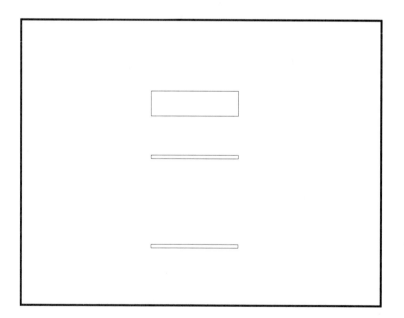

Figure P5–5 Result after stretching the top rectangle

Step 8 Draw a horizontal line through the top of the bottom rectangle, and then copy it five times up 1", up 1'-11", up 2'-0", up 2'-11" and up 3'-8". Your drawing should look like Figure P5–6.

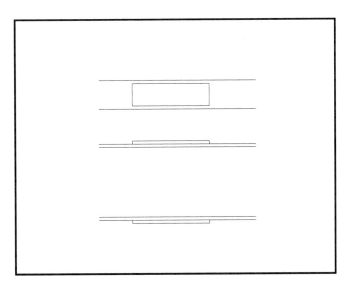

Figure P5–6 Basic Layout

Step 9 Use the SKETCH command to create the end "breaks" of the top and side views of the beam. Your drawing should look like Figure P5–7.

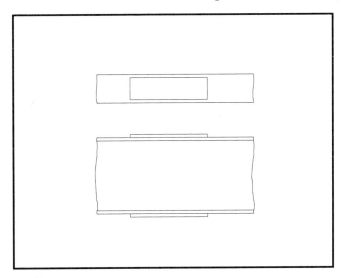

Figure P5–7 Drawing with sketch lines

Step 10 While the Object layer is still current, draw the added lines shown in Figure P5–8. Refer to Figure P5–1 for the size of the objects, and use the CHPROP command to change these lines to the Center and Hidden layers where indicated. When this step is completed, your drawing should look like Figure P5–9.

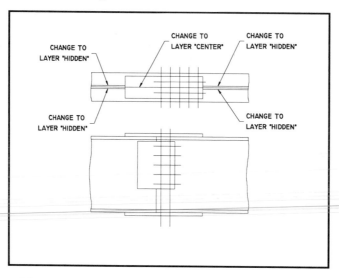

Figure P5–8 Additional objects added to the layout

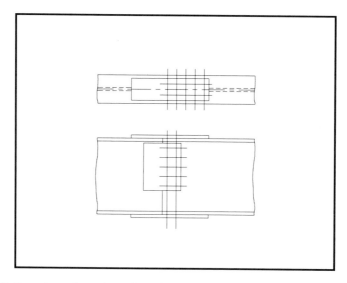

Figure P5–9 Drawing after changing the linetypes

Step 11   Set the Solid-Donut layer as the current layer. Create the solid-filled rectangles with the SOLID command. You can create each one individually, or you can create one and than COPY it to the required locations. Your drawing should then look like Figure P5–10.

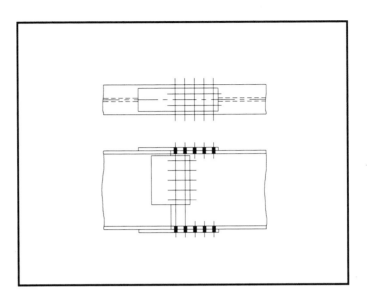

Figure P5–10 Drawing with the solid objects drawn

Step 12 Create the solid-filled circles with the DONUT command. The DONUT command permits you to place multiple created objects after you have specified the inside and outside diameters. These (the donuts) might be more easily created one by one simply by picking their individual insertion points without exiting the DONUT command. Your drawing should now look like Figure P5–11.

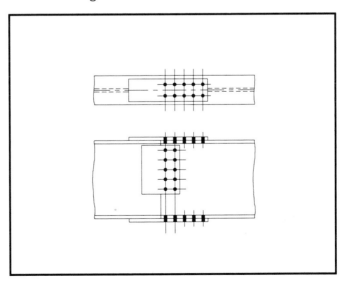

Figure P5–11 Drawing with the donut objects drawn

Step 13 Create the solid filled triangular arrowhead with the SOLID command. Draw the horizontal line and the circle as shown in Figure P5–12. Then use the ROTATE command to rotate the arrowhead, line, and circle by -45°, as shown in Figure P5–13.

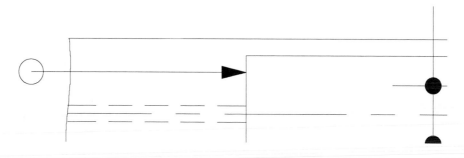

Figure P5–12 Drawing with the solid-filled triangular arrowhead

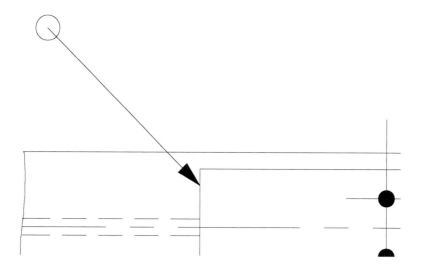

Figure P5–13 Result after rotating the arrowhead -45 degrees

Step 14 Copy and/or draw additional solid triangles, lines, circles, and open triangles as shown in Figure P5–14.

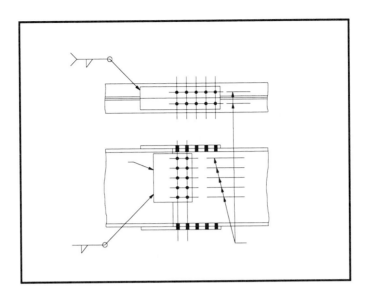

Figure P5–14 Drawing after additional solid triangles have been created

Step 15 Set the Text layer as the current layer. Using the TEXT or DTEXT command, draw the text objects shown in Figure P5–15. Note: You'll have to use the BREAK command to create a gap in the "break" sketch line on the left end of the lower view. This is to leave a clear space for the text objects. FigureP5–15 is the completed drawing.

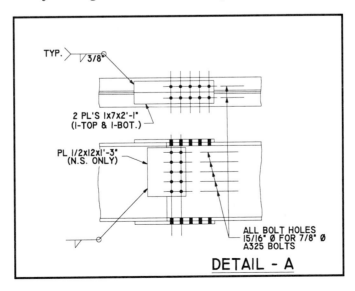

Figure P5–15 Completed drawing

EXERCISES 5–1 THROUGH 5–5

Exercise 5–1

Create the drawing shown according to the settings given in the following table:

Settings	Value		
1. Units	Architectural		
2. Limits	Lower left corner: 0',0'		
	Upper right corner: 9',6'		
3. Grid	4"		
4. Snap	2"		
5. Layers	*NAME*	*COLOR*	*LINETYPE*
	Construction	Cyan	Continuous
	Border	Red	Continous
	Backboard	Green	Continuous
	Rim	Magenta	Hidden
	Text	Blue	Continuous

Hints	
	Make sure to make each layer current before beginning to draw any objects that are on it.
	The border can be drawn from coordinates 3",3" to 8'-9",5'-6" using the RECTANG command.
	Draw a vertical construction line (xline) through a point whose **X** coordinate is 4'-0".
	Offset the verticle xline 2'-3" to each side of the line just created.
	Draw a horizontal construction line (xline) through a point whose **Y** coordinate is 2'-0".
	Offset the horizontal construction line 3" above and below the line just created. Offset the lower line 1'-2½" toward the bottom of the drawing.
	The construction lines just created will guide you in drawing the circles and lines required for completing the outline of the object.
	Using the intersections of the lines and/or circles, draw the sides and sloped bottom lines of the backboard on the Object layer.
	Using the TRIM command, trim the lines and circles to complete the shape.
	After the drawing is finished, either the Construction Layer can be turned OFF or the construction lines can be erased. Do *not* dimension.

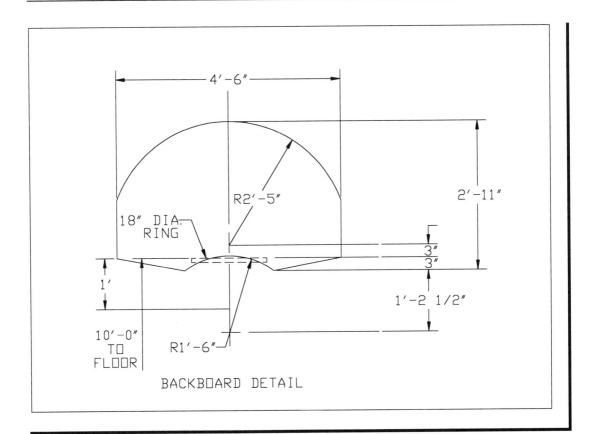

BACKBOARD DETAIL

Exercise 5-2

Create the drawing shown according to the settings given in the following table:

Settings	Value		
1. Units	Architectural		
2. Limits	Lower left corner: 0',0'		
	Upper right corner: 12',9'		
3. Grid	6"		
4. Snap	3"		
5. Layers	*NAME*	*COLOR*	*LINETYPE*
	Construction	Cyan	Continuous
	Border	Red	Continuous
	Object	Green	Continuous
	Center	Magenta	Center
	Text	Blue	Continuous
	Hidden	White	Hidden

Hints	Make sure to make each layer current before beginning to draw any objects that are on it.
	The border can be drawn from coordinates 3",3" to 11'-9",8'-6" using the RECTANG command.
	The front view of the wheel handle can be drawn using the PLINE command. The top of the handle is 8" above the top of the closure plate.
	The circle part of the top view of the wheel handle can be drawn using either the DONUT command or the PLINE command with the arc option, creating two 180-degree polyarcs with a width of 1".

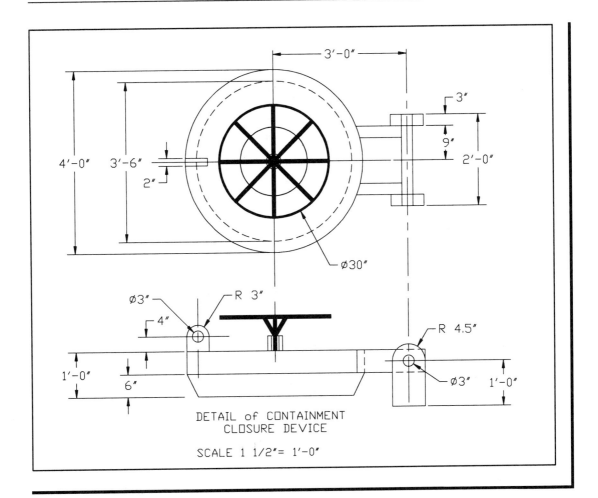

DETAIL of CONTAINMENT
CLOSURE DEVICE

SCALE 1 1/2″= 1′–0″

Exercise 5–3

Create the drawing shown according to the settings given in the following table:

Settings	Value		
1. Units	Architectural		
2. Limits	Lower left corner: 0',0'		
	Upper right corner: 70',50'		
3. Grid	12"		
4. Snap	3"		
5. Layers	*NAME*	*COLOR*	*LINETYPE*
	Construction	Cyan	Continuous
	Border	Red	Continuous
	Object	Green	Continuous
	Center	Magenta	Center
	Text	Blue	Continuous
	Hidden	White	Hidden

Hints	Open the drawing that you created in Exercise 5–2 and save as EX5-3. Change the limits. Resize the border. Erase the front view and centerlines connecting the views. Be sure to make each layer current before beginning to draw any objects that are on it.
	Now you can move the top view of the containment closure device to become the lower left object in the array, and use the ROTATE command to reorient the hinge from the right side to the top (+90°).
	Before using the ARRAY command to create the 11 other closure devices, the hidden-line rectangle can be created and arrayed with the closure device.

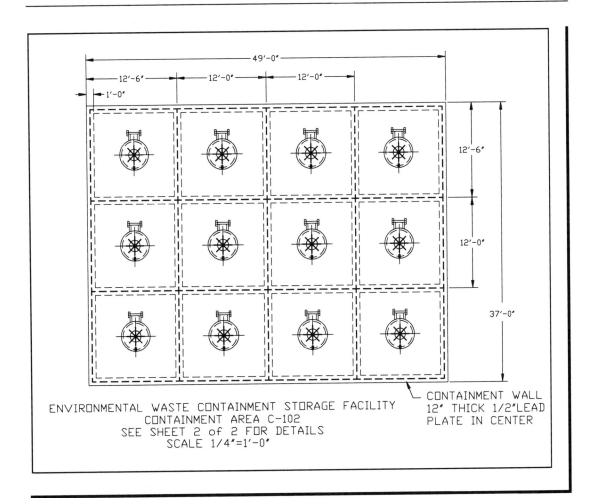

ENVIRONMENTAL WASTE CONTAINMENT STORAGE FACILITY
CONTAINMENT AREA C-102
SEE SHEET 2 of 2 FOR DETAILS
SCALE 1/4″=1′-0″

CONTAINMENT WALL
12″ THICK 1/2″LEAD
PLATE IN CENTER

Exercise 5–4

Create the drawing shown according to the settings given in the following table:

Settings	Value		
1. Units	Architectural		
2. Limits	Lower left corner: 0',0'		
	Upper right corner: 60',45'		
3. Grid	12"		
4. Snap	6"		
5. Layers	*NAME*	*COLOR*	*LINETYPE*
	Construction	Cyan	Continuous
	Border	Red	Continuous
	Object	Green	Continuous
	Text	Blue	Continuous

Hints	
	Be sure to make each layer current before beginning to draw any objects that are on it.
	The border can be drawn from coordinates 2',2' to 58',43' using the RECTANG command.
	The outline of the foundation wall can be drawn with the PLINE command. Then, by using the OFFSET command (set at 6"), create the additional three lines, each one from the previous.
	The Detail of Stair Riser and Sections "A" and "B" can be drawn to true dimensions. Then you can use the SCALE command to enlarge the view of the Detail by a factor of 1.5 and to enlarge the view of the Sections by a factor of 2.0.

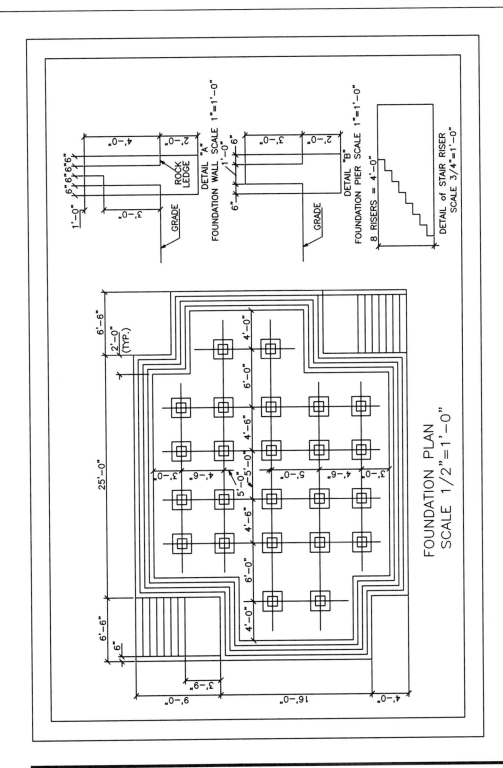

DETAIL "A"
FOUNDATION WALL SCALE 1"=1'–0"

DETAIL "B"
FOUNDATION PIER SCALE 1"=1'–0"

DETAIL of STAIR RISER
SCALE 3/4"=1'–0"

8 RISERS = 4'–0"

ROCK LEDGE

GRADE

GRADE

FOUNDATION PLAN
SCALE 1/2" = 1'–0"

Exercise 5-5

Create the drawing shown according to the settings given in the following table:

Settings	Value		
1. Units	Architectural		
2. Limits	Lower left corner: 0',0'		
	Upper right corner: 60',45'		
3. Grid	12"		
4. Snap	6"		
5. Layers	NAME	COLOR	LINETYPE
	Construction	Cyan	Continuous
	Border	Red	Continuous
	Object	Green	Continuous
	Text	Blue	Continuous

Hints	Open the drawing that you created in Exercise 5–4 and save as EX5-5. Erase the Detail of Stair Riser and Sections "A" and "B."
	Erase the internal double squares and the inside line of the foundation wall in the plan.
	Change the foundation wall lines to be on the Hidden layer.
	The roof lines can be drawn with polylines with a width of 1/2".

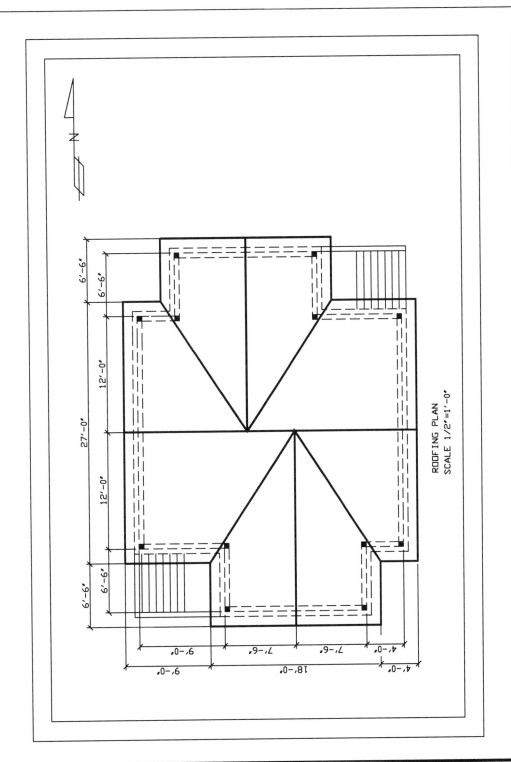

ROOFING PLAN
SCALE 1/2"=1'-0"

REVIEW QUESTIONS

1. The command that allows you to draw freehand lines is:
   a. SKETCH
   b. DRAW
   c. FLINE
   d. FREE

2. To create a six sided area which would select all the objects completely within it, you should respond to the "Select Objects:" prompt with:
   a. WP   c. W
   b. CP   d. C

3. The CHPROP command does not allow you to modify an object's:
   a. linetype
   b. line width
   c. color
   d. layer

4. By default, most selection set prompts default to which option:
   a. All   d. Window
   b. Auto   e. Crossing
   c. Box

5. The multiple option selection sets allows you to:
   a. select multiple objects which lie on top of each other
   b. scans the database only once to find multiple objects
   c. use the window or crossing options
   d. Both A and B
   e. Both B and C

6. In regard to using the SOLID command, which of the following statements is true:
   a. The order of point selection is unimportant
   b. FILL must be turned in order to use the SOLID command
   c. The points must be selected on existing objects
   d. The points must be selected in a clockwise order
   e. none of the above

7. What command is commonly used to create a filled rectangle?
   a. FILL-ON
   b. PLINE
   c. RECTANG
   d. LINE
   e. SOLID

8. To turn a series of line segments into a polyline, one uses which option of the PEDIT command?
   a. Join
   b. Fit curve
   c. Spline
   d. Connect
   e. Line segments cannot be connected.

9. Which command allows you to change the size of an object, where the X and Y scale factors re changed equally?
   a. ROTATE
   b. SALE
   c. SHRINK
   d. MODIFY
   e. MAGNIFY

10. The BOX option for creating selection sets is most useful for:
    a. creating custom functions
    b. creating rectangular selection areas
    c. extending a selection into 3D
    d. Nothing, it is not a valid option

11. Using the SCALE command, what number would you enter to enlarge an object by 50%?
    a. 0.5
    b. 50
    c. 3
    d. 1.5

12. To avoid changing the location of an object when using the scale command:
    a. the reference length should be less than the limits
    b. the scale factor should be less than one
    c. the base point should be on the object
    d. the base point should be at the origin

13. The ROTATE command is used to rotate objects around:
    a. any specified point
    b. the point -1,-1 only
    c. the origin
    d. is only usable in 3D drawings
    e. none of the above

14. The remove option for forming selection sets deletes objects from the drawing in much the same manner as the ERASE command.
    a. True
    b. False

15. Which of the following is not supported by the noun/verb feature?
    a. COPY
    b. MOVE
    c. TRIM
    d. ROTATE
    e. ERASE

16. When noun/verb selection is set to on, you may add objects to the selection set by:
    a. picking the objects
    b. windowing the objects
    c. using {shift} to add
    d. using {ctrl} to add

CHAPTER

6

FUNDAMENTALS V

INTRODUCTION

After completing this chapter, you will be able to:

✓ Construct geometric figures by means of the Multiline (MLINE) and SPLINE
   commands
✓ Modify multilines and splines
✓ Create or modify multiline styles
✓ Draw text in paragraph format, use special text character and symbol options,
   edit text, spell-check, and create or edit an existing text style
✓ Use grips to modify objects, group objects, and filter certain types of objects
   for modification
✓ Use inquiry commands
✓ Change the settings of system variables

MULTILINES

AutoCAD allows you to draw multiple parallel line segment with the MLINE
command. In addition, you can also modify the intersections of two or more multilines
or cut holes with the MLEDIT command. AutoCAD also allows you to create a new
multiline style or edit an existing one with the MLSTYLE command comprised of up
to 16 lines, called elements.

Drawing Multiple Parallel Lines

The MLINE command allows you to draw multiple parallel line segments, similar to polyline segments that have been offset one or more times. Examples of applying the MLINE command are shown in Figure 6–1.

The properties of each element of a multiline are determined by the style that is current when the multiline is drawn. The properties of the multiline that can be determined by the style include whether to display the line at the joints (miters) and ends and whether to close the ends with a variety of half circles, connecting inner and/or outer elements. In addition, the style controls the element properties, such as color, linetype, and offset distance between two paralle lines.

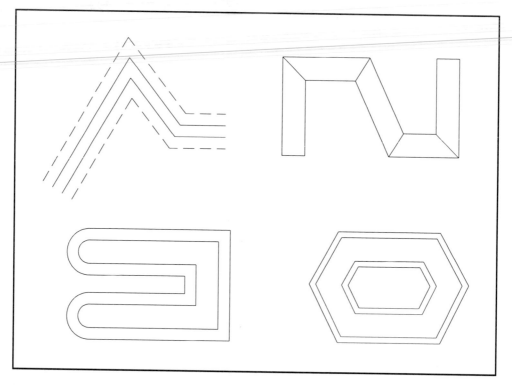

Figure 6–1 Examples of multilines

Invoke the MLINE command from:

Draw toolbar	Select the Multiline command (see Figure 6–2)
Pull-down menu	Draw > Multiline
Command: prompt	mline Enter

Figure 6–2 Invoking the Multiline command from the Draw toolbar

AutoCAD prompts:

> Command: **mline** Enter
> Justification/Scale/STyle/<From point>: *(specify a point or select one of the available options)*

From Point Option The From point option (default) lets you specify the starting point of the multiline, known as its origin. Once you specify the starting point for a multiline, AutoCAD prompts:

> <To point>:

When you respond by selecting a point, the first multiline segment is drawn according to the current style. You are then prompted:

> Undo/<To point>:

If you specify a point, the next segment is drawn, along with segments of all other elements specified by the current style. After two segments have been drawn the prompt will include the Close option:

> Close/Undo/<To point>:

Choosing the Close option causes the next segment to join the starting point of the multiline, fillets all elements, and exits the command.

Selecting Undo (u) after any segment is drawn (and the MLINE command has not been terminated) causes the last segment to be erased, and you are prompted again for a point.

Justification Option The Justification option determines the relationship between the elements of the multiline and the line you specify via the placement of the points. The justification is set by selecting one of the three available suboptions.

> Top/Zero/Bottom <current>:

Top Option The Top option causes the element with the greatest offset value to be drawn on the line of selected points. All other elements will be to the right of the line of points as viewed from the starting point to the ending point of each segment. In other words, if the line is drawn left to right, the line of points (and the element with the greatest offset value) will be on top of (above) all other elements.

Zero Option The Zero option causes the baseline to coincide with the line of selected points. Elements with positive offsets will be to the right of, and those with negative offsets to the left of, the line of selected points as viewed from the starting point to the ending point of the each segment.

Bottom Option The Bottom option causes the element with the least offset value to be drawn on the line of selected points. All other elements will be to the left of the line of points as viewed from the starting point to the ending point of each segment. In other words, if the line is drawn left to right, the line of points (and the element with the least offset value) will be on the bottom of (below) all other elements.

Figure 6–3 shows the location for various justifications.

Scale Option The Scale option determines the value used for offsetting elements when drawing them relative to the values assigned to them in the style. For instance, if the scale is changed to 3.0, elements that are assigned 0.5 and -1.5 will be drawn with offsets of 1.5 and -4.5, respectively. If a negative value is given for the scale, then the signs of the values assigned to them in the style will be changed

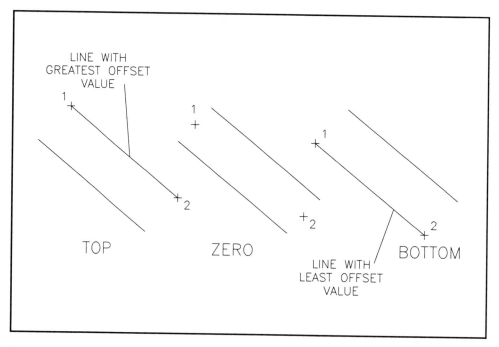

Figure 6–3 Location of various justifications

(positive to negative and negative to positive). The value can be entered in decimal form or as a fraction. A 0 (zero) scale value produces a single line.

STyle Option The Style option sets the current multiline style from the available styles. AutoCAD prompts:

Justification/Scale/STyle/<From point>: **ST** [Enter]
Multiline style name (or ?): *(specify the name of an existing style)*

Detailed explanation is provided later in this chapter for creating or modifying multiline styles.

Editing Multiple Parallel Lines

The MLEDIT command helps you modify the intersections of two or more multilines or cut holes in the lines of one multiline. The tools are available for the type of intersection operated on (cross, tee, or vertex) and if one or more elements needs to be cut or welded.

Invoke the MLEDIT command from:

Modify II toolbar	Select the Edit Multiline command (see Figure 6–4)
Pull-down menu	Modify > Object > Multiline...
Command: prompt	**mline** [Enter]

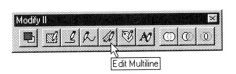

Figure 6–4 Invoking the Edit Multiline command from the Modify II toolbar

AutoCAD displays the Multiline Edit Tools image dialog box, as shown in Figure 6–5.

To select one of the available options, click on one of the image tiles. AutoCAD then prompts for appropriate information.

The first column in the Multiline Edit Tools image dialog box works on multilines that cross, the second works on multilines that form a tee, the third works on corner joints and vertices, and the fourth works on multilines to be cut or welded.

Closed Cross The Closed Cross option cuts all lines that make up the second multiline you select at the point where it crosses the first multiline, as shown in Figure 6–6. Click the Closed Cross image tile, as shown in Figure 6–7, to invoke the Closed Cross option. AutoCAD then prompts:

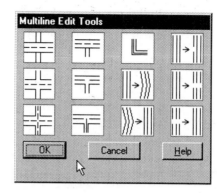

Figure 6-5 Multiline Edit Tools dialog box

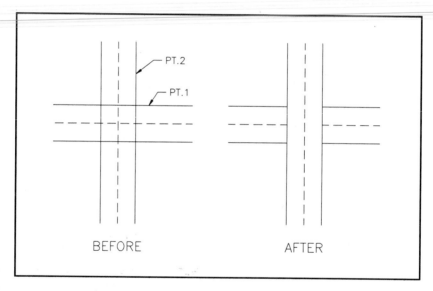

Figure 6-6 An example of a closed cross

Select first mline: *(select the first multiline, as shown in Figure 6-6)*
Select second mline: *(select the second multiline, as shown in Figure 6-6)*

After the closed cross intersection is created, AutoCAD prompts:

Select first mline (or Undo): *(select another multiline, enter **u**, or press ⏎)*

Selecting another multiline repeats the prompt for the second mline. Entering **u** undoes the closed cross just created.

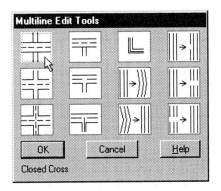

Figure 6–7 Invoking the Closed Cross option from the Multiline Edit Tools image dialog box

Open Cross The Open Cross option cuts all lines that make up the first multiline you select and cuts only the outside line of the second multiline, as shown in Figure 6–8. Click the Open Cross image tile, as shown in Figure 6–9, to invoke the Open Cross option; AutoCAD prompts:

Select first mline: *(select a multiline as shown in Figure 6–8)*
Select second mline: *(select a multiline that intersects the first multiline as shown in Figure 6–8)*

After the open cross intersection is created, AutoCAD prompts:

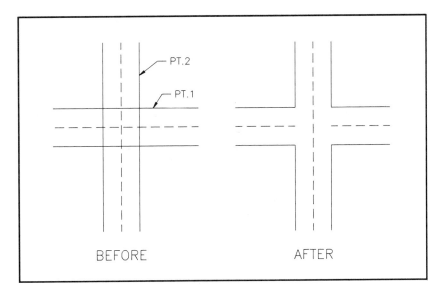

Figure 6–8 An example of an open cross

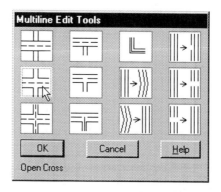

Figure 6–9 Invoking the Open Cross option from the Multiline Edit Tools image dialog box

Select first mline (or Undo): *(select another multiline, enter **u**, or press* Enter *)*

Selecting another multiline repeats the prompt for the second mline. Entering **u** undoes the open cross just created.

Merged Cross The Merged Cross option cuts all lines that make up the intersecting multiline you select except the centerlines, as shown in Figure 6–10. Click the Merged Cross image tile, as shown in Figure 6–11, to invoke the Merged Cross option; AutoCAD prompts:

Select first mline: *(select a multiline, as shown in Figure 6–10)*
Select second mline: *(select a multiline that intersects the first multiline, as shown in Figure 6–10)*

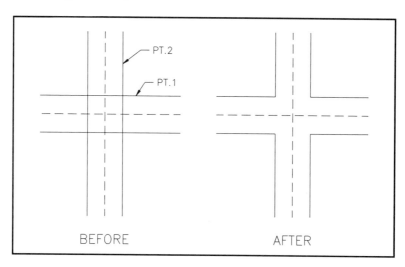

Figure 6–10 An example of a merged cross

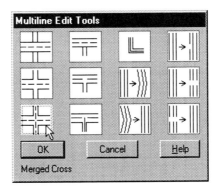

Figure 6–11 Invoking the Merged Cross option from the Multiline Edit Tools image dialog box

After the merged cross intersection is created, AutoCAD prompts:

Select first mline (or Undo): *(select another multiline, enter u, or press [Enter])*

Selecting another multiline repeats the prompt for the second mline. Entering **u** undoes the merged cross just created. The order in which the multilines are selected is not important

Closed Tee The Closed Tee option extends or shortens the first multiline you identify to its intersection with the second multiline, as shown in Figure 6–12. Click the Closed Tee image tile, as shown in Figure 6–13, to invoke the Closed Tee option; AutoCAD prompts:

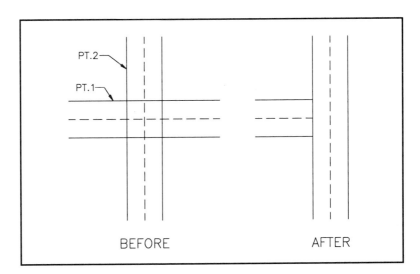

Figure 6–12 An example of a closed tee

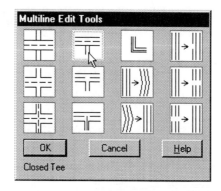

Figure 6–13 Invoking the Closed Tee option from the Multiline Edit Tools image dialog box

> Select first mline: *(select the multiline to trim or extend, as shown in Figure 6–12)*
> Select second mline: *(select the intersecting multiline, as shown in Figure 6–12)*

After the closed tee intersection is created, AutoCAD prompts:

> Select first mline (or Undo): *(select another multiline, enter u, or press* Enter *)*

Selecting another multiline repeats the prompt for the second mline. Entering **u** undoes the closed tee just created.

Open Tee The Open Tee option is similar to the Closed Tee option, except it leaves an open end at intersecting multiline, as shown in Figure 6–14. Click the

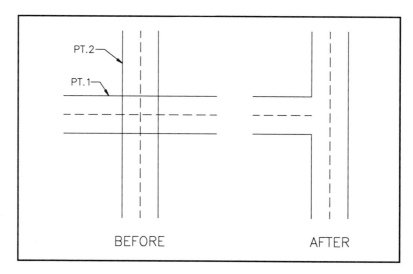

Figure 6–14 An example of an open tee

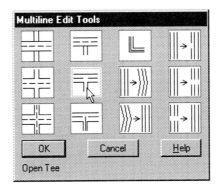

Figure 6–15 Invoking the Open Tee option from the Multiline Edit Tools image dialog box

Open Tee image tile, as shown in Figure 6–15, to invoke the Open Tee option; AutoCAD prompts:

> Select first mline: *(select the multiline to trim or extend, as shown in Figure 6–14)*
> Select second mline: *(select the intersecting multiline, as shown in Figure 6–14)*

After the open tee intersection is created, AutoCAD prompts:

> Select first mline (or Undo): *(select another multiline, enter **u**, or press Enter)*

Selecting another multiline repeats the prompt for the second mline. Entering **u** undoes the open tee just created.

Merged Tee The Merged Tee option is similar to the Open Tee option, except the centerline of the first multiline is extended to the center of the intersecting multiline, as shown in Figure 6–16. Click the Merged Tee image tile, as shown in Figure 6–17, to invoke the Merged Tee option; AutoCAD prompts:

> Select first mline: *(select the multiline to trim or extend, as shown in Figure 6–16)*
> Select second mline: *(select the intersecting multiline, as shown in Figure 6–16)*

After the merged tee intersection is created, AutoCAD prompts:

> Select first mline (or Undo): *(select another multiline, enter **u**, or press Enter)*

Selecting another multiline repeats the prompt for the second mline. Entering **u** undoes the merged tee just created.

Corner Joint The Corner Joint option lengthens or shortens each of the two multilines you select as necessary to create a clean intersection, as shown in Figure 6–18. Click the Corner Joint image tile, as shown in Figure 6–19, to invoke the Corner Joint option; AutoCAD prompts:

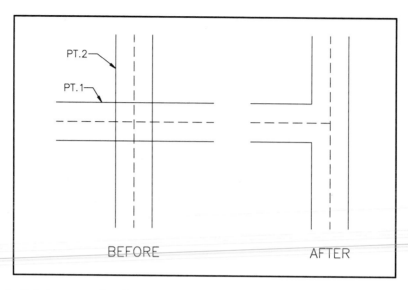

Figure 6-16 An example of a merged tee

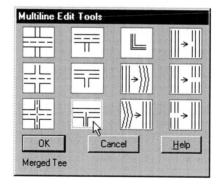

Figure 6-17 Invoking the Merged Tee option from the Multiline Edit Tools image dialog box

Select first mline: *(select the multiline to trim or extend, as shown in Figure 6–18)*
Select second mline: *(select the intersecting multiline, as shown in Figure 6–18)*

After the corner joint intersection is created, AutoCAD prompts:

Select first mline (or Undo): *(select another multiline, enter **u**, or press ⏎)*

Selecting another multiline repeats the prompt for the second mline. Entering **u** undoes the corner joint just created.

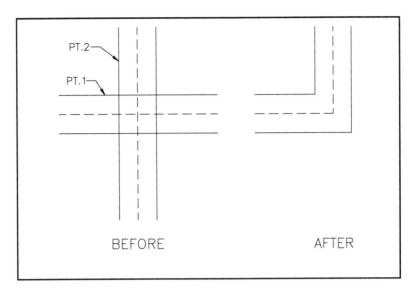

Figure 6–18 An example of a corner joint

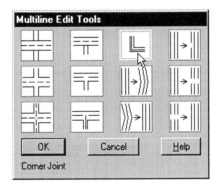

Figure 6–19 Invoking the Corner Joint option from the Multiline Edit Tools image dialog box

Add Vertex The Add Vertex option adds a vertex to a multiline, as shown in Figure 6–20. Click the Add Vertex image tile, as shown in Figure 6–21, to invoke the Add Vertex option; AutoCAD prompts:

Select mline: *(select a multiline to add a vertex, as shown in Figure 6–20)*

AutoCAD adds the vertex at the selected point and prompts:

Select mline (or Undo): *(select another multiline, enter **u**, or press ⏎)*

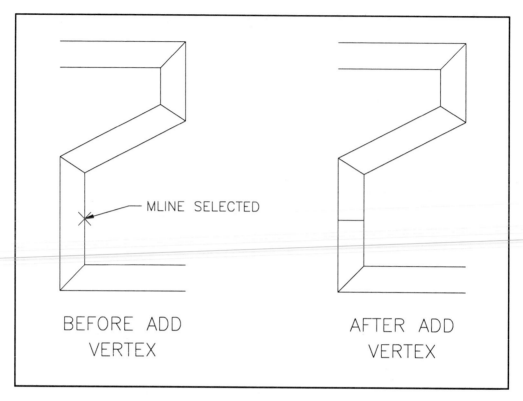

Figure 6-20 An example of adding a vertex

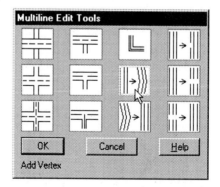

Figure 6-21 Invoking the Add Vertex option from the Multiline Edit Tools image dialog box

Selecting another multiline allows you to add another vertex. Entering **u** undoes the vertex just created.

Delete Vertex The Delete Vertex option deletes a vertex from a multiline, as shown in Figure 6–22. Click the Delete Vertex image tile, as shown in Figure 6–23, to invoke the Delete Vertex option, AutoCAD prompts:

Select mline: *(select a multiline to delete a vertex, as shown in Figure 6–22)*

AutoCAD deletes the vertex at the selected point and prompts:

Select mline (or Undo): *(select another multiline, enter **u**, or press* Enter *)*

Selecting another multiline allows you to delete another vertex. Entering **u** undoes the operation and displays the "Select mline:" prompt.

Cut Single The Cut Single option cuts a selected element of a multiline between two cut points, as shown in Figure 6–24. Click the Cut Single image tile, as shown in Figure 6–25, to invoke the Cut Single option; AutoCAD prompts:

Select mline: *(select a multiline and the selected point becomes the first cut point, as shown in Figure 6–24)*
Select second point: *(select the second cut point on the multiline, as shown in Figure 6–24)*

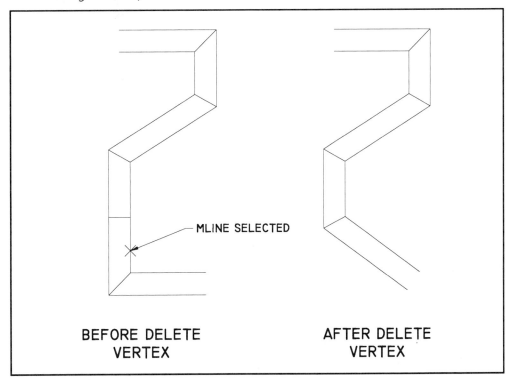

BEFORE DELETE
VERTEX

AFTER DELETE
VERTEX

MLINE SELECTED

Figure 6-22 An example of deleting a vertex

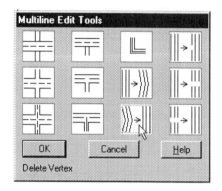

Figure 6-23 Invoking the Delete Vertex option from the Multiline Edit Tools image dialog box

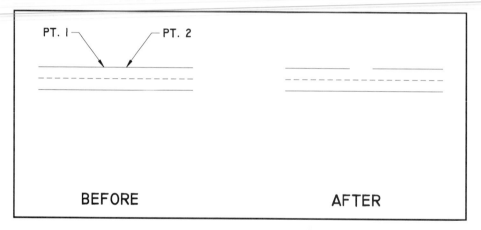

Figure 6-24 An example of removing a selected element of a multiline between two cut points

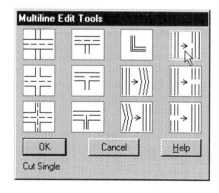

Figure 6-25 Invoking the Cut Single option from the Multiline Edit Tools image dialog box

AutoCAD cuts the multiline and prompts:

> Select mline (or Undo): *(select another multiline, enter **u**, or press* ⌨Enter *)*

Select another multiline to continue, or enter **u** to undo the operation and display the "Select mline:" prompt.

Cut All The Cut All option removes a portion of the multiline you select between two cut points, as shown in Figure 6–26. Click the Cut All image tile, as shown in Figure 6–27, to invoke the Cut All option; AutoCAD prompts:

> Select mline: *(select a multiline and the selected point becomes first cut point, as shown in Figure 6–26)*
> Select second point: *(select the second cut point on the multiline, as shown in Figure 6–26)*

AutoCAD cuts all the elements of the multiline and prompts:

> Select mline (or Undo): *(select another multiline, enter **u**, or press* ⌨Enter *)*

Select another multiline to continue, or enter **u** to undo the operation and display the "Select mline:" prompt.

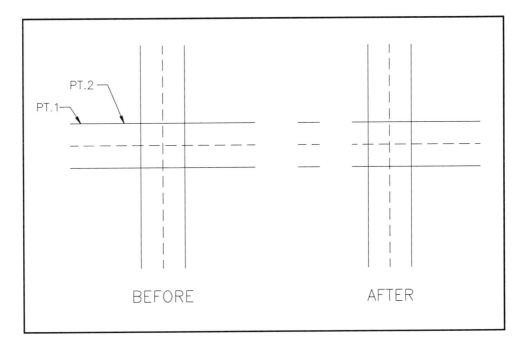

BEFORE   AFTER

Figure 6–26 An example of removing a portion of a multiline between two cut points

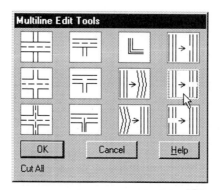

Figure 6–27 Invoking the Cut All option from the Multiline Edit Tools image dialog box

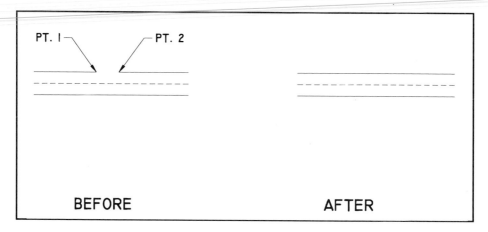

Figure 6–28 An example of rejoining multiline segments that have been cut

Weld All The Weld All option rejoins multiline segments that have been cut, as shown in Figure 6–28. Click the Weld All image tile, as shown in Figure 6–29, to invoke the Weld All option; AutoCAD prompts:

> Select mline: *(select the multiline, as shown in Figure 6–28)*
> Select second point: *(select the endpoint on the multiline to be joined, as shown in Figure 6–28)*

AutoCAD joins the multiline and prompts:

> Select mline (or Undo): *(select another multiline, enter **u**, or press* Enter *)*

Select another multiline to continue, or enter **u** to undo the operation and display the "Select mline:" prompt.

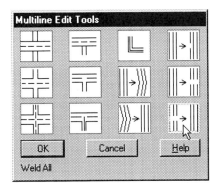

Figure 6–29 Invoking the Weld All option from the Multiline Edit Tools image dialog box

Creating and Modifying Multiline Styles

The MLSTYLE command is used to create a new multiline style or edit an existing one. You can define a multiline style comprised of up to 16 lines, called *elements*. The style controls the number of elements and the properties of each element. In addition you can specify the background color and the end caps of each multiline.

Invoke the MLSTYLE command from:

Pull-down menu	Format > Multiline Style...
Command: prompt	**mlstyle** Enter

AutoCAD displays the Multiline Styles dialog box shown in Figure 6–30.

Current The **Current:** list box allows you to select from the available multiline styles loaded in the current drawing. To make a specific multiline style current, first select the approrpiate multiline style from the list box and then choose OK to close the dialog box. If necessary, you can load additional multiline styles into the current drawing via the Load option.

Name The **Name:** edit field allows you to sepecify a name for a new multiline style or rename an existing one.

To create a new multiline style, first define the element and multiline properties, then specify a name for the newly created multiline in the Name: edit field. Click the **Save...** button, and AutoCAD displays the Save Multiline Style dialog box shown in Figure 6–31. By default, AutoCAD saves the multiline style definition in the ACAD.MLN library file. If necessary, you can select another file or provide a new

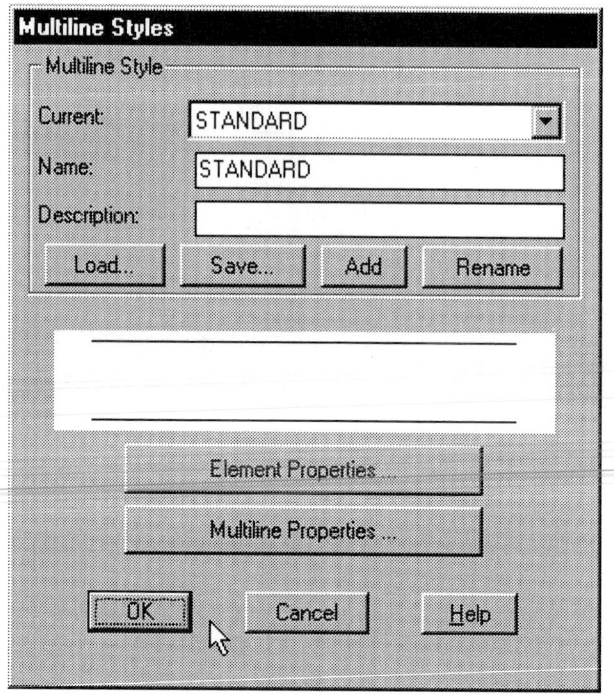

Figure 6–30 Multiline Styles dialog box

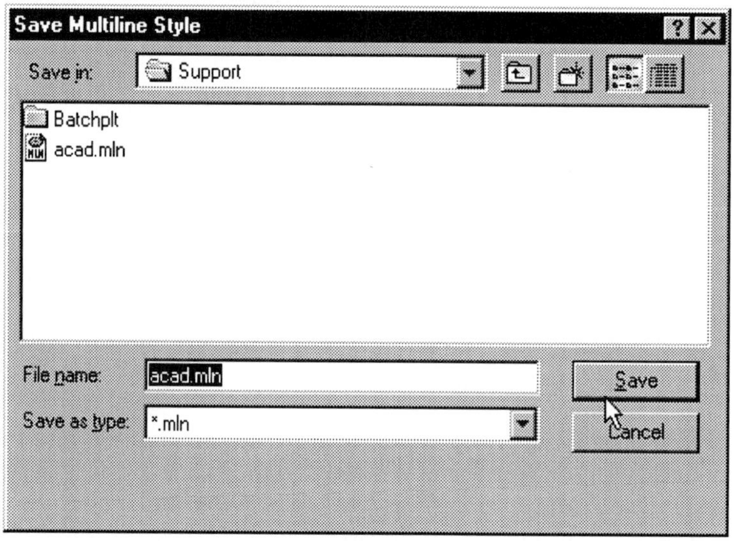

Figure 6–31 Save Multiline Style dialog box

file name with *mln* as the file extension. Click the Save button to save the multiline single *mln* library file.

To make the newly created multiline style current, click the Add button. AutoCAD then adds the newly created multiline style to the Current: list box and makes it the current multiline style.

Description The Description: edit field allows you to add a description of up to 255 characters, including spaces.

Load The Load... button allows you to load a multiline style from a multiline library file into the current drawing. To load a multiline style into the current drawing, click the Load... button. AutoCAD then displays the Load Multiline Styles dialog box shown in Figure 6–32. Select one of the available multiline styles from the list box. If you need to load a multiline style from a different library file, then click the File... button. AutoCAD lists the available multiline library files.

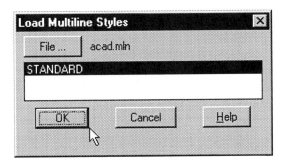

Figure 6–32 Load Multiline Styles dialog box

Select the approprate library file, and AutoCAD lists the multiline styles available from the library file selected. After selecting the multiline style, choose the OK button to close the dialog box.

Add As mentioned earlier, the Add button allows you to add the newly created multiline style to the Current: list box.

Element Properties Selecting the Element Properties... button displays an Element Properties dialog box similar to the one shown in Figure 6–33, with options to set or change the offset, number, line type or color of the multiline elements.

The Elements: list box displays existing elements along with the color and linetype of each.

Click the **Add** or **Delete** button to add a line element to the multiline style or delete a line element from the multiline style, respectively.

The **Offset** edit box sets the distance from the baseline for the elements selected from the Elements: list box. AutoCAD will use this distance to offset the element

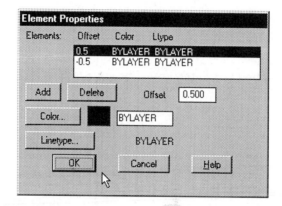

Figure 6–33 Element Properties dialog box

when the multiline is drawn and the scale factor is set to 1.0. Otherwise, the offset will be a ratio determined by the scale value.

Click the **Color...** button to display the Select Color dialog box and set the color for line elements (selected from Elements: list box) in the multiline style.

Click the **Linetype...** button to display the Select Linetype dialog box and set the linetype for line elements (selected from the Elements: list box) in the multiline style.

Multiline Properties Selecting the Multiline Properties... button displays a Multiline Properties dialog box similar to the one shown in Figure 6–34, with options to change the type of joints, end caps (and their angles), and background color for the multiline.

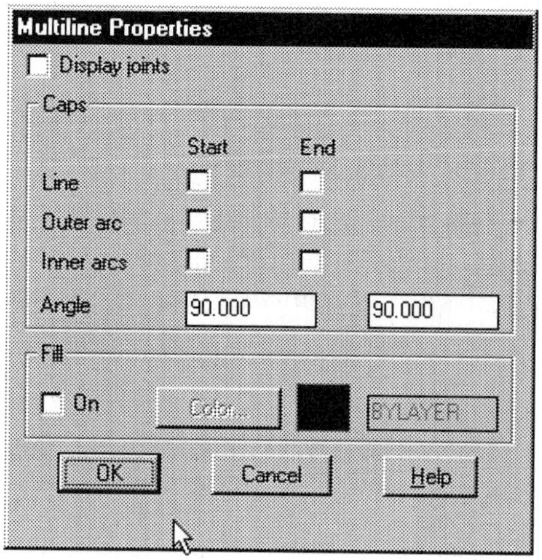

Figure 6–34 Multiline Properties dialog box

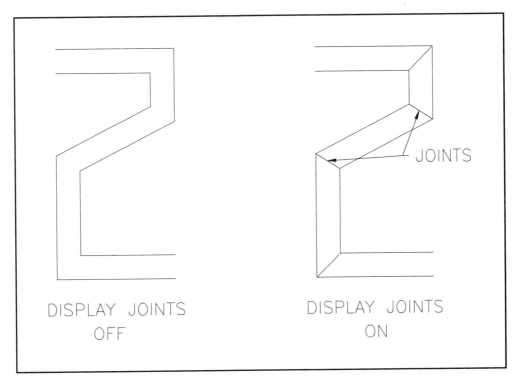

Figure 6-35 Display of the joints

The **Display joints** toggle button controls the display of the joints (miter) at the vertices of each multiline segment, as shown in Figure 6–35.

The **Caps** option has four suboptions to specify the appearance of multiline start and end caps. The Line toggle button controls the display of the start and end caps by a straight line, as shown in Figure 6–36.

The Outer arc toggle button controls the display of the start and end caps by connecting the ends of the outermost elements with a semicircular arc, as shown in Figure 6–37.

The Inner arcs toggle button controls the display of the start and end caps by connecting the ends of the innermost elements with a semicircular arc, as shown in Figure 6–38. For a multiline with an odd number of elements, the center element is not connected. For an even number of elements, connected elements are paired with elements that are the same number from each edge. For example, the second element from the left outer will be connected to the second element from the right outer, the third to the third, and so forth.

The Angle edit field sets the angle of endcaps, as shown in Figure 6–39.

The **Fill** toggle button controls the background fill of the multiline.

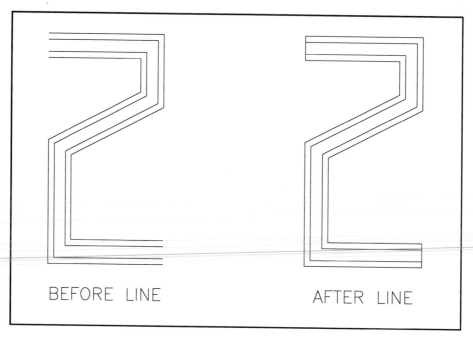

BEFORE LINE

AFTER LINE

Figure 6–36 Display of the line for start and end caps

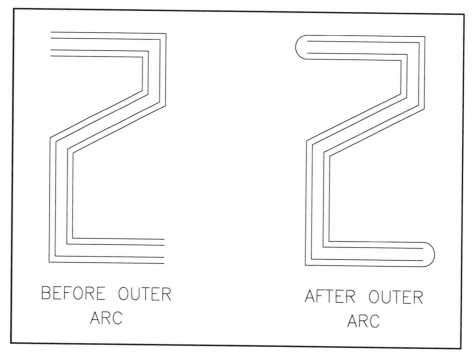

BEFORE OUTER
ARC

AFTER OUTER
ARC

Figure 6–37 Display of the outer arc for start end caps

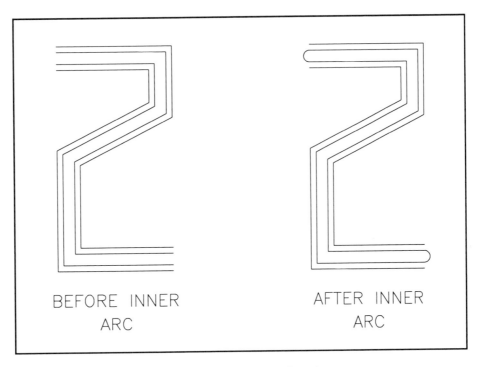

BEFORE INNER
ARC

AFTER INNER
ARC

Figure 6–38 Display of the inner arc for start and end caps

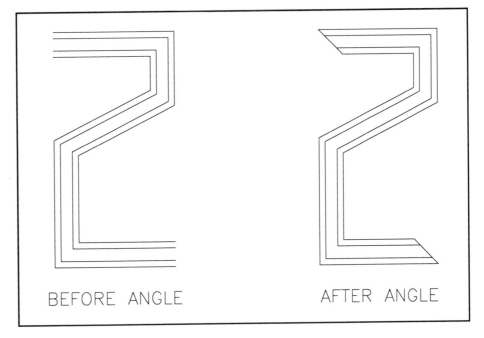

BEFORE ANGLE

AFTER ANGLE

Figure 6–39 Display of the end caps with an angular cap

The **Color...** button displays the Select Color dialog box and sets the color of the background fill.

Once you have set the appropriate element properties and multiline properties for a new multiline style, type the name and description in the Name: and Description: edit fields, respectively. Click the Save... button to save the newly created multiline style.

SPLINE CURVES

Drawing Spline Curves

The SPLINE command is used to draw a curve through or near a series of points. The type of curve is a nonuniform rational B-spline (NURBS). This type is used for drawing curves with irregularly varying radii, such as topographical contour lines.

The spline curve is drawn through a series of two or more points, with options either to specify end tangents or to use Close to join the last segment to the first. Another option lets you specify a tolerance, which determines how close to the selected points the curve is drawn.

Invoke the SPLINE command from:

Draw toolbar	Select the Spline command (see Figure 6–40)
Pull-down menu	Draw > Spline
Command: prompt	spline [Enter]

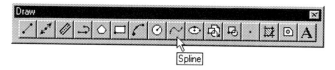

Figure 6–40 Invoking the Spline command from the Draw toolbar

AutoCAD prompts:

Command: **spline** [Enter]
Object/<Enter first point>: *(specify a point or select the Object option)*

The default option lets you specify the point from which the spline starts and to which it can be closed. After entering the first point, a rubber-band line appears. You will then be prompted:

Enter point:

When you respond by selecting a point, the spline segments are displayed as a rubber-band spline, curving from the first point, through the second point, and ending at the cursor. You are then prompted:

Close/Fit Tolerance/<Enter point>:

If you specify a point, the next segment is added to the spline. This will occur with each additional point selected until you use the Close option or enter a null response by pressing Enter.

Choosing a null response terminates the selection of segment determining points. You are then prompted for a start tangent determining point as follows:

Enter start tangent:

If you select a point (for tangency), its direction from the start point determines the start tangent. If you press Enter, the direction from the first point to the second point determines the tangency. After the start tangency is established, you are prompted:

Enter end tangent:

If you select a point (for tangency), its direction from the endpoint determines the end tangent. If you press Enter, the direction from the last point to the previous point determines the tangency.

If you choose the Close option instead of pressing Enter at the "Close/Fit Tolerance/<Enter point>:" prompt, AutoCAD uses the original starting point of the first spline segment as the endpoint of the last segment and terminates segment placing. You are then prompted:

Enter tangent:

You can select a point to determine the tangency at the connection of the first and last segments. If you press Enter, AutoCAD calculates the tangency and draws the spline accordingly. You can also use the Perp or Tan options to cause the tangency of the spline to be perpendicular or tangent to a specified object.

Instead, if you choose the Fit Tolerance option, you can vary how the spline is drawn relative to the selected points. You are then prompted:

Enter Fit Tolerance <current>:

Entering 0 (zero) causes the spline to pass through the selected points. A positive value causes the spline to pass within the specified value of the points.

Object Option The Object option is used to change spline-fit polylines into splines. This can be used for 2D or 3D polylines, which will be deleted depending on the setting of the DELOBJ system variable.

Editing Spline Curves

Splines created by means of the SPLINE command have numerous characteristics that can be changed with the SPLINEDIT command. These include quantity and location of fit points, end characteristics such as open/close and tangencies, and tolerance of the spline (how near the spline is drawn to fit points).

Splinedit operations on control points (which are different than fit points) of the selected spline include adding control points (with the Add or the Order option) and changing the weight of individual control points, which determines how close the spline is drawn to individual control points.

Invoke the SPLINEDIT command from:

Modify II toolbar	Select the Edit Spline command (see Figure 6–41)
Pull-down menu	Modify > Object > Spline
Command: prompt	splinedit Enter

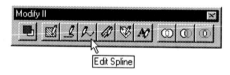

Figure 6–41 Invoking the Edit Spline command from the Modify II toolbar

AutoCAD prompts:

Command: **splinedit** Enter
Select Spline: *(select a spline curve)*
Fit Data/Close/Move Vertex/Refine/rEverse/Undo/eXit(X): *(select one of the available options)*

Control points appear in the grip color, and, if the spline has fit data, fit points also appear in the grip color. If you select a spline whose fit data is deleted, then the Fit Data option is not available. A spline can lose its fit data if you use the purge option while editing fit data, refine the spline, move its control vertices, fit the spline to a tolerance, or open or close the spline.

The Open option will replace Close if you select a closed spline, and vice versa.

Fit Data Option The Fit Data option allows you to edit the spline by providing the following suboptions:

Add/Close/Delete/Move/Purge/Tangents/toLerance/eXit <X>:

The **Add** suboption allows you to add fit points to the selected spline. AutoCAD prompts:

Select point: *(select a fit point)*

After you select one of the fit points, AutoCAD highlights it and you are prompted for the next point:

Enter new point: *(specify a point)*
Enter new point: *(specify another point or press* Enter *)*

Selecting a point places a new fit point between the highlighted ones.

The **Close** suboption closes an open spline smoothly with a segment or smoothes a spline with coincidental starting and ending points.

The **Open** suboption opens a closed spline, disconnecting it and changing the starting and ending points.

The **Delete** suboption deletes a selected fit point.

The **Move** suboption moves fit options to a new location by prompting:

Next/Previous/Select Point/eXit/<Enter new location> <N>:

The **Next** option steps forward through fit points.

The **Previous** option steps backwards through fit points.

The **Select** option permits you to select a fit point.

The **eXit** option exits this set of suboptions.

The **Enter new location** option moves the highlighted point to the point selected.

The **Purge** suboption deletes fit data for the selected spline.

The **Tangents** suboption edits the start and end tangents of a spline by prompting:

System Default/<Enter start tangent>: *(specify a point, enter an option, or press* Enter *)*
System Default/<Enter end tangent>: *(specify a point, enter an option, or press* Enter *)*

For a closed spline, the prompt is <Enter tangent>:.

If you choose the System Default, AutoCAD calculates the tangents. You can choose Tan or Perp and select an object for the spline tangent to be tangent to or perpendicular to the object selected.

The **toLerance** suboption refits the spline to the existing points with new tolerance values by prompting:

    Enter Fit Tolerance <current>: *(enter a value or press* Enter *)*

The value you enter determines how near the spline will be fit to the points.

The **eXit** suboption exits the Fit Data options and returns to the main prompt.

Close Option The Close option of the SPLINEDIT command causes the spline to be joined smoothly at its start point.

Open Option The Open option opens a closed spline. Previously open splines with coincidental starting and ending points will lose their tangency. Others will be restored to a previous state.

Move Vertex Option The Move Vertex option relocates a spline's control vertices by providing the following suboptions:

    Next/Previous/Select Point/eXit/<Enter new location> <N>:

The **Enter new location** suboption moves the highlighted point to the point selected.

The **Next** suboption steps forward through fit points.

The **Previous** suboption steps backwards through fit points.

The **Select Point** suboption permits you to select a fit point.

The **eXit** suboption exits this set of suboptions.

Refine Option The Refine option of the SPLINEDIT command allows you to fine tune a spline definition by providing the following suboptions:

    Add control point/Elevate Order/Weight/eXit <X>:

The **Add control point** suboption increases the number of control points that control a portion of a spline.

The **Elevate Order** suboption increases the order of the spline. You can increase the current order of a spline up to 26 (the default is 4), causing an increase in the number of control points.

The **Weight** suboption changes the weight at various spline control points by providing the following sub-options:

    Next/Previous/Select Point/eXit/<Enter new weight> <current> <N>:

    The **Next** suboption steps forward through fit points.

    The **Previous** suboption steps backwards through fit points.

The **Select Point** suboption permits you to select a fit point.

The **eXit** suboption exits this set of suboptions and returns you to the Refine prompt.

The default weight value for a control point is 1.0. Increasing it causes the spline to be drawn near the selected point. A negative or zero value is not valid.

The **eXit** suboption returns you to the main prompt.

rEverse Option The rEverse option of the SPLINEDIT command reverses the direction of the spline. Reversing the spline does not delete the Fit Data.

Undo Option The Undo option undoes the effects of the last subcommand.

eXit Option The eXit option terminates the SPLINEDIT command.

TEXT MANIPULATION

In addition to the TEXT and DTEXT commands, AutoCAD offers the MTEXT command, for drawing text by "processing" the words in paragraph form; the width of the paragraph is determined by the user-specified rectangular boundary. It is an easy way to have your text automatically formatted as a multiline group, with left, right or center justification as a group. Each multiline text object is a single object, regardless of the number of lines it contains. The text boundary remains part of the object's framework, although it is not plotted or printed. In this section, a detailed explanation is provided for drawing text with MTEXT command, drawing special characters, editing text, spell checking, creating and modifying text styles and controlling display of text.

Drawing Text with MTEXT

Invoke the MTEXT command from:

Draw toolbar	Select the Multiline Text command (see Figure 6–42)
Pull-down menu	Draw > Text > Multiline Text...
Command: prompt	**mtext** Enter

Figure 6–42 Invoking the Multiline Text command from the Draw toolbar

AutoCAD prompts:

> Command: **mtext** [Enter]
> Specify first corner: *(specify the first corner of the rectangular boundary)*
> Specify opposite corner or [Height/Justify/Rotation/Style/Width]: *(specify the opposite corner of the rectangular boundary, or select one of the available options)*

When you drag the cursor after specifying the first corner of the rectangular boundary, AutoCAD displays an arrow within the rectangle to indicate the direction of the paragraph's text flow. After you specify the opposite corner of the rectangular boundary, AutoCAD displays the Multiline Text Editor dialog box shown in Figure 6–43.

Enter the text in the text editor dialog box. If you click the return button on your pointing device while in the Multiline Text Editor dialog box, AutoCAD displays a button menu with options that include Undo, Cut, Copy, Paste, and Select All.

The Multiline Text Editor dialog box contains various control options, provided via three tabs: Character, Properties, and Find/Replace. The Character tab provides options to control character formatting for text entered in the Multiline Text Editor dialog box or imported into the text editor. The Properties tab provides the options to control the properties that apply to the multiline text object. And the Find/Replace tab provides the options to search for specified text strings and replace them with new text strings.

In AutoCAD Release 14, text can be highlighted in the following three ways: holding down the pick button while dragging across the selected text, double-clicking to select the entire word, or triple-clicking to select the paragraph.

Character Options The options provided in the Character tab (see Figure 6–43) include character formatting: Font, Height, Bold, Italic, Underline, Undo, Stack, Color, and Symbol.

The **Font** option allows you to specify a font for new text or changes the font of selected text. All of the available TrueType fonts and SHX fonts are listed in the drop-down list box.

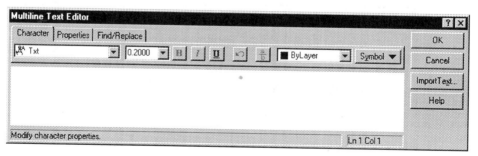

Figure 6–43 Multiline Text Editor dialog box

The **Height** option sets the character height in drawing units. The default value for the height is based on the current style. (A detailed discussion is provided later in the chapter on creating or modifying a text style.) If the current style is set to 0, then the value of the height is based on the value stored in the TEXTSIZE system variable. Each multiline text object can contain a text string of varying text size. When you highlight the text string in the dialog box, AutoCAD displays the selected text height in the list box. If necessary, you can specify a new height in addition to those listed.

You can also set the text height by selecting the Height option when AutoCAD prompts for the opposite corner of the rectangular boundary. Once the text height is specified, AutoCAD returns to the previous prompt until the opposite corner of the rectangular boundary is specified.

The **Bold** option allows you to turn ON and OFF bold formatting for new text or selected text. The Bold option is available only to the characters that belong to the TrueType font.

The **Italic** option allows you to turn ON and OFF italic formatting for new text or selected text. The Italic option is available only to the characters that belong to the TrueType font.

The **Underline** option allows you to turn ON and OFF underlining for new text or selected text.

The **Undo** option undoes the last edit action in the Multiline Text Editor dialog box that includes changes in the content of the text string or formatting.

The **Stack** option is used to place one part of a selected group of text over the remaining part. Before using the Stack option, the selected text must contain a forward slash (/) to separate the top part (to the left of the /) from the bottom part (to the right of the /). The slash will cause the horizontal bar to be drawn between the upper and lower parts, necessary for fractions with center justification. Instead of a slash (/), you can use the caret (^) symbol. In this case, AutoCAD will not draw a horizontal bar between the upper and lower parts with left justification, which is useful for placing tolerance values.

The **Color** option sets the color for new text or changes it for the selected text. You can assign the color by BYLAYER, BYBLOCK, or one of the available colors.

The **Symbol** option allows you to insert a listed symbol or nonbreaking space at the cursor position in the dialog box. In addition, you can also insert the symbols manually by means of the control characters.

Properties Options The options provided in the Properties tab (see Figure 6-44) control properties of the multiline text object such as Style, Justification, Width, and Rotation.

The **Style** option allows you to apply an existing style to new text or selected text. If you apply a new style to an existing text object, AutoCAD overrides character

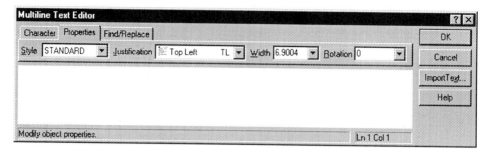

Figure 6–44 Multiline Text Editor dialog box displaying the Properties tab

formatting such as font, height, bold, and italic attributes. Styles that have backwards or upside-down effects are not applied.

You can also select the text style by means of the Style option when AutoCAD prompts for the opposite corner of the rectangular boundary. Once the text style is set, AutoCAD returns to the previous prompt until the opposite corner of the rectangular boundary is specified.

The **Justification** option sets the justification and alignment for new or selected text. Text is center, left, or right justified with respect to the left and right text boundaries, and aligned from the middle, top, or bottom of the paragraph with respect to the top and bottom text boundaries.

You can also set the justification by selecting the Justify option when AutoCAD prompts for the opposite corner of the rectangular boundary. The available justification options are the same as in the TEXT and DTEXT commands. Once justification is specified, AutoCAD returns to the previous prompt until the opposite corner of the rectangular boundary is specified.

The **Width** option sets the paragraph width for new or selected text. If it is set to the No Wrap option, the resulting multiline text object appears on a single line.

You can also set the width by selecting the Width option when AutoCAD prompts for the opposite corner of the rectangular boundary. Once the width is specified, AutoCAD returns to the previous prompt until the opposite corner of the rectangular boundary is specified.

The **Rotation** option sets the rotation angle for new or selected text, in the current unit of angle measurement.

You can also set the rotation by selecting the Rotation option when AutoCAD prompts for the opposite corner of the rectangular boundary. Once the rotation is specified, AutoCAD returns to the previous prompt until the opposite corner of the rectangular boundary is specified.

Find/Replace Options The options that are provided in the Find/Replace tab (see Figure 6–45) include Find, Replace with, Match Case, and Whole Word searches for specified text strings and replaces them with new text.

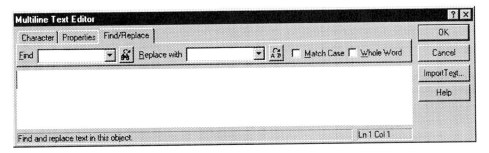

Figure 6–45 Multiline Text Editor dialog box displaying the Find/Replace tab

Type the text string to be searched for in the **Find** edit box, then choose the **Find** button to start the search. AutoCAD highlights the appropriate text string in the dialog box. To continue the search, choose the **Find** button again.

In the **Replace with** edit box type the text string that you want as replacement for the text string in the **Find** edit box. Then choose the **Replace with** button to replace the highlighted text with the text in the Replace with edit box.

When the **Match Case** toggle button is set to ON, AutoCAD finds text only if the case of all characters in the text object is matched to that of the text characters in the Find edit box. When it is set to OFF, AutoCAD finds a match for the specified text string regardless of the case of the characters.

When the **Whole Word** toggle button is set to ON, AutoCAD finds text only if the text string is a single word. If the text is part of another text string, it is ignored. When it is set to OFF, AutoCAD finds a match for the specified text string whether it is a single word or part of another word.

To import text into the Multiline Text Editor dialog box, choose the **Import Text...** button; AutoCAD displays the Open dialog box. Select the appropriate file (ASCII or RTF format) from the dialog box. Inserted text retains its original character formatting and style properties. If necessary, you can replace either selected text or all text of the current selection within the text boundary.

> **NOTE:** Imported text is limited to 16 KB file size.

To keep the settings and draw the paragraph text, click the OK button. AutoCAD closes the Multiline Text Editor dialog box and draws the paragraph text at the appropriate location.

Special Text Character and Symbol Options

In addition to the options provided in the Multiline Text Editor dialog box for drawing special characters, you can draw them by means of the control characters. The control characters for a symbol begin with a double percent sign (%%). The next character you enter represents the symbol. The control sequences defined by AutoCAD are presented in Table 6–1.

Table 6–1 Control Character Sequences for Drawing Special Characters and Symbols

Special Character or Symbol	Control Character Sequence	Example	
		Text String	Control Character Sequence
° (degree symbol)	%%d	104.5°F	104.5%%dF
± (plus/minus tolerance symbol)	%%p	34.5±3	34.5%%p3
Ø (diameter symbol)	%%c	56.06Ø	56.06%%c
% (single percent sign; necessary only when it must precede another control sequence	%%%	34.67%±1.5	34.67%%%%%P1.5
Special coded symbols (where nnn stands for a three-digit code)	%%nnn	@	%%064

Editing Text

The DDEDIT command allows you to edit text and attributes. An *attribute* is informational text associated with a block. See Chapter 10 for a detailed discussion of blocks and attributes.

Invoke the DDEDIT command from:

Modify II toolbar	Select the Edit Text command (see Figure 6–46)
Pull-down menu	Modify > Object > Text...
Command: prompt	ddedit [Enter]

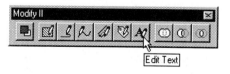

Figure 6–46 Invoking the Edit Text command from the Modify II toolbar

AutoCAD prompts:

> Command: **ddedit** `Enter`
> Select a TEXT or ATTDEF object>: *(select the text or attribute definition, or enter **u**, for undo)*

If you select a text string created by means of a TEXT or DTEXT command, AutoCAD displays the Edit Text dialog box, as shown in Figure 6–47. Make the necessary changes in the text string and choose the OK button to keep the changes.

If instead you select text created by means of the MTEXT command, AutoCAD displays the Multiline Text Editor dialog box shown in Figure 6–48. Make the necessary changes in the text string, and click the OK button to keep the changes.

AutoCAD continues to prompt you to select a new text string to edit, or you can enter **U** to undo the last change made to the text. To terminate the command sequence, give a null response.

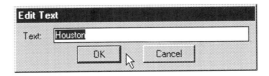

Figure 6–47 Edit Text dialog box

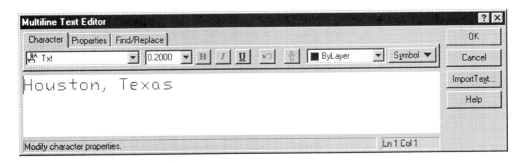

Figure 6–48 Multiline Text Editor dialog box

Spell-Checking

The SPELL command is used to correct the spelling of text objects created with the TEXT, DTEXT, or MTEXT command.

Invoke the SPELL command from:

Standard toolbar	Select the Spelling command (see Figure 6–49)
Pull-down menu	Tools > Spelling
Command: prompt	**spell** Enter

Figure 6–49 Invoking the Spelling command from the Standard toolbar

AutoCAD prompts:

Command: **spell** Enter
Select objects: *(select one or more text strings, and press Enter to terminate object selection)*

Only if AutoCAD finds a dubious word in the selected text objects does it display the Check Spelling dialog box, similar to Figure 6–50.

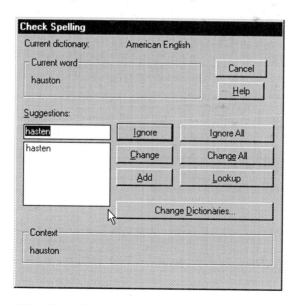

Figure 6–50 Check Spelling dialog box

AutoCAD displays the name of the current dictionary in the top of the Check Spelling dialog box. If necessary, you can change to a different dictionary by clicking the Change Dictionaries... button and selecting the appropriate dictionary from the Change Dictionaries dialog box.

AutoCAD displays each mispelled word in the **Current Word** section and lists the suggested alternate spellings in the **Suggestions:** list box. Click the **Change** button to replace the current word with the selected suggested work, or click the **Change All** button to replace all instances of the current word. Alternatively, click the **Ignore** button to skip the current word, or click the **Ignore All** button to ignore all subsequent entries of the current word.

The **Add** button allows you to include the current word (up to 63 characters) in the current or custom dictionary. The **Lookup** button allows you to check the spelling of the word in the suggestions box.

After completion of the spelling check, AutoCAD displays an AutoCAD message informing you that the spelling check is complete.

Creating and Modifying Text Styles

The Style option of the TEXT, DTEXT, and MTEXT commands (in conjunction with the STYLE command) lets you determine how text characters and symbols appear, other than adjusting the usual height, slant, and angle of rotation. To specify a text style from the Style option of the TEXT, DTEXT, and MTEXT commands, it must have been defined by using the STYLE command. In other words, the STYLE command creates a new style or modifies an existing style. The Style option under the TEXT, DTEXT, and MTEXT commands allow you to choose a specific style from the styles available.

There are three things to consider when using the STYLE command.

First, you must name the newly defined style. Style names may contain up to 31 characters, numbers, and special characters ($, -, and _). Names like "titleblock," "notes," and "billofmaterials" can remind you of the purpose for which the particular style was designed.

Second, you may apply a particular font to a style. The font that AutoCAD uses as a default is called TXT. It has blocky looking characters, which are economical to store in memory. But the TXT.SHX font, made up entirely of straight-line (noncurved) segments, is not considered as attractive or readable. Other fonts offer many variations in characters, including those for foreign languages. All fonts are stored for use in files of their font name with an extension of *.shx*. The most effective way to get a distinctive appearance in text strings is to use a specially designed font. You can also use TrueType fonts and Type 2 postscript. See Appendix F for a list of fonts that come with AutoCAD. If necessary, you can buy additional fonts from third-party vendors. AutoCAD can also read hundreds of PostScript fonts available in the marketplace.

The third consideration of the STYLE command is in how AutoCAD treats general physical properties of the characters, regardless of the font that is selected. These properties are the height, width-to-height ratio, obliquing angle, backwards, upside-down, and orientation (horizontal/vertical) options.

Invoke the STYLE command from:

Pull-down menu	Format > Text Style
Command: prompt	**style** Enter

AutoCAD displays the Text Style dialog box, similar to Figure 6-51.

Click the **New...** button to create a new style. AutoCAD displays the New Text Style dialog box shown in Figure 6-52. Type the appropriate name for the text style and choose the OK button to create the new style.

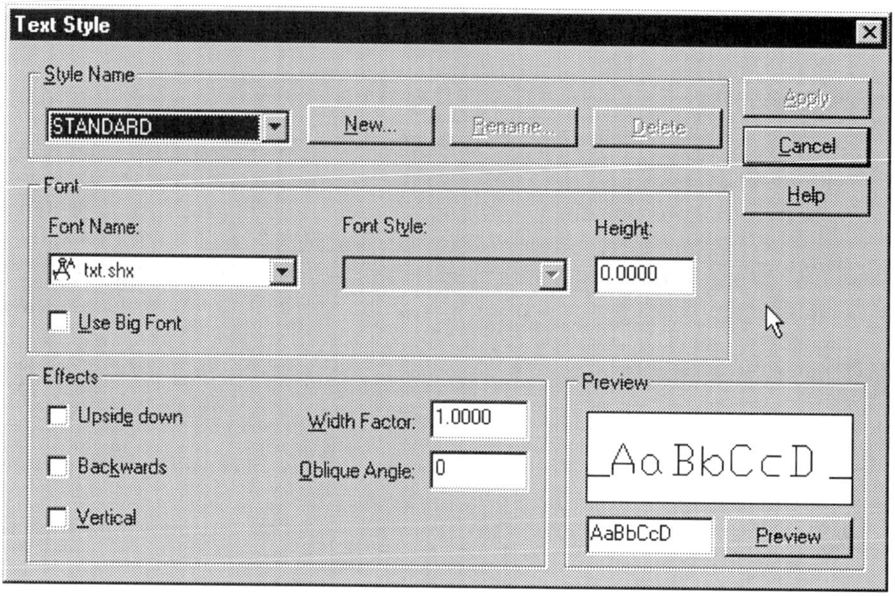

Figure 6-51 Text Style dialog box

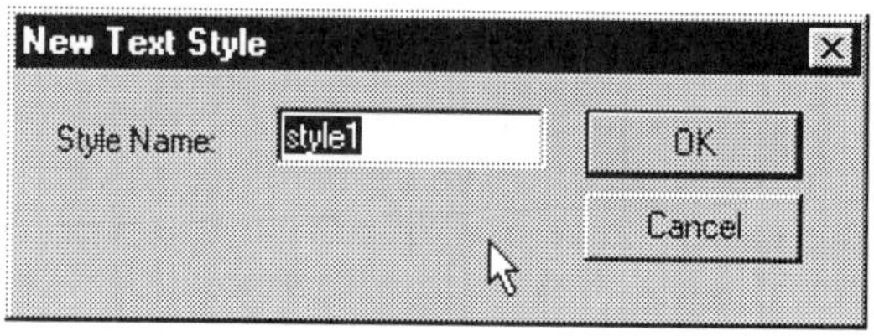

Figure 6-52 New Text Style dialog box

To rename an existing style, first select the style from the **Style Name** list box in the New Text Style dialog box, and then click the **Rename...** button. AutoCAD displays the Rename Text Style dialog box. Make the necessary changes in the name of the style, and choose the OK button to rename the text style.

To delete an existing style, first select the style from the **Style Name** list box in the Text Style dialog box, and then click the **Delete** button. AutoCAD displays the AutoCAD Alert dialog box to confirm the deletion of the selected style. Click the **Yes** button to confirm the deletion or the **NO** button to cancel the deletion of the selected style.

To assign a font to the selected text style, select the appropriate font from the **Font Name:** list box. Similarly, select a font style from the **Font Style:** list box. The font style specifies font character formatting, such as italic, bold, or regular.

The **Height:** edit field sets the text height to the value you enter. If you set the height to 0 (zero), then when you use this style in the TEXT, DTEXT, or MTEXT command, you are given an opportunity to change the text height with each occurrence of the command. If you set it to any other value, then that value will be used for this style and you will not be allowed to change the text height.

The **Upside down** and **Backwards** toggle buttons control whether the text is drawn right to left (with the characters backward) or upside down (left to right), respectively. See Figure 6–53.

The **Vertical** toggle button controls the display of the characters aligned vertically. The Vertical option is available only if the selected font supports dual orientation. See Figure 6–54 for an example of vertically oriented text.

The **Width Factor:** edit field sets the character width relative to text height. If it is set to more than 1.0, the text widens; if set to less than 1.0, it narrows.

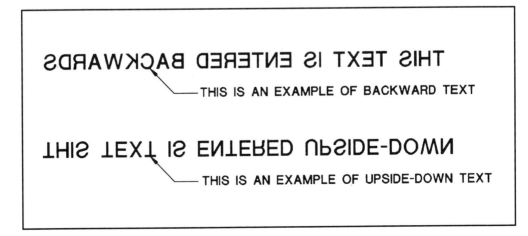

Figure 6–53 Examples of backward and upside-down text

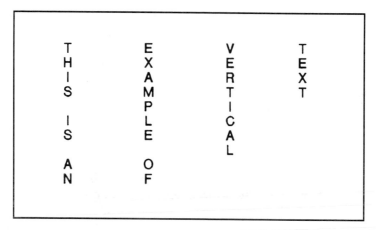

Figure 6–54 Example of vertically oriented text

The **Oblique Angle:** edit field sets the obliquing angle of the text. If it is set to 0 (zero) degrees, the text is drawn upright (or in AutoCAD, 90 degrees). A positive value slants the top of the characters toward the right, or in the clockwise direction. A negative value slants the characters in the counterclockwise direction. See Figure 6–55 for examples in oblique angle settings applied to a text string.

The **Preview** section of the Text Style dialog box displays sample text that changes dynamically as you change fonts and modify the effects. To change the sample text, enter characters in the box below the larger preview image.

After making the necessary changes in the Text Style dialog box, click the **Apply** button to apply the changes. Click the **Close** button to close the Text Style dialog box.

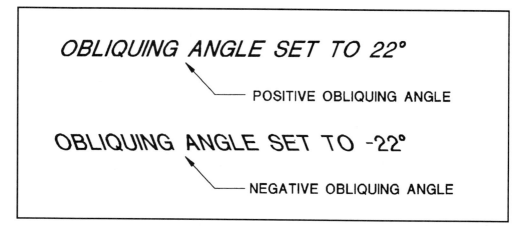

Figure 6–55 Example of oblique angle settings applied to a text string

Controlling the Display of Text

The QTEXT command is a utility command for TEXT, DTEXT, and MTEXT that is designed to reduce the redraw and regeneration time of a drawing. Regeneration time becomes a significant factor if the drawing contains a great amount of text and attribute information and/or if a fancy text font is used. Using QTEXT, the text is replaced with rectangular boxes of a height corresponding to the text height. These boxes are regenerated in a fraction of the time required for the actual text.

If a drawing contains many text and attribute items, it is advisable to set QTEXT to ON. However, before plotting the final drawing, or inspection of text details, the QTEXT command is set to OFF and followed by the REGEN command.

Invoke the QTEXT command from:

Command: prompt	**qtext** Enter

AutoCAD prompts:

Command: qtext Enter
ON/OFF <current>: *(select one of the two available options)*

EDITING WITH GRIPS

The grips feature allows you to edit AutoCAD drawings in an entirely different way than using the traditional AutoCAD modify commands. With grips you can move, stretch, rotate, copy, scale, and mirror selected objects without invoking one of the regular AutoCAD modify commands. When you select an object with grips enabled, small squares appear at specific points on the object that enable you to edit the selected objects.

To enable the grips feature, invoke the DDGRIPS command from:

Pull-down menu	Tools > Grips...
Command: prompt	**ddgrips** Enter

AutoCAD displays the Grips dialog box, similar to shown in Figure 6-56.

The **Enable Grips** toggle button controls the display of the grips. If it is set to ON, the grips display is enabled; if it is set OFF, the grips display is disabled.

You can also enable the grips feature by setting the system variable GRIPS to 1.

The **Enable Grips Within Blocks** toggle button controls the display of grips on objects within blocks. If it is set to ON, the grips are displayed on all objects within the block; if it is set to OFF, a grip is displayed only on the insertion point of the block.

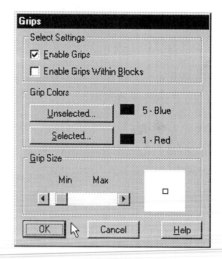

Figure 6–56 Grips dialog box

The **Grip Colors** area of the Grips dialog box allows you to change the colors to the selected and unselected grips. To change the colors, select the **Unselected...** and/or **Selected...** buttons. Each displays a standard color dialog box, allowing you to assign the color you want to use.

The **Grip Size** slider bar allows you to change the size of the grips. To adjust the size of grips, move the slider box left or right. As you move the slider, the size is illustrated to the right of the slider.

After making the necessary settings in the Grips dialog box, choose the OK button to keep the changes and close the Grips dialog box.

AutoCAD gives you a visual cue when grips are enabled by displaying a pick box at the intersection of the crosshairs, even when you are at the "Command:" prompt, as shown in Figure 6–57.

> **NOTE:** The pick box is also displayed on the crosshairs when the PICKFIRST (Noun/Verb selection) system variable is set to ON.

To place grips directly from the "Command:" prompt, select one or more objects you wish to manipulate.

> **NOTE:** To place grips, you can either select objects individually or select multiple objects by placing two points to specify the diagonally opposite corners of a rectangle.

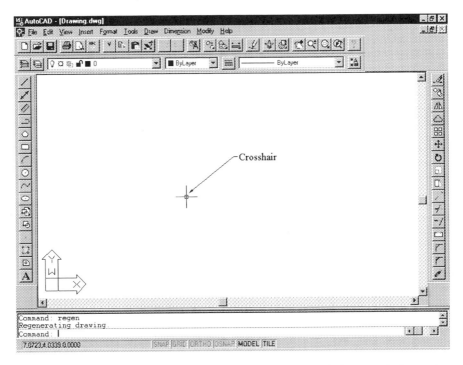

Figure 6-57 The pick box displayed at the intersection of the crosshairs at the "Command:" prompt

Grips appear on the endpoints and midpoint of lines and arcs, on the vertices and endpoints of polylines, on quadrants and the center of circles, on dimensions, text, solids, 3dfaces, 3dmeshes, and viewports, and on the insertion point of a block. Figure 6-58 shows location of the grips on some of the commonly used objects.

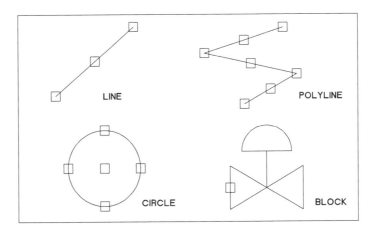

Figure 6-58 Locations of grips on commonly used objects

Using Grips

This section explains how to utilize grips in modifying your drawing. Learning to use grips speeds up the editing of your drawing while at the same time maintains accuracy of your work.

Snapping to Grips When you move your cursor over a grip, it automatically snaps to the grip point. This allows you to specify exact locations in the drawing without having to use grid, snap, ortho, object snap, or coordinate entry tools.

Condition of Grips Grips are categorized as being hot, warm, or cold, depending on their use.

A grip becomes *hot* when it is selected with your cursor. It has a solid-filled color and is the base point unless another is specified during a GRIP command. You can make more than one grip hot. Hold down the ⇧Shift key while selecting the grips.

A grip is said to be *warm* if it is on an object in the current selection set that you haven't picked with the cursor. The object(s) are highlighted to indicate that they are in the selection set.

A grip is said to be *cold* if it is on an object that is not in the current selection set. Although the objects with cold grips are not highlighted, they will look identical to those with warm grips, and you can still use the grips to snap to. Figure 6–59 shows examples of hot, warm, and cold grips.

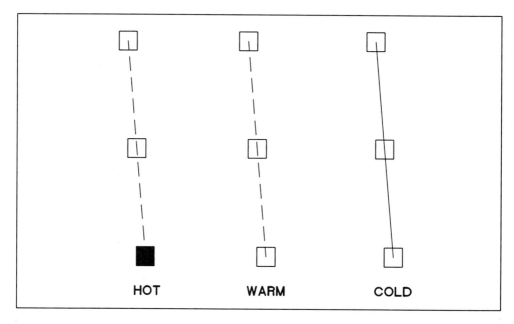

Figure 6–59 Examples of hot, warm, and cold grips

Clearing Grips To clear grips from a selection set, press ⎋ twice. The first time all the warm grips will turn to cold grips. The second time all the grips will clear. When you invoke a non-modifying AutoCAD command, such as LINE or CIRCLE, AutoCAD clears the grips from a selection set.

To use grips to edit the selected objects, at the "Command:" prompt pick a grip to act as the base point for the editing operation. Picking a grip starts the Grip modes, which includes STRETCH, MOVE, ROTATE, SCALE, and MIRROR. You can cycle through the Grip modes by pressing the Spacebar, ENTER, or entering a keyboard shortcut. Pressing the return mouse button, the grip mode cursor menu is displayed. To cancel Grip mode, enter **x** (for the mode's eXit option); AutoCAD returns to the "Command:" prompt. You can also use a combination of the current Grip mode and a multiple copy operation on the selection set.

You can also select the available Grip modes from a cursor menu when you pick a grip at the "Command:" prompt. Click the right button after picking a grip, AutoCAD displays the cursor menu with the listing of the Grip modes, as shown in Figure 6–60.

Stretch Mode The Stretch mode works similar to the STRETCH command. It allows you to stretch the shape of an object without affecting other crucial parts that remain unchanged. When you are in the Stretch Mode, the following prompt appears:

```
**STRETCH**
<Stretch to point>/Base point/Copy/Undo/eXit:
```

The default, <Stretch to point>, refers to the stretch displacement point. As you move the cursor, you see that the shape of the object is stretched dynamically from

Figure 6–60 Cursor menu displaying the Grip modes

the base point. You can specify the new point with the cursor or by entering coordinates. The displacement is applied to all selected hot grips.

If necessary, you can change the base point to be other than the base grip, by entering **base** or **b** at the prompt. Then pick the point with the cursor, or enter the coordinates.

To make multiple copies while stretching objects, enter **copy** or **c** to the prompt. Then specify destination copy points with the cursor, or enter their coordinates.

Move Mode The Move mode works similar to the MOVE command. It allows you to move one or more objects from their present location to a new one without changing their orientation or size. In addition, you can make copies of the selected objects at the specified displacement, leaving the original objects intact. To invoke the Move mode, cycle through the modes by entering a null response until it takes you to the Move mode, or enter **Move** or **m** from the keyboard. When you are in the Move mode, the following prompt appears:

```
**MOVE**
<Move to point>/Base point/Copy/Undo/eXit:
```

The default, <Move to point>, refers to the move displacement point. As you move the cursor, AutoCAD moves all the objects in the current selection set to a new point relative to the base point. You can specify the new point with the cursor or by entering the coordinates.

If necessary, you can change the base point to be other than the base grip, by entering **base** or **b** at the prompt. Then pick the point with the cursor or enter the coordinates.

To make multiple copies while moving objects, enter **copy** or **c** at the prompt and then specify the destination copy points with the cursor, or enter their coordinates.

Rotate Mode The Rotate mode works similar to the ROTATE command. It allows you to change the orientation of objects by rotating them about a specified base point. In addition, you can make copies of the selected objects and at the same time rotate them about a specified base point.

To invoke the Rotate mode, cycle through the modes by entering a null response until it takes you to the Rotate mode, or enter **Rotate** or **R** from the keyboard. When you are in the Rotate Mode, the following prompt appears:

```
**ROTATE**
<Rotation angle>/Base point/Copy/Undo/Reference/eXit:
```

The default, <Rotation angle>, refers to the rotation angle to which objects are rotated. As you move the cursor, AutoCAD allows you to drag the rotation angle, to position all the objects in the current selection set at the desired orientation. You can specify the new orientation with the cursor or from the keyboard. If you specify an angle by entering a value from the keyboard, this is taken as the amount that the objects should be rotated from their current orientation, around the base point. A positive angle rotates counterclockwise, and a negative angle rotates clockwise. Similar to the ROTATE command, you can use the Reference option to specify the current rotation and the desired new rotation.

If necessary, you can change the base point to be other than the base grip, by entering **base** or **b** to the prompt. Then pick the point with the cursor, or enter the coordinates.

To make multiple copies while rotating objects, enter **copy** or **c** at the prompt. Then specify destination copy points with the cursor, or enter the coordinates.

Scale Mode The Scale mode works similar to the SCALE command. It allows you to change the size of objects about a specified base point. In addition, you can make copies of the selected objects and at the same time change the size about a specified base point. To invoke the Scale mode, cycle through the modes by entering a null response until it takes you to the Scale mode, or enter **Scale** or **S** from the keyboard. When you are in the Scale mode, the following prompt appears:

```
**SCALE***
<Scale factor>/Base point/Copy/Undo/Reference/eXit:
```

The default, <Scale factor>, refers to the scale factor to which objects are made larger or smaller. As you move the cursor, AutoCAD allows you to drag the scale factor, to change all the objects in the current selection set to the desired size. You can specify the new scale factor with the cursor or from the keyboard. If you specify the scale factor by entering a value from the keyboard, this is taken as a relative scale factor by which all dimensions of the objects in the current selection set are to be multiplied. To enlarge an object, enter a scale factor greater than 1; to shrink an object, use a scale factor between 0 and 1. Similar to the SCALE command, you can use the Reference option to specify the current length and the desired new length.

If necessary, you can change the base point to be other than the base grip, by entering **base** or **b** at the prompt. Then pick the point with the cursor, or enter the coordinates.

To make multiple copies while scaling objects, enter **copy** or **c** at the prompt, and then specify the destination copy points with the cursor, or enter their coordinates.

Mirror Mode The Mirror mode works similar to the MIRROR command. It allows you to make mirror images of existing objects. To invoke the Mirror mode, cycle through the modes by entering a null response until it takes you to the Mirror mode, or enter **Mirror** or **M** from the keyboard. When you are in the Mirror Mode, the following prompt appears:

```
**MIRROR**
<Second point>/Base point/Copy/Undo/eXit:
```

Two points are required in AutoCAD to define a line about which the selected objects are mirrored. AutoCAD considers the base grip point as the first point; the second point is the one you pick or enter in response to the default, <Second point>.

If necessary, you can change the base point to be other than the base grip, by entering **base** or **b** at the prompt. Then pick the point with the cursor, or enter the coordinates.

To make multiple copies while retaining original objects, enter **copy** or **c** at the prompt. Then specify mirror points by picking the point(s) with the cursor, or enter the coordinates.

In AutoCAD Release 14, when you select an object at the "Command:" prompt with grips enabled, AutoCAD displays the selected object's layer, color, and linetype in the Object Properties toolbar, replacing the current settings. If you select more than one object having multiple properties, then the corresponding Object Properties drop-down list is displayed blank. For example, if you select objects from the Object and Text layers with different settings for Color and Linetype, all three drop-down lists are displayed blank.

From the Layer drop-down list, you can change the on/off, unlocked/locked, and thawed/frozen status, as well as the layer itself, for the selected object(s). It is like using the CHANGE or DDCHPROP command. Once you remove the display of the grips from the selected objects, AutoCAD returns the settings of the object properties, such as Layer, Color, and Linetype, to the default settings.

GROUPING OBJECTS

The GROUP command, introduced in AutoCAD Release 13, adds flexibility in modifying a group of objects. It allows you to name a selection set. Naming a selection set combines two powerful AutoCAD drawing features. One is being able to modify a group of unrelated objects as a group. It is similar to using "Previous" to select the last selection set when prompted to "Select object:" for a modify command. The advantage of using GROUP instead of "Previous" is that you are not restricted to only the last selection set. The other feature combined in the GROUP command is that of giving a name to a selected group of objects for recalling it later by the name of the group. This is similar to the BLOCK command. The advantage of using GROUP instead of BLOCK is that the GROUP command's "selectable" switch can be set to OFF for modifying an individual member without losing its "membership" in the group. Also, named groups, like blocks, are saved with the drawing.

A named group can be selected for modifying as a group only when its "selectable" switch is set to ON. Figure 6–61 shows the result of trimming an object with the selectable switch set to ON and to OFF. Modifying (such as with the MOVE or COPY command) objects that belong to a group can be selected by two methods. One is to select one of its members. The other method is to select the Group option by typing **g** at the "Select Objects:" prompt. AutoCAD prompts for the group's name.

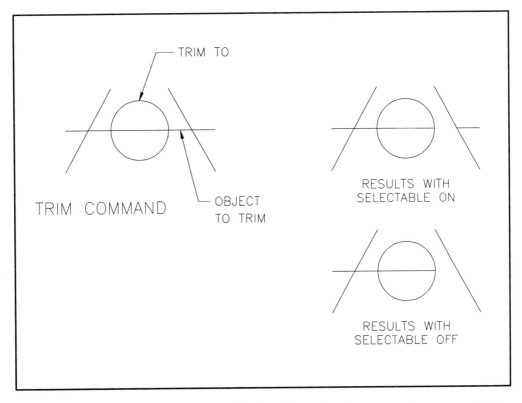

Figure 6–61 Trimming an object with the selectable switch set to ON and to OFF

Enter the group name and press 🄴🄽🅃🄴🅁 or the Spacebar. AutoCAD highlights the objects that belong to the selected group.

To create a new group or edit an existing group, invoke the GROUP command from:

Pull-down menu	Tools > Object Group...
Command: prompt	**group** 🄴🄽🅃🄴🅁

AutoCAD displays the Object Grouping dialog box, similar to Figure 6–62.

The dialog box is divided into four sections:

Group Name list box

Group Identification

Create Group

Change Group

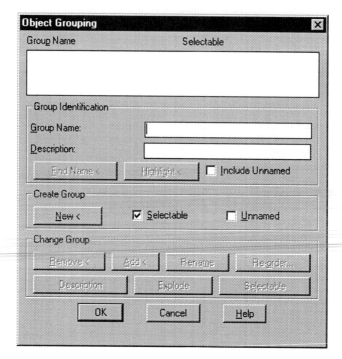

Figure 6–62 Object Grouping dialog box

Group Name List Box The Group Name list box lists the names of the existing groups defined in the current drawing. The Selectable column indicates whether a group is selectable. If it is listed as selectable, then selecting a single group member selects all the members except those on locked layers. If it is listed as unselectable, then selecting a single group member selects only that object.

Group Identification When a group is selected in the Group Name list, AutoCAD displays the group name and a description in the Group Identification section.

Choose the **Find Name** < button to list the groups to which an object belongs. AutoCAD prompts for the selection of an object and displays the Group Member List dialog box, which lists the group or groups to which the selected object belongs.

Choose the **Highlight** < button to see the members of the selected group from the Group Name list box.

The **Include Unnamed** toggle box controls the listing of the unnamed groups in the Group Name list box.

Create Group The Create Group section is used for creating a new group with or without a group name. In addition, you can set whether or not it is initially selectable.

To create a new group, type the group name and description in the Group Name: and Description: edit fields. Group names can be up to 31 characters long and can include letters, numbers, and the special charcters $, and _. To create an unnamed group, set the **Unnamed** toggle box to ON. AutoCAD assigns a default name, *An, to unnamed groups. The n represents a number that increases with each new group.

Set the **Selectable** box to ON or OFF, and then choose the **New <** button. AutoCAD prompts for the selection of objects. Select all the objects to be included in the new group, and press Enter or the Spacebar to complete the selection.

Change Group The Change Group section is for making changes to individual members of a group or to the group itself. The buttons are disabled until a group name is selected in the Group Name: list box.

The **Remove <** button allows you to remove selected objects from the selected group. To remove objects from the selected group, choose the **Remove <** button; AutoCAD prompts:

> Remove objects: *(select objects that are to be removed from the selected group and press* Enter *or the Spacebar)*

AutoCAD redisplays the Object Grouping dialog box.

The **Add <** button allows you to add the selected objects to the selected group. To add objects from the selected group, choose the Add < button; AutoCAD prompts:

> Select objects: *(select objects that are to be added to the selected group and press* Enter *or the Spacebar)*

AutoCAD redisplays the Object Grouping dialog box.

The **Rename** button allows you to change the name of the selected group to the name entered in the Group Name: edit box in the Group Identification section.

The **Re-order...** option allows you to change the numerical order of objects within the selected group. Initially, the objects are numbered in the order in which they were selected to form a group. Reordering is useful when creating tool paths. Choose the **Re-order...** button; AutoCAD displays the Order Group subdialog box shown in Figure 6–63.

> The **Group Name** list box gives the names of the groups defined in the current drawing. Members of a group are numbered sequentially starting with 0 (zero).
>
> **Remove from position (0 – *n*):** identifies the position number of an object.
>
> **Replace at position (0 – *n*):** identifies the new position number of the object.
>
> **Number of objects (1 – *n*):** identifies the number/range of objects to reorder.

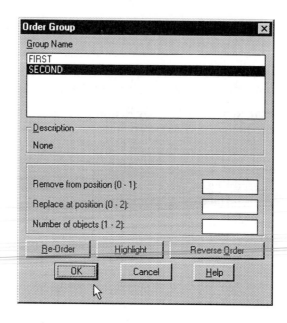

Figure 6–63 Object Group subdialog box

The **Re-Order** and **Reverse Order** buttons allow you to change the numerical order of objects as specified and reverses the order of all members, respectively.

The **Highlight** button allows AutoCAD to display the members of the selected group in the graphics area.

The **Description** button assigns an optional description up to 64 characters long.

The **Explode** button in the Change Group section of the Object Grouping dialog box deletes the selected group from the current drawing. Thus, the group no longer exists as a group. The members remain in the drawing and in any other group(s) of which they are members.

The **Description** button allows you to change the description of the selected group.

The **Selectable** button controls whether the group is selectable.

After making the necessary changes to the Object Grouping dialog box, click the **OK** button to keep the changes and close the dialog box.

FILTER—SELECTION SET

The FILTER command displays a dialog box that lets you create filter lists that you can apply to the selection set. With the FILTER command, you can select objects based on object properties, such as location, object type, color, linetype, layer, block name, text style, and thickness. For example, you could use the FILTER command to select all the blue lines and arcs with a radius of 2.0 units. You can even name filter lists and save them to a file.

The new selection set that is created by the FILTER command can be used as the Previous option at the next "Select object:" prompt. If you use the FILTER command transparently, then AutoCAD passes the new selection set directly to the command in operation. This will save you a considerable amount of time.

Invoke the FILTER command from:

Command: prompt	**filter** Enter

AutoCAD displays the Object Selection Filters dialog box shown in Figure 6–64.

The list box displays the filters currently being used as a selection set. The first time you use the FILTER command in the current drawing, the list box is empty.

The **Select Filter** section lets you add filters to the list box based on object properties. Select the object or logical operator from the pop-up list. You can use the grouping operators AND, OR, XOR, and NOT from the pop-up list. The grouping operators must be paired and balanced correctly in the filter list. For example, each Begin OR operator must have a matching End OR operator. If you select more than one filter, AutoCAD by default uses an AND as a grouping operator between each filter.

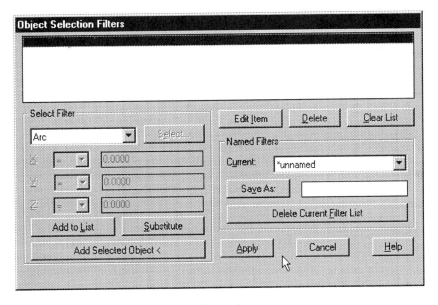

Figure 6–64 Object Selection Filters dialog box

The **Select...** button displays a dialog box that lists all items of the specified type within the drawing. From the list, you can select as many items as you want to filter. This process saves you from typing the specific filter parameters.

Click the **Add to List** button to add the current Select Filter selection to the filter list.

The **Add Selected Object <** button allows you to select an object from the drawing and add it to the filter list.

The **Substitute** button replaces the selected filter with the current one in the Select Filter box.

The **Edit Item** button moves the selected filter into the Select Filter area for editing. First select the filter from the filter list box and then click the **Edit Item** button. Make the necessary changes in the Select Filter section and click the **Substitute** button. The edited filter replaces the selected filter.

The **Delete** button allows you to delete the selected filter in the filter list box.

The **Clear List** button allows you to clear the filter list from the filter list box.

To save the current filter list, type the name for the filter list in the **Save As:** edit field, and click the **Save As:** button to save the list in the given name.

The **Current:** pop-up list displays the saved filter lists. Select a list to make it current.

The **Delete Current Filter List** button allows you to delete filter lists from the default filter file.

Click the **Apply** button to close the dialog box; AutoCAD displays the "Select Objects:" prompt, where you create a selection set. AutoCAD uses the filter list on the objects you select.

INFORMATION ABOUT OBJECTS

AutoCAD provides several commands for displaying useful information about the objects in the drawing. These commands do not create anything, nor do they modify or have any effect on the drawing or objects therein. The only effect on the AutoCAD editor is that on single-screen systems, the screen switches to the AutoCAD Text window (not to be confused with the TEXT command) and the information requested by the particular Inquiry command is then displayed on the screen. If you are new to AutoCAD, it is helpful to know the FLIP SCREEN feature that returns you to the graphics screen so you can continue with your drawing. On most systems this is accomplished with the F2 function key. You can also change back and forth between graphic and text screens with the GRAPHSCR and TEXTSCR commands typed in at the "Command:" prompt, respectively. The Inquiry commands include LIST, AREA, ID, DBLIST, and DIST.

LIST Command

The LIST comand displays information about individual objects stored by AutoCAD in the drawing database. The information includes:

The location, layer, object type, and space (model or paper) of selected object as well as the color and linetype if not set to BYLAYER or BYBLOCK.

The distance in the main axes between the endpoints of a line, that is, the delta-X, delta-Y, and delta-Z.

The area and circumference of a circle or the area of a closed polyline.

The insertion point, height, angle of rotation, style, font, obliquing angle, width factor, and actual character string of a selected text object.

The object handle, reported in hexadecimal.

Invoke the LIST command from:

Inquiry toolbar	Select the List command (see Figure 6–65)
Pull-down menu	Tools > Inquiry > List
Command: prompt	list Enter

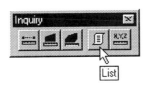

Figure 6–65 Invoking the List command from the Inquiry toolbar

AutoCAD prompts:

Command: list Enter
Select objects: *(select the objects and press Enter to terminate object selection)*

AutoCAD lists the information about the selected objects.

DBLIST Command

The DBLIST command lists the data about all of the objects in the drawing. It can take a long time to scroll through all the data in a large drawing. DBLIST can, like other commands, be terminated by canceling with Esc.

Invoke the DBLIST command from:

Command: prompt	**dblist** [Enter]

AutoCAD lists the information about all the objects in the drawing.

AREA Command

The AREA command is used to report the area (in square units) and perimeter of a selected closed geometric figure on the screen, such as a circle, polygon, or closed polyline. You may also specify a series of points that AutoCAD considers a closed polygon, compute, and report the area.

Invoke the AREA command from:

Inquiry toolbar	Select the Area command (see Figure 6–66)
Pull-down menu	Tools > Inquiry > Area
Command: prompt	**area** [Enter]

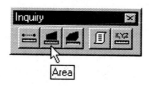

Figure 6–66 Invoking the Area command from the Inquiry toolbar

AutoCAD prompts:

Command: area [Enter]
<First point>/Object/Add/Subtract: *(specify a point or select one of the available options)*

The default option calculates the area when you select the vertices of the objects. If you want to know the area of a specific object such as a circle, polygon, or closed polyline, select the Object option.

The following command sequence is an example of finding the area of a polygon using the Object option, as shown in Figure 6–67.

Command: **area** [Enter]
<First point>/Object/Add/Subtract: **o** [Enter]
Select circle or polyline: *(select an object, as shown in Figure 6–67)*
Area = 12.21   Perimeter = 13.79

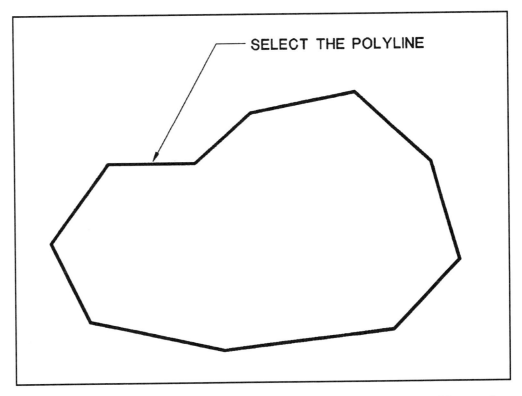

SELECT THE POLYLINE

Figure 6–67 Finding the area of a polygon using the AREA command Object option

The Add option allows you to add selected objects to form a total area; then you can use the Subtract option to remove selected objects from the running total.

The following example demonstrates the application of the Add and Subtract options. In this example, the area is determined for the closed shape after subtracting the area of the four circles, as shown in Figure 6–68.

Command: **Area** Enter
<First point>/Object/Add/Subtract: **a** Enter
<First point>/Object/Subtract: **o** Enter
(ADD mode) Select circle or polyline: *(select the polyline, as shown in Figure 6–68)*
Area = 12.9096, Perimeter = 15.1486
Total area = 12.9096
(ADD mode) Select circle or polyline: Enter
<First point>/Object/Subtract: **s** Enter
<First point>/Object/Add: **o** Enter
(SUBTRACT mode) Select circle or polyline: *(select circle A, as shown in Figure 6–68)*

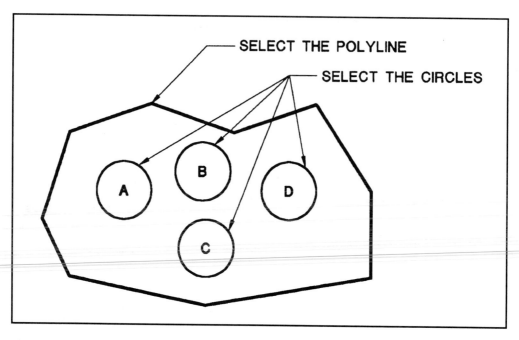

Figure 6–68 Using the Add and Subtract options of the AREA command

Area = 0.7125, Circumference = 2.9992
Total area = 12.1971
(SUBTRACT mode) Select circle or polyline: *(select circle B, as shown in Figure 6–68)*
Area = 0.5452, Circumference = 2.6175
Total area = 11.6179
(SUBTRACT mode) Select circle or polyline: *(select circle C, as shown in Figure 6–68)*
Area = 0.7125, Circumference = 2.9922
Total area = 10.9394
(SUBTRACT mode) Select circle or polyline: *(select circle D, as shown in Figure 6–68)*
Area = 0.5452, Circumference = 2.6175
Total area = 10.3942
(SUBTRACT mode) Select circle or polyline: `Enter`
<First point>/Object/Add: `Enter`

ID Command

The ID command is used to obtain the coordinates of a selected point. If you do not use an Object Snap mode to select a point that is not in the current construction plane, AutoCAD assigns the current elevation as the Z coordinate of the point selected.

Invoke the ID command from:

Inquiry toolbar	Select the Locate Point command (see Figure 6–69)
Pull-down menu	Tools > Inquiry > ID Point
Command: prompt	**id** Enter

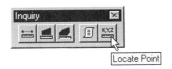

Locate Point

Figure 6–69 Invoking the Locate Point command from the Inquiry toolbar

AutoCAD prompts:

Command: id Enter
Point: *(select a point)*

AutoCAD displays the information about the selected point.

If the BLIPMODE system variable is set to ON (the default), a blip appears on the screen at the pick point, provided it is in the viewing area.

DIST Command

The DIST command prints out the distance, in the current units, between two points, either selected on the screen or keyed in from the keyboard. Included in the report are the horizontal and vertical distances (delta-X and delta-Y, respectively) between the points and the angles in and from the XY plane.

Invoke the DIST command from:

Inquiry toolbar	Select the Distance command (see Figure 6–70)
Pull-down menu	Tools > Inquiry > Distance
Command: prompt	**dist** Enter

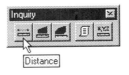

Distance

Figure 6–70 Invoking the Distance command from the Inquiry toolbar

AutoCAD prompts:

Command: distance `Enter`
First point: *(specify the first point to measure from)*
Second point: *(specify the endpoint to measure to)*

AutoCAD displays the distance between two selected points.

SYSTEM VARIABLES

AutoCAD stores the settings (or values) for its operating environment and some of its commands in system variables. Each system variable has an associated type: integer (for switching), integer (for numerical value), real, point, or text string. Unless they are read-only, you can examine and change these variables at the "Command:" prompt by typing the name of the system variable, or you can change them by means of the SETVAR command.

Integers (for Switching) System variables that have limited nonnumerical settings can be switched by setting them to the appropriate integer value. For example, the snap can be either ON or OFF. The purpose of the SNAPMODE system variable is to turn the snap on or off by using the AutoCAD SETVAR command or the AutoLISP (setvar) function.

Turning the snap ON or OFF is demonstrated in the following example by changing the value of its SNAPMODE system variable. First, its current value is set to "0", which is OFF.

Command: setvar `Enter`
Variable name or ?: **snapmode** `Enter`
New value for SNAPMODE (0): **1** `Enter`

This sequence may seem rather unnecessary because the snap mode is so easily toggled with a press of a function key. Changing the snap with the SETVAR command is inconvenient, but doing so does allow you to view the results immediately.

For any system variable whose status is associated with an integer, the method of changing the status is just like the preceding example. In the case of SNAPMODE, "0" turns it OFF and "1" turns it ON. In a similar manner, you can use SNAPISOPAIR to switch one isoplane to another by setting the system variable to one of three integers: 0 is the left isoplane, 1 is the top, and 2 is the right isoplane.

It should be noted that the settings for the Osnap system variable named OSMODE are members of the binomial sequence. The integers are 1, 2, 4, . . . , 512, 1024, 2048. See Table 6–2 for the meaning of OSMODE values. While the settings are switches, they are more than just ON and OFF. There may be several Object Snap modes active at one time. It is important to note that the value of an integer (switching) has nothing to do with its numerical value.

Table 6–2 Values for the OSMODE System Variable

NONe	0
ENDpoint	1
MIDpoint	2
CENter	4
NODe	8
QUAdrant	16
INTersection	32
INSert	64
PERpendicular	128
TANgent	256
NEArest	512
QUIck	1024
APP INT	2048

Integers (for Numerical Value) System variables such as APERTURE and AUPREC are changed by using an integer whose value is applied numerically in some way to the setting, rather than just as a switch. For instance, the size of the aperture (the target box that appears for selecting Osnap points) is set in pixels (picture elements) according to the integer value entered in the SETVAR command. For example, setting the value of APERTURE to 9 should render a target box that is three times larger than setting it to 3.

AUPREC is the variable that sets the precision of the angular units in decimal places. The value of the setting is the number of decimal places; therefore, it is considered a numerical integer setting.

Real System variables that have a real number for a setting, such as VIEWSIZE, are called real.

Point (X Coordinate, Y Coordinate) LIMMIN, LIMMAX, and VIEWCTR are examples of system variables whose settings are points in the form of the X coordinate and Y coordinate.

Point (Distance, Distance) Some system variables, whose type is point, are primarily for setting spaces rather than a particular point in the coordinate system. For instance, the SNAPUNIT system variable, though called a point type, uses its X and Y distances from (0,0) to establish the snap X and Y resolution, respectively.

String These variables have names like CLAYER, for the current layer name, and DWGNAME, for the drawing name.

PROJECT EXERCISE

This project exercise provides point-by-point instructions for the objects shown in Figure P6–1. In this exercise you will apply the skills acquired in Chapters 1 through 6. Do *not* create the dimensions in this exercise.

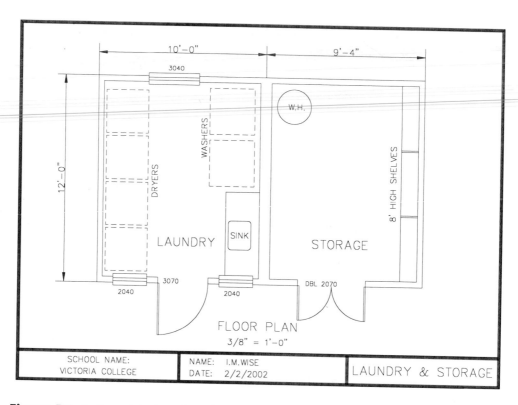

Figure P6–1 Completed project drawing (with dimensions added for reference)

In this project you will:

- Set up the drawing, including limits and layers.
- Use the XLINE, PLINE, and MLINE commands to create objects.
- Use the MLEDIT command for special joining of multilines.
- Use the TRIM and FILLET commands to modify objects.
- Use the TEXT and DTEXT commands to create text objects.

Set Up the Drawing and Draw a Border

Step 1   Start the AutoCAD program.

Step 2   To create a new drawing, invoke the NEW command from the Standard toolbar or select New from the pull-down menu File .

AutoCAD displays the Create New Drawing dialog box. Click the Start from Scratch button, and then set UNITS, LIMITS, SNAP, and GRID to the values shown in the nearby SETTINGS/VALUE table.

Step 3   Invoke the LAYER command from the Object Properties toolbar, or select Layer... from the pull-down menu Format. AutoCAD displays the Layer & Linetype Properties dialog box. Create five layers, and rename them as shown in the table, assigning appropriate color and linetype.

SETTINGS	VALUE		
UNITS	Architectural		
LIMITS	Lower left corner: -5'-0",-6'-0" Upper right corner: 24'-4",15'-4"		
GRID	4		
SNAP	4		
LAYERS	*NAME* Construction Border Object Hidden Text	*COLOR* Cyan Red White Magenta Blue	*LINETYPE* Continuous Continuous Continuous Hidden Continuous

Establishing Construction Lines

Step 4   Set Construction as the current layer, and set Ortho, Grid, and Snap all to ON. Invoke the ZOOM ALL command to display the screen to the limits.

Step 5   Invoke the XLINE command from the Draw toolbar. AutoCAD prompts:

Command: **xline** Enter
Hor/Ver/Ang/Bisect/Offset/<From point>:>: **v** Enter
Through point: *(place the cursor so that the X coordinate shown in the status bar is at -4'-8" and press the pick button)*
Through point: *(continue placing six additional vertical construction lines whose X coordinates are 0'-0", 5'-0", 10'-0", 15'-0", 19'-4", and 24'-0", and press* Enter *to terminate the command sequence)*

Command: *(press* Enter *to repeat the XLINE command)*
Command: _xline Hor/Ver/Ang/Bisect/Offset/<From point>: **h** Enter

Through point: *(place the cursor so that the Y coordinate shown in the status bar is at -5'-8" and press the pick button)*
Through point: *(continue placing four additional horizontal construction lines whose Y coordinates are -4'-0", 0'-0", 12'-0", and 15'-0", and press* Enter *to terminate the command sequence)*

The display should appear as shown in Figure P6–2.

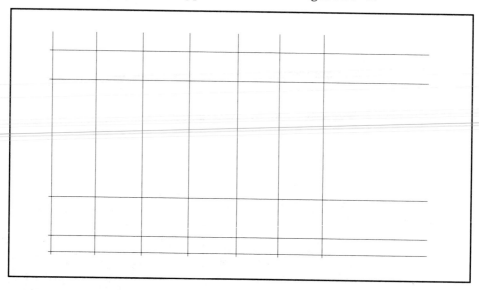

Figure P6–2 Drawing with construction lines

Step 6   Set Border as the current layer. Select Intersection as the Running Object mode.

Step 7   Invoke the PLINE command from the Draw toolbar. AutoCAD prompts:

Command: **pline** Enter
From point: *(select point 1 as shown in Figure P6–3)*
Current line-width is 0'-0"
Arc/Close/Halfwidth/Length/Undo/Width/<Endpoint of line>: **w** Enter
Starting width <0'-0">: **2** Enter
Ending width <0'-2">: Enter
Arc/Close/Halfwidth/Length/Undo/Width/<Endpoint of line>: *(select point 2 as shown in Figure P6–3)*
Arc/Close/Halfwidth/Length/Undo/Width/<Endpoint of line>: *(select point 3 as shown in Figure P6–3)*
Arc/Close/Halfwidth/Length/Undo/Width/<Endpoint of line>: *(select point 4 as shown in Figure P6–3)*
Arc/Close/Halfwidth/Length/Undo/Width/<Endpoint of line>: **c** Enter

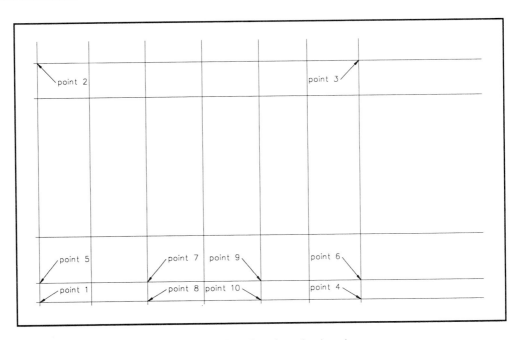

Figure P6–3 Points (intersections) for drawing the border

Command: (*press* Enter *to repeat the PLINE command*)
From point: (*select point 5 as shown in Figure P6–3*)
Current line-width is 0'-2"
Arc/Close/Halfwidth/Length/Undo/Width/<Endpoint of line>: (*select point 6 as shown in Figure P6–3*)
Arc/Close/Halfwidth/Length/Undo/Width/<Endpoint of line>: (*press* Enter *to terminate the command sequence*)

Command: (*press* Enter *to repeat the PLINE command*)
From point: (*select point 7 as shown in Figure P6–3*)
Current line-width is 0'-2"
Arc/Close/Halfwidth/Length/Undo/Width/<Endpoint of line>: (*select point 8 as shown in Figure P6–3*)
Arc/Close/Halfwidth/Length/Undo/Width/<Endpoint of line>: (*press* Enter *to terminate the command sequence*)

Command: (*press* Enter *to repeat the PLINE command*)
From point: (*select point 9 as shown in Figure P6–3*)
Current line-width is 0'-2"
Arc/Close/Halfwidth/Length/Undo/Width/<Endpoint of line>: (*select point 10 as shown in Figure P6–3*)
Arc/Close/Halfwidth/Length/Undo/Width/<Endpoint of line>: (*press* Enter *to terminate the command sequence*)

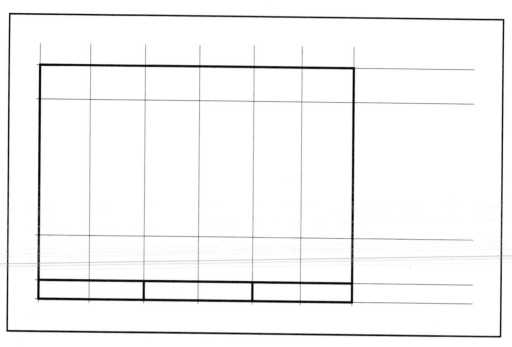

Figure P6–4 Drawing with the border

The display should appear as shown in Figure P6–4.

Drawing Text in the Title Block

Step 8   Set Construction as the current layer.

Step 9   To create additional construction lines for drawing text, invoke the LINE command from the Draw toolbar. AutoCAD prompts:

> Command: **line** [Enter]
> From point: *(select a point on line A, as shown in Figure P6–5, at coordinates -4'8",-4'8")*
> To point: *(invoke the Object Snap mode Perpendicular, and select line B as shown in Figure P6–5)*
> To point: *(press* [Enter] *to terminate the command sequence)*
>
> Command: *(press* [Enter] *to repeat the LINE command)*
> LINE From point: *(select a point on line A, as shown in Figure P6–5, at coordinates -4'8",-5,4")*
> To point: *(invoke the Object Snap mode Perpendicular, and select line B as shown in Figure P6–5)*
> To point: *(press* [Enter] *to terminate the command sequence)*

Command: *(press* Enter *to repeat the LINE command)*
LINE From point: *(invoke the Object Snap mode Midpoint, and select line C as shown in Figure P6–5)*
To point: *(use the Object Snap mode Perpendicular, and select line D as shown in Figure P6–5)*
To point: *(press* Enter *to terminate the command sequence)*

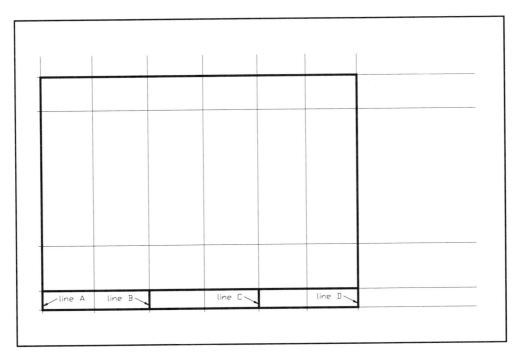

Figure P6–5 Points for creating lines to draw text objects

Step 10 Set Text as the current layer.

Step 11 Invoke the TEXT command from the Draw toolbar to draw the text. AutoCAD prompts:

Command: **text** Enter
Justify/Style/<Start point>: **j** Enter
Align/Fit/Center/Middle/Right/TL/TC/TR/ML/MC/MR/BL/BC/BR: **c** Enter
Center point: *(invoke the Object Snap mode Midpoint, and select the first construction line drawn in the previous step to establish point 1 as shown in Figure P6–6)*
Height <current>: **4** Enter
Rotation angle <current>: **0** Enter
Text: *(type in **SCHOOL NAME:**)*

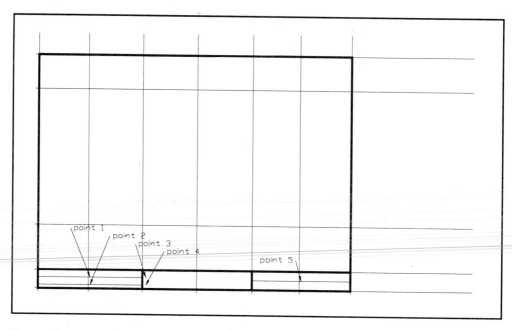

Figure P6-6 Points to draw text for the title block

Command: *(press* Enter *to repeat the TEXT command)*
TEXT Justify/Style/<Start point>: **j** Enter
Align/Fit/Center/Middle/Right/TL/TC/TR/ML/MC/MR/BL/BC/BR: **c** Enter
Center point: *(invoke the Object Snap mode Midpoint, and select the first*
    construction line drawn in the previous step to establish point 2 as
    shown in Figure P6-6)
Height <0'-4">: Enter
Rotation angle <0>: Enter
Text: *(type in the name of your school)*

Command: *(press* Enter *to repeat the TEXT command)*
TEXT Justify/Style/<Start point>: *(select point 3, as shown in Figure P6-6*
    at coordinates 5'-4",-4'-8")
Height <0'-4">: Enter
Rotation angle <0>: Enter
Text: NAME: *(type in **NAME:** followed by your name)*

Command: *(press* Enter *to repeat the TEXT command)*
TEXT Justify/Style/<Start point>: *(select point 4, as shown in Figure P6-6*
    at coordinates 5'-4", -5'-4")
Height <0'-4">: Enter
Rotation angle <0>: Enter
Text: *(type in **DATE:** followed by today's date)*

Command: *(press* Enter *to repeat the TEXT command)*
TEXT Justify/Style/<Start point>: **j** Enter
Align/Fit/Center/Middle/Right/TL/TC/TR/ML/MC/MR/BL/BC/BR: **m** Enter
Middle point: *(invoke the Object Snap mode Midpoint, and select the first construction line drawn in the previous step to establish point 5 as shown in Figure P6–6)*
Height <0'-4">: **6** Enter
Rotation angle <0>: Enter
Text: *(type in LAUNDRY & STORAGE)*

After drawing the text as indicated, the display should appear as shown in Figure P6–7.

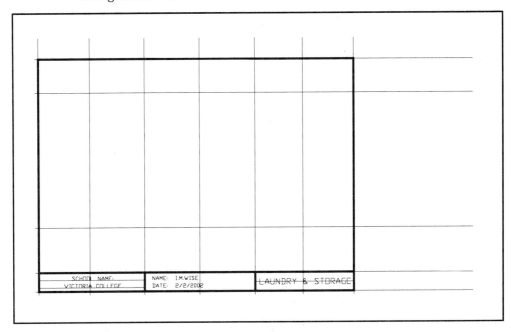

Figure P6–7 Drawing with the border and title block (Construction layer ON)

With the Construction layer set to OFF (do *not* turn it off at this time), the display would appear as shown in Figure P6–8.

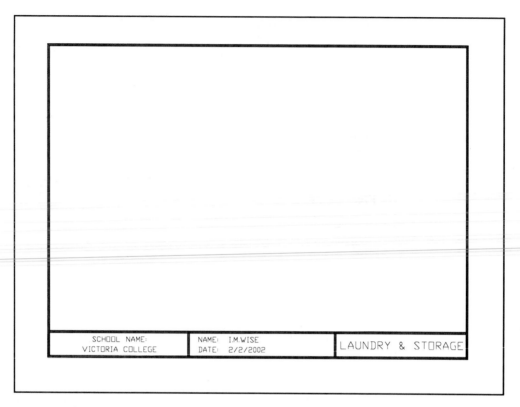

Figure P6–8 Drawing with the border and title block (Construction layer OFF)

Step 12   From the Standard toolbar, invoke the ZOOM Scale command. AutoCAD prompts:

Command: **zoom** `Enter`
All/Center/Dynamic/Extents/Left/Previous/Vmax/Window <Scale(X/XP)>: **.8** `Enter`

Step 13   Erase the construction lines that are not needed (see Figure P6–9) by invoking the ERASE, from the Modify toolbar. AutoCAD prompts:

Command: **erase** `Enter`
Select objects: (select all of the Construction lines with the designated symbol plus the xlines created for the title block text as shown in Figure P6–9).

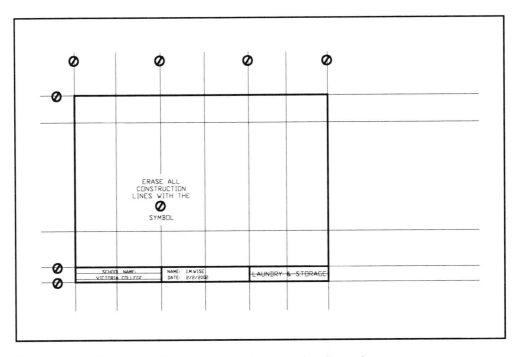

Figure P6-9 Drawing with the lines to be erased indicated

Invoke the ZOOM All command to display the whole drawing.

Drawing the Walls

Step 14 Set Object as the current layer. To draw the walls, invoke the MLINE command from the Draw toolbar. Set the Scale factor to 4, and draw the closed rectangle by selecting the points indicated in Figure P6–10. AutoCAD prompts:

```
Command: mline Enter
Justification = Top, Scale = 1.00, Style = X
Justification/Scale/STyle/<From point>: s Enter
Set Mline scale <1.00>: 4 Enter
Justification = Top, Scale = 4.00, Style = X
Justification/Scale/STyle/<From point>: (select point 1 as shown in Figure
     P6–10)
<To point>: (select point 2 as shown in Figure P6–10)
Undo/<To point>: (select point 3 as shown in Figure P6–10)
Close/Undo/<To point>: (select point 4 as shown in Figure P6–10)
Close/Undo/<To point>: c Enter
```

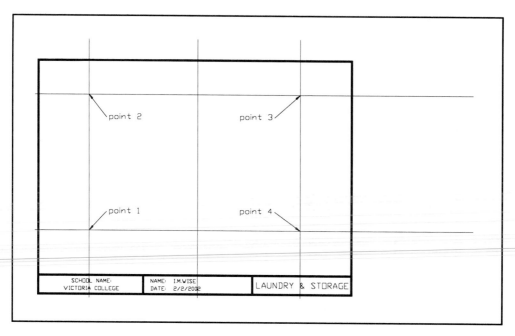

Figure P6–10 Points for drawing the walls

Step 15   To draw the interior wall, again invoke the MLINE command from the Draw toolbar. Set the Scale to 8 and the Justification to 0, and draw the interior wall by selecting the points indicated in Figure P6–11. AutoCAD prompts:

> Command: **mline** ⏎
> Justification = Top, Scale = 4.00, Style = X
> Justification/Scale/STyle/<From point>: **s** ⏎
> Set Mline scale <4.00>: **8** ⏎
> Justification = Top, Scale = 8.00, Style = X
> Justification/Scale/STyle/<From point>: **j** ⏎
> Top/Zero/Bottom <top>: **z** ⏎
> Justification = Zero, Scale = 8.00, Style = X
> Justification/Scale/STyle/<From point>: *(select point 1 as shown in Figure P6–11)*
> <To point>: *(select point 2 as shown in Figure P6–11)*
> Undo/<To point>: *(press ⏎ to terminate the command sequence)*

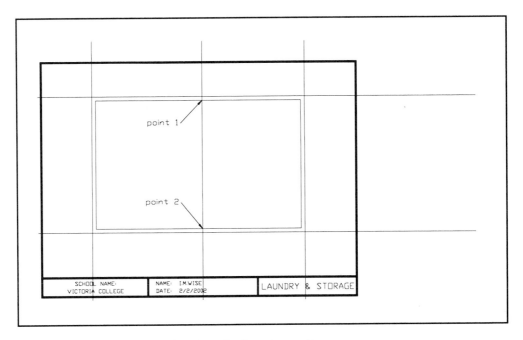

Figure P6-11 Points for drawing the interior walls

Step 16   Clear all of the Running Object Snap modes.

Step 17   To edit the multiline as shown in Figure P6–12, invoke the MLEDIT command from the Modify II toolbar. AutoCAD displays the Multiline Edit Tools dialog box. Select the Open Tee option, and then choose the OK button to close the dialog box. AutoCAD prompts:

> Command: **mledit** Enter
> Select first mline: *(select the interior wall at point A as shown in Figure P6–12)*
> Select second mline: *(select the exterior wall at point B as shown in Figure P6–12)*
> Select first mline (or Undo): *(select the interior wall at point C as shown in Figure P6–12)*
> Select second mline: *(select the exterior wall at point D as shown in Figure P6–12)*
> Select first mline (or Undo): *(press* Enter *to terminate the command sequence)*

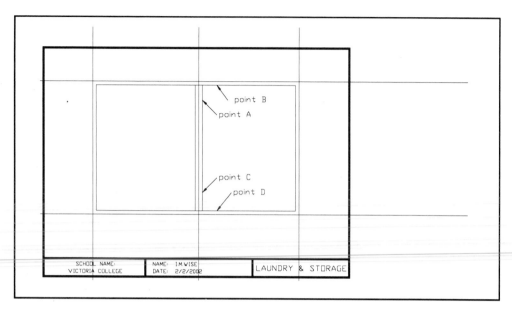

Figure P6–12 Points for editing multilines

After drawing the mline for the interior and exterior walls and "opening" the tees as indicated, the display should appear as shown in Figure P6–13.

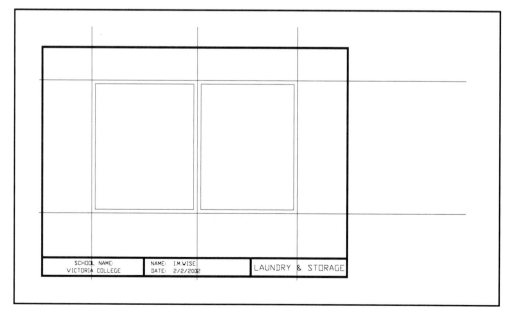

Figure P6–13 Drawing with interior and exterior walls

Step 18   Invoke the MOVE command from the Modify toolbar. AutoCAD prompts:

Command: **move** ⏎
Select objects: *(select the middle vertical construction line)*
Select objects: *(press ⏎ to complete the selection of objects)*
Base point or displacement: *(select a point on the selected line)*
Second point of displacement: *(select a point that is 2'-4" left of the line)*

Command: *(press ⏎ to repeat the MOVE command)*
Select objects: *(select the right vertical construction line)*
Select objects: *(press ⏎ to complete the selection of objects)*
Base point or displacement: *(select a point on the selected line)*
Second point of displacement: *(select a point that is 1'-4" left of the line)*

Command: *(press ⏎ to repeat the MOVE command)*
Select objects: *(select the lower horizontal construction line)*
Select objects: *(press ⏎ to complete the selection of the objects)*
Base point or displacement: *(select a point on the selected line)*
Second point of displacement: *(select a point that is 5'-4"above the line)*

Drawing the Counter for the Sink

Step 19   Set Intersection as the Running Object Snap mode. Invoke the LINE command from the Draw toolbar. AutoCAD prompts:

Command: **line** ⏎
From point: *(select point 1 as shown in Figure P6–14)*
To point: *(select point 2 as shown in Figure P6–14)*
To point: *(select point 3 as shown in Figure P6–14)*
To point: *(press ⏎ to terminate the command sequence)*

Command: *(press ⏎ to repeat the LINE command)*
LINE From point: *(select point 4 as shown in Figure P6–14)*
To point: *(select point 5 as shown in Figure P6-14)*
To point: *(press ⏎ to terminate the command sequence)*

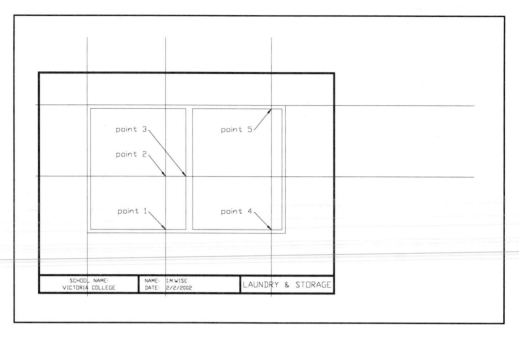

Figure P6–14 Points for drawing the counter for the sink

Step 20 Invoke the ERASE command from the Modify toolbar to erase the remaining construction lines. Clear all of the Running Object Snap modes.

Opening the Walls for Doors and Windows

Step 21 To create the opening of the walls, invoke the MLEDIT command from the Modify II toolbar. AutoCAD displays the Multiline Edit Tools dialog box, select the Cut All option, and then choose OK to close the dialog box. AutoCAD prompts:

Command: **mledit** [Enter]
Select mline: *(select the lower wall at point 1'-0",0'-0")*
Select second point: *(select the lower wall at point 3'-0",0'-0")*
Select mline (or Undo): *(select the lower wall at point 3'-8",0'-0")*
Select second point: *(select the lower wall at point 6'-8",0'-0")*
Select mline (or Undo): *(select the lower wall at point 7'-4",0'-0")*
Select second point: *(select the lower wall at point 9'-4",0'-0")*
Select mline (or Undo): *(select the lower wall at point 12'-0",0'-0")*
Select second point: *(select the lower wall at point 16'-0",0'-0")*
Select mline (or Undo): *(select the upper wall at point 3'-8",12'-0")*
Select second point: *(select the upper wall at point 6'-8",12'-0")*
Select mline (or Undo): *(press* [Enter] *to terminate the command sequence)*

Drawing the Windows and the Water Heater

Step 22   Invoke the ZOOM Window command to zoom in as shown in Figure P6–15.

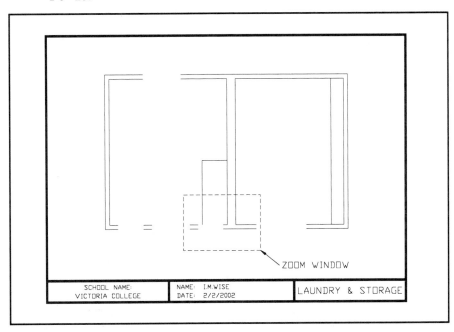

ZOOM WINDOW

| SCHOOL NAME: VICTORIA COLLEGE | NAME: I.M.WISE DATE: 2/2/2002 | LAUNDRY & STORAGE |

Figure P6-15 Drawing with ZOOM Window in the area indicated

Step 23   Change the SNAP setting to 2. Invoke the MLINE command from the Draw toolbar to draw the windows. AutoCAD prompts:

Command: **mline** `Enter`
Justification = Top, Scale = 4.00, Style = STANDARD
Justification/Scale/STyle/<From point>: **s** `Enter`
Set Mline scale <4.00>: **2** `Enter`
Justification = Top, Scale = 2.00, Style = STANDARD
Justification/Scale/STyle/<From point>: **j** `Enter`
Top/Zero/Bottom <top>: **z** `Enter`
Justification = Zero, Scale = 2.00, Style = STANDARD
Justification/Scale/STyle/<From point>: *(select point A, as shown in Figure P6–16, at coordinates 7'-4",0'-2")*
<To point>: *(select the endpoint at coordinates 9'-4",0'-2")*
Undo/<To point>: *(press* `Enter` *to terminate the command sequence)*

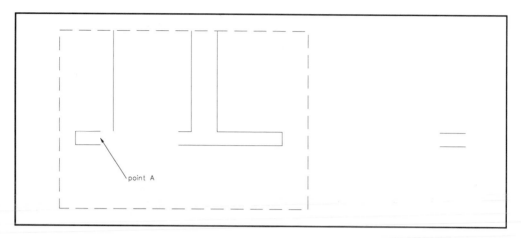

Figure P6–16 Points indicating where the starting point of the window has to be drawn

Command: *(press [Enter] to repeat the MLINE command)*
Justification = Zero, Scale = 2.00, Style = STANDARD
Justification/Scale/STyle/<From point>: **s** [Enter]
Set Mline scale <2.00>: **8** [Enter]
Justification = Zero, Scale = 8.00, Style = STANDARD
Justification/Scale/STyle/<From point>: *(select point A at coordinates 7'-4",0'-2")*
<To point>: *(select the endpoint at coordinates 9'-4",0'-2")*
Undo/<To point>: *(press [Enter] to terminate the command sequence)*

Step 24   Invoke the TRIM command from the Modify toolbar to trim the line for the counter even with the line for the window. AutoCAD prompts:

Command: **trim** [Enter]
Select cutting edges: *(select the mline for the cutting edge as shown in Figure P6–17)*
Select objects: *(press [Enter] to complete selection of the cutting edge)*
<Select object to trim>/Project/Edge/Undo: *(select the object to trim as shown in Figure P6–17)*
<Select object to trim>/Project/Edge/Undo: *(press [Enter] to complete selection of the object to trim)*

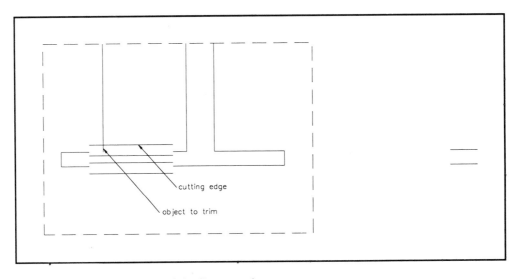

Figure P6–17 Indication of the lines to trim

Step 25 Use the LINE command to close the end of the multilines for the window openings and door jambs.

After trimming the line for the cabinet and drawing the lines for closing the ends of the window, the display should appear as shown in Figure P6–18.

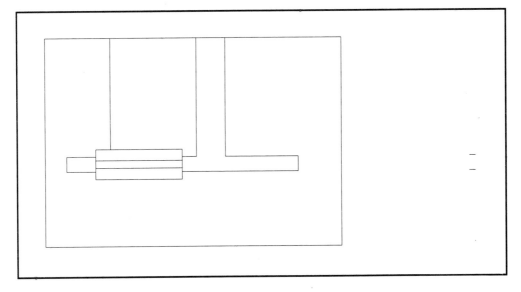

Figure P6–18 Drawing showing the window opening

Step 26   Draw two additional windows with the MLINE command with Scales 8 and 2 and Justification set to 0, and close the ends of the other multilines representing window and door jambs.

Step 27   Invoke the ZOOM All command to display the complete drawing. Draw the water heater with the CIRCLE command, with center at coordinates 11'-8",10'-4" and radius of 1'-0".

After drawing the remaining windows, closing the jambs, and drawing the water heater, the display should appear as shown in Figure P6–19.

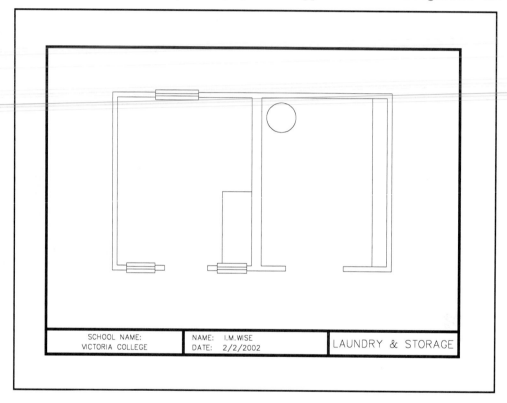

Figure P6–19 Drawing showing all the window openings and the water heater

Drawing the Doors

Step 28   Using the ZOOM Window option, enlarge the area as shown in Figure P6–20 to begin drawing doors.

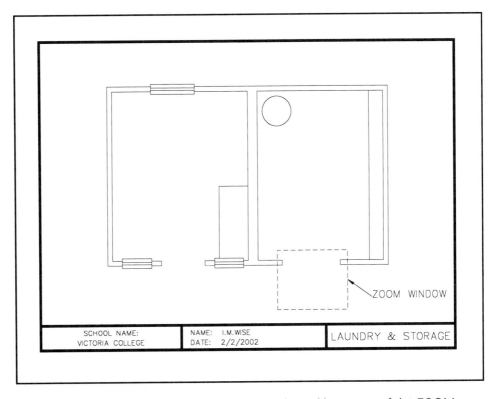

Figure P6–20 Points indicating the area to be enlarged by means of the ZOOM Window command

Step 29   Invoke the MLINE command from the Draw toolbar. Set the Scale to 1, and draw the double line representing the door on the right by selecting the points indicated in Figure P6–21. AutoCAD prompts:

> Command: **mline** Enter
> Justification = Zero, Scale = 2.00, Style = STANDARD
> Justification/Scale/STyle/<From point>: **j** Enter
> Top/Zero/Bottom <zero>: **t** Enter
> Justification = Top, Scale = 2.00, Style = STANDARD
> Justification/Scale/STyle/<From point>: **s** Enter
> Set Mline scale <2.00>: **1** Enter
> Justification = Top, Scale = 1.00, Style = STANDARD
> Justification/Scale/STyle/<From point>: *(select point A, as shown in Figure P6–21)*
> <To point>: *(select point B, as shown in Figure P6–21, at absolute coordinates 16'-0",-2'-0", or use the relative coordinates of @24<270)*
> Undo/<To point>: *(press* Enter *to terminate the command sequence)*

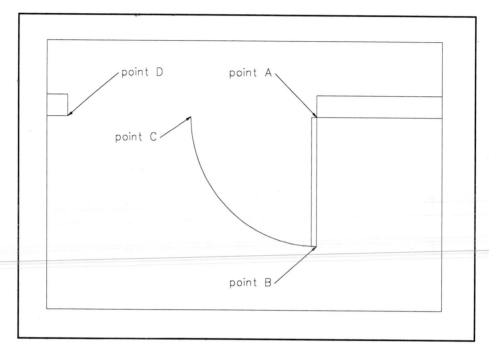

Figure P6-21 Points indicating the location of the door

Step 30   Invoke the LINE command from the Draw toolbar to close the ends of the "door" just drawn.

Step 31   Invoke the ARC command with Start/Center/Angle option to draw an arc to represent the swing of the door. AutoCAD prompts:

> Command: _arc Center/<Start point>: *(select point B, as shown in Figure P6-21)*
> Center/End/<Second point>: _c Center: *(select point A, as shown in Figure P6-21)*
> Angle/Length of chord/<End point>: Included Angle: **-90** Enter

Step 32   Invoke the MIRROR command from the Modify toolbar. AutoCAD prompts:

> Command: **mirror** Enter
> Select objects: *(select the multiline, end closing lines, and arc representing the door)*
> Select objects: *(press Enter to complete object selection)*
> First point of mirror line: *(select point C, as shown in Figure P6-21)*
> Second point: *(set Ortho to ON, and select a point above or below point C as shown in Figure P6-21)*
> Delete old objects? <N> Enter

Step 33 Use the PAN command to move to the viewing area to include the opening made in the wall on the left, and repeat the preceding method to draw the multiline, end lines, and arc to represent the 3'-0" door on the left as shown in Figure P6–22.

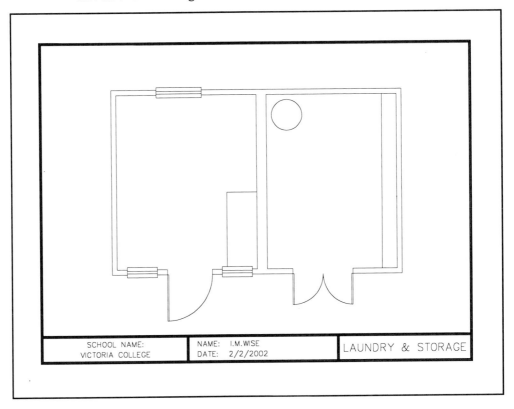

SCHOOL NAME:
VICTORIA COLLEGE

NAME: I.M.WISE
DATE: 2/2/2002

LAUNDRY & STORAGE

Figure P6–22 Drawing showing the doors and windows

Drawing the Sink

Step 34 Use the PAN and/or ZOOM command to move and resize the viewing area to include the counter, to draw a sink as shown in Figure P6–23.

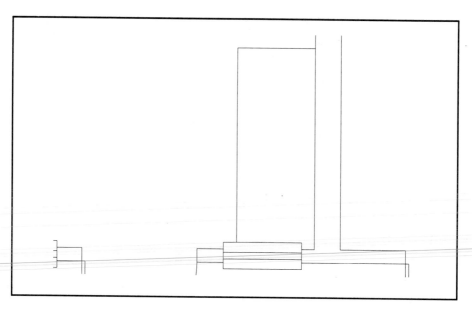

Figure P6–23 Drawing showing the closeup of the counter

Step 35 Invoke the RECTANGLE command from the Draw toolbar to draw the sink. AutoCAD prompts:

> Command: **rectang** [Enter]
> First corner: *(select the lower left point at 7'-10",2'-0")*
> Other corner: *(select the upper right point at 9'-2",3'-8")*

Step 36 Invoke the FILLET command from the Modify toolbar. AutoCAD prompts:

> Command: **fillet** [Enter]
> (TRIM mode) Current fillet radius = 0'-0"
> Polyline/Radius/Trim/<Select first object>: **r** [Enter]
> Enter fillet radius <0'-0">: **2** [Enter]
>
> Command: *(press* [Enter] *to repeat the FILLET command)*
> (TRIM mode) Current fillet radius = 0'-2"
> Polyline/Radius/Trim/<Select first object>: **p** [Enter]
> Select the polyline: *(select the rectangle drawn in the previous step)*

The results should appear as shown in Figure P6–24.

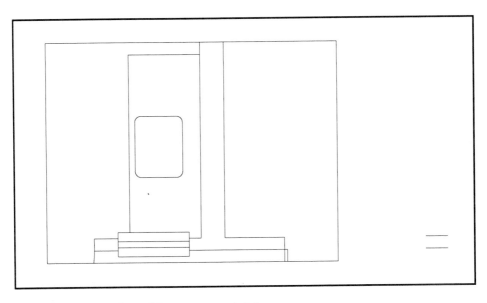

Figure P6–24 Drawing with counter and sink

Drawing the Washers and Dryers

Step 37 Invoke the ZOOM All command to display the complete drawing. Set Hidden as the current layer.

Step 38 Invoke the RECTANGLE command from the Draw toolbar. AutoCAD prompts:

> Command: **rectang** Enter
> First corner: *(select the lower left point at 0'-6",0'-8")*
> Other corner: *(select the upper right point at 3'-0",3'-2")*
>
> Command: *(press* Enter *to repeat the RECTANGLE command)*
> First corner: *(select the lower left point at 6'-8",5'-8")*
> Other corner: *(select the lower left point at 9'-4",8'-4")*

Step 39 Invoke the ARRAY command from the Modify toolbar. AutoCAD prompts:

> Command: **array** Enter
> Select objects: *(select the first rectangle drawn in step 38)*
> Select objects: *(press* Enter *to complete selection)*
> Rectangular or Polar array (R/P) <R>: **r** Enter
> Number of rows (—) <1>: **4**
> Number of columns (| | |) <1>: Enter
> Unit cell or distance between rows (—): *(select a point)*
> Other corner: *(select a point that is 2'-8" above the first point selected)*

Step 40   Invoke the COPY command from the Modify toolbar. AutoCAD prompts:

> Command: **copy** Enter
> Select objects: *(select the second rectangle drawn in step 38)*
> Select objects: *(press* Enter *to complete selection)*
> <Base point or displacement>/Multiple: *(select a point)*
> Second point of displacement: *(select a relative displacement point at 3'-0" at 90 degrees)*

Figure P6–25 shows the result after drawing the washers and dryers.

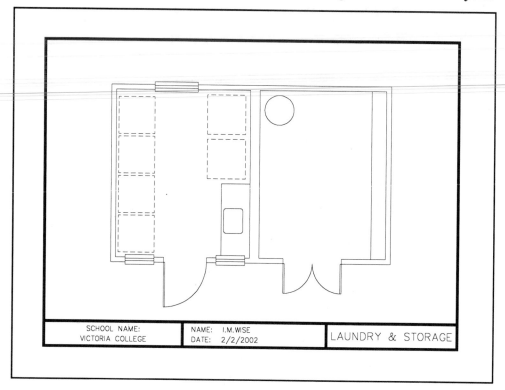

SCHOOL NAME:
VICTORIA COLLEGE

NAME: I.M.WISE
DATE: 2/2/2002

LAUNDRY & STORAGE

Figure P6–25 Drawing with washers and dryers

Completing the Shelves

Step 41   To draw the shelves, invoke the MLINE command from the Draw toolbar. AutoCAD prompts:

> Command: **mline** Enter
> Justification/Scale/STyle/<From point>: **j** Enter
> Top/Zero/Bottom <zero>: **z** Enter

Justification = Zero, Scale = 2.00, Style = STANDARD
Justification/Scale/STyle/<From point>: **s** [Enter]
Set Mline scale <2.00>: **1** [Enter]
Justification = Top, Scale = 1.00, Style = STANDARD
Justification/Scale/STyle/<From point>: *(select a point at 18'-0",8'-0")*

<To point>: *(select a point at 19'-0",8'-0")*

<To point>: *(press* [Enter] *to terminate the command sequence)*

Command: *(press* [Enter] *to repeat the MLINE command)*
Justification/Scale/STyle/<From point>: *(select a point at 18'-0",4'-0")*
<To point>: *(select a point at 19'-0",4'-0")*
<To point>: *(press* [Enter] *to terminate the command sequence)*

Figure P6–26 shows the result after drawing the shelves.

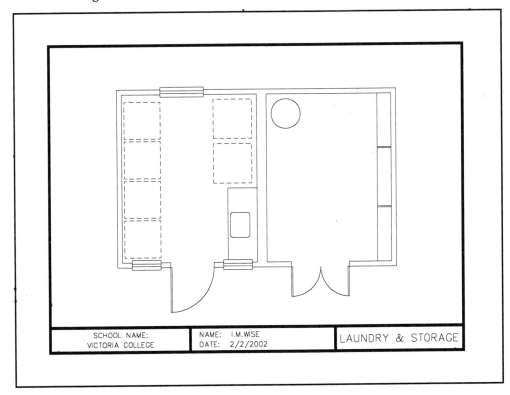

Figure P6–26 Drawing with shelves

Drawing Text Objects

Step 42   Set Text as the current layer. Invoke the DTEXT command, and draw the text at appropriate text size, as shown in Figure P6–27.

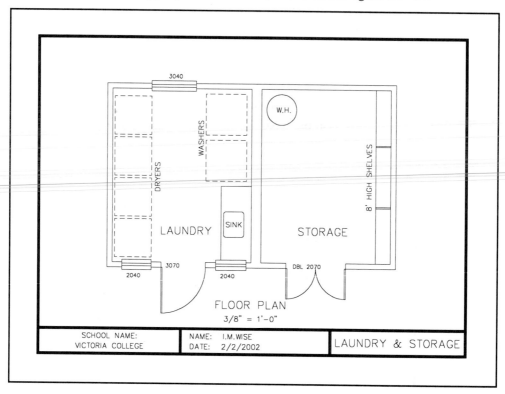

Figure P6–27 Drawing with text objects

Congratulations! You have just successfully applied several AutoCAD concepts in creating the drawing.

EXERCISES 6-1 THROUGH 6-6

Exercise 6-1

The drawing shown is typical of informational graphics/text drawings whose objects are not dimensioned but parametric in nature. This cross section of a reinforced concrete column is typical of those with varying dimensions and member of reinforcing bars. It is for reference only. The important information is given in the written text. Create the drawing shown according to the settings given in the following table.

Settings	Value		
1. Units	Decimal		
2. Limits	Lower left corner: 0",0"		
	Upper right corner: 12",9"		
3. Grid	.5		
4. Snap	.5		
5. Layers	*NAME*	*COLOR*	*LINETYPE*
	Center	Cyan	Continuous
	Border	Red	Continuous
	Object	Green	Continuous
	Text	Blue	Continous
	Hidden	Cyan	Continuous
	Pattern	White	Continuous

Hints	Make sure you are in the appropriate layer before you draw the objects.
	Use the DONUT command to draw two circles with large OD/ID and multiple circles with small OD and zero ID.
	The patterning in the cross section can be generated by drawing one small triangle with the PLINE command and then copying and rotating it randomly throughout the area. The stipples that are conventional in representing concrete can be created also randomly placed, by means of the POINT command. One of the conventions of patterning for concrete is that the stippling is usually more concentrated near the edges of the cross section than in the center.
	The MTEXT command is used to create blocks of text within prescribed rectangles. The justification determines where the block of text anchors and where the overage spills out of the rectangle.

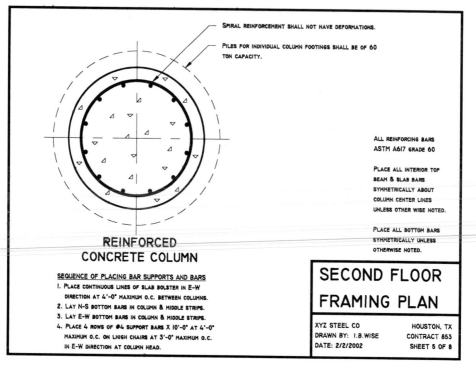

SPIRAL REINFORCEMENT SHALL NOT HAVE DEFORMATIONS.

PILES FOR INDIVIDUAL COLUMN FOOTINGS SHALL BE OF 60 TON CAPACITY.

ALL REINFORCING BARS
ASTM A617 GRADE 60

PLACE ALL INTERIOR TOP
BEAM & SLAB BARS
SYMMETRICALLY ABOUT
COLUMN CENTER LINES
UNLESS OTHER WISE NOTED.

PLACE ALL BOTTOM BARS
SYMMETRICALLY UNLESS
OTHERWISE NOTED.

REINFORCED
CONCRETE COLUMN

SEQUENCE OF PLACING BAR SUPPORTS AND BARS
1. PLACE CONTINUOUS LINES OF SLAB BOLSTER IN E-W
   DIRECTION AT 4'-0" MAXIMUM O.C. BETWEEN COLUMNS.
2. LAY N-S BOTTOM BARS IN COLUMN & MIDDLE STRIPS.
3. LAY E-W BOTTOM BARS IN COLUMN & MIDDLE STRIPS.
4. PLACE 4 ROWS OF #4 SUPPORT BARS X 10'-0" AT 4'-0"
   MAXIMUM O.C. ON LHIGH CHAIRS AT 3'-0" MAXIMUM O.C.
   IN E-W DIRECTION AT COLUMN HEAD.

SECOND FLOOR
FRAMING PLAN

XYZ STEEL CO	HOUSTON, TX
DRAWN BY: I.B.WISE	CONTRACT 853
DATE: 2/2/2002	SHEET 5 OF 8

Figure Ex6–1 Completed drawing

Exercise 6–2

Create the drawing shown according to the settings given in the following table. (Do *not* dimension this drawing.)

Settings	Value
1. Units	Architectural
2. Limits	Lower left corner: 0'-0,0'-0
	Upper right corner: 65'-0,54'-0
3. Grid	12
4. Snap	6
5. Layers	*NAME* *COLOR* *LINETYPE*
	Center Cyan Continuous
	Border Red Continuous
	Object Green Continuous
	Text Blue Continuous
	Hidden Cyan Hidden

Hints	
	Make sure you are in the appropriate layer before you draw the objects.
	Use the MLINE command to draw the beams in continuous linetype and the footings in hidden linetype.
	Use the MLEDIT command to connect the beams in open tees.
	The MTEXT command is used to create blocks of text within prescribed rectangles. The justification determines where the block of text anchors and where the overage spills out of the rectangle.

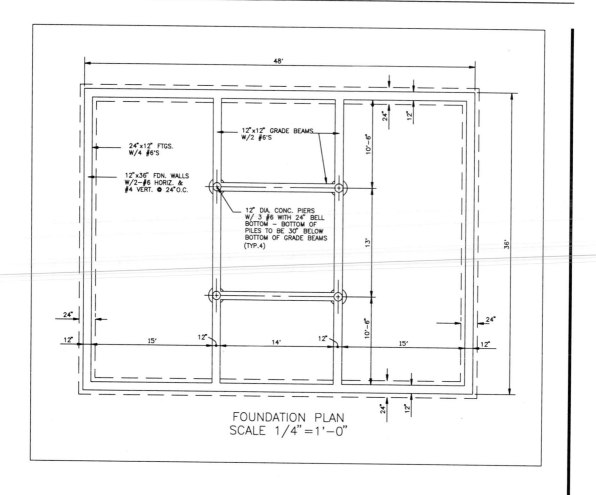

24"x12" FTGS.
W/4 #6'S

12"x36" FDN. WALLS
W/2-#6 HORIZ. &
#4 VERT. @ 24"O.C.

12"x12" GRADE BEAMS
W/2 #6'S

12" DIA. CONC. PIERS
W/ 3 #6 WITH 24" BELL
BOTTOM — BOTTOM OF
PILES TO BE 30" BELOW
BOTTOM OF GRADE BEAMS
(TYP.4)

FOUNDATION PLAN
SCALE 1/4"=1'-0"

Exercise 6-3

Create the drawing shown according to the settings given in the following table. (Do *not* dimension this drawing.)

Settings	Value
1. Units	Architectural
2. Limits	Lower left corner: 0'-0",0'-0"
	Upper right corner: 50'-0",40'-0"
3. Grid	12"
4. Snap	6"
5. Layers	

NAME	COLOR	LINETYPE
Center	Cyan	Continuous
Border	Red	Continuous
Object	Green	Continuous
Text	Blue	Continuous
Hidden	Cyan	Hidden

Hints	Make sure you are in the appropriate layer before you draw the objects.
	Use the MLINE command to draw the beam edges in continuous linetype and the webs in hidden linetype.
	Detail #1 can be drawn to true size and then the SCALE command used to increase its size by a factor of 1.5 (the scale ratio of 1/4" = 1'-0" to 3/8" = 1'-0").

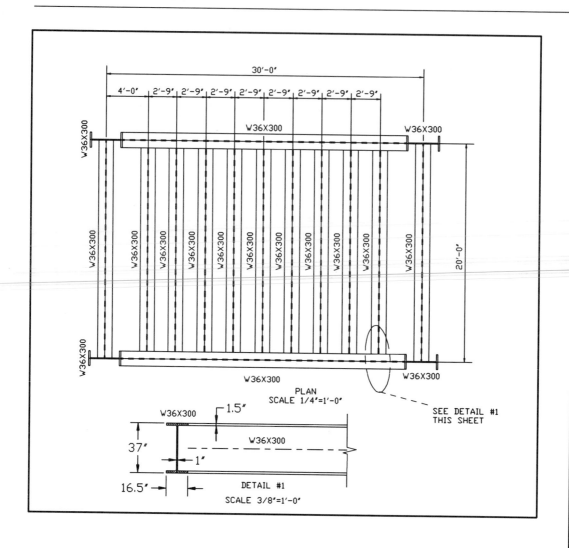

30'-0"

4'-0" | 2'-9" | 2'-9" | 2'-9" | 2'-9" | 2'-9" | 2'-9" | 2'-9" | 2'-9"

W36X300

W36X300

W36X300

20'-0"

W36X300

W36X300

PLAN
SCALE 1/4"=1'-0"

SEE DETAIL #1
THIS SHEET

W36X300

1.5"

W36X300

37"

1"

16.5"

DETAIL #1
SCALE 3/8"=1'-0"

Exercise 6–4

Create the drawing shown according to the settings given in the following table.

Settings	Value
1. Units	Architectural
2. Limits	Lower left corner: 10'-0",10'-0"
	Upper right corner: 132'-0",102'-0"
3. Grid	60"
4. Snap	12"
5. Added Layers	*NAME* *COLOR* *LINETYPE*
	Spline Green Continuous
	Text Blue Continuous

Hints	Use the SPLINE command to draw splines. They do *not* need to be drawn through exact points. Estimate their locations and reproduce the splines shown in the drawing. In the real world, the topographic point locations will be established by a surveying crew in the field and given to you to make your drawing.
	See Figure Ex6–4a for points showing the approximate locations used to draw the splines.

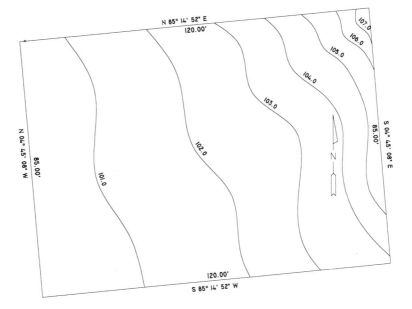

Figure Ex6–4 Topographic drawing

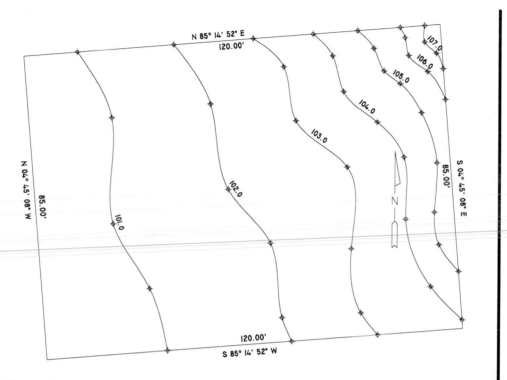

Figure Ex6-4a Topographic drawing showing the approximate locations

Exercise 6-5

Create the drawing shown according to the settings given in the following table. (Do *not* dimension this drawing.)

Settings	Value
1. Units	Architectural
2. Limits	Lower left corner: 0',0' Upper right corner: 12',9'
3. Grid	6"
4. Snap	3"
5. Layers	

NAME	_COLOR_	_LINETYPE_
Border	Red	Continuous
Object	Green	Continuous
Text	Blue	Continuous

Hints	
	Use the MLINE command to draw the door panel perimeters with a style that displays the joints. One of the top panels of the front door can be copied down. Then, using the STRETCH command, you can lengthen the copy and then copy the newly created longer panel. Repeat for the lower panels of all the doors.
	Draw the door handles with a style that closes the ends of the mline.
	The window inside the back door will have to be drawn using a style that does not display the joints or close the ends.
	Use the MLEDIT command to connect the window mullions in open tees.
	The MTEXT command is used to create text objects.

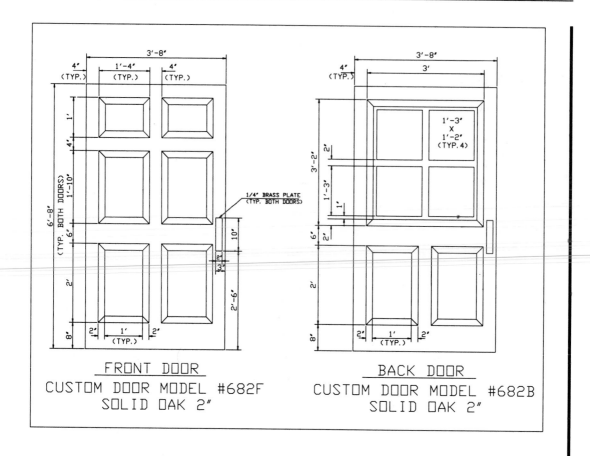

FRONT DOOR
CUSTOM DOOR MODEL #682F
SOLID OAK 2"

BACK DOOR
CUSTOM DOOR MODEL #682B
SOLID OAK 2"

Exercise 6–6

Create the drawing shown according to the settings given in the following table. (Do *not* dimension this drawing.)

Settings	Value		
1. Units	Architectural		
2. Limits	Lower left corner: 0',0'		
	Upper right corner: 12',9'		
3. Grid	6"		
4. Snap	3"		
5. Layers	*NAME*	*COLOR*	*LINETYPE*
	Border	Red	Continuous
	Object	Green	Continuous
	Text	Blue	Continuous

Hints	Use the MLINE command to draw the drawer perimeters with a style that displays the joints.
	Draw the drawer handles and desk top and bases with a style that closes the ends of the mline.
	Draw Details "A" and "B" to true size, and then use the SCALE command to make them larger, as in the drawing shown.

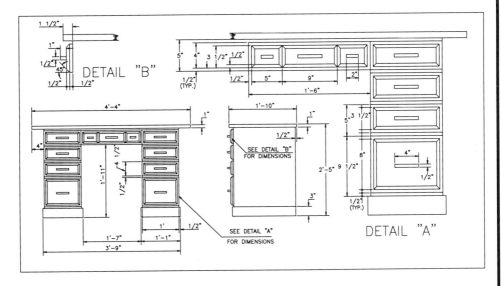

Figure Ex6–6 Detailed drawing of a desk

REVIEW QUESTIONS

1. The elements of a multiline can have different colors?
   a. True
   b. False

2. A SPLINE object:
   a. does not actually pass through the control points
   b. is always shown as a continuous line
   c. requires you to specify tangent information for each control point
   d. requires you to specify tangent information for the first and last points only

3. When spell checking a drawing, AutoCAD automatically checks the entire drawing.
   a. True
   b. False

4. To use incline lettering so that the vertical portions of the characters point to 2 o'clock for a horizontal line of text, the obliquing angle should be:
   a. -60
   b. -30
   c. 0
   d. 30
   e. 60

5. Once objects are GROUPed together, they can be ungrouped by:
   a. using the EXPLODE command
   b. using the UNGROUP command
   c. using the GROUP command
   d. they can not be ungrouped

6. To insert the diameter symbol into a string of text, you should type:
   a. %%d
   b. %%c
   c. %%phi
   d. %%dia

7. It is possible to force all text on a drawing to display as an open rectangle in order to speed up the redisplay of the drawing by using the:
   a. TEXT command
   b. RTEXT command
   c. QTEXT command
   d. DTEXT command

8. In order to select a different font for use in the DTEXT command, a text style must be created.
   a. True
   b. False

9. The grips dialog box allows you to change all of the following, except:
   a. grip size
   b. grip color
   c. toggle grips system variable on/off
   d. specify the location of the grips

10. Grips do not allow you to _____ an object.
    a. trim
    b. erase
    c. mirror
    d. move
    e. stretch

11. To edit a word in the middle of a string of text, a reasonable command to use would be:
    a. DDEDIT
    b. CHPROP
    c. DDCHPROP
    d. MODIFY
    e. CHANGE

12. Multiline styles can be saved to an external file, thus allowing their use in multiple drawings.
    a. True
    b. False

13. The ID command will:
    a. display the serial number of the AutoCAD program
    b. display the X, Y, and Z coordinate of a selected point
    c. allow you to password protect a drawing
    d. none of the above

14. A quick way to find the length of a line is to use what command?
    a. LIST
    b. DISTANCE
    c. DIMENSION
    d. LENGTH
    e. COORDINATES

15. To obtain a full listing of all the objects contained in the current drawing, you should use:
    a. LIST
    b. DBLIST
    c. LISTALL
    d. DBDUMP
    e. DUMP

16. When filleting multilines, you must specify:
    a. the radius of the innermost fillet
    b. the radius of the center line
    c. the radius of the outermost fillet
    d. multilines cannot be filleted

17. Which of the following are not valid options when creating a text style:
    a. width factor
    b. upside down
    c. vertical
    d. backwards
    e. none of the above (i.e. all are valid)

18. You can change the setting of a system variable by using the command:
    a. SYSVAR
    b. SETVAR
    c. VARSET
    d. VARSYS
    e. none of the above

19. Which of the following is not a valid type of system variable
    a. real
    b. integer
    c. point
    d. string
    e. double

20. To locate text such that it is centered exactly within a circle, a reasonable justification would be:
    a. Center
    b. Middle
    c. Full
    d. Both A and B
    e. none, simply zoom in and approximate it

• • • • • • • • • • • • • •

CHAPTER

7

DIMENSIONING

• •

INTRODUCTION

AutoCAD provides a full range of dimensioning commands and utilities to enable the drafter to comply with the conventions of most disciplines, including architecture and civil, electrical, and mechanical engineering, among many others.

After completing this chapter, you will be able to:

✓ Draw linear dimensioning
✓ Draw aligned dimensioning
✓ Draw angular dimensioning
✓ Draw diameter and radius dimensioning
✓ Draw leaders with annotation and geometric tolerance
✓ Draw ordinate dimensioning
✓ Draw baseline and continue dimensioning
✓ Edit dimension text
✓ Create and modify dimension styles

AutoCAD makes drawing dimensions easy. For example, the width of the rectangle shown in Figure 7–1 can be dimensioned by specifying the two endpoints of the top corners and then specifying a point to determine the location of the dimension line. AutoCAD drags a grayed image of the dimension to indicate how it will look while you move the cursor to specify the location of the dimension line. Another (even easier) method is to press Enter in response to the "First extension line or ENTER to select:" prompt and then to select the top line of the rectangle when prompted to select an object. AutoCAD acts as though you used an Object Snap feature to select the endpoints (or intersections) at the corners and again prompts for the location of the dimension line. This takes only two steps and does not require invoking one of the available object snap options.

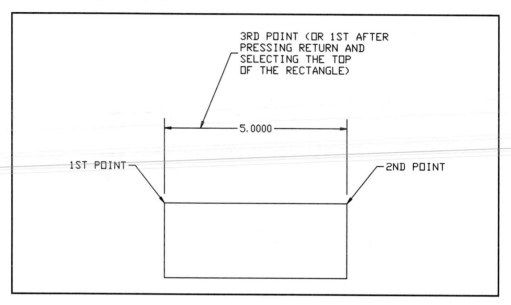

Figure 7-1 An example of linear dimensioning

Once linear dimensioning is mastered, other types of dimensions, such as diameter, radius, angular, baseline, and ordinate dimensioning, can be drawn quickly and accurately.

The dimension types available are linear, angular, diameter, radius, and ordinate. There are primary and secondary commands available for each of these types. There are also other general utility, editing, and style-related commands and subcommands that assist you in drawing the correct dimensions quickly and with accuracy.

The linear dimensioning command options include Horizontal, Vertical, Aligned, and Rotated.

Angular dimensioning is covered by the Angular command.

Diameter, radius and ordinate dimensioning are covered by the Diameter, Radius, and Ordinate commands, respectively.

Approximately 60 dimension variables are available specifically for dimensioning. Most of these have names that begin with "DIM," they are used for such purposes as determining the size of the gap between the extension line and the point selected on an object or whether one or both of the extension lines will be drawn or suppressed.

It is combinations of these variable settings that can be named and saved as dimension styles and later recalled for applying when needed.

Dimension utilities include Override, Center, Leader, Baseline, Continue, and Feature Control Frames for adding tolerancing information.

The dimension editing command options include Hometext, Newtext, Oblique, Tedit, and Trotate.

DIMENSION TERMINOLOGY

Following are the terms for the different parts that make up dimensions in AutoCAD.

Figure 7–2 shows the different components of a typical dimensioning.

Dimension Line The dimension line is offset from the measured feature. The dimension line (sometimes drawn into two segments outside the extension lines if a single line with its related text will not fit between the extension lines) indicates the direction and length of the measured distance but is usually offset for clarity. If the dimension is measured between parallel lines of one or two objects, then it may not be offset, but is drawn on the object or between two objects. Dimension lines are usually terminated with markers such as arrows or ticks (short slanted lines). Angular dimension lines become arcs whose centers are at the vertex of the angle.

Arrowhead The arrowhead is a mark at the end of the dimension line to indicate its termination. Shapes other than arrows are used in some styles.

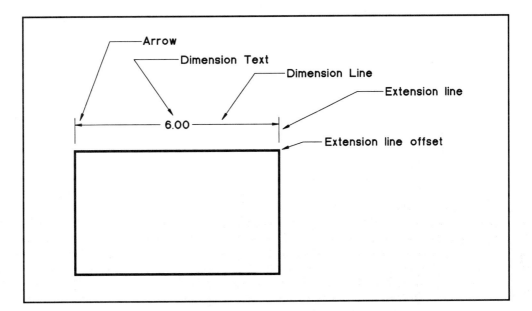

Figure 7–2 The different components of a typical dimensioning

Extension Line When the dimension line is offset from the measured feature, the extension lines (sometimes referred to as *witness lines*) indicate such offset. Unless you have invoked the Oblique option, the extension lines will be perpendicular to the direction of the measurement.

Dimension Text The dimension text consists of numbers, words, characters, and symbols used to indicate the measured value and type of dimension. When the text has been altered in the standard dimension style, the number/symbol format is decimal. This conforms to the same linear and angular units as the default settings of the units. The text style usually conforms to that of the current text style.

Leader The leader is a radial line used to point from the dimension text to the circle or arc whose diameter or radius is being dimensioned. A leader can also be used for general annotation.

Center Mark The center mark is made up of lines or a series of lines that cross in the center of a circle for the purpose of marking its center.

ASSOCIATIVE/NON-ASSOCIATIVE DIMENSIONS

Dimensions in AutoCAD can be drawn either as associative or non-associative, depending on the setting of the DIMASO dimensioning variable.

Associative The associative dimension drawn with the DIMASO dimensioning variable set to ON has all of its separate parts become members of a single associative dimension. Therefore, if any one of the members is selected for modifying, all members are highlighted and subject to being modified. This is similar to the manner in which member objects of a block are treated. In addition to the customary visible parts, AutoCAD draws point objects at the ends, where the measurement actually occurs on the object. If you have dimensioned the width of a rectangle with an associative dimension and then selected one end of the rectangle to stretch, the dimension will also be stretched, and the dimension text will be changed to correspond to the new measurement.

Non-Associative The non-associative dimensions are drawn while the DIMASO dimensioning variable is set to OFF, the members are drawn as separate objects. If one of the components of the dimension is selected for modifying, it will be the only one modified.

> **NOTE:** An associative dimension can be converted to a non-associative dimension with the EXPLODE command. Once the dimension is exploded, you cannot recombine the separate parts back into the associative dimension from which they were exploded (except by means of the UNDO command if feasible). Note that when you explode an associative dimension, the measurement-determining points (nodes) remain in the drawing as point objects.

DIMENSIONING COMMANDS

In AutoCAD two primary ways to enter dimensioning commands are available:

1. At the "Command:" prompt, enter **dim**. You will be shifted to the Dimensioning Command mode in which the prompt becomes "DIM:"; only those commands valid during this special mode will be acceptable. For example, you can enter **aligned** during this mode but not at the "Command:" prompt. And you cannot enter **line** while in the Dimensioning Command mode because it is not one of the dimensioning commands.

Other commands that are accessible while in the Dimensioning Command mode are Exit, Redraw, Style, Undo (or U), and Update.

2. At the "Command:" prompt, enter **dimaligned** (or some other special dimensioning command). This is acceptable during the standard Command mode but not in the Dimensioning Command mode.

Linear Dimensioning

Invoke the Linear Dimension command from:

Dimension toolbar	Select the Linear Dimension command (see Figure 7–3)
Pull-down menu	Dime<u>n</u>sion > <u>L</u>inear
Command: prompt	**dimlinear** ⏎
Dimensioning Command mode	**hor** (for horizontal) or **ver** (for vertical) ⏎

Figure 7–3 Invoking the Linear Dimension command from the Dimension toolbar

AutoCAD prompts:

Command: **dimlinear**
First extension line origin or press ENTER to select:

Specify a point and AutoCAD uses it as the start point (origin) for the first extension line. This point can be the endpoint of a line, the intersection of objects, the center point of a circle, or even the insertion point of a text object. You can select a point on the object itself. AutoCAD provides a gap between the object and the extension line that is equal to the value of the DIMEXE dimensioning variable, which you can change at any time. After you designate the start point (origin), AutoCAD prompts:

Second extension line origin:

Designate a point at which the second extension line should start.

Dynamic horizontal/vertical dimensioning is an option after you have selected two points in response to the DIMLINEAR command. If you select two points on the same horizontal line, moving the cursor above or below the line causes the grayed image of the dimension to appear. AutoCAD assumes you wish to draw a horizontal dimension. Likewise, AutoCAD assumes a vertical dimension if the selected points are on the same vertical line.

Dynamic drag, switching between horizontal and vertical, is more applicable when the two points specified are not on the same horizontal or vertical line. That is, they can be considered diagonally opposite corners of an imaginary rectangle with both width and height. After the two points are specified, you are prompted to select the location of the dimension line. You will also be shown a grayed image of where the dimension will be located, by where the cursor is located relative to the imaginary rectangle formed by the two points. If the cursor is above the top line or below the bottom line of the rectangle, then the dimension will be horizontal. If the cursor is to the right of the right side or to the left of the left side of the rectangle, then the dimension will be vertical. If the cursor is dragged to one of the outside quadrants or inside of the rectangle, it will maintain the type of dimension in effect before the cursor was moved.

After two points have been specified, AutoCAD prompts:

Dimension line location (Mtext/Text/Angle/Horizontal/Vertical/Rotated):

If necessary you can override the type of dimension to be drawn by typing **h** (for Horizontal), **v** (for Vertical), or **r** (for Rotated).

The **Rotated** option allows you to draw the dimension at a specified angle that is not horizontal, vertical, or at the angle determined by the two points specified in the case of aligned dimensioning (see the next section, on Aligned Dimensioning). When you select the Rotated option, AutoCAD prompts:

Dimension line angle <default>:

Specify the dimension line angle or specify two points on the drawing to rotate the dimension line. The points selected do not have to be parallel to the direction of the dimensioned distance.

The **Text** and **Mtext** options allow you to change the measured dimension text. The **Angle** option allows you to change the rotation angle of the dimension text. After responding appropriately for Text or Angle, AutoCAD repeats the prompts for the dimension line location.

Specify a point through which the dimension line is to be drawn. AutoCAD draws the line on which the dimension text is drawn. If there is enough room between the extension lines, the dimension text will be centered in or on this line. However, if the dimension line, arrows, and text do not fit between the extension lines, they are drawn outside. The text will be drawn near the second extension line.

The following command sequence is an example of placing linear dimensioning for a horizontal line by providing two data points for the first and second line origins, respectively, as shown in Figure 7–4.

> Command: **dimlinear**
> First extension line origin or press ENTER to select: *(specify the origin of the first extension line)*
> Second extension line origin: *(specify the origin of the second extension line)*
> Dimension line location (Mtext/Text/Angle/Horizontal/Vertical/Rotated): *(specify the location for the dimension line)*

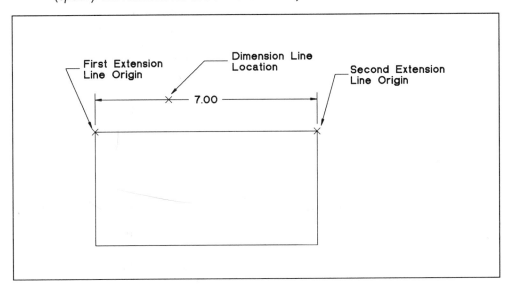

Figure 7–4 Placing linear dimensioning for a horizontal line

The following command sequence is an example of placing linear dimensioning for a vertical line by providing two data points for the first and second line origins, respectively, as shown in Figure 7–5.

> Command:**dimlinear**
> First extension line origin or press ENTER to select: *(specify the origin of the first extension line)*

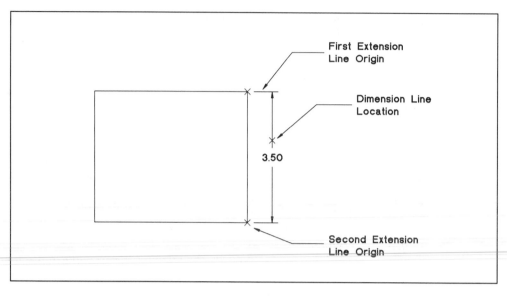

Figure 7–5 Placing linear dimensioning for a vertical line

Second extension line origin: *(specify the origin of the second extension line)*
Dimension line location (Mtext/Text/Angle/Horizontal/Vertical/Rotated):
    (specify the location for the dimension line)

Aligned Dimensioning

When dimensioning a line drawn at an angle, it may be necessary to align the dimension line with the object line.

Invoke the Aligned Dimension command from:

Dimension toolbar	Select the Aligned Dimension command (see Figure 7–6)
Pull-down menu	Dimension > Aligned
Command: prompt	**dimaligned** Enter
Dimensioning Command mode	**ali** Enter

Figure 7–6 Invoking the Dimaligned command from the Dimension toolbar

AutoCAD prompts:

> Command: **dimaligned**
> First extension line origin or press ENTER to select:

Designate a point at which the first extension line should start. AutoCAD prompts:

> Second extension line origin:

Designate a point at which the second extension line should start. After two points have been selected, AutoCAD prompts:

> Dimension line location (Mtext/Text/Angle):

The **Text** and **Mtext** options allow you to change the measured dimension text. The **Angle** option allows you to change the rotation angle of the dimension text. After you respond appropriately for Text or Angle, AutoCAD repeats the prompts for the dimension line location. Specify a point where the dimension line is to be drawn.

The following command sequence shows an example of placing aligned dimensioning for an angular line by providing two data points for the first and second line origins, respectively, as shown in Figure 7–7.

> Command: **dimaligned**
> First extension line origin or press ENTER to select: *(specify the origin of the first extension line)*
> Second extension line origin: *(specify the origin of the second extension line)*
> Dimension line location (Mtext/Text/Angle): *(specify the location of the dimension line)*

Linear Dimensioning of Objects

If you press ⏎ in response to the "First extension line origin or ENTER to select:" prompt, AutoCAD prompts:

> Select object to dimension:

If the object is a line object, AutoCAD automatically uses the line's endpoints as the first and second points to determine the distance to measure. You will be prompted to select the location of the dimension line. If you are in the Horizontal mode, a horizontal dimension is drawn accordingly. Likewise with the Vertical mode. If you have not yet determined the type of dimension to be drawn, then a horizontal dimension is drawn if the selection point for the dimension line is above or below the line object, and a vertical dimension is drawn if the selection point for the dimension line is to the right or left of the line object. If you are in the Aligned mode, AutoCAD

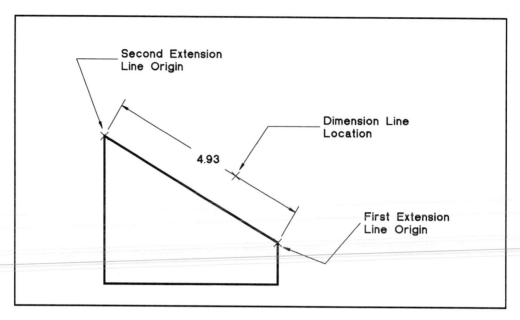

Figure 7–7 Placing aligned dimensioning for a line drawn at an angle

uses the endpoints of the selected line object as the first and second points and its direction as the direction to measure. If you are in the Rotated mode AutoCAD will use the first two points selected to determine the direction of the dimension and measure the distance between the two endpoints of the line object in that direction. The dimension line passes through the last point selected.

The following command sequence shows an example of placing a linear dimension to a single object, as shown in Figure 7–8.

> Command: **dimlinear**
> First extension line origin or ENTER to select: Enter
> Select object to dimension: *(identify the line)*
> Dimension line location (Mtext/Text/Angle/Horizontal/Vertical/Rotated): *(specify the location of the dimension line)*

If the object is a circle, AutoCAD automatically uses the diameter of the circle as the distance to measure and the point at which you selected the circle as one diameter endpoint for one end of the measured direction. If you are in the Horizontal mode, a horizontal dimension is drawn using the endpoints of the horizontal diameter. Likewise, with the Vertical mode the endpoints of the vertical diameter is used. If you are in the Rotated mode, AutoCAD uses the first two points selected to determine the direction of the dimension and measure the distance between the two endpoints of a diameter in that direction. The dimension line passes through the last point selected.

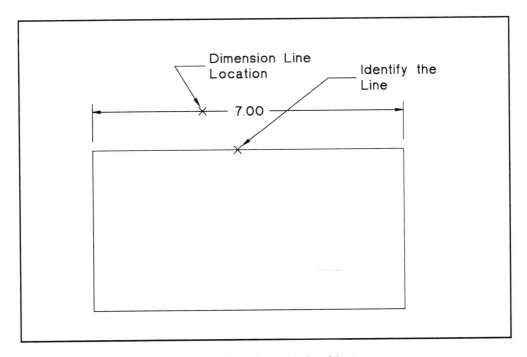

Figure 7–8 Placing a linear dimension for a single object

If the object is an arc, AutoCAD automatically uses the arc's endpoints for the first and second points in determining the distance to measure. You will be prompted to select the location of the dimension line. If you are in the Horizontal mode, a horizontal dimension is drawn accordingly. Likewise with the Vertical mode. If you have not yet determined the type of dimension to be drawn, then a horizontal dimension will be drawn if the selection point for the dimension line is above or below the arc, and a vertical dimension is drawn if the selection point for the dimension line is to the right or left of the arc. If you are in the Aligned mode, AutoCAD uses the endpoints of the selected arc as the first and second points and its direction as the direction to measure. If you are in the Rotated mode, AutoCAD uses the first two points selected to determine the direction of the dimension and measure the distance between the two endpoints of the arc in that direction. The dimension line passes through the last point selected.

Ordinate Dimensioning

AutoCAD uses the mutually perpendicular X and Y axes of the World Coordinate System or current User Coordinate System (see Chapter 15 for a detailed discussion of creating a User Coordinate System) as the reference lines from which to base the X or Y coordinate displayed in an ordinate dimension (sometimes referred to as a *datum dimension*).

Invoke the Ordinate Dimension command from:

Dimension toolbar	Select the Ordinate Dimension command (see Figure 7–9)
Pull-down menu	Dimension > Ordinate
Command: prompt	**dimordinate** Enter
Dimensioning Command mode	**ord** Enter

Ordinate Dimension

Figure 7–9 Invoking the Ordinate Dimension command from the Dimension toolbar

AutoCAD prompts:

Command: **dimordinate**
Select feature:

Although the default prompt is "Select feature:", AutoCAD is actually looking for a point that is significant in locating a feature point on an object, such as the endpoint/ intersection where planes meet or the center of a circle representing a hole or shaft. Therefore, an Object Snap mode, such as endpoint, intersection, quadrant, or center, will normally have to be invoked when responding to the "Select feature:" prompt. Selecting a point determines the origin of a single orthogonal leader that will point to the feature when the dimension is drawn. AutoCAD prompts:

Leader endpoint(Xdatum/Ydatum/Mtext/Text):

If the Ortho mode is set to ON, the leader will be a single horizontal line for a Ydatum ordinate dimension, as shown in Figure 7–10, or a single vertical line for an Xdatum ordinate dimension, as shown in Figure 7–11.

If the Ortho mode is set to OFF, the leader will be a three part-line consisting of orthogonal lines on each end joined by a diagonal line in the middle. It may be necessary to use the nonortho type of leader if the text has to be offset to keep from interferring with other objects in the drawing. The type of dimension drawn (Ydatum or Xdatum) depends on which is greater of the horizontal and vertical distances between the selected "feature" point and the "leader endpoint" point. A grayed image of the dimension is displayed during selection of the "leader endpoint".

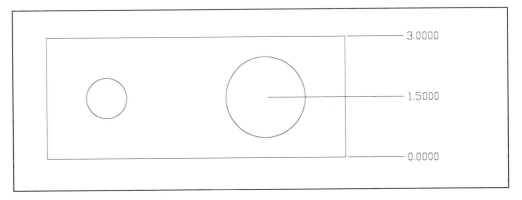

Figure 7–10 Ydatum dimension

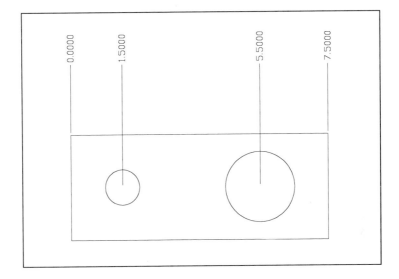

Figure 7–11 Xdatum dimension

Instead of providing a data point, type *X* or *Y*; AutoCAD then draws an Xdatum dimension or Ydatum dimension, respectively, regardless of the location of the "Leader endpoint" point relative to the "Select feature" point.

Radius Dimensioning

The radius dimensioning feature provides commands to create radius dimensions, as shown in Figure 7–12 for circles and arcs. The type of dimensions that AutoCAD utilizes depends on the dimension variable settings (see the later section on "Dimensioning Styles" for how to change the dimension variable settings to draw an appropriate radius dimensioning).

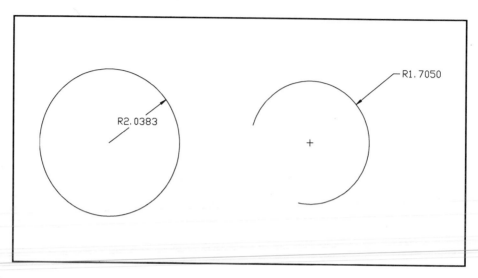

Figure 7–12 Radius dimensioning of circles and arcs

Invoke the Radius Dimension command from:

Dimension toolbar	Select the Radius Dimension command (see Figure 7–13)
Pull-down menu	Dime_nsion > _Radius
Command: prompt	**dimradius** ⏎Enter
Dimensioning Command mode	**rad** ⏎Enter

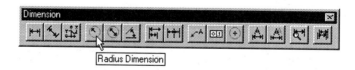

Figure 7–13 Invoking the Radius Dimension command from the Dimension toolbar

AutoCAD prompts:

Command: **dimradius**
Select arc or circle: *(specify an arc or a circle to dimension)*
Dimension line location (Mtext/Text/Angle):

The **Text** and **Mtext** options allow you to change the measured dimension text. The **Angle** option allows you to change the rotation angle of the dimension text. After you respond appropriately for Text or Angle, AutoCAD repeats the prompts for the dimension line location. Specify a point for the location of the dimension. Dimension text for radius dimensioning is preceded by the letter *R*.

The following command sequence shows an example of placing radius dimensioning for a circle, as shown in Figure 7–14.

Command: **dimradius**
Select arc or circle: *(specify the circle object)*
Dimension line location (Mtext/Text/Angle): *(specify a point to draw the dimension)*

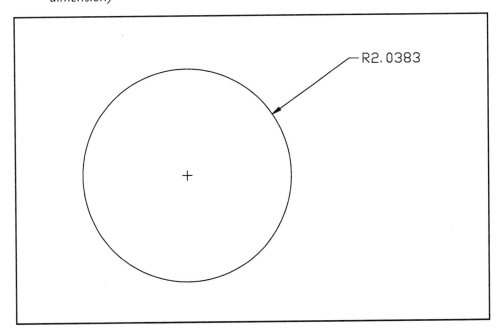

Figure 7–14 Radius dimensioning of a circle

Diameter Dimensioning

The diameter dimensioning feature provides commands to create diameter dimensions, as shown in Figure 7–15 for circles and arcs. The type of dimensions that AutoCAD utilizes depends on the dimension variable settings (see the later section on "Dimensioning styles" for how to change the dimension variable settings to draw an appropriate diameter dimensioning).

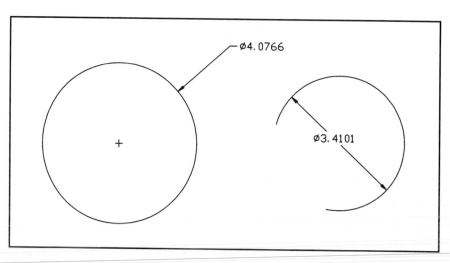

Figure 7–15 Diameter dimensioning of circles and arcs

Invoke the Diameter Dimension command from:

Dimension toolbar	Select the Diameter Dimension command (see Figure 7–16)
Pull-down menu	Dimension > Diameter
Command: prompt	**dimdiameter** Enter
Dimensioning Command mode	**dia** Enter

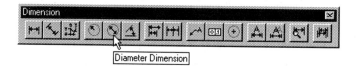

Diameter Dimension

Figure 7–16 Invoking the Diameter Dimension command from the Dimension toolbar

AutoCAD prompts:

Command: **dimdiamter**
Select arc or circle: *(select an arc or a circle to dimension)*
Dimension line location (Mtext/Text/Angle):

The **Text** and **Mtext** options allow you to change the measured dimension text. The **Angle** option allows you to change the rotation angle of the dimension text. After you respond appropriately for Text or Angle, AutoCAD repeats the prompts for the dimension line location. Specify a point for the location of the dimension.

Selecting a point determines the location of the diameter dimension. It will be on the same radius as the point selected. Note that the dimension for an arc of less than 180 degrees cannot be forced to where neither end of the dimension is on the arc.

The following command sequence shows an example of placing diameter dimensioning for a circle, as shown in Figure 7–17.

Command: **dimdiameter**
Select arc or circle: *(specify the circle object)*
Dimension line location (Text/Angle): *(specify a point to draw the dimension)*

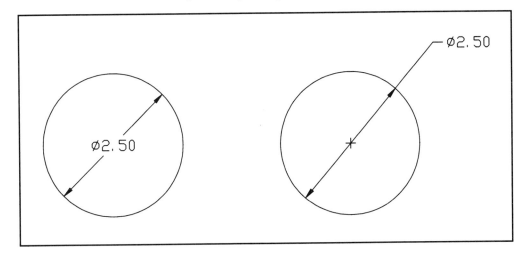

Figure 7–17 Diameter dimensioning of a circle

Angular Dimensioning

The Angular Dimension command allows you to draw angular dimensions using three points (vertex, point, point) between two nonparallel lines, on an arc (between two endpoints of the arc, with the center as the vertex), and on a circle (between two points on the circle, with the center as the vertex).

Invoke the Angular Dimension command from:

Dimension toolbar	Select the Angular Dimension command (see Figure 7–18)
Pull-down menu	Dimension > Angular
Command: prompt	**dimangular** ⏎
Dimensioning Command mode	**ang** ⏎

Figure 7–18 Invoking the Angular Dimension command from the Dimension toolbar

AutoCAD prompts:

Command: **dimangular**
Select arc, circle, line or press ENTER:

The default method of angular dimensioning is to select an object.

If the object selected is an arc, as shown in Figure 7–19, AutoCAD automatically uses the arc's center as the vertex and its endpoints for the first angle endpoint and second angle endpoint to use for determining the three points of a Vertex/Endpoint/Endpoint angular dimension. AutoCAD prompts:

Dimension line location (Mtext/Text/Angle):

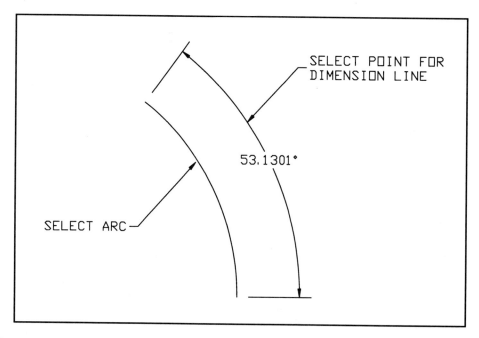

Figure 7–19 Angular dimensioning of an arc

The **Text** and **Mtext** options allow you to change the measured dimension text. The **Angle** option allows you to change the rotation angle of the dimension text. After you respond appropriately for Text or Angle, AutoCAD repeats the prompts for the dimension line location. Specify a point for the location of the dimension. AutoCAD automatically draws radial extension lines.

If the object selected is a circle, as shown in Figure 7–20, AutoCAD automatically uses the circle's center as the vertex and the point at which you selected the circle as the endpoint for the first angle endpoint and prompts:

Second angle endpoint:

Specify a point, and AutoCAD makes this point the second angle endpoint to use along with the previous two points as the three points of a Vertex/Endpoint/Endpoint angular dimension. Note that the last point does not have to be on the circle; however, it does determine the origin for the second extension line. Then, AutoCAD prompts:

Dimension line location (Mtext/Text/Angle):

The **Text** and **Mtext** options allow you to change the measured dimension text. The **Angle** option allows you to change the rotation angle of the dimension text. After

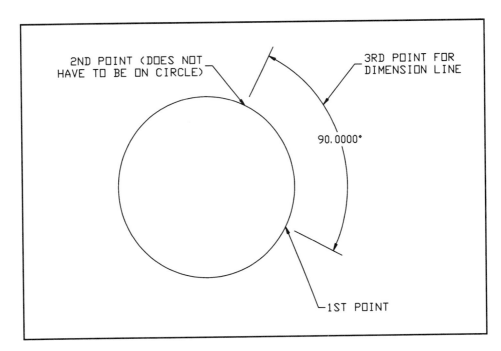

Figure 7–20 Angular dimensioning of a circle

you respond appropriately for Text or Angle, AutoCAD repeats the prompts for the dimension line location. Specify a point for the location of the dimension. AutoCAD automatically draws radial extension lines and draws either a minor or a major angular dimension, depending on whether the point used to select the location of the dimension arc is in the minor or major projected sector.

If the object selected is a line as shown in Figure 7–21, then AutoCAD prompts:

Second line:

Select another line, and AutoCAD uses the apparent intersection of the two lines as the vertex for drawing a Vertex/Vector/Vector angular dimension. You are then prompted to select the location of the dimension arc, which will always be less than 180 degrees.

If the dimension arc is beyond the end of the either line AutoCAD adds the necessary radial extension line(s). Then AutoCAD prompts:

Dimension line location (Mtext/Text/Angle):

The **Text** and **Mtext** options allow you to change the measured dimension text. The **Angle** option allows you to change the rotation angle of the dimension text. After you respond appropriately for Text or Angle, AutoCAD repeats the prompts for the dimension line location. Specify a point for the location of the dimension. AutoCAD automatically draws extension lines and draws the dimension text.

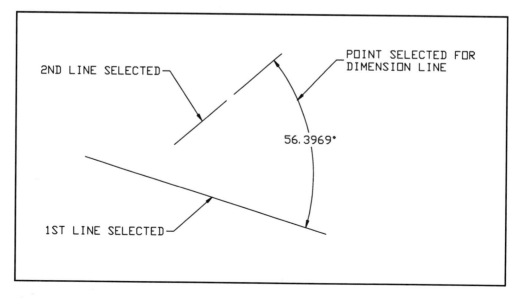

Figure 7–21 Angular dimensioning of a line

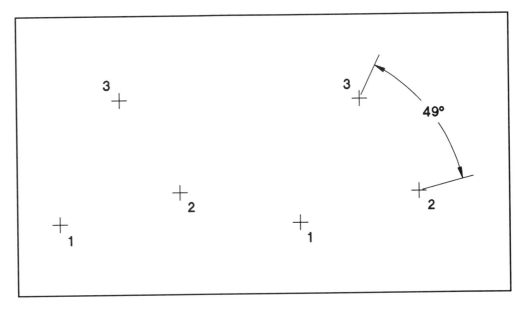

Figure 7–22 Using three points for angular dimensioning

If instead of selecting an arc, a circle, or two lines for angular dimensioning you press Enter, AutoCAD allows you to do three-point angular dimensioning. The following command sequence shows an example of placing angular dimensioning by providing three data points, as shown in Figure 7–22.

> Command: **dimangular**
> Select arc, circle, line or ENTER: Enter
> Angle Vertex: *(specify a point)*
> First angle endpoint: *(specify a point)*
> Second angle endpoint: *(specify a point)*
> Dimension arc line location (Mtext/Text/Angle): *(specify the dimension arc location)*

Baseline Dimensioning

Baseline dimensioning (sometimes referred to as *parallel dimensioning*) is used to draw dimensions, as shown in Figure 7–23, to multiple points from a single datum baseline. The first extension line origin of the initial dimension (it can be a linear, angular, or ordinate dimension) establishes the base from which the baseline dimensions are drawn. That is, all of the dimensions in the series of baseline dimensions will share a common first extension line origin. AutoCAD automatically draws a dimension line/arc beyond the initial (or previous baseline) dimension line/arc. The location of the new dimension line/arc is an offset distance established by the DIMDLI (for dimension line increment) dimensioning variable.

Dimensioning

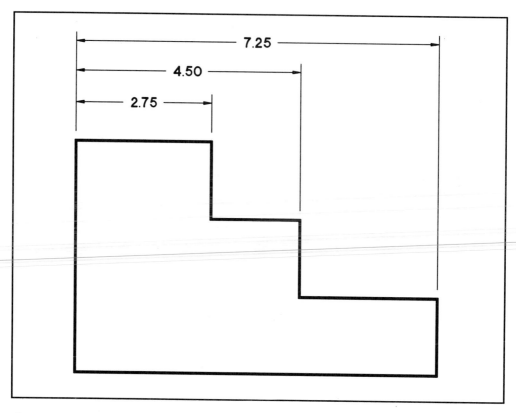

Figure 7–23 Baseline dimensioning

Invoke the Baseline Dimension command from:

Dimension toolbar	Select the Baseline Dimension command (see Figure 7–24)
Pull-down menu	Dimension > Baseline
Command: prompt	**dimbaseline** Enter
Dimensioning Command mode	**bas** Enter

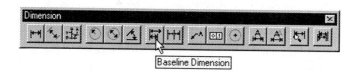

Figure 7–24 Invoking the Baseline Dimension command from the Dimension toolbar

AutoCAD prompts:

Command: **dimbaseline**
Specify a second extension line origin or (Undo/Select>): *(specify a point)*

After you select a point for the second extension line origin, AutoCAD will use the first extension line origin of the previous linear, angular, or ordinate dimension as the first extension line origin for the new dimension, and the prompt is repeated. Press ⌷Esc⌷ to exit the command.

For the Baseline Dimension command to be valid, there must be an existing linear, angular, or ordinate dimension. If the previous dimension was not a linear, angular, or ordinate dimension or if you press ⌷Enter⌷ without providing the second extension line origin, AutoCAD prompts:

Select base dimension:

You may select the base dimension, with the baseline being the extension line nearest to where you pick the dimension.

The following command sequence shows an example of placing baseline dimensioning for a circular object to an exising angular dimension, as shown in Figure 7–25.

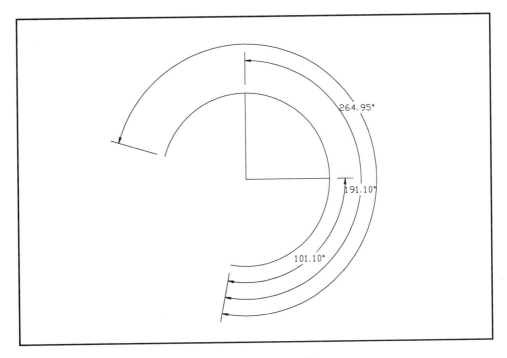

Figure 7–25 Baseline dimensioning of a circular object

Command: **dimbaseline**
Second extension line origin or (Undo<Select>): *(specify a point)*
Second extension line origin or (Undo<Select>): *(specify a point)*
Second extension line origin or (Undo<Select>): *(press* [Esc] *)*

Continue Dimensioning

Continue dimensioning, as shown in Figure 7–26, is used for drawing a string of dimensions each of whose second extension line origin coincides with the next dimension's first extension line origin.

Invoke the Continue Dimension command from:

Dimension toolbar	Select the Continue Dimension command (see Figure 7–27)
Pull-down menu	Dimension > Continue
Command: prompt	**dimcontinue** [Enter]
Dimensioning Command mode	**con** [Enter]

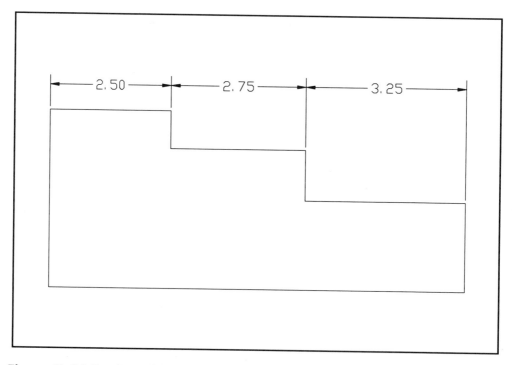

Figure 7–26 Continue dimensioning

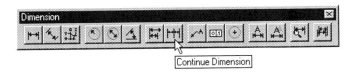

Figure 7–27 Invoking the Continue Dimension command from the Dimension toolbar

AutoCAD prompts:

Command: **dimcontinue**
Specify a second extension line origin or (Undo<Select>): *(specify a point)*

After you select a point for the second extension line origin, AutoCAD will use the second extension line origin of the previous linear, angular, or ordinate dimension as the first extension line origin for the new dimension, and the prompt is repeated. Press ⎋ to exit the command.

For the Continue Dimension command to be valid, there must be an existing linear, angular, or ordinate dimension. If the previous dimension was not a linear, angular, or ordinate dimension or if you press ⏎ without providing the second extension line origin, AutoCAD prompts:

Select continued dimension:

You may select the continued dimension, with the coincidental extension line origin being the one nearest to where the existing dimension is picked.

The following command sequence shows an example of placing continue dimensioning for a linear object to an existing linear dimension, as shown in Figure 7–28.

Command: **dimcontinue**
Specify a second extension line origin or (Undo<Select>): *(specify the right end of the 3.60-unit line)*
Specify a second extension line origin or (Undo<Select>): *(specify the right end of the right 1.80-unit line)*
Specify a second extension line origin or (Undo<Select>): *(press ⎋)*

Leader Dimensioning

The LEADER command minimizes the steps required to draw the text with the line(s) and arrowhead pointing to an object or feature on an object for annotations and callouts used to describe them.

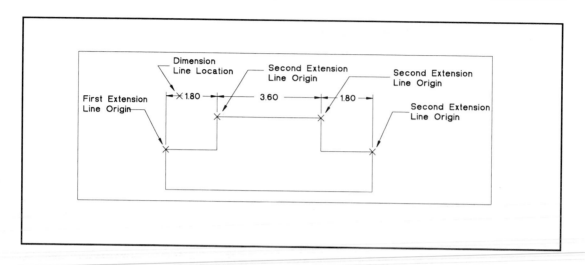

Figure 7–28 Continue dimensioning of a linear object

Invoke the LEADER command from:

Dimension toolbar	Select the Leader command (see Figure 7–29)
Pull-down menu	Dimension > Leader
Command: prompt	**leader** Enter
Dimensioning Command mode	**lea** Enter

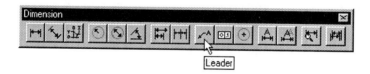

Figure 7–29 Invoking the Leader command from the Dimension toolbar

AutoCAD prompts:

Command: **dimleader**
From point: (*Specify a point for the arrowhead end of the leader*)
To point: (*Specify another point for the end of the leader at the opposite end from the arrowhead*)
To point (Format/Annotation/Undo)<Annotation>: (*specify a point or select one of the available options*)

If you specify another point, AutoCAD connects another leader segment to the previous one and repeats the last prompt.

To point (Format/Annotation/Undo)<Annotation>:

Annotation The Annotation option allows you to draw alphanumerics or symbols as text for the annotation at the end of the leader line opposite the arrowhead. AutoCAD prompts:

Annotation (or press ENTER for options):

Type the alphanumerics or symbols that will be used as text for the annotation at the end of the leader line opposite the arrowhead. If you press Enter instead, AutoCAD prompts:

Tolerance/Copy/Block/None/<Mtext>:

Selecting the **Mtext** option displays the Mtext dialog box, shown in Figure 7–30, for creating or editing single-line or multiline text for annotation.

AutoCAD places the primary dimension where it finds the < > (left arrow/right arrow) in a string of characters in the text box of the Mtext dialog box. If the measured dimension is 1/2" and **COPE < >** is displayed in the text box, the dimension would be drawn as **COPE 1/2"**. In a similar manner, [ ] (left bracket/right bracket) causes the secondary dimension to be drawn.

The **Tolerance** option allows you to draw a feature control frame for use in describing standard tolerances via the Geometric Tolerance dialog box, as described in the following section on "Tolerances."

The **Copy** option allows you to copy text, feature control frames, mtext, or blocks.

The **Block** option allows you to insert a named block. (Refer to Chapter 10 for a discussion Blocks).

The **None** option allows you to draw the leader without the annotation.

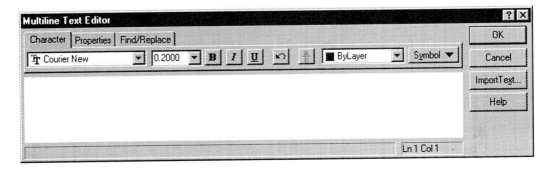

Figure 7–30 Multiline Text Editor dialog box

Format The Format option is used to determine the appearance of the leader and the arrowhead. AutoCAD prompts:

Spline/STraight/Arrow/None/<Exit>:

The **Spline** option allows you to draw a leader in a manner similar to the SPLINE command.

The **Straight** option allows you to draw a leader with straight-line segments.

The **Arrow** option allows you to draw an arrowhead at the first selected point of the leader.

The **None** option allows you to draw a leader without an arrowhead.

The **Exit** option exits the Format option.

Undo The Undo option undoes the last segment of the leader line.

If the leader radial direction is more than 15 degrees from horizontal, AutoCAD will add a horizontal segment pointing toward the annotation that is equal in length to an arrow as determined by the DIMASZ dimension variable.

Tolerances

Tolerance symbology and text can be included with the dimensions that you draw in AutoCAD. AutoCAD provides a special set of subcommands for the two major methods of specifying tolerances. One set is for the lateral method; the other is for the geometric method.

Lateral tolerances are the traditional tolerances. Though they are more often easier to apply, they do not always satisfy tolerancing in all directions (circularly and cylindrically), and are more subject to misinterpretations, especially in the international community.

Geometric tolerance values are the maximum allowable distances that a form or its position may vary from the stated dimension(s).

> **NOTE:** Lateral tolerance symbols and text are accessible from the Dimensioning Command mode and the Dimension Style dialog box. Geometric tolerance symbols and text are accessible from the Dimension toolbar, from the pull-down menu Dimension, and at the "Command:" prompt.

Lateral Tolerance Lateral tolerancing draws the traditional symbols and text for Limit, Plus or Minus (unilateral and bilateral), Single Limit, and Angular tolerance dimensioning.

Lateral tolerance is the range from the smallest to the greatest that a dimension is allowed to deviate and still be acceptable. For example, if a dimension is called out as 2.50 ± 0.05, then the tolerance is 0.1 and the feature being dimensioned may be anywhere between 2.45 and 2.55. This is the symmetrical plus-or-minus convention. If the dimension is called out as $2.50^{+0.10}_{-0.00}$, then the feature may be 0.1 greater than 2.50, but may not be smaller than 2.50. This is referred to as *unilateral*. The Limits tolerance dimension may also be shown as $^{2.55}_{2.45}$.

Invoke the Lateral Tolerance command from:

Dimensioning Command mode	**tol** Enter
Dimension Style dialog box	<u>A</u>nnotation > Tolerance

AutoCAD prompts:

Dim: **tol** (*invoking lateral tolerance*)
Current value <Off> New value: (*press* Enter *to accept the default, or type ON to set the tolerance to ON*)

A tolerance setting of ON applies only to lateral tolerancing. The particular mode of lateral tolerance that will be drawn depends on settings and values that have been specified in the Tolerance section of the Annotation dialog box, which is a subdialog box of the Dimension Styles dialog box. See the section on "Dimensioning Styles" later in this chapter.

Figure 7–31 shows the options available in the Annotation dialog box. Selecting the **Method:** list box in the Tolerance section of the Annotation dialog box displays the following options: None, Symmetrical, Deviation, Limits, and Basic. See Table 7–1 for examples of the various options. The **Upper Value:** and **Lower Value:** edit boxes allow you to preset the values where they apply. The **Justification:** selection box determines if the tolerance value that is drawn after the dimension will be at the top, middle, or bottom of the text space. The **Height:** box lets you set the height of the tolerance value text.

> ***NOTE:*** To get a preview of how your tolerance will appear in relation to the dimension, the format is set in the Primary Units section of the Annotation dialog box.

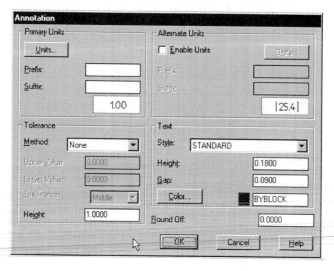

Figure 7–31 Annotation dialog box.

Table 7–1 Examples of Lateral Tolerances

Tolerance Method	Description	Example
Symmetrical	Only the Upper Value box is usable. Only one value is required.	1.00 ± 0.05
Deviation	Both Upper Value and Lower Value boxes are active. A 0.00 value may be entered in either box, indicating that the variation is allowed in only one direction.	$1.00 \begin{smallmatrix} +0.07 \\ -0.03 \end{smallmatrix}$ $\begin{smallmatrix} +0.10 \\ -0.00 \end{smallmatrix}$
Limits	Both Upper and Lower Value boxes are active. In this case, there is no base dimension. The Justification box is not active, because the values are not tolerance values but are actual dimensions to be drawn in full height-text. Using an upper Value of 0.0500 and a Lower Value of -0.0250 will cause annotation of a 1.000 basic dimension to be $\begin{smallmatrix} 0.0500 \\ 0.0250 \end{smallmatrix}$.	1.070 0.930
Basic	The dimension value is drawn in a box, indicating that it is the base value from which a general tolerance is allowed. The general tolerance is usually given in other notes or specifications on the drawing or other documents.	1.00

Geometric Tolerance Geometric tolerancing draws a feature control frame for use in describing standard tolerances according to the geometric tolerance conventions. Geometric tolerancing is applied to forms, profiles, orientations, locations, and runouts. Forms include squares, polygons, planes, cylinders, and cones.

Invoke the Geometric Tolerance command from:

Dimension toolbar	Select the Tolerance command (see Figure 7–32)
Pull-down menu	Dime_nsion > _Tolerance. . .
Command: prompt	**tolerance** Enter

Figure 7–32 Invoking the Geometric Tolerance command from the Dimension toolbar

AutoCAD displays the Symbol dialog box shown in Figure 7–33

The conventional method of expressing a geometric tolerance for a single dimensioned feature is in a feature control frame, which includes all necessary tolerance information for that particular dimension. A feature control frame has the geometric characteristic symbol box and the tolerance value box. Datum reference/material condition datum boxes may be added where needed. The feature control frame is shown in Figure 7–34. An explanation of the characteristic symbols is given in Figure 7–35.

Once you have selected the geometric characteristic symbol, the Geometric Tolerance dialog box will be displayed, as in Figure 7–36.

The supplementary material conditions of datum symbols are shown in Figure 7–37.

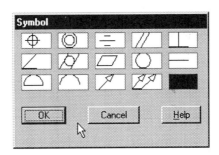

Figure 7–33 Symbol dialog box.

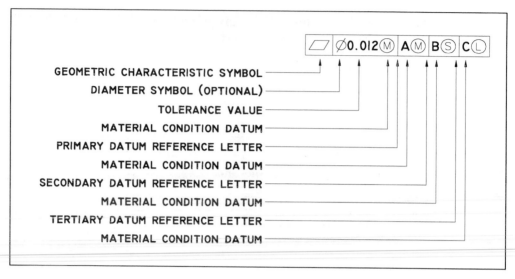

GEOMETRIC CHARACTERISTIC SYMBOL ──────────

DIAMETER SYMBOL (OPTIONAL) ──────────

TOLERANCE VALUE ──────────

MATERIAL CONDITION DATUM ──────────

PRIMARY DATUM REFERENCE LETTER ──────────

MATERIAL CONDITION DATUM ──────────

SECONDARY DATUM REFERENCE LETTER ──────────

MATERIAL CONDITION DATUM ──────────

TERTIARY DATUM REFERENCE LETTER ──────────

MATERIAL CONDITION DATUM ──────────

Figure 7–34 Feature control frame

CHARACTERISTIC SYMBOLS

FORM	▱	FLATNESS
	⎯	STRAIGHTNESS
	○	ROUNDNESS
	⌀	CYLINDRICITY
	⌒	LINE PROFILE
	⌓	SURFACE PROFILE
	∠	ANGULARITY
	//	PAREALLELISM
	⊥	PERPENDICULARITY
LOCATION	◎	CONCENTRICITY
	⊕	POSITION
	≡	SYMMETRY
RUNOUT	↗	CIRCULAR RUNOUT
	⇗	TOTAL RUNOUT

Figure 7–35 Geometric characteristics symbols

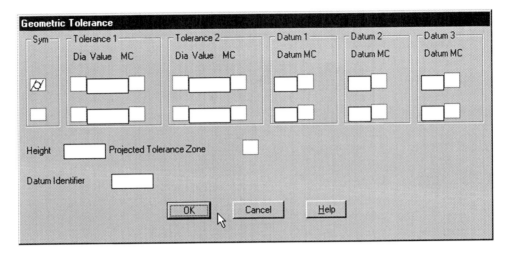

Figure 7-36 Geometric Tolerance dialog box

MATERIAL CONDITIONS OF DATUM SYMBOLS	
(M)	MAXIMUM MATERIAL CONDITIONS (MMC)
(S)	REGARDLESS OF FEATURE SIZE
⌀	DIAMETER

Figure 7-37 Material conditions of datum symbols

Maximum materials conditions (MMC) means a feature contains the maximum material permitted within the tolerance dimension, that is, minimum hole size, maximum shaft size.

Regardless of feature size (RFS) applies to any size of the feature within its tolerance. This is more restrictive. For example, RFS does not allow the tolernace of the center-to-center dimension of a pair of pegs fitting into a pair of holes greater leeway if the peg diameters are smaller and/or the holes are bigger, whereas MMC does.

The diameter symbol, ⌀, is used in lieu of the abbreviation DIA.

An application of geometric tolerancing is found in Exercise 7-1 at the end of this chapter. Geometric tolerancing is becoming widely accepted. The student is encouraged to study the latest drafting texts concerning the significance of the various symbols to be able to apply geometric tolerancing better.

Drawing Cross Marks For Arcs Or Circles

As shown in Figure 7–38, the Dimcenter command is used to draw the cross marks that indicate the center of an arc or circle.

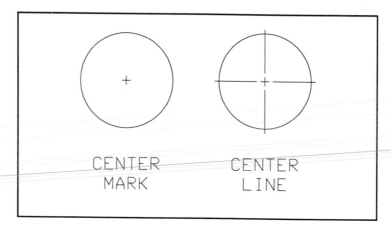

Figure 7–38 Circles with center cross marks

Invoke the Center Mark command from:

Dimension toolbar	Select the Center Mark command (see Figure 7–39)
Pull-down menu	Dimension > Center Mark
Command: prompt	**dimcenter** Enter
Dimensioning Command mode	**cen** Enter

Figure 7–39 Invoking the Center Mark command from the Dimension toolbar

AutoCAD prompts:

Command: **dimcenter**
Select arc or circle:

Select an arc or circle, and AutoCAD draws the cross marks in accordance with the setting of the DIMCEN dimensioning variable.

Oblique Dimensioning

The OBLIQUE command allows you to slant the extension lines of a linear dimension to a specified angle. The dimension line will follow the extension lines, retaining its original direction. This is useful for having the dimension stay clear of other dimensions or objects in your drawing. It is also a conventional method of dimensioning isometric drawings.

Invoke the OBLIQUE command from:

Pull-down menu	Dimension > Oblique
Dimensioning Command mode	**obl** Enter

AutoCAD prompts:

```
Command: oblique
Command: _dimedit Dimension Edit (Home/New/Rotate/Oblique)
     <Home>: _o
Select objects: (select the dimension(s) for obliquing)
Select objects: Enter
Enter obliquing angle (press ENTER for none): (specify an angle)
```

The extension lines of the selected dimension(s) will be slanted at the specified angle.

EDITING DIMENSION TEXT

AutoCAD allows you to edit dimensions with modify commands and grip editing modes. Also, AutoCAD provides two additional editing commands specifically designed to work on dimension objects, DIMEDIT and DIMTEDIT.

DIMEDIT Command

The options that are available in the DIMEDIT command allow you to replace the dimension text with new text, rotate the existing text, move the text to a new location, and if necessary restore the text back to its home position, which is the position defined by the current style. In addition, these options allow you to change the angle of the extension lines (normally perpendicular) relative to the direction of the dimension line (via the Oblique option).

Invoke the DIMEDIT command from:

Dimension toolbar	Select the Dimension Edit command (see Figure 7–40)
Command: prompt	**dimedit** Enter

Figure 7–40 Invoking the Dimension Edit command from the Dimension toolbar

AutoCAD prompts:

> Command: **dimedit**
> Dimension Edit (Home/New/Rotate/Oblique)<Home>: *(select one of the available options)*

Home The Home option returns the dimension text to its default position. AutoCAD prompts:

> Select objects: *(select the dimension objects and press the* Enter *key)*

New The New option allows you to change the original dimension text to the new text. AutoCAD prompts:

> Dimension text <text>: *(type in new text and press* Enter *)*
> Select objects: *(select the dimension objects for which the dimension text has to be replaced with new text)*

Rotate The Rotate option allows you to rotate the dimension text. AutoCAD prompts:

> Enter text angle: *(specify the rotation angle for text)*
> Select objects: *(select the dimension objects for which the dimension text has to be rotated)*

Oblique The Oblique option adjusts the obliquing angle of the extension lines for linear dimensions. This is useful to keep the dimension parts from interfering with other objects in the drawing. Also, it is an easy method by which to generate the slanted dimensions used in isometric drawings. AutoCAD prompts:

> Select objects: *(select the dimension objects)*
> Enter obliquing angle: *(specify the angle)*

DIMTEDIT Command

The DIMEDIT command is used to change the location of dimension text (with the Left/Right/Home options) along the dimension line and its angle (with the Rotate option).

Invoke the DIMEDIT command from:

Dimension toolbar	Select the Dimension Text Edit command (see Figure 7–41)
Command: prompt	**dimtedit** Enter
Dimensioning Command mode	**tedit** Enter

Figure 7–41 Invoking the Dimension Text Edit command from the Dimension toolbar

AutoCAD prompts:

Command: **dimtedit**
Select dimension:

Select the dimension to modify, and a grayed image of the dimension selected is displayed on the screen, with the text located at the cursor. You will be prompted:

Enter text location (Left/Right/Home/Angle):

By default, AutoCAD allows you to position the dimension text with the cursor, and the dimension updates dynamically as it drags.

Left The Left option will cause the text to be drawn toward the left extension line.

Right The Right option will cause the text to be drawn toward the right extension line.

Home The Home option returns the dimension text to its default position.

Angle The Angle option changes the angle of the dimension text. AutoCAD prompts:

Text angle:

The angle specified becomes the new angle for the dimension text.

Editing Dimensions with Grips If the grips feature is set to ON, you can pick an associative dimension object and its grips will be displayed at strategic points. The grips will be located at the object ends of the extension lines, the intersections of the dimension and extension lines, and at the insertion point of the dimension text. In addition to the normal grip editing of the dimension as a group (rotate, move, copy, etc.), each grip can be selected for editing the configuration of the dimension as follows: Moving the object end grip of an extension line will move that selection point, making the value change accordingly. Horizontal and vertical dimensions remain horizontal and vertical. Aligned dimensions follow the alignment of the relocated point. Moving the grip at the intersection of the dimension line and one of the extension lines causes the dimension line to be closer or farther away from the object dimensioned. Moving the grip at the insertion point of the text does the same as the intersection grip and also permits you to move the text back and forth along the dimension line.

DIMENSIONING STYLES

Each time a dimension is drawn it conforms to the settings of the dimension variables in effect at the time. The entire set of dimension variable settings can be saved in their respective states as a dimension style, with a name by which it can be recalled for application to a dimension later in the drawing session or in a subsequent session. Some dimension variables affect every dimension. For example, every time a dimension is drawn, the DIMSCALE setting determines the relative size of the dimension. But DIMDLI, the variable that determines the offsets for baseline dimensions, comes into effect only when a baseline dimension is drawn. However, when a dimension style is created and named, all dimension variable settings (except DIMASO and DIMSHO) are recorded in that dimension style, whether or not they will have an effect. The DIMASO and DIMSHO dimensioning variable settings are saved in the drawing separate from the dimension styles.

Parent Style and Style Families

A dimensioning style family lets different types of dimensions have variations on a parent style. That is, when you initially create a new style, you can make the settings of particular dimensioning variable different for linear dimensions than they are for angular dimensions. Though the settings may differ from one type to the other, they are still members of the same style family.

AutoCAD provides a comprensive set of dialog boxes for creating new dimension styles and managing existing ones. In turn, these dialog boxes compile and store dimension variable settings. Creating dimension styles through use of the DDIM command's dialog boxes allows you to make the desired changes to the appearance of dimensions without having to memorize or search for the names of the dimension variables in order to change the settings directly.

Invoke the DDIM command from:

Dimension toolbar	Select the Dimension Style command (see Figure 7–42)
Pull-down menu	Dime_n_sion > _S_tyle
Command: prompt	**dimstyle** Enter
Dimensioning Command mode	**style** Enter

Figure 7–42 Invoking the Dimension Style command from the Dimension toolbar

AutoCAD displays the **Dimension Styles** dialog box shown in Figure 7–43.

The **Dimension Style** section displays the name of the current style and provides a text box for entering names and buttons for saving and/or renaming a style.

The **Current:** list box displays the styles, with the current one highlighted. Its name is recorded as the DIMSTYLE value. Styles from externally referenced drawings are listed, though they are not changeable in the current drawing. Making any

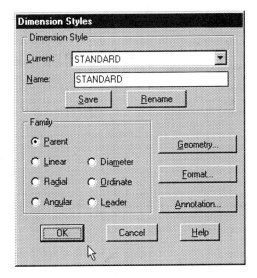

Figure 7–43 Dimension Styles dialog box

change creates a style formed from the current style and displays the current style name prefixed with a + (plus sign). For example, making changes to a style named ARCH1 causes the name +ARCH1 to be displayed.

The **Name:** text box lets you enter a name for a newly created style or rename the current style unless it is STANDARD, which cannot be renamed.

The **Save** button saves the settings in their current status as a style family by the name displayed in the **Name:** text box.

The **Rename** button renames the highlighted style family to the name displayed in the **Name:** text box.

Selecting one of the buttons in the **Family** section assigns the current set of dimension variable values to that family member.

The **Geometry. . .** button displays the Geometry dialog box.

The **Format. . .** button displays the Format dialog box.

The **Annotation. . .** button displays the Annotation dialog box.

Geometry Dialog Box

The Geometry dialog box, shown in Figure 7–44, lets you change the geometric appearance of a dimension, including its scale. Sections include Dimension Line, Extension Line, Scale, Arrowheads and Center (marks).

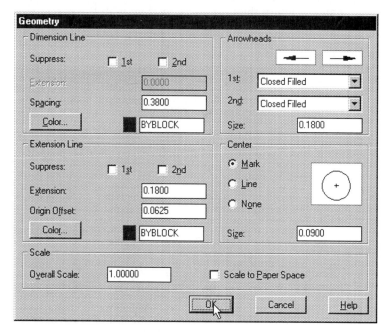

Figure 7–44 Geometry dialog box

Dimension Line The Dimension Line section includes the following choices.

The **Suppress:** options are 1st and 2nd, for suppressing the first and second dimension lines, respectively. Figure 7–45 shows an example. Values (1 for ON or 0 for OFF) for 1st and 2nd are recorded in DIMSD1 and DIMSD2, respectively.

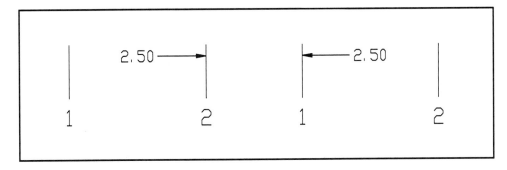

Figure 7–45 Suppressing the dimension line

The **Extension:** edit box determines how far the dimension line extends past the extension line when the termination marks are slashes. Values are recorded in DIMDLE.

The **Spacing:** edit box determines how far a baseline dimension line is drawn beyond the previous dimension line. Value is recorded in DIMDLI.

The **Color...** button determines the color of the dimension line.

Extension Line The Extension Line section includes the following options.

The **Suppress:** options are 1st and 2nd, for suppressing the first and second extension lines, respectively. Figure 7–46 shows an example. Values (1 for ON or 0 for OFF) for 1st and 2nd are recorded in DIMSE1 and DIMSE2, respectively.

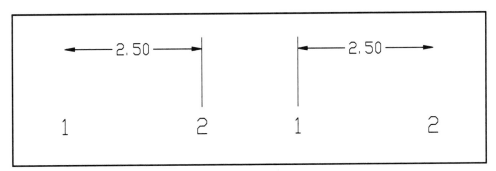

Figure 7–46 Suppressing the extension line

Dimensioning

The **Extension:** edit box determines how far the extension line extends past the dimension line. Values are recorded in DIMEXE.

The **Origin Offset:** edit box determines how far the extension line is offset from the origin point (selected when drawing the dimension). Values are recorded in DIMEXO.

The **Color...** button determines the color of the extension line.

Arrowheads The **Arrowheads** section lets you specify the type of arrowheads for the terminations of the dimension lines; see Figure 7–47. Unless you specify a different type for the second line end, it will default to the same type as the first line end. The types of arrowhead are recorded in DIMBLK if both the first and second are the same or in DIMBLK1 and DIMBLK2 if they are different. This section includes the following options.

The **1st:** list box shows the arrowheads available for the first line end and allows you to set one as current.

The **2nd:** list box lists the arrowheads available for the second line end and allows you to set one as current.

The standard library of arrowheads includes the following types: None, Closed, Dot, Closed Filled, Oblique, Open, Origin Indication, and Right-Angle. Figure 7–47 presents an example of each.

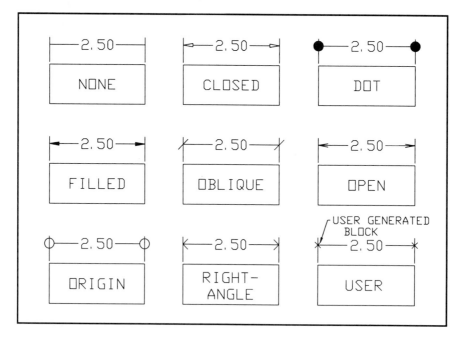

Figure 7–47 Arrowhead types

The **User Arrow** option lets you use a previously saved block by entering its name. Figure 7–48 shows the related dialog box. The block should be created as though it were drawn for the right end of a horizontal dimension line, with the insertion point at the intersection of the extension line and the dimension line.

The **Size:** edit box lets you determine the arrowhead size relative to the other dimension components. The value is recorded in DIMASZ.

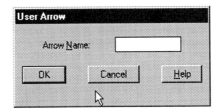

Figure 7–48 User Arrow dialog box

Center The **Center** section lets you specify how and whether center marks will be drawn for radius and diameter dimensions and the Center command. Center marks, when specified, will not be drawn if the dimensions are inside the circle or arc. This section includes the following choices.

Selecting the **Mark** button causes center cross marks to be drawn in accordance with the value in the Size: text box. It will be recorded as a positive value in DIMCEN.

Selecting the **Line** button causes crossed centerlines to be drawn in accordance with the value in the Size: text box. It will be recorded as a negative value in DIMCEN.

Selecting the **None** button causes no cross marks or centerlines to be drawn.

The **Size:** edit box lets you specify the size of the cross marks or centerlines. The value is recorded in DIMCEN.

Scale The **Scale** section lets you increase or decrease the size of all of the dimensioning components uniformly by the factor entered. For example, you have set the sizes of the components to plot at a scale factor of 1/4" = 1'- 0" (1:48) and wish to draw a detail to true size (including the dimensions) and then scale it up to 3/4" = 1'- 0" (1:16). You can set the dimensioning scale to 1/3 so that the components, when scaled up by a factor of 3, will plot at the same size as those not scaled up. This section includes the following options.

The **Overall Scale:** edit box lets you set the scale factor to be applied to the components of the dimensions. This does not include distances, coordinates, angles, or tolerances. The value is recorded in DIMSCALE.

The **Scale to Paper Space** check box lets you set the scale factor based on the ratio of the model space to the paper space in the current viewport.

Format Dialog Box

The **Format** dialog box, shown in Figure 7–49, lets you change where the dimension lines, extension lines, arrowheads, and leader lines are drawn. This dialog box includes the following choices.

User Defined The **User Defined** check box lets you determine where the text and/ or arrow are to be drawn regardless of the justification in effect. The value is recorded in DIMUPT.

Force Line Inside The **Force Line Inside** check box lets you force a line to be drawn inside the extension lines even if the dimension line and text are forced outside. The value is recorded in DIMTOFL.

Fit The **Fit:** list box lets you specify how and where arrows and text are drawn. The value is recorded in DIMFIT. It includes the following options.

Selecting the **Text and Arrows** option causes both the text and arrows to be drawn outside if the dimension lines are forced outside and both to be drawn inside if space is available. If you have selected the User Defined check box and are placing diameter/radius text, you can force the leader to be drawn outside the circle/arc by selecting outside with the cursor.

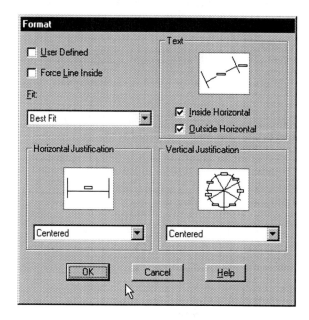

Figure 7–49 Format dialog box

Selecting the **Text Only** option causes the arrows to be drawn outside and the text inside the extension lines if there is room for the text only.

Selecting the **Best Fit** option causes the text to be drawn outside and the arrows inside the extension lines if there is room for the arrows only.

Selecting the **Leader** option causes the text (if there is not enough room for it between the extension lines) to be drawn above and to one side of the dimension line, with a leader to the dimension line where the text would normally be drawn.

Horizontal Justification The **Horizontal Justification** section lets you locate the text between the extension lines along the dimension line. The value is recorded in DIMJUST. This section includes the following options.

Selecting the **Centered** option causes the text to be centered between the extension lines.

Selecting the **1st Extension Line** option causes the text to be drawn near the 1st extension line.

Selecting the **2nd Extension Line** option causes the text to be drawn near the 2nd extension line.

Selecting the **Over 1st Extension Line** option causes the text to be drawn in line with and above the first extension line.

Selecting the **Over 2nd Extension Line** option causes the text to be drawn in line with and above the second extension line.

Text The **Text** section lets you specify whether the text is drawn inside or outside the extension lines. This section includes the following options.

Selecting the **Inside** option causes the text to be drawn horizontally between extension lines regardless of their angle.

Selecting the **Outside** option causes the text to be drawn outside the extension line, with a leader to an extension of the dimension line.

Vertical Justification The **Vertical Justification** section lets you specify the location of the text relative to the dimension line. This section includes the following options.

Selecting the **Centered** option causes the text to be drawn centered between the halves of a broken dimension line.

Selecting the **Above** option causes the text to be drawn above the dimesion line.

Selecting the **Outside** option causes the text to be drawn on the side of the dimension beyond the dimensioned object.

Selecting the **JIS** option causes the text to be drawn in accordance with the Japanese Industrial Standards.

Annotation Dialog Box

The **Annotation** dialog box, shown in Figure 7–50, lets you change how the dimension text or leader text appears. It includes sections for Primary Units, Tolerance, Alternate Units, and Text.

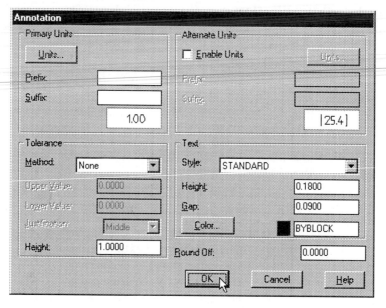

Figure 7–50 Annotation dialog box

Primary Units The **Primary Units** section of the Annotation dialog box includes Units, Prefix and Suffix options.

The **Prefix:** edit box allows you to include a prefix in the dimension text. The prefix text will override any default prefixes, such as those used in radius (R) dimensioning. The value is recorded in DIMPOST.

The **Suffix:** edit box allows you to include a suffix in the dimension text. If you specify tolerances, AutoCAD includes the suffix in the tolerances, as well as in the main dimension. The value is recorded in DIMPOST.

Selecting the **Units. . .** button causes the **Primary Units** dialog box to be displayed, as shown in Figure 7–51.

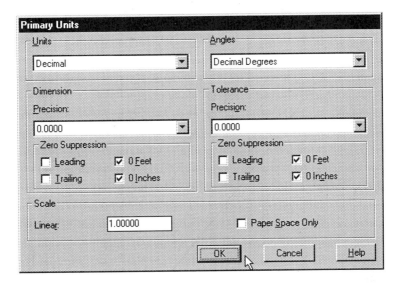

Figure 7-51 Primary Units dialog box

Primary Units Dialog Box The **Primary Units** dialog box lets you specify the format of the primary units. It includes the following sections.

The **Units** section is for setting the format of the units for linear, radial, diameter, ordinate, and leader dimension text. Options include Architectural, Decimal, Engineering, Fractional, and Scientific. The value is recorded in DIMUNIT.

The **Dimension** section lets you specify the precision of a dimension and whether leading or trailing zeros are displayed. This section includes the following choices.

The **Precision:** text box lets you determine to how many decimals the text will be shown in decimal units. This value is recorded in DIMDEC.

The **Zero Suppression** subsection of the Dimension section lets you specify whether or not zeros are displayed, as follows:

Selecting the **Leading** check box causes zeros ahead of the decimal point to be suppressed. *Example:* .700 is displayed instead of 0.700.

Selecting the **Trailing** check box causes zeros behind the decimal point to be suppressed. *Example:* 7 or 7.25 is displayed instead of 7.000 or 7.250, respectively.

Selecting the **0 Feet** check box causes zeros representing feet to be suppressed if the dimension text represents inches and/or fractions only. *Example:* 7" or 7 1/4" is displayed instead of 0'-7" or 0'-7 1/4".

Selecting the **0 Inches** check box causes zeros representing inches to be suppressed if the dimension text represents feet only. *Example:* 7' is displayed instead of 7'- 0".

The **Angles** section of the Primary Units dialog box is for setting the format of the units for the angular dimension text. Options include Decimal Degrees, Degrees/Minutes/Seconds, Grads, Radians, and Surveyor. The value is recorded in DIMAUNIT.

The **Tolerance** section lets you specify the precision of tolerance text and whether leading or trailing zeros are displayed. This section includes the following choices.

The **Precision:** text box lets you determine to how many decimals the text will be shown in decimal units. This value is recorded in DIMDEC.

The **Zero Suppression** subsection of the Tolerance section lets you specify whether or not zeros are displayed, as follows:

Selecting the **Leading** check box causes zeros ahead of the decimal point to be suppressed. *Example:* .700 is displayed instead of 0.700.

Selecting the **Trailing** check box causes zeros behind the decimal point to be suppressed. *Example:* 7 or 7.25 is displayed instead of 7.000 or 7.250, respectively.

Selecting the **0 Feet** check box causes zeros representing feet to be suppressed if the dimension text represents inches and/or fractions only. *Example:* 7" or 7 1/4" is displayed instead of 0'-7" or 0'-7 1/4".

Selecting the **0 Inches** check box causes zeros representing inches to be suppressed if the dimension text represents feet only. *Example:* 7' is displayed instead of 7'- 0".

The **Scale** section of the Primary Units dialog box lets you specify a scale factor for the linear measured distances of a dimension without affecting the components, angles, or tolerance values. This section includes the following options.

The **Linear:** text box lets you specify the linear scale factor. For example, you are drawing with the intention of plotting at the quarter-size scale, or 3" = 1'- 0". You have scaled up a detail by a factor of 4 so that it will plot to full scale. If you wish to dimension it after it has been enlarged, you can set the linear scale factor in this section of the Primary Units dialog box to .25 so that dimensioned distances will represent the dimension of the object features before it was scaled up. This method keeps the components at the same size as dimensions created without a scale change. The value is recorded in DIMLFAC.

Selecting the **Paper Space Only** check box causes the linear scale factor to apply to linear measured distances in dimensions drawn in paper space only. The value is recorded in DIMLFAC.

Tolerance The **Tolerance** section of the Annotation dialog box lets you specify whether or not a tolerance is drawn as part of the dimension text and what type of tolerance is drawn. This section includes the following choices.

The **Method:** list box lets you specify the type of tolerance. It includes the following options:

Selecting the **None** option suppresses tolerances. DIMTOL is set to 0.

Selecting the **Symmetrical** option causes the tolerance to be displayed in equal plus-and-minus values. DIMTOL is set to 1 and DIMLIM is set to 1.

Selecting the **Deviation** option causes the tolerance to be displayed in unequal plus-and-minus values. DIMTOL is set to 1 and DIMLIM is set to 0.

Selecting the **Limits** option causes the tolerance text to be represented as maximum and minimun distances. DIMTOL is set to 0 and DIMLIM is set to 1.

Selecting the **Basic** option causes the dimension text to be drawn within a rectangular box.

The **Upper Value:** text box lets you specify the upper value of the tolerance. The value is recorded in DIMTP.

The **Lower Value:** text box lets you specify the lower value of the tolerance. The value is recorded in DIMTM.

The **Justification:** list box lets you specify how tolerance text is drawn relative to the dimension text. It includes the following options:

The **Top** option aligns the top of the tolerance text with the top of the dimension text.

The **Middle** option aligns the middle of the tolerance text with the middle of the dimension text.

The **Bottom** option aligns the bottom of the tolerance text with the bottom of the dimension text.

The **Height:** text box lets you specify the height of the tolerance relative to the dimension text. For instance, a value of 0.5 makes the tolerance text half the height of the dimension text.

Alternate Units The **Alternate Units** section of the Annotation dialog box is similar to the Primary Units section, except for the **Enable Units** check box, which lets you enable (DIMALT set to 1) or disable (DIMALT set to 0) alternate units:

Text The **Text** section of the Annotation dialog box lets you change the style, heigth, text gap, and color of the text. It includes the following choices:

The **Style:** list box lets you specify the text style of the dimension text. The name is recorded in DIMTXSTY.

The **Height:** text box lets you specify the height of the dimension text. The value is recorded in DIMTXT.

The **Gap:** text box lets you specify the gap distance between dimension text and dimension lines that are broken for placing the text. The value is recorded in DIMGAP.

The **Color...** button lets you specify directly the color of the dimension text, or you can choose the Color button to display the Select Color dialog box.

Round Off The **Round Off:** text box lets you specify whether measured dimension distances will be rounded off for display. For example, a value of 0.5 causes dimensions to be rounded to the nearest 0.5 units.

OVERRIDING THE DIMENSION FEATURE

The DIMOVERRIDE command allows you to change one of the features in a dimension without having to change its dimension style or create a new dimension style. For example, you may wish to have one leader with the text centered at the ending horizontal line, rather than over the ending horizontal line in the manner that the current dimension style may call for. By invoking the Dimoverride command, you can respond to the prompt with the name of the dimension variable (DIMTAD in this case) and set the value to 0 rather than 1. Then you can select the dimension leader you wish to have overridden.

Invoke the **Dimoverride** command from:

Command: prompt	dimoverride Enter
Dimensioning Command mode	ove Enter

AutoCAD prompts:

Command: **dimoverride**
Dimension variable to override (or Clear to remove overrides): (*specify the dimension variable*)

If you specify a dimension variable, you are prompted:

Current value <current> New value: (*specify the new value*)
Dimension variable to override:

If you press Enter, you are prompted:

Select objects: (*select the dimension objects*)

The dimensions selected will have the dimension variable settings overridden in accordance with the value specified.

If you enter **c,** for Clear, you are prompted:

Select objects: *(select the dimension to clear the override)*

The dimensions selected will have the dimension variable setting overrides cleared.

UPDATING DIMENSIONS

The Dimension Update command permits you to make selected existing dimension(s) conform to the settings of the current dimension style.

Invoke the Dimension Update command from:

Dimension toolbar	Select the Dimension Update command (see Figure 7–52)
Pull-down menu	Dimension > Update
Dimensioning Command mode	**upd** Enter

Figure 7–52 Invoking the Dimension Update command from the Dimension toolbar

AutoCAD prompts:

Dimension Style Edit (Save/Restore/STatus/Variables/Apply/?) <Restore>:
　apply
Select objects: *(select any dimension(s) whose settings you wish to have updated to conform to the current dimension style).*

PROJECT EXERCISE

This project exercise provides point-by-point instructions for dimensioning the objects in the drawing shown in Figure P7–1.

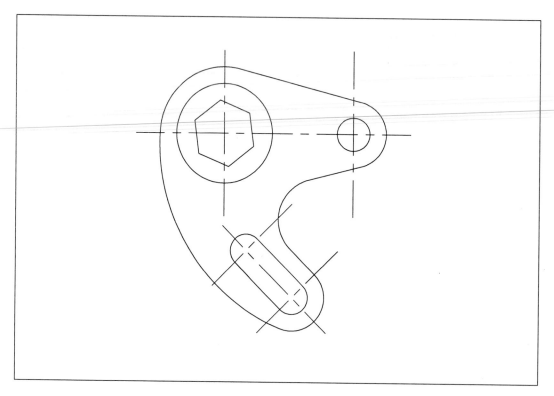

Figure P7–1 Completed project drawing

In this project you will use Dimension commands such as DIMLINEAR, DIMSTYLE, DIMALIGNED, DIMCONTINUE, DIMANGULAR, DIMRADIUS, and DIMDIAMETER to dimension objects.

Step 1   Start the AutoCAD program.

Step 2   Invoke the OPEN command from the Standard toolbar and select the drawing completed in the Chapter 4 Project Exercise.

Step 3 Invoke the LAYER command from the Object Properties toolbar, or select Layer... from the pull-down menu Format. AutoCAD displays the Layer & Linetype Properties dialog box.

Create one new layer, and rename it as shown in the following table, assigning appropriate color and linetype.

Layer Name	Color	Linetype
Dimension	Blue	Continuous

Set Dimension as the current layer, and close the Layer & Linetype Properties dialog box.

Step 4 Select Dimension Style... from the pull-down menu Format. AutoCAD displays the **Dimension Styles** dialog box.

Choose the **Geometry...** button to open the **Geometry** dialog box. Type **0.50** in the **Dimension Line Spacing:** edit box, **0.125** in the **Arrowheads Size:** edit box, and **0.125** in the **Extension Line Extension:** edit box. Choose **OK** to close the Geometry dialog box

Choose the **Annotation...** button in the **Dimension Styles** dialog box to open the **Annotation** dialog box. Choose the **Units...** button in the Primary Units section of the **Annotation** dialog box to open the **Primary Units** dialog box. Set **Precision:** to two decimal places and choose **OK** to close the **Primary Units** dialog box. Type **0.1250** in the **Height:** edit box in the Text section of the Annotation dialog box. Choose **OK** to close the **Annotation** dialog box.

Choose **OK** to close the **Dimension Styles** dialog box.

Step 5 Set the Running object snap to CENter.

Command: **osnap**
Object snap mode: **center**

Step 6 Invoke the DIMLINEAR command from the Dimension toolbar. Draw the linear dimension as shown in Figure P7–2.

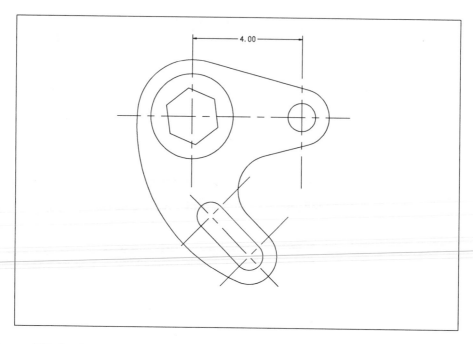

Figure P7–2 Completed linear dimension

Step 7   Invoke the Aligned Dimension command from the Dimension toolbar
(see Figure P7–3) to add the aligned dimensions to the drawing.

Figure P7–3 Invoking the DIMALIGNED command from the Dimension toolbar

Command: **dimaligned**
First extension line origin or press ENTER to select: *(select the arc at PT. 1
as shown in Figure P7–4)*
Second extension line origin: *(select the arc at PT. 2 as shown in Figure
P7–4)*
Dimension line location (Text/Angle): *(select PT. 3 to locate the dimen-
sion as shown in Figure P7–4)*

AutoCAD draws the dimension as shown in Figure P7–5.

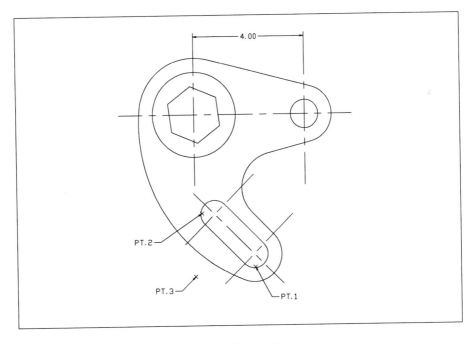

Figure P7–4   Selecting points for the aligned dimension

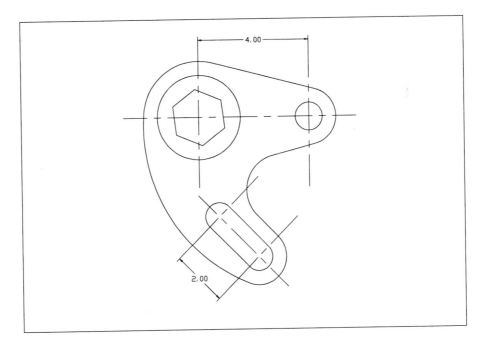

Figure P7–5   Completed aligned dimension

Invoke the DIMCONTINUE command from the Dimension toolbar.

Command: **dimcontinue**
Second extension line origin or (undo/<select>): *(select the large circle to continue the dimension as shown in Figure P7–6)*

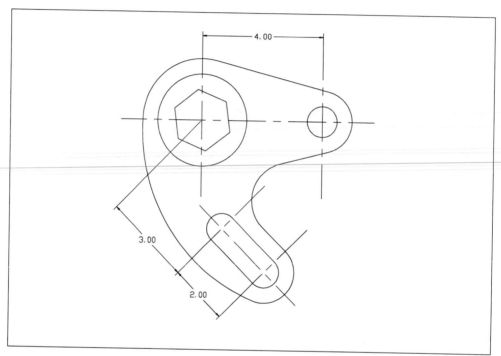

Figure P7–6 Aligned dimension

Step 8 Draw centerlines to assist in completing the dimensioning exercise. Set Centerline as the current layer. Invoke the LINE command from the Draw toolbar, and draw lines 1 and 2 as shown in Figure P7–7.

Command: **line**
From point: *7,8 (start point for line 1)*
To point: *@6.5<315*
To point: Enter

Command: Enter
From point: *7,8 (start point for line 2)*
To point: *(use the object snap tool "intersection" to draw the line to the intersection of the polygon as shown in Figure P7–7)*

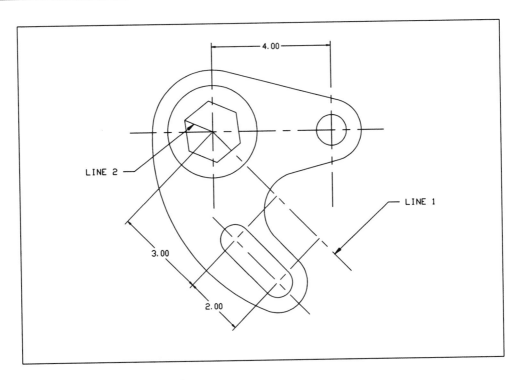

Figure P7–7 Lines 1 and 2

Step 9 Set Dimension as the current layer. Invoke the DIMALIGINED command from the Dimension toolbar to draw the remaining aligned dimensions for the drawing.

> Command: **dimaligned**
> First extension line origin or press ENTER to select: *(select the arc at PT. 1, as shown in Figure P7–8)*
> Second extension line origin: *(use the object snap tool "perpendicular" to select PT. 2, as shown in Figure P7–8)*
> Dimension line location (Text/Angle): *(select PT. 3 to locate the dimension as shown in Figure P7–8)*

AutoCAD draws the dimension as shown in Figure P7–9.

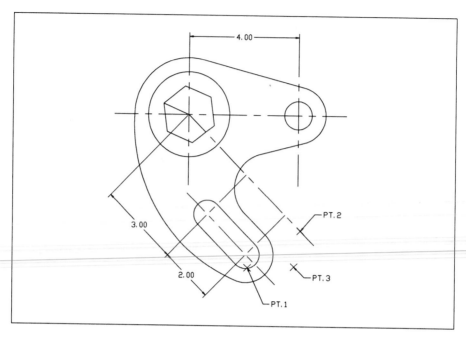

Figure P7-8 Drawing the aligned dimension

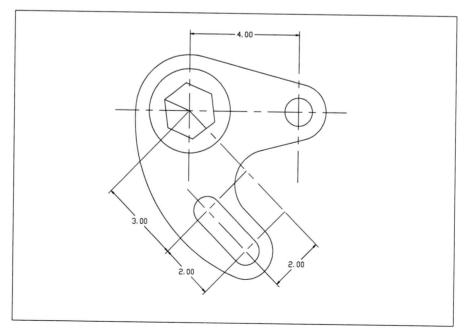

Figure P7-9 Completed dimension

Command: **dimaligned**
First extension line origin or press ENTER to select: *(use the object snap tool "intersection" to locate PT. 1 as shown in Figure P7–10)*
Second extension line origin: *(use the object snap tool "perpendicular" to select PT. 2 as shown in Figure P7–10)*
Dimension line location (Text/Angle): *(select PT. 3 to locate the dimension as shown in Figure P7–10)*

AutoCAD draws the dimension as shown in Figure P7–11.

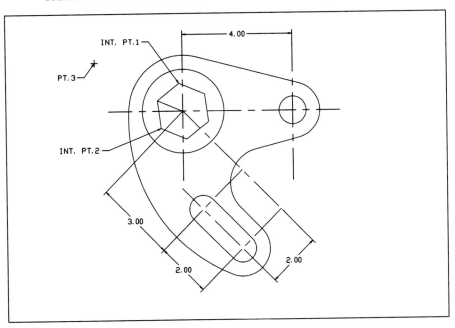

Figure P7–10 Drawing the aligned dimension

Step 10 Set the running object snap to NONE.

Command: **osnap**
Object snap mode: **none**

Step 11 Invoke the DIMANGULAR command from the Dimension toolbar to draw the angular dimensions.

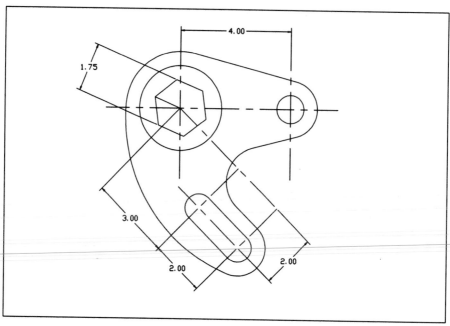

Figure P7–11 Completed dimension

Command: **dimangular**
Select arc,circle,line,or press ENTER: *(select line 1 as shown in Figure P7–12)*
Second line: *(select line 2 as shown in Figure P7–12)*
Dimension arc line location(Text,Angle): *(locate the dimension as at PT. 1 as shown in Figure P7–12)*

Command: **dimangular**
Select arc,circle,line,or press ENTER: *(select line 4 as shown in Figure P7–12)*
Second line: *(select line 5 as shown in Figure P7–12)*
Dimension arc line location(Text,Angle): *(locate the dimension as at PT. 2 in Figure P7–12)*

AutoCAD draws the dimensions as shown in Figure P7–13.

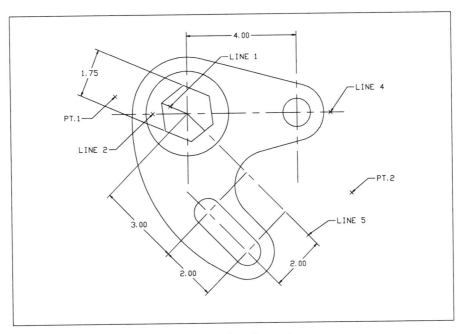

Figure P7–12 Selecting points for angular dimensions

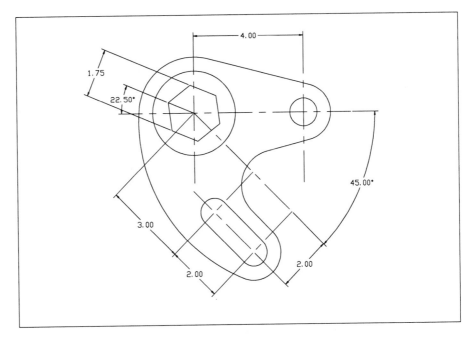

Figure P7–13 Completed angular dimensions

Step 12 Invoke the DIMRADIUS and DIMDIAMETER commands to draw the radius and diameter dimensions as shown in Figure P7–14.

> **NOTE:** Before using DIMRADIUS and DIMDIAMETER, open the Dimension Styles... dialog box from the pull-down menu Format. Select the **Format...** button, and turn on the User Defined option.

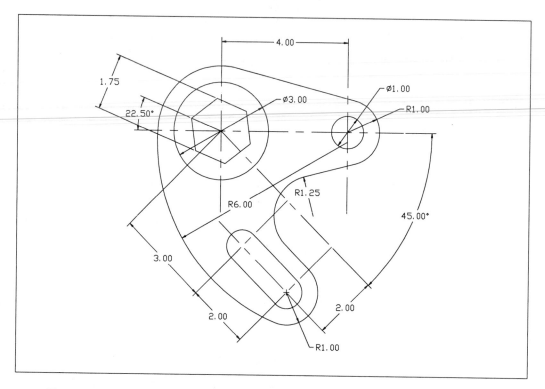

Figure P7–14 Completed dimensions

Step 13 End the drawing by invoking the END command.

Command: **end**

EXERCISES 7–1 THROUGH 7–5

Exercise 7–1

Create the drawing shown, with all the dimensions (includes both lateral tolerancing and geometric tolerancing symbology).

Settings	Value		
1. Units	Decimal		
2. Limits	Lower left corner: -250,-100		
	Upper right corner: 100,100		
3. Grid	5		
4. Snap	5		
5. Layers	*NAME*	*COLOR*	*LINETYPE*
	Dimension	White	Continuous
	Border	Red	Continuous
	Object	Green	Continuous
	Center	Magenta	Center
	Text	Blue	Continuous
	Hidden	White	Hidden

Hints	The border can be drawn from coordinates -245.00, -95.00 to 95.00, 95.00 using the RECTANG command. Create the drawing.
	In the Annotation section of the Dimension Styles dialog box, you can set the Methods to Limits, giving an Upper Value of 0.20 and a Lower Value of 0.10.
	For each feature control frame you can select Tolerance from the Dimension pull-down menu.
	In order to force the arrows inside the circle of diameter dimensions and the leader/text outside the circle, set the Fit: option to User Defined in the Format dialog box of the Dimension Styles dialog box.

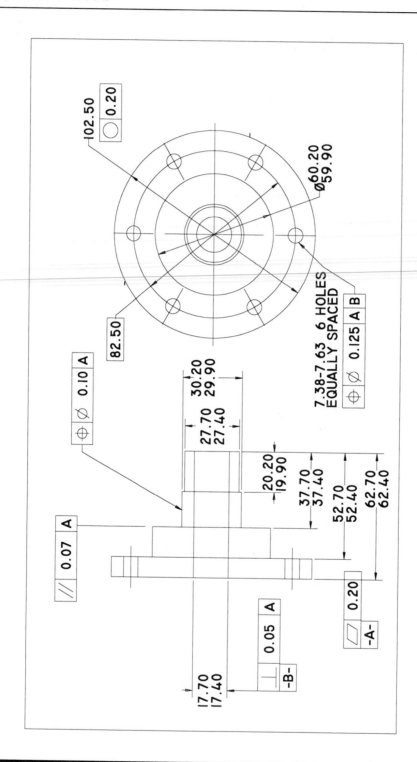

Figure Ex7–1 Completed drawing

Exercise 7-2

Open the drawing that was completed in Exercise 4–2 and add the dimensions shown in the drawing here.

Settings	Value		
1. Units	Architectural		
2. Limits	Lower left corner: 10'-0",-10',-0"		
	Upper right corner: 50'-0",35',-0"		
3. Grid	12"		
4. Snap	6"		
5. Layers	*NAME*	*COLOR*	*LINETYPE*
	Beam	White	Continuous
	Column	White	Continuous
	Dimension	White	Continuous
	Border	Red	Continuous
	Construction	Green	Continuous
	Text	Blue	Continuous

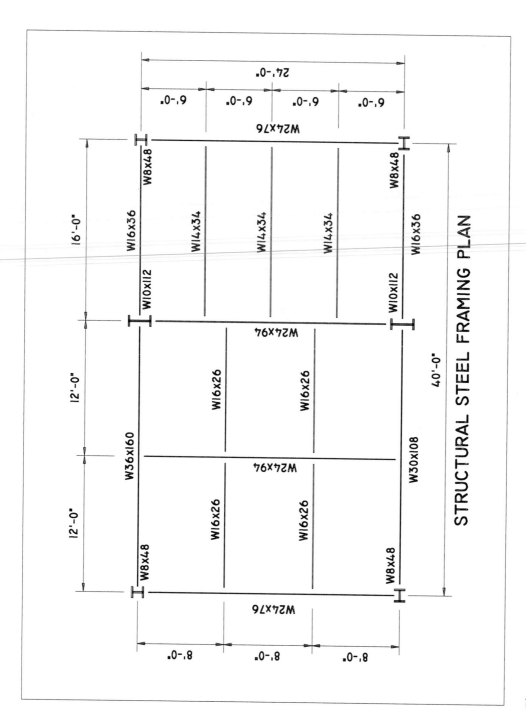

Figure Ex7–2 Completed drawing

Exercise 7–3

Open the drawing that was completed in Exercise 6–6 and add the dimensions shown in the drawing here.

Settings	Value		
1. Units	Architectural		
2. Limits	Lower left corner: 0',0'		
	Upper right corner: 12',9'		
3. Grid	6"		
4. Snap	3"		
5. Layers	*NAME*	*COLOR*	*LINETYPE*
	Border	Red	Continuous
	Object	Green	Continuous
	Text	Blue	Continuous

Hints	Detail B can be drawn to true scale and then increased in size by means of the SCALE command.
	In order to have the dimensions reflect the true sizes of features before their size was changed, set DIMLFAC to the reciprocal of the factor by which the object was scaled. For example, if the scale factor was 2, DIMLFAC should be set to 1/2.

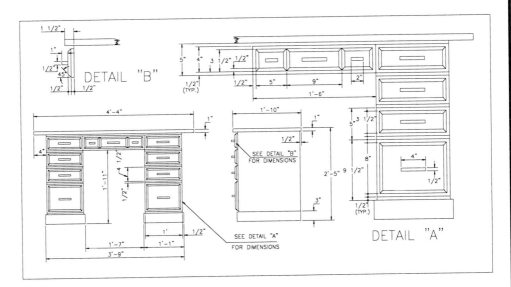

Figure Ex7–3 Completed drawing with dimensions

Exercise 7–4

The drawing of the instrument panel in Figure Ex7–4a has all the information needed to create your drawing. Add the dimensions shown in Figure Ex7–4b with the Baseline Dimension command.

Settings	Value		
1. Units	Decimal		
2. Limits	Lower left corner: 0,0		
	Upper right corner: 12,10.5		
3. Grid	.5"		
4. Snap	.25"		
5. Layers	*NAME*	*COLOR*	*LINETYPE*
	Border	Red	Continuous
	Object	Green	Continuous
	Text	Blue	Continuous
	Dimension	White	Continuous

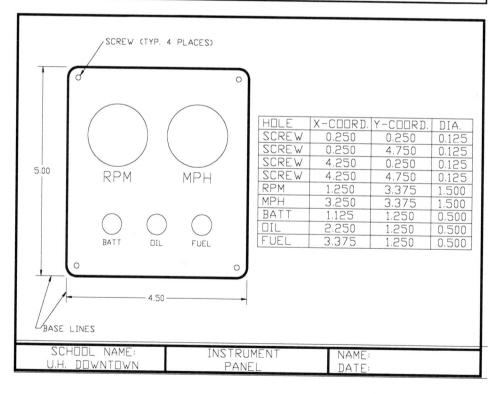

HOLE	X-COORD.	Y-COORD.	DIA.
SCREW	0.250	0.250	0.125
SCREW	0.250	4.750	0.125
SCREW	4.250	0.250	0.125
SCREW	4.250	4.750	0.125
RPM	1.250	3.375	1.500
MPH	3.250	3.375	1.500
BATT	1.125	1.250	0.500
OIL	2.250	1.250	0.500
FUEL	3.375	1.250	0.500

Figure Ex7–4a Layout of the drawing

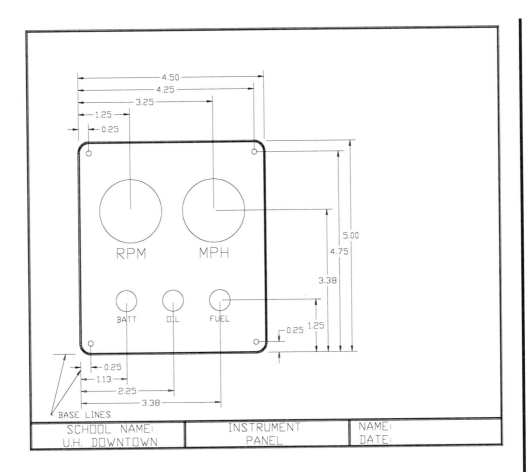

Figure Ex7–4b Layout of the drawing with baseline dimensions

Exercise 7–5

The drawing of the instrument panel in Figure Ex7–5a has all the information needed to create your drawing. Add the dimensions shown in Figure Ex7–5b with the Ordinate Dimension command.

Settings	Value
1. Units	Decimal
2. Limits	Lower left corner: -1.5,-2.5
	Upper right corner: 10.5,6.5
3. Grid	.5"
4. Snap	.25"
5. Layers	

NAME	COLOR	LINETYPE
Border	Red	Continuous
Object	Green	Continuous
Text	Blue	Continuous
Dimension	White	Continuous

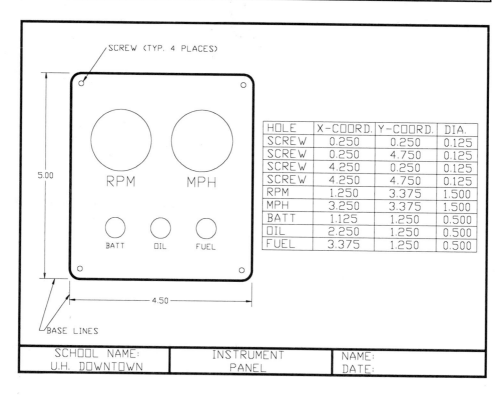

HOLE	X-COORD.	Y-COORD.	DIA.
SCREW	0.250	0.250	0.125
SCREW	0.250	4.750	0.125
SCREW	4.250	0.250	0.125
SCREW	4.250	4.750	0.125
RPM	1.250	3.375	1.500
MPH	3.250	3.375	1.500
BATT	1.125	1.250	0.500
OIL	2.250	1.250	0.500
FUEL	3.375	1.250	0.500

Figure Ex7–5a Layout of the drawing

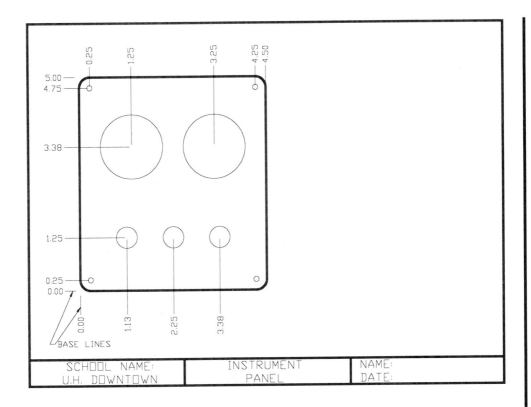

Figure Ex7–5b Layout of the drawing with ordinate dimensions

REVIEW QUESTIONS

1. Dimension types available in AutoCAD include:
   a. Linear
   b. Angular
   c. Diameter
   d. Radius
   e. All of the above

2. The associative dimension drawn with the DIMASO variable set to ON has all of its separate parts drawn as separate objects.
   a. True
   b. False

3. The Linear Dimensioning command allows you to draw horizontal, vertical, and aligned dimensions.
   a. True
   b. False

4. To place a linear dimension you must (1) select the first extension line origin, (2) locate the dimension line, and then (3) select the second extension line.
   a. True
   b. False

5. The angular dimension commands allows you to place angular dimensions between two parallel lines.
   a. True
   b. False

6. By default, the dimension text for a radius dimension is preceded by:
   a. Radius
   b. Rad
   c. R

7. Using DDMODIFY (modify properties) will allow you to override the dimension variable settings for a single dimension, without modifying the base dimensioning style.
   a. True
   b. False

8. The baseline dimensioning command is used to draw dimensions from a single datum baseline.
   a. True
   b. False

9. The DIMCENTER command allows you to place center cross marks or center lines in a circle.
   a. True
   b. False

10. You must explode a dimension before you can use the DIMTEDIT command to edit the dimension text.
    a. True
    b. False

11. The suppress option in the geometry sub-dialog box allows you to suppress only one extension line at a time.
    a. True
    b. False

12. The arrowhead section in the geometry sub-dialog box allows you to change the size and style of your arrowheads.
    a. True
    b. False

13. You must use the UNITS command to determine how many decimal places will be displayed in the dimension text.
    a. True
    b. False

For each of the following, select which of the dimensioning sub-dialog boxes the option can be found from the following list

   c. Geometry Sub-dialog box
   d. Format Sub-dialog box
   e. Annotation Sub-dialog box
   f. Units Sub-Sub-dialog box
   g. cannot be found in the dimensioning dialog boxes

14. Arrowhead size
15. Associative/Non-associative setting
16. Text height
17. Arrowhead style
18. Text location
19. Suppressing of extension lines
20. Linear tolerance settings
21. Number of decimal places for a linear dimension

PLOTTING/PRINTING

• •

INTRODUCTION

One task has not changed much in the transition from board drafting to CAD; obtaining a hard copy. The term "hard copy" describes a tangible reproduction of a screen image. The hard copy is usually a reproducible medium from which prints are made and can take many forms, including slides, videotape, prints, or plots. This chapter describes the most commonly used processes for getting a hard copy: plotting/printing.

In manual drafting, if you need your drawing to be done in two different scales, you physically draw the drawing for two different scales. In CAD, with minor modifications, you plot or print the same drawing in different scale factors on different sizes of paper. In AutoCAD, you can even compose your drawing in Paper Space with limits that equal the sheet size and plot it at 1:1 scale.

After completing this chapter, you will be able to:

✓ Plan the plotted sheet
✓ Change the display order of images and objects
✓ Set the plotting parameters and plot the drawing
✓ Import and export PostScript files

PLANNING THE PLOTTED SHEET

Planning ahead is still required in laying out the objects to be drawn on the final sheet. The objects drawn on the plotted sheet must be arranged. At least in CAD, with its true-size capability, an object can be started without first laying out a plotted sheet. But eventually, limits or at least a displayed area must be determined. For schematics, diagrams, and graphs, plotted scale is of little concern. But for architectural, civil, and mechanical drawings, plotting to a conventional scale is a professionally accepted practice that should not be abandoned just because it can be circumvented.

When setting up the drawing limits, you must take the plotted sheet into consideration to get the entire view of the object(s) on the sheet. So, even with all the power of the CAD system, some thought must still be given to the concept of scale, which is the ratio of true size to the size plotted. In other words, before you start drawing, you should have an idea at what scale the final drawing will be plotted or printed on a given size of paper.

The limits should correspond to some factor of the plotted sheet. If the objects will fit on a 24" × 18" sheet at full size with room for a border, title block, bill of materials, dimensioning, and general notes, then set up your limits to (0,0) (lower left corner) and (24,18) (upper right corner). This can be plotted or printed at 1:1 scale, that is, one object unit equals one plotted unit.

Plot scales can be expressed in several formats. Each of the following five plot scales is exactly the same; only the display formats differ.

> 1/4" = 1'-0"
> 1" = 4'
> 1 = 48
> 1:48
> 1/48

A plot scale of 1:48 means that a line 48 units long in AutoCAD will plot with a length of 1 unit. The units can be any measurement system, including inches, feet, millimeters, nautical miles, chains, angstroms, and light-years, but, by default, plotting units in AutoCAD are inches.

There are four variables that control the relationship between the size of objects in the AutoCAD drawing and their sizes on a sheet of paper produced by an AutoCAD plot:

- *Size of the object in AutoCAD.* For simplification it will be referred to as ACAD_size.
- *Size of the object on the plot.* For simplification it will be referred to as ACAD_plot.
- *Maximum available plot area for a given sheet of paper.* For simplification it will be referred to as ACAD_max_plot.
- *Plot scale.* For simplification it will be referred as to ACAD_scale.

The relationship between the variables can be described by the following three algebraic formulas:

ACAD_scale = ACAD_plot / ACAD_size

ACAD_plot = ACAD_size × ACAD_scale

ACAD_size = ACAD_plot / ACAD_scale

Example of Computing Plot Scale, Plot Size, and Limits

An architectural elevation of a building 48' wide and 24' high must be plotted on a 36" × 24" sheet. First, you determine the plotter's maximum available plot area for the given sheet size. This depends on the model of plotter you use.

Some experimentation is required to determine the actual size of the plotter's maximum available plot area. An easy way to determine the limits is to plot a long line drawn from (0,0) along the X axis, using the plot to FIT option. The resulting width of the plot will be the maximum width the plotter can address at the chosen size. To determine the maximum height for a chosen size, plot to FIT a long line drawn from (0,0) along the Y axis.

In the case of a Summagraphics/Houston Instruments plotter, the available area for 36" × 24" is 33.5" × 21.5". Next, you determine the area needed for the title block, general notes, and other items, such as an area for revision notes and a list of reference drawings. For the given example, let's say that an area of 27" × 16" is available for the drawing.

The objective is to arrive at one of the standard architectural scales in the form of x in. = 1 ft. The usual range is from 1/16" = 1'-0" for plans of large structures to 3" = 1'-0" for small details. To determine the plot scale, substitute these values for the appropriate variables in the formula:

ACAD_scale = ACAD_plot/ACAD_size

ACAD_scale = 27"/48' for X axis

= 0.5625"/1'-0" or 0.5625"=1'-0"

The closest standard architectural scale that can be used in the given situation is 1/2" = 1'-0" (0.5" = 1'-0", 1/24 or 1:24).

To determine the size of the object on the plot, substitute these values for the appropriate variables in the formula:

ACAD_plot = ACAD_size × ACAD_scale

ACAD_plot = 48' × (0.5"/1') for X axis

= 24" (less than the 27" maximum allowable space on the paper)

ACAD_plot = 24' × (0.5"/1') for Y axis

= 12" (less than the 16" maximum allowable space on the paper)

Plotting and Printing

If instead of 1/2" = 1'-0" scale, you wish to use a scale of 3/4" = 1'-0" then the size of the object on the plot will be 48' × (0.75"/1') = 36" for the X axis. This is more than the available space on the given paper, so the drawing will not fit on the given paper size. You must select a larger paper size.

Once the plot scale is determined and you have verified that the drawing fits on the given paper size, you can then determine the drawing limits for the plotted sheet size of 33.5" × 21.5".

To determine the limits for the X and Y axes, substitute the appropriate values in the formula:

$$\text{ACAD\_limits } (X \text{ axis}) = \text{ACAD\_max\_plot/ACAD\_scale}$$

$$= 33.5"/(0.5"/1'\text{-}0")$$

$$= 67'$$

$$\text{ACAD\_limits } (Y \text{ axis}) = 21.5"/(0.5"/1'\text{-}0")$$

$$= 43'$$

Appropriate limits settings in AutoCAD for a 36" × 24" sheet with a maximum available plot area of 33.5" × 21.5" at a plot scale of 0.5" = 1'-0" would be:

lower left corner: 0,0
upper right corner: 67',43'

Another consideration in setting up a drawing for user convenience is to have the (0,0) coordinates at some point other than the lower left corner of the drawing sheet. Many objects have a reference point from which other parts of the object are dimensioned. Being able to set that reference point to (0,0) is very helpful. In many cases, the location of (0,0) is optional. In other cases, the coordinates should coincide with real coordinates, such as those on an industrial plant area block. In still other cases, only one set of coordinates might be a governing factor.

In this example, the 48' wide × 24' high front elevation of the building is to be plotted on a 36" × 24" sheet at a scale of 1/2" = 1'-0". It has been determined that (0,0) should be at the lower left corner of the front elevation view, as shown in Figure 8–1.

Centering the view on the sheet requires a few minutes of layout time. Several approaches allow the drafter to arrive at the location of (0,0) relative to the lower left corner of the plotted sheet or limits. Having computed the limits to be 67' wide × 43' high, the half-width and half-height (dimensions from the center) of the sheet are 33.5' and 21.5' to scale, respectively. Subtracting the half-width of the building from the half-width of the limits will set the X coordinate of the lower left corner at –9.5' (from the equation, 24' – 33.5'). The same is done for the Y coordinate –9.5' (12' – 21.5'). Therefore, the lower left corner of the limits are at (–9.5',–9.5').

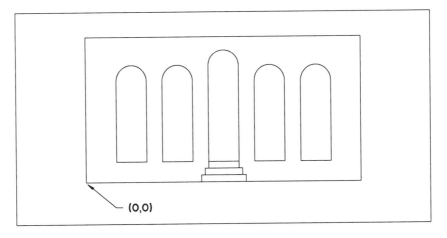

Figure 8–1 Setting the reference point to the origin (0,0) in a location other than the lower left corner

Appropriate limits settings in AutoCAD for a 36" × 24" sheet with a maximum available plot area of 33.5" × 21.5" by centering the view at a plot scale of 0.5" = 1'-0" (see Figure 8–2) is:

> lower left corner: -9.5',-9.5'
> upper right corner: 57.5',33.5'

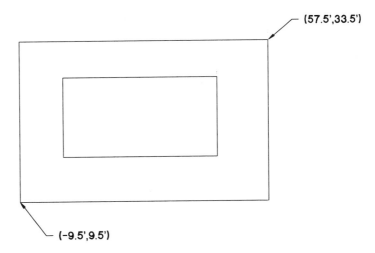

Figure 8–2 Setting the limits to the maximum available plot area by centering the view

Setting for LTSCALE

As explained in Chapter 3, the LTSCALE system variable provides a method of adjusting the linetypes to a meaningful scale for the drawing. This sets the length of dashes and spaces in linetypes. When the value of LTSCALE is set to the reciprocal of the plot scale, the linetypes provided with AutoCAD plot out on paper at the sizes they are defined in ACAD.LIN.

$$LTSCALE = 1/ACAD\_scale$$

Setting for DIMSCALE

As explained in Chapter 7, AutoCAD provides a set of dimensioning variables that control the way dimensions are drawn. The DIMSCALE dimension variable is applied globally to all dimensions that govern sizes or distances, as an overall scaling factor. The default DIMSCALE value is set to 1. When DIMSCALE is set to the reciprocal of the plot scale, it applies globally to all dimension variables for the plot scale factor.

$$DIMSCALE = 1/ACAD\_scale$$

If necessary, you can set individual dimensioning variables to the size that you want the dimension to appear on the paper by substituting the appropriate values in the following formula:

$$\text{size of the plotted dimvars\_value} = \text{dimvars\_value} \times ACAD\_scale \times DIMSCALE$$

As an example, here's how to determine the arrow size DIMASZ for a plot scale of 1/2" = 1'-0", DIMSCALE set to 1 and default DIMASZ of 0.18":

$$\text{size of the plotted arrow} = 0.18" \times (1/24) \times 1$$

$$= 0.0075"$$

Scaling Annotations and Symbols

How can you determine the size at which text and symbols (blocks) will plot? As mentioned earlier, you almost always draw objects actual size, that is, to real-world dimensions. Even in the case of text and blocks, you place them at the real-world dimensions. In the previous example, the architectural elevation of a building 48' × 24' is drawn to actual size and plotted to a scale of 1/2" = 1'-0". Let's say you wanted your text to plot at 1/4" high. If you were to create your text and annotations at 1/4", they would be so small relative to the elevation drawing itself that you could not read the character.

Before you begin placing the text, you need to know the scale at which you will eventually plot the drawing. In the previous example of an architectural elevation, the plot scale is 1/2" = 1'-0" and you want the text to plot 1/4" high. You need to find a relationship between 1/4" on the paper and the size of the text for the real-world dimensions in the drawing. If 1/2" on the paper equals 12" in the model, then 1/4"-high text on the paper equals 6", so text and annotations should be drawn at 6" high in the drawing to plot at 1/4" high at this scale of 1/2" = 1'-0". Similarly, you can calculate the various text sizes for a given plot scale. Table 8-1 shows the model text size needed to achieve a specific plotted text height at some common scales.

Composing the Border and Title Block

As mentioned earlier, you generally draw objects actual size, or to real-world dimensions. After completing the drawing, you can add a border and title block, just

Table 8-1 Text Size Corresponding to Specific Plotted Text Height at Various Scales

SCALE	FACTOR	PLOTTED TEXT HEIGHT								
		1/16"	3/32"	1/8"	3/16"	1/4"	5/16"	3/8"	1/2"	5/8"
1/16" = 1'-0"	192	12"	18"	24"	36"	48"	60"	66"	96"	120"
1/8" = 1'-0"	96	6"	9"	12"	18"	24"	30"	36"	48"	60"
3/16" = 1'-0"	64	4"	6"	8"	12"	16"	20"	24"	32"	40"
1/4" = 1'-0"	48	3"	4.5"	6"	9"	12"	15"	18"	24"	30"
3/8" = 1'-0"	32	2"	3"	4"	6"	8"	10"	12"	16"	20"
1/2" = 1'-0"	24	1.5"	2.25"	3"	4.5"	6"	7.5"	9"	12"	15"
3/4" = 1'-0"	16	1"	1.5"	2"	3"	4"	5"	6"	8"	10"
1" = 1'-0"	12	0.75"	1.13"	1.5"	2.25"	3"	3.75"	4.5"	6"	7.5"
1 1/2" = 1'-0"	8	0.5"	.75"	1"	1.5"	2"	2.5"	3"	4"	5"
3" = 1'-0"	4	0.25"	.375"	0.5"	0.75"	1"	1.25"	1.5"	2"	2.5"
1" = 10'	120	7.5"	11.25"	15"	22.5"	30"	37.5"	45"	60"	75"
1" = 20'	240	15"	22.5"	30"	45"	60"	75"	90"	120"	150"
1" = 30'	360	22.5"	33.75"	45"	67.5"	90"	112.5"	135"	180"	225"
1" = 40'	480	30"	45"	60"	90"	120"	150"	180"	240"	300"
1" = 50'	600	37.5"	56.25"	75"	112.5"	150"	187.5"	225"	300"	375"
1" = 60'	720	45"	67.5"	90"	135"	180"	225"	270"	360"	450"
1" = 70'	840	52.5"	78.75"	105"	157.5"	210"	262.5"	315"	420"	525"
1" = 80'	960	60"	90"	120"	180"	240"	300"	360"	480"	600"
1" = 90'	1080	67.5"	101.25"	135"	202.5"	270"	337.5"	405"	540"	675"
1" = 100'	1200	75"	112.5"	150"	225"	300"	375"	450"	600"	750"

like adding any other objects to the model. Instead of monotonously creating a border and title block for every new drawing in AutoCAD, you can create a stand-alone title block of appropriate paper size limits (electronic sheet) and insert it as a block to the proper scale factor.

Create the border and title block full size (12" × 9", 18" × 12", 24" × 18", 36" × 24", or 48" × 36"). When creating the border, make sure to set the limits to the plotter's maximum available plot area for the given sheet size. This depends on the kind of plotter you are using.

Once the plotter's maximum available plot area is determined for a given paper size, a border and title can be drawn that match these proportions. All text, attribute tags, logos, lines, and so forth should be drawn at the size they will plot. If necessary, you can also define attributes in the title block.

Insert the border and title into your drawing as a block, at a scale factor inverse of the scale that you use to plot the drawing. Let's look at an example.

We'll take the same example we used before—an architectural elevation of a building 48' wide and 24' high plotted on a 36" × 24" sheet to a plot scale of 1/2" = 1'-0" (1/24 or 1:24). Insert the border and title drawing and scale it 24 times larger (inverse of the plot scale factor 1/24) to fit around the elevation drawing. It scales back to the original size when the drawing is plotted.

If 1/8" plotted on the paper is to represent 1" of the drawing geometry, the scale factor of the border and title block insertion will be 8. If 1/8" plotted on the paper is to represent 1' of the drawing geometry, the scale factor of the border and title block insertion is 96. This method is used even when the object is very small and needs to be enlarged on the final plot. For a plot scale factor of 2" = 1", the scale factor of the border and title block insertion is 0.5.

The second approach is to scale the drawing down and insert it into the title block before you plot. This will allow you to plot at 1=1 scale, and "what you see is what you'll plot (WYSWYP)."

You create a 1=1 border and title drawing as explained earlier, and insert the drawing file into it at the appropriate scale. If you make changes to the drawing file, reinsert it with an equal sign to redefine it.

Create the drawing in real-size dimensions. Then, create a block of the entire drawing with the help of the BLOCK command. Next, insert your title block at 1=1 scale on its own layer and zoom to the title block. Then, insert your entire drawing into the border and title drawing at the scale that you would have used to plot in the previously discussed method. If you need to make changes in the drawing, you can explode, and then redefine it as a block with the same name.

Creating a Plot in Paper Space

One of the useful features of AutoCAD is the option to work on your drawing in two different environments, model space or paper space. In paper space you can arrange parts of the drawing at different scale factors and then plot it at a 1:1 scale. For a detailed explanation, refer to Chapter 12.

PLOTTING/PRINTING

To plot/print the current drawing, invoke the PLOT command from:

Standard toolbar	Select the Print command (see Figure 8–3)
Pull-down menu	File > Print...
Command: prompt	**plot** Enter

Figure 8–3 Invoking the Plot/Print command from the Standard toolbar

AutoCAD displays the Print/Plot configuration dialog box, similar to the Figure 8–4.

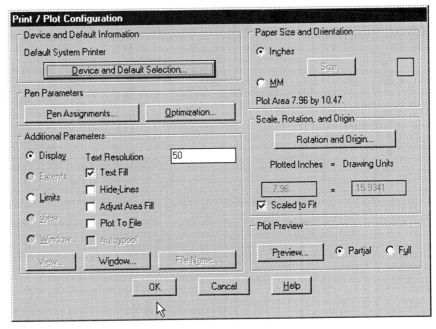

Figure 8–4 Print/Plot Configuration dialog box

Plotting and Printing

The dialog box is divided into six areas. The three on the left are:

1. Device and Default Information
2. Pen Parameters
3. Additional Parameters

The three on the right are:

4. Paper Size and Orientation
5. Scale, Rotation, and Origin
6. Plot Preview

The first time you plot, this Print/Plot Configuration dialog box displays the default parameters and basic plot specifications as set when AutoCAD was configured. If you want to use these values, press ⏎ or choose OK. If necessary, you can change any of the parameters as explained next.

1. Device and Default Information

In this section of the Print/Plot Configuration dialog box, AutoCAD displays the name of the manufacturer of the currently selected plotting device. If necessary, you can change the plotting device by clicking the **Device and Default Selection...** button. AutoCAD displays the Device and Default Selection dialog box, as shown in Figure 8–5.

In the Select a Device Configuration list box, AutoCAD describes all of the configured plotters. If necessary, you can change the current selection by picking another

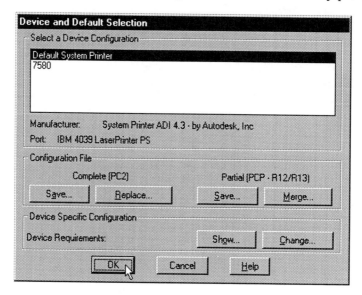

Figure 8–5 Device and Default Selection dialog box

one from the listed plotter descriptions. Selecting another plotter can change the settings of the parameters in the plotting dialog box. You can configure AutoCAD for up to 29 plotters, configure one plotter 29 different ways, or any combination.

AutoCAD allows you to save the plot configuration parameters and device-specific information as an ASCII file with .PC2 as file extension. The plot configuration parameters are device-independent information such as pen parameters, plot area, scale, paper size, and rotation. If you want to save just the plot configuration parameters, then you can save with the .PCP (partial plot configuration) file extension. The .PCP file information can be used with AutoCAD Releases 12 and 13.

To save plot configuration parameters and device-specific information, choose the **Save...** button in the Complete (PC2) section of the dialog box. AutoCAD displays the Save to File dialog box. Type in a new file name or select an existing file in which to save the current settings.

To use the values from an existing .PC2 file, chose the **Replace...** button, and AutoCAD displays the standard file dialog box, from which you can select the desired .PC2 file. AutoCAD replaces the current settings with settings from the selected .PC2 file. Current configuration information is lost unless it has been saved to a .PC2 file.

To save just the plot configuration parameters, choose the **Save...** button in the Partial (PCP -R12/R13) section of the dialog box. AutoCAD displays the Save to File dialog box. Type a new file name or select an existing file in which to save the current plot configuration parameters.

To use the values from an existing .PCP file, choose the **Merge...** button. AutoCAD displays the Merge from PCP File dialog box, from which you can select the desired existing .PCP file. AutoCAD replaces the current settings with settings from the selected .PCP file.

To display the current device-specific configuration, choose the **Show...** button in the Device Specific Configuration section of the dialog box. AutoCAD displays the configuration information for the current plotter.

To make changes to the current device-specific configuration, choose the **Change...** button in the Device Specific Configuration section of the dialog box. AutoCAD displays the Change Device Requirements dialog box, where you can make the necessary changes.

The options available in the various dialog boxes are different for different plotters.

After making the necessary changes in the Device and Default Selection dialog box, choose the OK button to close the dialog box.

2. Pen Parameters

In this section of the Print/Plat Configuration dialog box, you can assign a color, linetype, pen speed, and line weight to each pen. In addition, you can control the level of optimization and improve plot quality.

When you choose the **Pen Assignments...** button, the Pen Assignments dialog box appears, as shown in Figure 8-6. This is where you map the colors on the screen to the pens on the plotter. You can use up to 255 linetypes, colors, pen speeds, and line widths.

The first column is a list of the numbers (from 1 to 255) AutoCAD uses to define colors. An object is automatically assigned the color of the layer on which it is drawn; you can assign a color to an object independent of the layer on which it is drawn. It is highly recommended to have an object's color assigned by its layer.

The second column shows the assignment of pen numbers to the colors. You can have the plotter plot the object in either the same color you used in the drawing file or a different color. Generally, it is easier to keep track of colors and pens if they are the same color. If necessary, you can assign the same pen number to all of the colors, and the plotting will be done in one color. If you have a single-pen plotter and you want to do a multiple-pen plot, AutoCAD stops the plotter and prompts you to change pens whenever a different pen is required.

Some plotters are capable of generating linetypes. The third column shows the assignment of such non-AutoCAD linetypes to the colors. This feature is seldom used because it is simpler to assign linetypes to layers or to objects directly in the drawing.

The fourth column controls the pen speed setting. This is important for pen-based plotters because different pens have different speed requirements. Refillable technical pens generally require slower speeds, whereas roller pens are capable of very high speeds.

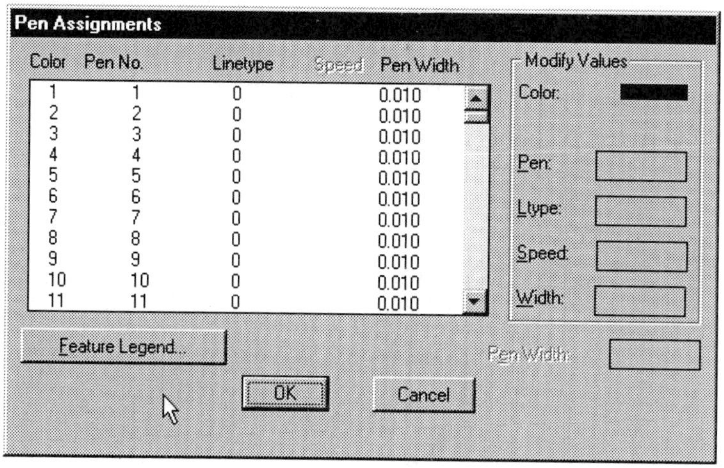

Figure 8-6 The dialog box that appears when the Pen Assignment... button is chosen

The fifth column allows you to select the thickness of individual lines being plotted in solidly filled areas. AutoCAD allows you specify the width of the pen used in the plotter. This setting affects how solid-filled areas (trace, pline, solid, and donut) are plotted. If the value you give here is too high, the solid areas come out like a hatch pattern; if it is too low, the plotter wastes time drawing over areas the pen has already covered. The 0.010 default pen width is adequate in most conditions.

To modify parameters, pick the entry you want to modify from the list box. The edit boxes in the Modify Values section will display the entry you selected. You can make the necessary changes for that entry.

> **NOTE:** Do not pick more than one entry. To deselect an entry, pick it again so that it is no longer highlighted.

If your plotter supports multiple linetypes, speeds, or pen widths, you can view the available information by choosing the **Feature Legend...** button. If it is not available, the Feature Legend... button will be grayed out. Chose OK to save the changes and close the dialog box.

> **NOTE:** If your current plotter doesn't support multiple pens, AutoCAD disables the list and edit boxes and displays the following message in the list box:
>
> Not available for this device.

When you choose the **Optimization...** button in the Print/Plot Configuration dialog box, the Optimizing Pen Motion dialog box appears, as shown in Figure 8–7. By checking the appropriate boxes in the dialog box, you can minimize wasted pen motion and reduce plot time. Each box checked will add that level of optimization

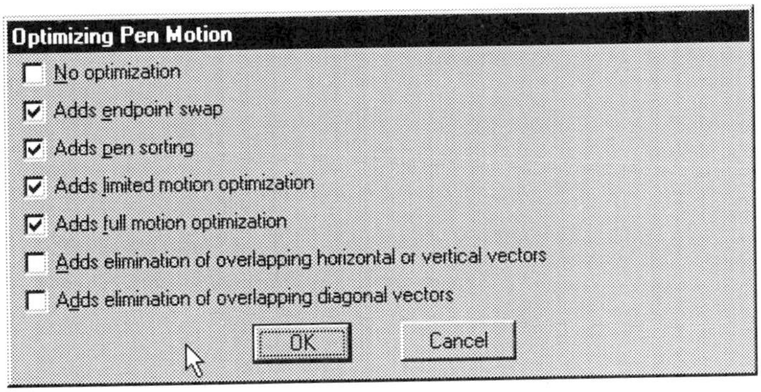

Figure 8–7 Optimizing Pen Motion dialog box

and may improve plot speed. The default settings are dependent on the plotting device you've configured. Choose OK to save the changes and close the Optimizing Pen Motion dialog box.

3. Additional Parameters

In this section of the Print/Plot Configuration dialog box, you can specify a rectangular area of the drawing to be plotted by selecting the appropriate radio buttons. In addition, you can control the removal of hidden lines from 3D drawings, adjust area fill, and create a plot file.

The following list describes the plotting options controlled by the radio buttons and check boxes in this area of the dialog box (Figure 8–8).

Display Option The Display option plots what is currently displayed on the screen. An important point to remember is that the lower left corner of the current display is the origin point of the plot. This option is useful if you want to plot only part of the drawing. Before you select this option, make sure the view you want to plot is displayed on the screen by using the ZOOM and PAN commands.

Extents Option The Extents option plots the entire drawing. It forces the lower left corner of the rectangle that includes all objects in the entire drawing, rather than the display, to become the origin of the plot. This option is similar to ZOOM Extents and ensures that the entire drawing is plotted, including any objects drawn outside the limits.

Limits Option The Limits option plots the drawing to its limits. In general, this makes the origin of the drawing equal to the origin of the plot.

View Option The View option plots a previously saved view. If you plot a previously created view, the plot is identical to the screen image after the VIEW Restore command is used to bring the view on-screen. View plotting makes it easy to plot predefined areas of a drawing. To select a view, choose the **View...** button. AutoCAD displays the View Name dialog box, as shown in Figure 8–9. Selecting a view name and choosing OK enables and selects the **View** radio button.

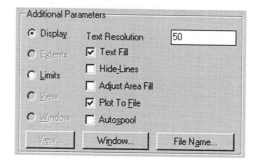

Figure 8–8 Additional Parameters section of the Print/Plot Configuration dialog box

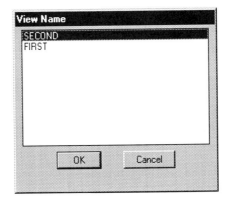

Figure 8–9 View Name dialog box

NOTE: If no view has been saved, both the **View** radio button and the **View...** button are not available.

Window Option The Window option allows you to pick a window on the screen and plot the objects that are inside the window. The lower left corner of the window becomes the origin of the plot. This is similar to using the ZOOM Window command to zoom into a specific portion of the drawing, and then using the Display option of the PLOT command to plot. To specify the Window, choose the **Window...** button. AutoCAD displays the **Window Selection** dialog box, as shown in Figure 8–10. Specify the coordinates of the two diagonal points or select the **Pick <** button from the dialog box and designate the window by means of your pointing device.

NOTE: If no window has been specified, the **Window** radio button is not available.

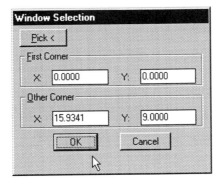

Figure 8–10 Window Selection dialog box

Hide Lines The Hide Lines option allows you to remove hidden lines from 3D drawings. Hidden lines are those that normally would be obscured by objects placed in front of them. This option is not applicable to 2D drawings.

> **NOTE:** For a complex drawing, removing hidden lines can add substantially to the time required for the plot.

Adjust Area Fill The Adjust Area Fill option allows you to compensate for pen width around the edges of a solid-filled area. When the plotter draws a solid-filled area, it finishes the area by drawing the boundary with the given pen width. If the plotter uses a wide pen, the solid area is too large. You can tell AutoCAD to compensate by selecting the check box for adjusting the area fill. Generally, compensation for pen width is critical only when you are producing drawings such as printed circuit artwork, photo etching, or similar artwork.

Plot to File The Plot to File option allows you to create a plot file rather than sending the drawing to the plotter directly. The creating of a plot file is useful if you need to use a plotter connected to another computer. You can copy the file to a floppy disk and then transfer the disk to the other computer. AutoCAD creates the plot file with *.PLT* as an extension to the given file name. Check the **Plot to File** check box to create a plot file. By default, the name of the plot file will be the same as the current drawing name and saved in the current folder. If you want to specify a different file name and/or save to a different folder, choose the **File Name...** button. AutoCAD displays a standard file dialog box, in which you can select or enter a new file name.

4. Paper Size and Orientation

In this section of the Print/Plot Configuration dialog box, you can specify the plot size and set the paper size of the plot. In addition, AutoCAD displays the current plot area and an icon to the right of the **Size...** button indicating portrait or landscape orientation.

AutoCAD lets you plot your drawing in inches or millimeters. Select the appropriate radio button to plot your drawing in inches or millimeters.

To select the plotting sizes, choose the **Size...** button. AutoCAD displays the Paper Size dialog box, similar to the one shown in Figure 8–11. AutoCAD lists the sizes that your current plotter accommodates. A special MAX size is included in the list. This is the maximum area that the plotter can handle. If you set the size to any size other than the standard size of MAX, then it will be listed with a USER label, as shown in Figure 8–11. To create a USER size, enter the appropriate width and height in a USER edit box. You can define up to five USER sizes. To select one of the sizes from the list, just select the entry you want from the list and click OK.

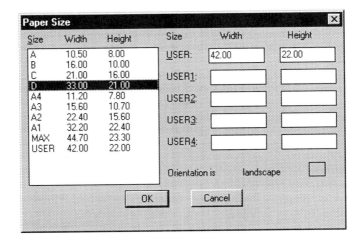

Figure 8-11 The Paper Size dialog box

Plotting and Printing

5. Scale, Rotation, and Origin

In this section of the Print/Plot Configuration dialog box, you can specify the plot rotation, origin, and plot scale.

To rotate the plot clockwise or to set a specific plot origin, pick the **Rotate and Origin...** button. AutoCAD displays the Plot Rotation and Origin dialog box, similar to the one shown in Figure 8-12. To rotate the plot, select the radio button for 0, 90, 180, or 270 degrees. AutoCAD will rotate the plot in the clockwise direction on the paper.

Specify the plot origin at another location by specifying X and Y coordinates in the edit boxes. The origin is the position on the plotter sheet where you tell AutoCAD to place the lower left corner of the drawing. By default, for most of the plotters the plot normally begins in the lower left corner of the paper and for a printer the plot begins

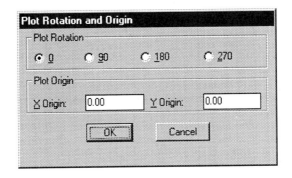

Figure 8-12 Plot Rotation and Origin dialog box

in the upper left corner of the paper. To change the location of the origin, and thus to change the location of the drawing on the sheet, you can give coordinates in inches or millimeters as appropriate. Choose OK to close the Plot Rotation and Origin dialog box.

Next, in the Print/Plot Configuration dialog box specify the plot scale in terms of plotted units = drawing units. Here, decide the scale at which you want to plot your drawing. There are two optional responses to the prompt. You can respond with a plot inches or millimeters (as previously chosen) = drawing units. As explained earlier, you can express the plot scale in several different formats. For example, if you want to plot your drawing to a scale of 1/4" = 1'-0", you enter 1:48 or .25 = 12. Or alternatively, you can respond by selecting the check box Scaled to Fit. This allows you to plot the drawing to fit on the given sheet of paper, no matter how large the drawing. If Scaled to Fit is set to ON, the edit boxes reflect the actual scale used to fit.

6. Plot Preview

In this section of the Print/Plot Configuration dialog box, AutoCAD allows you to preview your plot on your chosen paper size. It is helpful to see the plot before it is plotted, and a convenient way to save time and supplies.

There are two methods of plot preview: partial and full.

Partial Preview The partial preview displays a pair of rectangles: One rectangle represents the media; the other represents the plotted drawing extents. The partial preview can be displayed by selecting the radio button **Partial** and then choosing the **Preview...** button. It is displayed based on the settings you have selected, including:

    Drawing area to be plotted

    Paper size

    Plotting units to drawing units relationship

    Orientation and rotation

On color displays, the paper size is outlined in red and the effective area is outlined in blue. When the effective plotting area is the same as the paper size (in either the X and/or Y directions), AutoCAD displays the coincident outlines dashed in blue. In addition, you also see a small triangular rotation icon in the lower left corner when the default setting of zero rotation is in effect. If rotation is set to any of the other possible settings (90/180/270), the icon is moved to the other corners of the image area.

Partial preview will also give you advanced notice of any AutoCAD warnings that may be encountered when you plot the drawing.

Full Preview A full preview displays the drawing on the screen as it would appear when plotted. This takes much longer than the partial preview, but it takes less time than a regular plot regeneration. This is quicker than plotting wrong and starting all over again.

To get a full preview of your plot, select the radio button **Full** and then choose the **Preview...** button. AutoCAD temporarily clears the plotting dialog boxes, draws an outline of the paper size, and displays the drawing as it would appear on the paper when it is plotted (see Figure 8–13).

The cursor changes to a magnifying glass with plus and minus signs. Holding the pick button and dragging the cursor toward the top of the screen enlarges the preview image. Dragging it toward the bottom of the screen reduces the preview image. Right-click and AutoCAD displays a pop-up menu offering additional preview options: Zoom, Pan, and Zoom, Zoom Window, Zoom Previous, and Exit.

To end the full preview, choose the Exit option from the pop-up menu. AutoCAD returns to the Print/Plot Configuration dialog box.

> **Note:** You can also access a full preview by invoking the PREVIEW command from the pull-down menu File.

Plotting and Printing

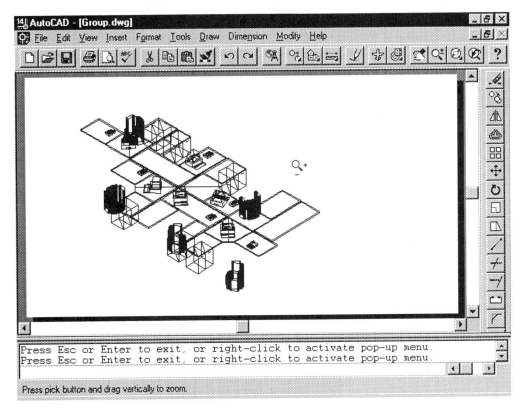

Figure 8–13 Plot Preview dialog box

When all plot specifications are satisfactory, choose the OK button. AutoCAD starts plotting and reports its progress as it converts the drawing into the plotter's graphics language by displaying the number of vectors processed.

If something goes wrong or if you want to stop immediately, press [Esc] at any time. AutoCAD cancels the plotting.

PLOTTING FROM THE COMMAND PROMPT

If you invoke the PLOT Command when the CMDDIA system variable is set to 0 (default is 1) the prompts will appear at the "Command:" prompt (text mode) instead of via an interaction with a dialog box. The options are similar to the options available with a Print/Plot Configuration dialog box.

POSTSCRIPT SUPPORT

PostScript is a graphical description language much like Hewlett Packard's HPGL. It enables programmers to write the programs that describe and manipulate graphic objects (lines, curves, boxes, etc.) as well as text through built-in and user-defined functions. These programs are then interpreted by an output device (either hard-copy or video) to render a graphic display.

Importing PostScript Images

PSIN is the AutoCAD command for importing PostScript files into AutoCAD. These files usually have the *.EPS* extension (AutoCAD accepts *.EPS* as the default extension) and may come from any program that produces standard encapsulated PostScript files or may be created manually by the not-so-faint of heart that wish to enter the world of PostScript programming.

Invoke the PSIN command from:

Pull-down menu	Insert > Encapsulated PostScript...
Command: prompt	**psin** [Enter]

AutoCAD displays a standard file dialog box, where you can enter a file name. After selecting the *EPS* file, AutoCAD displays either a box containing the *EPS* file name or a graphical representation, depending on the setting of the PSDRAG and PSQUALITY system variables. AutoCAD prompts for an insertion point followed by the scale factor. A copy of the specified PostScript file is inserted at the designated point in the current drawing to the specified scale.

> **NOTE:** AutoCAD imports these objects as anonymous blocks.

PSDRAG PSDRAG is the system variable that determines the look of the PostScript object during the initial placement or "dragging" process. If PSDRAG is set to 0 (zero), the object will appear as a box with the *EPS* file name inside. If PSDRAG is set to 1, the object appears graphically.

PSQUALITY The resolution at which PSIN operates is controlled by the PSQUALITY system variable. When PSQUALITY is set to 0 (zero), AutoCAD does not interpret the PostScript image but displays a box and file name scaled to represent the area of the image. When PSQUALITY is set to a value other than zero, that value is used to determine the resolution at which the PostScript image is rendered. Setting PSQUALITY to a positive value uses that value as the number of pixels per AutoCAD drawing unit and renders the image as filled polygons. The higher the positive value of PSQUALITY, the finer the resolution. If PSQUALITY is set to a negative value, the image is rendered in the same fashion as with the positive value, but images are rendered as unfilled objects, providing quicker drawing regeneration.

> **NOTE:** When PSQUALITY is set to zero, PSDRAG has no effect.

Exporting PostScript Images

The PSOUT command exports an AutoCAD drawing as an encapsulated PostScript *(EPS)* file. Once a drawing is placed in *EPS* format it can be used in many programs across numerous platforms. For example, a *DWG* file may be exported as an EPS file and then imported into an Aldus PageMaker desktop publishing program and then printed on a PostScript device attached to the AMIGA. As you can probably see, PostScript offers a great deal of flexibility.

Using PSOUT command is very similar to plotting to a file. The PSOUT command is invoked from:

Command: prompts	**psout** Enter

AutoCAD displays a standard file dialog box, where you enter a file name. AutoCAD exports the file as an *EPS* file with the specified file name.

The PSFILL Command

The PSFILL command complements the PSOUT command. It allows you to fill any 2D polyline with predefined as well as custom PostScript fill patterns. Patterns are defined in the *ACAD.PSF* (short for "Postscript Fill") file. To insert your own custom fill pattern, simply place the required PostScript code in the *ACAD.PSF* file. AutoCAD does not display these patterns but uses them to provide fills for polylines when exporting images.

Invoke the PSFILL command from:

Command: prompts	**psfill** `Enter`

AutoCAD prompts you to select the polyline and then specify the fill pattern you want to use. See Appendix E for the fill patterns available in AutoCAD.

EXERCISES 8–1 THROUGH 8–6

Exercise 8–1

Open the *ch2-proj.dwg* drawing that was completed in Chapter 2 and plot it at the following settings:

SECTION	SETTINGS
Device and Default Information	Select the available plotter to plot.
Pen Parameters	If the plotter is capable of plotting in color, make sure the Pen Assignments are set appropriately.
Additional Parameters	Select the **Display** radio button to plot the display of the drawing.
Paper Size and Orientation	Select the **Inches** radio button and Size A paper with landscape orientation.
Scale, Rotation, and Origin	Set Scale at 1 = 1; Origin at 0,0; and Plot Rotation at 0.
Plot Preview	Select the **Full** radio button and choose the **Preview...** button to preview the drawing for plotting.
Plot	Make the sure the appropriate paper is loaded in the plotter and choose **OK** to plot.

Hint	Before you invoke the PLOT command, set the display of the drawing in such a way that the complete drawing is plotted (WYSIWYG).

Plotting and Printing

Exercise 8–2

Open the *ch3-proj.dwg* drawing that was completed in Chapter 3 and plot it at the following settings:

SECTION	SETTINGS
Device and Default Information	Select the available plotter to plot.
Pen Parameters	If the plotter is capable of plotting in color, make sure the Pen Assignments are set appropriately.
Additional Parameters	Select the **Display** radio button to plot the display of the drawing.
Paper Size and Orientation	Select the **Inches** radio button and Size A paper with portrait orientation.
Scale, Rotation, and Origin	Set Scale at 1/2 = 1; Origin at 1,1; and Plot Rotation at 90.
Plot Preview	Select the **Full** radio button and choose the **Preview...** button to preview the drawing for plotting.
Plot	Make the sure the appropriate paper is loaded in the plotter and choose **OK** to plot.

Exercise 8–3

Open the *ch4-proj.dwg* drawing that was completed in Chapter 4 and plot it at the following settings:

SECTION	SETTINGS
Device and Default Information	Select the available plotter to plot.
Pen Parameters	If the plotter is capable of plotting in color, make sure the Pen Assignments are set appropriately.
Additional Parameters	Select the **Display** radio button to plot the display of the drawing.
Paper Size and Orientation	Select the **Inches** radio button and Size B paper with landscape orientation.
Scale, Rotation, and Origin	Set Scale at 1 = 1; Origin at 2,2; and Plot Rotation at 0.
Plot Preview	Select the **Full** radio button and choose the **Preview...** button to preview the drawing for plotting.
Plot	Make the sure the appropriate paper is loaded in the plotter and choose **OK** to plot.

Exercise 8-4

Open the *ch5-proj.dwg* drawing that was completed in Chapter 5 and plot it at the following settings:

SECTION	SETTINGS
Device and Default Information	Select the available plotter to plot.
Pen Parameters	If the plotter is capable of plotting in color, make sure the Pen Assignments are set appropriately.
Additional Parameters	Select the **Display** radio button to plot the display of the drawing.
Paper Size and Orientation	Select the **Inches** radio button and Size B paper with landscape orientation.
Scale, Rotation, and Origin	Set Scale at 1 = 1; Origin at 2,2; and Plot Rotation at 0.
Plot Preview	Select the **Full** radio button and choose the **Preview...** button to preview the drawing for plotting.
Plot	Make the sure the appropriate paper is loaded in the plotter and choose **OK** to plot.

Exercise 8–5

Open the *Ex6-4.dwg* drawing that was completed in Chapter 6 and plot it at the following settings:

SECTION	SETTINGS
Device and Default Information	Select the available plotter to plot.
Pen Parameters	If the plotter is capable of plotting in color, make sure the Pen Assignments are set appropriately.
Additional Parameters	Select the **Display** radio button to plot the display of the drawing.
Paper Size and Orientation	Select the **Inches** radio button and Size 42″ x 30″ paper with landscape orientation.
Scale, Rotation, and Origin	Set Scale at 1/4″ = 1′-0″; Origin at 0,0; and Plot Rotation at 0.
Plot Preview	Select the **Full** radio button and choose the **Preview...** button to preview the drawing for plotting.
Plot	Make the sure the appropriate paper is loaded in the plotter and choose **OK** to plot.

Exercise 8–6

Open the *ch6-proj.dwg* drawing that was completed in Chapter 6 and plot it at the following settings:

SECTION	SETTINGS
Device and Default Information	Select the available plotter to plot.
Pen Parameters	If the plotter is capable of plotting in color, make sure the Pen Assignments are set appropriately.
Additional Parameters	Select the **Display** radio button to plot the display of the drawing.
Paper Size and Orientation	Select the **Inches** radio button and Size 24" x 18" paper with landscape orientation.
Scale, Rotation, and Origin	Set Scale at 3/4" = 1'-0"; Origin at 0,0; and Plot Rotation at 0.
Plot Preview	Select the **Full** radio button and choose the **Preview...** button to preview the drawing for plotting.
Plot	Make the sure the appropriate paper is loaded in the plotter and choose **OK** to plot.

REVIEW QUESTIONS

1. If you were to plot a drawing at a scale of 1"=60', what should you set LTSCALE to?
   a. 60
   b. 1/60
   c. 720
   d. 1/720

2. If you want to plot a drawing requiring multiple pens and you are using a single pen plotter, AutoCAD will:
   a. not plot the drawing at all
   b. pause when necessary to allow you to change pens
   c. invoke an error message
   d. plot all the drawing using the single pen
   e. none of the above

3. The drawing created at a scale of 1:1 and plotted to "Fit", is plotted
   a. at a scale of 1:1
   b. to fit the specified paper size
   c. at the prototype scale
   d. none of the above

4. To plot a full scale drawing at a scale of 1/4"=1', use a plot scale of:
   a. 0.25=12
   b. 0.25=1
   c. 48=1
   d. 12=0.25
   e. 24=1

5. What is the file extension assigned to all files created when plotting to a file?
   a. DWG
   b. DRW
   c. DRK
   d. PLO
   e. PLT

6. When plotting, pen numbers are assigned to:
   a. colors
   b. layers
   c. thickness
   d. linetypes
   e. none of the above

Plotting and Printing

7. When plotting to a laser printer, line width is associated with:
   a. colors
   b. layers
   c. thickness
   d. linetypes
   e. none of the above

8. Options within the plot feature include:
   a. assignment of pen number and pen speed
   b. specification of plot origin, size, and scale
   c. rotation angle
   d. all of the above

If you need to draw three orthographic views of an airplane whose dimensions were: Wingspan of 102 feet, a total length of 118 feet, and a height of 39 feet. The drawing was to be done on a standard 12 x 9 inch sheet of paper. No dimensions will be added, so you will need only 1 inch between the views. For this drawing, answer the following questions:

9. What would be a reasonable scale for the paper plot?
   a. 1=5'
   b. 1=15'
   c. 1=25'
   d. 1=40'

10. What be a reasonable setting of LTSCALE?
   a. 1   d. 25
   b. 5   e. 300
   c. 60   f. 480

11. If you were plotting from paperspace, what ZOOM scale factor would you use?
   a. 1/5X
   b. 1/25X
   c. 1/60X
   d. 1/300X
   e. 1/5XP
   f. 1/25XP
   g. 1/60XP
   h. 1/300XP

12. When inserting your border in Paperspace, what scale factor should use:
   a. 1   d. 60
   b. 5   e. 300
   c. 25

13. Which of the following options will the plot preview give you?
    a. seeing what portion of your drawing will be plotted
    b. seeing the plotted size of your drawing
    c. seeing the plotted drawing relative to the page size
    d. seeing rulers around the edge of the plotted page for size comparison
    e. none of the above

HATCHING AND BOUNDARIES

· ·

INTRODUCTION

After completing this chapter, you will be able to:

✓ Use the BHATCH and HATCH commands.
✓ Fine-tune the hatching boundaries by means of the Boundary Hatch Advanced options dialog box.
✓ Modify hatch patterns via the HATCHEDIT command.

WHAT IS HATCHING?

Drafters and designers use repeating patterns, called *hatching*, to fill regions in a drawing for various purposes (see Figure 9–1). In a cutaway (cross-sectional) view, hatch patterns help the viewer differentiate between components of an assembly and indicate the material of each. In surface views, hatch patterns depict material and add to the readability of the view. In general, hatch patterns greatly help the drafter/designer achieve his or her purpose, that is, communicating information. Because drawing hatch patterns is a repetitive task, it is an ideal application of computer-aided drafting.

You can use patterns that are supplied in an AutoCAD support file called *ACAD.PAT*, or patterns in files available from third-party custom developers, or you can create

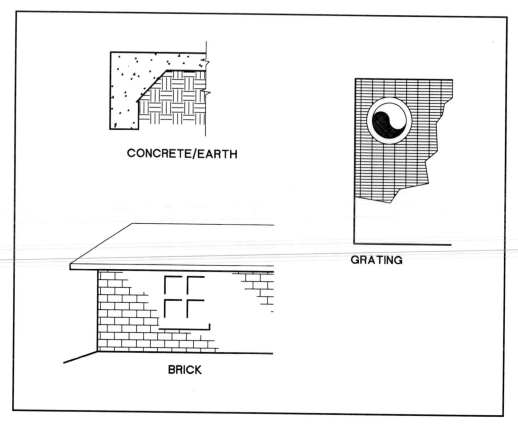

Figure 9–1 Examples of hatch patterns

your own custom hatch patterns. See Appendix E for the list of patterns supplied with *ACAD.PAT*.

AutoCAD Release 14 allows you to fill with a solid color in addition to a hatch pattern. AutoCAD creates an associative hatch, which updates when its boundaries are modified, or a nonassociative hatch, which is independent of its boundaries. Before AutoCAD draws the hatch pattern, it allows you to preview the hatching and to adjust the definition if necessary.

In AutoCAD Release 14, hatch patterns are considered as separate objects. This is different from AutoCAD Release 13, in which hatch patterns were considered anonymous blocks. The hatch pattern behaves as one object; if necessary, you can break it into individual objects with the EXPLODE command. Once it is broken into individual objects, the hatch pattern will no longer be associated with the boundary object.

Hatch patterns are stored with the drawing, so they can be updated, even if the pattern file containing the hatch is not available. You can control the display of the hatch pattern with the FILLMODE system variable. If FILLMODE is set to OFF, then the patterns are not displayed, and regeneration calculates only the hatch boundaries. By default, FILLMODE is set to ON.

The hatch pattern is drawn with respect to the current coordinate system, current elevation, current layer, color, linetype and current snap origin.

DEFINING THE HATCH BOUNDARY

A region of the drawing may be filled with a hatch pattern if it is enclosed by a boundary of connecting line, circle, or arc objects. Overlapping boundary objects can be considered as terminating at their intersections with other boundary objects. There must not be any gaps between boundary objects, however. Figure 9–2 illustrates variations of objects and the potential boundaries that might be established from them.

Note in Figure 9–2 how the enclosed regions are defined by their respective boundaries. A boundary might include all or part of one or more objects. In addition to lines, circles, and arcs, boundary objects can include 2D and 3D polylines, 3D faces, and viewports. Boundary objects should be parallel to the current UCS. You can also hatch the blocks inserted in the unequal X and Y scale factors.

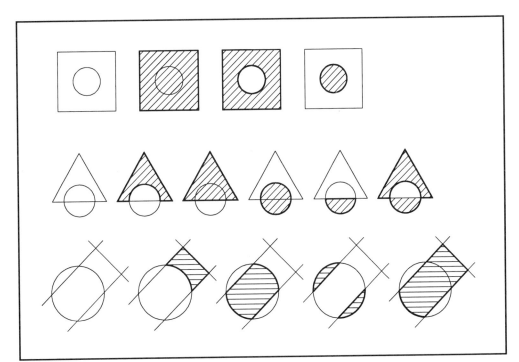

Figure 9–2 Allowed hatching boundaries made from different objects

BHATCH VERSUS HATCH

AutoCAD provides two commands for hatching: BHATCH and HATCH. The BHATCH command (introduced in AutoCAD Release 12) includes several features that greatly improve the ease of use over the HATCH command (introduced in Version 1.4). The BHATCH command automatically creates a boundary; conversely, with the HATCH command you must define a boundary or it allows you to create it. In Figure 9–3a, the HATCH command selects the four lines via the Window option. These four lines comprise the hatching boundary. These four objects are valid boundary segments for use by the HATCH command. They connect at their endpoints and do not overlap. Instead of using the Window option of the object selection process, you can select the four lines individually. This may be desirable if other unwanted objects were within a window used to select them.

In Figure 9–3b, the BHATCH command permits you to select a point in the region enclosed by the four lines. Then, AutoCAD creates a polyline with vertices that coincide with the intersections of the lines. There is also an option that allows you to retain or discard the boundary when the hatching is complete.

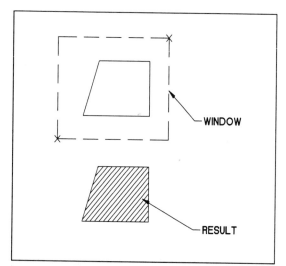

Figure 9–3a The HATCH command requires the user to select objects to define the boundary

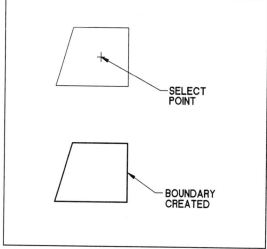

Figure 9–3b The BHATCH command allows the user to pick a single point and automatically creates the boundary

For example, if the four lines shown in Figure 9–3a had been segments of a closed polyline, then you could have selected that polyline by picking it with the cursor. Otherwise, all objects enclosing the region to be hatched must be selected when using the HATCH command, and those objects must be connected at their endpoints. For example, to invoke the HATCH command for the region in Figure 9–4, you would need to draw three lines (from 1 to 2, 2 to 3, and 3 to 4) and an arc from 4

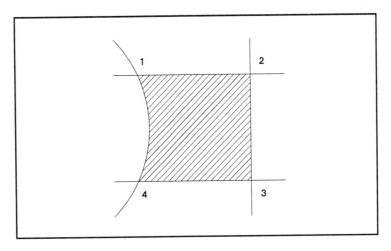

Figure 9–4 A Region bounded by three lines and an arc

to 1, select the four objects or connect them into a polyline, and select them (or it) to be the boundary.

The BHATCH command permits you to select a point in the region and have AutoCAD automatically create the needed polyline boundary. This ease of use and automation of the BHATCH command almost eliminates the need for the HATCH command except for rare, specialized applications. Also, the dialog boxes used by the BHATCH command provide a variety of easy-to-select options, including a means to preview the hatching before completing the command. This saves time. Consider the variety of effects possible, such as areas to be hatched, angle, spacing between segments in a pattern, and even the pattern selected. The Preview option lets you make necessary changes without having to start over.

Hatch Patterns with the BHATCH command

Invoke the BHATCH command from:

Draw toolbar	Select the Hatch command (see Figure 9–5)
Pull-down menu	Draw > Hatch...
Command: prompt	**bhatch** (Enter)

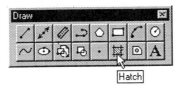

Figure 9–5 Invoking the BHATCH command from the Draw toolbar

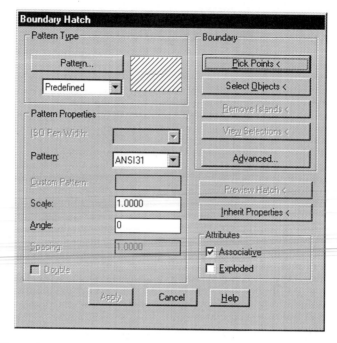

Figure 9–6 Boundary Hatch dialog box

AutoCAD displays the Boundary Hatch dialog box, similar to figure 9–6

Pattern Type The Pattern Type section of the Boundary Hatch dialog box enables you to select hatch patterns. The list box provided in the section allows you to select one of the three choices: Predefined, User-defined, or Custom.

The **Predefined** pattern type lets you select a pattern from those defined in the *ACAD.PAT* file. Select one of the available patterns by clicking the image tile located in the Pattern Type section of the dialog box. You can also select the pattern from the **Pattern:** list box located in the Pattern Properties section of the dialog box. The selected pattern becomes the value of the HPNAME system variable.

The **User-defined** pattern type allows you to define a simple pattern using the current linetype on the fly. Specify a simple pattern of parallel lines or two groups of parallel lines (crossing at 90 degrees) at the spacing and angle desired.

The **Custom** pattern type allows you to specify a custom pattern in a *.PAT* file other than the *ACAD.PAT* file.

You can also select one of the available hatch patterns by picking the **Pattern...** button located in the Pattern Type section of the dialog box. AutoCAD displays the Hatch pattern palette dialog box shown in Figure 9–7.

AutoCAD displays the images representing the hatch patterns and solid fill defined in the *ACAD.PAT* file. The images are displayed alphabetically in groups of

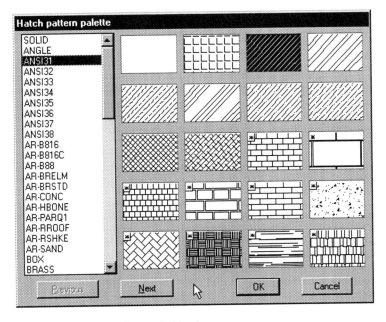

Figure 9–7 Hatch pattern palette dialog box

20. Select the desired pattern or solid fill, and choose the OK button to close the dialog box.

Pattern Properties The Pattern Properties section of the Boundary Hatch dialog box allows you to customize the selected hatch pattern.

If the pattern selected is a predefined pattern, then you can change the scale and angle in the **Scale:** and **Angle:** edit fields, respectively. The angle 0 corresponds to the positive X axis of the current UCS. The default scale is set to 1 and the default angle is set to 0 degrees. These settings can be changed to suit the desired appearance, as shown in Figure 9–8.

If the pattern selected is a user-defined pattern, then you can set the angle and spacing between parallel lines in the **Angle:** and **Spacing:** edit fields, respectively.

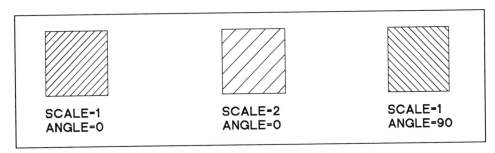

Figure 9–8 Hatch pattern with difference scale and angle values

If you want AutoCAD to draw a second set of lines at 90 degrees to the original lines, then set the **Double** check box to ON.

If the selected pattern is a custom pattern, then specify the name of the pattern in the **Custom Pattern:** edit field; in addition, you can set the scale and angle for the pattern in the **Scale:** and **Angle:** edit fields, respectively.

The **ISO Pen Width:** list box allows you to specify ISO-related pattern scaling based on the selected pen width. The option is available only if a predefined ISO hatch pattern is selected.

As mentioned earlier, AutoCAD considers the hatch pattern as one object, and if necessary you can separate it into individual line segments by setting the **Exploded** check box to ON. AutoCAD draws the hatch pattern as individual line segments and as nonassociative.

If you set the **Associative** check box to ON, AutoCAD draws the hatch pattern as an associative hatch and as a single object.

Boundary The Boundary section of the Boundary Hatch dialog box controls various aspects of boundary definition. AutoCAD provides two methods by which you can select the objects which determines the boundary for drawing hatch patterns: Pick Points and Select Objects.

The Pick Points method determines a boundary from existing objects that form an enclosed area. And the Select Objects methods selects specific objects for hatching.

To invoke the Pick Points method, select the **Pick Points <** button in the dialog box. AutoCAD prompts:

> Select internal point:*(specify a point within the hatched area)*
> Select internal point:*(specify a point, enter **u** to undo the selection, or press*
> Enter *to end point specification)*

See Figure 9–9 for an example of hatching by specifying a point inside a boundary.

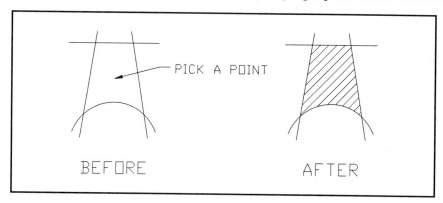

Figure 9–9 Hatching by specifying a point

Before you select the **Pick Points <** button to specify a point, it is very important to make sure an appropriate hatching style is selected. The styles available are: Normal, Outer, and Ignore. You can select one of the three available hatching styles from the **Boundary Style** list box located in the Advanced Options dialog box, as shown in Figure 9–10. The image tile in the **Boundary Style** list box shows an example of the selected hatching style. The image in Figure 9–10 shows a group of four nested objects: a circle, then inside the circle is a square, inside the square is a triangle, and inside the triangle is a text object.

The **Normal** style causes AutoCAD to hatch between alternate areas, starting with the outermost area. The **Outer** style hatches only the outermost area. The **Ignore** option causes AutoCAD to hatch the entire area enclosed by the outermost boundary, regardless of how you select the object, as long as its outermost objects comprise a closed polygon and are joined at their endpoints.

Before you specify the point for hatching, make sure the check box for **Island Detection** located in the Advanced Options dialog box is set appropriately. The Island Detection specifies whether objects within the outermost boundary are used as boundary objects. These internal objects are known as *islands*.

If Island Detection is set to ON (default setting), then islands are used as boundary objects. If Island Detection is set to OFF, then AutoCAD draws an imaginary line from the selected point to the nearest object and then traces the boundary in the counterclockwise direction, a process known as *ray casting*. AutoCAD expects you to select a point that is inside the boundary, and the point must be nearer to the boundary than to any other object.

For example, in Figure 9–11, specifying point P1 with Island Detetection set to ON in response to the **Pick Points <** option results in hatching for Normal style, as shown in the upper right, Outer style as shown in the lower left, and Ignore style as shown in the lower right.

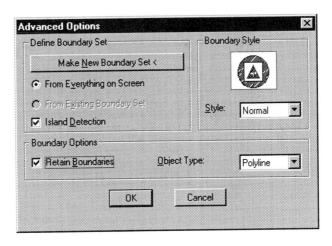

Figure 9–10 Advanced Options dialog box

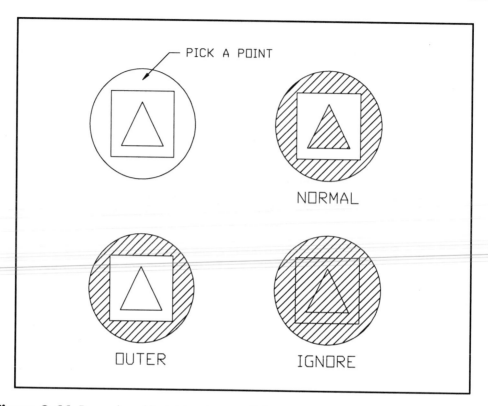

Figure 9–11 Examples of hatching by specifying a point for Normal, Outer, and Ignore style

Caution must be observed when hatching over dimensioning. Dimensions are not affected by hatching as long as the DIMASO dimension variable (short for "associative dimensioning") is set to ON when the hatching is created and the dimension has not been exploded. DIMASO toggles between associative and nonassociatvie dimensioning. If the dimensions are drawn with DIMASO set to OFF (or exploded into individual objects), then the lines (dimension and extension) have an unpredictable (and undesirable) effect on the hatching pattern. Therefore, selecting in this case should be done by specifying the individual objects on the screen.

Blocks are hatched as though they are separate objects. Note, however, that when you select a block, all objects that make up the block are selected as part of the group to be considered for hatching.

If the selected items include text, shape, and/or attribute objects, AutoCAD does not hatch through these items if identified in the selection process. AutoCAD leaves an unhatched area around the text objects so they can be clearly viewed, as shown in Figure 9–12. Using the Ignore style will negate this feature so that the hatching is not interrupted when passing through the text, shape, and attribute objects.

When a filled solid or trace with width is selected in a group to be hatched, AutoCAD does not hatch inside that solid or trace. However, the hatching stops right at the outline of the filled object, leaving no clear space around the object as it does around text, shape, and attributes.

To invoke the Select Objects option, select the **Select Objects <** button in the Boundary Hatch dialog Box. AutoCAD prompts:

Select objects: *(select the objects by one of the standard methods, and press* <kbd>Enter</kbd> *to terminate object selection)*

The **Select Objects <** option can be used to select an object, such as text, to cause AutoCAD *not* to hatch over the selected object and to leave a clear unhatched area around the text to provide better readability.

> **NOTE:** When you select objects individually (after selecting the **Select Objects <** button from the Boundary Hatch dialog box), AutoCAD no longer automatically creates a closed border. Therefore, any objects selected that will be part of the desired border must be either connected at their endpoints or a closed polyline.

The **Remove Islands <** button removes the boundary set objects defined as a boundary by the **Pick Points <** option. You cannot remove the outermost boundary.

The **View Selection <** option causes AutoCAD to highlight the defined boundary set. This option is not available when no selection or boundary has been made.

Figure 9–12 Hatching in an area where there is text

The **Preview Hatch** < option of the Boundary section of the Boundary Hatch dialog box causes AutoCAD to display the hatching resulting from your selections. After previewing the hatch, press [Enter] or click the Continue button to redisplay the Boundary Hatch dialog box to either accept (Apply) or modify your selections. This option is not available unless selections have been made.

The **Inherit Properties** < option allows you to apply the properties of an existing associative hatch to the current Pattern Type and Pattern Properties options. AutoCAD prompts:

Select hatch object: *(select an associative hatch pattern)*

AutoCAD sets the current Pattern Type and Pattern Properties options to the selected hatch pattern.

> **NOTE:** AutoCAD does not allow the properties of a nonassociative hatch pattern to be inherited.

Click the **Apply** Button to apply the hatch pattern. Before you pick the **Apply** button, if necessary you can fine-tune additional parameters related to the boundary set; these are accessible through the Advanced Options dialog box (see Figure 9–10).

Before describing how AutoCAD defines a boundary set, it is important to distinguish between a boundary set and a boundary. A *boundary set* is the group of objects from which AutoCAD creates a boundary. A boundary set is defined by selecting objects in a manner similar to selecting objects for some modify commands. Or the boundary set could be defined when you specify a point before the boundary is created and a particular set of objects is "assembled" in a group. The objects (or parts of them) in the group are used in the subsequent boundary. A *boundary* is created by AutoCAD after it has analyzed the objects (the boundary set) you have selected. It is the boundary that determines where the hatching begins and ends. The boundary consists of line/arc segments, which can be considered to be a closed polygon with segments that connect at their endpoints. If objects in the boundary set overlap, then in creating the boundary AutoCAD uses only the parts of objects that lie between intersections with other objects.

The **Object Type:** list box in the Advanced Options dialog box (see Figure 9–10) controls the type of the new boundary object. From the list box you can select either region or polyline to determine the type of boundary object. The Object Type list is enabled only when the check box for **Retain Boundaries** is set to ON. The Retain Boundaries check box specifies whether or not the boundary objects will be added to the drawing.

Define Boundary Set The Define Boundary Set section of the **Advanced Options** dialog box permits you to single out objects to be considered by AutoCAD when creating boundaries. This is especially useful when a region to be hatched is enclosed by a boundary with edge-determining objects that overlap (do not connect at endpoints) and the region has crossing objects that you do not wish to be considered during a **Pick Points <** option response.

Make New Boundary Set Choosing the **Make New Boundary Set <** button in the Advanced Options dialog box clears the dialog box and displays the drawing for normal object selection. AutoCAD creates a boundary set from those objects selected that are hatchable; existing boundary sets are abandoned. If hatchable objects are selected, they remain as a boundary set until you define a new one or exit the BHATCH command.

When you create a new boundary, AutoCAD enables the **From Existing Boundary Set** radio button in the Advanced Options dialog box. When you first invoke the BHATCH command, this option is *not* available, because by default AutoCAD selects the **From Everything on Screen** radio button to create a boundary set from everything visible on the screen. Enabling the **From Everything on Screen** radio button discards the current boundary set, if any, and allows you to select everything visible in the current viewport.

As mentioined earlier, the Island Detection toggle button in the Advanced Options dialog box specifies whether objects within the outermost boundary are used as boundary objects. If Island Detection is set to ON (default setting), then AutoCAD performs the hatching of the selected boundary depending on the Style setting (Normal, Outer, or Ignore). If Island Detection is set to OFF, then AutoCAD draws an imaginary line from the selected point to the nearest object and then traces the boundary in the counterclockwise direction.

For example, in Figure 9–13, point A is valid and point B is not when Island Detection is set to OFF. The object nearest to point A is the line that is part of a potential boundary (the square) of which point A is inside and AutoCAD considers

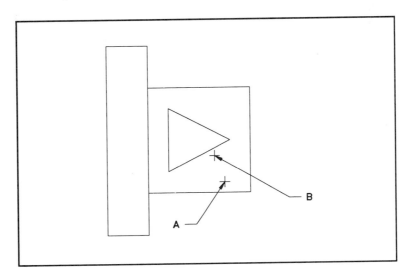

Figure 9–13 Selecting points for Hatching

the square as the hatch boundary. Conversely, point B is nearest a line that is part of a potential boundary (the triangle) of which point B is outside and AutoCAD displays an error message with the selected point as outside the boundary.

After making the neccesary changes to the Advanced Options dialog box, choose the **OK** button to close the dialog box.

Before you click the Apply button in the Boundary Hatch dialog box, if necessary preview the hatch pattern by picking the **Preview Hatch <** button. Pick the **Apply** button to apply the current hatch pattern settings to the selected objects, or click the **Cancel** button to cancel the settings and start all over again.

To create a solid fill in an enclosed area, select Solid pattern. The solid fill is drawn with the current color settings, and all pattern properties are disabled, such as scale, angle, and spacing.

In AutoCAD Release 14, when the GRIPS system variable is set to ON, and you select a hatch pattern, the grip appears at the centroid of the extent of the bounding box of the hatched area.

Hatch Patterns with the HATCH command

The HATCH command creates a nonassociative hatch or fill. As mentioned earlier, if the boundary is made of multiple objects, then endpoints must coincide for the hatch to be created properly with the HATCH command. AutoCAD allows you to create a polyline hatch boundary with the HATCH command if you do not have a closed boundary for drawing the hatch pattern.

Invoke the HATCH command from:

Command: prompt	hatch (Enter)

AutoCAD prompts:

Enter pattern name or [?/Solid/User defined] <current>: *(specify a predefined or custom pattern name, or select one of the available options)*

When you specify a predefined or custom pattern name, AutoCAD prompts:

Scale for pattern <current>: *(specify the scale for the selected pattern)*
Angle for pattern <current>: *(specify the angle for the selected pattern)*
Select objects: *(select the objects to draw the hatch pattern and press (Enter) to terminate object selection)*

AutoCAD draws the hatch pattern to the selected boundary objects.

Instead of selecting the objects, if you press (Enter) (null response) in responding to the "Select objects:" prompt, AutoCAD allows you to draw a polyline boundary with a combination of lines and arcs for drawing the hatch pattern. The prompt sequences are as follows:

Command: **hatch**
Enter pattern name or [?/Solid/User defined] <current>: *(specify a predefined or custom pattern name)*
Scale for pattern <current>: *(specify the scale for the selected pattern)*
Angle for pattern <current>: *(specify the angle for the selected pattern)*
Select objects: Enter
Retain polyline?<N>: *(press Enter to discard the hatching boundary, or enter y to retain the hatching boundary)*
From point: *(specify a start point for the polyline boundary)*
Arc/Close/Length/Undo/<Next point>: *(specify a point for the polyline boundary, or select an option)*

The options are similar to those for the PLINE command (see Chapter 4). When you've completed the polyline boundary, the HATCH command prompts you to create additional polyline boundaries.

When you specify the pattern name, you can select one of the three styles explained earlier. To invoke the Normal style, just type the name of the style. To invoke the Outermost style, type the name of the pattern followed by a comma (,) and the letter **o**. To invoke the Ignore style, type the name of the pattern followed by a comma (,) and the letter **i**.

? Option The ? option lists, and provides a brief description of, the hatch patterns defined in the *ACAD.PAT* file.

Solid Option The Solid option specifies a solid fill. As in drawing a hatch pattern, here also you can select objects to define a boundary or draw a polyline boundary with a combination of lines and arcs for a solid fill. The boundary of a solid fill must be closed and must not intersect itself. In addition, if the hatch area contains more than one loop, the loops must not intersect.

User-Defined Option The User-defined option draws a pattern of lines using the current linetype. You can specify a simple pattern of parallel lines or two groups of parallel lines (crossing at 90 degrees) at the specified spacing and angle. The prompt sequence are as follows:

Command: **hatch**
Enter pattern name or [?/Solid/User defined] <current>: *(specify u for user defined)*
Angle for crosshatch lines <current>: *(specify the angle for crosshatch lines)*
Spacing between lines <current>: *(specify the spacing for crosshatch lines)*
Double hatch area? <current>: *(specify y for a second set of lines to be drawn at 90 degrees or n to draw simple pattern of parallel lines)*
Select object: *(select objects or press Enter to define a polyline boundary)*

As in drawing a hatch pattern, here also you can select objects to define a boundary or draw a polyline boundary with a combination of lines and arcs for a user defined hatch pattern.

> **NOTE:** The selection of objects for hatching must be done with awareness of how each object will affect or be affected by the HATCH command. Complex hatching of large areas can be time consuming. Forgetting to select a vital object can change the whole effect of hatching. You can terminate hatching before it is completed by pressing ⎋.

Hatching Base Point and Angle Different areas hatched with the same (or a similar) pattern at the same scale and angle have corresponding lines lined up with each other in adjacent areas. This is because the families of lines were defined in the pattern(s) with the same basepoint and angle, no matter where the areas to be filled are in the drawing. This causes hatching lines to line up in adjacent hatched areas. But if you wish to offset the lines in adjacent areas, make the basepoint in one of the areas different from the basepoint in the adjacent area. Change the snap basepoint by either using the SNAP command and the Rotation option or by changing the SNAPBASE system variable. This is also useful for improving the appearance of hatching in any one area.

Changing the SNAPANG system variable or the base angle (from the SNAP/ Rotate command/option) affects the angles of lines in a hatching pattern. This capability is also possible when responding to the HATCH command's "Angle for pattern <default>:" prompt.

Multiple Hatching When you have finished hatching an area and press ⏎ to repeat the HATCH command, AutoCAD prompts only for the objects to be selected. The optional parameters of pattern, mode, scale, and angle remain unchanged. In order to change any options, you must invoke the **HATCH** command by typing HATCH at the "Command:" prompt. AutoCAD resumes prompting for the hatch options.

EDITING HATCHES

The HATCHEDIT command allows you to modify hatch patterns or choose a new pattern for an existing hatch. In addition, it allows you to change the pattern style of an existing pattern.

Invoke the HATCHEDIT command from:

Modify II toolbar	Select the Edit Hatch command (see Figure 9–14)
Pull-down menu	Modify > Object > Hatch...
Command: prompt	hatchedit ⏎

Figure 9–14 Invoking the Edit Hatch command from the Modify II toolbar

AutoCAD prompts:

Select hatch object: *(select a hatch pattern)*

AutoCAD displays the Hatchedit dialog box, similar to Figure 9–15.

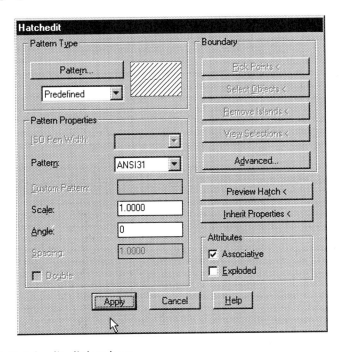

Figure 9–15 Hatchedit dialog box

Select one of the three options, Predefined, User-defined, or Custom, from the **Pattern Type** list box. To change the existing pattern to a new one, select one of the predefined patterns by clicking the image tile located in the Pattern Type section of the dialog box. You can also select a new pattern from the **Pattern:** list box located in the Pattern Properties section of the dialog box.

If necessary, you can change the Scale and Angle of the hatch pattern. Choose the **Advanced...** button to change the pattern style. To inherit properties of an existing hatch pattern, select the **Inherit Properties** < button, and then select an associative hatch pattern. The **Associative** check box controls whether or not selected hatching will be associative. If this option is selected, the modified hatch pattern is associative.

Once the necessary changes are made in the Hatchedit dialog box, choose the **Apply** button to modify the selected hatch pattern.

When selecting a solid fill to modify, pick an outer edge of the hatch pattern with your pointing device or select with Crossing Window selection over the solid fill.

CONTROLLING THE VISIBILITY OF HATCH PATTERNS

The FILL command controls the visibility of hatch patterns in addition to the filling of multilines, traces, solids, and wide polylines. Invoke the FILL command from:

Command: prompt	**fill** [Enter]

AutoCAD prompts:

Command: **fill**
ON?OFF <current>: *(specify ON to display the hatch pattern and OFF to turn off the display of hatch pattern)*

You have to invoke the REGEN command after changing the setting of FILL to see the effect.

PROJECT EXERCISE

This project exercise provides point-by-point instructions for the objects shown in Figure P9–1. In this exercise you will apply the skills acquired in Chapters 1 through 9.

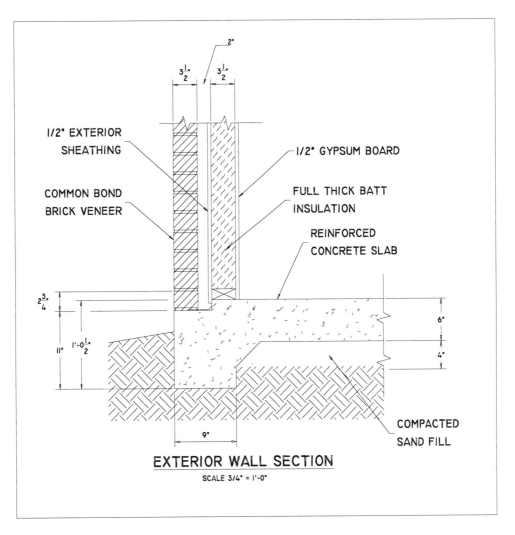

Figure P9–1 Completed project drawing

In this project you will:

■ Set up the drawing, including Limits, Units, and Layers.
■ Use the LINE, PLINE, and HATCH commands to create objects.
■ Use the ARRAY command to create objects from existing objects.
■ Use the FILLET and TRIM commands to modify objects.

Set Up the Drawing

Step 1 Start the AutoCAD program.

Step 2 To create a new drawing, invoke the NEW command from the Standard toolbar or select New from the pull-down menu File.

AutoCAD displays the Create New Drawing dialog box. Select the Start from Scratch button, and then set the Units, Limits, Snap, and Grid to the values shown in the SETTINGS/VALUE table.

Step 3 Invoke the LAYER command from the Object Properties toolbar, or select Layer... from the pull-down menu Format. AutoCAD displays the Layer & Linetype Properties dialog box. Create 10 layers, and rename them as shown in the table, and assign appropriate color and linetype.

SETTINGS	**VALUE**			
UNITS	Architectural			
LIMITS	Lower left corner: -2'-0",-2'-6" Upper right corner: 4'-0",3'-6"			
GRID	1"			
SNAP	1/2"			
LAYERS	*NAME*	*COLOR*	*LINETYPE*	
	Border	Cyan	Continuous	
	Slab	White	Continuous	
	Text	Blue	Continuous	
	Bricksection	White	Continuous	
	Concrete	White	Continuous	
	Earth	White	Continuous	
	Hatchboundry	Red	Continuous	
	Insulation	Green	Continuous	
	Sand	White	Continuous	
	Wall	White	Continuous	
HATCH PATTERNS	*NAME*	*LAYER*	*SCALE*	*ANGLE*
	AR-CONC	Concrete	0'-0 1/2"	0
	FLEX	Insulation	0'-3"	45
	ANSI31	Bricksection	0'-6"	0
	EARTH	Earth	0'-9"	45
	AR-SAND	Sand	0'-0 1/2"	0

Drawing the Concrete Slab, Brick Wall, and Frame Wall

Step 4   Set Slab as the current layer. Invoke the PLINE command with a width of 0.125 to draw the concrete perimeter and with a width of 0.0 to draw the "break" line, as shown in Figure P9–2. Figure P9–1 shows all the required dimensions to draw the layout. After you draw the layout, the drawing should look like Figure P9–2.

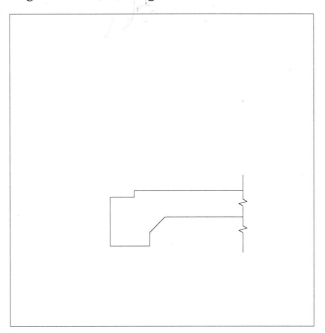

Figure P9–2 Layout of the drawing

Step 5   Set Wall as the current layer. Invoke the PLINE command to draw the bricks. The bottom brick is 2-3/8" x 3-1/2" and is 3/8" above the brick ledge.

Step 6   In order to create the arc that represents the mortar joints, invoke the CIRCLE command with the Three point option. Select the corners of the concrete and the brick that the desired arc touches, and then drag the cursor to a point that gives you a radius slightly larger than the joint gap. Then using the TRIM command, with the concrete and the brick as the objects to trim to, remove the outer part of the circle, leaving the desired arc. Invoke the MIRROR command to create an arc on the opposite edge of the brick, using the Midpoint Osnap mode on the bottom line of the brick as the basepoint about which to mirror. The completed drawing should look as shown in Figure P9–3.

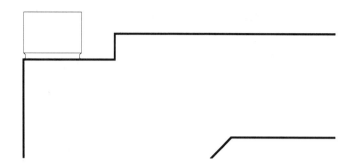

Figure P9–3 Layout of a brick to draw the wall

Step 7   Invoke the ARRAY command to duplicate the bricks and mortar joints and create a stack of 10 bricks. Draw a "break" line through the top brick, and use the TRIM command to trim off any brick extending past the "break" line, as shown in Figure P9–4.

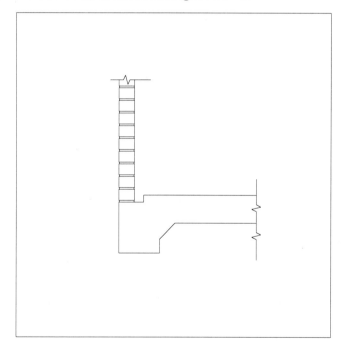

Figure P9–4 Layout of the wall

Step 8   Invoke the LINE command to draw the 1/2" gypsum board and the 1/2" exterior sheathing comprising the frame wall. The 2 × 4 sole plate is

1-1/2" thick and is shown by crossed lines. The heavy flashing at the bottom can be drawn with the PLINE command, with 0.125 width, then use the FILLET command to round the corner, as shown in Figure P9–5.

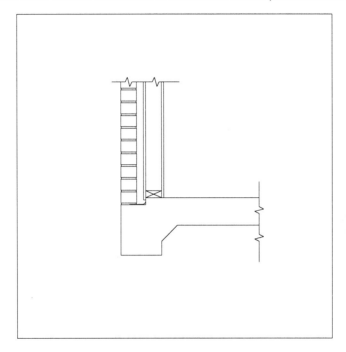

Figure P9–5 Layout of the gypsum board and exterior sheathing

Step 9   Set Hatchboundary as the current layer. Draw copies of the two faces of the bottom brick and the two bottom arcs representing the mortar joint. Set the Wall layer to OFF. The layout should look as shown in Figure P9–6.

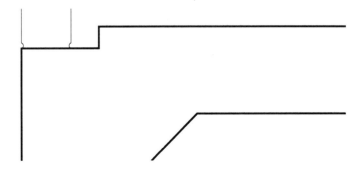

Figure P9–6 Layout of the brick and mortar joint

Step 10   Invoke the ARRAY command to duplicate the faces of the bricks and mortar joints into a stack of 10 double faces and double arcs. Set the Wall layer to ON and, using the "break" line through the top brick, invoke the TRIM command to trim off the brick faces extending past the "break" line. Invoke the PLINE command and trace over the parts of the "break" line between the brick faces. Set the Wall layer to OFF. The layout should look as shown in Figure P9–7.

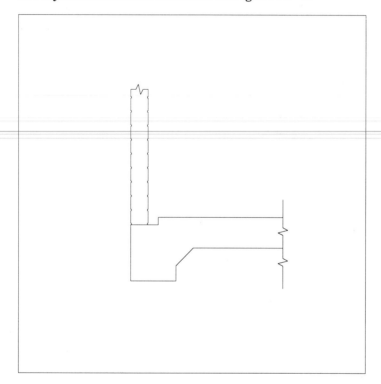

Figure P9–7 Layout of the brick wall with mortar joint

Step 11   Set Bricksection as the current layer. Invoke the BHATCH command and, using the ANSI31 pattern at a scale of 6 and a hatch angle of zero (0), select a point in the boundary just created of brick faces and mortar arcs. Invoke the LINE command, and draw the necessary lines as shown in Figure P9–8 to complete the boundaries for the Sand and Earth hatch patterns.

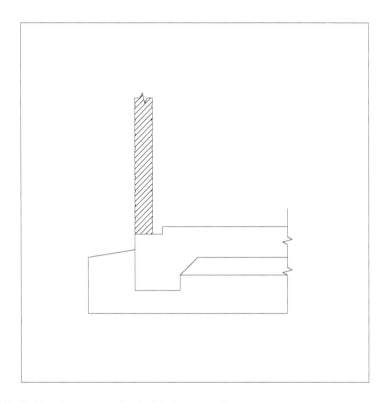

Figure P9–8 Hatch pattern for brick faces and mortar arcs

Step 12   Set Concrete as the current layer. Invoke the BHATCH command and, using the AR-CONC pattern at a scale of 1/2 and a hatch angle of zero (0), select a point in the boundary representing the concrete slab.

Step 13   Set Sand as the current layer. Invoke the BHATCH command and, using the AR-SAND pattern at a scale of 1/2 and a hatch angle of zero (0), select a point in the boundary representing the sand beneath the concrete slab.

Step 14   Set Earth as the current layer. Invoke the BHATCH command and using the EARTH pattern at a scale of 9 and a hatch angle of 45, select a point in the boundary representing the earth beneath the sand and concrete slab.

Step 15   Set Insulation as the current layer. Invoke the BHATCH command and, using the FLEX pattern at a scale of 3 and a hatch angle of 45, select a point in the boundary representing the frame wall between the exterior and interior sheathings. Set the Hatchboundary layer to OFF. The layout should look as shown in Figure P9–9.

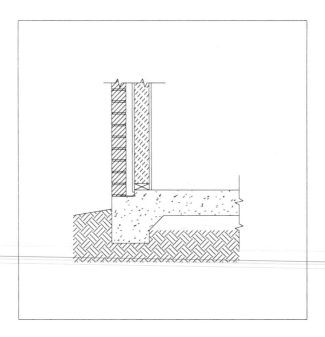

Figure P9–9 Layout of the exterior wall section

Step 16 Set Text as the current layer. Invoke the LEADER command, and draw the text object with the leader lines as shown in Figure P9–10.

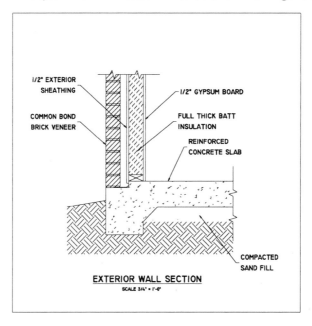

Figure P9–10 Layout of the exterior wall section with leader lines

Step 17 Set Dimension as the current layer. Draw all the required dimensioning to complete the exterior wall section as shown in Figure P9–11.

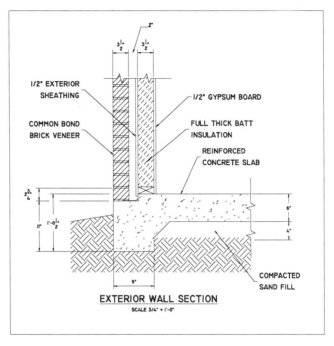

Figure P9–11 Layout of the exterior wall section with leader lines and dimensions

EXERCISES 9–1 THROUGH 9–6

Exercise 9–1

Create the drawing shown in accord with the settings given in the following table:

Settings	Value
1. Units	Decimal
2. Limits	Lower left corner: 0",0"
	Upper right corner: 12",9"
3. Grid	.5
4. Snap	.25
5. Layers	*NAME* *COLOR* *LINETYPE*
	Construction Cyan Continuous
	Object White Continuous
	Center Green Center

Hints	
	Use the PLINE command to draw half the object without the rounded corners. Grid lines are spaced at 0.5 in the figure.
	Use the FILLET command to round the corners of the object.
	Use the MIRROR command to complete the object.

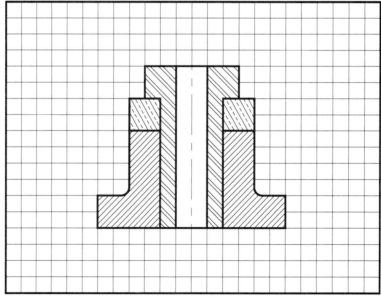

Figure Ex9–1 Completed project drawing (with grid added for reference)

Exercise 9–2

Create the drawing shown, including dimensions, in accord with the settings given in the following table:

Settings	Value			
1. Units	Architectural			
2. Limits	Lower left corner: –7'–0",–17'–0"			
	Upper right corner: 79'–0",27'–0"			
3. Grid	6"			
4. Snap	12"			
5. Layers	*NAME*	*COLOR*	*LINETYPE*	
	Border	Cyan	Continuous	
	Object	White	Continuous	
	Text	Blue	Continuous	
	Brick	White	Continuous	
6. Hatch Patterns	*NAME*	*LAYER*	*SCALE*	*ANGLE*
	BRICK	Brick	12"	0
	AR-RSHKE	Roof	1/2"	0

Hint	Use the dimensions in Figure Ex9–2a, draw the front elevation of the house. The main concern about being able to draw hatch patterns within the proper boundaries is to make sure the boundaries are closed. Overlapping at the intersections of the segments that make up the boundary is acceptable. But AutoCAD will not stop the hatch pattern if there is a gap between any of the boundary segments.

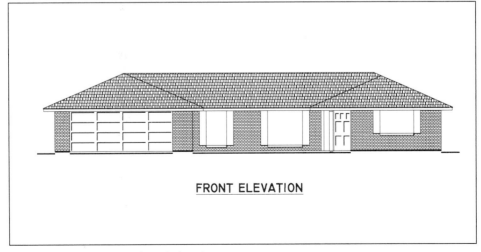

FRONT ELEVATION

Figure Ex9–2 Completed drawing

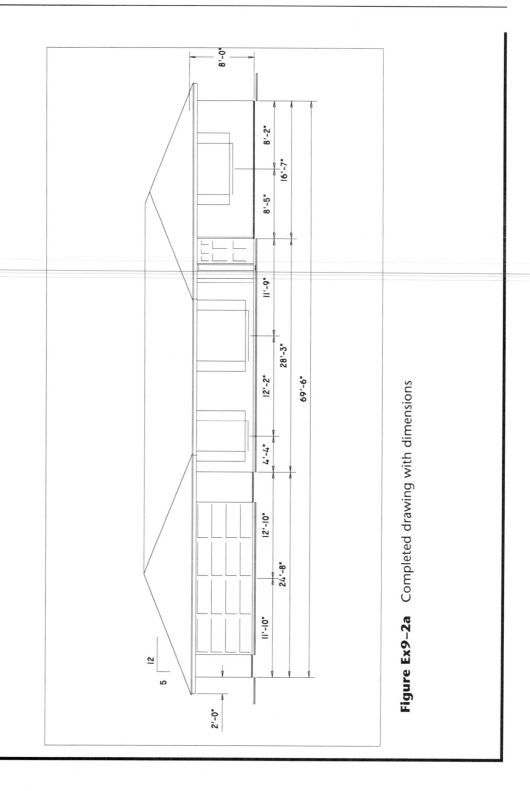

Figure Ex9–2a Completed drawing with dimensions

Exercise 9-3

Create the drawing shown, including dimensions, in accord with the settings given in the following table:

Settings	Value		
1. Units	Decimal		
2. Limits	Lower left corner: 0,0		
	Upper right corner: 17,11		
3. Grid	0.5		
4. Snap	0.25		
5. Layers	*NAME*	*COLOR*	*LINETYPE*
	Object	Green	Continuous
	Center	Red	Center
	Hidden	Magenta	Hidden
	Text	Blue	Continuous
	Hatch	White	Continuous
6. Hatch Pattern	*NAME*	*LAYER*	*SCALE* *ANGLE*
	ANSI31	Hatch	1.5" 0

Hint	All three areas can be selected at once, thus creating a single hatch object.

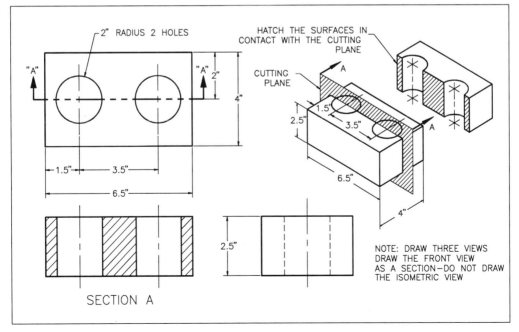

Figure Ex9–3   Completed project drawing

Exercise 9–4

Create the drawing shown, including dimensions, in accord with the settings given in the following table:

Settings	Value			
1. Units	Decimal			
2. Limits	Lower left corner: 0,0			
	Upper right corner: 17,11			
3. Grid	0.5			
4. Snap	0.25			
5. Layers	*NAME*	*COLOR*	*LINETYPE*	
	Object	Green	Continuous	
	Center	Red	Center	
	Hidden	Magenta	Hidden	
	Text	Blue	Continuous	
	Hatch	White	Continuous	
6. Hatch Pattern	*NAME*	*LAYER*	*SCALE*	*ANGLE*
	ANSI31	Hatch	1.5"	0

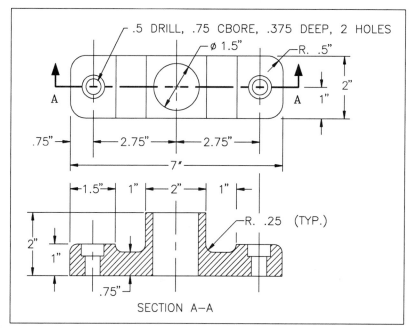

Figure Ex9–4 Completed drawing

Exercise 9–5

Create the drawing shown, including dimensions, in accord with the settings given in the following table:

Settings	Value		
1. Units	Decimal		
2. Limits	Lower left corner: 0,0		
	Upper right corner: 9,12		
3. Grid	0.1		
4. Snap	0.1		
5. Layers	*NAME*	*COLOR*	*LINETYPE*
	Object	Green	Continuous
	Center	Red	Center
	Hidden	Magenta	Hidden
	Text	Blue	Continuous
	Hatch1	White	Continuous
	Hatch2	White	Continuous
	Knurl	White	Continuous
6. Hatch Patterns	*NAME*	*LAYER*	*SCALE*	*ANGLE*
	ANSI31	Hatch1	0.75	0
	ANSI31	Hatch2	0.75	90
	ANSI37	Knurl	0.75	15

Hint	The angle pattern areas can use the same pattern, ANSI31, but with the hatch angles 90 degrees from each other.
	The knurled pattern needs added lines to close the boundary. These can be drawn on a separate layer. That layer can be set to OFF for viewing and plotting the drawing.

Hatching and Boundaries

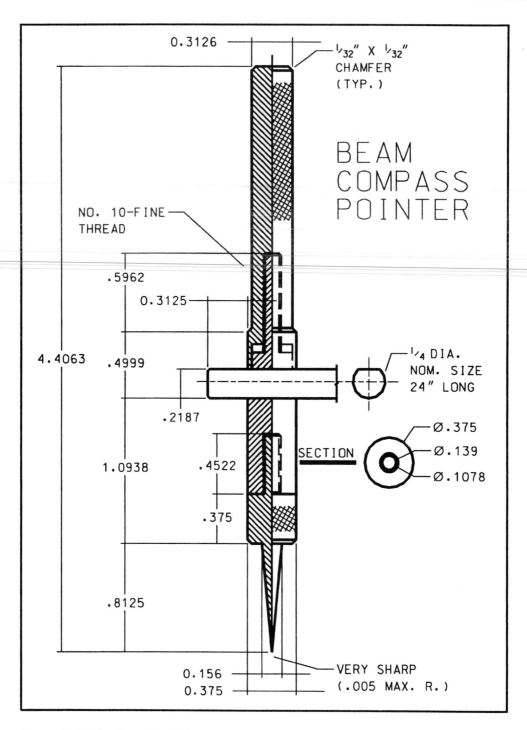

Figure Ex9–5 Completed drawing

Exercise 9–6

Create the drawing shown, including dimensions, in accord with the settings given in the following table:

Settings	Value			
1. Units	Decimal			
2. Limits	Lower left corner: 0,0			
	Upper right corner: 17,11			
3. Grid	0.5			
4. Snap	0.25			
5. Layers	*NAME*	*COLOR*	*LINETYPE*	
	Object	Green	Continuous	
	Center	Red	Center	
	Hidden	Magenta	Hidden	
	Text	Blue	Continuous	
	Hatch1	White	Continuous	
6. Hatch Pattern	*NAME*	*LAYER*	*SCALE*	*ANGLE*
	ANSI32	Hatch	0.5	0

Hint	All three areas can be selected at once, thus creating a single hatch object.

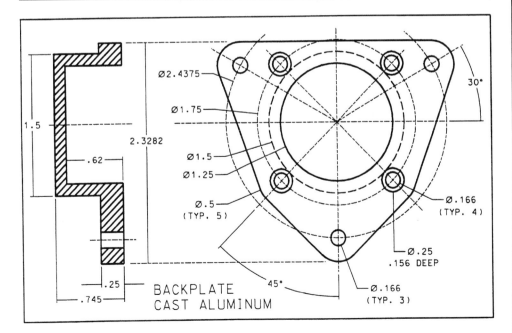

Figure Ex9–6 Completed drawing

REVIEW QUESTIONS

1. AutoCAD will ignore text within a crosshatching boundary.
   a. True
   b. False

2. The BHATCH command allows you to create an associative hatch pattern which updates when its boundaries are modified.
   a. True
   b. False

3. By default, hatch patterns are drawn at a 45 degree angle.
   a. True
   b. False

4. All of the following may be used as boundaries of the HATCH command, except:
   a. ARC
   b. LINE
   c. BLOCK
   d. CIRCLE
   e. TRACE

5. The following are all valid AutoCAD commands except:
   a. ANGLE
   b. POLYGON
   c. BHATCH
   d. ELLIPSE
   e. MULTIPLE

6. When using the BHATCH command with a named hatch pattern, one can change
   a. the color and scale of the pattern
   b. the angle and scale of the pattern
   c. the angle and linetype of the pattern
   d. the color and linetype of the pattern
   e. the color and angle of the pattern

7. Boundary hatch patterns inserted with an asterisk "*" preceding the name of the pattern will:
   a. exclude inside objects
   b. ignore inside objects
   c. be inserted as individual objects
   d. be inserted on layer 0
   e. none of the above

8. The AutoCAD hatch feature
   a. provides a selection of numerous hatch patterns
   b. allows you to change the color and linetype
   c. hatches over the top of text when the text is contained inside the boundary
   d. all of the above

9. The BHATCH command will allow you to create a polyline around the area being hatched and to retain that polyline upon completion of the command.
   a. True
   b. False

10

BLOCKS AND ATTRIBUTES

•••••••••••••••••••••••

INTRODUCTION

The AutoCAD BMAKE (block make) command feature is a powerful design/drafting tool. The BMAKE command enables a designer to create an object from one or more objects, save it under a user-determined name, and later place it back into the drawing. When blocks are inserted in the drawing they can be scaled up or down in both or either of the X and Y axes. They can also be rotated as they are inserted in the drawing. Blocks can best be compared with their manual drafting counterpart, the template. Even though an inserted block is more than one object, the block acts as a single unit when operated on by certain construction and modify commands, like MOVE, COPY, ERASE, ROTATE, ARRAY, and MIRROR. You can export a block to become a drawing file outside the current drawing and create a symbol library from which blocks are inserted into other drawings. Like the plastic template, blocks greatly reduce repetitious work.

The BMAKE command can save time because you don't have to draw the same object(s) more than once. Blocks save computer storage because the computer needs to store the object descriptions only once. When inserting blocks, you can change the scale and/or proportions of the original object(s).

After completing this chapter, you will be able to:

✓ Create and insert blocks in a drawing
✓ Convert individual blocks into drawing files
✓ Define attributes, edit attributes, and control the display of attributes
✓ Use the DIVIDE and MEASURE commands

CREATING BLOCKS

When you invoke the BMAKE command to create a block, AutoCAD refers to this as *defining* the block. The resulting definition is stored in the drawing database. The same block can be inserted as many times as needed.

Blocks may comprise one or more objects. The first step in creating blocks is to create a block definition. In order to do this, the objects that make up the block must be visible on the screen. That is, the objects that will make up the block definition must have already been drawn so you can select them when prompted to do so during the BMAKE command.

The layer the objects comprising the block are on is very important. Objects that are on layer 0 when the block is created will assume the color and linetype of the layer on which the block is inserted. Objects on any layer other than 0 when included in the block definition will retain the characteristics of that layer, even when the block is inserted on a different layer. See Figure 10–1 for an example.

You should be careful when invoking the CHPROP command to change the color or linetype of elements of a block. It is best to keep the color and linetype of blocks and the objects that comprise them in the BYLAYER state.

Examples of some common uses of blocks in various disciplines are shown in Figure 10–2.

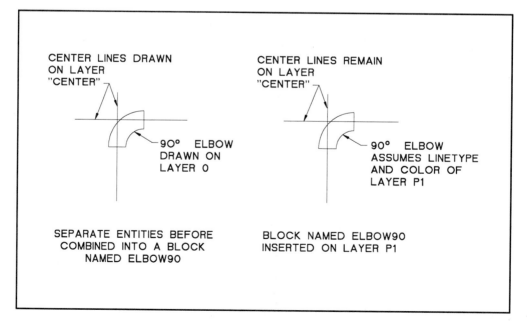

Figure 10–1 Example of inserting blocks drawn in different layers

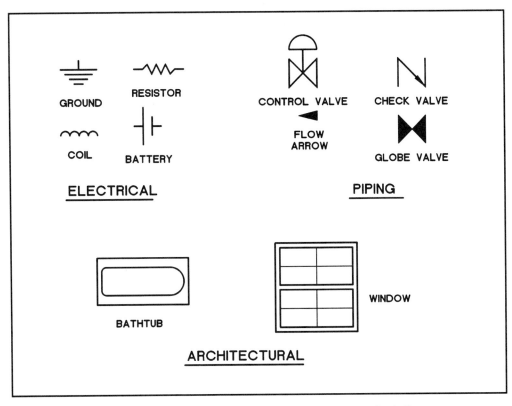

Figure 10–2 Examples of common uses of blocks in various disciplines

Creating a Block Definition

The BMAKE command creates a block definition for selected objects. Invoke the BMAKE command from:

Draw toolbar	Select the Make Block command (see Figure 10–3)
Pull-down menu	Draw > Block > Make...
Command: prompt	bmake Enter

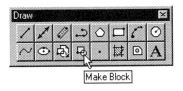

Figure 10–3 Invoking the Make Block command from the Draw toolbar

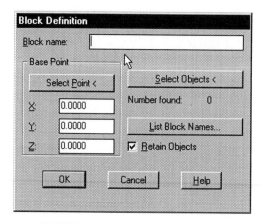

Figure 10–4 Block Definition dialog box

AutoCAD displays the Block Definition dialog box, similar to the Figure 10–4.

Block Name Specify the block name in the **Block name:** edit box. The block name can be up to 31 characters long and may contain letters, digits, and the special characters $ (dollar), - (hyphen), and _ (underscore).

Base Point In the Base Point section, you specify the insertion point for the block.

The insertion point specified during the creation of the block becomes the basepoint for future insertions of this block. It is also the point about which the block can be rotated or scaled during insertion. When determining where to locate the base insertion point it is important to consider what will be on the drawing *before* you insert the block. So you *must* anticipate this preinsertion state of the drawing. It is sometimes more convenient for the insertion point to be somewhere off of the object than on it.

You can specify the insertion point on the screen, or you can specify *X* and *Y* coordinates of the insertion point in the **X:** and **Y:** edit boxes, respectively, located in the Base Point section of the Block Definition dialog box. To specify the basepoint on the screen, select the **Select Point** < button in the Base Point section of the Block Definition dialog box. AutoCAD prompts:

> Insertion base point: *(specify the insertion point)*

Once you have specified the insertion point, the Block Definition dialog box reappears.

Selecting Objects To select objects to include in the block definition, select the **Select Objects** < button located in the Block Definition dialog box. AutoCAD prompts:

> Select objects: *(select objects via the AutoCAD object selection methods, and*
>   *press* Enter *to complete object selection)*

Once the objects are selected, the Block Definition dialog box reappears.

Listing Block Names To list the block names in the current drawing, choose the **List Block Names...** button located in the Block Definition dialog box. AutoCAD lists the blocks in the current drawing.

Retain Objects The Retain Objects check box controls whether the objects will be deleted or not after you create the block definition. If the Retain Objects check box is set to ON (default), then the objects will not be deleted from the drawing after the block definition is created. If it is set to OFF, then the objects will be deleted from the drawing after you create the block definition.

Choose the OK button to create the block definition to the given name. If the given name is the same as an existing block in the current drawing, AutoCAD displays a warning like that shown in Figure 10–5.

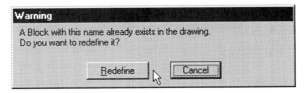

Figure 10–5 Warning dialog box regarding block definition

To redefine the block, select the **Redefine** button in the Warning dialog box. The block with that same name is then redefined. Once the drawing is regenerated, any insertion of this block on the drawing redefines to the new block definition with this name.

Select the **Cancel** button in the Warning dialog box to cancel the block definition. Then to create a new block definition, specify a different block name in the **Block Name:** edit box of the Block Definition dialog box and choose **OK**.

You can also create a block definition from selected objects by invoking the BLOCK command from:

Command: prompt	block [Enter]

AutoCAD prompts:

> Block name (or ?): *(specify a block name, or enter ? to list the block names in the current drawing)*
> Insertion base point: *(specify the insertion basepoint)*
> Select objects: *(select the objects to include in the block definition, and press [Enter] to complete object selection)*

AutoCAD creates the block with the given name and then erases the objects that make up the definition from the screen. You can restore the objects by entering the OOPS command immediately after the BLOCK command.

INSERTING BLOCKS

You can insert previously defined blocks into the current drawing by invoking the DDINSERT or INSERT command. If there is no block definition with the specified name in the current drawing, AutoCAD searches the drives and directories on the path for a drawing of that name and inserts it instead.

> **NOTE:** If blocks were created and stored in a template drawing, and you make your new drawing equal to the template, those blocks will be in the new drawing ready to insert. Any drawing inserted into the current drawing will bring with it all of its block definitions, whether they have been inserted or are only stored as definitions.

DDINSERT Command

Invoke the DDINSERT command from:

Draw toolbar	Select the Insert Block command (see Figure 10–6)
Pull-down menu	Insert>Block...
Command: prompt	**ddinsert** [Enter]

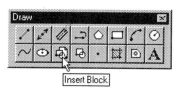

Figure 10–6 Invoking the Insert Block command from the Draw toolbar

AutoCAD displays the Insert dialog box, similar to Figure 10–7.

Specify a block name in the Block... edit box. Or choose the **Block...** button to display a dialog box that lets you select from a list of blocks defined in the current drawing (see Figure 10–8). Select the block you want to insert, and choose **OK** to close the dialog box.

You can specify the insertion point in terms of X, Y, and Z coordinates, the appropriate scale factor, and the rotation angle in the Insert dialog box. Choose the **OK** button, and a copy of the specified block is inserted at the designated point in the current drawing to the specified scale and rotation angle. The default scale factor is 1.0 (full scale). You can specify a scale factor between 0 and 1 to insert the block smaller than the original size of the block. If necessary, you can specify different X

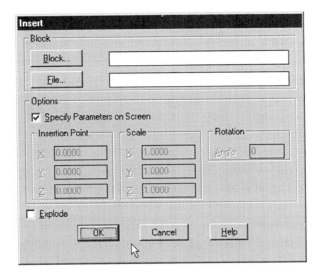

Figure 10-7 Insert dialog box

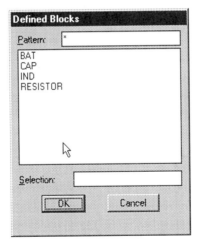

Figure 10-8 Listing of blocks defined in the current drawing

and Y scale factors for insertion of the block. It is possible to enter a negative value for the X and Y scale factors; this inserts a mirror image of the block about the insertion point. As a matter of fact, if -1 were used for both scale factors, it would "double mirror" the object, the equivalent of rotating it 180 degrees.

The rotation angle causes the block to be inserted at any desired angle. To rotate the block, give a positive or negative angle referencing the block in its original position, or drag the block to the correct angle and pick the position.

Instead of specifying the scale factor and rotation angle in the Insert dialog box, you can check ON for the **Specify Parameters on Screen** box. AutoCAD in turn prompts you for the insertion point, the scale factor, and the rotation angle. You can place the block at the appropriate insertion point. By dragging, you can place it at the correct angle and scale.

The **Explode** check box allows you to insert the block as a set of individual objects rather than as a single unit. The EXPLODE command is discussed later in this chapter.

To specify a drawing file to insert as a block definition, enter the drawing file name in the File... edit box. Or pick the **File...** button to display a standard file dialog box and select the appropriate drawing file.

> **NOTE:** The name of the last block inserted during the current drawing session is remembered by AutoCAD. The name becomes the default for subsequent use of the DDINSERT Command.

INSERT Command

Invoke the INSERT command from:

Command: prompt	insert [Enter]

AutoCAD prompts:

> Block name (or ?): *(specify a block name, or enter ? to list the block names in the current drawing)*
> Insertion point: *(specify the insertion point to insert the block)*
> X scale factor <1>/Corner/XYZ: *(specify a scale factor for the X axis, specify a point, or press [Enter] to accept the default scale factor)*
> Y scale factor (default=X): *(specify a scale factor for the Y axis, specify a point, or press [Enter] to accept the same scale factor as for the X axis)*
> Rotation angle <current>: *(specify a rotation angle, specify a point, or press [Enter] to accept the default rotation angle)*

Instead of specifying the insertion point to insert the block, you can invoke one of the following options at the "Insertion point:" prompt to preset the scale and rotation of a block before you specify its position:

Scale The Scale option sets the scale factor for the X, Y, and Z axes.

Xscale The Xscale option sets the X scale factor.

Yscale The Yscale option sets the Y scale factor.

Zscale The Zscale option sets the Z scale factor.

Rotate The Rotate option sets the rotation angle.

Pscale The Pscale option sets the scale factor for the X, Y, and Z axes to control the display of the block as it is dragged into position.

Pxscale The Pxscale option sets the scale factor for the X axis to control the display of the block as it is dragged into position.

Pyscale The Pyscale option sets the scale factor for the Y axis to control the display of the block as it is dragged into position.

Pzscale The Pzscale option sets the scale factor for the Z axis to control the display of the block as it is dragged into position.

PRotate The PRotate option sets the rotation angle of the block as its is dragged into position.

After you provide the appropriate information to the selected option, AutoCAD returns to the "Insertion point:" prompt. AutoCAD continues with the scale factor and rotation angle prompts. A copy of the specified block is inserted, with its defined insertion point located at the designated point in the current drawing to the specified scale and rotation angle.

NESTED BLOCKS

Blocks can contain other blocks. That is, when using the BLOCK command to combine objects into a single object, one or more of the selected objects can themselves be blocks. And the blocks selected can have blocks nested within them. There is no limitation to the depth of nesting. You may not, however, use the name of any of the nested blocks as the name of the block being defined. This would mean that you were trying to redefine a block, using its old definition in the new.

Any objects within blocks (as nested blocks) that were on layer 0 when made into a block will assume the color and linetype of the layer on which the block is inserted. If an object (originally on layer 0 when included in a block definition) is in a block that has been inserted on a layer other than layer 0, it will retain the color and linetype of the layer it was on when its block was included in a higher-level block. For example, you draw a circle on layer 0 and include it in a block named Z1. Then, you insert Z1 on layer R, whose color is red. The circle would then assume the color of layer R (in this case it will be red). Create another block called Y3 by including the block Z1. If you insert block Y3 on a layer whose color is blue, the block Y3 will retain the current color of layer R (in this case it will be red) instead of taking up the color of blue.

Blocks and Attributes

EXPLODE COMMAND

The EXPLODE command causes blocks, hatch patterns, and associative dimensioning to be turned into the separate objects from which they were created. It also causes polylines/polyarcs and multilines to separate into individual simple line and arc objects. The EXPLODE command causes 3D polygon meshes to become 3Dfaces, and 3D polyface meshes to become 3Dfaces and simple line and point objects. When an object is exploded, the new, separate objects are created in the space (model or paper) of the exploded objects.

Invoke the EXPLODE command from:

Modify toolbar	Select the Explode command (see Figure 10–9)
Pull-down menu	Modify > Explode
Command: prompt	explode [Enter]

Figure 10–9 Invoking the Explode command from the Modify toolbar

AutoCAD prompts:

Command: **explode**
Select objects: *(select objects to explode, and press [Enter] to complete object selection)*

You can use one or more object selection methods. The object selected must be eligible for exploding, or an error message will appear. An eligible object may or may not change its appearance when exploded.

Possible Changes Caused by the EXPLODE Command

A polyline segment having width will revert to a zero-width line and/or arc. Tangent information associated with individual segments is lost. If the polyline segments have width or tangent information, the EXPLODE command will be followed by the message:

Exploding this polyline has lost (width/tangent) information.
The UNDO command will restore it.

Individual elements within blocks that were on layer 0 when created (and whose color was BYLAYER) but were inserted on a layer with a color different than that of layer 0 will revert to the color of layer 0.

Attributes are special text objects that, when included in a block definition, take on the values (names and numbers) specified at the time the block is inserted. The power and usage of attributes are discussed later in this chapter. To understand the effect of the EXPLODE command on blocks that include attributes, it is sufficient to know that the fundamental object from which an attribute is created is called an *attribute definition*. It is displayed in the form of an *attribute tag* before it is included in the block.

An attribute within a block will revert to the attribute definition when the block is exploded and will be represented on the screen by its tag. The value of the attribute specified at the time of insertion is lost. The group will revert to those elements created by the ATTDEF command prior to combining them into a block via the MBLOCK command.

In brief, an attribute definition is turned into an attribute when the block in which it is a part is inserted; and conversely, an attribute is turned back into an attribute definition when the block is exploded.

Exploding Blocks with Nested Elements

Blocks containing other blocks and/or polylines are separated for one level only. That is, the highest-level block will be exploded, but any nested blocks or polylines will remain blocks or polylines. They in turn can be exploded when they come to the highest level.

Viewport objects in a block definition cannot be turned on after being exploded unless they were inserted in paper space.

Blocks with equal *X, Y,* and *Z* scales explode into their component objects. Blocks with unequal *X, Y,* and *Z* scales (nonuniformly scaled blocks) might explode into unexpected objects.

> **NOTE:** Blocks inserted via the MINSERT command or external references and their dependent blocks cannot be exploded.

MULTIPLE INSERTS OF BLOCKS

The MINSERT (multiple insert) command is used to insert blocks in a rectangular array. The total pattern takes the characteristics of a block, except the group cannot be exploded. This command works similar to the rectangular ARRAY command.

Invoke the MINSERT command from:

Command: prompt	minsert Enter

AutoCAD prompts:

Command: **minsert**
Block name (or ?): *(specify name of the block)*
Insertion point: *(specify the insertion point)*
X scale factor <1> / Corner / XYZ: *(type a number or specify a point)*
Y scale factor (default=X): *(type a number or null response)*
Rotation angle <0>: *(type a number or specify a point)*
Number of rows (—) <default>: *(specify the number of rows)*
Number of columns (||||) <default>: *(specify the number of columns)*
Unit cell or distance between rows (—): *(specify the distance between rows)*
Distance between columns (||||): *(specify the distance between columns)*

The row/column spacing can be specified by the delta-X/delta-Y distances between two points picked on the screen. For example, if, in response to the "Distance" prompt, you selected points 2,1 and 6,4 for the first and second points, respectively, the row spacing would be 3 (4 − 1) and the column spacing would be 4 (6 − 2).

INSERTING UNIT BLOCKS

Groups of objects often need to be duplicated within a drawing. We showed earlier how the AutoCAD MBLOCK command makes this task easier. The task of transferring blocks or groups of objects to another drawing is demonstrated in the section on the WBLOCK command. This section covers additional aspects of creating blocks in anticipation of inserting them later with a change in scale factors (sometimes with X and Y unequal). This is referred to as a *unit block*.

Doors and windows are a few of the objects that can be stored as blocks in a symbol library. But blocks can be used in different ways to suit differing situations. The following examples are offered as procedures that are used without customizing menus or AutoLISP routines to enhance the process. It should be noted that these procedures can be improved either with customization or possibly with some variations involving standard commands and features. Also, the symbology and names of items are subject to variation.

You can employ a variety of symbols to represent windows in an architectural plan view. Horizontal sliding windows may need to be distinguished from single-hung windows, as shown in Figure 10-10. You may also wish to have more than one option as to how you will insert a window. You may wish to make its insertion point the center of the window sometimes or one of its edges at other times.

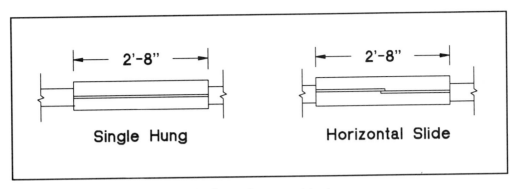

Figure 10–10 Two different windows shown as blocks

Because there are windows of varying widths, you might have to create a separate block for each width. A group of windows might be 1'-0", 1'-6", 2'-0", 2'-8", 3'-0", 3'-4", 4'-0", 5'-4", 6'-0", and 8'-0" and some widths in between. You would have to make a block for each width in addition to the different types. The symbol for the single-hung 2'-8"-wide window could be drawn with the snap set a 0.5 (1/2") to the dimensions shown in Figure 10–11. The objects in Figure 10–11 could be saved as a block named WDW32 (for a 32"-wide window). This window could be inserted from its corner, as shown, if you have established that intersection in the wall in which it is to be drawn.

The preceding method requires a separate block for each window width. Another method is to make a drawing of a window in which the X and/or Y dimension is 1 unit, in anticipation of making the final desired dimension the X and/or Y scale factor during insertion. The following Unit Block symbol for the window can be used for a window of any width, as shown in Figure 10–12. This group of objects might be made into a block named WDW1. Then, to use it for a 2'-8" window, the INSERT command would be:

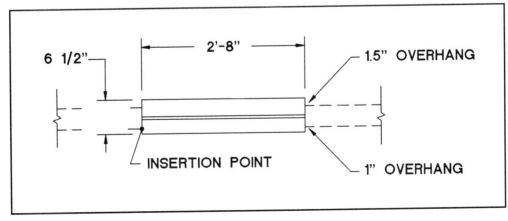

Figure 10–11 Single-hung 2'–8"-wide window

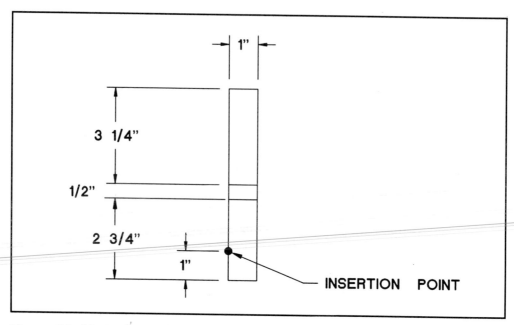

Figure 10–12 Creating a block for a window symbol

```
Command: insert
Block name: wdw1
Insertion point: (select insertion point)
X scale factor <1>: 32
Y scale factor <default=X>: 1
Rotation angle: Enter
```

Note that when you specify a value for the X scale factor, AutoCAD assumes you wish to apply the same value to the Y scale factor, making the resulting shape of the object(s) proportional to the unit block from which it was generated. That is why the Y scale factor defaults to the X scale factor. Therefore, if you wish to insert the block with an X scale factor different from the Y scale factor, you must input a Y scale factor even if it is to be a factor of 1. The block WDW1 can be used for a window of any width by making the desired width (in inches) the X scale factor and then using 1 as the Y scale factor. Figure 10–13 shows the window inserted in its location with the proper X scale factor. Also shown is the cleanup that can be done with the BREAK command.

Another variation on the unit block WDW1 would be to use the same shape for center insertion. It would be drawn the same, but the insertion point would be chosen as shown in Figure 10–14. Figure 10–15 shows the window inserted.

Window symbols in plan lend themselves to application of the one-way scaling unit block. As demonstrated, they vary in only the X scale and not the Y scale

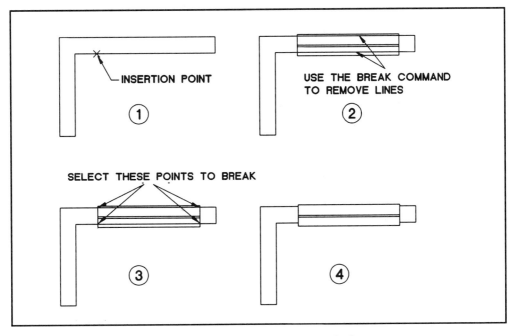

Figure 10–13 Inserting a unit block with a large *X* scale factor

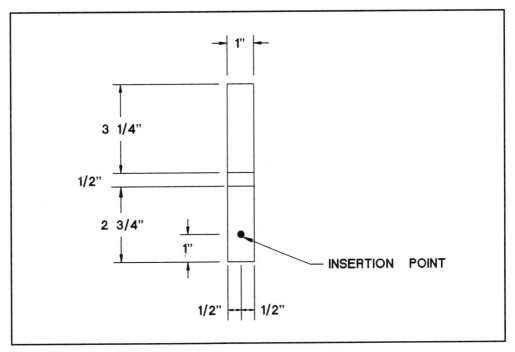

Figure 10–14 Using a unit block with a specified insertion point

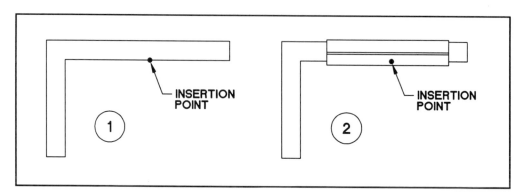

Figure 10–15 The unit block inserted as a window

from one size to another. Doors, however, present a special problem when we try to apply the unit block method. A symbol for a 2'-8"-wide door might look like that in Figure 10–16. The 2'-8"-wide door is drawn half open, that is, swung at 45 degrees to the wall. Therefore, if you used the same approach on the door and on the window unit block, some problems would be encountered.

First, a base block 1-unit-wide simplified door symbol would not be practical. For instance, if the unit block in Figure 10–17 were inserted with an X scale factor of 32 and a Y scale factor of 1, it would appear as in Figure 10–18. Even though the 4" lines that represent the jambs are acceptable, the "door" part of the symbol will not retain its 45-degree swing if not inserted with equal X and Y scale factors. Equal X and Y scale factors present another problem. Using a Y scale factor other than 1 would make the 4"-wide jamb incorrect. Therefore, combining the jambs with the door in the same symbol presents problems that might be impossible to overcome when trying to use a unit block approach to permit one block to serve for all sizes of doors.

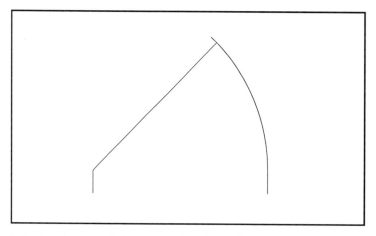

Figure 10–16 Creating a unit block symbol for a door

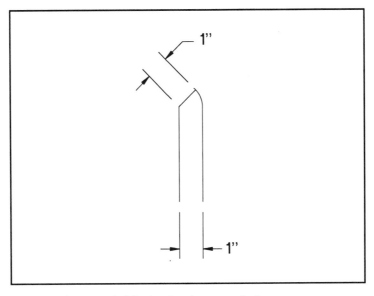

Figure 10–17 Creating a unit block of a door symbol

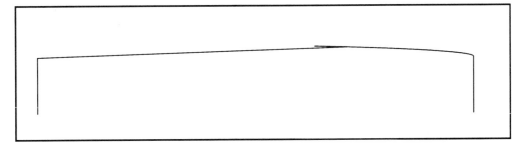

Figure 10–18 A unit block of the door inserted with *X* and *Y* scale factors

Separate Unit Blocks for One Symbol

The solution to the jambs' being adaptable to one-way scaling blocks while the door is not may be to make these two (jambs and door) into two blocks, as shown in Figure 10–19.

Now you can insert the blocks separately, as follows (see Figure 10–20):

```
Command: insert
Block name: jmb
Insertion point: (specify a point)
X scale factor <1>: 32
Y scale factor <default=X>: 1
Rotation angle <default>: Enter
```

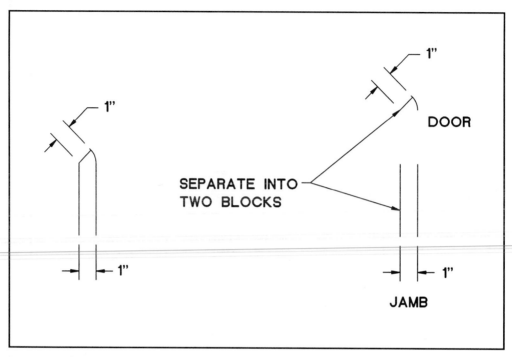

Figure 10–19 Creating one symbol from two unit blocks

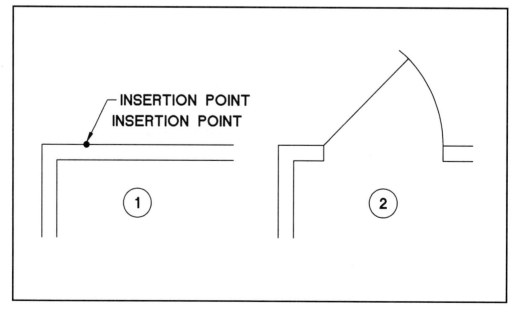

Figure 10–20 Two unit blocks inserted to create one symbol

Command: **insert**
Block name: **dr**
Insertion point: *(specify a point)*
X scale factor <1>: **32**
Y scale factor <default=X>: `Enter`
Rotation angle <default>: `Enter`

> **NOTE:** When you intend to apply the concept of the unit block, whether or not it is to be scaled uniformly (X scale equal to Y scale), be sure that shapes and sizes of all items in the symbol will be correct at their new scale.

Columns as Unit Blocks

Another unit block application is when both X and Y scale factors are changed, but not at the same factor. The column shown in Figure 10–21 is made into a block named COL1 and is inserted for a 10×8-wide flange symbol as follows:

Command:**insert**
Block name:**col1**
Insertion point:*(specify point)*
X scale factor <1>:**8**
Y scale factor (default=X>:**10**
Rotation angle:`Enter`

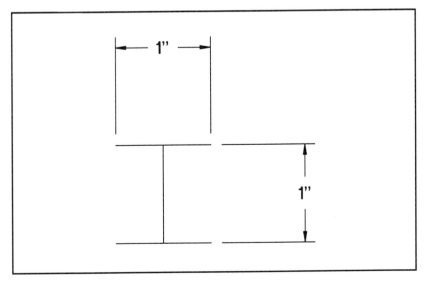

Figure 10–21 Creating a unit block of a column symbol

This can also be done for a 16 x 12 column rotated at 90 degrees, as shown in Figure 10–22.

    Command: **insert**
    Block name: **col1**
    Insertion point: *(specify a point)*
    X scale factor <1>: **12**
    Y scale factor <default=X>: **16**
    Rotation angle: **90**

Note the 90-degree rotation. But don't forget that the X and Y scale factors are applied to the block in the respective X and Y directions that were in effect when it was created, not to the X and Y directions after a rotated insertion.

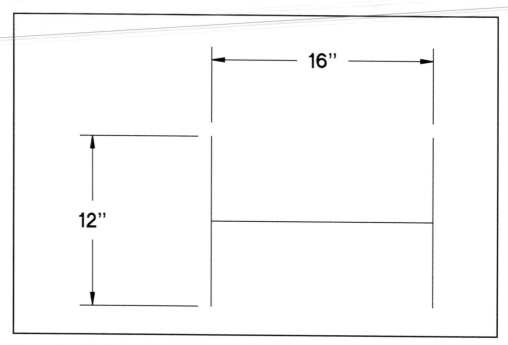

Figure 10–22 The 16 x 12 column symbol inserted and rotated 90 degrees

CREATING ONE DRAWING FROM ANOTHER

The WBLOCK command permits you to group objects in a manner similar to the MBLOCK command. But, in addition, WBLOCK exports the group to a file, which, in fact, becomes a new and separate drawing. The new drawing (created by the WBLOCK command) might consist of a selected block in the current drawing. Or it might be made up of selected objects in the current drawing. You can even export the complete current drawing to the new drawing file. Whichever of these you choose to WBLOCK, the new drawing assumes the layers, linetypes, styles, and other environmental items, such as system variable settings of the current drawing.

Invoke the WBLOCK command from:

Command: prompt	wblock ⏎

AutoCAD displays the Standard File dialog box, where you will provide a drawing name as you do when you begin a new drawing. You should type in only the file name and not the extension. AutoCAD appends the *.DWG* extension automatically. The name should comply with the operating system requirements of valid characters and should be unique for drawings on the specified directory/path. Otherwise you will get the message:

> Warning! Drawing (name) already exists. Do you want to replace it with the new drawing? <N>.

If you wish to use existing objects in the current drawing to create a new foundation drawing named "Slab1," your response would be as follows:

> Command: **wblock**
> Filename: **slab1**

After providing a valid file name (Slab1 in this case), you will be prompted:

> Block name:

Optional replies to the "Block name:" prompt include the following:

1. BLOCK (block name)
2. = (equal sign)
3. * (asterisk)
4. ⏎

Each of the four options are explained next:

> 1. Block name: *(specify the block name)*

If you had created a block from objects in the current drawing and named it Frame1, you could reply to the "Block name:" prompt with the name of the block as follows:

> Command: **wblock**
> Filename: **slab1**
> Block name: **frame1**

This sequence will create a new drawing named Slab1 that includes the objects in the block named Frame1. It should be noted that when the new drawing is called up for editing, the objects will no longer be combined into one block, but will be separate objects, just as they were in the current drawing before being made into the block. In addition, the new drawing, Slab1, will assume the settings of the current drawing in which the block named Frame1 is being created.

2. Block name: =

If you want to name the new drawing Frame1, the same as the block you had just created, you would respond as follows:

    Command: **wblock**
    Filename: **frame1**
    Block name: =

The difference between the = response and the previous Slab1 response is that the resulting name of the new drawing will be Frame1 instead of Slab1.

3. Block name: *

If you wish to have the entire current drawing duplicated into a new one (whether or not any objects have been made into a block), you respond as follows:

    Command: **wblock**
    File name: **slab1**
    Block name: *

If existing objects had been made into a block named Frame1 and it is the only object in the drawing, then responding with the asterisk (*) is similar to the equal sign (=) response. The asterisk response causes all objects to be written, whether visible or not and whether in blocks or not.

One advantage of using the WBLOCK command with the asterisk (*) response is that when the drawing is written to a file, all of the unused blocks, layers, linetypes, and other unused named objects are not written. That is, the drawing is automatically purged. This means that unused items will not be written to the new drawing file. For example, unused items include block definitions that have not been inserted, noncurrent layers that have no objects drawn on them, and styles that are not being used. This can be useful if you just wish to clean up a cluttered drawing, especially one that has had other drawing files inserted into it, each bringing with it various unused named objects.

4. Block name: `Enter`

If you do not wish to make a block in the current drawing, you can still make a separate drawing out of selected objects by pressing `Enter` in response to the "Block name:" prompt. You will then be prompted to select the objects to be written to the drawing file. As with the sequence of prompts in the BLOCK command, you are also be prompted for an insertion point, as shown here:

Command: **wblock**
Filename: **slab1**
Block name: Enter
Insertion point: *(specify a point)*
Select objects: *(select objects to be written to the new drawing)*

XRef and Model/Paper Space Considerations

Xrefs and model/paper space must be considered when using the WBLOCK command. A complete description of model/paper space is found in Chapter 12. A named block (to be written to the new drawing) will be written to model space. An external reference or one of its blocks cannot be blocked to a file via the WBLOCK command. Using the optional equal (=) response or selecting objects after an Enter response to the "Block name:" prompt also writes to model space. When you use the asterisk (*) option, writing the entire drawing to a file, model space objects are written to model space in the new drawing and paper space objects are written to paper space.

BASE COMMAND

The BASE command allows you to establish a base insertion point for the whole drawing in the same manner that you specify a base insertion point when using the MBLOCK command to combine elements into a block. The purpose of establishing this basepoint is primarily so that the drawing can be inserted into another drawing via the INSERT command and having the specified basepoint coincide with the specified insertion point. The default basepoint is the origin (0,0,0). You can specify a 2D point, and AutoCAD will use the current elevation as the base Z coordinate. Or you can specify the full 3D point.

Invoke the BASE command from:

Pull-down menu	Draw > Block > Base
Command: prompt	**base** Enter

AutoCAD prompts:

Command: **base**
Base point <current>: *(specify a point, or press* Enter *to accept the default)*

ATTRIBUTES

Attributes can be used for automatic annotation during insertion of a block. Attributes are special text objects that can be included in a block definition and must be defined beforehand and then selected when you are defining a block.

Attributes have two primary purposes:

The first use of attributes is to permit annotation during insertion of the block to which the attributes are attached. Depending on how you define an attribute, either it appears automatically with a preset (constant) text string or it prompts you (or other users) for a string to be written as the block is inserted. This feature permits you to insert each block with a string of preset text or with its own unique string.

The second (perhaps the more important) purpose of attaching attributes to a block is to have extractable data about each block insertion stored in the drawing database file. Then, when the drawing is complete (or even before), you can invoke the ATTEXT (short for "attribute extract") command to have attribute data extracted from the drawing and written to a file in a form that database-handling programs can use. You can have as many attributes attached to a block as you wish. As just mentioned, the text string that makes up an attribute can be either constant or user specified at the time of insertion.

A Definition Within a Definition

When creating a block, you select objects to be included. Objects such as lines, circles, and arcs are drawn by means of their respective commands. Normal text is drawn with the TEXT, DTEXT, or MTEXT command.

As with drawing objects, attributes must be drawn before they can be included in the block. This is complicated, and it requires additional steps to place them in the drawing; AutoCAD calls this procedure *defining the attribute*. Therefore, an attribute definition is simply the result of defining an attribute by means of the ATTDEF command. The attribute definition is the object that is selected during the BMAKE command. Later, when the block is inserted, the attributes that are attached to it and the manner in which they become a part of the drawing are a result of how you created (defined) the attribute definition.

Visibility and Plotting

If an attribute is to be used only to store information, then you can, as part of the definition of the attribute, specify whether or not it will be visible. If you plan to use an attribute with a block as a note, label, or callout, you should consider the effect of scaling (whether equal or unequal X/Y factors) on the text that will be displayed. The scaling factor(s) on the attribute will be the same as on the block. Therefore, be sure that it will result in the size and proportions desired. You should also be aware of the effect of rotation on visible attribute text. Attribute text that is defined as horizontal in a block will be displayed vertically when that block is inserted with a 90-degree angle of rotation.

Note that, like any other object in the drawing, the attribute must be visible on the screen (or would be if the plotted view were the current display) for that object to be eligible for plotting.

Tag, Value, Prompt, and Default

Four components associated with attributes should be understood before attempting a definition. The purpose of each is described as follows:

Tag An attribute definition has a tag, just as a layer or a linetype has a name. The tag is the identifier of the attribute definition and is displayed where this attribute definition is located, depicting text size, style, and angle of rotation. The tag cannot contain spaces. Two attribute definitions with the same tag should not be included in the same block. Tags appear in the block definition only, not after the block is inserted. However, if you explode a block, the attribute value (described herein) changes back into the tag.

If multiple attributes are used in one block, each must have a unique tag in that block. This restriction is similar to each layer, linetype, block, and other named object having a unique name within one drawing. An attribute's tag is its identifier at the time that attribute is being defined, before it is combined with other objects and attributes by the BMAKE command.

Value The value of an attribute is the actual string of text that appears (if the visibility mode is set to ON) when the block (of which it is a part) is inserted. Whether visible or not, the value is tied directly to the attribute, which, in turn, associates it with the block. It is this value that is written to the database file. It might be a door or window size or, in a piping drawing, the flange rating, weight, or cost of a valve or fitting.

> **NOTE:** When an extraction of attribute data is performed, it is the value of an attribute that is written to a file, but it is the tag that directs the extraction operation to that value. This will be described in detail in the later section on "Extracting Attributes."

Prompt The prompt is what you see when inserting a block with an attribute whose value is not constant or preset. During the definition of an attribute, you can specify a string of characters that will appear in the prompt area during the insertion of the block to prompt you to enter the appropriate value. What the prompt says to you during insertion is what you told it to say when you defined the attribute.

Default You can specify a default value for the attribute during the definition procedure. Then, during insertion of the block, it will appear behind the prompt in brackets, i.e., <default>. It will automatically become the value if Enter is pressed in response to the prompt for a value.

ATTRIBUTE COMMANDS

The four primary commands to manage Attributes are:

ATTDEF — attribute definition

ATTDISP — attribute display

ATTEDIT — attribute edit

ATTEXT — attribute extract

As explained earlier, the ATTDEF command is used to create an attribute definition. The attribute definition is the object that is selected during the BMAKE command.

The ATTDISP command controls the visibility of the attributes.

The ATTEDIT command provides a variety of ways to edit without exploding the block.

The ATTEXT command allows you to extract the data from the drawing and have it written to a file in a form that database-handling programs can use, as shown in the following:

DOORS

SIZE	THKNS	CORE	FINISH	LOCKSET	HINGES	INSET
3070	1.750	SOLID	PAINT	PASSAGE	4 X 4	¾
3070	1.750	SOLID	VARNISH	KEYED	4 X 4	20 X 20
2868	1.375	HOLLOW	PAINT	PRIVACY	3 X 3	¾

ROOM FINISHES

NAME	WALL	CEILING	FLOOR	BASE	REMARKS
LIVING	GYPSUM	GYPSUM	CARPET	NONE	PAINT
FAMILY	PANEL	ACOUSTICAL	TILE	STAIN	STAIN
BATH	PAPER	GYPSUM	TILE	COVE	4'_CERAMIC_TILE
GARAGE	GYPSUM	GYPSUM	CONCRETE	NONE	TAPE_FLOAT_ONLY

You can include an attribute in the WDW block to record the size of the window. A suggested procedure would be to zoom in near the insertion point and create an attribute definition with a tag that reads WDW-SIZE, as shown in Figure 10–23.

If, during the insertion of the WDW Block, you respond to the prompt for the SIZE attribute with 2054 for a 2'-0"-wide × 5'-4"-high window, the resulting block object would be as shown in Figure 10–24, with the normally invisible attribute value shown here for illustration purposes. Figure 10–25 shows the result of the attribute's being inserted with unequal scale factors.

Even though the value displayed is distorted, the string is not affected when extracted to a database file for a bill of materials.

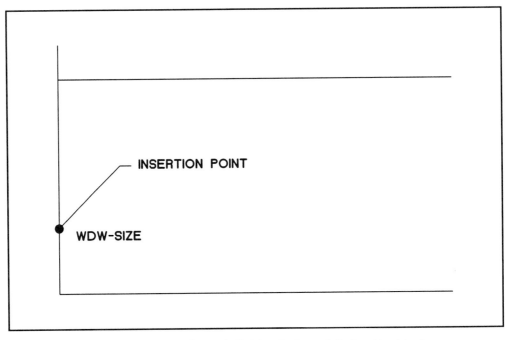

Figure 10–23 Create the attribute definition before defining the block

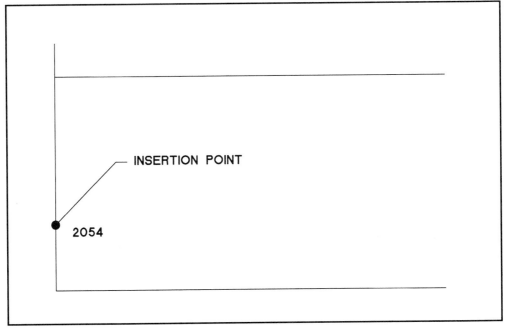

Figure 10–24 The attribute value (2054) visible with the block

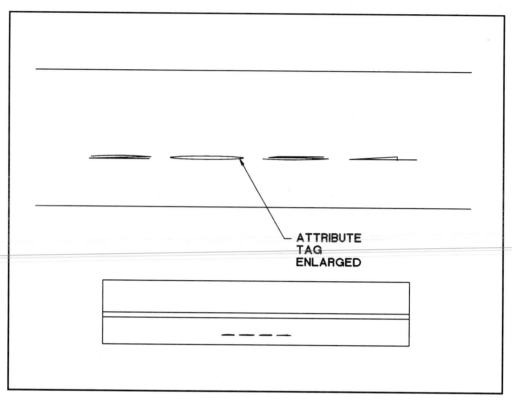

ATTRIBUTE
TAG
ENLARGED

Figure 10–25 The attribute in a block with exaggerated, unequal scale factors

To solve the distortion and rotation problem, if you wish to have an attribute displayed for rotational purposes, you can create a block that contains attributes only or only one attribute. Then it can be inserted at the desired location and rotated for readability to produce the results shown in Figure 10–26.

Attribute definitions would be created as shown in Figure 10–26 and inserted as shown in Figure 10–27.

The insertion points selected would correspond to the midpoint of the outside line that would result from the insertion of the WDW block. The SIZE attributes could be defined into blocks called WDWSIZE and inserted separately with each WDW block, thereby providing both annotation and data extraction.

> **NOTE:** The main caution in having an attribute block separate from the symbol (WDW) block is in editing. Erasing, copying, and moving the symbol block without the attribute block could mean that the data extraction results in the wrong quantity.

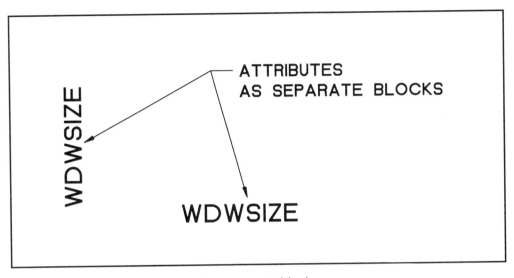

Figure 10–26 Attributes created as separate blocks

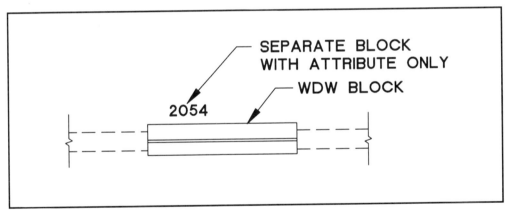

Figure 10–27 Attribute inserted separately for the window

There is another solution to the problem of a visible attribute's not being located or rotated properly in the inserted block. If the attribute is not constant, you can edit it independently after the block has been inserted via the ATTEDIT command. It permits changing an attribute's height, position, angle, value, and other properties. The ATTEDIT command is covered in detail in the later section on "Editing Attributes", but it should be noted here that the height editing option applies to the X and Y scales of the text. Therefore, for text in the definition of a block that was inserted with unequal X and Y scale factors, you will not be able to edit its proportions back to equal X and Y scale factors.

Creating an Attribute Definition

The DDATTDEF and ATTDEF commands allow you to create an attribute definition. The DDATTDEF command allows you to create an attribute definition through a dialog box; the ATTDEF command allows you to create an attribute definition at the Command: prompt.

Invoke the DDATTDEF command from:

Pull-down menu	Draw > Block > Define Attributes...
Command: prompt	**ddattdef** Enter

AutoCAD displays the Attribute Definition dialog box, similar to the Figure 10–28.

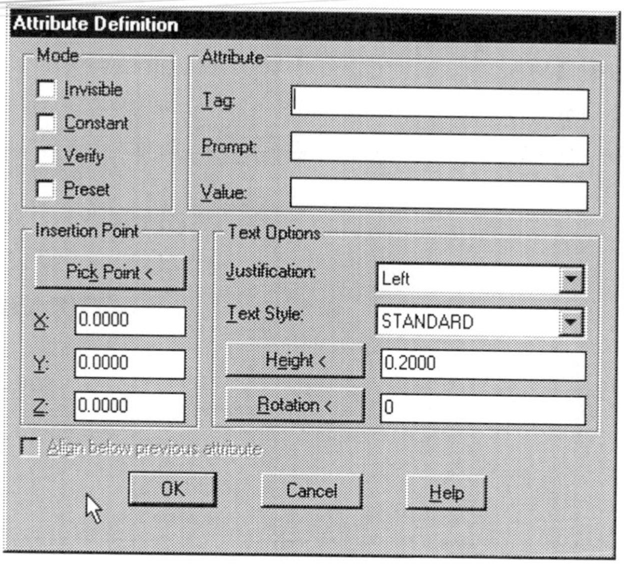

Figure 10–28 Attribute Definition dialog box

Set one or more of the available modes to ON in the MODE section of the Attribute Definition dialog box.

> **Invisible** — Setting the Invisible mode to ON causes the attribute value *not* to be displayed when the block insertion is completed. Even if visible, the value will not appear until the insertion is completed. Attributes needed only for data extraction should be invisible, to quicken regeneration and to avoid cluttering your drawing. You can use the ATTDISP command to override the Invisible mode setting. The Invisible mode's being Y (yes, or ON) does not affect the visibility of the tag in the attribute definition.

Constant — If the Constant mode is set to ON, you must enter the value of the attribute while defining it. That value will be used for that attribute every time the block to which it is attached is inserted. There will be no prompt for the value during insertion, and you cannot change the value.

Verify — If the Verify mode is set to ON, you will be able to verify its value when the block is inserted. For example, if a block with three (nonconstant value) attributes is inserted, once you have completed all prompt/value sequences that have displayed the original defaults, you will be prompted again, with the latest values as new defaults, giving you a second chance to be sure the values are correct before the INSERT command is completed. Even if you press Enter to accept an original default value, it appears as the second-chance default also. If, however, you make a change during the verify sequence, you will *not* get a third chance, that is, a second verify sequence.

Preset — If the Preset mode is set to ON, the attribute automatically takes the value of the default that was specified at the time of defining the attribute. During a normal insertion of the block, you will not be prompted for the value. You must be careful to specify a default during the ATTDEF command or the attribute value will be blank. A block consisting of only attributes whose defaults were blank when Preset modes were set to ON could be inserted, but it would not display anything and cannot be purged from the drawing. The only adverse effect would be that of adding to the space taken in memory. One way to get rid of a nondisplayable block like this is to use a visible entity to create a block with the same name, thereby redefining it to something that can be edited, i.e., erased and subsequently purged.

You can duplicate an attribute definition, with the COPY command, and use it for more than one block. Or you can explode a block and retain one or more of its attribute definitions for use in subsequent blocks.

The **Attribute** section of the Attribute Definition dialog box allows you to set attribute data. Enter the attribute's tag, prompt, and default value in the edit boxes.

The attribute's tag identifies each occurrence of an attribute in the drawing. The tag can contain any characters except spaces. AutoCAD changes lowercase letters to uppercase.

The attribute's prompt appears when you insert a block containing the attribute defintion. If you do not specify the prompt, AutoCAD uses the attribute tag as the prompt. If you turn on the Constant mode, the Prompt field is disabled.

The default Value specifies the default attribute value. This is optional, except if you turn on the Constant mode, for which the default value needs to be specified.

Blocks and Attributes

The **Insertion Point** section of the dialog box allows you to select a coordinate location for the attribute in the drawing, either by choosing the **Pick Point <** button to specify the location on the screen or by entering coordinates in the edit boxes provided.

The **Text Options** section of the dialog box allows you to set the justification, text style, height, and rotation of the attribute text.

The **Align below previous attribute** toggle button allows you to place the attribute tag directly below the previously defined attribute. If you haven't previously defined an attribute definition, this option is unavailable.

Choose the **OK** button to define the attribute definition.

After you close the Attribute Definition dialog box, the attribute tag appears in the drawing. Repeat the procedure to create additional attribute definitions.

Invoke the ATTDEF command from:

Command: prompt	attdef [Enter]

AutoCAD prompts:

Command: **attdef**
Attribute modes — Invisible:N Constant:N Verify:N Preset:N
Enter (ICVP) to change, ENTER when done: *(specify I, c, v, or p to change the current settings for attribute modes)*
Attribute tag: *(specify the attribute tag name, with no spaces or exclamation marks)*
Attribute prompt: *(specify the text for the prompt line, or press* [Enter] *to accept the attribute tag as the attribute prompt)*
Default Attribute value: *(specify a value for the default attribute value, or press* [Enter] *)*

This last prompt appears unless the Constant mode is set to Y (yes, or ON), in which case the prompt will be as follows:

Attribute value: *(specify ta value for the attribute value)*

After the foregoing ATTDEF prompts have been answered, you will be prompted to place the tag, in the same manner as you would for placing text, except AutoCAD will use the tag in place of the text string. Subsequent attributes can be placed in a manner similar to that for placing lines of text, using the insertion point and line spacing as left justified, centered, aligned, or right justified lines of text. Simply press [Enter] to invoke a repeating attribute definition.

Figure 10–29 shows a predrawn 2'-0"-wide door made into a block with attributes.

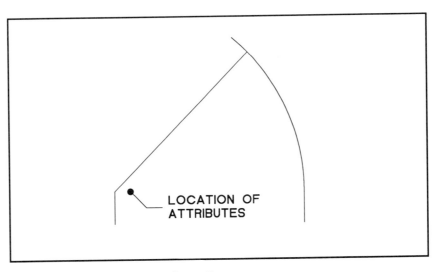

Figure 10–29 Predrawn door with attributes

NOTE: In this example the block is drawn to true size with jambs so it can be inserted with X and Y scale factors equal to 1 (one). But, the attributes will all be invisible, because the door might be inserted at a rotation incompatible with acceptable text orientations. The attributes can also be very small, located at a point that will be easy to find if they must be made visible in order to read (Figure 10–30).

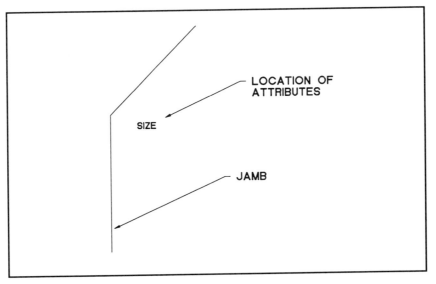

Figure 10–30 Predrawn jamb block with attributes

The Attributes are entered as follows (Figures 10–31 and 10–32):

Command: **attdef**
Attribute modes — Invisible:N Constant:N Verify:N Preset:N
Enter (ICVP) to change, RETURN when done: **i**
Attribute modes — Invisible:Y Constant:N Verify:N Preset:N
Enter (ICVP) to change, RETURN when done: **c**
Attribute modes — Invisible:Y Constant:Y Verify:N Preset:N
Enter (ICVP) to change, RETURN when done: Enter
Attribute tag: **size**
Attribute value: **26681.375** *(for 2'-6" × 6'-8" × 1-3/8")*
Justify/Style/<start point>: *(select point)*
Height <default>: **1/16**
Rotation angle <default>: Enter

Command: Enter
Attribute modes — Invisible:Y Constant:Y Verify:N Preset:N
Enter (ICVP) to change, RETURN when done: **c**
Attribute modes — Invisible:Y Constant:N Verify:N Preset:N
Enter (ICVP) to change, RETURN when done: Enter
Attribute tag: **matl**
Attribute prompt: **material**
Attribute default value: **mahogany**
Justify/Style/<start point>: *(select point)*
Command: Enter

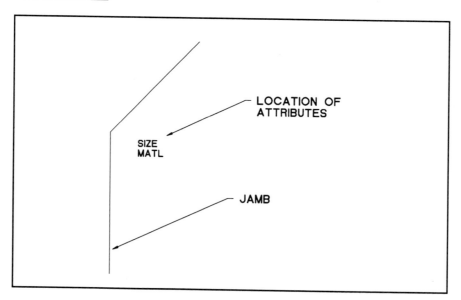

Figure 10–31 Predrawn jamb block with character attributes

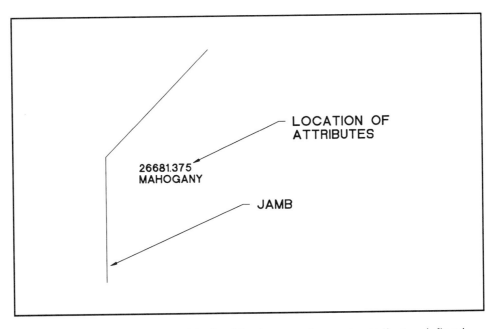

Figure 10–32 Predrawn jamb block with character/numeric attributes defined

NOTE: The values given for the various attributes can be written just as any string of text is written. You should note that these strings, when written to a database-handling file, might eventually need to be interpreted as numbers rather than characters. The difference is primarily of concern to the person who will use the data in a database-handling program. So, if you are not familiar with data types, such as numeric, character, and date, you might wish to consult with someone (or study a book on databases) if you are entering the values. For example, an architectural distance such as 12'-6 1/2" may need to be written in decimal feet (12.54) without the apostrophe or in decimal inches (150.5) without the inch mark if it is going to be used mathematically once extracted.

You can continue to define additional attributes in the same manner for the L.H./ R.H. SWING, PAINT/VARNISH FINISH, Type of HINGE, Type of LOCKSET, etc. (see Figure 10–33).

Inserting a Block with Attributes

Blocks with attributes may be inserted in a manner similiar to that for inserting reguar blocks. If there are any nonconstant attributes, you will be prompted to enter

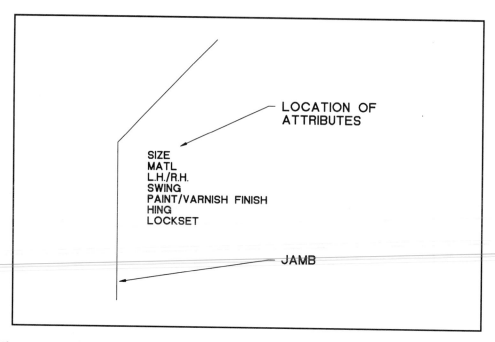

Figure 10–33 Predrawn jamb with additional attributes defined

the value for each. You may set the system variable called ATTREQ to 0 (zero), thereby suppressing the prompts for attribute values. In this case the values will either be blank or be set to the default values if they exist. You can later use either the DDATTE or ATTEDIT command to establish or change values.

You can set the ATTDIA system variable to a nonzero value, which will display a dialog box for attribute value input.

Controlling the Display of Attributes

The ATTDISP command controls the visibility of attributes. Attributes will normally be visible if the Invisible mode is set to N (normal) when they are defined.

Invoke the ATTDISP command from:

Pull-down menu	View > Display > Attribute Display
Command: prompt	attdisp Enter

AutoCAD prompts:

Command: **attdisp**
Normal / ON / OFF <current>: *(select one of the available options, or* Enter *to accept the default option)*

Responding ON makes all attributes visible; OFF makes all attributes invisible. The Normal option displays the attributes as you created them. The ATTMODE system variable is affected by the ATTDISP setting. If REGENAUTO is set to ON, changing the ATTDISP setting causes drawing regeneration.

Editing Attributes

Unlike other objects in an inserted block, attributes can be edited independent of the block. You can, however, edit groups of attributes collectively. This permits you to insert a block with generic attributes; that is, the default values can be used in anticipation of changing them to the desired values later. Or you can copy an existing block that may need only one or two attribute changes to make it correct for its new location. And, of course, there is always the chance that either an error was made in entering the value or design changes necessitate subsequent changes.

Editing an attribute is accomplished by invoking the DDATTE or ATTEDIT command. The DDATTE command edits individual, nonconstant attribute values associated with a specific block, whereas the ATTEDIT command edits both attribute values and attribute properties individually or globally, independent of the block.

Invoke the DDATTE command from:

Modify II toolbar	Select the Edit Attribute command (see Figure 10–34)
Pull-down menu	Modify > Object > Attribute > Single...
Command: prompt	**ddatte** Enter

Figure 10–34 Invoking the Edit Attribute command from the Modify II toolbar

AutoCAD prompts:

Command: **ddatte**
Select block: *(select the block)*

AutoCAD displays the Edit Attribute dialog box, similar to the one shown in Figure 10–35. Selecting objects that are not blocks or blocks that contain no attributes will cause an error message to appear.

The dialog box lists all the attributes defined with values for the selected block. Using the pointing device, you can select values to be changed in the dialog box.

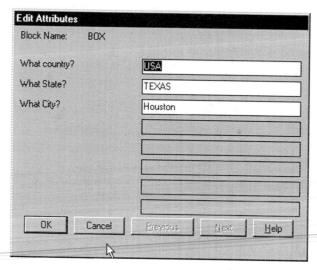

Figure 10–35 Edit Attributes dialog box

Type in the new values and accept the changes by clicking the OK button or pressing ⏎Enter. Selecting the CANCEL button terminates the command, returning all values to their original state.

You can use the DDATTE command to look at the values of a selected attribute without making changes. Or you can employ repeated editing or repeated inquiry looks at attribute values by modifying the DDATTE command with the MULTIPLE command, as follows:

Command: **multiple ddatte**

To change attribute properties such as position, height, and style, invoke the ATTEDIT command. The ATTEDIT command provides a variety of ways to specify attributes to be edited. It also allows various properties of the selected attributes to be edited. It should be noted that attributes with constant values cannot be edited in this manner.

Invoke the ATTEDIT command from:

Pull-down menu	Modify > Object > Attribute > Global
Command: prompt	attedit ⏎Enter

AutoCAD prompts:

Command: **attedit**
Edit attributes one at a time? <Y>:

Responding **Y** permits you to edit visible attributes individually. You can limit those attributes eligible for selection by specifying the block name, tag, or value. In addition to an attribute's value, other properties that can be changed during this one-at-a-time mode include its position, height, and angle of rotation.

Responding **N** permits global (or mass) editing of attributes. Again, you can limit those eligible for editing to a specified block name, tag, or value. However, this mode permits editing of attribute values only and no other properties.

After responding **Y** or **N**, you will be prompted to specify eligible attributes as follows:

> Block name specification <*>:
> Attribute tag specification <*>:
> Attribute value specification <*>:

For any attribute to be eligible for editing, the block name, attribute tag, and attribute value must all match the name, tag, and value specified. Use of "*" or "?" wild-card characters allows more than one string to match. Pressing Enter in response to the "Block name specification:" prompt defaults to the asterisk, which makes all attributes eligible with regard to the block name restriction. Attributes still have to match tag and value responses in order to be eligible for editing.

Global Editing If you responded to the "Edit attributes one at a time? <Y>:" prompt with **N** (no), thereby choosing global editing, and set the block name, tag, and value limitations, the following prompts appear:

> Global edit of Attribute values.
> Edit only Attributes visible on screen? <Y>

An **N** reply switches AutoCAD to the text window with the following message:

> Drawing must be regenerated afterwards.

When the editing for this command is completed (and if AUTOREGEN is set to ON) a drawing regeneration occurs.

If at the "Edit only Attributes visible on screen? <Y>:" prompt you respond **Y** (or default to **Y** by pressing Enter), you will be prompted as follows:

> Select Attributes:

Attributes may now be selected either by specifying them on the screen, or by the window, crossing, or last method. Eligible attributes are then highlighted and the following prompts appear:

> String to change: *(select a string to change)*
> New string: *(type a new text string)*

> **NOTE:** The changes you specify will affect a group of attributes all at one time. Take care that unintended changes do not occur.

The responses to the "String to change:" prompt cause AutoCAD to search eligible selected attribute strings for matching strings. Each matching string will be changed to your response to the "New string:" prompt. For example, blocks named WDW20, having tags named SIZE, and values of 2054 (for 2'-0" × 5'-4") can be changed to 2060 by the following sequence:

    String to change: **54**
    New string: **60**

If you did not limit the attributes by block name, tag, or value you might unintentionally change a window whose SIZE is 5440 (for 5'-4" × 4'-0") to 6040.

If you respond to "String to change:" by pressing `Enter`, it will cause any response to "New string:" to be placed ahead of all eligible attribute value strings. For example, if you specified only the block name WDW20 with an attribute value of 2054 to be eligible for editing, you can make an addition to the value by the following sequence:

    String to change: `Enter`
    New string: **dbl hung**

The value 2054 will be changed to read DBL HUNG 2054. Be sure to add a space behind the G if you do not want the result to be DBL HUNG2054.

Editing Attributes One at a Time If you responded to the "Edit attributes one at a time? <Y>:" prompt by pressing `Enter` (defaulting to **Y**), and have specified the eligible attributes through the block name, tag, and value sequences, you will be prompted:

    Select Attributes:

You may select attributes by specifying them on the screen or by the window, crossing, or last method. The eligible selected attributes with nonconstant values will be marked sequentially with an X. The next prompt is as follows:

    Value/Position/Height/Angle/Style/Layer/Color/Next <N>: (select one of the
        available options)

Angle is not an option for an attribute defined as fitted text, nor are the angle and height options for aligned attributes. Entering any option's initial letter permits a change relative to that option, followed by the repeated prompt for the list of options until you default to **N** for the next attribute.

The Value option, if chosen, will prompt you as follows:

    Change or Replace? <R>

Defaulting to **R** causes the following prompt:

New Attribute value:

Any string entered will become the new value. Even a null response will become a null (blank) value. Entering **C** at the "Change or Replace? <R>:" prompt will cause the following prompts to appear:

String to change:
New string:

Responses to these prompts follow the same rules described in the previous section on global editing. In addition to the Position/Height/Angle options normally established during attribute definition, you can change those preset properties such as Style/Layer/Color with the ATTEDIT command.

Extracting Attributes

Extracting data from a drawing is one of the foremost innovations in CAD. Paper copies of drawings have long been used to communicate more than just how objects look. In addition to dimensions, drawings tell builders or fabricators what materials to use, quantities of objects to make, manufacturers' names and models of parts in an assembly, coordinate locations of objects in a general area, and what types of finishes to apply to surfaces. But, until computers came into the picture (or pictures came into the computer), extracting data from manual drawings involved making lists (usually by hand) while studying the drawing, often checking off the data with a marker. The AutoCAD attribute feature and the ATTEXT command combine to allow complete, fast, and accurate extraction of (1) data consciously put in for the purpose of extraction, (2) data used during the drawing process, and (3) data that AutoCAD maintains about all objects (blocks in this case).

The CAD drawing in Figure 10–36 shows a piping control set. The 17 valves and fittings are a fraction of those that might be on a large drawing. Each symbol is a block with attributes attached to it. Values that have been assigned to each attribute tag record the type (TEE, ELL, REDUCER, FLANGE, GATE VALVE, or CONTROL VALVE), size (3", 4", or 6"), rating (STD or 150#), weld (length of weld), and many other vital bits of specific data. Keeping track of hundreds of valves, fittings, and even cut lengths of pipe is a time-consuming task subject to omissions and errors if done manually, even if the drawing is plotted from CAD. Just as important as extracting data from the original drawing is the need to update a list of data when the drawing is changed. Few drawings, if any, remain unchanged. The AutoCAD attribute feature makes the job fast, thorough, and accurate. Examples of some of the blocks with attribute definition are shown in Figures 10–37 to 10–39.

These are three examples of blocks as defined and inserted, each attribute having been given a value during the INSERT command. Remember, the value that will be extracted is in accordance with how the template specifies the tags. Figure 10–40

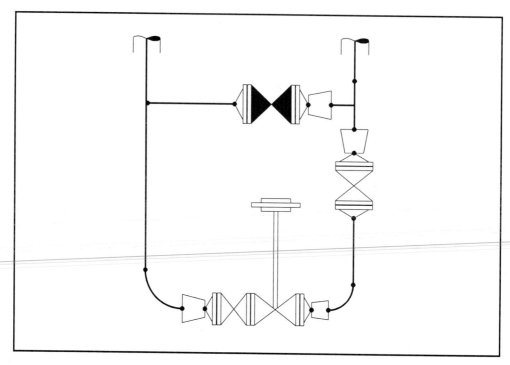

Figure 10–36 Piping control set

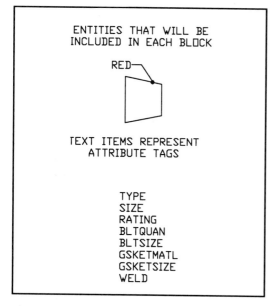

Figure 10–37 Reducer with attribute definition

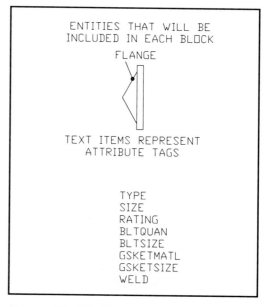

Figure 10–38 Flange with attribute definition

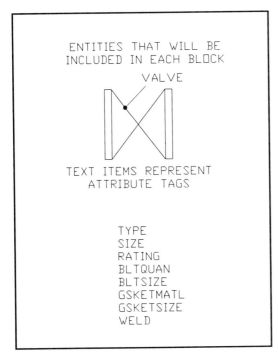

Figure 10–39 Valve with attribute definition

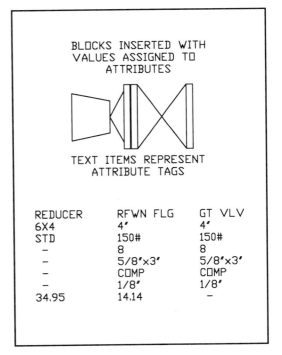

Figure 10–40 Inserted blocks with corresponding attribute values

shows the three blocks inserted, with corresponding attribute values in tabular form. By using the ATTEXT command, a complete listing of all valves and fittings in the drawing can be written to a file, as shown in Table 10–1.

The headings above each column in Table 10–1 are for your information only. These will not be written to the extract file by the ATTEXT command. They signify the tags whose corresponding values will be extracted.

When operated on by a database program, this file can be used to sort valves and fittings by type, size, or other value. The scope of this book is too limited to cover database applications. But generating a file like Table 10–1 that a database program can use is the important linkage between computer drafting and computer management of data for inventory control, material takeoff, flow analysis, cost, maintenance, and many other applications. The CAD drafter can apply the ATTEXT feature to perform this task.

Files Using the ATTEXT command involves concepts of computer applications other than CAD (although not necessarily more advanced). Some fundamental understanding of the computer's operating system is needed. The operating system is used to manipulate and store files.

Blocks and Attributes

Table 10-1 A List of Inventory as Specified by the ATTEXT Command and Tags

TYPE	SIZE	RATING	BLTQUAN	BLTSIZE	GSKETMATL	GSKETSIZE	WELD
TEE	6"	STD	4	5/8"X3"	COMP	1/8"	62.44
ELL	6"	STD	4	5/8"X3"	COMP	1/8"	41.63
ELL	4"	STD	4	5/8"X3"	COMP	1/8"	14.14
RED	6X4	STD	8	5/8"X3"	COMP	1/8"	34.95
RED	6X4	STD	8	5/8"X3"	COMP	1/8"	34.95
RED	6X3	STD	4	5/8"X3"	COMP	1/8"	31.81
RED	4X3	STD	8	5/8"X3"	COMP	1/8"	25.13
FLG	4"	150#	8	5/8"X3"	COMP	1/8"	14.14
FLG	4"	150#	8	5/8"X3"	COMP	1/8"	14.14
FLG	4"	150#	8	5/8"X3"	COMP	1/8"	14.14
FLG	4"	150#	8	5/8"X3"	COMP	1/8"	14.14
FLG	3"	150#	4	5/8"X3"	COMP	1/8"	11.00
FLG	3"	150#	4	5/8"X3"	COMP	1/8"	11.00
GVL	4"	150#	16	5/8"X3"	COMP	1/8"	11.00
GVL	4"	150#	16	5/8"X3"	COMP	1/8"	11.00
GVL	3"	150#	8	5/8"X3"	COMP	1/8"	11.00
CVL	3"	150#	8	5/8"X3"	COMP	1/8"	11.00

Many different types of files or groups of files are involved in using the ATTEXT command.

EXE and *DLL:* AutoCAD program files are being used to perform the attribute extraction.

DWG: The drawing file is a data file that contains the blocks and their associated attributes whose values are eligible for extraction.

TXT: A template file must be created to tell AutoCAD what type of data to extract.

A line editor or word processor is used to create the template file.

TXT or *DXF:* The extraction process creates a *FILENAME.TXT* file containing the data in accordance with the instructions received from the template file.

A set of database program files usually can operate on the extracted file.

Database Extracted data can be manipulated by a database application program. The telephone directory, a database, is an alphabetical listing of names, each followed by a first name (or initial), an address, and a phone number. A listing of pipe, valves, and fittings in a piping system can be a database if each item has essential data associated with it, such as its size, flange rating, weight, material of manufacture, product that it handles, cost, and location within the system, among many others.

The two elementary terms used in a database are the *record* and the *field*. A *record* is like a single listing in the phone book, made up of a name and its associated first name, address, and phone number. The name Jones with its data is one record. Another Jones with a different first name (or initials) is another record. Another Jones with the same first name or initials at a different address is still another record. Each listing is a record. The types of data that may be in a record come under the heading of a *field*. Name is a field. All the names in the list come under the name field. Address is a field. Phone number is a field. And even though some names may have first names and some may not, first name is a field. It is possible to take the telephone directory that is listed alphabetically by name, feed it into a computer database program, and generate the same list in numerical order by phone number. You can generate a partial list of all the Joneses sorted alphabetically by the first name. Or you can generate a list of everyone who lives on Elm Street. The primary purpose of the ATTEXT command is to generate the main list that includes all of the desired objects to which the database program manipulations can be applied.

Creating a Template

The template is a file saved in ASCII format; it lists the fields that specify the tags and determine which blocks will have their attribute data extracted. The template must be a file on an accessible path with the extension of *.TXT*. When you use a text editor or word processor in the ASCII mode, you must add this extension when you name the file.

Field Name The field name must correspond exactly to the attribute tag if you wish for that attribute's value to be extracted. If the attribute tag is called **type**, then there must be a field name in the template called **type**. A field name in the template called **ratings** will not cause a tag name called **rating** to have its values written to the extract file.

Character-Numeric The template tells the ATTEXT command to classify the data written to a particular field either as numeric or as character type. Characters (a, b, c, A, #, ", etc.) are always character type, but numbers do not always have to be numeric type. Characters occupy less memory space in the computer. Sometimes numbers, like an address and phone number, are better stored as characters unless they are to be operated on by mathematical functions (addition, subtraction, etc.). The only relative significance of numbers as characters is their order (1 2 3...) for sorting purposes by the database program. Characters (a b c...) have that same significance. The template contains two elements for each field. The first is the field name; the second is the character-numeric element.

Numbers in strategic spaces in the character-numeric element of the template file specify the number of spaces to allow for the values to be written in the extract file. Others also specify how many decimal places to carry numeric values.

The format is as follows:

fieldname	Nwwwddd	for numeric values with decimal allowance
fieldname	Nwww000	for numeric values without decimal allowance
fieldname	Cwww000	for character values

Each line in the template is one field. The w's and d's are to be filled in with the necessary digits when the template file is created. The order of fields listed in the template does not have to coincide with the order that attribute tags appear in a block. Any group of fields, in any order is acceptable. The only requirement for a block to be eligible for extraction by the ATTEXT command is that there be at least one tag–field match.

A template for the example in Figure 10–39 would be written as follows:

TYPE	C008000
SIZE	C008000
RATING	C006000
BLTQUAN	N004000
BLTSIZE	C010000
GSKETMATL	C006000
GSKETSIZE	C006000
WELD	N006002

NOTE: Word processors add coded characters (often hidden) to files unless specifically set up to write in the ASCII format. These coded characters are not acceptable in the template. Be sure that the text editor or word processor being used is in the proper mode. Also, do not use the [Tab] to line up the second column elements, but key in the necessary spaces, because the [Tab] involves coded characters.

From the extracted file in Table 10–1, a database program can generate a sorted list whose items correspond to selected values. The procedure (again, to explain would take another book entirely) might list only 3" flanges, or all 3" fittings, or all reducers, or any combination of available records required corresponding to tag–field association.

BL:xxxxxx Nonattribute Fields Available If necessary, additional data is also automatically stored with each inserted block. The suggested format in a template file and a description of each (in parentheses) follows:

Field Name	Field Format	Description
BL:LEVEL	Nwww000	(block nesting level)
BL:NAME	Cwww000	(block name)
BL:X	Nwwwddd	(X coordinate of block insertion point)
BL:Y	Nwwwddd	(Y coordinate)
BL:Z	Nwwwddd	(Z coordinate)
BL:NUMBER	Nwww000	(block counter; same for all members of a MINSERT)
BL:HANDLE	Cwww000	(block's handle; same for all members of a MINSERT)
BL:LAYER	Cwww000	(block insertion layer name)
BL:ORIENT	Nwwwddd	(block rotation angle)
BL:XSCALE	Nwwwddd	(X scale factor of block)
BL:YSCALE	Nwwwddd	(Y scale factor)
BL:ZSCALE	Nwwwddd	(Z scale factor)
BL:XEXTRUDE	Nwwwddd	(X component of block's extrusion direction)
BL:YEXTRUDE	Nwwwddd	(Y component)
BL:ZEXTRUDE	Nwwwddd	(*Z component*)

Note: The comments in parentheses are for your information and must not be included in the template file.

The first column lists the name of each field, for example. BL:ORIENT. The field format begins with a C or an N, denoting character or numeric data, respectively. The next three digits denote the width of the field, that is, how many spaces are to be allowed in the extract file for values to be written under this particular field. If the value to be written under this field for any record is too long for the width allowed, AutoCAD truncates the data written, proceeds with the extraction, and displays the following error message:

**Field overflow in record <record number>

The last three digits in the field format denote the number of decimal places to which numeric values will be written. Character fields should have zeros in these three places. When fields are specified as numeric, the attribute values must be numbers, or AutoCAD will display an error message.

You can use one of the two commands available to extract attributes. To extract attribute objects through the attributes extraction dialog box, use the DDATTEXT command. To extract objects at the "Command:" line, use the ATTEXT command.

Invoke the DDATTEXT command from:

Command: prompt	**ddattext** Enter

AutoCAD displays the Attribute Extraction dialog box, similar to Figure 10–41.

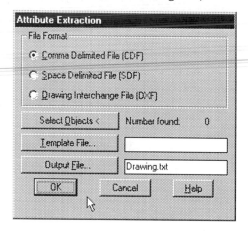

Figure 10–41 Attribute Extraction dialog box

Select one of the three radio buttons available in the **File Format** section of the Attribute Extraction dialog box.

The **Comma Delimited Format (CDF)** format generates a file containing no more than one record for each block reference in the drawing. The values written under the fields in the extract files are separated by commas, with the character fields enclosed in single quotes.

The **Space Delimited Format (SDF)** format writes the values lined up in the widths allowed. It is possible for adjacent mixed fields (characters and numeric) not to have spaces between them. It may be necessary to add dummy fields to provide spaces in these cases.

The AutoCAD **Drawing Interchange File** format is called DXF. Unlike the DXFOUT command, extraction files generated by the ATTEXT command contain only block reference, attribute, and end-of-sequence objects.

Specify the Template Filename in the **Template File...** edit box if you have selected either CDF or SDF file formats. AutoCAD appends the *.TXT* file type. If you select the DXF file format, the **Template File...** button and edit box are disabled.

Specify the output extract file name in the **Output File...** edit box. AutoCAD appends the *.TXT* file type for CDF and SDF file formats and DXX for DXF files. DOS permits a file name of *con,* for writing to the screen, or a file name of *prn,* for writing to a printer. In this case, a printer must be connected and ready to print.

Choose the **Select Objects <** button to select the objects to be included in the extraction of attributes. The dialog box will disappear, and AutoCAD allows you to select the attribute entities. After you have done so, the dialog box reappears, and the number of objects you selected is displayed after the **Number found:** *label.*

Choose the OK button to close the dialog box and extract the attributes from the selected blocks. The extracted information is stored in the output file specified in the Attribute Extraction dialog box. You can import the output file into a database program or open the output file with the help of a text editor and analyze the extracted information.

Invoke the ATTEXT command from:

Command: prompt	**attext** [Enter]

AutoCAD prompts:

> Command: **attext**
> CDF, SDF or DXF Attribute extract (or Entities)?<C>:

Select one of the three options: CDF, SDF, or DXF. You can also select the Entities option, which allows you to select the objects for extraction of their attributes. Once selection is complete, the prompt reverts to the CDF, SDF, or DXF prompt without the entities option. Then AutoCAD prompts for the template file name and extract file name, respectively.

Duplications The example extract file listed some records whose values in every field were the same. This would serve no purpose in a telephone directory but in a list of objects in a drawing it is possible that the only difference between two objects is their location in the drawing. In a bill of materials, the purchasing agent is not concerned with where, but how many duplicate objects there are. If it were essential to distinguish every object, the BL:X, BL:Y, and BL:Z fields could be included in the template to identify each object. Multiple insertions of the same block in the same location could still be distinguished by their BL:HANDLE field if the HANDLES system variable were set to ON, or by their BL:NUMBER if they were inserted with the MINSERT command.

Also, to the experienced pipe estimator (or astute novice) there are other duplications that are possible if not taken into account. Counting bolts and weld lengths for every fitting and valve could result in twice the quantities required. Mating flanges, each having 4 bolt holes, only require 4 bolts to assemble. An ell welded to a tee likewise requires the specified weld length only once. Therefore, Attribute value quantities associated with corresponding tags should take into account this and similar problems in mating assemblies.

Blocks and Attributes

Also, if the same fittings (in the form of blocks with attributes) are shown in more than one view in a drawing, some mechanism should be provided to prevent duplication of quantities. As you can see, advanced features (attributes) that provide solutions to complex problems (data extraction) often require carefully planned implementation.

Changing Objects in a Block Without Losing Attribute Values Sometimes it might be desirable to make changes to the objects within blocks that have been inserted with attributes and have had values assigned to the attributes. Remember that the values of the attributes can be edited with the DDATTE command. But, in order to change the geometry of a block, it is normally required that you explode the block, make the necessary changes, and then redefine the block. As long as the attribute definitions keep the same tags in the new definition, the redefined blocks that have already been inserted in the drawing will retain those attributes with the original definitions.

Another method of having a new block definition applied to existing blocks is to create a new drawing with the new block definition. This can be done by using the WBLOCK command to create a drawing that conforms to the old definition and then to edit that drawing. Or you can start a new drawing with the name of the block that you wish to change.

In order to apply the new definition to the existing block, you can call up the drawing from the OPEN command, and then use the INSERT command with the Block Name: option. For example, if you wish to change the geometry of a block named Part_1, and the changes have been made and stored in a separate drawing with the same name (Part_1), the sequence of prompts is as follows:

```
Command: insert
Block name <default>: part_1=
Block "Part_1" redefined
Regenerating drawing.
Insertion point: Esc
Command:
```

It is not necessary to specify an insertion point or to respond to scale factor and rotation angles. Simply inserting the block with the = (equals) behind the name will cause the definition of the drawing to become the new definition of the block with the same name residing in the current drawing.

Redefining a Block and Attributes The ATTREDEF command allows you to redefine a block and updates associated attributes. Invoke the ATTREDEF command from:

Command: prompt	**attredef** Enter

AutoCAD prompts:

> Command: **attredef**
> Name of block you wish to redefine: *(specify the block name to redefine)*
> Select objects: *(select objects for the block to redefine and press* Enter *)*
> Insertion base point of new block: *(specify the insertion basepoint of the new block)*

New attributes assigned to existing block references are given their default values. Old attributes in the new block definition retain their old values. Old attributes not included in the new block definition are deleted from the old block references.

DIVIDING OBJECTS

The DIVIDE command causes AutoCAD to divide an object into equal-length segments, placing markers at the dividing points. Objects eligible for application of the DIVIDE command are the line, arc, circle, ellipse, spline, and polyline. Selecting an object other than one of these will cause an error message to appear, and you will be returned to the "Command:" prompt.

Invoke the DIVIDE command from:

Pull-down menu	Draw > Point > Divide
Command: prompt	**divide** Enter

AutoCAD prompts:

> Command: **divide**
> Select object to divide: *(select a line, arc, circle, ellipse, spline, or polyline)*
> <Numer of segments>/Block: *(specify the number of segments, or type **b** for the Block option)*

You may respond with an integer from 2 to 32767, causing points to be placed along the selected object at equal distances but not actually separating the object. The Object Snap NODe can snap at the divided points. Logically, there will be one less point placed than the number entered, except in the case of a circle. The circle will have the first point placed at the angle from the center of the current snap rotation angle. A closed polyline will have the first point placed at the first point drawn in the polyline. The total length of the polyline will be divided into the number of segments entered without regard to the length of the individual segments that make up the polyline. An example of a closed polyline is shown in Figure 10–42.

> **NOTE:** It is advisable to set the PDSIZE and PDMODE system variables to values that will cause the points to be visible.

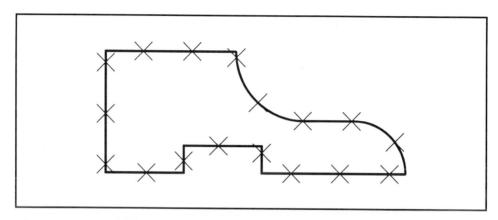

Figure 10–42 The DIVIDE command as used with a closed polyline

The Block option allows a named block to be placed at the dividing points instead of a point. The sequence of prompts is as follows:

Command: **divide**
Select object to divide: *(select a line, arc, circle, ellipse, spline, or polyline)*
<Number of segments>/Block: **block** *(or just b)*
Block name to insert: *(enter the name of the block)*
Align block with object? <Y>: *(press* Enter *to align the block with the object, or enter n, for not to align with the block)*
Number of segments: *(specify the number of segments)*

If you respond with **No** or **N** to the "Align block with object?" prompt, all of the blocks inserted will have a zero angle of rotation. If you default to **Yes**, the angle of rotation of each inserted block will correspond to the direction of the linear part of the object at its point of insertion or to the direction of a line tangent to a circular part of an object at the point of insertion.

MEASURING OBJECTS

The MEASURE command causes AutoCAD to divide an object into specified-length segments, placing markers at the measured points. Objects eligible for application of the MEASURE command are the line, arc, circle, ellipse, spline, and polyline. Selecting an object other than one of these will cause an error message to appear and you will be returned to the "Command:" prompt.

Invoke the MEASURE command from:

Pull-down menu	Draw > Point > Measure
Command: prompt	**measure** Enter

AutoCAD prompts:

Command: **divide**
Select object to divide: *(select a line, arc, circle, ellipse, spline, or polyline)*
<Segment length>/Block: *(specify the length of the segment, or type **b** for the Block option)*

If you reply with a distance, or show AutoCAD a distance by specifying two points, the object is measured into segments of the specified length, beginning with the closest endpoint from the selected point on the object. The Block option allows a named block to be placed at the measured point instead of a point.

PROJECT EXERCISE

This project exercise provides point-by-point instructions for creating the objects shown in Figure P10–1. In this exercise you will apply the skills acquired in Chapters 1 through 10.

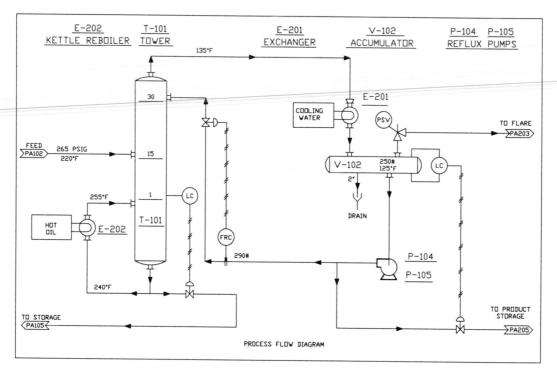

Figure P10–1 Completed project drawing

In this project you will:

■ Set up the drawing, including Limits, and Layers.
■ Use the LINE, PLINE, CIRCLE, ARC, and SOLID commands to create objects.
■ Use the BLOCK command to save objects for later insertion.
■ Use the ATTDEF command to create an attribute and include it in the block definition. This enables you to attach a text string to the block when it is inserted.
■ Use the INSERT command to insert the blocks created earlier.

Set Up the Drawing and Draw a Border

Step 1   Start the AutoCAD program.

Step 2   To create a new drawing, invoke the NEW command from the Standard toolbar or select New from the pull-down menu File. AutoCAD displays the **Create New Drawing** dialog box. Select the **Start From Scratch** option, and choose **OK** to create a new drawing.

Step 3   Invoke the LIMITS command, and set the limits to the lower left and upper right coordinates as shown in the SETTINGS/VALUES table. Set the grid and snap values as shown also.

SETTINGS	VALUE		
UNITS	Decimal		
LIMITS	Lower left corner: 0,0 Upper right corner: 18,12		
GRID	.5		
SNAP	.25		
LAYERS	*NAME*	*COLOR*	*LINETYPE*
	Blocks	Red	Continuous
	Border	Cyan	Continuous
	Equipment	Green	Continuous
	Instrument	Magenta	Continuous
	Pipeline	Blue	Continuous
	Text	White	Continuous

Step 4   Invoke the LAYER command from the Object Properties toolbar, or select Layer... from the pull-down menu Format. AutoCAD displays the Layer & Linetype Properties dialog box. Create five layers, rename them as shown in the table, and assign the appropriate color and linetype.

Step 5   Set Border as the current layer and set the Ortho, Grid, and Snap all to ON. Invoke the ZOOM ALL command to display the entire limits on screen.

Step 6   Invoke the RECTANG command from the Draw toolbar to draw the border (17" × 11") as shown in Figure P10–2.

> Command: **rectang**
> Chamfer/Elevation/Fillet/Thickness/Width/<First corner>: **.5,.5**
> Other corner: **@17,11**

Figure P10–2   Border for piping flowsheet

Step 7   Set Blocks as the current layer.

Step 8   Invoke the ZOOM command and use the Window option to zoom in on a small area of the display, as shown in Figure P10–3.

> Command: **zoom**
> All/Center/Dynamic/Extents/Left/Previous/Vmax/Window/<Scale(X/
>   XP)>: **window**
> First corner: **3,3**
> Other corner: **6,6**

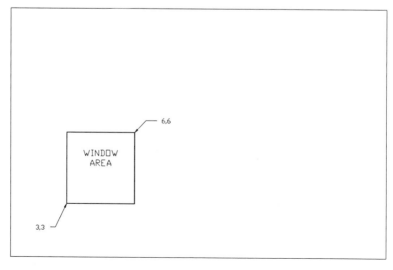

Figure P10–3   Zoom in on a portion of the display

Step 9 Open the Drawing Aids dialog box from the pull-down menu Tools, and set the grid to 0.125 and the snap to 0.0625, and set the grid and snap to ON.

Step 10 Draw the gate valve as shown in Figure P10–4.

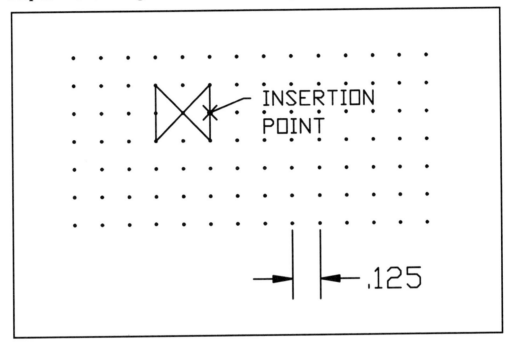

Figure P10–4 The gate valve

Step 11 Invoke the BMAKE command from the Draw toolbar, as shown in Figure P10–5.

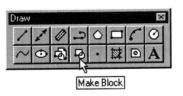

Figure P10–5 Invoking the Make Block command from the Draw toolbar

AutoCAD displays the Block Definition dialog box shown in Figure P10–6.

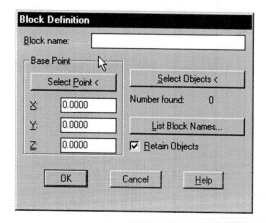

Figure P10–6 Block Definition dialog box

Type **GATE** in the Block name: edit box. Pick the **Select Point <** button. AutoCAD prompts:

Insertion base point: *(specify the insertion point as shown in Figure P10–4)*

Once you specify the insertion point, AutoCAD redisplays the Block Definition dialog box. Pick the **Select Objects <** button. AutoCAD prompts:

Select objects: *(select all the objects that comprise the gate valve)*

Once you select the objects, AutoCAD redisplays the Block Definition dialog box. Set the **Retain objects** check box to OFF. Choose the **OK** button to create the block called GATE and close the Block Definition dialog box.

Step 12   Draw the remaining symbols required for the piping flow sheet on the appropriate layers, as shown in the Figure P10–7.

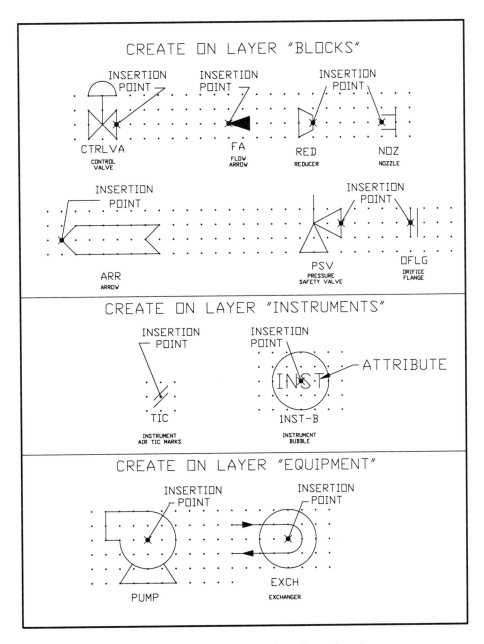

Figure P10–7 Required blocks for the piping flowsheet drawing

Create individual blocks for all the symbols by providing appropriate insertion points and block names (as shown in uppercase letters in Figure P10–7). If necessary, refer to Step 11 for the step-by-step procedure to create a block.

Before you create a block for the instrument bubble, define an attribute.

Invoke the DDATTDEF command. AutoCAD displays the Attribute Definition dialog box. Set appropriate attributes and the required prompts, as shown in Figure P10–8. Choose the **Pick Point <** button to place the attribute in the center of the instrument bubble, as shown in Figure P10–7.

Once you have defined the attribute, create the block for the instrument bubble. Make sure to include the attribute definition as part of the block when selecting objects.

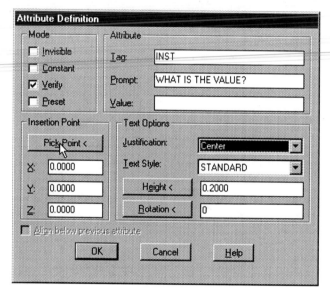

Figure P10–8 Attribute Definition dialog box

Step 13 Invoke the ZOOM ALL command to display the entire drawing.

Step 14 Open the Drawing Aids dialog box from the pull-down menu Tools and set the grid to 0.25, and the snap to 0.125, and set the grid and snap to ON.

Step 15 Set Equipment as the current layer.

Step 16 Draw the vertical and horizontal vessels and the boxes for the exchangers as shown in Figure P10–9. Following are the prompt sequences to draw the vessels and boxes for the exchangers.

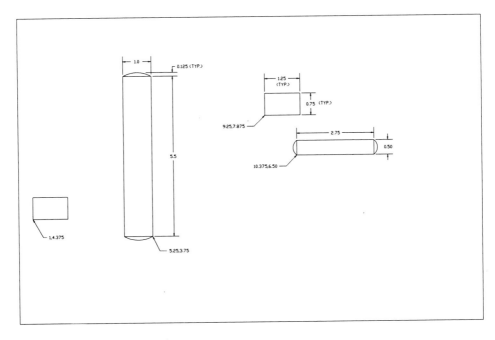

Figure P10–9 Equipment layout

To draw the vertical vessel:

Command: **rectang**
Chamfer/Elevation/Fillet/Thickness/Width/<First corner>: **5.25,3.75**
Other corner: **@-1,5.5**

Command: **arc**
Center/<Start point>: **4.25,3.75**
Center/End/<Second point>: **4.75,3.625**
Endpoint: **5.25,3.75**

Command:**arc**
Center/<Start point>: **5.25,9.25**
Center/End/<Second point>: **4.75,9.375**
Endpoint: **4.25,9.25**

To draw the horizontal vessel:

Command: **rectang**
Chamfer/Elevation/Fillet/Thickness/Width/<First corner>: **10.375,6.5**
Other corner: **@2.75,0.50**

Command: **arc**
Center/<Start point>: **10.375,7**
Center/End/<Second point>: **10.25,6.75**
Endpoint: **10.375,6.5**

Command: **arc**
Center/<Start point>: **13.125,6.5**
Center/End/<Second point>: **13.25,6.75**
Endpoint: **13.125,7**

To draw the boxes for the exchangers

Command: **rectang**
First corner: **9.25,7.875**
Other corner: **@1.25,0.75**

Command: **rectang**
First corner: **1,4.375**
Other corner: **@1.25,0.75**

Step 17 Insert the exchangers and pump as shown in Figure P10–10 by invoking the DDINSERT command from the Draw toolbar (Figure P10–11).

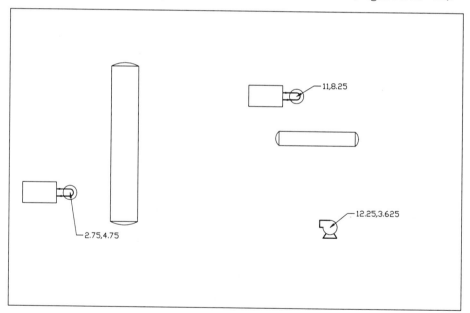

Figure P10–10 Layout with exchangers and pump

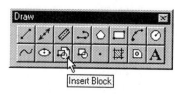

Figure P10–11 Invoking the Insert Block command from the Draw toolbar

AutoCAD displays the Insert dialog box shown in Figure P10-12.

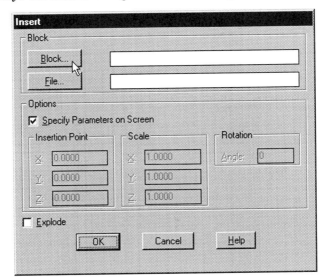

Figure P10-12 Insert dialog box

Pick the **Block...** button to list the available blocks in the current drawing. AutoCAD displays the **Defined Blocks** dialog box listing the available blocks in the current drawing. Select the **EXCH** block name, and choose **OK** to close the **Defined Blocks** dialog box. Set the **Specify Parameters on Screen** check box to OFF. In the Insertion Point section of the dialog box, type **2.75** in the X: edit box and **4.75** in the Y: edit box. In the Scale section of the dialog box, type **1.00** in the X: edit box and **1.00** in the Y: edit box. In the Rotation section of the dialog box, type **0** in the Angle: edit box. Choose the **OK** button to insert the block and close the dialog box.

Similarly, insert the EXCH block again at the insertion point **11,8.25**, with scale set to **1.00** and rotation to **0** degrees. Insert the PUMP block at the insertion point **12.25,3.625**, with scale set to **1.00** and rotation set to **0** degrees.

Step 18 Insert the NOZ block at the appropriate locations, as shown in Figure P10-13.

Draw a horizontal line (representing a tray) in the vessel just below the highest side, and then copy it three times, as shown in Figure P10-13.

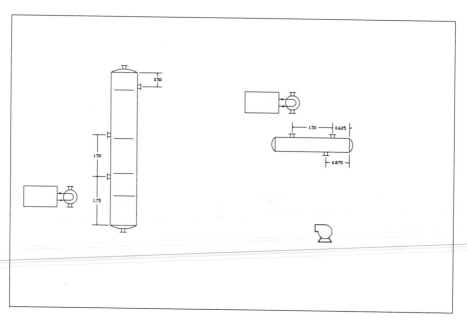

Figure P10–13 Layout with nozzles

Step 19   Set Pipeline as the current layer.

Step 20   Lay out the pipelines as shown in Figure P10–14 by invoking the LINE command.

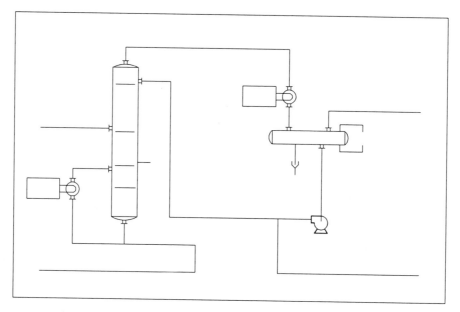

Figure P10–14 Layout with pipelines

Step 21   Insert the flowsheet symbols at the appropriate places, as shown in Figure P10–15 by invoking the DDINSERT command. Make sure to provide appropriate attribute values while inserting the instrument bubble block. After inserting the blocks, use the BREAK command to break out the pipeline passing through the valve symbols.

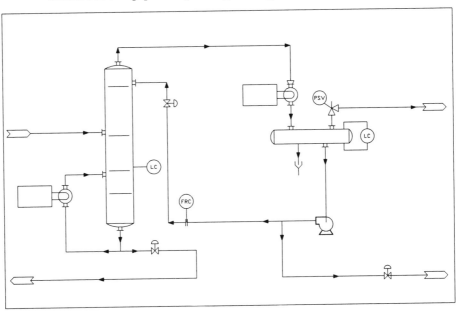

Figure P10–15 Layout with flowsheet symbols

Step 22   Set Instruments as the current layer.

Step 23   Invoke the PLINE command to draw line1, line2, and line3 instrument air lines as shown in Figure P10–16.

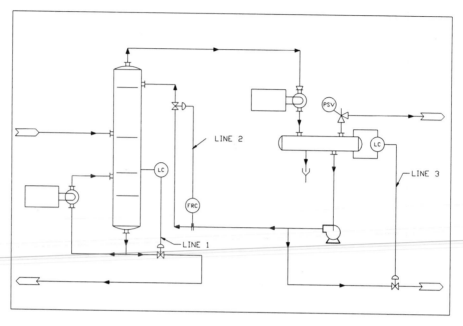

Figure P10–16 Layout with instrument air lines

Step 24   Invoke the DIVIDE command to insert the block tic on the instrument air lines as shown in Figure P10–17. AutoCAD prompts:

> Command: **divide**
> Select object to divide: *(select line 1)*
> <Number of segments>/Block: **b**
> Block name to insert: **tic**
> Align block with object? <Y>: **n**
> Number of segments: **5**

> Command: **divide**
> Select object to divide: *(select line 2)*
> <Number of segments>/Block: **b**
> Block name to insert: **tic**
> Align block with object? <Y>: **n**
> Number of segments: **7**

> Command: **divide**
> Select object to divide: *(select line 3)*
> <Number of segments>/Block: **b**
> Block name to insert: **tic**
> Align block with object? <Y>: **n**
> Number of segments: **8**

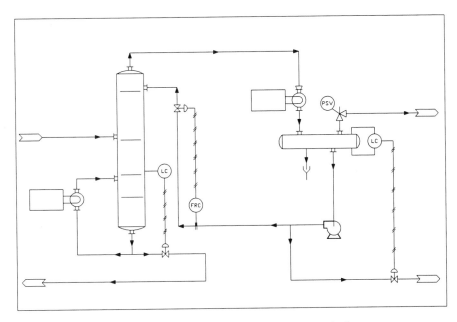

Figure P10–17 Layout with tic marks on the instrument air lines

Step 25 Set Text as the current layer.

Step 26 Invoke the DTEXT command to add the text as shown in Figure P10–18. The larger text height is set to 0.18 and the smaller text height is set to 0.125.

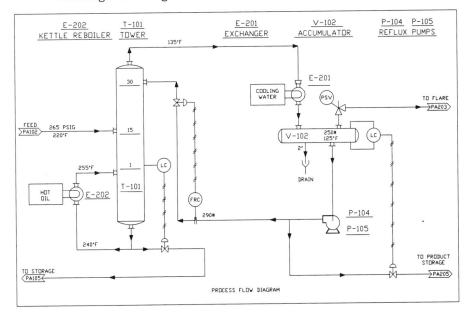

Figure P10–18 Layout with text

Step 27   Save the drawing as CH10-PROJ and exit the AutoCAD program.

Command: **end**

Congratulations! You have just successfully applied several AutoCAD concepts in creating a simple schematic drawing.

EXERCISES 10–1 THROUGH 10–4

Exercise 10–1

Create the drawing according to the settings given in the following table. Create all the required blocks by referring to the piping flowsheet symbols in Figure Ex10a–1. (Set the grid to 0.125 and the snap to 0.0625 to draw the symbols.)

Settings	Value		
1. Units	Decimal		
2. Limits	Lower left corner: 0,0		
	Upper right corner: 12,9		
3. Grid	.5		
4. Snap	.125		
5. Layers	*NAME*	*COLOR*	*LINETYPE*
	Blocks	Red	Continuous
	Border	Cyan	Continuous
	Equipment	Green	Continuous
	Lines	Magenta	Continuous
	Text	White	Continuous

Hints	Note that the insertion points are located on the symbol where they join the objects to which they are connected.
	In order to attach a nozzle to the curved top of the reactor, one of its legs will have to overlap. Then the block will have to be exploded before part of it can be trimmed.

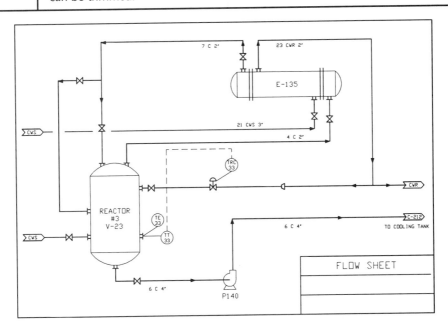

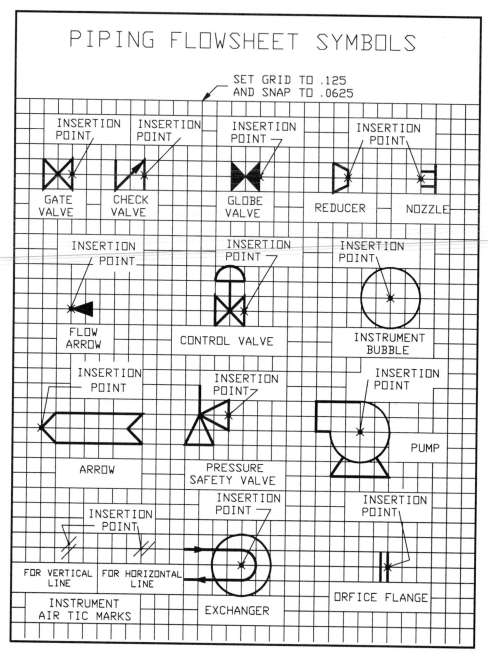

Figure Ex10a–1

Exercise 10–2

Create the drawing according to the settings given in the following table. Create all the required blocks by referring to the electrical symbols in Figure Ex10b–1. (Set the grid to 0.125 and the snap to 0.0625 to draw the symbols.)

Settings	Value		
1. Units	Decimal		
2. Limits	Lower left corner: 0,0		
	Upper right corner: 12,9		
3. Grid	.5		
4. Snap	.125		
5. Layers	*NAME*	*COLOR*	*LINETYPE*
	Blocks	Red	Continuous
	Border	Cyan	Continuous
	Lines	Magenta	Continuous
	Text	White	Continuous
	Construction	Red	Continuous

Hints	Note that the insertion points are located on the symbol where they join the objects to which they are connected.
	Draw the circuits with continuous lines on the Construction layer. Insert the blocks by using the Osnap mode Nearest. Then set the Construction layer to OFF and draw the lines between the symbols, connecting to their endpoints.

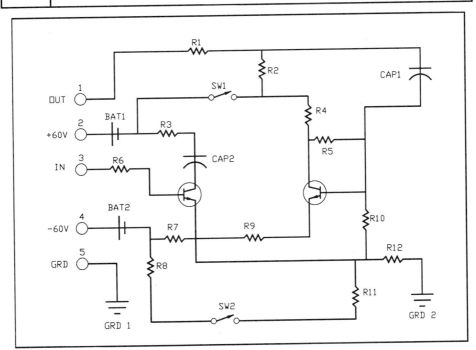

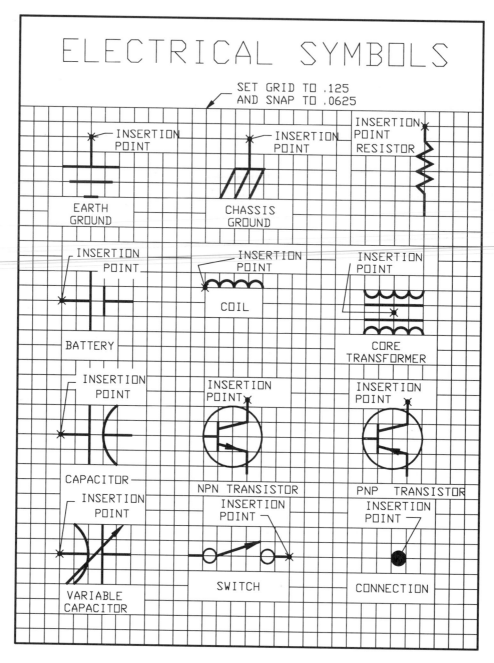

Figure Ex10b–1

Exercise 10–3

Create the drawing according to the settings given in the following table. Create all the blocks used in this drawing with an attribute tag. Create all the required blocks by referring to the electrical symbols in Figure Ex10b–1. (Set the grid to 0.125 and the snap to 0.0625 to draw the symbols.)

Settings	Value		
1. Units	Decimal		
2. Limits	Lower left corner: 0,0		
	Upper right corner: 12,9		
3. Grid	.5		
4. Snap	.125		
5. Layers	*NAME*	*COLOR*	*LINETYPE*
	Blocks	Red	Continuous
	Border	Cyan	Continuous
	Lines	Magenta	Continuous
	Text	White	Continuous
	Construction	Red	Continuous

Hints	Note that the insertion points are located on the symbol where they join the objects to which they are connected.
	Draw the circuits with continuous lines on the Construction layer. Insert the blocks by using the Osnap mode Nearest. Then set the Construction layer to OFF and draw the lines between the symbols, connecting to their endpoints.

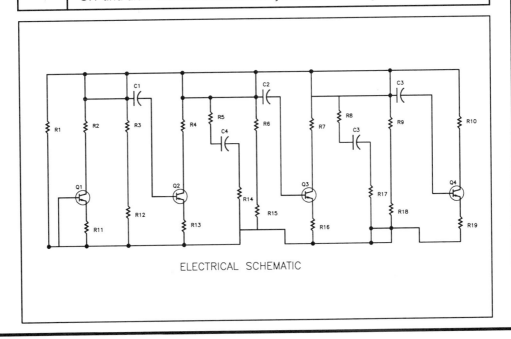

ELECTRICAL SCHEMATIC

Exercise 10–4

Create the drawing according to the settings given in the following table. Create all the required blocks by referring to the architectural symbols in Figure Ex10c–1.

Settings	Value		
1. Units	Architectural		
2. Limits	Lower left corner: 0'-0",0'-0"		
	Upper right corner: 64'-0",48'-0"		
3. Grid	1'-0"		
4. Snap	6"		
5. Layers	*NAME*	*COLOR*	*LINETYPE*
	Blocks	Red	Continuous
	Border	Cyan	Continuous
	Floorplan	Magenta	Continuous
	Text	White	Continuous
	Construction	Red	Continuous

Hint	Defining attributes is useful for labeling the desks as they are inserted.

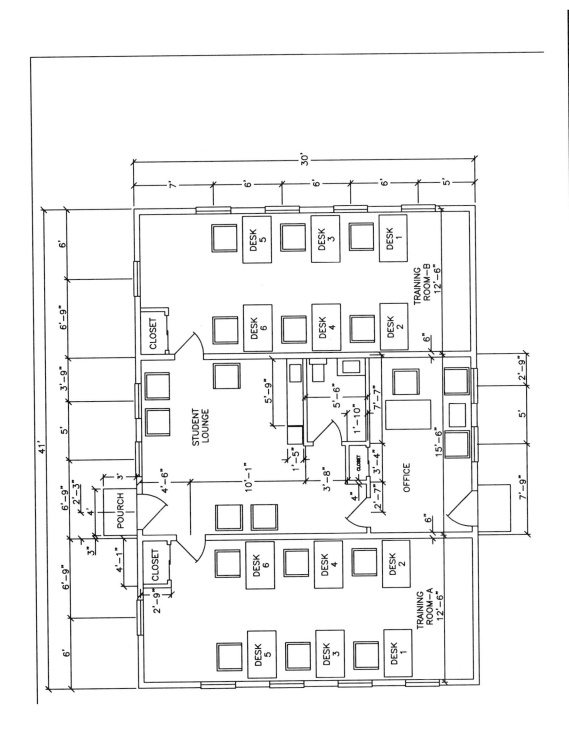

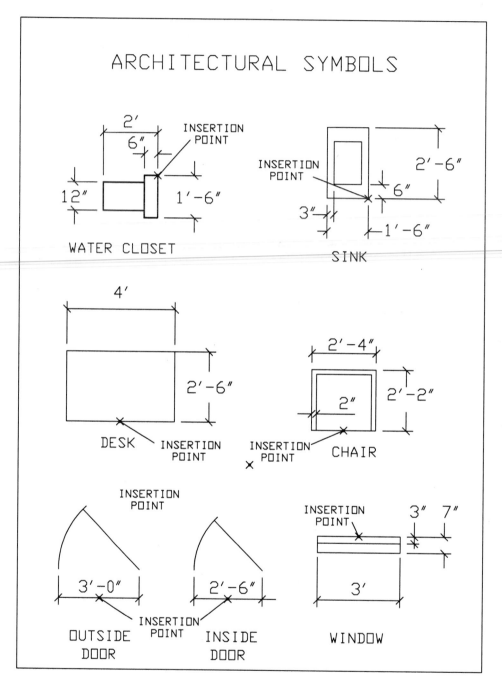

ARCHITECTURAL SYMBOLS

Figure Ex10c–1

REVIEW QUESTIONS

1. If you used "BL??7* as the pattern for listing blocks, which of the following block names would be listed?
   a. BL7
   b. BLOCK739
   c. BLUE727
   d. BLACK
   e. none of the above

2. It is possible to force invisible attributes to display on a drawing.
   a. True
   b. False

3. Which of the following forms of attribute extraction require template files?
   a. CDF   d. A and B
   b. SDF   e. none of the above
   c. DXF

4. The maximum number of characters for a block name is:
   a. 8   d. 31
   b. 16   e. 43
   c. 23

5. A block is:
   a. a rectangular-shaped figure available for insertion into a drawing
   b. a single element found in a block formation of a building drawn with AutoCAD
   c. one or more objects stored as a single object for later retrieval and insertion
   d. none of the above

6. A block cannot be exploded if it
   a. consists of other blocks (nested)
   b. has a negative scale factor
   c. has been moved
   d. has different X and Y scale factors
   e. none of the above

7. A new drawing may be created from an existing block by using the command:
   a. WBLOCK
   b. NEW
   c. BLOCK=
   d. SAVEAS
   e. none of the above

8. All of the following can be exploded, except:
   a. blocks
   b. associative dimensions
   c. polylines
   d. Blocks inserted with MINSERT command
   e. none of the above

9. To insert a block a called "TABLE" and have the block converted to individual object as it is inserted, what should you use for the block name?
   a. /TABLE
   b. *TABLE
   c. ?TABLE
   d. TABLE
   e. none of the above

10. The command used to write all or just part of a drawing out to a new drawing file is:
   a. SAVEAS
   b. BLOCK
   c. DXFOUT
   d. FILE
   e. WBLOCK

11. To return a block back to its original objects, use:
   a. EXPLODE
   b. BREAK
   c. CHANGE
   d. UNDO
   e. STRETCH

12. To identify a new insertion point for a drawing file which will be inserted into another drawing, invoke:
   a. BASE command
   b. INSERT command
   c. BLOCK command
   d. WBLOCK command
   e. DEFINE command

13. MINSERT places multiple copies of an existing block similar to the command:
   a. ARRAY
   b. MOVE
   c. INSERT
   d. COPY
   e. MIRROR

14. If one drawing is to be inserted into another drawing and editing operations are to be performed on the inserted drawing, you must first:
    a. use the PEDIT command
    b. EXPLODE the inserted drawing
    c. UNDO the inserted drawing
    d. nothing, it can be edited directly
    e. none of the above

15. The BASE command:
    a. can be used to move a block
    b. is a subcommand of PEDIT
    c. will accept 3D coordinates
    d. allows one to move a dimension baseline
    e. none of the above

16. Attributes are associated with:
    a. objects   d. layers
    b. blocks   e. shapes
    c. text

17. To merge two drawings, use:
    a. INSERT   d. BLOCK
    b. MERGE   e. IGESIN
    c. BIND

18. The WBLOCK command can be used to create a new block for use:
    a. in the current drawing
    b. in an existing drawing
    c. in any drawing
    d. only in a saved drawing
    e. none of the above

19. The DIVIDE command causes AutoCAD to
    a. divide an object into equal length segments
    b. divide an object into two equal parts
    c. break an object into two objects
    d. all of the above

20. One can not explode:
    a. polylines containing arcs
    b. blocks containing polylines
    c. dimensions incorporating leaders
    d. blocks inserted with different X, Y, and Z scale factors
    e. none of the above

21. The DIVIDE command will:
    a. place points along a line, arc, polyline, or circle
    b. accept 1.5 as segment input
    c. place markers on the selected object and separate it into different segments
    d. divide any object into the equal number of segments

22. When using the WBLOCK command to create a new block, one should respond to the block name with:
    a. a block name
    b. an equal sign
    c. an asterisk
    d. a file name
    e. none of the above

23. The WBLOCK commands creates:
    a. a drawing file
    b. a collection of blocks
    c. a symbol library
    d. an object file
    e. none of the above

24. The MEASURE command causes AutoCAD to divide an object
    a. into specified length segments
    b. into equal length segments
    c. into two equal parts
    d. all of the above

25. A command used to edit attributes is:
    a. DDATTE   d. ATTFILE
    b. EDIT   e. none of the above
    c. EDITATT

26. The WBLOCK command:
    a. means "Window Block" and allows for the use of a window to define a block
    b. allows you to send a previously defined block to a file, thus creating a drawing file of the block
    c. is used in lieu of the INSERT command when the block is stored in a separate disk file
    d. none of the above

27. Attributes are defined as the:
    a. database information displayed as a result of entering the LIST command
    b. X and Y values which can be entered when inserting a block
    c. coordinate information of each vertex found along a SPLINE object
    d. none of the above

CHAPTER

11

EXTERNAL REFERENCES

INTRODUCTION

One of the most powerful time-saving features of AutoCAD is the ability to combine one drawing with another. AutoCAD lets you display or view the contents of as many as 32,000 other drawing files while working in your current drawing file. This feature is provided by the XREF command, short for external reference.

After completing this chapter, you will be able to:

✓ Attach and detach reference files
✓ Change the path for reference files
✓ Load and unload reference files
✓ Decide whether to attach or overlay an external reference file
✓ Clip external reference files
✓ Control dependent symbols
✓ Manage external references
✓ Use the BIND command to add dependent symbols to the current drawing

USING EXTERNAL REFERENCES

Prior to Release 11, existing AutoCAD drawings could be combined in only one way: by means of the INSERT command to insert one drawing into another. When one drawing is inserted into another, the inserted drawing becomes a part of the drawing it is inserted into. The data from the inserted drawing is merged with the data of the current drawing. Once the drawing is inserted, no link or association remains between the original drawing from which the inserted drawing came and the drawing it has been inserted into.

The INSERT command and the XREF command give users a choice of methods for combining existing drawing files. The *external reference (xref)* feature does not make block insertion of drawings obsolete; users can decide which method is more appropriate for the current application.

When a drawing is externally referenced (instead of inserted as a block), the user can view and object snap to the referenced drawing from the current drawing, but each drawing's data is still stored and maintained in a separate drawing file. The only information in the reference drawing that becomes a permanent part of the current drawing is the name of the reference drawing and its directory path. If necessary, externally referenced files can be scaled, moved, copied, mirrored, or rotated by using the AutoCAD modify and construct commands. You can control the visibility, color, and linetype of the layers belonging to an external drawing file. This lets you control which portions of the external drawing file are displayed, and how. No matter how complex an external reference drawing may be, it is treated as a single object by AutoCAD. If you invoke the MOVE command and point to one line, for example, the entire object moves, not just the line you pointed to. You cannot explode the externally referenced drawing. All the manipulations performed on an external reference will not affect the original drawing file because an external reference is only an image, however scaled or rotated.

Borders are an excellent example of drawing files that are useful as external reference files. The objects that make up a border will use considerable space in a file, and commonly amount to around 20,000 bytes. If a border is drawn in each drawing file, this would waste a large amount of disk space when you multiply 20,000 bytes by 100 drawing files. If external reference files are used correctly, they can save 2 MB of disk space in this case.

Accuracy and efficient use of drawing time are other important design features that are enhanced through external reference files. When an addition or change is made to a drawing file that is being used as an external reference file, all the drawings that use the file will reflect the modifications. For example, if you alter the title block of a border, all the drawing files that use that border as an external reference file will automatically display the title block revisions. (Can you imagine accessing 100 drawing files to correct one small detail?) External reference files will save time and ensure the drawing accuracy required to produce a professional product. Figure 11–1 shows a drawing that externally references four other drawings to illustrate the doorbell detail. In fact, the drawing of the house is referenced twice: one for the right half and a second time for the mirrored left half.

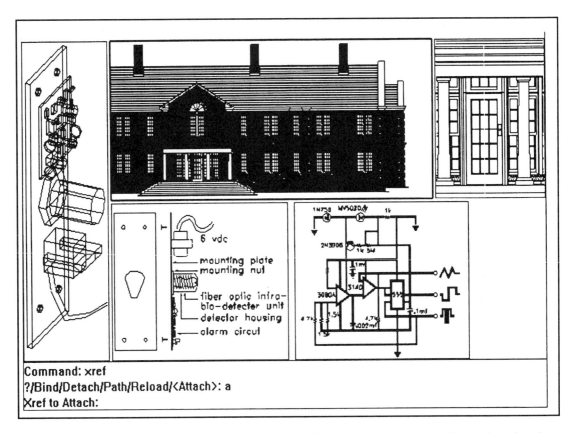

```
Command: xref
?/Bind/Detach/Path/Reload/<Attach>: a
Xref to Attach:
```

Figure 11–1 This drawing appears to be a single drawing but references four other drawings

There is a limit of 32,000 external references you can add to a drawing. In practice, this represents an unlimited number. If necessary, you can nest them so that loading one external reference automatically causes another external reference to be loaded. When you attach a drawing file as an external reference file, it is permanently attached until it is detached or bound to the current drawing. When you load the drawing with external references, AutoCAD automatically reloads each external reference drawing file; thus, each external drawing file reflects the latest state of the referenced drawing file.

The XREF command, when combined with the networking capability of AutoCAD, gives the project manager powerful new features to cope with the realities of file management. The project manager instantaneously sees the work of the departments and designers working on aspects of the contract. If necessary, you can overlay a drawing where appropriate, track the progress, and maintain document integrity. At the same time, departments need not lose control over individual designs and details.

In AutoCAD Release 14 you can control the display of the external reference file by means of clipping, so you can display only a specific section of the reference file.

EXTERNAL REFERENCES AND DEPENDENT SYMBOLS

The symbols that are carried into a drawing by an external reference are called *dependent symbols*, because they depend on the external file, not on the current drawing, for their characteristics. The symbols have arbitrary names and include blocks, layers, linetypes, text styles, and dimension styles.

When you attach an external reference drawing, AutoCAD automatically renames an xref's dependent symbols. AutoCAD forms a temporary name for each symbol by combining its original name with the name of the xref itself. The two names are separated by the vertical bar (I) character. Renaming the symbols prevents the xref's objects from taking on the characteristics of existing symbols in the drawing.

For example, you created a drawing called PLAN1 with layers 0, First-fl, Dim, and Text, in addition to blocks Arrow and Monument. If you attach the PLAN1 drawing as an external reference file, the layer First-fl will be renamed as PLAN1 I first-fl, Dim as PLAN1 I dim, and Text as PLAN1 I text, as shown in Figure 11–2. Blocks Arrow and Monument will be renamed as PLAN1 I Arrow and PLAN1 I Monument. The only exceptions to renaming are unambiguous defaults like layer 0 and linetype continuous. The information on layer 0 from the reference file will be placed on the active layer of the current drawing when the drawing is attached as an external reference of the current drawing. It takes on the characteristics of the current drawing.

This prefixing is carried to nested xrefs. For example, if the external file PLAN1 included an xref named "Title" that has a layer Legend, it would get the symbol name PLAN1 I Title I Legend if PLAN1 were attached to another drawing.

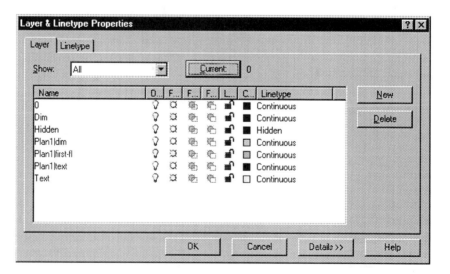

Figure 11–2 Attaching an external reference file

This automatic renaming of an xref's dependent symbols has two benefits:

■ It allows you to see at a glance which named objects belong to which external reference file.
■ It allows dependent symbols to have the same name in both the current drawing and an external reference, and coexist without any conflict.

The AutoCAD commands and dialog boxes for manipulating named objects do not let you select an xref's dependent symbols. Usually, dialog boxes display these entries in grayed-out text.

For example, you cannot insert a block that belongs to an external reference drawing in your current drawing, nor can you make a dependent layer the current layer and begin creating new objects.

You can control the visibility of the layers (ON/OFF, Freeze/Thaw) of an external reference drawing and, if necessary, you can change the color and linetype. When the VISRETAIN system variable is set to 0 (default), any changes you make to these settings, apply only to the current drawing session. They are discarded when you end the drawing. If VISRETAIN is set to 1, then the current drawing visibility, color, and linetype for xref dependent layers take precedence. They are saved with the drawing and are preserved during xref reload operations.

There may be times when you want to make your xref data a permanent part of your current drawing. To make an xref drawing a permanent part of the current drawing, use the Bind option of the XREF command. With the Bind option, all layers and other symbols, including the data, become part of the current drawing. This is similar to inserting a drawing via the INSERT command.

If necessary, you can make dependent symbols such as layers, linetypes, text styles, and dim styles part of the current drawing by using the XBIND command instead of binding the whole drawing. This allows you to work with the symbol just as if you had defined it in the current drawing.

ATTACHING AND MANIPULATING WITH THE XREF COMMAND

The XREF command provides various options for attaching and detaching external references files.

Invoke the XREF command from:

Reference toolbar	Select the External Reference command (see Figure 11–3)
Pull-down menu	Insert > External Reference...
Command: prompt	**xref** Enter

Figure 11-3 Invoking the External Reference command from the Reference toolbar

AutoCAD displays the External Reference dialog box, similar to Figure 11–4.

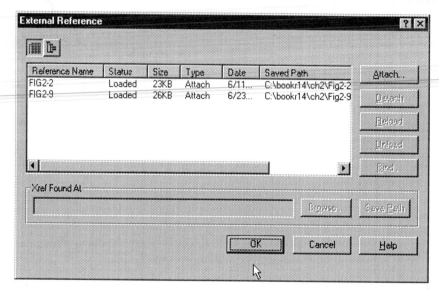

Figure 11-4 External Reference dialog box

> **NOTE:** Type **-XREF** and press `Enter` at the "Command:" prompt for all the options available at the Command: prompt level for attaching and manipulating external reference drawings. The available options are the same ones as in the External Reference dialog box.

AutoCAD provides two options for listing attached external reference drawings. By default, the List View option (see Figure 11–4) displays a list of the attached reference files and their associated data. To sort a column alphabetically, select the column heading. A second click sorts it in reverse order. To resize a column's width, select the separator between columns and drag the pointing device to the right or left.

The external file's **Reference Name** does not have to be the same as its original file name. To rename the external file, double-click the name or press `F2`. AutoCAD allows you to rename the file. The new name can be up to 31 characters and must be without any spaces.

The **Status** column displays the state of the external reference file, which can be Loaded, unLoaded, Unreferenced, Unresolved, Orphaned, Reload, or Not found. A detailed discussion is provided later in the chapter.

The **Size** column shows the file size of the corresponding external reference drawing. The size is not displayed if the external reference is unloaded, not found, or unresolved.

The **Type** column indicates whether the external reference is an attachment or an overlay.

The **Date** column displays the last date the associated drawing was modified. The date is not displayed if the external reference is unloaded, not found, or unresolved.

The **Saved Path** column shows the saved path of the associated external reference file.

Selecting any field highlights the external file's reference name.

You can also display the information as a tree view. To do so, click the Tree View button located at the top left of the dialog box, or press ⌐. To switch back to the List View, press ⌐.

In a Tree View listing, AutoCAD displays a hierarchical representation of the external reference in alphabetical order, as shown in Figure 11-5. Tree View shows the level of nesting relationship of the attached external references, whether they are attached or overlaid, whether they are loaded, unloaded, marked for reload or unload, or not found, unresolved, or unreferenced.

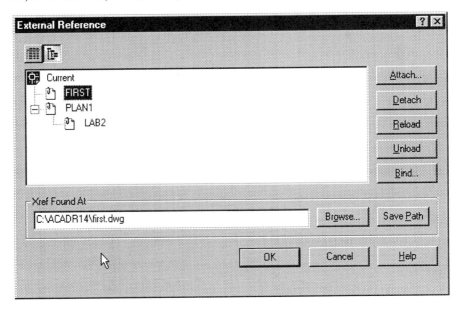

Figure 11-5 External Reference dialog box with Tree View listing

Attaching External Reference Drawings

The Attach option allows you attach a drawing as an external reference. Use it when you want to attach a new external reference file or a copy of the external reference file already attached to the current drawing. If you attach a drawing that itself contains an attached external reference, the attached external reference appears in the current drawing. If another person is currently editing the external reference drawing, the drawing attached is based on the most recently saved version.

To attach a drawing as an external reference, invoke the Attach option from:

External Reference dialog box	Select the **Attach...** button
Reference toolbar	Select the External Reference Attach command (see Figure 11–6)
Command: prompt	**xattach** Enter

Figure 11–6 Invoking the External Reference Attach command from the Reference toolbar

AutoCAD displays the Attach Xref dialog box similar to Figure 11–7.

Choose the **Browse...** button to display the **Select file to attach** dialog box. Select the appropriate drawing file to attach as a reference file to the current drawing.

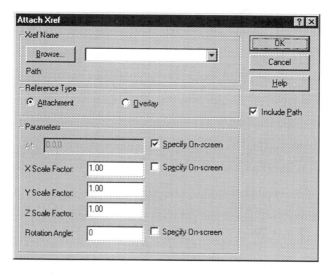

Figure 11–7 Attach Xref dialog box

> **NOTE:** Once you have attached your first external reference file to the current drawing, then whenever you invoke the Attach option, AutoCAD displays the **Select file to attach** dialog box instead of the **Attach Xref** dialog box.

Once an external reference drawing is attached to the current drawing, the external reference drawing name is added to the list box located next to the **Browse...** button. When an attached external reference file name is selected from the list box, its path is displayed below.

In the **Reference Type** section of the dialog box, select one of the two available options: **Attachment** or **Overlay**. When you attach an external reference in the **Attachment** mode, the external reference will be included in the drawing when the drawing itself is attached as an external reference to another drawing. If you attach an external reference in the **Overlay** mode, in contrast, an overlaid external reference is not included in a drawing when the drawing itself is attached as an external reference or overlaid external reference to another drawing.

For example, PLAN-A drawing is attached as an overlaid external reference to PLAN-B. Then PLAN-B is attached as an external reference to PLAN-C. PLAN-A is not seen in PLAN-C because it is overlaid in PLAN-B, not attached as an external reference. But, if PLAN-A is attached an external reference in PLAN-B, and in turn PLAN-B is attached in PLAN-C, both PLAN-A and PLAN-B will be seen in PLAN-C.

So, the only behavioral difference between overlays and attachments is how nested references are handled. Overlaid external references are designed for data sharing. If necessary, you can change the status from Attach to Overlay, or vice versa, by clicking the mode in the Type column in the External Reference dialog box.

The **Include Path** check box in the Attach Xref dialog box determines whether or not the full path to the external reference is saved. If Include Path is set to ON, then the external reference path is saved in the drawing database; if it is set to OFF, the name of the external reference drawing is saved without a path in the database. AutoCAD searches for the external reference drawing in the AutoCAD Support File Search Path and in the paths associated with the PROJECTNAME in the Files tab of the Preferences dialog box.

In the **Parameters** section of the Attach Xref dialog box, you can specify the insertion point, **X Scale Factor**, **Y Scale Factor**, and **Z Scale Factor**, and the **Rotation Angle,** similar to the insertion of a block explained in Chapter 10.

Detaching External Reference Drawings

The Detach option allows you detach one or more external reference drawings from the current drawing. Only the external reference drawings attached or overlaid directly to the current drawing can be detached. You cannot detach an external reference drawing referenced by another external reference drawing. If the external reference is currently being displayed as part of the current drawing, it disappears when you detach it.

To detach an external reference drawing from the current drawing, first select the drawing name from the displayed list in the External Reference dialog box, and then select the **Detach** button. AutoCAD detaches the selected external reference drawing(s) from the current drawing. You can select several files at once by using the standard Windows methods (holding down ⇧Shift or Ctrl while selecting).

Reloading External Reference Drawings

The Reload option allows you to update one or more external reference drawings any time while the current drawing is in AutoCAD. When you load a drawing into AutoCAD, it automatically reloads any external references attached. The Reload option has been provided to reread the external drawing from the external drawing file whenever it is desirable to do so from within AutoCAD. The Reload option is helpful in a network environment to get the latest version of the reference drawing while you are in an AutoCAD session.

To reload external reference drawing(s), first select the drawing name(s) from the displayed list in the External Reference dialog box, and then select the **Reload** button. AutoCAD reloads the selected external reference drawing(s). You can select several files at once by using the standard Windows methods (holding down ⇧Shift or Ctrl while selecting).

Unloading External Reference Drawings

The Unload option allows you to unload one or more external reference drawings from the current drawing. Unlike the Detach option, the Unload option merely suppresses the display and regeneration of the external reference definition, to help current session editing and improve performance. This option can also be useful when a series of external reference drawings needs to be viewed during a project on an as-needed basis. Rather than having the referenced files displayed at all times, you can reload the drawing when you require the information.

To unload external reference drawing(s), first select the drawing name(s) from the displayed list in the External Reference dialog box, then select the **Unload** button. AutoCAD turns off the display of the selected external reference drawing(s). You can select several files at once by using the standard Windows methods (holding down ⇧Shift or Ctrl while selecting).

The effects of Unload and Reload take effect after you close the dialog box.

Binding External Reference Drawings

The Bind option allows you to make your external reference drawing data a permanent part of the current drawing. To bind external reference drawing(s), first select the drawing name(s) from the displayed list in the External Reference dialog box,

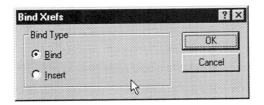

Figure 11–8 Bind Xrefs dialog box

then select the **Bind...** button. AutoCAD displays the Bind Xrefs dialog box shown in Figure 11–8. Select one of the two available bind types: **Bind** or **Insert**. You can select several files at once by using the standard Windows methods (holding down Shift or Ctrl while selecting).

With **Bind**, the external reference drawing becomes an ordinary block in your current drawing. It also adds the dependent symbols to your drawing, letting you use them as you would any other named objects. In the process of binding, AutoCAD renames the dependent symbols. The vertical bar symbol (|) is replaced with three new characters: a $, a number, and another $. The number is assigned by AutoCAD to ensure that the named object will have a unique name.

For example, if you bind an external reference drawing named PLAN1 that has a dependent layer PLAN1|FIRST-FL, AutoCAD will try to rename the layer to PLAN1$0$FIRST-FL. If there is already a layer by that name in the current drawing, then AutoCAD tries to rename the layer to PLAN1$1$FIRST-FL, incrementing the number until there is no duplicate.

If you do not want to bind the entire external reference drawing, but only specific dependent symbols, such as a layer, linetype, block, dimension style, or text style, then you can use the XBIND command, explained later in this chapter, in the section on "Adding Dependent Symbols to the Current Drawing."

With **Insert**, the external reference drawing is inserted in the current drawing just like inserting a drawing with the INSERT command. AutoCAD adds the dependent symbols to the current drawing by stripping off the external reference drawing name.

For example, if you insert an external reference drawing named PLAN1 that has a dependent layer PLAN1|FIRST-FL, AutoCAD will rename the layer to FIRST-FL. If there is already a layer by that name in the current drawing, then the layer FIRST-FL would assume the properties of the layer in the current drawing.

Changing the Path

To change to a different path or file name for the currently selected external reference file, choose the **Browse...** button in the External dialog box. AutoCAD displays the Select New Path dialog box, in which you can select a different path or file name.

Saving the Path

To save the path as it appears in the **Xref Found At** field of the currently selected external reference file, select the **Save Path** button. AutoCAD saves the path of the currently selected external reference file.

After making the necessary changes in the External Reference dialog box, choose the OK button to keep the changes and close the dialog box.

ADDING DEPENDENT SYMBOLS TO THE CURRENT DRAWING

The XBIND command lets you permanently add a selected subset of external reference dependent symbols to your current drawing. The dependent symbols include the block, layer, linetype, dimension style, and text style. Once the dependent symbol is added to the current drawing, it behaves as if it were created in the current drawing and saved with the drawing when you ended the drawing session. While adding the dependent symbol to the current drawing, AutoCAD removes the vertical bar symbol (I) from each dependent symbol's name, replacing it with three new characters: a $, a number, and another $ symbol.

For example, you might want to use a block that is defined in an external reference. Instead of binding the entire external reference with the Bind option of the XREF command, it is advisable to use the XBIND command. With the XBIND command, the block and the layers associated with the block will be added to the current drawing. If the block's definition contains reference to an external reference, AutoCAD binds that xref and all its dependent symbols as well. After binding the necessary dependent symbols, you can detach the external reference file.

Invoke the XBIND command from:

Reference toolbar	Select the External Reference Bind command (see Figure 11–9)
Pull-down menu	Modify > Object > External Reference > Bind...
Command: prompt	**xbind** Enter

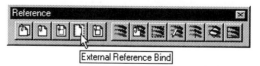

Figure 11–9 Invoking the External Reference Bind command from the Reference toolbar

AutoCAD displays the Xbind dialog box, similar to the Figure 11–10.

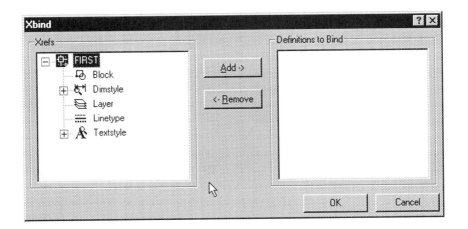

Figure 11–10 Xbind dialog box

> **NOTE:** To invoke the XBIND command at the "Command:" prompt level, type **-XBIND** and press ⏎ at the "Command:" prompt. The available options are the same ones as in the Xbind dialog box.

On the left side of the Xbind dialog box AutoCAD lists the external reference files currently attached to the current drawing. Double-click on the name of the external reference file, and AutoCAD expands the list by listing the dependent symbols. Select the dependent symbol from the list and choose the **Add->** button. AutoCAD moves the selected dependent symbol into the **Definitions to Bind** list. If necessary, return it back to the external reference dependent list from the **Definitions to Bind** list by choosing the **<-Remove** button after selecting the appropriate dependent symbol.

Click **OK** to bind the definitions to the current drawing.

CONTROLLING THE DISPLAY OF EXTERNAL REFERENCES

The XCLIP command allows you to control the display of unwanted information by clipping the external reference drawings and blocks. Clipping does not edit or change the external reference or block; it just prevents part of the object from being displayed. The defined clipping boundary can be visible or hidden. You can also define the front and back clipping planes.

The clipping boundary consists of planar straight-line segments. You can also generate the clip boundary from polylines. If the polyline is fit-curved or has arcs, the clip boundary is displayed as if the polyline had been decurved prior to being used as a clip boundary.

The XCLIP command can be applied to one or more external references or blocks. If you set the clip boundary to OFF, the entire external reference or block is displayed. If you subsequently set the clip boundary to ON, the clipped drawing is displayed again. If necessary, you can delete the clipping boundary; AutoCAD redisplays the entire external reference or block. In addition, AutoCAD also allows you to generate a polyline from the clipping boundary.

Invoke the XCLIP command from:

Reference toolbar	Select the External Reference Clip command (see Figure 11–11)
Pull-down menu	Modify > Object > Clip
Command: prompt	xclip Enter

Figure 11–11 Invoking the External Reference Clip command from the Reference toolbar

AutoCAD prompts:

Command: **xclip**
Select objects: *(select one or more external references and/or blocks to be included in the clipping and press* Enter *to complete the selection)*
ON/OFF/Clipdepth/Delete/generate Polyline/<New boundary>: *(select one of the available options)*

Creating a New Clipping Boundary The **New boundary** option (default) allows you to define a rectangular or polygonal clip boundary or generates a polygonal clipping boundary from a polyline. AutoCAD prompts:

Select polyline/Polygonal/<Rectangular>: *(select one of the available options)*

The **Rectangular** option (default) allows you to define a rectangular boundary by specifying the opposite corners of a window. The clipping boundary is applied in the current UCS and is independent of the current view.

The **Select polyline** option defines the boundary by using a selected polyline. The polyline can be open or closed, can be made of straight-line segments, but cannot intersect itself.

The **Polygonal** option defines a polygonal boundary by specifying points for the vertices of a polygon.

Once the clipping boundary is defined, AutoCAD displays only the portion of the drawing that is within the clipping boundary and then exits the command.

If you already have a clipping boundary of the selected external reference drawing, and you invoke the **New Boundary** option, then AutoCAD prompts:

> Delete old boundary? No/<Yes> *(select one of the two available options)*

If you choose Yes, the entire reference file is redrawn and the command continues; if you choose No, the command sequence is terminated.

> **NOTE:** The display of the boundary border is controlled by the XCLIPFRAME system variable. If it is set to 1 (ON), then AutoCAD displays the boundary border; if it is set to 0 (OFF), then AutoCAD does not display the boundary border.

Controlling the Display of the Clipped Boundary The ON/OFF option controls the display of the clipped boundary. The **OFF** option displays all of the geometry of the external reference or block, ignoring the clipping boundary. The **ON** option displays the clipped portion of the external reference or block only.

Setting the Front and Back Clipping Planes The **Clipdepth** option sets the front and back clipping planes on an external reference or block. Objects outside the volume defined by the boundary and the specified depth are not displayed.

Deleting the Clipping Boundary The **Delete** option removes the clipping boundary for the selected external reference or block. To turn off the clipping boundary temporarily, use the OFF option explained earlier. The Delete option erases the clipping boundary and the clipdepth and displays the entire reference file.

> **NOTE:** The ERASE command cannot be used to delete clipping boundaries.

Generating a Polyline AutoCAD draws a polyline coincident with the clipping boundary. The polyline assumes the current layer, linetype, and color settings. When you delete the clipping boundary, AutoCAD deletes the polyline. If you need to keep a copy of the polyline, then invoke the **Generate Polyline** option. AutoCAD makes a copy of the clipping boundary. You can use the PEDIT command to modify the generated polyline, and then redefine the clipping boundary with the new polyline. To see the entire external reference while redefining the boundary, use the **OFF** option to turn off the clipping boundary.

MANAGING EXTERNAL REFERENCES

Several tools are available to help in the management and tracking of external references.

One of the tracking mechanisms is an external ASCII log file that is maintained on each drawing that contains external references. This file, which AutoCAD generates and maintains automatically, has the same name as the current drawing and a file extension *.XLG*. You can examine the file with any text editor and/or print it. The log file registers each Attach, Bind, Detach, and Reload of each external reference for the current drawing. AutoCAD writes a title block to the log file that contains the name of the current drawing, the date and time, and the operation being performed. Once a log file has been created for a drawing, AutoCAD continues to append to it. The log file is always placed in the same directory as the current drawing. The log file is maintained only if the XRECTL system variable is set to 1. The default setting for XRECTL is 0.

External references are also reported in response to the ? option of the XREF command and the BLOCK command. Because of the external reference feature, the contents of a drawing may now be stored in multiple drawing files. This means that new backup procedures are required to handle drawings linked in external reference partnerships. Three possible solutions are:

1. Make the external reference drawing a permanent part of the current drawing prior to archiving with the Bind option of the XREF command.
2. Modify the current drawing's path to the external reference drawing so that they are both stored in the same directory, and then archive them together.
3. Archive the directory location of the external reference drawing with the drawing which references it. Tape backup machines do this automatically.

In AutoCAD Release 14, a combination of demand loading and the saving of drawings with indexes helps you increase the performance of drawing with external references. In conjunction with the **XLOADCTL** and **INDEXCTL** system variables, demand loading provides a method of displaying only those parts of the referenced drawing that are necessary.

The **XLOADCTL** system variable controls whether demand loading is set to ON or OFF and whether it opens the original drawing or a copy. If **XLOADCTL** set to **0**, then AutoCAD turns off demand loading, and the entire reference file is loaded. If **XLOADCTL** is set to **1**, then AutoCAD turns on the demand loading, and the reference file is kept open. AutoCAD loads only the objects that are necessary to display on the current drawing. AutoCAD places a lock on all reference drawings that are set for demand loading. Other users can open those reference drawings, but they cannot save changes to them. If **XLOADCTL** is set to **2**, then AutoCAD turns on demand loading and a copy of the reference file is opened. AutoCAD makes a temporary copy of the externally referenced file and demand-loads the temporary file. Other users are allowed to edit the original drawing. When you disable demand loading, AutoCAD reads in the entire reference drawing regardless of layer visibility or clip instances.

The **INDEXCTL** system variable determines whether Layer, Spatial, or Layer & Spatial indexes are created when a drawing file is saved. Using layer and spatial indexes increases performance when AutoCAD is demand-loading external references. If **INDEXCTL** is set to **0**, then indexes are not created; if **INDEXCTL** is set to **1**, a layer index is created. The layer index maintains a list of objects that are on specific layers, and with demand loading it determines which objects need to be read in and displayed. If **INDEXCTL** is set to **2**, then a spatial index is created. The spatial index organizes lists of objects based on their location in 3D space, and it determines which objects lie within the clip boundary and reads only those objects into the current session. If **INDEXTCTL** is set to **3**, both layer and spatial indexes are created and saved with the drawing. If you intend to take full advantage of demand loading, then **INDEXCTL** should be set to **3**.

> **NOTE:** If the drawing you are working on is not going to be referenced by another drawing, it is recommended that you set the **INDEXCTL** to **0** (OFF).

AutoCAD provides another system variable, VISRETAIN, to control the visibility of layers in the external reference drawing. If the VISRETAIN system variable is set to **0** (OFF), any changes you make to settings of the external reference drawing's layers, such as ON/OFF, Freeze/Thaw, Color, and Linetype, apply to the current drawing session only. If VISRETAIN is set to **1** (ON), then any changes you make to settings of the external reference drawing's layers takes precedence over the external reference layer definition.

INSERTING IMAGES INTO THE CURRENT DRAWING

The IMAGE command allows you insert a raster or bit-mapped bitonal, 8-bit gray, 8-bit color, or 24-bit color image file into the drawing. The image formats that can be inserted into AutoCAD include BMP, TIF, RLE, FLI, PCX, and TGA. More than one image can be displayed in any viewport, and the number and size of images is not limited.

Invoke the IMAGE command from:

Reference toolbar	Select the Image command (see Figure 11–12)
Pull-down menu	Insert > Raster Image...
Command: prompt	**image** Enter

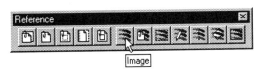

Figure 11–12 Invoking the Image command from the Reference toolbar

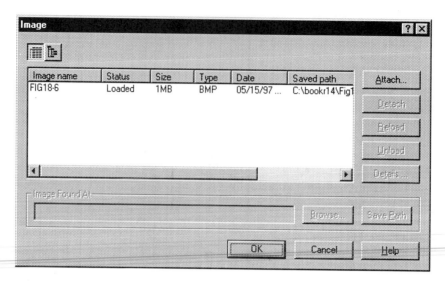

Figure 11–13 Image dialog box

AutoCAD displays the Image dialog box, similar to Figure 11–13.

The Image dialog box looks a lot like the External Reference dialog box. In the Image dialog box, AutoCAD lists the images attached to the current drawing. The information provided in the list box of the Image dialog box, such as Image name, Status, Size, Type, Data, and Saved path, is similar to the information provided in the External Reference dialog box. You can switch between List View and Tree View, as in the External Reference dialog box, by clicking the two buttons at the top left of the Image dialog box.

Attaching an Image to the Current Drawing

The **Attach** option allows you attach an image object to the current drawing. Invoke the Attach option from:

Image dialog box	Select the **Attach...** button
Reference toolbar	Select the Image Attach command (see Figure 11–14)
Command: prompt	**imageattach** Enter

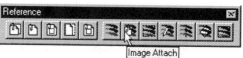

Figure 11–14 Invoking the Image Attach command from the Reference toolbar

AutoCAD displays the Attach Image dialog box. Select the image file and pick the open button. AutoCAD displays Attach Image dialog box, similar to Figure 11–15.

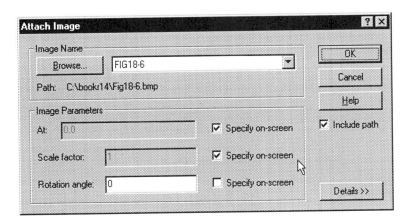

Figure 11–15 Attach Image dialog box

To select a different image choose the **Browse...** button to display the Attach Image File dialog box. Select the appropriate image file to attach to the current drawing.

> **NOTE:** Once you have attached your first image file to the current drawing, then whenever you invoke the Attach option, AutoCAD displays the Attach Image File dialog box instead of Attach Image dialog box.

Once an image file is attached to the current drawing, the image file name is added to the list box located next to the **Browse...** button. When an attached image file name is selected from the list box, its path is displayed below.

The **Include Path** check box determines whether or not the full path to the image file is saved. If Include Path is set to ON, then the image file path is saved in the drawing database; if it is set to OFF, the name of the image file is saved without a path in the database. AutoCAD searches for the image file in the AutoCAD Support File Search Path and in the paths associated with the PROJECTNAME in the Files tab of the Preferences dialog box.

In the **Image Parameters** section of the Attach Image dialog box, you can specify the **Insertion Point** coordinates, the **Scale Factor**, and the **Rotation Angle,** similar to insertion of a block explained in Chapter 10.

Choose the **Details>>** button to display the image information for the selected image file. This information includes image resolution in horizontal and vertical units, image size by width and height in pixels, and image size by width and height in the current selected units.

Detaching an Image from the Current Drawing

The **Detach** option removes the selected image definitions from the drawing database and erases all the associated image objects from the drawing and from the display. To detach an image file from the current drawing, first select the image file name from the displayed list in the Image dialog box, and then select the **Detach** button. AutoCAD detaches the selected image file from the current drawing.

Reloading an Image into the Current Drawing

The Reload option loads the most recent version of an image. To reload the image file to the current drawing, first select the image file name from the displayed list in the Image dialog box, and then select the **Reload** button. AutoCAD reloads the selected image file into the current drawing.

Unloading an Image from the Current Drawing

The **Unload** option unloads the image data from working memory without erasing the image objects from the drawing. It is highly recommended that you unload images that are no longer needed for editing. By unloading the images, you can improve performance by reducing the memory requirement for AutoCAD. To unload the image file from the current drawing, first select the image file name from the displayed list in the Image dialog box, and then select the **Unload** button. AutoCAD unloads the selected image file from the current drawing.

Details of the Image File

The Details option provides detailed information about the selected image; including the image name, saved path, active path, file creation date and time, file size and type, color, color depth, width and height in pixels, resolution, default size in units, and a preview image. To display the detailed information of the selected image file, first select the image file name from the displayed list in the Image dialog box, then select the **Details...** button. AutoCAD displays the detailed information of the selected image file in the Image File Details dialog box, similar to the Figure 11–16.

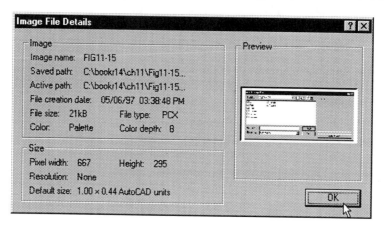

Figure 11–16 Image File Details dialog box

Changing the Path

To change to a different path or file name for the currently selected image file, choose the **Browse...** button in the Image dialog box. AutoCAD displays the Attach Image dialog box, in which you can select a different path or file name.

Saving the Path

To save the path as it appears in the **Image Found At** field of the currently selected image file, select the **Save Path** button. AutoCAD saves the path of the currently selected image file.

After making the necessary changes in the Image dialog box, choose the OK button to keep the changes and close the dialog box.

CONTROLLING THE DISPLAY OF THE IMAGE OBJECTS

The IMAGECLIP command allows you to control the display of unwanted information by clipping the image object; this is similar to the use of the XCLIP command for external references and blocks.

Invoke the IMAGECLIP command from:

Reference toolbar	Select the Image Clip command (see Figure 11–17)
Pull-down menu	Modify > Object > Image Clip
Command: prompt	imageclip Enter

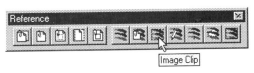

Figure 11–17 Invoke the Image Clip command from the Reference toolbar

AutoCAD prompts:

Command: **imageclip**
Select image to clip: *(select the image to clip)*
ON/OFF/Delete/<New boundary>: *(select one of the available options)*

Creating a New Clipping Boundary The **New boundary** option (default) allows you to define a rectangular or polygonal clip boundary. AutoCAD prompts:

Polygonal/<Rectangular>: *(select one of the available options)*

The **Rectangular** option (default) allows you to define a rectangular boundary by specifying the opposite corners of a window. The rectangle is always drawn parallel to the edges of the image.

The **Polygonal** option defines a polygonal boundary by specifying points for the vertices of a polygon.

Once the clipping boundary is defined, AutoCAD displays only the portion of the image that is within the clipping boundary and then exits the command.

> **NOTE:** The display of the boundary border is controlled by the IMAGEFRAME system variable. If it is set to 1 (ON), then AutoCAD displays the boundary border; if it is set to 0 (OFF), then AutoCAD does not display the boundary border.

Controlling the Display of the Clipped Boundary The ON/OFF option controls the display of the clipped boundary. The **OFF** option displays all of the image, ignoring the clipping boundary. The **ON** option displays the clipped portion of the image only.

ADJUSTING THE IMAGE SETTINGS

The IMAGEADJUST command controls the brightness, contrast, and fade values of the selected image. Invoke the IMAGEADJUST command from:

Reference toolbar	Select the Image Adjust command (see Figure 11–18)
Pull-down menu	Modify > Object > Image > Adjust...
Command: prompt	imageadjust Enter

Figure 11–18 Invoking the Image Adjust command from the Reference toolbar

AutoCAD prompts:

Command: **imageadjust**
Select image to adjust: *(select an image object)*

AutoCAD displays the Image Adjust dialog box, similar to Figure 11–19.

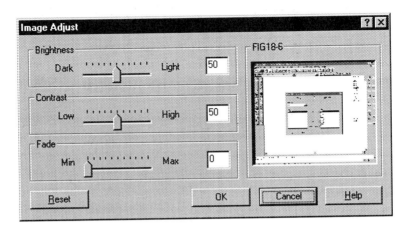

Figure 11–19 Image Adjust dialog box

You can adjust the Brightness, Contrast, and Fade within the range of 0 to 100.

Select the **Reset** button to reset values for the brightness, contrast, and fade parameters to the default settings of 50, 50, and 0, respectively.

ADJUSTING THE DISPLAY QUALITY OF IMAGES

The IMAGEQUALITY command controls the display quality of images. The quality setting affects display performance. A high-quality image takes longer to display. Changing the setting updates the display immediately without causing a regeneration. Images are always plotted using a high-quality display.

Invoke the IMAGEQUALITY command from:

Reference toolbar	Select the Image Quality command (see Figure 11–20)
Pull-down menu	Modify > Object > Image > Quality
Command: prompt	**imagequality** Enter

Figure 11–20 Invoking the Image Quality command from the Reference toolbar

AutoCAD prompts:

Command: **imagequality**
High/Draft <current>: *(select one of the two available options)*

The **High** option produces a high-quality image on screen. And the **Draft** option produces a lower-quality image on screen.

CONTROLLING THE BACKGROUND IMAGE

The TRANSPARENCY command controls whether the background pixels in an image are transparent or opaque. Invoke the TRANSPARENCY command from:

Reference toolbar	Select the Image Transparency command (see Figure 11–21)
Pull-down menu	Modify > Object > Image > Transparency
Command: prompt	**transparency** Enter

Figure 11–21 Invoking the Transparency command from the Reference toolbar

AutoCAD prompts:

Command: **transparency**
Select image: *(select the images, and press* Enter *to complete selection)*
ON/OFF <current>: *(select one of the two available options)*

The **ON** option turns transparency on so that objects beneath the image are visible. The **OFF** option turns transparency off so that objects beneath the image are not visible.

PROJECT EXERCISE

This project exercise provides point-by-point instructions for creating two drawings and then using them as external references in the third drawing, shown in Figure P11–1.

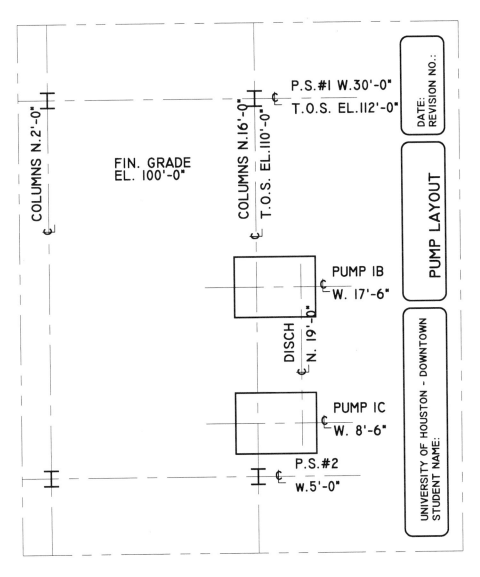

Figure P11–1 Completed project drawing

Step 1   Start the AutoCAD program.

Step 2   Create a new drawing with the parameters given in the following table.

SETTINGS	VALUE		
UNITS	Architectural		
LIMITS	Lower left corner: 0,0 Upper right corner: 28'-0",35'-0"		
GRID	1'		
SNAP	6"		
LAYERS	*NAME* Centerline Object Text Border	*COLOR* Green White Blue Red	*LINETYPE* Center Continuous Continuous Phantom

Set Centerline as the current layer and set up LTSCALE factor to 32.

Step 3   Invoke the LINE command from the Draw toolbar and draw the centerlines as shown in Figure P11–2.

Command: **line**
From point: **2',0**
To point: **@35'<90**
To point: Enter
Command: **line**
From point: **0,5'**
To point: **@23'<0**
To point: Enter

Invoke the OFFSET command from the Modify toolbar, and offset the vertical line 14' to the right and the horizontal line 25' upward.

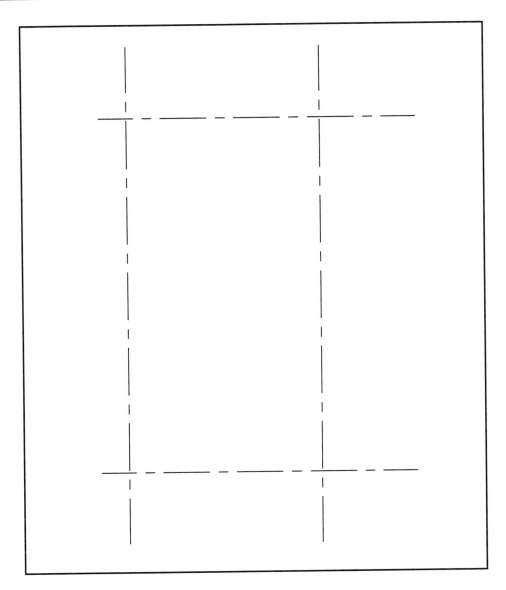

Figure P11–2 Centerlines

Step 4 Set Object as the current layer, and use the PLINE command with the width set to 1" to draw the steel columns at the points shown in Figure P11–3. The steel columns are 12" × 12".

NOTE: Draw one column and then copy it to the other locations. Make sure the grid and snap are set to ON.

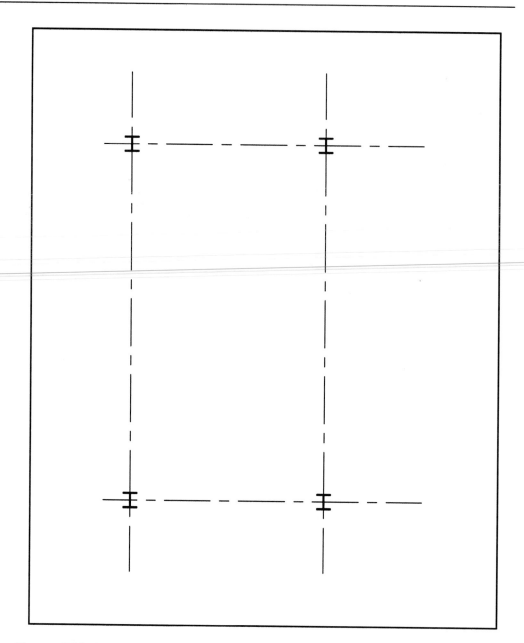

Figure P11–3 Steel columns

Step 5 Set Text as the current layer, and invoke the DTEXT command to draw
in the coordinate callouts as shown in Figure P11–4. Set the text height
to 8"; this will cause the text to be plotted out 0.25" high when plotted at
0.375" = 12".

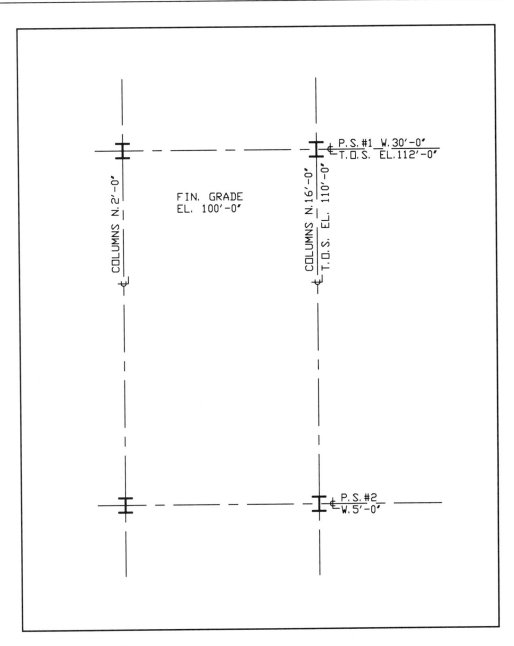

Figure P11–4 Add text to the drawing

Step 6   Save the drawing with the name "Piperack" and end the session.

Step 7   Create another new drawing with the parameters given earlier in the settings table. Set Centerline as the current layer.

Step 8 Invoke the LINE command from the Draw toolbar and draw the centerlines as shown in Figure P11–5.

> Command: **line**
> From point: **12'-6",8'-6"**
> To point: **@10'<0**
> To point: Enter
> Command: **line**
> From point: **19',7'**
> To point: **@12'<90**
> To point: Enter

Invoke the OFFSET command from the Modify toolbar and offset the horizontal centerline 9' upward.

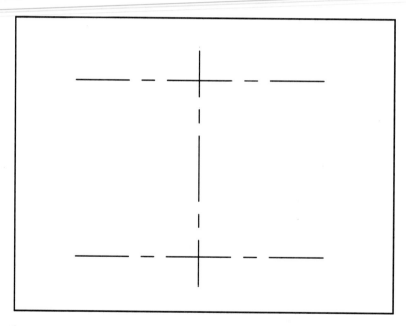

Figure P11–5 Pump centerlines

Step 9 Set Object as the current layer and use the LINE command to draw the pump foundation as shown in Figure P11–6.

> Command: **line**
> From point: **14'-6",6'-6"**
> To point: **@5'-6"<0**
> To point: **@4'<90**

To point: **@5'-6"<180**
To point: **c**

Command: **line**
From point: **14'-6",15'-6"**
To point: **@5'-6"<0**
To point: **@4'<90**
To point: **@5'-6"<180**
To point: **c**

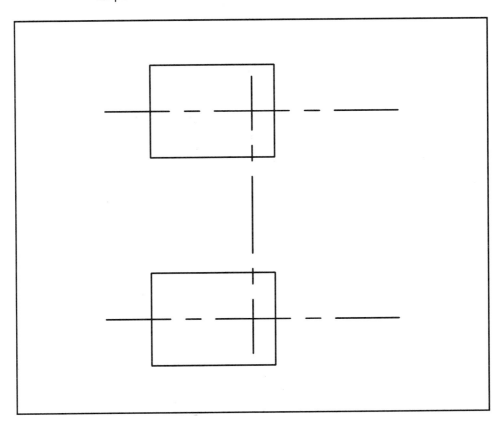

Figure P11–6 Pump foundations

Step 10   Set Text as the current layer and invoke the DTEXT command from the Draw toolbar to draw in the coordinate callouts as shown in Figure P11–7. Set the text height to 8". This will cause the text to be plotted out 0.25" high when plotted at 0.375" = 12".

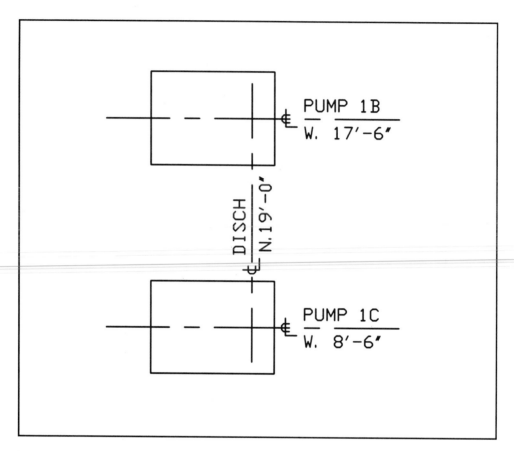

Figure P11–7 Add text to the drawing

Step 11   Save the drawing with the name "Pump" and end the session.

Step 12   Create another new drawing with the parameters given earlier in the settings table. Set Border as the current layer.

Step 13   Invoke the LINE command from the Draw toolbar and draw the border line as shown in Figure P11–8.

Command: **line**
From point: **0,0**
To point: **@28'<0**
To point: **@35'<90**
To point: **@28'<180**
To point: **c**

Figure P11-8 Border drawing

Step 14   Attach the pipe rack drawing as a reference file to the current drawing with an insertion point of 0,0, a scale factor of 1.0, and a rotation angle of 0 degrees.

After attaching the pipe rack drawing, your drawing will appear as shown in Figure 11–9.

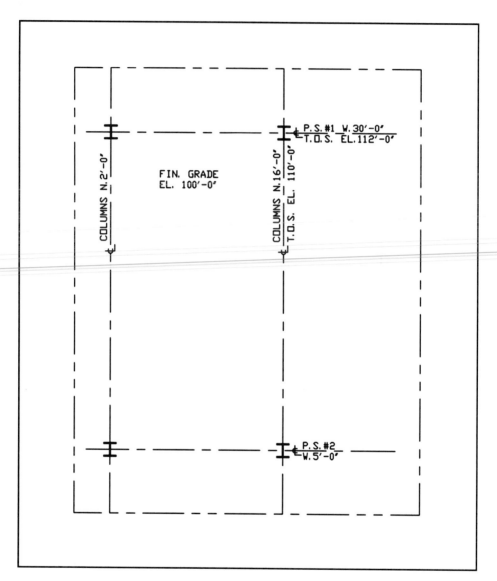

Figure P11–9 Attach the pipe rack drawing

Step 15   Attach the pump drawing as a reference file to the current drawing with an insertion point of 0,0, a scale factor of 1.0, and a rotation angle of 0 degrees.

After you attach the pump drawing, your drawing will appear as shown in Figure P11–10.

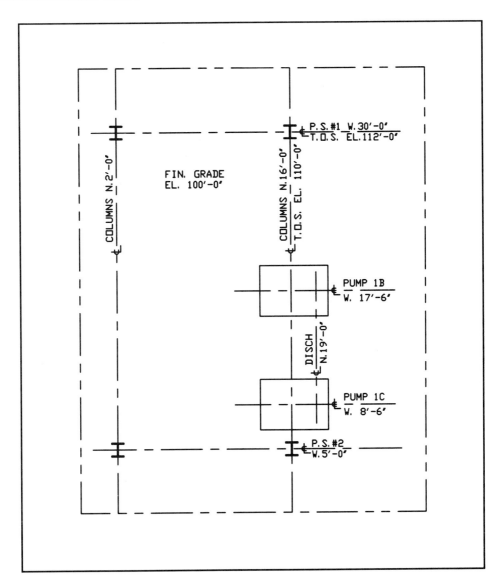

Figure P11–10 Attach the pump drawing

Step 16 Complete the title block as shown in Figure P11–11, with your name and the date filled in. Save the drawing as PROJCH11.DWG, and end the session.

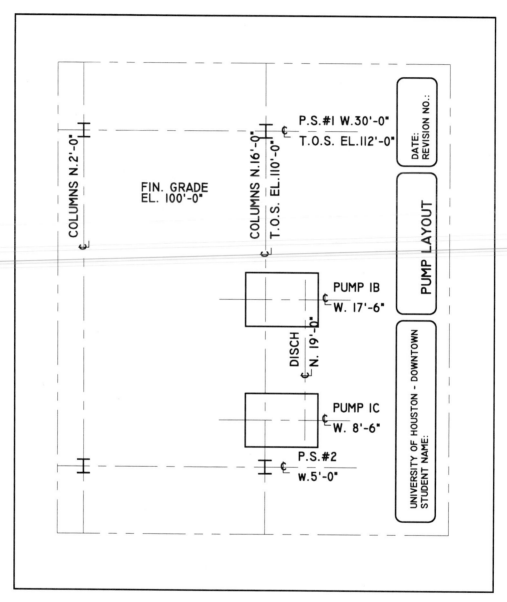

Figure P11–11 Completed drawing

EXERCISES 11–1 THROUGH 11–5

Exercise 11–1

Create a new drawing according to the parameters given in the table, and draw the column layout as shown in Figure Ex11–1a. Add the necessary dimensions and save the drawing as EX11-1a.

Settings	Value		
1. Units	Architectural		
2. Limits	Lower left corner: -10'-0",-10'-0"		
	Upper right corner: 50'-0",35'-0"		
3. Grid	12"		
4. Snap	6"		
5. Layers	*NAME*	*COLOR*	*LINETYPE*
	Border	Red	Continuous
	Beams	Cyan	Continuous
	Columns	Green	Continuous
	Text	Blue	Continuous
	Dimension	White	Continuous

Hint	The columns on the corners are 8" × 8", and the remaining columns are 10" × 10". They can be drawn as polylines with a width of 0.5.

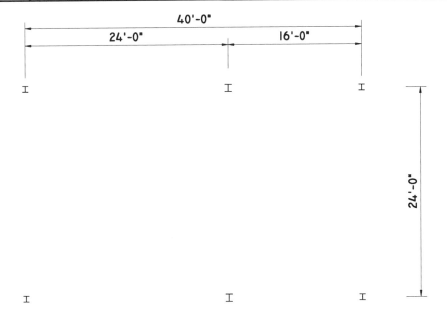

Figure Ex11–1a Layout of the columns

Create another new drawing according to the parameters given in the table. Attach the file EX11–1a as a reference file. Draw the walls and doors as shown in Figure Ex11–1b. Add text for the view name and for labeling the doors. Add the necessary dimensions, and save the drawing as EX11-1b.

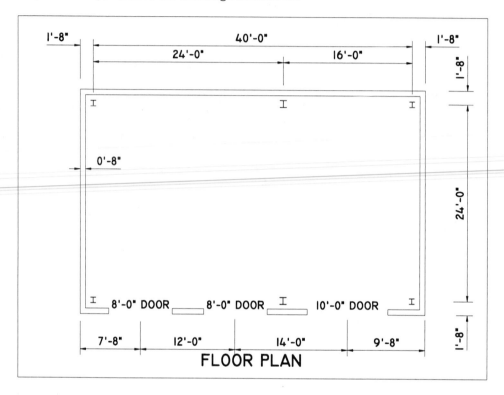

Figure Ex11–1b Layout of the walls, doors, and columns

Open the drawing EX11–1a and make the necessary changes for column spacing as shown in Figure Ex11–1c. Save the drawing.

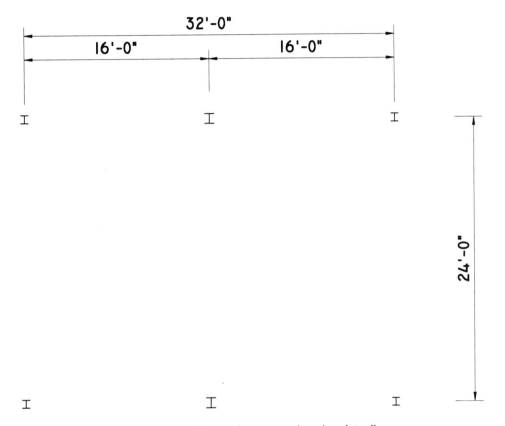

Figure Ex11–1c Layout of the column spacing (updated)

Open the drawing EX11–1b; the changes in the column layout show up automatically. The walls and doors will have to be altered to conform to the revised external reference column layout. Make the necessary changes, including eliminating one of the doors, as shown in Figure Ex11–1d. The wall along the column line on the left has to be relocated, and the dimension of the remaining door in the left bay changed from 8'-0" to 10'-0".

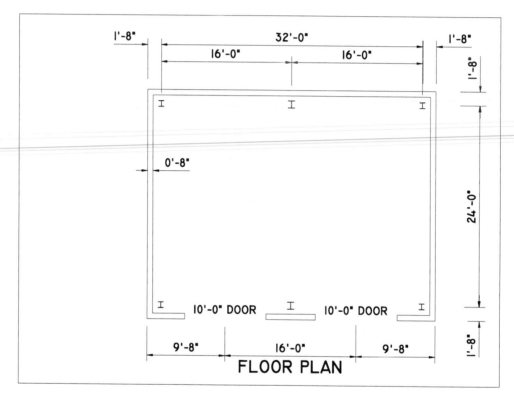

Figure Ex11–1d Layout of the columns (final revision)

Exercise 11–2

Open the drawing of the laundry and storage floor plan, *P6-1.dwg*, that was completed in Chapter 6. Set the Construction, Dim, Hidden, and Text layers to OFF. The drawing should appear as shown in Figure Ex11–2a. Save the drawing with the name EX11-2a.

Settings	Value		
1. Units	Architectural		
2. Limits	Lower left corner: -5'-0",-6'-0"		
	Upper right corner: 24'-4",15'-4"		
3. Grid	6"		
4. Snap	2"		
5. Layers	*NAME*	*COLOR*	*LINETYPE*
	Border	Red	Continuous
	Beams	Cyan	Continuous
	Columns	Green	Continuous
	Text	Blue	Continuous
	Dimension	White	Continuous
	Electrical	Magenta	Continuous
	Lighting	Red	Continuous

Hint	The outlet symbols (110V and 220V) can each be drawn one time and then copied to the other locations. The curved line from the switch to the light fixture can be drawn on the same layer as the switch and the fixture. You can then use the Properties button on the standard toolbar and change the Linetype to hidden.

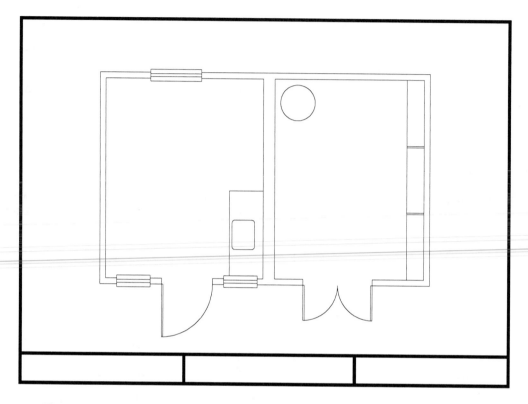

Figure Ex11–2a Laundry and storage floor plan with the Construction, Dim, Hidden, and Text layers set to OFF

Create a new drawing according to the parameters given in the table. Attach the file EX11-2a as a reference file. Draw the lighting and electrical symbols as shown in Figure Ex11–2b. Save the drawing as EX11-2b.

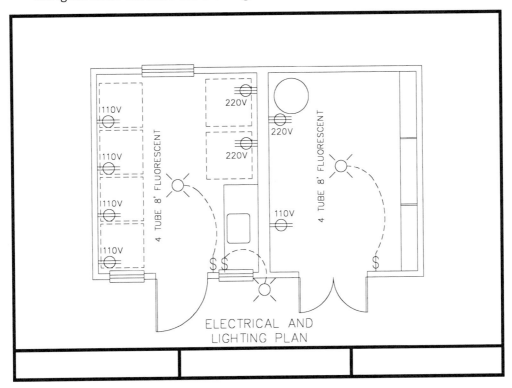

Figure Ex11–2b   Layout of the walls, doors, and columns

Exercise 11–3

Open the drawing *EX5-4.dwg* that was completed in Chapter 5. Erase the Detail A, Detail B, and the details of the stair riser. Also erase the interior footings (the 24 double rectangles inside the perimeter grade beams), the dimensions, and one interior line of the four perimeter lines. Change the linetype of the perimeter grade beam lines to hidden linetype. The drawing should appear as shown in Figure Ex11–3a. Save the drawing with the name EX11-3a.

Settings	Value		
1. Units	Architectural		
2. Limits	Lower left corner: 0'-0",0'-0"		
	Upper right corner: 60'-0",45'-0"		
3. Grid	12"		
4. Snap	6"		
5. Layers	*NAME*	*COLOR*	*LINETYPE*
	Construction	Cyan	Continuous
	Border	Red	Continuous
	Object	Green	Continuous
	Text	Blue	Continuous

Hint	The foundation layout can be used from the external reference as the basis for the walls and stair for the roofing plan. Once the roofing plan is completed, the layers in the external reference can be turned off. If any later changes are made in the foundation layout, they will automatically show up in the roofing plan, which can then be revised to suit the changes.

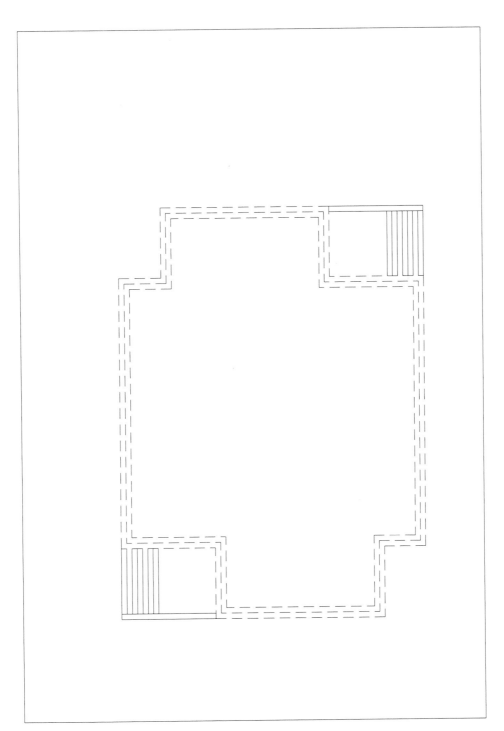

Figure Ex11-3a Foundation plan

Create a new drawing according to the parameters given in the table. Attach the file EX11-3a as a reference file, with an insertion point of 0,0, a scale factor of 1.0, and a rotation angle of 0 degrees. Draw the roof as shown in Figure Ex11–3b. Save the drawing as EX11-3b.

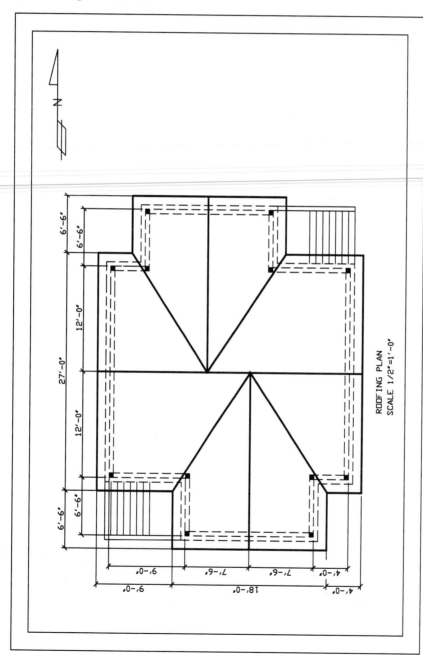

Figure Ex11–3b Roof layout

Exercise 11–4

Create a new drawing according to the parameters given in the table, and draw the floor plan as shown in Figure Ex11–4a. Do *not* add the dimensions, which are provided here only for reference. Save the drawing as EX11-4a.

Settings	Value		
1. Units	Architectural		
2. Limits	Lower left corner: –2'-0",–2'-0"		
	Upper right corner: 70'-0",50'-0"		
3. Grid	6"		
4. Snap	2"		
5. Layers	*NAME*	*COLOR*	*LINETYPE*
	Walls	Red	Continuous
	Ductwork	White	Continuous
	Text	Blue	Continuous

Hint	The ductwork can be drawn with the MLINE command.

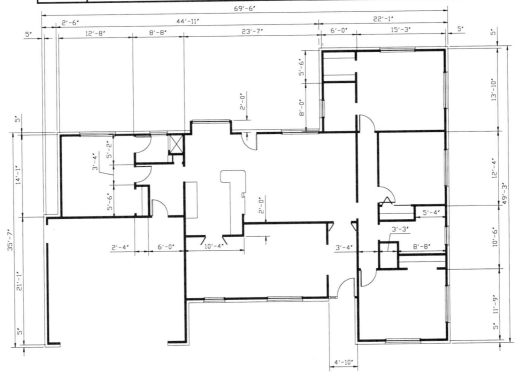

Figure Ex11–4a Floor plan

Create a new drawing according to the parameters given in the table. Attach the file EX11-4a as a reference file. Draw the A/C duct layout as shown in Figure Ex11–4b. Save the drawing as EX11-4b.

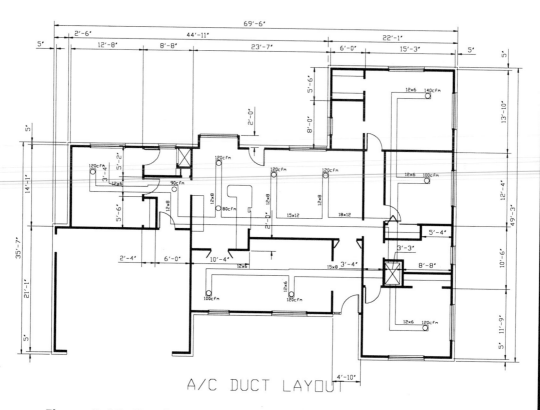

Figure Ex11–4b   Floor plan with the A/C duct layout

Exercise 11-5

Create a new drawing according to the parameters given in the table, and draw the vessel shown in Figure Ex11–5a. Save the drawing with the name EX11-5a.

Settings	Value
1. Units	Architectural
2. Limits	Lower left corner: 0,0
	Upper right corner: 28'-0",35'-0"
3. Grid	1'
4. Snap	6"
5. Layers	

NAME	COLOR	LINETYPE
Centerline	Green	Center
Object	White	Continuous
Text	Blue	Continuous
Border	Red	Phantom

Hint	This exercise uses a drawing that already has external references attached to it, and those external references must also be accessible for this exercise.

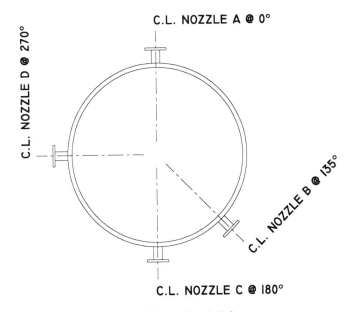

Figure Ex11–5a   Vessel layout

Create another new drawing according to the parameters given in the table, and draw an octagonal foundation as shown in Figure Ex11–5b. Do *not* add the dimensions, which are provided here only for reference.

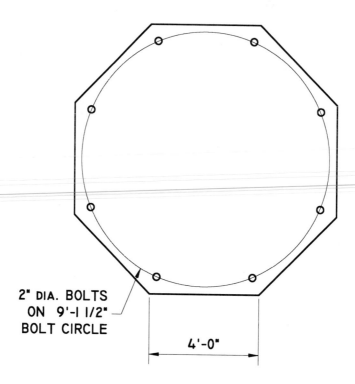

2" DIA. BOLTS
ON 9'-1 1/2"
BOLT CIRCLE

4'-0"

FOUNDATION PLAN

Figure Ex11–5b   Octagonal foundation

Attach the file Ex11-5a as a reference file, with an insertion point of 0,0, a scale factor of 1.0, and a rotation of 0 degrees. The drawing should appear as shown in Figure Ex11–5c. Save the drawing as EX11-5c.

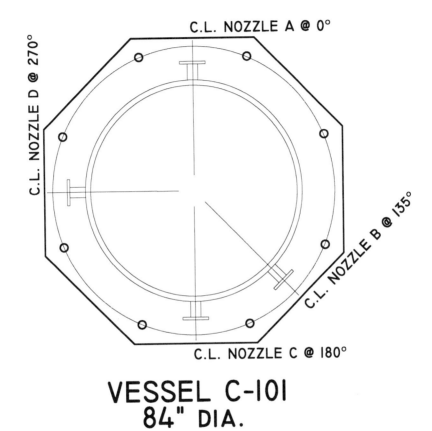

Figure Ex11–5c   Vessel in an octagonal foundation

Open the drawing of the vessel and pump plan, PROJCH11.DWG, the project exercise completed in Chapter 11. Attach the file Ex11-5c as a reference file, with an insertion point of 7'-0",8'-0", a scale factor of 1.0, and a rotation of 0 degrees. The drawing should appear as shown in Figure Ex11–5d. Save the drawing as EX11-5d.

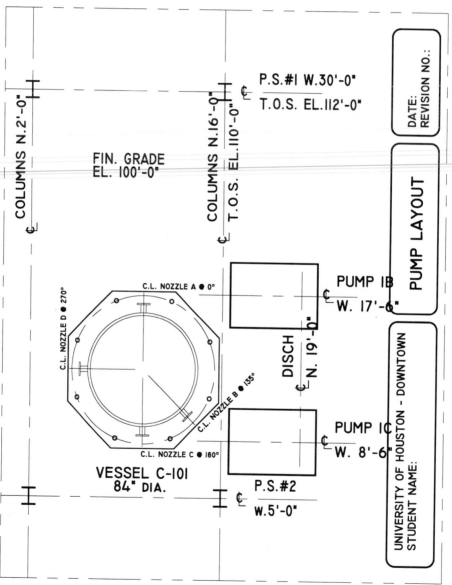

Figure Ex11–5d Layout of the vessel and pump with a vessel in an octagonal foundation

REVIEW QUESTIONS

1. If an externally referenced drawing called "FLOOR.DWG" contains a block called "TABLE" and is permanently bound to the current drawing, the new name of the block is:
   a. FLOOR0TABLE
   b. FLOOR I TABLE
   c. FLOOR$0TABLE
   d. FLOOR_TABLE
   e. FLOOR$ I $TABLE

2. If an externally referenced drawing called "FLOOR.DWG" contains a block called "TABLE" name of the block is listed as:
   a. FLOOR0TABLE
   b. FLOOR I TABLE
   c. FLOOR$0TABLE
   d. FLOOR_TABLE
   e. FLOOR$ I $TABLE

3. The maximum number of files which can be externally referenced into a drawing is:
   a. 32
   b. 1024
   c. 8000
   d. 32000
   e. only limited by memory

4. If you want to retain, from one drawing session to another, any changes you make to the color or visibility of layers in an externally referenced file, the system variable that controls is:
   a. XREFRET
   b. RETXREF
   c. XREFLAYER
   d. VISRETAIN
   e. these changes cannot be saved from one session to another

5. XREF's are converted to blocks if you detach them.
   a. True
   b. False

6. When detaching XREF's from your drawing, it is acceptable to use wild cards to specify which XREF should be detached.
   a. True
   b. False

7. Overlaying XREF's rather than attaching them causes AutoCAD to display the file as a bit map image, rather than a vector based image.
   a. True
   b. False

8. To make a reference file a permanent part of the current drawing database, use the XREF command with the :
   a. Attach option
   b. Bind option
   c. ? option
   d. Reload option
   e. Path option

9. The XREF command is invoked from the toolbar:
   a. Draw
   b. Modify
   c. External Reference
   d. Any of the above
   e. None of the above

10. The Attach option of the XREF command is used to:
    a. bind the external drawing to the current drawing
    b. to attach a new external reference file to the current drawing
    c. reload an external reference drawing
    d. all of the above

11. The following are the dependent symbols that can be made a permanent part of your current drawing, except:
    a. Blocks
    b. Dimstyles
    c. Text Styles
    d. Linetypes
    e. Grid and Snap

12. Including an image file in a drawing will incorporate the image similar to the way a drawing file is merged by using:
    a. INSERT
    b. XREF
    c. WBLOCK

13. Which of the following is not a valid file type to use with the IMAGE command is:
    a. BMP   d. JPG
    b. TIF   e. GIF
    c. WMF

14. Which of the following parameter can be adjusted on a bitmapped image:
    a. Brightness
    b. Contrast
    c. Fade
    d. all of the above
    e. none of the above

CHAPTER

12

DRAWING ENVIRONMENTS

INTRODUCTION

The option to draw in two different environments, model space and paper space, is one the most useful features of AutoCAD. Most of your drafting and design work will be done in the 3D environment of model space, even though your objects may have been drawn only in a two-dimensional plane. Paper space is a 2D environment used for arranging various views of what was drawn in model space and then adding such things as borders, title blocks, notes, and dimensions. Model space (3D) objects can be represented in paper space only as projections on a 2D plane.

After completing this chapter, you will be able to:

✓ Create viewports—Tiled and Untiled (floating)
✓ Set the Tilemode system variable
✓ Use the VPORTS and MVIEW commands
✓ Use the MSPACE and PSPACE commands
✓ Use the VPLAYER (Viewport Layer) command
✓ Set the PSLTSCALE (paper space linetype scaling)
✓ Dimension in model space and paper space
✓ Plot from model space and paper space

VIEWPORTS

The ability to split the display into two or more separate viewports is one of the most useful features of AutoCAD. Multiple viewports divide your drawing screen into rectangles, permitting several different areas for drawing instead of just one. It is like having multiple zoom lens cameras, with each camera being used to look at a different portion of the drawing. You can have up to 32,000 viewports (or cameras) visible at once. You retain your pull-down menus and "Command:" prompt area.

Each viewport maintains a display of the current drawing independent of the display shown by other viewports. You can simultaneously display a viewport showing the entire drawing, and another viewport showing a part of the drawing in greater detail. A view in one viewport can be from a different point of view than those in other viewports. You can draw as well as modify the objects from one viewport to another. For example, three viewports could be used in a 2D drawing, two of them to zoom in on two separate parts of the drawing, showing two widely separated features in great detail on the screen simultaneously, and the third to show the entire drawing (see Figure 12–1). In a 3D drawing, four viewports could be

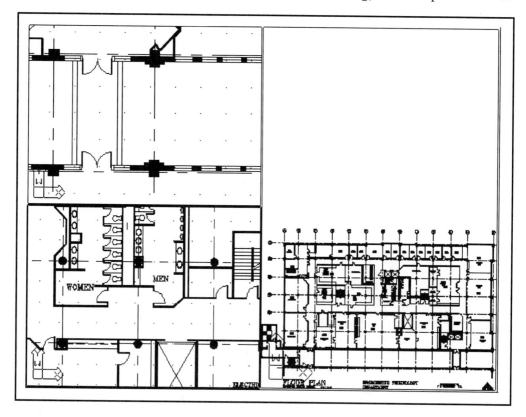

Figure 12–1 Multiple viewports show different parts of the same 2D drawing

used to display simultaneously four views of a wireframe model; top, front, right side, and isometric, as in Figure 12–2.

You can create and manipulate two different types of viewports: tiled viewports and untiled, or overlapping, viewports.

Tiled Viewports

When the TILEMODE system variable is set to 1 (ON), you can divide the graphics area of your display screen into multiple, nonoverlapping (tiled) viewports, as in Figures 12–1 and 12–2. You can create the tiled viewports using the VPORTS command.

You can work in only one viewport at a time. It is considered the current viewport. A viewport is set to current by picking in it with your pointing device. You can even switch viewports in midcommand (except during the ZOOM command). When a viewport is current, its border will be thicker than the other borders. The cursor is active only in the current viewport; when you move your pointing device outside the current viewport, the cursor appears as an arrow pointer.

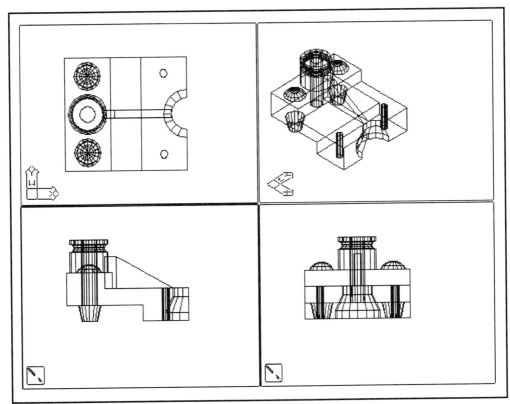

Figure 12–2 Using viewports to show four views simultaneously for a 3D wireframe model

Display commands like ZOOM and PAN and drawing tools like GRID, SNAP, and ORTHO are set independently in each viewport. The most important thing to remember is that the images shown in multiple viewports are all of the same drawing. An object added to or modified in one viewport will affect its image in the other viewports. You are not making copies of your drawing, just viewing its image in different viewports.

When you are working in tiled viewports, visibility of the layers is controlled globally in all the viewports. If you turn off a layer, AutoCAD turns it off in all the viewports. You can work only in the model space environment when you are in tiled viewports.

Untiled Viewports

If the TILEMODE system variable is set to 0 (OFF), you can divide the graphics area of your display screen into multiple, overlapping, contiguous, or separated untiled viewports, as shown in Figure 12–3. You can create untiled viewports by using the MVIEW command.

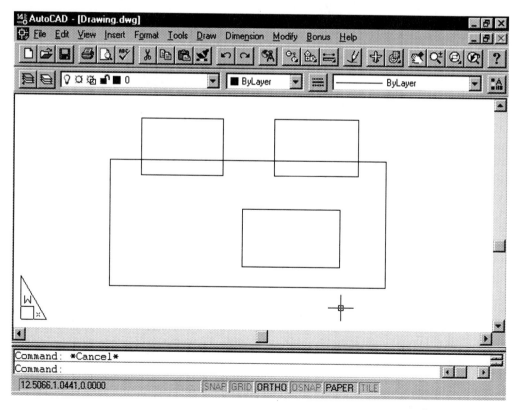

Figure 12–3 When TILEMODE is set to OFF, you can create multiple overlapping viewports

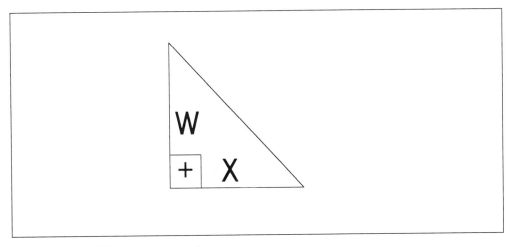

Figure 12–4 The paper space icon

AutoCAD treats an untiled viewport like any other object, such as a line, arc, or text object. You can use any of the standard AutoCAD modify or construction commands, such as MOVE, COPY, STRETCH, SCALE, and ERASE, to manipulate the untiled viewports. For example, you can use the MOVE command to grab one viewport and move it around the screen without affecting other viewports. A viewport can be of any size and can be located anywhere in paper space.

When working in untiled viewports, you can switch back and forth between model space and paper space by using the MSPACE and PSPACE commands, respectively. When you are in model space, you can work in only one viewport at a time, similar to tiled viewports.

When you are working in paper space, the cursor crosshairs span the entire graphics screen and do not change when you position the cursor over a viewport. AutoCAD displays at the bottom of the screen the current environment you are currently working in (MODEL or PAPER), see Figure 12–3. Doubleclick the image tile to switch back and forth between model and paper space. In addition, AutoCAD displays the paper space icon, as shown in Figure 12–4 (unless the icon has been turned off by invoking the UCSICON command).

What is drawn in paper space appears only in untiled viewports. It will disappear if you change to tiled viewports. What is drawn in model space will be seen when you switch to tiled viewports.

By using the VPLAYER command you can control layer visibility by viewport, rather than globally, when working in untiled viewports model space. You can freeze a layer in one viewport while leaving it thawed in another. All the drawing features found in tiled viewports, like the ability to draw from one viewport to another, are possible while working in untiled viewports model space. You cannot use the MVIEW, VPLAYER, MSPACE, and PSPACE commands unless the TILEMODE variable is set to OFF (0).

SETTING THE TILEMODE SYSTEM VARIABLE

The TILEMODE system variable allows you to work on either tiled or untiled viewports when the variable is set to ON (1) or OFF (0), respectively. To change the value of the TILEMODE system variable, type **TILEMODE** at the "Command:" prompt, press Enter or the spacebar, and change the appropriate value.

For example, the following command sequence shows steps to change the TILEMODE system variable from 1 (ON) to 0 (OFF):

```
Command: tilemode
New value for TILEMODE <1>: 0
Command:
```

When you set TILEMODE to 0 (OFF) in a drawing for the first time, AutoCAD switches to paper space, clears the graphics area, and prompts you to create one or more viewports. Since no viewport objects are then in the drawing, objects are not visible until you create at least one viewport. Use the MVIEW command to create one or more viewports. If subsequently you set TILEMODE to 1 (ON) and then to 0 (OFF) again, AutoCAD displays the paper space view that was current before TILEMODE was set to 1 (ON).

You can also change the TILEMODE setting by invoking from:

Pull-down menu	View > Model Space (Tiled) *(to set the TILEMODE system variable to 1)*
	View > Model Space (Floating) *(To set the TILEMODE system variable to 0 and switch to model space)*
	View > Paper Space *(To set the TILEMODE system variable to 0 and switch to paper space)*

CREATING TILED VIEWPORTS

The VPORTS (or VIEWPORTS) command allows you to create tiled viewports. It can be invoked only when TILEMODE is set to 1 (ON). The VPORTS command offers several options for adding, deleting, and joining viewports to the screen display.

Invoke the VPORTS command from:

Pull-down menu	View > Tiled Viewports
Command: prompt	**vports** Enter

AutoCAD prompts:

Command: **vports**
Save/Restore/Delete/Join/SIngle/2/<3>/4: *(select one of the available options)*

Save Option The Save option allows you to save the current viewport configuration. The configuration includes the number and placement of active viewports and their associated settings. You can save any number of configurations with the drawing, to be recalled at any time. When you select this option, AutoCAD prompts:

?/Name for new viewport configuration:

You can use the same naming conventions for your configuration as for layer names. Instead of providing the name, you can respond with **?** to request a list of saved viewport configurations.

Restore Option The Restore option allows you to display a saved viewport configuration. When you select this option, AutoCAD prompts:

?/Name of viewport configuration to restore:

Provide the name of the viewport configuration you want to restore.

Delete Option The Delete option deletes a named viewport configuration. When you select this option, AutoCAD prompts:

?/Name of viewport configuration to delete:

Provide the name of the viewport configuration you want to delete.

Join Option The Join option combines two adjoining viewports into a single viewport. The view for the resulting viewport is inherited from the dominant viewport. When you select this option, AutoCAD prompts:

Select dominant viewport <current>:

You can give a null response to show the current viewport as the dominant viewport, or you can move the cursor to the desired viewport and press the pick button. Once you identify the dominant viewport, then AutoCAD prompts:

Select viewport to join:

Drawing Environments

Move the cursor to the desired viewport to join, and press the pick button. If the two viewports selected are not adjacent or do not form a rectangle, AutoCAD displays an error message and reissues the prompts.

SIngle Option The Single option allows you to make the current viewport the single viewport.

? Option The ? option displays the identification numbers and screen positions of the active viewports. When you select this option, AutoCAD prompts:

Viewport configuration(s) to list <*>:

To list all saved configurations, give a null response. You also can use wild cards to list saved viewport names. All viewports are given an identification number by AutoCAD. This number is independent of any name you might give the viewport configuration. Each viewport is given a coordinate location, with respect to 0.0000,0.0000 as the lower left corner of the graphics area and 1.0000,1.0000 as the upper right corner.

2 Option The 2 option splits the current viewport in half. When you select this option, AutoCAD prompts:

Horizontal/<Vertical>:

You can select a horizontal or a vertical split, as shown in Figure 12–5. Vertical is the default.

3 Option The 3 option divides the current viewport into three viewports. This is the default option. When you select this option, AutoCAD prompts:

Horizontal/Vertical/Above/Below/Left/<Right>:

You can select the Horizontal or Vertical option to split the current viewport into thirds by horizontal or vertical division, as shown in Figure 12–6. The other options let you split into two small ones and one large one, specifying whether the large is to be placed above, below, or to the left or right (see Figure 12–6).

Figure 12–5 Using the 2 option to split a current viewport in half by vertical or horizontal division

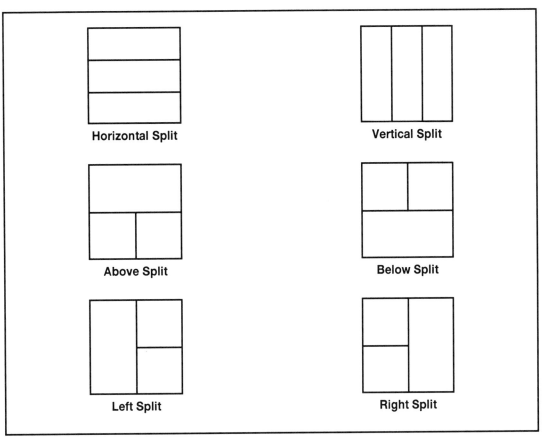

Figure 12-6 Using the 3 option to split a current viewport into various three-way divisions

4 Option The 4 option divides the current viewport into four viewports of equal size both horizontally and vertically, as shown in Figure 12–7.

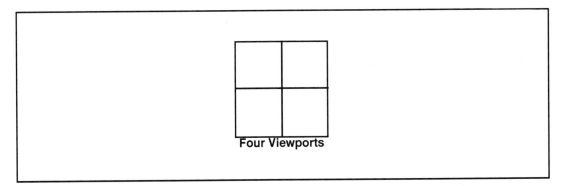

Figure 12-7 Using the 4 option to split a current viewport into four viewports of equal size

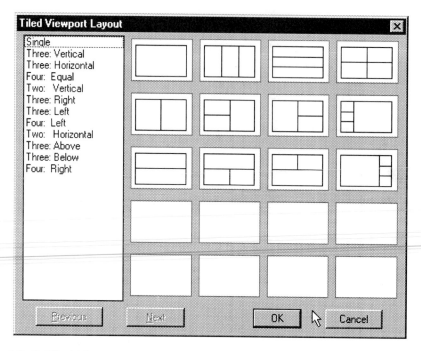

Figure 12–8 Tiled Viewport Layout icon menu

> **NOTE:** You can also select the viewports layout from an icon menu. Select Layout. . . located in the Tiled Viewports submenu from the pull-down menu View to display the Tiled Viewport Layout icon menu. The icon menu is displayed with various options to select layout configuration or tiled viewports (see Figure 12–8).

When you are working in multiple viewports, the REDRAW and REGEN commands will affect only the current viewport. To redraw or regenerate all the viewports simultaneously, use the REDRAWALL or REGENALL commands, respectively.

CREATING UNTILED VIEWPORTS

The MVIEW command is used to create new untiled viewports, to turn their display on or off, and to instruct AutoCAD to perform hidden-line removal on a viewport's contents during a paper space plot. This command can be invoked only when TILEMODE is set to OFF (0).

Invoke the MVIEW command from:

Pull-down menu	View > Floating Viewports
Command: prompt	**mview** Enter

AutoCAD prompts:

Command: **mview**
ON/OFF/Hideplot/Fit/2/3/4/Restore/<First Point>: *(select one of the available options)*

First Point Option The First Point option lets you create a single new viewport by specifying two diagonal data points. Specify two points to define a rectangular boundary, and the viewport is created to fill that area.

ON Option The ON option turns on a model view inside the viewport. When you create a viewport, the model view is turned on by default. If it is on, AutoCAD automatically regenerates. When you select this option, AutoCAD prompts you to select the viewport to turn on.

OFF Option The OFF option turns off a model view inside the viewport. This clears the model space view and does not regenerate it again until the model view inside the viewport is turned on again. By turning the model view off, you can move, resize, and otherwise modify the viewport in paper space. When you select this option, AutoCAD prompts you to select the viewport to turn off.

Hideplot Option The Hideplot option instructs AutoCAD to turn on or off the hidden-line removal on the contents of the selected viewport when plotting in Paper Space. When you select this option, AutoCAD prompts for on or off. Then, AutoCAD prompts you to select the viewport.

Fit Option The Fit option creates a single viewport to fill the display. This can be convenient when you simply want the new viewport to fill the available display area.

2 Option The 2 option lets you create two viewports within a rectangular area you specify. When you select this option, AutoCAD prompts:

Horizontal/<Vertical>:

You can divide the display horizontally or vertically. Vertical is the default.

3 Option The 3 option lets you create three viewports in a rectangular area. When you select this option, AutoCAD prompts:

Horizontal/Vertical/Above/Below/Left/<Right>:

You can select the Horizontal or Vertical option; AutoCAD creates three viewports stacked on top of each other or side by side. The other options let you create two small ones and one large one, specifying whether the large one is to be placed above, below, or to the left, or right of the two small ones.

4 Option The 4 option lets you create four viewports in a rectangular area, either by specifying the area or by fitting the four viewports to the display.

SWITCHING BETWEEN MODEL SPACE AND
PAPER SPACE ENVIRONMENTS

The MSPACE command lets you switch from paper space to model space. The TILEMODE system variable must be set to 0 (OFF) before this command can be invoked. In order for AutoCAD to switch from paper space to model space, at least one viewport must be on and active.

Invoke the MSPACE command from:

Pull-down menu	View > Model Space (Floating)
Command: prompt	**mspace** Enter

AutoCAD switches to model space. If at least one viewport is ON and active, AutoCAD switches to the last active viewport.

The PSPACE command lets you switch from model space to paper space. The TILEMODE system variable must be set to 0 (OFF) before this command can be invoked.

Invoke the PSPACE command from:

Pull-down menu	View > Paper Space
Command: prompt	**pspace** Enter

AutoCAD switches from model space to paper space.

CONTROLLING THE VISIBILITY OF LAYERS
WITHIN VIEWPORTS

As described earlier, the VPLAYER (short for ViewPort LAYER) command controls the visibility of layers in a single viewport or in a set of viewports. This enables you to select a viewport and freeze a layer in it while still allowing the contents of that layer to appear in another viewport. See Figure 12–9, in which two viewports contain the same view of the drawing, but in one viewport the layer containing the dimensioning is on, and in another it is off by using the VPLAYER

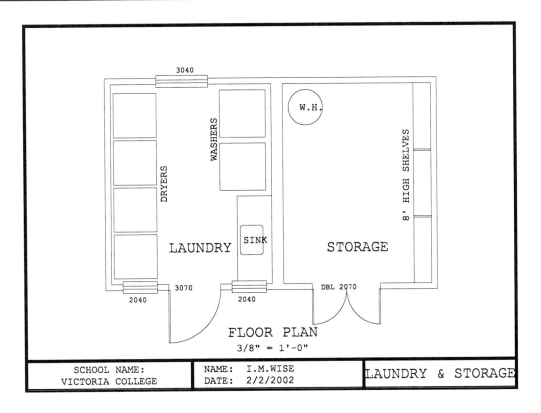

Figure 12–9 One viewport with DIMLAYER ON and another with DIMLAYER OFF

command. To invoke the **VPLAYER** command, the TILEMODE system variable must be set to 0 (OFF).

The VPLAYER command can be invoked from either model space or paper space. Several options in the VPLAYER command require you to select one or more viewports in which to make your changes. AutoCAD prompts:

All/Select/<Current>:

To accept the default option, you have to be in model space; AutoCAD applies changes in the current viewport. If you choose the **Select** option and are in model space, AutoCAD temporarily switches to paper space so you can select a viewport. The **All** option applies your changes to all paper space viewports.

If you set TILEMODE to 1 (ON), the global layer settings take precedence over any VPLAYER settings.

Invoke the VPLAYER command from:

Command: prompt	**vplayer** Enter

AutoCAD prompts:

```
Command: vplayer
?/Freeze/Thaw/Reset/Newfrz/Vpvisdflt: (select one of the available options)
```

? Option The ? option displays the names of layers in a specific viewport that are frozen. When you select this option, AutoCAD prompts:

```
Select a viewport:
```

Pick a single viewport. If you are in model space, AutoCAD switches temporarily to paper space to let you select a viewport.

Freeze Option The Freeze option allows you to specify one or more layers to freeze in the selected viewport. When you select this option, AutoCAD prompts:

```
Layer(s) to freeze:
```

You can respond to this prompt with a single layer name, a list of layer names separated by commas, or any valid wild-card specification. Then AutoCAD prompts:

```
All/Select/<current>:
```

Select the viewport(s) in which to freeze the selected layers.

Thaw Option The Thaw option allows you to specify one or more layers to thaw that were frozen by the VPLAYER command in selected viewports. When you select this option, AutoCAD prompts:

```
Layer(s) to thaw:
```

You can respond to this prompt with a single layer name, a list of layer names separated by commas, or any valid wild-card specification. Then AutoCAD prompts:

```
All/Select/<current>:
```

Select the viewport(s) in which to thaw the selected layers.

Reset Option The Reset option allows you to restore the default visibility setting for a layer in a given viewport. The default visibility is controlled by the Vpvisdflt option (explained shortly). When you select this option, AutoCAD prompts:

```
Layer(s) to Reset:
```

You can respond to this prompt with a single layer name, a list of layer names separated by commas, or any valid wild-card specification. Then AutoCAD prompts:

All/Select/<current>:

Select the viewport(s) in which to reset the selected layers.

Newfrz (New Freeze) Option The New Freeze option allows you to create new layers that are frozen in all viewports. If you create a new viewport, the layers that are created by the Newfrz option will be frozen by default. (The layer can be thawed in the chosen viewport by using the Thaw option). When you select this option, AutoCAD prompts:

New viewport frozen layer name(s):

You can respond to this prompt with a single layer name or a list of layer names separated by commas.

Vpvisdflt (Viewport Visibility Default) Option The Viewport Visibility Default option allows you to set a default visibility for one or more existing layers. This default determines the frozen/thawed state of an existing layer in newly created viewports. When you select this option, AutoCAD prompts:

Layer name(s) to change default viewport visibility:

You can respond to this prompt with a single layer name, a list of layer names separated by commas, or any wild-card specification. Then AutoCAD prompts:

Change default viewport visibility to Frozen/<Thawed>:

You can respond to this prompt with a null response to set the default visibility to thaw, or enter **F** to set the default visibility to freeze.

You can control the visibility of layers in viewports from the Layer & Linetype Properties dialog box. Invoke the LAYER command, and AutoCAD displays the Layer & Linetype Properties dialog box, similar to Figure 12–10.

The Freeze in Current Viewports column (fourth column from the left) toggles between freezing and thawing of selected layer(s). Similarly, the Freeze in New Viewports column (fifth column from left) toggles between freezing and thawing of selected layer(s) for new viewports.

In Figure 12–10, the layers Dim, Object, and Text are frozen in the current viewport, and Elevation and Hidden are frozen in all the new viewports.

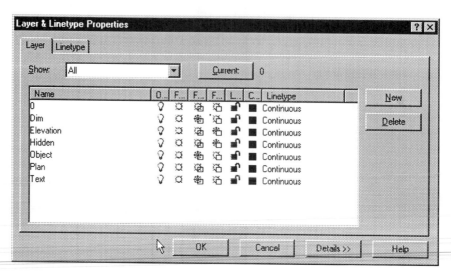

Figure 12–10 Layer & Linetype Properties dialog box

SETTING PAPER SPACE LINETYPE SCALING

Linetype dash lengths and the space lengths between dots and/or dashes are based on the drawing units of the model or paper space in which the objects were created. They can be scaled globally by the LTSCALE factor, as explained earlier. If you want to display objects in viewports at different scales when TILEMODE is set to OFF (0), the linetype objects by default would be scaled to model space rather than paper space. However, by setting paper space linetype scaling (PSLTSCALE) to 1, dash and space lengths are based on paper space drawing units, including the linetype objects that are drawn in model space. For example, a single linetype definition with a dash length of 0.30 and displayed in several viewports with different zoom factors, would be displayed in paper space with dashes of length 0.30, regardless of the scale of the viewpoint in which it is being displayed (PSLTSCALE set to 1).

Invoke the PSLTSCALE command from:

Command: prompt	**psltscale** Enter

AutoCAD prompts:

Command: **psltscale**
New value for PSLTSCALE <current>: *(specify the new value, or press* Enter *to accept the current value)*

> **NOTE:** When you change PSLTSCALE value to 1, the linetype objects in the viewport are not automatically regenerated. Use the REGEN or REGENALL command to update the linetypes in the viewports.

DIMENSIONING IN MODEL SPACE AND PAPER SPACE

Dimensioning can be done in both model space and paper space. There are no restrictions placed on the dimensioning commands by the current mode. It is advisable to draw associative dimensions in model space, since AutoCAD places the defining points of the dimension in the space where the dimension is drawn. If the model geometry is modified with a command such as STRETCH, EXTEND, or TRIM, the dimensions are updated automatically. In contrast, if the dimensions are drawn in paper space, the paper space dimension does not change if the model geometry is modified.

For dimensioning in model space, the DIMSCALE factor should be set to 0.0. This causes AutoCAD to compute a scale factor based on the scaling between paper space and the current model space viewport. If dimensioning that describes model geometry should be created in paper space, then the DIMLFAC dimension variable scale factor should be based on the model space viewport. It is important that the length scaling be set to a value that is appropriate for the view being dimensioned.

PLOTTING FROM MODEL SPACE AND PAPER SPACE

In model space, the plot is based on how much of the drawing in the current viewport falls within the plot option chosen. In paper space, the plot is based on how much of the drawing, including any viewports and their contents, falls within the plot option chosen.

Following are the Ten Golden Steps for plotting a drawing from Paper Space at 1=1 scale after drawing the model in model space to real-world dimensions.

1. Set the Limits in paper space equal to the plotter's maximum available plot area for the given sheet size.

2. After setting the Limits, use the ZOOM All Command in paper space.

3. Set appropriate Grid and Snap values (this may be different from the values in model space).

4. Insert a border and title block, if you already have one, at 1=1, scale, or attach it as an external reference. If you have border and title blocks, draw the appropriate border and title on its own layer so you can freeze it as you work on your drawing.

5. Create as many viewports as you need, using the MVIEW command on a separate layer for the various views and details you want to plot.

6. If necessary, resize, stretch, and move the viewports to be plotted to match your planned arrangement in the sheet.

7. Enter model space to create or modify your drawing. You can control the layers independently in each viewport by the VPLAYER command.

8. Establish the proper model-to-paper display units scale for each viewport. This can be done with the ZOOM XP command. Entering a scale factor followed by **XP** will cause the image to display relative to your paper space units. Typing **1/24XP** or **0.04167XP** (1/24=0.04167) will display an image to a scale of 1/2" = 1'-0", which is the same as 1:24 or 1/24. You determine the ZOOM XP scale factor as a reciprocal of the plot scale you would use if you plotted from model space when TILEMODE is set to 1 (ON). For example, to display an image to plot scale 1/4" = 1'-0", you would enter a scale factor of **1/48** followed by **XP** to cause the image to display relative to your paper space units. See Table 12–1 for factors for the XP option to various plotting scale factors.

   After you use ZOOM XP, be careful not to do other Zooms in or out in model space. Panning is safe and good for fine-tuning the view. The important thing to remember is that it is the viewport display that is scaled, not the plot.

9. Enter paper space. Add any annotations or dimensions you wish to do in paper space. Fill in your title block information.

10. Plot at a scale of 1:1.

> **NOTE:** Partially visible viewports are not plotted. Viewports that have been turned off are not plotted. The "remove hidden lines" option applies only to model space objects, and each viewport is processed for hidden lines according to its own HIDEPLOT setting.

Table 12–1 Typical Architectural Display Scaling for Paper Space Viewports

PLOTTING SCALE	DISPLAY FACTOR
3" = 1'	ZOOM 1/4XP
3/4" = 1'	ZOOM 1/16XP
1/2" = 1'	ZOOM 1/24XP
3/8" = 1'	ZOOM 1/32XP
1/4" = 1'	ZOOM 1/48XP
1/8" = 1'	ZOOM 1/96XP

EXERCISES 12–1 THROUGH 12–3

Exercise 12–1

Plot the drawing from Exercise 4–2 (chapter 4) by displaying the drawing to 3/16" = 1'-0" in paper space and plotting to 1=1 (what you see is what you get) on an A-size sheet via the following steps.

Step 1   Open drawing *EX4-2.DWG*. Set TILEMODE to 0 to get into paper space.

Step 2   Set the Limits in paper space with the lower left corner at 0,0 and the upper right corner at 12,9.

Step 3   Set the Grid and Snap resolutions to 0.5 and 0.25, respectively.

Step 4   Create a border and title block (size A), as shown in Figure Ex12–1.

UNIVERSITY OF HOUSTON-D
STUDENT NAME:

STEEL PLAN

DATE:

Figure Ex12–1 Title Block

Step 5   Create a viewport using the MVIEW command with a size of 7.5" × 4.5".

Step 6   Enter model space using the MSPACE command.

Step 7 Set the display of the model as shown in Figure Ex12–1a by using the ZOOM command to a scale factor of 1/64XP, and save the drawing as *EX12-1.DWG*

NOTE: Do *not* zoom in or out in model space after setting the display to the appropriate display factor.

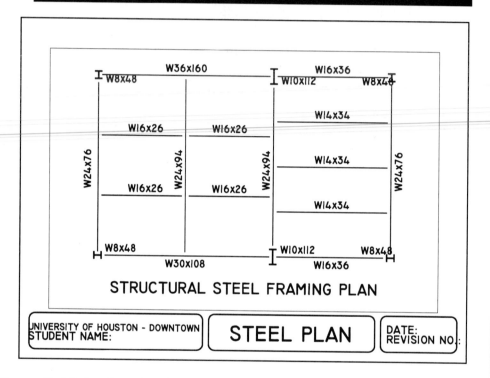

Figure Ex12–1a Completed drawing

Step 8 Enter paper space using the PSPACE command.

Step 9 Plot the drawing to a scale of 1=1 on an A-size sheet.

Exercise 12–2

Plot the drawing from Exercise 11–5 (Chapter 11) by displaying the drawing to 1/2" = 1'-0" in paper space and plotting to 1=1 (what you see is what you get) on a C-size sheet in portrait mode via the following steps.

Step 1 Open drawing *EX11-5.DWG.* Set TILEMODE to 0 to get into paper space.

Step 2 Set the Limits in paper space with the lower left corner at 0,0 and the upper right corner at 18,24.

Step 3 Set the Grid and Snap resolutions to 2 and 1, respectively. Draw the title block.

Step 4 Create a viewport using the MVIEW command with a size of 15" × 21".

Step 5 Enter model space using the MSPACE command.

Step 6 Set the display of the model as shown in Figure Ex12–2 by using the ZOOM command to a scale factor of 1/24XP.

NOTE: Do *not* zoom in or out in model space after setting the display to the appropriate display factor.

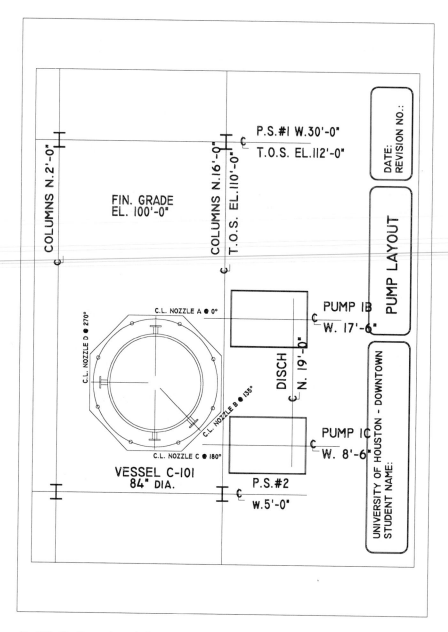

Figure Ex12–2 Completed drawing

Step 7   Enter paper space using the PSPACE command.

Step 8   Plot the drawing to a scale of 1=1 on an C-size sheet in portrait mode.

Exercise 12–3

Plot the drawing from Exercise 11–2 (Chapter 11) by displaying the drawing to 3/8" = 1'-0" in paper space and plotting to 1=1 (what you see is what you get) on a B-size sheet via the following steps.

Step 1   Open drawing *EX11-2.DWG*. Set TILEMODE to 0 to get into paper space.

Step 2   Set the Limits in paper space with the lower left corner at 0,0 and the upper right corner at 18,12.

Step 3   Set the Grid and Snap resolutions to 1.0 and 0.5, respectively.

Step 4   Create a title block.

Step 5   Create a viewport using the MVIEW command with a size of 15" × 9".

Step 6   Change to model space using the MSPACE command.

Step 7   Set the display of the model as shown in Figure Ex12–3 by using the ZOOM command to a scale factor of 1/32XP.

> **NOTE:** Do *not* zoom in or out in model space after setting the display to the appropriate display factor.

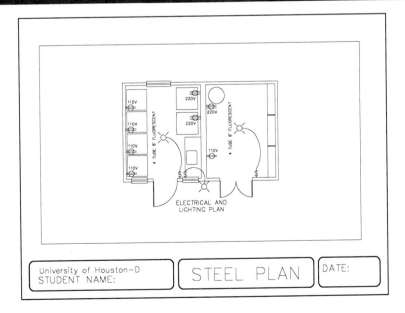

Figure Ex12–3 Completed drawing

Step 8   Enter paper space using the PSPACE command.

Step 9   Plot the drawing to a scale of 1=1 on a C-size sheet in portrait mode.

Step 10   Attach drawing *EX11-5.DWG*. Set the layer that contains the border and title block to OFF.

Step 11   Change the drawing name to "Lighting/Electrical."

REVIEW QUESTIONS

1. When working in Paperspace, it is possible to object snap to objects which are drawn in Modelspace.
   - a. True
   - b. False

2. To force a redraw of all visible viewports on the display screen, use:
   - a. REDRAW
   - b. REGEN
   - c. REDRAWALL
   - d. ZOOMALL
   - e. none of the above

3. To set up multiple viewports windows, use:
   - a. VPORT
   - b. VPORTS
   - c. VIEWPORT
   - d. VIEWPORTS
   - e. none of the above

4. Paperspace allows:
   - a. display of details at different scales on the same drawing
   - b. plotting of multiple viewports
   - c. insertion of such items as title blocks for annotating drawings
   - d. all of the above

5. To create viewports in Paperspace, use:
   - a. VPORT   d. MVIEWS
   - b. VPORTS   e. none of the above
   - c. MVIEW

6. While in Paperspace, to make a layer visible in one viewport, but invisible in all other viewports, use:
   - a. LAYER
   - b. VPLAYER
   - c. MVIEW
   - d. VIEWPORTS
   - e. none of the above

7. When TILEMODE is set to zero, you
   - a. can go back and forth between Paperspace and Modelspace
   - b. can use the MVIEW command
   - c. can use the VPLAYER command
   - d. all of the above

8. If you want to display an object in two untiled viewports at different scales, but want the dashed lines within each viewport to plot with the same dash lengths, you should set
   a. LTSCALE=0
   b. PSLTSCALE=0
   c. PSLTSCALE=1
   d. LTSCALE=-1
   e. none of the above

9. To scale the objects contained in a Paperspace viewport, from floating Modelspace use the ZOOM command with what option?
   a. All
   b. Extents
   c. XP
   d. Vmax
   f. none of the above

10. You can create and manipulate viewports when TILEMODE is set to?
    a. tiled
    b. untiled
    c. A and B
    d. none of the above

11. The number of viewports is limited by the size of your monitor.
    a. True
    b. False

12. The most logical place to draw a border is in:
    a. Modelspace
    b. Paperspace

13. When you switch from tiled modelspace to untiled modelspace, AutoCAD will automatically create a viewport if none currently exist.
    a. True
    b. False

UTILITY COMMANDS

. . . .

INTRODUCTION

After completing this chapter, you will be able to:

✓ Use the geometric calculator to perform geometric calculations
✓ Manage named objects
✓ Delete unused named objects
✓ Use the utility display commands
✓ Use object properties
✓ Use X, Y, Z filters
✓ Use the Shell command
✓ Set up a drawing by means of the MVSETUP utility
✓ Use the Time and Audit commands
✓ Customize AutoCAD settings
✓ Export and Import data
✓ Use object linking and embedding
✓ Use Internet utilities

GETTING TO KNOW THE GEOMETRIC CALCULATOR (CAL)

The CAL is an on-line calculator that evaluates real, integer, and vector expressions. The CAL command, when entered at the "Command:" prompt (or 'cal transparently when prompted for input) switches you to the calculator mode. When the "Command:" prompt is preceded by double angle brackets (>>), AutoCAD is awaiting input, which must be in the acceptable calculator format. For example, you can solve a simple algebraic equation by entering the following:

```
Command: cal
Initializing. . .
>>Expression:  A=pi*4^2 Enter
```

producing the following response:

```
50.2655
```

This sequence might be used to derive the area of a circle with a radius of 4. The variable A and the equal sign are not required to arrive at the solution. Entering **pi*4^2** will suffice. However, the **A=** serves to give a user-defined name (the letter A in this case) to a variable so that the result of the equation can be set as the value of the named variable for later use in AutoLISP or in another calculator expression. In the built-in calculator, "pi" has been assigned a preset value of approximately 3.141592654, which is the ratio of a circle's circumference to its diameter. The "*" and the "^" are the symbols for multiply and exponent, respectively, as is noted later in the listing of arithmetic operators you may use in calculator expressions.

You may also enter the built-in calculator transparently (while in the middle of another command), as shown here during the LINE command (see Figure 13–1):

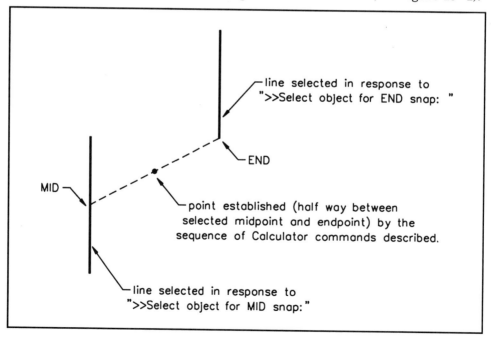

Figure 13–1 Using the CAL command transparently during the LINE command

Command: **line**
From point: **'cal**
>>Expression: **(mid+end)/2**
>>Select object for MID snap: *(pick one line)*
>>Select object for END snap: *(pick other line)*
To point: (Enter)

This expression causes AutoCAD to pause while the user selects points by object snapping to a midpoint and an endpoint. Then AutoCAD uses the midpoint between those two points as the starting point of the line to be drawn.

Responses to the ">>Expression:" and other calculator (with leading >>'s) prompts vary according to the desired function.

In addition to using CAL (and 'CAL transparently) while in AutoCAD, you can use CAL as an operator within an AutoLISP expression, followed by a calculator expression enclosed in double quotes.

CAL can be considered an AutoLISP subroutine with an argument of a calculator expression-string. In the following example, CAL finds the midpoint between two other midpoints of parallel and equal-length lines 1 and 2 (see Figure 13-2).

Command: **(setq pt1 (cal "(mid+mid)/2"))**
>>Select object for MID snap: *(pick one line)*
>>Select object for MID snap: *(pick other line)*
(4.5 5.0 0.0)

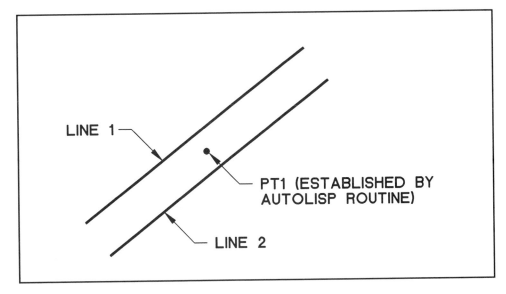

Figure 13-2 CAL finds the midpoint between two other midpoints parallel and equal-length lines 1 and 2

> **NOTE:** The AutoLISP expression works only if the calculator program has been loaded. This is done as follows:
>
> Command: **(xload "cal")**

Things you can do directly or interactively (with AutoLISP) through this programmable calculator include the following:

- Use expressions similar to common algebra to solve equations.
- Name and store values directly (or indirectly through expressions) to variables for later use in expressions, by AutoLISP or in AutoCAD commands.
- Derive information about the existing geometry, or use available data to generate or analyze geometric constructs such as points, vectors, components (x, y, and z coordinates) of a point, coordinate systems, and axes.
- Apply Object Snap modes.

Notations and Format

Calculator expressions are entered in a format similar to algebra, known as *infix notation*. Operational precedences are as follows:

1. Left to right for operators of equal precedence
2. Parentheses, from innermost out
3. Exponents first; multiplication and division second; addition and subtraction last

Numeric operators that can be used are:

+	add
-	subtract
*	multiply
/	divide
^	raise to a power
[ ]	signifies expression

Vector operators that can be used are:

+	add vectors
-	subtract vectors
*	multiply a vector by a real number or scaler product of vectors
/	divide a vector by a real number
&	vector product of vectors
[ ]	signifies expression

Point/vector operators and symbols that can be used are:

[ ] encloses point or vector

, separates coordinate values

< precedes angle

@ precedes distance

* denotes WCS (overrides UCS)

Architectural distances can be entered as either feet'-inches" or feet'inches".

Angles can be entered in degrees/minutes/seconds as degrees d, minutes', seconds", radians r, or gradians g. Degrees must be entered as 0d if the angle in d/m/s is less than one degree.

Points and vectors are entered by enclosing the coordinate values in square brackets, separated by commas. Zero values can be omitted as long as the commas are there. For example, the following values are valid point/vectors:

[,,]   equals   [0,0,0]

[8,9,]   equals   [8,9,0]

[,,7]   equals   [0,0,7]

Coordinate systems can be entered in the following formats:

System	Format	Example
polar	=[dist<angle]	[7<45]
cylindrical	=[dist<angle,z]	[3<0.57r,1.0]
spherical	=[dist<angle1,angle2]	[7<30<60]
relative	=[@x,y,z]	[@1.0,2.5,3.75]
WCS	=[*x,y,z]	[*5,6,20]

Conversion of point/vectors between the User Coordinate System and the World Coordinate System can be achieved by the following functions:

W2U converts from the WCS to the UCS

U2W converts from the UCS to the WCS

A point/vector expression can include arithmetic operators, as the following example shows:

[4+3<45]
[3<3.14/6,0.5*2]

Other point/vector operators include the following:

sin, asin	sine and arcsine of angle
cos, acos	cosine and arccosine of angle
tang, atan	tangent and arctangent of angle
ln	natural log of the number
log	base-10 log of the number
exp	natural exponent of the number
exp10	base-10 exponent of the number
sqr, sqrt	square and square root
abs	absolute value
round	number rounded to nearest integer
trunc	integer with decimal portion removed
r2d	converts angle in radians to degrees
d2r	converts angle in degrees to radians
pi	quotient of circumference divided by diameter
vec	obtains the vector between two points
vec1	obtains a unit vector between two points

Coordinate values of point/vectors can be obtained singly and in pairs by using one of the following operators:

xyof(point)	returns new point with x and y coordinates of point
xzof(point)	returns new point with x and z coordinates of point
yzof(point)	returns new point with y and z coordinates of point
xof(point)	returns new point with x coordinate of point
yof(point)	returns new point with y coordinate of point
zof(point)	returns new point with z coordinate of point
rxof(point)	returns real that is x coordinate of point
ryof(point)	returns real that is y coordinate of point
rzof(point)	returns real that is z coordinate of point

Cur The cur command pauses and prompts the user to pick a point with the cursor, using that point in the expression.

@ The @ symbol causes the last point to be used in the expression. This is similar to the relative coordinate method of specifying points.

Object Snap Using the first three letters of any of the Object Snap modes in an expression causes AutoCAD to pause and prompt the user for a point subject to the Object Snap mode specified.

Finding Points You can obtain a point on a line by entering the two endpoints and either a distance or a scaler value, as follows:

> **pld(pt1,pt2,distance)** returns a point that is the given distance from pt1 in the direction of pt2 from pt1

> **pld([1,2,3], [5,5,3],3.5)** obtains pt3, as shown in Figure 13–3.

> **plt(pt1,pt2,proportion)** returns a point that is in the direction of pt2 from pt1; and its distance from pt1 will be the product of the proportion multiplied by the distance between pt1 and pt2

> **plt(pt1,pt2, 0.5)** obtains pt 3, as shown in Figure 13–4.

> **plt(pt1, pt2, 7/8)** obtains pt3, as shown in Figure 13–5.

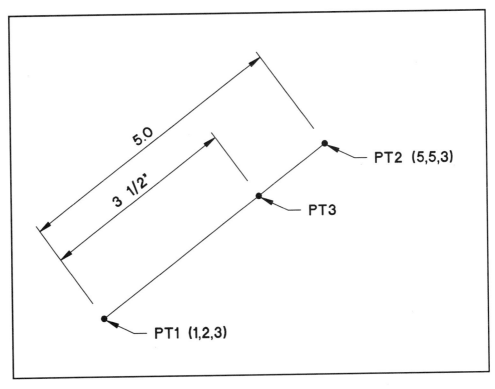

Figure 13–3 Obtaining a point on a line by entering the two endpoints

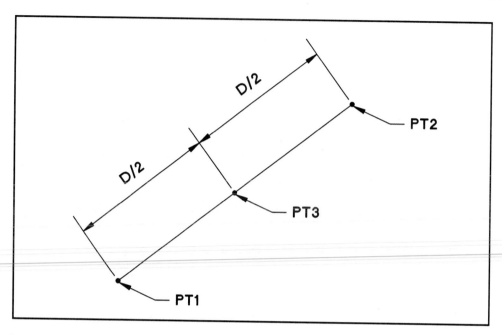

Figure 13–4 Obtaining a point on a line by entering the two endpoints and a distance

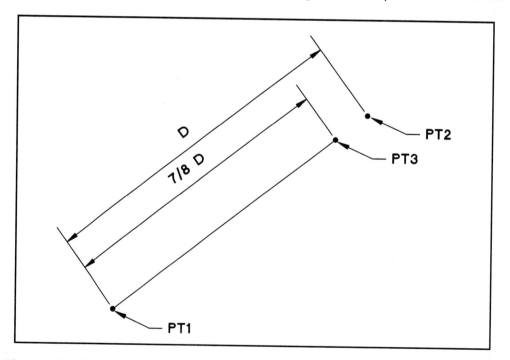

Figure 13–5 Obtaining a point on a line by entering the two endpoints and a scaler value

Additional Geometric Functions

Special points, vectors, distances, radii, and angles can be derived by using the calculator functions described in this section.

Rotation of a point about an axis.

> **rot(p,origin,angle)**   returns the point *p* rotated *ang* angle about an axis through the origin in the *y* direction, as shown in Figure 13–6.

> **rot(p,Axpt1,Axpt2,ang)**   returns the point *p* rotated *ang* angle about an axis through Axpt1 and Axpt2. as shown in Figure 13–7.

Intersection Point **Ille(pt1,pt2)** returns the distance between points pt1 and pt2.

> **dpl(pt1,pt2,pt3)**   returns the distance (shortest) between point pt1 and a line through pt2 and pt3

> **dpp(pt1,pt2,pt3,pt4)**   returns the distance (shortest) between point pt1 and a plane defined by the three points pt2, pt3, and pt4

Radius Rad pauses for the user to select an arc, circle, or 2D polyline arc segment and returns its radius.

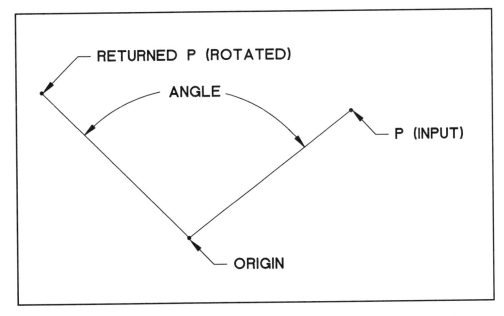

Figure 13–6 Rotation of a point about an axis through the origin in the y direction

Utility Commands

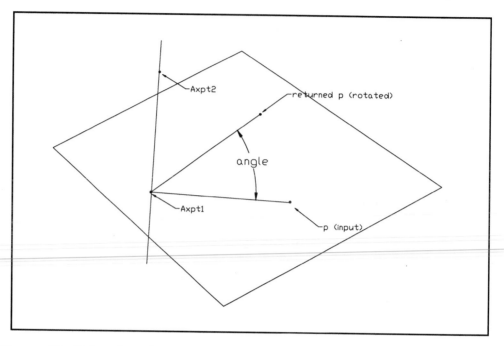

Figure 13–7 Rotation of a point about an axis through Axpt1 and Axpt2

Angle Ang(v) returns the angle between the X axis and a line defined by the vector **v**.

> **ang(pt1,pt2)**   returns the angle between the X axis and a line defined by points pt1 and pt2

> **ang(apex,pt1,pt2)**   returns the angle between lines defined by apex to pt1 and apex to pt2

> **ang(apex,pt1,pt2,pt3)**   returns the angle between lines defined by apex to pt1 and apex to pt2 and measured counterclockwise about the axis defined by apex to pt3

Normal Vector

> **nor**   returns the unit normal vector (3D) of a selected arc, circle, or polyline arc segment

> **nor(v)**   returns the unit normal vector (2D) to the vector **v**

> **nor(pt1,pt2)**   returns the unit normal vector (2D) to the line through pt1 and pt2

> **nor(pt1,pt2,pt3)**   returns the unit normal vector (3D) to the plane defined by the three points pt1, pt2, and pt3

Shortcut Operations

Following are the shortened versions of calculator operators:

dee	=	dist(end,end)
ille	=	ill(end,end,end,end)
mee	=	(end+end)/2
nee	=	nor(end,end)
vee	=	vec(end,end)
vee1	=	vec1(end,end)

MANAGING NAMED OBJECTS

The RENAME command allows you to change the names of blocks, dimension styles, layers, linetypes, text styles, views, User Coordinate Systems, or viewport configurations.

Invoke the RENAME command from:

Command: prompt	**rename** Enter

AutoCAD prompts:

Command: **rename**
Block/Dimstyle/LAyer/LType/Style/Ucs/VIew/VPort: *(select one of the available options to rename)*
Old (object) name: *(specify the old name)*
New (object) name: *(specify the new name)*

Except for the layer named 0 and the linetype named Continuous, you can change the name of any of the named objects.

You can also rename the named objects from the Rename dialog box. To open the Rename dialog box, invoke the DDRENAME command from:

Pull-down menu	Format > Rename...
Command: prompt	**ddrename** Enter

AutoCAD displays the Rename dialog box, similar to Figure 13–8.

In the **Named Objects** list box, select the object name you want to change. The **Items** list box displays the names of all objects that can be renamed. To change the object's name, pick the name in the Items list box or type it into the **Old Name:** edit

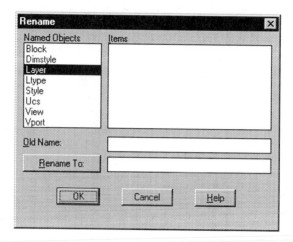

Figure 13–8 Rename dialog box

box. Enter the new name in the **Rename To:** edit box, and select the **Rename To:** button to update the object's name in the Items list box. To close the dialog box, choose the **OK** button.

DELETING UNUSED NAMED OBJECTS

The PURGE command is used to delete selectively any unused named objects.

Invoke the PURGE command from:

Pull-down menu	File > Drawing Utilities > Purge
Command: prompt	**purge** Enter

AutoCAD prompts:

Command: **purge**
Purge unused Blocks/Dimstyles/LAyers/LTypes/SHapes/STyles/APpids/
    Mlinestyles/All: *(select one of the available options to purge)*
Names to purge <*>: *(specify the names of the objects to purge, or with wild-
    card characters specify the objects to purge)*
Verify each name to be purged? <Y>: *(press Enter for AutoCAD to prompt for
    verification of each symbol name displayed before it is purged, or enter n,
    for not to purge each symbol name without verification)*

Depending on the response, AutoCAD prompts for verification of each symbol before it is purged.

The PURGE command removes only one level of reference. For instance, if a block has nested blocks, the PURGE command removes the outer block definition only. To remove the second-, third-, or deeper-level blocks within blocks, you must repeat the PURGE command until there are no referenced objects. You can use the PURGE command at any time during a drawing session.

Individual shapes are part of a *.SHX* file. They cannot be renamed, but references to those that are not being used can be purged. Views, User Coordinate Systems, and viewport configurations cannot be purged, but the commands that manage them provide options to delete those that are not being used.

COMMAND MODIFIER—MULTIPLE

MULTIPLE is not a command, but when used with another AutoCAD command, it causes automatic recalling of that command when it is completed. You must press [Esc] to terminate this repeating process. Here is an example of using this modifier to cause automatic repeating of the ARC command:

Command: **multiple arc**

You can use the MULTIPLE command modifier with any of the draw, modify, and inquiry commands. PLOT, however, will ignore the MULTIPLE command modifier.

UTILITY DISPLAY COMMANDS

The utility display commands include VIEW, REGENAUTO, DRAGMODE, and BLIPMODE.

Saving Views

The VIEW command allows you to give a name to the display in the current viewport and have it saved as a view. You can recall a view later by using the VIEW command and responding with the name of the view desired. This is useful for moving back quickly to needed areas in the drawing without having to resort to zoom and pan.

Invoke the VIEW command from:

Command: prompt	view [Enter]

AutoCAD prompts:

Command: **view**
?/Delete/Restore/Save/Window: *(select one of the available options)*

? Option The ? option causes AutoCAD to display a list of named views according to the response to the next prompt:

View(s) to list <*>:

The default response is the global symbol, the asterisk, which will cause all the named views to be listed. Other typical restrictions of the names can be specified by using whole names or combinations of characters and wild-card symbols, such as the asterisk and/or the question mark. AutoCAD includes in the list the space (M for model or P for paper) in which each view was defined.

Delete Option The Delete option allows you to delete specified views according to names or character/wild-card specifications given.

Restore Option The Restore option causes the named view to replace the current display in a manner similar to the combined action of the VPOINT command and the ZOOM Dynamic command.

Model space views restored to paper space are placed in the viewport of your choice by responding to the following prompt:

Restoring model space View.
Select viewport:

The desired viewport (which must be on and active) can be chosen by specifying its border. AutoCAD automatically changes to model space. Restoring a paper space view while working in model space causes AutoCAD to change automatically to paper space. The TILEMODE system variable must be set to OFF to restore a paper space view.

Save Option The Save option prompts for a name and saves the display in the current viewport to the given name.

Window Option The Window option prompts for two points to specify the diagonally opposite corners of a rectangle, which will be the display used in the same manner as the Save option.

You can also create a new view and restore a view from the View Control dialog box. To open the View Control dialog box, invoke the DDVIEW command from:

Viewpoint toolbar	Select the Named Views command (see Figure 13–9)
Pull-down menu	View > Named Views...
Command: prompt	**ddview** Enter

Figure 13–9 Invoking the Named Views command from the Viewpoint toolbar

AutoCAD displays View Control dialog box, similar to Figure 13–10. AutoCAD lists the saved view, if any, in the Views list box. To create a new view, choose the **New...** button. AutoCAD displays the Define New View dialog box. Provide an appropriate view name and choose the **Save View** button.

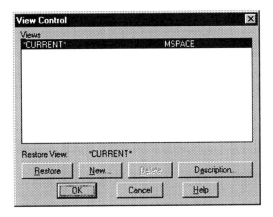

Figure 13–10 View Control dialog box

To restore a saved view, first select from the list box the view name, and then choose the **Restore** button. AutoCAD restores the selected view.

To delete a saved view, first select from the list box the view name to delete, and choose the **Delete** button. AutoCAD deletes the selected view.

Controlling the Regeneration

The REGENAUTO command controls automatic regeneration. When the REGENAUTO is set to ON, AutoCAD drawings regenerate automatically. When it is set to OFF, then you may have to regenerate the drawing manually to see the current status of the drawing.

Invoke the REGENAUTO command from:

Command: prompt	**regenauto** ⏎

AutoCAD prompts:

Command: **regenauto**
ON/OFF<current>: *(select one of the two available options)*

When you set REGENAUTO to OFF, what you see on the screen may not always represent the current state of the drawing. When changes are made by certain commands, the display will be updated only after you invoke the REGEN command. But waiting time can be avoided as long as you are aware of the status of the display. Turning the REGENAUTO setting back to ON will cause a regeneration. If a command should require a regeneration while REGENAUTO is set to OFF, you will be prompted:

About to regen, proceed? <Y>

Responding with **No** will abort the command. Exceptions to this are the ZOOM Vmax command, which does not require a regeneration, and ZOOM All, ZOOM Extents, REGEN, and VIEW Restore, which do require regeneration.

Regeneration during a transparent command will be delayed until a regeneration is performed after that transparent command. The following message will appear:

REGEN QUEUED

Controlling the Drawing of Objects

The DRAGMODE command controls the way dragged objects are displayed. Certain draw and modify commands display highlighted dynamic (cursor-following) representations of the objects being drawn or edited. This can slow down the drawing process if the objects are very complex. Setting DRAGMODE to OFF turns off dragging.

Invoke the DRAGMODE command from:

Command: prompt	**dragmode** [Enter]

AutoCAD prompts:

Command: **dragmode**
ON/OFF/Auto<current>: *(select one of the three available options)*

When DRAGMODE is set to OFF, all calls for dragging are ignored. Setting DRAGMODE to ON allows dragging by use of the DRAG command modifier. Setting DRAGMODE to Auto causes dragging wherever possible.

When DRAGMODE is set to OFF, the DRAG command modifier can be used wherever dragging is permitted. For example, during the MOVE prompt you can use the following:

Command: **move**
Select objects: *(select the objects)*
Base point or displacement: *(specify the basepoint)*
Second point of displacement: **drag**

At this point the selected objects follows the cursor movement.

Controlling the Display of Marker Blips

The BLIPMODE command controls the display of marker blips. When BLIPMODE is set to ON, a small cross mark is displayed when points on the screen are specified with the cursor or by entering their coordinates. After you edit for a while, the drawing can become cluttered with these blips. They have no effect other than visual reference and can be removed at any time by using the REDRAW, REGEN, ZOOM, or PAN command. Any other command requiring regeneration causes the blips to be removed.

When BLIPMODE is set to OFF, the blips marks are not displaced. Invoke the BLIPMODE command from:

Command: prompt	**blipmode** Enter

AutoCAD prompts:

Command: **blipmode**
ON/OFF<current>: *(select one of the two available options)*

CHANGING THE DISPLAY ORDER OF OBJECTS

The DRAWORDER command allows you to change the display order of objects as well as images. This will ensure proper display and plotting output when two or more objects overlay one another. For instance, when a raster image is attached over an existing object, AutoCAD obscures them from view. With the help of the DRAWORDER command you can make the existing object display over the raster image.

Invoke the DRAWORDER command from:

Modify II toolbar	Select the Draworder command (see Figure 13–11)
Pull-down menu	Tools > Display Order
Command: prompt	**draworder** Enter

Figure 13–11 Invoking the Draworder command from the Modify II toolbar

AutoCAD prompts:

Command: **draworder**
Select objects: *(select the objects for which you want to change the display order, and press* Enter *to complete object selection)*
Above object/Under object/Top/<Bottom>: *(select one of the available options)*
Select reference object: *(select the reference object for changing the order of display)*

When multiple objects are selected for reordering, the relative display order of the objects selected is maintained.

Above Object The Above object option moves the selected object(s) above a specified reference object.

Under Object The Under object option moves selected object(s) below a specified reference object.

Top The top option moves selected object(s) to the top of the drawing order.

Bottom The bottom option moves selected object(s) to the bottom of the drawing order.

> **NOTE:** The DRAWORDER command terminates when selected object(s) are reordered. The command does not continue to prompt for additional objects to reorder.

OBJECT PROPERTIES

There are two important properties that control the appearance of objects: color and linetype. You can specify the color and linetype for the objects to be drawn with the help of the LAYER command, as explained in Chapter 3. You can do the same thing by means of the COLOR and LINETYPE commands.

COLOR Command

The COLOR command allows you to specify a color for the objects to be drawn, separate from the layer color.

Invoke the COLOR command from:

Object Properties toolbar	Select one of the colors available from the option menu (see Figure 13–12)
Command: prompt	color Enter

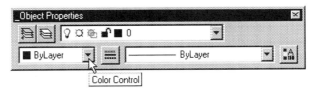

Figure 13-12 Selecting one of the available colors from the option menu in the Object Properties toolbar

AutoCAD prompts:

> Command: **color**
> New object color <current>: *(specify one of the colors, or press* Enter *to accept the current color selection)*

The color may be entered as a standard name (red, green, cyan, yellow, magenta, blue, white, or green) or by the number code (1 through 255). Or you can respond with BYLAYER or BYBLOCK. BYLAYER is the default. If you reply with a standard name or number code, this becomes the current color. All new objects you create are drawn with this color, regardless of which layer is current, until you again set the color to BYLAYER or BYBLOCK. BYLAYER causes the objects drawn to assume the color of the layer on which it is drawn. BYBLOCK causes objects to be drawn in white until selected for inclusion in a block definition. Subsequent insertion of a block that contains objects drawn under the BYBLOCK option causes those objects to assume the color of the current setting of the COLOR command. You can use the DDMODIFY command to change the color of the existing objects.

> **NOTE:** As noted in Chapter 3, the options to specify colors by both layer and the COLOR command can cause confusion in a large drawing, especially one containing blocks and nested blocks. You are advised not to mix the two methods of specifying colors in the same drawing.

LINETYPE Command

The LINETYPE command allows you to draw lines with different dash/dot/space combinations. It is used to load linetype definitions from a library or lets you create custom linetypes.

A linetype must exist in a library file and be loaded before you can apply it to an object or layer. Standard linetypes are in the library file called *ACAD.LIN* and are not loaded with the LAYER command. You have to load the linetype before you assign it to a specific layer.

Linetypes are combinations of dashes, dots, and spaces. Customized linetypes permit "out of line" objects in a linetype such as circles, wavy lines, blocks, and skew segments.

Dash, dot, and space combinations eventually repeat themselves. For example, a six-unit-long dash, followed by a dot between two one-unit-long spaces repeats itself according to the overall length of the line drawn and the LTSCALE setting.

Lines with dashes (not all dots) usually have dashes at both ends. AutoCAD automatically adjusts the lengths of end dashes to reach the endpoints of the adjoining line. Intermediate dashes will be the lengths specified in the definition. If the overall length of the line is not long enough to permit the breaks, the line is drawn continuous.

There is no guarantee that any segments of the line fall at some particular location. For example, when placing a centerline through circle centers, you cannot be sure that the short dashes will be centered on the circle centers as most conventions call for. To achieve this effect, the short and long dashes have to be created by either drawing them individually or by breaking a continuous line to create the spaces between the dashes. This also creates multiple in-line lines instead of one line of a particular linetype. Or you can use the DIMENSION command Center option to place the desired mark.

Individual linetype names and definitions are stored in one or more files whose extension is *.LIN*. The same name may be defined differently in two different files. Selecting the desired one requires proper responses to the prompts in the Load option of the LINETYPE command. If you redefine a linetype, loading it with the LINETYPE command will cause objects drawn on layers assigned to that linetype to assume the new definition.

Mastering the use of linetypes involves using the LAYER command, and the LINETYPE command, the LTSCALE command and knowing which files contain the linetype definition(s) desired. Also, with the LINETYPE command you can define custom linetypes.

Invoke the LINETYPE command from:

Object Properties toolbar	Select the Linetype command (see Figure 13–13)
Pull-down menu	Format > Linetype
Command: prompt	**linetype** Enter

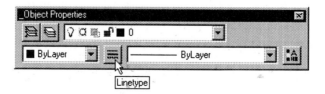

Figure 13–13 Invoking the Linetype command from the Object Properties toolbar

AutoCAD displays the Layer & Linetype Properties dialog box, similar to Figure 13–14.

AutoCAD lists the available linetypes for the current drawing and displays the current linetype setting next to the **Current:** button. By default, it is set to ByLayer. To change the current linetype setting, select the appropriate linetype from the Linetype list box and select the **Current:** button. All new objects you create will be drawn with the selected linetype, irrespective of the layer you are working, until you again set the linetype to ByLayer or ByBlock. ByLayer causes the object drawn to assume the linetypes of the layer on which it is drawn. ByBlock causes objects to be drawn in Continuous linetype until selected for inclusion in a block definition. Subsequent insertion of a block that contains objects drawn under the ByBlock option will cause those objects to assume the linetype of the block.

To load a linetype explicitly into your drawing, choose the **Load...** button. AutoCAD displays the Load or Reload Linetypes dialog box, as shown in Figure 13–15.

By default, AutoCAD lists the available linetypes from the *ACAD.LIN* file. Select the linetype to load from the **Available Linetypes** list box, and choose the **OK** button.

If you need to load linetypes from a different file, choose the **File...** button in the Load or Unload Linetypes dialog box. AutoCAD displays the Select Linetype File dialog box. Select the appropriate linetype file and choose the **OK** button. In turn, AutoCAD lists the available linetypes from the selected linetype file in the Load or Unload Linetypes dialog box. Select the appropriate linetype to load from the Available Linetypes list box, and choose the **OK** button.

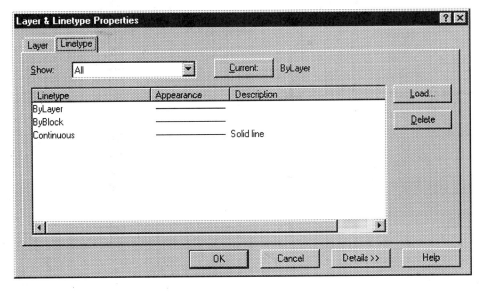

Figure 13–14 Layer & Linetype Properties dialog box

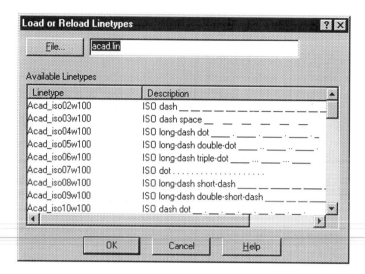

Figure 13-15 Load or Reload Linetypes dialog box

To delete a linetype that is currently loaded in the drawing, first select the linetype from the list box in the Layer & Linetype Properties dialog box, and then select the **Delete** button. You can delete only linetypes that are not referenced in the current drawing. You can not delete linetype Continuous, ByLayer, or ByBlock. Deleting is the same as using the PURGE command to purge unused linetypes from the current drawing.

To display additional information of a specific linetype, first select the linetype from the Linetype list box in the Layer & Linetype Properties dialog box, and then choose the **Details >>** button. AutoCAD displays an extension of the dialog box, listing additional settings, as shown in Figure 13-16.

The **Name:** and **Description:** edit fields display the selected linetype name and description, respectively.

The **Global scale factor:** edit field displays the current setting of the LTSCALE factor. The **Current object scale:** edit field displays the current setting of the CELTSCALE factor. If necessary, you can change the values of the LTSCALE and CELTSCALE factors.

The **ISO pen width:** box sets the linetype scale to one of a list of standard ISO values. The resulting scale is the global scale factor multiplied by the object's scale factor.

Setting the **Use paper space units for scaling** check box to ON scales linetypes in paper space and model space identically.

After making the necessary changes, click the **OK** button to keep the changes and close the Layer & Linetype Properties dialog box.

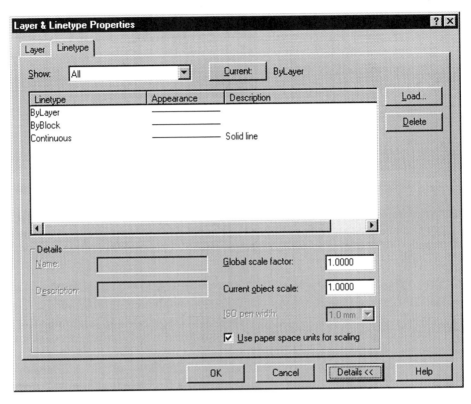

Figure 13–16 Extended Layer & Linetype Properties dialog box

NOTE: As noted in Chapter 3, the options to specify linetypes by both layer and the LINETYPE command can cause confusion in a large drawing, especially one containing blocks and nested blocks. You are advised not to mix the two methods of specifying linetypes in the same drawing.

X, Y, AND *Z* FILTERS—AN ENHANCEMENT TO OBJECT SNAP

The AutoCAD filters feature allows you to establish a 2D point by specifying the individual (X and Y) coordinates one at a time in separate steps. In the case of a 3D point you can specify the individual (X, Y, and Z) coordinates in three steps. Or you can specify one of the three coordinate values in one step and a point in another step, from which AutoCAD extracts the other two coordinate values for use in the point being established.

The filters feature is used when being prompted to establish a point, as in the starting point of a line, the center of a circle, drawing a node with the POINT command, or specifying a basepoint or second point in displacement for the MOVE or COPY command, to mention just a few.

> **NOTE:** During the application of the filters feature there are steps where you can input either single coordinate values or points, and there are steps where you can input only points. It is necessary to understand these restrictions and options and when one type of input is more desirable than the other.

When selecting points during the use of filters, you need to know which coordinates of the specified point are going to be used in the point being established. It is also essential to know how to combine Object Snap modes with those steps that use point input.

The filters feature is actually an enhancement to either the object snap or the @ (last point) feature. The AutoCAD ability to establish a point by snapping to a point on an existing object is one of the most powerful features in CAD, and being able to have AutoCAD snap to such an existing point and then filter out selected coordinates for use in establishing a new point adds to that power. Therefore, in most cases you will not use the filters feature if it is practical to type in all of the coordinates from the keyboard, because typing in all the coordinates can be done in a single step. The filters feature is a multistep process, and each step might include substeps, one to specify the coordinate(s) to be filtered out and another to designate the Object Snap mode involved.

Filters with @

When AutoCAD is prompting for a point, the filters feature is initiated by entering a period followed by the letter designation for the coordinate(s) to be filtered out. For example, if you draw a point starting at (0,0) and use the relative polar coordinate response @3<45 to determine the endpoint, you can use filters to establish another point whose X coordinate is the same as the X coordinate of the end of the line just drawn. It works for Y and Z coordinates and combinations of XY, XZ, and YZ coordinates also. The following command sequence shows how to apply filter to a line that needs to be started at a point whose X coordinate is the same as that of the end of the previous line and whose Y coordinate is 1.25. The line will be drawn horizontally 3 units long. The sequence is as follows:

Command: **line**
From point: **0,0**
To point: **@3<45**
To point: Enter

Command: **line** *(or* Enter *)*
From point: **.x**
of **@**
(need YZ): **0,1.25**
To point: **@3<0**

Entering **.x** initiates the filters feature. AutoCAD then prompts you to specify a point from which it can extract the *X* coordinate. The @ (last point) does this. The new line has a starting point whose *X* coordinate is the same as that of the last point drawn. By using the filters feature to extract the *X* coordinate, that starting point will be on an imaginary vertical line through the point specified by @ in response to the "of" prompt.

When you initiate filters with a single coordinate (.x in our example) and respond with a point (@), the prompt that follows asks for a point also. From it (the second point specified) AutoCAD extracts the other two coordinates for the new point.

Even though the prompt is for "YZ," the point may be specified in 2D format as 0,1.25 (the *X* and *Y* coordinates), from which AutoCAD takes the second value as the needed *Y* coordinate. The *Z* coordinate is assumed to be the elevation of the current coordinate system.

You can use the two-coordinate response to initiate filters. Then specify a point, and all that AutoCAD requires is a single value for the final coordinate. An example of this follows.

Command: **line**
From point: **0,0**
To point: **@3<45**
To point: Enter

Command: **line** *(or* Enter *)*
From point: **.xz**
of **@**
(need Y): **1.25**
To point: **@3<0**

You can also specify a point in response to the "(need Y):" prompt:

(need Y): **0,1.25** *(or pick a point on the screen)*

In this case, AutoCAD uses the *Y* coordinate of the point specified as the *Y* coordinate of the new point.

Remember, it is an individual coordinate in 2D (one or two coordinates in 3D) of an existing point that you wish AutoCAD to extract and use for the new point. In most cases you will be object snapping to a point for the response. Otherwise, if you knew the value of the coordinate needed, you would probably type it in at the keyboard.

Filters with Object Snap

Without filters, an Object Snap (Osnap) mode establishes a new point to coincide with one on an existing object. With filters, an Osnap mode establishes selected coordinates of a new point to coincide with corresponding coordinates of one on an existing object.

Extracting one or more coordinate values to be applied to corresponding coordinate values of a point that you are being prompted to establish is shown in the following example.

In Figure 13–17, a 2.75" × 7.1875" rectangle has a 0.875"-diameter hole in its center. A board drafter would determine the center of a square or rectangle by drawing diagonals and centering the circle at their intersection. AutoCAD drafters (without filters) could do the same, or they might draw orthogonal lines from the midpoint of a horizontal line and from the midpoint of one of the vertical lines to establish a centering intersection. The following command sequence shows steps in drawing a rectangle with a circle in the center using filters.

```
Command: line
From point:  (select point p1)
To point:  @2.75<90
To point:  @7.1875<0
To point:  @2.75<270
To point:  c
```

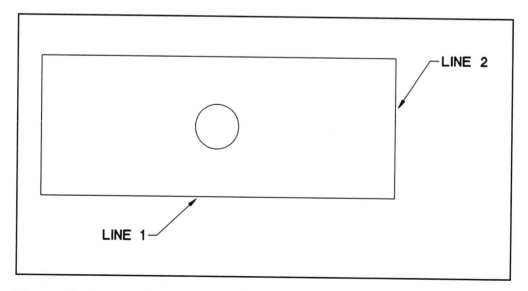

Figure 13-17 Extracting coordinate values to be applied to corresponding coordinate values

Command: **circle**
3P/2P/TTR/<Center point>: **.x**
of **mid**
of *(select line 1)*
(need YZ): **mid**
of *(select line 2)*
Diameter/<Radius>: **d**
Diameter: **.875**

SHELL COMMAND

The SHELL command allows you to execute operating system programs without leaving AutoCAD. You can execute any operating system program as long as there is sufficient memory to execute.

Invoke the SHELL command from:

Command: prompt	**shell** Enter

AutoCAD prompts:

Command: **shell**
OS Command: *(invoke one of the available operating system's utility programs)*

When the utility program is finished, AutoCAD takes you back to the "Command:" prompt. If you need to execute more than one operating system program, give a null response to the "OS command:" prompt. AutoCAD responds with the appropriate operating system prompt. You can now enter as many operating system commands as you wish. When you are finished, you may return to AutoCAD by typing **EXIT**. It will take you back to the "Command:" prompt.

If there is not enough free memory for the SHELL command, the following message will appear:

Shell error: insufficient memory for command.

Where there is insufficient memory, you can execute the SH command instead of the SHELL command. SH requires less memory than the SHELL command and can be used to access internal DOS commands, such as DIR, COPY, and TYPE. If the need arises, you can adjust the amount of memory required for the SH and SHELL commands by modifiying the *ACAD.PGP* file. For additional information, see Chapter 18 on "Customizing AutoCAD."

In the Windows 95 and Windows NT 4.0 operating system, instead of invoking the SHELL command, you can switch between programs by selecting the appropriate program from the task bar. Depending on the memory available in the computer, you can open multiple programs and switch between the programs by selecting appropriate open programs from the task bar. In the Windows NT 4.0 operating system, you can even open multiple sessions of AutoCAD Release 14 and switch between them.

> **NOTE:** Do *not* delete the AutoCAD lock files or temporary files created for the current drawing when you are at the operating system prompt.

SETTING UP A DRAWING

The MVSETUP command is used to control and set up the view(s) of a drawing, including the choice of standard plotted sheet sizes with a border, the scale for plotting on the selected sheet size, and multiple viewports. MVSETUP is an AutoLISP routine that can be customized to insert any type of border and title block.

Options and associated prompts depend on whether the TILEMODE system variable is set to ON (1) or OFF (0). When TILEMODE is set to ON, Tiled Viewports is enabled. When TILEMODE is set to OFF, the Floating Viewports menu item is enabled. Other paper space–related drawing setup options are available.

Invoke the MVSETUP command from:

Command: prompt	**mvsetup** [Enter]

AutoCAD prompts depend on the current TILEMODE settings. If TILEMODE is set to 1, then AutoCAD prompts:

> Enable paper space?(No/<Yes>): *(press* [Enter] *to enable paper space, and in turn AutoCAD changes the TILEMODE setting to 0, or type **n** and press* [Enter] *to stay in the TILEMODE setting of 1)*

If TILEMODE is set to 0, then AutoCAD prompts:

> Align/Create/Scale viewports/Options/Title block/Undo: *(select an option)*

The following is the procedure for setting up the drawing with TILEMODE set to 1. AutoCAD prompts:

> Enable paper space?(No/<Yes>): *(type **n** and press* [Enter] *)*
> Units type (Scientific/Decimal/Engineering/ Architectural/ Metric): *(select a unit type. Depending on the units selected, AutoCAD lists the available scales. Select one of the available scales, or you can even specify a custom scale factor)*

Enter the scale factor: *(specify a scale factor)*
Enter the paper width: *(specify the paper width at which the drawing will be plotted)*
Enter the paper height: *(specify the paper height at which the drawing will be plotted)*

AutoCAD sets up the appropriate limits to allow you to draw to full scale and also draws a bounding box enclosing the limits. Draw the drawing to full scale; and when you ready to plot, specify the scale mentioned earlier to plot the drawing.

Following is the procedure for setting up the drawing with TILEMODE set to 0. AutoCAD prompts:

Align/Create/Scale viewports/Options/Title block/Undo: *(select an option)*

The options are explained here in the order that is logical to complete the drawing setup.

Title Block The title block option allows you to select an appropriate title block. First, AutoCAD lists the available title blocks and prompts you to select one of the available title blocks as follows:

0: None
1. ISO A4 Size(mm)
2. ISO A3 Size(mm)
3. ISO A2 Size(mm)
4. ISO A1 Size(mm)
5. ISO A0 Size(mm)
6. ANSI-V Size(in)
7. ANSI-A Size(in)
8. ANSI-B Size(in)
9. ANSI-C Size(in)
10. ANSI-D Size(in)
11. ANSI-E Size(in)
12. Arch/Engineering (24 x 36in)
13. Generic D size Sheet (24 x 36in)

Add/Delete/Redisplay/<Number of entry to load>: *(select one of the available title blocks and press* Enter *, AutoCAD inserts a border and title block, as shown in Figure 13–18, or enter an option)*

The **Add** option allows you to add a title block drawing to the available list.

The **Delete** option allows you to delete an entry from the available list.

The **Redisplay** option redisplays the list of title block options.

Create The Create option allows you to establish viewports. AutoCAD prompts:

Delete objects/Undo/<Create viewports>: *(press* Enter *to create viewports and AutoCAD lists the available viewport layout options, or enter an option)*
Available Mview viewport layout options:

0: None
1: Single
2: Std. Engineering
3: Array of Viewports

Redisplay/<Number of entry to load>: *(select one of the available layout options or select an option)*

The **None** selection creates no viewports. The **1** selection creates a single viewport whose size is determined during subsequent prompts responses. The **2** selection creates four viewports with preset viewing angle by dividing a specified area into quadrants. The size is determined by response to subsequent prompt. The **3** selection creates a matrix of viewports along the X and Y axes.

The **Delete objects** option deletes the existing viewports.

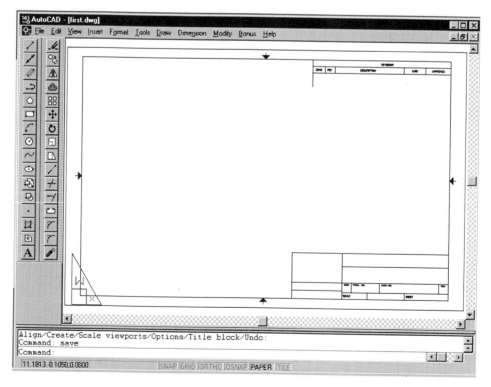

Figure 13–18 Title block and border for ANSI-B Size

The **Undo** option reverses operations performed in the current MVSETUP session.

Scale Viewports The Scale Viewports option adjusts the scale factor of the objects displayed in the viewports. The scale factor is specified as a ratio of paper space to model space. For example, 1:48 is 1 paper space unit for 48 model space units (scale for 1/4" = 1'0").

Options The Options option lets you establish several different environment settings that are associated with your layout. AutoCAD prompts:

> Set Layer/LImits/Units/Xref: *(enter an option)*

The **Set Layer** option permits you to specify a layer for placing the title block.

The **LImits** option permits you to specify whether or not to reset the limits to drawing extents after the title block has been inserted.

The **Units** option permits you to specify whether sizes and point locations will be translated to inch or millimeter paper units.

The **Xref** option permits you to specify whether the title block is to be inserted or externally referenced.

Align The Align option causes AutoCAD to pan the view in one viewport so that it aligns with a basepoint in another viewport. Whichever viewport the other point moves to becomes the active viewport. AutoCAD prompts:

> Angled/Horizontal/Vertical alignment/Rotate view/Undo: *(select an option)*

The **Angled** option causes AutoCAD to pan the view in a viewport in a specified direction.

The **Horizontal** option causes AutoCAD to pan the view in one viewport, aligning it horizontally with a basepoint in another viewport.

The **Vertical Alignment** option causes AutoCAD to pan the view in one viewport, aligning it vertically with a basepoint in another viewport.

The **Rotate View** option causes AutoCAD to rotate the view in a viewport around a basepoint.

The **Undo** option causes AutoCAD to undo the results of the current MVSETUP command.

TIME COMMAND

The TIME command displays the current time and date related to your current drawing session. In addition, you can find out how long you have been working in AutoCAD. This command uses the clock in your computer to keep track of the time functions and displays to the nearest millisecond using 24-hour military format.

Utility Commands

Invoke the TIME command from:

Pull-down menu	Tools > Inquiry > Time
Command: prompt	time Enter

The following listing is displayed in the text screen followed by a prompt:

Current time:	11 July 1997 at 11:54:15.340
Time for this drawing:	
Created:	11 July 1997 at 10:31:12.230
Last updated:	11 July 1997 at 10:31:12.230
Total editing time:	0 days 01:23:03:110
Elapsed timer (on):	0 days 01:23:03:110
Next automatic save in:	0 days 01:03:17:350

Display/ON/OFF/Reset:

The first line gives today's date and time.

The third line gives the date and time the current drawing was initially created. The drawing time starts when you initially begin a new drawing. If the drawing was created by means of the WBLOCK command, it is the date and time the command was executed that is displayed here.

The fourth line gives the date and time the drawing was last updated. Initially set to the drawing creation time; this is updated each time you use the END or SAVE command.

The fifth line gives the length of time you are in AutoCAD. This timer is continuously updated by AutoCAD while you are in the program, excluding plotting and printer plot time. This timer cannot be stopped or reset.

The sixth line provides information about the stopwatch timer. You can turn this timer ON or OFF and reset it to zero. This timer is independent of other functions.

The seventh line provides information about when the next automatic save will take place.

Display Option The Display option redisplays the time functions, with updated times.

ON Option The ON option turns the stopwatch timer to ON, if it is OFF. By default it is ON.

OFF Option The OFF option turns the stopwatch timer to OFF and displays the accumulated time.

Reset Option The RESET option resets the stopwatch timer to zero.

To exit the TIME command at the prompt, give a null response or press Esc .

AUDIT COMMAND

The AUDIT command serves as a diagnostic tool to correct any errors or defects in the database of the current drawing. AutoCAD generates an extensive report of the problems, and for every error detected AutoCAD recommends action to correct it.

Invoke the AUDIT command from:

Pull-down menu	File > Drawing Utilities >Audit
Command: prompt	**audit** Enter

AutoCAD prompts:

Command: **audit**
Fix any errors detected? <current>: *(specify **y** for yes or **n** for no)*

If you respond with **Y** or **Yes**, AutoCAD will fix all the errors detected and display an audit report with detailed information about the errors detected and fixing them. If you answer with **N** or **No**, AutoCAD will just display a report and will not fix any errors.

In addition, AutoCAD creates an ASCII report file (AUDITCLT system variable should be set to ON) describing the problems and the actions taken. It will save the file in the current directory, using the current drawing's name with the file extension *.ADT*. You can use any ASCII editor to display the report file on the screen or print it on the printer, respectively.

> **NOTE:** If a drawing contains errors that the AUDIT command cannot fix, open the drawing with the RECOVER command to retrieve the drawing and correct its errors.

OBJECT LINKING AND EMBEDDING (OLE)

Object linking and embedding (OLE) is a Microsoft Windows feature that combines various application data into one compound document. AutoCAD Release 14 has client as well as server capability. As a client, AutoCAD now permits you to have objects from other Windows applications either embedded in or linked to your drawing.

When an object is inserted into an AutoCAD drawing from an application that supports OLE, the object can maintain a connection with its source file. If you insert an embedded object into AutoCAD (client), it is no longer associated with the source (server). If necessary, you can edit the embedded data from inside the AutoCAD drawing by using the original application. But at the same time, this editing does not change the original file.

Utility Commands

If, instead, you insert an object as a linked object in AutoCAD (client), the object remains associated with its source (server). When you edit a linked object in AutoCAD by using the original application, the original file as well as the object inserted in AutoCAD change.

Linked or embedded objects appear on the screen in AutoCAD and can be printed or plotted using Windows system drivers. If you open the drawing using a DOS or UNIX version of AutoCAD, you do not see the OLE objects.

Let's look at an example of object linking between an AutoCAD (server) drawing and Microsoft Word (client). Figure 13–19 shows a drawing of a desk, a computer, and a chair that contains various attribute values. We are going to link this drawing to a Microsoft Word document.

From the pull-down menu Edit select the Copy option and AutoCAD prompts you to select objects. Select the computer, the table, and the chair and press [Enter]. This will copy the selection to the Windows clipboard. Minimize the AutoCAD program.

Invoke Microsoft Word from the Desktop by double-clicking the Word program icon. The Microsoft Word program is displayed, as shown in Figure 13–20.

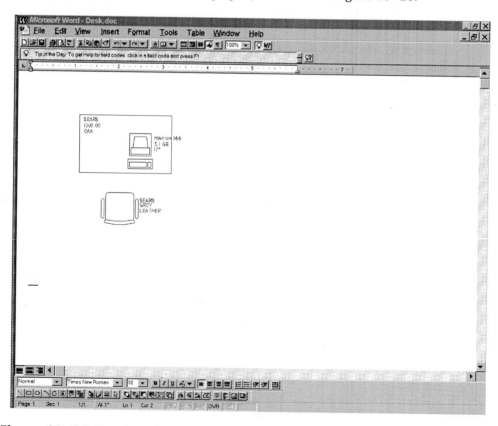

Figure 13–19 Drawing of a desk, a computer, and a chair with attribute values

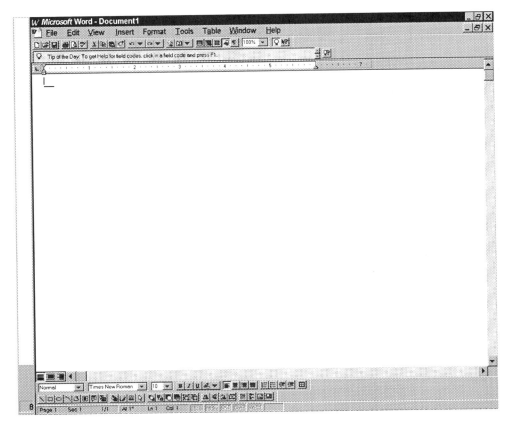

Figure 13–20 Microsoft Word program

Utility Commands

From the pull-down menu Edit in Microsoft Word, select Paste Special..., and Word displays the Paste Special dialog box shown in Figure 13–21. Select the Paste Link button. This will insert the AutoCAD drawing object into Microsoft Word, as shown in Figure 13–22.

Minimize the Word program and maximize AutoCAD (or if the AutoCAD program is not open, double-click the drawing image in the Word document, which will launch the AutoCAD program with the image drawing open). Edit the values of the attributes in the computer block to 166, 3.1 GB, 17", which represent a Pentium 166 computer with a 3.1 GB hard drive and a 17" monitor.

Switch back to the Word program, and from the Edit pull-down menu select the Links... option. The Word program will display the Links dialog box shown in Figure 13–23.

Select the Update Now button and then choose the OK button. The image in the Word document is updated, as shown in Figure 13–24.

In our example, AutoCAD is the server and Microsoft Word is the client.

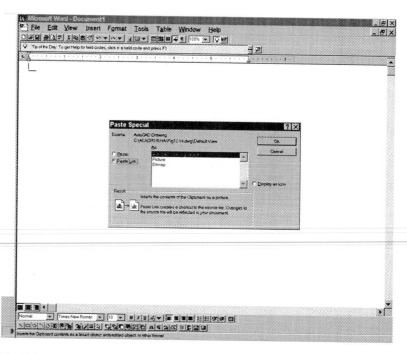

Figure 13–21 Paste Special dialog box

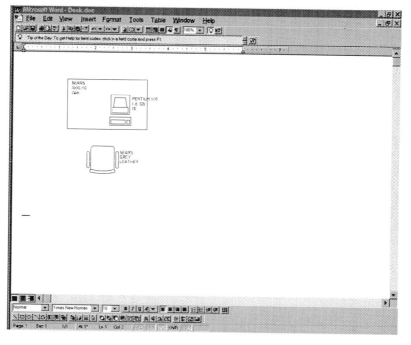

Figure 13–22 Microsoft Word document with the AutoCAD drawing

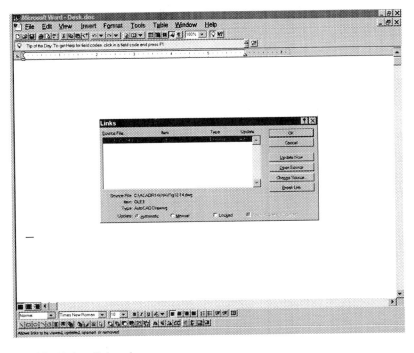

Figure 13-23 Links dialog box

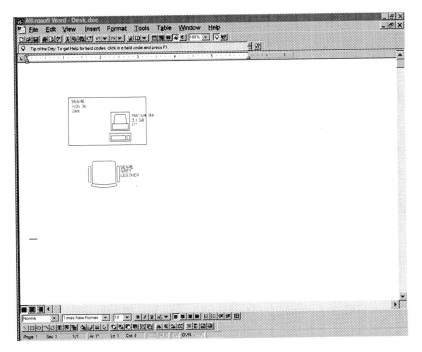

Figure 13-24 AutoCAD drawing updated in the Word is the client

Alternatively, you can place a linked object into AutoCAD, where AutoCAD is the client and another application is the server. Let's look an example in which AutoCAD is the client and Excel is the server.

From the pull-down menu Edit in AutoCAD, select the Paste Special... option. AutoCAD displays the Paste Special dialog box shown in Figure 13–25. Select the Paste Link radio button and Microsoft Excel Worksheet from the list box and click the OK button.

The Excel spreadsheet will be linked to the drawing, as shown in Figure 13–26. AutoCAD is now the client and Microsoft Excel is the server.

To edit the spreadsheet, double-click anywhere on the spreadsheet, which in turn will launch Excel with the spreadsheet document open. Any changes made to the spreadsheet will be reflected in the drawing. Figure 13–27 shows the changes that were made in the spreadsheet.

Here is another example in which an AutoCAD drawing is the client, for both embedding to WORD and linking from EXCEL.

Figure 13–28 shows both an AutoCAD screen and an Excel spreadsheet, in which the spreadsheet is being used for area calculations. The AREA cells are formulas that calculate the product of the corresponding WIDTH and LENGTH cells. In turn, the TOTAL cell is the sum of the AREA cells.

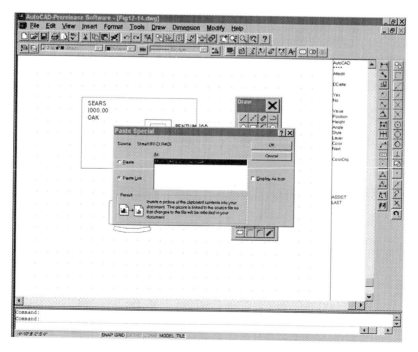

Figure 13–25 Paste Special dialog box

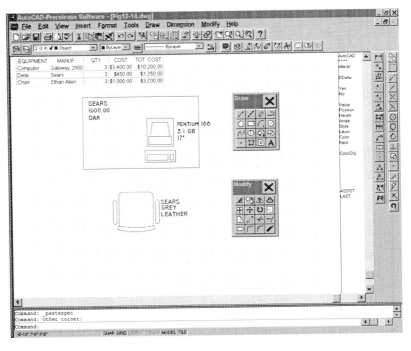

Figure 13–26 Excel spreadsheet in the AutoCAD drawing

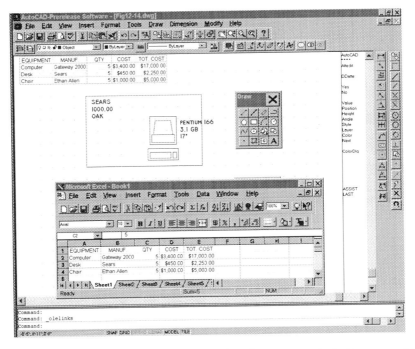

Figure 13–27 AutoCAD drawing showing the changes made in the spreadsheet

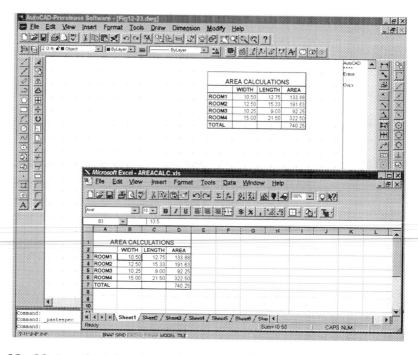

Figure 13–28 AutoCAD drawing screen and an Excel spreadsheet

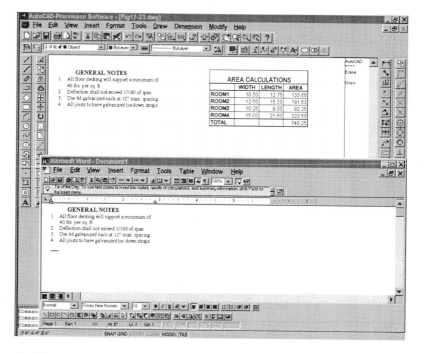

Figure 13–29 AutoCAD drawing and a Word document

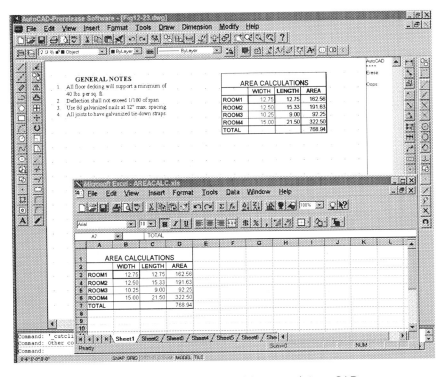

Figure 13–30 Changes shown in the spreadsheet and AutoCAD screen

Figure 13–29 shows the same AutoCAD screen and a Word document that was used for typing the GENERAL NOTES, which were in turn embedded into the AutoCAD drawing.

Figure 13–30 shows how the cell value in the WIDTH for ROOM1 has been changed, resulting in changes in the AREA and TOTAL cells. Because this object (the spreadsheet consisting of four columns and seven rows, including the title) was paste linked into the AutoCAD drawing, the linked object automatically reflects the changes.

CUSTOMIZING THE AUTOCAD SETTINGS

The Preferences dialog box allows you to customize the AutoCAD settings. AutoCAD Release 14 allows you to save and restore a set of custom preferences called a *profile*. A profile can include preference settings that are not saved in the drawing, with the exception of pointer and printer driver settings. By default, AutoCAD stores your current preferences in a profile named <Unnamed Profile>.

To open the Preferences dialog box, invoke the PREFERENCES command from:

Pull-down menu	Tools > Preferences
Command: prompt	**preferences** Enter

AutoCAD displays the Preferences dialog box, similar to Figure 13–31. From the Preferences dialog box, the user can control various aspects of the AutoCAD environment. The Preferences dialog box is divided into eight sections; to make changes to any of the sections, select the cooresponding tab from the top of the Preferences dialog box.

Files The Files section, shown in Figure 13–31, specifies the directory in which AutoCAD searches for support files, driver files, project files, template drawing file location, temporary drawing file location, temporary external reference file location, and texture maps. It also specifies the location of the files for menu, help, log, text editor, and dictionary files.

When you choose the **Browse...** button, AutoCAD displays the Browse for Folder or Select a File dialog box, depending on what you selected from the list.

When you choose the **Add...** button, AutoCAD adds a search path for the selected directory.

When you choose the **Remove** button, AutoCAD removes the selected search path or file.

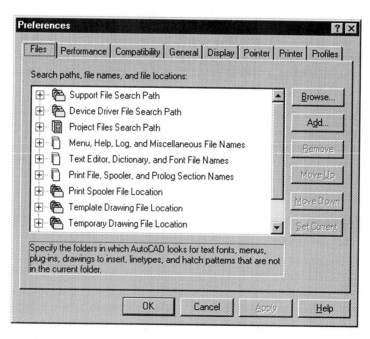

Figure 13–31 Preferences dialog box (with the Files tab selected)

When you select the **Move Up** button, AutoCAD moves the selected search path above the preceding search path.

When you select the **Move Down** button, AutoCAD moves the selected search path below the following search path.

When you select the **Set Current** button, AutoCAD makes the selected project or spelling dictionary current.

Performance The Performance section of the Preferences dialog box, shown in Figure 13–32, controls preferences that relate to AutoCAD performance.

The **Solid model object display** section of the dialog box controls the quality of the display of solid objects.

The **Display object being dragged** section of the dialog box controls the way dragged objects are displayed. It sets the DRAGMODE system variable.

The check box for **Show text boundary frame only** controls the display of the frames for text objects. It sets the QTEXTMODE system variable. The setting can also be changed with QTEXT command.

The check box for **Show raster image content** controls the display of raster images when you use Realtime PAN or ZOOM. It sets the RTDISPLAY system variable.

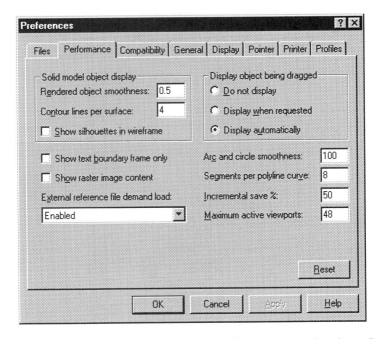

Figure 13–32 Preferences dialog box (with the Preferences tab selected)

The **External reference file demand load:** option menu controls the method of loading external references and whether indexes are used.

The **Arc and circle smoothness:** edit field controls the smoothness of circles, arcs, and ellipses. A higher number produces smoother objects, but AutoCAD requires more time to regenerate them. The setting can also be changed with the VIEWRES command.

The **Segments per polyline curve:** edit field controls the number of line segments to be generated for each polyline curve. The higher the number you specify, the greater the performance impact. Here you set the SPLINESEGS system variable.

The **Incremental save %:** edit field sets the percentage of wasted space allowed in a drawing file. When the specified percentage is reached, AutoCAD performs a full save instead of an incremental save. A low percentage setting lowers performance, because AutoCAD performs time-consuming full saves more often. The default setting is 50%. Here you are setting the ISAVEPERCENT system variable.

The **Maximum active viewports:** edit field sets the maximum number of active viewports. It sets the MAXACTVP system variable.

Select the **Reset** button to reset back to system defaults.

Compatibility The Compatibility section of the Preferences dialog box, shown in Figure 13–33, maintains compatibility with earlier versions of AutoCAD

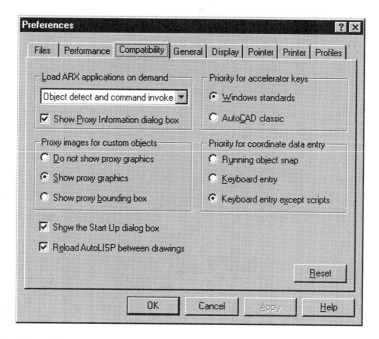

Figure 13–33 Preferences dialog box (with the Compatibility tab selected)

The **Load ARX applications on demand** option menu sets whether and when AutoCAD demand loads a third-party application if a drawing contains custom objects created in that application.

The options provided in the **Priority for accelerator keys** section determine how AutoCAD interprets keystrokes. With the **Windows standards** (default) option, AutoCAD interprets keyboard accelerators by Microsoft Windows standards; for instance, ⌨Ctrl+⌨C equals COPYCLIP, not cancel, as it used to be in the earlier versions of AutoCAD. With the **AutoCAD classic** option, AutoCAD interprets keyboard accelerators using AutoCAD standards rather than Microsoft Windows standards; for instance ⌨Ctrl+⌨C equals cancel, not COPYCLIP as in Microsoft Windows.

The options provided in the **Proxy images for custom objects** section control the display of objects in a drawing that were created in a third-party application.

The options provided in the **Priority for coordinate data entry** section control how AutoCAD responds to input of coordinate data. Selection of **Running object snap** means that at all times, running object snaps are used instead of specific coordinates. Selection of **Keyboard entry** means that at all times, the specific coordinates you enter are used, overriding any running object snap. Selection of **Keyboard entry except scripts** (default) means the specific coordinates you enter are used rather than running objects snaps, except in scripts.

The **Show the Start Up dialog box** check box controls whether the Start Up dialog box is displayed when you start the AutoCAD program.

The **Reload AutoLISP between drawings** check box specifies whether AutoLISP defined functions and variables are preserved when you open a new drawing or whether they are valid in the current drawing only.

Select the **Reset** button to reset back to system defaults.

General The General section of the Preferences dialog box, shown in Figure 13–34, sets a number of general operating preferences.

The **Drawing session safety precautions** section sets the parameters for the safety precautions required during a drawing session. The **Automatic save** check box (by default set to ON) controls whether automatic save will take place at specified intervals. The **Minutes between saves:** edit field specifies the interval in minutes for automatic saving of the current drawing. The **Create backup copy with each save** check box (by default set to ON) specifies whether a backup copy of a drawing is created when you save the drawing. Here you are setting the ISAVEBAK system variable. The **Full-time CRC validation** check box (by default set to OFF) specifies whether a cyclic redundancy check (CRC), an error-checking mechanism, is to be performed each time an object is read into the drawing. The **Audit after each DXFIN or DXBIN** check box (by default set to OFF) specifies whether AutoCAD should do an audit after you use the DXFIN or DXBIN command. The **Maintain a log file** check box (by default set to OFF) specifies whether the contents of the text window are written to a log file.

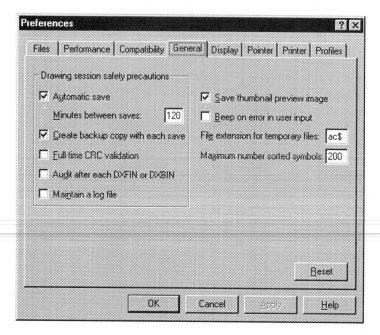

Figure 13–34 Preferences dialog box (with the General tab selected)

The **Save thumbnail preview image** check box (by default set to ON) specifies whether the image of the current drawing is saved as thumbnail image so that it can be displayed in the Preview area of the Select File dialog box when the drawing is selected. Here you are setting the RASTERPREVIEW system variable.

The **Beep on error in user input** check box (by default set to OFF) specifies whether AutoCAD should sound an alarm beep when it detects an invalid entry.

The **File extension for temporary files:** edit field sets the unique file extension for temporary files.

The **Maximum number sorted symbols:** edit field (default value 200) specifies the maximum number of items to sort. Items are sorted in alphabetical order.

Select the **Reset** button to reset back to system defaults.

Display The Display section of the Preferences dialog box, shown in Figure 13–35, customizes the AutoCAD display.

The **Drawing window parameters** section controls the parameters of the AutoCAD drawing window. The **Display AutoCAD screen menu in drawing window** check box (by default set to OFF) specifies whether to display the screen menu on the right side of the drawing window. The **Display scroll bars in drawing window** check box (by default set to OFF) specifies whether to display scroll bars at the bottom and right sides of the drawing window. The **Maximize the AutoCAD**

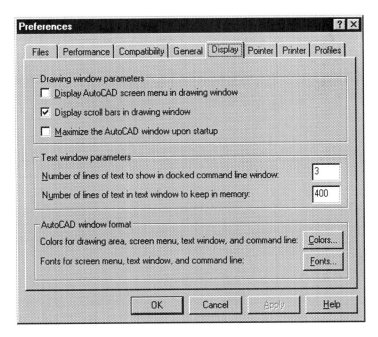

Figure 13–35 Preferences dialog box (with the Display tab selected)

window upon startup check box (by default set to OFF) specifies whether AutoCAD should fill the entire screen area when you start.

The **Text window parameters** section controls the parameters of the AutoCAD text window. The **Number of lines of text to show in docked command line window:** edit field (by default set to 3) specifies the number of lines of text you want to display in the docked command window. You can set the value to any integer from 1 to 100. The **Number of lines of text in text window to keep in memory:** edit field (by default set to 400) specifies the number of lines of text you want the text window to keep in memory. You can set the value anywhere from 25 to 2048.

The **AutoCAD window format** section controls the format of the AutoCAD drawing window. Choose the **Colors...** button and AutoCAD displays the AutoCAD Window Colors dialog box, which can be used to set the colors for drawing area, screen menu, text window, and command line. Choose the **Fonts...** button and AutoCAD displays the Graphics Window Font dialog box, which can be used to specify the font AutoCAD uses for the screen menu and command line and in the text window.

Pointer The Pointer section, shown in Figure 13–36, sets the current AutoCAD pointing device. In addition, you can set the cursor size. The cursor size is specified in terms of percentage of the total screen in the **Percentage of screen size** edit field. The allowable range is from 1 to 100 percent of the total screen. When it is set

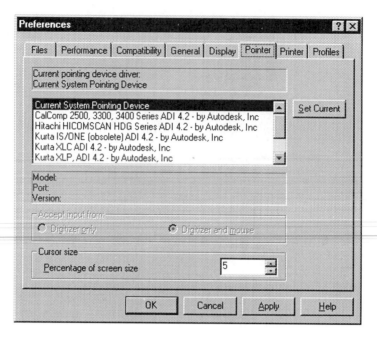

Figure 13–36 Preferences dialog box (with the Pointer tab selected)

to 100%, the ends of the crosshairs are never visible. If it is set to less than 100%, then you can see the ends of the crosshairs. The default setting is 5%.

Printer The Printer section, shown in Figure 13–37, customizes printer or plotter settings and sets the current printer. You can add a printer to the list of available printers, or you can remove a printer from the available printers. You can customize the settings of any of the available printers in the Printer section.

Profile The Profiles section, shown in Figure 13–38, saves and restores user preference settings called as a profile. AutoCAD displays the name of the current profile in the **Current profile:** section and lists the available profiles just below the Current profile: section. To make a specific profile the current profile, first select the profile name from the list box, and then select the **Set Current** button. AutoCAD restores the preference settings from the selected profile name. Choose the **Copy...** button to copy an existing profile. Choose the **Rename...** button to rename the selected profile name. Select the **Delete** button to delete the selected profile. Choose the **Export...** button to export a profile as a *REG* file. Choose the **Import...** button to import a profile creasted using export. Select the **Reset** button to reset the values in the selected profile to the default settings.

After making all the necessary changes, select the **Apply** button to apply the changes. Then choose **OK** to close the Preferences dialog box.

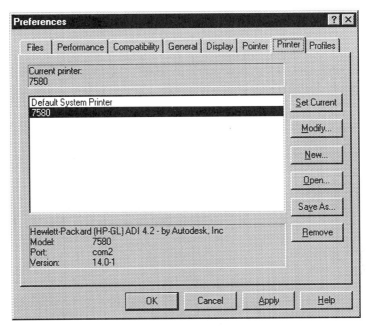

Figure 13–37 Preferences dialog box (with the Printer tab selected)

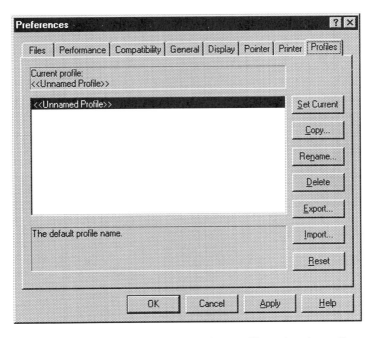

Figure 13–38 Preferences dialog box (with the Profiles tab selected)

Utility Commands

SAVING OBJECTS IN OTHER FILE FORMATS (EXPORTING)

The EXPORT command allows you to save a selected object in other file formats, such as *.BMP*, *.DXF*, *.DWF*, *.SAT*, *.3DS*, and *.WMF*. Invoke the EXPORT command from:

Pull-down menu	File > Export
Command: prompt	**export** Enter

AutoCAD displays the Export Data dialog box, similar to Figure 13–39. In the **Save as type:** list box select the format type in which you wish to export objects. Type the file name in the **File name:** edit box. Select the **Save** button and AutoCAD prompts:

Select objects: *(select the objects to export, and press* Enter *to complete object selection)*

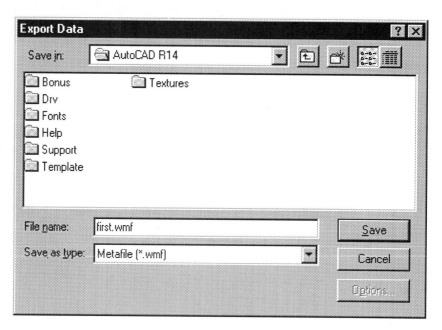

Figure 13–39 Export Data dialog box

AutoCAD exports the selected objects in the specified file format using the specified file name.

Table 13–1 lists the format types available in AutoCAD for exporting the current drawing.

Table 13–1 Exportable Format Types

Format Type	Description
3DS	3D Studio file
BMP	Device-independent bitmap file
DWG	AutoCAD drawing file (same as invoking the WBLOCK command)
DWF	AutoCAD drawing web format file
DXF AutoCAD R14	AutoCAD Release 14 drawing interchange file
DXF AutoCAD R13/LT95	AutoCAD R13/LT95 drawing interchange file
DXF AutoCAD R12/LT2	AutoCAD R12/LT2 drawing interchange file
DXX	AutoCAD attribute extract DXF file (same as invoking the ATTEXT command)
EPS	Encapsulated PostScript file
SAT	ACIS solid-object file
STL	Solid object stereo-lithography file
WMF	Windows metafile

IMPORTING VARIOUS FILE FORMATS

The IMPORT command allows you to import various file formats, such as *.3DS*, *.DXF*, *.EPS*, *.SAT*, and *.WMF*, into AutoCAD. Invoke the IMPORT command from:

Insert toolbar	Select Import command (see Figure 13–40)
Command: prompt	**insert** Enter

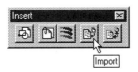

Figure 13–40 Invoking the Import command from the Insert toolbar

AutoCAD displays the Import File dialog box, similar to Figure 13–41. In the **Files of Type:** list box select the format type you wish to import into AutoCAD. Select the file from the appropriate directory from the list box and pick the Open button. AutoCAD imports the file into the AutoCAD drawing.

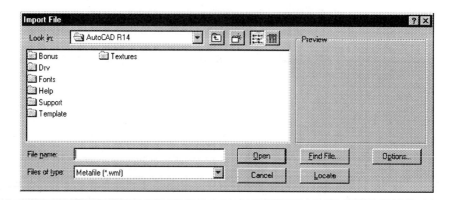

Figure 13–41 Import File dialog box

Table 13–2 Lists the format types available to import into AutoCAD

Format Type	Description
3DS format:	Imports a 3D Studio file
DXF format:	Imports drawing interchange file
EPS format:	Imports Encapsulated PostScript file
SAT format:	Imports ACIS solid object file
WMF format:	Imports Windows Metafile

INTERNET UTILITIES

The Internet is the most important way to convey digital information around the world. You are probably already familiar with the best-known uses of the Internet: e-mail (electronic mail) and the Web (short for "World Wide Web"). E-mail lets users exchange messages and data at very low cost. The Web brings together text, graphics, audio, and movies in an easy-to-use format. Other uses of the Internet include FTP (file transfer protocol, for effortless binary-file transfer), Gopher (presents data in a structured, subdirectory-like format), and Usenet, a collection of more than 10,000 news groups.

AutoCAD allows you to interact with the Internet in several ways. AutoCAD Release 14 is able to launch a Web browser from within AutoCAD. Release 14 can create DWF (short for "drawing Web format") files for viewing drawings in 2D format on Web pages. Release 14 can open, insert, and save drawings to and from the Internet.

Launching the Default Web Browser

The BROWSER command lets you start a Web browser from within AutoCAD. By default, the BROWSER command uses whatever brand of Web browser program is registered in your computer's Windows operating system. AutoCAD lists the name of the browser before prompting you for the URL (short for "uniform resource locator").

The URL is the Web site address, such as http://www.autodesk.com. (More about URLs in the next section.) The BROWSER command can be used in scripts, toolbar or menu macros, and AutoLISP routines to access the Internet automatically.

Invoke the BROWSER command from:

Standard toolbar	Select the Launch Browser command (see Figure 13–42)
Command: prompt	**browser** Enter

Figure 13–42 Invoking the Launch Browser command from the Standard Toolbar

AutoCAD prompts:

Command: **browser**
Default Browser: C:\INTERNET\NETSCAPE\PROGRAM\NETSCAPE.EXE
Browse <www.autodesk.com>: *(specify a new location, or press* Enter *to accept the default location)*

The default URL is Autodesk's own Web site. After you type the URL and press Enter, AutoCAD launches the Web browser, which contacts the Web site. Figure 13–43 shows Netscape Communicator and the Autodesk Web site.

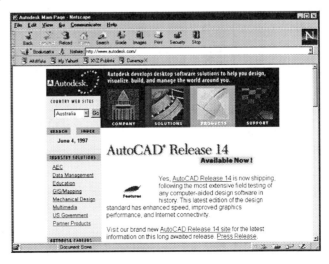

Figure 13–43 Netscape Communicator displaying the Autodesk Web site

Utility Commands

> **NOTE:** If the BROWSER command (or any other command mentioned in this chapter) does not work on your computer, you need to load it into AutoCAD. The BROWSER command is located in the program file called *Browser.Arx*. Use the AppLoad command to locate and load the program, as shown in the Figure 13–44. Table 13–3 presents four programs that contain Internet-related commands for AutoCAD Release 14.

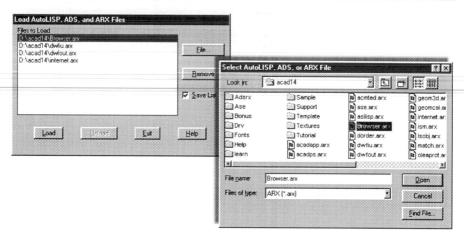

Figure 13–44 AppLoad dialog boxes

Table 13–3 ObjectArx Programs Containing Internet-Related Commands

Program	Command Names
Browser.Arx	Browser
Dwfiu.Arx	Attachurl
	Detachurl
	Listurl
	Selecturl
Dwfout.Arx	Dwfout
	Dwfoutd
Internet.Arx	Inectfg
	Inethelp
	Inserturl
	Openurl
	Saveurl

Uniform Resource Locator

As mentioned earlier, the file-naming system of the Internet is known as URL, short for "uniform resource locator." The URL system allows you to find any resource (a file) on the Internet. Example resources include a text file, a Web page, a program file, an audio or movie clip—in short, anything you might also find on your own computer. The primary difference is that these resources are located on somebody else's computer. A typical URL looks like the examples in Table 13–4.

Table 13–4 Example URLs

Example	Meaning
http://www.autodesk.com	Autodesk primary Web site
http://data.autodesk.com	Autodesk data publishing Web site
news://adesknews.autodesk.com	Autodesk news server
ftp://ftp.autodesk.com	Autodesk FTP server

The "http://" prefix is not required. Most of today's Web browsers automatically add in this routing prefix, which saves you a few keystrokes. URLs can access several different kinds of resources—such as Web sites, e-mail, news groups—but always take on the following format:

    scheme://netloc

The "scheme" accesses the specific resource on the Internet, including those in Table 13–5.

Table 13–5 URL Prefix Meanings

Scheme Prefix	Meaning
file://	Files on your computer's hard drive or local network
ftp://	File transfer protocol (downloading files)
http://	Hypertext transfer protocol (Web sites)
mailto://	Electronic mail (e-mail)
news://	Usenet news (news groups)
telnet://	Telnet protocol
gopher://	Gopher protocol

The ":///" characters indicate a network address. Table 13-6 lists the formats recommended for specifying URL-style file names with the BROWSER command. *Servername* is the name of the server, such as "www.autodesk.com." The *pathname* is the same as a subdirectory or folder name. The *drive:* is the driver letter, such as C: or D:. A *local file* is a file located on your computer. The *localhost* is the name of the network host computer.

Table 13-6 Recommended Formats for Specifying URL-Style File Names

Drawing Location	Template URL
Web site	http://servername/pathname/filename
FTP site	ftp://servername/pathname/filename
Local file	file:///drive:/pathname/filename
	file:///drive|/pathname/filename
	file://\\localPC\pathname\filename
	file:////localPC/pathname/filename
Network file	file://localhost/drive:/pathname/filename
	file://localhost/drive|/pathname/filename

URLs are used indirectly by the Web browser in several different ways. The first way places URLs in the drawing for use by the browser when the drawing is exported in DWF format. To help make the process clearer, here are the steps you need to take to make use of URLs:

Step 1: Open a drawing in AutoCAD.

Step 2. Place URLs in the drawing with the ATTACHURL command.

Step 3: Export the drawing with the DWFOUT command.

Step 4: Copy the DWF file to your Web site.

Step 5: Start your Web browser with the BROWSER command.

Step 6: View the DWF file and click on a hyperlink spot.

The second method employs URLs to access drawings over the Internet. For example, the INSERTURL command uses the URL typed in to locate and insert a drawing as a block. If the Web site contains both the DWF files (that you are viewing) and the original DWG file, then you can drag the DWG file into the current AutoCAD drawing.

A third purpose of URLs is to let you create links between files. By simply clicking on a link, you automatically access additional information. For example, clicking on the parts list in the drawing might bring up the original Excel file used to create the parts list. Clicking on a standard detail might bring up the local building code. Clicking on a side view might bring up the 3D perspective view.

However, there is one significant limitation to URLs in AutoCAD. You cannot use a URL directly within a drawing to create hyperlinks inside of AutoCAD. Following are additional limitations you may come across working with URLs in AutoCAD:

■ AutoCAD does not check that the URL you type is valid.
■ If you attach a URL to a block, the URL data will be lost when you scale the block unevenly, stretch the block, or explode it.
■ You cannot attach a URL to rays and xlines, since the URL would be infinitely long, something the DWF format cannot handle.
■ Wide polylines have a URL that is only one-pixel wide, not the full width of the polyline.

Attaching URLs

The ATTACHURL command allows you to attach one or more URLs to objects and rectangular areas in a drawing. Note that you cannot use URLs in a drawing. Instead, after one or more URLs are inserted in the drawing, you must export the drawing in DWF format using the DWFOUT command. Then, when the DWF file is displayed by a Web browser, the URL locations take on special meaning. The location of the URL is sometimes called a *hyperlink*. When you click on the hyperlink, the Web browser automatically accesses the related URL file location.

The "object" URL is best for attaching hyperlinks to one or more objects. The "area" URL is best for placing a hyperlink around a group of objects or in an area where there are no objects.

Invoke the ATTACHURL command from:

Internet Utilities toolbar	Select Attach URL command (see Figure 13–45)
Command: prompt	**attachurl** [Enter]

Figure 13–45 Invoking the Attach URL command from the Internet Utilities toolbar

AutoCAD prompts:

Command: **attachurl**
URL by (Area/<Objects>): *(select one of the two available options)*

Objects Option The Objects option allows you to select an object to which to attach a URL. If you select multiple objects, then AutoCAD attaches the URL to all the selected objects. AutoCAD gives no indication that an object has a URL attached. Attaching a URL to an object is sometimes called a *ID link*. It is a one-dimensional link because you pick a single object to activate it within the Web browser. (Technically, the URL is stored in that object's extended entity data, or *xdata* for short.)

Area Option The Area option allows you to define an area around which AutoCAD creates a rectangle. Since AutoCAD gives no visible indication which objects contain a URL, you might prefer to place the URL in a rectangular area, which shows up in the drawing as a red rectangle.

Attaching the URL to an area is sometimes called a *2D link*. It is a two-dimensional link because you can pick anywhere in that area to activate the hyperlink. When the URL is an area, AutoCAD creates a layer named URLLAYER (with the color red), places the rectangle, and stores the URL as xdata of that rectangle.

Be careful that you do not overlap URLs (either objects or areas), since you could hyperlink to the wrong URL. If you find the URL rectangles distracting, turn off the URLLAYER layer. Do not delete or freeze that layer, since it will not be exported by the DWFOUT command.

Selecting URLs

Although you can see the rectangle of area URLs, object URLs and the URLs themselves are invisible. For this reason, AutoCAD has the SELECTURL command, which highlights all objects and areas that have URLs attached. Invoke the SELECTURL command from:

Internet Utilities toolbar	Select the Select URLs command (see Figure 13–46)
Command: prompt	**selecturl** Enter

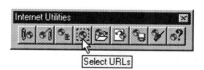

Figure 13–46 Invoking the Select URLs command from the Internet Utilities toolbar

AutoCAD highlights all objects that have a URL, including URL area rectangles. Depending on your computer's display system, the highlighting shows up as dashed lines or another color.

Listing URLs

The LISTURL command lists any URLs attached to an object in a drawing. Invoke the LISTURL command from:

Internet Utilities toolbar	Select the List URLs command (see Figure 13–47)
Command: prompt	**listurl** Enter

Figure 13–47 Invoking the List URLs command from the Internet Utilities toolbar

AutoCAD prompts:

Command: **listurl**
Select objects: *(select the objects that have URLs attached, and press* Enter *to complete object selection)*

You cannot use the LIST command, since it does not display xdata. If you really want to see the full details, use the XDLIST command found in the Bonus menu. This program lists all extended entity data found in the selected objects.

Detaching URLs

The DETTACHURL command removes the hyperlink to a Web site identified by the attached URL from an object or area. Invoke the DETACHURL command from:

Internet Utilities toolbar	Select the Detach URLs command (see Figure 13–48)
Command: prompt	**detachurl** Enter

Figure 13–48 Invoking the Detach URLs command from the Internet Utilities toolbar

AutoCAD prompts:

Command: **detachurl**
Select objects: *(select one or more objects or an area to which an URL is attached, and press* Enter *to complete object or area selection)*

When you select the rectangle of an area URL, AutoCAD erases the rectangle and reports, "DetachURL, deleting the area." If there are no more area URLs remaining, AutoCAD also purges the URLLAYER layer name.

Drawing Web Format

To display AutoCAD drawings on the Internet, Autodesk invented a new file format called *Drawing Web Format*, or *.DWF* for short. The *.DWF* file has several benefits and some drawbacks. The *.DWF* file is compressed and is as small as 1/8 of the original *.DWG* drawing file so that it takes less time to transmit over the Internet, particularly with the relatively slow telephone modem connections. The *.DWF* format is more secure, since the original drawing is not being displayed. Another user cannot tamper with the original *.DWG* file.

However, the *.DWF* format has drawbacks. You must go through the extra step of translating from *.DWG* to *.DWF*. *.DWF* files cannot display rendered or shaded drawings. *.DWF* is a flat, 2D file format; therefore, it does not preserve 3D data, although you can export a 3D view. The early versions of *.DWF* (version 2.x and earlier) did not handle paper space objects.

To view a *.DWF* file on the Internet, your Web browser needs a *plug-in*. A plug-in is a software extension that lets a Web browser handle a variety of file formats. Autodesk makes the *.DWF* plug-in freely available from its Web site. It's a good idea to check regularly the following URL for updates to the *.DWF* plug-in, which is updated about twice a year at http://www.autodesk.com. (The exact location of the *.DWF* plug-in is not given, since Autodesk changes its Web site around every year. Simply use the Web site's Index to search for the plug-in.)

To view AutoCAD *.DWG* and *.DXF* files on the Internet, your Web browser needs a *.DWG-.DXF* plug-in from a third-party developer, since Autodesk does not make one available. The plug-ins are available free for noncommercial use from the following vendors:

SoftSource   http://www.softsource.com/

California Software Labs   http://www.cswl.com

To create a *.DWF* file, invoke the DWFOUT command from:

Command: prompt	**dwfout** Enter

AutoCAD displays the Create .DWF File dialog box shown in Figure 13–49. Select the directory in which you want to save the *.DWF* format file, and type the file name in the File name: edit field. To set the options for conversion to *.DWF* format, choose the **Options...** button. AutoCAD displays the .DWF Export Options dialog box shown in Figure 13–50.

In the DWF Export Options dialog box, select one of the three available radio buttons for Precision. Unlike AutoCAD *.DWG* files, which are based on real numbers, *.DWF* files are saved using integer numbers. With the **Low** precision setting AuotCAD saves the drawing using 16-bit integers, which is adequate for all but the most complex drawings. The file is about 40% smaller than High precision, which means a 40% faster transmission time over the Internet. **Medium** precision saves the *.DWF* file using 20-bit integers. **High** precision saves *using* 32-bit integers.

The **Use File Compression** check box controls whether or not to compress the *.DWF* file. Compression further reduces the size of the *.DWF* file. You should always use compression, unless you know that another application cannot decompress the *.DWF* file.

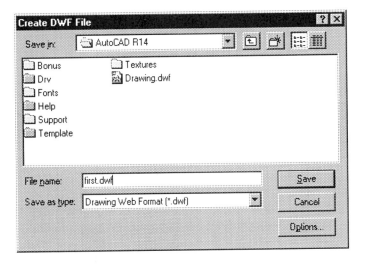

Figure 13–49 Create DWF File dialog box

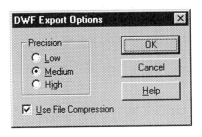

Figure 13–50 DWF Export Options dialog box

Utility Commands

AutoCAD itself cannot display *DWF* files, nor can *DWF* files be converted back to *DWG* format without using file translation software from a third-party vendor.

Viewing *DWF* Files

In order to view a *DWF* file, you need a Web browser with a special plug-in that allows the browser to interpret the file correctly. (Remember: You cannot view a *DWF* file with AutoCAD.) Autodesk has named their *DWF* plug-in *Whip!*, short for "Windows HIgh Performance." The plug-in should not be confused with the AutoCAD display driver, even though both are named Whip! Table 13–7 summarizes the differences between the two products. To help reduce confusion, we'll call the Whip plug-in the *DWF* plug-in.

Table 13–7 Differences Between Whip Plug-in and Whip Display Driver

	Whip Plug-in	**Whip Display Driver**
Meant for:	Viewing *DWF* files	Displaying AutoCAD drawings
Works in:	Web browsers	AutoCAD Releases 13 and 14
DWF file:	Read, view, and print	Export only
Available from:	Autodesk Web site	Included with AutoCAD

Autodesk updates the DWF plug-in approximately twice a year. Each update includes some new features. In summary, all versions of the Whip plug-in perform the following functions:

■ View *DWF* files created by AutoCAD within a browser.
■ Right-clicking the DWF image displays a cursor menu with commands.
■ Real-time pan and zoom lets you change the view of the *DWF* file as quickly as a drawing file in AutoCAD R14.
■ Embedded hyperlinks let you display other documents and files.
■ File compression means that a *DWF* file appears in your Web browser faster than the equivalent *DWG* drawing file would.
■ Print the *DWF* file alone or along with the entire Web page.
■ Work with Netscape Navigator v3.x or Microsoft Internet Explorer v3.x. A separate plug-in is required, depending which of the two browsers you use.

At the time of writing this book, *DWF* plug-in Release 2 was current. Here are some the features:

■ Views DWF files created by AutoCAD R14 and R13.
■ Allows you to "drag and drop" a *DWG* file from a Web site into AutoCAD R14 as a new drawing or as a block.

- Views percentage- or pixel-specified *DWF* files; views a *DWF* file in a specified browser frame; views a named view stored in the *DWF* file; and can specify a view using X, Y coordinates.
- Turns the user interface on and off.
- Sends *DWF* file information to CGI scripts.
- Supports Netscape Communicator v4.0 (previously named Navigator) and Microsoft Internet Explorer v4.0 Web browsers. A separate plug-in is required for each browser.
- Supports raster images in *DWF* files; renders images as a purple outline during pans and zooms to help speed up the display.
- Supports TrueType fonts.

To use the Whip plug-in with a Web browser, your computer should have a fast CPU, such as an 80486, Pentium, or Pentium Pro. Your computer must be running Windows 95, Windows NT v3.51 (with service pack 5), or Windows NT v4.0. The computer should display at least 256 colors. The Web browser must be at least Netscape v3.0x or Explorer v3.0x.

If you don't know whether the *DWF* plug-in is installed in your Web browser, select Help > About Plug-ins from the browser's menu bar. You may need to scroll through the list of plug-ins to find something like this:

```
WHIP!
File name: C:\INTERNET\NETSCAPE\PROGRAM\plugins\npdwf.dll
Autodesk Drawing Web Format File
Mime Type        Description              Suffixes    Enabled
Drawing/x-dwf    Drawing Web Format file  dwf         Yes
```

If the plug-in is not installed or is an older version, then you need to download it from Autodesk's Web site at http://www.autodesk.com/products/. For Netscape users, the file is quite large at 3.5 MB and takes about a half hour to download using a typical 28.8-Kbaud modem. The file you download from the Autodesk Web site is a self-extracting installation file with a name such as *Whip2.Exe*. After the download is complete, start the program and follow the instructions on the screen.

> **NOTE:** If your computer has an older version of the *DWF* plug-in for Netscape, you must uninstall it before installing the newer version. If the Netscape Web browser is running, close it before installing the *DWF* plug-in.

For Internet Explorer users, the *DWF* plug-in is an ActiveX control. Explorer's auto-download feature automatically installs the control the first time your browser accesses a Web page that includes a *DWF* file. The download time is about 10 minutes with a 28.8-Kbps modem.

DWF Plug-in Commands

To display the DWF plug-in's commands, move the cursor over the DWF image and press the mouse's right button. This displays a cursor menu with the commands Pan, Zoom, NAMED VIEWS. To select a command, move the cursor over the command name and press the left mouse button.

Pan Pan is the default command. Press the left mouse button and move the mouse. The cursor changes to an open hand to signal that you can pan the view around the drawing. This is exactly the same as real-time panning in AutoCAD. Panning works only when you are zoomed in; it does not work in Full View mode.

Zoom Zoom is like the ZOOM Realtime command in AutoCAD. The cursor changes to a magnifying glass. Hold down the left mouse button and move the cursor up (to zoom in) or down (to zoom out).

Zoom to Rectangle Zoom to Rectangle is the same as ZOOM Window in AutoCAD. The cursor changes to a plus sign. Click the left mouse button at one corner, and then drag the rectangle to specify the size of the new view.

Fit to Window Fit to Window is the same as the AutoCAD ZOOM Extents command. You see the entire drawing.

Full View Full View causes the Web browser to display the *DWF* image as large as possible by itself. This is useful for increasing the physical size of a small DWF image. When you are done viewing the large image, right-click and select the BACK command or click the browser's BACK button to return to the previous screen.

Named Views NAMED VIEWS works only when the original *DWG* drawing file contained named views created with the VIEW command. Selecting NAMED VIEWS displays a *nonmodal* dialog box that allows you to select a named view. (A *nonmodal* dialog box remains on the screen; unlike AutoCAD modal dialog boxes, you do not need to dismiss a nonmodal dialog box to continue working.) Double-click a named view to see it; click OK to dismiss the dialog box.

Highlight URLs Highlight URLs displays a highlight box around all objects and areas with URLs in the image. This helps you see where the hyperlinks are. To read the associated URL, pass the cursor over a highlight area and look at the URL on the browser's status line. (A shortcut is to hold down `Shift`, which causes the URLs to highlight until you release `Shift`).

Print The Print option prints the *DWF* image. To print the entire Web page (including the *DWF* image), use the browser's Print button.

SaveAs SaveAs saves the *DWF* file in one of three formats to your computer's hard drive: *DWF*, *BMP* (Windows bitmap), or *DWG*. Saving in *DWG* (AutoCAD drawing file) format works only when a copy of the *DWG* file is available at the same subdirectory as the *DWF* file. You cannot use the SAVEAS command until the entire *DWF* file has finished being transmitted to your computer.

About WHIP About WHIP displays information about the *DWF* file, including the *DWF* file revision number, description, author, creator, source file name, creation time, modification time, source creation time, source modification time, current view left, current view right, current view bottom, and current view top.

Back Back is almost the same as clicking the browser's Back button. It works differently when the *DWF* image is displayed in a frame.

Forward Forward is almost the same as clicking the browser's Forward button. When the *DWF* image is in a frame, only that frame goes forward.

Drag-and-Drop

The *DWF* plug-in allows you to perform several drag-and-drop functions. Drag-and-drop is when you use the mouse to drag an object from one application to another.

Hold down ⌁Ctrl⌁ to drag a *DWF* file from the browser into AutoCAD. Recall that AutoCAD cannot translate a *DWF* file into *DWG* drawing format. For this reason, this form of drag-and-drop works only when the originating *DWG* file exists in the same subdirectory as the *DWF* file. (This may change in a future release of the *DWF* plug-in when *DWG* directory and *DWF* directory options are implemented.) Note that this drag-and-drop function works only for AutoCAD Release 14; it does not work with AutoCAD Release 13 or earlier.

Another drag-and-drop function is to drag a *DWF* file from the Windows Explorer (or File Manager) into the Web browser. This causes the Web browser to load the *DWF* plug-in and, then to display the *DWF* file. Once the file is displayed, you can execute all of the commands listed in the previous section.

Finally, you can also drag-and-drop a *DWF* file from the Windows Explorer (or File Manager) into AutoCAD. This causes AutoCAD to launch another program that is able to view the *DWF* file. This does not work if you have no other software on your computer system capable of viewing *DWF* files.

Embedding a *DWF* File

To let others view your *DWF* file over the Internet, you need to embed the *DWF* file in a Web page. There are several approaches to embedding a *DWF* file in a Web page.

The quickest way is to use the <embed> tag in a very simple manner. <Embed> is an HTML (hypertext markup language) code for embedding an object in a Web page.

```
<embed src="filename.dwf">
```

Replace "filename.dwf" with the name of the *DWF* file. Remember to keep the quotation marks in place. To specify the size of the *DWF* image on the Web page, include the Width and Height options.

```
<embed width=800 height=600 name=description src="filename.dwf">
```

Replace 800 and 600 with any appropriate numbers, such as 100 and 75 for a "thumbnail" image, 300 and 200 for a small image, or 640 and 480 for a medium-size image. These width and height values are measured in pixels.

The Name option displays a textual description of the image when the browser does not load images. For example, you might replace *description* with the *DWF* file name.

If you use Netscape Navigator, you can include a description of where to get the Whip plug-in if it is not available with the Web browser.

```
<embed width=800 height=600 name=description src="filename.dwf"
pluginspage=http://www.autodesk.com/products/autocad/whip/
    whip.htm>
```

If you use Microsoft Internet Explorer, you must add the <object> and <param> tags.

```
<object width=600 height=400 classid="clsid:b2be75f3-9197-11cf-abf4-
    08000996e931"
codebase="ftp://ftp.autodesk.com/pub/autocad/plugin/
    whip.cab#Version=2,0,0,0">
<param name="description" value="filename.dwf">
<embed width=600 height=400 name=description src="filename.dwf"
pluginspage=http://www.autodesk.com/products/autocad/whip/
    whip.htm>
    </object>
```

Opening a Drawing from a URL

When a drawing is stored on the Internet, you can access it from within AutoCAD with the OPENURL command. Instead of specifying the file's location with the usual drive-subdirectory-file name format, such as C:\ACAD14\FILENAME.DWG, you use the URL format. Recall that the URL is the universal file-naming system by which the Internet accesses any file located on any computer hooked up to the Internet.

Invoke the OPENURL command from:

Internet Utilities toolbar	Select the Open from URL command (see Figure 13–51)
Command: prompt	**openurl** Enter

Open from URL

Figure 13–51 Invoking the Open from URL command from the Internet Utilities toolbar

AutoCAD displays the Open DWG from URL dialog box, similar to Figure 13–52. The dialog box prompts you to type the URL. For your convenience, AutoCAD fills in the preliminary "http://," which is needed to access Web pages. If you plan to access a different resource on the Internet, erase the http:// and replace it. For example, you might want to replace it with ftp:// to access a drawing at an FTP site. Table 13–8 lists templates for typing the URL for opening a drawing file.

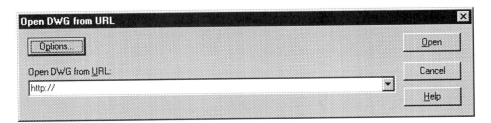

Figure 13–52 Open DWG from URL dialog box

Table 13–8 Template URLs for Opening a Drawing File

Drawing Location	Template URL
Web or http site	http://servername/pathname/filename.dwg
FTP site	ftp://servername/pathname/filename.dwg
Local file	file:///drive:/pathname/filename.dwg
Network file	file://localhost/drive:/pathname/filename.dwg

When you want AutoCAD to deal with "secure" sites that ask you for a user name and password, open the Internet Configuration dialog box shown in Figure 13–53 by choosing the Options button in the Open DWG from URL dialog box. Very often, you do not need such secure sites. For example, most FTP sites allow *anonymous* logins, for which you need no password and the user name is *anonymous*. Most Web sites require no login at all. For security reasons, the passwords are not retained once you exit AutoCAD.

To access a secure FTP site, turn OFF the Anonymous Login check box and type in your user name and password.

To access a secure Web site (also called an http site), type your user name and password. If you prefer, you can leave them blank; later, AutoCAD will display a User Authentication dialog box, where you can enter the user name and password.

Select the Direct Connection radio button when your computer connects with the Internet via an Internet service provider. When your computer connects to the Internet through a proxy server, select the Proxy Server button. (Most typically,

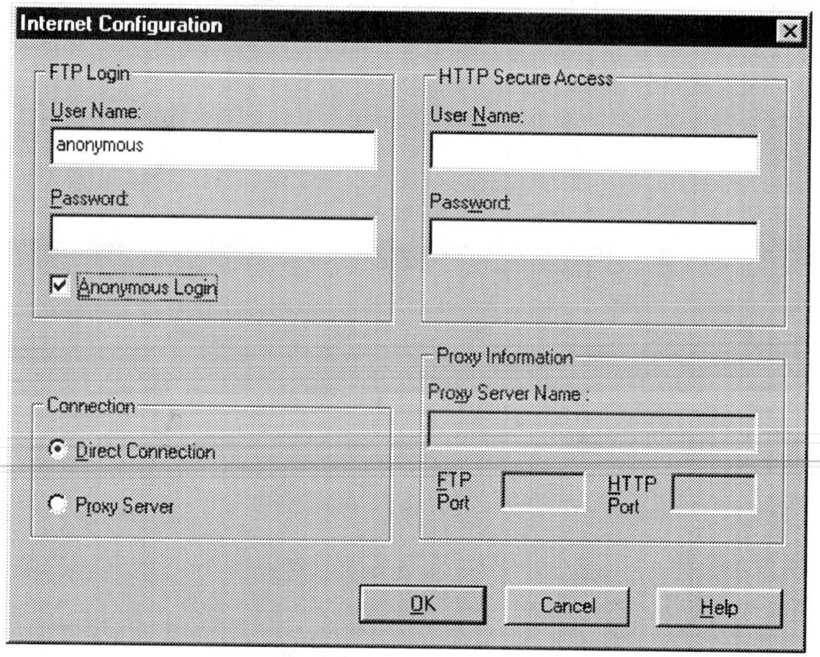

Figure 13-53 Internet Configuration dialog box

larger firms have a *proxy server* that acts as a gateway between the firm's internal network and the external Internet. Ask your system administrator for the details of how to configure the proxy server, including the proxy server name, default FTP port, and default http port.

Choose the **OK** button to close the Internet Configuration dialog box.

To open the drawing, choose the **Open** button in the Open DWG from URL dialog box. If necessary, AutoCAD prompts you to save the current drawing before opening the drawing from the Internet. During file transfer, AutoCAD displays a dialog box to report the progress. If your computer uses a 28.8K-bps modem, you should allow about 10 minutes per megabyte of drawing file size. If your computer has access to a faster T1 connection to the Internet, you should expect a transfer speed of about 1 minute per megabyte.

It may be helpful to understand that the OPENURL command does not copy the file from the Internet location directly into AutoCAD. Instead, it copies the file from the Internet to your computer's designated Temporary subdirectory, such as C:\WIN95\TEMP (and then loads the drawing from the hard drive into AutoCAD). This is known as *caching*. It helps to speed up the processing of the drawing, since the drawing file is now located on your computer's fast hard drive instead of on the relatively slow Internet.

Inserting a Block from a URL

When a block (symbol) is stored on the Internet, you can access it from within AutoCAD by means of the INSERTURL command. The INSERTURL command works just like the OPENURL command, except that the external block is inserted into the current drawing.

Invoke the INSERTURL command from:

Internet Utilities toolbar	Select the Insert from URL command (see Figure 13–54)
Command: prompt	**inserturl** Enter

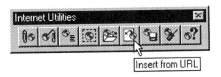

Figure 13–54 Invoking the Insert from URL command from the Internet Utilities toolbar

AutoCAD displays the Insert DWG from URL dialog box, similar to Figure 13–55. The dialog box prompts you to type the URL. After you choose the Insert button, AutoCAD retrieves the file and continues with the INSERT command's familiar prompts.

```
_.insert Block name (or ?): c:\win95\temp\filename.dwg
Insertion point: (pick insertion point)
X scale factor <1> / Corner / XYZ: (specify the X scale factor)
Y scale factor (default=X): (specify the Y scale factor)
Rotation angle <0>: (specify the rotation angle)
```

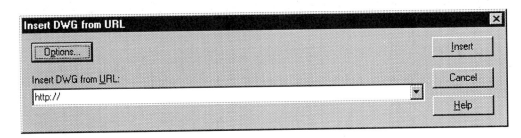

Figure 13–55 Insert DWG from URL dialog box

Saving a Drawing to a URL

When you are finished editing a drawing in AutoCAD, you can save it to a file server on the Internet with the SAVEURL command. If you inserted the drawing from the Internet (using INSERTURL) into the default *DRAWING.DWG* drawing, AutoCAD insists that you first save the drawing to your computer's hard drive.

Invoke the SAVEURL command from:

Internet Utilities toolbar	Select the Save to URL command (see Figure 13–56)
Command: prompt ˜	**openurl** Enter

Figure 13–56 Invoking the Save to URL command from the Internet Utilities toolbar

AutoCAD displays the Save DWG from URL dialog box, similar to Figure 13–57. The dialog box prompts you to type the URL. For your convenience, AutoCAD fills in the preliminary "ftp://," which is needed to write a file to an FTP site. The reason that "http://" is not displayed is that you have to write a file to a Web site using FTP (file transfer protocol). And AutoCAD will not allow you to use "file://" or other URL prefixes.

When a drawing with the same name already exists at that URL, AutoCAD warns you, just like when you use the SAVEAS command. Recall from our discussion on the OPENURL command that AutoCAD uses your computer system's Temporary subdirectory, hence the reference to it in the dialog box.

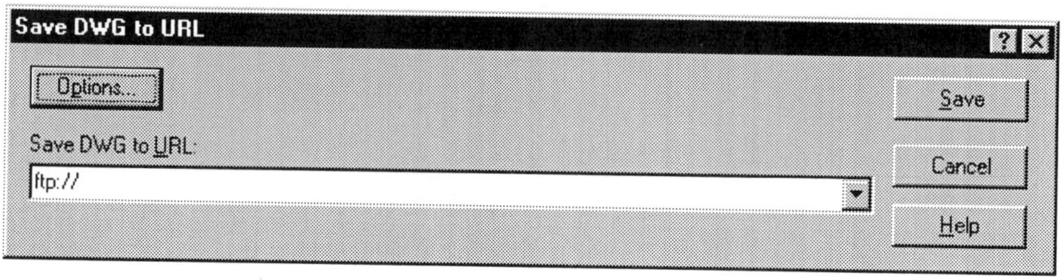

Figure 13–57 Save DWG to URL dialog box

PROJECT EXERCISE

In this project, you use AutoCAD URL tools to place several URLs in a drawing. The URLs are listed, one is deleted, and then the drawing is exported in *DWF* format. If your computer system has a Web browser installed with the *DWF* plug-in, then in this project you drag a *DWF* file into the browser. Finally, if your computer can access the Internet, this project has you open a drawing from the Autodesk Press Web site.

Step 1   Start AutoCAD and open any drawing file.

Step 2   Place an area URL anywhere in the drawing. Invoke the ATTACHURL command; AutoCAD prompts:

> Command: **attachurl**
> URL by (Area/<Objects>): **a**
> First corner: *(specify a point)*
> Other corner: *(specify point)*
> Enter URL: **http://www.autodesk.com**

AutoCAD places a red rectangle in the drawing similar to Figure P13–1

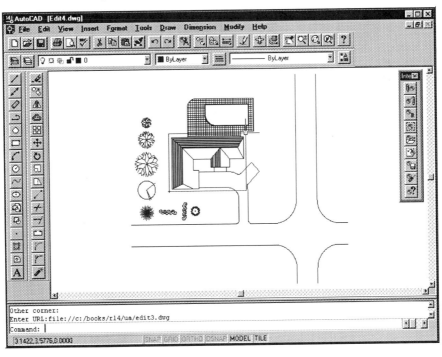

Figure P13–1 URL placed in a drawing

Step 3   Attach a URL to an object in the drawing by invoking the ATTACHURL command; AutoCAD prompts:

> Command: **attachurl**
> URL by (Area/<Objects>): **o**
> Select objects: *(select an object)*
> Select objects: *(press* Enter *to terminate the selection of objects)*
> Enter URL: **http://data.autodesk.com**

Step 4   To highlight the areas and objects that have URLs, invoke the SELECTURL command; AutoCAD prompts:

> Command: **selecturl**

AutoCAD highlights the area URLs and object URLs, similar to Figure P13–2.

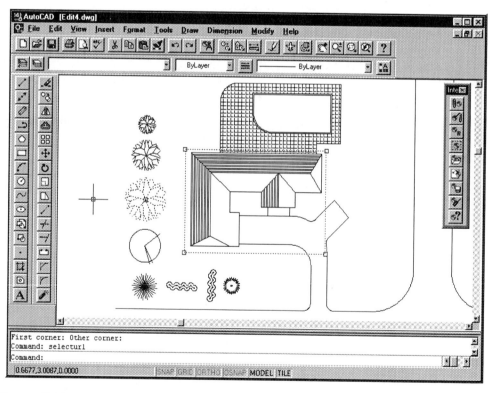

Figure P13–2 Highlighted URLs

Step 5   To list the names of the URLs, invoke the LISTURL command; AutoCAD prompts:

Command: **listurl**
URL for selected object is: http://www.autodesk.com
URL for selected object is: http://data.autodesk.com

Since the URL objects were already selected (highlighted), the LISTURL command did not prompt you to select objects. To remove the highlighting of the objects and the areas that have URLs, press ⎋ twice.

Step 6   Invoke the DETACHURL command to delete the URL attached to an object. AutoCAD prompts:

Command: **detachurl**
Select objects: *(select the object that contains the URL)*
Select Objects: *(press ⏎ to terminate object selection)*

Step 7   Invoke the DWFOUT command to export the current drawing as a *DWF* file.

Command: **dwfout**

AutoCAD displays the Create DWF File dialog box. Choose the Options button, AutoCAD displays the DWF Export Options dialog box. Select Low precision and choose **OK** to close the DWF Export Options dialog box. Select the Save button to save the current drawing as a *DWF* file.

Step 8   If your Web browser has the *DWF* plug-in installed, start the Web browser.

Step 9   Switch to Windows Explorer (or File Manager) and locate the *DWF* file you created in the previous step. If necessary, use the Search function to find *.*DWF*.

Step 10   Drag the *DWF* file from Windows Explorer (or the File Manager) into the browser. The browser will take several seconds first to load the plug-in and then to load and display the *DWF* file.

Step 11   Place the cursor in the image and right-click the mouse button to open the cursor menu. Practice selecting several commands, such as Zoom, Pan, and Print.

Step 12   To remove the image, click the browser's Back button.

Step 13   Switch back to AutoCAD and start a new drawing by selecting the Start from Scratch option.

Step 14   If your computer is not logged on to the Internet, do so now. For example, if you access the Internet through an Internet service provider, use the Dial-up Networking feature of Windows to access the Internet service provider.

Utility Commands

Step 15 Switch back to AutoCAD and invoke the OPENURL command to open a drawing using a URL. AutoCAD displays the Open DWG from URL dialog box. Type the following URL:

http://www.practicewrench.autodeskpress.com

Choose the Open button. AutoCAD displays the Remote Transfer in Progress dialog box. The file is 25 KB in size and should take a few seconds to download.

Once the Wrench drawing appears, as shown in Figure P13–3, it looks just like any drawing you open from your computer's hard drive.

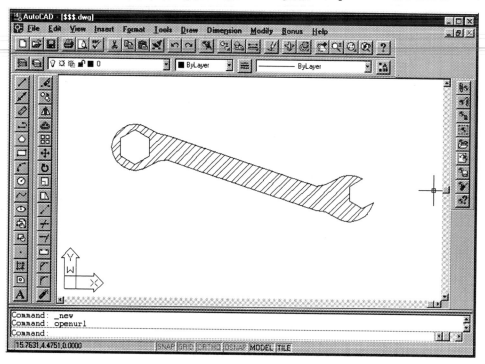

Figure P13–3 *Wrench.Dwg* opened from the Internet

Save the drawing in your local drive and exit AutoCAD.

REVIEW QUESTIONS

1. All of the following can be renamed using the RENAME command, except:
   a. current drawing name
   b. named views within the current drawing
   c. block names within the current drawing
   d. text style names within the current drawing

2. The PURGE command can be used:
   a. after an editing session
   b. at the beginning of the editing session
   c. at any time during the editing session
   d. A and B only

3. To calculate the product of 4 times 21.5 times pi and store it for use with later AutoCAD commands, you should respond to the ">>Expression" prompt of the CAL command with:
   a. A=* 4 21.5 pi
   b. A= 4 * 21.5 * 3.14
   c. A= 4 * 21.5 * pi
   d. A= (* 4 21.5 pi)
   e. none of the above

4. To use the product from the previous question to respond to a scale factor in the SCALE command you would type:
   a. %A
   b. ^A
   c. !A
   d. A
   e. (A)

5. The most common setting for the current drawing color is:
   a. Red
   b. Bylayer
   c. Byblock
   d. White
   e. none of the above

6. Which of the following are not valid color names in AutoCAD:
   a. Brown
   b. Red
   c. Yellow
   d. Magenta
   e. none of the above (i.e. all are valid)

7. To change the background color for the graphics drawing area, you should use:
   a. COLOR
   b. BGCOLOR
   c. PREFERENCES
   d. SETTINGS
   e. CONFIG

8. The command to invoke the internet browser in AutoCAD is:
   a. INTERNET
   b. BROWSER
   c. HTTP
   d. WWW
   e. none of the above

9. AutoCAD release 13 can be used to edit a drawing saved as an AutoCAD release 14 drawing?
   a. True
   b. False

10. AutoCAD release 14 can be used to edit a drawing that is saved in an AutoCAD release 13 drawing?
    a. True
    b. False

11. All the following items can be purged from a drawing file, except:
    a. Text styles
    b. Blocks
    c. System variables
    d. Views
    e. Linetypes

12. The following can be deleted with the purge command, except:
    a. blocks not referenced in the current drawing

    b. linetypes that are not being used in t he current drawing
    c. layer 0, if it is not being use
    d. Named views
    e. none of the above (i.e. All can be purged)

13. With the OLE (object linking and embedding) , you can copy or move information from one application to another while retaining the ability to edit the information in the original application.
    a. True
    b. False

14. If the TIME command is not turned off during lunch break, the TIME command will
    a. include the lunch break time
    b. exclude the lunch break time
    c. turn itself off after 10 minutes of inactivity
    d. automatically subtract one hour for lunch
    e. none of the above

15. The VIEW command
    a. servers a purpose similar to the PAN command
    b. will restore previously saved views of your drawing
    c. is normally used on very small drawings
    d. none of the above

16. When using a .X point filter, AutoCAD will request you to complete the point selection process by entering:
    a. An X coordinate
    b. A Y and Z coordinate
    c. An OSNAP mode
    d. Nothing, .X is not a valid filter

17. The geometric calculator function MEE will:
    a. calculate the midpoint of a selected line
    b. calculate the midpoint between the endpoints of any two objects
    c. Return the node name for the computer you are working on
    d. average a string of numbers
    e. none of the above

18. DWF is short for:
    a. DraWing Format.
    b. Drawing Web Format.
    c. DXF Web Format.

19. The purpose of DWF files is to view:
    a. 2D drawings on the Internet.
    b. 3D drawings on the Internet.
    c. 3D drawings in another CAD system.
    d. All of the above.

20. URL is short for:
    a. Union Region Lengthen.
    b. Earl.
    c. Useful Resource Line.
    d. Uniform Resource Locator.

Utility Commands

21. Which of the following URLs are valid:
    a. www.autodesk.com
    b. http://www.autodesk.com
    c. All of the above.
    d. None of the above.

22. What is the purpose of a URL?
    a. Accesses files on computers, networks, and the Internet.
    b. Is a universal filenaming system for the Internet.
    c. Creates a link to another file.
    d. All of the above.

23. FTP is short for:
    a. Forwarding Transfer Protocol
    b. File Transfer Protocol
    c. File Transference Protocol
    d. File Transfer Partition

24. URLs be used in an AutoCAD drawing.
    a. True
    b. False

25. The purpose of URLs is to let you create _____ between files.
    a. Backups.
    b. Links.
    c. Copies.
    d. Partitions.

26. You can attach a URL to rays and xlines.
    a. True
    b. False

27. The Attachurl command allows you to attach a URL to _____ and
    _____.
    a. Objects and files.
    b. Files and folders.
    c. Files and subdirectories.
    d. Areas and objects.

28. To see the location of URLs in a drawing, use the _____ command.
    a. SelectURL
    b. OpenURL
    c. InsertURL
    d. ListURL

29. Rectangular URLs are stored on layer _____.
    a. URLLAYER
    b. LAYERURL
    c. URL
    d. LAYER

30. Compression in the DWF file causes it to take _____ time to transmit over the Internet
    a. More.
    b. Less.
    c. All of the above.
    d. None of the above.

31. A "plug-in" lets a Web browser:
    a. Plug into the Internet.
    b. Display a file format.
    c. Log in to the Internet.
    d. Display a URL.

32. A Web browser can view DWG drawing files over the Internet.
    a. True
    b. False

33. The Whip plug-in and the Whip display driver are the same.
    a. True
    b. False

34. The SAVEURL command saves the _____ to the Internet via _____.
    a. URL; HTTP.
    b. Drawing file; FTP.
    c. DWF file; HTTP.
    d. URL; FTP.

Utility Commands

CHAPTER

14

SPECIAL FEATURES—
SLIDES AND SCRIPTS

INTRODUCTION

Slides are quickly viewable, noneditable views of a drawing or parts of a drawing. There are two primary uses for slides. One is to have a quick and ready picture to display symbols, objects, or written data for information purposes only. The other very useful application of slides is to be able to display a series of pictures, organized in a prearranged sequence for a timed slide show. This is a very useful tool for demonstrations to clients or in a showroom. This feature supplements the time-consuming calling up of views required when using the ZOOM, PAN, or other display commands. The "slide show" is implemented through the SCRIPT command (described later in this chapter).

It should be noted that a slide merely masks the current display. Any cursor movement or editor functions employed while a slide is being displayed affects the current drawing under the slide and not the slide itself.

After completing this chapter, you will be able to:

✓ Make and view a slide
✓ Create a slide library
✓ Create and modify a script file
✓ Create utility commands to use in a script file

Special Features—
Slides and Scripts

MAKING A SLIDE

The current display can be made into a slide with the MSLIDE command. The current viewport becomes the slide while you are working in model space. The entire display, including all viewports, becomes the slide when using MSLIDE while you are working in paper space. The MSLIDE command takes a picture of the current display and stores it in a file, so be sure it is the correct view.

Invoke the MSLIDE command from:

Command: prompt	**mslide** Enter

The **Create Slide File** dialog box appears, as shown in Figure 14–1. The default is the drawing name, which can be used as the slide file name by pressing Enter. Or you can type any other name, as long as you are within the limitations of the operating system file-naming convention. AutoCAD automatically appends the extension *.SLD*. Only objects that are visible in the screen drawing area (or in the current viewport when in model space) are made into the slide.

If you plan to show the slide on different systems, you should use a full-screen view with a high-resolution display for creating the slide.

SLIDE LIBRARIES

The SLIDELIB program provided with AutoCAD is used in conjunction with a list of slide file names. Each slide file name must correspond to an actual slide whose extension is *.SLD*. The list of file names is in a separate file, written in ASCII format, with each slide file name on a separate line by itself. The file names in the list may or may not include the *.SLD* extension, but they must include the path (drive and/or directory) for the SLIDELIB command to access the proper file for inclusion in the library.

A file named *SLDLIST* could read as follows:

        pic_1
        A:pic_2.sld
        c:\dwgs\pic_3.sld
        b:\other\pic_6

Each line represents a slide name, some with extensions, some without. Each one has a different path. When the SLIDELIB command is used to address this file, all the slides listed will be included in the library you specify. The paths are not included when used with the SLIDELIB program. If there were a *PIC_2.SLD* on another path, it would not be included or it would conflict with the one specified for

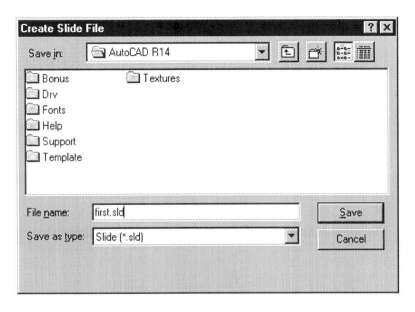

Figure 14-1 Create Slide File dialog box

its particular library file. This allows for control of which slides will be used if the same slide file name exists in several drive/directory locations. The SLIDELIB program appends *.SLB* to the library file it creates from the slide list.

The preceding listing file can be used to create a library file named *ALLPICS.SLB*.

VIEWING A SLIDE

The VSLIDE command displays a slide in the current viewport. Invoke the VSLIDE command from:

Command: prompt	**vslide** Enter

The **Select Slide File** dialog box appears. Select the slide to display in the current viewport. If you have stored the slide in a library file and are calling it up for view, you can use the library file keyname followed by the slide name in parentheses. For example, if a slide named PIC_1 (actually stored under the filename *pic_1.sld*) is in a library file called *ALLPICS.SLB*, you can use the following format:

Command: **vslide**
Slide file <default>: **allpics(pic_1)**

> **NOTE:** The library file lists only the address of each slide. It can be on a path or directory other than that of the slide(s) listed in it. It is not necessary to specify the path in front of the slide name. For example, the *ALLPICS.SLB* file might be on the working directory, while the slide PIC_1 is on drive F in the directory SL1, and the slide PIC_2 is on drive F in the directory SL2. The sequences to call them into view would be as follows:
>
> Command: **vslide**
> Slide file <default>: **allpics(pic_1)**
>
> Command: **vslide**
> Slide file <default>: **allpics(pic_2)**

If the *ALLPICS.SLB* file is on drive F in the subdirectory SLB, the sequences are as follows:

Command: **vslide**
Slide file <default>: **f:\slb\allpics(pic_1)**

Command: **vslide**
Slide file <default>: **f:\slb\allpics(pic_2)**

SCRIPTS

Of the many means available to enhance AutoCAD through customization, scripts are among the easiest to create. Scripts are similar to the macros that can be created to enhance word processing programs. They permit you to combine a sequence of commands and data into one or two entries. Creating a script, like most enhancements to AutoCAD, requires that you use a text editor to write the script file (with the extension *.SCR*), which contains the instructions and data for the SCRIPT command to follow.

Because script files are written for use at a later time, you must anticipate the conditions under which they will be used. Therefore, familiarity with sequences of prompts that will occur and the types of responses required is necessary to have the script function properly. Writing a script is a simple form of programming.

The Script Text

A script text file must be written in ASCII format. That is, it must have no embedded print codes or control characters that are automatically written in files when created with a word processor in the document mode. If you are not using one of the available line editors, be sure you are in the nondocument, programmer, or ASCII mode of your word processor when creating or saving the file. Save the script with the file extension *.SCR.*

Each command can occupy a separate line, or you can combine several command/ data responses on one line. Each space between commands and data is read as an Enter, just as is pressing the Spacebar while in AutoCAD. The end of a line of text is also the same as an Enter.

Spaces and Ends of Lines in Script Files

The following script file contains several commands and data. The commands are GRID, LINE, CIRCLE, LINE, and CIRCLE again. The data are the response ON, coordinates (such as 0,0 and 5,5) and distances, such as radius 3.

```
GRID ON LINE 0,0 5,5  CIRCLE 3,3 3
LINE 0,5 5,0
CIRCLE 5,2.5 1
```

The first line includes the GRID, LINE, and CIRCLE commands and their responses. Note the two spaces after 5,5; these are required to simulate the double Enter. Not obvious is the extra space following the 5,0 response in the second LINE command. This extra space and the invisible CR-LF (carriage-return, linefeed) code that ends every line in a text file combine to simulate pressing the spacebar twice. This is necessary, again, to exit the LINE command.

Some text editors automatically remove blank spaces at the end of text lines. To guard against that, an alternative is to have a blank line indicate the second Enter, as follows:

```
GRID ON LINE 0,0 5,5  CIRCLE 3,3 3
LINE 0,5 5,0

CIRCLE 5,2.5 1
```

Invoke the SCRIPT command from:

Pull-down menu	Tools > Run Script...
Command: prompt	script Enter

AutoCAD displays the **Select Script File** dialog box. Select the appropriate script file from the list box and choose the **Open** button. AutoCAD executes the command sequence from the script file.

Changing Block Definitions with a Script File

Using a script to perform a repetitive task is illustrated in the following example. This application also offers some insight on changing the objects in an inserted block with attributes without affecting the attribute values.

Figure 14-2 shows a group of drawings all of which utilize a common block with attribute values in one insertion that are different from the attribute values of those in other drawings. In this case, the border/title block is a block named BRDR. It was originally drawn with the short lines around and outside of the main border line. It was discovered that these lines interfered with the rollers on the plotter and needed to be removed. The BRDR block definition is shown in Figure 14-3. Remember, the inserted block has different attribute values in each drawing, such as drawing number, date and title.

You want to change objects in the block but maintain the attribute values as they are. There are two approaches to redefinition. One is to find a clear place in the drawing and insert the block with an asterisk (*). This is the same as inserting and exploding the block. Then you make the necessary changes in the objects and make the revised group into a block with the same block name. This redefines all insertions of blocks with that same name in the drawing. In this case there is only one insertion. You must be attentive to how any changes to attributes might affect the already inserted block of that name.

The second method is to use the WBLOCK command to place a copy of the block in a file with the same name. This makes a new and separate drawing of the block. Then you exit the current drawing, call up the newly created drawing, make the required changes in the objects, and end the drawing that was created by the WBLOCK command. Then you re-enter the drawing in which the block objects need to be changed. You now use the INSERT command and respond with "blockname=" and have the block redefined without losing the attribute values. For example, if the block name is BRDR, the sequence would be as follows:

Command: **insert**
Block name: **BRDR=**
Block BRDR redefined
Regenerating drawing.
Insertion point: Esc *(cancels the command sequence)*

The key to this sequence is the equal sign (=) following the block name. This causes AutoCAD to change the definition of the block named BRDR to be that of the drawing named BRDR, but maintains the attribute values as long as attribute definitions remain unchanged.

If the preceding procedure must be repeated many times, this is where a script file can be employed to automate the process. In the following example, we show how to apply the script to a drawing named PLAN_1. The sequence included an Enter as it was described to be used while in AutoCAD. This expedited the operation by not

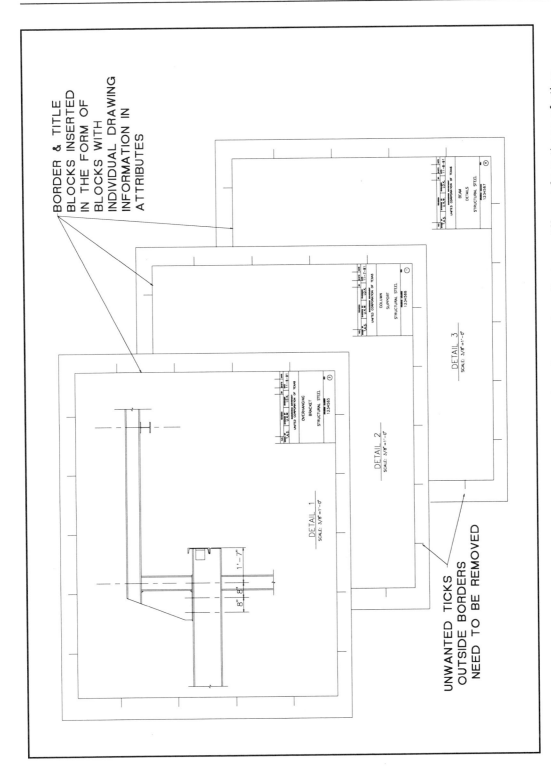

Figure 14–2 Drawings utilizing common block and attribute values that are different from those of other drawings

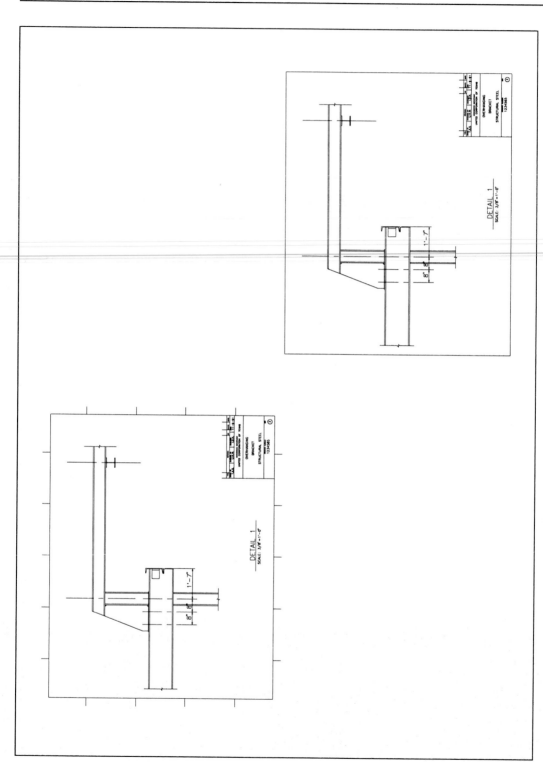

Figure 14–3 A block definition

actually having the block inserted, but only having its definition brought into the drawing. Because an ⌨Enter or ⌨Esc during the running of a script file causes the script to terminate, those keystrokes cannot be in the middle of a script; besides, invoking ⌨Esc in a SCRIPT command requires using the AutoLISP function "(command)." The script can be written in a file (called *BRDRCHNG.SCR* for this example) in ASCII format as follows:

```
INSERT
BRDR=
0,0   (the 0,0 is followed by six spaces)
ERASE L  (the L is followed by one space)
REDRAW
```

Now, from the "Command:" prompt, you can apply the script to drawing PLAN_1 by responding as follows:

Command: **script**

There are several important aspects of this sequence:

Lines 1–2 This is where you might enter ⌨Esc if you were not in the SCRIPT command and have the definition of the block named BRDR take on that of the drawing BRDR without actually having to continue with the insertion in the drawing.

Line 3 In this case, 0,0 as the insertion point is arbitrary because the inserted block is going to be erased anyway. Special attention is to given to the six spaces following the insertion point. These are the same as pressing the Spacebar or ⌨Enter six times in response to the "X-scale," "Y-scale," and "Rotation angle" prompts, and the number of spaces that follow must correspond to the number of attributes that require responses for values. In this example there were three attributes. Again, the fact that the responses are null is immaterial, because this insertion will not be kept.

Line 4 The ERASE L is self-explanatory, but do not forget that after the "L" you must have another space (press the Spacebar again) to terminate the object selection process and complete the ERASE command.

Line 5 The REDRAW command is not really required except to show the user for a second time that the changes have been made before the script ends.

Utility Commands for a Script

Following are the utility commands that may be used within a script file.

DELAY The DELAY command causes the script to pause for the number of milliseconds that have been specified by the command. To set the delay in the script for five seconds, you would write:

DELAY 5000

RESUME The RESUME command causes the script to resume running after the user has pressed either Esc or Backspace to interrupt the script. It may be entered as follows:

Command: **resume**

GRAPHSCR and TEXTSCR The GRAPHSCR and TEXTSCR commands are used to flip or toggle the screen to the graphics or text mode, respectively, during the running of the script. Each is simply entered as a command in the script, as follows:

Command: **graphscr**

or

Command: **textscr**

These two screen toggle commands can be used transparently by preceding them with an apostrophe.

RSCRIPT The RSCRIPT command, when placed at the end of a script, causes the script to repeat itself. With this feature you can have a slide show run continuously until terminated by Esc or a Backspace.

A repeating demonstration can be set up to show some sequences of commands and responses as follows:

```
GRID ON
LIMITS 0,0 24,24
ZOOM A
CIRCLE 12,12 4
DELAY 2000
COPY L  M 12,12 18,12 12,18 6,12 12,6 (an extra space at the end)
DELAY 5000
ERASE W 0,0 24,24 (an extra space at the end)
DELAY 2000
LIMITS 0,0 12,9
ZOOM A

GRID OFF
TEXT 1,1 .5 0 THAT'S ALL FOLKS!
ERASE L (an extra space at the end)
RSCRIPT
```

This script file utilizes the DELAY and RSCRIPT subcommands. Note the extra spaces where continuation of some actions must be terminated.

The SCRIPT command can be used to show a series of slides, as in the following sequence:

```
VSLIDE SLD_A
VSLIDE *SLD_B
DELAY 5000
VSLIDE
VSLIDE *SLD_C
DELAY 5000
VSLIDE
DELAY 10000
RSCRIPT
```

This script uses the asterisk (*) before the slide name prior to the delay. This causes AutoCAD to load the slide, ready for viewing. Otherwise, there would be a blank screen between slides while the next one is being loaded. The RSCRIPT command repeats the slide show.

REVIEW QUESTIONS

1. To load a script file called "SAMPLE.SCR", use:
   a. SCRIPT, then SAMPLE
   b. LOAD, then SAMPLE
   c. LOAD, SCRIPT, then SAMPLE
   d. none of the above

2. The AutoCAD command used for viewing a slide is:
   a. VSLIDE
   b. VIEWSLIDE
   c. SSLD
   d. SLIDE
   e. MSLIDE

3. If a REDRAW is performed while viewing a slide:
   a. the command will be ignored
   b. the current slide will be deleted
   c. the current drawing will be displayed
   d. AutoCAD will load the drawing the slide was created from
   e. none of the above

4. A script file is identified by the following extension:
   a. SCR   d. SPT
   b. BAK   e. none of the above
   c. DWK

5. A slide file is identified by the following extension:
   a. SLD   d. SLU
   b. SCR   e. none of the above
   c. SLE

6. Slides can be removed from the display with the command:
   a. ZOOM ALL
   b. REGEN
   c. OOPS
   d. Both A and B
   e. none of the above

7. The SCRIPT command cannot be used to:
   a. insert blocks
   b. create layers
   c. place text
   d. create another script file
   e. none of the above (i.e. all are possible)

8. To create a slide library, you must:
    a. use the AutoCAD command SLIDELIB
    b. add slides to the library one at a time
    c. create an ASCII text file listing all slides to be included in the library
    d. have all slide files in a common directory

9. To cause a script file to execute in an infinite loop, you should place what command at the end of the file?
    a. REPEAT
    b. RSCRIPT
    c. GOTO:START
    d. BEGIN
    e. none of the above

10. If AutoCAD is executing in an infinite script file loop, how can you terminate the loop?
    a. press {backspace}
    b. press {ctrl} + {c}
    c. press {alt} + {c}
    d. press {F1}
    e. none of the above

15

AUTOCAD 3D

· ·

INTRODUCTION

After completing this chapter, you will be able to:

✓ Define a User Coordinate System
✓ View in 3D using the VPOINT and DVIEW commands
✓ Create 3D objects
✓ Use the REGION command
✓ Use the 3DPOLY and 3DFACE commands
✓ Create meshes
✓ Edit in 3D using the ALIGN, ROTATE3D, MIRROR3D, 3DARRAY, EXTEND, and TRIM commands
✓ Create solid shapes: solid box, solid cone, solid cylinder, solid sphere, solid torus, and solid wedge
✓ Create solids from existing 2D objects and regions
✓ Create solids by means of revolution
✓ Create composite solids
✓ Edit 3D solids via the CHAMFER, FILLET, SECTION, SLICE, and INTERFERE command
✓ Obtain the mass properties of a solid
✓ Place a multiview in paper space
✓ Generate Views in viewports
✓ Generate profiles

WHAT IS 3D?

In 2D drawings you have been working with two axes, X and Y. In 3D drawings you work with the the Z axis, in addition to the X and Y axes, as shown in Figure 15–1. Plan views, sections, and elevations represent only two dimensions. Isometric, perspective, and axonometric drawings, on the other hand, represent all three dimensions. For example, to create three views of a cube, the cube is simply drawn as a square with thickness. This is referred to as extruded 2D. Only objects that are extrudable can be drawn by this method. Other views are achieved by rotating the viewpoint or the object, just as if you were physically holding the cube. You can get an isometric or perspective view by simply changing the viewpoint.

Whether you realize it or not, all drawings you have done in previous chapters were created by AutoCAD in true 3D. What this means is that every line, circle, or arc that you have drawn, even if you think you have drawn it in 2D, is really stored with three coordinates. By default, AutoCAD stores the Z value as your current elevation with a thickness of zero. What you think of now as 2D is really only one of an infinite number of views of your drawing in 3D space.

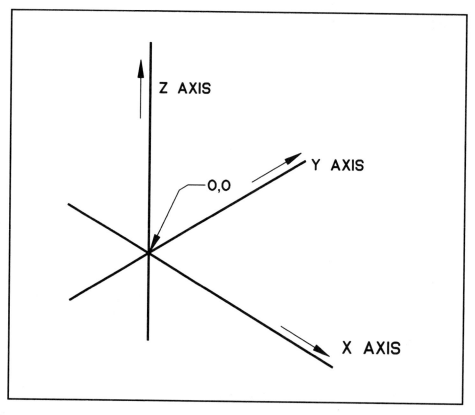

Figure 15–1 The X, Y, and Z axes for 3D drawing

Drawing objects in 3D provides three major advantages:

■ An object is drawn once and then can be viewed and plotted from any angle (viewpoint).
■ A 3D object holds mathematical information that can be used in engineering analysis such as finite element analysis and computer numerical control (CNC) machinery.
■ Shading and rendering enhances the visualization of an object.

There are two major limitations in working in 3D: (1) Whenever you want to input 3D coordinates whose Z coordinate is different from the current construction plane's elevation, you have to use the keyboard instead of your pointing device. One exception is to object snap to an object not in the current construction plane. The input device (mouse or digitizer) can supply AutoCAD with only two of the three coordinates at a time. Three-dimensional-input devices exist, but there is no practical support by AutoCAD for them at this time. So you are limited to using the keyboard. (2) Determining where you are in relationship to an object in 3D space is difficult.

COORDINATE SYSTEMS

AutoCAD provides two types of coordinate systems. One is a single fixed coordinate system called the World Coordinate System, and the other is an infinite set of user-defined coordinate systems available through the User Coordinate System.

The **World Coordinate System (WCS)** is fixed and cannot be changed. In this system (when viewing the origin from 0,0,1), the X axis starts at the point 0,0,0 and values increase as the point moves to the operator's right; the Y axis starts at 0,0,0 and values increase as the point moves to the top of the screen; and finally, the Z axis starts at the 0,0,0 point and values get larger as it comes toward the user. All drawings from previous chapters are created with reference to the WCS. The WCS is still the basic system in virtually all 2D AutoCAD drawings. However, because of the difficulty in calculating 3D points, the WCS is not suited for many 3D applications.

The **User Coordinate System (UCS)** allows you to change the location and orientation of the X, Y, and Z axes to reduce the number of calculations needed to create 3D objects. The UCS command lets you redefine the origin of your drawing and establish the positive X and the positive Y axes. New users think of a coordinate system simply as the direction of positive X and positive Y. But once the directions of X and Y are defined, the direction of Z will be defined as well. Thus, the user has only to be concerned with X and Y. As a result, when you are drawing in 2D, you are also somewhere in 3D space. For example, if a sloped roof of a house is drawn in detail using the WCS, each endpoint of every object on the inclined roof plane must be calculated. On the other hand, if the UCS is set to the same plane as the roof, each object can be drawn as if it were in the plan view. You can define any number of

UCSs within the fixed WCS and save them, assigning each a user-determined name. But at any given time, only one coordinate system is current and all coordinate input and display is relative to it. This is unlike a rotated snap grid in which direction and coordinates are based on the WCS. If multiple viewports are active, they all share the same current UCS.

Right-hand Rule

The directions of the X, Y, and Z axes change when the UCS is altered; hence, the positive rotation direction of the axes may become difficult to determine. The right-hand rule helps in determining the rotation direction when changing the UCS or using commands that require object rotation.

To remember the orientation of the axes, do the following:

1. Hold your right hand with the thumb, forefinger, and middle finger pointing at right angles to each other, as shown in Figure 15–2.
2. Consider the thumb to be pointing in the positive direction of the X axis.
3. The forefinger points in the positive direction of the Y axis.
4. The middle finger points in the positive direction of the Z axis.

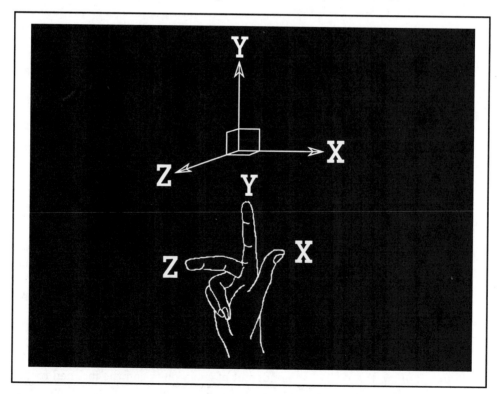

Figure 15–2 The correct hand position when using the right-hand rule

Setting the Display of the UCS Icon

The UCS icon provides a visual reminder of how the UCS axes are oriented, where the current UCS origin is, and the viewing direction relative to the UCS *XY* plane. AutoCAD displays a different coordinate system icon in paper space and in model space. When model space is current, AutoCAD displays the icon shown in Figure 15–3; when paper space is current, AutoCAD displays the icon as shown in Figure 15–3.

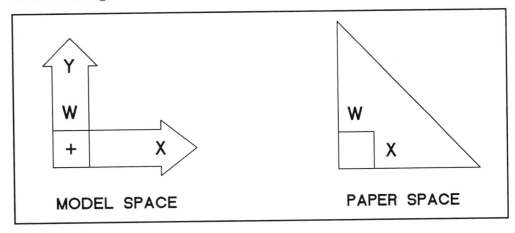

Figure 15–3 The UCS icon for model space and for paper space

The *X* and *Y* axis directions are indicated with arrows labeled appropriately, and the *Z* axis is indicated by the placement of the icon. The icon displays a W in the *Y* axis arrow if the current UCS is the World Coordinate System, and a "+" appears at the base of the arrows if the icon is placed at the origin of the current coordinate system. When looking straight up or down on the *Z* plane, the icon seems flat. When viewed at any other angle, the icon looks skewed. The orientation of the *Z* axis is indicated further by the presence or absence of a box at the base of the arrows that create the icon. If the box is visible, you are looking down on the *XY* plane; if the box is not present, the bottom of the *XY* plane is being viewed. See Figure 15–4 for all the different orientations of the UCS icon.

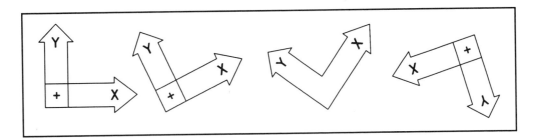

Figure 15–4 The UCS icon in different orientations

AutoCAD 3D

NOTE: If the viewing angle comes within 1 degree of the Z axis, the UCS icon will change to a "broken pencil," as shown in Figure 15–5. When this icon is showing in a view, it is recommended that you avoid trying to use the cursor to specify points in that view, because the results may be unpredictable.

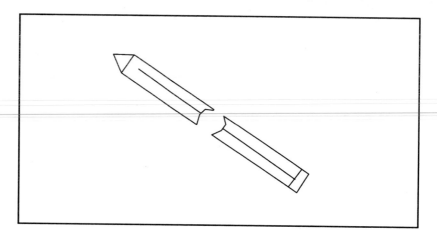

Figure 15–5 The UCS icon becomes a broken pencil when the viewing angle is within 1 degree of the Z axis

The display and placement on the origin of the UCS icon is handled by the UCSICON command. Invoke the UCSICON command from:

Pull-down menu	View > Display > UCS icon
Command: prompt	ucsicon Enter

AutoCAD prompts:

Command: **ucsicon**
ON/OFF/All/Nooring/ORigin<default>: *(select one of the available options)*

ON Option The ON option allows you to set the icon to ON if it is OFF in the current viewport.

OFF Option The OFF option allows you to set the icon to OFF if it is ON in the current viewport.

Noorigin Option The Noorigin option tells AutoCAD to display the icon at the lower left corner of the viewport, regardless of the location of the UCS origin. This is like parking the icon in the lower left corner. This is the default setting.

ORigin Option The ORigin option forces the icon to be displayed at the origin of the current coordinate system.

> **NOTE:** If the origin is off screen, the icon is displayed at the lower left corner of the viewport.

All Option The All option determines whether the options that follow affect all of the viewports or just the current active viewport. This option is issued before each and every option if you want to affect all viewports. For example, to turn ON the icon in all the viewports and display the icon on the origin, the following sequence of prompts is displayed:

Command: **ucsicon**
ON/OFF/All/Noorigin/ORigin <default>: **all**
ON/OFF/Noorigin/ORigin: **on**
Command: Enter
ON/OFF/All/Noorigin/ORigin: **all**
ON/OFF/Noorigin/ORigin: **origin**

Defining a New UCS

The UCS is the key to almost all 3D operations in AutoCAD, as mentioned earlier. Many commands in AutoCAD are traditionally thought of as 2D commands. They are effective in 3D because they are always relative to the current UCS. For example, the ROTATE command rotates in only the X and Y directions, if you want to rotate an object in the Z direction, change your UCS so that X or Y is now in the direction of what was previously Z. Then you could use the 2D ROTATE command.

The UCS command lets you redefine the origin in your drawing. Broadly, you can define the origin by four methods:

■ Specify a data point for an origin, specify a new XY plane by providing three data points, or provide a direction for the Z Axis.
■ Define an origin relative to the orientation of an existing object.
■ Define an origin by aligning with the current viewing direction.
■ Define an origin by rotating the current UCS around one of its axes.

Invoke the UCS command from:

UCS toolbar	Select the UCS command (see Figure 15–6)
Pull-down menu	Tools > UCS
Command: prompt	ucs Enter

Figure 15–6 Invoking the UCS command from the UCS toolbar

AutoCAD prompts:

Command: **ucs**
Origin/ZAxis/3point/OBject/View/X/Y/Z/Prev/Restore/Save/Del/?/<World>:
(select one of the available options)

Origin Option The Origin option defines a new UCS by shifting the origin of the current UCS, leaving the directions of the *X*, *Y*, and *Z* axes unchanged. When you select this option, AutoCAD prompts:

Origin point (0,0,0):

Specify a new origin point relative to the origin of the current UCS, as shown in Figure 15–7.

ZAxis Option The ZAxis option allows you to define an origin by giving a data point and the direction for the *Z* axis. AutoCAD arbitrarily, but consistently, sets the direction of the *X* and *Y* axes in relation to the given *Z* axis. When you select this option, AutoCAD prompts:

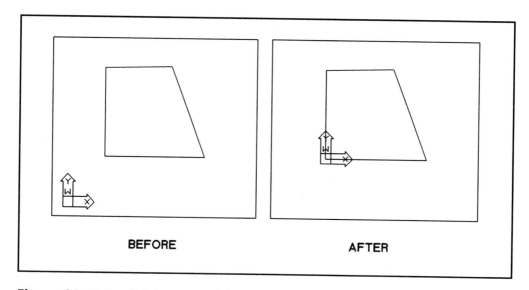

BEFORE   AFTER

Figure 15–7 Specifying a new origin point relative to the origin of the current UCS

Origin point (0,0,0):
Point on positive portion of the Z axis <default>:

Specify a data point and the direction for the positive Z axis. If you give a null response to the second prompt, the Z axis of the new coordinate system will be parallel to the previous one. This is similar to using the Origin option.

3point Option The 3point option is the easiest and most often used option for controlling the orientation of the UCS. This option allows the user to select three points to define the origin and the directions of the positive X and Y axes. The origin point acts as a base for the UCS rotation, and when a point is selected to define the direction of the positive X axis, the direction of the Y axis is limited because it is always perpendicular to the X axis. When the X and Y axes are defined, the Z axis is automatically placed perpendicular to the XY plane. When you select this option, AutoCAD prompts:

Origin point (0,0,0): *(specify the origin point)*
Point on positive portion of the X-axis <default>: *(specify a point for the*
  positive X axis)
Point on positive-Y portion of the UCS XY plane <default>: *(specify a point*
  for the positive Y axis)

Specify a data point and the direction for the positive X and Y axes, as shown in Figure 15–8. The points must not form a straight line. If you give a null response to the first prompt, the new UCS will have the same origin as the previous UCS. If you give a null response to the second or third prompt, then that axis direction will be parallel to the corresponding axis in the previous UCS.

OBject Option The OBject option lets you define a new coordinate system by pointing to an object. The actual orientation of the UCS depends on how the object was created. When the object is selected, the UCS origin is placed at the first point used to create the object (in the case of a line, it will be the closest endpoint; for a circle, it will be the center point of the circle); the X axis is determined by the direction from the origin to the second point used to define the object. And the Z axis direction is placed perpendicular to the XY plane in which the object sits. Table 15–1 lists the location of the origin and its X axis for different types of objects.

When you select this option, AutoCAD prompts:

Select object to align UCS: *(identify an object to define a new coordinate*
  system)

Identify an object to define a new coordinate system, as shown in Figure 15–9.

View Option The View option places the XY plane parallel to the screen, and makes the Z axis perpendicular. The UCS origin remains unchanged. This method is used mainly for labeling text, which should be aligned with the screen rather than with objects.

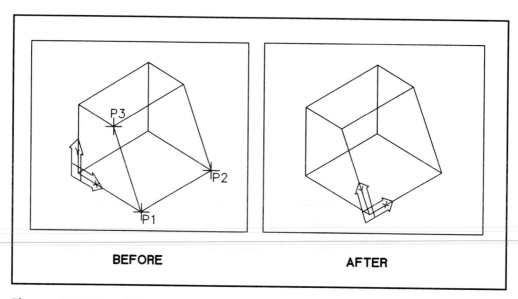

BEFORE　　　　　　　　　　　**AFTER**

Figure 15–8 Specifying a data point and the direction for the positive X and Y axes via the 3Point Option

Table 15–1 Location of the Origin and Its X Axis for Different Types of Objects

Object	Method of UCS Determination
Line	The endpoint nearest the specified point becomes the new UCS origin. The new X axis is chosen so that the line lies in the XZ plane of the new UCS.
Circle	The circle's center becomes the new UCS origin, and the X axis passes through the point specified.
Arc	The arc's center becomes the new UCS origin, and the X axis passes through the endpoint of the arc closest to the pick point.
2D polyline	The polyline's start point becomes the new UCS origin, with the X axis extending from the start point to the next vertex.
Solid	The first point of the solid determines the new UCS origin, and the X axis lies along the line between the first two points.
Dimension	The new UCS origin is the middle point of the dimension text, and the direction of the X axis is parallel to the X axis of the UCS in effect when the dimension was drawn.

X/Y/Z Rotation Option The X/Y/Z rotation option lets you define a new coordinate system by rotating the X, Y, and Z axes independent of each other. You can show AutoCAD the desired angle by specifying two points, or you can enter the rotation angle from the keyboard. In either case, the new angle is specified relative

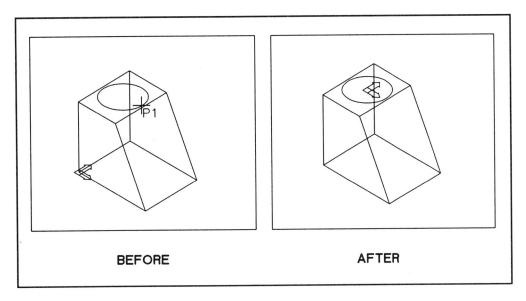

Figure 15–9 Defining a new coordinate system

to the X axis of the current UCS. See Figures 15–10, 15–11, and 15–12 for examples of rotating the UCS around the X, Y, and Z axes, respectively.

Previous Option The Previous option is similar to the Previous option of the ZOOM command. AutoCAD saves the last 10 coordinate systems in both model

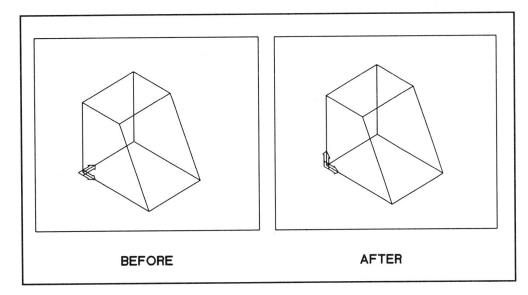

Figure 15–10 Example of rotating the UCS around the X axis

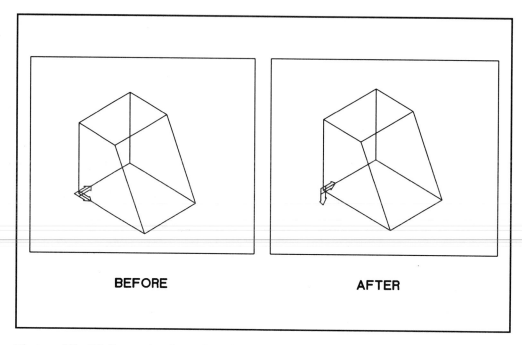

BEFORE   AFTER

Figure 15-11 Example of rotating the UCS around the *Y* axis

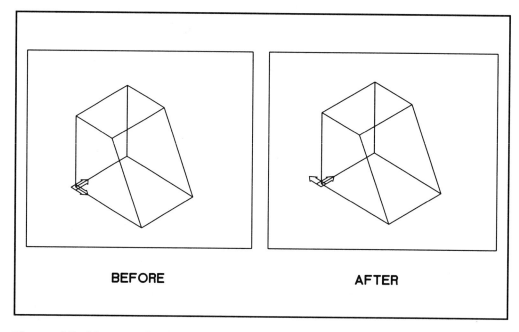

BEFORE   AFTER

Figure 15-12 Example of rotating the UCS around the *Z* axis

space and paper space. You can step back through them by using repeated Previous options.

Restore Option The Restore option allows you to restore any previously saved UCS.

> **NOTE:** You can also restore a previously saved UCS by invoking the DDUCS command, which in turn displays a dialog box listing the previously saved UCS.

Save Option The Save option allows you to save the current UCS under a user-defined name.

Delete Option The Delete option allows you to delete any saved UCS.

? Option The ? option lists the name of the UCS you specify, the origin, and the X, Y, and Z axes for each saved coordinate system, relative to the current UCS. To list all the UCS names, accept the default, or you can specify wild cards.

World Option The World option returns the drawing to the WCS.

Selecting a Preset UCS

The DDUCSP command is used to make a preset coordinate system orientation current. Invoke the DDUCSP command from:

UCS toolbar	Select the Preset UCS command (see Figure 15–13)
Pull-down menu	Tools > UCS > Preset UCS...
Command: prompt	**dducsp** Enter

Figure 15–13 Invoking the Preset UCS command from the UCS toolbar

AutoCAD displays the UCS Orientation dialog box, similar to Figure 15–14. The UCS Orientation dialog box displays tiles showing the standard view from preset orientations from which to select. If you select one of the tiles, the current UCS will be reoriented to align with the displayed view. The orientation will be **Relative to Current UCS** or **Absolute to WCS**, depending on the option selected.

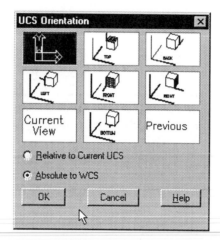

Figure 15-14 UCS Orientation dialog box

Viewing a Drawing from Plan View

The PLAN command provides a convenient means of viewing a drawing from plan view. The definition of plan means that you are at positive Z and looking perpendicularly down on X to the right, and Y pointing up. You can select the plan view of the current UCS, a previously saved UCS, or the WCS.

Invoke the PLAN command from:

Pull-down menu	View > 3D Viewpoint > Plan View
Command: prompt	plan Enter

AutoCAD prompts:

Command: **plan**
<Current UCS>/Ucs/World: *(select one of the available options)*

Current UCS Option The Current UCS option displays the plan view of the current UCS. This is the default option.

Ucs Option The Ucs option displays a plan view of a previously saved UCS. When you select this option, AutoCAD prompts for a name of the UCS.

World Option The World option displays the plan view of the WCS.

VIEWING IN 3D

Until now, you have been working on the plan view, or the XY plane. You have been looking down at the plan view from a certain distance along the Z axis. The direction from which you view your drawing or model is called the viewpoint. You can view a drawing from any point in model space. From your selected viewpoint, you can add objects, modify existing objects, or suppress the hidden lines from the drawing.

The VPOINT and DVIEW commands are used to control viewing of a model from any point in model space.

Viewing a Model by Means of the VPOINT Command

To view a model in 3D, you may have to change the viewpoint. The location of the viewpoint can be controlled by means of the VPOINT command. The default viewpoint is 0,0,1; i.e., you are looking at the model from 0,0,1 (on the positive Z axis above the model) to 0,0,0 (origin).

Invoke the VPOINT command from:

Pull-down menu	View > 3D Viewpoint > Tripod
Command: prompt	**vpoint** Enter

AutoCAD prompts:

Command: **vpoint**
Rotate/<Viewpoint><current>: *(select one of the available options)*

The default method requires you to enter X, Y, and Z coordinates from the keyboard. These coordinates establish the viewpoint. From this viewpoint, you will be looking at the model in space toward the model's origin. For example, a 1,-1,1 setting gives you a -45-degree angle projected in the XY plane and 35.264-degree angle above the XY plane (top, right, and front views); looking at the model origin (0,0,0). You can set the viewpoint to any X, Y, Z location. Table 15–2 lets you experiment with the rotation of 3D objects.

If instead of entering coordinates you give a null response (press Enter or the Spacebar), a compass and axes tripod appear on the screen, as shown in Figure 15–15. The compass, in the upper right of the screen, is a 2D representation of a globe. The center point of the circle represents the north pole (0,0,1), the inner circle represents the equator, and the outer circle represents the south pole (0,0,-1), as shown in Figure 15–16. A small cross is displayed on the compass. You can move the cross with your pointing device. If the cross is in the inner circle, you are above the equator looking down on your model. If the cross is in the outer circle, you are looking from beneath your drawing, or from the southern hemisphere. Move the cross, and the axes tripod rotates to conform to the viewpoint indicated on the compass. When you achieve the desired viewpoint, press the pick button on your pointing device or press Enter. The drawing regenerates to reflect the new viewpoint position.

Rotate Option The Rotate option allows you to specify the location of the viewpoint in terms of two angles. The first angle determines the rotation in the XY plane

Table 15–2 Various Viewpoint Settings for Rotating 3D objects

Viewpoint Setting	Displayed View(s)
0,0,1	Top
0,0,-1	Bottom
0,-1,0	Front
0,1,0	Rear
1,0,01	Right side
-1,0,0	Left side
1,-1,1	Top, Front, Right side
-1,-1,1	Top, Front, Left side
1,1,1	Top, Rear, Right side
-1,1,1	Top, Rear, Left side
1,-1,-1	Bottom, Front, Right side
-1,-1,-1	Bottom, Front, Left sdie
1,1,-1	Bottom, Rear, Right side
-1,1,-1	Bottom, Rear, Left side

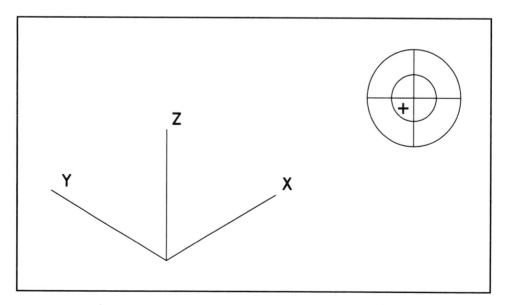

Figure 15–15 The VPOINT command's compass and axes tripod

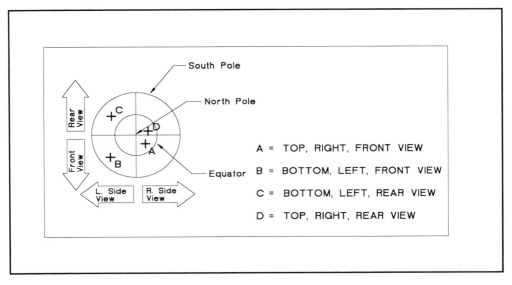

Figure 15–16 Components of the VPOINT command's compass and its poles

from the X axis (0 degrees) clockwise or counterclockwise. The second angle determines the angle from the XY plane up or down. When you select the Rotate option, AutoCAD prompts:

> Enter angle in X-Y plane from X axis <current>: *(specify the angle in the XY plane from the X axis)*
> Enter angle from X-Y plane <current>: *(specify the angle from the XY plane)*

Specify the angles, and your drawing regenerates to reflect the new viewpoint position.

Viewpoint Presets AutoCAD provides a **Viewpoint Presets** dialog box when you invoke the DDVPOINT command. The dialog box lets you set a 3D viewing direction by specifying an angle from the X axis and an angle from the XY plane. This is similar to using the Rotate option of the VPOINT command.

Invoke the DDVPOINT command from:

Pull-down menu	View > 3D Viewpoint > Select...
Command: prompt	**ddvpoint** Enter

AutoCAD displays the **Viewpoint Presets** dialog box, similar to the one shown in Figure 15–17. Specify viewing angles from the image tile, or enter their values in the edit boxes. You specify the view direction relative to the current UCS or the WCS, the viewing angles are updated accordingly. The new angle is indicated by the white arm; the current viewing angle is indicated by the red arm. By selecting the

AutoCAD 3D

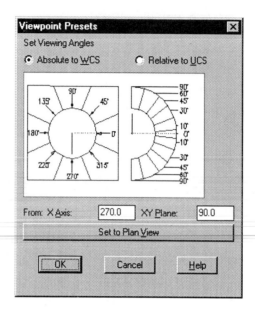

Figure 15–17 Viewpoint Presets dialog box

Set to Plan View button, you can set the viewing angles to display the plan relative to the selected coordinate system.

> **NOTE:** By default, AutoCAD always places the model to your current viewpoint position in reference to the WCS, not the current UCS. If necessary, you can change the WORLDVIEW system variable from 1 (default) to 0; AutoCAD then places the model in reference to the UCS for your current viewpoint position. It is recommended that you keep the WORLDVIEW set to 1 (default). Regardless of the WORLDVIEW setting, you are always looking through your view-point to the WCS origin.

Viewing a Model by Means of the DVIEW Command

The DVIEW command is an enhanced VPOINT command. Here you visually move around an object on the screen, dynamically viewing selected objects as the view changes. The DVIEW command provides either parallel or perspective views, whereas the VPOINT command provides only parallel views. In the case of a parallel view, parallel lines always remain parallel, whereas in perspective view, parallel lines converge from your view to a vanishing point. Figures 15–18a and 15–18b show parallel and perspective views, respectively, of a model. The viewing direction is the same in each case.

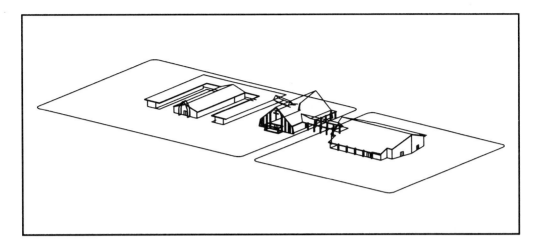

Figure 15-18a The DVIEW command displaying a model with parallel projection

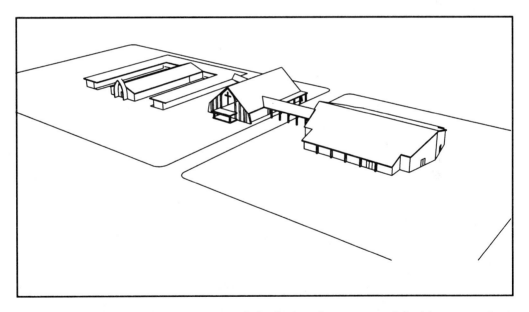

Figure 15-18b The DVIEW command displaying the same model with perspective projection

Invoke the DVIEW command from:

Pull-down menu	View > 3D Dynamic View
Command: prompt	**dview** Enter

AutoCAD prompts:

> Command: **dview**
> Select objects: *(select objects or press Enter)*

All or any part of the objects in the drawing can be selected for viewing during the DVIEW command process. But once you exit the DVIEW command, all objects in the drawing are represented in the new view created. If your drawing is too large to display quickly in the DVIEW display, small portions can be selected and used to orient the entire drawing. The purpose of this is to save time on slower machines and still give dynamic rotation so that you can quickly and effortlessly adjust the view of your object before you begin working with it.

If you give a null response to the "Select objects:" prompt, AutoCAD provides you with a picture of a 3D house. Whatever you do to the 3D house under DVIEW will be done to your current drawing when you exit the DVIEW command.

Each time you exit the DVIEW command, AutoCAD performs an unconditional regeneration. No matter what the current setting for REGENAUTO is, AutoCAD automatically performs a regeneration.

After selecting the objects, give a null response. AutoCAD prompts with the following options:

> CAmera/TArget/Distance/POints/PAn/Zoom/TWist/CLip/Hide/Off/Undo/
> <eXit>: *(select one of the available options)*

CAmera Option The Camera option is one of the six options that adjusts what is seen in the view. With the Camera option, the drawing is stationary while the camera moves in two directions. It can move up and down (above or below) or it can move around the target to the left or right (clockwise or counterclockwise). When you are moving the camera, the target is fixed.

When you enter the Camera option, AutoCAD prompts:

> Toggle angle in/Enter angle from X-Y plane <default>:

You can specify the amount of rotation you want by positioning the graphics cursor in the graphics area. When you move the cursor, you will see the object begin to rotate dynamically vertically, and the AutoCAD status line displays a continuous readout of the new angle. Move the cursor to the desired angle and then press the pick button. Or you could type the desired angle from the keyboard. Either way, you have selected an angle of view above or below the target.

Next, AutoCAD prompts for the desired rotation angle of the camera around the target:

> Toggle angle from/Enter the angle in the X-Y plane from X axis <default>:

You can move the camera 180 degrees clockwise and 180 degrees counterclockwise around the target. You specify the angle by using the cursor to specify a point on the screen. Or you could type in the desired angle from the keyboard. Either way, you have selected an angle of view around the target clockwise or counterclockwise.

The toggle angle option allows you to move between two angle input modes.

AutoCAD takes you back to the 12-option prompt of the DVIEW command. When the new angle of view is correct, you exit by giving a null response or by selecting the Exit option. This takes you back to the "Command:" prompt.

When you exit DVIEW, your entire drawing will rotate to the same angle of view as the few objects that you selected.

The following command sequence shows an example of using the CAmera option of the DVIEW command.

```
Command: dview
Select objects: (select the objects)
CAmera/TArget/Distance/POints/PAn/Zoom/TWist/CLip/Hide/Off/Undo/
    <eXit>: ca
Toggle angle in/Enter angle from X-Y plane <default>: 45
Toggle angle from/Enter angle in X-Y plane from X axis <default>: 45
CAmera/TArget/Distance/POints/PAn/Zoom/TWist/CLip/Hide/Off/Undo/
    <eXit>: Enter
```

TArget Option The TArget option is similar to the CAmera option, but in this case the target is rotated around the camera. The camera remains stationary except for maintaining its lens on the target point. The prompts are similar to those for the CAmera option. There may seem to be no difference between the CAmera and TArget options, but there is a difference in the actual angle of view. For instance, if you elevate the camera 75 degrees above the target, you are then looking at the target from the top down. On the other hand, if you raise the target 75 degrees above the camera, you are then looking at the target from the bottom up. The angles of view are reversed. The real difference comes when you are typing in the angles rather than visually picking them.

The following command sequence shows an example of using the TArget option of the DVIEW command.

```
Command: dview
Select objects: (select the objects)
CAmera/TArget/Distance/POints/PAn/Zoom/TWist/CLip/Hide/Off/Undo/
    <eXit>: ta
Toggle angle in/Enter angle from X-Y plane <default>: 75
Toggle angle from/Enter angle in X-Y plane from X axis <default>: 75
CAmera/TArget/Distance/POints/PAn/Zoom/TWist/CLip/Hide/Off/Undo/
    <eXit>: Enter
```

Distance Option The Distance option creates a perspective projection from the current view. The only information required for this option is the distance from the camera to the target point. Once AutoCAD knows the distance, it will apply the correct perspective. When perspective viewing is on, a box icon appears on the screen, as shown in Figure 15–19, in place of the UCS icon. Some commands (like ZOOM and PAN) will not work while perspective is on. You turn on the perspective just for visual purposes or for plotting.

When you select the Distance option, AutoCAD prompts:

New camera/target distance <default>:

In addition to the prompt, you also see a horizontal bar at the top of the screen. The bar goes from 0x to 16x. These are factor distances times your current distance from the object. Moving the slider cursor toward the right increases the distance between the target and the camera. Moving the slider cursor toward the left reduces the distance between the target and the camera. The current distance is represented by 1x. For instance, moving the slider cursor to 3x makes the new distance three times the previous distance. Or you could also type the desired distance in the current linear units from the keyboard.

The following command sequence shows an example of using the Distance option of the DVIEW command.

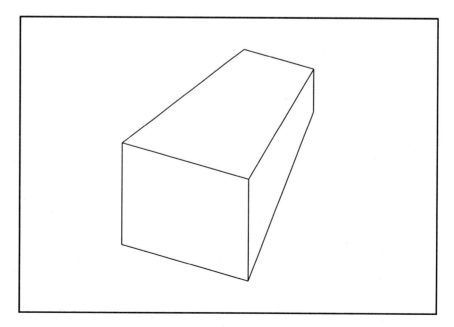

Figure 15–19 The perspective box icon appears when perspective mode is on

Command: **dview**
Select objects: *(select the objects)*
CAmera/TArget/Distance/POints/PAn/Zoom/TWist/CLip/Hide/Off/Undo/
    <eXit>: **d**
New camera/target distance <default>: **75'**
CAmera/TArget/Distance/POints/PAn/Zoom/TWist/CLip/Hide/Off/Undo/
    <eXit>: Enter

Off Option The Off option turns off the perspective view. The following command sequence shows an example of using the Off option of the DVIEW command.

Command: **dview**
Select objects: *(select the objects)*
CAmera/TArget/Distance/POints/PAn/Zoom/TWist/CLip/Hide/Off/Undo/
    <eXit>: **o**
CAmera/TArget/Distance/POints/PAn/Zoom/TWist/CLip/Hide/Off/Undo/
    <eXit>: Enter

> **NOTE:** To turn the perspective on again, select the Distance option and press Enter for all the defaults. There is no option called On for turning on the perspective view.

POints Option The POints option establishes the location of the camera as well as the target points. This gives AutoCAD the basic information needed to create the view. The location of the camera and target points must be specified in a parallel projection. If perspective is set to ON, AutoCAD temporarily turns it off while you specify the new location for camera and target points, and then redisplays the image in perspective.

When you select the POints option, AutoCAD prompts:

Enter target point: *(specify the target location)*
Enter camera point: *(specify the camera location)*

After the locations are defined, the screen shows the new view immediately.

The following command sequence shows an example of using the POints option of the DVIEW command.

Command: **dview**
Select objects: *(select the objects)*
CAmera/TArget/Distance/POints/PAn/Zoom/TWist/CLip/Hide/Off/Undo/
    <eXit>: **po**
Enter Target point: *(specify a point)*
Enter Camera point: *(specify a point)*
CAmera/TArget/Distance/POints/PAn/Zoom/TWist/CLip/Hide/Off/Undo/
    <eXit>: Enter

AutoCAD 3D

PAn Option The PAn option allows you to view a different location of the model by specifying the pan distance and direction. This option is similar to the regular PAN command. The following command sequence shows an example of using the PAn option of the DVIEW command.

Command: **dview**
Select objects: *(select the objects)*
CAmera/TArget/Distance/POints/PAn/Zoom/TWist/CLip/Hide/Off/Undo/
    <eXit>: **pa**
Displacement base point: *(specify a point)*
Second point: *(specify a point)*
CAmera/TArget/Distance/POints/PAn/Zoom/TWist/CLip/Hide/Off/Undo/
    <eXit>: Enter

Zoom Option The Zoom option lets you zoom in on a portion of the model. This option is similar to the regular AutoCAD ZOOM Center command, with the center point lying at the center of the current viewport. This option is controlled by a scale factor value.

When you select the Zoom option, AutoCAD prompts:

Adjust zoom scale factor <default>: *(specify the zoom scale factor)*

In addition to the prompt, you see a horizontal bar at the top of the screen. The slider bar lets you specify a zoom scale factor, with 1x being the current zoom level. Any value greater than 1 increases the size of the objects in the view; any decimal value less than 1 decreases the size.

> **NOTE:** When the perspective is set to ON, the Zoom option prompts for a lens size rather than a zoom factor, but the effect is similar. The larger the lens size, the closer the object.

TWist Option The TWist option rotates or twists the view. It allows you to rotate the image around the line of sight at a given angle from zero, with zero being to the right. The angle is measured counterclockwise.

The following command sequence shows an example of using the TWist option of the DVIEW command.

Command: **dview**
Select objects: *(select the objects)*
CAmera/TArget/Distance/POints/PAn/Zoom/TWist/CLip/Hide/Off/Undo/
    <eXit>: **tw**
New view twist <default>: *(select a point)*
CAmera/TArget/Distance/POints/PAn/Zoom/TWist/CLip/Hide/Off/Undo/
    <eXit>: Enter

CLip Option The CLip option hides portions of the object in view so that the interior of the object can be seen or parts of the complex object can be more clearly identified.

The CLip option has three suboptions, Back, Front, and Off. The Back suboption eliminates all parts of the object in view that are located beyond the designated point along the line of sight. The Front suboption eliminates all parts of the object in view that are located between the camera and the front clipping plane. The Off suboption turns off front and back clipping.

The following command sequence shows an example of using the CLip option of the DVIEW command.

> Command: **dview**
> Select objects: *(select the objects)*
> CAmera/TArget/Distance/POints/PAn/Zoom/TWist/CLip/Hide/Off/Undo/
>   <eXit>: **cl**
> Back/Front/<Off>: **b**
> On/Off/<Distance from Target> <default>: *(specify the distance, or turn on
>   and off the previously defined clipping plane)*
> CAmera/TArget/Distance/POints/PAn/Zoom/TWist/CLip/Hide/Off/Undo/
>   <eXit>: Enter

Hide Option The Hide option is similar to the regular AutoCAD HIDE command.

Undo Option The Undo option will undo the last DVIEW operation. You use it to step back through multiple DVIEW operations.

eXit Option The eXit option ends the DVIEW command and returns you to the "Command:" prompt. It is the default option of the DVIEW command.

CREATING 3D OBJECTS

As mentioned earlier, there are several advantages to drawing objects in 3D, including viewing the model at any angle, automatic generation of standard and auxiliary 2D views, rendering and hidden-line removal, interference checking, and engineering analysis.

AutoCAD supports three types of 3D modeling: wireframe, surface, and solid.

The wireframe model consists of only points, lines, and curves that describe the edges of the object. In AutoCAD you can create a wireframe model by positioning 2D (planar) objects anywhere in 3D space. In addition, AutoCAD provides additional commands, such as 3DPOLY, for creating a wireframe model.

The surface model is more sophisticated than the wireframe model. It defines not only the edges of a 3D object but also its surfaces. The AutoCAD surface modeler defines faceted surfaces by using a polygonal mesh. It is possible to create a mesh to a flat or curved surface by locating the boundaries or edges of the surface.

Solid modeling is the easiest type of 3D modeling. Solids are the unambiguous and informationally complete representation of the shape of a physical object. Fundamentally, solid modeling differs from wireframe or surface modeling in two ways:

■ The information is more complete in the solid model.
■ The method of construction of the model itself is inherently straightforward.

In wireframe or surface modeling, objects are created by positioning lines or surfaces in 3D space. In solid modeling, you build the model as you would with building blocks; from beginning to end, you think, draw, and communicate in 3D. One of the main benefits of solid modeling is its ability to be analyzed. You can calculate the mass properties of a solid object, such as its mass, center of gravity, surface area, and moments of intertia.

Each modeling type uses a different method for constructing 3D models, and the use of each editing method varies among model types. It is recommended not to mix modeling methods. It is possible in AutoCAD to convert between model types from solids to surfaces and from sufaces to wireframe; however, you cannot convert from wireframes to surfaces or surfaces to solids.

2D DRAW Commands in 3D Space

You can use most of the draw commands discussed in previous chapters with a Z coordinate value. But 2D objects such as polylines, circles, arcs, and solids are constrained to the XY plane of the current UCS. For these objects, the Z value is accepted only for the first coordinate to set the elevation of the 2D object above or below the current plane. When you specify a point by using an Object Snap mode, it assumes the Z value of the point to which you snapped.

Setting Elevation and Thickness

You can create new objects by first setting up a default elevation (Z value). Subsequently, all the objects drawn assume the current elevation as the Z value whenever a 3D point is expected but you supply only the X and Y values. The current elevation is maintained separately in model space and paper space.

Similarly, you create new objects with extrusion thickness by presetting a value for the thickness. Subsequently, all the objects drawn, such as lines, polylines, arcs, circles, and solids, assume the current thickness and extrude in their Z direction. For example, you can draw a cylinder by drawing a circle with preset thickness, or you can draw a cube simply by drawing a square with preset thickness.

> **NOTE:** Thickness can be positive or negative. Thickness is in the Z axis direction for 2D objects. For 3D objects that can accept thickness, it is always relative to the current UCS. They will appear oblique if they do not lie in or parallel to the current UCS. If thickness is added to a line drawn directly in the Z direction, the line appears to extend beyond its endpoint in the positive or negative thickness direction. Text and dimensions ignore the thickness setting.

Invoke the ELEV command from:

Command: prompt	**elev** Enter

AutoCAD prompts:

Command: **elev**
New current elevation <current>: *(specify the elevation, and press* Enter *to*
  accept the current elevation setting)
New current thickness <current>: *(specify the thickness, and press* Enter *to*
  accept the current thickness setting)

For example, the following are the command sequences to draw a six-sided polygon
at zero elevation with a radius of 2.5 units and a height of 4.5 units and to place a
cylinder at the center of the polygon with a radius of 1.0 unit at an elevation of 2.0
units with a height of 7.5 units, as shown in Figure 15-20.

Command: **elev**
New current elevation <0.0000>: Enter
New current thickness <0.0000>: **4.5**

Command: **polygon** *(draw a polygon with a radius of 2.5 units)*
Command: **elev**
New current elevation <0.0000>: **2.0**
New current thickness <0.0000>: **7.5**
Command: **circle** *(draw a circle with a radius of 1.0 unit)*

You can change the thickness of the existing objects by invoking the CHANGE or
CHPROP command.

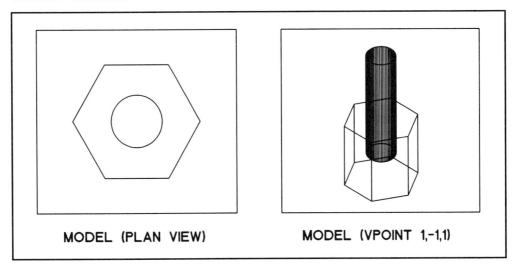

MODEL (PLAN VIEW)   MODEL (VPOINT 1,-1,1)

Figure 15-20 Specifying a new current elevation and thickness

AutoCAD 3D

Creating a Region Object

The REGION command creates a region object from a selection set of objects. Closed polylines, lines, curves, circular arcs, circles, elliptical arcs, ellipses, and splines are valid selections. Once you create a region, you can extrude it with the EXTRUDE command to make a 3D solid. You can also create a composite region with the UNION, SUBTRACTION, and INTERSECTION commands. If necessary, you can hatch a region with the BHATCH command.

AutoCAD converts closed 2D and planar 3D polylines in the selection set to separate regions and then converts polylines, lines, and curves that form closed planar loops. If more than two curves share an endpoint, the resultant region might be arbitrary. Each object retains its layer, linetype, and color. AutoCAD deletes the original objects after converting them to regions and, by default, does not hatch the regions.

Invoke the REGION command from:

Draw toolbar	Select the Region command (see Figure 15–21)
Pull-down menu	<u>D</u>raw > Regio<u>n</u>
Command: prompt	**region** Enter

Figure 15–21 Invoking the Region command from the Draw toolbar

AutoCAD prompts:

Command: region
Select objects: *(select the objects, and press* Enter *to complete object selection)*

Drawing 3D Polylines

The 3DPOLY command draws polylines with independent *X*, *Y*, and *Z* axis coordinates. The 3DPOLY command works similar to the PLINE command, with a few exceptions. Unlike the PLINE command, 3DPOLY draws only straight-line segments without variable width. Editing a 3D polyline with the PEDIT command is similar to editing a 2D polyline, except for some options. 3D Polylines cannot be joined, curve-fit with arc segments, or given a width or tangent.

Invoke the 3DPOLY command from:

Pull-down menu	Draw > 3D Polyline
Command: prompt	**3dpoly** Enter

AutoCAD prompts:

Command: **3dpoly**
From point: (specify a point)
Close/Undo/<Endpoint of line>: (specify a point or select one of the available options)

The available options are similar to those for the PLINE command, described earlier in Chapter 4.

Creating 3D Faces

When you create a 3D model, it is often necessary to have solid surfaces for hiding and shading. These surfaces are created with the 3DFACE command. The 3DFACE command creates a solid surface, and the command sequence is similar to that for the SOLID command. Unlike the SOLID command, you can give differing Z coordinates for the corner points of a face, forming a section of a plane in space. Unlike the SOLID command, a 3DFACE is drawn from corner to corner clockwise or counterclockwise around the object (and it does not draw a "bow tie"). A 3D face is a plane defined by either three or four points used to represent a surface. It provides a means of controlling which edges of a 3D face will be visible. You can describe complex, 3D polygons using multiple 3D faces, and you can tell AutoCAD which edges you want to be drawn. If you have an object with curved surfaces, then the 3DFACE command is not suitable. One of the mesh commands is more appropriate, as explained later in the chapter.

Invoke the 3DFACE command from:

Surfaces toolbar	Select the 3D Face command (see Figure 15–22)
Pull-down menu	Draw >Surfaces > 3D Face
Command: prompt	**3dface** Enter

Figure 15–22 Invoking the 3D Face command from the Draw toolbar

AutoCAD 3D

AutoCAD prompts:

Command: **3dface**
From point: *(specify the first point)*

Specify the first point, and AutoCAD prompts you for the second, third, and fourth points in sequence. Then AutoCAD closes the face from the fourth point to the first point and prompts for the third point. If you give a null response to the prompt for the third point, AutoCAD closes the 3Dface with three sides, terminates the command, and takes you to the "Command:" prompt.

If you want to draw additional faces in one command sequence, the last two points of the first face become the first two points for the second face. And the last two points of the second face become the first two points of the third face, and so on. You have to be very careful in drawing several faces in one command sequence, since AutoCAD does not have an Undo option that works inside the 3DFACE command. A single mistake can cause the entire face to be redrawn. For this reason, it is a good idea to draw 3D faces one at a time.

For example, the following command sequence demonstrates the placement of 3D faces, as in Figure 15–23.

Command: **3dface**
First point: *(select point A1)*
Second point: *(select point A2)*
Third point: *(select point A3)*
Fourth point: *(select point A4)*
Third point: *(select point A5)*
Fourth point: *(select point A6)*
Third point: *(select point A7)*
Fourth point: *(select point A8)*
Third point: *(select point A1)*
Fourth point: *(select point A2)*
Third point: Enter

The surface created, as shown in Figure 15–23, required four faces to cover it. Some of the faces are overlapping, which is not acceptable when viewing the object. The 3DFACE command allows face edges to be "invisible." To create an invisible edge, the letter **I** must be entered at the prompt for the first point of the edge to be invisible, and then the point can be entered.

The following command sequence shows the placement of 3D faces for invisible edges, as shown in Figure 15–23.

Command: **3dface**
First point: *(select point A1)*
Second point: *(select point A8)*
Third point: *(select point A5)*
Fourth point: *(select point A4)*

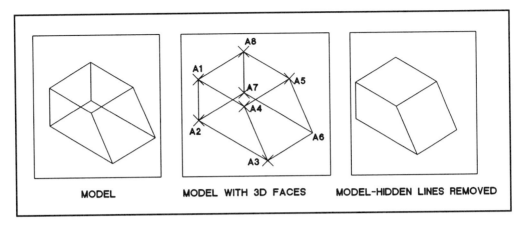

Figure 15–23 Drawing a 3D object with the 3DFACE command

Third point: *(select point A3)*
Fourth point: *(select point A6)*
Third point: *(select point A7)*
Fourth point: **i** « *(select point A8)*
Third point: *(select point A1)*
Fourth point: *(select point A2)*
Third point: *(select point A3)*
Fourth point: *(select point A4)*
Third point: Enter

3DFACE commands ignore thickness. The SPLFRAME system variable controls the display of invisible edges in 3D faces. If SPLFRAME is set to a nonzero value, all invisible edges of 3D faces are displayed.

Controlling the Visibility of a 3D Face The EDGE command allows you to change the visibility of 3D face edges. You can selectively set the edges to ON/OFF.

Invoke the EDGE command from:

Surfaces toolbar	Select the Edge command (see Figure 15–24)
Pull-down menu	Draw >Surfaces > Edge
Command: prompt	**edge** Enter

Figure 15–24 Invoking the Edge command from the Draw toolbar

AutoCAD prompts:

> Command: **edge**
> Display/<Select edge>: *(select the edges and press* Enter *to complete selection, or select the Display option)*

The **Display** option highlights invisible edges of 3D faces so you can change the visibility of the edges. AutoCAD prompts:

> Select/<All>:

The default option displays all the invisible edges. Once the edges are displayed, AutoCAD allows you to change the status of the visibility.

The **Select** option allows you selectively to identify hidden edges to be displayed. Then, if necessary, you can change the status of the visibility.

Modifying a 3D Face The DDMODIFY command allows you to modify a selected 3D face.

Invoke the DDMODIFY command from:

Pull-down menu	Modify > Properties...
Command: prompt	**ddmodify** Enter

AutoCAD prompts:

> Command: **ddmodify**
> Select one to modify: *(select a 3D face)*

AutoCAD displays the Modify 3D Face dialog box, similar to Figure 15–25.

The **Point 1**, **Point 2**, **Point 3**, and **Point 4** sections display the vertex coordinates of the selected 3D face. If necessary, you change the vertex coordinates by selecting the appropriate **Pick Point <** button or typing coordinates in the appropriate X/Y/Z edit fields. From the Modify 3D Face dialog box you can also change the color, linetype, and layer of the selected 3D face.

The check boxes located in the **Visibility** section of the dialog box allow you to change the visibility of the four edges.

> **NOTE:** All edges are visible regardless of the visibility setting if the SPLFRAME system variable is set to 1 (ON).

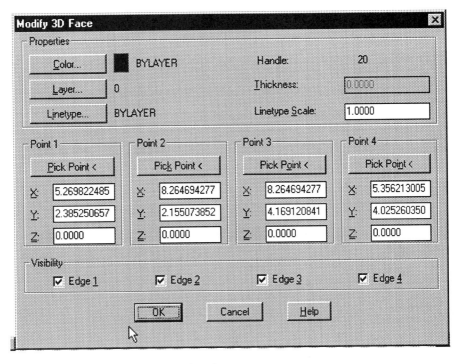

Figure 15–25 Modify 3D Face dialog box

CREATING MESHES

A 3D mesh is a single object. It defines a flat surface or approximates a curved one by placing multiple 3D faces on the surface of an object. It is a series of lines consisting of columns and rows. AutoCAD lets you determine the spacing between rows (*M*) and columns (*N*).

It is possible to create a mesh for a flat or curved surface by locating the boundaries or edges of the surface. Surfaces created in this fashion are called *geometry-generated* surfaces. Their size and shape depend on the boundaries used to define them and on the specific formula (or command) used to determine the location of the vertices between the boundaries. AutoCAD provides four different commands to create geometry-generated surfaces: RULESURF, REVSURF, TABSURF, and EDGESURF. The differences between these types of meshes depend on the types of objects connecting the surfaces. In addition, AutoCAD provides two other commands for creating polygon mesh: 3DMESH and PFACE. The key to using meshes effectively is to understand the purpose and requirement of each type of mesh and to select the appropriate one for the given condition.

AutoCAD 3D

Creating a Free-form Polygon Mesh

You can define a free-form 3D polygon mesh by means of the 3DMESH command. Initially, it prompts you for the number of rows and columns, in terms of mesh M and mesh N, respectively. Then it prompts for the location of each vertex in the mesh. The product of $M \times N$ gives the number of vertices for the mesh.

Invoke the 3DMESH command from:

Surfaces toolbar	Select 3D Mesh command (see Figure 15–26)
Pull-down menu	Draw >Surfaces > 3D Mesh
Command: prompt	**3dmesh** Enter

Figure 15–26 Invoking the 3D Mesh command from the Surfaces toolbar

AutoCAD prompts:

Command: **3dmesh**
Mesh M Size: *(specify an integer value between 2 and 256)*
Mesh N Size: *(specify an integer value between 2 and 256)*

The points for each vertex must be entered separately, and the M value can be considered the number of lines that will be connected by faces, while the N value is the number of points each line consists of. Vertices may be specified as 2D or 3D points, and may be any distance from each other.

The following command sequence creates a simple 5×4 polygon mesh. The mesh is created between the first point of the first line, the first point of the second line, and so on, as shown in Figure 15–27.

Command: **3dmesh**
Mesh M Size: **5**
Mesh N Size: **4**
Vertex (0,0): *(select point A1)*
Vertex (0,1): *(select point A2)*
Vertex (0,2): *(select point A3)*
Vertex (0,3): *(select point A4)*
Vertex (1,0): *(select point B1)*
Vertex (1,1): *(select point B2)*
Vertex (1,2): *(select point B3)*
Vertex (1,3): *(select point B4)*

Vertex (2,0): *(select point C1)*
Vertex (2,1): *(select point C2)*
Vertex (2,2): *(select point C3)*
Vertex (2,3): *(select point C4)*
Vertex (3,0): *(select point D1)*
Vertex (3,1): *(select point D2)*
Vertex (3,2): *(select point D3)*
Vertex (3,3): *(select point D4)*
Vertex (4,0): *(select point E1)*
Vertex (4,1): *(select point E2)*
Vertex (4,2): *(select point E3)*
Vertex (4,3): *(select point E4)*

NOTE: Specifying 3D mesh of any size can be time-consuming and tedious. It is preferable to use one of the commands for geometry-generated surfaces, such as RULESURF, TABSURF, REVSURF, or EDGESURF. The 3DMESH command is designed primarily for AutoLISP and ADS applications.

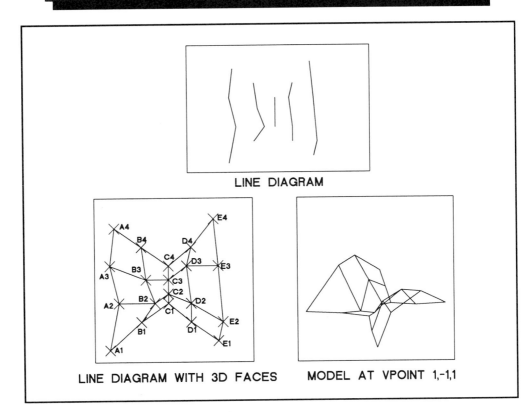

LINE DIAGRAM

LINE DIAGRAM WITH 3D FACES   MODEL AT VPOINT 1,-1,1

Figure 15–27 Creating a 3D mesh

AutoCAD 3D

Creating a 3D Polyface Mesh

The PFACE command allows you to construct a mesh of any topology you desire. This command is similar to the 3DFACE command, but it creates surfaces with invisible interior divisions. You can specify any number of vertices and 3D faces, unlike the other meshes. Producing this kind of mesh lets you conveniently avoid creating many unrelated 3D faces with the same vertices.

AutoCAD first prompts you to pick all the vertex points, then you can create the faces by entering the vertex numbers that define their edges.

Invoke the PFACE command from:

Command: prompt	pface [Enter]

AutoCAD prompts:

Command: **pface**
Vertex 1: *(specify a point)*

One by one, specify all the vertices used in the mesh, keeping track of the vertex numbers shown in the prompts. You can specify the vertices as 2D or 3D points and place them at any distance from one another. Enter a null response (press [Enter]) after specifying all the vertices, and AutoCAD prompts for a vertex number that has to be assigned to each face. You define any number of vertices for each face, and enter a null response (press [Enter]). AutoCAD prompts for the next face. After all the vertex numbers for all the faces are defined, enter a null reponse (press [Enter]), and AutoCAD draws the mesh.

The following command sequence creates a simple polyface for a given six-sided polygon, with a circle of 1" radius drawn at the center of the polygon at a depth of -2, as shown in Figure 15–28.

Command: **pface**
Vertex 1: *(select point A1)*
Vertex 2: *(select point A2)*
Vertex 3: *(select point A3)*
Vertex 4: *(select point A4)*
Vertex 5: *(select point A5)*
Vertex 6: *(select point A6)*
Vertex 7: [Enter]
Face 1, Vertex 1: **1**
Face 1, Vertex 2: **2**
Face 1, Vertex 3: **1**
Face 1, Vertex 4: **2**
Face 1, Vertex 5: **1**
Face 1, Vertex 6: **2**

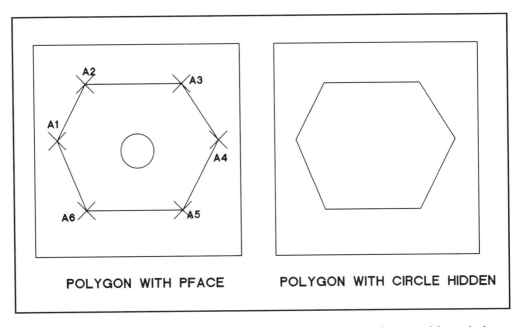

Figure 15–28 Creating a polyface for a given six-sided polygon with a circle at the center

Face 1, Vertex 7: `Enter`
Face 2, Vertex 1: `Enter`

If necessary, you can make an edge of the polyface mesh invisible by entering a negative number for the beginning vertex of the edge. By default, the faces are drawn on the current layer and with the current color. However, you can create the faces in layers and colors different from the original object. You can assign a layer or color by responding to the "Face m, Vertex n:" prompt with **L** for layer or **c** for color. AutoCAD then prompts for the name of the layer or color, as appropriate. It will continue with the prompts for vertex numbers. The layer or color you enter is used for the face you are currently defining and for any subsequent faces created.

> **NOTE:** Specifying the layer or color within the PFACE command does not change object properties for subsequent commands. Specifying PFACE of any size can be time-consuming and tedious. It is preferable to use one of the commands for geometry-generated surfaces, such as RULESURF, TABSURF, REVSURF, or EDGESURF. The PFACE command is designed primarily for AutoLISP and ADS applications.

Creating a Ruled Surface Between Two Objects

The RULESURF command creates a polygon mesh between two objects. The two objects can be lines, points, arcs, circles, 2D polylines, or 3D polylines. If one object is open, such as a line or an arc, the other must be open too. If one is closed, such as a circle, so must the other be. A point can be used as one object, regardless of whether the other object is open or closed. But only one of the objects can be a point.

RULESURF creates an $M \times N$ mesh, with the value of mesh M a constant 2. The value of mesh N can be changed depending on the required number of faces. This can be done with the help of the SURFTAB1 system variable. By default, SURFTAB1 is set to 6.

The following command sequence shows how to change the value of SURFTAB1 from 6 to 20:

Command: **surftab1**
New value for SURFTAB1 <6>: **20**

Invoke the RULESURF command from:

Surfaces toolbar	Select the Ruled Surface command (see Figure 15–29)
Pull-down menu	Draw >Surfaces > Ruled Surface
Command: prompt	**rulesurf** [Enter]

Figure 15–29 Invoking the Ruled Surface command from the Surfaces toolbar

AutoCAD prompts:

Command: **rulesurf**
Select first defining curve: *(select the first defining curve)*
Select second defining curve: *(select the second defining curve)*

Identify the two objects to which a mesh has to be created. See Figure 15–30, in which an arc (A1–A2) and a line (A3–A4) were selected and a mesh was created with SURFTAB1 set to 15. Two lines (B1–B2 and B3–B4) were selected and a mesh was created with SURFTAB1 set to 20. A cone was created by drawing a circle at an elevation of 0 and a point (C1) at an elevation of 5, followed by the application of the RULESURF command with SURFTAB1 set to 20.

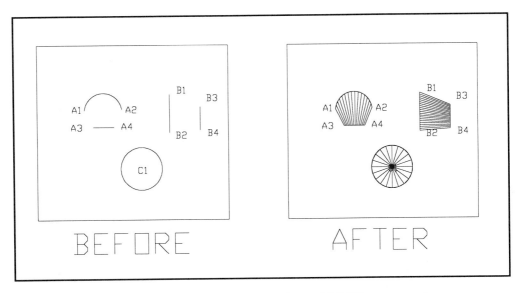

Figure 15–30 Creating ruled surfaces with the RULESURF command

NOTE: When you identify the two objects, make sure to select on the same side of the objects, left or right. If you pick the left side of one of the sides and the right side of the other, you will get a bow-tie effect.

Creating a Tabulated Surface

The TABSURF command creates a surface extrusion from an object with a length and direction determined by the direction vector. The object is called the *defining curve* and can be a line, arc, circle, 2D polyline, or 3D polyline. The direction vector can be a line or open polyline. The endpoint of the direction vector nearest the specified point will be swept along the path curve, describing the surface. Once the mesh is created, the direction vector can be deleted. The number of intervals along the path curve is controlled by the SURFTAB1 system variable, similar to the RULESURF command. By default, SURFTAB1 is set to 6.

Invoke the TABSURF command from:

Surfaces toolbar	Select the Tabulated Surface command (see Figure 15–31)
Pull-down menu	Draw >Surfaces > Tabulated Surface
Command: prompt	**tabsurf** Enter

Figure 15-31 Invoking the Tabulated Surface command from the Surfaces toolbar

AutoCAD prompts:

Command: **tabsurf**
Select path curve: *(select the path curve)*
Select direction vector: *(select the direction vector)*

The location at which the direction vector is selected determines the direction of the constructed mesh. The mesh is created in the direction from the selection point to the nearest endpoint of the direction vector. In Figure 15-32, a mesh was created with SURFTAB1 set to 16 by identifying a polyline as the path curve and the line as the direction vector.

> **NOTE:** The length of the 3D mesh is the same as that of the direction vector.

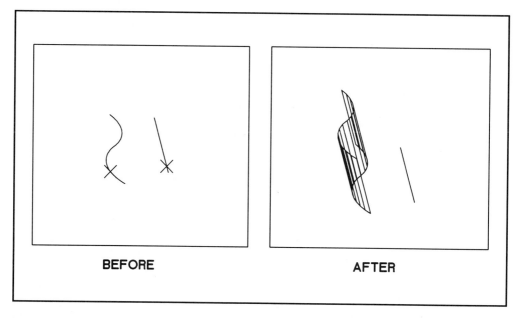

BEFORE   **AFTER**

Figure 15-32 Creating a tabulated surface with the TABSURF command

Creating a Revolved Surface

The REVSURF command creates a 3D mesh that follows the path defined by a path curve and is rotated around a centerline. The object used to define the path curve may be an arc, circle, line, 2D polyline, or 3D polyline. Complex shapes consisting of lines, arcs, or polylines can be joined into one object using the PEDIT command, and then you can create a single rotated mesh instead of several individual meshes.

The centerline can be a line or polyline that defines the axis around which the faces are constructed. The centerline can be of any length and at any orientation. If necessary, you can erase the centerline after the construction of the mesh. Thus it is recommended that you make the axis longer than the path curve so that it is easy to erase after the rotation.

In the case of REVSURF, both the mesh M size as well as mesh N are controlled by the SURFTAB1 and SURFTAB2 system variables, respectively. The SURFTAB1 value determines how many faces are placed around the rotation axis and can be an integer value between 3 and 1024. SURFTAB2 determines how many faces are used to simulate the curves created by arcs or circles in the path curve. By default, SURFTAB1 and SURFTAB2 are set to 6.

The following command sequence shows how to change the value of SURFTAB1 from 6 to 20 and that of SURFTAB2 from 6 to 15:

Command: **surftab1**
New value for SURFTAB1 <6>: **20**

Command: **surftab2**
New value for SURFTAB1 <6>: **15**

Invoke the REVSURF command from:

Surfaces toolbar	Select the Revolved Surface command (see Figure 15–33)
Pull-down menu	Draw >Surfaces > Revolved Surface
Command: prompt	revsurf Enter

Figure 15–33 Invoking the Revolved Surface command from the Surfaces toolbar

AutoCAD prompts:

Command: **revsurf**
Select path curve: (select the path curve)

Select axis of revolution: *(select the axis of revolution)*
Start angle<0>: *(specify the start angle, or press* Enter *to accept the default angle)*
Included angle (+=ccw,-=cw)<Full circle>: *(specify the included angle, or press* Enter *to accept the default)*

For the "Start Angle:" prompt, it does not matter if you are going to rotate the curve 360 degrees (full circle). If you want to rotate the curve only a certain angle, you must provide the start angle in reference to three o'clock (default) and then indicate the angle of rotation in the counterclockwise (positive) or clockwise (negative) direction. See Figure 15–34, in which a mesh was created with SURFTAB1 set to 16 and SURFTAB2 set to 12, by identifying a closed polyline as the path curve and the vertical line as the axis of revolution, and then rotated 360 degrees.

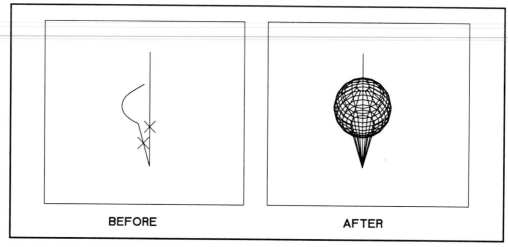

BEFORE   AFTER

Figure 15–34 Creating a meshed surface with the REVSURF command

Creating an Edge Surface with Four Adjoining Sides

The EDGESURF command allows a mesh to be created with four adjoining sides defining its boundaries. The only requirement for EDGESURF is that the mesh have exactly four sides. The sides can be lines, arcs, or any combination of polylines and polyarcs. Each side must join the adjacent one to create a closed boundary.

In EDGESURF, both the mesh M size and mesh N can be controlled by the SURFTAB1 and SURFTAB2 system variables, respectively, just as in REVSURF.

Invoke the EDGESURF command from:

Surfaces toolbar	Select the Edge Surface command (see Figure 15–35)
Pull-down menu	Draw >Surfaces > Edge Surface
Command: prompt	**edgesurf** Enter

Figure 15–35 Invoking the Edge Surface command from the Surfaces toolbar

AutoCAD prompts:

Command: **edgesurf**
Select edge 1: *(select the first edge)*
Select edge 2: *(select the second edge)*
Select edge 3: *(select the third edge)*
Select edge 4: *(select the fourth edge)*

When picking four sides, you must be consistent in picking the beginning of each polyline group. If you pick the beginning of one side and the end of another, the final mesh will cross and look strange. See Figure 15–36, in which a mesh was created with SURFTAB1 set to 25 and SURFTAB2 set to 20 by identifying four sides.

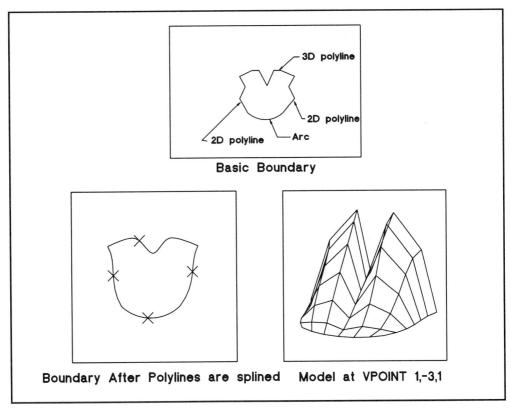

Figure 15–36 Creating a meshed surface with the EDGESURF command

Editing Polymesh Surfaces

As with blocks, polylines, hatch, and dimensioning, you can explode a mesh. When you explode a mesh it separates into individual 3D faces. Meshes can also be altered by invoking the PEDIT command, similar to editing polylines using the PEDIT command. Most of the options under the PEDIT command can be applied to meshes, except giving width to the edges of the polymesh. For a detailed explanation of the PEDIT command, refer to Chapter 5.

EDITING IN 3D

This section describes how to perform various 3D editing operations, such as aligning, rotating, mirroring, arraying, extending, and trimming.

Aligning Objects

The ALIGN command allows you to translate and rotate objects in 3D space regardless of the position of the current UCS. The move is defined by three source points and three destination points. ALIGN lets you select the objects to move, and then subsequently prompts for three source points and three destination points. Invoke the ALIGN command from:

Pull-down menu	Modify > 3D Operation > Align
Command: prompt	align [Enter]

AutoCAD prompts:

Command: **align**
Select objects: *(select the objects)*

Select the objects to move and press [Enter]. AutoCAD then prompts for three source points and three destination points. Temporary lines are displayed between the matching pairs of source and destination points. If you enter all six points, the move consists of a translation and two rotations based on the six points. The translation moves the 1st source point to the 1st destination point. The first rotation aligns the line defined by the 1st and 2nd source points with the line defined by the 1st and 2nd destination points. The second rotation aligns the plane defined by the three source points with the plane defined by the three destination points.

If instead of entering three pairs of points you enter two pairs of points, the transformation reduces to a translation from the 1st source point to the 1st destination point and a rotation such that the line passing through the two source points aligns with the line passing through the two destination points. The transformation occurs in either 2D or 3D, depending on your response to the following prompt:

<2d> or 3d transformation:

If you enter **2d** or press Enter, the rotation is performed in the *XY* plane of the current UCS. If you enter **3d**, the rotation is in the plane defined by the two destination points and the 2nd source point.

If you enter only one pair of points, the transformation reduces to a simple translation from the source to the destination point. This is similar to using the AutoCAD regular MOVE command without the dynamic dragging.

Rotating Objects About a 3D Object

The ROTATE3D command lets you rotate an object about an arbitrary 3D axis. Invoke the ROTATE3D command from:

Pull-down menu	Modify > 3D Operation > Rotate 3D
Command: prompt	**rotate3D** Enter

AutoCAD prompts:

Command: **rotate3d**
Select objects: *(select objects)*

AutoCAD lists the options for selecting the axis of rotation:

Axis by Entity/Last/View/Xaxis/Yaxis/Zaxis/<2points>: *(select one of the available options)*

2points Option The 2points option prompts you for two points. The axis of rotation is the line that passes through the two points, and the positive direction is from the first to the second point.

Axis by Object Option The Axis by Object option lets you select an object and then derives the axis of rotation based on the type of object selected. Valid objects include: line, circle, arc, and pline.

Last Option The Last option specifies the last-used axis. If there is no last axis, a message to that effect is displayed and the axis selection prompt is redisplayed.

View Option The View option prompts you to select a point. The axis of rotation is perpendicular to the view direction and passes through the selected point. The positive axis direction is toward the viewer.

X/Y/Zaxis Option The X/Y/Z option prompts you to select a point. The axis of rotation is parallel to standard axis of the current UCS and passes through the selected point.

Once you have selected the axis of rotation, AutoCAD prompts:

<Rotation angle>/Reference: *(specify the rotation angle, or enter r, for reference)*

AutoCAD rotates the selected object(s) to the specified rotation angle. The **Reference** option allows you to specify the current orientation as the reference angle or to show AutoCAD the angle by pointing to the two endpoints of a line to be rotated and then specifying the desired new rotation. AutoCAD automatically calculates the rotation angle and rotates the selected object appropriately.

See Figure 15–37 for an example of rotating a cylinder around the Z axis.

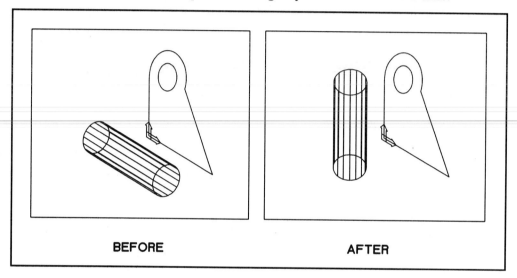

BEFORE   **AFTER**

Figure 15–37 Rotating a cylinder about the Z axis with the ROTATE3D command

Mirroring About a Plane

The MIRROR3D command lets you mirror a selected object about a plane. Invoke the MIRROR3D command from:

Pull-down menu	Modify > 3D Operation > Mirror 3D
Command: prompt	**mirror3D** Enter

AutoCAD prompts:

Command: **mirror3d**
Select objects: *(select the objects)*

Select the objects to mirror and press Enter. AutoCAD then lists the options for selecting the mirroring plane:

Plane by Object/Last/Normal/View/XY/YZ/XZ/<3points>: *(select one of the options to specify the mirroring plane)*

Delete old objects? <No>: *(enter **y** to delete the objects or **n** not to delete the objects)*

3points Option The 3points option prompts you for three points. The mirroring plane is the plane that passes through the three selected points.

Plane by Object Option The Plane by Object option lets you select an object, and the mirroring plane is aligned with the plane of the object selected. Valid objects include: circle, arc, and pline.

Last Option The Last option specifies the last used plane. If there is no last plane, a message is displayed to that effect and the plane selection prompt is redisplayed.

Normal Option The Normal option prompts you to select two points. The mirroring plane is the plane specified by a point on the plane and a point on the plane's normal (perpendicular to the plane).

View Option The View option prompts you to select a point. The mirroring plane is created perpendicular to the view direction and passes through the selected point.

XY/YZ/XZ The XY/YZ/XZ option prompts you to select a point. The mirroring plane is created parallel to the standard plane of the current UCS and passes through the selected point.

See Figure 15–38 for an example of mirroring a cylinder aligned with the plane of the object selected (pline).

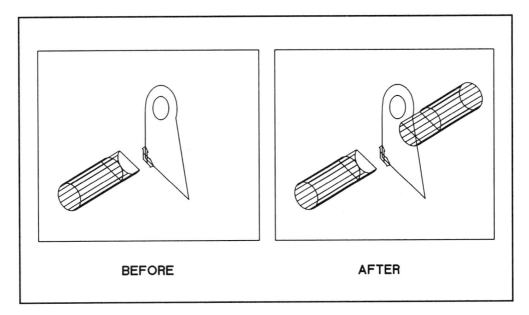

Figure 15–38 Mirroring a cylinder about a polyline object

Creating a 3D Array

The 3DARRAY command is used to make multiple copies of selected objects in either rectangular or polar array in 3D. In the rectangular array, specify the number of columns (*X* direction), the number of rows (*Y* direction), the number of levels (*Z* direction), and the spacing between columns, rows, and levels. In the polar array, specify the number of items to array, the angle that the arrayed objects are to fill, the start point and endpoint of the axis about which the objects are to be rotated, and whether or not the objects are rotated about the center of the group.

Invoke the ARRAY3D command from:

Pull-down menu	<u>M</u>odify > <u>3</u>D Operation > <u>3</u>D Array
Command: prompt	**3DARRAY** Enter

AutoCAD prompts:

> Command: **3Darray**
> Select objects: *(select the objects to array)*
> Rectangular or Polar array (R/P): *(select one of the two available options)*

Rectangular Array To generate a rectangular array, enter **R** (for rectangular array) and AutoCAD prompts:

> Number of rows(---)<1>: *(specify the number of rows or press* Enter *or the Spacebar)*
> Number of columns(|||)<1>: *(specify the number of columns or press* Enter *or the Spacebar)*
> Number of levels(...)<1>: *(specify the number of levels or press* Enter *or the Spacebar)*
> Distance between rows(---)<1>: *(specify a distance)*
> Distance between columns(---)<1>: *(specify a distance)*
> Distance between levels(---)<1>: *(specify a distance)*

Any combination of whole numbers of columns, rows, and levels may be entered. AutoCAD includes the original object in the number you enter. An array must have at least two columns, two rows, or two levels. Specifying one row requires that more than one column be specified, or vice versa. Specifying one level creates a 2D array. Column, row, and level spacing can be different from one another. They can be entered separately when prompted, or you can select two points and let AutoCAD measure the spacing. Positive values for spacing generate the array along the positive *X*, *Y*, and *Z* axes. Negative values generate the array along the negative *X*, *Y*, and *Z* axes.

Polar Array To generate a polar array, enter **p** (for polar array) and AutoCAD prompts:

Number of items: *(specify the number of items in the array; include the original object)*
Angle to fill <360>: *(specify an angle, or press* Enter *for 360 degrees)*
Rotate objects as they are copied <Y>: *(enter **y** to rotate the objects as they are copied, or enter **n** not to rotate the objects as they are copied)*
Center point of array: *(specify a point)*
Second point on axis of rotation: *(specify a point for the axis of rotation)*

Extending and Trimming in 3D

AutoCAD allows you to extend an object by means of the EXTEND command (explained in chapter 4) to any object in 3D space or to trim an object to any other 3D space by means of the TRIM command (explained in chapter 4), regardless of whether the objects are on the same plane or parallel to the cutting or boundary edges. Before you select an object to extend or trim in 3D space, specify one of the three available projection modes: None, UCS, or View. The **None** option specifies no projection. AutoCAD extends/trims only objects that intersect with the boundary/ cutting edge in 3D space. The **UCS** option specifies projection onto the *XY* plane of the current UCS. AutoCAD extends/trims objects that do not intersect with the boundary/cutting objects in 3D space. The **View** option specifies projection along the current view direction. the PROJMODE System variable allows you to set one of the available projection modes. You can also set the projection mode by selecting the Project option available in the EXTEND command.

In addition to specifying the projection mode, you have to specify one of the two available options for the edge. The edge determines whether the object is extended/ trimmed to another object's implied edge or only to an object that actually intersects it in 3D space. The available options are Extend and No Extend. The **Extend** option extends the boundary/cutting object/edge along its natural path to intersect another object or its implied edge in 3D space. The **No Extend** option specifies that the object is extended/trimmed only to a boundary/cutting object/edge that actually intersects it in 3D space. The EXTEDGE system variable allows you to set one of the available modes. You can also set the Edge by selecting the Edge option available in the EXTEND command.

CREATING SOLID SHAPES

As mentioned earlier, solids are the most informationally complete and least ambiguous of the modeling types. It is easier to edit a complex solid shape than to edit wireframes and meshes.

You create solids from one of the basic solid shapes: box, cone, cylinder, sphere, torus, or wedge. The user-defined solids can be created by extruding or revolving 2D objects and regions to define a 3D solid. In addition, you can create more complex solid shapes by combining solids together by performing a boolean operation— union, subtraction, or intersection.

Solids can be further modified by filleting and chamfering their edges. AutoCAD provides commands for slicing a solid into two pieces or obtaining a 2D cross section of a solid.

Like meshes, solids are displayed as a wireframe until you hide, shade, or render them. AutoCAD provides commands to analyze solids for their mass properties (volume, moments of inertia, center of gravity, etc.). AutoCAD allows you to export data about a solid object to applications such as NC (numerical control) milling and EXTEDGE FEM (finite element method) analysis. If necessary, you can use the AutoCAD EXPLODE command to explode solids into mesh and wireframe objects.

> **NOTE:** The ISOLINES system variable controls the number of tessellation lines used to visualize curved portions of the wireframe. The default value for ISOLINES is set to 4.

Creating a Solid Box

The BOX command creates a solid box or cube. The base of the box is defined parallel to the current UCS by default. The solid box can be drawn by one of two options: by providing a center point or a starting corner of the box. Invoke the BOX command from:

Solids toolbar	Select the Box command (see Figure 15–39)
Pull-down menu	Draw > Solids > Box
Command: prompt	box Enter

Figure 15–39 Invoking the BOX command from the Solids toolbar

AutoCAD prompts:

Command: **box**
Center/<Corner of box><0,0,0>: *(specify a point, or type c for the Center option)*

First, by default, you are prompted for the starting corner of the box. Once you provide the starting corner, the box's dimensions can be entered in one of three ways.

The default option lets you create a box by locating the opposite corner of its base rectangle first, and then its height. The following command sequence defines a box, as in Figure 15–40, using the default option:

Command: **box**
Center/<Corner of box>: **3,3**
Cube/Length/<Other corner>: **7,7**
Height: **4**

The **Cube** option allows you to create a box in which all edges are of equal length. The following command sequence defines a box using the Cube option:

Command: **box**
Center/<Corner of box>: **3,3**
Cube/Length/<Other corner>: **c**
Length: **3**

The **Length** option lets you create a box by defining its length, width, and height. The following command sequence defines a box using the Length option:

Command: **box**
Center/<Corner of box>: **3,3**
Cube/Length/<Other corner>: **l**
Length: **3**
Width: **4**
Height: **3**

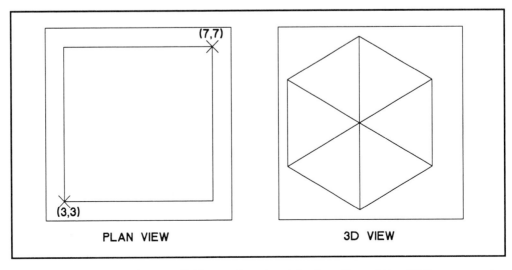

Figure 15–40 Creating a solid box using the default option of the BOX command

Center Option The Center option allows you to create a box by locating its center point. Once you locate the center point, a line rubberbands from this point to help you visualize the size of the rectangle. Then AutoCAD prompts you to define the size of the box by entering one of the following options:

Cube/Length/<Other corner>: *(select one of the available options)*

NOTE: Once you create a box you cannot stretch it or change its size.

Creating a Solid Cone

The CONE command creates a cone, either round or elliptical. By default, the base of the cone is parallel to the current UCS. Solid cones are symmetrical and come to a point along the *Z* axis. The solid cone can be drawn two ways: by providing a center point for a circular base or by selecting the elliptical option to draw the base of the cone as an elliptical shape.

Invoke the CONE command from:

Solids toolbar	Select the Cone command (see Figure 15–41)
Pull-down menu	Draw > Solids > Cone
Command: prompt	cone Enter

Figure 15–41 Invoking the Cone command from the Solids toolbar

AutoCAD prompts:

Command: **cone**
Elliptical/<Center point><0,0,0>: *(specify a point, or type e for the Elliptical option)*

By default, AutoCAD prompts you for the center point of the base of the cone and assumes the base to be a circle. Subsequently, you are prompted for the radius (or enter **D**, for diameter). Enter the appropriate value and then it prompts for the apex/height of the cone. The height of the cone is the default option, and it allows you to set the height of the cone, not the orientation. The base of the cone is parallel to the current base plane. The apex option, in contrast, prompts you for a point. In turn, it sets the height and orientation of the cone. For example, the following command sequence shows steps in drawing a cone, as in Figure 15–42, using the default option:

Command: **cone**
Elliptical/<Center point>: **5,5**
Diameter/<Radius>: **3**
Apex/<Height>: **4**

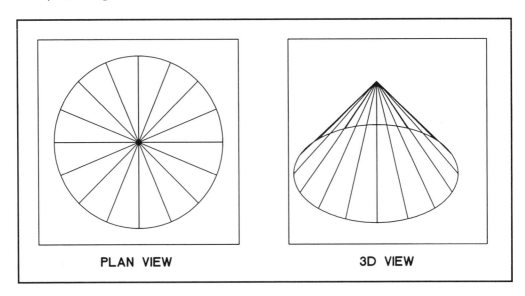

PLAN VIEW   3D VIEW

Figure 15–42 Creating a solid cone using the default option of the CONE command

Elliptical Option Selecting the Elliptical option indicates that the base of the cone is an ellipse. The prompts are identical to the regular AutoCAD those for ELLIPSE command. For example, the following command shows steps in drawing a cone using the Elliptical option:

Command: **cone**
Elliptical/<Center point>: **e**
<Axis endpoint 1>/Center: **3,3**
Axis endpoint 2: **6,6**
Other axis distance: **5,7**
Apex/<Height>: **4**

Creating a Solid Cylinder

The CYLINDER command creates a cylinder of equal diameter on each end and similar to an extruded circle or an ellipse. The solid cylinder can be by means of one of with two options: by providing a center point for a circular base or by selecting the elliptical option to draw the base of the cylinder as an elliptical shape.

Invoke the CYLINDER command from:

Solids toolbar	Select Cylinder command (see Figure 15–43)
Pull-down menu	Draw > Solids > Cylinder
Command: prompt	cylinder Enter

Figure 15–43 Invoking the Cylinder command from the Solids toolbar

AutoCAD prompts:

Command: **cylinder**
Elliptical/<Center point><0,0,0>: *(specify a point, or type **e** for the Elliptical option)*

The prompts are identical to those for a cone. For example, the following command sequence shows steps in drawing a cylinder, as in Figure 15–44, using the default option:

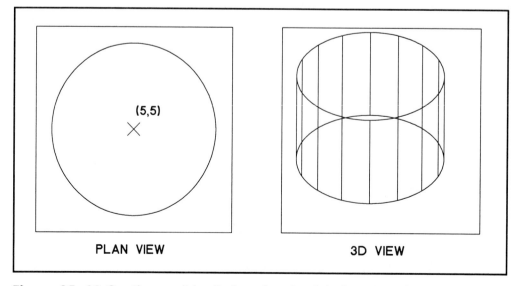

PLAN VIEW   3D VIEW

Figure 15–44 Creating a solid cylinder using the default option of the CYLINDER command

Command: **cylinder**
Elliptical/<Center point>: **5,5**
Diameter/<Radius>: **3**
Center of other end/<Height>: **4**

Creating a Solid Sphere

The SPHERE command creates a 3D body in which all surface points are equidistant from the center. The sphere is drawn in such a way that its central axis is coincident with the Z axis of the current UCS.

Invoke the SPHERE command from:

Solids toolbar	Select the Sphere command (see Figure 15–45)
Pull-down menu	Draw > Solids > Sphere
Command: prompt	**sphere** Enter

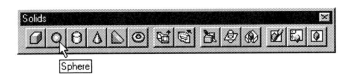

Figure 15–45 Invoking the Sphere command from the Solids toolbar

AutoCAD prompts:

Command: **sphere**
Center of sphere<0,0,0>: *(specify a point)*

First, AutoCAD prompts for the center point of the sphere; then you can provide the radius or diameter to define a sphere.

For example, the following command sequence shows steps in drawing a sphere, as in Figure 15–46:

Command: **sphere**
<Center point>: **5,5**
Diameter/<Radius> of sphere: **3**

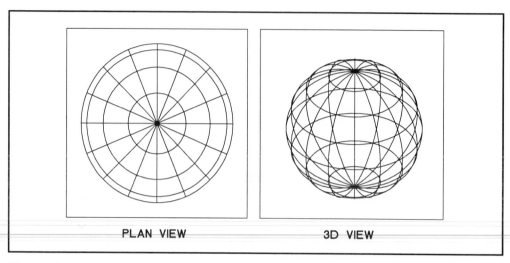

PLAN VIEW   3D VIEW

Figure 15–46 Creating a solid sphere using the default option of the SPHERE command

Creating a Solid Torus

The TORUS command creates a solid with a donutlike shape. If a torus were a wheel, the center point would be the hub. The torus is created lying parallel to and bisected by the *XY* plane of the current UCS. Invoke the TORUS command from:

Solids toolbar	Select the Torus command (see Figure 15–47)
Pull-down menu	Draw > Solids > Torus
Command: prompt	torus Enter

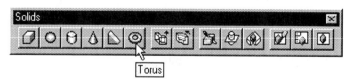

Torus

Figure 15–47 Invoking the Torus command from the Solids toolbar

AutoCAD prompts:

Command: **torus**
Center of torus<0,0,0>: *(specify a point)*

AutoCAD prompts for the center point of the torus and then subsequently for the diameter or radius of the torus and the diameter or radius of the tube, as in Figure

15–48. You can also draw a torus without a center hole if the radius of the tube is defined as greater than the radius of the torus. A negative torus radius would create a football-shaped solid.

For example, the following command sequence shows steps in drawing a torus, as in Figure 15–49:

Command: **torus**
<Center of torus>: **5,5**
Diameter/<Radius> of torus: **3**
Diameter/<Radius> of tube: **0.5**

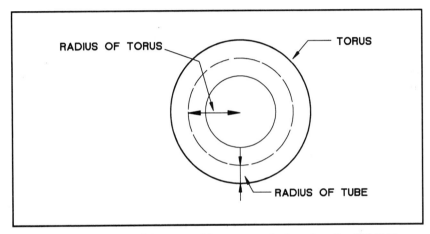

Figure 15–48 Creating a solid torus with a center hole using the TORUS command

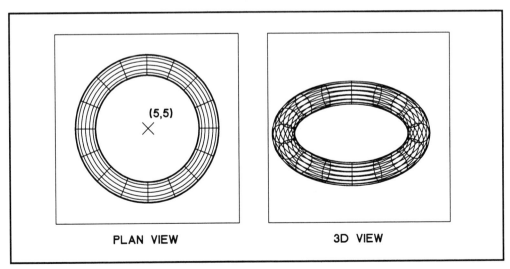

Figure 15–49 Creating a torus by specifying the baseplane and central axis direction using the TORUS command

Creating a Solid Wedge

The WEDGE command creates a solid like a box that has been a cut in half diagonally along one face. The face of the wedge is always drawn parallel to the current UCS, with the sloped face tapering along the *Z* axis. The solid wedge can be drawn by one of two options: by providing a center point of the base or by providing starting corner of the box.

Invoke the WEDGE command from:

Solids toolbar	Select the Wedge command (see Figure 15–50)
Pull-down menu	Draw > Solids > Wedge
Command: prompt	**wedge** [Enter]

Figure 15–50 Invoking the Wedge command from the Solids toolbar

AutoCAD prompts:

Command: **wedge**
Center/<Corner of wedge><0,0,0>: *(specify a point, or type* **C** *for the corner of the wedge)*

First, by default you are prompted for the starting corner of the box. Once you provide the starting corner, AutoCAD prompts:

Cube/Length/<corner of wedge>: *(select one of the available options)*

The wedge dimensions can be specified by using one of the three options. The **other corner** option lets you create a wedge by locating first the opposite corner of its base rectangle and then its height. The **Cube** option allows you to create a wedge in which all edges are of equal length. The **Length** option lets you create a box by defining its length, width, and height.

Center Option The Center option allows you to create a wedge by first locating its center point. Once you locate the center point, a line rubber-bands from this point to help you visualize the size of the rectangle. Then AutoCAD prompts you to define the size of the box by entering one of the following options:

Cube/Length/<corner of wedge>: *(select one of the available options)*

Creating Solids from Existing 2D Objects

The EXTRUDE command creates a unique solid by extruding circles, closed polylines, polygons, ellipses, closed splines, donuts, and regions. Because a polyline can have virtually any shape, the EXTRUDE command allows you to create irregular shapes. In addition, AutoCAD allows you to taper the sides of the extrusion.

> **NOTE:** A polyline must contain at least 3 but not more than 500 vertices and none of the segments can cross each other. See Figure 15–51 for examples of shapes that cannot be extruded. If the polyline has width, AutoCAD ignores the width and extrudes from the center of the polyline path. If a selected object has thickness, AutoCAD ignores the thickness.

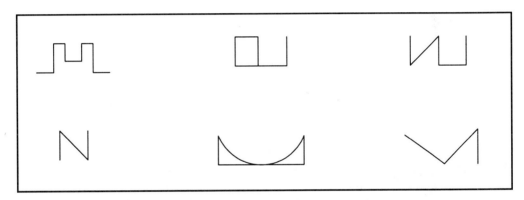

Figure 15–51 Shapes (shown in plan view) that cannot be extruded using the EXTRUDE command

Invoke the EXTRUDE command from:

Solids toolbar	Select the Extrude command (see Figure 15–52)
Pull-down menu	Draw > Solids > Extrude
Command: prompt	**extrude** Enter

Figure 15–52 Invoking the Extrude command from the Solids toolbar

AutoCAD prompts:

Command: **extrude**
Select objects: *(select the objects to extrude)*

Select the objects to extrude (you can select multiple objects in a single use of the command), AutoCAD prompts:

Path/<Height of Extrusion>: *(select one of the two available options)*

Height of Extrusion Option The Height of Extrusion option (default) allows you to specify the distance for extrusion. Specifying a positive value extrudes the objects along the positive Z axis of the current UCS, and a negative value extrudes along the negative Z axis.

Path Option The Path option allows you to select the extrusion path based on a specified curve object. All the profiles of the selected object are extruded along the chosen path to create solids. Lines, cirles, arcs, ellipses, elliptical arcs, polylines, or splines can be paths. The path should not lie on the same plane as the profile, nor should it have areas of high curvature. The extruded solid starts from the plane of the profile and ends on a plane perpendicular to the path's endpoint. One of the endpoints of the path should be on the plane of the profile. Otherwise, AutoCAD moves the path to the center of the profile.

Once you specify the Height of Extrusion and path appropriately, AutoCAD prompts:

Extrusion taper angle <0>: *(specify the angle)*

Specify an angle between –90 and +90 degrees, or press Enter or the Spacebar to accept the default value of 0 degrees. If you specify 0 degrees as the taper angle, AutoCAD extrudes a 2D object perpendicular to its 2D plane, as shown in Figure 15–53. Positive angles taper in from the base object; negative angles taper out.

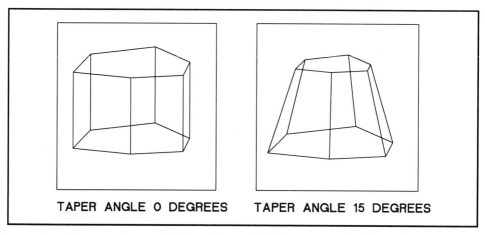

TAPER ANGLE 0 DEGREES   TAPER ANGLE 15 DEGREES

Figure 15–53 Creating a solid with the EXTRUDE command with 0 degrees and with 15 degrees of taper angle

NOTE: It is possible for a large taper angle or a long extrusion height to cause the object, or portions of the object, to taper to a point before reaching the extrusion height.

Creating Solids by Means of Revolution

The REVOLVE command creates a unique solid by revolving or sweeping a closed polyline, polygons, circles, ellipses, closed splines, donuts, and regions. Polylines that have crossing or self-intersecting segments cannot be revolved. The REVOLVE command is similar to the REVSURF command. The REVSURF command creates a surface of revolution, whereas REVOLVE creates a solid of revolution. The REVOLVE command provides several options for defining the axis of revolution.

Invoke the REVOLVE command from:

Solids toolbar	Select the Revolve command (see Figure 15–54)
Pull-down menu	Draw > Solids > Revolve
Command: prompt	**revolve** Enter

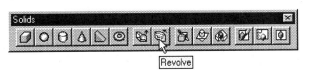

Figure 15–54 Invoking the Revolve command from the Solids toolbar

AutoCAD prompts:

Command: **revolve**
Select objects: *(select the object to revolve)*

Select the object to revolve. (You cannot select more than one object.) AutoCAD prompts:

Axis of revolution – Object/X/Y/<Start point of axis>: *(select one of the available options)*

Start Point of Axis Option The Start point of axis option (default) allows you to specify two points for the start point and the endpoint of the axis, and the positive direction of rotation is based on the right-hand rule.

Object Option The Object option allows you select an existing line or single polyline segment that defines the axis about which to revolve the object. The positive axis direction is from the closest to the farthest endpoint of this line.

X Axis Option The X axis option uses the positive *X* axis of the current UCS as the axis of the revolution.

Y Axis Option The Y axis option uses the positive *Y* axis of the current UCS as the axis of the revolution.

Once you specify the axis of revolution, AutoCAD prompts:

Angle of revolution <full circle>:

Specify the angle for revolution. The default is for a full circle. You can specify any angle between 0 and 360 degrees.

CREATING COMPOSITE SOLIDS

As mentioned earlier in this chapter, you can create a new composite solid or region by combining two or more solids or regions via boolean operations. Although the term *boolean* implies that only two objects can be operated upon at once, AutoCAD lets you select many solid objects in a single boolean command. There are three basic boolean operations that can be performed in AutoCAD:

Union

Subtraction

Intersection

The UNION, SUBTRACTION, and INTERSECTION commands let you select both the solids and regions in a single use of the commands, but solids are combined with solids, and regions combined only with regions. Also, in the case of regions you can make composite regions only with those that lie in the same plane. This means that a single command creates a maximum of one composite solid, but might create many composite regions.

Union Operation

Union is the process of creating a new composite object from one or more original objects. The union operation joins the original solids or regions in such a way that there is no duplication of volume. Therefore, the total resulting volume can be equal to or less than the sum of the volumes in the original solids or regions.

The UNION command performs the union operation. You can invoke the UNION command from:

Modify II toolbar	Select the Union command (see Figure 15–55)
Pull-down menu	Modify > Boolean > Union
Command: prompt	**union** Enter

Figure 15-55 Invoking the Union command from the Modify II toolbar

AutoCAD prompts:

    Command: **union**
    Select objects: *(select the objects to union)*

You can select more than two objects at once. The objects (solids or regions) can be overlapping, adjacent, or nonadjacent.

For example, the following command sequence shows steps in creating a composite solid by joining two cylinders, as in Figure 15-56:

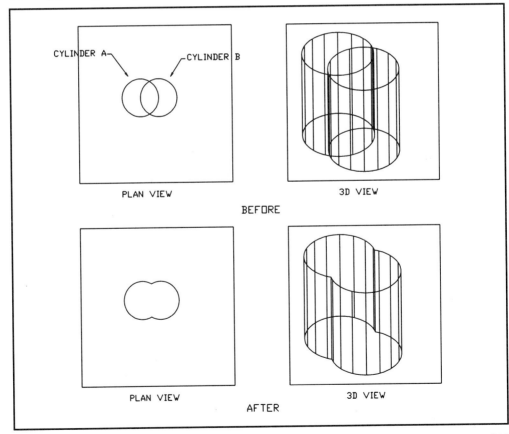

Figure 15-56 Creating a composite solid by joining two cylinders using the UNION command

Command: **union**
Select objects: *(select cylinders A and B and press* Enter *)*

Subtraction Operation

Subtraction is the process of forming a new composite object by starting with one object and removing from it any volume that it has in common with a second object. In the case of solids, they are created by subtracting the volume of one set of solids from another set. If the entire volume of the second solid is contained in the first solid, then what is left is the first solid minus the volume of the second solid. However, if only part of the volume of the second solid is contained within the first solid, then only the part that is duplicated in the two solids is subtracted. Similarly, in the case of regions, they are created by subtracting the common area of one set of existing regions from another set.

The SUBTRACT command performs the subtraction operation . You can invoke the SUBTRACT command from:

Modify II toolbar	Select the Subtract command (see Figure 15–57)
Pull-down menu	Modify > Boolean > Subtract
Command: prompt	**subtract** Enter

Figure 15–57 Invoking the Subtract command from the Modify II toolbar

AutoCAD prompts:

Command: **subtract**
Source objects...
Select objects: *(select the objects from which you will subtract other objects)*

You can select one or more objects as source objects. If you select more than one, they are automatically unioned. After selecting the source objects, press Enter or the Spacebar, and AutoCAD prompts you to select the objects to subtract from the source object.

Objects to subtract from them...
Select objects: *(select the objects to subtract)*

If necessary, you can select one or more objects to subtract from the source object. If you select several, they are automatically unioned before they are subtracted from the source object.

> **NOTE:** Objects that are neither solids nor regions are ignored.

For example, the following command sequence shows steps in creating a composite solid by subtracting cylinder B from A, as in Figure 15–58.

Command: **subtract**
Select objects: *(select cylinder A and press* Enter *or the Spacebar)*

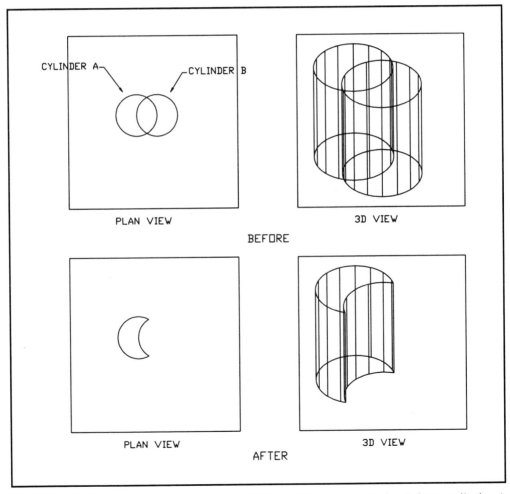

CYLINDER A⌐   ⌐CYLINDER B

PLAN VIEW   3D VIEW
BEFORE

PLAN VIEW   3D VIEW
AFTER

Figure 15–58 Creating a composite solid by subtracting cylinder B from cylinder A using the SUBTRACT command

Objects to subtract from them...
Select objects: *(select cylinder B and press* [Enter] *or the Spacebar)*

Intersection Operation

Intersection is the process of forming a composite object from only the volume that is common to two or more original objects. In the case of solids, you can create a new composite solid by calculating the common volume of two or more existing solids. Whereas in the case of regions, it is done by calculating the overlapping area of two or more existing regions.

The INTERSECT command performs the intersection operation. You can invoke the INTERSECT command from:

Modify II toolbar	Select the Intersect command (see Figure 15–59)
Pull-down menu	Modify > Boolean > Intersect
Command: prompt	intersect [Enter]

Figure 15–59 Invoking the Intersect command from the Modify II toolbar

AutoCAD prompts:

Command: **intersect**
Select objects: *(select the objects for intersection)*

Only two objects can be selected at a time.

For example, the following command sequence shows steps in creating a composite solid by intersecting cylinder A with cylinder B, as shown in Figure 15–60:

Command: **intersect**
Select objects: *(select cylinders A and B and press* [Enter] *or the Spacebar)*

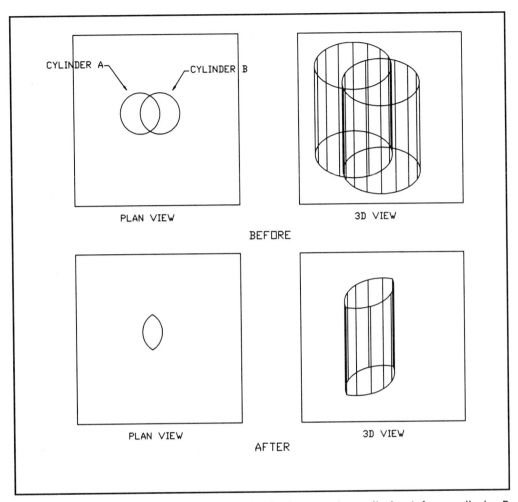

Figure 15–60 Creating a composite solid by intersecting cylinder A from cylinder B using the INTERSECTION command

EDITING 3D SOLIDS

AutoCAD makes the work of creating solids a little easier by providing editing tools, including chamfering or filleting the edges, creating a cross section through a solid, creating a new solid by cutting the existing solid and removing a specified side, and creating a composite solid from the interference of two or more solids. If necessary, you can always use the AutoCAD modify and construct commands, such as MOVE, COPY, ROTATE, SCALE, and ARRAY, to edit solids.

Chamfering Solids

The CHAMFER command (explained in Chapter 4) can also be used to bevel the edges of an existing solid object.

Invoke the CHAMFER command from:

Modify toolbar	Select the Chamfer command (see Figure 15–61)
Pull-down menu	Modify > Chamfer
Command: prompt	**chamfer** Enter

Figure 15–61 Invoke the Chamfer command from the Modify toolbar

AutoCAD prompts:

Command: **chamfer**
Polyline/Distances/Angle/Trim/Method/<Select first line>: (select an edge on a 3D solid)

If you pick an edge that is common to two surfaces, AutoCAD highlights one of the surfaces and prompts:

Next/<OK>:

If this is the surface you want, press Enter or the Spacebar to accept it. If it is not, enter **N** (for next) to highlight the adjoining surface and then press Enter or the Spacebar. AutoCAD prompts:

Enter base surface distance <default>: (specify a distance, or press Enter or the Spacebar to accept the default)
Enter adjacent surface distance <default>: (specify a distance, or press Enter or the Spacebar to accept the default)

Once you provide the chamfer distances, AutoCAD prompts:

Loop/<Select edge>:

Select the edges of the highlighted surface you want chamfered, and then press Enter or the Spacebar. The **Loop** option allows you to select one of the edges on the base surface, and AutoCAD automatically selects all edges on the base surface for chamfering.

The following command sequence draws a chamfer for a solid object, as shown in Figure 15–62.

Command: **chamfer**
Polyline/Distances/Angle/Trim/Method/<Select first line>:*(select the edge)*
Next/<OK>: Enter
Enter base surface distance <current>:**0.25**
Enter adjacent surface distance <current>:**0.5**
Loop/<Select edge>: *(select the first edge)*
Loop/<Select edge>: *(select the second edge)*

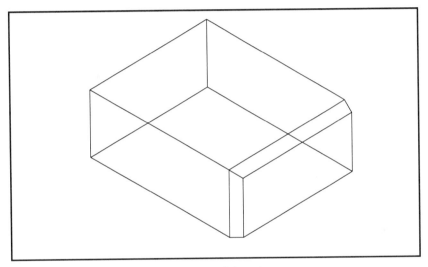

Figure 15–62 Example of chamfering a solid surface

Filleting Solids

The FILLET command (explained in Chapter 4) can also be used to round the edge of an existing solid object. Invoke the FILLET command from:

Modify toolbar	Select the Fillet command (see Figure 15–63)
Pull-down menu	Modify > Fillet
Command: prompt	**fillet** Enter

Fillet

Figure 15–63 Invoking the Fillet command from the Modify toolbar

AutoCAD prompts:

Command: **fillet**
Polyline/Radius/Trim/<Select first object>: *(select an edge in a 3D solid)*

If necessary, you can select multiple edges; but you must select the edges individually after specifying the radius for the fillet. AutoCAD prompts:

Enter radius <default>: *(specify a distance for a radius, or press* Enter *or the Spacebar to accept the default)*

AutoCAD prompts:

Chain/Radius<Select edge>:

Select additional edges. Once you are through with selection of edges for filleting, press Enter or the Spacebar to complete the command sequence.

The following command sequence draws a fillet for a solid object, as in Figure 15–64.

Command: **fillet**
Polyline/Radius/Trim/<Select first object>: *(select the solid edge)*
Enter radius<current>:**0.5**
Chain/Radius/<Select edge>: *(select the second edge)*
Chain/Radius/<Select edge>: Enter

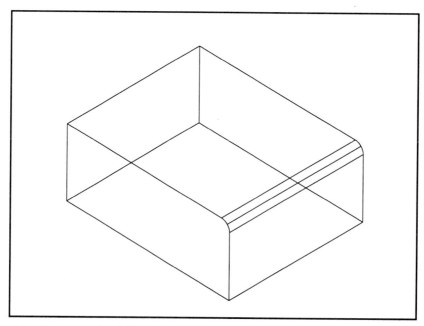

Figure 15–64 Example of filleting a solid surface

Sectioning Solids

The SECTION command creates a cross section of one or more solids. The cross section is created as one or more regions. The region is created on the current layer and is inserted at the location of the cross section. If necessary, you can use the MOVE command to move the cross section.

Invoke the SECTION command from:

Solids toolbar	Select the Section command (see Figure 15–65)
Pull-down menu	Draw > Solids > Section
Command: prompt	section Enter

Figure 15–65 Invoking the Section command from the Solids toolbar

AutoCAD prompts:

Command: **section**
Select objects: *(select the objects from which you want the cross section to be generated)*

After selecting the objects, press Enter or the Spacebar. AutoCAD prompts you to define the sectioning plane:

Sectioning plane by Object/Zaxis/View/XY/YZ/ZX/<3points>: *(select one of the available options)*

3points Option The 3points option (default) allows you to define a section plane by locating three points. The first point is the origin, the second point determines the positive direction of the X axis for the section plane, and the third point determines the positive Y axis of the section plane. This option is similar to the 3point option of the AutoCAD UCS command.

Object Option The Object option aligns the sectioning plane with a circle, ellipse, circular or elliptical arc, 2D spline, or 2D polyline segment.

Zaxis Option The Zaxis option defines the section plane by locating its origin point and a point on the Z axis (normal) to the plane.

View Option The View option aligns the section plan with the viewing plane of the current viewport. Specifying a point defines the location of the sectioning plane.

XY Option The XY option aligns the sectioning plane with the XY plane of the current UCS. Specifying a point defines the location of the sectioning plane.

YZ Option The YZ option aligns the sectioning plane with the *XY* plane of the current UCS. Specifying a point defines the location of the sectioning plane.

ZX Option The ZX option aligns the sectioning plane with the *XY* plane of the current UCS. Specifying a point defines the location of the sectioning plane.

See Figure 15–66 for a hatched section produced with the SECTION command.

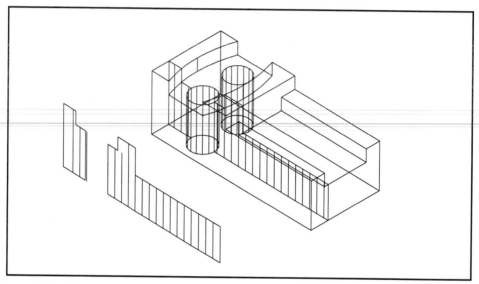

Figure 15–66 Creating a 2D hatched cross section using the SECTION command

Slicing Solids

The SLICE command allows you to create a new solid by cutting the existing solid and removing a specified side. If necessary, you can retain both halves of the sliced solids or just the half you specify. The sliced solids retain the layer and color of the original solids.

Invoke the SLICE command from:

Solids toolbar	Select the Slice command (see Figure 15–67)
Pull-down menu	Draw > Solids > Slice
Command: prompt	slice [Enter]

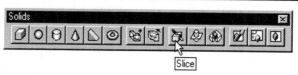

Figure 15–67 Invoking the Slice command from the Solids toolbar

AutoCAD prompts:

Command: **slice**
Select objects: *(select the objects to create a new solid by slicing)*

After selecting the objects, press Enter or the Spacebar. AutoCAD prompts you to define the slice plane:

Slicing plane by Object/Zaxis/View/XY/YZ/ZX/<3points>:

The options are the same as those for the SECTION command explained earlier in this chapter.

After defining the slicing plane, AutoCAD prompts you to indicate which part of the cut solid is to be retained:

Both sides/<Point on desired side of the plane>:

The default option allows you to select with your pointing device the side of the slice that has to be retained in your drawing.

The **Both sides** option allows you to retain both sides of the sliced solids.

Figure 15–68 shows two parts of a solid model that have been cut using the SLICE command and moved apart using the MOVE command.

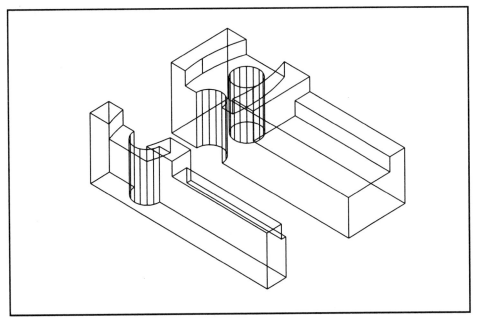

Figure 15-68 Cutting a solid model into two parts using the SLICE command

Solid Interference

The INTERFERE command checks the interference between two or more solids and creates a composite solid from their common volume.

There are two ways to determine the interference between solids:

- Select two sets of solids. AutoCAD determines the interference between the first and second sets of solids.
- Select one set of solids instead of two. AutoCAD determines the interference between all of the solids in the set. They are checked against each other.

Invoke the INTERFERE command from:

Solids toolbar	Select the Interfere command (see Figure 15–69)
Pull-down menu	Draw > Solids > Interference
Command: prompt	interfere [Enter]

Figure 15–69 Invoking the Interfere command from Solids toolbar

AutoCAD prompts:

> Command: **interfere**
> Select the first set of solids: *(select the first set of solids and press [Enter] or the Spacebar)*
> Select the second set of solids: *(select the second set of solids or press [Enter])*

The second selection set is optional. Press [Enter] or the Spacebar if you do not want to define the second selection set. If the same solid is included in both the selection sets, it is considered part of the first selection set and ignored in the second selection set. AutoCAD highlights all interfering solids and prompts:

> Create interference solids? <N>:

Entering **y** creates and highlights a new solid on the current layer that is the intersection of the interfering solids. If there are more than two interfering solids, AutoCAD prompts:

> Highlight pairs of interfering solids?<N>: *(Specify y or **n**)*

Enter **y**, and if there is more than one interfering pair, AutoCAD prompts:

> eXit/<Next pair>: *(Specify x or n)*

Pressing [Enter] cycles through the interfering pairs of solids, and AutoCAD highlights each interfering pair of solids. Enter **x** to complete the command sequence.

MASS PROPERTIES OF A SOLID

The MASSPROP command calculates and displays the mass properties of selected solids and regions. The mass properties displayed for solids are mass, volume, bounding box, centroid, moments of inertia, products of inertia, radii of gyration, and principal moments with corresponding principal directions. The mass properties are calculated based on the current UCS.

Invoke the MASSPROP command from:

Inquiry toolbar	Select the Mass Properties command (see Figure 15–70)
Pull-down menu	Tools > Inquiry > Mass Properties
Command: prompt	**massprop** [Enter]

Figure 15–70 Invoking the Mass Properties command from the Inquiry toolbar

AutoCAD prompts:

Command: **massprop**
Select objects: *(select the objects you want displayed as mass properties)*

The MASSPROP command displays the object mass properties in the text window, as shown in Figure 15–71. AutoCAD prompts:

Write to file<N>:

If you enter **y**, AutoCAD prompts for a file name and saves the file in ASCII format.

> **NOTE:** You can also use the AutoCAD LIST and AREA commands to obtain information about individual solid(s) (coordinates) and the area(s) of the solid(s), respectively.

AutoCAD 3D

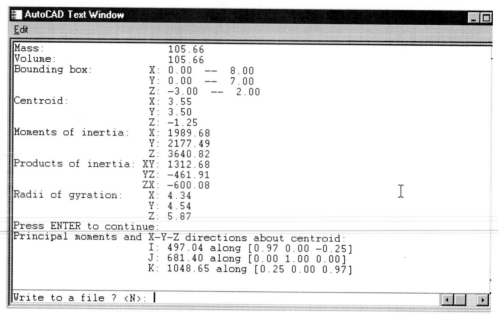

```
AutoCAD Text Window
Edit
Mass:                      105.66
Volume:                    105.66
Bounding box:       X:  0.00  --   8.00
                    Y:  0.00  --   7.00
                    Z: -3.00  --   2.00
Centroid:           X:  3.55
                    Y:  3.50
                    Z: -1.25
Moments of inertia:  X: 1989.68
                     Y: 2177.49
                     Z: 3640.82
Products of inertia: XY: 1312.68
                     YZ: -461.91
                     ZX: -600.08
Radii of gyration:   X:  4.34
                     Y:  4.54
                     Z:  5.87
Press ENTER to continue:
Principal moments and X-Y-Z directions about centroid:
                     I:  497.04 along [0.97 0.00 -0.25]
                     J:  681.40 along [0.00 1.00 0.00]
                     K: 1048.65 along [0.25 0.00 0.97]

Write to a file ? <N>: |
```

Figure 15–71 Mass properties listing

Hiding Objects

The HIDE command hides objects or displays in different colors that are behind other objects in the current viewport. Complex models are difficult to read in wireframe form, and benefit in clarity when the model is displayed with hidden lines removed. HIDE considers circles, solids, traces, wide polyline segments, 3D faces, polygon meshes, and the extruded edges of objects with a thickness to be opaque surfaces hiding objects that lie behind them. The HIDE command remains active only until the next time the display is regenerated. Depending on the complexity of the model, hiding may take from a few seconds to even several minutes.

Invoke the HIDE command from:

Render toolbar	Select the Hide command (see Figure 15–72)
Pull-down menu	View > Hide
Command: prompt	hide [Enter]

Hide

Figure 15–72 Invoking the Hide command from the Render toolbar

AutoCAD prompts:

Command: **hide**

There are no prompts to be answered. The current viewport goes blank for a period of time, depending on the complexity of the model, and is then redrawn with hidden lines removed temporarily. Hidden-line removal is lost during plotting unless you specify that AutoCAD remove hidden lines in the plotting configuration.

PLACING MULTIVIEWS IN PAPER SPACE

The SOLVIEW command creates untiled viewports using orthographic projection to lay out orthographic views and sectional views. View-specific information is saved with each viewport as you create it. The information that is saved is used by the SOLDRAW command, which does the final generation of the drawing view. The SOLVIEW command automatically creates a set of layers that the SOLDRAW command uses to place the visible lines, hidden lines, and section hatching for each view. In addition, the SOLVIEW command creates a specific layer for dimensions that are visible in individual viewports. The AutoCAD SOLVIEW command applies the following conventions in naming the layers:

	Layer Name
For visible lines	VIEW NAME-VIS
For hidden lines	VIEW NAME-HID
For dimensions	VIEW NAME-DIM
For sections	VIEW NAME-HAT6

The viewport objects are drawn on the VPORTS layer. The SOLVIEW command creates the VPORTS layer if it does not already exist. All the layers created by SOLVIEW are assigned the color white and the linetype continuous. The stored information is deleted and updated when you run the SOLDRAW command, so do not draw any objects on these layers.

Invoke the SOLVIEW command from:

Solids toolbar	Select the Setup View command (see Figure 15–73)
Pull-down menu	Draw > Solids > Setup > View
Command: prompt	**solview** Enter

AutoCAD 3D

Figure 15–73 Invoking the Setup View command from Solids toolbar

AutoCAD prompts:

Command: **solview**
Ucs/Ortho/Auxiliary/Section/<eXit>: *(select one of the available options)*

Ucs Option The Ucs option creates a profile view relative to a User Coordinate System. AutoCAD prompts:

Named/World/?/<Current>: *(select one of the available options)*

The **Named** option uses the *XY* plane of a named UCS to create a profile view. After prompting for the name of the view, AutoCAD prompts as follows:

Enter view scale <1.0>: *(specify the scale factor for the view to be displayed)*
View center: *(specify the center location for the viewport to be drawn in the paper space)*
Clip first corner: *(specify a point for one corner of the viewport)*
Clip other corner: *(specify a point for the opposite corner of the viewport)*
View name: *(specify a name for the newly created view)*

The **World** option uses the *XY* plane of the WCS to create a profile view. The prompts are the same as just described for the Named option.

The **?** option lists the names of existing User Coordinate Systems. After the list is displayed, press any key to return to the first prompt.

The **Current** option, which is the default option, uses the *XY* plane of the current UCS to create a profile view. The prompts are the same as explained earlier for the Named option.

If no untiled viewports exist in your drawing, the UCS option allows you to create an initial viewport from which other views can be created.

Ortho Option The Ortho option creates a folded orthographic view from an existing view. AutoCAD prompts:

Pick side of viewport to project: *(select the one of the edges of a viewport)*

View center: (specify the center location for the viewport to be drawn in the paper space)
Clip first corner: (specify a point for one corner of the viewport)
Clip other corner: (specify a point for the opposite corner of the viewport)
View name: (specify a name for the newly created view)

Auxiliary Option The Auxiliary option creates an auxiliary view from an existing view. An auxiliary view is one that is projected onto a plane perpendicular to one of the orthographic views and inclined in the adjacent view. AutoCAD prompts:

Inclined plane's 1st point: (specify a point)
Incline plane's 2nd point: (specify a point)
Side to view from: (specify a point that determines the side from which you will view the plane)
View center: (specify the center location for the viewport to be drawn in the paper space)
Clip first corner: (specify a point for one corner of the viewport)
Clip other corner: (specify a point for the opposite corner of the viewport)
View name: (specify a name for the newly created view)

Section oOption The Section option creates a sectional view of solids with cross-hatching. AutoCAD prompts:

Cutting plane 1st point: (specify a point to define the first point of the cutting plane)
Cutting plane 2nd point: (specify a point to define the second point of the cutting plane)
Side of cutting plane to view from: (specify a point to define the side of the cutting plane from which to view)
Enter view scale: (specify the scale factor for the view to be displayed)
View center: (specify the center location for the viewport to be drawn in the paper space)
Clip first corner: (specify a point for one corner of the viewport)
Clip other corner: (specify a point for the opposite corner of the viewport)
View name: (specify a name for the newly created view)

eXit Option The eXit option terminates the SOLVIEW command and returns you to the "Command:" prompt.

GENERATING VIEWS IN VIEWPORTS

The SOLDRAW command generates sections and profiles in viewports that have been created with the SOLVIEW command. Visible and hidden lines representing the silhouette and edges of solids in the viewports are created and then projected to a plane perpendicular to the viewing direction. AutoCAD deletes any existing profiles and sections in the selected viewports, and new ones are generated. In addition, AutoCAD freezes all the layers in each viewport, except those required to display the profile or section.

Invoke the SOLDRAW command from:

Solids toolbar	Select the Setup Drawing command (see Figure 15–74)
Pull-down menu	<u>D</u>raw > Sol<u>i</u>ds > Set<u>u</u>p > <u>D</u>rawing
Command: prompt	**soldraw** Enter

Figure 15–74 Invoking the Setup Drawing command from the Solids toolbar

AutoCAD prompts:

Command: **soldraw**
Viewports to draw...
Select objects: *(select the viewports)*

AutoCAD generate views in the selected viewports.

GENERATING PROFILES

The SOLPROF (alias PROF) command creates a profile image of a solid, including all of its edges, according to the view in the current viewport. The profile image is created from lines, circles. arcs, and/or polylines. SOLPROF will not give correct results in perspective view; it is designed for parallel projections only.

The SOLPROF command will work only when TILEMODE is set to 0 (OFF) and you are in model space.

Invoke the SOLPROF command from:

Solids toolbar	Select the Setup Profile command (see Figure 15–75)
Pull-down menu	<u>D</u>raw > Sol<u>i</u>ds > Set<u>u</u>p > <u>P</u>rofile
Command: prompt	**solprof** Enter

Figure 15–75 Invoking the Setup Profile command from the Solids toolbar

AutoCAD prompts:

Command: **solprof**
Select objects: *(select one or more objects)*

Select one or more solids and press «. The next prompt lets you decide the placement of hidden lines of the profile on a separate layer:

Display hidden profile lines on separate layer? <Y>:

Enter **Yes** or **No**. If you answer **Yes** (default option), two block inserts are created—one for the visible lines in the same linetype as the original and the other for hidden lines in the hidden linetype. The visible lines are placed on a layer whose name is PV-(viewport handle of the current viewport). The hidden lines are placed on a layer whose name is PH-(viewport handle or the current viewport). If these layers do not exist, AutoCAD will create them. For example, if you create a profile in a viewport whose handle is 6, then visible lines will be placed on a layer PV-6 and hidden lines on layer PH-6. To control the visibility of the layers, you can turn the appropriate layers on and off.

The next prompt determines whether 2D or 3D entities are used to represent the visible and hidden lines of the profile:

Project profile lines onto a profile? <Y>:

Enter **Yes** or **No**. If you answer **Yes** (default option), AutoCAD creates the visible and hidden lines of the profile with 2D AutoCAD entities; **No** creates the visible and hidden lines of the profile with 3D AutoCAD entities.

Finally, AutoCAD asks if you want tangential edges deleted. A *tangential edge* is an imaginary edge at which two facets meet and are tangent. In most of the drafting applications, the tangential edges are not shown. The prompt sequence is as follows for deleting the tangential edges:

Delete tangential edges? <Y>:

Enter **Yes** to delete the tangential edges and **No** to retain them.

PROJECT EXERCISE

This project creates the bracket shown in Figure P15–1. The bracket is drawn entirely by means of AutoCAD solid modeling features. Follow the steps, and you will be able to build the model by using various commands available in AutoCAD solid modeling.

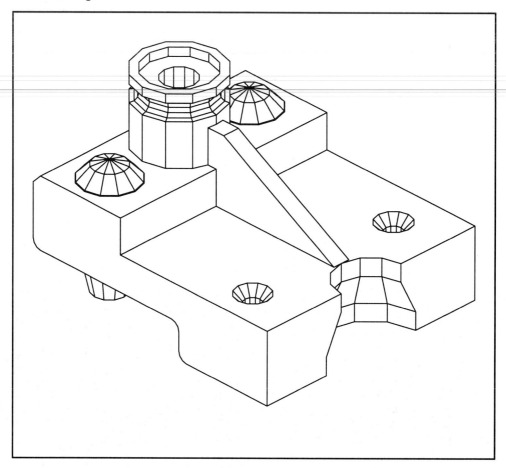

Figure P15–1 Creating a bracket using solid modeling

Step 1   Begin a new drawing.

Step 2   Set TILEMODE to 0. This automatically places you in paper space.

Step 3   Set UNITS to 2 decimal places. Set LIMITS to 0,0 and 22,17. ZOOM All.

Step 4 Create the following layers with appropriate colors and linetypes:

Layer Name	Color	Linetype
Object	Red	Continuous
Border	Green	Continuous
Dim	Blue	Continuous
Viewports	Cyan	Continuous

Set Border as the current layer.

Step 5 Draw the border and the title block.

Step 6 Set Viewports as the current layer. Make four viewports.

Command: **mview**
On/OFF/Hideplot/Fit/2/3/4/Restore/<First Point>: **3.5,10**
Other corner: **9.5,16**

Command: Enter
On/OFF/Hideplot/Fit/2/3/4/Restore/<First Point>: **11,10**
Other corner: **17,16**

Command: Enter
On/OFF/Hideplot/Fit/2/3/4/Restore/<First Point>: **3.5,2.5**
Other corner: **9.5,8.5**

Command: Enter
On/OFF/Hideplot/Fit/2/3/4/Restore/<First Point>: **11,2.5**
Other corner: **17,8.5**

Step 7 Change to model space.

Command: **mspace**

Make the upper right viewport current. Set Vpoint to 1,-1,1.

Step 8 Make the upper left viewport current. Set Grid to 0.5 and Snap to 0.25.

Step 9 Make the lower left viewport current. Set Vpoint to 0,-1,0.

Step 10 Make the lower right viewport current. Set Vpoint to 1,0,0.

Step 11 Set Object as the current layer.

Begin the layout of the drawing by drawing four boxes using the BOX command:

Command: **box**
Center/<Corner of box> <0,0,0>: **0,0,-2**
Cube/Length/<Other corner>: **I**

AutoCAD 3D

Length: **8**
Width: **7**
Height: **1**

Command: **box**
Center/<Corner of box> <0,0,0>: **0,0,-1**
Cube/Length/<Other corner>: **l**
Length: **3**
Width: **7**
Height: **1**

Command: **box**
Center/<Corner of box><0,0,0>: **5,0,-3**
Cube/Length/<Other corner>: **l**
Length: **3**
Width: **7**
Height: **1**

Command: **box**
Center/<Corner of box><0,0,0>: **2.5,3.25,-1**
Cube/Length/<Other corner>: **l**
Length: **.75**
Width: **.5**
Height: **2**

The preceding box constructions form the basic shape of the bracket, as shown in Figure P15–2.

Step 12   Use the CYLINDER command to create a cylinder:

Command: **cylinder**
Elliptical/<Center point> <0,0,0>: **1.5,3.5**
Diameter/<Radius>: **1.25**
Center of other end/<Height>: **2**

Step 13   Use the WEDGE command to create a wedge as shown in Figure P15–3:

Command: **wedge**
Center/<Corner of wedge> <0,0,0>: **3.25,3.25,-1**
Cube/Length/<Other corner>: **l**
Length: **3.75**
Width: **.5**
Height: **2**

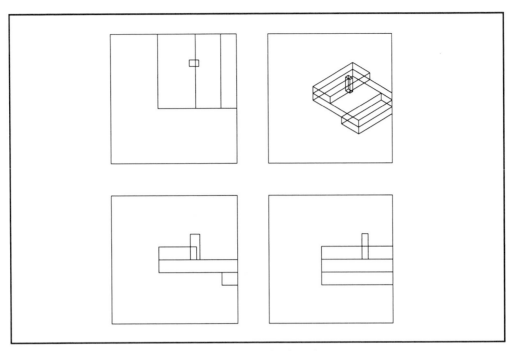

Figure P15–2 Creating the basic shape of the bracket

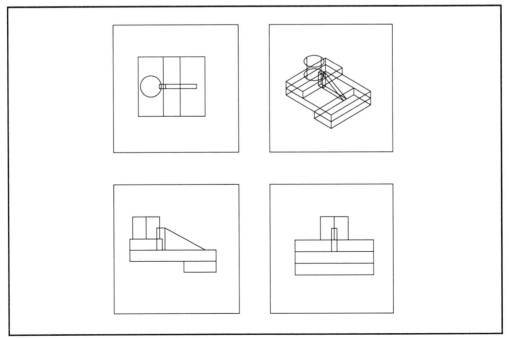

Figure P15–3 Creating the basic shape of the bracket

Step 14   Setup a UCS as follows:

> Command: **ucs**
> Origin/ZAxis/3point/OBject/View/X/Y/Z/Prev/Restore/Save/Del/?/
>   <World>: **3**
> Origin point <0,0,0>:*(select point 1 by using object snap ENDpoint as
>   shown in Figure P15–4)*
> Point on positive portion of the x-axis:*(select point 2 by using object snap
>   ENDpoint as shown in Figure P15–4)*
> Point on positive portion of the y-axis:*(select point 3 by using object snap
>   ENDpoint as shown in Figure P15–4)*

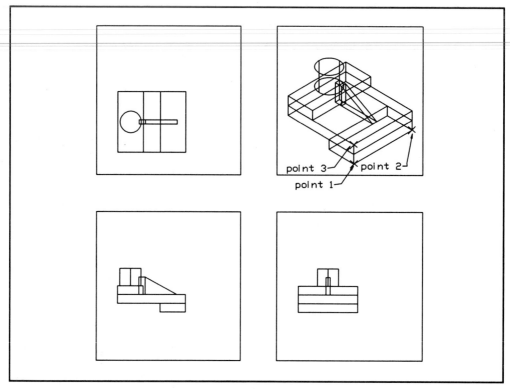

Figure P15–4 Defining a UCS

Step 15   Draw a polyline to the given coordinates, as shown in Figure P15–5:

> Command: **pline**
> From point: **3.5,2**
> Current line-width is 0.000
> Arc/Close/Halfwidth/Length/Undo/Width/<Endpoint of line>:
>   **@1.0<180**

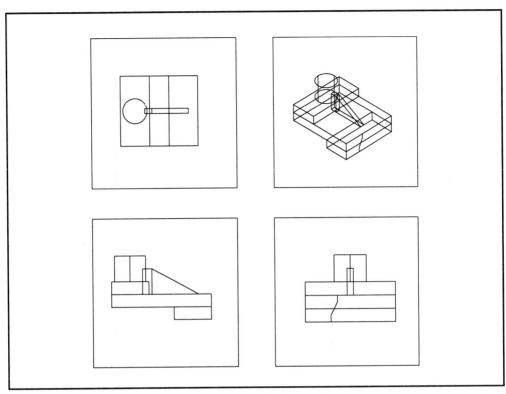

Figure P15–5 Drawing a polyline to specified coordinates

Arc/Close/Halfwidth/Length/Undo/Width/<Endpoint of line>:
  @0.5<270
Arc/Close/Halfwidth/Length/Undo/Width/<Endpoint of line>:
  @-0.5,-1
Arc/Close/Halfwidth/Length/Undo/Width/<Endpoint of line>:
  @0.5<-90
Arc/Close/Halfwidth/Length/Undo/Width/<Endpoint of line>: **@1.5<0**
Arc/Close/Halfwidth/Length/Undo/Width/<Endpoint of line>: **c** Enter

Step 16 Revolve the polyline just created into a solid, as shown in Figure P15–6:

Command: **revolve**
Select objects: **l**
Select object: Enter
Axis of revolution - Object/X/Y/<Start point of axis>: **3.5,2**
Endpoint of axis: **@2<270**
Included angle <full circle>: **180**

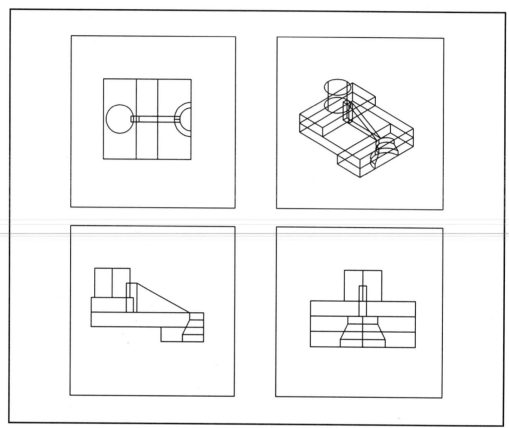

Figure P15–6 Revolving a polyline into a solid

Step 17 Create two spheres in reference to the WCS.

Command: **ucs**
Origin/ZAxis/3point/Entity/View/X/Y/Z/Prev/Restore/Save/Del/?/
    <world>: Enter
Command: **sphere**
<Center of sphere> <0,0,0>: **1.5,1.125,-0.05**
Diameter/<Radius of sphere>: **1**

Copy the sphere to a displacement of 0,4.75, as shown in Figure P15–7.

Command: **copy**
Select objects: **I**
Select objects: Enter
<Base point or displacement>/Multiple: **0,0**
Second point of displacement: **0,4.75**

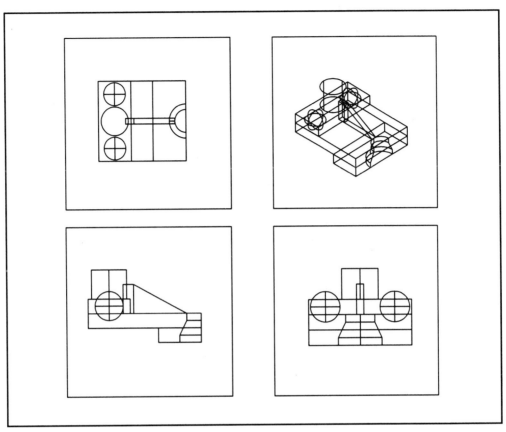

Figure P15–7 Copying a sphere to a specified displacement

Step 18 Place two cones by using the CONE command, as shown in Figure P15–8.

> Command: **cone**
> Elliptical/<Center point> <0,0,0>: **1.5,1.125,-2**
> Diameter/<Radius>: **0.75**
> Apex/<Height>: **-3**

Copy the cone to a displacement of 0,4.75.

Step 19 Starting at 0,0,-5, create a box that is $3 \times 7 \times 2$, as shown in Figure P15–9.

Step 20 Create a 0.5-radius cylinder, centered at 1.5,3.5,-2, to a height of 4, as shown in Figure P15–10.

Step 21 Create a cylinder with radius 1, centered at 1.5,3.5,1.75 to a height of 0.25, as shown in Figure P15–11.

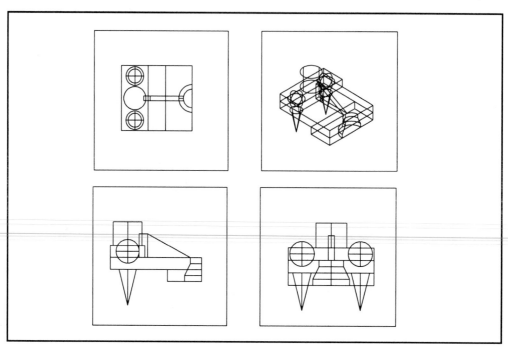

Figure P15–8 Placing two cones using the CONE command

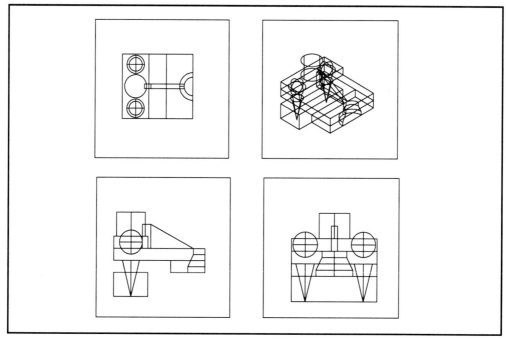

Figure P15–9 Creating a box with starting point 0,0,-5 and dimensions of 3 × 7 × 2

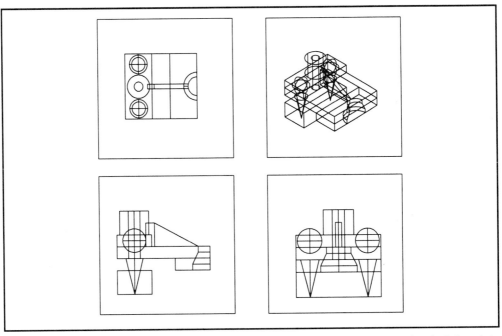

Figure P15–10 Creating a 0.5 cylinder centered at 1.5,3.5,-2 and with a height of 4

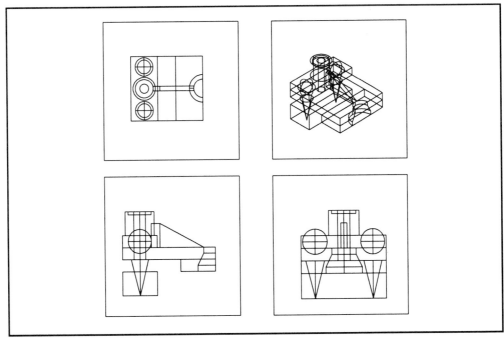

Figure P15–11 Creating a 0.5 cylinder centered at 1.5,3.5,1.75, with a height of 0.25 and a radius of 1

Step 22 Create a cylinder with radius 0.25, centered at 6.5,1.0,-3 to a height of 2, as shown in Figure P15–12.

Copy the cylinder to a displacement of 0,5.

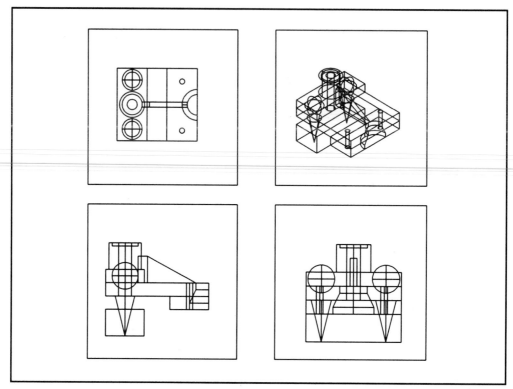

Figure P15–12 Creating a cylinder centered at 6.5,1.0,-3, with a height of 2 and a radius of 0.25

Step 23 Use the TORUS command to create a torus, as shown in Figure P15–13:

Command: **torus**
<Center of torus> <0,0,0>: **1.5,3.5,1.5**
Diameter/<Radius> of torus: **1.25**
Diameter/<Radius> of tube: **0.25**

Step 24 Select the connected boxes (except the box that was drawn in Step 19), the wedge, the large cylinder, the spheres, and the cones for use with the UNION command.

Command: **union**
Select objects: *(select the boxes, wedge, large cylinder, spheres, cones and press* Enter *)*

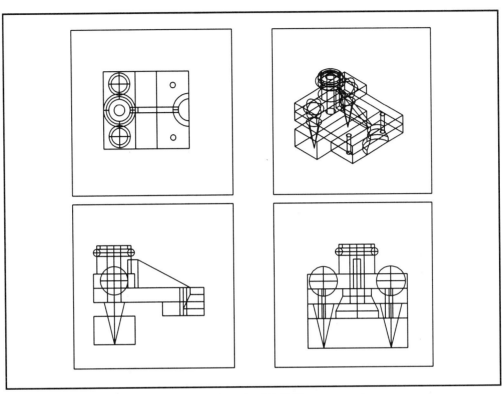

Figure P15–13 Creating a torus using the TORUS command

Step 25 Select the resulting solid in response to the first SUBTRACT prompt, and then selecting the remaining primitives to be subtracted from it.

> Command: **subtract**
> Select solids and regions to subtract from...
> Select objects: *(select the solid resulting from Step 24)*
> Select objects: ⏎Enter
> Select solids and regions to subtract from...
> Select objects: *(select the remaining primitives)*
> Select objects: ⏎Enter

The drawing should look like Figure P15–14.

Step 26 Select the faces, as shown in Figure P15–15, for chamfer and fillet. Use the CHAMFER and FILLET commands with 0.25 as the chamfer values and the radii on the respective selected objects. The end result should look like Figure P15–16.

Step 27 After invoking the HIDE command, the result is as shown in Figure P15–17.

AutoCAD 3D

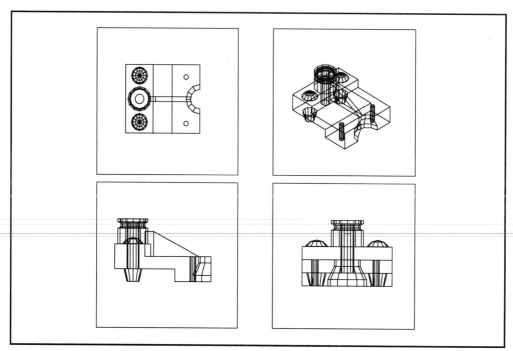

Figure P15–14 Subtracting the primitives from the newly created solid using the SUBTRACT command

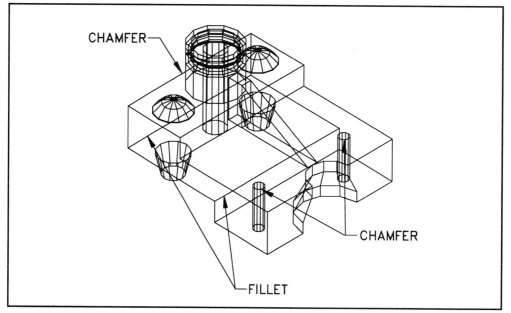

Figure P15–15 Using the CHAMFER and FILLET commands to chamfer and fillet the faces

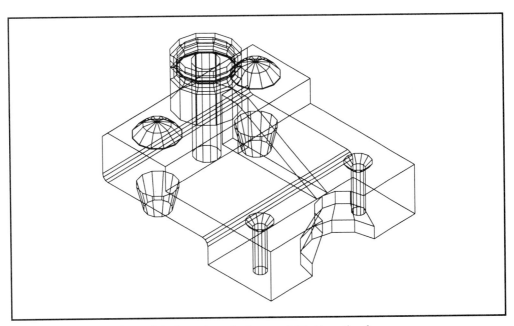

Figure P15–16 The solid after chamfering and filleting the faces

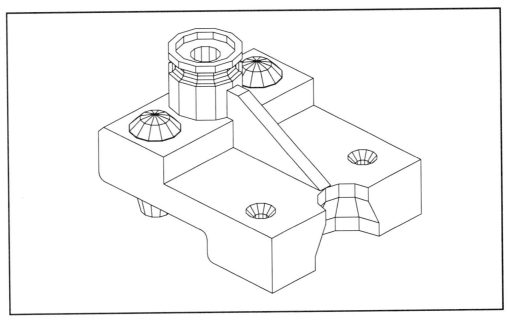

Figure P15–17 The completed solid after using the HIDE command

Step 28   End the drawing.

EXERCISES 15-1 THROUGH 15-5

Exercise 15-1

Layout the objects shown in 3D form. Create the drawings to the given dimension. Display the drawing with VPOINT in four different views. Select the HIDE command for one of the views.

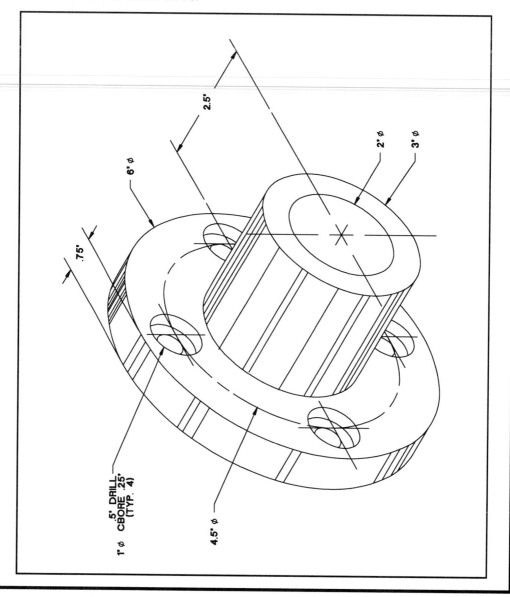

Exercise 15–2

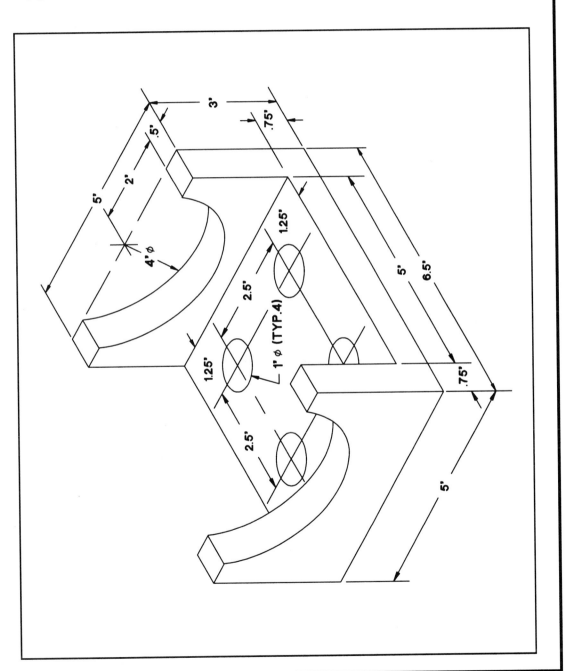

Exercise 15-3

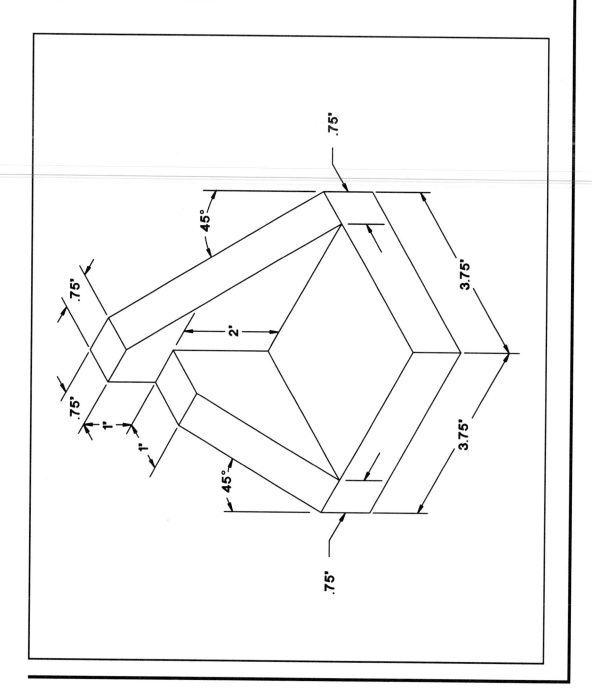

Exercise 15–4

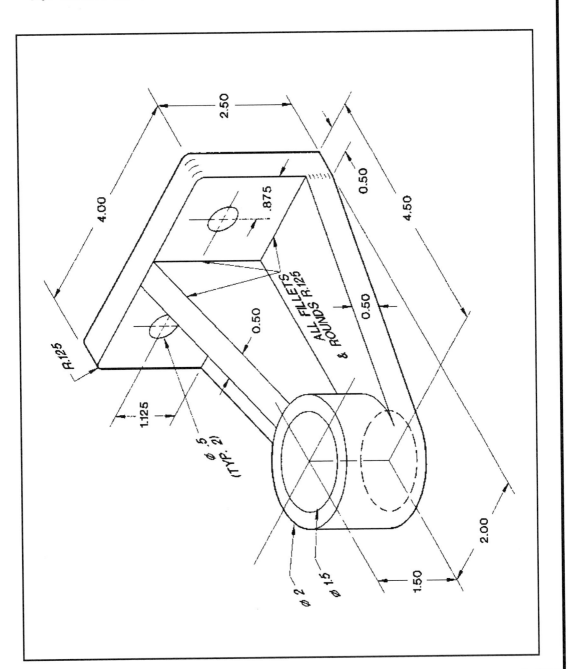

Exercise 15–5

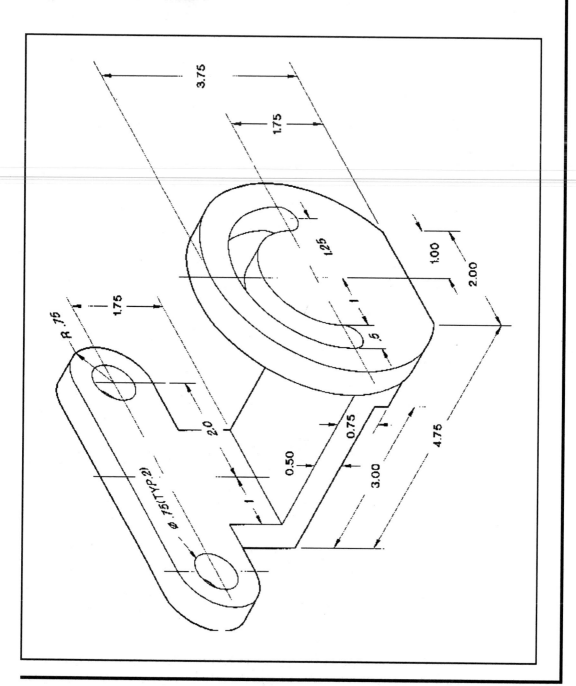

REVIEW QUESTIONS

1. What type of coordinate system does AutoCAD use?
   a. Lagrangian System
   b. Right hand system
   c. Left hand system
   d. Maxwellian system

2. If the origin of the current coordinate system is off screen, then the UCSICON, if it is set to Origin, will:
   a. Appear in the lower left corner of the screen
   b. Will attempt to be at the origin, and will therefore not be on screen
   c. Will appear at the center of the screen
   d. Force AutoCAD to perform a ZOOM so that it will be on screen

3. Which of the following UCS options will perform a translation only on the coordinate system:
   a. Rotate
   b. Z-axis
   c. Origin
   d. View
   e. none of the above

4. Which of the following UCS options will perform only a rotation of the coordinate system.
   a. Rotate
   b. Z-axis
   c. Origin
   d. View
   e. none of the above

5. Which of the following UCS options will perform both a rotation and a translation of the coordinate system.
   a. Rotate
   b. Z-axis
   c. Origin
   d. View
   e. none of the above

6. The command used to generate a perspective view of a 3D model is:
   a. VPOINT
   b. PERSPECT
   c. VPORT
   d. DVIEW
   e. none of the above

7. The VPOINT command will allow you to specify the viewing direction in all of the following methods except:
   a. 2 points
   b. 2 angles
   c. 1 point
   d. Dynamically dragging the X, Y, and Z axes
   e. none of the above (i.e. all are valid)

8. Objects can be assigned a negative thickness?
   a. True   b. False

9. Regions:
   a. Are 3 dimensional objects
   b. Can be created from any group of objects
   c. Can be used in conjunction with Boolean operations
   d. Cannot be crosshatched

10. Which of the following mesh commands is primarily used in a user defined function, rather than from the keyboard:
    a. 3Dmesh
    b. Rulesurf
    c. Tabsurf
    d. Edgemesh
    e. 3Dface

11. The PFACE command:
    a. generates a mesh
    b. requests the vertexes of the object
    c. can create an opaque (will hide) flat polygon
    d. all of the above

12. To align two objects in 3D space, invoke the command called:
    a. ALIGN
    b. ROTATE
    c. 3DROTATE
    d. TRANSFORM
    e. 3DALIGN

13. 3D arrays are limited to rectangular patterns (i.e. rows, columns, and layers).
    a. True   b. False

14. The union command will allow you to select more than two solid objects concurrently.
    a. True   b. False

15. Which of the following is not a standard solid primitive shape used by AutoCAD:
    a. SPHERE
    b. BOX
    c. DOME
    d. WEDGE
    e. CONE

16. Fillets on solid objects are limited to planar edges:
    a. True   b. False

17. A command which will split a solid object into two solids is:
    a. TRIM
    b. SLICE
    c. CUT
    d. SPLIT
    e. DIVIDE

18. To display a more realistic view of a 3D object, use:
    a. HIDE
    b. VIEW
    c. DISPLAY3D
    d. MAKE3D
    e. VIEWEDIT

19. To force invisible edges of 3DFACEs to display, what system variable should be set to 1?
    a. 3DEDGE
    b. 3DFRAME
    c. SPLFRAME
    d. EDGEFACE
    e. EDGEVIEW

20. Advantages of solid modeling include:
    a. Creation of objects which are manufacturable
    b. Interfaces with Computer Aid Manufacturing
    c. Analysis of physical properties of objects
    d. All of the above

21. The SECTION command:
    a. Creates a region
    b. Creates a polyline
    c. Crosshatches the area where a plane intersects a solid
    d. Is an alias for the HATCH command
    e. Will give you a choice of either A or B

•••••••••••••

CHAPTER

16

RENDERING

••••••••••••••••••••••••••

INTRODUCTION

S hading or rendering turns your 3D model into a realistic (eye-catching) image. The AutoCAD SHADE command allows you to produce quick, shaded models. However, the AutoCAD RENDER command gives you more control over the appearance of the final image. You can add lights and control lighting in your drawing and define the reflective qualities of surfaces in the drawing, making objects dull or shiny. You can create the rendered image of your 3D model entirely within AutoCAD.

After completing this chapter, you will be able to:

✓ Render a 3D model
✓ Create and modify lighting—ambient light, distant light, point light, and spotlight
✓ Create and modify a scene
✓ Create and modify a material
✓ Save and replay an image

SHADING A MODEL

The AutoCAD SHADE command lets you produce a shaded picture of the 3D model in the current Viewport. You have little control over lighting. Shade uses a single light that is logically placed just over your right shoulder in the current viewport.

Invoke the SHADE command from:

Render toolbar	Select the Shade command (see Figure 16–1)
Pull-down menu	View > Shade
Command: prompt	**shade** [Enter]

Shade

Figure 16–1 Invoking the Shade command from the Render toolbar

There are no prompts to answer. The current viewport goes blank for a period of time. When the entire drawing is being shaded, AutoCAD redraws sections of it on the screen and then reports that the shading is complete.

The shaded image remains until the next regeneration occurs and the original drawing is displayed on the screen. The shaded image can be displayed only on the screen; you can't plot it. You can make a slide by means of the MSLIDE command.

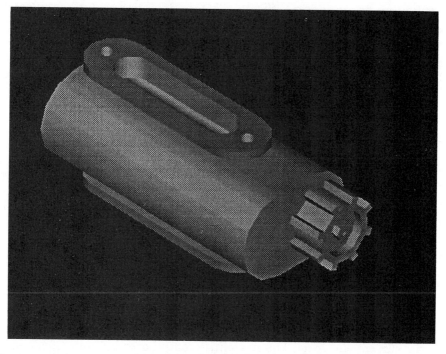

Figure 16–2 A 3D model rendered by AutoCAD *(Courtesy Autodesk)*

AutoCAD shading is controlled by two system variables, SHADEDGE and SHADEDIF. SHADEDGE defines how your object is shaded in relation to the edges of your model. SHADEDIF allows you to adjust the ratio of ambient light to diffuse light. You may change the way the SHADE command shades your model by changing the SHADEDGE and SHADEDIF system variables.

SHADEDGE allows you to set one of four configurations.

0   Faces shaded, edges not highlighted

1   Faces shaded, edges drawn in current background color

2   Faces not filled, edges in object color (default)

3   Faces in object color, edges in background color

SHADEDIF allows you to change the ratio of diffuse reflective light to ambient light. In other words, the higher the setting of SHADEDIF, the greater the difference you see between different surfaces. You can set the SHADEIF value between 0 and 100. The default value is 70.

RENDERING A MODEL

The AutoCAD render facility allows you to create realistic models from your AutoCAD drawings. With the AutoCAD RENDER command you can adjust lighting factors, material finishes, and camera placement. All these options give you a great deal of flexibility. If you wish to take rendering "to the max," you may wish to purchase AutoVision or 3D Studio Max to gain the greatest flexibility and photorealism.

The tools available for rendering allow you to adjust the type and quality of the rendering, set up lights and scenes, and save and replay images. But you can always use the RENDER command without any other AutoCAD render setup. By default, RENDER uses the current view if no scene or selection is specified. If there are no lights specified, the RENDER command assumes a default over-the-shoulder distant light source with an intensity of 1.

Invoke the RENDER command from:

Render toolbar	Select the Render command (see Figure 16–3)
Pull-down menu	View > Render > Render...
Command: prompt	**render** Enter

Figure 16–3 Invoking the Render command from the Render toolbar

AutoCAD displays the Render dialog box, similar to Figure 16–4.

The **Rendering Type:** scroll box lists the available rendering types, including AutoCAD Render, Photo Real, Photo Raytrace, and AutoVision if installed. The default type is set to AutoCAD Render.

The **Screen to Render** box lists the scenes available in the current drawing, including the current view, from which you can select the screen/view for rendering.

The **Rendering Procedure** section of the dialog box sets the default value for rendering. Three settings are available:

> The **Query for Selections** check box controls whether or not to display a prompt to select objects to render.

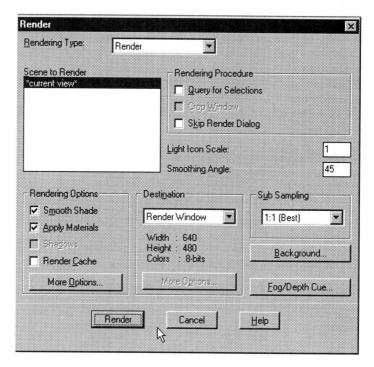

Figure 16–4 Render dialog box

The **Crop Window** check box controls the prompts for whether or not to pick an area on the screen for rendering.

The **Skip Render Dialog** check box controls whether or not to skip the Render dialog box and render the current view.

The **Light Icon Scale:** edit field controls the size of the light blocks inserted in the drawing. The default is set to a scale factor of 1.0. If necessary, you can change the value to some other real number to rescale the blocks. Overhead, Direct, and Sh_spot are the blocks affected by the scale factor.

The **Smoothing Angle:** edit field sets the angle at which AutoCAD interprets an edge. The default value is 45 degrees. Angles greater than 45 degrees are considered edges and those less than 45 degrees as smoothed.

The **Rendering Options** section of the dialog box controls the rendering display. Four main settings plus additional options are available:

The **Smooth Shade** option yields a smooth appearance. Depending on the object's surfaces and the direction of the screen's lights, smooth shading adds a cleaner, more realistic appearance to a rendering.

The **Apply Materials** option applies surface materials you have defined and attaches them by color or to specific object(s). If the Apply Materials option is not selected, then all objects in the drawing assume the color, ambient, reflection, transparency, refraction, bump map, and roughness attribute values defined for the *GLOBAL* material.

The **Shadows** option generates shadows when selected. This option is applicable only when Photo Real or Photo Raytrace rendering is selected.

The **Render Cache** option specifies that rendering information be written to a cache file on the hard disk. As long as the drawing or view is unchanged, the cached file is used for subsequent renderings, eliminating the need for AutoCAD to retessellate.

For fine-tuning the Rendering quality, choose the **More Options...** button. AutoCAD displays the Windows Render Options dialog box. The options available vary depending on whether you have selected Render, Photo Real, Photo Raytrace, or a third-party application as your rendering type.

The **Destination** section of the dialog box controls the image output setting. Three options can be selected from the list box:

The **Viewport** option allows AutoCAD to render to a viewport.

The **File** option renders to a file. When the File option is selected in the scroll box, you must choose the **More Options...** button to select the file type, set the colors in the output file and setting the postscript options, if necessary.

The **Render Window** option renders the model in a window, as shown in Figure 16–5.

The Open command available from the File pull-down menu in the Render window allows you to open two types of files: bitmap (*.BMP*) files and clipboard (*.CLP*) files. The Save command available from the File pull-down menu in the render window allows you to save an image to a bitmap file. If necessary, you can also use the Print command available from the File pull-down menu to print the image. The Copy command available from the Edit pull-down menu can be used to copy an image from the active render window to the clipboard. The Options command available from the File pull-down menu displays the Windows Render Options dialog box, as shown in Figure 16–6, from which you can select aspect ratios and resolutions for bitmap images.

The **Sub Sampling** section of the Render dialog box controls the rendering time and image quality without abandoning effects such as shadows by rendering a fraction of all pixels. The available ratios include 1:1 (for best quality) to 8:1 (fastest).

The **Background...** button allows you to set the background for your scene. Choose the Background button to display the Background dialog box, similar to Figure 16–7. Following are the four options available to select the type of background for rendering:

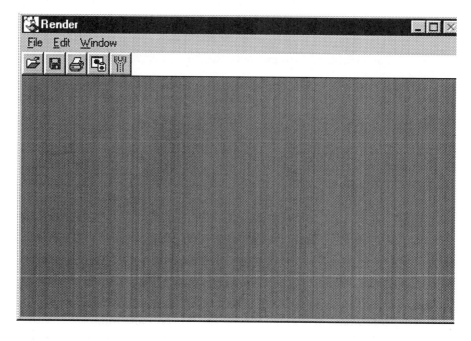

Figure 16–5 Render window

Figure 16–6 Windows Render Options dialog box

The **Solid** option selects a one-color background. Use the controls in the **Colors** section to specify the color.

The **Gradient** option lets you specify a two- or three-color gradient background. Use the Colors section controls and the Horizon, Height, and Rotation controls on the lower right of the dialog box to define the gradient.

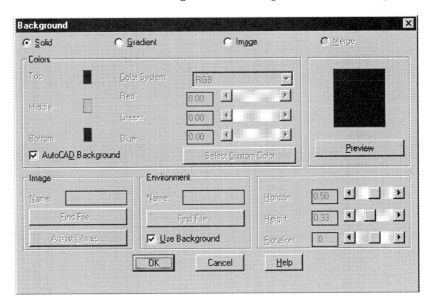

Figure 16–7 Background dialog box

The **Image** option enables you to use a bitmap *(BMP)* file for the background. Manipulate the controls in the **Image** and **Environment** sections to define the bitmap.

The **Merge** option enables you to use the current AutoCAD image as the background.

The **Fog/Depth Cue...** button in the Render dialog box provides settings for visual cues for the apparent distance of objects. Choose the Fog/Depth Cue... button to display the Fog/Depth Cue dialog box, similar to Figure 16–8.

The **Enable Fog** check box sets the fog to ON and OFF without affecting the settings in the dialog box. The **Fog Background** check box controls whether or not to apply the fog to the background as well as to the geometry. The **color controls** section of the dialog box controls whether AutoCAD uses the red-green-blue color system or the hue-lightness-saturation color system. The **Near/Far Distance** section of the dialog box defines where the fog starts and ends. Each value is a

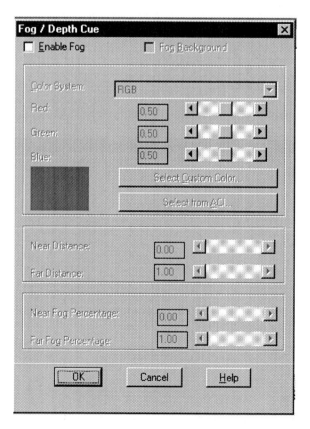

Figure 16–8 Fog/Depth Cue dialog box

percentage of the distance from the camera to the back clipping plane. The **Near/ Far Fog Percentage** section of the dialog box defines the percentage of fog at the near and far distances, ranging from 0% fog to 100% fog.

After making all the necessary changes in the Render dialog box, choose the **Render** button. AutoCAD renders the selected objects in the selected destination window.

SETTING UP LIGHTS

The AutoCAD render facility gives you great control over four types of lights in your renderings.

Ambient light can be thought of as background light that is constant and distributed equally among all objects.

Distant light gives off a fairly straight beam of light that radiates in one direction. Another property of distant light is that its brilliance remains constant, so an object close to the light receives as much light as a distant object.

Point light can be thought of as a ball of light. A point light radiates beams of light in all directions. Point lights also have more natural characteristics. Their brilliance may be diminished as the light moves away from its source. An object that is near a point light appears brighter; an object that is farther away will appear darker.

An AutoCAD **Spotlight** is very much like the kind of spotlight you might be accustomed to seeing at a theater or auditorium. Spotlights produce a cone of light toward a target that you specify.

Invoke the LIGHT command from:

Render toolbar	Select the Lights command (see Figure 16–9)
Pull-down menu	View > Render > Light...
Command: prompt	**light** Enter

Figure 16-9 Invoking the Lights command from the Render toolbar

AutoCAD displays the Lights dialog box, similar to Figure 16–10.

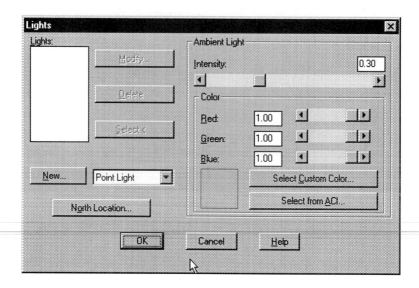

Figure 16–10 Lights dialog box

Creating a New light

In the Lights dialog box, select one of the three available light types from the list box located to the right of the **New...** button. Then, choose the **New...** button. Depending on the type of light selected, AutoCAD displays the **New Point Light** dialog box shown in Figure 16–11, **New Distant Light** dialog box shown in Figure 16–12, or the **New Spotlight** dialog box as shown in Figure 16–13.

Light Name Type the name of the light in the **Light Name:** edit box. The name must be eight or fewer characters.

Intensity The slider bar located below the **Intensity:** edit box changes the brightness of the light, with 0 turning the light off. Distant light intensity values may range from 0 to 1. Point lights have a more complex intensity setting. This setting can be any real number. The factors that control the maximum intensity are the extents of the drawing and the current rate of falloff. Spotlight intensity factors are the same as for point lights except that the falloff is always inverse linear.

Position The **Modify <** and **Show...** buttons located in the **Position** section let you modify or look at the *X,Y,Z* coordinate location of the light and its target.

Color The **Color** section controls the current color of the light. To set the color you can either adjust the Red, Green, and Blue slider bars or choose the **Select Custom Color...** button.

Attenuation The setting of the attenuation controls how light diminishes over distance. The attenuation applies to both point light as well as spotlight. Select one of

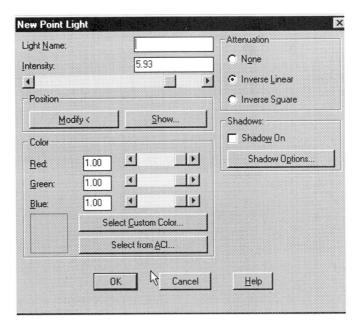

Figure 16-11 New Point Light dialog box

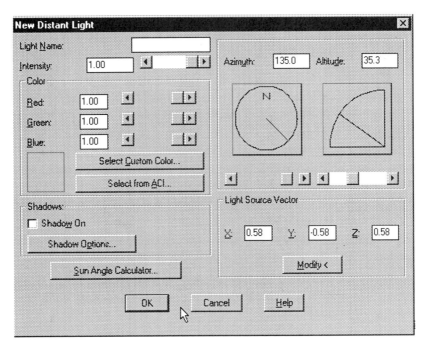

Figure 16-12 New Distant Light dialog box

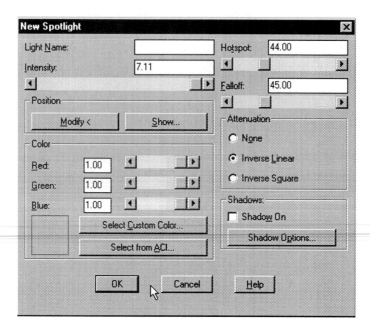

Figure 16–13 New spotlight dialog box

the three radio buttons. Selection of **None** sets no attenuation. Objects far from the point light are as bright as objects close to the light. Selection of **Inverse Linear** falloff decreases the light intensity linearly as the distance increases. For example, an object 10 units away from the light source will be 1/10 as illuminated as an object adjacent to the light source. Selection of **Inverse Square** falloff decreases the light intensity by the inverse of the squared distance. An object 10 units away from the light source receives 1/100 the amount of light of an item adjacent to the light source. This function provides rapid falloff so that a point light can be more localized.

Azimuth and Altitude The **Azimuth and Altitude** edit boxes in the New Distant Light dialog box specify the position of the distant light by using the site-based coordinates. Azimuth can be set at any value between -180 and 180. Altitude can be set at any value between -90 and 90.

Light Source Vector The **Light Source Vector** section displays the coordinates of the light vector that results from the light position you set using Azimuth and Altitude. You can also enter values directly in the edit boxes. AutoCAD updates the corresponding Azimuth and Altitude values.

Hotspot and Falloff The **Hotspot and Falloff** edit fields in the New Spotlight dialog box specify the angle that defines the brightness cone of light and the full cone of light, respectively.

Once you set the appropriate values in the dialog box, choose the **OK** button to create a new light and close the dialog box. AutoCAD lists the name of the light in the Lights: list box of the Lights dialog box.

Ambient Light

The Ambient Light slider bar allows you to adjust the intensity of the ambient (background) light from a value of (off) to 1 (bright). The **Color** sub-section controls the current color of the ambient light. To set the color you can adjust either the Red, Green, and Blue slider bars or choose the **Select Custom Color...** button. Choose the **OK** button to accept the changes and close the **Lights** dialog box.

Modifying a Light

In the Lights dialog box, first select from the Lights: list box the light name to modify. Then choose the **Modify...** button. AutoCAD displays the appropriate Modify dialog box, depending on the light type selected. Make the necessary changes, and choose the **OK** button to accept the changes. You *cannot* change a light type. For example, you *cannot* make a point light a distant light. But you can delete the point light and insert a new distant light in the same location.

Deleting a Light

First, select from the Lights: list box the light name to delete. Then choose the **Delete** button. AutoCAD deletes the selected light.

Selecting a Light

The **Select <** button allows you to select a light from the screen. AutoCAD temporarily dismisses the dialog box while you specify a light on screen using the pointing device. The **Lights** dialog box returns, with the selected light highlighted in the Lights: list.

SETTING UP A SCENE

Inserting and adjusting lights allows you to render images from an unlimited number of viewpoints. If necessary, you can save a certain combination of lights and a particular view as a scene, which you can recall at anytime. A scene represents a particular view of the drawing together with one or more lights. Making a scene avoids re-creating a particular set of conditions every time you need to render that image. The VPOINT and DVIEW commands are used to control viewing of a model from any point in model space, and the LIGHT command allows you to add one or more lights to the model or modify lights. The SCENE command allows you to save a scene. You can have an unlimited number of scenes in a drawing.

> **NOTE:** The VIEW command allows you to save a view but doesn't save the lights, whereas the scene can include both the view and the light positions.

Invoke the SCENE command from:

Render toolbar	Select the Scenes command (see Figure 16–14)
Pull-down menu	View > Render > Scene
Command: prompt	scene [Enter]

Figure 16–14 Invoking the Scenes command from the Render toolbar

AutoCAD displays the Scenes dialog box, similar to Figure 16–15.

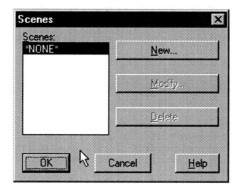

Figure 16–15 Scenes dialog box

AutoCAD lists the scenes available in the current drawing in **Scenes:** list box.

Creating a New Scene

The **New...** button in the Scenes dialog box allows you to add a new scene to the current drawing. When you choose the **New...** button, AutoCAD displays the New Scene dialog box, similar to Figure 16–16. (A similar dialog box is displayed when you select the **Modify...** button, except that dialog box is entitled Modify Scene).

Scene Name Type in the name of the scene, which may be up to eight characters long.

Views The **Views** list box displays the list of the views in the current drawing. *CURRENT* is the current view in the active viewport. The active view in the

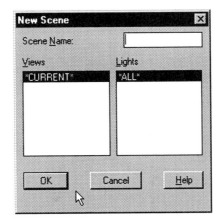

Figure 16–16 New Scene dialog box

current scene is highlighted. Selecting another view makes it the new view of the scene. You can have only one view in a scene.

Lights The **Lights** list box displays the list of lights in the current drawing. *ALL* represents all the lights in the drawing. When you select the *ALL* option, all the lights in the drawing are added to the scene. The lights in the current scene are highlighted. Selecting a nonhighlighted light adds that light to the scene. Selecting a highlighted light deselects that light and removes it from the scene.

> **NOTE:** You can create a scene with no lights, which in this case, the only lighting in the scene is ambient light.

Choose the **OK** button to create a new scene.

Modifying an Existing Scene

The **Modify...** button in the Scenes dialog box allows you to modify an existing scene. Choosing this button invokes the **Modify Scene** dialog box and allows you to add or delete views and lights.

Deleting a Scene

The **Delete** button in the Scenes dialog box deletes the selected scene from the current drawing.

MATERIALS

The RMAT command gives you the power to modify the light reflection characteristics of the objects you will render. By modifying these characteristics, you make objects appear rough or shiny. These finish characteristics are stored in the drawing via surface property blocks. The drawing contains one surface property block for each finish you create, an attribute from the name, and AutoCAD color index (ACI) if assigned. You can modify materials by manipulating ambient, diffuse, specular, and roughness factors.

Invoke the RMAT command from:

Render toolbar	Select the Materials command (see Figure 16–17)
Pull-down menu	View > Render > Materials...
Command: prompt	**rmat** Enter

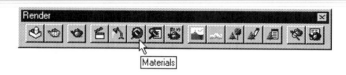

Figure 16–17 Invoking the Materials command from the Render toolbar

AutoCAD displays the Materials dialog box, similar to Figure 16–18.

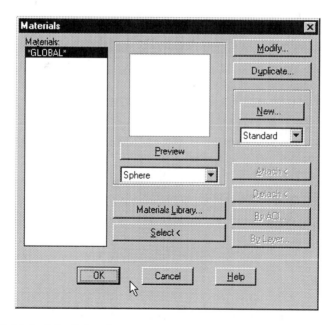

Figure 16–18 Materials dialog box

The **Materials:** list box lists the available materials. The default for objects with no other material attached is *GLOBAL*.

Materials Library... Choosing the **Materials Library...** button displays the Materials Library dialog box shown in Figure 16-19, from which you can select a material.

The **Materials Library** dialog box allows you to import a predefined material from an .*MLI* materials library into the current drawing. The **Materials List:** box in the dialog box lists the materials currently in the drawing. The **Library List:** box lists the materials available in the library file. If necessary, you can preview a sample of the material selected in the list. The sample is applied to a sphere. You can preview only one material at a time. To import materials from the Library List: box into the current drawing, first select the materials you want to import from the Library List: box and then click the **<-Import** button. AutoCAD adds the selected materials to the Materials List: box. Choose the **OK** button to close the Materials Library dialog box, and AutoCAD returns control to the Materials dialog box.

Select < The **Select <** button temporarily removes the Materials dialog box and displays the graphics area so you can select an object and display the attached material. After you select the object, the Materials dialog box reappears, with the method of attachment displayed at the bottom of the dialog box.

Modify... The **Modify...** button allows you to modify a material by displaying the Modify Standard Material dialog box.

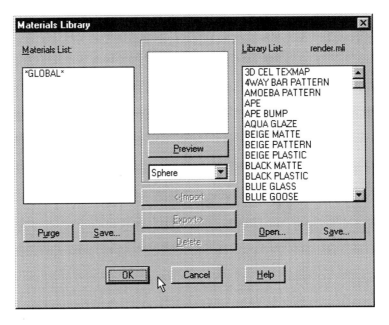

Figure 16-19 Materials Library dialog box

Duplicate... The **Duplicate...** button duplicates a selected material and displays the New Standard Material dialog box with the Material Name text box. Make the necessary changes, and save the material with a new material name.

New... The **New...** button allows you to create a new material by displaying the New Standard Material dialog box.

Attach < The **Attach** < button displays the graphics area so you can select an object and attach the current material to it.

Detach < The **Detach** < button displays the graphics area so you can select an object and detach the material from it.

By ACI... The **By ACI...** button displays the Attach by AutoCAD Color Index (ACI) dialog box, from which you can select the available ACI to attach to a material.

By Layer... The **By Layer...** button displays the Attach by Layer dialog box, from which you can select a layer by which to attach a material.

Choose the **OK** button to accept the changes and close the Materials dialog box.

SETTING PREFERENCES FOR RENDERING

The Rendering Preferences dialog box allows you to establish the default settings for rendering. Invoke the RPREF command from:

Render toolbar	Select the Render Preferences command (see Figure 16–20)
Pull-down menu	View > Render > Preferences...
Command: prompt	**rpref** Enter

Figure 16–20 Invoking the Render Preferences command from the Render toolbar

AutoCAD displays Rendering Preferences dialog box similar to Figure 16–21. The available settings in the Rendering Preferences dialog box are same as in the Render dialog box. For detailed explanation on the available settings refer to the earlier section on "Rendering a Model."

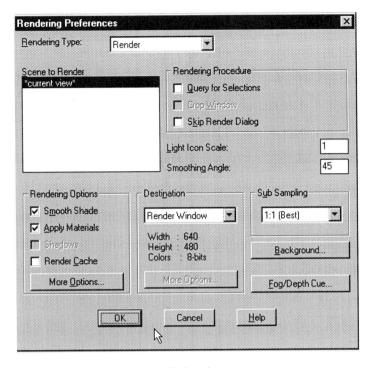

Figure 16–21 Rendering Preferences dialog box

SAVING AN IMAGE

You can save the contents of the frame buffer to a GIF, TIFF, or TGA file format by invoking the SAVEIMG command.

Invoke the SAVEIMG command from:

Pull-down menu	Tools > Display Image > Save...
Command: prompt	**saveimg** Enter

AutoCAD displays the Save Image dialog box, similar to Figure 16–22.

Format   Choose the file format for the output image. You can save an image in any one of the three industry standard file formats: GIF, TGA, or TIFF.

Portion   The Portion section specifies the portion of the image to be rendered.

Choose the **OK** button to save the image. AutoCAD displays the Image File dialog box. Select the file type to save from the **Save as type:** list box. Select the appropriate directory in which to save the file, and type the file name in the **File name:** edit field. Choose the **Save** button to save the image to the given file name.

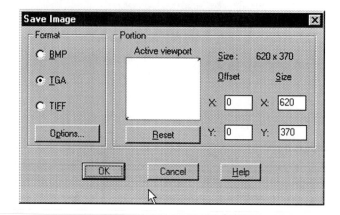

Figure 16–22 Save Image dialog box

Viewing an Image

The REPLAY command allows you to load a GIF, TIFF, or TGA file into the frame buffer for viewing, converting, or using as a background for a composite rendering.

Invoke the REPLAY command from:

Pull-down menu	Tools > Display Image > View...
Command: prompt	**replay** Enter

AutoCAD displays the standard File dialog box. Select a file or enter a file name. After you select an image file and choose the **OK** button, an Image Specifications dialog box is displayed as shown in Figure 16–23.

Image The image tile in the Image Specifications dialog box lets you select a smaller part of the image you want to display. The default size of the image in the image tile reflects the entire display size in pixel measurement, with offset set to 0,0, the lower left corner of the image. To resize the image, specify two points, one for the lower left corner and the other for the upper right corner of the image in the image tile. AutoCAD automatically draws a box to mark the bounds of the reduced image area and updates the values in the X and Y Image Size coordinates.

Screen The screen tile lets you adjust the offset location of the selected, sized image in relation to your screen. The tile displays the size of your screen or your current viewport. To change the offset, select a point in this tile to offset the center of the image to that point. AutoCAD automatically redraws the image size boundaries to mark the new offsets and updates the values in the X and Y Screen Offset coordinates.

Reset Resets the size and offset values to the original values.

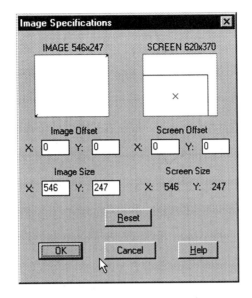

Figure 16–23 Image Specifications dialog box

STATISTICS

The STATS command gives detailed information on your last rendering. This can be useful for diagnosing problems with your drawing.

Invoke the STATS command from:

Render toolbar	Select the Statistics command (see Figure 16–24)
Pull-down menu	View > Render > Statistics...
Command: prompt	**stats** Enter

Figure 16–24 Invoking the Statistics command from the Render toolbar

AutoCAD displays a Statistics dialog box. If necessary, you can save the information in the Statistics dialog box to a file.

REVIEW QUESTIONS

1. Text is ignored by the SHADE command.
   a. True
   b. False

2. The SHADEDGE system variable will cause the faces of an object to be shaded in the objects color and the edges in the background color if it is set to:
   a. 0   d. 3
   b. 1   e. 4
   c. 2

3. Approximately where is the light source for the SHADE command?
   a. Pure ambient light (i.e. all around)
   b. Just behind your right shoulder
   c. Directly behind the object
   d. In the upper right corner of the screen

4. It is possible to make a slide of a shaded image.
   a. True
   b. False

5. If you save your drawing while a shaded view is displayed, the preview of the drawing will appear shaded.
   a. True
   b. False

6. Which of the following is not a valid type of light you can add to a drawing for the RENDER command?
   a. Point
   b. Spot
   c. Distant
   d. Ambient
   e. none of the above (i.e. all are valid)

7. It is possible to make a slide of a rendered image.
   a. True
   b. False

8. If there is a single point light source in your drawing, object will be darker if you set the attenuation for that light to:
   a. None
   b. Inverse Linear
   c. Inverse Square

9. Distant light sources do not attenuate (i.e. get dimmer with distance).
   a. True
   b. False

10. The SCENE command operates much like the VIEW command, but it also saves all the lights you have added to the drawing.
    a. True
    b. False

11. The maximum number of scenes which can be saved in a drawing is:
    a. 8
    b. 64
    c. 256
    d. 32000
    e. unlimited (except by memory)

12. Material finishes are assigned based on the color of the object in AutoCAD.
    a. True
    b. False

13. Which of the following file types is not available to the SAVEIMG command:
    a. BMP
    b. GIF
    c. TGA
    d. TIF

14. All lights emit white light.
    a. True
    b. False

15. The smoothing angle is the minimum angle:
    a. between faces which AutoCAD will ignore
    b. between the viewing angle and the face which AutoCAD will display the face
    c. between the incident light and the face which AutoCAD will still reflect the light
    d. none of the above

· · · · · · · · · · · · · · ·

CHAPTER

17

THE TABLET AND DIGITIZING

· ·

INTRODUCTION

The AutoCAD program consists of several major components in the form of program files along with many other supporting files. One major part of the program, the menu (in the form of a *filename.MNU* file), determines how various devices work with the program. The devices controlled by the menu include the buttons on the pointing device (mouse or tablet puck), the toolbars, pull-down menus, function box keys (not commonly used), and tablet. This chapter covers configuring and using the tablet menu.

First, using the tablet part of any menu requires that the AutoCAD program be installed and configured for the particular make and model of digitizing tablet that is properly connected to the computer.

> **NOTE:** The installation configuration (in Release 14) permits using a mouse as well as a digitizing tablet. But because a mouse and a tablet are both pointing devices, you must choose one or the other at any one time. This prestartup configuration is not to be confused with configuring the installed tablet with the TABLET command while in AutoCAD.

Second, a preprinted template with up to four rectangular menu areas should be used that has properly arranged columns and rows of pick areas within each menu area. Each pick area corresponds to a command or line of programming in the *filename.MNU* menu file in effect. It is also necessary to set aside a screen area on the tablet if you wish to control the screen cursor with the tablet's puck. See Figure 17–1.

After completing this chapter, you will be able to:

✓ Configure the tablet menu
✓ Calibrate the tablet for digitizing

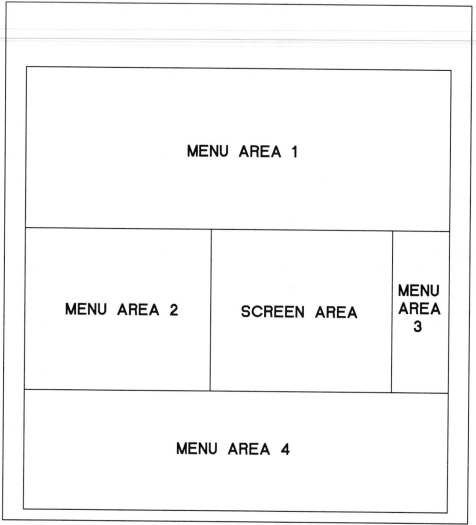

Figure 17–1 The four screen areas of the overlay

TABLET OPERATION

When a *filename.MNU file*, a digitizing tablet, and an overlay have been installed and properly set up to work together, you can use the attached puck on the tablet surface to achieve the following results.

Normal operation   The most common use of a tablet is to allow the user to move the puck and press the pick button while pointing to one of the various commands or symbols on a preprinted overlay and be able to invoke that particular command or initiate a program (perhaps written by that user) that will draw that symbol. In addition, when the puck is moved within the overlay's designated screen area, the screen cursor will mimic the puck movement, thereby permitting the user to specify points or select objects on the screen.

Mouse movement   Some tablets have an option that causes the puck to emulate mouse-type movement rather than absolute movement. Mouse emulation means that if you pick the puck up off of the tablet surface and move it to another place in the screen area, the screen cursor does not move. The cursor moves only with puck movement while it is on the tablet and in the screen area. Absolute (normal) tablet-puck operation means that, once configured, each point in the tablet's screen area corresponds to only one point on the screen. So, while in the normal mode, if you pick up the puck and put it down at another point in the tablet screen area, the cursor will immediately move to the screen's corresponding point.

Paper copying   By switching Tablet mode to ON, you can cause points on the tablet to correspond to drawing coordinates rather than to screen pixel locations as it does in the normal or Mouse operations just described. This allows you to fix a drawing (like a map) on the tablet surface, select two points on the map, specify their coordinate locations on the map, after which the puck movement around the map will cause screen cursor movement to correspond to the same coordinates in the computer-generated drawing. Options and precautions for using this feature (referred to as *digitizing*) are discussed in this chapter.

Tablet Configuration

The intended procedure is to have a preprinted template (the overlay) arranged on a sheet that can be fixed to the tablet. Tablet menu area(s) can then be configured to coincide with the template. Although you could try to configure a bare tablet, it would be difficult to select the required points for rectangular menu areas and also impractical to try and place a template on the tablet after it was configured in such a manner. However, if a tablet has been configured for one template, you can use another template in the same location without reconfiguring as long as the areas are the same. One benefit of this is being able to change from one set of icons/symbols or commands to another set without having to configure again. However, a change in the menu must be made in order to accommodate changes in the template, even if the configuration is the same.

The *ACAD.MNC* (compiled from *ACAD.MNU*) menu file supports a multibutton pointing device and the tablet overlay that is provided with the AutoCAD program package. That overlay is approximately 11" × 11" and has four areas for selecting icon/commands and a screen area, as shown in Figure 17–1.The pointing device (the puck furnished with every tablet) usually has three or more buttons (the menu supports up to a 10-button puck or mouse) and the cursor movement on the screen mimics the puck's movement in the tablet's configured screen area.

CUSTOM MENUS

Chapter 18 describes how to customize a menu file. Most of the explanations and examples refer to the screen menu, primarily because of its complexity. The same principles of customizing the tablet portion of a menu can be applied.

TABLET COMMAND

The TABLET command is used to switch between digitizing paper drawings and normal command/icon/screen area selecting on a configured overlay. The TABLET command is also used to calibrate a paper drawing for digitizing or to configure the overlay to suit the current menu.

Invoke the TABLET command from:

Pull-down menu	Tools > Tablet
Command: prompt	**tablet** Enter

AutoCAD prompts:

Command: **tablet**
Option (ON/OFF/CAL/CFG): *(select one of the available options)*

CFG (Configuration) Option The CFG option is used to set up the individual tablet menu areas and the screen pointing area. At this time a preprinted overlay should have been fixed to the tablet. Its menu areas should suit the menu you wish to use. The sequence of prompts is as follows:

Command: **tablet**
Option (ON/OFF/CAL/CFG): **cfg**
Enter number of tablet menus desired (0-4) <default>:

Select the number of individual menu areas desired (with a limit of 4). The next prompt asks:

Do you want to realign tablet menu areas? <N>:

If you respond **No** (**N** or press Enter), the prompts will skip to selecting rows and columns. If you respond **Yes** (or **Y**), then for each of the menu areas specified you will be prompted to "point and pick" three corners, as follows:

Digitize upper left corner of menu area n:
Digitize lower left corner of menu area n:
Digitize lower right corner of menu area n:

The "n" refers to tablet menu areas of the corresponding tablet number in the menu. If the three corners you digitize do not form a right angle (90 degrees), you will be prompted to try again. Individual areas may be skewed on the tablet and with respect to each other, but such an arrangement usually does not provide the most efficient use of total tablet space. Tablet areas should not overlap.

The next prompts are:

Enter the number of columns for menu area n:
Enter the number of rows for menu area n:

Enter the numbers from the keyboard. The area will be subdivided into equal rectangles determined by the row and column values you have entered. If the values you enter do not correspond to the overlay row/column values, the results will be unpredictable when trying to use the tablet. Remember also that the overlay must suit the menu being used.

The standard AutoCAD overlay is installed as follows:

Command: **tablet**
Option (ON/OFF/CAL/CFG): **cfg**
Enter number of tablet menus desired (0-4) <default>: **4**
Do you want to realign tablet menu areas? <N>: **y** (if required)

At this time, digitize areas 1 through 4, as shown in Figure 17–2. The values for columns and rows must be entered as follows:

MENU AREA	COLUMN	ROW
1	25	9
2	11	9
3	9	7
4	25	7

These values are for the *ACAD.MNC* menu. Other menus may vary. To simplify the installation of the standard menu tablet, an option called RE-CFG automatically responds with the correct values for columns and rows as long as areas 1 through 4 are selected in the proper sequence.

Once the tablet menu areas have been configured, you will be prompted to digitize the corners of the screen pointing area. With the overlay that accompanies the standard *ACAD.MNC* is an area set aside for screen pointing. Because there is no

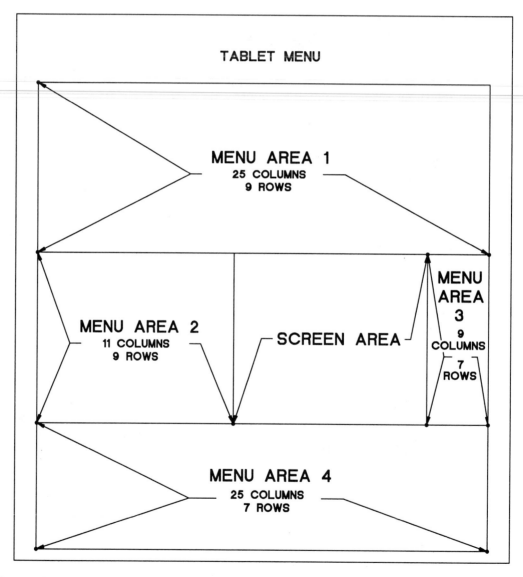

Figure 17–2 Digitizing the screen areas of the tablet menu

command/icon programming associated with the screen pointing area, it is not necessary to specify this particular area. It is, however, positioned for maximum productivity in tablet usage. You may specify a rectangular area anywhere on the tablet, as long as it does not overlap any of the tablet menu areas. On a large (table-sized) tablet, a large screen area may be specified. Too large an area, however, can become tiresome to use. An area about the size of the pad supplied with a mouse (8" × 6") is recommended. The drafting-table-sized tablets are used primarily for digitizing large maps and paper drawings without having to move and recalibrate. The prompt for specifying the screen area is:

Do you want to respecify the Fixed Screen Pointing Area? <N>

If you reply **Yes** (or **Y**), you will be prompted as follows:

Digitize lower left corner of screen pointing area:
Digitize upper right corner of screen pointing area:

ON/OFF Option The default setting of the Tablet mode is OFF. The OFF setting does not incapacitate the tablet as you might think; rather, it means that you are not going to use the tablet for digitizing (making copies of paper drawings). With the Tablet mode set to OFF you can use the tablet to select command/icons in the areas programmed accordingly. You may also use the puck in the screen area of the tablet to control the screen cursor.

In order to digitize paper drawings, you must respond to the prompt as follows:

Command: **tablet**
Option (ON/OFF/CAL/CFG): **on**

Most systems have a toggle key to switch the Tablet mode ON and OFF. With many PCs, the toggle is either F10 or Ctrl + T.

CAL Option If the tablet has been calibrated already, the last calibration coordinates will still be in effect. If not, or if you wish to change the calibration (necessary when you move the paper drawing on the tablet), you can respond as follows:

Option (ON/OFF/CAL/CFG): **cal**
Digitize point #1: *(digitize the first known point)*

The point you select on the paper drawing must be one whose coordinates you know. The next prompt asks you to enter the actual paper drawing coordinates of the point you just digitized:

Enter coordinates point #1: *(enter those known coordinates)*

You are then prompted to digitize and specify coordinates for the second known point:

Digitize point #2: *(digitize the second known point)*
Enter coordinates point #2: *(enter those known coordinates)*
Digitize point #3 (or RETURN to end): *(digitize the third known point*
or press Enter *)*

An example of a drawing that might be digitized is a map, as shown in Figure 17–3.

If, for example, the map in Figure 17–3 has been printed on an 11" × 17" sheet and you wish to digitize it on a 12" × 12" digitizer, you can overlay and digitize on one-half of the map at a time. You may use the coordinates 10560,2640 and 7920,5280 for two calibrating points. But because X coordinates increase toward the left, you must consider them as negative values in order to make them increase to the right. Therefore, in calibrating the map, you may use coordinates –10560,2640 and –7920,5280 to calibrate the first half and coordinates –7920,2640 and –5280,5280 for the second half.

The points on the paper should be selected so that the X values increase toward the right and the Y values increase upward.

Once calibration has been initiated in a particular space (model or paper), turning on the Tablet mode must be done while in that particular space.

Transformation Options

Tablet Calibration can be done by one of several transformation methods. These include Orthogonal, Affine, Projective, and Multiple-Point. The method you choose may depend on the condition of the map/drawing that is to be digitized and the desired accuracy.

Orthogonal This option involves two points. It results in uniform scaling and rotation. The translation is arbitrary. Orthogonal (two-point) translation is most suitable for tracing paper drawings that are dimensionally and rotationally accurate (right angles are not skew). It is advisable to use this option for long, narrow applications (a pipeline, for example).

Affine This option involves three points and can be applied to a paper drawing with scale factors, rotation, and right angle representations that are not to an acceptable accuracy in two dimensions. This can be applied to drawings with parallel lines that are represented parallel, but with an X direction scale/Y direction scale differential that is out of tolerance. Right angles may not be represented by right angles.

Whether or not you should use the Affine option depends on whether or not those lines that should be parallel are represented by parallel lines on the paper drawing. You can check the report displayed (in the form of a table) when you have digitized

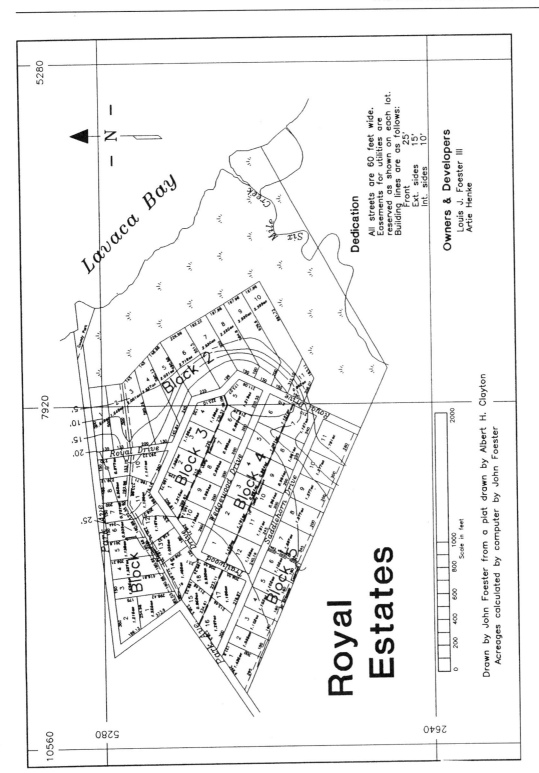

Figure 17-3 An example of a drawing digitized as a map

at least three points. If the RMS error (described in this section) is small, then the Affine option should be acceptable.

Projective This option involves four points, to simulate a translation comparable to a perspective in which points from one plane converge while passing through another plane (skew to the first) to one point of view. This option is applicable to copying paper sheets with irregularities that differ from one area to another (known as rubber-sheeting) and parallel lines that are not always represented as parallel. However, lines do project as lines.

Multiple-Point The Multiple-Point option will accept more than four points to be digitized and specified. AutoCAD will use the "least squares" method to optimize the calibration to compensate for imperfections in the paper drawing. The accuracy of this method is proportional to the number of points used.

The Calibration Table

If you use three or more points during calibration, AutoCAD computes the range or error (if any) and reports the results and displays information designed to help you determine if the paper copying process is acceptable. An example of a calibration table follows:

Four Calibration Points

Transformation type:	Orthogonal	Affine	Projective
Outcome of fit:	Success	Success	Exact
RMS Error:	143'-6.2"	73'-4.1"	
Standard deviation:	62'-2.7"	1'-7.8"	
Largest residual:	193'-1"	74'-1"	
At point:	2	3	
Second largest residual:	177'-9"	7'-7"	
At point:	3	2	

Outcome of Fit

Cancelled Cancelled occurs only with projective transformations. It indicates the fit has been cancelled.

Exact The number of points used was exactly correct and the transformation defined from them was valid.

Failure Points selected, though the correct number, were probably collinear or coincidental.

Impossible Insufficient points were selected for the transformation type under which "Impossible" is reported.

Success The transformation defined was valid and more points were used than was required.

RMS Error If the transformation is reported as a "Success," then the RMS (root mean square) error is reported. This is the square root of the average of the squares of the distances (called *residuals*) of each selected point from their respective targets.

Standard Deviation This reports the standard deviation of all residuals (the distance each point misses its target).

Point(s)/Residual(s) The two points whose residuals (see "RMS Error" and "Standard Deviation") are largest and second largest are reported along with their respective residual values.

TABLET MODE AND SKETCHING

Sketching while in Tablet mode operates similar to sketching with a mouse or on a tablet with the Tablet mode off. The difference is that the entire tablet surface is used for digitizing while the Tablet mode is on, making the maximum area available for tracing but making the pull-down menus inaccessible.

Editing Sketches

Once sketched lines have been recorded and the SKETCH command has been terminated, you can use regular editing commands (like COPY, MOVE, ERASE) to edit the individual line segments or sketched polylines (discussed next) just as though they had been drawn by the LINE or PLINE command. In the case of sketched polylines, the PEDIT command can be used for editing.

Sketching in Polylines

You can cause AutoCAD to make the created sketch segments into polylines instead of lines by setting the SKPOLY system variable to a nonzero value.

Linetypes in Sketching

You should use the Continuous linetype while sketching, whether with regular lines or polylines.

REVIEW QUESTIONS

1. What filename extension is used to store the menu command entries for a tablet menu?
   a. TAB   d. PGP
   b. MNX   e. INI
   c. CMD

2. How many different tablet menu areas can be specified on a digitizing pad?
   a. 1   d. 4
   b. 2   e. 5
   c. 3

3. When aligning a tablet menu with the digitizing pad, how many points are required?
   a. 1   d. 4
   b. 2   e. 5
   c. 3

4. To toggle the digitizing pad between menu functions and paper copying, you press:
   a. {F10}   d. {ctrl} + {O}
   b. {F11}   e. none of the above
   c. {F12}

5. The minimum number of points required to calibrate a digitizing pad using an Affine calibration is:
   a. 1   d. 4
   b. 2   e. 5
   c. 3

6. If you have an isometric drawing on paper and wished to digitize an orthographic view of the top, what type of calibration would you use?
   a. 2 point (Orthogonal)
   b. 3 point (Affine)
   c. 4 point (Projective)
   d. cannot be done

7. If you have photograph of a building and wished to digitize an the front elevation, what type of calibration would you use?
   a. 2 point (Orthogonal)
   b. 3 point (Affine)
   c. 4 point (Projective)
   d. cannot be done

8. What does RMS stand for in RMS error?
   a. Real Measure Statistic
   b. Root Mean Square
   c. Radical Motion Setting
   d. ReMainder Sum
   e. none of the above

9. If you select three points in a straight line to calibrate the digitizing pad, what "Outcome of Fit" will AutoCAD report for an Affine fit:
   a. Canceled
   b. Exact
   c. Failure
   d. Impossible
   e. Success

10. When using the SKETCH command, what system variable determines if lines segments or polylines?
    a. SKLINE
    b. SKPOLY
    c. SKTYPE
    d. LINESEG
    e. POLYGEN

11. What command will allow you to generate freehand lines when digitizing a paper drawing?
    a. DIGITIZE
    b. TABLET
    c. SKETCH
    d. FREEHAND
    e. DRAW

2. The option of the TABLET command which allows for the configuration of a tablet menu is:
   a. ON   d. CFG
   b. OFF   e. MENU
   c. CAL

13. The RMS error will always be lower (or equal) for a projective fit versus an orthogonal fit when 6 points are selected.
    a. True
    b. False

14. AutoCAD's default menu template has how many menu areas?
    a. 1   d. 4
    b. 2   e. 5
    c. 3

CHAPTER

18

CUSTOMIZING AUTOCAD

INTRODUCTION

Off the shelf, AutoCAD is extremely powerful. But, like many popular engineering and business software programs, it does not automatically do all things for all users. It does (probably better than any software available) permit users to make changes and additions to the core program to suit individual needs and applications. Word processors offer a feature by which you can save a combination of many keystrokes and invoke them at any time with just a few keystrokes. This is known as a *macro*. Database management programs (as well as other types of programs) have their own library of user functions that can also be combined and saved as a user-named, custom-designed command. These programs also allow you to create and save standard blank forms for use later to be filled out as needed. Using these features to make your copy of a generic program unique and more powerful for your particular application is known as *customizing*.

Customizing AutoCAD can include several facets requiring various skill levels. The topics include creating command aliases, linetypes, shapes, hatch patterns, menu customization, and command macros. A text editor is required (MS-DOS *EDIT.COM* and Microsoft Windows *NOTEPAD.EXE* are examples) in order to customize AutoCAD menus. A macro is a sequence of commands executed by a single user selection from a custom menu. A macro will automatically maintain the office standard, allowing the user to concentrate on the specifics of drafting and design.

After completing this chapter, you will be able to:

✓ Create command aliases
✓ Create modify, and understand AutoCAD Menu Structure
✓ Create custom linetypes, hatch patterns, and fonts

EXTERNAL COMMANDS AND ALIASES

AutoCAD allows you to run certain programs, this includes internal and external DOS commands. Windows 95 brings true multitasking by making it possible to use AutoCAD simultaneously with word processors, database and spreadsheet programs, and many other applications. In order to make it possible to use these external programs from within AutoCAD, you must first list them, with certain specifications, in an ASCII file called *ACAD.PGP*.

Because Microsoft Windows is a multitasking environment, the external commands really pertain to the DOS version of AutoCAD. They will work in Windows, but it is much easier to run the applications as separate programs. You can also include aliases in the *ACAD.PGP* file for regular AutoCAD commands. An alias is nothing but a nickname.

Command aliasing provides an alternate keystroke for invoking a command, not options of the command. The ZOOM command has a Window option; however, you cannot define an alias ZW for ZOOM Window. There is an alias for ZOOM, the letter Z. Prior to modifying the *ACAD.PGP* file, it is recommended that you make a backup copy of the file, such as *XACAD.PGP*, so that if you make a mistake, you can restore the original version. Following is an extract from the *ACAD.PGP* file.

```
;   AutoCAD Program Parameters File For AutoCAD Release 14
;   External Command and Command Alias Definitions

;   External command format:
;   <Command name>,[<DOS request>],<Bit flag>,[*]<Prompt>,

;   Examples of external commands for command windows

CATALOG,    DIR /W, 0,File specification: ,
DEL,DEL,            0,File to delete: ,
DIR, DIR,           0,File specification: ,
EDIT,START EDIT,    1,File to edit: ,
SH,,                1,*OS Command: ,
```

```
SHELL,,              1,*OS Command: ,
START,START,         1,*Application to start: ,
TYPE,TYPE,           0,File to list: ,

; Examples of external commands for Windows
; See also the STARTAPP AutoLISP function for an alternative
method.

EXPLORER, START EXPLORER, 1,,
NOTEPAD,  START NOTEPAD,  1,*File to edit: ,
PBRUSH,   START PBRUSH,   1,,

; Command alias format:
; <Alias>,*<Full command name>

; Sample aliases for AutoCAD commands
; These examples include most frequently used commands.

3A,    *3DARRAY
3F,    *3DFACE
3P,    *3DPOLY
A,     *ARC
AA,    *AREA
AL,    *ALIGN
AP,    *APPLOAD
AR,    *ARRAY
AAD,   *ASEADMIN
AEX,   *ASEEXPORT
ALI,   *ASELINKS
ASQ,   *ASESQLED
ARO,   *ASEROWS
ASE,   *ASESELECT
AT,    *DDATTDEF
-AT,   *ATTDEF
ATE,   *DDATTE
-ATE,  *ATTEDIT
B,     *BMAKE
-B,    *BLOCK
BH,    *BHATCH
BO,    *BOUNDARY
-BO,   *-BOUNDARY
BR,    *BREAK
C,     *CIRCLE
CH,    *DDCHPROP
```

The External Commands are defined at the top of the *ACAD.PGP* file.

The format for a command line is as follows:

```
<Command  name>,<executable>,<Memory  reserve>,[*]<Prompt>,
    <Return code>
```

An example of lines in an *ACAD.PGP* file for specifying external commands is as follows:

```
SH,,0, *OS Command: ,0
SHELL,,0, *OS Command: ,0
TYPE,TYPE, 0, File to type: ,0
CATALOG,DIR/W,0, File specification: ,0
DEL,DEL, 0, File to erase: ,0
DIR,DIR, 0, File specification: ,0
EDIT,, 0, File to edit: ,0
```

The command name (to be entered at the "Command:" prompt) should not be the same as an AutoCAD command and should be in uppercase characters.

The executable string is sent to the operative system as the name of a command. It can contain parameters and switches.

The memory amount must contain a number (usually 0). It maintains compatibility with previous versions of AutoCAD.

The prompt (optional) is used to inform the operator if additional input is necessary. If the prompt is preceded by an asterisk (*), then the user response may contain spaces. The response must be terminated by pressing Enter. Otherwise, pressing the Spacebar or Enter will terminate the response.

The return code is a bit-coded specification. The number you specify will represent one or more of the bitcodes. For example, if you specify 3, then bitcodes 1 and 2 will be in effect. If you specify 5, then bitcodes 1 and 4 will be in effect. The values are as follows:

0: Return to text screen.

1: Load *DXB* file. This causes a file named *$cmd.dxb* to be loaded into the drawing at the end of the command.

2: Construct block from DXB file. This causes the response to the prompt to become the name of a block to be added to the drawing, consisting of objects in the *$cmd.dxb* file written by the file command. This code must be used in conjunction with bitcode 1. This may not be used to redefine a previously defined block.

4: Restore text/graphics mode. If this bitcode is included, the mode you were in (text or graphics) will be returned to when the command is completed; otherwise, you will be in text mode.

The format to define an alias is as follows:

```
<Alias>,*<Full command name>
```

The abbreviation preceding the comma is the character or characters to be entered at the "Command:" prompt. The asterisk (*) must precede the command you wish invoked. It may be a standard AutoCAD command name, a custom command name that has been defined in and loaded with AutoLISP or ADS, or a display or machine driver command name. Aliases cannot be used in scripts. You can prefix a command in an alias with the underscore that causes a command line version to be used instead of a dialog box, as shown here:

```
BH, *_BHATCH
```

CUSTOMIZING MENUS

When you launch the standard version of AutoCAD for Windows, you are presented with the standard menu. Selecting an item from a menu might execute a command, an AutoLISP routine, or a macro or cause another menu to be displayed. Menus are user definable and are created/edited using text editors. Menu files also define the functionality and appearance of the menu area. If you perform an application-specific task on a regular basis that requires multiple steps to accomplish this task, you can place this in a menu macro and have AutoCAD complete all the required processes in a single step while pausing for input if necessary. Menu macros are similar to script files (files ending with *.SCR). Script files are also capable of executing many commands in sequence but have no decision-making capability and cannot pause for interactive user input.

AutoCAD for Windows and DOS supports the following kinds of menus:

- Pull-down and cursor menus
- Screen menus
- Image tile menus
- Pointing device menus
- Tablet menus

AutoCAD for Windows has additional menu functionality as follows:

- Toolbars
- Keyboard accelerators
- Help strings and tool tips
- Menu groups

Menu File Types

Prior to AutoCAD Release 13 for Windows, there were two types of menu files, ASCII text files ending with the file extension .MNU and a compiled version of the same file with the extension *.MNX*. The *ACAD.MNU* file is provided with the AutoCAD program, and if, when you launch AutoCAD, the *ACAD.MNX* file is not present or any changes were made to the *ACAD.MNU* file, AutoCAD automatically compiles and, creates a new *ACAD.MNX*. If you created your own custom menu—for example, *CUSTOM.MNU*—then upon loading the menu, AutoCAD automatically creates *CUSTOM.MNX*. The *ACAD.MNU* and *ACAD.MNX* files are still applicable in the DOS and UNIX versions of AutoCAD Release 14. Because of the additional functionality of the Windows version of AutoCAD Release 14, a new menu scheme exists.

The following table lists the menu files used by AutoCAD for Windows Release 14 version:

Menu File Type	Description
.MNU	Template menu file, ASCII text
.MNC	Compiled menu file. This binary file contains the command strings and menu syntax that defines the functionality and appearance of the menu.
.MNR	Menu resource file. This binary file contains the bitmaps used by the menu.
.MNS	Source menu file (AutoCAD generated)

AutoCAD Release 14 comes with the *ACAD.MNU* file. This is located in the "AutoCAD R14\SUPPORT" directory, assuming AutoCAD is installed on the C: drive, and AutoCAD R14 is the subdirectory. If your location is different, substitute the drive and path location for your case. The *.MNS* file is similar in structure to the *.MNU* file and is created automatically and dynamically updated by AutoCAD when you add new toolbars. The *.MNC* file compiles when you reload AutoCAD or dynamically update the menu. The *.MNR* file is created automatically when *.MNS* is completed and when buttons on the toolbars are created, changed, or added. The *.MNR* menu resource file is used for storing bitmaps (*.BMP*) for the icons and is a binary file.

When you add toolbar information to the menu, the *.MNS* file is the file that is updated. The toolbars are denoted in the ***TOOLBARS major section. If you delete the *.MNS* file, you will lose the newly created toolbars, because AutoCAD creates a new *.MNS* file based on the *.MNU* file. If you want to add the toolbars to your *.MNU* file, copy the ***TOOLBARS section from your *.MNS* file and paste it into your *.MNU* file. If you delete your *.MNS* file, AutoCAD rebuilds it based on the information found in the *.MNU* file. AutoCAD has another file that is constantly updated, called the *ACAD.INI* file. Windows applications contain many *.INI* files. This is where the initialization and configuration is kept for Windows applications. When you move toolbars and dock menus, the information is read to the *ACAD.INI* file so that when you launch AutoCAD, the menus are located in their new positions.

Another new feature in AutoCAD for Windows with respect to flyout menus is that over a period of time, AutoCAD will figure which menu items you use most often; these items are placed at the top level of the menu.

Menu File Structure

Menus are divided into sections relating to specific menu areas. Menu sections can contain submenus that you can reference and display as needed. The command strings and macro syntax that define the result of a menu selection are called *menu macros*. The Windows NOTEPAD editor program can only open a file size less than 64K in memory. To view the contents of the *ACAD.MNU* file, use the Windows WordPad program, which is located in the Accessories group. Prior to opening the *ACAD.MNU* file, copy it and save it as *XACAD.MNU*. Then if something should happen, you can restore the original. It is important that files remain as text files without any formatting codes.

Following are the major sections in menu files for DOS and Windows versions. (Major sections are denoted by ***):

BUTTONS*n Pointing device button menu, where *n* is either 1 or 2.

> ***BUTTONS1 is the normal menu used by a mouse or tablet cursor (puck).

> ***BUTTONS2 Holding down [Shift] and pressing the right mouse button (or on a three button mouse pressing the middle button) activates the menu.

AUX*n Auxiliary device button, where *n* is a number either 1 or 2.

POP*n Pull-down and cursor menus, where *n* is a number from 0 to 16 (Note: 0 is used only for cursor menus).

> ***POP0 is the cursor menu, which follows the crosshairs. Pressing [Shift] and the left mouse button, (or pressing button 3 on a digitizing puck) activates this menu.

> ***POP1 through ***POP16 are the pull-down menus. The AutoCAD regular menu file does not use all the available pull-down menus.

SCREEN Screen menu area, which slowly and surely is disappearing from AutoCAD for Windows. It may not be supported in future versions.

IMAGE Image menu tile areas (formerly called ***ICON; will not be supported in the next release of the AutoCAD program)

TABLET*n Tablet menu area, where *n* is a number from 1 to 4.

> ***TABLET1 through ***TABLET4 are for the four menu areas of a digitizing tablet.

***TOOLBARS** Toolbar menus are the most flexible and easily customized method of interface now available for the AutoCAD user. Groups of buttons can be placed around or on the screen in changeable proportions in toolbars. These buttons can be used to invoke commands, macros, or user-defined programs that can make drawing easier and more accurate.

You can use the find feature of Windows WordPad to locate the major sections.

Menu system does not have to use all of the preceding major menu sections. AutoCAD for Windows has additional major sections explained later in the chapter.

Following is the menu code taken from the *ACAD.MNU* file.

```
***POP1
ID_File      [&File]
ID_New       [&New...\tCtrl+N]^C^C_new
ID_Open      [&Open...\tCtrl+O]^C^C_open
ID_Save      [&Save\tCtrl+S]^C^C_qsave
ID_Saveas    [Save &As...]^C^C_saveas
             [--]
ID_Print     [&Print...\tCtrl+P]^C^C_plot
             [--]
ID_Import    [&Import...]^C^C_import
ID_Export    [&Export...]^C^C_export
ID_Ioopts    [->Op&tions]
ID_Wmfopt      [WMF Op&tions...]^C^C_wmfopts
ID_Psqual      [PostScript &Quality]'_psquality
ID_Psdisp      [PostScript &Display]'_psdrag
               [--]
ID_Psprol      [<-&PostScript Prolog]'_psprolog
             [--]
ID_Mngt        [->&Management]
ID_Unlock      [&Unlock File...]^C^C_files
ID_Audit       [&Audit]^C^C_audit
ID_Recov       [<-&Recover...]^C^C_recover
             [--]
ID_MRU       [Drawing History]
             [--]
ID_Exit      [E&xit]^C^C_quit
```

POP1 is the major section, which is the File (first) menu on the menu bar of AutoCAD for Windows. All the words that begin with ID_ are menu tag names. These are specific to AutoCAD for Windows and are discussed later. Labels are enclosed in square brackets []. The ampersand (&) is how you underscore the following letter, which allows menu selections from the keyboard, with the ALT + "letter" combination common to all Windows programs. The label (or letters between the brackets) is what appears in the pull-down menu. The first label in the menu is what appears on the menu bar as "<u>F</u>ile"; all other labels appear on the menu itself. This is only for POP menus 1 to 16 and IMAGE menus. The text following the closing bracket is the command macro that AutoCAD will execute.

Here is the syntax:

```
[&Open...\tCtrl+O]^C^C_open
```

The ^C^C is the cancel command which is followed by the open command. The symbol ^ before the C is a caret, which is Ⓢⁿⁱᵗᵗ + 6 on the keyboard. This combination of characters executes the "ESC" sequence to cancel any previous command. Note that there are two of them. This is because some AutoCAD commands require the user to press Esc twice before cancelling a command. After the cancellation, the OPEN command will execute. This is an example of a simple macro.

Menu Macro Syntax

Following is a partial list of the codes you will encounter in menu macros:

Syntax	Description
***	Denotes major sections of the menu
**	Denotes subsections located between major sections
[ ]	Menu label
;	Semicolon; equivalent to pressing Enter on the keyboard
space	A space character; equivalent to pressing Enter on the keyboard
\	Pause for user input
'	Issue a command transparently while in another command
*	Repeat a command until user cancels
+	Allows the long macros to be continued onto the next line

The following example macro will create a layer called "EL_OFFEQ" (Electrical Office Equipment), assign the color "RED", and make it the current layer:

```
[EL_OFFEQ]^C^C-LAYER;M;EL-EQUIP;C;RED;;;
```

This is the equivalent of typing the -LAYER command, selecting the Make option, typing "EL-OFFEQ" as the desired layer name, selecting the Color option to assign the color Red, and finally, pressing Enter three times to exit the command. Selecting this macro will execute all of this in one operation. Use the Make option of the -LAYER command in case the layer does not yet exist. If the layer does exist it will become the current layer. Note that there is no space after the ^C^C.

Example of Creating a Menu File

Let's go through the sequence of steps in creating a menu file incorporating all the facets of menu sections. In order to create the menu file, first create the blocks with attributes shown in Figure 18–1, and save the drawing in your current working directory.

Figure 18–1 shows three blocks: a computer, a table, and a chair. Create the objects on layer 0 and the attribute definitions on layer ATTRIB. Make layer 0 "white" and layer ATTRIB "yellow." Define the attributes as visible, and verify. Following is the list of attribute tags with the corresponding block names:

Block Name	Attribute Flag
COMPUTER	CPU
	HD
	MONITOR
TABLE	MANUF
	COST
	FINISH
CHAIR	MANUF
	COLOR
	MATL

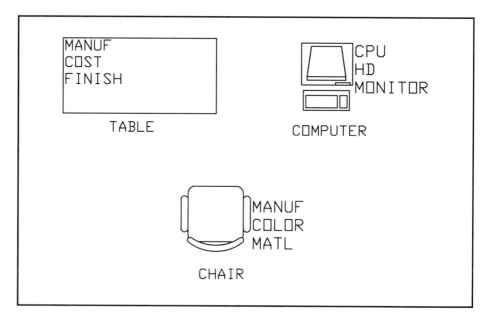

Figure 18–1 Drawing showing the three blocks required to complete the menu exercise

Save the blocks as separate drawing files, *COMP.DWG, CHAIR.DWG,* and *TABLE1.DWG,* by using the WBLOCK command.

Create a menu system file called *TEST.MNU* that will insert various items of furniture into a drawing using either a standard set of values or a custom set of values. The purpose of the menu system is to insert the blocks with a single pick from a menu that will automatically create the standard layer for insertion of the block, allow for custom values (if the Custom option is selected), and set layer 0 as the current layer.

Invoke the AutoCAD program from the Windows file manager. Begin a new drawing, and launch the Windows NOTEPAD editor from the Accessories group. Type the following code, and save the file as *TEST.MNU* in your current working directory.

```
***POP1
**Furniture
[&Furniture]
[->&Standard Furniture]
 [&Computer]^C^C^CATTREQ;0;-LAYER;M;EL_OFFEQ;COLOR;1;;;+
INSERT;COMP;\;;\ATTREQ;1;-LAYER;SET;0;;
 [&Table]^C^C^CATTREQ;0;-LAYER;M;FR_OFF;COLOR;3;;;+
INSERT;TABLE1;\;;\ATTREQ;1;-LAYER;SET;0;;
 [<-C&hair]^C^C^CATTREQ;0;-LAYER;M;FR_OFF;COLOR;3;;;+
INSERT;CHAIR;\;;\ATTREQ;1;-LAYER;SET;0;;
[->Custo&m Furniture]
 [Com&uter]^C^C^CATTDIA;0;-LAYER;M;EL_OFFEQ;COLOR;1;;;+
INSERT;COMP;\;;\\\\-LAYER;S;0;;ATTDIA;1
 [Tab&le]^C^C^CATTDIA;0;-LAYER;M;FR_OFF;COLOR;3;;;+
INSERT;TABLE1;\;;\\\\-LAYER;S;0;;ATTDIA;1
 [<-Chai&r]^C^C^CATTDIA;0;-LAYER;M;FR_OFF;COLOR;3;;;+
INSERT;CHAIR;\;;\\\\-LAYER;S;0;;ATTDIA;1
[--]
[Layer EL_OFFEQ]^C^C^C-LAYER;M;EL_OFFEQ;COLOR;1;;;
[Layer FR_OFF]^C^C^C-LAYER;M;FR_OFF;COLOR;3;;;
[--]
[Layer 0]^C^C^C-LAYER;SET;0;;
```

Get back to the AutoCAD program, and load the *TEST.MNU* menu file by typing **MENU** at the "Command:" prompt and then pressing Enter or the Spacebar. The Select Menu File dialog box appears, as shown in Figure 18-2.

Select the *TEST.MNU* file from the appropriate drive and directory, and choose the **Open** button. *TEST.MNU* will replace *ACAD.MNU*. The right mouse button on your tablet puck/mouse (or Enter) will not respond to any action because in the *TEST.MNU* file the ***BUTTONS1 major section is not defined. Only the pull-down menu Furniture is displayed, as shown in Figure 18-3.

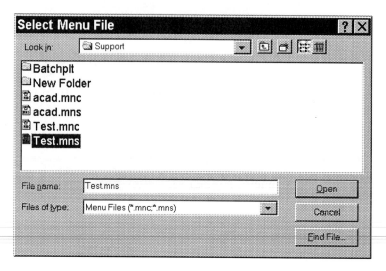

Figure 18-2 Select Menu File dialog box

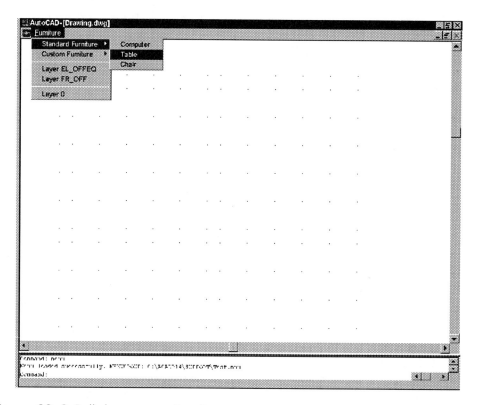

Figure 18-3 Pull-down menu Furniture

To test the menu, select the Computer option from the Standard Furniture cascading menu. AutoCAD prompts for an insertion point and rotation angle. From the Custom Furniture cascading menu, select the Computer option. AutoCAD prompts for the insertion point and rotation angle, and in addition prompts for three attribute values. If you come across an error message, go back to the *TEST.MNU* file, check the syntax, and make the necessary changes. Reload the *TEST.MNU* file, invoke the commands again, and make sure it is working properly. Let's examine some of the unique features of the TEST.MNU file line by line.

```
***POP1
```

Indicates that this is a pull-down menu located at position 1.

```
[&Furniture]
```

This is the title that will appear on the menu bar. The ampersand before the F will underline the letter F, allowing the menu to be selected using the Alt + F combination.

```
[->&Standard Furniture]
```

This is the beginning of the cascading menu, as noted by the "->." The letter S will be underscored and "Standard Furniture" will appear as the first item in the "Furniture" pull-down menu.

```
[&Computer]^C^C^CATTREQ;0;-LAYER;M;EL_OFFEQ;COLOR;1;;;+
INSERT;COMP;\;;\ATTREQ;1;-LAYER;SET;0;;
```

This is the first item available in the cascaded menu. The ^C 's will cancel any previous command. It is advisable to use three ^C combinations, because some commands require more than two exits to terminate. Following the ^C is ATTREQ, a SETVAR variable whose function is to control attribute requests. If it has a value of 0, the block will be inserted without prompting for attributes using standard values, which, in this case, is what we want. Note the use of the semicolon which is equivalent to pressing Enter. Next, the -LAYER command is invoked, creates an "EL_OFFEQ" layer and sets the color to "RED" (1 is RED), followed by three returns to terminate the LAYER command. The use of the "+" symbol at the end of the line is to allow the code to continue onto the next line. There are no spaces between the final return ";" and the "+". The macro continues by invoking the INSERT command and inserting a block called COMP. The first "\" backslash character after the block name is to pause, which allows the user to pick an insertion point. The two semicolons (;;) that follow the backslash character is to accept the default scale factors. The next backslash character is for the user to pick a rotation angle. The ATTREQ SETVAR variable is reset to the default value of 1. The final command is to restore layer 0 as the current layer.

```
[->Custo&m Furniture]
[Com&puter]^C^C^CATTDIA;0;-LAYER;M;EL_OFFEQ;COLOR;1;;;+
INSERT;COMP;\;;\\\\-LAYER;S;0;;ATTDIA;1
```

This code is for a custom Computer option from the Custom Furniture cascading menu. In the Custom menu, the intent is to allow the operator to insert a block and at the same time allow the user to input nonstandard values for the attributes of the block. ATTDIA (Attribute dialog box), which is a SETVAR variable, is set to 0. This will disable the Attribute Dialog Box from popping up on the screen. Instead, the user can input attribute values from the "Command:" prompt. The layer command creates the "EL_OFFEQ" layer, whose color is set to "RED." The "+" is used to allow the continuation of the command onto the next line. The INSERT command is invoked, and the COMP block is inserted, pausing for the user to pick an insertion point. The macro is followed by two semicolons ";;", which accepts the default scale factor. The following four "\\\\" backslash characters is to pause for the operator to pick the rotation angle of the block and input the three attribute values for the block. The final command is to restore layer 0 as the current layer.

> **NOTE:** It is considered good programming practice to reset the SETVAR variables to their default values.

```
[Layer EL_OFFEQ]^C^C^C-LAYER;M;EL_OFFEQ;COLOR;1;;;
[Layer FR_OFF]^C^C^C-LAYER;M;FR_OFF;COLOR;3;;;
[--]
[Layer 0]^C^C^C-LAYER;SET;0;;
```

This macro creates new layers if they do not already exist and assigns the appropriate colors. The [--] code draws a line (separator) on the pull-down menu to group similar elements visually.

Menugroups and Partial Menu Loading

One of the problems with the *TEST.MNU* file menu is that in order to use it, you have to replace the AutoCAD default menu file (*ACAD.MNU*) even though *TEST.MNU* is incomplete, containing only one major section. One method around this problem is to rename the major section in *TEST.MNU* from ***POP1 to ***POP11 and to append this menu to the AutoCAD default *ACAD.MNU* file. Then you can use the all the available standard menu commands in addition to the custom menu. The *ACAD.MNU* file that comes standard with AutoCAD uses ***POP1 to ***POP10. This has been the traditional approach, which causes rather large menu files just to use the additional functionality. If AutoCAD changes the default menu file, the user will sometimes be forced to make necessary changes to additional functionality to accommodate the *ACAD.MNU* file changes. Windows NOTEPAD can only edit a file that is less the 64K in size. You would have to use some other editor to append the ***POP11 to the copy of the standard AutoCAD menu. But AutoCAD Release 14 provides the ability for partial loading of menus so you can mix and match the functionality of various menus. Changes in one menu will not affect the other menus. AutoCAD achieves this new functionality with addition of a new major section group called ***MENUGROUP. Each menu file can only have one major section called MENUGROUP.

The ***MENUGROUP= major section is how AutoCAD tracks which menus are loaded and referenced. A MENUGROUP string definition can be up to 32 alphanumeric characters (spaces and punctuation marks are not allowed). The ***MENUGROUP= label must proceed all menu definitions that use the name-tag mechanism, which will be covered later. This applies only to AutoCAD Release 14; it is not supported by any other platform. Open the *TEST.MNU* file in the NOTEPAD editor, make the following changes, and save the file as *TEST.MNU* to demonstrate partial menu loading.

```
//This is a test menu file and it demonstrates the basic new
//functionality of the new menu name tag syntax.

***MENUGROUP=test
***POP1
**Furniture
ID_Furn [&Furniture]
ID_Furns [->&Standard Furniture]
ID_Comps    [&Computer]^C^C^CATTREQ;0;-LAYER;M;EL_OFFEQ;COLOR;1;;;+
INSERT;COMP;\;;\ATTREQ;1;-LAYER;SET;0;;
ID_Tables   [&Table]^C^C^CATTREQ;0;-LAYER;M;FR_OFF;COLOR;3;;;+
INSERT;TABLE1;\;;\ATTREQ;1;-LAYER;SET;0;;
ID_Chairs   [<-C&hair]^C^C^CATTREQ;0;-LAYER;M;FR_OFF;COLOR;3;;;+
INSERT;CHAIR;\;;\ATTREQ;1;-LAYER;SET;0;;
ID_Furnc [->Custo&m Furniture]
ID_Compc    [Com&uter]^C^C^CATTDIA;0;-LAYER;M;EL_OFFEQ;COLOR;1;;;+
INSERT;COMP;\;;\\\\-LAYER;S;0;;ATTDIA;1
ID_Tablec   [Tab&le]^C^C^CATTDIA;0;-LAYER;M;FR_OFF;COLOR;3;;;+
INSERT;TABLE1;\;;\\\\-LAYER;S;0;;ATTDIA;1
ID_Chairc   [<-Chai&r]^C^C^CATTDIA;0;-LAYER;M;FR_OFF;COLOR;3;;;+
INSERT;CHAIR;\;;\\\\-LAYER;S;0;;ATTDIA;1
[--]
[Layer EL_OFFEQ]^C^C^C-LAYER;M;EL_OFFEQ;COLOR;1;;;
[Layer FR_OFF]^C^C^C-LAYER;M;FR_OFF;COLOR;3;;;
[--]
ID_Lyr0 [Layer 0]^C^C^C-LAYER;SET;0;;
```

The text that follows the \\ is considered comment lines by the AutoCAD program and is ignored in menu file compilation.

The name tags before the labels in the menu begin with "ID_". This can be any string; however, AutoCAD recommends using "ID_" as part of the string. The other requirement is that name tags be unique. Details on how name tags are used is provided later in the chapter. To partially load the menus, invoke Customize Menus...

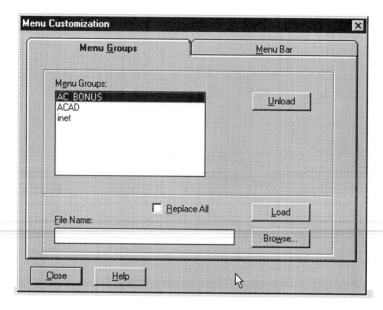

Figure 18-4 Menu Customization dialog box

from the pull-down menu Tools. AutoCAD displays the Menu Customization dialog box, as shown in Figure 18-4.

Choose the Browse... button, and AutoCAD displays the Select Menu file dialog box. Select the *TEST.MNU* file from the appropriate drive and directory, and click the OK button to close the dialog box. AutoCAD displays the name of the menu file selected in the **File Name:** edit box. Select the Load button. *TEST.MNU* will be added to the Menu Groups: list box. The functionality of the TEST.MNU menu is added to the AutoCAD menu. If the *TEST.MNU* file had toolbars, then they would have appeared on the screen. To display the *TEST.MNU* group as part of the AutoCAD menu bar, first select *TEST.MNU* from the Menu Groups: list box. Then choose the Menu Bar tab, as shown in Figure 18-5. AutoCAD displays the Menu Bar page shown in Figure 18-6.

The Menu Bar page of the dialog box shows the Furniture item menu on the left side and the AutoCAD menu bar on the right side. Select Furniture on the left side and Help on the right side, and then select the Insert>> button. AutoCAD inserts the Furniture item before the Help item on the right side of the dialog box. Choose the Close button to accept the configuration. AutoCAD adds the Furniture menu item to the standard AutoCAD menu bar between the Tools and Help menus, complete with its own functionality, as shown in Figure 18-7.

Partial menu loading gives you the ability to blend menus together and achieve the functionality as if the menu system were one menu. Test the menu items from the AutoCAD menu and from the Furniture menu. The system works as if dealing with

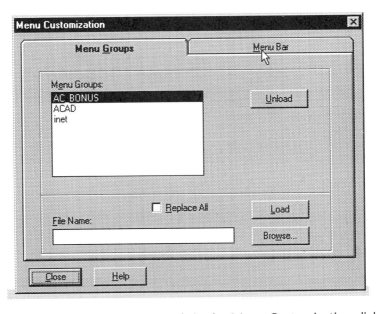

Figure 18-5 Choosing the Menu Bar tab in the Menu Customization dialog box

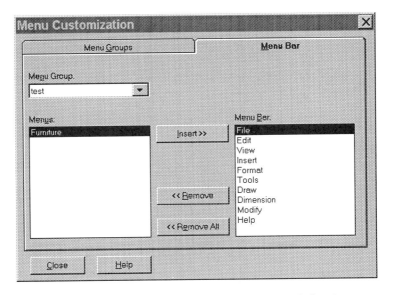

Figure 18-6 Menu Bar page of the Menu Customization dialog box

one menu. To unload the *TEST.MNU* menugroup, open the Menu Customization dialog box (Menu Groups page), select the "test" menu group from the Menu Groups: list box, and then select the Unload button.

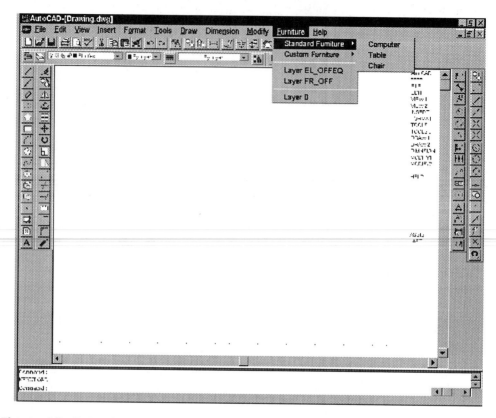

Figure 18-7 Furniture menu item as part of the AutoCAD standard menu

Helpstrings

In the menu file, you can also include help strings that will be displayed in the status bar whenever a command is selected from the pull-down menu. Open the *TEST.MNU* file in the NOTEPAD editor and add the ***HELPSTRINGS section, as shown next. Save the file as *TEST.MNU* to demonstrate the display of help strings.

```
//This is a test menu file and it demonstrates the basic new
//functionality of the new menu name tag syntax.

***MENUGROUP=test
***POP1
**Furniture
ID_Furn [&Furniture]
ID_Furns [->&Standard Furniture]
ID_Comps    [&Computer]^C^C^CATTREQ;0;-LAYER;M;EL_OFFEQ;COLOR;1;;;+
INSERT;COMP;\;;\ATTREQ;1;-LAYER;SET;0;;
```

```
ID_Tables    [&Table]^C^C^CATTREQ;0;-LAYER;M;FR_OFF;COLOR;3;;;+
INSERT;TABLE1;\;;\ATTREQ;1;-LAYER;SET;0;;
ID_Chairs    [<-C&hair]^C^C^CATTREQ;0;-LAYER;M;FR_OFF;COLOR;3;;;+
INSERT;CHAIR;\;;\ATTREQ;1;-LAYER;SET;0;;
ID_Furnc [->Custo&m Furniture]
ID_Compc    [Com&uter]^C^C^CATTDIA;0;-LAYER;M;EL_OFFEQ;COLOR;1;;;+
INSERT;COMP;\;;\\\\-LAYER;S;0;;ATTDIA;1
ID_Tablec    [Tab&le]^C^C^CATTDIA;0;-LAYER;M;FR_OFF;COLOR;3;;;+
INSERT;TABLE1;\;;\\\\-LAYER;S;0;;ATTDIA;1
ID_Chairc    [<-Chai&r]^C^C^CATTDIA;0;-LAYER;M;FR_OFF;COLOR;3;;;+
INSERT;CHAIR;\;;\\\\-LAYER;S;0;;ATTDIA;1
[--]
[Layer EL_OFFEQ]^C^C^C-LAYER;M;EL_OFFEQ;COLOR;1;;;
[Layer FR_OFF]^C^C^C-LAYER;M;FR_OFF;COLOR;3;;;
[--]
ID_Lyr0 [Layer 0]^C^C^C-LAYER;SET;0;;


***HELPSTRINGS
ID_Furn [Office Furniture]
ID_Furns [Standard Office Furniture]
ID_Comps [Standard Computer]
ID_Tables [Standard Table]
ID_Chairs [Standard Chair]
ID_Furnc [Custom Office Furniture]
ID_Compc [Custom Computer]
ID_Tablec [Custom Table]
ID_Chairc [Custom Chair]
```

The text inside the square brackets next to the tag name will appear on the status bar when the command is invoked from the pull-down menu bar. For example, selecting the Computer option from the Custom Furniture menu, causes the text inside the square brackets to appear on the status bar, as shown in Figure 18–8.

To load the menu with changes, select Customize Menu... from the pull-down menu Tools. Unload the *TEST.MNU* file if it is already loaded, and then reload the updated file with changes. Select the Browse... button, and AutoCAD displays the Select Menu file dialog box. Select the *TEST.MNU* file from the appropriate directory, and click the OK button to close the dialog box. AutoCAD displays the name of the menu file selected in the **File Name:** edit box. Select the Load button. *TEST.MNU* will be added to the Menu Groups: list box. The functionality of the *TEST.MNU* menu is added to the AutoCAD menu.

To display the *TEST.MNU* group as part of the AutoCAD menu bar, first select *TEST.MNU* from the Menu Groups: list box. Then choose the Menu Bar tab. The Menu Bar page of the dialog box shows the Furniture menu on the left side and the

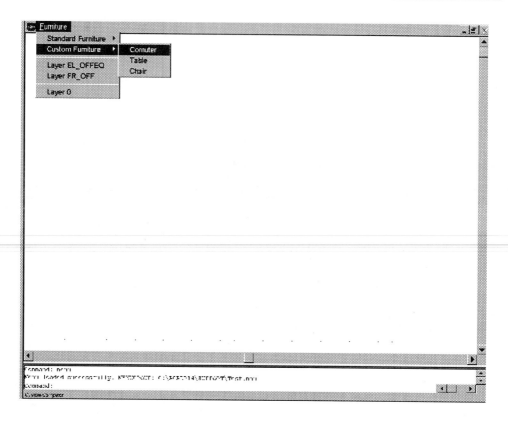

Figure 18-8 Status bar displaying the helpstring

AutoCAD menu bar on the right side. Select the Furniture item on the left side and Help on the right side, and then select the Insert>> button. AutoCAD inserts the Furniture item before the Help item on the right side of the dialog box. Choose the Close button to accept the configuration. AutoCAD adds the Furniture menu item to the standard AutoCAD menu bar between the Tools and Help menus, complete with its own functionality. Test the Furniture pull-down menu to see whether the help string appears on the status bar.

Creating and Modifying Toolbars

The easiest way is to create toolbars while you are working in AutoCAD is to let AutoCAD add the code automatically to the *.MNS file. If you want to add this information to the *.MNU file, copy and paste this information into the *.MNU file, and then delete the *.MNS file. AutoCAD will rebuild the *.MNS file based on the information found in the *.MNU file.

In this section, you will create three new toolbars, as shown in Figure 18–9, as part of the *TEST.MNU* file: one for custom and standard computers, one for custom and

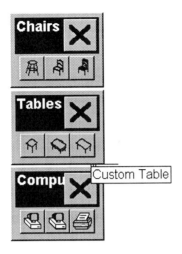

Figure 18–9 Toolbars for a custom menu

standard tables, and finally one for custom and standard chairs. Make sure the TEST menu file is still partially loaded into the AutoCAD menu.

To create a new toolbar, select Toolbars... from the pull-down menu View. AutoCAD displays the Toolbars dialog box shown in Figure 18–10.

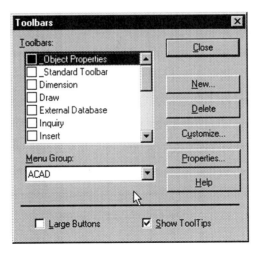

Figure 18–10 Toolbars dialog box

From the Toolbars dialog box, select the New... button. AutoCAD displays the New Toolbar dialog box shown in Figure 18–11.

From the Menu Group: drop-down list box, select the "test" group. In the Toolbar Name: edit box, type **Chairs** and choose the OK button. AutoCAD displays the

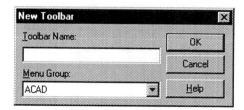

Figure 18–11 New Toolbar dialog box

new toolbar Chairs, as shown in Figure 18–12. If you cannot see the newly created toolbar on the screen, you may have to move the Toolbars dialog box out of the way to find it.

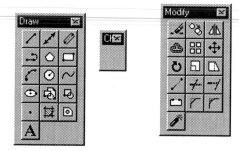

Figure 18–12 Chairs toolbar

To add buttons to the empty Chairs toolbar, choose the Customize... button in the Toolbars dialog box. The Customize Toolbars dialog box appears, as shown in Figure 18–13.

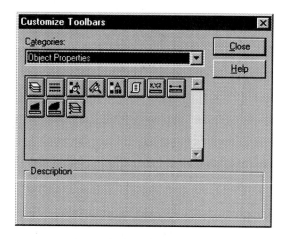

Figure 18–13 Customize Toolbars dialog box

AutoCAD lists various types of button groups in the **Categories:** drop-down list box. Select any button from the button groups and, while holding down your left mouse button, drag the outline of the button to the empty Chairs toolbar and release the mouse button. A copy of this button together with its associated code is attached to the toolbar.

Place the cursor on the button located in the Chairs toolbar, and click the right button on your pointing device. AutoCAD displays the Button Properties dialog box shown in the Figure 18–14.

Type **Custom Chair** in the **Name:** edit box. This is the tooltip that will be displayed when the mouse pointer passes over the button. In the **Help:** edit box, type **"Custom Office Furniture"**. This will be the message displayed on the status bar when the mouse pointer passes over the button. In the **Macro:** edit section, delete the existing code and replace it with the following code taken from the *TEST.MNU* file created earlier for Custom Chair:

```
^C^C^CATTDIA;0;-LAYER;M;FR_OFF;COLOR;3;;;INSERT;CHAIR;\;;\\\\
-LAYER;S;0;;ATTDIA;1
```

Do not add "+" in the macro. Although this will work for the POP menus, it will not work in the Button Property dialog box. Remember that spaces and semicolons are considered Returns by AutoCAD. You may now wish to edit the Button Icon by choosing the Edit... button in the Button Properties dialog box. AutoCAD displays the Button Editor dialog box shown Figure 18–15.

Make the necessary changes to the icon by using the tools provided in Button Editor dialog box. Select the Save or Save As... button to save the changes. This will allow you to save the icon as a bitmap (files with the *.BMP* extension). Choose the Close button to return to the Button Properties dialog box. For the changes to take effect, select the Apply button in the Button Properties dialog box. Once again AutoCAD will save the changes to the *TEST.MNS* file.

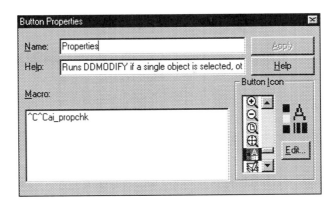

Figure 18–14 Button Properties dialog box

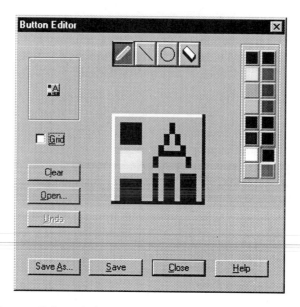

Figure 18–15 Button Editor dialog box

Repeat the procedure to add another button to the Chairs toolbar, adding a chair as standard furniture. Make sure to copy the appropriate code from the *TEST.MNU* file. In addition, create two more toolbars: one called Tables and the other called Computers, as shown in Figure 18–16.

Let's look at an example of creating a flyout toolbar called Office Furniture, as shown in Figure 18–17. In order to create a flyout toolbar, we need to reference existing toolbars.

Figure 18–16 Table and Computer toolbars

Figure 18–17 Flyout toolbar

The Office Furniture toolbar will include three flyout icons, namely, Computers, Chairs, and Tables. The Computers flyout will include macros for Standard Computer and Custom Computer. Similarly, Chairs and Tables flyout will include Standard Chair and Custom Chairs and Standard Table and Custom Table, respectively.

To create a new toolbar, select Customize Toolbars... from the pull-down menu Tools. AutoCAD displays the Toolbars dialog box. From the Toolbars dialog box select the New... button. AutoCAD displays the New Toolbar dialog box.

From the **Menu Group:** drop-down list box select the "test" group. In the **Toolbar Name:** edit box, type **Office Furniture** and select the OK button. AutoCAD displays the new Office Furniture toolbar. If you cannot see the newly created toolbar on the screen, you may have to move the Toolbar dialog box out of the way to find it. To add buttons to the empty Office Furniture toolbar, click the Customize... button in the Toolbars dialog box. AutoCAD displays the Customize Toolbars dialog box. From the Categories drop-down list box, select the Custom option. AutoCAD provides a choice of two types of buttons; a standard button and a flyout button, indicated by the small block triangle in the lower right corner of the button, as shown in Figure 18–18.

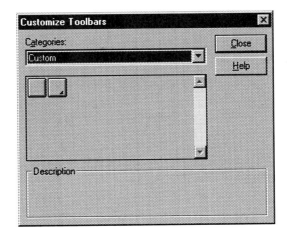

Figure 18–18 Flyout button box

Select the flyout button and drag it to the Office Furniture toolbar. Place two additional flyout buttons in the Office Furniture toolbar. Move your mouse pointer to the Office Furniture toolbar and right-click on the left button. The Flyout Properties dialog box appears, as shown in Figure 18–19.

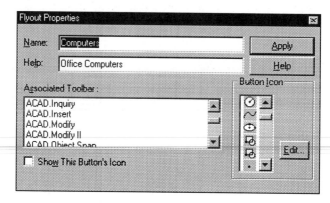

Figure 18–19 Flyout Properties dialog box

In the **Name:** edit box, type **Computers**. In the **Help:** edit box, type **"Office Computers"**. From the Associated Toolbar: drop-down list select test.Computer and then select the Apply button. Repeat this process for the Tables and Chairs. Make sure the check box for Show this Button's Icon is turned off in the Flyout Properties dialog box. If it is set to ON, AutoCAD will not allow swapping of the icons to reflect the last toolbar icon selected. Once all the flyout buttons are defined, close the Toolbars dialog box.

Choose Customize Menus... from the pull-down menu Tools, unload the TEST menu group, and then reload the updated test menu group. On the Menu Bars page, add the Furniture menu bar item before the AutoCAD Help item. Various toolbars will be displayed on the screen. Select the various buttons from the newly created toolbars and verify that the associated macros work.

When you create the toolbars, AutoCAD adds all descriptions of the toolbars to the *TEST.MNS* file under a major section called ***TOOLBARS. AutoCAD creates and maintains the *.*MNS* files. You can add the ***TOOLBARS section to your *.*MNU* template file. From the Program Manager Accessories Group start the NOTEPAD editor program and open the *TEST.MNS* file. From the *TEST.MNS* file select the ***TOOLBARS major section and paste it into the *TEST.MNU* file. You can have multiple copies of the NOTEPAD editor open at the same time. Following is the line-by-line listing of the code of the *TEST.MNU* file after button bars are added.

```
//This is a test menu file and it demonstrates the basic new
//functionality of the new menu name tag syntax.
```

```
***MENUGROUP=test
***POP1
**Furniture
ID_Furn [&Furniture]
ID_Furns [->&Standard Furniture]
ID_Comps     [&Computer]^C^C^CATTREQ;0;-
LAYER;M;EL_OFFEQ;COLOR;1;;;+
INSERT;COMP;\;;\ATTREQ;1;-LAYER;SET;0;;
ID_Tables    [&Table]^C^C^CATTREQ;0;-LAYER;M;FR_OFF;COLOR;3;;;+
INSERT;TABLE1;\;;\ATTREQ;1;-LAYER;SET;0;;
ID_Chairs    [<-C&hair]^C^C^CATTREQ;0;-LAYER;M;FR_OFF;COLOR;3;;;+
INSERT;CHAIR;\;;\ATTREQ;1;-LAYER;SET;0;;
ID_Furnc [->Custo&m Furniture]
ID_Compc     [Com&uter]^C^C^CATTDIA;0;-
LAYER;M;EL_OFFEQ;COLOR;1;;;+
INSERT;COMP;\;;\\\\-LAYER;S;0;;ATTDIA;1
ID_Tablec    [Tab&le]^C^C^CATTDIA;0;-LAYER;M;FR_OFF;COLOR;3;;;+
INSERT;TABLE1;\;;\\\\-LAYER;S;0;;ATTDIA;1
ID_Chairc    [<-Chai&r]^C^C^CATTDIA;0;-LAYER;M;FR_OFF;COLOR;3;;;+
INSERT;CHAIR;\;;\\\\-LAYER;S;0;;ATTDIA;1
[--]
[Layer EL_OFFEQ]^C^C^C-LAYER;M;EL_OFFEQ;COLOR;1;;;
[Layer FR_OFF]^C^C^C-LAYER;M;FR_OFF;COLOR;3;;;
[--]
ID_Lyr0 [Layer 0]^C^C^C-LAYER;SET;0;;

***HELPSTRINGS
ID_Furn [Office Furniture]
ID_Furns [Standard Office Furniture]
ID_Comps [Standard Computer]
ID_Tables [Standard Table]
ID_Chairs [Standard Chair]
ID_Furnc [Custom Office Furniture]
ID_Compc [Custom Computer]
ID_Tablec [Custom Table]
ID_Chairc [Custom Chair]

***TOOLBARS
**COMPUTER
ID_Computer [_Toolbar("Computer", _Floating, _Show, 200, 100,0)]
ID_Layers     [_Button("Standard Computer", ICON2580.bmp,
     ICON_32_-LAYERS)]^C^C^CATTREQ;0;-
LAYER;M;EL_OFFEQ;COLOR;1;;;INSERT;COMP;\;;
   \ATTREQ;1;-LAYER;SET;0;;
```

```
ID_Layers_0      [_Button("Custom Computer", ICON7216.bmp,
    ICON_32_-LAYERS)]^C^C^CATTDIA;0;-LAYER;M;EL_OFFEQ;COLOR;1;;;INSERT;COMP;\;;
    \\\\-LAYER;S;0;;ATTDIA;1


**TABLES
ID_Tables_0  [_Toolbar("Tables", _Floating, _Show, 200, 200, 0)]
ID_StandardComputer [_Button("Standard Table", ICON1629.bmp,
    ICON499.bmp)]^C^C^CATTREQ;0;-LAYER;M;FR_OFF;COLOR;3;;;INSERT;TABLE1;\;;
    \ATTREQ;1;-LAYER;SET;0;;
ID_CustomComputer [_Button("Custom Table", ICON5498.bmp,
    ICON8877.bmp)]^C^C^CATTDIA;0;-LAYER;M;FR_OFF;COLOR;3;;;INSERT;TABLE1;\;;
    \\\\-LAYER;S;0;;ATTDIA;1


**CHAIRS
ID_Chairs      [_Toolbar("Chairs", _Floating, _Show, 200, 300, 0)]
ID_StandardTable [_Button("Standard Chair", ICON2854.bmp,
    ICON5060.bmp)]^C^C^CATTREQ;0;-LAYER;M;FR_OFF;COLOR;3;;;INSERT;CHAIR;\;;
    \ATTREQ;1;-LAYER;SET;0;;
ID_CustomTable [_Button("Custom Chair", ICON665.bmp,
    ICON4474.bmp)]^C^C^CATTDIA;0;-LAYER;M;FR_OFF;COLOR;3;;;INSERT;CHAIR;\;;
    \\\\-LAYER;S;0;;ATTDIA;1


**OFFICE_FURNITURE
**TB_OFFICE_FURNITURE
                [_Toolbar("Office Furniture", _Floating, _Show,
200, 400, 0)]
ID_            [_Flyout("Computer", ICON8617.bmp, ICON_32_BLANK,
_OtherIcon, test.COMPUTER)]
ID__0          [_Flyout("Tables", ICON3090.bmp, ICON_32_BLANK,
_OtherIcon, test.TABLES)]
ID__1          [_Flyout("Chairs", ICON9328.bmp, ICON_32_BLANK,
_OtherIcon, test.CHAIRS)]
```

Make sure you save the *TEST.MNU* file. If you deleted the *TEST.MNS* file without copying the ***TOOLBARS section to the *TEST.MNU* file, you will lose the newly created toolbars. During the process of adding new toolbars, it is always recommended to copy the ***TOOLBARS sections to the *.MNU* file. Remember, if there is no *.MNS* file, AutoCAD creates it for you based on the *.MNU* template file.

You can manually insert the ***TOOLBARS section of code into your *TEST.MNU* file, but let AutoCAD do the job and then copy it into the *.MNU* template file. Let's examine, line by line, some of the unique features of the code in the ***TOOLBARS section of the *TEST.MNU* file.

***TOOLBARS

Defines the major section for toolbars.

`**COMPUTER`

Menu subsection.

`ID_Computer [_Toolbar("Computer", _Floating, _Show, 200, 100, 0)]`

`ID_Computer`

Tag name by which the item on the menu is referenced.

`_Toolbar`

Signifies that the menu is dealing with a toolbar definition.

`"Computer"`

Name that appears above the toolbar

`_Floating`

Indicates that the toolbar is floating and not docked. Possible values are _Top, _Bottom, _Left, _Right, or _Floating. The underscore character in front of the keywords is not required; however, it is used for the international versions of AutoCAD. The keywords are not case sensitive.

`_Show`

Visibility keyword, available options include _Show or _Hide

`200, 100, 0`

The first number is the distance in pixels from the left edge of the screen. The second number is the distance in pixels from the top edge. The final number is the number of rows in the toolbar.

`ID_Layers    [_Button("Standard`
`    Computer",ICON2580.bmp,ICON_32_-LAYERS)]macro`

`ID_Layers`

Tag name by which this item on the menu is referenced.

`_Button`

Signifies that the menu is dealing with a button definition.

`"Standard Computer"`

This is the tooltip text that is displayed when the mouse pointer passes over the button.

`ICON2580.bmp`

ID of the small-icon (16×16) bitmap.

`ICON_32_-LAYERS`

ID of the large-icon (32×32) bitmap.

`macro`

Command sequence required to complete the macro.

Customizing AutoCAD

Flyout Section of the Menu

```
**TB_OFFICE_FURNITURE
        [_Toolbar("Office Furniture", _Floating, _Show, 200, 400,
0)]
ID_    [_Flyout("Computer", ICON8617.bmp, ICON_32_BLANK, _OtherIcon,
test.COMPUTER)]
ID__0 [_Flyout("Tables", ICON3090.bmp, ICON_32_BLANK, _OtherIcon,
test.TABLES)]
ID__1 [_Flyout("Chairs", ICON9328.bmp, ICON_32_BLANK, _OtherIcon,
test.CHAIRS)]


  [_Toolbar("Office Furniture", _Floating, _Show, 200, 400, 0)]
```

The toolbar menu item is the same as for the toolbar description explained earlier.

```
ID_    [_Flyout("Computer", ICON8617.bmp, ICON_32_BLANK, _OtherIcon,
test.COMPUTER)]
```

   ID_

   Tag name by which the item on the menu is referenced.

   Flyout

   Signifies that the menu is dealing with a flyout definition.

   "Computer"

   Tooltip text that is displayed when the mouse pointer passes over the button.

   ICON8617.bmp

   ID of the small-icon (16×16) bitmap.

   ICON_32_BLANK

   ID of the large-icon (32×32) bitmap.

   _OtherIcon

   Has one of two possible values: _OtherIcon or _OwnIcon. The OtherIcon value allows the button to switch icons and displays the last icon selected. The OwnIcon value will not permit this switching.

Accelerator Keys

AutoCAD supports user-defined accelerator keys. Add the following major section (***ACCELERATORS) to the *TEST.MNU* file.

```
***ACCELERATORS
ID_Comps   [SHIFT+"F1"]
ID_Tables [SHIFT+"F2"]
```

```
ID_Chairs [SHIFT+"F3"]
ID_Lyr0   [SHIFT+"L"]
```

The first item is the name tag followed, in brackets, by the accelerator key combination. Type the keyboard combination (for example: Shift + F1), the menu item identified by ID_Comps will be executed. The accelerator key combination will not work if the menu is partially loaded as part of the *ACAD.MNU* file. Only when the menu is loaded in place of the AutoCAD menu will these key combinations work.

Apart from including macros, you can also include AutoLISP code in the menus (refer to Chapter 19) or have the menu macros load and run AutoLISP applications.

DIESEL

As mentioned earlier, a macro is a string of commands that AutoCAD executes when the menu item is selected. You can also add AutoLISP in a macro and call an AutoLISP routine from a macro. AutoCAD provides a macro language alternative to AutoLISP, called DIESEL. DIESEL is an acronym for Direct Interpretively Evaluated String Expression Language. The subject of DIESEL is beyond the scope of this book, but let's go through an example to see the application of DIESEL.

DIESEL allows you to customize the AutoCAD status line through the use of the MODEMACRO SETVAR variable, and it also allows modification of the appearance of pull-down menus. DIESEL, though a macro language and similar in style to AutoLISP, does not have the power and flexibility of AutoLISP.

The simplest use of DIESEL is through the MODEMACRO SETVAR variable. At the AutoCAD "Command": prompt type **MODEMACRO** and press Enter or the Spacebar. AutoCAD prompts:

New value for MODEMACRO, or . for none <"">: Captain CAD

Type in a text string as shown in this example and press Enter. AutoCAD displays the text string in the status bar, as shown in Figure 18–20.

To return to the default value, type **MODEMACRO** at the "Command:" prompt and press Enter or the Spacebar. Type in a single period to the prompt and press Enter or the Spacebar. The status bar returns to the default settings.

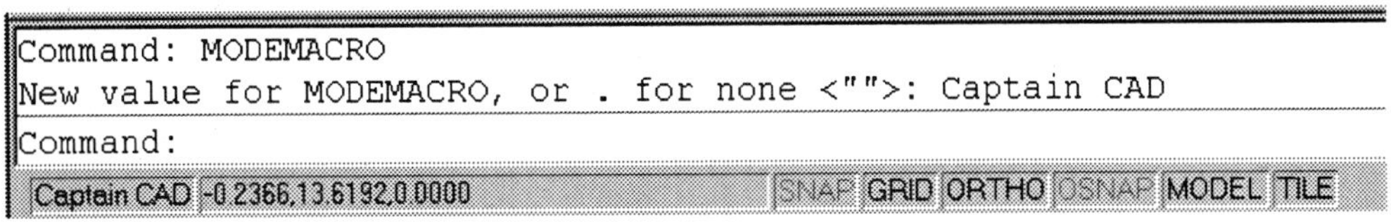

```
Command: MODEMACRO
New value for MODEMACRO, or . for none <"">: Captain CAD
Command:
```
Captain CAD -0.2366,13.6192,0.0000   SNAP GRID ORTHO OSNAP MODEL TILE

Figure 18–20 Display of the text string in the status bar

As another example, a string with arguments is provided in response to the MODEMACRO prompt:

```
New value for MODEMACRO, or . for none <"">:-LAYER =
$(getvar,clayer)
```

AutoCAD gets the current layer name and displays it in the status bar, as shown in Figure 18–21.

DIESEL expressions can also be placed as part of the menus.

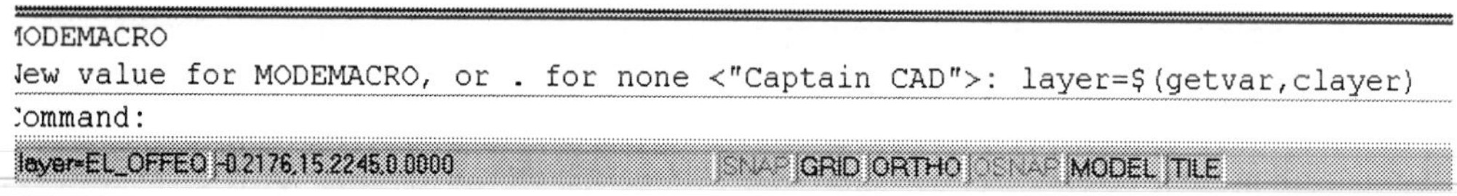

```
1ODEMACRO
Jew value for MODEMACRO, or . for none <"Captain CAD">: layer=$(getvar,clayer)
Command:
layer=EL_OFFEO -0.2176,15.2245,0.0000        SNAP GRID ORTHO OSNAP MODEL TILE
```

Figure 18–21 Display of the current layer name in the status bar

CUSTOMIZING TABLET MENUS

The previous descriptions and examples of menu customization can be applied to customizing the tablet menu area. One problem not encountered in a tablet menu is that of the display. The brackets that enclose nonactive items will not be visible except to someone who is reading the *filename.MNU* file from which the *filename.MNX* file was compiled.

The main concern in customizing the tablet part of the menu is in placing the programming lines in the right order and in the right area so they will correspond to the preprinted overlay that will be configured on the tablet for use with the menu.

A menu may have up to four tablet areas. They will have the headings ***TABLET1, ***TABLET2, ***TABLET3, and ***TABLET4. The first program line following a heading will correspond to the configured overlay's upper left column/row rectangle. Subsequent program lines will correspond the rectangle to the right in the same row as its predecessor until the end of the row is reached. Then the next program line will be on the extreme left rectangle of the next row. For example, a tablet menu area with 12 program lines might be in any one of the six following arrangements:

1	2	3	4	5	6	7	8	9	10	11	12

1	2	3	4	5	6
7	8	9	10	11	12

1	2	3	4
5	6	7	8
9	10	11	12

1	2	3
4	5	6
7	8	9
10	11	12

1	2
3	4
5	6
7	8
9	10
11	12

1
2
3
4
5
6
7
8
9
10
11
12

If there are more rectangles specified in the tablet configuration than there are program lines, the extras will be nonactive when picked. If there is an excess of program lines in the menu, they will, of course, not be accessible.

DIALOG CONTROL LANGUAGE

AutoCAD Release 12 introduced programmable dialog boxes, and this feature is continued in AutoCAD Release 14. Programming dialog boxes requires a thorough knowledge of AutoLISP and/or C/C++. The description of the dialog box is a text file known as a *DCL* (Dialog Control Language) file. The *DCL* file is a description of the various parts of the dialog and of the elements the dialog contains. The following is an example of a *DCL* file.

```
cesdoor : dialog
{
    label = "CESCO Doors";
    : row
    {
        : radio_cluster
        {
            key = "thick";
            : boxed_radio_column
            {
                label = "Thickness";
                : radio_button
                {
                    key = "t1";
                    label = "1\"";
                    value = "1";
                }
                : radio_button
                {
                    key = "t2";
                    label = "2\"";
                }
                : radio_button
                {
                    key = "t4";
                    label = "4\"";
                }
            }//boxed radio column - Thickness
        }//radio cluster - Thick
        : radio_cluster
        {
            key = "hinge";
            : boxed_radio_column
            {
                label = "Hinge";
                spacer;
                : radio_button
                {
                    key = "rt";
                    label = "Right";
```

```
            }
            : radio_button
            {
               key = "lt";
               label = "Left";
               value = "1";
            }
            spacer;
         }//boxed radio column - Hinge location
      }//radio_cluster - Hinge
}// row - top
: row
{
      : radio_cluster
      {
         key = "opng";
         : boxed_radio_column
         {
            label = "Open";
            width = 9;
            : radio_button
            {
               key = "in";
               label = "In";
            }
            : radio_button
            {
               key = "out";
               label = "Out";
               value = "1";
            }
         }//boxed radio column - Opening
      }//radio_cluster - opng
      : radio_cluster
      {
         key = "hand";
         : boxed_radio_column
         {
            label = "Handles";
            : radio_button
            {
               key = "hndl2";
               label = "2";
```

```
                value = "1";
            }
            : radio_button
            {
                key = "hnd13";
                label = "3";
            }
        }//boxed radio column - Number of handles
    }//radio_cluster - hand
}//row - 2nd row
spacer_1;
ok_cancel;
}
```

When AutoCAD is loaded into memory, it automatically loads two files: *ACAD.DCL* and *BASE.DCL*. These files contain various attributes on which you can build your dialogs. Each element (:radio_button, for example) contains a key (key = "hnd13"). These keys are the names to which AutoLISP and C/C++ refer in order to retrieve values from them and act upon them. Figure 18–22 shows a sample dialog box.

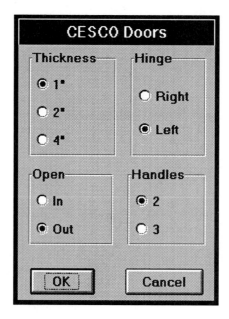

Figure 18–22 Sample dialog box

Selecting the OK button causes AutoLISP or C/C++ to read the various keys to determine which values the user selected and pass the results to the calling program. When writing programs that utilize dialog boxes, a certain portion of the code is dedicated to reading and responding to the dialog box (apart from the DCL file describing the dialog box itself). This provides the user with a more detailed view of all the inputs and can be used to limit the user inputs to the program. Dialog boxes can utilize radio buttons, toggle boxes, horizontal and vertical sliders, list boxes, edit boxes, buttons, image tiles, and more to enhance the front end to any program requiring user input.

A complete discussion of programming dialog boxes is beyond the scope of this book. Refer to AutoCAD's Customization Guide for more details.

EXERCISES

1. What extension must a file have when you are writing a custom menu?

2. How many menus may be active simultaneously?

3. What AutoCAD command sequence will activate a menu written as a file named *XYZ.MNU*?

4. Under the ***BUTTONS menu, which program line corresponds to the second button on the mouse/puck?

5. Placing three blank spaces in a menu program line is equivalent to what action from the keyboard?

6. What is the purpose of the caret (^) in a menu program line?

7. What is the purpose of the "^C" at the beginning of a menu program line?

8. Create a menu file to include a program line that will draw a rectangle whose opposite corners are points with coordinates 1,1 and 5,2.

9. Create a menu file to include a program line that will draw a circle of diameter 2 units and whose center point has the coordinates 3,3.

10. Create a menu file to include a program line that will array the circle in Exercise 9 in a polar array every 30 degrees, with the center of the array at a point whose coordinates are 4,3.

11. Create a menu file to include a program line that will permit a line-arc-line continuation starting at point 1,1, with user picks for the second, third, and fourth points.

12. Write lines that set UNITS as follows:

   a. Decimal to four-place display

   b. Architectural to 1/8" display

   c. Each of the above to include a mechanism to return to the graph screen

CUSTOMIZING HATCH PATTERNS

Certain concepts about hatch patterns should be understood before learning to create one.

1. Hatch patterns are made up of lines or line segment\space combinations. There are no circles or arcs available in hatch patterns like there are in shapes and fonts (which will be covered next).

2. A hatch pattern may be one or more series of repeated parallel lines or repeating dot or line segment/space combinations. That is, each line in one so-called family is like every other line in that same family. And each line has the same offset and stagger (if it is a segment/space combination), relative to its adjacent sibling, as every other line.

3. One hatch pattern can contain multiple families of lines. One family of lines may or may not be parallel to other families. With properly specified basepoints, offsets, staggers, segment/space combinations, lengths, and relative angles, you can create a hatch pattern from multiple families of segment/space combinations that will display repeated closed polygons.

4. Each family of lines is drawn with offsets and staggers based on its own specified basepoint and angle.

5. All families of lines in a particular hatch pattern will be located (basepoint), rotated, and scaled as a group. These factors (location, angle of rotation, and scale factor) are determined when the hatch pattern is loaded by the HATCH command and used to fill a closed polygon in a drawing.

6. The pattern usually can be achieved by different ways of specifying parameters.

Hatch patterns are created by including their definition in a file whose extension is *.PAT*. This can be done by using a line editor such as EDLIN (EDIT in DOS 6.xx) or a word processor in the nondocument (or programmer) mode, which will save the text in ASCII format. Your hatch pattern definition can also be added to the *ACAD.PAT* file. You can also create a new file specifically for a pattern.

Each pattern definition has one header line giving the pattern name/description and a separate specification line describing each family of lines in the pattern.

The header line has the following format:

```
*pattern-name[,description]
```

The pattern name will be the name for which you will be prompted when using the HATCH command. The description is optional and is there so someone reading the *.PAT* file can identify the pattern. The description has no effect, nor will it be displayed while using the HATCH command. The leading asterisk denotes the beginning of a hatch pattern.

The format for a line family is as follows:

```
angle, x-origin, y-origin, delta-x, delta-y [,dash-1, dash-2...]
```

The brackets "[]" denote optional segment/space specifications used for noncontinuous-line families. Note also that any text following a semicolon (;) is for comment only and will be ignored. In all definitions, the angle, origins, and deltas are mandatory (even if their values are zero).

An example of continuous lines that are rotated at 30 degrees and separated by 0.25 units is as follows (see Figure 18–23):

```
*P30, 30 degree continuous
30, 0,0, 0,.25
```

The 30 specifies the angle.

The first and second zero specify the coordinates of the origin.

The third zero, though required, is meaningless for continuous lines.

The 0.25 specifies the distance between lines.

A pattern of continuous lines crossing at 60 degrees to each other could be written as follows (see Figure 18–24):

```
*PX60,x-ing @ 60
30, 0,0, 0,.25
330, 0,0, 0,.25
```

A pattern of lines crossing at 90 degrees but having different offsets is as follows (see Figure 18–25):

```
*PX90, x-ing @ 90 w/ 2:1 rectangles
0, 0,0, 0,.25
90, 0,0, 0,.5
```

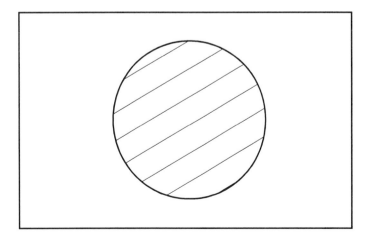

Figure 18–23 A hatch pattern with continuous lines rotated at 30 degrees and separated by 0.25 units

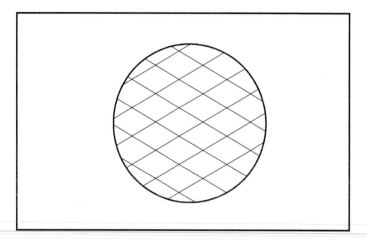

Figure 18–24 A hatch pattern with continuous lines crossing at 60 degrees to each other and separated by 0.25 units

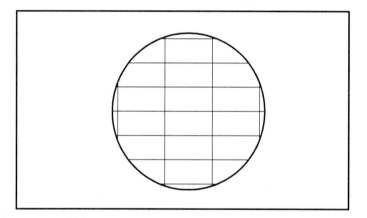

Figure 18–25 A hatch pattern with lines crossing at 90 degrees and having different offsets

Note the effect of the delta-Y. It is the amount of offset between lines in one family. Hatch patterns with continuous lines do not require a value (other than zero) for delta-X. Orthogonal continuous lines also do not require values for the X origin unless used in a pattern that includes broken lines.

To illustrate the use of a value for the Y origin, two parallel families of lines can be written to define a hatch pattern for steel as follows (see Figure 18–26):

```
*steel
45, 0,0, 0,1
45, 0,.25, 0,1
```

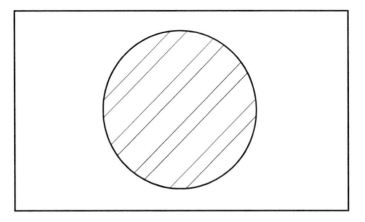

Figure 18–26 Defining a hatch pattern for steel

Three concepts are worthy of note in this example.

- If the families were not parallel, then specifying origins other than zero would serve no purpose.
- Parallel families of lines should have the same delta-Y offsets. Different offsets would serve little purpose.
- Most important, the delta-Y is at a right angle to the angle of rotation, but the Y origin is in the Y direction of the coordinate system. The steel pattern as written in the example would fill a polygon, as shown in Figure 18–27. Note the dimensions when used with no changes to the scale factor of 1.0 or rotation angle of zero.

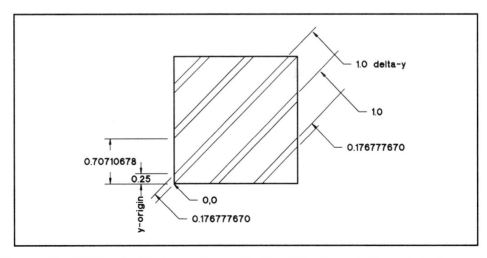

Figure 18–27 The steel hatch pattern with the delta-Y at a right angle to the angle of rotation and the Y origin in the Y direction of the coordinate system

Customizing AutoCAD

Custom Hatch Patterns and Trigonometry

The dimensions in the hatch pattern resulting from a 0.25 value for the delta-Y of the second line-family definition may not be what you expected, as shown in Figure 18–28. If you wished to have a 0.25 separation between the two line families (see Figure 18–29), then you must either know enough trigonometry/geometry to predict accurate results or else put an additional burden on the user to reply to prompts with the correct responses to achieve those results. For example, you could write the definition as follows:

```
*steel
0, 0,0, 0,1
0, 0,.25, 0,1
```

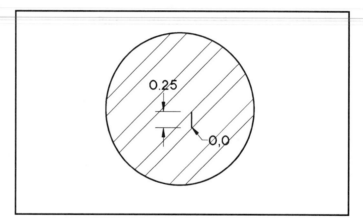

Figure 18–28 Hatch pattern dimensions resulting from a 0.25 value for the delta Y of the second line-family definition

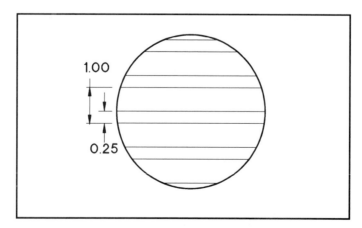

Figure 18–29 Steel hatch pattern defined with a 0.25 separation between the two line families

In order to use this pattern as shown, the user will have to specify a 45-degree rotation when using it. This will maintain the ratio of 1 to .25 between the offset (delta-*Y*) and the spacing between families (*Y* origin). However, if you wish to avoid this inconvenience to the user, but still wish to have the families separated by .25, you can write the definition as follows:

```
*steel
45, 0,0, 0,1
45, 0,.353553391, 0,1
```

The value for the *Y* origin of .353553391 was obtained by dividing .25 by the sine (or cosine) of 45 degrees, which is .70710678. The *X* origin and *Y* origin specify the coordinates of a point. Therefore, setting the origins of any family of continuous lines merely tells AutoCAD that the line must pass through that point. See Figure 18–30 for the trigonometry used.

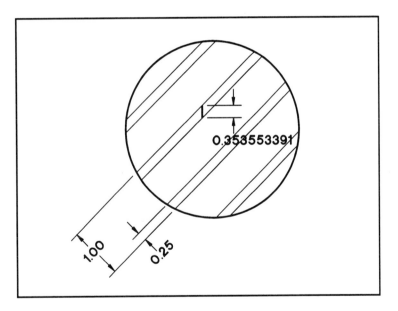

Figure 18–30 Steel hatch pattern defined with a 45 degree rotation to maintain a 1:25 offset ratio

For families of lines that have segment/space distances, the point determined by the origins can tell AutoCAD not only that the line passes through that point, but that one of the segments will begin at that point. A dashed pattern can be written as follows (see Figure 18–31):

```
*dashed
0, 0,0, 0,.25, .25,-.25
```

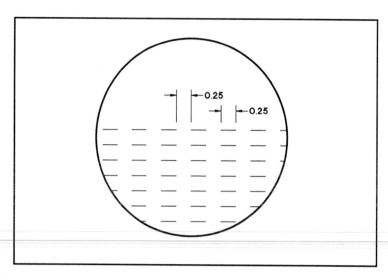

Figure 18–31 Writing a dashed pattern

Note that the value of the *X* origin is zero, thus causing the dashes of one line to line up with the dashes of other lines. Staggers can be produced by giving a value to the *X* origin as follows (see Figure 18–32):

```
*dashstagger
0, 0,0, .25,.25, .25,-.25
```

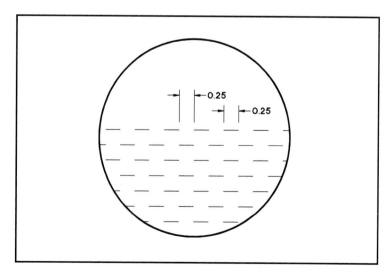

Figure 18–32 Writing a staggered dashed pattern

In a manner similar to defining linetypes, you can cause lines in a family to have several lengths of segments and spaces (see Figure 18–33).

```
*simple
0, 0,0, 0,.5
90, 0,0, 0,1, .5,-.5
```

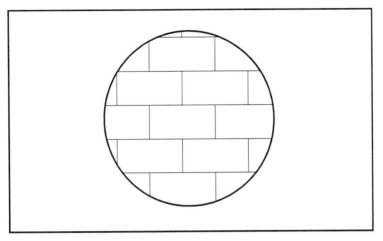

Figure 18–33 A pattern with several lengths of segments and spaces

A similar, but more complex hatch pattern could be written as follows (see Figure 18–34):

```
*complex
45, 0,0, 0,.5
-45, 0,0, 0,1.414213562, 0,1.41421356
```

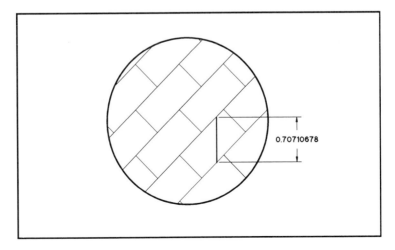

Figure 18–34 A pattern with more complex hatch patterns

Repeating Closed Polygons

Creating hatch patterns with closed polygons requires planning. For example, a pattern of 45/90/45-degree triangles, as shown in Figure 18–35, should be started by first extending the lines, as shown in Figure 18–35a. Extend the construction lines through points of the object parallel to other lines of the object. Note the grid that emerges when you use the lines and distances obtained to determine the pattern.

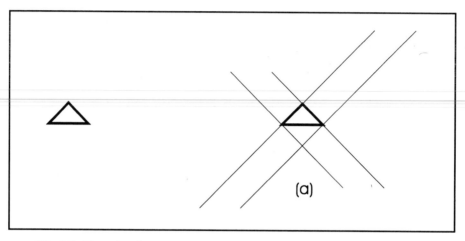

Figure 18–35 Closed polygons

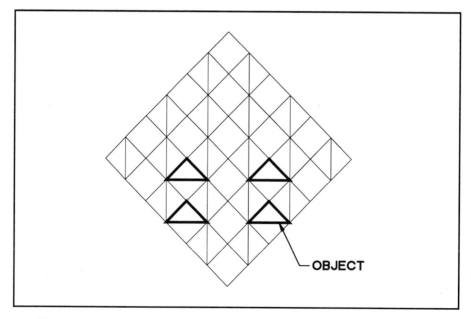

Figure 18–36 Creating triangular hatch patterns — method #1

It is also helpful to sketch construction lines that are perpendicular to the object lines. This will assist you in specifying segment/space values. In the example, two of the lines are perpendicular to one another, thus making this easier. Figures 18–36 through 18–39 illustrate potential patterns of triangles. Once the pattern is selected, the grid, and some knowledge of trigonometry, will assist you in specifying all of the values in the definition for each line family.

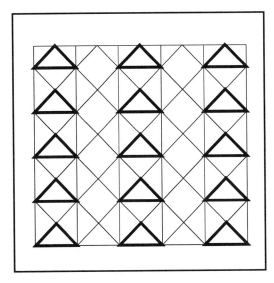

Figure 18–37 Creating triangular hatch patterns—method 2

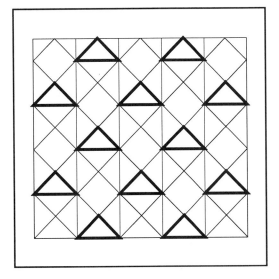

Figure 18–38 Creating triangular hatch patterns—method 3

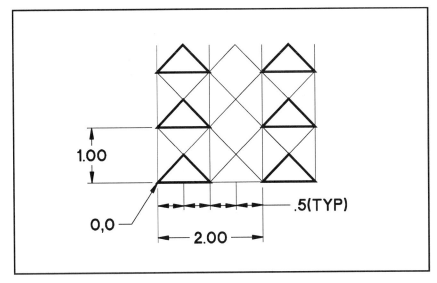

Figure 18–39 Creating triangular hatch patterns—method 4

For pattern PA the horizontal line families can be written as follows (see Figure 18–40):

```
0, 0,0, 0,1, 1,-1
```

The specifications for the 45-degree family of lines can be determined by using the following trigonometry:

```
sin 45 degrees = 0.70710678
S = 1
L = S times sin 45 degrees
L = 1 times sin 45 degrees = 0.70710678
```

Note that the trigonometry function is applied to the hypotenuse of the right triangle. In the example, the hypotenuse is 1 unit. A different value would simply produce a proportional result; i.e., a hypotenuse of .5 would produce $L = S \times 0.70710678 = 0.353553391$. The specifications for the 45-degree family of lines could be written as follows:

```
45, 0,0 0.70710678,0.70710678, 0.70710678,-2.121320343
angle,origin,offset,   stagger,              segment,       space
```

For the 135-degree family of lines, the offset, stagger, segment, and space have the same values (absolute) as for the 45-degree family. Only the angle, the X origin, and the sign (+ or –) of the offset or stagger may need to be changed.

The 135-degree family of lines could be written as follows:

```
135, 1,0,  -0.70710678,-0.70710678, 0.70710678,-2.121320343
```

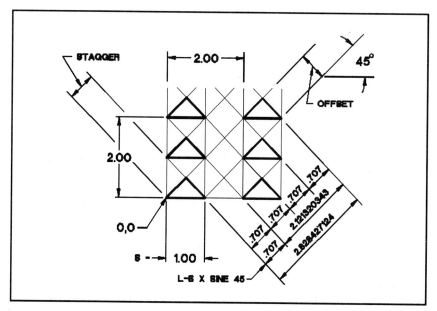

Figure 18–40 Triangular patterns

Putting the three families of lines together under a header could be written as follows, and as shown in Figure 18–41.

```
*PA,45/90/45 triangles stacked
0, 0,0, 0,1, 1,-1
45, 0,0 0.70710678,0.70710678, 0.70710678,-2.121320343
135, 1,0,  -0.70710678,-0.70710678, 0.70710678,-2.121320343
```

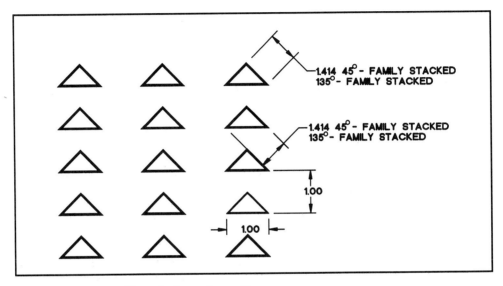

Figure 18–41 Families of triangular patterns

In the preceding statement, "could be written" tells you that there may be other ways to write the definitions. As an exercise, write the descriptions using 225 degrees instead of 45 degrees and 315 instead of 135 for the second and third families, respectively. As a hint, you determine the origin values of each family of lines from the standard coordinate system. But, to visualize the offset and stagger, orient the layout grid so that the rotation angle coincides with the zero angle of the coordinate system. Then the signs and the values of delta-X and delta-Y will be easier to establish along the standard plus for right/up and negatives for left/down directions. Examples of two hatch patterns, PB and HONEYCOMB, follow.

The PB pattern can be written as follows, and as shown in Figure 18–42.

```
*PB, 45/90/45 triangle staggered
0, 0,0, 1,1, 1,-1
45, 0,0, 0,1.414213562, 0.70710678,0.70710678
135, 0,0, 0,1.414213562, 0.70710678,0.70710678
```

Note that this alignment simplifies the definitions of the second and third families of lines over the PA pattern.

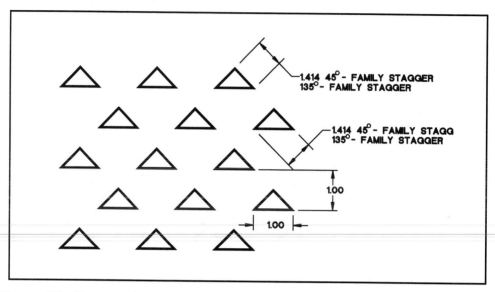

Figure 18–42 Example of the pattern

The HONEYCOMB pattern can be written as follows, and as shown in Figure 18–43.

```
*HONEYCOMB
90, 0,0, 0,1, 0.577350264,-1.154700538
330, 0,0, 0,1, 0.577350264,-1.154700538
30, 0.5,-0.288675135, 0,1, 0.577350264,-1.154700538
```

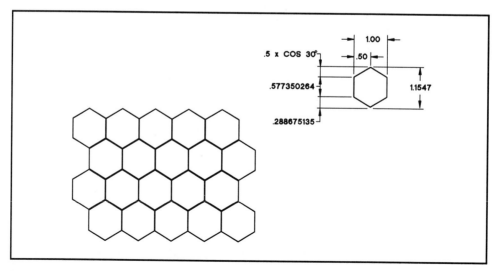

Figure 18–43 Example of the HONEYCOMB pattern

CUSTOMIZING SHAPES AND TEXT FONTS

Shapes and fonts are written in the same manner, and are both stored in files with the *.SHP* file extension. The *.SHP* files must be compiled into *.SHX* files. This section covers how to create and save *.SHP* files and how to compile *.SHP* files into *.SHX* files. To compile an *.SHP* file into an *.SHX* file for shapes or fonts, enter:

Command: **compile**

From the Select Shape File dialog box, select the file to be compiled. If the file has errors they will be reported; otherwise, you will be prompted:

Compilation successful
Output file name .SHX contains nnn bytes

The main difference between shapes and fonts is in the commands used to place them in a drawing. Shapes are drawn by using the SHAPE command, and fonts are drawn using commands that insert text, such as TEXT or DIM. Whether or not an object in an *.SHP/.SHX* file can be used with the SHAPE command or as a font character is partly determined by whether its shape name is written in uppercase or lowercase (explained herein).

Each shape or character in a font in an *.SHP* or *.SHX* file is made up of simplified objects. These objects are simplified lines, arcs, and circles. The reason they are referred to as simplified is because in specifying their directions and distances, you cannot use decimals or architectural units. You must use only integers or integer fractions. For example, if the line distance needs to be equal to 1 divided by the square root of 2 (or .7071068), the fraction 70 divided by 99 (which equals .707070707) is as close as you can get. Rather than call the simplified lines and arcs "objects," we will refer to them as "primitives."

Individual shapes (and font characters) are written and stored in ASCII format. *.SHP/.SHX* files may contain up to 255 SHAPE-CHARACTERS. Each SHAPE-CHARACTER definition has a header line, as follows:

```
*shape number, defbytes, shapename
```

The codes that describe the SHAPE-CHARACTER may take up one or more lines following the header. Most of the simple shapes can be written on one or two lines. The meaning of each item in the header is as follows:

The shape number may be from 1 to 255 with no duplications within one file.

Defbytes is the number of bytes used to define the individual SHAPE-CHARACTER, including the required zero that signals the end of a definition. The maximum allowable bytes in a SHAPE-CHARACTER definition is 2000. Defbytes (the bitcodes) in the definition are separated by commas. You may enclose pairs of bitcodes within parentheses for clarity of intent, but this does not affect the definition.

The *shapename* should be in uppercase if it is to be used by the SHAPE command. Like a block name is used in the BLOCK command, you enter the shapename when prompted to do so during the SHAPE command. If the shape is a character in a font file, you may make any or all of the shapename characters lowercase, thereby causing the name to be ignored when compiled and stored in memory. It will serve for reference only in the *.SHP* file for someone reading that file.

Pen Movement Distances and Directions

The specifications for pen movement distances and directions (whether the pen is up or down) for drawing the primitives that will make up a SHAPE-CHARACTER are written in bitcodes. Each bitcode is considered one defbyte. Codes 0 through 16 are not DISTANCE-DIRECTION codes, but special instructions-to-AutoCAD codes (to be explained shortly, after DISTANCE-DIRECTION codes).

DISTANCE-DIRECTION codes have three characters. They begin with a zero. The second character specifies distance. More specifically, it specifies vector length, which may be affected by a scale factor. Vector length and scale factor combine to determine actual distances. The third character specifies direction. There are 16 standard directions available through use of the DISTANCE-DIRECTION bitcode (or defbyte). Vectors 1 unit in length are shown in the 16 standard directions in Figure 18–44.

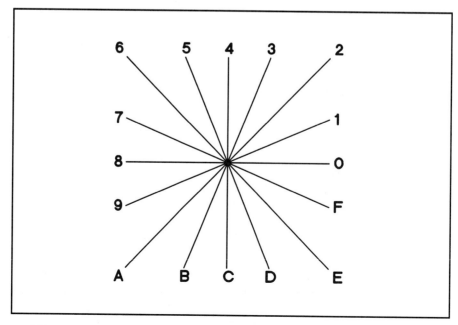

Figure 18–44 DISTANCE-DIRECTION bitcodes

Directions 0, 4, 8, and C are equivalent to the default 0, 90, 180, and 270 degrees, respectively. Directions 2, 6, A, and E are 45, 135, 225, and 315 degrees, respectively. But the odd-numbered direction codes are *not* increments of 22.5 degrees, as you might think. They are directions that coincide with a line whose delta-*X* and delta-*Y* ratio are 1 unit to 2 units. For example, the direction specified by code 1 is equivalent to drawing a line from 0,0 to 1,.5. This equates to approximately 26.56505118 degrees (or the arctangent of 0.5). The direction specified by code 3 equates to 63.434494882 degrees (or the arctangent of 2) and is the same as drawing a line from 0,0 to .5,1.

Distances specified will be measured on the nearest horizontal or vertical axis. For example, 1 unit in the 1 direction specifies a vector that will project 1 unit on the horizontal axis. Three units in the D direction will project 3 units on the vertical axis (downward). So the vector specified as 1 unit in the 1 direction will actually be 1.118033989 units long at an angle of 26.65606118 degrees, and the vector specified as 3 units in the D direction will be 3.354101967 units long at an angle of 296.5650512 degrees. See Figure 18-45 for examples of specifying direction.

To illustrate the codes specifying the DISTANCE-DIRECTION vector, the following example is a definition for a shape called "oddity" that will draw the shape shown in Figure 18-46.

```
*200,7,ODDITY
014,012,020,029,02C,016,0
```

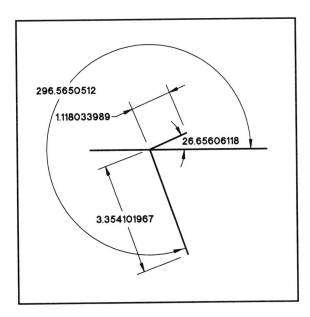

Figure 18-45 Specified distances

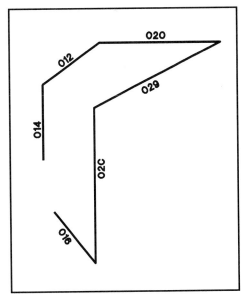

Figure 18-46 DISTANCE-DIRECTION vector specifying codes

To draw the shape named "oddity", you would first load the shape file that contains the definition and then use the SHAPE command as follows:

Command: **shape**
Name (or ?): **oddity**
Starting point: *(specify a point)*
Height <default>: *(specify a scale factor)*
Rotation angle <default>: *(specify a rotation angle)*

> **NOTE:** An alternative to the standard DISTANCE-DIRECTION codes is to use codes 8 and 9 to move the pen by paired (delta-X,delta-Y) ordinate displacements. This is explained next, in the section on "Special Codes".

Special Codes

Special codes can be written in decimal or hexadecimal. You can specify a special code as 0 through 16 or as 000 through 00E. A three-character defbyte with two leading zeros will be interpreted as a hexadecimal special code. A code 10 is a special code in decimal. However, 010 is equivalent to decimal 16. But more important, it will be interpreted by AutoCAD as a DISTANCE-DIRECTION code with a vector length of 1 and a direction of 0. The hexadecimal equivalent to 10 is 00A. The code functions are as follows.

Code 0: End of Shape The end of each separate shape definition must be marked with the code 0.

Codes 1 and 2: Pen Up and Down The "PEN DOWN" (or DRAW) mode is on at the beginning of each shape. Code 2 turns the DRAW mode off or lifts the pen. This permits moving the pen without drawing. Code 1 turns the DRAW mode on.

Note the relationship between the insertion point specified during the SHAPE command and where you wish the object and its primitives to be located. If you wish for AutoCAD to begin drawing a primitive in the shape at a point remote from the insertion point, then you must lift the pen with a code 2 and move the pen (with the proper codes) and then lower the pen with a code 1. Movement of the pen (directed by other codes) after a "PEN DOWN" code 1 is what causes AutoCAD to draw primitives in a shape.

Codes 3 and 4: Scale Factors Individual (and groups of) primitives within a shape can be increased or decreased in size by integer factors as follows: code 3 tells AutoCAD to divide the subsequent vectors by the number that immediately follows the code 3. Code 4 tells AutoCAD to multiply the subsequent vectors by the number that immediately follows the code 4.

CAUTION!

Scale factors are cumulative. The advantage of this is that you can specify a scale factor that is the quotient of two integers. A two-thirds scale factor can be achieved by a code 4 followed by a factor of 2 followed by a code 3 followed by a factor of 3. But, the effects of scale factor codes must be reversed when they are no longer needed. They do not go away by themselves. Therefore, at the end of the definition (or when you wish to return to normal or other scaling within the definition), the scale factor must be countered. For example, when you wish to return to the normal scale from a two-thirds scale, you must use code 3 followed by a factor of 3 followed by a code 4 followed by a factor of 2. There is no law that states you must always return to normal from a scaled mode. You can, with codes 3 and 4 and the correct factors, change from a two-thirds scale to a one-third scale for drawing additional primitives within the shape. You should *always*, however, return to the normal scale at the end of the definition. A scale factor in effect at the end of one shape will carry over to the next shape.

Codes 5 and 6: Saving and Recalling Locations Each location in a SHAPE definition is specified relative to a previous location. However, once the pen is at a particular location, you can store that location for later use within that SHAPE definition before moving on. This is handy when an object has several primitives starting or ending at the same location. For example, a wheel with spokes would be easier to define by using code 5 to store the center location, drawing a spoke, and then using code 6 to return to the center.

Storing and recalling locations are known as *pushing* and *popping* them, respectively, in a stack. The stack storage is limited to four locations at any one time. The order in which they are popped is the reverse of the order in which they were pushed. Every location pushed must be popped.

More pushes than pops will result in the following error message:

    Position stack overflow in shape nnn

More pops than pushes will result in the following error message:

    Position stack underflow in shape nnn

Code 7: Subshape One shape in an *.SHP/.SHX* file can be included in the definition of another shape in the same file by using the code 7 followed by the inserted shape's number.

Codes 8 and 9: X-Y Displacements Normal vector lengths range from 1 to 15 and can be drawn in one of the 16 standard directions unless you use a code 8 or code 9 to specify X-Y displacements. A code 8 tells AutoCAD to use the next two bytes as the X and Y displacements, respectively. For example, 8, (7,–8) tells AutoCAD to move the pen a distance that is 7 in the X direction and 8 in the Y direction. The parentheses are optional, for viewing effects only. After the displacement bytes, specifications revert to normal.

Code 9 Code 9 tells AutoCAD to use all following pairs of bytes as X-Y displacements until terminated by a pair of zeros. For example; 9,(7,–8),(14,9),(–17,3),(0,0) tells AutoCAD to use the three pairs of values for displacements for the current mode and then revert to normal after the (0,0) pair.

Code 00A: Octant Arc Code 00A (or 10) tells AutoCAD to use the next two bytes to define an arc. It is referred to as an octant (an increment of 45 degrees) arc. Octant arcs start and end on octant boundaries. Figure 18–47 shows the code numbers for the octants. The specification is written in the following format:

```
10, radius. (-)OSC
```

The radius may range from 1 to 255. The second byte begins with zero and specifies the direction by its sign (clockwise if negative, counterclockwise otherwise), the starting octant (S) and the number of octants it spans (C), which may be written as 0 to 7, with 0 being 8 (a full circle). Figure 18–48 shows an arc drawn with the following codes:

```
10,(2,-043)
```

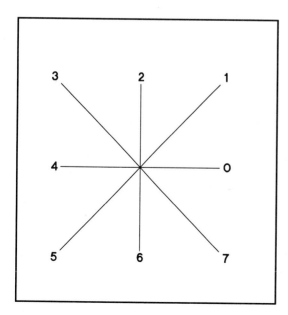

Figure 18–47 Code numbers for octants

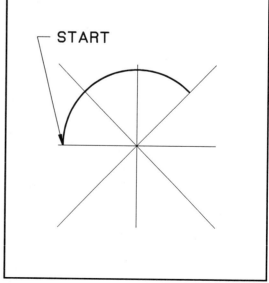

Figure 18–48 An arc drawn with code 10,(2, –043)

The arc has a radius of 2, begins at octant arc 4, and turns 135 degrees (3 octants) clockwise.

Code 00B: Fractional Arc Code 00B (11) can be used to specify an arc that begins and ends at points other than the octants. The definition is written as follows:

```
11,start-offset, end-offset, high-radius, low-radius, (-)0SC
```

Start and end offsets specify how far from an octant the arc starts and ends. The high-radius, if not zero, specifies a radius greater than 255. The low-radius is specified in the same manner as the radius in a code 10 arc, as are the starting octant and octants covering specifications in the last byte. The presence of the negative also signifies a clockwise direction.

The units of offset from an octant are a fraction of 1 degree times 45 divided by 256, or approximately .17578125 degrees. For example, if you wish to specify the starting value near 60 degrees, the equation would be:

```
offset = (60-45)*(256/45) = 85.333333
```

So the specification value would be 85.

To end the arc at 102 degrees, the equation would be:

```
offset = (102-90)*(256/45) = 68.2666667
```

So the specification value would be 68.

To draw an arc with a radius of 2 that starts near 60 degrees and ends near 102 degrees, the specifications would be as follows:

```
11,(85,68,0,2,012)
```

The last byte (012) specifies the starting octant to be 1 (45 degrees) and the ending octant to be 2 (90 degrees).

Codes 00C and 00D: Bulge-Specified Arc Codes 00C and 00D (12 and 13) are used to specify arcs in a different manner from octant codes. Codes 00C and 00D call out bulge factors to be applied to a vector displacement. The effect of using code 00C or 00D involves specifying the endpoints of a flexible line by the X-Y displacement method and then specifying the bulge. The bulge determines the distance from the straight line between the endpoints and the extreme point on the arc. The bulge can range from −127 to 127. The maximum/minimum values (127 or −127) define a 180-degree arc (half circle). Smaller values define proportionately smaller-degree arcs. That is, an arc specified some value, say x, will be x times 180 divided by 127 degrees. A bulge value of zero will define a straight line.

Code 00C precedes a single-bulge-defined arcs; 00D precedes multiple arcs. This is similar to the way codes 008 and 009 work on X-Y displacement lines. Code 00D, like 009, must be terminated by a 0,0 byte pair. You can specify a series of bulge arcs and lines without exiting the code 00D by using the zero bulge value for the lines.

Code 00E: Flag Vertical Text Command Code 00E (14) is only for dual-orientation text font descriptions, where a font might be used in either horizontal or vertical orientations. When code 00E is encountered in the SHAPE definition, the next code will be ignored if the text is horizontal.

Text Fonts

Text fonts are special SHAPE files written for use with AutoCAD TEXT drawing commands. The shape numbers should correspond to ASCII codes for characters. Table 18–1 shows the ASCII codes. Codes 1 through 31 are reserved for special control characters. Only code 10 (line feed) is used in AutoCAD. In order to be used as a font, the file must include a special shape number, 0, to describe the font. Its format is as follows:

```
*0,4,fontname
above, below, modes, 0
```

"Above" specifies the number of vector lengths that uppercase letters extend above the baseline, and "below" specifies the number of vector lengths that lowercase letters extend below the baseline. A modes byte value of zero (0) defines a horizontal (normal) mode, and a value of two (2) defines dual-orientation (horizontal or vertical). A value of 2 must be present in order for the special code 00E (14) to operate.

Standard AutoCAD fonts include special shape numbers 127, 128, and 129 for the degrees symbol, plus/minus symbol, and diameter dimensioning symbol, respectively.

The definition of a character from the *TXT.SHP* file is as follows:

```
*65,21,uca
2,14,8,(-2,-6),1,024,043,04D,02C,2,047,1,040,2,02E,14,8,(-4,
-3),0
```

Note that the number 65 corresponds to the ASCII character that is an uppercase "A." The name "uca" (for uppercase a) is in lowercase to avoid taking up memory. As an exercise, you can follow the defbytes to see how the character is drawn. The given character definition starts by lifting the pen. A font containing the alphanumeric characters must take into consideration the spaces between characters. This is done by having similar starting and stopping points based on each character's particular width.

CUSTOM LINETYPES

Linetype definitions are stored in files with an *.LIN* extension. Approximately 40 standard linetype definitions are stored for use in the *acad.lin* file. The definitions are in ASCII format and can be edited, or you can add new ones of your own by using either a text editor in the nondocument mode or the Create option of the

Table 18–1 ASCII Codes for Text Fonts

Code	Character	Code	Character	Code	Character
32	space	64	@	96	left apostrophe
33	!	65	A	97	a
34	" double quote	66	B	98	b
35	#	67	C	99	c
36	$	68	D	100	d
37	%	69	E	101	e
38	&	70	F	102	f
39	' apostrophe	71	G	103	g
40	(	72	H	104	h
41	)	73	I	105	i
42	*	74	J	106	j
43	+	75	K	107	k
44	, comma	76	L	108	l
45	- hyphen	77	M	109	m
46	. period	78	N	110	n
47	/	79	O	111	o
48	0	80	P	112	p
49	1	81	Q	113	q
50	2	82	R	114	r
51	3	83	S	115	s
52	4	84	T	116	t
53	5	85	U	117	u
54	6	86	V	118	v
55	7	87	W	119	w
56	8	88	X	120	x
57	9	89	Y	121	y
58	: colon	90	Z	122	z
59	; semicolon	91	[	123	{
60	<	92	\ backslash	124	| vertical bar
61	=	93	]	125	}
62	>	94	^ caret	126	~ tilde
63	?	95	_ underscore		

Codes 1 to 31 are for control characters, only one of which is used in AutoCAD text fonts.

LINETYPE command. Or you can save new or existing linetype definitions in another *filename.lin* file.

Simple linetypes consist of series of dashes, dots, and spaces. Their definitions are considered the in-line pen-up/pen-down type. Complex linetypes have repeating "out-of-line" objects, such as text and shapes, along with the optional in-line dashes, dots, and spaces. These are used in mapping/surveying drawings for such things as topography lines, fences, utilities, and many other descriptive lines. Instrumentation/control drawings also use many lines with repeating shapes to indicate graphically the purpose of each line.

Each linetype definition in a file comprises two lines. The first line must begin with an asterisk, followed by the linetype name and an optional description, in the following format:

```
*ltname,description
```

The second line gives the alignment and description by using proper codes and symbols, in the following format:

```
alignment,patdesc-1,patdesc-2,...
```

A simple linetype definition for two dashes and a dot, called DDD, could be written as follows:

```
*DDD,____  ____  .  ____  ____  .  ____  ____  .
A,.75,-.5,.75,-.5,0,-.5
```

The linetype name is DDD. A graphic description of underscores, spaces, and periods follow. The dashes are given as .75 in length (positive for pen down) separated by spaces -.5 in length (negative for pen up), with the 0 specifying a dot. No character other than the A should be entered for the alignment; it is the only one applicable at this time. This type of alignment causes the lines to begin and end with dashes (except for linetypes with dots only).

The complex linetype definitions include a descriptor (enclosed in square brackets) in addition to the alignment and dash/dot/space specification. A shape descriptor will include the shape name, shape file, and optional transform specification, as follows:

```
[shapename,filename,transform]
```

A text descriptor will include the actual text string (in quotes), the text style, and optional transform specification, as follows:

```
["string",textstyle,transform]
```

Transform specifications (if included) can be one or more of the following:

```
A=##     absolute rotation
R=##     relative rotation
```

```
S=##      scale
X=##      X offset
Y=##      Y offset
```

The ## for rotation is in decimal degrees (plus or minus), for scale and offset it is in decimal units.

The following example of an embedded shape in a line for an instrument air line (with repeating circles) could be written as follows:

```
*INSTRAIR, ____  [CIRC]  ____   [CIRC] ____
A,2.0,-.5,[CIRC,ctrls.shx],-.5
```

If the *ctrls.shx* file contains a proper shape description of the desired circle, it will be repeated in the broken line (with spaces on each side) when applied as the INSTRAIR linetype. If the scale of the circle needed to be doubled in order to have the proper appearance, it could be written as follows:

```
*INSTRAIR, ____  [CIRC]  ____   [CIRC] ____
A,2.0,-.5,[CIRC,ctrls.shx,S=2],-.5
```

The following example of an embedded text string in a line for a storm sewer (with repeating SS's) could be written as follows:

```
*STRMSWR,____   SS  ____   SS  ____
A,3.0,-1.0,["SS",simplex,S=1,R=0,X=0,Y=-0.125],-1.0
```

CUSTOMIZING AND PROGRAMMING LANGUAGE

There are various other topics with respect to the customization of AutoCAD, some of which are beyond the scope of this book. AutoCAD provides a programming language called AutoLISP (refer to Chapter 19). AutoLISP is a structured programming language similar in a number of ways to other programming languages. However, it is an interpreted language. Because it is an interpreted language, you can type an AutoLISP statement at the "Command:" prompt in AutoCAD and AutoCAD will execute it. AutoLISP code is created with a text editor. A compiled language (AutoCAD supports a number of these too) is first converted into object code (this is called compiling) or machine language and then linked with various other compiled object code modules (this is called linking) to form an executable file. The executable file is then loaded into memory and executed. C/C++ and ARx (AutoCAD Runtime Extension) are examples of compiled programming languages, and they require additional software to create their executable files.

Customizing AutoCAD

REVIEW QUESTIONS

1. The purpose of the ACAD.PGP file is to:
   a. allow other programs to be accessed while editing a drawing
   b. enable shape files to be complied
   c. store system configurations
   d. serve as a "file manager" for system variables
   e. none of the above

2. The standard AutoCAD screen menu:
   a. is stored in a file named ACAD.MNU
   b. can be viewed using the DOS TYPE command
   c. contains the screen menu items found in the AutoCAD screen menus
   d. all of the above

3. In an AutoCAD menu file, a semicolon contained in a menu item will tell the computer to:
   a. prompt the user for input
   b. press {ENTER}
   c. press {ctrl}
   d. ignore the rest of the line as a comment
   e. none of the above

4. AutoCAD menu files are stored with what type of file extension?
   a. DWG   d. MEN
   b. DXF   e. none of the above
   c. MNU

5. When developing screen menus, the information you would like to see displayed in the screen menus should be:
   a. typed in uppercase letters only
   b. enclosed with brackets "[]"
   c. longer than four characters, but shorter than ten characters
   d. all of the above

6. How many characters between brackets will display in a screen menu?
   a. 2   d. 8
   b. 4   e. 10
   c. 6

7. What symbology signifies the heading of a menu device such as a digitizer or table area?
   a. ****   c. **S
   b. ***   d. none of the above

8. What is the purpose of the backslash "\" in a menu line?
   a. Pause for user input
   b. Terminate a command
   c. press E
   d. none of the above

9. What file defines external commands and their parameters?
   a. ACAD.DWK
   b. ACAD.EXT
   c. ACAD.PGP
   d. ACAD.LSP
   e. ACAD.CMD

10. The system variable used in conjunction with DIESEL to modify the contents of status line is:
    a. STATUSLINE
    b. MACRO
    c. MODEMACRO
    d. MODESTATUS

11. AutoCAD allows you to create your own icons for use in toolbar menus.
    a. True
    b. False

12. To specify a cascade menu on a pulldown menu, you should use:
    a. \   c. ->
    b. >   d. #>

13. Command aliases are stored in what file?
    a. ACAD.INI   d. ACAD.MNU
    b. ACAD.ALS   e. none of the above
    c. ACAD.PGP

14. If you define a help string for a menu entry, it will display:
    a. On the status line
    b. as a small label by the icon
    c. if you invoke the help command
    d. at the command prompt
    e. none of the above

15. When creating a partial menu, the one entry which be included is:
    a. PARTIAL   d. MENU
    b. MENUGROUP   e. ENTRYNUMBER
    c. SECTION

16. Which of the following would not be a valid line is a definition of a custom crosshatching pattern?
    a. 0,0,1,0,1
    b. 90,1,0,1,0
    c. 180,0,0,1,1,-1,1
    d. 270,1,2,0,1,1,-1,0,-1
    e. 360,1,2,1,-1

17. The first line of a custom crosshatching definition always begins with:
    a. *   d. !
    b. **   e. !!
    c. ***

18. To define a custom linetype with three elements, a 1 unit dash, a 0.5 unit dash, and a dot, all separated by 0.25 unit spaces what would the definition look like:
    a. A,1,0.25,0.5,0.25,0
    b. A,1,.25,0.5,0.25,0,0.25
    c. A,1,-0.25,0.5,-0.25,0
    d. A,1,-0.25,0.5,-0.25,0,-0.25
    e. A,1,0.5,0,-0.25

19. The bit code which specifies a direction of 12 o'clock in a shape file is:
    a. 0   d. 12
    b. 4   e. C
    c. 8

20. When specifying the name of a shape character, in order to conserve memory you should:
    a. use upper-case
    b. use lower-case
    c. preface the name with an *
    d. use a short name
    e. it does not matter, all shape require the same amount of memory regardless of their name

19

AUTOLISP

•••••••••••••••••••••

INTRODUCTION

This chapter will cover the fundamental concepts of the AutoLISP programming language, including writing, storing, and loading *.LSP* files; variables
and expressions; lists; custom functions; and file handling.

After completing this chapter, you will be able to:

✓ Grasp fundamental concepts of the AutoLISP programming language
✓ Decipher program files written by others
✓ Establish a basis for more advanced programming

AUTOLISP BASICS

In Version 2.1 of AutoCAD (Release 6, May 1985), Autodesk first introduced
AutoLISP, its embedded programming language. It provided on-board computa-
tional power for the operator while in AutoCAD. It also permitted true programming routines to be used by way of menu devices, including interactive functions to
receive input from the operator in the form of keyboard entries and screen picks for
use in the routine. Version 2.18 (January 1986) included a full implementation of
user-defined functions and custom commands, which added a whole new world of
open architecture to AutoCAD (meaning you can customize the program to suit your
needs).

Loading AutoLISP Into Your Drawing

You do not have to learn how to write AutoLISP programs in order to be able to use them. AutoLISP programs are available from several sources. They are in the form of *filename.LSP* files. AutoCAD comes with program files that are ready to load and use in your drawing.

An AutoLISP file named *RECTANG.LSP* (which facilitates drawing a square or rectangle) can be loaded for use during the current editing session by means of the AutoLISP function called "load" as follows:

Command: **(load "rectang")**

> **NOTE:**
>
> 1. The use of the parentheses distinguishes AutoLISP functions and routines. This is especially important when using a function, such as "load," for which there is an AutoCAD command of the same name.
>
> 2. Do *not* include the *.LSP* extension. AutoCAD appends it automatically.
>
> 3. You may also specify a path if necessary. For example, if the *RECTANG.LSP* file is on the A: drive in a directory called Lisp, the following response can be used:
>
> Command: **(load "a:/lisp/rectang")**
>
> Notice the use of the nonstandard forward slashes to specify the directory path.

Expressions and Variables

Expressions in AutoLISP should be understood before getting into variables. The simplest application of AutoLISP is to evaluate an equation by just typing it in and pressing ⌷Enter⌷. Of course, you must enter the equation in the proper format, which is somewhat different from ordinary algebraic notation. It involves a format that is unique among those used in other, more popular computer programming languages. For example, if you wish to add 5 and 3, simply enter the following expression:

Command: **(+ 5 3)**

The integer 8 will be displayed in the prompt area. That is, AutoLISP evaluates the expression and returns the integer 8. Throughout this chapter, the word *return* will be used to describe the result of an evaluation. The following expression returns the integer 108:

Command: **(+ 5 3 1 99)**

NOTE:

1. When AutoCAD sees an open parenthesis (unless responding to a prompt to enter text), it knows that it is entering an AutoLISP expression to be evaluated. The AutoLISP evaluator remains in effect until it encounters the closing parenthesis that is the mate of the first open parenthesis.

2. AutoLISP uses prefix notation, which means that expressions begin with the operator (after the opening parenthesis, of course). In the preceding examples, the plus sign (+) is the arithmetic operator. The *operator* tells AutoLISP what operation to perform on the items that follow. The items that follow the operator are known as the *arguments*.

3. As you can see by the second example, the plus operator can have more than the usual two arguments to which an algebraic plus sign is restricted.

4. Elements in an AutoLISP expression are separated by one or more spaces. Multiple adjoining spaces (unlike spaces in a menu line) are considered one space in an AutoLISP routine.

Variables as Symbols and Symbols that Should Not Vary   Just as algebra uses letter names for the unknown-at-the-time values in an equation, AutoLISP utilizes symbols as variables, whose name you may select during the writing of the program. In algebra, for example, a sequence might be written as follows:

Algebra	**AutoLISP**
$a = 3$	(setq a 3)
$b = 7$	(setq b 7)
therefore	
$a + b = 10$	(+ a b) returns 10
and	
$ab = 21$	(* a b) returns 21

Assigning Names   There are three situationss for assigning names:

Expressions: for example, pi is the name for 3.14159. . .

Variables: A variable is an expression whose value is not known when originally written into the program. Variables will take on some value after the program has been called into use. The value of the variable is usually determined by some operation on some other value that the user has been prompted to enter while the program is in progress.

Custom-Defined Functions: AutoCAD permits users to create and name a customized function and then to use it in AutoCAD in a manner similar to a standard AutoCAD command.

Terminology And Fundamental Concepts

Lists, operators, arguments, types, parentheses, the exclamation point, and the concept of the function-list comprise the basis of AutoLISP.

Lists Practically everything in AutoLISP is a list of one sort or another. Functions are usually represented as a list of expressions enclosed in parentheses. For example, (+ 1 2.0) is an AutoLISP function with three elements in it, the "+," the "1," and the "2.0." Other lists can be established by applying a function called list or by applying the single quote, as in '(1 2 3.0 a "b").

Operators and Arguments Arguments are those items in a function-list on which the operator operates. For example, in the function-list (+ 1 2), the operator is (+) and the arguments are "1" and "2."

Types Arguments are classified by their type. The arguments in the example (+ 1 2) are of the type called integer. In the function-list (+ 1.0 2.0), the arguments are of the type called real, signifying a real number.

Parentheses The primary mechanisms for entering and leaving AutoLISP and entering expressions within AutoLISP are the open and close parentheses.

CAUTION!

For every open parenthesis [(] there must be a close parenthesis [).] If AutoCAD encounters a condition where the close parentheses are one fewer than the open ones, the prompt will display the following:

1>

Most often this is caused by the need for one close parenthesis. A display of 3> could indicate the need for three close parentheses. The problem is usually remedied by just entering the specified number of close parentheses. This type of error message can also be caused by having an odd number of double quotation marks inside of an AutoLISP expression, in which case one double quotation mark must be entered, followed by the required number of close parentheses, in order to eliminate the error message in the prompt area. Further examination will usually reveal that the program line needs to be corrected to prevent the message from recurring.

Exclamation Point A leading exclamation point in response to a prompt is another mechanism for entering AutoLISP. This tells AutoCAD that the symbol that follows the exclamation point is an AutoLISP variable that has been set equal to some value and that AutoCAD should use the value of the variable as a response to the prompt.

The terms and concepts just described are explained in detail, with examples, in the sections that follow.

Functions The first function-list to be introduced involves three expressions: the operator SETQ, the variable that we have arbitrarily named x and the real number 2.5. Within this function SETQ will perform a special operation on the variable x and the real number 2.5. SETQ is probably the most common AutoLISP function. It means "set equal." Using SETQ as the first of three expressions will set the second expression equal to the third. We are accustomed to performing this operation by the conventional expression $x = 2.5$. But as you will see in the next example, in order to write $x = 2.5$ in AutoLISP you must write in a special format: SET x EQUAL 2.5. It is done by writing three expressions in parentheses, with the first being the operator SETQ, the second being x, and the third being the value to which the variable named x is to be equal, for example:

Command: **(setq x 2.5)**

Having $x = 2.5$, or, more properly, to have SET x EQUAL 2.5, is necessary only if you wish to use the value of the real number 2.5 later by just entering its name x. If, earlier, you have entered (setq x 2.5) at the "Command:" prompt, then any time during that current editing session you could re-enter AutoLISP right from the keyboard by using ! before the name of the value in response to a prompt for some real number. If the prompt is asking for a name of something (like a layer name, which requires responding with something called a *string variable*), then trying to use a variable that has been set equal to a real number will cause an error message. The use of ! is another way to enter AutoLISP directly from the keyboard or in a string of custom menu commands and responses.

For example, if you create a unit block named UB and wish to Insert it with a scale factor of 2.5, the sequence of prompts and responses would be as follows:

Command: **insert**
Block name (or ?): **ub**
Insertion point: *(pick an insertion point)*
X scale factor <1> / Corner / XYZ: **!x**

Note at this point that the use of the name x and the fact that it is being applied to the X scale is purely coincidental.

By using the ! in front of the x, you will have the value of x (or 2.5 in this case) used as a response to the prompt asking for the X scale.

AutoLISP

This example is not very efficient. Entering **!x** *appears* to take only two keystrokes, whereas entering **2.5** takes three. True, this would save a keystroke. But because entering the exclamation point requires the shift key, it is a double stroke requiring both hands. Along with the *x* it is actually less convenient than entering 2.5, which has three one-hand strokes. Additionally, the characters "2," ".," and "5" are all accessible on the AutoCAD tablet overlay, while the ! is not. Entering 2.5 will, however, give the same accuracy as entering 2.50000000000000.

> **NOTE:** If *x* has not previously been set equal to a value, then entering **!x** will return "nil." Believe it or not, advanced programming does make use of the nil. Normally, variables and expressions retain their names and values only during the current editing session. The names are lost when a drawing is ended. At the beginning of each session they must be re-established. But even this problem of saving variable values from one session to another can be addressed by a custom program.

Naming and SETQING the Value of an Expression Suppose the value you wish to enter is 1 divided by the square root of 2. This could be written as 0.7071068 depending on the accuracy desired. Now compare three keystrokes using AutoLISP versus 9 or 10 from the keyboard or tablet. Not only will a variable having a short name (and having been set equal to that value) save time in entering, but it will decrease the probability of errors in both reading and keying-in a long string of characters, for example:

Command: **(setq x 0.7071068)**

If the value 0.7071068 is needed in response to a prompt, simply enter **!x**. Programming begins to appear both expedient and practical.

> ### CAUTION!
> You may respond with .7071068 outside AutoLISP, but while in AutoLISP you must use some value (even if zero) on both sides of the decimal point. Expressions beginning or ending with a dot (.) have another special meaning.

Before leaving this example, additional power of AutoLISP can be seen in a demonstration of using an expression within an expression within an expression. Two other AutoLISP operators will be introduced at this time. They are the SQRT and the "/" functions. SQRT returns the square root of the argument following (it must be only one argument and must be a nonnegative real number). The "/"

function requires two arguments and returns the quotient of the first divided by the second, for example, the following returns 1.414213562373...

Command: **(setq y (sqrt 2))**

You may now use this value as follows:

Command: **(sqrt 2)**

This does two things. It sets *y* equal to the expression that follows, which is the square root of 2, and returns 1.414213562.

Having entered this, you may operate on *y* as follows:

Command: **(/ 1.0 y)**

This expression will return the quotient of 1 divided by the value of y, which was previously set equal to the square root of 2. Therefore, the expression evaluates to 0.7071068.

Using an AutoLISP function in this fashion neither sets values nor gives them names. It is of little use later but does return (display in the prompt area) the result of the prescribed computation for immediate viewing. Sometimes this is handier than picking up a hand-held calculator.

A two-step use of AutoLISP could be written as follows:

Command: **(setq y (sqrt 2))**
Command: **(setq x (/ 1 y))**

The first step sets *y* equal to the square root of 2. The second step sets *x* equal to the inner expression, which uses the "/" operator (for division) and returns the value of 1 divided by the value of *y*. This two-step sequence involves four operators (SQRT, /, and SETQ twice). It names y and sets it equal to the square root of 2. It names *x* and sets it equal to the reciprocal of *y*.

Instead of this two-step routine, a simpler one-step routine is as follows:

Command: **(setq x (/ 1 (sqrt 2)))**

So in one step you can name an expression *x* and set it equal to the reciprocal of the square root of 2. It allows you then to respond to any prompt for a real number and apply this value by simply entering **!x**. This saves time and ensures accuracy to 14 decimal places, which is what CAD is all about in the first place—speed and accuracy.

AutoLISP

Example

At the "Command:" prompt enter the following expression:

Command: **(setq a 1 b 2 c 99 d pi e 2.5)**

This expression is a function-list using the operator SETQ. Note the opening and closing parentheses that distinguish it as an individual expression. Unlike the (+ . . .) function that performs a single operation of as many Arguments as you wish to furnish, the (setq . . .) must have pairs of Arguments. SETQ operates on each pair of Arguments individually. After entering the preceding, you can have AutoLISP evaluate equations by entering them as follows:

Command: **(setq x (+ a b))** *(returns 3)*
Command: **(setq y (- a c))** *(returns -98)*
Command: **(setq z (* b d))** *(returns 6.283185308)*
Command: **(setq q (/ c e))** *(returns 39.6)*

Perform the following exercise:

Name and give values to variables corresponding to the following algebraic equations:

$a = 4$
$b = 7$
$c = a \times b$
$d = b^2$ *(with 2 as exponent)*
$e = \sqrt{a^2 + b^2}$ *(square root of a-squared plus b-squared)*

Exercises from the Keyboard

Line After first drawing a random line (with the Snap mode off), establish variables for the points p1 and p2 as follows (see Figure 19–1). Type in **(setq p1 (getpoint))**. Use the Osnap mode Endpoint to pick one end of the line. Type in **(setq p2 (getpoint)),** and use the Osnap mode Endpoint to pick the other endpoint of the line. Do not be alarmed that the prompt area is blank. When the points have been returned, record the X and Y coordinates on paper for use in the following exercises. For example, if (1.2345 6.7890 0.0000) is returned for p1, enter the following:

Command: **(setq X1 1.2345)** *(returns 1.2345)*
Command: **(setq Y1 6.7890)** *(returns 6.7890)*

> **NOTE:** Enter the numbers you obtain, not the 1,2345 and 6,789 from the example!

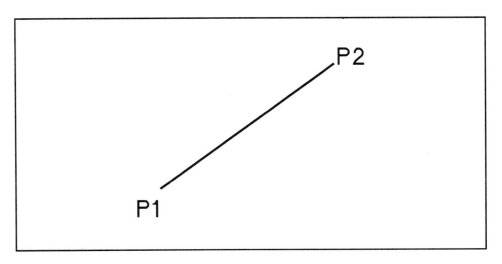

Figure 19–1 The line for writing a routine

Write in from the keyboard routines to perform the following:

1. Set dx equal to the horizontal distance between p1 and p2.
2. Set dy equal to the vertical distance between p1 and p2.
3. Set d equal to the distance between p1 and p2.
4. Set a equal to the angle between p1 and p2 in radians.

Circle After first drawing a random circle (with the Snap mode off), set variables to the center c of the circle and to one point p on the circle (see Figure 19–2). Write routines to perform the following:

1. Set r equal to the radius of the circle.
2. Set d equal to the diameter of the circle.
3. Set p equal to the perimeter of the circle.
4. Set a equal to the area of the circle.

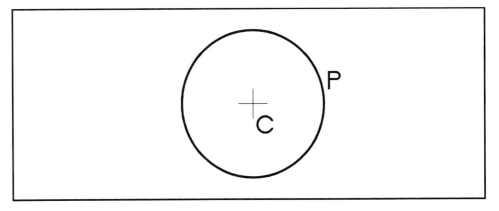

Figure 19–2 The circle for writing a routine

Arc Establish endpoints p1 and p2 and the center *c* of the arc (see Figure 19–3) as in the exercises. Write routines to perform the following:

1. Set *r* equal to the radius of the arc.
2. Set *lc* equal to the chord length of the arc.
3. *(A doozie)* Set *la* equal to the arc length of the arc.

Computation Write routines to perform the following (see Figure 19–4):

1. Given *a* = 1 and *b* = 2, find *c*.
2. Given *b* = 2 and *c* = 3, find *a*.
3. Find the area of the triangle for question 1.
4. Find the area of the triangle for question 2.

According to Ben Shneiderman in his preface to Dan Friedman's *The Little LISPer,* "The fundamental structure of the LISP programming language was derived from the abstract notions of lambda calculus and recursive function theory by John McCarthy. His goal was to produce a programming language with a powerful notation for defining and transforming functions. Instead of operating on numeric quantities, LISP was designed to manipulate abstract symbols, called atoms, and combinations of symbols, called lists. The expressive power was recognized by a small number of researchers who were primarily concerned with difficult symbolic manipulation problems in artificial intelligence."

Translating an algebraic word problem into a true algebraic expression demands a certain symbol classification and list processing also. Many algebra students who can learn how to solve an algebraic expression (or at least memorize the procedures) once it is in the proper structure reach a complete impasse when asked to "interpret" the word problem into that proper structure.

Words in a sentence or paragraph have characteristics similar to AutoLISP functions or expressions. Verbs act on subjects like subroutines act on variables and expressions. The conjunction *and* joins phrases like the "+" joins real numbers. A phrase like *out of here* has the subphrase *of here* in it.

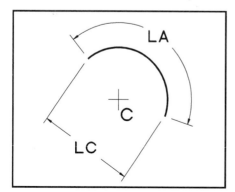

Figure 19–3 The arc for writing a routine

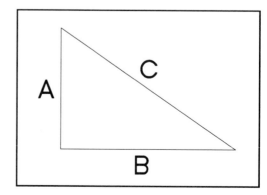

Figure 19–4 The triangle for writing a routine

LISTS

Types of Arguments

Although an argument is defined, in part, by *The American Heritage Dictionary* as "A quarrel; contention," it also is defined under the heading of math as "The independent variable of a function." The AutoCAD Programmer's Reference consistently describes the variables on whose value the function value depends as arguments.

The List in AutoLISP Is an Argument   When is a list not a list? As mentioned earlier, almost every function in AutoLISP is some form of a list.The AutoLISP interpreter operates on lists as they occur in a routine or program. The AutoLISP expression (setq x (/ 1 (sqrt 2))) is a list. To the AutoCAD lisp interpreter it is a list to be evaluated according to the operator SETQ. Likewise, (/ 1 (sqrt 2)) and (sqrt 2) are a sublist and subsublist, respectively, to be evaluated. But none of these would be considered as the type of defined list (known as list to the type function) that some of the AutoLISP function-lists, like (CAR <list>), normally require as their argument. The lists that are acceptable arguments to these certain functions might be looked upon as special lists within lists. They must take on a special format in order to satisfy the main function-list as the required argument(s).

AutoLISP function-lists that require lists as one of their arguments include the CAR, CADR, LAST, LENGTH, NTH, and REVERSE functions.

Whenever an AutoLISP function-list requires a list as one of its arguments, you must use one of the following procedures:

1. You may use the function-list that has as its operator the function called list. This function-list is written in the format (list <expr>...) as described in the AutoCAD Programmer's Reference. Typing in **(list 1.0 2.0)** will return (1.000000 2.000000). But more importantly, it will satisfy the requirements of this special list when needed for data input. Other function-lists (such as the one with the operator SQRT) most likely will *not* satisfy the special requirement of an argument that must be of the type called list.

2. If you must respond within AutoLISP with the special form of list required, writing **(list 1.0 2.0)** every time becomes laborious (like writing 3.14159 and so forth when the use of pi will do). Therefore, it is convenient to use the SETQ function and write:

(setq p (list 1.0 2.0))

The name *p* is strictly arbitrary in this case. Any unique variable name you want to use will suffice. Then whenever your routine requires you to respond with a point whose *X* and *Y* coordinates are 1.0 and 2.0, respectively, you can respond with *p* within AutoLISP or **!p** directly from the keyboard while in AutoCAD.

Try this exercise for an illustration of the preceding: The default limits of 0,0 and 12,9 as in the *ACAD.DWG* file will be helpful. Type in at the "Command:" prompt the following:

> Command:(setq p (list 1.0 2.0)) *((1.000000 2.000000) will be displayed)*
> Command: line
> From point: (list 6.0 7.0)
> To point: !p

Creating a List

As explained earlier in this chapter, the (list <expr>...) function-list is often used under restrictive conditions. For example, using it as a response to certain commands requiring a 2D point, the "<expr>..." part of the overall expression must be "<expr> <expr>," where both <expr>'s are real numbers.

Remember that an integer can be entered in AutoLISP and that AutoCAD will translate it into a real number under certain conditions. For a 3D point, the form of the response must be "<expr> <expr> <expr>." Using "<real> <real>," "<real> <int>," or "<int> <int>" may be considered as proper responses to a prompt for the starting point of a 2D line. This coincides with the type of entry required for a point even while *not* in AutoLISP.

For example, the following are considered appropriate while in AutoCAD:

> Command: line
> From point: 1.5, .7081068
>   *or*
> From point: 3.1415, 5
>   *or*
> From point: 1, 1

A similar mixture of reals and integers is evident in the following example from within AutoLISP:

> Command: line
> From point: (list 1.5 0.7071068)
>   *or*
> From point: (list pi 5)
>   *or*
> From point: (list 1 1)

Note two subtle differences (not the parentheses, because they are not subtle): (1) From within AutoLISP, any real number must begin with an integer, *not* a decimal point. (2) The two expressions comprising the list within each function are separated by a space, as in the last examples (within AutoLISP), instead of a comma, as in the first examples (not in AutoLISP).

A List That Doesn't Look Like a List Once a symbol (name of your choice) has been SETQed (set equal) to a list by the (setq <sym> (list <expr> <expr>...)) function, then that symbol becomes a defined list. It will evaluate to that (<expr> <expr>...) for use as a response within AutoLISP or out of AutoLISP by using the ! prefix. For example, entering **(setq p1 (list 2.0 3.0))** returns (2.0000 3.0000). Using the type command, as in entering **(type p1)**, will return "list." It will work for the following response to the LINE command:

   From point: **!p1**

But if **(setq p1 (list 2.0 "z"))** has been entered as the prior routine instead of (setq p1 (list 2.0 3.0)), the preceding sequence will *not* accept !p1 as a valid response, even though (type p1) still returns "list." Its argument, (<expr> <expr>..), as a list is not (<real> <real>..), as points require.

Before you even considered programming in AutoLISP, you were using lists. If, in response to the "From point:" prompt, you entered **2,3.75** from the keyboard (or any form of "real,real," "real,integer," or "integer, integer") then you used a list. Even if you had entered **x1,2.5** or **3,y,** you would have been using a list. But you would have found out that even though it was in a similar format, the elements of the entry were not of the proper classification. Once you understood that AutoCAD rejected anything except certain classifications of elements, you learned to work using that knowledge (or went back to the drawing board, literally!).

A disguised use of the list input is when you specify a point on the screen. AutoCAD defines that specification as a list in the proper format, (*X* coordinate, *Y* coordinate), and enters it for you. It is a list in the acceptable format.

Association List The following is a list, but it is a very special list:

   ((a 097) (b 098) (c 099) (d 100)...(x 120) (y 121) (z 122))

Each expression in the list similarly has two expressions enclosed in parentheses (making each of them a list), with the first being a lowercase letter and the second being an integer.

What makes the last list special is that it satisfies the requirements of an association list. It may be used (like other qualified association lists) as an argument in the AutoLISP function ASSOC. It takes the form (assoc <item> <alist>).

EXERCISES

Determine if the following evaluation results below satisfy the requirements of the expression of the type list. If not, explain why.

a. 1 , 2
b. 1 2
c. (12)
d. (1 2)
e. (1.0 2)
f. (1.0 2.0)
g. ((1 2))
h. ((1 2)
i. (1 .2)
j. (1.0 0.2)
k. (1.0 2.0 3.0 x)
l. (1.0 2.0x3.0)
m. (* 2 4)
n. (-2 -4)

PAUSING FOR USER INPUT

There are very few AutoCAD commands that begin and end just by entering the command name. Except for END, REGEN, REDRAW, OOPS, UNDO, and the like, most commands pause for user input before they are completed. You can include this interactive capability in your AutoLISP routines through several input functions. The exercises in this section will introduce two such functions, (getpoint) and (getreal). The (getpoint) function pauses for input of a point (either from the keyboard or on screen) and returns that point in the form of a list of two reals. The (getreal) function pauses for user input of a real number and returns that real number.

AutoLISP Functions — The COMMAND Function

The function-list (command <args>...) provides a method of invoking an AutoCAD command from within AutoLISP. It is usually the culmination of the routine. The <args> are written in the same sequence as if entered from the keyboard from AutoCAD. The AutoCAD command name that follows the (command ...) function must be enclosed in quotation marks, as in the following example:

```
(setq p1 (list 1.0 1.0))
(setq p2 (list 2.0 2.75))
(command "line" p1 p2 "")
```

When included in an AutoLISP routine, this sequence will draw a line from 1,1 to 2,2.75.

Note that the double-double quotation mark is the equivalent of pressing [Enter] while in AutoLISP. It is referred to as the null string (""). It simulates pressing the Spacebar.

In the (command ...) function-list, the arguments that are AutoCAD entries are enclosed within quotation marks, while AutoLISP symbols and expressions are *not*. One of the notable differences is illustrated in responding to a prompt for an angle. Remember, AutoLISP requires radians, whereas AutoCAD normally uses degrees (unless the units are set for angle input to be in radians). For this illustration, certain symbols were named and SETQed to values, as shown here:

```
(setq ublkname "UB1")
(setq inspt (list 2.0 2.0))
(setq xscal 2.5)
(setq yscal 2.5)
(setq ang 90)
```

Then a routine could be written in two different ways with the same results, as follows:

```
(command "insert" ublkname inspt xscal yscal ang)
```

or

```
(command "insert" "UB1" "2,2" "2.5" "" "90")
```

Although angular responses to normal AutoLISP functions must be in radians, this is an angular response while temporarily back in the AutoCAD screen and therefore must be 90, for degrees.

The first program line uses AutoLISP symbols as responses to the INSERT command that the (command ...) function invoked. The second line uses AutoCAD equivalents of the same responses. In the latter, the responses must be enclosed within quotation marks. This use of the quotation marks is different from their use to mark characters as a string type of argument in function-lists other than the (command ...) function.

Two subtle lessons can be gleaned from the foregoing:

- The use of quotation marks returns you to AutoCAD types of responses.
- The double-double quotation marks (null string) is used to cause the *Y* scale factor to default to the *X* scale factor. This would not be appropriate if the *Y* scale needed to be different, of course. Using the null string in this manner is equivalent to returning to the AutoCAD screen, striking the Spacebar, and then returning to AutoLISP.

AutoLISP

Pause Symbol

During a (command...) function you can cause a pause if you wish to allow the user input during the particular AutoCAD command that you have called up. This is done by using the pause symbol in lieu of a variable or of a fixed value where a particular response is required. For example, in the preceding program line you could have allowed the user to input a name and an angle:

```
(command "insert" pause inspt xscal yscal pause)
```

or

```
(command "insert" pause "2,2" "2.5" "" pause)
```

Symbology Used in This Chapter to Describe Functions

The function descriptions in this section include the operator (+ or − , for example), and the elements (arguments) that must (or may) follow the operator. If the arguments following the operator in the description are enclosed with angle <> brackets only, then those arguments must follow the operator and must be of the type specified. An argument in square [ ] brackets following the operator (not necessarily immediately) is optional. When an argument is followed by an ellipsis "...," then the operator will accept multiplearguments of the type specified.

ELEMENTARY FUNCTIONS

(+ <number> <number>...) This function returns the sum of the <number>s. There may be any quantity of <number>s.

(- <number> <number>...) This function returns the difference of the <number>s. There may be any quantity of <number>s.

(* <number> <number>...) This function returns the product of any quantity of <number>s.

(\ <number> <number>...) This function returns the quotient of the first <number> divided by the second <number>. If there are more than two arguments, the quotient of the first and second will be divided by the third, and so on.

Rules of Promotion of an Integer to a Real

As noted in the Reference Manual, integers may range from −32768 to 32767, depending on the platform. Adding or multiplying integers whose sum or product exceeds 32,767 (or is less than −32,768) will not provide an acceptable result.

1. If any argument in one of the functions is entered as an integer and that integer is outside the integer limits, then the result is not usable.

2. If all of the number arguments entered are integers, then the result will be an integer, and if that result is outside the integer limits, the result will be subject to error.

3. If any of the arguments is entered as a real (and none is an integer exceeding the integer limits), then the result will be a real without limits.

More Elementary Functions

(1+ <number>) and (1- <number>) These functions are just different methods of writing (+ <number> 1) and (- <number> 1), respectively. For example:

```
(1+7) returns 8
(1-7) returns 6
```

(abs <number>) This function returns the absolute value of the <number>. For example:

```
(abs (- 4 7)) returns 3
```

(ascii <string>) This function returns the ASCII value of the first character of the <string>. For example:

```
(ascii "All") returns 65
(ascii "a")   returns 97
(ascii "B")   returns 66
```

(chr <number>) This function returns the character (as a one-character string whose ASCII code is <number>. For example:

```
(chr 65)  returns "A"
(chr 97)  returns "a"
(chr 100) returns "d"
```

(eval <expr>) This function returns the result of evaluating <expr>, where <expr> is any LISP expression. For example:

```
(setq z 6)
(setq q 'z)
(eval z) returns 6
(eval q) returns 6
```

(exp <number>) This function returns e raised to the <number> power (natural antilog). It returns a real. For example:

```
(exp 1.0)   returns 2.718282
(exp -0.2)  returns 0.818730753
```

AutoLISP

(expt <base> <power>) This function returns <base> raised to the specified <power>. If both arguments are integers, the result is an integer; otherwise, the result is a real. For example:

```
(expt 3 4) returns 81
```

(log <number>) This function returns the natural log of <number> as a real. For example:

```
(log 3.74) returns 1.32175584
(log 1.025) returns 0.024692613
```

(sqrt <number>) This function returns the square root of <number> as a real. For example:

```
(sqrt 16) returns 4.000000
(sqrt 2.0) returns 1.414213562
```

(type <item>) This function returns the type of <item>, where type is one of the following (as an atom):

REAL	floating point numbers
FILE	file descriptors
STR	strings
INT	integer
SYM	symbol
list	lists (and user functions)
SUBR	internal AutoLISP functions
PICKSET	AutoCAD selection sets
ENAME	AutoCAD entity names
PAGETB	Function paging table

Trigonometry Functions

(sin <angle>) This function returns the sine of <angle>, where <angle> is expressed in radians.

(cos <angle>) This function returns the cosine of <angle>, where <angle> is expressed in radians. For example:

```
(cos 1)        returns .540302306
(sin (/ pi 2)) returns 1.00000
```

(atan <num1> [<num2>]) If only <num1> is present, then (atan ...) returns the angle (in radians) whose tangent is <num1>. If <num1> and <num2> are present, then (atan ...) returns the angle whose tangent is the dividend of <num1> divided by <num2>. For example:

```
(atan 0.75)    returns 0.643501109
(atan 1.0 2.0) returns 0.463647609
```

LIST HANDLING FUNCTIONS

(list <expr>...) This function has expression(s) as its arguments. It is included in this section because it is the function that creates the lists that the other functions in this section require as arguments.

(list ...) This function takes any number of expressions and makes them into a list. For example:

```
(list 1 1) returns (1 1)
```

Remember! A created list is enclosed in parentheses.

A specific application of the (list ...) function is to combine two or three reals in the format required by a function whose argument is <pt>, which is a 2D or 3D point. The point is a special form of a list. For example:

```
(setq p1 (list 1.0 1.0))
(setq p2 (list 2.0 2.0))
```

allows the following:

```
(setq a (angle p1 p2))
```

which returns 0.785398163.

But

```
(setq p1 (list "you" 1.0))
(setq p2 (list 2.0 2.0))
(setq a (angle p1 p2))
```

returns

    error: bad point value

(angle <pt1> <pt2>) This function returns the angle (in radians) between the baseline of angle zero and the line from pt1 to pt2.

(distance <pt1> <pt2>) This function returns the distance in decimal units from pt1 to pt2. If the units are set to architectural and the distance between two points is 6'-3", the (distance ...) function will return 75.000000.

(polar <pt> <angle> <distance>) This function returns a point. It can be one of the most useful tools in the AutoLISP tool kit. The arguments must be of the proper type. The <pt> must evaluate to a list of two reals. The <angle> and <distance> are each a real. The value of the <angle> is in radians.

(osnap <pt> <mode-string>) This function returns a point. It allows object snapping to a point while in AutoLISP. Like the (polar ...) function, it returns a point in the form of a list of two or three real s. For example, if a circle has been drawn using p1 and p2 in the 2P method as follows:

```
(setq p1 (list 1.0 3.0))
(setq p2 (list 4.0 3.0))
(command "circle" "2P" p1 p2)
```

then

```
(command "line" "0,0" (setq c (osnap p1 "center")) "")
```

returns (2.5 3.0), or the list or two reals representing the center of the circle as the endpoint of the line.

(inters <pt1> <pt2> <pt3> <pt4> [<onseg>]) This function returns a point. It can be used for the following:

1. To determine if two nonparallel lines intersect.

2. If they intersect, the location of that point.

3. If they do not intersect, where they would intersect if one or both were extended until they intersected.

If the optional <onseg> argument is present and is nil, the lines will be considered infinite in length and the function will return a list of three reals designating that intersection point.

If the optional <onseg> argument is not present or is not nil, then their intersection must be on both segments in order for a point to be returned; otherwise, the function will return nil.

CAR, CDR, and Combinations

CAR and CDR are the primary functions that select and return element(s) of a list. Unlike the (angle ...) function and (distance ...) function, these functions will operate on a list comprised of elements of any type. The elements can be atoms or lists within the list. The atoms can be reals, integers, strings, or symbols. The argument to the CAR and CDR functions can even be a list of mixed types of elements. These were the foundation functions designed to analyze a list of symbols (which is what language is). In AutoLISP, these functions break down points into coordinates. For example:

```
(setq p1 '(1.0 2.0)) returns (1.0 2.0)
```

Then

```
(car p1)                    returns 1.0, a real
```

But

```
(cdr p1)                    returns (2.0), a list
```

Note the parentheses enclosing 2.0. If

    (setq L1 (list 1.0 2.0)) and (setq L2 (list L1 3.0))
then

    (car L2) returns (1.0 2.0), a list

Here is a list within a list. Or in the function-list (setq L2 (list L1 3.0)), L1 is a list within a list within a function-list.

The preceding expression is not used very often in AutoLISP, but its capability is worthy of note.

(car <list>) returns the first element of <list>.

(cdr <list>) returns <list> without the first element.

The type of the return of the (car <list>) function depends on the type of the first element.

If

    (setq L (list 1.0 2.0))

then

    (car L) returns 1.0, a real

If

    (setq L (list 1 2.0))

then

    (car L) returns 1, an integer

If

    (setq L (list "1" 2))

then

    (car L) returns "1," a string

If the symbol "a" evaluates to nil and

    (setq L (list a 2))

then

    (car L) returns the symbol "a"

But if

```
(setq a 1.0) and (setq L (list a 2.0))
```

then

```
(car L) returns 1.0, a real
```

Whereas (car <list>) can return any type of expression, (cdr <list>) always returns a list. The return may not look like a list, but its type will be a list (even if nil). For example:

```
(setq L1 (1.0 2.0))
(cdr L1)
```

returns (2.0), a list. Remember, the parentheses designate the list and (car L1) returns 1.0, a real. So how can the list (2.0) be used as a real? By using the following combination:

```
(car (cdr L1))
```

which is the same as

```
(car (2.0))
```

which returns 2.0, a real. Note how (car <list>) breaks the first expression out of the <list> and returns it evaluated to its type.

Although (car <list>) and (cdr <list>) operate on the same list, (cdr <list>) always returns a list. Consider the following:

```
(setq L1 (list 1.0))   returns (1.0), a list
(car L1)               returns 1.0, a real
(cdr L1)               returns nil
```

This is the null list, or the same as (list ( )).

If

```
(setq L1 (list 1.0 2.0))
```

then

```
(car L1)        returns 1.0
(cdr L1)        returns (2.0)
(car (cdr L1))  returns 2.0
```

A shortcut for this is: (cadr <list>), or

```
(cadr L1)
```

which returns 2.0, a real. CADR is one of several short forms of combinations of CAR and CDR.

NOTE: (car <list>) may return any type

(cdr <list>) is a list

The short forms of CAR and CDR begin with C and end with R. The characters between will be either an A or a D and will determine the sequence of combined CAR(s) and CDR(s). Here are some short forms:

CAAR	(car (car <list>))
CDDR	(cdr (cdr <list>))
CADR	(car (cdr <list>))
CDAR	(cdr (car <list>))

Any form that begins with CA will return an expression.

Any form that begins with CD will return a list.

All CARs and CDRs represented by A's and D's in such forms as CADAR and CDDAR, however deep, must have lists as their individual arguments.

For example: If

```
(setq L1 (list (1.0 2.0) 3.0))   returns ((1.0 2.0) 3.0)
(car L1)                          returns (1.0 2.0), a list
(cdr L1)                          returns (3.0), also a list
```

(list (1.0 2.0) 3.0) makes a list out of the list (1.0 2.0) and the atom 3.0. That is why (car L1) returned a list, even though 3.0 is a real in the list "L1;" (cdr <list>) always returns a list. The first element of L1 is (1.0 2.0), when it is removed from ((1.0 2.0) 3.0), (3.0) remains. And that is the function of (cdr L1), to return a list with its first element removed.

So

```
(caar L1) is the same as (car (car L1))
```

and returns 1.0, a real. But

```
(cdar L1), which is the same as (cdr (car L1))
```

returns (2.0), a list. Because 2.0 and 3.0 are not first elements, in order to return their values as reals, they must first be returned as the first elements of a list, as follows:

```
(cadar L1) means (car (cdr (car L1)))
```

and returns 2.0, which is the same as

```
(car (cdr (1.0 2.0)))
```

and the same as

```
(car (2.0))
```

And

```
(cadr L1) means (car (cdr L1))
```

and returns 3.0, or

```
(car (3.0))
```

CAR and CADR Mainly for Graphics

(car ...) and (cadr ...) are the primary functions for accessing the X and Y coordinates of a point in AutoCAD. Remember, if **(setq L1 (list 1.0 2.0))** is entered, **(cdr L1)** returns the not-so-useful list (2.0). But by using **(cadr L1)**, which means **(car (cdr L1))**, then in the following manner **(cadr L1)** returns 2.0, which is no longer a list but a real.

Review

All forms of the CAR-CDR combination that begin with CA will return the first expression. All forms that begin with CD will return a list.

For graphics applications, lists represent the X and Y coordinates of a 2D point and the X, Y, and Z coordinates of a 3D point. Therefore, the more useful CAR-CDR combination forms are as follows:

In a 2D point:

```
(setq p2d (list 1.0 2.0))
(car p2d)        returns 1.0, the X coordinate
(cadr p2d)       returns 2.0, the Y coordinate
(caddr p2d)      returns nil
```

In a 3D point:

```
(setq p3d (list 1.0 2.0 3.0))
(car p3d)        returns 1.0, the X coordinate
(cadr p3d)       returns 2.0, the Y coordinate
(caddr p3d)      returns 3.0, the Z coordinate
(cdr p2d)        returns (2.0), a list
(cdr p3d)        returns (2.0 3.0), a list
```

Neither of the last two statements is very useful unless the programmer wishes to project all of the 3D points on the *Y-Z* plane.

(last <list>) This function returns the last expression in the <list>. Although (last <list>) can be used to return the *Y* coordinate of a 2D point and the *Z* coordinate of a 3D point, it is not recommended for that purpose. Because there might be an erroneous return, it is recommended that (cadr <list>) be used for the *Y* coordinate and (caddr <list>) for the *Z* coordinate.

(cons <new first element> <list>) This function returns the <first new element> and <list> combined into a new list, as in the following:

```
(setq a 2.0)
(setq b 3.0)
(setq L1 (list a b))
(cons 1.0 L1)  returns (1.0 2.0 3.0)
```

(cons ...) This function will also return what is known as a "dotted pair" when there is an atom in place of the <list> argument, as in the following:

```
(cons 1.0 2.0)  returns (1.000000 . 2.000000)
```

This special form of a list requires less memory than ordinary lists.

(length <list>) returns the number of elements in <list> as in the following:

```
(setq L1 (list "you" (1.0 2.0) 3.0))
returns ("you" (1.0 2.0) 3.0)
(length L1)          returns 3
(length (car L1))    returns nil, because (car L1) is an atom
(length (cdr L1))    returns 2
(length (cadr L1))   returns 2
(length (caddr L1))  returns nil
```

If

```
(setq L1 (list "you" (1.0) 2.0))
(length L1)          returns 3
(length (cadr L1))   returns 1
```

(nth <n> <list>) This function returns the *n*th element of <list>. (Zero is the first element.) For example:

```
(setq L1 (list "you" (1.0 2.0) 3))
(nth 0 L1)              returns "you," a string
(nth 1 L1)              returns (1.0 2.0), a list
(nth 2 L1)              returns 3, an integer
(nth 0 (cadr L1))       returns 1.0, a real
(nth 1 (cadr L1))       returns 2.0, a real
(nth 3 L1)              returns nil
```

(reverse <list>) This function returns the <list> with the elements in reverse order, as in the following:

```
(setq L1 (list (1.0 2.0) 3.0))
(reverse L1)            returns (3.0 (1.0 2.0))
(reverse (car L1))      returns (2.0 1.0)
```

TYPE-CHANGING FUNCTIONS

In order for the AutoCAD operator, AutoCAD, and AutoLISP to communicate properly between (and within) themselves, data is constantly exchanged. Of the different data types (as classified by AutoLISP) there are three types that can be stored as one type but need to be communicated as another type: integer, the real, and the string.

Some AutoLISP functions are designed to take data of one type as their argument and return that data as another type. The basic outline below, Figure 19–5, shows the functions and the types that they are designed to translate from and to.

(angtos <angle> [<mode> [<precision>]]) This function takes <angle> input as a real in radians and returns a string in the format determined by <mode>. The values of <mode> and their corresponding format are as follows:

		FROM		
		INTEGER	REAL	STRING
TO	INTEGER	(FIX)	FIX	ATOI
	REAL	FLOAT	(FLOAT)	ATOF
	STRING	ITOA	ANGTOS	
			RTOS	

Figure 19–5 The basic translation for communication between AutoCAD and AutoLISP

Angtos Mode	Format
0	degrees
1	degrees/minutes/seconds
2	grads
3	radians
4	surveyor's units

For example: If

```
(setq p1 (1.0 1.0))
(setq p2 (2.0 2.0))
(setq a (angle p1 p2)) returns 0.78539816
```

then

```
(angtos a 0) returns "45"
(angtos a 1) returns "45.000000"
(angtos a 2) returns "45d0'0.0000""
(angtos a 3) returns "0.78539816r"
(angtos a 4) returns "N 45d0'0.0000 W""
```

The optional <precision> determines the decimal places to be displayed.

(atof <string>) This function takes a <string> and returns a real. For example:

```
(atof "3.75")    returns 3.750000
(atof "4")       returns 4.000000
```

(atoi <string>) This function takes a <string> and returns an integer. For example:

```
(atoi "3.75")    returns 3
(atoi "4")       returns 4
```

(itoa <int>) This function takes an <integer> and returns a string. For example:

```
(itoa 33) returns "33"
(itoa -4) returns "-4"
```

(rtos <number> [<mode> [<precision>]]) This function takes a real input and returns a string in the format determined by <mode>. The values of <mode> and their corresponding format is as follows:

Rtos Mode	Format
1	scientific
2	decimal
3	engineering
4	architectural
5	arbitrary Fractional Units

AutoLISP

The optional <precision> determines the decimal places to be displayed.

(fix <number>) This function takes a real or integer and returns an integer. For example:

```
(fix 4)          returns 4
(fix 4.25)       returns 4
```

(float <number>) This function takes a real or integer and returns a real. For example:

```
(float 4)        returns 4.000000
(float 4.25)     returns 4.250000
```

INPUT FUNCTIONS

The input functions cause a program to pause for user input of a particular type and return data in the format of a specified type.

The optional [<prompt>] in all (get ...) functions allows the programmer to display the <prompt> message in the prompt area on the screen. It will be demonstrated in the first (get ...) function description.

> **NOTE:** The (getvar ...) function is *not* a function for user input.

> **CAUTION!**
> For all (get ...) functions, the user input *cannot* be in the form of an AutoLISP function.

(getangle [<pt>] [<prompt>]) This function will return an angle, in radians, between two points, the first of which may be the optional [<pt>] in the function. Note the option of either selecting two points or inputting the first point into the AutoLISP function and selecting the second point. This method is used in the (getdist ...) and the (getorient ...) functions and will be referred to in their descriptions. For example:

```
(setq a (getangle "PICK TWO POINTS: "))
```

will pause for the user to input two points, either of which may be typed in at the keyboard (as in 1'2,3'6-1/2 if in the architectural units mode) or picked on the screen. If the response to the preceding (getangle ...) function were 1,1 and 2,2, then the function would return 0.785398. Or if

```
(setq p1 (list 14.0 42.5))
```

then

```
(setq a (getangle p1 "PICK SECOND PT: "))
```

will use p1 for the first point and pause for the user to input the second point from the keyboard or on the screen.

If

(setq p1 (list 1 1)) and (setq a (getangle p1 "PICK SECOND PT: "))

and **2,2** were entered, it would return 0.785398.

CAUTION!

Unlike the (angle ...) function, the angle returned by the (getangle ...) function is affected by a change in the ANGBASE system variable. If ANGBASE were changed from 0 degrees to 45 degrees, the preceding (getangle p1 ...) function with a response of 2,2 would return 0.000000. (See the upcoming (getorient ...) function description.)

(getcorner <pt> [<prompt>]) This function returns a point selected during the pause. As the user places the cursor for selection, a rectangle is displayed with the <pt> as one corner of the rectangle and the cursor location as the diagonally opposite corner.

(getdist [<pt>] [<prompt>]) This function returns the distance between two points in the same manner and with the same options as the (getangle ...) function returns an angle. The return will be a real. If the units are set to architectural a length of 3'-6 1/2" would be returned as 42.500000.

(getint [<prompt>]) This function pauses for an integer input and returns that integer.

(getkword [<prompt>]) This function pauses for user input of a keyword that must correspond to a word on a list set up by the (initget ...) function prior to using the (getkword ...) function. If the response is not appropriate, AutoCAD will retry. This function prevents a program from terminating prematurely due to the wrong type of data being input by mistake, and gives the user another chance. It also permits returning a string by just inputting initial letters. For example:

```
(initget 1 "SET Make New")
(setq g (getkword "LAYER CHOICES? (SET, M, or N): "))
```

AutoCAD will reject any response that does not comprise the initial uppercase characters of the options in the list set by (initget ...). The response may also include any and all of the lowercase characters in the string, but nothing in addition to the characters of any of the options. The responses that are valid to the example here are: SET, M, Ma, Mak, Make, N, Ne, and New, with any of the preceding in uppercase.

```
(initget 1 "SET MaKe New")
(getkword)
```

will accept *m* because the *K* was preceded by a lowercase *a*.

```
(initget 1 "SET MAke New")
(getkword)
```

will not accept *m*, but will accept *ma*, *mak*, or *make*, but not *makeup*.

(getorient [<pt>] [<prompt>]) This function will pause for the user to input two points, and will return an angle, in radians, between two points.

The point selection options are the same as for the (getangle ...) function. Unlike the (getangle ...) function, the (getorient ...) function is not affected by an ANGBASE system variable change. It will return an angle determined by the line connecting the two input points. The angle will be measured between that line and the zero East baseline regardless of the ANGBASE setting.

(getpoint [<pt>] [<prompt>]) This function pauses for input of a point (either from the keyboard or a pick on the screen), and returns that point in the form of a list of two reals.

The optional <pt>, if used, will cause a rubberband line from <pt> to the placement of the cursor until a pick is made.

(getreal [<prompt>]) This function pauses for user input of a real number and returns that real number.

(getstring [<cr>] [<prompt>]) This function pauses for keyboard characters to be entered and returns them as a string. It is not necessary to enclose the input in quotation marks. AutoLISP will do that automatically. The optional <cr>, if present and not nil, will permit the string to have blank spaces. The string must be terminated by striking ⏎. Otherwise, if <cr> is present and nil, striking the Spacebar will terminate the entry.

(initget [<bits>] [<string>]) This function offers the programmer a one-time control of the user's response to the next (get ...) function, and that (get ...) function only.

This means that anytime control is needed for a (get ...) function, a new (initget ...) function must precede it.

The type of control that is offered by the (initget ...) function is as follows:

> The program can be set up to reject responses of a certain unwanted type or value (without terminating the program) and offer the user a second chance to enter an acceptable response.

The program can be made to accept points outside of the limits even when LIMCHECK is on.

The program can be made to return 3D points rather than 2D points.

Dashed lines can be used when drawing a rubberband or a box.

The program can be made to accept a string when the (get ...) function normally requires a specific type, such as point or real.

The controls offered by using the <bits> option are shown in Figure 19–6. The <bits> may be a sum of whichever values in Figure 19–6 correspond to the controls desired for the next (get ...) function. For example:

```
(setq p1 (list 0 0))
(initget 9)
(setq d (getdist p1 "SECOND POINT: "))
```

The bits in the next to last line are a sum of 1 (rejects null input) and 8 (allows input outside limits). This will allow the second point to be outside the limits even if the LIMITS mode is ON. It also will not accept a null return.

CONDITIONAL AND LOGIC FUNCTIONS

AutoLISP conditional and logic functions allow the user to have a program test certain conditions and proceed according to the result of those tests. Or, by using the WHILE function, a programmer's LOOP situation will allow iteration of a changing variable between the extents of a specified range.

BITS VALUE	MEANING
1	REJECTS NULL INPUT
2	REJECTS ZERO VALUES
4	REJECTS NEGATIVE VALUES
8	ALLOWS INPUT OUTSIDE LIMITS
16	RETURNS 3D POINTS RATHER THAN 2D
32	USES DASHED LINES FOR RUBBERBAND/BOX

Figure 19–6 The Controls offered by the Bits option

AutoLISP

The symbol T is used when an expression is needed that will never evaluate to nil.

(if <testexpr> <thenexpr> [<elseexpr>]) This function evaluates <testexpr>. If <textexpr> does not return nil, then the function returns the evaluation of <thenexpr>. If the optional <elseexpr> is present and <testexpr> evaluates to nil, then the function returns the evaluation of <elseexpr>. Otherwise, the function returns nil. For example:

```
(setq q (getint "ENTER QUANTITY FROM 1-99: " ))
(if (< q 10)
    (setq c q)
    (setq c (fix (/ q 10)))
)
```

This program will take a number (from user input) and test to see if it is less than 10. If so, it will SETQ the symbol *c* to that number. If it is 10 or greater, it will divide the number by 10 and SETQ *c* to the whole number of the result; for instance, 37 becomes 3.7 becomes 3.

(cond (<test1> <result1> ...) ...) This function accepts any number of arguments. The first item in each list is evaluated, and when one returns not nil, the following expressions in that list are evaluated and the function returns the value of the last expression. For example, a routine could be written to return the angle of a line to be only in the first or fourth quadrants, regardless of how it was originally selected. Note the four possibilities shown in Figure 19–7.

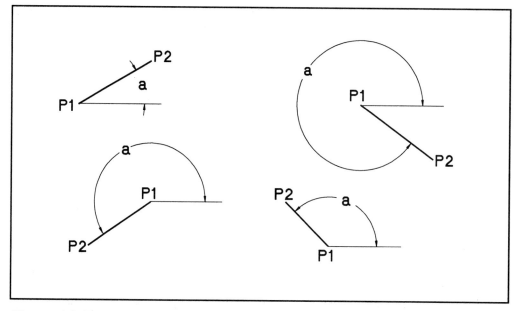

Figure 19–7 Conditional and logic function return possibilities

We will not consider the four ortho directions, N, E, S, or W, in this example. If an angle is returned that was determined by the function (setq a (angle p1 p2)), then it could be in one of four quadrants. Then to ensure that no matter which angle was set by p1-p2, the function would return an angle in the first or fourth quadrant. For example:

```
(setq a (angle p1 p2))
(cond
   ((and (> a pi) (< a (* 3 (/ pi 2)))) (setq a (- a pi))
   ((and (> a (/ pi 2)) (< a pi)) (setq a (+ a pi))
)
```

(while <testexpr> <expr>...) This function evaluates <textexpr>, and, if it is not nil, evaluates the following expressions and then repeats the procedure again with <testexpr>.

This repetition continues until <textexpr> evaluates to nil; the function then returns the evaluation of <lastexpr>.

Test Expressions

(if ...), (cond ...), and (while ...) These functions normally use one of the logic functions as <textexpr>. For example, the following program lines were previously entered:

```
(setq a 10.0)
(if (null a) (setq a 6.0))
```

This sequence will not change the value of the symbol *a* because the evaluation of the expression (null *a*) is nilintegerTherefore, the following expression will not be evaluated. Had *a* not been previously SETQed, the expression (null *a*) would evaluate to T (for TRUE), and the expression following would be evaluated and would have SETQed the symbol *a* to 6.0.

(= <atom> <atom> ...) This expression returns T if all of the <atom>s evaluate to the same thing.

(/= <atom1> <atom2>) This expression returns T if <atom1> is "not equal to" <atom2>. It is nil otherwise.

(< <atom> <atom> ...) This expression returns T if each <atom> is "less than" the <atom> to its right. It is nil otherwise.

(<= <atom> <atom> ...) This expression returns T if each <atom> is "less than or equal to" the <atom> to its right. It is nil otherwise.

(> <atom> <atom> ...) This expression returns T if each <atom> is "greater than" the <atom> to its right. It is nil otherwise.

(>= <atom> <atom> ...) This expression returns T if each <atom> is "greater than or equal to" the <atom> to its right. It is nil otherwise.

(and <expr>...) This expression returns T if all <expr>s return T. It is nil otherwise.

(boundp <atom>) This expression returns T if <atom> has a value bound to it. It is nil otherwise.

(eq <expr1> <expr2>) This expression returns T if <expr1> and <expr2> are identical and are bound to the same object. It is nil otherwise.

(equal <expr1> <expr2>) This expression returns T if <expr1> and <expr2> evaluate to the same thing. It is nil otherwise.

(not <expr>) This expression returns T if <expr> is nil. Otherwise the function returns nil.

(null <item>) This expression returns T if <item> is bound to nil. The function returns nil otherwise.

(or <expr>...) This expression returns T if any of the <expr>s evaluate to something that is not nil. Otherwise the function returns nil.

EXERCISES

1integer Identify the atoms in the following expressions:

```
(if (not (null dfr)) (setq dfr (rtos rad)) (setq dfr "0"))
```

Write the AutoLISP expression equivalent to each of the following:

2. $a = 1$
3. $b = 2.0$
4. $c = a$
5. $d = 1 + 2$
6. $e = \sqrt{2}$
7. $f = 1 + b^2$
8. $g = 7 + 9 + 3 + 7$
9. $h = (3 + 5 + 6) + 7$
10. $i = (7\ \ 3) + (4 - (6\ \ 3))$

11. $j = 3\ (7 + 6)$
12. $k = 3 + (7 \times 6)$
13. $l = 5 - (7 + 2)$
14. $m = \sin\ 0.75$
15. $n = \cos\ 1.75$
16. $o = \sin\ (\text{pi} \div 2)$
17. $p = $ absolute value of a
18. $q = x^3$
19. $r = \tan^{-1}((3\ \text{pi}) + 4)$

In the rectangle shown in Figure Ex19–1, write the expressions that evaluate to the following:

20. the vertical distance between p1 and p3
21. the distance between p1 and p3
22. the horizontal distance between p2 and p4
23. the distance between p1 and p4
24. p2 in terms of p1 and p3
25. p3 in terms of p2 and p4
26. the sum of the four sides (perimeter)
27. the area enclosed by the four sides

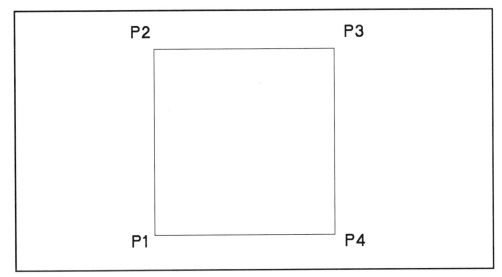

Figure Ex19–1 The rectangle for writing expressions

28. the area of a triangle whose vertices are p1, p2, and p3
29. the angle between lines from p1 to p3 and from p1 to p4

Answer the following:

30. In (setq L1 (list 1.0 2.0)) what is (car L1)?
31. In (setq L2 (list 3.0 4.0)) what is (cdr L2)?
32. In (setq L3 (list 5.0 6.0)) what is (cadr L3)?

For the following expression, write the combination of CAR and CDR that will return the given values from list L5:

```
(setq L5 (list 1.0 '(2.0 (3.0 4.0)) 5.0))
```

33. 1.0
34. 2.0
35. 3.0
36. 4.0
37. 5.0

Give the evaluations of the following expressions:

40. (+ 5 6.0)
41. (- 7 6)
42. (- 8 9)
43. (+ 1 20 300)
44. (- 1 20 300)
45. (- 300 20 1)
46. (- 30000 1.0)
47. (+ 30000 30000)
48. (* 1 2)
49. (* 1.0 2.0)
50. (* 3 4)
51. (* 5.0 6)
52. (* 1 2 3)
53. (* 4 4 6.0)
54. (* 7 8000)
55. (* 8.0 9000)
56. (* 3 pi)
57. (* pi pi)
58. (/ 2.0 1.0)
59. (/ 2.0 1)
60. (/ 2 1)
61. (/ 1 2)
62. (/ 3 2)
63. (/ 3.0 2)
64. (/ 3 2.0)
65. (/ 1.0 2)
66. (/ 40000 2)

67. (/ 2 40000)
68. (abs (+ 4 2))
69. (abs (- 4 2))
70. (ascii "ABC")
71. (ascii "aBC")
72. (chr 66)
73. (chr 98)
74. (expt 3 2)
75. (expt 2 3)
76. (sqrt 9)
77. (sqrt (* 2 8))
78. (type 1)
79. (type pi)
80. (type 3.0)
81. (type T)
82. (sin 0)
83. (cos (/ pi 2))
84. (atan 1)
85. (angle (list 1.0 1.0) (list 2.0 2.0))
86. (angle (list 2.0 1.0) (list 0.0 1.0))
87. (distance (list 1.0 1.0) (list 3.5 1.0))
88. (distance (list 6.0 5.0) (list 2.0 2.0))
89. (polar (list 1.0 1.0) 0 2.0)
90. (polar (list 2.0 3.0) pi 1)
91. (inters (list 0.0 0.0) (list 3.0 3.0)
     (list 3.0 0.0) (list 0.0 3.0))

CUSTOM COMMANDS AND FUNCTIONS

(defun ...) and (defun C: ...) This is an AutoLISP function called DEFUN that will create a custom-designed function. Its format is:

(defun <sym> <argument list> <expr>...)

The DEFUN function operates in a manner similar to the SETQ function. SETQ names a variable and sets it equal to a value. DEFUN names a new function so that when its name is entered in a routine, it will evaluate to the subsequent expression(s). In addition, it allows variables to be operated on by the function by entering the name of that defined function followed by a variable or group of variables.

The customizing power of this feature cannot be emphasized enough. What this means to the programmer is that when a routine has been worked out in AutoLISP, the entire routine can be given a name. Then when the routine needs to be used again, the programmer simply enters the name of the routine. This makes it a user-defined or custom-defined function.

The name of a custom-defined function can also be entered while in AutoCAD, or it can be included in a menu string by entering its name enclosed in parentheses.

In addition to having a one-word entry perform the task of many lines of programming, there is an optional feature that makes the custom-defined function even more effective. The user can define the custom function to perform the prescribed task on a dummy variable in the definition and then enter the defined function followed by some real variable later and have the task performed on the real variable. The dummy variables are listed in the <argument list>.

Arguments and Local Symbols

Every custom-defined function and command must include the parentheses used to enclose the arguments. Even if there are no arguments or local symbols (which means the opening and closing parentheses would be empty), those opening and closing parentheses must follow the user-designated function name. Remember, however, that arguments (the dummy variables) are not permitted in custom commands using the "C:FNAME" format. The following forms are examples of how function and command definitions may be written:

(defun fname ( )...def exprs...)	No arguments or local symbols
(defun C:FNAME ( )...def exprs...)	No arguments or local symbols
(defun fname (/ x y z)...def exprs...)	Three local symbols only
(defun C:FNAME (/ x y z)...def exprs...)	Three local symbols only

AutoLISP

(defun fname (a b)...def exprs...)   Two arguments only

(defun fname (a b / x y z)...def exprs...)   Two arguments and three local symbols

---

CAUTION!

If the arguments enclosing parentheses are inadvertently omitted, AutoLISP will take whatever is in the first parentheses of the definition expressions and try to use them as arguments and/or local symbols. Naturally, this will not operate as expected and will result in an error message. Therefore, include parentheses as shown, even if empty.

Also, within the <argument list>, optional local symbols may be listed (after the slash) to name symbols to be used within the function definition only, without having any effect on the same symbol name outside the defined function. This form of creating a defined function is for use within AutoLISP and cannot be entered without the enclosing parentheses. An added feature, to be discussed later, will allow the same user-defined function to be invoked in the same manner as AutoCAD commands. That is, with the added feature, the user-defined functions can be entered from the keyboard or in the menu without parentheses and then recalled immediately afterward by simply striking Enter.

Defined Functions and Commands

When one starts to delve into custom programs in many graphic applications, one of the first geometric-trigonometric stumbling blocks to overcome is the use of radians to measure angles. AutoCAD is no exception. Even if the use of radians is second nature to someone, using degrees seems to be first nature with almost all designer-drafters. The main problem is in converting from one to the other. This is often necessary because AutoCAD uses degrees for the screen and radians in AutoLISP. Therefore, one of the first AutoLISP routines introduced in articles and books on AutoLISP is one that converts the value of an angle in degrees to its value in radians. The second routine is usually one that converts from radians back to degrees. The usual name for the degrees-to-radians function is the abbreviation *dtr*. The dtr function is written as follows:

```
(defun dtr (a)
  (* pi (/ a 180.0))
)
```

In the format (defun <sym> <argument list> <expr>...), dtr is the symbol (<sym>), a is the only argument in the argument list, and (* pi (/ a 180.0)) is the expression (<expr>).

Though (/ a 180.0) is an expression, it resides within the expression (* pi (/ a 180.0)), and is not considered one of the separate <expr> expressions in the format: (defun <sym> <argument list> <expr>...). The <expr>... indicates there is no limit to the number of expressions possible in a defined function. Although this is a rather minor point, it may help in understanding what an expression is and how AutoLISP looks at them.

Writing a Defined Function

The dtr function may be typed in from the keyboard while in the AutoCAD screen, as follows:

Command: **(defun dtr (a) (* pi (/ a 180.0)))**

This function may be used and applied to any real number in the following manner:

Command: **(dtr 90.0)** *(returns 1.570796327) or* Command: **(dtr 180.0)**
(returns 3.141592654) or Command: **(dtr 7.5)** *(returns 0.130899694)*

Although entering this function from the keyboard will define the dtr function for use at any time during the current editing session, the definition will be lost when the drawing is ended. Although writing this routine is fairly simple, it is still not very economical. There is a better way.

Writing and Storing a Defined Function

Usually, any function that needs to be defined in one drawing will be useful enough to warrant saving the definition for instant reuse later in any drawing without having to type it in repeatedly. Therefore, defined functions may be saved for loading into a drawing. By using a text editor or word processor in the programmer mode, the custom programmer can create a file having the file extension of *.LSP* and then type in the routine. The following example is similar to the first example, only with a slight variation in format:

Filename: **ANGLE.LSP**

```
(defun dtr (a)              ;degrees to radians
  (* pi (/ a 180.0))        ;pi times "a" divided by 180
)                           ;leave function definition
```

The indentation is permissible in writing a defined function in a *FILENAME.LSP* file (unlike the program lines in a *FILENAME.MNU* file). It is even desirable in order to be able to identify easily the distinct elements and subelements of the function definition. The value of this procedure will become more evident with more elaborate definitions. The closing parenthesis, on a line by itself, is lined up with the opening parenthesis. This is an example of how indentation coincides with the depth of nesting of expressions.

In this last example, remarks have been written to the right, following semicolons. AutoLISP ignores anything on a line following a semicolon.

Function Names   The name of the file may or may not be the same as any of the function names it includes. It may even be the same as a function in another file, although that would not be logical. Uniqueness of names is critical within a group of named items, such as files, functions, variables, and drawings on one directory. But in most cases it is not a problem to duplicate names across groups, such as having a *FILENM1.LSP* and a *FILENM1.DWG*, and a *FILENM1.SHP* at the same time along with defining a custom function as follows:

```
(defun filenm1 (...
```

Duplication in this case is not only acceptable but sometimes desirable in coordinating a group of specially named custom files and functions that are all in a single enhancement program being used for a singular purpose.

Loading a Defined Function   As mentioned earlier in this chapter, custom-defined functions must be written into a *FILENAME.LSP* file in order to be saved and usable later. Once a custom-defined function is stored in that file, the user must load the file in order to use it. For example, the file named *ANGLE.LSP* has been created to store the custom-defined function named dtr as follows:

Filename: **ANGLE.LSP**

```
(defun dtr (a)         ;degrees to radians
  (* pi (/ a 180.0)) ;pi times a divided by 180
)                      ;leave function definition
```

In order to make dtr usable, the user must invoke the AutoLISP function named LOAD. It has the format of:

```
(load <filename>)
```

with <filename> being a string without the extension of *.LSP*. Therefore, the file name must be enclosed within quotations, as follows:

```
(load "angle")
```

CAUTION!

Be aware of the distinction between the AutoLISP load function and the AutoCAD load command. The AutoCAD command named LOAD is used to load *FILENAME.SHP* (shape) files and is entered without the parentheses, in the following manner:

Command: **LOAD**

The AutoLISP function named "load" is used to load *FILENAME.LSP* (AutoLISP) files and is entered with the parentheses, in the following manner:

Command: **(load "angle")**

The preceding sequence will make the custom-defined function named dtr usable in the current editing session. The user must be careful when trying to load *.LSP* files from some other drive or directory. If the file named *ANGLE.LSP* is stored on the directory named LISPFILE then the format would be as follows:

Command: **(load "/lispfile/angle")**

Special note should be made of the forward slash versus the backslash. The file name is a string, and a leading backslash in a string is itself a special control character used in conjunction with other code characters for specific operations on the string. Thus, in order to have a backslash read as a backslash in a string, there must be a double backslash. Therefore, the forward slash is recommended in designating a directory path in PC-DOS/MS-DOS.

Drive specifications can also be included in the AutoLISP LOAD function format as follows:

Command: **(load "a:angle")**

or

Command: **(load "a:/lispfile/angle")**

The last entry may be used if the *ANGLE.LSP* file is in the lispfile directory on the A: drive.

If the custom programmer has created custom-defined functions in a file called ACAD.LSP and that file is accessible when a drawing is edited, AutoCAD will "load" that file automatically. Only functions that might be used in all drawings should be included in that file if it is created.

AutoLISP

SIN and COS, but not TAN! Sometimes designer-drafters wish to determine some distances in the all-powerful right triangle (from which trigonometry is derived) by using the opposite and adjacent sides instead of the hypotenuse. So why doesn't AutoLISP have the TAN (tangent) function in addition to the SIN and COS? First of all, an angle is defined in *Webster's New Collegiate Dictionary* as "a measure of the amount of turning necessary to bring one line or plane into coincidence with or parallel to another." Two special cases exist in computing the tangent of an angle, one of which causes a problem that the sine and cosine do not cause. When two lines exist, it is assumed that they must have length and therefore have a nonzero value. When considering the sine or cosine of an angle, the hypotenuse is always one of the existing nonzero lines. And in the sine and cosine of any angle the hypotenuse is always the divisor. So, even if the opposite side (in the case of the sine) or the adjacent side (in the case of the cosine) turn out to be zero, the worst that can happen is that the function will result in zero. In the case of the tangent, where the divisor is the adjacent side, if it is zero the result approaches infinity and is therefore not valid for use within the program. This occurs, of course, at 90 degrees.

The other special case is where the angle is zero and the tangent is zero. Zero may be a valid entry, whereas infinity cannot be. This problem does not occur in the sine and cosine functions because the results of either range from 1 to 0 to -1 and back to 1. All results within this range are valid for use within programs.

An approach to arriving at the tangent is possible by using existing AutoLISP functions named SIN and COS. The tangent can be expressed as the quotient of the sine divided by the cosine. But here again is the possibility of the divisor being zero because the cosine of 90 degrees is just that. If used for specific purposes where it is known that the value of the adjacent side involved is nonzero, then a custom-defined function that will return the tangent of an angle (along with a radians-to-degrees function) might be included in the *ANGLE.LSP* file, as follows:

Filename: **ANGLE.LSP**

```
(defun dtr (a)           ;degrees to radians
  (* pi (/ a 180.0))     ;pi times a divided by 180
)                        ;leave function definition

(defun rtd (b)           ;radians to degrees
  (* 180.0 (/ b pi))     ;180 times b divided by pi
)                        ;leave function definition

(defun tan (c)           ;tangent
  (/ (sin c) (cos c))    ;sine divided by cosine
)                        ;leave function definition
```

Defined AutoLISP Commands   AutoCAD programming features allow the creation of custom-defined AutoLISP commands with two characteristics similar to regular AutoCAD commands.

■ AutoLISP commands can be entered from the keyboard or within a menu string by just entering the name of the custom command without having to enclose it in parentheses.

■ If a particular AutoLISP command was the last command used, then striking « will recall that same command for immediate use.

> **NOTE:** AutoLISP commands cannot operate on external variables (arguments) of an <argument list>. However, local symbols are allowed.

Writing an AutoLISP Function   The format used in creating an AutoLISP command is as follows:

(defun C:CMDNAME </ local symbols> <expr>...)

where CMDNAME can be a name of your choice and can duplicate the name of an existing AutoCAD command or function, if your purpose is to override that command with a definition of your own.

WHAT IS THE DATABASE?

The file that stores information about the drawing has tables and Block sections that include data associated with linetype, layer, style (for text), view, UCS, viewport, and blocks. These are accessible through the (tblnext...) and (tblsearch...) functions.

The Entities section contains data associated individually with each entity in the drawing. There are functions that point to the entity data and that can use or manipulate that data.

Entity Names, Entity Data, and Selection Sets

Information is continually being updated during an editing session. An ongoing record is being kept for each new, modified, or deleted entity. The information or data concerning each entity is stored at some particular location in the drawing file. (This location is not to be confused with its X, Y, and Z coordinates.)

AutoLISP gains access to an entity's data through its entity name, which points to the location of the entity's data within the drawing file. The entity name is the address of that entity's data. You must grasp the concepts of entity name and entity data and be able to distinguish between the two.

Entity Name Functions

Entity name functions evaluate to an item whose data type is called AutoCAD entity name. An entity name can be used as a response when an AutoCAD command prompts you to "Select object:."

The (entnext [<ename>]) function, if performed with no arguments, returns the entity name of the first nondeleted entity in the database. If (entnext...) is performed with an entity name (which we will arbitrarily call en1, for illustration purposes) as the argument, it returns the entity name of the first nondeleted entity that follows en1, in the database.

Walking Through the Data Base

Certain functions can search through the database. The (entlast) function returns the entity name of the last nondeleted main entity in the database. It may be used to return the entity name of a new entity that has just been added by a previous (command...) function.

The (entsel [<prompt>]) function returns a list that has the entity name as the first element and the point by which the entity was selected as the second element. Note that the second element (a point) is a list itself. For example:

```
Command: line
From point: 1,1
to point: 4,4
to point: Enter
Command: (setq es (entsel "Select an Entity: "))
Select an Entity: 2.5,2.5 (returns (<Entity name: 60000018> (2.5 2.5 0.0)))
```

While the evaluation of (entsel...) is a list and not an AutoCAD entity name, its first element is an entity name, obtainable by using the following:

```
Command: (car es) (returns <Entity name: 60000018>, an entity name)
```

Note that the address of this entity is displayed in hexadecimal form, 60000018, and is different for each different entity name. It will also differ from one editing session to the next for the same entity.

Point data is also obtainable by:

```
Command: (cadr es) (returns (2.5 2.5 0.0),a list)
```

And the X coordinate is obtainable by:

```
Command: (caadr es) (returns 2.5, a real)
```

Note that

Command: **(cdr es)**

returns ((2.5 2.5 0.0)), which is a list whose only element is also the list (2.5 2.5 0.0).

The (handent <handle>) function returns the entity name associated with the specified handle. This more advanced concept will not be covered within this section. It is noteworthy, however, that the (handent...) function does assist in the problem of entities changing their names from one editing session to the next.

Entity Data Functions

Entity data functions have entity names as their arguments.

ENTGET Function The primary entity data function is (entget <ename>). This function returns a list of entity data describing <ename> in that special format called an *association list*.

Data Types for DataBase Functions Before continuing with detailed descriptions of the entity data functions and even before introducing selection sets, it would be convenient to discuss certain data types that AutoLISP has set aside especially for use when accessing the database. Some of the concepts used in this discussion of data types will not be described in detail until later in this section. Therefore, the student will probably wish to refer back here later for review after studying those concepts.

In a manner similar to integers, reals, strings, and lists, the special data types called AutoCAD selection sets and AutoCAD entity names can be used as arguments required by certain AutoLISP functions. It should be noted that the special functions designed to operate on these data types can operate on them only. For example; having performed the following sequence:

```
(setq en1 (entnext))
(setq ss1 (ssget "w" '(0 0) '(12 9)))
(setq od1 (list 1.0 2.0))
(setq od2 "HELLO")
```

the following are valid entries:

(setq ed1 (entget en1)) **and** (setq en2 (ssname ss1 0))

But the following are not valid:

(setq ed2 (entget od1)) **and** (setq ed3 (entget od2))

The first two are valid entries because en1 is an AutoCAD entity name, which is the required data type for an argument to the (entget...) function. The second two are not valid entries because od1 and od2 are other data types and so are not valid as arguments. Od1 is a list and od2 is a string.

Similarly, ss1 is a special data type called AutoCAD selection set and is valid as an argument to the (ssname...) function.

Further study will show that the (ssname...) function returns a value in the form of that special data type called AutoCAD entity name. Therefore, if the preceding entries had been performed, then the following is a valid entry:

```
(setq ed4 (entget (ssname ss1 0)))
```

returning the data (as an association list) about the first entity in the drawing file that is included in a window whose corners are 0,0 and 12,9integerEven if no entities had been found, and the operation had returned nil, the operation would still have been proper, having had the required data type as an argument to the (entget...) function.

Back to Entget For an example let's say a newly created drawing had the following as the first entries:

```
Command: line
From point: 1,1
To point: 4,4
To point: Enter
```

```
Command: line
From point: 1,4
To point: 4,1
To point: Enter
```

then

```
(setq L1 (entget (entnext))
```

returns

```
((-1 . <Entity name: 60000018>) (0 . "LINE") (8 . "0")
    (10 1.0 1.0 0.0) (11 4.0 4.0 0.0) (210 0.0 0.0 1.0))
```

and

```
(setq L2 (entget (entlast)) or (setq L2 (entget (entnext L1))
```

returns

((-1 . <Entity name: 60000030>) (0 . "LINE") (8 . "0")
(10 1.0 4.0 0.0) (11 4.0 1.0 0.0) (210 0.0 0.0 1.0))

Also note the syntax in the following example:

Having entered

```
(setq en1 (entnext))
(setq en2 (entlast))
```

then

```
(setq L1 (entget en1))
```

returns the same as

```
(setq L1 (entget (entnext)))
```

and

```
(setq L2 (entget en2))
```

returns the same as

```
(setq L2 (entget (entlast))) or (setq L2 (entget (entnext L1)))
```

This is to emphasize that the entity names en1 and en2 are only addresses (or pointers) to where the data associated with the entities are located within the drawing file. The data list itself is gotten through the (entget...) function, which must have that address or entity name as its argument.

The Association List

Once the concepts of <ename>s and <elist>s are understood and the throes of creating those first routines to extract them are survived, the custom programmer must now deal with how to make use of the results.

The (assoc <item> <alist>) function is the primary mechanism used to extract specific data associated with a selected entity. In order to store data in an organized, efficient, and economical fashion, each common group of data is assigned what is called a group code. That group code is simply an integer. For example, the starting point for a line is a group code 10 and its layer is a group code 8.

Using the first entity in the previous example, you may then enter the following sequence:

Command: **(setq ed1 (entget (entnext)))**

AutoLISP

This returns the association list we saw earlier, which we will display as follows:

```
((-1 . <Entity name:60000018>)
 (0 . "LINE")
 (8 . "0")
 (10 1.0 1.0 0.0)
 (11 4.0 4.0 0.0)
 (210 0.0 0.0 1.0)
)
```

Dotted Pairs The first and last parentheses enclose the association list. Each of the other matched pairs of parentheses enclose lists, with each list comprising a specific group code integer as the first element followed by its associated value. In the case of the group code 8, its value is the string "0," which is the name of the layer that this entity is on. Likewise, the value of the group code 0 is the entity type, which is the string "LINE." Note that these two sublists have a period between the group code and its associated value (separated by spaces). This is a special list called a *dotted pair*, that requires less memory in storage. For economy, AutoCAD uses these dotted pairs where feasible. Some group codeS, like the starting point, may be in the more common form of the list, such as (10 1.0 1.0 0.0) with the group code as the first element followed by the X, Y, and Z coordinates, respectively.

Group codes are broken down as shown in Tables 19–1 and 19–2.

Table 19–1 Group Codes and their Respective Following Value

GROUP CODE RANGE	FOLLOWING VALUE
0 - 9	String
10 - 59	Floating-point
60 - 79	Integer
210 - 239	Floating-point
999	Comment (String)

Table 19–2 Group Codes and Their Respective Value Type

GROUP CODE RANGE	VALUE TYPE
0	Identifies the start of an entity, table entry, or file separator. The text value that follows indicates which
1	The primary text value for an entity
2	A name, attribute tag, block name, etc.
3–4	Other textual or name values

5	Entity handle expressed as a hexadecimal string
6	Linetype name (fixed)
7	Text style name (fixed)
8	Layer name (fixed)
9	Variable name identifier (used only in the Header section of the *DXF* file)
10	Primary point (start point of a line or text entity, center of a circle, etc.)
11–18	Other points
39	This entity's thickness if nonzero (fixed)
40–48	Floating-point values (text height, scale, etc.)
49	Repeated value—multiple 49 groups may appear in one entity for variable-length tables (such as the dash lengths in the Ltype table)
50–58	Angles
62	Color number (fixed)
66	"Entities follow" flag (fixed)
70–78	Integer values, such as repeat counts, modes.
210,220,230	*X, Y,* and *Z* components of extrusion direction.
999	Comments

Extracting Data from a list

```
((-1 . <Entity name:60000018>)
  (0 . "LINE")
  (8 . "0")
  (10 1.0 1.0 0.0)
  (11 4.0 4.0 0.0)
  (210 0.0 0.0 1.0)
)
```

If the preceding list had been SETQed to the variable named ed1 then examples of the (assoc...) function would be as follows:

Command: **(assoc 0 ed1)** *(returns (0 . "LINE"))* Command: **(assoc 8 ed1)** *(returns (8 . "0"))* Command: **(assoc 10 ed1)** *(returns (10 1.0 1.0 0.0))*

These results are lists. The first two are dotted pairs. In order to extract data from these, the following may be entered:

Command: **(cdr (assoc 0 ed1))** *(returns "LINE," a string)* Command: **(cdr (assoc 8 ed1))** *(returns "0," also a string)*

But the following returns (1.0 1.0 0.0),a list:

Command: **(cdr (assoc 10 ed1))**

Therefore, in order to extract the *X* coordinate, enter:

Command: **(cadr (assoc 10 ed1))**

which returns 1.0, a real. Note how CDR returns the second element of a dotted pair as an atom, whereas it requires CADR to return the second element of an ordinary list as an atom. CDR applied to an ordinary list returns a list (unless it is applied to a single-element list).

Other Entity Data Functions

The (entdel <ename>) function deletes the entity specified by <ename> from the drawing or restores the entity previously deleted during the current editing session.

The (entmod <elist>) updates the database information for the entity specified. Using this function in conjunction with the AutoLISP (subst...) function is a convenient way to make specific changes to selected entities.

The (entupd <ename>) function is used for more advanced handling of block and polyline subentities. The student is referred to the AutoLISP Programmer's Reference for use of this function.

Selection Sets

A *selection set* is a collection of entity names. It is the programmer's equivalent to a group of entities selected by one or more of the optional methods of selecting objects from the screen; except that, by using the selection set functions, certain entities not visible on the screen may even be included in the group. It should be emphasized that a selection set comprises the entity names of the entities in the group. The selection set can be used in response to any AutoCAD command where selection by "Last" is valid. It also is a valid argument to selection set functions that supply entity names to the (entget) function, which then returns entity data in the form of an association list.

The (ssget [<mode>] [<pt1> [<pt2>]]) function returns the selection set and prompts something like <Selection set: 1>. This indicates that the selection set contains one or more entities. If no objects meet the selection method, then nil will be returned.

The <mode>, if included, determines by what method the selection process is made. The "W," "L," "C," and "P" correspond to the window, last, crossing, and previous selection modes, respectively. Examples are as follows:

(ssget)	Asks the user for entity selection with one or more standard options
(ssget "W" '(2 2) '(8 9))	Selects the entities inside the window from 2,2 to 8,9
(ssget "L")	Selects the last entity added to the database
(ssget "C" '(0 0) '(5 3))	Selects the entities crossing the box from 0,0 to 5,3
(ssget "P")	Selects the most recently selected objects
(ssget '(1.0 1.0))	Selects the entity passing through the point 1,1
(ssget "X" <filter-list>)	Selects the entities matching the "filter-list"

SSGET Filters The **(ssget "X" <filter-list>)** function provides a method of scanning the entire drawing file and selecting the entities having certain values associated with specified group codes. This function is used in conjunction with the (cons...) function. Note that while the (ssget...) function returns a group of entity names, it scans a group of association lists (the drawing file, that is). So the filter will be constructed in a manner that can be tested against entity data. Examples are as follows:

(ssget "X"(list(cons 0 "CIRCLE")))	Returns a selection set consisting of all the circles in the drawing
(ssget "X"(list(cons 8 "0")))	returns all entities on layer "0"
(ssget "X"(list(cons 0 "CIRCLE") (cons 8 "0")))	returns all circles on layer "0"

Note that the (ssget "X"...) function selects only from main entities. Special methods must be used to gain data about subentities such as attributes and polyline vertices.

The **(sslength <ss>)** function returns an integer containing the number entities in selection set <ss>. For example, the following returns 1:

```
(setq sset (ssget "L"))
(sslength sset)
```

The **(ssname <ss> <index>)** function returns the entity name of the <index>'th element of selection set <ss>. The first element begins with number 0. For example, let's say that (setq sset (ssget)) results in five items:

```
(setq en1 (ssname sset 0)) (returns the first entity)
(setq en3 (ssname sset 2)) (returns the third entity)
```

The **(ssadd [<ename> [<ss>]])** function without arguments constructs a selection set with no members. If performed with a single-entity-name argument, it constructs a new selection set containing that single entity name. If performed with an entity name and a selection set, it adds the named entity to the selection set.

The **(ssdel <ename> <ss>)** function deletes entity name <ename> from selection set <ss>.

The **(ssmemb <ename> <ss>)** function tests whether entity name <ename> is a member of selection set <ss>.

Advanced Association List and (Scanning) Functions

Examples of (assoc <item> <alist>) have been presented previously in this section. It will now be used in our custom-designed command.

The (subst <newitem> <olditem> <list>) function searches <list> for <olditem>, and returns a copy of <list> with <newitem> substituted in every place where <olditem> occurred.

Two sample routines are listed next. The TSAVE routine redefines the REDRAW command and then uses a time-checking part to cause the newly defined REDRAW command to invoke a SAVE command after a predetermined time has passed. The PARAB routine draws a parabola.

Saved in the file named *TSAVE.LSP:*

```
;-Autosave-
(defun S::STARTUP ( )
     (command "undefine" "redraw")
     (setq savetime 0.25)
)

(defun C:TSAVE ( )
     (setq temptime (getreal "ENTER INTERVAL OF TIME IN MINUTES
     FOR SAVING: "))
     (setq savetime (/ temptime 60.0))
)

(defun C:REDRAW ( )
```

```
    (if (null cdate1)
      (setq cdate1 (decihr (getvar "cdate"))))
    (setq cdate2 (decihr (getvar "cdate")))
    (if (or (> (- cdate2 cdate1) savetime)
      (> cdate1 cdate2)
      )
      (progn
             (setq tempex (getvar "expert"))
             (setvar "expert" 2)
                 (command "save" "c:backup")
             (setq cdate1 cdate2)
             (setvar "expert" tempex)
        )
    )
      (command ".redraw")
)

(defun decihr (dt / hms dh dm ds hd)
    (setq hms (* (- dt (fix dt)) 10000.0))
    (setq dh (/ (fix hms) 100.0))
    (setq dm (/ (- dh (fix dh)) 0.6))
    (setq ds (/ (- hms (fix hms)) 36.0))
    (setq hd (+ (fix dh) dm ds))
)
```

Saved in the file named PARAB.LSP:

---------------------------- PARABOLA ---

```
(defun c:parab ( )
    (setq point1 (getpoint "ENTER POINT: " ))
    (setq number (getint "ENTER ITERATIONS: "))
    (setq i (getreal "ENTER INCREMENTS: "))
    (setq p1 point1 p (car point1) counter 0)
    (while (< counter number)
      (setq p2
        (list
             (+ (car point1) i)
             (+ (cadr point1) (* 2.0 (sqrt (* p i)))))
        )
    )
    (command "line" p1 p2 "")
    (setq p1 p2 counter (1+ counter) i (+ i i))
```

)
)

AUTOCAD DEVELOPMENT SYSTEM (ADS)

The AutoCAD Development System (ADS) is a programming interface that, like AutoLISP, permits you to write or use applications for AutoCAD in high-level languages such as C. The applications are loaded in a similar manner to AutoLISP. AutoLISP is more appropriate for smaller applications, whereas ADS makes use of an extensive, powerful, and more complex library of programming functions. ADS, because of the large library, demands more of your system. ADS is not stand-alone, but is tied to AutoLISP; therefore, it is not a good substitute for simpler tasks that can be so easily implemented with AutoLISP.

REVIEW QUESTIONS

1. To load the LISP file "SETUP" into the current AutoCAD drawing, type in the following at the "Command:" prompt:
   a. SETUP
   b. LOAD SETUP
   c. (LOAD SETUP)
   d. (LOAD "SETUP")
   e. none of the above

2. The command used to easily select and load AutoLISP and ADS routines is:
   a. APPLOAD
   b. LOAD
   c. DBLIST
   d. ADS
   e. none of the above

3. What does the (CADR L) function do?
   a. returns the first element of list L
   b. returns the second element of list L
   c. returns the third element of list L
   d. none of the above

4. What does the (atan N) function do?
   a. Returns the angle, in degrees, whose tangent is N
   b. Draws a line tangent to the last object drawn
   c. Returns the tangent of the angle N, where N is in radians
   d. none of the above

5. What does the function (/ A B) do?
   a. Returns the quotient of A divided by B
   b. Returns the quotient of B divided by A
   c. Returns the remainder of A divided by B
   d. Returns the remainder of B divided by A

6. In (+ a 7) the + is called the:
   a. operand
   b. operator
   c. symbol
   d. none of the above

7. The following are acceptable AutoLISP data types except:
   a. Real   d. Storage
   b. Integer e. Symbol
   c. String

AutoLISP

8. If (setq a 7), what does (list 4 a) return?
   a. (4 7)
   b. (7 4)
   c. (11)
   d. an error message
   e. none of the above

9. What does (/ 3 7) return?
   a. 10
   b. 0
   c. 0.4285714285714
   d. 4
   e. none of the above

10. The expression to add 7 to 3 is:
    a. (7 + 3)
    b. (+ 7 3)
    c. (7 3 +)
    d. none of the above

11. The expression (* 10 .5) returns:
    a. 5
    b. 20
    c. An error
    d. (5)

12. The statement (setq pi 3) will:
    a. Redefine the symbol PI
    b. give an error message
    c. be ignored by AutoCAD since PI is a predefined symbol
    d. none of the above

13. To associate a LISP file with a menu file, so that it will be automatically loaded when the menu file is loaded you must use the same file name for both, with only the extensions varying. The proper extension for the LISP file is:
    a. MLP   d. LSM
    b. MNL   e. LLP
    c. LSP

14. When working in AutoCAD and you get the prompt "1>", it means:
    a.you have one minute until the network shuts down
    b.you need to specify one more argument for the previous function
    c. you need to enter 1 more right parenthesis ")"

HARDWARE REQUIREMENT

• •

INTRODUCTION

The configuration of your CAD system is a combination of the hardware and software you have assembled to create your system. There are countless PC configurations available on the market. The goal for a new computer user should be to assemble a PC workstation that does not block future software and hardware upgrades. This section lists the essential hardware required to run AutoCAD Release 14.

When you install AutoCAD Release 14 it automatically configures itself to the various drivers already set up for Windows 95/Windows NT. The **Preferences...** dialog box can be used to custom configure your installation, as explained in Chapter 13.

RECOMMENDED CONFIGURATION

The configuration recommended by Autodesk for a personal computer CAD workstation includes the following:

1. Intel Pentium® (recommended) or compatible processor.
2. Operating System: Windows NT® version 3.51 or 4.0 or Windows® 95.

3. RAM and Hard-Disk Space: 32MB of RAM recommended, plus 10MB (recommended) of additional RAM for each concurrent AutoCAD session. 50MB of free hard-disk space (minimum), plus additional 2.5MB of free hard-disk space during installation only (this space is used for temporary files that are removed when installation is complete). 64MB of disk swap space (minimum).

> **NOTE:** An additional 8MB to 15MB of disk space may be required for files installed in the system folder. This space does not need to be on the same drive as the program folder where you load AutoCAD.

4. Video 1024 x 768 VGA video display recommended, with Windows-supported display adapter.
5. Peripherals: CD ROM drive required for initial installation only; mouse/ pointing device.

Optional Peripherals: Printer or plotter, digitizer

WINDOWS: THE OPERATING ENVIRONMENT

Windows 95 or Windows NT is the name of the operating environment. Windows 95 or Windows NT provides the graphical user interface and device independence, and lets you run more than one program at a time.

The *graphical user interface* (or GUI, for short) consists of the windows, icons, scroll bars, menu bar, button bar, and other graphical elements you see on the Windows screen. The GUI lets you use the mouse to control most aspects of a software program, including selecting commands, resizing windows, clicking on icons, and drawing.

Device independence means that all software applications running under Windows use the same device drivers, such as for the display, the mouse, and the printer. AuotCAD uses the Windows 95 or Windows NT device driver.

The multitasking and task switching feature of Windows 95 or Windows NT lets you be more productive. *Multitasking* means that Windows can run more than one program at a time, unlike DOS which runs just one program at a time. *Task switching* means that you can quickly switch from task to task (or from one program to another).

INPUT DEVICES

AutoCAD supports several input device configurations. Data may be entered via the keyboard, the mouse, or a digitizing tablet.

Keyboard

The keyboard is one of the primary input methods. It can be used to enter commands and responses.

Mouse

The mouse is used with the keyboard as a tracking device to move the crosshairs on the screen. This method is fast and far surpasses the keyboard for positioning the screen crosshairs.

The mouse is equipped with two or more buttons. The left button is the pick button; the other buttons can be programmed to perform any of the AutoCAD commands.

Digitizer

The digitizer is another means of input supported by AutoCAD, but is not well supported by Windows. Hence, Autodesk provides a "mole" mode that lets the mouse and digitizer work at the same time in Windows while AutoCAD is running.

The digitizing tablet is a flat, sensitized electromechanical device that can recognize the location of the tablet cursor. The tablet cursor moves over the surface of the digitizing tablet, causing a corresponding movement of the screen cursor.

Another use of the digitizing tablet is to overlay a tablet menu, configured to enter commands when they are selected by placing the crosshairs of the puck at the corresponding digitizer coordinates. This process automates any AutoCAD command options that are represented on the menu, and eliminates the use of the keyboard except to enter an occasional command value.

The tablet cursor (puck) may have from 4 to 16 buttons. Except for the first button, the current menu can be programmed to cause the remaining buttons to perform any of the regular AutoCAD commands. The first button is always the pick button.

PLOTTERS AND PRINTERS

AutoCAD supports several types of output devices for producing hard copies of drawings. The most common devices are the thermal plotter, pen plotter, inkjet printer, and laser printer.

Thermal Plotters

The thermal plotter heats up the drawing paper, changing the color to black to create a hard copy of the drawing. The resolution of the output, which is measured in dots per inch (dpi), may range from a low-quality (100 dpi) product to medium-quality (400 dpi) product.

Appendix A

Pen Plotters

The pen plotter draws continuous lines on the paper. The drawing pen is driven by vector commands that correspond to the X and Y coordinates on the drawing paper. Drawing media varies between mylar, vellum, and bond. The pens used in such plotters also vary in size and quality, thus affecting the drawing resolution. Resolution is typically between the equivalent of 1000 and 2000 dpi.

Pen plotters come in all shapes and sizes, and over the years pen plotters have improved in the areas of speed, accuracy, and price. The pen plotter is an established favorite for those who demand clear line and shape definition. Although prices vary on the different types of pen plotters, it is possible to get a good desktop pen plotter in the area of $2000. Contact your dealer to find out if a particular model is supported.

Inkjet Printers

AutoCAD supports the ability to generate a hard copy of your drawing with an inkjet printer, either in black-white or in color. Inkjet printers form characters and graphics by squirting ink onto standard paper. Inkjet printers provide the most inexpensive means for color printing. They are generally used to provide rough draft hard copies for graphics and text data. They are an excellent and cost-effective way to produce check plots in A-, B-, and C-size.

Laser Printers

Laser printers are the newest printing device on the CAD market. They deliver a low-cost, medium- to high-resolution hard copy that can be driven from a personal computer. Laser printers boast resolutions from 300 dpi to 1200 dpi and printing speeds of about 4–12 pages per minute (ppm) for text and 1–2 pages per minute for graphics.

As with any raster device, laser printers require a vector-to-raster conversion to generate most graphics. AutoCAD can plot design files on laser printers that support the HP LaserJet PCL and PostScript graphic output languages. The cost of laser printers ranges from under $1000 to over $12,000, yet the increase in resolution makes the price a good investment for many serious CAD users.

• • • • • • • • • • • • • •

APPENDIX

B

ALPHABETICAL LISTING OF AUTOCAD COMMANDS

• •

COMMANDS

Command (Aliases)	Explanation	Options	Toolbar	Pull-Down Menu
'About	Displays a dialog box with the AutoCAD version and serial numbers, a scrolling window with the text of the *acad.msg* file, and other information			TYPE IN
Acisin	Imports an ACIS file			File
Acisout	Exports AutoCAD solid objects to an ACIS file			File
Align	Moves and rotates objects to align with other objects			Modify
Ameconvert	Converts AME solid models to AutoCAD solid objects			TYPE IN
Aperture	Regulates the size of the object snap target box	Select (1–50 pixels) to increase or reduce size of box		TYPE IN
Appload	Loads AuotLISP, ADS, and ARX applications			Tools
Arc (A)	Draws an arc of any size	A Included angle C Center point D Starting direction E Endpoint L Length of chord R Radius S Start point Enter Continues arc from endpoint of line or arc	Draw	Draw

Command (Aliases)	Explanation	Options		Toolbar	Pull-Down Menu
Area	Calculates the area of a polygon, pline, or circle	A S E	Sets add mode Sets subtract mode Calculates area of the circle or pline selected	Object Properties	Tools
Array	Copies selected objects in circular or rectangular pattern	P R	Polar (circular) arrays about a center point Rectangular arrays objects in horizontal rows and vertical columns	Modify I	Modify
Arx	Loads, unloads, acquaints you with ARX applications				
Asexxx	Related to Structured Query Launguage applications				
Attdef	Creates an attribute definition that assigns (tags) textual information to a block	I C V P	Regulates visibility Regulates constant/variable mode Regulates verify mode Regulates preset mode		TYPE IN
Attdisp	Regulates the visibility of attributes in the drawing	ON OFF N	Makes all attribute tags visible Makes all attributes invisible Normal visibility set individually		View
Attedit	Permits the editing of attributes				Modify
Attext	Extracts attribute information from a drawing	C D S E	CDF comma-delimited format DXF format SDF format Select objects		TYPE IN
Attredef	Redefines a block and updates associated attributes				TYPE IN
Audit	Performs drawing integrity check while in AutoCAD	Y N	Fixes errors encountered Reports, but does not fix, errors		File
Base	Defines the origin point for insertion of one drawing into another				Draw
Bhatch	Fills an automatically defined boundary with a hatch pattern through the use of dialog boxes; also allows previewing and repeated adjustments without starting over each time			Draw	Draw
Blipmode	Turns blip markers on and off				TYPE IN
Block	Makes a compound object from a group of objects	?	Lists names of defined blocks	Draw	Draw
Bmake	Uses a dialog box to define a block				
Bmpout	Exports selected objects to bitmap format				

Command (Aliases)	Explanation	Options		Toolbar	Pull-Down Menu
Boundary	Creates a polyline of a closed boundary				Draw
Box	Creates a 3D solid box			Solids	Draw
Break	Breaks out (erases) part of an object or splits it into parts	F	Allows you to reselect the first point again	Modify I	Modify
Browser	Launches the Web browser				
Cal	Evaluates mathematical and geometric expressions				TYPE IN
Chamfer	Makes a chamfer at the intersection of two lines	D P	Sets chamfer distance Chamfers all intersections of a pline figure	Modify I	Modify
Change	Makes changes in the location, size, orientation, and other properties of selected objects; is very helpful for editing text	P E C LA LT F	Changes properties of objects Elevation Color Layer Linetype Thickness		TYPE IN
Chprop	Makes changes in the properties of selected objects	C LA LT T	Color Layer Linetype Thickness		TYPE IN
Circle (C)	Draws a circle of any size; default is center point and radius	2P 3P D TTR R	Two endpoints on diameter Three points on circle. Enters circle diameter Tangent, Tangent, Radius Enter radius	Draw	Draw
Color 1. Red 2. Yellow 3. Green 4. Cyan 5. Blue 6. Magenta 7. White	Sets color for objects by name or number; also sets color to be by block or layer	number name BYBLOCK BYLAYER	Sets color by number Sets a color by name Retains color of block Uses color of layer		TYPE IN
Compile	Compiles shape and font files				TYPE IN
Cone	Creates a 3D solid cone			Solids	Solids
Config	Displays options in the text window to reconfigure the video display, digitizer, plotter, and operating parameters				TYPE IN
Convert	Converts associative hatches and 2D polylines to Release 14 optimized format				
Copy (CP)	Makes one or more copies of selected objects	M	Makes more than one copy of the selected object	Modify I	Modify
Copyclip	Copies selected objects to the Windows clipboard				

Command (Aliases)	Explanation	Options	Toolbar	Pull-Down Menu
Copyhist	Text in command line history is copied to the clipboard			
Copylink	Current view is copied to the clipboard for OLE applications			
Cutclip	Cuts and copies selected objects from the drawing to the clipboard			
Cylinder	Creates a 3D solid cylinder		Solids	Solids
Dblist	Makes a listing of every object in the drawing database		Inquiry	Tools
Ddattdef	Displays a dialog box that creates an attribute definition object for textual information to be associated with a block definition			Draw
Ddatte	Edits attributes via a dialog box			
Ddattext	Displays a dialog box that extracts data from a drawing; available formats are DXF, CDF, SDF, and selected objects			TYPE IN
Ddchprop	Displays a dialog box that modifies the color, layer, linetype, and thickness of selected objects			TYPE IN
Ddcolor	Sets the color for new objects			Format
Ddedit	Edits text and attributes via a dialog box		Modify II	Modify
'Ddgrips	Allows you to enable grips and set their colors and size via a dialog box			Tools
'Ddim	Controls dimensioning through a series of dialog boxes; see also *Dim*		Dimension	Format
Ddinsert	Displays a dialog box that inserts a copy of a previously drawn part or a drawing file into a drawing, and lets you set an insertion point, scale, rotate, or explode the part; see also *Insert*		Insert	Insert
Ddmodify	Controls object properties			Modify
Ddptype	Specifies the display mode and size of point objects			Format
'Ddptype	Specifies point object display mode and sizes			
'Ddrename	Displays a dialog box that renames text styles, layers, linetypes, blocks, views, User Coordinate Systems, viewport configurations, and dimension styles; see also *Rename*			Format

Command (Aliases)	Explanation	Options	Toolbar	Pull-Down Menu
'Ddrmodes	Allows drawing aids to be set via a dialog box			Tools
'Ddselect	Displays a dialog box that sets object selection modes, the size of the pickbox, and the object sort method			Tools
Dducs	To control the User Coordinate System via a dialog box		UCS	Tools
Dducsp	Selects a preset User Coordinate System		UCS	Tools
'Ddunits	Displays a dialog box that sets coordinate and angle display formats and precision; see also *Units*			Format
Ddview	Creates and restores views		Viewpoint	View
Ddvpoint	Sets the 3D viewing direction			View
Delay	Sets the timing for a sequence of commands used in a script file			TYPE IN
Dim	Accesses the dimensioning mode			TYPE IN
Dist	Determines the distance between two points		Inquiry	Tools
Divide	Places markers along selected objects, dividing them into a specified number of parts	B Sets a specified block as a marker		Draw
Doughnut (Donut)	Draws a solid circle or a ring with a specified inside and outside diameter		Draw	Draw
Dragmode	Allows control of the dynamic specification (dragging) feature for all appropriate commands	ON Honors drag requests when applicable OFF Ignores drag requests A Sets Auto mode: drags whenever possible		TYPE IN
Draworder	Changes the display order of images and objects			
Dtext	Enters text on the display as it is typed in	See Text command for options	Draw	Draw

Command (Aliases)	Explanation	Options		Toolbar	Pull-Down Menu
Dview (DV)	Defines parallel or visual perspective views dynamically	CA	Selects the camera angle relative to the target		View
		CL	Sets front and back clipping planes		
		D	Sets camera-to-target distance, turns on perspective		
		H	Removes hidden lines on the selection set		
		OFF	Turns perspective off		
		PA	Pans the drawing across the screen		
		PO	Specifies the camera and target points		
		TA	Rotates the target point about the camera		
		TW	Twists the view around your line of sight		
		U	Undoes a Dview subcommand		
		X	Exits the Dview command		
		Z	Zooms in/out, or sets lens length		
Dwviewer	Opens aerial viewer				
Dwfout	Exports a drawing web format file				
Dxbin	Inserts specially coded binary files into a drawing				File
Dxfin	Loads a drawing interchange file				File
Dxfout	Writes a drawing interchange file	B	Writes binary *DXF* file		File
		E	Outputs selected entities only		
		0-16	Floating point precision		
Edge	Changes the visibility of 3D face edges			Surfaces	Draw
Edgesurf	Constructs a 3D polygon mesh approximating a Coons surface patch (a bicubic surface interpolated between four adjoining edges)			Surfaces	Draw
Elev	Sets the elevation and extrusion thickness for entities to be drawn in 3D drawings				TYPE IN
Ellipse	Draws ellipses using any of several methods	C	Selects center point	Draw	Draw
		R	Selects rotation rather than second axis		
		I	Draws isometric circle in current isoplane		
End	Exits after saving the updated drawing				TYPE IN
Erase (E)	Deletes objects from the drawing			Modify I	Modify

Command (Aliases)	Explanation	Options	Toolbar	Pull-Down Menu
Explode	Changes a block or polyline back into its original objects		Modify I	Modify
Export	Saves objects to other file formats			
Extend	Extends a line, arc, or polyline to meet another object	U Undoes last extension	Modify I	Modify
Extrude	Creates unique solid primitives by extruding existing 2D objects		Solids	Draw
Fill	Determines if solids, traces, and wide polylines are automatically filled	ON Solids, traces, and wide polylines filled OFF Solids, traces, and wide polylines outlined		TYPE IN
Fillet	Constructs an arc of specified radius between two lines, arcs, or circles	P Fillets an entire polyline; sets fillet radius R Sets fillet radius	Modify I	Modify
Filter	Creates lists to select objects based on properties			TYPE IN
Graphscr [F2]	Flips to the graphics display on single-screen systems; used in command scripts and menus			TYPE IN
Grid [F7] On/Off toggle	Displays a grid of dots, at desired spacing, on the screen	ON Turns grid on OFF Turns grid off S Locks grid spacing to snap resolution A Sets grid aspect (differing X–Y spacings) number Sets grid spacing (0 = use snap spacing) number X Sets spacing to multiple of snap spacing	Status bar	
Group	Creates a named selection set of objects		Standard	Tools
Hatch	Creates crosshatching and patternfilling	name Uses hatch pattern name from library file U Uses simple user-defined hatch pattern ? Lists selected names of available hatch patterns NAME and U can be followed by a comma and a hatch style from the following list: I Ignores internal structure N Normal style: turns hatch lines off and on when internal structure is encountered O Hatches outermost portion only		TYPE IN
Hatchedit	Modifies an existing associative hatch block		Modify II	Modify

Command (Aliases)	Explanation	Options		Toolbar	Pull-Down Menu
"Help or '?	Displays a list of valid commands and data entry options or obtains help for a specific command or prompt	To get a set of Help modes, use Esc and F2 for flip screen		Standard	Help
Hide	Regenerates a 3D visualization with hidden lines removed			Render	View
Id	Displays the coordinates of a point selected on the drawing				Tools
Imagexxx	Commands used for modifying and displaying images to the clipboard				
Import	Imports various file formats into AutoCAD				
Insert	Inserts a copy of a block or Wblock complete drawing into the current drawing	fname	Loads fname as block	Draw	Draw
		fname=f	Creates block fname from file f		
		*name	Retains individual part objects		
		C	(as reply to X scale prompt) Specifies scale via two points (Corner specification of scale)		
		XYZ	(as reply to X scale prompt) Readies Insert for X,Y, and Z scales		
		~	Displays a File dialog box		
		?	Lists names of defined blocks		
Insertobj	Inserts embedded or linked objects				
Interfere	Finds the interference of two or more solids and creates a composite solid from their common volume			Solids	Solids
Intersect	Creates composite solids or regions from the intersection of two or more solids or regions			Modify II	Modify
Isoplane Ctrl + E	Changes the location of the isometric crosshairs to left, right, and top plane	L	Left plane		TYPE IN
		R	Right plane		
		T	Top plane		
		Enter	Toggle to next plane		

Command (Aliases)	Explanation	Options		Toolbar	Pull-Down Menu
Layer (LA)	Allows for the creation of drawing layers and the assigning of color and linetype properties	C F LT M N ON OFF S T ? L U	Sets layers to color selected Freezes layers Sets specified layers to linetype Makes a layer the current layer, creating it if necessary Creates new layers Turns on layers Turns off layers Sets current layer to existing layer Thaws layers Lists specified layers and their associated colors, linetypes, and visibility Lock Unlock	Object Properties	Format
Leader	Draws a line from an object to, and including an annotation				
Lengthen	Lengthens an object			Modify I	Modify
Light	Manages lights and lighting effects			Render	View
Limits	Sets up the drawing size	2 points ON OFF	Sets lower left/upper right drawing limits Enables limits checking Disables limits checking		Format
Line (L)	Draws straight lines of any length	Enter C U	(as reply to "From point:") Starts at end of previous line or arc (as reply to "To point:") Closes polygon (as reply to "To point:") Undoes segment	Draw	Draw
Linetype	Defines, loads, and sets the linetype	? C L S name BYBLOCK BYLAYER ?	Lists a linetype library Creates a linetype definition Loads a linetype definition Sets current object linetype; *set suboptions:* Sets object linetype name Sets floating object linetype Uses layer's linetype for objects Lists specified loaded linetypes		TYPE IN
List	Provides database information for objects that are selected			Inquiry	Tools
Load	Loads a file of user-defined shapes to be used with the SHAPE command	?	Lists the names of loaded shape files		TYPE IN

Command (Aliases)	Explanation	Options		Toolbar	Pull-Down Menu
Logfileoff	Closes the log file opened by LOGFILEON				TYPE IN
Logfileon	Writes the text window contents to a file				TYPE IN
Ltscale	Regulates the scale factor to be applied to all linetypes within the drawing				TYPE IN
Massprop	Calculates and displays the mass properties of regions or solids			Inquiry	Tools
Matchprop	Causes properties of one object to be assigned to selected objects				
Matlib	Imports and exports materials to and from a library of materials				Tools
Measure	Inserts markers at measured distances along a selected object	B	Uses specified block as marker	Inquiry	Tools
Menu	Loads a menu into the menu areas (screen, pull-down, tablet, and button)				Tools
Menuload	Loads partial menu files				TYPE IN
Menuunload	Unloads partial menu files				TYPE IN
Minsert	Inserts multiple copies of a block in a rectangular array	fname	Loads fname and forms a rectangular array of the resulting block	Draw	Draw
		fname=f	Creates block fname from file f and forms a rectangular array		
		?	Lists names of defined blocks		
		C	(as reply to X scale prompt) Specifies scale via two points (Corner specification of scale)		
		XYZ	(as reply to X scale prompt) Readies Multiple Insert for $X, Y,$ and Z scales		
		~	Displays a File dialog box		
Mirror	Reflects selected objects about a user-specified axis, vertical, horizontal, or inclined			Modify I	Modify
Mirror3D	Creates a mirror image copy of objects about a plane				Modify
Mledit	Edits multiple parallel lines			Modify II	Modify
Mline	Draws multiple parallel lines				
Mlstyle	Defines a style for multiple parallel lines				Format

Command (Aliases)	Explanation	Options		Toolbar	Pull-Down Menu
Move (M)	Moves selected objects to another location in the drawing			Modify I	Modify
Mslide	Creates a slide of what is displayed on the screen				TYPE IN
Mspace (MS)	Switches to model space from paper space			Status bar	View
Mtext	Creates paragraph text			Draw	Draw
Multiple	Allows the next command to repeat until canceled				TYPE IN
Mview	Sets up and controls viewports	ON	Turns selected viewport(s) on; causes model to be regenerated in the selected viewport(s)		View
		OFF	Turns selected viewport(s) off; causes model not to be displayed in the selected viewport(s)		
		Hideplot	Causes hidden lines to be removed in selected viewport(s) during paper space plotting		
		Fit	Creates a single viewport to fit the current paper space view		
		2	Creates two viewports in specified area or to fit the current paper space view		
		4	Creates four equal viewports in specified area or to fit the current paper space view		
		Restore	Translates viewport configurations saved with the VPORTS command into individual viewport objects in paper space		
		<point>	Creates a new viewport within the area specified by two points		
Mvsetup	Sets up the specifications of a drawing				TYPE IN
New	Creates a new drawing			Standard	File
Offset	Reproduces curves or lines parallel to the one selected	number T	Specifies offset distance Through: allows specification of a point through which the offset curve is to pass	Modify I	Modify
Olelinks	Cancels, changes, updates OLE links				
Oops	Recalls last set of objects previously erased				TYPE IN

Command (Aliases)	Explanation	Options	Toolbar	Pull-Down Menu
Open	Opens an existing drawing		Standard	File
Ortho [F8]	Restricts the cursor to vertical or horizontal use	ON Forces cursor to horizontal or vertical use OFF Does not constrain cursor movement	Status bar	
Osnap	Allows for selection of precise points on existing objects	CEN Center of arc or circle END Closest endpoint of arc or line INS Insertion point of text/block/shape INT Intersection of line/arc/circle MID Midpoint of arc or line NEA Nearest point of arc/circle/line/point NOD Node (point) NON None (off) PER Perpendicular to arc/line/circle QUA Quadrant point of arc or circle QUI Quick mode (first find, not closest) TAN Tangent to arc or circle	Object Snap	Tools
'Pan (P)	Moves the display window		Standard	View
Pasteclip	Inserts clipboard data			
Pastespec	Specifies fomat of data imported from the clipboard			
Pedit (2D)	Permits editing of 2D polylines	C Closes to start point D Decurves, or returns a spline curve to its control frame F Fits curve to polyline J Joins to polyline O Opens a closed polyline S Uses the polyline vertices as the frame for a spline curve (type set by SPLINETYPE) U Undoes one editing operation W Sets uniform width for polyline X Exits PEDIT command E Edits vertices B Sets first vertex for Break G Go (performs Break or Straighten operation) I Inserts new vertex after current one M Moves current vertex N Makes next vertex current P Makes previous vertex current R Regenerates the polyline S Sets first vertex for Straighten T Sets tangent direction for current vertex W Sets new width for following segment X Exits vertex editing, or cancels Break/Straighten	Modify II	Modify

Command (Aliases)	Explanation	Options		Toolbar	Pull-Down Menu
Pedit (3D)	Allows editing of 3D polylines	C	Closes to start point.	Modify II	Modify
		D	Decurves, or returns a spline curve to its control frame		
		O	Opens a closed polyline		
		S	Uses the polyline vertices as the frame for a spline curve (type set by SPLINETYPE)		
		U	Undoes one editing operation		
		X	Exits PEDIT command		
		E	Edits vertices		
		During vertex editing:			
		B	Sets first vertex for Break		
		G	Go (performs Break or Straighten operation)		
		I	Inserts new vertex after current one		
		M	Moves current vertex		
		N	Makes next vertex current		
		P	Makes previous vertex current		
		R	Regenerates the polyline		
		S	Sets first vertex for Straighten		
		X	Exits vertex editing, or cancels Break/Straighten		
Pedit (mesh)	Allows editing of 3D polygon meshes	D	Desmoothes-restores original mesh	Modify II	Modify
		M	Opens (or closes) the mesh in the *M* direction		
		N	Opens (or closes) the mesh in the *N* direction		
		S	Fits a smooth surface as defined by SURFTYPE		
		U	Undoes one editing operation		
		X	Exits PEDIT command		
		E	Edits mesh vertices		
		D	Moves down to previous vertex in *M* direction		
		L	Moves left to previous vertex in *N* direction		
		M	Repositions the marked vertex		
		N	Moves to next vertex		
		P	Moves to previous vertex		
		R	Moves right to next vertex in *N* direction		
		RE	Redisplays the polygon mesh		
		U	Moves up to next vertex in *M* direction		
		X	Exits vertex editing		
Pface	Creates a 3D mesh of arbitrary complexity and surface characteristics				TYPE IN

Command (Aliases)	Explanation	Options		Toolbar	Pull-Down Menu
Plan	Puts the display in plan view (Vpoint 0,0,1) relative to either the current UCS, a specified UCS, or the WCS	C	Establishes a plan view of the current UCS		View
		U	Establishes a plan view of the specified UCS		
		W	Establishes a plan view of the WCS		
Pline (PL)	Draws 2D polylines	H	Sets new half-width	Draw	Draw
		U	Undoes previous segment		
		W	Sets new line width		
		Enter	Exits PLINE command		
		C	Closes with straight segment		
		L	Segment length (continues previous segment)		
		A	Switches to arc mode		
		In arc mode:			
		A	Included angle		
		CE	Center point		
		CL	Closes with arc segment		
		D	Starting direction		
		L	Chord length, or switches to line mode		
		R	Radius		
		S	Second point of three-point arc		
Plot (Print)	Plots a drawing to a plotting device or a file		Standard	Standard	File
Point	Draws single points on the drawing			Draw	Draw
Polygon	Creates regular polygons with the specified number of sides indicated	E	Specifies polygon by showing one edge	Draw	Draw
		C	Circumscribes around circle		
		I	Inscribes within circle		
Preferences	Customizes the AutoCAD settings				Tools
Preview	Displays plotted view of drawing				
Psdrag	Controls the appearance of an imported PostScript image that is being dragged (that is, positioned and scaled) into place by the PSIN command	0	Only the image's bounding box is displayed as you drag it into place		File
		1	The rendered PostScript image is displayed as you drag it into place		
Psfill	Fills 2D polyline outlines with PostScript fill patterns defined in the AutoCAD PostScript support file *(acad.psf)*				TYPE IN
Psin	Imports encapsulated PostScript (EPS) files				File
Psout	Exports the current view of your drawing to an encapsulated Postscript (EPS) file				File

Command (Aliases)	Explanation	Options	Toolbar	Pull-Down Menu
Pspace (PS)	Switches to paper space		Status bar	View
Purge	Removes unused Blocks, text styles, layers, linetypes, and dimension styles from the drawing	A Purges all unused named objects B Purges unused blocks D Purges unused dimstyles LA Purges unused layers SH Purges unused shape files ST Purges unused text styles LT Purges linetypes		File
Qsave	Saves the drawing without requesting a file name		Standard	File
Qtext	Enables text objects to be identified without drawing the test detail	ON Quick text mode on. OFF Quick text mode off		TYPE IN
Quit	Exit AutoCAD			File
Ray	Creates a semi-infinite line		Draw	
Recover	Attempts to recover damaged or corrupted drawings			File
Rectang	Draws a rectangular polyline		Draw	Draw
Redefine	Restores a built-in command deleted by UNDEFINE			TYPE IN
Redo	Reverses the previous command if it was U or Undo		Standard	Edit
'Redraw (R)	Refreshes or cleans up the current viewport		Standard	View
'Redrawall	Redraws all viewports		Standard	View
Regen	Regenerates the current viewport			TYPE IN
Regenall	Regenerates all viewports			TYPE IN
Regenauto	Controls automatic regeneration performed by other commands	ON Allows automatic regenerations OFF Prevents automatic regenerations		TYPE IN
Region	Creates a region object from a selection set of existing objects		Draw	Draw
Reinit	Allows the I/O ports, digitizer, display, plotter, and *PGP* file to be reinitialized			TYPE IN
Rename	Changes the names associated with text styles, layers, linetypes, blocks, views, UCSs, viewport configurations, and dimension styles	B Renames block. D Renames dimension style LA Renames layer LT Renames linetype S Renames text style U Renames UCS VI Renames view VP Renames viewport configuration		TYPE IN

Command (Aliases)	Explanation	Options		Toolbar	Pull-Down Menu
Render	Creates a realistically shaded image of a 3D wireframe or solid model			Render	View
Replay	Displays a GIF, TGA, or TIFF image				Tools
'Resume	Resumes an interrupted command script				TYPE IN
Revolve	Creates a solid by revolving a 2D object about an axis			Solids	Draw
Revsurf	Creates a 3D polygon mesh approximating a surface of revolution, by rotating a curve around a selected axis			Surfaces	Draw
Rmat	Manages rendering materials			Render	View
Rotate	Rotates existing objects to the angle selected	R	Rotates with respect to reference angles	Modify I	Modify
Rotate3D	Moves objects about a 3D axis				
Rpref	Sets rendering preferences			Render	View
Rscript	Restarts a command script from the beginning				TYPE IN
Rulesurf	Creates a 3D polygon mesh approximating a ruled surface between two curves			Surfaces	Draw
Save	Updates the current drawing file without exiting the Drawing Editor			Standard	File
Saveas	Same as SAVE, but also renames the current drawing				File
Saveimg	Saves a rendered image to a file				Tools
Scale	Changes the size of existing objects to the selected scale factor	R	Resizes with respect to reference size	Modify I	Modify
Scene	Manages scenes in model space			Render	View
Script	Executes a command script				Tools
Section	Uses the intersection of a plane and solids to create a region			Section	Modify
Select	Groups objects into a selection set for use in subsequent commands				TYPE IN
'Setvar	Allows you to display or change the value of system variables	?	Lists specified system variables		TYPE IN
Shade	Shades the model in the current viewport			Render	View
Shape	Draws predefined shapes	?	Lists available shape names		TYPE IN
Shell	Allows access to other programs while running AutoCAD				TYPE IN

Command (Aliases)	Explanation	Options		Toolbar	Pull-Down Menu
Showmat	Lists material type and method of attachment for the selected object				
Sketch	Allows freehand sketching	C	Connect: restarts sketch at endpoint	Draw	Draw
		E	Erases (backs up over) temporary lines		
		P	Raises/lowers sketching pen		
		Q	Discards temporary lines, remains in SKETCH		
		R	Records temporary lines, remains in SKETCH		
		X	Records temporary lines, exits SKETCH; draws line to current point		
Slice	Slices a set of solids with a plane			Solids	Draw
Snap [F9]	Allows for precision alignment of points	number	Sets snap resolution	Status bar	
		ON	Aligns designated points		
		OFF	Does not align designated points		
		A	Sets aspect (differing X–Y spacing)		
		R	Rotates snap grid		
		S	Selects style, standard or isometric		
Soldraw	Generates sections and profiles in viewports created with SOLVIEW				
Solid	Creates filled-in polygons			Draw	Draw
Solprof	Creates a profile image of a 3D solid				
Solview	Creates floating viewports for 3D solid objects				
Spell	Checks the spelling in a drawing			Standard	Tools
Sphere	Creates a 3D solid sphere			Solids	Draw
Spline	Creates a quadratic or cubic spline (NURBS) curve			Draw	Draw
Splinedit	Edits a spline object			Modify II	Modify
Stats	Displays rendering statistics			Render	View
Status	Displays drawing setup				Tools
Stlout	Stores a solid in ASCII or binary file				File
Stretch	Allows you to move a portion of a drawing while retaining connections to other parts of the drawing			Modify I	Modify
Style	Sets up named text styles, with various combinations of font, mirroring, obliquing, and horizontal scaling	?	Lists specified currently defined text style		Format

Command (Aliases)	Explanation	Options	Toolbar	Pull-Down Menu
Subtract	Creates a composite region or solid by subtracting the area of one set of regions from another and subtracting the volume of one set of solids from another		Modify II	Modify
Syswindows	Arranges windows			
Tablet	Allows for configuration of a tablet menu or digitizing of an existing drawing	ON Turns tablet mode on OFF Turns tablet mode off CAL Calibrates tablet for use in the current space		Tools
Tabsurf	Creates a polygon mesh approximating a general tabulated suface defined by a path and a direction vector		Surfaces	Draw
Text	Enters text on the drawing	J Prompts for justification options S Lists or selects text style A Aligns text between two points, with style-specified width factor; AutoCAD computes appropriate height C Centers text horizontally F Fits text between two points, with specified height; AutoCAD computes an appropriate width factor M enters text horizontally and vertically R Right-justifies text BL Bottom left BC Bottom center BR Bottom right ML Middle left MC Middle center MR Middle right TL Top left TC Top center TR Top right	Draw	Draw
'Textscr F1	Flips to the text display on singlescreen systems; used in command scripts and menus			TYPE IN
Tiffin	Imports a TIFF-format raster image file			File
Time	Indicates total elapsed time for each drawing	D Displays current times ON Starts user elapsed timer OFF Stops user elapsed timer R Resets user elapsed timer		Tools
Tolerance	Creates geometric tolerances		Dimension	Draw
Toolbar	Customizes, hides, and displays toolbars			

Command (Aliases)	Explanation	Options		Toolbar	Pull-Down Menu
Torus	Creates a donut-shaped solid			Solids	Draw
Trace	Creates solid lines of specified width			Draw	Draw
Transparency	Determines transparency of opacity of bitonal image background				
Treestat	Displays information on the drawing's current spatial index, such as the number and depth of nodes in the drawing's database; use this information with the TREEDEPTH system variable setting to fine-tune performances for large drawings				TYPE IN
Trim	Deletes portions of selected entities that cross a selected boundary edge	U	Undoes last trim operation	Modify I	Modify
U	Reverses the effect of the previous command			Standard	Edit
UCS	Defines or modifies the current User Coordinate System	D	Deletes one or more saved coordinate systems	Standard	View
		E	Sets a UCS with the same extrusion direction as that of the selected object		
		O	Shifts the origin of the current coordinate system		
		P	Restores the previous UCS		
		R	Restores a previously saved UCS		
		S	Saves the current UCS		
		V	Establishes a new UCS whose Z Axis is parallel to the current viewing direction		
		W	Sets the current UCS equal to the WCS		
		X	Rotates the current UCS around the X axis		
		Y	Rotates the current UCS around the Y axis		
		Z	Rotates the current UCS around the Z axis		
		ZA	Defines a UCS using an origin point and a point on the positive portion of the Z axis		
		3	Defines a UCS using an origin point, a point on the positive portion of the X axis, and a point on the positive Y portion of the X plane		
		?	Lists specified saved coordinate systems		

Command (Aliases)	Explanation	Options		Toolbar	Pull-Down Menu
Ucsicon	Controls visibility and placement of the UCS icon, which indicates the origin and orientation of the current UCS; the options normally affect only the current viewport	A N OR ON	Changes settings in all active viewports Displays the icon at the lower-left corner of the viewport Displays the icon at the origin of the current UCS if possible Enables the coordinate system icon		Tools
Undefine	Deletes the definition of a built-in AutoCAD command				TYPE IN
Undo	Reverses the effect of multiple commands, and provides control over the Undo facility	number A B C E G M	Undoes the number most recent commands Auto: controls treatment of menu items as Undo groups Back: undoes back to previous Undo mark Control: enables/disables the Undo mark End: terminates an Undo group Group: begins sequence to be treated as one command Mark: places marker in Undo file (for back)	Standard	Edit
Union	Creates a composite region or solid			Modify II	Modify
Units	Selects coordinate and angle display formats and precision				Format
'View	Saves the current graphics display and space as a named view, or restores a saved view and space to the display	D R S W ?	Deletes named view Restores named view to screen Saves current display as named view Saves specified window as named view Lists specified named views		View
Viewports or Vports	Divides the AutoCAD graphics display into multiple viewports, each of which can contain a different view of the current drawing	D J R S S1 2 3 4 ?	Deletes a saved viewport configuration Joins (merges) two viewports Restores a saved viewport configuration Saves the current viewport configuration Displays a single viewport filling the entire graphics area Divides the current viewport into viewports Divides the current viewport into three viewports Divides the current viewport into four viewports Lists the current and saved viewport configurations		View

Command (Aliases)	Explanation	Options		Toolbar	Pull-Down Menu
Viewres	Adjusts the precision and speed of circle and arc drawing on the monitor				Format
Vplayer	Sets viewport visibility for new and existing layers	?	Lists layers frozen in a selected viewport		Type In
		Freeze	Freezes specified layers in selected viewport(s)		
		Thaw	Thaws specified layers in selected viewport(s)		
		Reset	Resets specified layers to their default visibility		
		Newfz	Creates new layers that are frozen in all viewports		
		Vpvisdfit	Sets the default viewport visibility for existing layers		
Vpoint	Selects the viewpoint for a 3D visualization	R	Selects viewpoint via two rotation angles		View
		Enter	Selects viewpoint via compass and axes tripod		
		x,y,z	Specifies viewpoint		
Vslide	Displays a previously created slide file	file	Views slide		Tools
		*file	Preloads next Vslide you will view		
Wblock	Creates a block as a separate drawing	name	Writes specified block definition		File
		=	Block name same as file name		
		*	Writes entire drawing		
		Enter	Writes selected objects		
Wedge	Creates a 3D solid with a tapered sloping face			Solids	Draw
Wmxxx	Controls windows metafiles				
Xattach	Attaches an external reference				
Xbind	Permanently adds a selected subset of an external reference's dependent symbols to your drawing	Block	Adds a Block.	Reference	Modify
		Dimstyle	Adds a dimstyle		
		Layer	Adds a layer		
		Ltype	Adds a linetype		
		Style	Adds a style		
Xclip	Defines and external reference				
Xline	Creates an infinite line			Draw	Draw
Xplode	Breaks a compound object into its component objects				TYPE IN

Command (Aliases)	Explanation	Options		Toolbar	Pull-Down Menu
Xref	Allows you to work with other AutoCAD drawings without adding them permanently to your drawing and without altering their contents	Attach	Attaches a new Xref or inserts a copy of an Xref that you have already attached	Reference	Insert
		Bind	Makes an Xref a permanent part of your drawing		
		Detach	Removes an Xref from your drawing		
		Path	Allows you to view and edit the file name AutoCAD uses when loading a particular Xref		
		Reload	Updates one or more Xrefs at any time, without leaving and re-entering the Drawing Editor		
		?	Lists Xrefs in your drawing and the drawing associated with each one		
'Zoom (Z)	Enlarges or reduces the display area of a drawing	number	Multiplier from original scale	Standard	View
		numberX	Multiplier from current scale		
		number XP	Scale relative to paper space		
		A	All		
		C	Center		
		D	Dynamic Pan Zoom		
		E	Extents ("drawing uses")		
		L	Lower left corner		
		P	Previous		
		V	Virtual screen maximum		
		W	Window		
3Dface	Draws 3D plane sections	I	Makes the following edge invisible	Surfaces	Draw
3Dmesh	Defines a 3D polygon mesh (by specifying its size in terms of *M* and *N*) and the location of each vertex in the mesh			Surfaces	Draw
3Dpoly	Creates a 3D polyline	C	Closes the Polyline back to the first point	Draw	Draw
		U	Undoes (deletes) the last segment entered		
		Enter	Exits 3Dpoly command		

DIMENSIONING COMMANDS

Command	Explanation
Dimaligned	Aligns dimension parallel with objects
Dimangular	Draws an arc to show the angle between two nonparallel lines or three specified points
Dimbaseline	Continues a linear dimension from the baseline (first extension line) of the previous or selected dimension
Dimcenter	Draws a circle/arc center mark or centerlines
Dimcontinue	Continues a linear dimension from the second extension line of the previous dimension
Dimdiameter	Dimensions the diameter of a circle or arc
Dimedit	Edits dimensions
Dimordinate	Creates ordinate point associative dimensions
Dimoverride	Overrides a subset of the dimension variable settings associated with selected dimension objects
Dimradius	Dimensions the radius of a circle or arc, with an optional center mark or centerlines
Dimstyle	Switches to a new text style
Dimtedit	Allows repositioning and rotation of text items in an associative dimension without affecting other dimension subentities
Leader	Draws a line with an arrowhead placement of dimension text

DIMENSIONING VARIABLES

Name	Description	Type	Default
DIMADEC	Controls number of places of precision displayed for angular dimension text		
DIMALT	Alternate units	Switch	Off
DIMALT	Alternate units decimal places	Integer	2
DIMALTF	Alternate units scale factor	Scale	25.4
DIMALTTD	Alternate units tolerance value	Integer	2
DIMALTTZ	Toggles suppression of zeros for tolerance values	Integer	0
DIMALTU	Sets unit format for alternate units	Integer	2
DIMALTZ	Toggles suppression of zeros for alternate values	Integer	0
DIMAPOST	Alternate units text suffix	String	None
DIMASO	Associative dimensioning	Switch	On
DIMASZ	Arrow size.	Distance	0.18
DIMAUNIT	Angle format	Integer	0
DIMBLK	Arrow block	String	None
DIMBLK1	Separate arrow block 1	String	None
DIMBLK2	Separate arrow block 2	String	None
DIMCEN	Center mark size	Distance	0.09
DIMCLRD	Dimension line color	Color number	BYBLOCK
DIMCLRE	Extension line color	Color number	BYBLOCK
DIMCLRT	Dimension text color	Color number	BYBLOCK
DIMDEC	Decimal place for tolerance values	Integer	4
DIMDLE	Dimension Line extension	Distance	0.0
DIMDLI	Dimension line increment	Distance	0.38
DIMEXE	Extension line extension	Distance	0.18
DIMEXO	Extension line offset	Distance	0.0625
DIMFIT	Placement of text and arrowheads	Integer	3

Name	Description	Type	Default
DIMGAP	Dimension line gap	Distance	0.09
DIMJUST	Controls horizontal text position	Imteger	0
DIMLFAC	Length factor	Scale	1.0
DIMLIM	Limits dimensioning	Switch	Off
DIMPOST	Dimension text suffix	String	None
DIMRND	Rounding value	Scaled distance	0.0
DIMSAH	Separate arrow blocks	Switch	Off
DIMSCALE	Dimension feature scale factor	Switch	1.0
DIMSD1	Suppresses first dimension line	Switch	Off
DIMSD2	Suppresses second dimension line	Switch	Off
DIMSE1	Suppresses extension line 1	Switch	Off
DIMSE2	Suppresses extension line 2	Switch	Off
DIMSHO	Shows dragged dimension	Switch	On
DIMSOXD	Suppresses outside dimension lines	Switch	Off
DIMSTYLE	Dimension style	Name	*UNNAMED
DIMTAD	Text above dimension line	Switch	Off
DIMTDEC	Tolerance values	Integer	4
DIMTFAC	Tolerance text scale factor	Scale	1.0
DIMTIH	Text inside horizontal	Switch	On
DIMTIX	Text inside extension lines	Switch	Off
DIMTM	Minus tolerance value	Scaled distance	0.0
DIMTOFL	Text outside, force line inside	Switch	Off
DIMTOH	Text outside horizontal	Switch	On
DIMTOL	Tolerance dimensioning	Switch	Off
DIMTOLJ	Tolerance dimensioning justification	Integer	1
DIMTP	Plus tolerance value	Scaled distance	0.0
DIMTSZ	Tick size	Distance	0.0
DIMTVP	Text vertical position	Scale	0.0
DIMTXSTY	Dimension text style	String	Standard

Name	Description	Type	Default
DIMTXT	Text size	Distance	0.18
DIMTZIN	Controls suppression of zeros in tolerance values		
DIMUNIT	Sets unit format	Integer	2
DIMUPT	User-positioned text	Switch	Off
DIMZIN	Zero suppression	Integer	0

OBJECT SELECTION

Object Selection Option	Meaning
point	Selects one object that crosses the small pick box. If no object crosses the pick box and Auto mode has been selected, this designated point is taken as the first corner of a Crossing or Window box
Multiple	Allows selection of multiple objects using a single search of the drawing. The search is not performed until you give a null response to the "Select objects:" prompt
Window	Selects all objects that lie entirely within a window
WPolygon	Selects objects that lie entirely within a polygon shaped selection area
Crossing	Selects all objects that lie within *or cross* a window
CPolygon	Selects all objects that lie within and crossing a polygon-shaped selection area
Fence	Selects all objects that cross a selection fence line
BOX	Prompts for two points. If the second point is to the right of the first point, selects all objects inside the box (like "Window"); otherwise, selects all objects within or crossing the box (like "Crossing")
AUto	Accepts a point, which can select an object using the small pick box; if the point you pick is in an empty area, it is taken as the first corner of a BOX (see above)
ALL	Selects all entities in the drawing except entities on frozen or locked layers
Last	Selects the most recently drawn object that is currently visible
Previous	Selects the previous selection set
Add	Establishes Add mode to add following objects to the selection set
Remove	Sets Remove mode to remove following objects from the selection set
SIngle	Sets single selection mode; as soon as one object (or one group of objects via Window/Crossing box) is selected, the selection set is considered complete and the editing command uses it without further user interaction
Undo	Undoes (removes objects last added)

(See figures on the following pages)

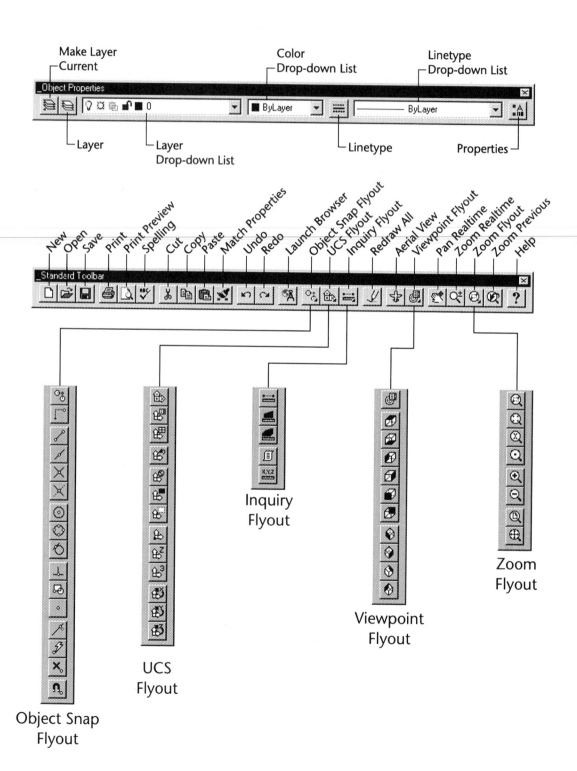

Make Layer
Current

Color
Drop-down List

Linetype
Drop-down List

Object Properties

ByLayer

ByLayer

Layer

Layer
Drop-down List

Linetype

Properties

New
Open
Save
Print
Print Preview
Spelling
Cut
Copy
Paste
Match Properties
Undo
Redo
Launch Browser
Object Snap Flyout
UCS Flyout
Inquiry Flyout
Redraw All
Aerial View
Viewpoint Flyout
Pan Realtime
Zoom Realtime
Zoom Flyout
Zoom Previous
Help

Standard Toolbar

Object Snap
Flyout

UCS
Flyout

Inquiry
Flyout

Viewpoint
Flyout

Zoom
Flyout

Draw
Toolbar

Modify
Toolbar

Modify II
Toolbar

Dimensioning
Toolbar

Reference
Toolbar

Appendix C

Solids
Toolbar

Surfaces
Toolbar

Render
Toolbar

External Database
Toolbar

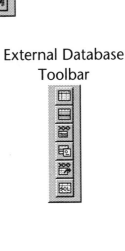

INTRODUCTION

This is a complete listing of AutoCAD system variables. Each variable has an associated type: integer, real, point, or text string. These variables can be examined and changed (unless read-only) by means of the SETVAR command and AutoLISP (getvar and setvar) functions. Many of the system variables are saved across editing sessions; as indicated in the table, some are saved in the drawing itself, while others are saved in the AutoCAD general configuration file, *ACAD.CFG*.

Variable	Default Setting	Type	Saved In	Explanation
ACADPREFIX	" "	String	Read-only	The directory path, if any specified by the ACAD environment variable, with path separators appended if necessary (read-only)
ACADVER		String		This is the AutoCAD version number, which can have values only like "12" or "12a" (read-only). Note that this differs from the *DXF* file $ACADVER header variable, which contains the drawing database level number.
AFLAGS	0	Integer		Attribute flags bit-code for ATTDEF command (sum of the following): 1 = Invisible 2 = Constant 4 = Verify 8 = Preset
ANGBASE	0	Real	Drawing	Angle 0 direction (with respect to the current UCS)
ANGDIR	0	Integer	Drawing	1 = clockwise angles, 0 = counterclockwise (with respect to the current UCS)

Variable	Default Setting	Type	Saved In	Explanation
APERTURE	10	Integer	Config	Object Snap target height, in pixels (default value = 10)
APBOX				Sets AutoSnap aperture box to ON or OFF
AREA		Real		True area computed by Area, List, or Dblist (read-only)
ATTDIA	0	Integer	Drawing	1 causes the INSERT command to use a dialog box for entry of attribute values; 0 to issue prompts
ATTMODE	1	Integer	Drawing	Attribute display mode (0 = OFF, 1 = normal, 2 = ON)
ATTREQ	1	Integer	Drawing	0 assumes defaults for the values of all attributes during insert of blocks; 1 enables prompts (or dialog box) for attribute values, as selected by ATTDIA
AUDITCTL	0	Integer	Config	Controls whether an .adt log file (audit report file) is created 0 = Disables (or prevents) the writing of adt log files 1 = Enables the writing of .adt log files by the AUDIT command
AUNITS	0	Integer	Drawing	Angular units mode (0 = decimal degrees, 1 = degrees/minutes/seconds, 2 = grads, 3 = radians, 4 = surveyor's units)
AUPREC	0	Integer	Drawing	Angular units decimal places
AUTOSNAP	'			Controls the display of the AutoSnap marker and SnapTips and sets the AutoSnap magnet to ON or OFF
BACKZ	0.0000	Integer	Drawing	Back clipping plane offset for the current viewport, in drawing units. Meaningful only if the back clipping bit in VIEWMODE is on. The distance of the back clipping plane from the camera point can be found by subtracting BACKZ from the camera-to-target distance (read-only).
BLIPMODE	1	Integer	Drawing	Marker blips ON if 1, OFF if 0
CDATE		Real		Calendar date/time (read-only)
CECOLOR	"BY-LAYER"	String	Drawing	Current object color (read-only)
CELTSCALE	1	Real	Drawing	Sets the current global linetype scale for objects
CELTYPE	"BY-LAYER"	String	Drawing	Current object linetype (read-only)
CHAMFERA	0.0000	Real	Drawing	First chamfer distance
CHAMFERB	0.0000	Real	Drawing	Second chamfer distance
CHAMFERC	0.0000	Real	Drawing	Sets the chamfer length
CHAMFERD	0.0000	Real	Drawing	Sets the chamfer angle

Variable	Default Setting	Type	Saved In	Explanation
CHAMMODE	0	Integer		Sets the input method by which AutoCAD creates chamfers 0 = Requires two chamfer distances 1 = Requires one chamfer length and an angle
CIRCLERAD	0.0000	Real	Drawing	Sets the default circle radius; to specify no default, enter 0 (zero)
CLAYER	"0"	String	Drawing	Sets the current layer (read-only)
CMDACTIVE		Integer		Bitcode that indicates whether an ordinary command, transparent command, script, or dialog box is active (read-only). It is the sum of the following: 1 = Ordinary command is active 2 = Ordinary command and a transparent command are active 4 = Script is active 8 = Dialog box is active
CMDDIA	1	Integer	Config	1 = Use dialog boxes for PLOT commands 0 = Don't use dialog boxes for PLOT command
CMDECHO	1	Integer		When the AutoLISP (command) function is used, prompts and input are echoed if this variable is 1 but not if it is 0
CMDNAMES		String		Displays in English the name of the command (and transparent command) that is currently active, for example; LINE'ZOOM indicates that the ZOOM command is being used transparently during the LINE command
CMLJUST	0	Integer		Specifies multiline justification 0 = Top 1 = Middle 2 = Bottom
CMSCALE	1.0000	Real	Config	Controls the overall width of a multiline
CMSTYLE		String	Config	Sets the name of the multiline style that AutoCAD uses to draw the multiline
COORDS	1	Integer	Drawing	If 0, coordinate display is updated on point picks only; if 1, display of absolute coordinates is continuously updated; if 2, distance and angle from last point are displayed when a distance or angle is requested
CURSORSIZE				Sets the size of the crosshairs as a percentage of screen size
CVPORT	2	Integer	Drawing	The identification number of the current viewport
DATE		Real		Julian date/time (read-only)

Appendix D

Variable	Default Setting	Type	Saved In	Explanation
DBMOD		Integer		Bitcode that indicates the drawing modification status (read-only); it is the sum of the following: 1 = Entity database modified 2 = Symbol table modified 4 = Database variable modified 8 = Window modified 16 = View modified
DCTCUST		String	Config	Displays the current custom spelling dictionary path and file name
DCTMAIN		String	Config	Displays the current main spelling dictionary file name
DELOBJ	1	Integer	Drawing	Controls whether objects used to create other objects are retained or deleted from the drawing database 0 = Objects are deleted 1 = Objects are retained
DEMANDLOAD				Determines demand loading of a third-party application if a drawing contains custom objects created in that application
DIASTAT		Integer		Dialog box exit status: if 0, the most recent dialog box was exited via CANCEL; if 1, the most recent dialog box was exited via OK (read-only)
DIMxxx		Assorted	Drawing	All the dimensioning variables are also accessible as system variables (see Dimensioning Variables, Appendix C)
DISPSILH				Sets display of silhouette curves of body objects in wireframe mode
DISTANCE	0.0000	Real		Distance computed by DIST command (read-only)
DONUTID	0	Real		Default donut inside diameter; can be zero
DONUTOD		Real		Default donut outside diameter; must be nonzero. If DONUTID is larger than DONUTOD, the two values are swapped by the next command
DRAGMODE	2	Integer	Drawing	0 = no dragging, 1 = on if requested, 2 = auto
DRAGP1	10	Integer	Config	Regeneration-drag input sampling rate
DRAGP2	25	Integer	Config	Fast-drag input sampling rate
DWGCODEPAGE		String	Drawing	Drawing code page: This variable is set to the system code page when a new drawing is created, but otherwise AutoCAD doesn't maintain it. It should reflect the code page of the drawing and you can set it to any of the values used by the SYSCODEPAGE system variable or to "undefined." It is saved in the header

Variable	Default Setting	Type	Saved In	Explanation
DWGNAME		String		Drawing name as entered by the user; if the user specified a drive/directory prefix, it is included as well (read-only)
DWGPREFIX		String		Drive/directory prefix for drawing (read-only)
DWGTITLED		Integer		Bitcode that indicates whether the current drawing has been named (read-only) 0 = The drawing hasn't been named 1 = The drawing has been named
EDGEMODE				Sets how TRIM and EXTEND determine cutting and boundary edges
ELEVATION	0.0000	Real	Drawing	Current 3D elevation, relative to the current UCS for the current space
EXPERT	0	Integer		Controls the issuance of certain "are you sure?" prompts: 0 = Issues all prompts normally 1 = Suppresses "About to regen, proceed?" and "Really want to turn the current layer off?" 2 = Suppresses the preceding prompts and Block's "Block already defined. Redefine it?" and Save/Wblock's "A drawing with this name already exists. Overwrite it?" 3 = Suppresses the preceding prompts and those issued by linetype if you try to load a linetype that is already loaded or create a new linetype in a file that already defines it 4 = Suppresses the preceding prompts and those issued by "Ucs Save" and "Vports Save" if the name you supply already exists 5 = Suppresses the preceding prompts and those issued by "Dim Save" and "Dim Override" if the dimension style name you supply already exists (the entries are redefined) When a prompt is suppressed, EXPERT, the operation in question, is performed as though you had responded Y to the prompt. In the future, values greater than 5 may be used to suppress additional safety prompts. The setting of EXPERT can affect scripts, menu macros, AutoLISP, and the command functions. The default value is 0.
EXPLMODE				Determines whether EXPLODE supports nonuniformly scaled (NUS) blocks
EXTMAX		3D point	Drawing	Upper right drawing uses extents. Expands outward as new objects are drawn; shrinks only by ZOOM All or ZOOM Extents. Reported in World coordinates for the current space (read-only)

Appendix D

Variable	Default Setting	Type	Saved In	Explanation
EXTMIN		3D point	Drawing	Lower left drawing uses extents. Expands outward as new objects are drawn; shrinks only by ZOOM All or ZOOM Extents. Reported in World coordinates for the current space (read-only)
FACETRES	0.5	Real	Drawing	Adjusts smoothness of shaded and hidden-line-removed objects
FFLIMIT	0	Integer	Config	Limits numbers of PostScript and TrueType fonts in memory
FILEDIA	1	Integer	Config	1 = Use file dialog boxes if possible; 0 = do not use File dialog boxes unless requested via ~ (tilde)
FILLETRAD	0.0000	Real	Drawing	Fillet radius
FILLMODE	1	Integer	Drawing	Fill mode ON if 1, OFF if 0
FONTALT	" "	String	Config	Specifies alternate font
FONTMAP		String	Config	Specifies font mapping file
FRONTZ	0.0000	Real	Drawing	Front clipping plane offset for the current viewport, in drawing units. Meaningful only if the front clipping bit in VIEWMODE is ON and the "Front clip not at eye" bit is also ON. The distance of the front clipping bit from the camera point can be found by subtracting FRONTZ from the camera-to-target distance (read-only)
GRIDMODE		Integer	Drawing	1 = Grid on for current viewport, X and Y
GRIDUNIT		2D point	Drawing	Grid spacing for current viewport, X and Y
GRIPBLOCK	0	Integer	Config	Controls the assignment of grips in blocks 0 = Assigns grip only to the insertion point of the block 1 = Assigns grips to entities within the block
GRIPCOLOR	5	Integer (1–255)	Config	Color of nonselected grips; drawn as a box outline
GRIPHOT	1	Integer (1–255)	Config	Color of selected grips; drawn as a filled box
GRIPS	1	Integer	Config	Allows the use of selection set grips for the Stretch, Move, Rotate, Scale, and Mirror modes 0 = Disables grips 1 = Enables grips
GRIPSIZE	3	Integer (1–255)	Config	The size in pixels of the box drawn to display the grip
HANDLES	0	Integer	Drawing	If 0, entity handles are disabled; if 1, handles are on (read-only)
HIGHLIGHT	1	Integer		Object selection highlighting ON if 1, OFF if 0
HPANG		Real		Default hatch pattern angle
HPBOUND				Controls BHATCH and BOUNDARY object types

Variable	Default Setting	Type	Saved In	Explanation
HPDOUBLE	0	Integer		Default hatch pattern doubling for "U" user defined patterns 0 = Disables doubling 1 = Enables doubling
HPNAME	" "	String		Default hatch pattern name. Up to 34 characters no spaces allowed. Returns " " if there is no default. Enter . (period) to set no default
HPSCALE		Real		Default hatch pattern scale factor; must be nonzero
HPSPACE		Real		Default hatch pattern line spacing for "U" user defined simple patterns; must be nonzero
INDEXCTL				Controls whether layer and spatial indexes are created and saved in drawing files
INETLOCATION				Saves the Browser location used by the Internet
INSBASE		3D point	Drawing	Insertion basepoint (set by BASE command) expressed in UCS coordinates for the current space
INSNAME	" "	String		Default block name for DDINSERT or INSERT. The name must conform to symbol-naming conventions. Returns " " if there is no default. Enter . (period) to set no default
ISAVEBAK				Optimizes the speed of periodic saves, especially for large drawings in Windows
ISAVEPERCENT				Specifies the amount of wasted space tolerated in a drawing file
ISOLINES		Real		Stores the end angle of the last arc entered
LASTANGLE	0	Real		The end angle of the last arc entered, relative to the XY plane of the current UCS for the current space (read-only)
LASTPOINT	0.0000, 0.0000, 0.0000	3D point		The last point entered, expressed in UCS coordinates for the current space; referenced by @ during keyboard entry
LASTPROMPT				Saves the last string echoed to the command line
LENSLENGTH	50.0000	Real	Drawing	Length of the lens (in millimeters) used in perspective viewing, for current viewport (read-only)
LIMCHECK	0	Integer	Drawing	Limits checking for the current space: ON if 1, OFF if 0
LIMMAX	12,000, 9,000	2D point	Drawing	Upper right drawing limits for the current space, expressed in World coordinates
LIMMIN	0.0000, 0.0000	2D point	Drawing	Lower left drawing limits for the current space, expressed in World coordinates

Appendix D

Variable	Default Setting	Type	Saved In	Explanation
LISPRINT				Detrmines whether names and values of AutoLISP-defined functions and variables are preserved when you open a new drawing
LOCALE	"en"	String		Displays the ISO language code of the current AutoCAD version
LOGFILEMODE				Determines whether the contents of the text window are written to a log file
LOGFILENAME				Determines the path for the log file
LOGINNAME		String		Displays the user's name as configured or input when AutoCAD is loaded (read-only)
LTSCALE	1.000	Real	Drawing	Linear units mode (1 = scientific, 2 = decimal, 3 = engineering, 4 = architectural, 5 = fractional)
LUNITS	2	Integer	Drawing	Linear units decimal places or denominator
LUPREC	4	Integer	Drawing	Sets linear units decimal places
MAXACTVP	16	Integer		Maximum number of viewports to regenerate at one time (read-only)
MAXOBJMEN				Controls the object pager
MAXSORT	200	Integer	Config	Maximum number of symbol/file names to be sorted by listing commands; if the total number of items exceeds this number, then none of the items are sorted (default value is 200)
MEASUREMENT				Sets drawing units as English or metric
MENUCTL	1	Integer	Config	Controls the page switching of the screen menu 0 = Screen menu doesn't switch pages in response to keyboard command entry 1 = Screen menu switches pages in response to keyboard command entry
MENUECHO	0	Integer		Menu echo/prompt control bits (sum of the following): 1 = Suppresses echo of menu items (^P in a menu item toggles echoing) 2 = Suppresses printing of system prompts during menu 4 = Disables ^P toggle of menu echoing The default value is 0 (all menu items and style prompts are displayed)
MENUNAME	"Acad"	Integer	Drawing	The name of the currently loaded menu file; includes a drive/path prefix if you entered it (read-only)
MIRRTEXT	1	Integer	Drawing	Mirror reflects text if nonzero, retains text direction if 0

Variable	Default Setting	Type	Saved In	Explanation
MODEMACRO		String		Allows you to display a text string in the status line, such as the name of the current drawing, time/date stamp, or special modes. You can use MODEMACRO to display a simple string of text, or use special text strings written in the DIESEL macro language to have AutoCAD evaluate the macro from time to time and base the status line on user-selected conditions
MTEXTED	" "	String	Config	Sets the name of the program to use for editing mtext objects
OFFSETDIST	0.0000	Real		Sets the default offset distance; if you enter a negative value, it defaults to Through mode
OLEHIDE				Controls the display of OLE objects in AutoCAD
ORTHOMODE	0	Integer	Drawing	Ortho mode ON if 1, OFF if 0
OSMODE	0	Integer	Drawing	Object Snap modes bitcode (sum of the following): 1 = Endpoint 2 = Midpoint 4 = Center 8 = Node 16 = Quadrant 32 = Intersection 64 = Insertion 128 = Perpendicular 256 = Tangent 512 = Nearest 1024 = Quick
OSNAPCOORD				Controls whether coordinates entered on the command line override running object snaps
PDMODE	0	Integer	Drawing	Point entity display mode
PDSIZE	0.0000	Real	Drawing	Point entity display size
PELLIPSE	0	Integer	Drawing	Controls the ellipse type created with ELLIPSE 0 = Creates a true ellipse object 1 = Creates a polyline representation of an ellipse
PERIMETER		Real		Perimeter computed by Area, List, or Dblist (read-only)
PFACEMAX	4	Integer		Maximum number of vertices per face (read-only)

Appendix D

Variable	Default Setting	Type	Saved In	Explanation
PICKADD	1	Integer	Config	Controls additive selection of objects 0 = Disables PICKADD. The most recently selected objects, either by an individual pick or windowing, become the selection set. Previously selected objects are removed from the selection set. You can add more objects to the selection set, however, by holding down [Shift] while selecting 1 = Enables PICKADD. Each object you select, either individually or by windowing, is added to the current selection set. To remove objects from the selection set, hold down [Shift] while selecting
PICKAUTO	1	Integer	Config	Controls automatic windowing when the "Select objects:" prompt appears 0 = Disables PICKAUTO 1 = Allows you to draw a selection window (both window and crossing window) automatically at the "Select objects:" prompt
PICKBOX	10	Integer	Config	Object selection target height, in pixels
PICKDRAG	0	Integer	Config	Controls the method of drawing a selection window 0 = You draw the selection window by clicking the mouse at one corner and then at the other corner 1 = You draw the selection window by clicking at one corner, holding down the mouse button, dragging, and releasing the mouse button at the other corner
PICKFIRST	1	Integer	Config	Controls the method of object selection so that you can select objects first and then use an edit/inquiry command 0 = Disables PICKFIRST 1 = Enables PICKFIRST
PICKSTYLE	3	Integer	Drawing	Controls group selection and associative hatch selection
PLATFORM		String		Read-only message that indicates which version of AutoCAD is in use
PLINEGEN	1	Integer	Drawing	Sets the linetype pattern generation around the vertices of a 2D polyline. When set to 1, PLINEGEN causes the linetype to be generated in a continuous pattern around the vertices of the polyline. When set to 0, polylines are generated with the linetype to start and end with a dash at each vertex. PLINEGEN doesn't apply to polylines with tapered segments
PLINETYPE				Determines whether AutoCAD uses optimized 2D polylines
PLINEWID	0.0000	Real	Drawing	Default polyline width; it can be zero

Variable	Default Setting	Type	Saved In	Explanation
PLOTID		String	Config	Changes the default plotter, based on its assigned description
PLOTROTMODE	1	Integer	Drawing	Controls orientation of plots
PLOTTER		Integer	Config	Changes the default plotter, based on its assigned integer (0–maximum configured); you can create up to 29 configurations
POLYSIDES	8	Integer		Default number of sides for the POLYGON command; the range is 3–1024
POPUPS	1	Integer		1 if the currently configured display driver supports dialog boxes, the menu bar, pull-down menus, and icon menus; 0 if these advanced user interface features are not available (read-only)
PROJECTNAME				Saves the current project name
PROJMODE	1	Integer	Config	Sets the current Projection mode for Trim or Extend operations
PROXYGRAPHICS				Determines whether images of proxy objects are saved in the drawing
PROXYNOTICE				Displays a notice when you open a drawing containing custom objects created by an application that is not present
PROXYSHOW				Controls the display of proxy objects in a drawing
PSLTSCALE	0	Integer	Drawing	Controls paper space linetype scaling 0 = No special linetype scaling 1 = Viewport scaling governs linetype scaling
PSPROLOG		String	Config	Assigns a name for a prolog section to be read from the *acad.psf* file when using the PSOUT command
PSQUALITY		Integer	Config	Controls the rendering quality of PostScript images and whether they are drawn as filled objects or as outlines. A zero setting disables PostScript image generation and a nonzero setting enables PostScript generation *Positive setting:* Sets the number of pixels per AutoCAD drawing unit for the PostScript resolution *Negative setting:* Still sets the number of pixels per drawing unit, but uses the absolute value; causes AutoCAD to show the PostScript paths as outlines, and doesn't fill them
QTEXTMODE	0	Integer	Drawing	Quick text mode ON if 1, OFF if 0
RASTERPREVIEW	0	Integer	Drawing	Controls whether drawing preview images are saved with the drawing
REGENMODE	1	Integer	Drawing	Regenauto ON if 1, OFF if 0

Variable	Default Setting	Type	Saved In	Explanation
RE-INIT		Integer		Reinitializes the I/O ports, digitizer, display, plotter, and *acad.pgp* file using the following bit codes. To specify more than one reinitialization, enter the sum of their values, for example, 3 to specify both digitizer port (1) and plotter port (2) reinitialization 1 = Digitizer port reinitialization 2 = Plotter port reinitialization 4 = Digitizer reinitialization 8 = Display reinitialization 16 = PGP file reinitialization (reload)
RTDISPLAY				Controls the display of raster images during Realtime ZOOM
SAVEFILE		String	Config	Current auto-save file name (read-only)
SAVENAME		String		The file name you save the drawing to (read-only)
SAVETIME	120	Integer	Config	Automatic save interval, in minutes (or 0 to disable automatic saves). The SAVETIME timer starts as soon as you make a change to a drawing, and is reset and restarts by a manual SAVE, SAVEAS, or QSAVE. The current drawing is saved to *auto.sv$*
SCREENBOXES		Integer	Config	The number of boxes in the screen menu area of the graphics area. If the screen menu is disabled (configured off), SCREENBOXES is zero. On platforms that permit the AutoCAD graphics window to be resized or the screen menu to be reconfigured during an editing session, the value of this variable might change during the editing session (read-only)
SCREENMODE		Integer	Config	A (read-only) bit code indicating the graphics/text state of the AutoCAD display. It is the sum of the following bit values: 0 = Text screen is displayed 1 = Graphics mode is displayed 2 = Dual-screen display configuration
SCREENSIZE		2D point		Current viewpoint size in pixels, X and Y (read-only)
SHADEDGE	3	Integer	Drawing	0 = Faces shaded, edges not highlighted 1 = Faces shaded, edges drawn in background color 2 = Faces not filled, edges in object color 3 = Faces in entity color, edges in background color
SHADEDIF	70	Integer	Drawing	Ratio of ambient to diffuse light (in percentage of ambient light)
SHPNAME	" "	String		Default shape name; must conform to symbol-naming conventions. If no default is set, it returns a " ". Enter . (period) to set no default.
SKETCHINC	0.1000	Real	Drawing	Sketch record increment

Variable	Default Setting	Type	Saved In	Explanation
SKPOLY	0	Integer	Drawing	Sketch generates lines if 0, polylines if 1
SNAPANG	0	Real	Drawing	Snap/Grid rotation angle (UCS-relative) for the current viewport
SNAPBASE	0.0000, 0.0000	2D point	Drawing	Snap/Grid origin point for the current viewport (in UCS *XY* coordinates)
SNAPISOPAIR	0	Integer	Drawing	Current isometric plane (0 = left, 1 = top, 2 = right) for the current viewport
SNAPMODE	0	Integer	Drawing	1 = Snap on for current viewport; 0 = Snap off
SNAPSTYL	0	Integer	Drawing	Snap style for current viewport (0 = standard, 1 = isometric)
SNAPUNIT	1.0000, 1.0000	2D point	Drawing	Snap spacing for current viewport, *X* and *Y*
SORTENTS		Integer	Config	Controls the display of objects sort order operations using the following codes. To select more than one, enter the sum of their codes; for example, enter 3 to specify codes 1 and 2 The default, 96, specifies sort operations for plotting and PostScript output 0 = Disables SORTENTS 1 = Sort for object selection 2 = Sort for object snap 4 = Sort for redraws 8 = Sort for MSLIDE slide creation 16 = Sort for regenerations 32 = Sort for plotting 64 = Sort for PostScript output
SPLFRAME	0	Integer	Drawing	*If = 1:* – the control polygon for spline-fit polylines is to be displayed – only the defining mesh of a surface-fit polygon mesh is displayed (the fit surface is not displayed) – invisible edges of 3D faces are displayed *If = 0:* – does not display the control polygon for spline-fit polylines – displays the fit surface of a polygon mesh, not the defining mesh – does not display the invisible edges of 3D faces
SPLINESEGS	8	Integer	Drawing	The number of line segments to be generated for each spline patch
SPLINETYPE	6	Integer	Drawing	Type of spline curve to be generated by PEDIT Spline. The valid values are: 5 = Quadratic B-spline 6 = Cubic B-spline
SURFTAB1	6	Integer	Drawing	Number of tabulations to be generated for Rulesurf and Tabsurf; also mesh density in the *M* direction for Resurf and Edgesurf

Variable	Default Setting	Type	Saved In	Explanation
SURFTAB2	6	Integer	Drawing	Mesh density in the *N* direction for Revsurf and Edgesurf
SURFTYPE	6	Integer	Drawing	Type of surface fitting to be performed by PEDIT Smooth. The valid values are: 5 = Quadratic B-spline surface 6 = Cubic B-spline surface 8 = Bezier surface
SURFU	6	Integer	Drawing	Surface density in the *M* direction
SURFV	6	Integer	Drawing	Surface density in the *N* direction
SYSCODEPAGE		String	Drawing	Indicates the system code page specified in *acad.xmf* (read-only)
TABMODE	0	Integer		Controls the use of tablet mode 0 = Disables tablet mode 1 = Enables tablet mode
TARGET	0.0000, 0.0000, 0.0000	3D point	Drawing	Location (in UCS coordinates) of the target (look-at) point for the current viewport (read-only)
TDCREATE		Real	Drawing	Time and date of drawing creation (read-only)
TDINDWG		Real	Drawing	Total editing time (read-only)
TDUPDATE		Real	Drawing	Time and date of last update/save (read-only)
TDSURTIMER		Real	Drawing	User elapsed timer (read-only)
TEMPPREFIX	" "	String		Contains the directory name (if any) configured for placement of temporary files, with a path separator appended if necessary (read-only)
TEXTEVAL	0	Integer		If = 0, all responses to prompts for text strings and attribute values are taken literally. If = 1, text starting with "(" or "!" is evaluated as an AutoLISP expression, as for nontextual input. *Note:* The DTEXT command takes all input literally, regardless of the setting of TEXTEVAL
TEXTFILL				Controls the filling of Bitstream, TrueType, and Adobe Type 1 fonts
TEXTQLTY				Sets the resolution of Bitstream, TrueType, and Adobe Type 1 fonts
TEXTSIZE	0.2000	Real	Drawing	The default height for new text objects drawn with the current text style (meaningless if the style has a fixed height)
TEXTSTYLE	"STANDARD"	String	Drawing	Contains the name of the current text style (read-only)
THICKNESS	0.0000	Real	Drawing	Current 3D thickness
TILEMODE	1	Integer	Drawing	1 = Release 10 compatibility mode (uses Vports) 0 = Enables paper space and viewport entities (uses MVIEW)

Variable	Default Setting	Type	Saved In	Explanation
TOOLTIPS	1	Integer	Config	Controls the display of Tool Tips
TRACEWID	0.0500	Real	Drawing	Default trace width
TREEDEPTH		Integer	Drawing	A 4-digit (maximum) code that specifies the number of times the tree-structured spatial index may divide into branches, hence affecting the speed in which AutoCAD searches the database before completing an action. The first two digits refer to the depth of the model space nodes, and the second two digits refer to the depth of paper space nodes. Use a positive setting for 3D drawings and a negative setting for 2D drawings
TREEMAX	10000000	Integer	Config	Limits memory consumption during drawing regeneration
TRIMMODE	1	Integer		Controls whether AutoCAD trims selected edges for chamfers and fillets
UCSFOLLOW	0	Integer	Drawing	The setting is maintained separately for both spaces and can be accessed in either space, but the setting is ignored while in paper space (it is always treated as if set to 0)
UCSICON	0	Integer	Drawing	The coordinate system icon bitcode for the current viewport (sum of the following): 1 = On — icon display enabled 2 = Origin — if icon display is enabled, the icon floats to the UCS origin if possible
UCSNAME	" "	String	Drawing	Name of the current coordinate system for the current space; returns a null string if the current UCS is unnamed (read-only)
UCSORG	0.0000, 0.0000, 0.0000	3D point	Drawing	The origin point of the current coordinate system for the current space; this value is always returned in World coordinates (read-only)
UCSXDIR	1.0000, 0.0000, 0.0000	3D point	Drawing	The X direction of the current UCS for the current space (read-only)
UCSYDIR	0.0000, 1.0000, 0.0000	3D point	Drawing	The Y direction of the current UCS for the current space (read-only)
UNDOCTL	1	Integer		A (read-only) code indicating the state of the UNDO feature; it is the sum of the following values: 1 = Set if UNDO is enabled 2 = Set if only one command can be undone 4 = Set if Auto-group mode is enabled 8 = Set if a group is currently active
UNDOMARKS		Integer		The (read-only) number of marks that have been placed in the UNDO control stream by the UNDO command Mark option. The Mark and Back options are unavailable if a group is currently active

Variable	Default Setting	Type	Saved In	Explanation
UNITMODE	0	Integer	Drawing	0 = Displays fractional, feet and inches, and surveyor's angles as previously 1 = Displays fractional, feet and inches, and surveyor's angles in input format
USERI1-5				Saves and recalls integer values
USERR1-5				Saves and recalls real numbers
USERS1-5				Saves and recalls text string data
VIEWCTR		3D point	Drawing	Center of view in current viewport, expressed in UCS coordinates (read-only)
VIEWDIR		3D point	Drawing	The current viewport's viewing direction expressed in World coordinates; this describes the camera point as a 3D offset from the TARGET point (read-only)
VIEWMODE	0	Integer	Drawing	Viewing mode bitcode for the current viewport (read-only); the value is the sum of the following: 1 = Perspective view active 2 = Front clipping on 4 = Back clipping on 8 = UCS follow mode 16 = Front clip not at eye. If On, the front clip distance (FRONTZ) determines the front clipping plane. If Off, FRONZ is ignored and the front clipping is set to pass through the camera point (i.e., vectors behind the camera are not displayed). This flag is ignored if the front clipping bit (2) is off
VIEWSIZE		Real	Drawing	Height of view in current viewport, expressed in drawing units (read-only)
VIEWTWIST	0	Real	Drawing	View twist angle for the current viewport (read-only)
VISRETAIN	1	Integer	Drawing	If = 0, the current drawing's On/Off, Freeze/Thaw, color, and linetype settings for Xref-dependent layers take precedence over the Xref's layer definition; if = 1, these settings don't take precedence
VSMAX		3D point		The upper right corner of the current viewport's virtual screen, expressed in UCS coordinates (read-only)
VSMIN		3D point		The lower left corner of the current viewport's virtual screen, expressed in UCS coordinates (read-only)
WORDDUCS	1	Integer		If = 1, the current UCS is the same as the WCS; if = 0, it is not (read-only)

Variable	Default Setting	Type	Saved In	Explanation
WORLDVIEW	1	Integer	Drawing	Dview and Vpoint command input is relative to the current UCS. If this variable is set to 1, the current UCS is changed to the WCS for the duration of a DVIEW or VPOINT command. Default value = 1
XCLIPFRAME				Sets visibilty of Xref clipping boundaries
XLOADPATH				Creates a path for storing temporary copies of demand-loaded Xref files
XREFCTL	1	Integer	Config	Controls whether .xlg files (external reference log files) are written 0 = Xref log (.xlg) files not written 1 = Xref log (.xlg) files written

Appendix D

E

HATCH AND FILL PATTERNS

· ·

INTRODUCTION

AutoCAD supports two types of hatch patterns: vector patterns and PostScript fill patterns. Vector patterns are made of straight lines and dots; they are defined in the *Acad.Pat* pattern file. You can create custom hatch patterns or purchase patterns created by third-party vendors. You place a hatch pattern with the HATCH and BHATCH commands.

PostScript fill patterns are made via PostScript PDL (page description language); they are defined in the *Acad.Psf* file. To create a custom fill pattern, you need to know PostScript programming. You place a fill pattern with the PSFILL command.

Over 60 hatch patterns and 12 PostScript fills are supplied with the AutoCAD package. Some are shown on the following pages.

HATCH PATTERNS

ANGLE

ANSI31

ANSI32

ANSI33

ANSI34

ANSI35

ANSI36

ANSI37

ANSI38

AR-B816

AR-B816C

AR-B88

AR-BRELM

AR-BRSTD

AR-CONC

AR-HBONE

AR-PARQ1

AR-RROOF

AR-RSHKE

AR-SAND

BOX

BRASS

BRICK

BRSTONE

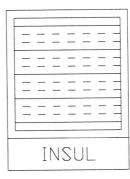
HONEY

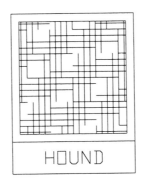
HOUND

INSUL

LINE

MUDST

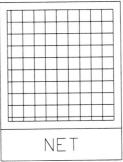
NET

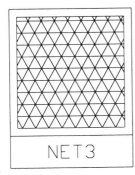
NET3

PLAST

PLASTI

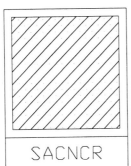
SACNCR

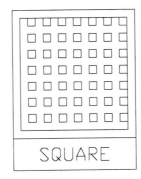
SQUARE

STARS

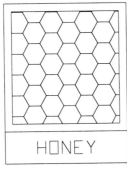

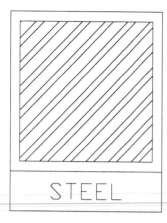

STEEL

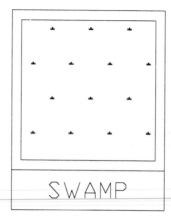

SWAMP

TRANS

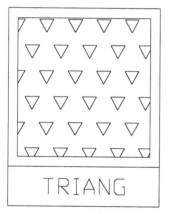

TRIANG

ZIGZAG

POSTSCRIPT FILL PATERNS

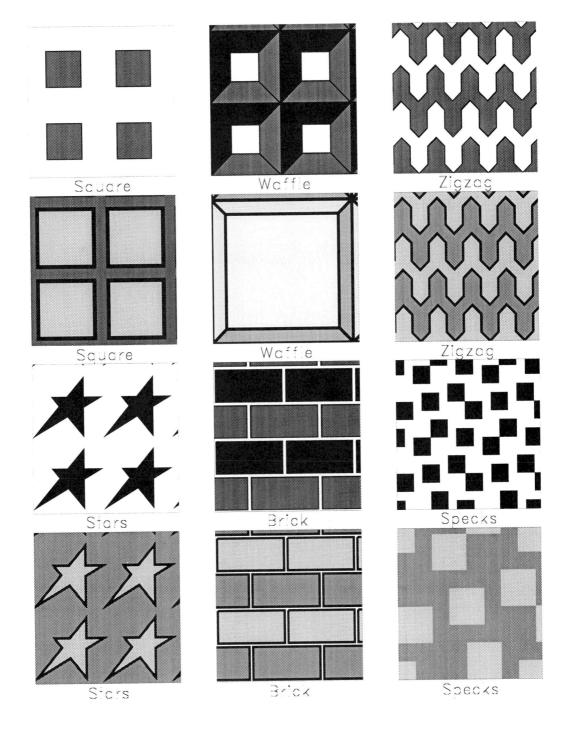

Square

Waffle

Zigzag

Square

Waffle

Zigzag

Stars

Brick

Specks

Stars

Brick

Specks

FONTS

INTRODUCTION

AutoCAD works with two types of text fonts: the original SHX-format font files and PFB PostScript font files. The AutoCAD package includes 17 SHX text fonts, five SHX symbol fonts, and 16 PFB text fonts. Some of the available fonts are shown on the following pages.

USING SHX AND PFB FILES

Other SHX font files are available from third-party developers. In addition, AutoCAD can use PostScript fonts from any source, many of which are included free with other software packages. Postscript fonts are usually stored in the \Psfonts subdirectory.

AutoCAD does not store text fonts in the drawing file. Instead, the *DWG* file references SHX font definition files stored elsewhere on the hard drive. Thus, if you receive a drawing from another AutoCAD system, you might have to tell AutoCAD where to find the font files on your system.

PostScript fonts placed in an AutoCAD drawing have two anomilies: the fonts are unfilled and they are drawn 30% too small. To compensate for the reduced size, specify a text height 50% larger.

STANDARD TEXT FONTS

FAST FONTS

TXT   ABCDEFGHIJKLMNOPQRSTUVWXYZ 1234567890

MONOTXT   ABCDEFGHIJKLMNOPQRSTUVWXYZ 1234567890

SIMPLEX FONTS

ROMANS   ABCDEFGHIJKLMNOPQRSTUVWXYZ 1234567890

SCRIPTS   ABCDEFGHIJKLMNOPQRSTUVWXYZ 1234567890

GREEKS   ABXΔEΦΓHIϑKΛMNOΠΘΡΣΤΥΩΞΨZ 1234567890

DUPLEX FONTS

ROMAND   ABCDEFGHIJKLMNOPQRSTUVWXYZ 1234567890

COMPLEX FONTS

ROMANC   ABCDEFGHIJKLMNOPQRSTUVWXYZ 1234567890

ITALICC   ABCDEFGHIJKLMNOPQRSTUVWXYZ 1234567890

SCRIPTC   ABCDEFGHIJKLMNOPQRSTUVWXYZ 1234567890

GREEKC   ABXΔEΦΓHIϑKΛMNOΠΘΡΣΤΥΩΞΨZ 1234567890

TRIPLEX FONTS

ROMANT   ABCDEFGHIJKLMNOPQRSTUVWXYZ 1234567890

ITALICT   ABCDEFGHIJKLMNOPQRSTUVWXYZ 1234567890

STANDARD TEXT FONTS

GOTHIC FONTS

GOTHICE   ABCDEFGHIJKLMNOPQRSTUVWXYZ 1234567890

GOTHICG   ABCDEFGHIJKLMNOPQRSTUVWXYZ 1234567890

GOTHICI   ABCDEFGHIJKLMNOPQRSTUVWXYZ 1234567890

SYMBOL FONTS

A B C D E F G H I J K L M N O P Q R S T U V W X Y Z
a b c d e f g h i j k l m n o p q r s t u v w x y z

SYASTRO

⊙ ☿ ♀ ⊕ ♂ ♃ ♄ ♅ ♆ ♇ ☽ ... ∗ ☊ ☋ ♈ ♉ ♊ ♋ ♌ ♍ ♎ ♏ ♐ ♑ ♒
∗ ... ... ⌣ ∪ ⊃ ∩ ∈ → ↑ ← ↓ ∂ ∇ ⌢ ´ ` ˘ ✕ § † ‡ ∃ ℒ ® ©

SYMAP

○ □ △ ◇ ☆ + × ∗ ● ■ ▲ ◀ ▼ ▶ ★ ... ... † ✕ ... ... ✦ ☪ ✡ ... ⌂ ✡ ♿ 🔔
... ... ∘ ∘ ∘ ○ ○ ○ ◯ ◯ ⬯ ⬭ ... || ⊥ 丁 / ... ... ♠ ♡ ◇ ♣ ... ...

SYMATH

א ′ | ‖ ± ∓ × · ÷ = ≠ ≡ < > ≦ ≧ ∝ ~ √ ∪ ⊃ ∩ ∈ → ↑
← ↓ ∂ ∇ √ ∫ ∮ ∞ § † ‡ ∃ ∏ Σ ( ) [ ] { } ( ) √ ∫ ≈ ≅

SYMETEO

. , · ▲ ▗ ⌃ ⌃ ∩ ∪ ˙ ‥ ... S ∿ ∞ R 9 — / | \ — ∕ ∖
| \ ∖ — ∕ ∖ ⌢ ⌒ ⌣ ⌣ ( ) ⌒ ⌇ ∿ ∿ ⊓ ⌐ ⌐ α σ ϕ ◦ ●

SYMUSIC

. , ♪ ♩ ∘ ● # ♮ ♭ — - ∗ ... 𝄞 ⊚: ‖| · · ⋯ ⌐ ∧ ⇌ ▽
. , ♪ ♩ ∘ ● # ♮ ♭ — - ∗ ... 𝄞 ⊙: ℟ ⊙ ☿ ♀ ⊕ ♂ ♃ ♄ ♅ ♆ ♇

STANDARD TEXT FONTS

POSTSCRIPT FONTS

CIBT.PFB   ABCDEFGHIJKLMNOPQRSTUVWXYZ 1234567890

COBT.PFB   ABCDEFGHIJKLMNOPQRSTUVWXYZ 1234567890

EUR.PFB   ABCDEFGHIJKLMNOPQRSTUVWXYZ 1234567890

EURO.PFB   *ABCDEFGHIJKLMNOPQRSTUVWXYZ 1234567890*

PAR.PFB   ABCDEFGHIJKLMNOPQRSTUVWXYZ 1234567890

ROM.PFB   ABCDEFGHIJKLMNOPQRSTUVWXYZ 1234567890

ROMB.PFB   ABCDEFGHIJKLMNOPQRSTUVWXYZ 1234567890

ROMI.PFB   *ABCDEFGHIJKLMNOPQRSTUVWXYZ 1234567890*

SAS.PFB   ABCDEFGHIJKLMNOPQRSTUVWXYZ 1234567890

SASB.PFB   ABCDEFGHIJKLMNOPQRSTUVWXYZ 1234567890

SASBO.PFB   *ABCDEFGHIJKLMNOPQRSTUVWXYZ 1234567890*

SASO.PFB   *ABCDEFGHIJKLMNOPQRSTUVWXYZ 1234567890*

SUF.PFB   ABCDEFGHIJKLMNOPQRSTUVWXYZ 1234567890

TE.PFB   ABCDEFGHIJKLMNOPQRSTUVWXYZ 1234567890

TEB.PFB   ABCDEFGHIJKLMNOPQRSTUVWXYZ 1234567890

CYRILLIC FONTS

CYRILLIC   АБВГДЕЖЗИЙКЛМНОПРСТУФХЦЧШЩ 1234567890

CYRILTLC   АБЧДЕФГХИЩКЛМНОПЦРСТУВШЖЙЗ 1234567890

· · · · · · · · · · · · · ·

APPENDIX

G

LINETYPES

· ·

INTRODUCTION

Linetypes are defined by the *ACAD.LIN* file. In addition to the continuous linetype, the AutoCAD program comes with the 45 linetypes. Some of them are listed on the next page. You can add custom linetypes to the *ACAD.LIN* file.

Before you can use a linetype in a drawing, it must be loaded by means of the LINETYPE command. Set the linetype scale with the LTSCALE command; set independent linetype scaling in paper space with the PSLTSCALE system variable; control the generation of linetype along a polyline with the PLINEGEN system variable.

STANDARD LINETYPES

BORDER

BORDER2

BORDERX2

CENTER

CENTER2

CENTERX2

DASHDOT

DASHDOT2

DASHDOTX2

DASHED

DASHED2

DASHEDX2

DIVIDE

DIVIDE2

DIVIDEX2

DOT

DOT2

DOTX2

HIDDEN

HIDDEN2

HIDDENX2

PHANTOM

PHANTOM2

PHANTOMX2

INDEX